PLANNING AND CONTROL OF LAND DEVELOPMENT: CASES AND MATERIALS

FIFTH EDITION

By

Daniel R. Mandelker
Howard A. Stamper Professor of Law
Washington University

John M. Payne
Professor of Law & Justice Hall Scholar
Rutgers University — Newark

LEXIS Publishing™

LEXIS®·NEXIS®· MARTINDALE-HUBBELL®
MATTHEW BENDER®· MICHIE™· SHEPARD'S®

Library of Congress Cataloging-in-Publication Data

Mandelker, Daniel R.
    Planning and control of land development : cases and materials /
Daniel R. Mandelker,
John M. Payne.--5th ed.
    p. cm.
Includes index.
ISBN 0-8205-5035-3
    1. Land use--Law and legislation--United States--Cases. 2. Real estate
development--Law and legislation--United States--Cases. I. Payne, John M.,
1941- II.
Title.
KF5698.A4 M36 2001
346.7304'5—dc21
00-054455

Editorial Offices
2 Park Avenue, New York, NY 10016-5675 (212) 448-2000
201 Mission St., San Francisco, CA 94105-1831 (415) 908-3200
701 East Water Street, Charlottesville, VA 22902-7587 (804) 972-7600
www.lexis.com

For Nicky, Alison and Susan

For Adam, Matt and Petie

Preface

A book in its fifth edition needs no introduction. As we have said before, if this edition retains the acceptance of its predecessors, an honor that the Editors have endeavored to earn, it will largely speak for itself, and we have therefore foregone the customary statement of purposes by way of preface. Instructors are invited to turn to the accompanying Teacher's Manual for a more detailed description of the changes we have made in this edition and our proposals for how this book might be used.

With this edition, however, Roger A. Cunningham, the late James V. Campbell Professor of Law at the University of Michigan Law School, no longer appears as co-author. This does not diminish his contributions to this book, which will reflect his wisdom and learning for many years to come.

We wish to confirm our dedication to this important area of the law. Land use law is democracy at the grass roots. We firmly believe that teachers and students who study it need to know how it is practiced, how planners and local decision makers, as well as lawyers, contribute to its making, and how it reflects the expectations we have about the environment around us. This book is dedicated to this purpose.

January 15, 2001

Daniel R. Mandelker
John M. Payne

Acknowledgments

The American Planning Association, for permission to reprint from Douglas Porter, Maryland's "Smart Growth" Program: An Evaluation and Recommendations, Planning Advisory Service Memo, August 1999. Copyright 1999 by the American Planning Association. Reprinted with permission.

The American Planning Association, for permission to reprint from Growing Smart Legislative Guidebook (Phases I & II Interim Edition, 1998). Copyright 1998 by The American Planning Association. Reprinted with permission.

Harvard Law Review for permission to reprint from Michelman, *Property, Utility, and Fairness: Comments on the Ethical Foundations of Just Compensation Law,* 80 Harv. L. Rev. 1165, 1172–77, 1181–83 (1967). Copyright 1967 by the Harvard Law Review Association.

International City Management Association and John Kriken for permission to reprint San Antonio Corridor Design Plan from The Practice of Local Government Planning, ed. Frank S. So et al. (1979); and to reprint from R. Drucker, Land Subdivision Regulation, in the Practice of Local Government Planning, ed. Frank S. So & Judith Getzels (1988).

Island Press, for material excerpted from Land Use and Society: Geography, Law and Public Policy by Rutherford Platt. Copyright © 1996 by Island Press. Reprinted with permission of Island Press. Also for material excerpted from Managing Growth in America's Communities by Douglas R. Porter. Copyright © 1997 by Island Press. Reprinted by permission of Island Press.

The Johns Hopkins University Press, for permission to reprint from Fischel, William A., The Economics of Zoning Laws: A Property Rights Approach to American Land Use Controls pp. 4, 7-8, 18-19. © 1985, The Johns Hopkins University Press. Reprinted with permission of The Johns Hopkins University Press.

Land Use Law and Zoning Digest, for permission to reprint from Garvin and Leitner, *Drafting Interim Development Ordinances: Creating Time to Plan,* 48 Land Use Law & Zoning Digest, No. 6 (1996).

Lincoln Institute of Land Policy, for permission to reprint from Richard Babcock & Charles Siemon, The Zoning Game Revisited (1985). Copyright 1985 by Lincoln Institute of Land Policy. Reprinted with permission.

Acknowledgments

Ohio State Law Journal and Professor Mark Cordes, for permission to reprint from Mark Cordes, *Takings, Fairness and Farmland Preservation,* 60 Ohio St. L.J. 1033 (1999). Originally published in 60 Ohio St. L. J. 1033 (1999).

Rutgers Center for Urban Policy Research, for permission to reprint from Eric Heikkila, The Economics of Planning (New Brunswick, N.J.: Center for Urban Policy Research). Copyright 2000 by Rutgers The State University of New Jersey. Reprinted with permission.

Urban Affairs Review, for permission to reprint from Susan Fainstein, *New Directions in Planning Theory,* 35 Urban Affairs Review 451, 452-53, 472-73 (2000). Copyright © 2000 by Sage Publications, Inc. Reprinted with permission.

Urban Land Institute, for permission to reprint from Douglas R. Porter, Patrick L. Phillips & Terry J. Lassar, Flexible Zoning: How It Works. Washington, D.C., 1988. ULI Catalog No.: F14.

Washington University Law Quarterly for permission to reprint from Mandelker, *Delegation of Power and Function in Zoning Administration,* 1963 Wash. U.L.Q. 60, 61, 63. Copyright 1963.

William & Mary Environmental Law & Policy Review, for permission to reprint from Daniel Mandelker, *Managing Space to Manage Growth,* 23 William and Mary Environmental Law and Policy Review 801 (1999). Copyright 1999 by The Marshall-Wythe School of Law College of William & Mary. Reprinted with permission.

Unless otherwise indicated in the text, the emphasis in all quoted materials is as in the original.

NOTES ON A BIBLIOGRAPHY

Treatises. In addition to Professor Mandelker's one-volume treatise on Land Use Law (4th ed. 1997, with supplements), other one-volume books are J. Juergensmeyer & T. Roberts, Land Use Planning and Control Law (1998), and Professor Kmiec's Zoning and Planning Deskbook, which is periodically updated. There are a number of multi-volume treatises. These include the late Professor Norman Williams' American Land Planning Law; P. Rohan, Zoning and Land Use Controls, presently edited by Professor Eric Kelly as General Editor; and Rathkopf's Law of Zoning and Planning, now thoroughly updated by Professor Ed Ziegler as the principal revision author. Anderson's Law of Zoning is presently under revision. Federal law is covered by D. Mandelker, J. Gerard & T. Sullivan, Federal Land Use Law, which is updated annually.

Periodicals. The Urban Lawyer, which is the official publication of the Urban, State and Local Government Law Section of the American Bar Association, and the Florida State University Journal of Land Use and Environmental Law, regularly contain articles on land use topics. The Southwestern Legal Foundation publishes an annual Institute on Planning, Zoning and Eminent Domain that carries articles based on speeches presented at the Institute.

Two monthly periodicals are devoted entirely to land use law. The American Planning Association publishes the Land Use Law & Zoning Digest. Each issue contains a lead article and digests of recent cases and statutes. The Association also publishes a monthly Zoning News that reports on new developments in zoning around the country. Clark Boardman publishes a monthly Zoning and Planning Law Report that contains a lead article, case digests and reports on new developments. Clark Boardman also publishes an annual Land Use and Environment Law Review that reproduces leading articles published during the previous year and an annual Zoning and Planning Law Handbook that contains articles on land use topics. The Journal of the American Planning Association carries articles on land use planning and controls. Urban Land, published by the Urban Land Institute, has a section on regulatory problems that often covers land use issues. Land Development, a publication of the National Association of Homebuilders, is another useful publication.

Several journals are devoted to environmental law. Of these, the Ecology Law Quarterly, Environmental Law, the Harvard Environmental Law Review, and the Natural Resources Journal often carry articles on land use law.

NOTES ON A BIBLIOGRAPHY

The Journal of Planning Literature, edited at Ohio State University's planning school and published by Sage Publications, is a quarterly publication that contains bibliographies of articles on land use and related topics as well as abstracts of the more important articles. It also contains individual bibliographies and review articles on land use topics that are extremely helpful.

Publications and Services. The American Planning Association publishes a periodic Planning Advisory Service. Each issue is a report on a land use or planning topic. The reports often discuss land use control problems and techniques. Both the Association and the Urban Land Institute have an active publications program that includes books and other publications on land use topics.

SUMMARY TABLE OF CONTENTS

TABLE OF CONTENTS

———

CHAPTER 5: THE ZONING PROCESS: EUCLIDEAN ZONING GIVES WAY TO FLEXIBLE ZONING 423

Chapter 1

AN INTRODUCTION TO LAND USE CONTROLS

A. WHY LAND USE CONTROLS?

Cities and other places don't just happen. The use of land requires the coming together of a complex set of social, economic and physical forces, held together by a vision (often inchoate) of the desired outcome. This was true even in the days of the mythic American frontier, when the rugged individualism of pioneer families was supported by government policy making: homestead grants, the Indian wars, and the transcontinental railroad. Planning for the use of land as we know it today began with the first European arrivals on the North American continent, and it continues in modern times. Consider Boston:

R. PLATT, LAND USE AND SOCIETY: GEOGRAPHY, LAW AND PUBLIC POLICY, pp. 47–50 (Island Press, 1996)

A short walk across central Boston traverses an archive of different stages of public involvement in the city-shaping process. Starting in the vicinity of the waterfront on Boston Harbor, one wanders through the North End and financial district whose irregular street pattern dates from the mid-17th century. (It is Boston folklore that these streets originated as cow paths.) These lead eventually to the city's open core, the Boston Common and the Public Garden, set aside from private development by public action respectively in the 1630s and the 1830s. Adjoining the Public Garden to the west are the rectilinear streets and bowfront brick row houses of Back Bay, Boston's mid-19th century expansion onto newly filled land bordering the Charles River. Crossing Boyleston Street from Back Bay, one enters the high-rise complex of multiple-use structures in Prudential Center and adjacent areas.

How does one account for the perceived differences in urban form between the North End, Back Bay, and Prudential Center? [Changing social and economic circumstances, as well as new transportation and construction technologies are partial explanations, according to Platt.—Eds.] But there is an additional explanation for the contrasting patterns of the three districts, namely *the extent and form of public intervention in the private building process*. Boston's early growth was largely organic. Actions by the town selectmen to constrain individual freedom in building were limited to measures concerned with fire, as in specifying materials to be used in roofing and chimneys and in requiring the possession by householders of fire-fighting implements. Otherwise, the town placed few restrictions on the layout and construction of individual structures.

Back Bay, by contrast, was a totally preconceived expansion of Boston. New land, created through filling of the malodorous fens, vested legally in the Commonwealth of Massachusetts, which historically holds tidelands in trust

1

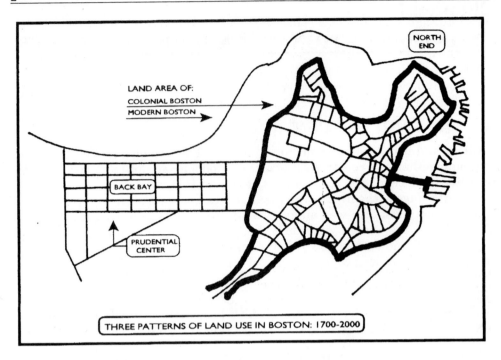

THREE PATTERNS OF LAND USE IN BOSTON: 1700-2000

for the public. In 1856, a multipartite agreement to govern the filling and development of the fens was executed between the Commonwealth, the City of Boston, and various private proprietors. Pursuant to this agreement, the Commissioners on the Back Bay, a legal entity created by the legislature in 1852, exercised total control over the layout of streets and disposition of parcels. Purchasers of building lots were required to accept deed restrictions limiting the use, height, and external appearance of structures. Municipal land use zoning would not appear in Boston until after World War I. Meanwhile, private deed restrictions provided strict legal control to ensure harmonious development of Back Bay.

Prudential Center legally resembles the Back Bay project to the extent that public authorities promoted the development of an underutilized site (in this case a railroad yard) and controlled its form and usage through deed restrictions. But Prudential Center involved other legal devices as well. The site (including the newly recognized property interest in "air rights") had to be acquired from the private owner using public eminent domain power. It was then reconveyed at a lower cost to the redevelopment corporation. The latter was required to provide an auditorium and convention hall, as well as public ways and parking spaces, as a condition to constructing private commercial space.

1. THE CHALLENGE OF LAND USE POLICY

If land use inevitably leads to land use planning, land use planning in turn inevitably requires the formulation of land use policy. Not everyone wants to live in cities, even so charming a one as Boston. (Frank Lloyd Wright, never one to mince words, observed that "[t]o look at the plan of any great city is to look at the cross section of some fibrous tumor." F. L. Wright, The Disappearing City 26 (1932)). Nor do we lack alternatives. The same process of policy planning that has informed the evolution of Boston over three centuries has, for better or worse, produced the ubiquitous post-World War Two pattern of dispersed homes, offices and shops, dependent on the automobile, now often criticized as "sprawl." This pattern, in turn, has in recent years produced its own reaction, the "smart growth" movement, which emphasizes preservation of farmland and open space by accommodating population growth in compact new developments or (bringing the issue full circle) in revitalized, redeveloped cities.

How is one to choose between these (and many more) possibilities? Even in a free-market society where most planning and policymaking is, by definition, assigned to the incremental decisions made by countless private individuals and groups, the description of Boston's evolution demonstrates that public planning and policymaking can play a significant role in determining the pattern of land uses. By what criteria should government act (or refrain from acting)? There are many possible answers to that question, some overlapping, some mutually exclusive. A number of these perspectives will be suggested in the remainder of this chapter. To start at the beginning, however, consider the two excerpts that follow, which consider the most basic of questions: how much land is available for use, are we in any danger of running out, and should we be concerned about controlling the land use decisions that private individuals make? Rutherford Platt, the author of the description of Boston which opens this chapter, is a geographer who is sympathetic to the need for land use controls. William Fischel, an economist, approaches land use controls skeptically because of their interference with free market principles, and he often finds that the case for specific regulations has not been made with sufficient rigor.

We begin with an academic parlor game:

> Divide the current U.S. population into households of four persons and house them at the "suburban sprawl" density of one acre per household. (An acre is $\frac{1}{640}$ of a square mile, or approximately the size of a football field without the end zones.) What percentage of the total land area of the contiguous forty-eight states would be taken up? [W. Fischel, The Economics of Zoning Laws: a Property Rights Approach to American Land Use Controls, pp. 1–2 (The Johns Hopkins University Press, 1985).]

Try to answer Professor Fischel's question before reading on.

R. PLATT, LAND USE AND SOCIETY: GEOGRAPHY, LAW AND PUBLIC POLICY, pp. 6–7, 26–27 (Island Press, 1996)

How Much Land Do We Have?

> In the United States, there is more land where nobody is than where anybody is. That is what makes America what it is. [Gertrude Stein, The Geographical History of America, 1936.]

Three decades ago, the noted resource economist Marion Clawson observed that the total land area of the United States, about 2.1 billion acres, theoretically amounted to a "share" of 12.5 acres for every living American at that time. In 1920, this figure stood at 20 acres per capita; it would further decline, in Clawson's estimate, to 7.5 acres in the year 2000. Clawson's prediction is on track. In 1984, U.S. land area per capita was 9.3 acres and shrinking. It nevertheless remained 14 times higher than that of the world as a whole and was at least three times the total for most other industrial nations.

Acreage per capita, however, is not a very meaningful figure. In the first place, it masks regional variation and is a poor measure of social well-being. At a state level, the citizens of Connecticut have one acre per capita (dividing its land by its population) and New Jerseyites have only two-thirds of an acre each, while the 686,000 residents of North Dakota "claim" 64 acres apiece. But does this mean that the people of North Dakota are better off than those of Connecticut? Clearly not in economic terms: Connecticut ranks second in income per capita while North Dakota ranks 33d. In terms of quality of life, this is a matter of personal judgment: windy open spaces versus the pains and pleasures of Megalopolis.

Second, a large proportion of the nation's wealth of land resources is distant from the everyday habitat of most of us. Three-quarters of the U.S. population (192 million in 1990) live in the nation's 341 metropolitan statistical areas (MSAs) that have been designated by the U.S. Bureau of the Census. . . . MSAs occupy about 16 percent of the nation's land area and have an average density of 2.1 acres per capita. But even within MSAs most of the population that does not live at the urban-rural fringe feels remote from "the country," which is apt to be privately owned and inaccessible in any case. . . .

A third limitation on the acres-per-capita measure of land wealth is the diversity of physical capacities and use categories into which land resources may be classified. Overall totals of land area reveal little about the sufficiency of land for particular purposes such as production of food and fiber, forest products, water resources, recreation, natural habitat, and urban uses. . . . Even [the] raw data reveal little about the sufficiency of the land for the purposes listed. Assessments must be tempered by the potential for interchange among various categories, that is, the degree of reversibility of land use changes. Also, the growing importance of the global economy, the rise of the U.S. trade deficit, the effect of currency exchange rates, and the flow of commodities and people across national borders vastly complicate the task of appraising the adequacy of U.S. land resources.

Finally, land differs as to its ownership status. About one-third of the U.S. land area is owned by the Federal government and is thus removed from the operation of the private land market, although federal lands do accommodate a variety of private activities.

. . .

A clear dichotomy exists between rural land uses on the one hand and urban and built-up uses on the other. . . . Reversible conversion of rural land from one use to another is a normal response to changing economic circumstance. Irreversible transformation of productive rural land, either to a degraded condition (due to soil erosion, salinization, or inundation) or to an urban or built-up condition, poses important public policy issues.

The spatial growth of urban land is the mirror image of the loss of rural land to development. But the implications of such growth are not limited to the loss of productive or potentially productive rural land. Urbanization involves a spectrum of public issues including environmental quality, adequacy of water supply, equity in housing and economic opportunity, energy consumption, traffic congestion, visual blight, natural hazards, and rising public costs per capita for providing utilities and services to a vastly expanded region of urban habitation.

W. FISCHEL, THE ECONOMICS OF ZONING LAWS: A PROPERTY RIGHTS APPROACH TO AMERICAN LAND USE CONTROLS, pp. 4, 7–8, 18–19 (The Johns Hopkins University Press, 1985)

A . . . measure of urban land is the Urbanized Area (UA). The UA is, roughly speaking, the built-up, contiguous part of an SMSA [Standard Metropolitan Statistical Area]. This does not mean just the central city of the SMSA; it includes surrounding suburbs. But its extent is based on population density rather than political boundaries. . . . The density criteria for being included in a UA are not too demanding: a suburban housing development that had one house for every two acres would be included so long as it was adjacent to the rest of the UA.

Urbanized Areas include about 60 percent of the U.S. population, and they take up only 1.2 percent of the land area. But this sanguine statistic does not address the concerns that many express about "suburban sprawl" or about development in smaller towns and rural areas.

Suburban sprawl data can be examined easily. It is true that suburban areas are less densely populated than central cities, but the difference is less than one might suspect. Since the problem of suburban sprawl most frequently focuses on the largest urban areas, I subtracted the population and land area of the central city (or cities, where there were two or more) of the twenty-five largest UAs and computed their gross-population density. It turns out to be 4.9 persons per acre. If we all lived at these 1970 suburban densities, we would take up less than 2.5 percent of the forty-eight states' land area.

. . .

[T]here is no danger that development will impinge on the stock of land for nonurban uses. . . . [A]lthough land may not be crucial, *use* is.

Zoning and other land use controls influence the location and combination of labor and capital. They can have a far greater influence on economic and other social activity than might be indicated by the fraction of land affected or the share of rent in national income. Land *use* controls can affect the quality of the environment, the provision of public services, the distribution of income and wealth, the pattern of commuting, development of natural resources, and the growth of the national economy. The notion that zoning is just a matter of local concern is incorrect when the cumulative effect of these regulations is considered.

NOTES AND QUESTIONS

1. *Categories of land.* Professors Platt and Fischel agree that most Americans live in urbanized areas on a relatively small percentage of the country's total land, and that the supply of non-urban land for agriculture and related uses is, as Platt puts it, "abundant." Implicit in their discussions, moreover, is the assumption that land can, will, and perhaps should migrate between one category and the other over time. The battleground of this process is sometimes characterized as the urban "fringe." The "can" and "will" of changing land uses is susceptible to objective study of historical trends and future projections although, by way of caution, note that by using different data units (MSA and SMSA, respectively) a decade apart, the two authors arrive at different absolute numbers about the extent of urbanization. When accepting claims of "objectivity," both planners and lawyers need to be alert to the nuances of data.

2. *Land use policy.* The "should" of land use change is the concern of policymakers. With respect to rural uses, Platt emphasizes in his book principles of sustainability and reversibility, whereas for urbanized areas both he and Fischel note a long list of relevant factors: preserving some (unspecified) level of environmental quality, providing adequate public services (Platt is more specific), encouraging social and economic equity. As to equity issues, Platt mentions "economic opportunity" while Fischel stresses economic growth; Platt singles out equity in housing, while Fischel highlights income equity. Fischel (but not Platt) mentions development of natural resources; Platt (but not Fischel) lists protection against visual blight and natural hazards. How would you change these lists of policy criteria, if at all?

3. *"Sprawl."* Low-density extensions of urbanized areas, or "sprawl," has much concerned land use policy makers in recent years. What can you glean about Platt's and Fischel's attitudes towards sprawl? These issues are discussed in detail in Ch. 7, *infra.*

4. *Land use policy, taxation and public services.* Although our formal concern in this book is with land use controls, the policy connections to taxation (particularly property taxation at the local level) and the provision of public services cannot be overstressed. Recognition of these linkages can be seen in both the Platt and Fischel excerpts, and is elaborated by the American Planning Association in its Growing Smart Legislative Handbook pp. xxv-xxvi (Phases I & II Interim Edition, 1998):

> The late Norman Williams, Jr., . . . observed in two influential articles that there is not one system of land-use control, but rather three, with each tending to work against the others. Williams noted that in most parts of the country, the property tax system supports major public services but does not bring in enough revenue to meet local needs. Inevitably, local officials are driven to take into account the revenue-raising capacities of various proposed land uses. This leads to a situation where "good ratables," such as industrial, most commercial, and high-value residential development—which bring in significant real property taxes and require little in the way of public services—are encouraged, but "bad ratables," such as quality affordable housing, are discouraged.

The second system concerns the impact of major public services, particularly transportation facilities, such as highway interchanges, and those for sewer collection and disposal. Williams observed that, while the construction of some facilities, such as schools, depends primarily on the type and intensity of land use in the area, other public facilities, such as water and sewers, can have such a strong influence on adjacent land use that they actually may dominate the official set of controls.

The third official system of land-use control that Williams identified is comprised of zoning, subdivision control, official mapping, and other devices. Counter-intuitively, Williams pointed out that the official system may actually be the least important. If the first two systems work to produce unbalanced development in search of good ratables or development in the wrong place due to lack of forethought and coordination, the third system, in Williams' words, "comes out third best."

The two articles referred to by the American Planning Association are Norman Williams, Jr., *The Three Systems of Land Use Control*, 25 Rutgers L. Rev. 80 (1970), and *id. Planning Law in the 1980s: What Do We Know About It?*, 7 Vt. L. Rev. 205 (1982).

At least in the case of infrastructure, the interrelationship identified by Professor Williams can also work in reverse. For instance, to be cost-effective without unrealistically large public subsidies, most forms of mass transit require a certain density of surrounding uses in order to provide a sufficient base of paying riders. Once land develops at low densities, policymakers are for all practical purposes precluded from recommending mass transit solutions at a later date.

5. *Utopia as policy.* Land use policymaking reaches its ultimate form in proposals for utopian alternatives to urban life, which invariably link planning to some overarching intellectual principle of social organization. While it would be an overstatement to say that land use planning has produced utopia in America, utopian ideas have nonetheless influenced the actual course of land use. In the twentieth century, perhaps the most famous, and also the most influential, was Ebenezer Howard's "Garden City," designed to reflect Howard's belief that relatively small communities organized around cooperative land ownership could mitigate the 19th century conflict between capital and labor.

This approach resulted in a compact village pattern surrounded and protected by a working greenbelt of fields, the prototype of which was constructed at Letchworth in England, beginning in 1903. See R. Fishman, Urban Utopias in the Twentieth Century 64–75 (1982). Letchworth in turn influenced the first wave of suburban-style development in the United States between the world wars, such as Radburn, New Jersey. Frank Lloyd Wright's utopian urban alternative, Broadacre City, fared less well in the 1930s. His followed Thomas Jefferson's belief that true democracy would reside in the virtues of a decentralized, self-sufficient, agrarian society of yeomen rather than capitalists. (Distrust of capitalism links Letchworth and Broadacres). When adapted to the technology of the automobile age, however, Wright's design produced a far-flung, low density blanket of semi-urbanization. See Fishman, *id.*, at 122–134. No part of Broadacre City was ever built in anything resembling the form that Wright imagined it, but in the decades after World War Two, critics, somewhat unfairly, saw Levittown as its alter ego.

2. CONFLICT AND CONFLICT RESOLUTION IN THE USE OF LAND

The preceding materials demonstrate that the use of land necessarily involves the development, consciously or otherwise, of a land use policy. If this were all, there would be little need for the evolution of land use controls. Imagine, for instance, that each of us actually occupied the statistical 7.5 acres that Rutherford Platt reports to be our predicted lot in the year 2000, and that we did so in complete isolation from our neighbors. Putting aside the obvious bleakness of a life lived this way, there would be no reason to interfere with each other's completely autonomous choices about how to use our allotted land. We would each have a land use "policy," but no matter.

Just the slightest relaxation of the assumption that we would live in *complete* isolation from our neighbors totally changes the picture, however. If I generate noxious fumes on my 7.5 acre island, for instance, the prevailing winds will blow them towards my neighbors just as, in the real world, smokestack pollution from the U.S. middle west ends up as toxic rain over New England forests. Inevitably, preferred land use policies can come into conflict with each other, as we seek to implement policies that maximize our own values. One function of the system of land use controls is to evolve policies that reduce the amount of conflict over land uses before conflict arises. Another is to provide a framework for resolving those conflicts that do occur.

Before beginning to introduce the system of land use controls that actually prevails in this country, based on comprehensive planning and local land use ordinances, the materials in this section invite you to notice that law is neither the only nor, on occasion, the best mechanism for resolution of land use disputes. Here, we will explore market mechanisms for resolution of land use controversies, as well as other forms of collective decisionmaking besides conventional zoning. It is true that regulation of the use of land has become pervasive in America, but only the most impassioned partisans will insist that either purely private or purely public control of land use decisionmaking will produce the best results. For thoughtful commentators, finding the proper balance between collective and individual decisionmaking, between "land use controls" on the one hand and "free markets" on the other, is the essence of the policy choice to be made.

It might be thought that posing this question is irrelevant at the start of a coursebook on the *law* of land use, for resort to law, by its very nature, suggests that the choice has already been made to collectivize the decision-making process. This is only partially true, however, for two interrelated reasons. Understanding the alternatives to the system of land use law (or to any particular law) is important because, as law students using this book already know, and others will soon come to realize, legal rules are often susceptible to multiple interpretations. Persuading decisionmakers to accept one interpretation and reject others is what lawyers do, and an understanding of how and why collective decisionmaking might or might not be preferable to private decisionmaking about a land use issue will sometimes be the key to effective analysis of an issue of land use law. And, for the same reasons, a persuasive critique might well convince legislators or administrators to add a law, amend a law, or repeal a law to make the system of land use work better.

To put these matters in perspective, consider the following problem, which is based on *PA Northwest Distributors, Inc. v. Township of Moon*, 584 A.2d 1372 (Pa. 1991). Relatively few land use disputes involve pornographic books, but Moon Township's commonplace decision to use "law" to resolve this community conflict over land use preferences is typical of the American way of land use practice. Do you agree with this approach? Is "law" the best way to resolve land use disputes? What are the alternatives?

PROBLEM

Blue owns property located on Beers School Road in the Township of Moon. Beers School Road is adjacent to the Greater Pittsburgh International Airport and is characterized by hotels, motels, restaurants, shopping centers, automobile dealerships, auto rental lots, gas stations, parking lots, and other commercial establishments. The zoning permits commercial uses, broadly defined. Blue leased the property to a tenant who opened an "adult" bookstore.

Four days later, the Moon Township Board of Supervisors published a public notice of its intention to amend the Moon Township Zoning Ordinance to regulate "adult commercial enterprises." On May 23, 1985, following a public hearing on the matter, the Moon Township Board of Supervisors adopted Ordinance No. 243, which ordinance imposes extensive restrictions on the location and operation of "adult commercial enterprises." The bookstore, by definition, is an adult commercial enterprise under the ordinance, and it does not and cannot meet the place restrictions set forth in the ordinance. Section 803 of the ordinance requires that no adult commercial enterprise can operate within 500 feet of a pre-existing school, hospital, nursing home, group care facility, park, church, establishment selling alcoholic beverages, or another adult commercial enterprise. Section 804 requires that no adult commercial enterprise can operate within 1,000 feet of an area zoned residential. Blue and his tenant contend that there is no site in Moon where the bookstore can operate legally.

The Zoning Officer of Moon Township has informed the bookstore that it is out of compliance with the ordinance and, as the ordinance requires, has ordered it to comply or move within 90 days. (After losing in various administrative and judicial proceedings, the Moon ordinance was invalidated by the Pennsylvania Supreme Court. The legal issues presented by the case are raised in Chapter 3, *infra*.)

A NOTE ON VARIOUS APPROACHES TO THE RESOLUTION OF LAND USE DISPUTES

Consider the range of ways that this conflict over the use of land in Moon Township might have been resolved. In doing so, we will put aside a world utterly without "law," land use or otherwise, where the disputants would simply square off and the one with superior force would win, at least until someone stronger came along. With the condition of minimal civility thus imposed, those who object to the dirty bookstore had at least three options available to them (can you think of others?):

Option 1. *Voluntary change.* Lawyers and politicians tend to overlook this option, because it doesn't normally require our services, but it is the option of choice for countless numbers of land use conflicts every day. Here, residents of Moon might have approached the owner of the bookstore and asked that he consider their preferences. If they did this early enough in the planning of the venture, the owner might have chosen to locate elsewhere, rather than face community opposition. Or, in a slightly less friendly approach to voluntary change, the community might have picketed the store once it opened, or picketed Blue's home or other business locations. Think of examples from your own experience where neighbors across the backyard fence or elevator lobby have resolved land use preferences either amicably or at least without resort to more formal mechanisms.

Option 2. *Purchase the right to change the offending use.* A well-heeled citizen might buy out the bookstore's lease, or buy the underlying fee from the landlord and evict the tenant, paying damages as necessary. Or a group of less affluent citizens might pool their resources to do the same. Why might an individual or a group of individuals be reluctant to do so, even if they could otherwise raise the money? Alternatively, the citizens could persuade Moon Township to use its power of eminent domain to "condemn" the lease or the underlying fee simple title, paying the lessee and lessor "just compensation" as necessary and putting the property to some other, public, purpose. Would this be more (or less?) effective than having private parties complete the buyout?

(Purchasing the right to change land uses need not be as confrontational as in the Moon Township example. Every time farm land is sold to a real estate developer for residential subdivision or for a suburban office park, the buyer is expressing a belief that the land can and should be put to better use than the farmer is making of it. A local government or the state acts similarly when it buys (through condemnation or otherwise) the land for an interstate highway, or a new community college.)

Option 3. *Compel the owner to change the offending use.* This is the approach taken in the actual case. Rather than persuasion (or after it had failed) and rather than outright purchase, the citizens of Moon expressed their preference that the land be used for something other than a dirty bookstore by amending the zoning code (the form of regulation that dominates the field) to prohibit the offending use. Under some circumstances, the citizens of Moon might have resorted to the governmental power of the courts to compel the discontinuance of the offending use, rather than going to the local legislature. Consider, for instance, a state whose common law would recognize this type of use as a "public nuisance"; or perhaps the objectors get lucky and discover an enforceable covenant running with the land that restricts the use of the land to single-family residents. Judicial enforcement of unwritten common-law rules is every bit as compulsory as enforcement of legislation, and the rules are often sufficiently flexible to give the judge a good deal of discretion in deciding what range of land uses is permissible.

Of these possible strategies, the purest example of a "market" approach is to purchase the change of use, as suggested in Option Two. Note, however, that either a single private individual, a group of individuals acting privately but in concert, or the government acting on behalf of all the individuals in the community can pursue this strategy. Does it matter which individual or group acts, so long as "compensation" is paid?

Option One, informal negotiation, is similar to a market transaction except that inducements other than a cash price are used as the medium of exchange. Do these inducements qualify as "prices"? Note further that Option One does not include the government as one of the entities that could offer inducements to voluntary change. Is this omission appropriate? Why might we insist that governments act only through more formal mechanisms?

Compelling change, the approach of Option Three, almost of necessity requires governmental involvement, because in our society only government has legitimate access to the power to compel compliance under most circumstances. Note, however, that the nuisance and covenants approaches to compulsory change start with private decisionmaking and become coercive only when courts (which are agencies of government) are willing to enforce private norms or contracts. Indeed, an informal threat to bring a nuisance or covenant lawsuit may be sufficient to induce "voluntary" compliance, taking us full circle back to Option One.

We now turn to the specifics, beginning with the pros and cons of market-based strategies. These materials may help reinforce your intuitive sense of the strengths and weaknesses of the various options, they may suggest additional options, or they may cause you to rethink your views. There are no certifiably "correct" answers. When you are done with the chapter (or perhaps later in the semester), you may want to reread the Moon Township problem to see how, if at all, you would answer differently.

a. Efficiency and Equity: Government Intervention and its Alternatives

In recent years, one of the most powerful critiques of the existing system of land use controls has been put forward by economists who argue that free markets operate best to resolve competition over the uses of land, and that the contemporary emphasis on land use *regulation* unduly interferes with this process. While not claiming that the private market, unaided, can resolve all land use conflicts, free market economists nonetheless advocate major changes to achieve a much less intrusive role for governments. What is the basis for the claim that free markets work best? Are there offsetting problems with the market approach that can be solved by regulation? How are we to know whether regulation is or is not appropriate in any given circumstance?

An important caution is in order at the outset. Ten pages do not an economist make. The study of economics is a major intellectual discipline, and scholarly work in the special field of land use economics is both extensive and complex. In the excerpts which follow, virtually all technical elaboration of the basic concepts has been eliminated; we paint with the broadest brush, simplifying the outline of the topic and filling in with only the primary colors. As lawyers, you must be able to recognize when expertise other than your own can be useful, and then know enough to ask the right questions so that the experts can help you reach your conclusion. Spotting the questions is the purpose of this section.

E. HEIKKILA, THE ECONOMICS OF PLANNING, pp. 25–26, 37, 39, 43–47 (Rutgers University, Center for Urban Policy Research, 2000)

To the economist, land use zoning is seen as an exercise in resource allocation, even if it may not normally be viewed in those terms by planners themselves. One of the most fundamental issues addressed by micro-economics [as it applies to land use markets.—Eds.] is how to allocate scarce resources in an efficient manner. If the quantity of land is fixed, as it is in most urban settings, then one is forced to make trade-offs. One more acre of land devoted to nonresidential uses, for example, results in one less acre devoted to residential use. From this perspective, zoning maps represent the planners' "solution" to the resource allocation problem. In preparing these plans (as zoning maps are sometimes called), planners must balance a range of considerations, among these economic efficiency. An efficient solution is defined as one that yields the greatest possible output (such as social benefit) for a given amount of input (such as land). An inefficient solution, by this same reasoning, is one that uses more inputs than necessary to achieve a given level of output. While there may be room for legitimate debate about what outputs are important (for example, whose benefits should count?), one would be hard pressed to argue in favor of an *inefficient* solution! After all, if we can receive more benefit from the same amount of land, why not do so?

. . . [U]nder certain conditions planners may expect the market to generate an allocation of land among competing uses in an efficient or benefit-maximizing manner. In other cases, such as in the case of externalities (effects that are not priced by the market), we may expect that the market solution is inefficient by the same definition. Where markets fail to generate optimal solutions there is the possibility that planning intervention may be warranted. Land use zoning represents a quantity-oriented mode of intervention, where zoning assigns each land use category a set quota of land as indicated by the land use maps referred to above. An alternative mode of intervention is price-based intervention, an option that planners would do well to consider to attain planning ends more effectively.

Market Failure

The term market failure applies to any situation where the market outcome does not produce the maximum social benefit. . . . [T]he market demand curves provide the marginal valuation of each parcel of land from *the owner's perspective*. This should be apparent because the market demand curve registers willingness to pay, and . . . willingness to pay is the standard measure of individual benefit in cost-benefit analysis. If the owner of the good is the only one who is affected by its consumption, then the owner's benefit is equal to the overall social benefit. However, it is not rare to encounter situations where the benefits or costs of the use of a good extend beyond the owner of the good in question. This is particularly so in the case of land use, as is evidenced by all the attention given to land use issues in public hearings on parcel-specific rezoning issues. In many such cases the general public is quite affected by visual distractions, traffic noise, "undesirable elements," noxious fumes, quality-of-life issues, or other environmental impacts that are not encapsulated in the market price of the parcel in question. These and similar effects are not internalized in or reflected by market prices and so they are termed *externalities*. They are effects that are external to market prices.

. . . [Externalities] provide a potential justification for intervention by planners into the land use market. The market develops the "highest and best use" of properties from the owners' perspectives, but this may not coincide with the land use allocation that maximizes social benefit. However tempting it may be, as planners we must resist the temptation to leap in at this point with cries of "market failure!" as a justification for wanton intervention in land use markets by way of zoning [because] market failure does not preclude the possibility of even worse regulatory failure.. . .

Price-Based versus Quantity-Based Intervention

The question remains whether price or quantity intervention in urban land markets is preferable from an economic perspective. As one might expect, the answer is not quite that simple, and there are persuasive arguments to be considered from either perspective. Relevant considerations include the relative information requirements of these two modes of intervention, the desirability of spatial contiguity of land uses, and issues of fairness or political process. There are also issues of institutional inertia, political palatability, and professional training to consider.

[As to information requirements, Heikkila argues that both zoning and price intervention pose a serious risk of acting on imperfect information, because it is difficult to ascertain the benefit-maximizing point for each land use choice. He then concludes as follows:] For price-based intervention, however, the market is left to uncover the new allocation . . . once the correct tax or subsidy has been specified. Moreover, as market conditions change, the market continues to adjust itself, while zoning intervention requires recalculation of the optimum allocation each time there is a fundamental change in market conditions.

As we have seen, price intervention has the potential advantage of allowing market allocations to evolve over time in response to changing market conditions. Built form, however, is durable and costly to alter to any great extent. Hence, decisions of the past may display considerable inertia whether quotas are in place or not. And if land uses are allowed to evolve in response to price signals, an additional element of uncertainty is thereby introduced into urban land markets. Moreover, zoning is often undertaken with an explicitly spatial or geographical frame of reference. Many of the advantages of price intervention mean very little unless there is careful reasoning behind the manner in which [price intervention through] fees or subsidies vary across the map. It is also very difficult to capture the interactive effects of land use externalities. For example, the externality costs imposed by nonresidential land may depend on what the surrounding land uses are. It may become very cumbersome and difficult to design a set of taxes or subsidies that properly accounts for such interactive effects.

Another issue is one of fairness and political process. [With respect to zoning, the author points out that if a zoning regulation requires the "wrong," i.e. inefficient, use of land, the market would eventually move the use to the most efficient, price-maximizing point, except for the fact that land use regulations cannot normally be bought and sold.] This potential gain is sorely tempting, and local newspapers in virtually every city are replete with stories about individuals who have interests in a particular parcel of land and who are alleged to have made unseemly if not illegal contributions to the political campaigns of the local elected officials who are charged with approving or denying applications to rezone specific parcels of land from one use category to another. . . . Similar arguments may be made regarding taxes and subsidies, for they too cater to specific interests (for example, homeowners who receive mortgage interest tax subsidies) who may be tempted to appeal in dubious ways to the political decision makers who enact legislation or bylaws that determine the scope and extent of those taxes and subsidies. From this perspective, seeking a rezoning of a specific parcel is akin to seeking special exemption from a tax that applies broadly to owners of a particular class of land. This line of reasoning suggests that the issue of undue or unfair influence over the political decision-making process is not specific to zoning regulation or to taxes and subsidies, but is instead more broadly applicable to a general class of circumstances where public officials hold discretionary powers over legislation that impacts specific individuals in favorable or unfavorable ways, and where this situation may open the way to influence peddling. . . . [T]hese issues should not be overlooked completely by planners nor by economists. . . .

A final observation is appropriate regarding the trade-off between quantity-based modes of intervention in land markets (such as zoning) and price-based modes (such as taxes or subsidies). . . . [I]t does not necessarily follow that intervention is called for at all. In light of the many costs associated with intervention of any kind, one might reasonably conclude that the burden of loss implied by [a demonstration of economic] inefficiency is less than the burden or cost implied by the very act of intervention. One such cost is of course the maintenance of a regulatory staff that draws its salary from the public purse. Additionally, as we have already seen, the information requirements for intervention are quite onerous; it may not be reasonable to expect that planners have sufficient information or knowledge to intervene wisely, and so the welfare or benefit gains from intervention may be more illusory than real. And finally, some might also argue that the infringement of freedom and the intrusion into the public domain inherent in government intervention represent a significant cost to social welfare. Based on these considerations, the range of choices may best be cast as quantity-based intervention, price-based intervention, and nonintervention.

NOTES AND QUESTIONS

1. *Efficiency.* The holy grail of economic analysis is to find the most "efficient" allocation of resources, which Heikkila defines as "one that yields the greatest possible output (such as social benefit) for a given amount of input (such as land)." Assuming, for the moment, that efficiency is an appropriate goal (as he points out, who will be so bold as to champion a policy of inefficiency?), what does it mean to be "efficient?" Heikkila's summary answer, "social benefit" is hardly a self-defining concept. Further elaboration is necessary:

> Economists' notion of efficiency is much more than the idea of cost minimization. A second and equally important component requires that resources that could produce two different products be assigned to the good that would add most to society's well-being. Controversy arises in determining which goods are most valuable to society.

> Economists' analysis of this controversy has three aspects. [A discussion of marginal pricing is omitted.—Eds.]

> The second aspect of economists' analysis of value is *consumer sovereignty*. They argue that individuals are best able to choose which goods will most improve their well-being. Thus, economists look to individual choices to determine which goods are most valued.

> Finally, economists use *willingness to pay* as a measure of how much individuals value any good [and hence their preference]. If resources could be used to produce either of two goods, efficiency requires that the good produced be the one for which individuals are willing to pay more.

> The concept of highest and best use of land is based on this idea of efficiency. If a developer is willing to pay more for land for conversion from agricultural to urban use than anyone is willing to pay to maintain a parcel in agriculture, the criterion of most highly valued use implies that the conversion would be an efficient use of land. . . . [Brown, *Market Failure: Efficiency or Equity?* in The Land Use Policy Debate in the United States 143, 144–145 (J. deNeufville ed., 1981).]

2. *"Whose benefits should count?"* Heikkila carefully qualifies his introduction to the efficiency principle by noting "legitimate debate" about which "outputs" should count. A moment's reflection will identify things, in addition to Heikkila's examples, that individual consumers might value, but which cannot readily be reduced to a "price": "visual distractions, traffic noise, 'undesirable elements,' noxious fumes, quality-of-life issues, or other environmental impacts . . ."

Many land use conflicts involve benefits that cannot be monetized easily, because there is no ready way to exclude any individual from enjoying the benefit at the same time as others. Economists call this kind of valuable asset a "public good"; the air we breathe is the classic example, because it can be shared without competition. Since supply is not affected by consumption, there can be no price in the conventional sense, and no price vehicle to measure "willingness to pay." In theory, of course, it would be possible to determine the market price each of us places on, say, the existence of an unspoiled coastal view by asking us how much we would be willing to pay for it, but the diffused and widespread enjoyment of this "asset,"and the fact that my coastal demand doesn't affect yours, makes it extremely unlikely that an accurate "price" could be determined. For one thing, the (immense) cost of finding out everyone's preference, which economists call a "transaction cost," has to be factored into the measure of whether a given allocation of resources is efficient; transaction costs are considered further in the following article. For another, each of us has an incentive to become what economists call a "free rider," concealing our true preference, knowing that we can get a "free ride" if someone else is foolish enough to fess up and pay.

3. *Wealth effects.* Elaborating on "willingness to pay" later in his treatise, Professor Heikkila observes that "willingness to pay may be constrained by ability to pay." He continues:

> For example, suppose that we are undertaking a cost-benefit analysis of a flood control project where the chief potential beneficiaries are low-income families living in housing of inferior quality. Their willingness to pay, in principle if not in fact, may be constrained by their low incomes. This is a common phenomenon, termed "wealth effect," where a person's marginal valuation of a benefit is colored by his or her wealth or lack thereof. In principle, what a cost-benefit analysis should strive for is a wealth-adjusted assessment of willingness to pay. In other words, how much would this person be willing to pay assuming that he or she had an average level of income or wealth? It is particularly important for the analyst to make this kind of adjustment . . . in cases where the distribution of costs and benefits is highly differentiated by income class or other categories of ability to pay. [Heikkila, *supra*, pp. 186–87.]

Although the problem of wealth effects is usually illustrated by impacts on low-income consumers, note that Heikkila's "average level of income" approach would significantly erode the advantage upper-income persons have to freely bid their preferences. How is one to make the adjustment he says is necessary? (He does not say.) Would doing so substantially undercut the "objectivity" of the market-based approach?

4. *Doing business in "the real world": the limits of economic modeling.* Microeconomic analysis is usually conducted in an abstract model of the world, rather than the real world itself. Modeling is a reasonable approach for economists to take, because the real world is far too complex to be understood all at once, even with modern computers to process data. Some of the other modeling assumptions that economists use to simplify analysis are identified in the following excerpt [the items have been renumbered to reflect omission of some technical details]:

> . . . The list of attributes essential to a perfectly functioning market is demanding: (1) many buyers and sellers, (2) good information about prices and quality, (3) ease of entry and exit for both buyers and sellers, (4) the ability to exclude individuals from making use of the service if they are unwilling to pay the price, (5) no cost to a transaction in the market, [and] (6) buyers and sellers fully internalize the

consequences of production and consumption. [Lee, *Land Use Planning as a Response to Market Failure* in The Land Use Policy Debate in the United States 149, 152 (J. deNeufville ed., 1981).]

Properly done, economic modeling with limiting assumptions such as these can provide valuable insights about the way things work in the "real world," but care must always be taken not to mistake the idealized world of the hypothetical for the messy reality of a world in which everything is connected.

All responsible economists, Heikkila included, acknowledge freely that perfect markets are unobtainable, and that "market failure" may justify intervention in the form of public regulation. In a classic article, Frank Michelman explored (among many other things), why this might be so, expanding on the concept of "transaction costs" introduced above.

MICHELMAN, PROPERTY, UTILITY AND FAIRNESS: COMMENTS ON THE ETHICAL FOUNDATIONS OF "JUST COMPENSATION" LAW, 80 Harvard Law Review 1165, 1174–1176 (1967)

[I]t will be useful to dwell briefly on the reasons why collective action should ever be necessary to the attainment of efficiency as above defined. For if an efficient change in the use of resources benefits gainers more than it costs losers, it might seem that gainers could be relied upon to make offers (directly to losers or indirectly through third-party enterprisers) which would suffice to induce losers to quit their objections to the change and, if they are in the way, to step aside. Conversely, if an inefficient change is one which costs losers more than it benefits gainers, it might seem that losers could be relied upon to make offers to induce gainers to abandon their proposal even if the losers could not directly block it.

This reasoning overlooks the extreme difficulty of arranging human affairs in such a way that each person is both enabled and required to take account of all the costs, or all the missed opportunities for mutual benefit, entailed by his proposed course of action before he decides whether he will embark on it. In addition, it overlooks the extreme difficulty of concluding voluntary arrangements to take account of such costs, or to exploit such opportunities, even after they become evident — a difficulty which stems from inertia, the expense (in time and effort) of bargaining, and strategic concealment. . . .

[A] government's regulatory activity may claim an efficiency justification. Consider an enactment requiring A to desist from operating a brickyard on land surrounded by other people's homes. The proposition implicit in the law (if we take efficiency to be its goal) is that A's neighbors stand to gain more from A's moving or altering his technology so as to reduce the nuisance than A or his customers would lose. It might, then, be argued that the measure is unnecessary because, if its premises are sound, we should expect the neighbors to offer A an acceptable sum in return for his agreement to cooperate. Conversely, the very fact that no such transaction has spontaneously evolved may be said to prove that A's operation, granting that the neighbors are sustaining some of its costs, is efficient. Apparently, it is worth more to A to continue than it would be worth to the neighbors collectively to have him stop. The argument, however, is imperfect. A sufficient criticism, for present purposes, is that the failure of the neighbors to make an offer may indicate, not that it would not be worthwhile for each of them to contribute some sum to a fund whose total would be acceptable to A in exchange for his moving, but only that they are unable to arrive (except by the expenditure of more time and effort than it would be worth) at a settlement with A, and among themselves, about what the total price should be and how the burden should be distributed. The situation will be complicated by the impulse of each neighbor to be secretive about his true preferences because he hopes that others will take up the whole burden, thereby yielding him a free benefit. And A, dealing with a group instead of with an individual, may turn more than usually cagey himself. There will, in addition, be side costs of drafting agreements, checking on their legality, and so forth.

NOTES AND QUESTIONS

1. *The Coase Theorem.* Professor Michelman's discussion of transaction costs is in part a reply to another classic article, Coase, *The Problem of Social Cost,* 3 J.L. & Econ. 1 (1960). In a situation similar to the brickyard example that Michelman gives (using neighboring landowners, a cattle rancher and a farmer), Professor Coase argued that the two would voluntarily resolve this land use conflict by the one buying out part or all of \the other's use until an "efficient" level of adjustment had been reached, one in which the benefits of the bargain are maximized for both parties. Coase's crucial insight, which supplies an important argument for a markets-based approach to land use policy, is that it doesn't matter whether the rancher or the farmer is given the initial legal entitlement to prevent the other's use. So long as the two are free to bargain, they will work themselves away from an initial all-or-nothing result to an economically "correct" solution.

At first glance, what has come to be called "the Coase Theorem" (a term Professor Coase did not use) might seem to have little practical applicability, since economists uniformly agree with Michelman that the transaction costs associated with the Coasean bargain are almost always too high to justify the effort. (Coase explicitly assumed zero transaction costs in his model, and acknowledged how limiting that assumption was.) In addition (as Professor Coase also recognized), we can only be indifferent to the initial allocation of rights under the "theorem" if both parties are similarly situated financially, i.e., that there is no "wealth effect." This problem may not occur so uniformly as does the transaction cost problem, but it will be more than widespread enough to be of serious practical concern. Moreover, both problems-transaction costs and wealth effects, actually suggest ways to justify collective action.

2. *Entitlements.* Consider first a regime in which the *a priori* zoning rule is merely the starting point for bargaining between the farmer and rancher, or between the brickyard and the homeowners, rather than a fixed rule that can only be altered by formal legislative action. (The latter, of course, is the most typical situation in "the real world.") Wealth effects can be mitigated, if not eliminated altogether, by taking care to assign the initial entitlement in some equitable way so as to equalize the bargaining power of the two parties. Doing so, of course, requires a more subjective judgment about what is "fair" than classical microeconomic theory would prefer. Consider this further suggestion from Professor Michelman's article:

> But we cannot stand on the assumption that efficiency is the only goal. Few people any longer doubt that governments are properly engaged in controlling the distribution of wealth and income among members of society, as well as in controlling resource use so as to maximize the aggregate social product. . . . For the purposes of this essay I propose to rely on a proposition which will, I believe, command general and intuitive agreement. The proposition is that a designed redistribution by government action will surely be regarded as arbitrary unless it has a general and apparent "equalizing" tendency — unless its evident purpose is to redistribute from the better off to the worse off. Progressive income taxes and social welfare programs are, of course, excellent examples of such measures. . . .
>
> [M]easures such as the restriction on foundry operations in residential areas and the conversion of a neighborhood street into an arterial highway may be accompanied by accidental losses which, while not justified by any recognized distributional precept, are universally admitted to be noncompensable. It appears, then, that a redistribution which would have been unacceptable if undertaken for its own sake may be tolerated if it is the accidental consequence of a measure claiming the independent justification of efficiency. . . .[Michelman, *supra*, at 1183]

3. *Collective markets.* Two other adaptations of the Coase Theorem become possible if we substitute collective action—the government—for one or both of the parties in the paradigmatic private market. First, as the representative of the community's welfare, the government could bargain with the adversely affected landowner for a shift from the initial entitlement represented by the zoning ordinance to a rule preferred by the landowner, by way of a variance, for instance, or a zoning amendment. By what mechanism would such a bargain be struck, it being contrary to accepted norms for the government to "sell" legislation? Would it matter how the initial entitlement was stated? Chapter 5, which details the law of variances, zoning amendments, and so forth, will demonstrate to you that as a practical matter, local governments often establish regulations a notch or two below what the market will probably prefer, with a view towards extracting concessions when a change in the "entitlement" is bargained for. See also the materials later in this chapter, dealing with alternative forms of dispute resolution.

The other way in which the Coasean bargain can be adapted to collective action is to see the zoning ordinance (or other form of regulation), not as establishing the initial entitlement, but as the community's collective judgment about what it thinks the ultimate private bargain would have been, had the parties been able to surmount transaction costs and other barriers to the smooth functioning of the market. Of course, the question then becomes, can collective decision making adequately represent the myriad components of the private bargain and therefore reach a demonstrably "efficient" solution? Not all legislators will accurately gauge the public will (nor, on all occasions, should they, if The Federalist #10 is to be believed). Power and money influence governmental deliberations (a point that Heikkila emphasizes, *supra*). Do lessened transaction costs and wealth effects problems come at the expense of heightened subjectivity, exactly what the impersonal "market" ideally avoids? Even those sympathetic to collective action concede the problem: "Governmental regulation requires collectively agreeable land use policies whose formulation presents severe difficulties. These policies must be based on what economists call an interpersonal comparison of personal utility — the collective compromise of widely variant social preferences. These comparisons are difficult to make because they require subjective value judgments." D. Mandelker, Environment and Equity 6 (1981).

4. *Public choice theory.* One way around this problem is suggested by what over the last thirty years has come to be called "public choice" theory. Public choice posits that there is a market for citizens' votes, a market within which political representatives bargain for votes by offering the most acceptable packages of positions on public issues. [See J. Buchanan & G. Tullock, The Calculus of Consent (1962).] If a politician accurately discerns the mood of the public, he or she is returned to office by an objective majority that speaks in roughly the same way as the market's equilibrium price. Of course, it may take several rounds of "bargaining" for this consensus to emerge, but that is also true of market transactions, which do not necessarily arrive at the "efficient" solution immediately. For a variant on this, see Fischel, The Economics of Zoning Laws § 5.5 (1985), suggesting a "median voter" model, in which government officials act as if a public referendum were held on every public issue. Another variant argues that competition between *municipalities*, as opposed to individuals, might serve to maintain regulation at "efficient" levels. It has been suggested, for instance, that the ability of an individual or business to "exit" a jurisdiction or refuse to enter it, may make it less urgent for courts to review and possibly strike down regulations that are perceived as inefficient. Under some circumstances, other municipalities might simply "compete" for these "consumers" of regulations by offering them a more attractive regulatory environment. See Been, *"Exit" as a Constraint on Land Use Exactions: Rethinking the Unconstitutional Conditions Doctrine*, 91 Colum. L. Rev. 473 (1991). Are all actors equally able to exercise their right of "exit?" Is there a risk that market imperfections in the competition between municipalities might drive regulation to sub-optimal levels under some circumstances?

5. *Judicial review.* Is there a legitimate role for courts to play in seeing that initial entitlements are assigned in ways that facilitate efficient bargains? (Recall that in the Problem based on the *Moon Township* case, *supra*, one set of choices to be made was to invoke "collective action" in the form of the courts.) Later in these materials, you will encounter varying styles of deferential or non-deferential judicial review given to different types of land use controversies. In *Krause*, *infra* Ch. 3, sec. C2b, for instance, a "garden variety" dispute between neighboring residential uses, the court gives substantial deference to the allocation of entitlements determined by the municipality. By contrast, in the celebrated *Mount Laurel* cases, *infra* Ch. 4, which involve claims that affordable housing is excluded from more affluent communities, the court

shifts a very heavy burden of persuasion against the municipality's allocations. The correctness of these decisions will be considered later; for now it suffices to see the linkage between such conventional legal techniques as burden of proof and the grander themes of microeconomics.

6. *Tradeoffs.* Although freely noting that market failure could justify collective action, Heikkila nonetheless hastens to warn us that the "temptation" to "leap in" with "unwarranted regulation" must be resisted. The foregoing suggests that while his warning may be a bit too categorical, it nonetheless captures the tradeoffs that must be made between the self-executing virtues of the hypothetical free market on the one hand, and the potentially more equitable, but error-prone process of regulation on the other. At the very least, the free market critique of land use controls must give the proponent of such controls pause from time to time. Is this regulation truly necessary? Does it facilitate efficient results? If not, how securely can we articulate the justification for departing from what we think the market would do? Conversely, those who admire the objectivity and dispassion with which a smoothly operating market functions (particularly when graphed) must constantly remind themselves to take a reality check from time to time, especially when market results favor (as they frequently tend to do) those with power and money over those without. On balance, does Professor Heikkila make a persuasive case for price-based intervention to address equity problems? How does Professor Michelman address this point?

Or is it a mistake to argue on the economist's terms? Some have suggested that we should simply reject the efficiency test as the basis for determining whether governmental regulation of land use is justified? Dean William Hines has written that the "ethical force" of an idea may provide a basis for governmental protection of natural resource areas even though the destruction of the resource area through development may be the efficient solution. Hines, *A Decade of Nondegradation Policy in Congress and the Courts: The Erratic Pursuit of Clean Air and Clean Water,* 62 Iowa L. Rev. 643 (1977):

> [U]nless restrained by some external force or internal command, mankind incessantly exploits and ultimately despoils or destroys natural environments. . . . [S]omewhere in the frenzied pursuit of more material possessions and a higher living standard it is morally necessary to think about what kind of world will be passed along to future generations. It is a sobering thought to reflect on the possibility that nature may not continue to exist as we know it. [*Id.* at 649.]

Hines was writing about programs in the national Clean Air and Clean Water Acts that protect "pure air" and "pure water" from further degradation. To what extent are his comments applicable to the land use conflict and control problems discussed in these notes? That question should accompany you as you traverse the rest of this book.

7. *Sources.* Richard Posner's treatise, Economic Analysis of Law (1998), now in its fifth edition, has heavily influenced this field for thirty years. For extensive collections of essays, see *Public Choice Theme Issue*, 6 Geo. Mason L. Rev. 709 (1998); *Symposium on Law and Economics of Local Government,* 67 Chi.-Kent L. Rev. 707 (1991). See also Stearns, *The Misguided Renaissance of Social Choice,* 103 Yale L.J. 1219 (1994); Elhauge, *Does Interest Group*

Theory Justify More Intrusive Judicial Review?, 101 Yale L.J. 31 (1991); Simon, *Social Republican Property*, 38 UCLA L. Rev. 1335 (1991); Hovenkamp, *Marginal Utility and the Coase Theorem*, 75 Cornell L. Rev. 783 (1990); Kelman, *On Democracy Bashing: A Skeptical Look at the Theoretical and "Empirical" Practice of the Public Choice Movement*, 74 Va. L. Rev. 199 (1988). For a set of earlier readings, see Economic Foundations of Property Law (B. Ackerman ed., 1975).

b. Other Private Ordering Solutions to Land Use Conflict Problems

As the preceding materials demonstrate, totally private ordering of land use decision making through market mechanisms is not a realistic option, but at the same time, dissatisfaction with the results achieved by conventional zoning regulations has led to a steady stream of alternative proposals that embrace, to a greater or lesser extent, elements of private ordering. In addition, the evolution in recent years of alternative dispute resolution techniques has added the possibility of "private order" dispositions even within the existing regulatory system. Note how these various devices fit into the framework of alternatives discussed in connection with the *Moon Township* case, *supra*. Consider, also, how well they should appeal to an enthusiast of market solutions, on the one hand, or of collective decision making on the other.

i. Covenants and Nuisance

One of the best-known of the proposed alternatives to zoning was outlined by Professor Robert Ellickson in an extensive article, *Alternatives to Zoning: Covenants, Nuisance Rules, and Fines as Land Use Controls*, 40 U. Chi. L. Rev. 681, 713–14 (1973). Ellickson offers a trenchant critique of the zoning approach and he makes a spirited case for a heavy infusion of private ordering, which he suggests could be based on venerable common-law concepts of covenants and nuisance:

> Existing property law provides for enforcement of many [private] agreements of this type, including covenants, leases, easements and defeasible fees. Covenants serve as a representative example of these consensual transactions between landowners; this category encompasses affirmative and negative obligations and is perhaps the most prevalent type of private agreement between neighbors.

Ellickson also notes that "[c]ovenants negotiated between landowners will tend to optimize resource allocation among them" because they "will enhance a developer's profit only if they increase his land values by more than the cost of imposing them. His land values will rise only if his home buyers perceive that the covenants will reduce the future nuisance costs they might suffer by an amount greater than the sum of their loss of flexibility in use and future administrative costs. . . .[A]ssuming equal bargaining power and information, consensual covenants will not involve inequitable gains or losses to any party."

He then suggests ways in which administration and judicial review could be modernized to better adapt devices such as covenants to modern conditions, but he also concludes that "[e]ven if covenant law were sensibly modernized, . . . covenants could play only a limited role in older established neighborhoods where land ownership is highly fractionated. Except for the simplest problems involving a few neighbors, land owners rarely meet as a group to draft agreements governing land use. . . . [T]he costs of organizing many people are apparently too high, and the risk of freeloaders too great, for private bargaining to take place." *Id.* at 718. Note the echoes of the Coase Theorem and its limitations.

To supplement covenants and other private ordering devices, Ellickson turns to nuisance rules in a modification of the Coase theorem:

> In order to promote economically productive behavior that cannot easily be achieved by bargaining and to satisfy community desires to reward virtuous activities, legal rules should seek to transfer wealth from those whose actions have unusually harmful external impacts and to those whose actions are usually beneficial to others. [*Id.* at 729–30.]

He provides the following rule for nuisance liability:

> [A]n aggrieved landowner establishes a prima facie case for nuisance when he shows that his neighbor has damaged him by carrying on activities, or harboring natural conditions, perceived as unneighborly under contemporary community standards. [*Id.* at 733.]

Even without Ellickson's imaginative proposal, common law nuisance is a rich and fertile bed of doctrine from which much of contemporary land use law arises. As part of that evolution, its main outlines are traced in Chapter 2, sec. A, *infra*.

NOTES AND QUESTIONS

1. *Covenants and equity.* Elsewhere in his article, Professor Ellickson acknowledges that efficiency solutions do not guarantee equitable ones, and he takes care to argue that private ordering through devices such as covenants "usually" will not produce unfair gains or losses. Is his assumption of equal bargaining power a realistic one in the type of covenant situations he describes? Ellickson also points out, correctly, that covenants can be misused to enforce racial segregation, a problem of market failure that justifies governmental regulation. *Id.* at 714–15. But he argues that income-restrictive covenants are acceptable absent monopoly power, because income level, unlike race, is not necessarily a permanent condition, and he doubts that a sufficient number of private homeowners would agree to income restrictive covenants, "opting instead for freedom to devote their holdings to more dense residential developments in the future." *Id.* at 715. He then concludes, "Zoning is clearly more effective than restrictive covenants in achieving class exclusions." *Id.* These issues are considered at greater length in Chapter 4.

2. *Uncertainty as a problem.* Jan Krasnowiecki also agrees that zoning is unworkable but believes that Ellickson's solution would "be even more costly and chaotic than zoning." Krasnowiecki, *Abolish Zoning,* 31 Syracuse L. Rev. 719, 721 (1980). His concern is with the developer. "[O]ne of my complaints about zoning is that it does not offer assurances early enough or with sufficient finality to protect the developer from unexpected expenditures." *Id.* at 721–22. He does not believe that Professor Ellickson's expanded nuisance law would help with this problem. For another alternative, see Kmiec, *Deregulating Land Use: An Alternative Free Enterprise Development System,* 130 U. Pa. L. Rev. 28 (1981) (use of preestablished performance standards).

3. *Does private ordering work?* Houston, Texas, is an unzoned city, the largest urbanized place in American without conventional land use controls. Instead, covenants are widely used, thus offering a field test of at least part of Professor Ellickson's approach. In Land Use Without Zoning (1972), Bernard Siegan argued that zoning does not make a difference because housing prices in Houston were lower than in comparable zoned cities. His study is questionable. As Professor Fischel points out, *supra,* ch. 11, housing prices reflect a variety of housing attributes, including access to employment as well as the effect of an adjacent undesirable use. Lower transportation costs to employment may offset the price effect of the undesirable use. Lower house prices in Houston could actually indicate the presence of undesirable uses that zoning may have prevented. See Fischel, *supra,* § 11.1. See also M. Goldberg & P. Horwood, Zoning: Its Costs and Relevance for the 1980s (1980) (reviewing the empirical studies and the Houston experience). Professor Seigan updated his argument and offered a Houston-Dallas comparison in Seigan, *Conserving and Developing the Land,* 27 San Diego L. Rev. 279, 295–304 (1990). See also MacDonald, *Houston Remains Unzoned,* 71 Land Econ. 137 (1995) (analyzing voting pattern in 1993 election in which Houston again rejected zoning proposal, and concluding that the "pattern of zoning suggests that the demand for zoning stems from its use as a device for excluding lower-income people from certain areas.").

4. *Does zoning work?* The Houston question can be reversed by asking whether there is any empirical evidence that zoning really works, as measured by its positive impact on housing prices. Earlier studies produced mixed results, and Fischel doubts their value, for the same types of reasons summarized in Note 3, above. More recently Pollakowski and Wachter, *The Effects of Land Use Constraints on Housing Prices,* 66 Land Econ. 315 (1990), found that zoning increased prices in Montgomery County, Md., particularly when combined with growth controls. See also McDonald and McMillen, *Land Values, Land Use, and the First Chicago Zoning Ordinance,* 16 J. Real Est. Fin. & Econ. 135 (1998) (ordinance had no effect on land values). Thorson, *An Examination of the Monopoly Zoning Hypothesis,* 72 Land Econ. 43 (1996), found higher prices in towns with monopoly power, but no clear evidence that it was used to limit housing production. Do Fischel's criticisms apply to these studies as well?

ii. Informal Dispute Resolution

What it is.—Considering the popularity of "alternative dispute resolution" systems in such other fields as disparate as contracts and divorce, it is surprising that ADR has yet to take hold extensively in land use disputes. Both governmental regulators and private landowners might well conclude that the high transaction costs of disputing the regulation could be lowered, and welfare gains realized (i.e., that a more "efficient" solution will result), by using informal, often private instrumentalities to search for a mutually agreeable resolution. Note that, in doing so, the government would serve essentially as the representative of the community at large in something like the bargaining from initial entitlements described by the Coase Theorem, *supra*. For a collection of land use case studies, see Lampe and Kaplan, *Resolving Land-Use Conflicts Through Mediation: Challenges and Opportunities*, Lincoln Institute of Land Policy Working Paper (1999).

Alternative dispute resolution encompasses a bewildering variety of techniques. Professor Menkel-Meadow summarized them as follows:

> [S]ome disputes involving parties with long-term relationships (such as neighbors, employees, family members) might go to mediation, whereas others would seek arbitration and a faster and cheaper award. Still others might get directed to a governmental ombudsman, and some disputants would opt for a full trial. . . . Skilled facilitators might improve communications between parties or help them discover their underlying needs and interests. Or, perhaps someone might give the parties a neutral evaluation of the facts in dispute or an analysis of the legal claims and rights they are demanding. [Menkel-Meadow, *Introduction: Symposium on AD*, 44 UCLA L. Rev. 1613, 1616 (1997).]

Lampe and Kaplan, *supra,* conclude that mediation can be successful in resolving land use disputes, provided that the disputants are motivated to resolve the issue and commit themselves to good-faith efforts to do so, using whatever ADR process is invoked. Motivation is present when the parties perceive either that they have no option, or that they stand to gain more than could be assured by conflict or adversarial processes. Initial legal rules, as Coase would predict, often contribute to creating the necessary motivation. In general, parties to land use dispute resolution find the process less costly and more personally satisfying than formal alternatives.

Almost everywhere in America, local land use bodies — planning boards and boards of adjustment — are made up of local citizens with little or no professional planning expertise, but with close knowledge of the local scene and an instinct for informality. As you become more familiar with the work of these boards, particularly in the many small communities that exercise land use powers, you may want to ask yourself whether such homegrown institutions alleviate the need for ADR or, on the contrary, make it even more urgent to have the ADR option.

Some examples.—For a description of several examples of informal dispute resolution see Susskind, et al., *Resolving Disputes the Kindler, Gentler Way*, Plan., Vol. 61, No. 5, at 16 (1995). In one example, a Virginia city proposed a new east-west connector road in its comprehensive plan to serve the northern, less-developed part of the city and relieve congestion on a heavily traveled primary road. Residents of the area rose up in arms, and the city agreed with neighborhood demands to put a hold on the new road until a consensus was reached, and to open up the road proposal for discussion. However, neighborhood leaders also agreed to join the planning staff in a training program on collaborative problem solving.

The training was held, and after all participants agreed on a process, a consensus committee met for a year to develop a new plan. The result was the development of a linear park that preserves the right-of-way for the connector road. The road would be built once traffic on the primary connector reached capacity.

This example raises a number of problems. The negotiation process was over a plan, so the question is whether this was an appropriate way to resolve the public interest questions that the adoption of a plan raises. You can reconsider this question after you review the materials on planning that follow. Negotiation of this type may be more justifiable in resolving conflicts between a neighborhood and a new use that seeks to locate in the neighborhood. Recall the Moon Township problem, *supra*. Which techniques might have worked there?

Sources.—See Netter, *Mediation in a Land Use Context*, 1995 Inst. on Plan. Zoning & Eminent Domain; M. Fulton, *Reaching Consensus in Land Use Negotiations*, Am. Plan. Ass'n, Plan. Advisory Serv. Rep. No. 417 (1989). For case studies of mediation in land use disputes that illustrate how mediation works, see D. Lampe & M. Kaplan, Resolving Land-Use Conflicts Through Mediation: Challenges and Opportunities, 51–53 (Lincoln Institute of Land Policy Working Paper, 1999). Mediation in land use disputes is encouraged in some state legislation. Cal. Gov't Code § 66031(a)(9); Pa. Stat. Ann. tit. 53, § 10908.1.

B. LAND USE CONTROLS: AN INTRODUCTION TO PLANNING

In Section A, we explored the interaction between private and public solutions to land use controversies, represented by the tension between the free market and government regulation. Implicit has been a focus on the short term, on solving the problem at hand within the facts as they presently exist. Keep in mind, however, that formulation of land use *policy* is an unavoidable consequence of land use itself, even if the "policy" is no more than to do whatever one is doing at the moment. There is, of course, a better way of approaching land use policy, and that is to *plan* in advance so that problems, if not eliminated, are at least minimized and, when they do arise, can be resolved within a well-thought-out set of criteria and preferences.

The most important characteristic of land use planning is that it is a method of collective decision making imposed to control private land use choices. Thus, land use planning is like zoning, subdivision review, historic preservation, and a host of other legal devices that will be introduced in this book; as opposed to these other topics, planning is distinguished only by its emphasis on future events, as opposed to the near term. Because land use planning thus emphasizes collective action, it arguably partakes of all the strengths and weaknesses of other forms of collective action. As you read the practical and theoretical discussions of planning issues which follow in this section, consider how they relate to the market versus regulation philosophies presented earlier in this chapter.

1. PLANNING THEORY AND THE PLANNING PROCESS

a. The Planning Concept

Is planning simply a response to market failure? As the following excerpt indicates, planning can seek to do much more than achieve an efficiency goal that cannot be achieved in the marketplace.

> Some of the arguments offered in support of comprehensive land use planning — reducing conflicts between incompatible land uses, coordinating private development and public infrastructure, preserving open space, programming capital improvements, emphasizing long-range alternatives as a balance to the short time horizons of entrepreneurs and politicians — can be related to evidence of market failure. . . . The arguments are used, however, to justify the traditional methods of plan making rather than to seek the best ways for solving the problems. Reducing incompatibilities between adjacent land uses could be accomplished through regulation of the land market, but that would not require land use plans.
>
> When land use policy emphasizes comprehensive planning, it implicitly forces a choice between accepting the outcomes of land markets or replacing land market decisions with political ones. Because market failure can be corrected without land use plans, the plan-making method can only be justified as a policy instrument on the basis of public objectives that override market performance. [Lee, *Land Use Planning as a Response to Market Failure,* in The Land Use Policy Debate in the United States 149, 158–59 (J. deNeufville ed., 1981).]

That planning modifies market outcomes through the application of policy judgments is not always stressed in the literature. Consider the following definition of the land use plan, which appears in the leading textbook on planning published by the American Planning Association, the national organization of planners:

HOLLANDER, POLLOCK, RECKINGER & BEAL, GENERAL DEVELOPMENT PLANS in The Practice of Local Government Planning 60 (F. So & J. Getzels eds., 2d ed. 1988)

City plans have masqueraded under a variety of names — development plan, urban plan, master plan, general plan, growth management plan, comprehensive plan, policy plan, and many more. These name changes reflect, in part, the evolution of what the plan is supposed to do. . . . Largely for convenience, this chapter will use the term *general plan.*

Despite changes in name and concept, some consistent threads characterize the general plan. First, it is a *physical plan.* Although a reflection of social and economic values, the plan is fundamentally a guide to the physical development of the city. It is the translation of values into a scheme that describes how, why, when, and where to build, rebuild, or preserve the city. This emphasis on the physical has been the source of much controversy and debate. Some planners have argued that the physical emphasis ignores people, but this argument has by and large been put to rest. A consensus has developed in the field that the general development plan is not a social service delivery plan, or a health plan, or a plan for economic promotion, although it may reflect or incorporate elements of all of these.

A second characteristic of the general plan is that it is *long range*. By that we mean it covers a time period greater than one year, usually five years or more. In years past the general plan was largely a snapshot or frozen image of what the city would look like twenty, thirty, or forty years later, but there was, unfortunately, little guidance as to how to get from the present to the utopian future. It is now recognized that an effective plan will express current policies that will shape the future rather than show a rigid image of the future itself. Nevertheless, a good plan should be slightly utopian. It should challenge and inspire us with a vision of what might be. It should also tell us how to get there.

A third characteristic of a general development plan is that it is *comprehensive*. It covers the entire city geographically — not merely one or more sections of the city. It also encompasses all the functions that make a city work, such as transportation, housing, land use, utility systems, and recreation. Moreover, the plan considers the interrelationships of functions.

Fourth, the general plan is a *statement of policy*, covering such community desires as quantity, character, location, and rate of growth (be it no growth, slow growth, rapid growth, or decline) and indicates how these desires are to be achieved. . . .

Finally, a plan is a guide to decision making by the planning commission, the city council, and the mayor or manager.

NOTES AND QUESTIONS

1. *A contrary view.* Perhaps the key to this excerpt is the observation that planning "is the translation of values into a scheme." Market-oriented economists and planning critics naturally are skeptical that collective community decision making through planning can produce the necessary values for the scheme. They argue that plans may violate the market-based efficiency test and produce socially undesirable outcomes. The following excerpt from an article by Professor Dan Tarlock forcefully makes this point:

> The legitimacy of a planning choice rests on the assertion that collective intervention produces a net gain in society's aggregate welfare. The planner's claim is that his or her proposal will promote the most efficient location of available resources. A planning choice would be readily perceived as legitimate if, by curing market imperfections, it achieved an allocation equivalent to that produced by a perfectly competitive market. Too often, however, the aggregate gains of a planning choice cannot be demonstrated. The planning choice is not designed to force internalization of external costs, which are difficult enough to quantify, but is based upon the assumption that the planner's re-distributive values are superior to those of the market and will result in a net gain to the aggregate welfare.

Planners assert that land use allocation is amenable to rational evaluation, that collective goals can be evaluated and welded into a single hierarchy of community objectives, and that planners can expertly resolve goal conflicts. The planner's choices derived from their overall perspective, however, risk being arbitrary since planners bear little responsibility for distribution of the costs or benefits of their activity. Furthermore, the choices are unlikely to rest upon a widespread consensus that would silence those adversely affected by short-term losses with the assurance of long-term efficiency gains. Thus the choices may be unacceptable to many members of the community because they appear unfair. The failure to consider the opportunity costs of the decision will make the planner's efficiency claims vulnerable to disproof. [Tarlock, *Consistency With Adopted Land Use Plans as a Standard of Review: The Case Against,* 9 Urb. L. Ann. 69, 75–76 (1975).]

2. *The coordination function.* Note also the statement in the planning association's textbook that the plan should be comprehensive and that it should consider "the interrelationship of functions." The last statement suggests that one function of planning is to serve a coordinating role, a function presumably as neutral as its role in promoting efficiency. Professor Alan Altshuler examined the coordinating role of planning in his classic, The City Planning Process (1965). He doubted whether the coordinating role of planning really is neutral:

One might say that the planner needs coordinative power only because some specialists stupidly or obstinately refuse to cooperate with others in the interests of "simple efficiency," even though no significant values are threatened. The answer is that . . . cooperation and isolation in themselves have important effects on organizations. . . . If an agency head claims that a measure advanced in the name of efficiency actually threatens important values . . . no outsider can refute him until he examines the bases of his arguments in detail. . . . In the end, no act of coordination is without its effect on other values than efficiency. [*Id.* at 331–32.]

3. *Types of plans.* Kaiser & Godschalk, *Twentieth Century Land Use Planning: A Stalwart Family Tree,* 61 J. Am. Plan. Ass'n 365 (1995), trace the evolution of planning and identify several types of plans. Planning began with a plan for physical development, which the authors call a "land use design plan," which now usually includes action strategies and identification of planning policies. It often proposes an "end-state," or a mapped depiction of where the community will be after a period of years.

A second type of plan, "a land classification plan, a more general map of growth policy areas rather than a detailed land use pattern, is now also common, particularly for counties, metropolitan areas, and regions that want to encourage urban growth in designated development areas and to discourage it in conservation or rural areas." Verbal policy plans focus "on written statements of goals and policy, without mapping specific land use patterns or implementation strategy." They can avoid the problem of keeping mapped plans up to date as a community grows, and also avoid the difficulty of

applying general policy to specific parcels of property. A development management plan "lays out a specific program of actions to guide development, such
as a public investment program, a development code, and a program to extend
infrastructure and services; and it assumes public sector initiative for influencing the location, type, and pace of growth."

As you read the zoning and other cases in this casebook, see if a comprehensive plan was involved and try to decide where it fits in this typology. Chapter
3 considers the requirement that land use regulations must be consistent with
a comprehensive plan. How does the type of plan adopted affect that problem?

4. The new edition of the book from which the selection on planning was
taken is The Practice of Local Government Planning (C. Hoch, L. Dalton &
F. So ed., 3d ed. 2000). Part Three of the book contains several chapters on
functional planning elements, including development planning.

b.   Planning Styles: "Rational Planning" and Its Alternatives

Current debate in planning theory focuses on what might be called planning
"style." At issue is the extent to which planning can and should be carried
out in an objective, fact-based, quasi-scientific mode. This is often referred to
as the "Rational Model" or "Rational Planning." Burby's excerpt, which
follows, was written while Rational Planning was, as he puts it, "in vogue,"
and while he, too, is critical of it, his description nonetheless gives a clear view
of how Rational Planning worked.

R. BURBY III, PLANNING AND POLITICS: TOWARD A MODEL OF PLANNING-RELATED POLICY OUTPUTS IN AMERICAN LOCAL GOVERNMENT (1968) (U.N.C. Envtl. Policies & Urb. Dev. Thesis Series No. 12)

The Rational model of planning, though currently in vogue, has been subject
to searching criticisms. The most pervasive of these has been that Rational
planning is irrelevant to a pluralist political system and as a consequence is
ineffective. Factors which contribute to this apparent ineffectiveness have
been attributed to almost every aspect of the Rational model.

First, the Rational model requires that goals be clearly and unambiguously
specified by policy-makers. This is the major task of the political system, but
there is mounting evidence that participants in the political process are not
likely to either specify social goals or limit their policy involvement to this
level of abstraction. . . .

The second step in the Rational model specifies that goals be translated into
design criteria (objectives). . . . Since physical objects and processes are infi-
nitely easier to measure than social objects and processes, it is sometimes
claimed that the Rational planner ignores the social aspects of program
design. As Perloff suggests, objectives originally defined in physical terms
have proven "difficult to 'translate' into meaningful social and human resource
terms." This problem is reinforced by the tendency of planners to be "method"
rather than "goal" oriented. . . .Thus, by focusing on proximate objectives

which can be measured, the planner may well achieve functional rationality, but be substantively irrational since there is no way of knowing whether a course of action is consistent or inconsistent with "higher order" goals. Further, since the Rational planning method is most effective when objectives are clearly and narrowly defined, the Rational model may lead to partial planning of the kind where normative choices can be reduced to a minimum and "expert" solutions to problems can be determined. This, in turn, can be seen to strengthen planners who are responsible for various disparate governmental functions to the detriment of coordinated public policy.

The problems inherent in devising a plan to maximize objectives, the third step in the Rational model, have been widely discussed. For instance, Braybrooke and Lindblom claim that limited intellectual capacity, limited knowledge, limited funds for analysis, limited ability to construct complete rational deductive systems, interdependence between fact and value, the openness of analytic systems, and the diversity of forms in which problems actually arise all conspire against "synoptic" rationality. . . . In recognition of these limitations, planning technicians tend to simplify the problem of devising courses of action to achieve even narrowly defined proximate objectives. Hitch and McKean write:

> . . . analyses must be piecemeal, since it is impossible for a single analysis to cover all problems of choice simultaneously in a large organization. Thus, comparisons of alternative courses of action always pertain to a part of the government's (or corporation's) problem. Other parts of the over-all problem are temporarily put aside, possible decisions about some matters being ignored, specific decisions about others being taken for granted. The resulting analyses are intended to provide assistance in finding optimal, or at least good, solutions to sub-problems: in the jargon of systems and operations research, they are sub-optimizations. . . .

The final phase of the Rational model consists of implementation of the plan or course of action which best achieves the stated objectives. However, deviation from any of the plan's specifications for public action will tend to upset the plan's internal consistency such that the extent that objectives will be obtained becomes indeterminate. Most empirical studies of public decision-making suggest that deviation from planned courses of action tends to be the rule rather than the exception. . . .

NOTES AND QUESTIONS

1. *Rationality and irrationality.* Responding to the type of Rational Planning approach described by Burby, one planner has observed that "[t]he strictly means-ends calculating approach to rational action, then, may lead to embarrassing . . . results. If instrumental rationality cannot address the issue of desirable goals and norms — if it must rather assume those as standards with respect to which to calculate streams of benefits and costs, pleasures and pains — then the purpose for which rationality is used is nonrational, perhaps irrational." Forester, *Practical Rationality in Planmaking,* in Rationality in Planning 48–49 (M. Breheny & A. Hooper eds., 1985).

2. *Values and variables.* In The City Planning Process ch. 6 (1965), Professor Altshuler points out that professionals are very careful in selecting the variables that define their competence. The most successful professionals narrow the variables they claim to define their professional role. Highway engineers, for example, limit themselves to the solution of traffic engineering problems. Perhaps planners suffer because the range of variables they must consider is so wide.

Altshuler suggests that the selection of the variables professionals consider critical to professional competence implies a selection of the values they are attempting to implement. "In practical affairs . . . men easily slip into treating familiar variables as ultimate values." *Id.* at 337. Value judgment appears to be inherent, even in a rational planning process.

Altshuler also points out that the law has adopted a judicial decisionmaking process that does not claim legitimacy through the selection of a limited number of variables and is conducted under conditions of great value uncertainty. The judicial process avoids the problem of value selection by slipping around them, basing its credibility on a process of collective decisionmaking through incremental change. Is there a lesson here for planners?

One commentator has indicated how the origins of planning led to a value-free approach to the planning process:

> The municipal reform arm of the Progressive Movement was one of the major forces shaping the new profession of planning. The Progressives had considerable faith in the capacity of professional expertise to solve problems ranging from environmental degradation caused by speculative resource extraction to the ugliness and disorder resulting from speculative urban development. But in adopting this paradigm, planners accepted the ideas that politics can be separate from planning or administration and that professionals would provide nonpartisan, expert advice to elected officials or municipal elites. This was the dominant image of professional planners into the period after World War II. [Howe, *Professional Roles and the Public Interest in Planning*, 6 J. Plan. Lit. 230, 231 (1992).]

3. *Planning for the "public interest."* It is sometimes suggested that a conception of the "public interest" can supply the values otherwise missing in the Rational Planning approach. Professor Howe notes that a value-neutral planner could draw on existing laws and policies adopted by elected decision makers for a "formal" definition of the public interest. She then goes on to explore other conceptions of the public interest that planners might use, such as utilitarian definitions that mirror market economics (public interest as the aggregation of expressed individual preferences, for instance), or a definition based on a (quasi-objective) identification of collective interests that override individual preferences, and, finally, what she calls the "good reasons" approach, essentially a process by which the planner can "refute emotivism through detailed analysis of how we actually talk and think about value judgments in general and ethical judgments in particular." Howe, *Professional Roles and the Public Interest in Planning*, 6 J. Plan. Lit. 230, 234–40 (1992).

Is anything gained by using the public interest label to describe one or another of these approaches? Is it simply another way of formulating the value choice problem? Reread the comments by Professor Tarlock, *supra,* on this point and see the excellent discussion in Steiner, *The Public Sector and the Public Interest,* in U.S. Congress, Joint Econ. Comm., 91st Cong., 1st Sess., The Analysis and Evaluation of Public Expenditures: The PPB System 13 (1969). Consider the link to the use of substantive due process in constitutional law. When a court tests a land use regulation against the general welfare principle, is it engaging the same kinds of issues as when the "public interest" paradigm is raised?

4. *Alternatives.* One commentator argues that the attack on Rational Planning discredited it and led to its collapse, but that none of the alternative planning theories that rose to replace it achieved a consensus among planners. Sanyal, Planning's Three Challenges in The Profession of City Planning 312, 324 (L. Rodwin & B. Sanyal eds., 2000). The following selection discusses recent trends in planning theory:

S. FAINSTEIN, NEW DIRECTIONS IN PLANNING THEORY, 35 Urban Affairs Review 451, 452–53, 472–73 (2000)

In this article, I discuss and critique contemporary planning theory in terms of its usefulness in addressing what I believe to be its defining question: What is the possibility of consciously achieving widespread improvement in the quality of human life within the context of a global capitalist political economy? I examine . . . three approaches referred to earlier under the rubrics of (1) the communicative model, (2) the new urbanism, and (3) the just city. In my conclusion, I defend the continued use of the just-city model and a modified form of the political economy mode of analysis that underlies it.

The first type, sometimes called the collaborative model, emphasizes the planner's role in mediating among "stakeholders" within the planning situation; the second, frequently labeled neotraditionalism, paints a physical picture of a desirable city to be obtained through planning; and the third, which derives from the political economy tradition, although also outcome oriented, is more abstract than the new urbanism, presenting a model of spatial relations based on equity. This typology of planning theories is not exhaustive — there remain defenders of the traditionally dominant paradigm of the rational model, as well as incrementalists who base their prescriptions on neoclassical economics, and Corbusian modernists, who still promote formalist physical solutions to urban decay. Nor are the types wholly mutually exclusive — each contains some elements of the others, and some theorists cannot be fit easily into one of the types. Nevertheless, each type can claim highly committed proponents, and each points to a distinctive path for both planning thought and planning practice.

Differences among the types reflect the enduring tension within planning thought between a focus on the planning process and an emphasis on desirable outcomes. In the recent past, neither tendency has fully dominated because theoretical orientations toward process and outcome have respectively affected different aspects of practice. Thus the concept of the rational model represented an approach based wholly on process, with little regard either to political conflict or to the specific character of the terrain on which it was working. As Beauregard put it, "In its fullest development, the Rational Model had neither subject nor object. It ignored the nature of the agents who carried out planning and was indifferent to the object of their efforts [i.e., the built environment]." This model has provided the metatheory for planning activity in the decades since the 1960s, incorporating the faith in scientific method that swept through the social sciences during the cold war period. Within planning practice, it has primarily been used for forecasting impacts and for program evaluation. . . . Outcome-oriented physical planning has left its mark on metropolitan areas in the form of urban renewal, low-density development, and spatial and functional segregation. . . .

The recent theoretical moves involved in the typology sketched earlier represent a reaction both to previously dominant modes of thought and also to events "on the ground." Thus the communicative model responds to imposition of top-down planning by experts deploying an Enlightenment discourse that posits a unitary public interest to be achieved through application of the rational model, the new urbanism is a backlash to market-driven development that destroys the spatial basis for community, and the just-city formulation reacts to the social and spatial inequality engendered by capitalism. In common with earlier critics of the rational model, . . . theorists within all three schools doubt the applicability of the scientific method to urban questions; none of the three approaches relies on scientific justification as the rationale for its vision. Whatever their differences, they are all three postpositivist.

. . .

RESURRECTING OPTIMISM

The three types of planning theory described in this article all embrace a social reformist outlook. They represent a move from the purely critical perspective that characterized much theory in the 1970s and 1980s to one that once again offers a promise of a better life. . . .Communicative planning theory has evaded the issue of universalism by developing a general procedural ethic without substantive content. The new urbanists claim that their design prescriptions incorporate diversity and provide people what they really want rather than what archaic zoning laws and greedy developers impose on them. Thus, even though they have been criticized for imposing a particular formula on others, they defend themselves by arguing that their conception incorporates difference. Just-city theorists work from "the basic premise . . . that any distributional conception of social justice will inevitably be linked to the broader way of life in which people engage". The argument is that although there may be no universal standards of good and bad, there are criteria for judging better and worse.

The Progressives of the previous period spent much of their energy condemning traditional planning for authoritarianism, sexism, the stifling of diversity, and class bias. More recent theorizing has advanced from mere critique to focusing instead on offering a more appealing prospect of the future. For communicative planning, this means practices that allow people to shape the places in which they live; for new urbanists, it involves an urban form that stimulates neighborliness, community involvement, subjective feelings of integration with one's environment, and aesthetic satisfaction. For just-city theorists, it concerns the development of an urban vision that also involves material well-being but that relies on a more pluralistic, cooperative, and decentralized form of welfare provision than the state-centered model of the bureaucratic welfare state.

At the millennium's end, then, planning theorists have returned to many of the past century's preoccupations. Like their nineteenth-century predecessors, they are seeking to interpose the planning process between urban development and the market to produce a more democratic and just society. The communicative theorists have reasserted the moral preoccupations that underlay nineteenth-century radicalism, the new urbanists have promoted a return to concern with physical form, and just-city theorists have resurrected the spirit of utopia that inspired Ebenezer Howard and his fellow radicals. Although strategic and substantive issues separate the three schools of thought described here, they share an optimism that had been largely lacking in previous decades. Sustaining this optimism depends on translating it into practice.

NOTES AND QUESTIONS

1. *The communicative model.* This planning model bears a strong family resemblance to the (small-*r*) "republican tradition" in American political thought, which contrasts the individualism of utilitarian and market philosophies with a search for "civic virtue":

> . . . [R]epublicanism offers the hope that freedom might encompass an ability to share a vision of a good life or a good society with others. We are thus empowered to engage in collective, deliberate, active intervention in our fate, in what would otherwise be the by-product of private decisions. Where liberalism embraces or at least accepts the politics of self-interest, republicanism expects citizens to place the general good ahead of personal gratification. [Pope, *Republican Moments: The Role of Direct Popular Power in the American Constitutional Order*, 139 U. Pa. L. Rev. 287, 296–97 (1990) (internal quotations and citations omitted).]

Critiquing the concept of communicative planning, Professor Fainstein says that it "should not be faulted for its ideals of openness and diversity. Rather, its vulnerability lies in a tendency to substitute moral exhortation for analysis. . . . [When] ideal speech becomes the objective of planning, the argument takes a moralistic tone, and its proponents seem to forget the economic and social forces that produce endemic social conflict and domination by the powerful." Fainstein, *supra*, at 455. Innes, *Information in Communicative Planning*, 64 J. Am. Plan. Ass'n 52 (1998), makes the obvious but often overlooked point that planners themselves need communicative skills. See also Anderson, *Doing the Impossible: Notes for a General Theory of Planning*, 25 Envt. & Plan. Bull. 667 (1998).

2. *Citizen participation and advocacy planning.* The War on Poverty programs of the 1960s required "citizen participation" in community development programs, which eventually led to the more general use of participatory techniques in many local planning programs. For an early study of several cities that includes a review of citizen participation in planning, see The State of the Art in Local Planning in Housing for All Under Law 5–1 (R. Fishman ed., 1978). Day, *Citizen Participation in the Planning Process: An Essentially Contested Concept?*, 11 J. Plan. Lit. 421, 432 (1997), surveys current participation practices, concluding that the issue is "a very complex one."

Citizen participation initially was seen as a means of involving lower income and disadvantaged groups in governmental decision making, but middle and upper income groups have been quick to realize the advantages of participation. This trend and its effect on planning were reviewed in a brilliant study of growth-management planning in Fairfax County, Virginia, which included a review of the citizen participation effort. G. Dawson, No Little Plans (1977). Dawson concluded that active citizens organized in small groups and backed by their local politician could be effective in blocking unwanted development close to their homes, over the opposition of professional planners. "Ironically, the considerable citizen involvement was the major factor in the county's failure to channel growth." *Id.* at 110–11.

3. *"The new urbanism."* If communicative planning can be criticized for elevating process over substance the new urbanism, also called by names such as "neotraditionalism" and "traditional neighborhood developments" (TNDs), risks the reverse: it starts with an *a priori* substantive conclusion — neighborliness is best — and then seeks to achieve that goal through physical design standards. The new urbanism takes inspiration from one of the most influential planning books of the 20th century, The Death and Life of Great American Cities (1961), in which Jane Jacobs applied meticulous techniques of observation to conclude that the "life" of urban places lies in their unplanned spontaneity of diverse uses. By contrast, to Jacobs the "death" of cities occurred in the rigidly planned tower-in-the-park utopias championed by the great European architect Le Corbusier, whose watered-down realization became the American urban renewal program of the 1950s and 60s.

4. *Designing neighborliness.* Exemplars of the new urbanism such as two Florida new towns, Seaside and Celebration (the latter sponsored by the Walt Disney Company as an outgrowth of its Orlando ventures), seek to emulate older forms and relationships in technically up-to-date buildings for modern life. Developments are kept to the scale of a traditional neighborhood to facilitate local travel without an automobile, building lots are relatively small, covenants require design features such as front porches to encourage street life, and public squares group civic and commercial usages. The most prominent popularizers of the new urbanism are the architects of the Seaside plan, Andres Duany and Elizabeth Plater-Zyberk. See Suburban Nation: The Rise of Sprawl and the Decline of the American Dream (2000) (with Jeff Speck). See also Foruseth, *Neotraditional Planning: A New Strategy for Building Neighborhoods?*, 14 Land Use Pol'y 201 (1997). Two recent books on Celebration are critical. D. Frantz and C. Collins, Celebration U.S.A.: Living in Disney's Brave New Town (1999); A. Ross, The Celebration Chronicles: Life, Liberty and the Pursuit of Property Values in Disney's New Town (1999).

Critics uniformly note that for a model that embraces diversity as a value, new urbanist communities such as Seaside and Celebration have made little, if any, progress towards either racial or economic integration. For a guide to 80 "new urbanist" communities in 29 states, see R. Arendt, Crossroads, Hamlet, Village, Town: Design Characteristics of Traditional Neighborhoods, Old and New (American Planning Association 2000).

5. *The new urbanism and zoning.* A frequent complaint of the "new urbanists" is that conventional zoning makes it difficult, if not impossible, to achieve TNDs. Nor, they say, does it help to allow neotraditional developments as an alternative to conventional zoning, using such techniques as conditional use permits or planned unit developments, if conventional developments can be built "as of right." Why might this be so? Edward Ziegler and Greg Byrne claim that "[if] TND projects continue to be accommodated by a PUD rezoning process that may involve any number of variances, and take as long as three or four years for final development approval, conventional suburban development will remain unchanged." *Zoning, New Urbanist Development, and the Fort Collins Plan,* American Planning Association Zoning News, Sept. 1998 (citing three unused Florida ordinances).

They argue that new urbanist standards must be mandated by the zoning code, including the following: mixed uses permitted in all zones, higher minimum densities (5–12 dwelling units per acre), small block size (4–12 acres), prohibition of gated communities, and design standards for streets, commercial buildings and both single-and multi-family residential developments that emphasize neighborhood integration. Tight, mandated standards are typical in TND ordinances. Can they create their own problems? A Connecticut statute authorizes a zoning district with design objectives similar to those for TND. Conn. Gen. Stat. § 8-2j.

6. *The "just city."* Professor Fainstein's sympathies are with this approach, which grows out of earlier arguments for "equity planning" as an antidote to the rigorous objectivity of Rational Planning. See Metzger, *The Theory and Practice of Equity Planning: An Annotated Bibliography,* 11 J. Plan. Lit. 112 (1996). Fainstein recognizes the tendency of her model to "identify unfairness without positing what was fair," 35 Urb. Aff. Q. at 467, and she argues that one solution is to "judge results," *id.* at 470, by identifying and studying cities that have achieved relatively equitable societies. For a provocative argument that planning's "sinister dark side" is its capacity for use as a tool of social control and oppression, see Yiftachel, *Planning and Social Control: Exploring the Dark Side,* 12 J. Plan. Lit. 395 (1998).

One difficulty with theories of planning that are based on ethical precepts (and a persuasive explanation of why "objective" models such as "rational planning" have persisted for so long), is that it is very difficult to get from the normative to the real. Fainstein concedes that "[in] applying the just-city perspective, one must judge results." Still, she is vague about how one *plans* to achieve this outcome. Compare Knaap, *The Determinants of Residential Property Values: Implications for Metropolitan Planning,* 12 J. Plan. Lit. 267 (1998) (planning may have contributed to the problem of housing affordability, suggesting solutions).

7. *Planning or plan?* In *Does Planning Need the Plan?*, 64 J. Am. Plan. Ass'n 208 (1998), Michael Neuman notes the powerful criticisms of traditional planning theory, but asks rhetorically

> [C]an planning go plan-less, naked and exposed? If the latter, why not call our profession "ning" and leave out "plan" entirely? As it is, planning is blessed with an active verb for its name, a characteristic it shares with other professions that nurture and bring things into being: nursing, engineering, design. City planners bring cities to life and life to cities, and have done so for centuries using plans.

He argues that "persuasive plans possess the power of the dream [that] can stir minds, arouse hopes, and inspire action," and that plans serve as the "loci of conflict" to engage various participants in civic life to articulate their own visions for the community.

8. *Sources.* For additional reading on planning theory, see Sager, *Planning and the Liberal Paradox: A Democratic Dilemma in Social Choice*, 12 J. Plan. Lit. 16 (1997); Johnson, Urban Planning and Politics (1997); See also Shipley and Newkirk, *Visioning: Did Anybody See Where It Came From?*, 12 J. Plan. Lit. 407 (1998); M. Branch, Comprehensive Planning for the 21st Century: General Theory and Principles (1998) (linking public and private planning processes); Beatley, Ethical Land Use (1994). On plan implementation and evaluation, see Forsyth, *Administrative Discretion and Urban and Regional Planners' Values*, 14 J. Plan. Lit. 5 (1999); Baer, *General Plan Evaluation Criteria: An Approach to Making Better Plans*, 63 J. Am. Plan. Ass'n 329 (1997); Talen, *Do Plans Get Implemented? A Review of Evaluation in Planning*, 10 J. Plan. Lit. 248 (1996); J. Grant, *On Some Public Uses of Planning "Theory,"* 66 Town Plan. Rev. 59 (1994) (Halifax, N.S. case studies). H. Smith, Planning America's Communities: Paradise Found? Paradise Lost? (1991) is a readable collection of case studies and commentaries by a non-academic practicing planner.

2. PLANNING PRACTICE

Some (but not all) of the planning theorists whose work was canvassed in the preceding materials acknowledged the tricky business of converting theory into practice. Indeed, until recently, the conventional lay wisdom about land use planning would have focused on old-fashioned "master plans," windy, visionary documents decorated with pretty maps and graphs, but mostly destined to sit on the shelf because of their irrelevance to everyday decision making. Even professional planners sometimes have had this attitude. See Krumholtz and Forester, Making Equity Planning Work 60 (1990) (describing new Cleveland Planning Director's surprise to find that his staff had not thought to consult the city's master plan while reviewing a major development proposal on land suitable for a city park).

The profession of planning is actively practiced on a daily basis, however, and increasingly the fruits of that practice are influencing the way land use controls are created and administered through zoning and other familiar controls at the "retail" level. We present here a brief introduction to state and regional planning, and to the preparation of "comprehensive plans" at the local level, as a foundation for considering further the relationship between planning and zoning in the rest of the book.

a. State and Regional Planning

Many land use problems extend beyond local government boundaries. As such, they clearly generate serious externalities when observed from a local perspective, and just as clearly cannot be regulated effectively (using either an efficiency or an equity criterion) in a series of local plans and ordinances. At the same time, the tradition of home rule governance, which is particularly strong with respect to land use issues, has generated strong political resistance to the adoption of statewide or regional planning and zoning systems. English planner Peter Self explains:

> As the government framework widens, the planning of urbanization becomes theoretically and functionally more rational but tends to lose its political base and to become entangled with other policy issues. It seems that popular identification of a common metropolitan existence and set of interests declines steadily with distance from the main center, although this may be due to the political separatism of suburbanites rather than to their failure to recognize the existence of common problems. Few people, however, appear to recognize their membership of an entity called an urban or city region or to appreciate its functional importance except for transportation — and popular interest in that subject grows spottier as one moves outward. The influence of other regional interests of an economic or ethnic character will in some circumstances be perceived much more strongly. [P. Self, Planning the Urban Region 147 (1982).]

Many states have land use programs for environmental areas, such as coastal areas, but comprehensive state and regional planning and land use control programs that cover more than just environmental resources also have a long history. Regional planning, as opposed to state planning, usually refers to a component part of a state, such as a metropolitan area; regional planning on occasion also crosses state boundaries, as in the [Lake] Tahoe Regional Planning Agency. As used here, the term "state and regional" refers to planning and land use controls that are comprehensive in scope and not limited to environmental protection. These programs are explored in more detail in Chapter 7.

State planning agencies and plans.—State planning has a long history, and can be said to have flourished modestly prior to World War II by keeping to a narrow agenda that focused on conservation of natural resources. When it revived beginning with pioneering efforts in Hawaii and New York in the late 1950s and early 1960s, the emphasis was broadened to comprehensive planning. The federal government also stimulated the creation of new state-level planning organization with grants and what came to be known as the A-95 program, a regulation that gave state and regional agencies the ability to review federal grant applications for consistency with state and regional plans, goals and policies. Although these programs have dwindled, state-level planning is today perhaps at its historical peak, driven by the increasing recognition that failure to deal with externalities-based problems burdens every level of government and every corner of society.

AMERICAN PLANNING ASSOCIATION, GROWING SMART LEGISLATIVE GUIDEBOOK: MODEL STATUTES FOR PLANNING AND THE MANAGEMENT OF CHANGE 4-11-4-15 (Phases I and II Interim Edition 1998)

TWO STATE PLANNING MODELS

Two general approaches in state planning have emerged and pose useful paradigms for drafting legislation. One has been called the *"civic model"* and is derived from the heritage and assumptions of city planning. The second has been termed the *"management model"* and draws its orientation and techniques from the science of organization management. Under the civic model, the state would engage in a goal-setting process, develop an inventory of resources and an appraisal of existing conditions that affect the ability to achieve those goals, identify a set of alternative actions, and compile a list of implementing measures. The civic model would produce plans affecting land use and critical areas management or addressing functional topics like transportation, water, and economic development. The plans would have regulatory impact and/or affect the programming of infrastructure to support particular growth strategies. . . .

[T]he purpose of the management model is to ensure that state agencies operate in an efficient and coordinated manner consistent with the priorities of the chief executive. Under the management model, the governor, who is the state's chief executive, implements policies and measures enacted by the state legislature and uses the planning system to exert administrative control over state agencies by establishing operational guidelines and directions for them.

Five main approaches to state land-use planning programs have been identified. . .

State planning—the state plans and zones land, develops and maintains a statewide land-use plan, and implements the plan through permits and regulations (Hawaii is the only state that comes close to this model).

State-mandated planning—the state sets mandatory standards, some of which apply to regional agencies and local governments, for those aspects of land use planning and control that involve state interests (e.g., Oregon, Florida).

State-promoted planning—the state sets guidelines for those aspects of planning that involve state interests, establishing incentives for local governments to meet the guidelines (e.g., Georgia).

State review (the "mini-NEPA system")—the state requires environmental impact reports for certain types of development, thus superimposing a second tier of review on the traditional local planning model. The state agency reviews the reports for conformance with state standards. (e.g., California, Washington).

State permitting—the state requires permits for certain types of development, thus preempting local review and permitting for those types of development. (e.g., Vermont).

NOTES AND QUESTIONS

1. *From state planning to state regulation.* As the Growing Smart commentary indicates, only Hawaii has come even close to following up state planning with direct state regulation of land uses. See Callies, *Land Use Planning in the Fiftieth State,* in State and Regional Comprehensive Planning 125 (P. Buchsbaum and L. Smith eds., 1993). Everywhere else, the thrust of the state planning process is to guide decisions made by the tangle of state, regional and local agencies that have pre-existing jurisdiction over various aspects of the land use process.

Several exceptions to this generalization are evolving, however, in which direct state involvement is becoming greater. These are: undesirable or controversial facilities that serve a broad area, sometimes called LULUs (Locally Unwanted Land Uses); areas of critical state concern, often (but not necessarily) environmentally sensitive areas; and developments that have a regional impact, or DRIs. A common thread is that local governments, where the authority to regulate is commonly placed, have little if any incentive to recognize either the positive or negative benefits that result outside their boundaries when these types of decisions are made. Unless control is shifted to a higher level to capture these externalities in the decision making process, sub-optimal results are likely to occur. See generally, American Planning Association, Growing Smart Legislative Handbook ch.5 (Interim Ed. 1998).

2. *"Environmental justice."* Scholars and community activists have argued for some time that a disproportionate share of society's most necessary but least pleasant land uses — toxic waste facilities or prisons, for example — end up in the least powerful cities or neighborhoods, often in communities of color. The "environmental justice" movement seeks to redress this imbalance and has raised concerns across a range of land use issues broader than environmental concerns alone. See Dubin, *From Junkyards to Gentrification: Explicating a Right to Protective Zoning in Low-Income Communities of Color,* 77 Minn. L. Rev. 739 (1993). The American Planning Association Legislative Guidebook at 5–8 through 5–11 recommends shifting responsibility to the state level, but there is little reason to think that this alone would change the political dynamic. Professor Dubin canvasses theories of judicial enforcement, including a right to "protective zoning." Professor Arnold advocates a different, locally focused strategy:

> The next frontier for both the movement and the focus of environmental justice scholarship, however, is land use planning by communities of color and low-income communities. Local neighborhoods can use land use planning to articulate visions for what they want their communities to be, and negotiate land use regulations to implement these visions. In other words, they would not be merely late participants in using existing rules to stop (or attempt to stop) current proposals for unwanted land uses, but also pre-siting participants in

developing the rules that will determine what will and will not go in their neighborhoods. . . . [T]he law is about more than litigation, rights, courts, and jurisprudence. The law is about problem-solving, policy making, participation, and regulation, all of which are part of the land use regulatory model. [Arnold, *Planning Milagros: Environmental Justice and Land Use Regulation*, 76 Denv. U. L. Rev. 1 (1998).]

For a careful but controversial study questioning some of the premises of the environmental justice movement, see Been, *What's Fairness Got to Do With It? Environmental Justice and the Siting of Locally Undesirable Land Uses*, 78 Cornell L. Rev. 1001 (1993).

3. *Areas of state concern.* Some states have created regional planning agencies with significant regulatory powers for critical natural resource areas. The extensive 1600 square mile Pine Barrens in southeast New Jersey are an example. The transfer of development rights program for this area is described in Ch. 7, *infra*. The state created a Pinelands Commission, which prepared a comprehensive management plan for the area. N.J. Stat. Ann. §§ 13:18A-8, 9. Local master plans and land use ordinances must conform to the Commission's comprehensive management plan, § 13:18A-12, and the Commission may disapprove any development not in compliance with the plan. § 13:18A-15. The approach has survived judicial scrutiny. See *Hovson's, Inc. v. Secretary of Interior*, 519 F. Supp. 434 (D.N.J. 1981), *aff'd on other grounds*, 711 F.2d 1208 (3d Cir. 1983). Appraisals include Collins, *How Is the Pineland Program Working?*, in Protecting the New Jersey Pinelands 274, 278–280 (B. Collins & E. Russell eds., 1988); R. Mason, Contested Lands 191 (1992). The Commission maintains an informative website at www.state.nj.us/pinelands/ which includes, inter alia, the most recent annual report; see also N.J. Pinelands Comm., The Pinelands Development Credit Program (1996). New York has a similar system for the 9375-square-mile Adirondack Park area in the northern part of the state, which was upheld against objections that it violated local home rule. *Wambat Realty Corp. v. State,* 362 N.E.2d 581 (N.Y. 1977), noted, 16 Urb. L. Ann. 389 (1979). See R. Liroff & G. Davis, Protecting Open Space: Land Use Control in the Adirondack Park 68–73 (1981), reviewed in 70 Cornell L. Rev. 361 (1985). For studies of special management areas that include the Pinelands and Adirondack Park, see Managing Land Use Conflicts (D. Brower & D. Carol eds., 1987).

4. *Sources.* American Planning Association, Growing Smart Legislative Handbook 4–7 through 4–11 (Interim Ed. 1998) contains an excellent short summary of the evolution of state and regional planning programs. A permanent edition of the Guidebook will be published. On early state planning, see Wise, *History of State Planning—An Interpretive Commentary* (Washington: Council of State Planning Agencies, 1977). The classic description of the rebirth of state planning, whose title has given a name to the modern movement, is Bosselman and Callies, The Quiet Revolution in Land Use Control (1971). See also Wickersham, *Note, The Quiet Revolution Continues: The Emerging New Model for State Growth Management Statutes*, 18 Harv. Envtl. L. Rev. 489 (1994). Deyle and Smith, *Local Government Compliance with State Planning Mandates: The Effects of State Implementation in Florida,*

64 J. Am. Plan. Ass'n 457 (1998), finds highly variable compliance, attributable to weakness in implementation at the state level. State programs that regulate land use are considered in Ch. 7, *infra*.

b. Regional Planning Agencies and Plans

Regional planning also has a respectable history, although many of the notable early efforts were privately sponsored (including the landmark New York City Regional Plan of the 1920s). As with state plans, the New Deal had some success encouraging the adoption of regional plans, but the real era of growth began in the 1950s and 1960s, when Congress added regional planning requirements to a number of federal assistance programs, such as housing, transportation, and environmental protection, and when federal funding became available. During its first term, the Reagan Administration substantially dismantled the federal programs that funded regional planning, because of the administration's emphasis on increasing the responsibilities of state governments. Federally mandated regional planning survives, but now concentrates almost entirely on transportation planning for transportation projects funded under federal legislation. Like state plans (and for the same reasons), regional plans became an increasingly important factor in land use regulation in the 1990s, particularly in larger states where there was political value in recognizing distinct sub-areas of the jurisdiction.

AMERICAN PLANNING ASSOCIATION, GROWING SMART LEGISLATIVE GUIDEBOOK: MODEL STATUTES FOR PLANNING AND THE MANAGEMENT OF CHANGE 6-5—6-6 (Phases I and II Interim Edition 1998)

WHAT IS REGIONAL PLANNING?

Regional planning is planning for a geographic area that transcends the boundaries of individual governmental units but that shares common social, economic, political, natural resource, and transportation characteristics. A regional planning agency prepares plans that serve as a framework for planning by local governments and special districts.

Throughout the United States, there are regional planning agencies that are either voluntary associations of local government or mandated or authorized by state legislation (e.g., the Metropolitan Council in the Twin Cities or the Metropolitan Services District in Portland, Oregon). These exist for purposes of undertaking plans that are typically advisory in nature; providing information, technical assistance, and training; coordinating efforts among member governments, especially efforts that involve federal funding; and providing a two-way conduit between member governments and the state and federal agencies. Regional planning agencies may also serve as a forum to discuss complex and sometimes sensitive issues among member local governments and to try to find solutions to problems that affect more than one jurisdiction. Sometimes these organizations have direct regulatory authority in that they not only prepare plans, but also administer land-use controls through subdivision review and zoning recommendations, review proposals for major developments whose impacts may cross jurisdictional borders, and review and certify local plans.

States authorize the establishment of these regional planning agencies in different ways. In some parts of the country, the regional agencies take their structure from general enabling legislation (e.g., for regional planning commissions or councils of government). In other places, they are the product of intergovernmental or joint powers agreements, as in California, or interstate compacts, as with the Delaware Regional Planning Commission in the Philadelphia, Pennsylvania/Camden, New Jersey area, or the Tahoe Regional Planning Agency in Nevada and California. In some states, regional agencies are created by special state legislation that applies only to one particular agency (e.g., the Northeastern Illinois Planning Commission in the Chicago area, or the Cape Cod Commission in Massachusetts). In still others, they may exist as private, voluntary organizations that seek to provide a regional perspective through independently prepared plans and studies. Examples of such agencies are the Regional Plan Association in New York City and Bluegrass Tomorrow in the Lexington, Kentucky area.

NOTES AND QUESTIONS

1. *Defining regions.* State plans, by definition, follow existing state boundaries, but sub-state (regional) plans require choices. McDowell offers general criteria and examples:

> The region . . . should have a clear organizing concept which sets the theme for planning. A metropolitan area and a river basin are good examples. The former is a continuously urbanized community cut by numerous local jurisdictional boundaries but struggling to function as a single entity for many purposes. The second is a large interdependent land and water resource — also cut by many local jurisdictional boundaries as well as state lines — whose long-term preservation and productivity depends heavily upon its management as a single system. The stronger the organizing concept, the clearer will be the purposes of the region — and the benefits to be planned for. [McDowell, *Regional Planning Today,* in The Practice of State and Regional Planning 133, 151, 152 (F. So, I. Hand & B. McDowell eds., 1986).]

Note that McDowell's examples generate different regions for different purposes (a river basin may extend beyond a metropolitan area, for instance, or the latter may sprawl across more than one basin). Functional regions may also exert reciprocal influences on each other. For example, a housing region will be defined in part by how long it takes to travel to work, while a transportation region will be defined in part by where people live and at what densities. How are overlapping functional regions to coordinate their planning?

2. *Councils of Government and Metropolitan Planning Organizations.* In the 1960s and 1970s most of the old-style regional planning commissions, dominated by private citizens who were community leaders, gave way to Councils of Governments (COGs) made up of elected, politically accountable officials of local governments in the region. Instead of enabling powerful leaders to

collectively make significant policy commitments and back them up with action, often just the opposite occurred, as political tensions in the COGs led to logrolling and timid or no action on regional plans. By the late 1970s there were 39 federal programs that required or supported COGs, and many states established counterpart statewide systems for state programs. A reduction in federal aid has led to a substantial drop in the number of regional councils. For a discussion of regional planning see D. Rothblatt & A. Sancton, Metropolitan Governance Revisited (1998).

3. *Transportation planning.* The importance of transportation facilities, such as highways, to land use and development and the availability of federal funding has made transportation planning the most important planning function regional agencies exercise today. The Transportation Planning Act for the 21st Century (TEA-21), delegates the planning functions to MPOs. There is a similar program for transportation planning at the state level. See 23 U.S.C. § 134. The statement of purpose in proposed regulations for regional transportation planning indicates the scope of this planning process:

> The purpose of this subpart is to implement 23 U.S.C. 134 and 49 U.S.C. 5303–5306 which require that a Metropolitan Planning Organization (MPO) be designated for each urbanized area (UZA) and that the metropolitan area have a continuing, cooperative, and comprehensive transportation planning process that results in plans and programs that consider all transportation modes and support metropolitan community development and social goals. The transportation plan and program shall facilitate the development, management and operation of an integrated, intermodal transportation system that enables the safe, efficient, economic movement of people and goods. [23 C.F.R. § 141.300.]

Transportation issues as they relate to land use planning are considered further in Chapter 7. The Clean Air Act adds another element by requiring regional transportation plans to comply with plans the state adopts to implement the Clean Air Act. 42 U.S.C. § 7506. This provision has proved highly controversial in areas where it has led EPA to block highway projects because of air quality violations.

4. *Metropolitan agencies with land use powers.* Two metropolitan areas, the Twin Cities area in Minnesota and the Portland, Oregon metropolitan area, have metropolitan planning agencies that have land use powers. The Minnesota legislation requires the Metropolitan Council, which is an appointed body, to prepare a development guide and to "review the comprehensive plans of local government units . . . to determine their compatibility with each other and conformity with metropolitan system plans." *Id.,* § 473.175. For a case applying the consistency requirement to uphold a city's rejection of a conditional use permit see *BBY Investors v. City of Maplewood,* 467 N.W.2d 631 (Minn. App. 1991).

The powers of the Portland agency, which are exercised under the state land use program, are even more extensive. See Ch. 7, *infra.*

c. The Local "Comprehensive Plan"

The comprehensive land use plan is the analog at the local level of state and regional planning. It provides a statement of goals and objectives for the future development of the community and a map that translates the goals and policies of the plan into land use designations indicating where different types of development should be located. The planning policies and plan map together provide a basis for decisions on land use in the land use regulation process. The plan also provides policies and locations for the public facilities, such as highways, which are required to serve future land uses. The Pennsylvania planning legislation that follows is an example of a modern local planning enabling statute.

PENNSYLVANIA STATUTES ANNOTATED TIT. 53

§ 10301(a) The comprehensive plan consisting of maps, charts and textual matter, shall include, but need not be limited to, the following related basic elements:

(1) A statement of objectives of the municipality concerning its future development, including, but not limited to, the location, character and timing of future development. . . .

(2) A plan for land use, which may include the amount, intensity, character and timing of land use proposed for residence, industry, business, agriculture, major traffic and transit facilities, utilities, community facilities, public grounds, parks and recreation, preservation of prime agricultural lands, flood plains and other areas of special hazards and other similar uses.

(2.1) A plan to meet the housing needs of present residents and of those individuals and families anticipated to reside in the municipality, which may include conservation of presently sound housing, rehabilitation of housing.in declining neighborhoods and the accommodation of expected new housing in different dwelling types and at appropriate densities for households of all income levels.

(3) A plan for movement of people and goods, which may include expressways, highways, local street systems, parking facilities, pedestrian and bikeway systems, public transit routes, terminals, airfields, port facilities, railroad facilities and other similar facilities or uses.

(4) A plan for community facilities and utilities which may include public and private education, recreation, municipal buildings, fire and police stations, libraries, hospitals, water supply and distribution, sewage and waste treatment, solid waste management, storm drainage, and flood plain management, utility corridors and associated facilities, and other similar facilities or uses.

(4.1) A statement of the interrelationships among the various plan components, which may include an estimate of the environmental, energy conservation, fiscal, economic development and social consequences on the municipality.

(4.2) A discussion of short- and long-range plan implementation strategies, which may include implications for capital improvements programming, new or updated development regulations, and identification of public funds potentially available.

(5) A statement indicating the relationship of the existing and proposed development of the municipality to the existing and proposed development and plans in contiguous municipalities, to the objectives and plans for development in the county of which it is a part, and to regional trends.

NOTES AND QUESTIONS

1. *History.* The basis for modern local planning is found in a Standard City Planning Enabling Act (1928), proposed by the Department of Commerce. In a crucial misstep, however, the Act provided that the planning function should be optional at the local level, not mandatory, and many fewer jurisdictions adopted formal comprehensive (or "master" plans) than adopted zoning ordinances. The legal status of the plan has been much changed in recent years by the adoption of a mandatory planning requirement in many states, sometimes accompanied by a requirement that zoning be consistent with the plan.

The drafters of the Act were explicit that adoption by the legislature was not required. In notes to the Act, they pointed out that the plan should cover a period of years longer than the term of any council; that the council deals with "pressing and immediate needs" and not with long-term policy; that the plan in any event will presumptively be binding on the council when it determines public expenditures (see § 9); and that a hostile council may overturn a plan adopted by an earlier council. Some modern planning enabling acts require adoption by the council and some do not. To what extent do the various theories of planning discussed in this chapter suggest that legislative adoption is preferable?

The model act makes the plan applicable to both public and private development, with little recognition that the role of the planning process and the problems of legal implementation are very different in these two situations. While the plan's proposals that affect private development are to be directly implemented through legal techniques such as zoning, the model act provides only a weak veto over public development (requiring a two-thirds vote in the planning commission). Title II of the model act does provide a link between the plan and the approval of subdivisions, however.

A puzzling provision in the Act authorizes municipalities to prepare a "zoning plan" as well as other plan elements. The purpose of the zoning plan is not clear, and this provision no longer appears in state land use legislation.

All states now have planning enabling legislation, but the original model provided by the model act has been substantially modified in most states. Certain elements, such as the optional nature of the plan, adoption by the legislative body and its application to public and private development, are still present.

2. *Optional and mandatory plan elements.* The Pennsylvania legislation also requires an "energy conservation plan element," which is to detail the impact of each plan element on energy use and measures to reduce energy consumption and promote the "effective utilization of renewable energy resources." *Id.,* § 10201.2. For a similar list of planning elements contained in the 1975 New

Jersey Municipal Land Use Law, see N.J. Stat. Ann. § 40:55D-28. New Jersey also requires a housing element, a recreation element, a conservation element, a historic preservation plan, and "[a]n economic plan element considering all aspects of economic development and sustained economic vitality." Many states are less specific, however. The American Planning Association Legislative Guidebook recommends that land use, housing, transportation and community facilities elements be mandatory, along with a statement of issues and opportunities, and a program for implementation. It would provide an "opting-out" procedure for elements dealing with economic development, critical and sensitive areas, and natural hazards, and it would make other elements (e.g., human services, community design, historic preservation) optional. See *id.* at 7--61.

3. *Improving planning legislation.* The American Planning Association's model enabling act for local planning is based on a series of important premises: that different types of communities (e.g., mature suburbs, developing areas) will require different types of plans; that planning must be done in a regional context and with citizen participation; that plan elements must be consistent with each other; and that planning must be an on-going process. The Guidebook also warns that plans must be drafted with realistic assumptions about local and regional land markets, and with due concern for constitutional takings limits. The American Planning Association strongly recommends that local planning be mandated by the state, but it also acknowledges political constraints on some states' ability to do so. See generally, American Planning Association, Growing Smart Legislative Guidebook (Interim Ed. 1998) at 7–61 to 7–67; *id.* at 7–54 to 7–61 (history of model acts); *id.* at 7–9 to 7–18 (organizational structures for local planning).

For discussion of the organizational structure for planning see *id.*, 7–9 to 7–18. The model act authorizes the creation of a local land planning agency, but its philosophy is that "the local government should be given as much discretion as possible in structuring the planning function."

4. *Substantive plan requirements.* Notice that the Pennsylvania legislation is neutral with respect to the content of most planning "elements," such as land use, but mandates substantive planning policies for other elements, such as housing. The Standard Planning Act did not contain substantive policies for any of the elements for which it authorized planning. This was a critical decision that allowed local self-determination in planning and land use regulation, a legislative delegation only weakly corrected by paragraph (5) of the Pennsylvania legislation. This provision, which is also common to other state planning acts, has had very little practical effect.

The substantive affordable housing requirements in the Pennsylvania planning legislation are an attempt to prevent exclusionary suburban zoning, which is one of the negative social consequences of the failure to provide substantive planning policies. This issue is discussed in Chapter 4, *infra.* Are there any other areas of planning concern where the statute should provide substantive policies? California requires a "local open-space plan for comprehensive and long-range preservation and conservation of open-space land within its jurisdiction." Cal. Gov't Code § 65563. Is this substantive? A Supreme Court case considered taking problems raised by this uncommon planning requirement. See Ch. 2, *infra.*

5. *Internal consistency.* Paragraph 4.1 of the Pennsylvania legislation requires "a statement of the interrelationships among the various plan components." California's planning legislation has a similar provision, which requires the general plan to "comprise an integrated, internally consistent and compatible statement of policies." Cal. Gov't Code § 65300.5. These provisions attempt to remedy the failure of the Standard Planning Act to require plans to state an internally consistent planning policy. The California courts have applied this requirement to invalidate plans found to have internally inconsistent elements. See *Concerned Citizens of Calaveras County v. Board of Supvrs.,* 212 Cal. Rptr. 273 (Cal. App. 1985).

7. *Planning and discretion.* Courts have begun to use plans to curb abuse of the freewheeling discretion that characterizes modern land use practice. This can have unintended but important consequences.

> One of the key issues that arises in the design of a planning system for local government is the tension between the need for flexibility to make decisions and the need to limit discretion. A city council, which must deal with a dynamic environment and must enter into a political bargaining process in which the final outcome is unpredictable, requires discretion to make decisions as problems and opportunities materialize. On the other hand there is pressure . . . [to] want the city council to adopt plans and stick to them. . . .Reduction of the city council's discretionary authority is intended to minimize capricious decisions. [Rider, *Local Government Planning: Prerequisites of an Effective System,* 18 Urb. Aff. Q. 271 (1982).]

One consequence of the use of planning to curb discretion is that policy decisions are pushed forward to the plan making stage, perhaps before true consensus has been reached, rather than delayed to the decision making stage. The plan may be overly generalized as a result. As Rider states, "[t]he adoption of a plan, far from signaling the arrival at a consensus . . . will more likely signal the opening of a new round of negotiations." *Id.* at 276. In a later article he urges "rejection of the plan as a standard and rejection of the related concept of 'consistency' which requires decisions to be consistent with a plan." Rider, *Planning as a Multicentric Process,* 57 Town Plan. Rev. 159, 161 (1986). Note that the rational planning model, with its emphasis on objectivity, may be most useful in limiting discretion. Is this an argument for or against rational planning?

7. *Sources.* For historical treatment of the Standard Planning Enabling Act, see Black, *The Comprehensive Plan* in Principles and Practice of Urban Planning at 349, 353–55 (W. Goodman & E. Freund eds., 1968). For additional background on the adoption of the Standard Planning Act, see T. Kent, The Urban General Plan 28–38 (1964). For a modern treatment see R. Burby & P. May, Making Governments Plan: State Experiments in Managing Land Use (1997). For a comprehensive text on planning, see E. Kelly & B. Becker, Community Planning: An Introduction to the Comprehensive Plan.

3. AN INTRODUCTION TO LAND USE CONTROLS

a. Why Enabling Legislation Is Important

It is only a slight exaggeration to say (as many have) that local governments exist for two purposes: to operate public schools, and to control the use of land. It thus becomes important to understand how state and local law — constitutional and statutory — shapes the exercise of zoning power at the local level. Indeed, a thorough study of state and local government law, a task well beyond the scope of this book, is essential for anyone contemplating practice in the field of land use controls. A brief introduction is in order, however.

b. Delegation Doctrine

In the United States, local governments ("municipal corporations") possess no inherent right of self government. They exist as creatures of the state, created for the purpose of carrying out tasks at the local level that are assigned to them by the state legislature. When this is done, the state is said to have "delegated" authority to the municipality to act on a certain subject. Because the municipality has no inherent legislative power of its own, when disputes arise about the scope of local regulation, it often becomes important to determine whether a given power has in fact been "delegated" to it by the legislature. If the municipality has acted outside its delegated authority, the act will fail.

In virtually all states, the legislature is required to act with respect to municipalities by "general laws" whenever possible, a reform which limits the possibility of specific meddling in the affairs of individual municipalities. Second, in about half the states, the constitution provides for "home rule," which allows individual municipalities to act with respect to local matters without a delegation of authority from the state legislature.

Some states have held that their home rule powers authorize the adoption of zoning ordinances, but all states have passed enabling legislation that authorizes zoning.

Mention was made earlier of the Standard Zoning Enabling Act of 1926. This model act was, in fact, a draft "general law" offered for use by state legislatures to delegate to municipalities the power to zone. In the years after 1926, using the SZEA as a guide, most states did exactly that. It might be thought that the SZEA or something like it might not be necessary in "home rule" states, but as a general rule this is not so. Home rule power is granted to municipalities only to the extent that "local" matters are affected, and most states have concluded that zoning is of sufficient statewide concern that the state legislature may continue to control the subject.

As one might suspect, this matter of delegating power to local governments, particularly in the form of "general laws" that must cover a myriad of different situations, offers rich opportunity for interpretation of the scope of the grant. "Dillon's Rule," named after a prominent 19th century treatise writer (and judge), posited that grants should be narrowly construed. Most states have reversed Dillon's Rule by statute, judicial interpretation, or specific constitutional command (for the latter see N.J. Const. Art. IV, § 7, ¶11). Broad delegations broadly interpreted are now the rule, but it is important to recognize that the underlying doctrinal structure remains. Courts can sometimes rein in an abuse of delegated power at the local level by holding that it violates an ambiguous provision of the zoning enabling act. They can also focus political attention on an issue by refusing to construe a power as within the grant, meaning that the legislature will have to amend the law (with attendant political debate) if it wants a given result. You should be alert to these and other uses of delegation doctrine as you proceed.

c. Zoning Enabling Legislation

All of the fifty states have zoning enabling legislation for municipalities, and many states also have zoning enabling legislation for counties. As has been mentioned, the most influential early form was the Standard State Zoning Enabling Act (SZEA), which was prepared under the aegis of the United States Department of Commerce and first published in mimeographed form in 1923. Zoning legislation is described more fully in Chapter 3, *infra*, but at this point, as you move forward to discuss takings doctrine, it is essential to know that most states have authorized zoning through legislation.

d. The Practice of Local Zoning

To a considerable extent, the remainder of this book addresses "the practice of local zoning." As you proceed, you will begin to develop a feel for the rich tapestry of people, institutions, and events that are involved. To help you get started, however, we will suggest here some of the things to be watching for.

Zoning ordinances and zoning change.—The zoning ordinance is the basic tool of land use regulation. The ordinance itself is normally enacted as local legislation by the governing body of the municipality according to general state law and the applicable zoning enabling act. Although there is an increasing tendency to place the relevant regulations in a single, comprehensive, well-indexed ordinance, significant rules affecting the use of land, such as subdivision and site planning rules, will often be found scattered throughout the local code, as well as in the laws of separate regulatory bodies (a county or a water conservation district, for instance).

For many reasons, the enacted zoning ordinance will frequently serve as a starting point for discussion about the use of a particular piece of land, rather than a self-executing "rule." Euclidean zoning is static, in that it describes a fixed state of permitted uses, and changing circumstances over time may render it obsolete. This is particularly a problem in smaller jurisdictions (which is to say, most jurisdictions with zoning powers) that do not have the budget or the professional staff to monitor and update regularly. If a would-be developer uncovers an attractively out-of-date provision affecting a piece of land and takes steps to develop "as of right," the municipality may find itself scrambling to prevent an inappropriate (or at least undesired) use. Some of the least attractive misuses of public power can occur under these circumstances, as well as some of the most opaque judicial decisions.

The zoning "game."—The late Richard Babcock gave our topic an indelible label in his 1966 book, The Zoning Game. Two decades later, with Charles

Siemon, he "revisited" the zoning game with a collection of highly readable
stories about zoning fights he had participated in as a developer's lawyer.
Babcock and Siemon, The Zoning Game Revisited (1985). Here are some of
the book's concluding thoughts, edited into a single excerpt, to carry with you
as you begin your own study. (The case names refer to the episodes in the
book.)

> Often, zoning is put down as political. So, what else is new? Of
> course, it is highly political; perhaps that is why it is so exciting a
> game. Some planners seem not to understand this or, if they do, they
> are appalled, as though it were a cockroach in the cola bottle. But that
> is a circumstance one must anticipate before the game begins. The
> lawyer for the developer or landowner must always expect to lose in
> the trial court. A trial judge, after all, is part of the home scene and
> may not be able to avoid the infection of "neighborism" that permeates
> the community. As one observer of the trial court's decision in *Her-
> nandez* notes, "Bumpy [the judge's nickname] wasn't going to let the
> Mayor get away with it."
>
> Corruption is not the fundamental problem in land use, although
> it does exist. Rather benign manipulation continues to affect the
> system. The problem lies with the parochialism, the NIMBY complex,
> with which the process is festooned. It is this intellectual corruption
> that has saturated land use regulation for fifty years and shows little
> sign of abating. The locals are too selfish or bloody close to the actions
> to bring any objectivity to their judgment. Recall the old gentleman
> in Palm Beach who testified against any further adjacent high-rises
> because the high-rise buildings they lived in were enough. [*Id.* at 259,
> 260–61, 262.]

Of course, the "neighbors" would say many of the same things (and more)
about developers and their lawyers. Who has the better of it is for you to
consider as you read on.

Chapter 2

THE CONSTITUTION AND LAND USE CONTROLS: ORIGINS, LIMITATIONS AND FEDERAL REMEDIES

This chapter traces, roughly in chronological order, the origins and changing treatment of land use law pursuant to the federal constitution. We begin, however, with a brief review of the common law of nuisance, because it is the critical legal antecedent for land use regulation, federal and otherwise. As you read these nuisance cases, consider how they deal with the market/regulation and rationality/values dichotomies that were explored in Ch. 1.

A. NUISANCE LAW

BOVE v. DONNER-HANNA COKE CORP.

236 App. Div. 37, 258 N.Y.S. 229 (1932)

EDGCOMB, J.:

The question involved upon this appeal is whether the use to which the defendant has recently put its property constitutes a private nuisance, which a court of equity should abate.

In 1910 plaintiff purchased two vacant lots at the corner of Abby and Baraga streets in the city of Buffalo, and two years later built a house thereon. The front of the building was converted into a grocery store, and plaintiff occupied the rear as a dwelling. She rented the two apartments on the second floor.

Defendant operates a large coke oven on the opposite side of Abby street. The plant runs twenty-four hours in the day, and three hundred and sixty-five days in the year. Of necessity, the operation has to be continuous, because the ovens would be ruined if they were allowed to cool off. The coke is heated to a temperature of around 2,000 degrees F., and is taken out of the ovens and run under a "quencher," where 500 or 600 gallons of water are poured onto it at one time. This is a necessary operation in the manufacture of coke. The result is a tremendous cloud of steam, which rises in a shaft and escapes into the air, carrying with it minute portions of coke, and more or less gas. This steam and the accompanying particles of dirt, as well as the dust which comes from a huge coal pile necessarily kept on the premises, and the gases and odors which emanate from the plant, are carried by the wind in various directions, and frequently find their way onto the plaintiff's premises and into her house and store. According to the plaintiff this results in an unusual amount of dirt and soot accumulating in her house, and prevents her opening the windows on the street side; she also claims that she suffers severe headaches by breathing the impure air occasioned by this dust and these offensive

53

odors, and that her health and that of her family has been impaired, all to her very great discomfort and annoyance; she also asserts that this condition has lessened the rental value of her property, and has made it impossible at times to rent her apartments.

Claiming that such use of its plant by the defendant deprives her of the full enjoyment of her home, invades her property rights, and constitutes a private nuisance, plaintiff brings this action in equity to enjoin the defendant from the further maintenance of said nuisance, and to recover the damages which she asserts she has already sustained.

As a general rule, an owner is at liberty to use his property as he sees fit, without objection or interference from his neighbor, provided such use does not violate an ordinance or statute. There is, however, a limitation to this rule; one made necessary by the intricate, complex and changing life of today. The old and familiar maxim that one must so use his property as not to injure that of another (*sic utere tuo ut alienum non laedas*) is deeply imbedded in our law. An owner will not be permitted to make an unreasonable use of his premises to the material annoyance of his neighbor if the latter's enjoyment of life or property is materially lessened thereby. This principle is aptly stated by Andrews, Ch. J., in *Booth v. R., W. & O.T.R.R. Co.* (35 N.E. 592, 594, N.Y.) as follows:

> The general rule that no one has absolute freedom in the use of his property, but is restrained by the co-existence of equal rights in his neighbor to the use of his property, so that each in exercising his right must do no act which causes injury to his neighbor, is so well understood, is so universally recognized, and stands so impregnably in the necessities of the social state, that its vindication by argument would be superfluous. The maxim which embodies it is sometimes loosely interpreted as forbidding all use by one of his own property, which annoys or disturbs his neighbor in the enjoyment of his property. The real meaning of the rule is that one may not use his own property to the injury of any legal right of another.

Such a rule is imperative, or life to-day in our congested centers would be intolerable and unbearable. If a citizen was given no protection against unjust harassment arising from the use to which the property of his neighbor was put, the comfort and value of his home could easily be destroyed by any one who chose to erect an annoyance nearby, and no one would be safe, unless he was rich enough to buy sufficient land about his home to render such disturbance impossible. When conflicting rights arise, a general rule must be worked out which, so far as possible, will preserve to each party that to which he has a just claim.

While the law will not permit a person to be driven from his home, or to be compelled to live in it in positive distress or discomfort because of the use to which other property nearby has been put, it is not every annoyance connected with business which will be enjoined. Many a loss arises from acts or conditions which do not create a ground for legal redress. *Damnum absque injuria* is a familiar maxim. Factories, stores and mercantile establishments are essential to the prosperity of the nation. They necessarily invade our cities, and interfere more or less with the peace and tranquility of the neighborhood in which they are located.

One who chooses to live in the large centers of population cannot expect the quiet of the country. Congested centers are seldom free from smoke, odors and other pollution from houses, shops and factories, and one who moves into such a region cannot hope to find the pure air of the village or outlying district. A person who prefers the advantages of community life must expect to experience some of the resulting inconveniences. Residents of industrial centers must endure without redress a certain amount of annoyance and discomfiture which is incident to life in such a locality. Such inconvenience is of minor importance compared with the general good of the community. . . .

Whether the particular use to which one puts his property constitutes a nuisance or not is generally a question of fact, and depends upon whether such use is reasonable under all the surrounding circumstances. What would distress and annoy one person would have little or no effect upon another; what would be deemed a disturbance and a torment in one locality would be unnoticed in some other place; a condition which would cause little or no vexation in a business, manufacturing or industrial district might be extremely tantalizing to those living in a restricted and beautiful residential zone; what would be unreasonable under one set of circumstances would be deemed fair and just under another. Each case is unique. No hard and fast rule can be laid down which will apply in all instances. . . .

The inconvenience, if such it be, must not be fanciful, slight or theoretical, but certain and substantial, and must interfere with the physical comfort of the ordinarily reasonable person. . . .

Applying these general rules to the facts before us, it is apparent that defendant's plant is not a nuisance *per se,* and that the court was amply justified in holding that it had not become one by reason of the manner in which it had been conducted. Any annoyance to plaintiff is due to the nature of the business which the defendant conducts, and not to any defect in the mill, machinery or apparatus. The plant is modern and up to date in every particular. It was built under a contract with the Federal government, the details of which are not important here. The plans were drawn by the Kopperas Construction Company, one of the largest and best known manufacturers of coke plants in the world, and the work was done under the supervision of the War Department. No reasonable change or improvement in the property can be made which will eliminate any of the things complained of. If coke is made, coal must be used. Gas always follows the burning of coal, and steam is occasioned by throwing cold water on red hot coals.

The cases are legion in this and other States where a defendant has been held guilty of maintaining a nuisance because of the annoyance which he has caused his neighbor by reason of noise, smoke, dust, noxious gases and disagreeable smells which have emanated from his property. But smoke and noisome odors do not always constitute a nuisance. I find none of these cases controlling here; they all differ in some particular from the facts in the case at bar.

It is true that the appellant was a resident of this locality for several years before the defendant came on the scene of action, and that, when the plaintiff built her house, the land on which these coke ovens now stand was a hickory grove. But in a growing community changes are inevitable. This region was never fitted for a residential district; for years it has been peculiarly adapted for factory sites. This was apparent when plaintiff bought her lots and when she built her house. The land is low and lies adjacent to the Buffalo river, a navigable stream connecting with Lake Erie. Seven different railroads run through this area. Freight tracks and yards can be seen in every direction. Railroads naturally follow the low levels in passing through the city. Cheap transportation is an attraction which always draws factories and industrial plants to a locality. It is common knowledge that a combination of rail and water terminal facilities will stamp a section as a site suitable for industries of the heavier type, rather than for residential purposes. In 1910 there were at least eight industrial plants, with a total assessed valuation of over a million dollars, within a radius of a mile from plaintiff's house.

With all the dirt, smoke and gas which necessarily come from factory chimneys, trains and boats, and with full knowledge that this region was especially adapted for industrial rather than residential purposes, and that factories would increase in the future, plaintiff selected this locality as the site of her future home. She voluntarily moved into this district, fully aware of the fact that the atmosphere would constantly be contaminated by dirt, gas and foul odors; and that she could not hope to find in this locality the pure air of a strictly residential zone. She evidently saw certain advantages in living in this congested center. This is not the case of an industry, with its attendant noise and dirt, invading a quiet, residential district. It is just the opposite. Here a residence is built in an area naturally adapted for industrial purposes and already dedicated to that use. Plaintiff can hardly be heard to complain at this late date that her peace and comfort have been disturbed by a situation which existed, to some extent at least, at the very time she bought her property, and which condition she must have known would grow worse rather than better as the years went by.

To-day there are twenty industrial plants within a radius of less than a mile and three-quarters from appellant's house, with more than sixty-five smoke-stacks rising in the air, and belching forth clouds of smoke; every day there are 148 passenger trains, and 225 freight trains, to say nothing of switch engines, passing over these various railroad tracks near to the plaintiff's property; over 10,000 boats, a large portion of which burn soft coal, pass up and down the Buffalo river every season. Across the street, and within 300 feet from plaintiff's house, is a large tank of the Iroquois Gas Company which is used for the storage of gas.

The utter abandonment of this locality for residential purposes, and its universal use as an industrial center, becomes manifest when one considers that in 1929 the assessed valuation of the twenty industrial plants above referred to aggregates over $20,000,000, and that the city in 1925 passed a zoning ordinance putting this area in the third industrial district, a zone in which stockyards, glue factories, coke ovens, steel furnaces, rolling mills and other similar enterprises were permitted to be located.

One has only to mention these facts to visualize the condition of the atmo-sphere in this locality. It is quite easy to imagine that many of the things of which the plaintiff complains are due to causes over which the defendant has no control. At any rate, if appellant is immune from the annoyance occasioned by the smoke and odor which must necessarily come from these various sources, it would hardly seem that she could consistently claim that her health has been impaired, and that the use and enjoyment of her home have been seriously interfered with solely because of the dirt, gas and stench which have reached her from defendant's plant.

It is very true that the law is no respecter of persons, and that the most humble citizen in the land is entitled to identically the same protection accorded to the master of the most gorgeous palace. However, the fact that the plaintiff has voluntarily chosen to live in the smoke and turmoil of this industrial zone is some evidence, at least, that any annoyance which she has suffered from the dirt, gas and odor which have emanated from defendant's plant is more imaginary and theoretical than it is real and substantial.

I think that the trial court was amply justified in refusing to interfere with the operation of the defendant's coke ovens. No consideration of public policy or private rights demands any such sacrifice of this industry.

Plaintiff is not entitled to the relief which she seeks for another reason.

Subdivision 25 of section 20 of the General City Law gives to the cities of this State authority to regulate the location of industries and to district the city for that purpose. Pursuant to such authority the common council of the city of Buffalo adopted an ordinance setting aside the particular area in which defendant's plant is situated as a zone in which coke ovens might lawfully be located.

After years of study and agitation it has been found that development in conformity with some well-considered and comprehensive plan is necessary to the welfare of any growing municipality. The larger the community the greater becomes the need of such plan. Haphazard city building is ruinous to any city. Certain areas must be given over to industry, without which the country cannot long exist. Other sections must be kept free from the intrusion of trade and the distraction of business, and be set aside for homes, where one may live in a wholesome environment. Property owners, as well as the public, have come to recognize the absolute necessity of reasonable regulations of this character in the interest of public health, safety and general welfare, as well as for the conservation of property values. Such is the purpose of our zoning laws.

After due consideration the common council of Buffalo decreed that an enterprise similar to that carried on by the defendant might properly be located at the site of this particular coke oven. It is not for the court to step in and override such decision, and condemn as a nuisance a business which is being conducted in an approved and expert manner, at the very spot where the council said that it might be located. A court of equity will not ordinarily assume to set itself above officials to whom the law commits a decision, and reverse their discretion and judgment, unless bad faith is involved. No such charge is made here . . . .

I see no good reason why the decision of the Special Term should be disturbed. I think that the judgment appealed from should be affirmed.

All concur.

Judgment affirmed, with costs.

NOTES AND QUESTIONS

1. *The nature of a nuisance action.* The late William L. Prosser, the dean of American tort scholars, metaphorically threw up his hands when he reached the topic of nuisance in his influential treatise: "There is perhaps no more impenetrable jungle in the entire law than that which surrounds the word 'nuisance.'" W. Page Keeton, ed., Prosser and Keeton on Torts § 86 (5th ed. 1984). Fortunately, for the purpose of understanding zoning and planning law, we need not fully penetrate that jungle (at least until we reach the *Lucas* case, *infra*). We offer the briefest sketch of nuisance law in these notes; the reader is cautioned that a wonderful web of intricate detail lies beneath the surface and must be mastered through study of other sources if nuisance figures prominently in any particular case or problem. The summary which follows draws on the Prosser and Keeton treatise.

Nuisances may be private or public. A private nuisance is one that affects the use or enjoyment of land, and normally is privately enforced through a tort action for damages. A public nuisance affects the public at large, need not be connected to land, and is normally enforceable by public officials, although the same conduct may give rise to a parallel private nuisance if private lands are also affected. Prosser and Keeton on Torts § 86. See Beuscher & Morrison, *Judicial Zoning Through Recent Nuisance Cases,* 1955 Wis. L. Rev. 440 (concluding that the distinction between public and private nuisance is illusory when an activity affects the property of a large number of individuals). Some, but not all, nuisance actions may support an injunction instead of, or in addition to, damages. Prosser & Keeton, § 87 at 623. Nuisance is distinguishable from trespass (often tenuously) in that the latter affects the exclusive possession of land, rather than use and enjoyment. *Id*. at 622. Private nuisance rules, which seek to adjust the relationship between adjoining land users, are of primary interest to zoning lawyers.

The plaintiff in a private nuisance action must show intentional conduct, actual interference with use and enjoyment (although the interference may not have been intended), and substantial harm (normally including provable reduction in value of the property). Most importantly, it must be shown that "[t]he interference that came about under such circumstances was of such a nature, duration or amount as to constitute unreasonable interference with the use and enjoyment of the land." *Id*. at 623. While classic examples of private nuisance involve physical interference with the plaintiff's land, the smoke and grit in the principal case, for instance, physical or mental harm to the occupants of the land may also support an action, provided that it meets the requisites of intent, substantiality and unreasonableness; in practice, this means that if the harm is of a type that would offend a person of average sensibility and is of a continuing nature, it would adversely affect the value of the land itself, and a nuisance may be found. *Id*. § 88. The maintenance of a structure or the carrying on of an activity that offends the plaintiffs' aesthetic sense may, in fact reduce the value of their property as well as cause mental discomfort, but most courts have refused to find a nuisance because of the difficulty of establishing generally acceptable aesthetic standards. The leading case recognizing the possibility of an aesthetic nuisance is *Parkersburg Bldrs. Material Co. v. Barrack,* 191 S.E. 368 (W. Va. 1937). See also *Allison v. Smith,* 695 P.2d 791 (Colo. App. 1984). Aesthetic regulation is considered further in Ch. 8 *infra.*

Most nuisance cases involve recurrent activity rather than an isolated wrongful act, because the latter conduct is less likely to meet the substantial interference test. Recurrent activity is also usually necessary before injunctive relief can be obtained by the plaintiff. And if the harm was neither foreseeable in the first instance nor a result of ultra-hazardous activity, some continuance of the defendant's activity is necessary to establish his fault and consequent liability. Moreover, the duration or frequency of the invasion of the plaintiff's interest certainly has a bearing on the reasonableness of his conduct. For a contemporary review of nuisance law see Saxer, *Untangling the Nuisance Knot,* 26 B.C. Envtl. Aff. L. Rev. 89 (1998).

2. *Courts, markets and planners.* Ultimately, the utility of the defendant's conduct depends upon the social value the courts attach to it. In an earlier edition of his treatise, Prosser observed that

> [t]he plaintiff must be expected to endure some inconvenience rather than curtail the defendant's freedom of action, and the defendant must so use his own property that he causes no unreasonable harm to the plaintiff. The law of private nuisance is very largely a series of adjustments to limit the reciprocal rights and privileges of both. In every case the court must make a comparative evaluation of the conflicting interests according to objective legal standards, and the gravity of the harm to the plaintiff must be weighed against the utility of the defendant's conduct. [Prosser, Torts 596 (4th ed. 1971).]

If the defendant's conduct has little or no social value, or is a result of pure malice or spite, should there be liability for causing a nuisance although the harm to the plaintiff is relatively slight? Most courts answer yes.

Note that it is *judges* who are making these decisions. Could they equally well be made in the free market, without the assistance of law? Are there impediments to bargained-for solutions between neighbors (are the trespassing cows in Coase's famous theorem a nuisance)? How would rational planners and the critics of rational planning handle nuisance-type problems? Some commentators argue that parties to a nuisance suit will bargain as Coase predicts after a court judgment fixing liability, but one study found this did not occur. Farnsworth, *Do Parties to Nuisance Cases Bargain After Judgment? A Glimpse Inside the Cathedral,* 66 U. Chi. L. Rev. 373 (1999). Animosity between the parties as a result of litigation, rather than transaction costs, was the problem.

3. *Judicial zoning.* Modern society requires factories, smelters, oil refineries, chemical plants, power stations, and use of explosives for blasting. Such activities may not be nuisances even though they cause substantial discomfort or inconvenience to neighboring landholders, if they are carried on in suitable localities and the adverse impact upon neighboring landholders is avoidable only at prohibitive expense. This has led to the judicially developed doctrine that some activities are *per se* unreasonable in certain localities. Courts have come to recognize that certain localities, because of their physical character or the pattern of community development (or both) are properly and primarily devoted to certain activities and that the introduction of incompatible activities must be deemed unreasonable. In short, to the extent that adjudication on a case-by-case basis permits, courts have engaged in "judicial zoning." See Beuscher & Morrison, *Judicial Zoning Through Recent Nuisance Cases,* 1955 Wis. L. Rev. 440.

4. *The limits of nuisance.* Nuisance theory is of limited use in the areas in which it could be most valuable — slum and mixed fringe areas in which the patterns of land use are less than desirable and do not provide an acceptable measure against which an intruding and offensive use may be judged. Moreover, even where the nuisance *per se* approach allows a court to concentrate on the character of the neighborhood involved, the result of a litigated case is difficult to predict. In part this is because there is no universally accepted standard of social value or suitability; hence different courts will necessarily vary in their appraisal of the reasonableness of particular land uses in particular localities. And in part the difficulty of prediction results from uncertainty as to the availability of injunctive relief. This uncertainty exists both in cases where the plaintiff seeks to enjoin a proposed new land use on the ground that it will be a nuisance and in cases where the court finds that an established land use is a nuisance.

5. *Injunctive relief.* As was the case in *Bove,* the plaintiff in a nuisance case usually seeks injunctive relief. As Professor Robert Ellickson has observed,

> [c]ommentators have traditionally offered four primary rationales for injunctions. First, since market values do not reflect the subjective losses a plaintiff suffers and since those losses are hard to monetize by any other means, the remedy of damages is said to be inadequate. . . . A second justification for . . . [the injunctive remedy] is the moral assertion that a landowner should not be able in effect to exercise a private power of eminent domain and force others to exchange basic property rights for damages. . . . The third rationale used for injunctions is that damages are inadequate when the defendant is judgment-proof.
>
> . . . A fourth justification for . . . injunctions is that administrative factors can make granting an injunction more efficient than awarding damages. [Ellickson, *Alternatives to Zoning: Covenants, Nuisance Rules, and Fines as Land Use Controls,* 40 U. Chi. L. Rev. 681, 739–42 (1973).]

Most courts will not enjoin a proposed land use in advance of its establishment unless it can be shown that it will constitute a nuisance per se at the locus in quo. If the plaintiff waits to sue until an offensive land use is established nearby, however, the court may deny injunctive relief on the basis of estoppel. More important, even if the court determines that the defendant is causing a nuisance, most courts will try to "balance the hardship," and will refuse to grant an injunction if there is a great disparity between the economic consequences of the nuisance and the injunction — i.e., if the plaintiff's economic loss is small in comparison to the economic loss that the injunction would visit upon the defendant and upon the community at large. See, e.g., *City of Harrisonville v. W.S. Dickey Clay Mfg. Co.*, 289 U.S. 334 (1933); *Koseris v. J.R. Simplot Co.*, 352 P.2d 235 (Idaho 1960) (over 1,000 employees); *Dundalk Holding Co. v. Easter*, 137 A.2d 667 (Md.), *cert. denied*, 358 U.S. 821 (1958); *Antonik v. Chamberlain*, 78 N.E.2d 752 (Ohio Ct. App. 1947) ("life and death of a legitimate and necessary business"); *Storey v. Central Hide & Rendering Co.*, 225 S.W.2d 615 (Tex. 1950) (only plant in county).

6. *Priority in time.* Some courts consider priority in time as an important factor in nuisance cases and may hold against a plaintiff who "came to a nuisance." Is there an economic rationale for this doctrine? Did the plaintiff in the *Bove* case "come" to the nuisance? If not, why did she lose?

The Prosser and Keeton text argues that to award an injunction or damages to a plaintiff who came to a nuisance would confer "a windfall capital gain to which he is not entitled." Prosser & Keeton on Torts § 88B at 635 (5th ed. 1984). The reason is that the plaintiff would have purchased the property at a depressed value and then would have increased its value by enjoining the nuisance. But the authors conclude that:

> The prevailing rule is that in the absence of a prescriptive right, the defendant cannot condemn the surrounding premises to endure his operation, and that the purchaser is entitled to a reasonable use and enjoyment of his land to the same extent as any other owner, so long as he buys in good faith and not for the sole purpose of a vexatious lawsuit. [*Id.*]

For an analysis of this problem that "focuses on the efficiency of market activities as they unfold through time, rather than on static allocative effects," see Cordato, *Time Passage and the Economics of Coming to the Nuisance: Reassessing the Coasean Perspective*, 20 Campbell L. Rev. 273 (1998).

7. *The Boomer case and injunctive relief.* From an early date, some American courts have held that whenever the damage resulting from a nuisance is substantial, the plaintiff is entitled to injunctive relief as a matter of right. See, e.g., *Hulbert v. California Portland Cement Co.*, 118 P. 928 (Cal. 1911); *Sullivan v. Jones*, 57 A. 1065 (Pa. 1904). When the *Bove* case was decided the New York courts adhered to the rule that injunctive relief is a matter of right once the court determines that the defendant is maintaining a nuisance. See, e.g., *Whalen v. Union Bag & Paper Co.*, 101 N.E. 805 (N.Y. 1913). Do you think the court would have been more likely to find that Donner-Hanna was maintaining a nuisance in the *Bove* case if New York had adopted the balancing approach to the question whether injunctive relief should be granted?

The New York Court of Appeals abandoned the rule that injunctive relief is a matter of right in an important case, *Boomer v. Atlantic Cement Co.*, 257 N.E.2d 870 (N.Y. 1970), where the loss to the defendant cement company if the operation of its cement plant were enjoined would apparently have been in excess of $45,000,000, while the amount required to compensate all the plaintiffs for their permanent loss (if the injunction were refused) would clearly be less than $1,000,000. The New York court expressly adopted the rule that a court should exercise its equitable discretion to refuse injunctive relief when there is a gross disparity between the economic consequences of the nuisance and the injunction. In addition, the court said,

> Effective control of air pollution is a problem presently far from solution even with the full public and financial powers of government. In large measure adequate technical procedures are yet to be developed and some that appear possible may be economically impracticable.
>
> It seems apparent that amelioration of air pollution will depend on technical research in great depth; on a carefully balanced consideration of the economic impact of close regulation; and of the actual effect on public health. It is likely to require massive public expenditure and to demand more than any local community can accomplish and to depend on regional and interstate controls.
>
> A court should not try to do this on its own as a by-product of private litigation, and it seems manifest that the judicial establishment is neither equipped in the limited nature of any judgment it can pronounce nor prepared to lay down and implement an effective policy for the elimination of air pollution. This is an area beyond the circumference of one private lawsuit. It is a direct responsibility for government and it should not thus be undertaken as an incident to solving a dispute between property owners and a single cement plant — one of many — in the Hudson River valley. [*Id.* at 871.]

The New York court ordered the trial court to "grant an injunction which shall be vacated upon payment by defendant of such amounts of permanent damage to the respective plaintiffs as shall for this purpose be determined by the court." One judge dissented, contending that the award of permanent damages instead of an injunction would amount to an inverse condemnation that "may not be invoked by a private person or corporation for private gain or advantage" and should "only be permitted when the public is primarily served in the taking or impairment of property," because the New York constitution forbids the taking of private property when it is not to be put to a public use.

8. *What happened in Boomer.* After *Boomer* was remanded for further proceedings, two of the plaintiffs (including Boomer) settled with the defendant cement company; the trial court then undertook to determine the permanent damages to be awarded to the remaining plaintiff, Kinley, who owned a 238-acre dairy farm. The court received testimony that the defendant had converted the primary fuel of its plant from coal to oil, had added a spray system to the apparatus used to convey raw material from the quarry to the plant, and had replaced the multiclone dust collectors on the clinker cooler with a fiberglass bag type collector, all at a total cost of $1,600,000. The court then fixed Kinley's permanent damages at $140,000 after finding that the value of his farm without the nuisance was $265,000 and that its value with the nuisance would be only $125,000. 340 N.Y.S.2d 97 (Sup. Ct. 1972).

The appellate division affirmed the trial court's judgment. *Kinley v. Atlantic Cement Co.,* 349 N.Y.S.2d 199 (App. Div. 1973). A majority of the panel agreed that the proper measure of permanent damages in a nuisance case is "the difference between the market value of the property before and after the nuisance." One judge, in a concurring opinion, took a different view. He asserted that, although the before and after measure of damages is proper in eminent domain cases, it is not necessarily proper in private nuisance cases where

> it would be unrealistic to assume that the defendant could acquire a servitude of the present nature simply by paying the price which a willing seller could accept. . . . . While the public interest may dictate that the defendant be afforded an opportunity to acquire a servitude, there is no apparent reason to assume that the purchase is being made either by or on behalf of the public and, accordingly, the value of the servitude should reflect the private interest of the parties to this lawsuit [*Id.* at 202.]

The concurring opinion then concluded that defendants in such cases should be required to pay the holdup price required to persuade an unwilling landowner to sell an "easement to pollute." Do you think the judge who wrote the concurring opinion would have taken a different view if the air pollution produced by the defendant's cement plant had been considered a public nuisance? Was the concurring judge applying the Coase Theorem?

9. *Change in circumstances post-judgment.* Suppose that the defendant paid Kinley the permanent damages of $140,000 and that the defendant were later able to reduce or eliminate the air pollution found to constitute a nuisance, or that a state or federal air pollution control agency later closed down or substantially curtailed the operation of the defendant's cement plant. Would the defendant then be entitled to restitution of some part of the permanent damages it paid to Kinley? Could the problem of determining the amount of restitution be avoided by awarding Kinley, instead of permanent damages, a right to recover on a periodic basis all damages up to the time of suit? The latter would result, in substance, in the defendant's being required to pay a periodic "rent" for its "easement to pollute."

10. *Effect of zoning.* In *Bove* the zoning ordinance allowed the defendant's use. What effect did the court give to the ordinance? The majority rule is that a zoning ordinance cannot legalize the creation of a nuisance, although most courts mean by this that the ordinance cannot preclude a court from holding a use a *nuisance per accidens* (a nuisance in fact). See, e.g., *Armory Park Neighborhood Ass'n v. Episcopal Community Serv.,* 712 P.2d 914 (Ariz. 1985). Is this correct? Some courts will give some effect to the uses allowed by a zoning ordinance in nuisance actions. *Harrison v. Indiana Auto Shredders Co.,* 528 F.2d 1107 (7th Cir. 1976). Why should land use regulations adopted by a municipality be allowed to affect a trial court judgment in a nuisance case?

Another possible alternative in cases like *Boomer* would be to enjoin the nuisance and require the plaintiff to compensate the defendant for its financial loss by paying money damages. The court adopted this remedy in the following case.

SPUR INDUSTRIES, INC. v. DEL E. WEBB DEVELOPMENT CO.

108 Ariz. 178, 494 P.2d 700 (1972)

CAMERON, VICE CHIEF JUSTICE

From a judgment permanently enjoining the defendant, Spur Industries, Inc., from operating a cattle feedlot near the plaintiff Del E. Webb Development Company's Sun City, Spur appeals. Webb cross-appeals. Although numerous issues are raised, we feel that it is necessary to answer only two questions. They are:

1. Where the operation of a business, such as a cattle feedlot is lawful in the first instance, but becomes a nuisance by reason of a nearby residential area, may the feedlot operation be enjoined in an action brought by the developer of the residential area?

2. Assuming that the nuisance may be enjoined, may the developer of a completely new town or urban area in a previously agricultural area be required to indemnify the operator of the feedlot who must move or cease operation because of the presence of the residential area created by the developer?

The facts necessary for a determination of this matter on appeal are as follows. The area in question is located in Maricopa County, Arizona, some 14 to 15 miles west of the urban area of Phoenix, on the Phoenix-Wickenburg Highway, also known as Grand Avenue. About two miles south of Grand Avenue is Olive Avenue which runs east and west. 111th Avenue runs north and south as does the Agua Fria River immediately to the west. See Exhibits A and B below.

Farming started in this area about 1911. In 1929, with the completion of the Carl Pleasant Dam, gravity flow water became available to the property located to the west of the Agua Fria River, though land to the east remained dependent upon well water for irrigation. By 1950, the only urban areas in the vicinity were the agriculturally related communities of Peoria, El Mirage, and Surprise located along Grand Avenue. Along 111th Avenue, approximately one mile south of Grand Avenue and 1½ miles north of Olive Avenue, the community of Youngtown was commenced in 1954. Youngtown is a retirement community appealing primarily to senior citizens.

In 1956, Spur's predecessors in interest, H. Marion Welborn and the Northside Hay Mill and Trading Company, developed feedlots, about ½ mile south of Olive Avenue, in an area between the confluence of the usually dry Agua Fria and New Rivers. The area is well suited for cattle feeding and in 1959 there were 25 cattle feeding pens or dairy operations within a 7 mile radius of the location developed by Spur's predecessors. In April and May of 1959, the Northside Hay Mill was feeding between 6,000 and 7,000 head of cattle and Welborn approximately 1,500 head on a combined area of 35 acres.

In May of 1959, Del Webb began to plan the development of an urban area to be known as Sun City. For this purpose, the Marinette and the Santa Fe Ranches, some 20,000 acres of farmland, were purchased for $15,000,000 or

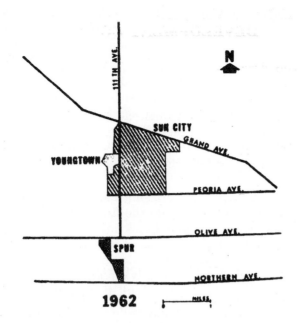

Exhibit A

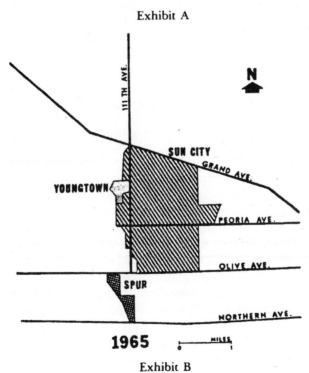

Exhibit B

$750.00 per acre. This price was considerably less than the price of land located near the urban area of Phoenix, and along with the success of Youngtown was a factor influencing the decision to purchase the property in question.

By September 1959, Del Webb had started construction of a golf course south of Grand Avenue and Spur's predecessors had started to level ground for more feedlot area. In 1960, Spur purchased the property in question and began a rebuilding and expansion program extending both to the north and south of the original facilities. By 1962, Spur's expansion program was completed and had expanded from approximately 35 acres to 114 acres. See Exhibit A above.

Accompanied by an extensive advertising campaign, homes were first offered by Del Webb in January 1960 and the first unit to be completed was south of Grand Avenue and approximately 2½ miles north of Spur. By 2 May 1960, there were 450 to 500 houses completed or under construction. At this time, Del Webb did not consider odors from the Spur feed pens a problem and Del Webb continued to develop in a southerly direction, until sales resistance became so great that the parcels were difficult if not impossible to sell. . . .

By December 1967, Del Webb's property had extended south to Olive Avenue and Spur was within 500 feet of Olive Avenue to the north. See Exhibit B above. Del Webb filed its original complaint alleging that in excess of 1,300 lots in the southwest portion were unfit for development for sale as residential lots because of the operation of the Spur feedlot.

Del Webb's suit complained that the Spur feeding operation was a public nuisance because of the flies and the odor which were drifting or being blown by the prevailing south to north wind over the southern portion of Sun City. At the time of the suit, Spur was feeding between 20,000 and 30,000 head of cattle, and the facts amply support the finding of the trial court that the feed pens had become a nuisance to the people who resided in the southern part of Del Webb's development. The testimony indicated that cattle in a commercial feedlot will produce 35 to 40 pounds of wet manure per day, per head, or over a million pounds of wet manure per day for 30,000 head of cattle, and that despite the admittedly good feedlot management and good housekeeping practices by Spur, the resulting odor and flies produced an annoying if not unhealthy situation as far as the senior citizens of southern Sun City were concerned. There is no doubt that some of the citizens of Sun City were unable to enjoy the outdoor living which Del Webb had advertised and that Del Webb was faced with sales resistance from prospective purchasers as well as strong and persistent complaints from the people who had purchased homes in that area.

Trial was commenced before the court with an advisory jury. The advisory jury was later discharged and the trial was continued before the court alone. Findings of fact and conclusions of law were requested and given. The case was vigorously contested, including special actions in this court on some of the matters. In one of the special actions before this court, Spur agreed to, and did, shut down its operation without prejudice to a determination of the matter on appeal. On appeal the many questions raised were extensively briefed.

Public
Private Nuisance

It is noted, however, that neither the citizens of Sun City nor Youngtown are represented in this lawsuit and the suit is solely between Del E. Webb Development Company and Spur Industries, Inc.

May Spur Be Enjoined?

The difference between a private nuisance and a public nuisance is generally one of degree. A private nuisance is one affecting a single individual or a definite small number of persons in the enjoyment of private rights not common to the public, while a public nuisance is one affecting the rights enjoyed by citizens as a part of the public. To constitute a public nuisance, the nuisance must affect a considerable number of people or an entire community or neighborhood.

Where the injury is slight, the remedy for minor inconveniences lies in an action for damages rather than in one for an injunction. Moreover, some courts have held, in the "balancing of conveniences" cases, that damages may be the sole remedy. See *Boomer v. Atlantic Cement Co.*, 26 N.Y.2d 219, 309 N.Y.S.2d 312, 257 N.E.2d 870, 40 A.L.R.3d 590 (1970), and annotation comments, 40 A.L.R.3d 601.

Thus, it would appear from the admittedly incomplete record as developed in the trial court, that, at most, residents of Youngtown would be entitled to damages rather than injunctive relief.

We have no difficulty, however, in agreeing with the conclusion of the trial court that Spur's operation was an enjoinable public nuisance as far as the people in the southern portion of Del Webb's Sun City were concerned.

§ 36-601, subsec. A reads as follows:

§ 36-601. Public nuisances dangerous to public health

A. The following conditions are specifically declared public nuisances dangerous to the public health:

1. Any condition or place in populous areas which constitutes a breeding place for flies, rodents, mosquitoes and other insects which are capable of carrying and transmitting disease-causing organisms to any person or persons.

By this statute, before an otherwise lawful (and necessary) business may be declared a public nuisance, there must be a "populous" area in which people are injured:

. . . [I]t hardly admits a doubt that, in determining the question as to whether a lawful occupation is so conducted as to constitute a nuisance as a matter of fact, the locality and surroundings are of the first importance. (citations omitted) A business which is not per se a public nuisance may become such by being carried on at a place where the health, comfort, or convenience of a populous neighborhood is affected. . . . What might amount to a serious nuisance in one locality by reason of the density of the population, or character of the neighborhood affected, may in another place and under different surroundings be deemed proper and unobjectionable. . . . *MacDonald v. Perry,* 255 P. 494, 497 (Ariz. 1927).

It is clear that as to the citizens of Sun City, the operation of Spur's feedlot was both a public and a private nuisance. They could have successfully maintained an action to abate the nuisance. Del Webb, having shown a special injury in the loss of sales, had a standing to bring suit to enjoin the nuisance. The judgment of the trial court permanently enjoining the operation of the feedlot is affirmed.

Must Del Webb Indemnify Spur?

A suit to enjoin a nuisance sounds in equity and the courts have long recognized a special responsibility to the public when acting as a court of equity:

> § 104. Where public interest is involved.
>
> Courts of equity may, and frequently do, go much further both to give and withhold relief in furtherance of the public interest than they are accustomed to go when only private interests are involved. Accordingly, the granting or withholding of relief may properly be dependent upon considerations of public interest. . . . 27 Am. Jur. 2d, Equity, page 626.

In addition to protecting the public interest, however, courts of equity are concerned with protecting the operator of a lawfully, albeit noxious, business from the result of a knowing and willful encroachment by others near his business.

In the so-called "coming to the nuisance" cases, the courts have held that the residential landowner may not have relief if he knowingly came into a neighborhood reserved for industrial or agricultural endeavors and has been damaged thereby:

> Plaintiffs chose to live in an area uncontrolled by zoning laws or restrictive covenants and remote from urban development. In such an area plaintiffs cannot complain that legitimate agricultural pursuits are being carried on in the vicinity, nor can plaintiffs, having chosen to build in an agricultural area, complain that the agricultural pursuits carried on in the area depreciate the value of their homes. The area being *primarily agricultural,* any opinion reflecting the value of such property must take this factor into account. The standards affecting the value of residence property in an urban setting, subject to zoning controls and controlled planning techniques, cannot be the standards by which agricultural properties are judged.
>
> People employed in a city who build their homes in suburban areas of the county beyond the limits of a city and zoning regulations do so for a reason. Some do so to avoid the high taxation rate imposed by cities, or to avoid special assessments for street, sewer and water projects. They usually build on improved or hard surface highways, which have been built either at state or county expense and thereby avoid special assessments for these improvements. It may be that they desire to get away from the congestion of traffic, smoke, noise, foul air and the many other annoyances of city life. But with all these

advantages in going beyond the area which is zoned and restricted to protect them in their homes, they must be prepared to take the disadvantages. *Dill v. Excel Packing Company,* 331 P.2d 539, 548, 549 (Kan. 1958).

And:

> . . . a party cannot justly call upon the law to make that place suitable for his residence which was not so when he selected it. . . . *Gilbert v. Showerman,* 23 Mich. 448, 455, 2 Brown 158 (1871).

Were Webb the only party injured, we would feel justified in holding that the doctrine of "coming to the nuisance" would have been a bar to the relief asked by Webb, and, on the other hand, had Spur located the feedlot near the outskirts of a city and had the city grown toward the feedlot, Spur would have to suffer the cost of abating the nuisance as to those people locating within the growth pattern of the expanding city:

> The case affords, perhaps, an example where a business established at a place remote from population is gradually surrounded and becomes part of a populous center, so that a business which formerly was not an interference with the rights of others has become so by the encroachment of the population. . . . *City of Ft. Smith v. Western Hide & Fur Co.,* 239 S.W. 724, 726 (Ark. 1922).

We agree, however, with the Massachusetts court that:

> The law of nuisance affords no rigid rule to be applied in all instances. It is elastic. It undertakes to require only that which is fair and reasonable under all the circumstances. In a commonwealth like this, which depends for its material prosperity so largely on the continued growth and enlargement of manufacturing of diverse varieties, "extreme rights" cannot be enforced. . . . *Stevens v. Rockport Granite Co.,* 104 N.E. 371, 373 (Mass. 1914).

There was no indication in the instant case at the time Spur and its predecessors located in western Maricopa County that a new city would spring up, full-blown, alongside the feeding operation and that the developer of that city would ask the court to order Spur to move because of the new city. Spur is required to move not because of any wrongdoing on the part of Spur, but because of a proper and legitimate regard of the courts for the rights and interests of the public.

Del Webb, on the other hand, is entitled to the relief prayed for (a permanent injunction), not because Webb is blameless, but because of the damage to the people who have been encouraged to purchase homes in Sun City. It does not equitably or legally follow, however, that Webb, being entitled to the injunction, is then free of any liability to Spur if Webb has in fact been the cause of the damage Spur has sustained. It does not seem harsh to require a developer, who has taken advantage of the lesser land values in a rural area as well as the availability of large tracts of land on which to build and develop a new town or city in the area, to indemnify those who are forced to leave as a result.

Having brought people to the nuisance to the foreseeable detriment of Spur, Webb must indemnify Spur for a reasonable amount of the cost of moving or shutting down. It should be noted that this relief to Spur is limited to a case wherein a developer has, with foreseeability, brought into a previously agricultural or industrial area the population which makes necessary the granting of an injunction against a lawful business and for which the business has no adequate relief.

It is therefore the decision of this court that the matter be remanded to the trial court for a hearing upon the damages sustained by the defendant Spur as a reasonable and direct result of the granting of the permanent injunction. Since the result of the appeal may appear novel and both sides have obtained a measure of relief, it is ordered that each side will bear its own costs.

Affirmed in part, reversed in part, and remanded for further proceedings consistent with this opinion.

NOTES AND QUESTIONS

1. *More about Spur.* Do you understand the court in *Spur Industries* to hold that an injunction will be more readily granted when the defendant is found to be maintaining a public rather than only a private nuisance? Could Del E. Webb Development Co. have secured any relief at all if the court had classified the nuisance as solely private in character? Suppose the action had been brought by the Sun City municipal attorney, or as a class action by a substantial number of Sun City residents? Would the relief granted have been the same? Upon remand, how should the trial court frame its judgment? Should the injunction be conditioned on tender of the damages assessed by the court to Spur Industries, or should payment of the damages be conditioned on compliance with the injunction against continued operation of Spur Industries' feedlot? For an update on Sun City, see Shetter, *Sun City Holds On,* Planning, Vol. 62, No. 1, at 16 (1996) (huge success of development leads to construction of eight more cities by Del Webb in other areas; average age of residents is 74.4 years).

2. *Compensated injunctions.* The court says this remedy is available only in very narrow circumstances: "wherein a developer has, with foreseeability, brought into a previously agricultural or industrial area the population which makes necessary the granting of an injunction against a lawful business and for which the business has no adequate relief"? Why this limitation? Are the differences between *Spur* and *Boomer* significant? Would the Arizona court refuse to follow *Boomer*?

3. *A compensation model.* In an article contemporaneous with the decision in *Spur Industries* (neither cites the other) Calabresi and Melamed worked out a general model based on the Coase Theorem that led to the same result. They posited that an entitlement (i.e., a property right) to use a natural resource (e.g., clean air) may be allocated either to the plaintiff or the defendant in a nuisance case, and that this entitlement may be protected either by an injunction (a property rule) so that the entitlement may be taken away only by one who obtains the permission of the owner of the entitlement, or by an award of damages (a liability rule) so that the entitlement may be taken away by one who pays judicially determined compensatory damages.

Problems with Nuisance cases [handwritten note]

The authors reasoned that, since an entitlement may initially be allocated to either of the parties and can be protected either by an injunction or by an award of damages, there must be four possible outcomes in nuisance cases, rather than only the three traditionally found in court decisions. Thus in addition to finding no nuisance, or finding nuisance and granting an injunction, or finding nuisance and awarding only damages, Calabresi and Melamed concluded that courts should be free to grant an injunction and require the plaintiff to pay damages to compensate the defendant for the loss caused by the injunction, arguing that through choice among all four possible outcomes, courts can do a better job in achieving both economic efficiency and fairness than is possible when they limit themselves to the three traditional outcomes. See Calabresi & Melamed, *Property Rules, Liability Rules, and Inalienability: One View of the Cathedral,* 85 Harv. L. Rev. 1089 (1972). For commentary on the thesis advanced by Calabresi and Melamed, see Kaplow & Shavell, *Property Rules Versus Liability Rules: An Economic Analysis,* 109 Harv. L. Rev. 713 (1996); Krier & Schwab, *The Cathedral at Twenty-Five: Citations and Impressions,* 106 Yale L.J. 2121 (1997); Rose, *The Shadow of the Cathedral,* 106 Yale L.J. 2175 (1997).

Ellickson, *supra,* argues that "[n]uisance law would function better if, in general, a plaintiff in a nuisance case were limited to choosing between the remedies of . . . damages . . . [or] compensated injunction," which would permit the plaintiff

> to enjoin the defendant's conduct, but only if he compensates the defendant for the defendant's losses caused by the injunction. . . . A rebuttable presumption against . . . injunctions [without compensation] should exist in nuisance cases, and be overcome only when the plaintiff can show that his personal safety or fundamental freedoms are vitally threatened by the defendant's activity. [*Id.* at 738–48.]

4. *An economic model.* We might now try to develop an economic model of nuisance-based land use conflicts along the following lines: Land use conflicts adjudicated in a nuisance setting present a classic case of legal intervention to modify externalities. Let us assume a developing residential area; a factory now seeks to locate in that area. If that location is the best location possible for that industry, then we can consider the location optimal if the gains to society from that location are greater than the costs that location imposes on existing uses. Unfortunately, the private market has no way to force the intruding use to compensate those already in the neighborhood for negative externalities which its location imposes.

Nuisance law provides a method for imposing a duty to compensate on the intruding use. It does this either by awarding damages, or by granting equitable relief that will force the intruder to make improvements minimizing the effect on surrounding properties. If the harm cannot be minimized through improvements, the intruder will be compelled to relocate. The nuisance remedy may not always work well, however: (1) It ignores the fact that a land use conflict is two-sided, and arises as much from the fact that existing uses may be harm-sensitive as from the fact that the intruder may be harm-productive; (2) the judicial context of the nuisance lawsuit is not conducive to a full consideration of aggregate social and economic costs and benefits;

(3) to assume that existing uses are entitled to preempt any given spatial location improperly ratifies private land use decisions; (4) relocation of the existing use may be less costly and impose less economic dislocation than relocation of the intruding use; and (5) the intruder may bring positive as well as negative externalities. Thus a new factory may attract other related and economically desirable uses to the area. In view of these considerations, what alternative decision model would you construct for nuisance litigation? See D. Mandelker, The Zoning Dilemma, ch. 2 (1971); Note, *An Economic Analysis of Land Use Conflicts,* 21 Stan. L. Rev. 293 (1969).

5. *Buffers.* Nuisance adjudication can also have a spatial component. The classic example is the "brickyard in the wilderness," a noxious activity that is socially useful and does no harm because there are no neighbors. Trouble arises when a neighborhood springs up, as in *Hadacheck v. Sebastian,* the next principal case. Can the new neighbors enjoin the brickyard? What do *Bove* and *Spur Industries* have to say about this? Either the brickyard or the new neighbors could mitigate at least some of the conflict by providing a buffer between the incompatible uses. Whose responsibility is this? Recall the *Spur Industries* court's emphasis on the foreseeability of future residential development. For a scholarly discussion, see Michelman, *Property, Utility and Fairness: Comments on the Ethical Foundations of "Just Compensation" Law,* 80 Harv. L. Rev. 1165, 1242–44 (1967).

An instructive case is *Patton v. Westwood Country Club,* 247 N.E.2d 761 (Ohio Ct. App. 1969), where an abutting landowner brought a nuisance action to enjoin the operation of a golf and country club. The court dismissed the action, relying in part on the fact that when the plaintiff constructed her residence the club was already there. But it also pointed out that the club had taken steps to protect the plaintiff. The club had changed the sprinkling system on the nearest fairway, moved the fairway farther away from the plaintiff's residence, and planted twenty pine trees adjacent to plaintiff's lot. The cost of these changes was approximately $2,000.

Location may make a difference. Courts are likely to find a nuisance in an established area (can you see why?), but in these areas the intruder may have no opportunity to buffer. The court will have to accept existing patterns of landownership as their legal reference point, and in established residential neighborhoods the ownership pattern will be fragmented and small, externalities will be aggravated, and mitigation will be difficult if not impossible. This in turn helps make the case for collective control through zoning, though zoning may have to take established development into account as nonconforming uses. Buffering may also raise problems in undeveloped areas. For example, if an industrial use is required to buffer first by acquiring excess land, is the area appropriate for conflicting (e.g., residential) uses? How can a court make this assumption? Recall *Bove.* But if one takes a "wait and see" attitude, then later buffering may become impractical. Again, the case for collective controls.

B. THE TAKINGS ISSUE

Among the inherent powers of sovereignty recognized since ancient common law times is the power of "eminent domain," the power to take private property

5th + 14th AMEND

for public use, a power possessed by federal and state governments. In addition, the states possess a general power to regulate, called "the police power," to protect "the public health, safety, morals, or general welfare," on which the power to regulate land use and development is based. The federal government possesses no general police power, but through the grant of enumerated powers in U.S. Const. Art. I, § 8, it also possesses a large power to regulate in ways that affect land use and development. Exercise of the powers delegated to the federal government is limited by the Fifth Amendment: "No person shall be deprived of life, liberty, or property, without due process of law; nor shall private property be taken for public use without just compensation." The exercise of the powers reserved to the states is limited by state constitutional provisions and by the Fourteenth Amendment to the United States Constitution, which provides, *inter alia*, "No state shall . . . deprive any person of life, liberty, or property, without due process of law; nor deny to any person within its jurisdiction the equal protection of the laws."

These constitutional provisions require the federal government to pay "just compensation" when private property is taken for public use. The constitutions of all but three states expressly prohibit the taking of private property for public use without compensation, and in these three states the constitutions have been judicially interpreted to require compensation. Moreover, the United States Supreme Court has held that the due process clause of the Fourteenth Amendment makes the compensation clause of the Fifth Amendment applicable to the states. *Chicago, B. & Q.R.R. v. Chicago,* 166 U.S. 226 (1897).

There is no constitutional requirement to pay compensation for the exercise of the "police power," the power to regulate (as opposed to the power to "take" property), even if a regulation causes actual or potential economic loss. (Your land might be more valuable, for example if a zoning ordinance permitted a ten story building, rather than a five story one.) Recall the efficiency and equity considerations presented in Chapter 1. Is the traditional no-compensation rule justifiable? When state or local regulatory legislation is found not to be a proper exercise of the police power, it can be enjoined as a deprivation of liberty or property, or both, without due process of law in violation of the Fourteenth Amendment. The Supreme Court has also concluded that under some circumstances, a regulation can affect land so significantly that it is the functional equivalent of a taking of property — a "regulatory taking," to use the current terminology.

This simplistic summary of the constitutional framework will be elaborated in complex detail in the materials that follow. Most commentators (to say nothing of novice students of land use law) have concluded that the cases are far from internally consistent, and that the Supreme Court has from time to time steered an erratic course. However, by keeping in sight these guideposts — police power regulation versus takings, substantive due process versus compensation (and occasionally equal protection) — you should be able eventually to frame your own conclusions about what the law is and what it ought to be.

1. THE EARLY SUPREME COURT CASES

Both the compensation and due process issues were resolved squarely in *Mugler v. Kansas,* 123 U.S. 623 (1887), an important early case interpreting the Fourteenth Amendment. Upholding a Kansas statute prohibiting the manufacture of intoxicating liquors, the Supreme Court concluded that the Fourteenth Amendment did not abrogate the police powers of the states. It concluded "that all property in this country is held under the implied obligation that the owner's use of it shall not be injurious to the community" [*id.* at 669]. However, the Amendment also imposed on all courts a duty to strike down legislative acts purportedly enacted pursuant to the police power of a state when such acts have "no real or substantial relation" to the proper objects of the police power — protection of "the public health, the public morals, or the public safety." [*Id.* at 662.]

A few years after *Mugler,* in *Lawton v. Steele,* 152 U.S. 133 (1894), the Supreme Court, in upholding a New York statute authorizing seizure and destruction of illegal fishing nets without payment of compensation to their owners, confirmed the "no compensation" principle of *Mugler* and laid down the classic test for substantive due process: a purported exercise of the police power does not violate the Fourteenth Amendment's due process clause if it appears, "first that the interests of the public . . . require such interference; second, that the means are reasonably necessary for the accomplishment of the purpose, and not unduly oppressive on individuals." *Id.* at 137. This has long been considered the classic statement of the requirements of substantive due process. But *Lawton* did not indicate the relative weight to be attached to each of the designated factors. This question was addressed in the following Supreme Court case, one of the first to consider the takings issue as applied to land use controls.

HADACHECK v. SEBASTIAN

239 U.S. 394 (1915)

JUSTICE MCKENNA delivered the opinion of the court:

Habeas corpus prosecuted in the Supreme Court of the State of California for the discharge of plaintiff in error from the custody of defendant in error, Chief of Police of the City of Los Angeles.

Plaintiff in error, to whom we shall refer as petitioner, was convicted of a misdemeanor for the violation of an ordinance of the City of Los Angeles which makes it unlawful for any person to establish or operate a brick yard or brick kiln, or any establishment, factory or place for the manufacture or burning of brick within described limits in the city. Sentence was pronounced against him and he was committed to the custody of defendant in error as Chief of Police of the City of Los Angeles.

Being so in custody he filed a petition in the Supreme Court of the State for a writ of *habeas corpus.* The writ was issued. Subsequently defendant in error made a return thereto supported by affidavits, to which petitioner made sworn reply. The court rendered judgment discharging the writ and remanding petitioner to custody. The Chief Justice of the court then granted this writ of error. . . .

[Petitioner alleged that he was the owner of land within the limits described in the ordinance, on which land there was a valuable bed of clay worth about $800,000 for brick-making purposes, but worth only about $60,000 for any purpose other than the manufacture of brick; that he had made excavations of considerable depth and extent on his land, so that the land could not be used for residential purposes or any purpose other than extraction of the clay and manufacture of brick; that he purchased the land because of the bed of clay located thereon, at a time when the land was outside the limits of the city and distant from any dwellings; that he had erected expensive machinery for the manufacture of bricks on the land; that if the ordinance should be declared valid he would be compelled entirely to abandon his business and would be deprived of the use of his property because the manufacture of brick must necessarily be carried on where suitable clay is found and the clay cannot be transported to some other location; that there was no reason for the prohibition of the brick-making business because it was so conducted as not to be a nuisance; that the district described in the ordinance included only about three square miles, was sparsely settled and contained large tracts of unsubdivided and unoccupied land; that there were at the time of the adoption of the ordinance in other districts of the city thickly built up with residences brick yards maintained more detrimental to the inhabitants of the city, but permitted to be maintained without prohibition or regulation; that no ordinance had been passed at any time regulating or attempting to regulate brick yards or inquiry made whether they could be maintained without being a nuisance or detrimental to health; and that the ordinance in question was enacted for the sole and specific purpose of prohibiting and suppressing the business of petitioner and that of the other brick yard within the district described in the ordinance.

[The City of Los Angeles denied the charge that the ordinance was arbitrarily directed against the business of petitioner and alleged that there was another district in which brick yards were prohibited. There was a denial of the allegations that the brick yard was or could be conducted sanitarily and so as not to be offensive to health, with supporting affidavits alleging that the fumes, gases, smoke, soot, steam and dust arising from petitioner's brick factory had from time to time caused sickness and serious discomfort to those living in the vicinity. There was no specific denial of petitioner's allegations as to the value of his property and his inability to move the brick factory elsewhere, but there was a general denial that enforcement of the ordinance would "entirely deprive petitioner of his property and the use thereof."

[The Supreme Court of California considered the petitioner's business one which could be regulated and that regulation was not precluded by the fact "that the value of investments made in the business prior to any legislative action will be greatly diminished" or that petitioner had been engaged in brick-making in that locality for a long period. The California court said the evidence tended to show that the district had become primarily a residential section and that the residents were seriously incommoded by petitioner's operation of his factory; and that such evidence, "when taken in connection with the presumptions in favor of the propriety of the legislative determination, overcame the contention that the ordinance was a mere arbitrary invasion of private right, not supported by any tenable belief that the continuance of the business was so detrimental to the interests of others as to require suppression." The court thus rejected the contention that the ordinance was not in good faith enacted as a police measure, and that it was intended to discriminate against petitioner. With respect to the charge of discrimination between localities, the court said that the determination as to where brick-making should be prohibited was for the local legislative body — Eds.]

We think the conclusion of the court is justified by the evidence and makes it unnecessary to review the many cases cited by petitioner in which it is decided that the police power of a state cannot be arbitrarily exercised. The principle is familiar, but in any given case it must plainly appear to apply. It is to be remembered that we are dealing with one of the most essential powers of government, one that is the least limitable. It may, indeed, seem harsh in its exercise, usually is on some individual, but the imperative necessity for its existence precludes any limitation upon it when not exerted arbitrarily. A vested interest cannot be asserted against it because of conditions once obtaining. To so hold would preclude development and fix a city forever in its primitive conditions. There must be progress, and if in its march private interests are in the way they must yield to the good of the community. The logical result of petitioner's contention would seem to be that a city could not be formed or enlarged against the resistance of an occupant of the ground and that if it grows at all it can only grow as the environment of the occupations that are usually banished to the purlieus.

The police power and to what extent it may be exerted we have recently illustrated in *Reinman v. Little Rock,* 237 U.S. 171. The circumstances of the case were very much like those of the case at bar and give reply to the contentions of petitioner, especially that which asserts that a necessary and lawful occupation that is not a nuisance *per se* cannot be made so by legislative declaration. There was a like investment in property, encouraged by the then conditions; a like reduction of value and deprivation of property was asserted against the validity of the ordinance there considered; a like assertion of an arbitrary exercise of the power of prohibition. Against all of these contentions, and causing the rejection of them all, was adduced the police power. There was a prohibition of a business, lawful in itself, there as here. It was a livery stable there; a brick yard here. They differ in particulars, but they are alike in that which cause and justify prohibition in defined localities — that is, the effect upon the health and comfort of the community.

The ordinance passed upon prohibited the conduct of the business within a certain defined area in Little Rock, Arkansas. This court said of it: granting that the business was not a nuisance *per se,* it was clearly within the police power of the State to regulate it, "and to that end to declare that in particular circumstances and in particular localities a livery stable shall be deemed a nuisance in fact and in law." And the only limitation upon the power was stated to be that the power could not be exerted arbitrarily or with unjust discrimination. There was a citation of cases. We think the present case is within the ruling thus declared.

Attorneys

There is a distinction between *Reinman v. Little Rock* and the case at bar. There a particular business was prohibited which was not affixed to or dependent upon its locality; it could be conducted elsewhere. Here, it is contended, the latter condition does not exist, and it is alleged that the manufacture of brick must necessarily be carried on where suitable clay is found and that the clay on petitioner's property cannot be transported to some other locality. This is not urged as a physical impossibility but only, counsel say, that such transportation and the transportation of the bricks to places where they could be used in construction work would be prohibitive "from a financial standpoint." But upon the evidence the Supreme Court considered the case, as we understand its opinion, from the standpoint of the offensive effects of the operation of a brick yard and not from the deprivation of the deposits of clay, and distinguished *Ex parte Kelso,* 147 Cal. 609, 82 P. 241, wherein the court declared invalid an ordinance absolutely prohibiting the maintenance or operation of a rock or stone quarry within a certain portion of the city and county of San Francisco. The court there said that the effect of the ordinance was "to absolutely deprive the owners of real property within such limits of a valuable right incident to their ownership, — *viz.,* the right to extract therefrom such rock and stone as they might find it to their advantage to dispose of." The court expressed the view that the removal could be regulated but that "an absolute prohibition of such removal under the circumstances," could not be upheld.

In the present case there is no prohibition of the removal of the brick clay; only a prohibition within the designated locality of its manufacture into bricks. And to this feature of the ordinance our opinion is addressed. Whether other questions would arise if the ordinance were broader, and opinion on such questions, we reserve.

Petitioner invokes the equal protection clause of the Constitution and charges that it is violated in that the ordinance (1) "prohibits him from manufacturing brick upon his property while his competitors are permitted, without regulation of any kind, to manufacture brick upon property situated in all respects similarly to that of plaintiff in error"; and (2) that it "prohibits the conduct of his business while it permits the maintenance within the same district of any other kind of business, no matter how objectionable the same may be, either in its nature or in the manner in which it is conducted."

If we should grant that the first specification shows a violation of classification, that is, a distinction between businesses which was not within the legislative power, petitioner's contention encounters the objection that it depends upon an inquiry of fact which the record does not enable us to determine. It is alleged in the return to the petition that brickmaking is prohibited in one other district and an ordinance is referred to regulating business in other districts. To this plaintiff in error replied that the ordinance attempts to prohibit the operation of certain businesses having mechanical power and does not prohibit the maintenance of any business or the operation of any machine that is operated by animal power. In other words, petitioner makes his contention depend upon disputable considerations of classification and upon a comparison of conditions of which there is no means of judicial determination and upon which nevertheless we are expected to reverse legislative action exercised upon matters of which the city has control.

To a certain extent the latter comment may be applied to other contentions, and, besides, there is no allegation or proof of other objectionable businesses being permitted within the district, and a speculation of their establishment or conduct at some future time is too remote.

In his petition and argument something is made of the ordinance as fostering a monopoly and suppressing his competition with other brickmakers. The charge and argument are too illusive. It is part of the charge that the ordinance was directed against him. The charge, we have seen, was rejected by the Supreme Court, and we find nothing to justify it.

It may be that brick yards in other localities within the city where the same conditions exist are not regulated or prohibited, but it does not follow that they will not be. That petitioner's business was first in time to be prohibited does not make its prohibition unlawful. And it may be, as said by the Supreme Court of the State, that the conditions justify a distinction. However, the inquiries thus suggested are outside of our province.

There are other and subsidiary contentions which, we think, do not require discussion. They are disposed of by what we have said. It may be that something else than prohibition would have satisfied the conditions. Of this, however, we have no means of determining, and besides we cannot declare invalid the exertion of a power which the city undoubtedly has because of a charge that it does not exactly accommodate the conditions or that some other exercise would have been better or less harsh. We must accord good faith to the city in the absence of a clear showing to the contrary and an honest exercise of judgment upon the circumstances which induced its action.

We do not notice the contention that the ordinance is not within the city's charter powers nor that it is in violation of the state constitution, such contentions raising only local questions which must be deemed to have been decided adversely to petitioner by the Supreme Court of the State.

Judgment affirmed.

NOTES AND QUESTIONS

1. *Substantive due process. Lawton* established a three-factor balancing test: proper governmental purpose, reasonable means to achieve the purpose, and the extent of the burden imposed upon the person subject to the police power regulation. How are those factors employed in *Hadacheck?*

2. *The nuisance rationale.* It is clear that the *Hadacheck* Court thought the Los Angeles ordinance intended to protect the public health and comfort by eliminating the nuisance-like effects of a brick factory in a primarily residential area, although the area was sparsely populated when the brick factory was established. Could the neighboring residential landowners have persuaded a court that the factory was a common-law public nuisance in light of the fact that they "came to the nuisance"? Is the legislative power to regulate land use under the police power greater than the judicial power to do so by means of nuisance adjudication? Even if so, must there be a "nuisance-like" basis for the law? This problem recurs. See, e.g., the *Euclid* and *Lucas* cases, *infra.*

Takings

3. *Presuming validity.* The *Hadacheck* case asserted that "the imperative necessity" for the existence of the police power "precludes any limitation upon it when not exerted arbitrarily." *Reinman*, cited and relied on in *Hadacheck*, adds that the only limitation is that the police power may not be exerted arbitrarily or with unjust discrimination. But how did the court in these cases determine that the legislative exercise of the police power was not arbitrary or unjustly discriminatory? Did the Court in *Hadacheck* independently weigh the reasonableness and social utility of the petitioner's use of his land for manufacturing bricks against the gravity of the harm to, and the social utility of, the residential land uses in the neighborhood of the brick factory, as it would have done in a nuisance case? If not, why not? The reason — not articulated in *Hadacheck* — is that the courts have traditionally accorded a presumption of validity to legislative acts — even those of a municipal governing body — regulating land use. See, e.g., *Village of Euclid v. Ambler Realty Co.,* reproduced *infra*.

4. *Evenhanded means.* The Court's acceptance of the city's purpose was foreshadowed by *Mugler* and *Lawton*, but it rejects the petitioner's equal protection claims. The inadequate fact record may have been sufficient to justify this conclusion, but the Court goes on to say that there would be no denial of equal protection even if it were shown "that brickyards in other localities within the city where the same conditions exist are not regulated or prohibited," because "it does not follow that they will not be" regulated at some future time. If such were the case, would the city's prohibition of Hadacheck's (but not others') brick manufacturing satisfy modern rational basis tests? To the extent that most regulations are aided by a strong presumption of constitutionality and can pass a weak rational basis test, the "burden" factor becomes crucial, a progression that largely explains today's emphasis on takings doctrine.

Future
Regulation

5. *Economic burden.* Did the *Hadacheck* Court seriously address the petitioner's allegation that the effect of the Los Angeles ordinance was to reduce the value of his clay deposits from about $800,000 to about $60,000? If this allegation was true, did not the ordinance violate the *Lawton* requirement that the legislative act must not be "unduly oppressive on individuals"? Are you satisfied with the *Hadacheck* Court's statement that "[i]n the present case there is no prohibition of the removal of the brick clay; only a prohibition within the designated locality of its manufacture into bricks," and the Court's conclusion that it was legally irrelevant that transport of the clay to some other locality for manufacture and further transport of the bricks to "places where they could be used in construction work" would be prohibitive from a financial standpoint?

Takings doctrine may have influenced the Court's thinking here: the traditional rule in formal eminent domain cases (recall the "regulatory takings" analog to eminent domain) is that just compensation does not include payment for consequential business losses, even if the business is completely destroyed, because the business on the land is distinct from the value of the land itself. Although *Hadacheck* precedes the development of a "regulatory takings" theory by the Court, its analysis of Hadacheck's losses plays a major role in later takings cases. See also Michelman, *Property and Fairness: Comments on the Ethical Foundations of "Just Compensation" Law,* 80 Harv. L.

Rev. 1165, 1198, 1237, 1242–44 (1967). The next case famously began the evolution of the "regulatory takings" doctrine:

PENNSYLVANIA COAL CO. v. MAHON

260 U.S. 393 (1922)

JUSTICE HOLMES delivered the opinion of the Court:

This is a bill in equity brought by the defendants in error to prevent the Pennsylvania Coal Company from mining under their property in such way as to remove the supports and cause a subsidence of the surface and of their house. The bill sets out a deed executed by the Coal Company in 1878, under which the plaintiffs claim. The deed conveys the surface, but in express terms reserves the right to remove all the coal under the same, and the grantee takes the premises with the risk, and waives all claim for damages that may arise from mining out the coal. But the plaintiffs say that whatever may have been the Coal Company's rights, they were taken away by an Act of Pennsylvania, approved May 27, 1921, P.L. 1198, commonly known there as the Kohler Act. The Court of Common Pleas found that if not restrained the defendant would cause the damage to prevent which the bill was brought, but denied an injunction, holding that the statute if applied to this case would be unconstitutional. On appeal the Supreme Court of the State agreed that the defendant had contract and property rights protected by the Constitution of the United States, but held that the statute was a legitimate exercise of the police power and directed a decree for the plaintiffs. A writ of error was granted bringing the case to this Court.

The statute forbids the mining of anthracite coal in such way as to cause the subsidence of, among other things, any structure used as a human habitation, with certain exceptions, including among them land where the surface is owned by the owner of the underlying coal and is distant more than one hundred and fifty feet from any improved property belonging to any other person. As applied to this case the statute is admitted to destroy previously existing rights of property and contract. The question is whether the police power can be stretched so far.

Government hardly could go on if to some extent values incident to property could not be diminished without paying for every such change in the general law. As long recognized, some values are enjoyed under an implied limitation and must yield to the police power. But obviously the implied limitation must have its limits, or the contract and due process clauses are gone. One fact for consideration in determining such limits is the extent of the diminution. When it reaches a certain magnitude, in most if not in all cases there must be an exercise of eminent domain and compensation to sustain the act. So the question depends upon the particular facts. The greatest weight is given to the judgment of the legislature, but it always is open to interested parties to contend that the legislature has gone beyond its constitutional power.

This is the case of a single private house. No doubt there is a public interest even in this, as there is in every purchase and sale and in all that happens within the commonwealth. Some existing rights may be modified even in such a case. But usually in ordinary private affairs the public interest does not warrant much of this kind of interference. A source of damage to such a house is not a public nuisance even if similar damage is inflicted on others in different places. The damage is not common or public. The extent of the public interest is shown by the statute to be limited, since the statute ordinarily does not apply to land when the surface is owned by the owner of the coal. Furthermore, it is not justified as a protection of personal safety. That could be provided for by notice. Indeed the very foundation of this bill is that the defendant gave timely notice of its intent to mine under the house. On the other hand the extent of the taking is great. It purports to abolish what is recognized in Pennsylvania as an estate in land — a very valuable estate — and what is declared by the Court below to be a contract hitherto binding the plaintiffs. If we were called upon to deal with the plaintiffs' position alone, we should think it clear that the statute does not disclose a public interest sufficient to warrant so extensive a destruction of the defendant's constitutionally protected rights.

But the case has been treated as one in which the general validity of the act should be discussed. The Attorney General of the State, the City of Scranton, and the representatives of other extensive interests were allowed to take part in the argument below and have submitted their contentions here. It seems, therefore, to be our duty to go farther in the statement of our opinion, in order that it may be known at once, and that further suits should not be brought in vain.

It is our opinion that the act cannot be sustained as an exercise of the police power, so far as it affects the mining of coal under streets or cities in places where the right to mine such coal has been reserved. As said in a Pennsylvania case, "For practical purposes, the right to coal consists in the right to mine it." *Commonwealth v. Clearview Coal Co.,* 256 Pa. St. 328, 331. What makes the right to mine coal valuable is that it can be exercised with profit. To make it commercially impracticable to mine certain coal has very nearly the same effect for constitutional purposes as appropriating or destroying it. This we think that we are warranted in assuming that the statute does.

It is true that in *Plymouth Coal Co. v. Pennsylvania,* 232 U.S. 531, it was held competent for the legislature to require a pillar of coal to be left along the line of adjoining property, that, with the pillar on the other side of the line, would be a barrier sufficient for the safety of the employees of either mine in case the other should be abandoned and allowed to fill with water. But that was a requirement for the safety of employees invited into the mine, and secured an average reciprocity of advantage that has been recognized as a justification of various laws.

The rights of the public in a street purchased or laid out by eminent domain are those that it has paid for. If in any case its representatives have been so short sighted as to acquire only surface rights without the right of support, we see no more authority for supplying the latter without compensation than there was for taking the right of way in the first place and refusing to pay for it because the public wanted it very much. The protection of private property in the Fifth Amendment presupposes that it is wanted for public use, but provides that it shall not be taken for such use without compensation.

A similar assumption is made in the decisions upon the Fourteenth Amendment. When this seemingly absolute protection is found to be qualified by the police power, the natural tendency of human nature is to extend the qualification more and more until at least private property disappears. But that cannot be accomplished in this way under the Constitution of the United States.

The general rule at least is, that while property may be regulated to a certain extent, if regulation goes too far it will be recognized as a taking. It may be doubted how far exceptional cases, like the blowing up of a house to stop a conflagration, go — and if they go beyond the general rule, whether they do not stand as much upon tradition as upon principle. In general it is not plain that a man's misfortunes or necessities will justify his shifting the damages to his neighbor's shoulders. We are in danger of forgetting that a strong public desire to improve the public condition is not enough to warrant achieving the desire by a shorter cut than the constitutional way of paying for the change. As we already have said, this is a question of degree — and therefore cannot be disposed of by general propositions. But we regard this as going beyond any of the cases decided by this Court. The late decisions upon laws dealing with the congestion of Washington and New York, caused by the war, dealt with laws intended to meet a temporary emergency and providing for compensation determined to be reasonable by an impartial board. They went to the verge of the law but fell far short of the present act. *Block v. Hirsh,* 256 U.S. 135; *Marcus Brown Holding Co. v. Feldman,* 256 U.S. 170; *Levy Leasing Co. v. Siegel,* 258 U.S. 242.

We assume, of course, that the statute was passed upon the conviction that an exigency existed that would warrant it, and we assume that an exigency exists that would warrant the exercise of eminent domain. But the question at bottom is upon whom the loss of the changes desired should fall. So far as private persons or communities have seen fit to take the risk of acquiring only surface rights, we cannot see that the fact that their risk has become a danger warrants the giving to them greater rights than they bought.

Decree reversed.

JUSTICE BRANDEIS, dissenting. . . . [Most of Justice Brandeis' dissent is omitted. He would have upheld the statute as a restriction on a noxious use. The following paragraphs contain his views on the "whole parcel" issue and the relevance of "reciprocity of advantage" to taking questions:]

It is said that one fact for consideration in determining whether the limits of the police power have been exceeded is the extent of the resulting diminution in value; and that here the restriction destroys existing rights of property and contract. But values are relative. If we are to consider the value of the coal kept in place by the restriction, we should compare it with the value of all other parts of the land. That is, with the value not of the coal alone, but with the value of the whole property. The rights of an owner as against the public are not increased by dividing the interests in his property into surface and subsoil. The sum of the rights in the parts can not be greater than the rights in the whole. The estate of an owner in land is grandiloquently described as extending *ab orco usque ad coelum.* But I suppose no one would contend that by selling his interest above one hundred feet from the surface he could prevent the State from limiting, by the police power, the height of

Average Reciprocity of Advantage

structures in a city. And why should a sale of underground rights bar the State's power? For aught that appears the value of the coal kept in place by the restriction may be negligible as compared with the value of the whole property, or even as compared with that part of it which is represented by the coal remaining in place and which may be extracted despite the statute. . . .

A prohibition of mining which causes subsidence of such structures and facilities is obviously enacted for a public purpose; and it seems, likewise, clear that mere notice of intention to mine would not in this connection secure the public safety. Yet it is said that these provisions of the act cannot be sustained as an exercise of the police power where the right to mine such coal has been reserved. The conclusion seems to rest upon the assumption that in order to justify such exercise of the police power there must be "an average reciprocity of advantage" as between the owner of the property restricted and the rest of the community; and that here such reciprocity is absent. Reciprocity of advantage is an important consideration, and may even be an essential, where the State's power is exercised for the purpose of conferring benefits upon the property of a neighborhood, as in drainage projects, or upon adjoining owners, as by party wall provisions. But where the police power is exercised, not to confer benefits upon property owners, but to protect the public from detriment and danger, there is, in my opinion, no room for considering reciprocity of advantage. There was no reciprocal advantage to the owner prohibited from using [his brickyard in the *Hadacheck* case and similar uses in similar cases where use prohibitions were upheld] unless it be the advantage of living and doing business in a civilized community. That reciprocal advantage is given by the act to the coal operators.

NOTES AND QUESTIONS

1. *What Pennsylvania Coal did.* Given the *Mugler* line of cases, culminating in *Hadacheck*, how does Justice Holmes justify his holding that the Pennsylvania statute in the principal case should be "recognized as a taking" that could not be sustained unless compensation were paid to the coal mine owners? Do you understand Holmes to hold that protection of a large number of human habitations, factories, mercantile establishments, public buildings, streets and roads, bridges, and public service facilities of municipal corporations and private corporations was not a significant "public purpose"? Or that destruction of such properties by causing subsidence of the surface of the land was not a "noxious" use of the area below the surface? Or that prohibition of mining so as to cause subsidence was not a "reasonable means" of protecting the public safety, wealth, and property? What is the significance of the court's pointing out that "[t]his is the case of a single private house"? If that is so, why does the Court also consider "the general validity of the act?"

2. *The property interest taken.* If Holmes was correct in holding that the Pennsylvania statute in the principal case amounted to a de facto "taking" of private property for public use, what kind of a "property interest" was "taken"? At oral argument, counsel for the Pennsylvania Coal Company identified three distinct estates in mining property: surface, subsurface, and a distinctive Pennsylvanian "right to have the surface supported by the subjacent strata." 260 U.S. at 395. The statute certainly "deprived" the coal companies of what might be called the "privilege" to destroy this support "estate," but Pennsylvania clearly did not "acquire" it. How, therefore, could the statute be deemed to effect a "taking" of private property for public use? Why should the deprivation of the privilege in question be "recognized as a taking" simply because the resulting economic loss to the coal companies would be substantial? Recall the language in *Hadacheck* indicating that substantial economic loss is irrelevant when the police power is exerted non-arbitrarily against property owners. Review the facts in *Pennsylvania Coal.* Might the case have been decided differently if the coal company had acquired its interest in the property *after* the Kohler Act came into force, even if the economic consequences were the same?

3. *The denominator problem.* Even if we accept the Holmes thesis that "while property may be regulated to a certain extent, if regulation goes too far it will be recognized as a taking," on what basis did Holmes find that the regulation went "too far" in *Mahon*? Was Brandeis not right in arguing that "[i]f we are to consider the value of the coal kept in place by the restriction, we should compare it with the value of all other parts of the [coal company's] land"? In ignoring this point, did Holmes implicitly hold that requiring "pillars" of coal to be kept in place to support the surface was ipso facto a "taking," without regard to the relative value of the "pillars" and "all other parts of the land"? This problem has come to be known as the "denominator" problem and has an important place in modern takings law.

4. *Financial loss.* In *Mahon*, Holmes said that "[t]o make it commercially impracticable to mine certain coal [i.e., the "pillars" required for surface support] has very nearly the same effect for constitutional purposes as appropriating or destroying it." This statement was based on the fact the cost of providing artificial support in lieu of the "pillars" of coal would exceed the value of the "pillars." See the coal company's argument, 260 U.S. at 395. Is Holmes's statement consistent with the Court's conclusion in *Hadacheck v. Sebastian* that there was no "taking" despite the fact that transportation of Hadacheck's brick clay to some other locality for manufacturing would be impractical "from a financial standpoint," since the Los Angeles ordinance only prohibited the manufacture of bricks and not the removal of the clay? *Keystone Bituminous Coal Ass'n v. De Benedictis,* 480 U.S. 470 (1987), which is discussed *infra,* sustained a Pennsylvania statute very similar to the Kohler Act and distinguished *Pennsylvania Coal.*

5. *Pennsylvania Coal as history.* Friedman, *A Search for Seizure: Pennsylvania Coal Co. v. Mahon in Context,* 4 L. & Hist. Rev. 1 (1986), provides background. Noting that the Mahons (or their predecessors) had sold the "support estate" and that "[n]o doubt, these risks looked small at the time," he points out that by 1922

> the times . . . had changed radically. . . .The surface now supported a large population; nine counties, with about 1,000,000 people. . . . Moreover, "pillar robbing" had become a serious problem, partly, it was said, because courts had upheld the clauses which waived rights to damages for subsidence. Whole chunks of Scranton were on the verge of collapse. [*Id.* at 2.]

Was the situation in Scranton any different from that in Los Angeles at the time of *Hadacheck*? Was the coal company, in the eyes of the court, in a stronger moral or legal position than Hadacheck? Friedman also notes that a companion Pennsylvania law, the Fowler Act, ignored by both Holmes and Brandeis, provided for an optional fund to compensate victims, supported by

> a tax or, if you will, a kind of private eminent domain. The companies would pay for what they took; the original contracts were in a sense renegotiated. . . . If the state had taxed the public generally, rather than solely the companies, there is little question the scheme would have worked. The companies wanted their cake and eat it too. Pennsylvania Coal Co. refused to pay the Fowler tax [which was optional]; this brought it under the tough terms of the Kohler Act—the iron fist designed to force companies to accept . . . the Fowler Act.

6. *Sources.* For some fascinating recent scholarship on *Pennsylvania Coal* see Brauneis, *The Foundation of Our 'Regulatory Takings' Jurisprudence: The Myth and Meaning of Justice Holmes's Opinion in Pennsylvania Coal Company v. Mahon,* 106 Yale L.J. 613 (1996) (arguing that *Pennsylvania Coal* was not a takings case); Rose, *Mahon Reconstructed: Why the Takings Issue is Still a Muddle,* 57 S. Cal. L. Rev. 561 (1984) (questioning decision); Treanor, *Jam for Justice Holmes: Reassessing the Significance of Mahon,* 86 Geo. L.J. 813 (1998).

———

Four years after *Pennsylvania Coal,* the Supreme Court considered the constitutionality of a modern comprehensive zoning ordinance for the first time in *Euclid v. Ambler Realty.* The decision is the leading case on the constitutionality of zoning. The District Court had held the Euclid ordinance unconstitutional, approaching the question from a different perspective than that later taken by the Supreme Court. Faced with the prospect that the nascent movement to plan and control land uses would be snuffed out by the high court, the proponents of zoning rallied with amicus support. To give you the flavor of the fight, we first set out the facts of the *Euclid* case, taken verbatim from the Supreme Court opinion, followed by excerpts from the District Court opinion and finally the legal analysis of the Supreme Court. The amicus brief is described in the notes following. As you read, note how the doctrinal themes of earlier cases are used (or ignored).

VILLAGE OF EUCLID v. AMBLER REALTY CO.

272 U.S. 365 (1926)

[Justice Sutherland stated the facts as follows:] The Village of Euclid is an Ohio municipal corporation. It adjoins and practically is a suburb of the City of Cleveland. Its estimated population is between 5,000 and 10,000, and its area from twelve to fourteen square miles, the greater part of which is farm lands or unimproved acreage. It lies, roughly, in the form of a parallelogram measuring approximately three and one-half miles each way. East and west it is traversed by three principal highways: Euclid Avenue, through the southerly border, St. Clair Avenue, through the central portion, and Lake Shore Boulevard, through the northerly border in close proximity to the shore of Lake Erie. The Nickel Plate railroad lies from 1,500 to 1,800 feet north of Euclid Avenue, and the Lake Shore railroad 1,600 feet farther to the north. The three highways and the two railroads are substantially parallel.

Appellee is the owner of a tract of land containing 68 acres, situated in the westerly end of the village, abutting on Euclid Avenue to the south and the Nickel Plate railroad to the north. Adjoining this tract, both on the east and on the west, there have been laid out restricted residential plats upon which residences have been erected.

On November 13, 1922, an ordinance was adopted by the Village Council, establishing a comprehensive zoning plan for regulating and restricting the location of trades, industries, apartment houses, two-family houses, single family houses, etc., the lot area to be built upon, the size and height of buildings, etc.

The entire area of the village is divided by the ordinance into six classes of use districts, denominated U-1 to U-6, inclusive; three classes of height districts, denominated H-1 to H-3, inclusive; and four classes of area districts, denominated A-1 to A-4, inclusive. The use districts are classified in respect of the buildings which may be erected within their respective limits, as follows: U-1 is restricted to single family dwellings, public parks, water towers and reservoirs, suburban and interurban electric railway passenger stations and rights of way, and farming, non-commercial greenhouse nurseries and truck gardening; U-2 is extended to include two-family dwellings; U-3 is further extended to include apartment houses, hotels, churches, schools, public libraries, museums, private clubs, community center buildings, hospitals, sanitariums, public playgrounds and recreation buildings, and a city hall and courthouse; U-4 is further extended to include banks, offices, studios, telephone exchanges, fire and police stations, restaurants, theaters and moving picture shows, retail stores and shops, sales offices, sample rooms, wholesale stores for hardware, drugs and groceries, stations for gasoline and oil (not exceeding 1,000 gallons storage) and for ice delivery, skating rinks and dance halls, electric substations, job and newspaper printing, public garages for motor vehicles, stables and wagon sheds (not exceeding five horses, wagons or motor trucks) and distributing stations for central store and commercial enterprises; U-5 is further extended to include billboards and advertising signs (if permitted), warehouses, ice and ice cream manufacturing and cold storage plants, bottling works, milk bottling and central distribution stations, laundries, carpet cleaning, dry cleaning and dyeing establishments, blacksmith, horseshoing, wagon and motor vehicle repair shops, freight stations, street car barns, stables and wagon sheds (for more than five horses, wagons or motor trucks), and wholesale produce markets and salesrooms; U-6 is further extended to include plants for sewage disposal and for producing gas, garbage and refuse incineration, scrap iron, junk, scrap paper and rag storage, aviation fields, cemeteries, crematories, penal and correctional institutions, insane and feeble minded institutions, storage of oil and gasoline (not to exceed 25,000 gallons), and manufacturing and industrial operations of any kind other than, and any public utility not included in, a class U-1, U-2, U-3, U-4 or U-5 use. There is a seventh class of uses which is prohibited altogether.

Class U-1 is the only district in which buildings are restricted to those enumerated. In the other classes the uses are cumulative; that is to say, uses in class U-2 include those enumerated in the preceding class, U-1; class U-3 includes uses enumerated in the preceding classes, U-2 and U-1; and so on. In addition to the enumerated uses, the ordinance provides for accessory uses, that is, for uses customarily incident to the principal use, such as private garages. Many regulations are provided in respect of such accessory uses.

The height districts are classified as follows: In class H-1, buildings are limited to a height of two and one-half stories or thirty-five feet; in class H-2, to four stories or fifty feet; in class H-3, to eighty feet. To all of these, certain exceptions are made, as in the case of church spires, water tanks, etc.

The classification of area districts is: In A-1 districts, dwellings or apartment houses to accommodate more than one family must have at least 5,000 square feet for interior lots and at least 4,000 square feet for corner lots; in A-2 districts, the area must be at least 2,500 square feet for interior lots, and 2,000 square feet for corner lots; in A-3 districts, the limits are 1,250 and 1,000 square feet, respectively; in A-4 districts, the limits are 900 and 700 square feet, respectively. The ordinance contains, in great variety and detail, provisions in respect of width of lots, front, side and rear yards, and other matters, including restrictions and regulations as to the use of bill boards, sign boards and advertising signs.

A single family dwelling consists of a basement and not less than three rooms and a bathroom. A two-family dwelling consists of a basement and not less than four living rooms and a bathroom for each family; and is further described as a detached dwelling for the occupation of two families, one having its principal living rooms on the first floor and the other on the second floor.

Appellee's tract of land comes under U-2, U-3 and U-6. The first strip of 620 feet immediately north of Euclid Avenue falls in class U-2, the next 130 feet to the north, in U-3, and the remainder in U-6. The uses of the first 620 feet, therefore, do not include apartment houses, hotels, churches, schools, or other public and semi-public buildings, or other uses enumerated in respect of U-3 to U-6, inclusive. The uses of the next 130 feet include all of these, but exclude industries, theaters, banks, shops, and the various other uses set forth in respect of U-4 to U-6, inclusive. *

---

* The court below seemed to think that the frontage of this property on Euclid Avenue to a depth of 150 feet came under U-1 district and was available only for single family dwellings. An examination of the ordinance and subsequent amendments, and a comparison of their terms with the maps, shows very clearly, however, that this view was incorrect. Appellee's brief correctly interpreted the ordinance: "The northerly 500 feet thereof immediately adjacent to the right of way of the New York, Chicago & St. Louis Railroad Company under the original ordinance was classed as U-6 territory and the rest thereof as U-2 territory. By amendments to the ordinance a strip 630 [620] feet wide north of Euclid Avenue is classed as U-2 territory, a strip 130 feet wide next north as U-3 territory and the rest of the parcel to the Nickel Plate right of way as U-6 territory."

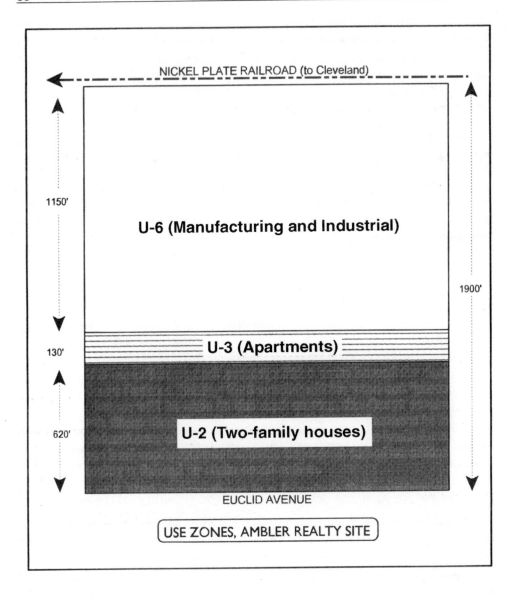

Annexed to the ordinance, and made a part of it, is a zone map, showing the location and limits of the various use, height and area districts, from which it appears that the three classes overlap one another; that is to say, for example, both U-5 and U-6 use districts are in A-4 area districts, but the former is in H-2 and the latter in H-3 height districts. The plan is a complicated one and can be better understood by an inspection of the map, though it does not seem necessary to reproduce it for present purposes.

The lands lying between the two railroads for the entire length of the village area and extending some distance on either side to the north and south, having an average width of about 1,600 feet, are left open, with slight exceptions, for industrial and all other uses. This includes the larger part of appellee's tract. Approximately one-sixth of the area of the entire village is included in

U-5 and U-6 use districts. That part of the village lying south of Euclid Avenue is principally in U-1 districts. The lands lying north of Euclid Avenue and bordering on the long strip just described are included in U-1, U-2, U-3 and U-4 districts, principally in U-2.

The enforcement of the ordinance is entrusted to the inspector of buildings, under rules and regulations of the board of zoning appeals. Meetings of the board are public, and minutes of its proceedings are kept. It is authorized to adopt rules and regulations to carry into effect provisions of the ordinance. Decisions of the inspector of buildings may be appealed to the board by any person claiming to be adversely affected by any such decision. The board is given power in specific cases of practical difficulty or unnecessary hardship to interpret the ordinance in harmony with its general purpose and intent, so that the public health, safety and general welfare may be secure and substantial justice done. Penalties are prescribed for violations, and it is provided that the various provisions are to be regarded as independent and the holding of any provision to be unconstitutional, void or ineffective shall not affect any of the others.

AMBLER REALTY CO. v. VILLAGE OF EUCLID

297 F. 307, 313–16 (N.D. Ohio 1924)

WESTENHAVER, J. The argument supporting this ordinance proceeds both on a mistaken view of what is property and of what is police power. Property, generally speaking, defendant's counsel concedes, is protected against a taking without compensation, by the guaranties of the Ohio and United States Constitutions. But their view seems to be that so long as the owner remains clothed with the legal title thereto and is not ousted from the physical possession thereof, his property is not taken, no matter to what extent his right to use is invaded or destroyed or its present or prospective value is depreciated. This is an erroneous view. The right to property, as used in the Constitution, has no such limited meaning. As has often been said in substance by the Supreme Court: "There can be no conception of property aside from its control and use, and upon its use depends its value." . . .

In defendants' view, the only difference between the police power and eminent domain is that the taking under the former may be done without compensation and under the latter a taking must be paid for. It seems to be the further view that whether one power or the other is exercised depends wholly on what the legislative department may see fit to recite on that subject. Such, however, is not the law. If police power meant what is claimed, all private property is now held subject to temporary and passing phases of public opinion, dominant for a day, in legislative or municipal assemblies. . . . Obviously, police power is not susceptible of exact definition. . . . And yet there is a wide difference between the power of eminent domain and the police power; and it is not true that the public welfare is a justification for the taking of private property for the general good. . . .

Nor can the ordinances here be sustained by invoking the average reciprocity of advantage rule. . . . It is a futile suggestion that plaintiff's present and obvious loss from being deprived of the normal and legitimate use of its property would be compensated indirectly by benefits accruing to that land from the restrictions imposed by the ordinance on other land. It is equally futile to suppose that other property in the village will reap the benefit of the damage to plaintiff's property and that of others similarly situated. The only reasonable probability is that the property values taken from plaintiff and other owners similarly situated will simply disappear, or at best be transferred to other unrestricted sections of the Cleveland industrial area, or at the worst, to some other and far distant industrial area. So far as plaintiff is concerned, it is a pure loss. In the average reciprocity of advantage there is a measureless difference between adjoining property owners as regards a party wall or a boundary pillar, and the owners of property restricted as in this case. In the former there may be some reciprocity of advantage, even though unequal in individual cases. In the present case, the property values are either dissipated or transferred to unknown and more or less distant owners.

The plain truth is that the true object of the ordinance is to place all of the property in an undeveloped area of 16 square miles in a straitjacket. The purpose to be accomplished is really to regulate the mode of living of persons who may hereafter inhabit it. In the last analysis, the result to be accomplished is to classify the population and segregate them according to their income or situation in life. . . .

VILLAGE OF EUCLID v. AMBLER REALTY CO.

272 U.S. 365 (1926)

JUSTICE SUTHERLAND delivered the opinion of the Court:

The ordinance is assailed on the grounds that it is in derogation of § 1 of the Fourteenth Amendment to the Federal Constitution in that it deprives appellee of liberty and property without due process of law and denies it the equal protection of the law, and that it offends against certain provisions of the Constitution of the State of Ohio. The prayer of the bill is for an injunction restraining the enforcement of the ordinance and all attempts to impose or maintain as to appellee's property any of the restrictions, limitations or conditions. The court below held the ordinance to be unconstitutional and void, and enjoined its enforcement. 297 F. 307.

Before proceeding to a consideration of the case, it is necessary to determine the scope of the inquiry. The bill alleges that the tract of land in question is vacant and has been held for years for the purpose of selling and developing it for industrial uses, for which it is especially adapted, being immediately in the path of progressive industrial development; that for such uses it has a market value of about $10,000 per acre, but if the use be limited to residential purposes the market value is not in excess of $2,500 per acre; that the first 200 feet of the parcel back from Euclid Avenue, if unrestricted in respect of use, has a value of $150 per front foot, but if limited to residential uses, and ordinary mercantile business be excluded therefrom, its value is not in excess of $50 per front foot.

It is specifically averred that the ordinance attempts to restrict and control the lawful uses of appellee's land so as to confiscate and destroy a great part of its value; that it is being enforced in accordance with its terms; that prospective buyers of land for industrial, commercial and residential uses in the metropolitan district of Cleveland are deterred from buying any part of this land because of the existence of the ordinance and the necessity thereby entailed of conducting burdensome and expensive litigation in order to vindicate the right to use the land for lawful and legitimate purposes; that the ordinance constitutes a cloud upon the land, reduces and destroys its value, and has the effect of diverting the normal industrial, commercial and residential development thereof to other and less favorable locations.

The record goes no farther than to show, as the lower court found, that the normal, and reasonably to be expected, use and development of that part of appellee's land adjoining Euclid Avenue is for general trade and commercial purposes, particularly retail stores and like establishments, and that the normal, and reasonably to be expected, use and development of the residue of the land is for industrial and trade purposes. Whatever injury is inflicted by the mere existence and threatened enforcement of the ordinance is due to restrictions in respect of these and similar uses; to which perhaps should be added — if not included in the foregoing — restrictions in respect of apartment houses. Specifically, there is nothing in the record to suggest that any damage results from the presence in the ordinance of those restrictions relating to churches, schools, libraries and other public and semi-public buildings. It is neither alleged nor proved that there is, or may be, a demand for any part of appellee's land for any of the last named uses; and we cannot assume the existence of facts which would justify an injunction upon this record in respect of this class of restrictions.

For present purposes the provisions of the ordinance in respect of these uses may, therefore, be put aside as unnecessary to be considered. It is also unnecessary to consider the effect of the restrictions in respect of U-1 districts, since none of appellee's land falls within that class.

We proceed, then, to a consideration of those provisions of the ordinance to which the case as it is made relates, first disposing of a preliminary matter.

A motion was made in the court below to dismiss the bill on the ground that, because complainant [appellee] had made no effort to obtain a building permit or apply to the zoning board of appeals for relief as it might have done under the terms of the ordinance, the suit was premature. The motion was properly overruled. The effect of the allegations of the bill is that the ordinance of its own force operates greatly to reduce the value of appellee's lands and destroy their marketability for industrial, commercial and residential uses; and the attack is directed, not against any specific provision or provisions, but against the ordinance as an entirety. Assuming the premises, the existence and maintenance of the ordinance, in effect, constitutes a present invasion of appellee's property rights and a threat to continue it. Under these circumstances, the equitable jurisdiction is clear.

It is not necessary to set forth the provisions of the Ohio Constitution which are thought to be infringed. The question is the same under both Constitutions, namely, as stated by appellee: Is the ordinance invalid in that it violates the constitutional protection "to the right of property in the appellee by attempted regulations under the guise of the police power, which are unreasonable and confiscatory?"

Building zone laws are of modern origin. They began in this country about twenty-five years ago. Until recent years, urban life was comparatively simple; but with the great increase and concentration of population, problems have developed, and constantly are developing, which require, and will continue to require, additional restrictions in respect of the use and occupation of private lands in urban communities. Regulations, the wisdom, necessity and validity of which, as applied to existing conditions, are so apparent that they are now uniformly sustained, a century ago, or even half a century ago, probably would have been rejected as arbitrary and oppressive. Such regulations are sustained, under the complex conditions of our day, for reasons analogous to those which justify traffic regulations, which, before the advent of automobiles and rapid transit street railways, would have been condemned as fatally arbitrary and unreasonable. And in this there is no inconsistency, for while the meaning of constitutional guaranties never varies, the scope of their application must expand or contract to meet the new and different conditions which are constantly coming within the field of their operation. In a changing world, it is impossible that it should be otherwise. But although a degree of elasticity is thus imparted, not to the *meaning,* but to the *application* of constitutional principles, statutes and ordinances, which, after giving due weight to the new conditions, are found clearly not to conform to the Constitution, of course, must fall.

The ordinance now under review, and all similar laws and regulations, must find their justification in some aspect of the police power, asserted for the public welfare. The line which in this field separates the legitimate from the illegitimate assumption of power is not capable of precise delimitation. It varies with circumstances and conditions. A regulatory zoning ordinance, which would be clearly valid as applied to the great cities, might be clearly invalid as applied to rural communities. In solving doubts, the maxim *sic utere tuo ut alienum non laedas,* which lies at the foundation of so much of the common law of nuisances, ordinarily will furnish a fairly helpful clew. And the law of nuisances, likewise, may be consulted, not for the purpose of controlling, but for the helpful aid of its analogies in the process of ascertaining the scope of, the power. Thus the question whether the power exists to forbid the erection of a building of a particular kind or for a particular use, like the question whether a particular thing is a nuisance, is to be determined, not by an abstract consideration of the building or of the thing considered apart, but by considering it in connection with the circumstances and the locality. A nuisance may be merely a right thing in the wrong place, — like a pig in the parlor instead of the barnyard. If the validity of the legislative classification for zoning purposes be fairly debatable, the legislative judgment must be allowed to control.

There is no serious difference of opinion in respect of the validity of laws and regulations fixing the height of buildings within reasonable limits, the character of materials and methods of construction, and the adjoining area which must be left open, in order to minimize the danger of fire or collapse, the evils of over-crowding, and the like, and excluding from residential sections offensive trades, industries and structures likely to create nuisances.

Here, however, the exclusion is in general terms of all industrial establishments, and it may thereby happen that not only offensive or dangerous industries will be excluded, but those which are neither offensive nor dangerous will share the same fate. But this is no more than happens in respect of many practice-forbidding laws which this Court has upheld although drawn in general terms so as to include individual cases that may turn out to be innocuous in themselves. The inclusion of a reasonable margin to insure effective enforcement, will not put upon a law, otherwise valid, the stamp of invalidity. Such laws may also find their justification in the fact that, in some fields, the bad fades into the good by such insensible degrees that the two are not capable of being readily distinguished and separated in terms of legislation. In the light of these considerations, we are not prepared to say that the end in view was not sufficient to justify the general rule of the ordinance, although some industries of an innocent character might fall within the proscribed class. It can not be said that the ordinance in this respect "passes the bounds of reason and assumes the character of a merely arbitrary fiat." *Purity Extract Co. v. Lynch,* 226 U.S. 192. Moreover, the restrictive provisions of the ordinance in this particular may be sustained upon the principles applicable to the broader exclusion from residential districts of all business and trade structures, presently to be discussed.

It is said that the Village of Euclid is a mere suburb of the City of Cleveland; that the industrial development of that city has now reached and in some degree extended into the village and, in the obvious course of things, will soon absorb the entire area for industrial enterprises; that the effect of the ordinance is to divert this natural development elsewhere with the consequent loss of increased values to the owners of the lands within the village borders. But the village, though physically a suburb of Cleveland, is politically a separate municipality, with powers of its own and authority to govern itself as it sees fit within the limits of the organic law of its creation and the State and Federal Constitutions. Its governing authorities, presumably representing a majority of its inhabitants and voicing their will, have determined, not that industrial development shall cease at its boundaries, but that the course of such development shall proceed within definitely fixed lines. If it be a proper exercise of the police power to relegate industrial establishments to localities separated from residential sections, it is not easy to find a sufficient reason for denying the power because the effect of its exercise is to divert an industrial flow from the course which it would follow, to the injury of the residential public if left alone, to another course where such injury will be obviated. It is not meant by this, however, to exclude the possibility of cases where the general public interest would so far outweigh the interest of the municipality that the municipality would not be allowed to stand in the way.

We find no difficulty in sustaining restrictions of the kind thus far reviewed. The serious question in the case arises over the provisions of the ordinance excluding from residential districts, apartment houses, business houses, retail stores and shops, and other like establishments. This question involves the validity of what is really the crux of the more recent zoning legislation, namely, the creation and maintenance of residential districts, from which business and trade of every sort, including hotels and apartment houses, are excluded. Upon that question this Court has not thus far spoken. The decisions of the state courts are numerous and conflicting; but those which broadly sustain the power greatly outnumber those which deny altogether or narrowly limit it; and it is very apparent that there is a constantly increasing tendency in the direction of the broader view. . . .

As evidence of the decided trend toward the broader view, it is significant that in some instances the state courts in later decisions have reversed their former decisions holding the other way. . . .

The decisions enumerated in the first group cited above agree that the exclusion of buildings devoted to business, trade, etc., from residential districts, bears a rational relation to the health and safety of the community. Some of the grounds for this conclusion are — promotion of the health and security from injury of children and others by separating dwelling houses from territory devoted to trade and industry; suppression and prevention of disorder; facilitating the extinguishment of fires, and the enforcement of street traffic regulations and other general welfare ordinances; aiding the health and safety of the community by excluding from residential areas the confusion and danger of fire, contagion and disorder which in greater or less degree attach to the location of stores, shops and factories. Another ground is that the construction and repair of streets may be rendered easier and less expensive by confining the greater part of the heavy traffic to the streets where business is carried on. . . .

The matter of zoning has received much attention at the hands of commissions and experts, and the results of their investigations have been set forth in comprehensive reports. These reports, which bear every evidence of painstaking consideration, concur in the view that the segregation of residential, business, and industrial buildings will make it easier to provide fire apparatus suitable for the character and intensity of the development in each section; that it will increase the safety and security of home life; greatly tend to prevent street accidents, especially to children, by reducing the traffic and resulting confusion in residential sections; decrease noise and other conditions which produce or intensify nervous disorders; preserve a more favorable environment in which to rear children, etc. With particular reference to apartment houses, it is pointed out that the development of detached house sections is greatly retarded by the coming of apartment houses, which has sometimes resulted in destroying the entire section for private house purposes; that in such sections very often the apartment house is a mere parasite, constructed in order to take advantage of the open spaces and attractive surroundings created by the residential character of the district. Moreover, the coming of one apartment house is followed by others, interfering by their height and bulk with the free circulation of air and monopolizing the rays of the sun which otherwise would fall upon the smaller homes, and bringing, as their necessary accompaniments, the disturbing noises incident to increased traffic and business, and the occupation, by means of moving and parked automobiles, of larger portions of the streets, thus detracting from their safety and depriving children of the privilege of quiet and open spaces for play, enjoyed by those in more favored localities, — until, finally, the residential character of the neighborhood and its desirability as a place of detached residences are utterly destroyed. Under these circumstances, apartment houses, which in a different environment would be not only entirely unobjectionable but highly desirable, come very near to being nuisances.

If these reasons, thus summarized, do not demonstrate the wisdom or sound policy in all respects of those restrictions which we have indicated as pertinent to the inquiry, at least, the reasons are sufficiently cogent to preclude us from saying, as it must be said before the ordinance can be declared unconstitutional, that such provisions are clearly arbitrary and unreasonable, having no substantial relation to the public health, safety, morals, or general welfare.

It is true that when, if ever, the provisions set forth in the ordinance in tedious and minute detail, come to be concretely applied to particular premises, including those of the appellee, or to particular conditions, or to be considered in connection with specific complaints, some of them, or even many of them, may be found to be clearly arbitrary and unreasonable. But where the equitable remedy of injunction is sought, as it is here, not upon the ground of a present infringement or denial of a specific right, or of a particular injury in process of actual execution, but upon the broad ground that the mere existence and threatened enforcement of the ordinance, by materially and adversely affecting values and curtailing the opportunities of the market, constitute a present and irreparable injury, the court will not scrutinize its provisions, sentence by sentence, to ascertain by a process of piecemeal dissection whether there may be, here and there, provisions of a minor character, or relating to matters of administration, or not shown to contribute to the injury complained of, which, if attacked separately, might not withstand the test of constitutionality. In respect of such provisions, of which specific complaint is not made, it cannot be said that the land owner has suffered or is threatened with an injury which entitles him to challenge their constitutionality. . . .

. . . What would be the effect of a restraint imposed by one or more of the innumerable provisions of the ordinance, considered apart, upon the value or marketability of the lands is neither disclosed by the bill nor by the evidence, and we are afforded no basis, apart from mere speculation, upon which to rest a conclusion that it or they would have any appreciable effect upon those matters. Under these circumstances, therefore, it is enough for us to determine, as we do, that the ordinance in its general scope and dominant features, so far as its provisions are here involved, is a valid exercise of authority, leaving other provisions to be dealt with as cases arise directly involving them.

And this is in accordance with the traditional policy of this Court. In the realm of constitutional law, especially, this Court has perceived the embarrassment which is likely to result from an attempt to formulate rules or decide questions beyond the necessities of the immediate issue. It has preferred to follow the method of a gradual approach to the general by a systematically guarded application and extension of constitutional principles to particular cases as they arise, rather than by out of hand attempts to establish general rules to which future cases must be fitted. This process applies with peculiar force to the solution of questions arising under the due process clause of the Constitution as applied to the exercise of the flexible powers of police, with which we are here concerned.

Decree reversed.

Justice Van Devanter, Justice McReynolds and Justice Butler, dissent.

NOTES AND QUESTIONS

1. *A change of heart.* "Justice Sutherland . . . was writing an opinion for the majority in *Village of Euclid v. Ambler Realty Co.,* holding the zoning ordinance unconstitutional, when talks with his dissenting brethren (principally Stone, I believe) shook his convictions and led him to request a reargument, after which he changed his mind and the ordinance was upheld." McCormack, *A Law Clerk's Recollections,* 46 Colum. L. Rev. 710, 712 (1946). In view of the district court's opinion, the powerful argument of Newton D. Baker, a highly capable attorney, on behalf of Ambler Realty, and the decision in favor of the Euclid ordinance after the rehearing, the Court's opinion by the conservative Justice Sutherland was rather surprising. The three dissenting justices did not write an opinion.

2. *Euclid as a "test case."* One of the factors strongly influencing the Court toward a favorable decision on the broad issue of constitutionality of zoning was undoubtedly the brief filed by Alfred Bettman as counsel for several *amici curiae,* including the National Conference on City Planning, the Ohio State Conference on City Planning, the National Housing Association, and the Massachusetts Federation of Town Planning Boards. Alfred Bettman was a leading national land use attorney in the years between the two world wars. His views on the *Euclid* case after the decision of the federal district court were expressed in the following letter:

> Regarding the Euclid Village zoning decision, the case was unfortunate. . . . The City made no scientific survey, and in an effort to keep the village entirely residential, the local authorities zoned all as residential and business, except a very narrow piece along the railroads, too narrow for a practical industrial development. It was a piece of arbitrary zoning and on the facts not justifiable. . . . Everybody advised against an appeal [from the District Court decision], because on appeal the decision is sure to be affirmed, even though the upper court disagrees with the opinion. [Letter from A. Bettman to D.J. Underwood, City Attorney, Tulsa, Oklahoma, Sept. 29, 1924.]

The views thus expressed by Bettman in 1924 no doubt account for his decision to ask the Supreme Court, on rehearing the *Euclid* case, to decide only "the constitutionality of comprehensive zoning" *in principle,* and not to consider "the reasonableness or arbitrariness of that detail of the ordinance which . . . placed appellee's land in a residential rather than an industrial zone." For an extensive discussion of the motivations for single family residential zoning in the years before *Euclid,* see Lees, *Preserving Property Values? Preserving Proper Homes? Preserving Privilege?: the Pre-Euclid Debate over Zoning for Exclusively Private Residential Areas, 1916–1926,* 56 U. Pitt. L. Rev. 367 (1994). She finds the expected concerns about preserving residential quality as well as discriminatory motives.

3. *A critique of Euclid.* For all its celebrity, *Euclid* is not without its critics. Professor Tarlock uses the Bettman brief as his starting point.

TARLOCK, EUCLID REVISITED, Land Use Law & Zoning Digest, Vol. 34, No. 1, at 4, 6–8 (1982) *

The Taking Issue

. . . Bettman's argument rested on a factual assumption that was unwarranted and proceeded to a theory that would read the taking clause out of the Constitution. Ambler Realty Co.'s claim that the value of its property had been taken was called "speculative" and thus not entitled to compensation because "one may not speculate upon a community's not exercising its constitutional police power and then claim a property right in the community's non-action. In truth the old value for which protection is claimed may have been produced, in whole or in part, by the very evil against which the legislation is directed."

Bettman quickly went on to point out what the court held two years later in *Nectow v. City of Cambridge*: the fact that a specific line drawing may be unconstitutional does not impair the validity of the plan as a whole.

Then, to bolster the basic argument that the Court should focus on comprehensive zoning in the abstract, Bettman distinguished Ambler's best case, *Pennsylvania Coal v. Mahon,* first on the technical ground that zoning was an exercise of the police power and not the power of eminent domain, and, second, that the property rights asserted by Ambler Realty Co., unlike the property rights created by deed in *Pennsylvania Coal,* were "simply those which inhere generally in all owners of land: and it is axiomatic that all property is held subject to the general right of the public to regulate its use for the protection of public health, safety, convenience, welfare."

Average Reciprocity of Advantage

These arguments that the ordinance was not a taking are essentially negative, but at two points in the brief Bettman advanced a powerful affirmative abstract argument in favor of the ordinance. The strongest general justification for zoning is that it is a publicly imposed restrictive covenant scheme; thus, restrictions on one lot can be justified by the average reciprocity of advantage that the complaining lot receives from similar restrictions imposed on adjoining lots. . . . Bettman argued that a comprehensive ordinance was constitutional because "each piece of property pays, in the shape of reasonable regulation of its use, for the protection which the plan gives to all property lying within its boundaries." Later in the brief, he asserted that a comprehensive zoning ordinance "gives to each piece of property its share of the general health, order, convenience, and security which the whole plan brings to the community."

Comprehensive zoning ordinances

---

* Reprinted by permission.

Public Nuisance Analogy

The core of [Bettman's] argument is found in a paragraph [from his brief]:

> The law of nuisance operates by way of prevention as well as by suppression. The zoning ordinance, by segregating the industrial districts from the residential districts, aims to produce, by a process of prevention applied over the whole territory of the city throughout an extensive period of time, the segregation of the noises and odors and turmoils necessarily incident to the operation of industry from those sections of the city in which the homes of the people are or may be appropriately located. The mode of regulation may be new; but the purpose and the fundamental justification are the same. . . .

[Bettman anticipated an argument that], if the purpose of zoning is to segregate nuisance-like activities, [shouldn't an owner have the opportunity] to prove that his use would not in fact be a nuisance? Bettman answered this objection by denying that a zoning ordinance was "restricted to or identical with nuisance regulation." He argued that nuisance law had become so confused that it was impossible to advise a client about the fate of a proposed use, and thus it was proper to make use segregations in advance of construction based on the probable nuisance like characteristics of a proposed use.

Market Allocation

[Bettman's final argument was] . . . that (1) zoning is necessary to correct a market failure that prevents the market from achieving an efficient allocation of land uses; (2) it is quite possible for cities to predict the course of the market and to draw a zoning map that will be filled in efficiently over time; and (3) therefore, a comprehensive zoning ordinance is entitled to the full presumption of constitutionality.

The end result was to be a tidy zoning map with everything in its proper place. "[T]he zone plan is one consistent whole, with parts adjusted to each other, carefully worked out on the basis of actual facts and tendencies, including actual economic factors, so as to secure development of all the territory within the city in such a way as to promote the public health, safety, convenience, order, and general welfare." . . .

Justice Sutherland's Response

Bettman's analysis of nuisance law seems to have been directly incorporated in three places in Justice Sutherland's opinion. . . . "In solving doubts [Sutherland says], the maxim *sic utere tuo ut alienum non laedes,* which lies at the foundation of so much of the common law of nuisances, ordinarily will furnish a fairly helpful clew." This is simply another way of stating that in nuisance law everything depends on the context of the dispute.

Bettman's "margin of safety" argument . . .impressed Sutherland. After advancing the nuisance analogy as a justification for zoning, Justice Sutherland quickly concluded that zoning ordinances need be no more over-inclusive than other types of regulation that had been held constitutional. Thus, the risk that inoffensive uses would be kept out of an area was not a sufficient reason to invalidate a comprehensive ordinance.

The hardest problem for Justice Sutherland was the constitutionality of segregating one type of residential use from another, but he resolved it in favor of zoning by characterizing apartment houses as parasites robbing single-family neighborhoods of value.

Conclusion

. . . On the basis of published accounts of the circumstances that led to the case, as well as the evidence presented at trial and the famous Bettman *amicus* brief that influenced the court on rehearing, the case at best validates a limited and flawed vision of zoning. Thus *Euclid* is not a sufficient basis for much contemporary zoning. The most difficult issues in zoning were glossed over or ignored by most parties to the litigation, and they continue to plague the courts. There is nothing very surprising in this conclusion. Most land use scholars have known it for years.

NOTES AND QUESTIONS

1. *Repositioning Euclid as a facial challenge.* It is quite clear that Justice Sutherland decided only "the constitutionality of comprehensive zoning" and not "the reasonableness or arbitrariness of that detail of the ordinance which . . . placed appellee's land in a residential rather than an industrial zone," as Bettman urged in the part of his brief quoted above. Thus the Court was able to avoid any serious consideration of the appellee's contention that the Euclid zoning ordinance reduced the value of its land so greatly as to result in a "taking" without compensation, in violation of the Fourteenth Amendment's "due process" clause.

2. *Zoning "as applied."* Had the case been decided "as applied," it is more likely that Ambler Realty would have won. (On what theory: takings; substantive due process; equal protection?) Had Ambler Realty won, would the inevitable result have been to cast constitutional doubt on *all* zoning schemes? Conversely, because the Village of Euclid won, did that imply that *all* zoning was constitutional? Two years later, in *Nectow v. City of Cambridge*, 277 U.S. 183 (1928), the Court took an "as applied" case and held against the city. *Nectow* is discussed further in Ch. 3, *infra*.

3. *Euclid and Pennsylvania Coal.* Lacking confidence in the professional quality of Euclid's ordinance, it is understandable why Bettman was so anxious to have it facially reviewed. Even so, why did the court completely ignore *Pennsylvania Coal Co. v. Mahon*, decided only four years earlier? Under the holding in *Pennsylvania Coal*, wouldn't Ambler Realty's allegations about the diminution in value as a result of the *adoption* of the ordinance, if supported by evidence, tend strongly to show that the zoning regulations "went too far" and amounted to a *de facto* "taking"? Does the court's failure to even cite *Pennsylvania Coal* imply that a comprehensive zoning ordinance can never amount to a regulatory taking? This question informs much of the modern constitutional law of land use controls.

4. *Average reciprocity of advantage.* Note that Justice Sutherland's opinion does not refer to, much less rely on, the "average reciprocity of advantage" argument included in the Bettman brief. Justices Holmes and Brandeis each discussed this concept in *Pennsylvania Coal,* but Bettman cites neither. Holmes used the concept narrowly; Brandeis, whose dissenting position would have been supported by the broad concept that Bettman stated, apparently thought that such a broad use of "average reciprocity" was untenable, as did Judge Westenhaver in the *Euclid* trial opinion. Justice Sutherland no doubt agreed with Justice Brandeis and Judge Westenhaver. But consider Professor Michelman's point:

> [W]e might choose to view majoritarian collective action not as a succession of unrelated particular measures, each having an independently calculable distributional impact, but — more faithfully to the facts of political life — as an ongoing process of accommodation leaving in its wake a deposit of varied distributional impacts which significantly offset each other. [Michelman, *Property and Fairness: Comments on the Ethical Foundations of "Just Compensation" Law,* 80 Harv. L. Rev. 1165, 1177 (1967).]

Does Michelman embrace Bettman's argument? If (for sake of argument) Holmes' narrow use is correct and Bettman's broad use is untenable, where is the dividing line? Would the average reciprocity of advantage concept be applicable, for instance, within a built-up urban residential area "zoned" exclusively for residential use?

5. *Understanding Euclid.* As Professor Tarlock notes, *Euclid* was a poor vehicle for setting the 20th century course of American land use law. Consider the following factors: (1) the case arose in a middle-class suburban community, and the court did not review the policy basis for that community's zoning ordinance; (2) while much of Euclid was not built up at the time of this decision, the case projects an image of the community that assumes a closely developed suburb at fairly high densities; (3) judicial notice was taken of techniques of apartment building, now outmoded, that provided an important factual backdrop for the opinion; (4) what worried the court most was the separation of incompatible uses; and (5) an implied hierarchy of land use categories was erected that placed single-family residential at the top of the pyramid. But the Court completely failed to notice that if, e.g., single-family dwellings were built at the same density as apartments, the parking problems would be the same; and that, if apartments were built at the same height as single-family dwellings, the light and air problems would disappear. By ignoring the possibilities for accommodation between "uses" that more sophisticated site and density controls might have provided, the Supreme Court in the *Euclid* case ratified a control technique based on the separation of mutually incompatible land uses, and thus the exclusion of the less desirable "intruding" uses from what might be called "harm-sensitive" land. The "zoning" technique of land use regulation is treated in detail in Chs. 3, 4, and 5, *infra.*

6. *Sources.* For additional discussion of the *Euclid* decision and arguments to the Court, see the collection of essays in Zoning and the American Dream (C. Haar & J. Kayden eds., 1989), especially Brooks, *The Office File Box —*

Emanations from the Battlefield, at 3; Knack, *Return to Euclid*, Planning, Vol. 62, No. 11 at 4 (1996), sketches the post-decision planning history of Euclid (bleak), with useful photographs.

2. *PENN CENTRAL*: THE BALANCING TEST

The next major Supreme Court case on the taking issue did not come until the late 1970s, and it was a highly charged case arising out of an attempt to construct what many considered an ugly skyscraper on the roof of Grand Central Station in New York City, a national icon. Justice Brennan's opinion for the majority follows:

PENN CENTRAL TRANSPORTATION CO. v. CITY OF NEW YORK

438 U.S. 104 (1978)

[The following statement of facts is taken from the official Syllabus.] Under New York City's Landmarks Preservation Law (Landmarks Law), which was enacted to protect historic landmarks and neighborhoods from precipitate decisions to destroy or fundamentally alter their character, the Landmarks Preservation Commission (Commission) may designate a building to be a "landmark" on a particular "landmark site" or may designate an area to be a "historic district." The Board of Estimate may thereafter modify or disapprove the designation, and the owner may seek judicial review of the final designation decision. The owner of the designated landmark must keep the building's exterior "in good repair" and before exterior alterations are made must secure Commission approval.

Under two ordinances owners of landmark sites may transfer development rights from a landmark parcel to proximate lots. Under the Landmarks Law, the Grand Central Terminal (Terminal), which is owned by the Penn Central Transportation Co. and its affiliates (Penn Central), was designated a "landmark" and the block it occupies a "landmark site." Appellant Penn Central, though opposing the designation before the Commission, did not seek judicial review of the final designation decision. Thereafter appellant Penn Central entered into a lease with appellant UGP, whereby UGP was to construct a multistory office building over the Terminal. (UGP agreed to pay Penn Central $1 million annually during construction and a minimum of $3 million annually thereafter.) After the Commission had rejected appellants' plans for the building as destructive of the Terminal's historic and aesthetic features, with no judicial review thereafter being sought, appellants brought suit in state court claiming that the application of the Landmarks Law had "taken" their property without just compensation in violation of the Fifth and Fourteenth Amendments and arbitrarily deprived them of their property without due process of law in violation of the Fourteenth Amendment. The trial court's grant of relief was reversed on appeal. . .

JUSTICE BRENNAN delivered the opinion of the Court:

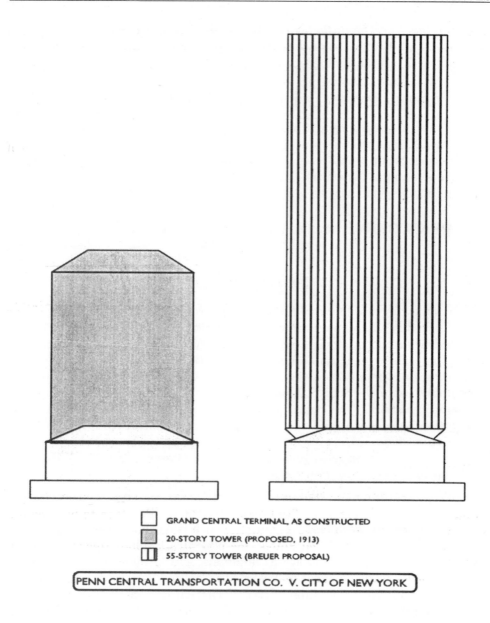

GRAND CENTRAL TERMINAL, AS CONSTRUCTED

20-STORY TOWER (PROPOSED, 1913)

55-STORY TOWER (BREUER PROPOSAL)

PENN CENTRAL TRANSPORTATION CO. V. CITY OF NEW YORK

I

[Justice Brennan noted that Grand Central station, erected in 1913, was "a magnificent example of the French beaux-art style." It faces 42nd Street at its intersection with Park Avenue. "Although a 20-story office tower, to have been located above the Terminal, was part of the original design, the planned tower was never constructed." The Terminal was one of many buildings owned by Penn Central in the area, including a number of hotels and office buildings.

[Penn Central presented two proposals. "The first, Breuer I, provided for the construction of a 55-story office building, to be cantilevered above the existing facade and to rest on the roof of the Terminal. The second, Breuer II Revised, called for tearing down a portion of the Terminal that included the 42d Street facade, stripping off some of the remaining features of the Terminal's facade, and constructing a 53-story office building." The Commission denied both proposals. It concentrated on the view of the building from Park Avenue. Although a high-rise office building 375 feet away to the north had already destroyed this view, the commission found "majestic approach from the south to be still unique in the city." A 55-story building on top of the Terminal would be far more detrimental and "nothing more than an aesthetic joke."]

II

The issues presented by appellants are (1) whether the restrictions imposed by New York City's law upon appellants' exploitation of the Terminal site effect a "taking" of appellants' property for a public use within the meaning of the Fifth Amendment, which of course is made applicable to the States through the Fourteenth Amendment, and, (2) if so, whether the transferable development rights afforded appellants constitute "just compensation" within the meaning of the Fifth Amendment. We need only address the question whether a "taking" has occurred.[25]

A

Before considering appellants' specific contentions, it will be useful to review the factors that have shaped the jurisprudence of the Fifth Amendment injunction "nor shall private property be taken for public use, without just compensation." The question of what constitutes a "taking" for purposes of the Fifth Amendment has proved to be a problem of considerable difficulty. While this Court has recognized that the "Fifth Amendment's guarantee [is] designed to bar Government from forcing some people alone to bear public burdens which, in all fairness and justice, should be borne by the public as a whole," *Armstrong v. United States,* 364 U.S. 40, 49 (1960), this Court, quite simply, has been unable to develop any "set formula" for determining when "justice and fairness" require that economic injuries caused by public action be compensated by the Government, rather than remain disproportionately concentrated on a few persons. See *Goldblatt v. Hempstead,* 369 U.S. 590, 594 (1962). Indeed, we have frequently observed that whether a particular restriction will be rendered invalid by the Government's failure to pay for any losses proximately caused by it depends largely "upon the particular circumstances [in that] case." *United States v. Central Eureka Mining Co.,* 357 U.S. 155, 168 (1958).

In engaging in these essentially ad hoc, factual inquiries, the Court's decisions have identified several factors that have particular significance. The economic impact of the regulation on the claimant and, particularly, the extent to which the regulation has interfered with distinct investment backed

---

[25] As is implicit in our opinion, we do not embrace the proposition that a "taking" can never occur unless Government has transferred physical control over a portion of a parcel.

expectations are of course relevant considerations. See *Goldblatt v. Hemp-stead, supra,* at 594. So too is the character of the governmental action. A "taking" may more readily be found when the interference with property can be characterized as a physical invasion by Government, see, e.g., *Causby v. United States,* 328 U.S. 256 (1946), than when interference arises from some public program adjusting the benefits and burdens of economic life to promote the common good.

"Government could hardly go on if to some extent values incident to property could not be diminished without paying for every such change in the general law." *Pennsylvania Coal Co. v. Mahon,* 260 U.S. 393, 413 (1922), and this Court has accordingly recognized, in a wide variety of contexts, that Government may execute laws or programs that adversely affect recognized economic values. Exercises of the taxing power are one obvious example. A second are the decisions in which this Court has dismissed "taking" challenges on the ground that, while the challenged Government action caused economic harm, it did not interfere with interests that were sufficiently bound up with the reasonable expectations of the claimant to constitute "property" for Fifth Amendment purposes. See, e.g., *United States v. Willow River Power Co.,* 324 U.S. 499 (1945) (interest in high water level of river for run off for tail waters to maintain power head is not property); *United States v. Chandler-Dunbar Water Power Co.,* 229 U.S. 53 (1913) (no property interest can exist in navigable waters); see also Sax, *Takings and the Police Power,* 74 Yale L.J. 36, 61–62 (1963).

More importantly for the present case, in instances in which a state tribunal reasonably concluded that "the health, safety, morals or general welfare" would be promoted by prohibiting particular contemplated uses of land, this Court has upheld land use regulations that destroyed or adversely affected recognized real property interests. Zoning laws are of course the classic example, see *Euclid v. Ambler Realty Co.,* 272 U.S. 365 (1926) (prohibition of industrial use); *Gorieb v. Fox,* 274 U.S. 603, 608 (1927) (requirement that portions of parcels be left unbuilt); *Welch v. Swasey,* 214 U.S. 91 (1909) (height restriction), which have been viewed as permissible governmental action even when prohibiting the most beneficial use of the property.

Zoning laws generally do not affect existing uses of real property, but taking challenges have also been held to be without merit in a wide variety of situations when the challenged governmental actions prohibited a beneficial use to which individual parcels had previously been devoted and thus caused substantial individualized harm. *Miller v. Schoene,* 276 U.S. 272 (1928), is illustrative. In that case, a state entomologist, acting pursuant to a state statute, ordered the claimants to cut down a large number of ornamental red cedar trees because they produced cedar rust fatal to apple trees cultivated nearby. Although the statute provided for recovery of any expense incurred in removing the cedars, and permitted claimants to use the felled trees, it did not provide compensation for the value of the standing trees or for the resulting decrease in market value of the properties as a whole. A unanimous Court held that this latter omission did not render the statute invalid. The Court held that the State might properly make "a choice between the preservation of one class of property and that of the other" and since the apple industry was important in the State involved, concluded that the State had not exceeded "its constitutional powers by deciding upon the destruction of one class of property [without compensation] in order to save another, which, in the judgment of the legislature, is of greater value to the public." *Id.*, at 279.

Again, *Hadacheck v. Sebastian*, 239 U.S. 394 (1915), upheld a law prohibiting the claimant from continuing his otherwise lawful business of operating a brickyard in a particular physical community on the ground that the legislature had reasonably concluded that the presence of the brickyard was inconsistent with neighboring uses. See also *United States v. Central Eureka Mining Co., supra* (government order closing gold mines so that skilled miners would be available for other mining work held not a taking); *Atchison, T. & S.F.R. Co. v. Public Utilities Comm.*, 346 U.S. 346 (1953) (railroad may be required to pay cost of constructing railroad grade crossing); *Walls v. Midland Carbon Co.*, 254 U.S. 300 (1920) (law prohibiting manufacture of carbon black upheld); *Reinman v. Little Rock*, 237 U.S. 171 (1915) (law prohibiting livery stable upheld); *Mugler v. Kansas*, 123 U.S. 623 (1887) (law prohibiting liquor business upheld).

Goldblatt v. Hempstead, supra, is a recent example. There, a 1958 city safety ordinance banned any excavations below the water table and effectively prohibited the claimant from continuing a sand and gravel mining business that had been operated on the particular parcel since 1927. The Court upheld the ordinance against a "taking" challenge, although the ordinance prohibited the present and presumably most beneficial use of the property and had, like the regulations in *Miller* and *Hadacheck,* impacted severely on a particular owner. The Court assumed that the ordinance did not prevent the owner's reasonable use of the property since the owner made no showing of an adverse effect on the value of the land. Because the restriction served a substantial public purpose, the Court thus held no taking had occurred. It is of course implicit in *Goldblatt* that a use restriction on real property may constitute a "taking" if not reasonably necessary to the effectuation of a substantial public purpose, see *Nectow v. Cambridge,* [277 U.S. 183 (1928)]; cf. *Moore v. City of East Cleveland,* 431 U.S. 494, 513–514 (1977) (Stevens, J., concurring), or perhaps if it has an unduly harsh impact upon the owner's use of the property.

Pennsylvania Coal Co. v. Mahon, 260 U.S. 393 (1922), is the leading case for the proposition that a state statute that substantially furthers important public policies may so frustrate distinct investment-backed expectations as to amount to a "taking." There the claimant had sold the surface rights to particular parcels of property, but expressly reserved the right to remove the coal thereunder. A Pennsylvania statute, enacted after the transactions, forbade any mining of coal that caused the subsidence of any house, unless the house was the property of the owner of the underlying coal and was more than 150 feet from the improved property of another. Because the statute made it commercially impracticable to mine the coal, *id.,* at 414, and thus had nearly the same effect as the complete destruction of rights claimant had purchased from the owners of the surface land, see *id.,* at 414–415, the Court held that the statute was invalid as effecting a "taking" without just compensation. See also *Armstrong v. United States, supra.* (Government's complete destruction of a materialman's lien in certain property held a "taking"); *Hudson Water Co. v. McCarter,* 209 U.S. 349, 355 (1908) (if height restriction makes property wholly useless "the right of property prevails over the public interest" and compensation is required). See generally Michelman, *Property, Utility, and Fairness: Comments on the Ethical Foundations of "Just Compensation" Law,* 80 Harv. L. Rev. 1165, 1229–1234 (1967).

Finally, Government actions that may be characterized as acquisitions of resources to permit or facilitate uniquely public functions have often been held to constitute "takings." *Causby v. United States, supra,* is illustrative. In holding that direct overflights above the claimant's land, that destroyed the present use of the land as a chicken farm, constituted a "taking," *Causby* emphasized that Government had not "merely destroyed property [but was] using a part of it for the flight of its planes." *Id.,* at 262–263, n. 7. See also *Griggs v. Allegheny County,* 369 U.S. 84 (1962) (overflights held a taking); *Portsmouth Co. v. United States,* 260 U.S. 327 (1922) (United States' military installations repeated firing of guns over claimant's land is a taking); *United States v. Cress,* 243 U.S. 316 (1917) (repeated floodings of land caused by water project is taking); but see *YMCA v. United States,* 395 U.S. 85 (1969) (damage caused to building when federal officers who were seeking to protect building were attacked by rioters held not a taking). See generally Michelman, 80 Harv. L. Rev. 1165, 1226–1229 (1967); Sax, 74 Yale L.J. 36 (1963).

B

In contending that the New York City law has "taken" their property in violation of the Fifth and Fourteenth Amendments, appellants make a series of arguments, which, while tailored to the facts of this case, essentially urge that any substantial restriction imposed pursuant to a landmark law must be accompanied by just compensation if it is to be constitutional. Before considering these, we emphasize what is not in dispute. Because this Court has recognized, in a number of settings, that States and cities may enact land use restrictions or controls to enhance the quality of life by preserving the character and desirable aesthetic features of a city, see *New Orleans v. Dukes,* 427 U.S. 297 (1976); *Young v. American Mini Theaters, Inc.,* 427 U.S. 50 (1976); *Village of Belle Terre v. Boraas,* 416 U.S. 1, 9–10 (1974); *Berman v. Parker,* 348 U.S. 26, 33 (1954); *Welch v. Swasey, supra,* at 108, appellants do not contest that New York City's objective of preserving structures and areas with special historic, architectural, or cultural significance is an entirely permissible governmental goal. They also do not dispute that the restrictions imposed on its parcel are appropriate means of securing the purposes of the New York City law. Finally, appellants do not challenge any of the specific factual premises of the decision below. They accept for present purposes both that the parcel of land occupied by Grand Central Terminal must, in its present state, be regarded as capable of earning a reasonable return, and that the transferable development rights afforded appellants by virtue of the Terminal's designation as a landmark are valuable, even if not as valuable as the rights to construct above the Terminal. In appellants' view none of these factors derogate from their claim that New York City's law has effected a "taking."

They first observe that the air space above the Terminal is a valuable property interest, citing *United States v. Causby, supra.* They urge that the Landmark Law has deprived them of any gainful use of their "air rights" above the Terminal and that, irrespective of the value of the remainder of their parcel, the city has "taken" their right to this superadjacent air space, thus entitling them to "just compensation" measured by the fair market value of these air rights.

Apart from our own disagreement with appellants' characterization of the effect of the New York law, see *infra,* the submission that appellants may establish a "taking" simply by showing that they have been denied the ability to exploit a property interest that they heretofore had believed was available for development is quite simply untenable. Were this the rule, this Court would have erred not only in upholding laws restricting the development of air rights, see *Welch v. Swasey, supra,* but also in approving those prohibiting both the subjacent, see *Goldblatt v. Hempstead, supra,* and the lateral development, see *Gorieb v. Fox, supra,* of particular parcels.[27] "Taking" jurisprudence does not divide a single parcel into discrete segments and attempt to determine whether rights in a particular segment have been entirely abrogated. In deciding whether a particular governmental action has effected a taking, this Court focuses rather both on the character of the action and on the nature and extent of the interference with rights in the parcel as a whole, here, the city tax block designated as the "landmark site."

Secondly, appellants, focusing on the character and impact of the New York City law, argue that it effects a "taking" because its operation has significantly diminished the value of the Terminal site. Appellants concede that the decisions sustaining other land use regulations, which, like the New York law, are reasonably related to the promotion of the general welfare, uniformly reject the proposition that diminution in property value, standing alone, can establish a taking, see *Euclid v. Ambler Realty Co., supra* (75% diminution in value caused by zoning law); *Hadacheck v. Sebastian, supra* (87½% diminution in value), and that the taking issue in these contexts is resolved by focusing on the uses the regulations permit. See also *Goldblatt v. Hempstead, supra.* Appellants, moreover, also do not dispute that a showing of diminution in property value would not establish a taking if the restriction had been imposed as a result of historic district legislation, see generally *Maher v. City of New Orleans,* 516 F.2d 1051 (CA5 1975), but appellants argue that New York City's regulation of individual landmarks is fundamentally different from zoning or from historic district legislation because the controls imposed by New York City's law apply only to individuals who own selected properties.

Stated baldly, appellants' position appears to be that the only means of ensuring that selected owners are not singled out to endure financial hardship

---

[27] These cases dispose of any contention that might be based on *Pennsylvania Coal Co. v. Mahon supra,* that full use of air rights is so bound up with the investment backed expectations of appellants that Governmental deprivation of these rights invariably — *i.e.,* irrespective of the impact of the restriction on the value of the parcel as a whole — constitutes a "taking." Similarly, *Welch, Goldblatt,* and *Gorieb* illustrate the fallacy of appellants' related contention that a "taking" must be found to have occurred whenever the land use restriction may be characterized as imposing a "servitude" on the claimant's parcel.

for no reason is to hold that any restriction imposed on individual landmarks pursuant to the New York scheme is a "taking" requiring the payment of "just compensation." Agreement with this argument would of course invalidate not just New York City's law, but all comparable landmark legislation in the Nation. We find no merit in it.

It is true, as appellants emphasize, that both historic district legislation and zoning laws regulate all properties within given physical communities whereas landmark laws apply only to selected parcels. But, contrary to appellants' suggestions, landmark laws are not like discriminatory, or "reverse spot," zoning: that is, a land use decision which arbitrarily singles out a particular parcel for different, less favorable treatment than the neighboring ones. In contrast to discriminatory zoning, which is the antithesis of land use control as part of some comprehensive plan, the New York City law embodies a comprehensive plan to preserve structures of historic or aesthetic interest wherever they might be found in the city,[28] and as noted, over 400 landmarks and 31 historic districts have been designated pursuant to this plan.

Equally without merit is the related argument that the decision to designate a structure as a landmark "is inevitably arbitrary or at least subjective because it basically is a matter of taste," Reply Brief of Appellant 22, thus unavoidably singling out individual landowners for disparate and unfair treatment. The argument has a particularly hollow ring in this case. For appellants not only did not seek judicial review of either the designation or of the denials of the certificates of appropriateness and of no exterior effect, but do not even now suggest that the Commission's decisions concerning the Terminal were in any sense arbitrary or unprincipled. But, in any event, a landmark owner has a right to judicial review of any Commission decision, and, quite simply, there is no basis whatsoever for a conclusion that courts will have any greater difficulty identifying arbitrary or discriminatory action in the context of landmark regulation than in the context of classic zoning or indeed in any other context.[29]

Next, appellants observe that New York City's law differs from zoning laws and historic district ordinances in that the Landmark Law does not impose identical or similar restrictions on all structures located in particular physical communities. It follows, they argue, that New York City's law is inherently incapable of producing the fair and equitable distribution of benefits and burdens of governmental action which is characteristic of zoning laws and historic district legislation and which they maintain is a constitutional

[28] Although the New York Court of Appeals contrasted the New York City Landmark Law with both zoning and historic district legislation and stated at one point that landmark laws do not "further a general community plan," 42 N.Y.2d, at 330, it also emphasized that the implementation of the objectives of the landmark law constitutes an "acceptable reason to single out one particular parcel for different and less favorable treatment." *Ibid.* Therefore, we do not understand the New York Court of Appeals to disagree with our characterization of the Act.

[29] When a property owner challenges the application of a zoning ordinance to his property, the judicial inquiry focuses upon whether the challenged restriction can reasonably be deemed to promote the objectives of the community land use plan, and will include consideration of the treatment of similar parcels. See generally *Nectow v. Cambridge, supra.* When a property owner challenges a landmark designation or restriction as arbitrary or discriminatory, a similar inquiry presumably will occur.

requirement if "just compensation" is not to be afforded. It is of course true that the Landmark Law has a more severe impact on some landowners than on others, but that in itself does not mean that the law effects a "taking." Legislation designed to promote the general welfare commonly burdens some more than others. The owners of the brickyard in *Hadacheck,* of the cedar trees in *Miller v. Schoene,* and of the gravel and sand mine in *Goldblatt v. Hempstead,* were uniquely burdened by the legislation sustained in those cases. [30] Similarly, zoning laws often impact more severely on some property owners than others but have not been held to be invalid on that account. For example, the property owner in *Euclid* who wished to use his property for industrial purposes was affected far more severely by the ordinance than his neighbors who wished to use their land for residences.

In any event, appellants' repeated suggestions that they are solely burdened and unbenefited is factually inaccurate. This contention overlooks the fact that the New York City law applies to vast numbers of structures in the city in addition to the Terminal — all the structures contained in the 31 historic districts and over 400 individual landmarks, many of which are close to the Terminal. [31] Unless we are to reject the judgment of the New York City Council that the preservation of landmarks benefits all New York citizens and all structures, both economically and by improving the quality of life in the city as a whole — which we are unwilling to do — we cannot conclude that the owners of the Terminal have in no sense been benefited by the Landmark Law. Doubtless appellants believe they are more burdened than benefited by the law, but that must have been true too of the property owners in *Miller, Hadacheck, Euclid,* and *Goldblatt.* [32]

Appellants' final broad-based attack would have us treat the law as an instance, like that in *United States v. Causby, supra,* in which Government, acting in an enterprise capacity, has appropriated part of their property for some strictly governmental purpose. Apart from the fact that *Causby* was a

---

[30] Appellants attempt to distinguish these cases on the ground that, in each, Government was prohibiting a "noxious" use of land and that in the present case, in contrast, appellants' proposed construction above the Terminal would be beneficial. We observe that the uses in issue in *Hadacheck, Miller,* and *Goldblatt* were perfectly lawful in themselves. They involved no "blameworthiness, . . . moral wrongdoing, or conscious act of dangerous risk-taking which induce[d society] to shift the cost to a particular individual." Sax, 74 Yale L.J. 36, 50 (1964). These cases are better understood as resting not on any supposed "noxious" quality of the prohibited uses but rather on the ground that the restrictions were reasonably related to the implementation of a policy — not unlike historic preservation — expected to produce a widespread public benefit and applicable to all similarly situated property.

Nor, correlatively, can it be asserted that the destruction or fundamental alteration of a historic landmark is not harmful. The suggestion that the beneficial quality of appellants' proposed construction is established by the fact that construction would have been consistent with applicable zoning laws ignores the development in sensibilities and ideals reflected in landmark legislation like New York City's.

[31] There are some 53 designated landmarks and three historic districts or scenic landmarks in Manhattan between 14th and 59th Streets. See Landmarks Preservation Commission, Landmarks and Historic Districts (1977).

[32] It is of course true that the fact the duties imposed by zoning and historic district legislation apply throughout particular physical communities provides assurances against arbitrariness, but the applicability of the landmarks law to large numbers of parcels in the city, in our view, provides comparable, if not identical, assurances.

case of invasion of airspace that destroyed the use of the farm beneath and this New York City law has in no wise impaired the present use of the Terminal, the Landmark Law neither exploits appellants' parcel for city purposes nor facilitates nor arises from any entrepreneurial operations of the city. The situation is not remotely like that in *Causby* when the airspace above the Terminal was in the flight pattern for military aircraft. The Landmarks Law's effect is simply to prohibit appellants or anyone else from occupying portions of the airspace above the Terminal, while permitting appellants to use the remainder of the parcel in a gainful fashion. This is no more an appropriation of property by Government for its own uses than is a zoning law prohibiting, for "aesthetic" reasons, two or more adult theaters within a specified area, see *Young v. American Mini Theaters, Inc., supra,* or a safety regulation prohibiting excavations below a certain level. See *Goldblatt v. City of Hempstead, supra.*

C

Rejection of appellants' broad arguments is not however the end of our inquiry, for all we thus far have established is that the New York law is not rendered invalid by its failure to provide "just compensation" whenever a landmark owner is restricted in the exploitation of property interests, such as air rights, to a greater extent than provided for under applicable zoning laws. We now must consider whether the interference with appellants' property is of such a magnitude that "there must be an exercise of eminent domain and compensation to sustain [it]." *Pennsylvania Coal Co. v. Mahon,* 260 U.S., at 413. That inquiry may be narrowed to the question of the severity of the impact of the law on appellants' parcel, and its resolution in turn requires a careful assessment of the impact of the regulation on the Terminal site.

Unlike the governmental acts in *Goldblatt, Miller, Causby, Griggs,* and *Hadacheck,* the New York City law does not interfere in any way with the present uses of the Terminal. Its designation as a landmark not only permits but contemplates that appellants may continue to use the property precisely as it has for the past 65 years: as a railroad terminal containing office space and concessions. So the law does not interfere with what must be regarded as Penn Central's primary expectation concerning the use of the parcel. More importantly, on this record, we must regard the New York City law as permitting Penn Central not only to profit from the Terminal but to obtain a "reasonable return" on its investment.

Appellants, moreover, exaggerate the effect of the Act on its ability to make use of the air rights above the Terminal in two respects.[33] First, it simply cannot be maintained, on this record, that appellants have been prohibited from occupying *any* portion of the airspace above the Terminal. While the Commission's actions in denying applications to construct an office building in excess of 50 stories above the Terminal may indicate that it will refuse to issue a certificate of appropriateness for any comparably sized structure,

---

[33] Appellants of course argue at length that the transferable development rights, while valuable, do not constitute "just compensation."

nothing the Commission has said or done suggests an intention to prohibit _any_ construction above the Terminal. The Commission's report emphasized that whether any construction would be allowed depended upon whether the proposed addition "would harmonize in scale, material, and character with [the Terminal]." Since appellants have not sought approval for the construction of a smaller structure, we do not know that appellants will be denied any use of any portion of the airspace above the Terminal.[34]

Second, to the extent appellants have been denied the right to build above the Terminal, it is not literally accurate to say that they have been denied _all_ use of even those pre-existing air rights. Their ability to use these rights has not been abrogated; they are made transferable to at least eight parcels in the vicinity of the Terminal, one or two of which have been found suitable for the construction of new office buildings. Although appellants and others have argued that New York City's transferable development rights program is far from ideal, the New York courts here supportably found that, at least in the case of the Terminal, the rights afforded are valuable. While these rights may well not have constituted "just compensation" if a "taking" had occurred, the rights nevertheless undoubtedly mitigate whatever financial burdens the law has imposed on appellants and, for that reason, are to be taken into account in considering the impact of regulation. Cf. _Goldblatt v. Hempstead, supra,_ at 594 n.3.

On this record we conclude that the application of New York City's Landmark Preservation Law has not effected a "taking" of appellants' property. The restrictions imposed are substantially related to the promotion of the general welfare and not only permit reasonable beneficial use of the landmark site but afford appellants opportunities further to enhance not only the Terminal site proper but also other properties.[36]

Affirmed.

JUSTICE REHNQUIST, with whom THE CHIEF JUSTICE and JUSTICE STEVENS join, dissenting. . . . [The following excerpts from then-Justice Rehnquist's opinion explain his view on the nuisance basis for taking law and the role of average reciprocity of advantage:]

1

As early as 1887, the Court recognized that the government can prevent a property owner from using his property to injure others without having to compensate the owner for the value of the forbidden use. . . . [Citing and quoting from _Mugler v. Kansas,_ 123 U.S. 623, 668–69 (1887) — Eds.]

---

[34] Counsel for appellants admitted at oral argument that the Commission has not suggested that it would not, for example, approve a 20-story office tower along the lines of that which was part of the original plan for the Terminal.

[36] We emphasize that our holding today is on the present record which in turn is based on Penn Central's present ability to use the Terminal for its intended purposes and in a gainful fashion. The city conceded at oral argument that if appellants can demonstrate at some point in the future that circumstances have changed such that the Terminal ceases to be, in the city's counsel's words, "economically viable," appellants may obtain relief.

Appellees are not prohibiting a nuisance. The record is clear that the proposed addition to the Grand Central Terminal would be in full compliance with zoning, height limitations, and other health and safety requirements. Instead, appellees are seeking to preserve what they believe to be an outstanding example of Beaux Arts architecture. Penn Central is prevented from further developing its property basically because it did *too good* of a job in designing and building it. The city of New York, because of its unadorned admiration for the design, has decided that the owners of the building must preserve it unchanged for the benefit of sightseeing New Yorkers and tourists.

Unlike in the case of land use regulations, appellees are not prohibiting Penn Central from using its property in a narrow sense. Instead, appellees have placed an affirmative duty on Penn Central to maintain the Terminal in its present state of "good repair." Appellants are not free to use their property as they see fit within broad outer boundaries but must strictly adhere to their past use except where appellees conclude that alternative uses would not detract from the Landmark. While Penn Central may continue to use the Terminal as it is presently designed, appellees otherwise "exercise complete dominion and control over the surface of the land," *United States v. Causby,* 328 U.S. 256, 262 (1946), and must compensate the owner for his loss. . . .

2

Even where the government prohibits a noninjurious use, the Court has ruled that a taking does not take place if the prohibition applies over a broad cross section of land and thereby "secure[s] an average reciprocity of advantage." *Pennsylvania Coal Co. v. Mahon,* 260 U.S. 393, 415 (1922). While zoning at times reduces *individual* property values, the burden is shared relatively evenly and it is reasonable to conclude that on the whole an individual who is harmed by one aspect of the zoning will be benefited by another.

Here, however, a multimillion dollar loss has been imposed on appellants; it is uniquely felt and is not offset by any benefits flowing from the preservation of some 500 other "Landmarks" in New York. Appellees have imposed a substantial cost on less than one-tenth of one percent of the buildings in New York for the general benefit of all its people. It is exactly this imposition of general costs on a few individuals at which the "taking" protection is directed. . . .

NOTES AND QUESTIONS

1. *Penn Central* is a critical case in takings jurisprudence. For the first time the Court attempted to integrate its "essentially ad hoc, factual inquiries" by providing a comprehensive three-factor balancing test. But does Justice Brennan then apply his own test? Penn Central lost a valuable business opportunity under a law that postdated its acquisition of the Terminal, facts which fit comfortably with two of the three factors in his test ("physical invasion" was not an issue). Shouldn't the case have come out the other way? Is *Hadacheck v. Sebastian* still good law? Is economic impact, the three-factor test notwithstanding, still the only test that really matters? And if so, what about *Pennsylvania Coal*?

2. *Nuisance.* What has happened to the nuisance rationale for land use regulation so explicitly endorsed in *Euclid*? Reread footnote 30 in the majority opinion. Justice Brennan's apparent rejection of the harm-benefit rule was confirmed in the Court's *Lucas* decision, reproduced *infra*.

3. *Average reciprocity of advantage.* The railroad argued that the landmark law "is inherently incapable of producing the fair and equitable distribution of benefits and burdens of governmental action," to which Justice Brennan replied that the landmark owners benefit as "citizens" of New York. Has Alfred Bettman's theory finally been adopted by the Court? Arguably, Brennan's approach, if pushed far enough, could read the takings clause out of the constitution. See Mandelker, Waiving the Taking Clause: Conflicting Signals from the Supreme Court, in 1994 Proceedings of the Institute on Planning, Zoning, and Eminent Domain (1995). Despite the reappearance of "average reciprocity" in the *Agins* case, reproduced *infra*, this maxim appears more recently to have lost importance as the court has fashioned new and more restrictive takings theories. See generally Oswald, *The Role of the "Harm/ Benefit" and "Average Reciprocity of Advantage" Rules in a Comprehensive Takings Analysis,* 50 Vand. L. Rev. 1449 (1997).

4. *Investment-backed expectations. Penn Central* is the first Supreme Court opinion to embrace this concept, which seemed to introduce a tilt in takings law that favors landowners. Can you see why? Justice Brennan never really defines the term, however, except to note where it would not apply. An example is his statement that a landowner does not have an investment-backed expectation in the "ability to exploit" a property interest he believed was available for development. Another is his statement that "unilateral" expectations are not protected. This takings factor remains unclear almost a quarter-century after *Penn Central*, although courts have applied it to uphold takings claims when a landowner had a vested property right. See *Pace Resources, Inc. v. Shrewsbury Township,* 808 F.2d 1023 (3d Cir. 1987). They also apply it to uphold takings claims to protect a landowner's expectations at the time she purchased the land. See *Gil v. Inland Wetlands & Watercourses Agency,* 593 A.2d 1368, 1372 (Conn. 1991) (accepting "fact-bound determination" that landowner had reasonable investment-backed expectations that he could build on lot).

5. *Notice.* Should a landowner lose her investment-backed expectations if a restrictive land use regulation is adopted after she purchases her property? Wouldn't this approach read the takings clause out of the constitution? In *Ruckelshaus v. Monsanto Co.,* 467 U.S. 986 (1984), the Court said yes in a non-land use context. It held that a statute giving notice that disclosure of trade secrets would be required when applying to register a pesticide was not a taking. The Court went even further and held that the "force" of the investment-backed expectations factor partly defeated the takings claim, suggesting that proof of expectations is a necessary condition to a takings suit. Lower federal courts applied the notice rule to reject takings claims when property owners purchased land that was subject to wetlands and similar regulation that restricted the use of their property, see, e.g., *Claridge v. New Hampshire Wetlands Bd.,* 485 A.2d 287 (1984), but the *Nollan* case, reproduced *infra,* and especially footnote 2, cast doubt on these holdings. In the

Lucas case, also reproduced *infra,* Justice Kennedy referred to the investment-backed expectations factor as circular. Is he right?

6. *Whole parcel rule.* Justice Brennan stated in *Penn Central* that "[t]aking jurisprudence does not divide a single parcel into discrete segments and attempt to determine whether rights in a particular segment have been entirely abrogated," but "focuses rather both on the character of the action and on the nature and extent of the interference with rights in the parcel as a whole." Is this statement consistent with the majority opinion in *Mahon*? Would it be accurate to say that the majority opinion in *Penn Central* adopts, in general, the views stated by Justice Brandeis in *Mahon,* and that the dissent in *Penn Central* adopts the views stated by Justice Holmes in *Mahon*? The whole parcel rule, sometimes called the denominator rule, has become important in takings law, and is discussed in more detail *infra.*

7. *A critique of Penn Central.* John Echeverria, in *Is the Penn Central Three-Factor Test Ready for History's Dustbin?,* Land Use L. & Zoning Dig., Vol. 60, No. 1, at 3 (2000), answered his own question yes. He argued that none of the factors identified in the case are meaningful. The economic impact test provides no guidance on when a taking occurs. The "character" factor was clearly intended to distinguish cases where a physical occupation occurred, but is no longer meaningful because the Court subsequently held that physical occupation is a per se taking. See the Note on physical occupation, *infra.* Investment-backed expectations, the final factor, is equally problematic because it is not clear whether a takings claim will be successful if a landowner has investment-backed expectations, and doomed if he does not. Reconsider these arguments after you have studied the *Lucas* decision.

8. *Burden sharing.* Significant by its absence from Justice Brennan's three-factor analysis is a point that the Court has long made clear, namely that the takings clause "is designed to bar Government from forcing some people alone to bear burdens which, in all fairness and justice, should be borne by the populace as a whole." *Armstrong v. United States,* 346 U.S. 40, 49 (1960). This rule instead forms the core of Justice Rehnquist's dissent, which takes off from the plaintiffs' contrast between the narrow impact of the Landmark Preservation Law and the broader way in which "zoning laws and historic-district ordinances" operate. Should this approach be seen as an alternate to Brennan's three-factor test? Ought it to be another one of the "factors"? Why do the plaintiffs (and Justice Rehnquist) focus on "disparate and unfair treatment" under the "taking" rubric instead of invoking the equal protection clause of the Fourteenth Amendment? How does this approach relate to the "average reciprocity" theory?

9. *Cross references.* We will look at "zoning laws" in detail in Ch. 3 and take a closer look at "historic district" and "landmark preservation" ordinances in Ch. 8. The transfer of development rights technique is considered in Chs. 7 and 8.

A few years after *Penn Central* the Court decided another takings case that was to have an important effect on land use takings law:

AGINS v. CITY OF TIBURON

447 U.S. 255 (1980)

Mr. Justice Powell delivered the opinion of the Court.

I

After the appellants acquired five acres of unimproved land in the city of Tiburon, Cal., for residential development, the city . . . placed the . . . property in "RPD-1," a Residential Planned Development and Open Space Zone. RPD-1 property may be devoted to one-family dwellings, accessory buildings, and open-space uses. Density restrictions permit the appellants to build between one and five single-family residences on their 5-acre tract. The appellants never have sought approval for development of their land under the zoning ordinances.[1]

The appellants filed a two-part complaint against the city in State Superior Court. The first cause of action sought $2 million in damages for inverse condemnation. The second cause of action requested a declaration that the zoning ordinances were facially unconstitutional. The gravamen of both claims was the appellants' assertion that the city had taken their property without just compensation in violation of the Fifth and Fourteenth Amendments. The complaint alleged that land in Tiburon has greater value than any other suburban property in the State of California. The ridgelands that appellants own "possess magnificent views of San Francisco Bay and the scenic surrounding areas [and] have the highest market values of all lands" in Tiburon. Rezoning of the land "forever prevented [its] development for residential use. . . ." Therefore, the appellants contended, the city had "completely destroyed the value of [appellants'] property for any purpose or use whatsoever. . . ."

The city demurred, claiming that the complaint failed to state a cause of action. The Superior Court sustained the demurrer, and the California Supreme Court affirmed. 598 P. 2d 25 (1979). The State Supreme Court first considered the inverse condemnation claim. It held that a landowner who challenges the constitutionality of a zoning ordinance may not "sue in inverse condemnation and thereby transmute an excessive use of the police power into a lawful taking for which compensation in eminent domain must be paid." 598 P. 2d, at 28. The sole remedies for such a taking, the court concluded, are mandamus and declaratory judgment. Turning therefore to the appellants' claim for declaratory relief, the California Supreme Court held that the zoning ordinances had not deprived the appellants of their property without compensation in violation of the Fifth Amendment.

We noted probable jurisdiction. 444 U.S. 1011 (1980). We now affirm the holding that the zoning ordinances on their face do not take the appellants' property without just compensation.

---

[1] Shortly after it enacted the ordinances, the city began eminent domain proceedings against the appellants' land. The following year, however, the city abandoned those proceedings, and its complaint was dismissed. The appellants were reimbursed for costs incurred in connection with the action.

II

The Fifth Amendment guarantees that private property shall not "be taken for public use, without just compensation." The appellants' complaint framed the question as whether a zoning ordinance that prohibits all development of their land effects a taking under the Fifth and Fourteenth Amendments. The California Supreme Court rejected the appellants' characterization of the issue by holding, as a matter of state law, that the terms of the challenged ordinances allow the appellants to construct between one and five residences on their property. The court did not consider whether the zoning ordinances would be unconstitutional if applied to prevent appellants from building five homes. Because the appellants have not submitted a plan for development of their property as the ordinances permit, there is as yet no concrete controversy regarding the application of the specific zoning provisions. Thus, the only question properly before us is whether the mere enactment of the zoning ordinances constitutes a taking. The application of a general zoning law to particular property effects a taking if the ordinance does not substantially advance legitimate state interests, see *Nectow v. Cambridge,* 277 U.S. 183, 188 (1928), or denies an owner economically viable use of his land, see *Penn Central Transp. Co. v. New York City,* 438 U.S. 104, 138, n. 36 (1978). The determination that governmental action constitutes a taking is, in essence, a determination that the public at large, rather than a single owner, must bear the burden of an exercise of state power in the public interest. Although no precise rule determines when property has been taken, the question necessarily requires a weighing of private and public interests. The seminal decision in *Euclid v. Ambler Co.,* 272 U.S. 365 (1926), is illustrative. In that case, the landowner challenged the constitutionality of a municipal ordinance that restricted commercial development of his property. Despite alleged diminution in value of the owner's land, the Court held that the zoning laws were facially constitutional. They bore a substantial relationship to the public welfare, and their enactment inflicted no irreparable injury upon the landowner.

In this case, the zoning ordinances substantially advance legitimate governmental goals. The State of California has determined that the development of local open-space plans will discourage the "premature and unnecessary conversion of open-space land to urban uses." Cal. Govt. Code Ann. § 65561(b). The specific zoning regulations at issue are exercises of the city's police power to protect the residents of Tiburon from the ill effects of urbanization.[8] Such governmental purposes long have been recognized as legitimate.

The ordinances place appellants' land in a zone limited to single-family dwellings, accessory buildings, and open-space uses. Construction is not permitted until the builder submits a plan compatible with "adjoining patterns of development and open space." In passing upon a plan, the city also will consider how well the proposed development would preserve the surrounding

---

[8] The City Council of Tiburon found that "[it] is in the public interest to avoid unnecessary conversion of open space land to strictly urban uses, thereby protecting against the resultant adverse impacts, such as air, noise and water pollution, traffic congestion, destruction of scenic beauty, disturbance of the ecology and environment, hazards related to geology, fire and flood, and other demonstrated consequences of urban sprawl."

environment and whether the density of new construction will be offset by adjoining open spaces. The zoning ordinances benefit the appellants as well as the public by serving the city's interest in assuring careful and orderly development of residential property with provision for open-space areas. There is no indication that the appellants' 5-acre tract is the only property affected by the ordinances. Appellants therefore will share with other owners the benefits and burdens of the city's exercise of its police power. In assessing the fairness of the zoning ordinances, these benefits must be considered along with any diminution in market value that the appellants might suffer. Although the ordinances limit development, they neither prevent the best use of appellants' land, nor extinguish a fundamental attribute of ownership. The appellants have alleged that they wish to develop the land for residential purposes, that the land is the most expensive suburban property in the State, and that the best possible use of the land is residential. The California Supreme Court has decided, as a matter of state law, that appellants may be permitted to build as many as five houses on their five acres of prime residential property. At this juncture, the appellants are free to pursue their reasonable investment expectations by submitting a development plan to local officials. Thus, it cannot be said that the impact of general land-use regulations has denied appellants the "justice and fairness" guaranteed by the Fifth and Fourteenth Amendments.

III

The State Supreme Court determined that the appellants could not recover damages for inverse condemnation even if the zoning ordinances constituted a taking. The court stated that only mandamus and declaratory judgment are remedies available to such a landowner. Because no taking has occurred, we need not consider whether a State may limit the remedies available to a person whose land has been taken without just compensation.

The judgment of the Supreme Court of California is Affirmed.

NOTES AND QUESTIONS

1. *Ripeness. Agins* was the first takings case to seriously apply a ripeness test. Because the ordinance on its face permitted between one and five dwellings on the property, the Court could hold any as-applied takings claim in abeyance until the city actually granted or denied permission to build. It then could dismiss the facial takings claim because the ordinance served a legitimate purpose. Notice how the Court's broad language protects land use regulation that protects open space for a variety of purposes. Ripeness rules, which have become important in this area, are discussed *infra* in this chapter.

2. *Average reciprocity.* Note the holding that the landowner "will share with other owners the benefits and burdens of the city's exercise of its police power." The Agins stand to lose much of the exploitation value of a uniquely scenic property so that others can have a less obstructed view. What do they gain in return? Is this the correct frame of reference within which to assess "average reciprocity"?

3. *A two-part takings test.* The most important holding in *Agins* is its adoption of a two-part takings test. There is a taking if "the ordinance does not substantially advance legitimate state interests, or denies an owner economically viable use of his land." This is an about face from the three-factor test the Court adopted in *Penn Central,* which is not mentioned though the case is cited. What is even more striking is that the first part of the test looks very much like the test courts impose when they decide whether a land use regulation violates substantive due process. The Court in *Penn Central* did say that "a use restriction may constitute a 'taking' if [it is] not reasonably necessary to the effectuation of a substantial government purpose," 438 U.S. at 127, but this was not identified as one of the "factors that have particular significance."

Most state courts recognize that the *Agins* takings test is disjunctive: either prong is enough for a taking. E.g., *Clajon Prod. Corp. v. Petera,* 70 F.3d 1566, 1576 (10th Cir. 1995); *Bevan v. Brandon Township,* 475 N.W.2d 37, 40 (Mich. 1991); *McFillan v. Berkeley County Planning Comm'n,* 438 S.E.2d 801, 809 (W. Va. 1993). However, the more important question is whether the first prong properly belongs in takings law.

4. *Does the Agins first prong belong in takings law?* A number of commentators have argued that it does not. Echeverria, *Does a Regulation That Fails to Advance a Legitimate Governmental Interest Result in a Regulatory Taking?,* 29 Envtl. L. 853 (1999), argues that the first prong of *Agins* is derived from substantive due process, not takings, precedents; that the "plain meaning" of "take" has nothing to do with the legitimacy of the government's interest; that the first prong is inconsistent with the "original understanding"; and that it violates the understanding that the function of regulatory takings doctrine is to fairly distribute the burdens of legitimate government activity. He particularly notes *Hawaii Housing Authority v. Midkiff,* 467 U.S. 229 (1984), which held that the question whether a governmental purpose is legitimate is antecedent to the question of whether it is a taking. Therefore, he concludes, if a land use regulation does not serve a legitimate purpose it cannot be a taking. See also Kayden, *Land Use Regulations, Rationality, and Judicial Review: The RSVP in the Nollan Invitation (Part I),* 23 Urb. Law. 301, 316–25 (1991).

5. *Del Monte Dunes.* The Court had an opportunity to clarify the status of the first *Agins* prong in *City of Monterey v. Del Monte Dunes,* 526 U.S. 687 (1999). A developer proposed a residential development on a 37.6 acre beachfront property that had previously been used for industrial purposes. It reduced the number of proposed dwelling units several times in response to objections from the city, but the city council, shifting votes at the last minute, overruled the planning commission and rejected the proposal. The council's denial raised several concerns, including the adequacy of access, traffic congestion and the impact on an endangered species, the Smith's Blue Butterfly, which feeds on a buckwheat plant that grows on the property.

After trial, the jury delivered a general verdict on a takings claim, a separate verdict on an equal protection claim, and awarded temporary taking damages of $ 1.45 million. Among other questions, the jury was asked whether the city's "particular decision to deny Del Monte Dunes' final development proposal was reasonably related to the city's proffered justifications." 526 U.S. at 706. This and related instructions essentially put the case to the jury on the first prong of *Agins,* and because it was a general verdict, it had to be presumed that the jury had decided on this theory. The city appealed and numerous amici urged that *Agins* be reconsidered. In the end, the Supreme Court upheld the verdict but ducked the *Agins* issue, on the technical ground that the city could not now challenge instructions it had drafted originally. On whether the first *Agins* prong was a correct statement of takings law, five justices joined or wrote opinions concluding that it did not provide a definitive statement or a thorough explanation of when a taking occurs in cases other than exaction cases. See Stroud, *A Review of Del Monte Dunes v. City of Monterey and its Implications For Local Government Exactions,* 15 J. Land Use & Envtl. Law 195 (1999).

See also *Eastern Enters. v. Apfel,* 524 U.S. 498 (1998), not a land use case, where the Court divided sharply on whether to use substantive due process or takings as the basis for invalidating a retroactive pension statute. Four justices rejected the use of substantive due process but held that there was a taking. Four justices required the use of substantive due process, but held that there was no constitutional violation. Justice Kennedy split the difference, rejecting the takings theory but finding a due process violation. The only majority in *Apfel* was for rejecting the takings theory.

6. *Inverse condemnation.* The landowner's claim was for inverse condemnation, which the court described, citing *United States v. Clarke,* 445 U.S. 253, 255–258 (1980), as "a shorthand description of the manner in which a landowner recovers just compensation for a taking of his property when condemnation proceedings have not been instituted." In the *First English* case, reproduced *infra,* the Court later held that inverse condemnation is available in land use cases.

A NOTE ON THE *KEYSTONE* CASE

The decision.—Keystone Bituminous Coal Ass'n v. De Benedictis, 480 U.S. 470 (1987), which involved a modern version of the coal mining subsidence law struck down in *Pennsylvania Coal,* was a replay of that landmark case. The act prohibited mining that causes subsidence below three categories of structures and as interpreted by the state required that 50 percent of the coal beneath these structures remain in place to provide surface support. The Court upheld the act.

The Court cited the two-part *Agins* test as a basis for distinguishing *Pennsylvania Coal.* Unlike the earlier statute, the act under review prevented "a significant threat to the public welfare." In addition it did not make it "impossible for petitioners to profitably engage in their business" and there had been no "undue interference with their investment-backed expectations."

On the first point, the Court found that "important public interests are served by enforcing a policy that is designed to minimize subsidence in certain areas." It added that its "hesitance to find a taking when the state merely restrains uses of property that are tantamount to public nuisances is consistent with the notion of 'reciprocity of advantage' that Justice Holmes referred to in *Pennsylvania Coal.*" It then cited *Mugler v. Kansas* for the proposition that "all property in this country is held under the implied obligation that the owner's use of it shall not be injurious to the community."

On the second point, the Court turned to a discussion of "diminution in value and investment-backed expectations." It held that the plaintiffs here, unlike the plaintiff in *Pennsylvania Coal,* had not shown that the act made coal mining commercially impracticable. The Court applied the whole parcel rule to hold that the plaintiffs could not segment the coal that had to be left in place, so that they could claim that a taking of this segment of their property had occurred. The Court also rejected an argument that a taking occurred because the plaintiffs' support estate had been taken, noting that "in *Penn Central,* the Court rejected the argument that the 'air rights' above the terminal constituted a separate segment of property for Takings Clause purposes."

The rationale.—In applying the first prong of the *Agins* test, the *Keystone* majority arguably did no more than restate the views of Justice Brandeis in his *Pennsylvania Coal* dissent. Brandeis had argued that the Kohler Act was "merely the prohibition of a noxious use" —"a use which interferes with paramount rights of the public" —similar to the uses prohibited in *Mugler v. Kansas,* and *Hadacheck v. Sebastian.* Following these cases it should not have been necessary to consider the economic impact argument. Here too, however, the court seemed to accept without acknowledgment Justice Brandeis' argument, in his *Pennsylvania Coal* dissent, that "if we are to consider the value of the coal kept in place by the restriction, we should compare it with the value of all other parts of the land" owned by the coal company. This is an application of the whole parcel rule. Note also the invocation of *Penn Central's* broad application of the average reciprocity rule.

Keystone was one of three takings cases decided in 1987 that came to be known as the "1987 Trilogy," and it was the only one won by government. (The others are *Nollan* and *First English,* reproduced *infra.*) All were decided by 5-4 majorities. Whether a majority of the present Court would accept all of the broad holdings in the *Keystone* decision is not clear. The nuisance basis for the decision has also limited its value as a takings precedent.

A NOTE ON PHYSICAL OCCUPATION AS A PER SE TAKING

In *Penn Central,* Justice Brennan said "A 'taking' may more readily be found when the interference with property can be characterized as a physical invasion by Government . . . than when interference arises from some public program adjusting the benefits and burdens of economic life to promote the common good," citing *Causby v. United States,* 328 U.S. 256 (1946). In *Causby* the Court held that repeated and long-continued overflights by military aircraft that destroyed the existing use of plaintiffs' land as a chicken farm amounted to a *de facto* "taking."

Loretto.—In *Loretto v. Teleprompter Manhattan CATV Corp.,* 458 U.S. 419 (1982), the Court held that a New York statute requiring landlords to allow CATV carriers to run cables across and attach the cables to apartment buildings effected a "per se taking" because it resulted in a "permanent physical occupation" of less than one-eighth of a cubic foot of space on plaintiff's apartment building. In an opinion by Justice Marshall, the Court said that "our cases uniformly have found a taking to the extent of the occupation, without regard to whether the action achieves an important public benefit or has only minimal economic impact on the owner." Marshall explained that "[s]uch an appropriation is perhaps the most serious form of invasion of an owner's property interests" because "the government does not simply take a single 'strand' from the 'bundle' of property rights" but "chops through the bundle, taking a slice of every strand," and also because it triggers the property owner's "historically rooted expectation of compensation." In a footnote, Justice Marshall also said that "[t]he permanence and absolute exclusivity of a physical occupation distinguish it from temporary limitations on the right to exclude. Not every physical *invasion* is a taking. . . . [S]uch temporary limitations are subject to a more complex balancing process to determine whether they are a taking. The rationale is evident: they do not absolutely dispossess the owner of his rights to use, and exclude others from his property."

Justices Blackmun (joined by Justices Brennan and White) dissented in *Loretto*. They argued that (1) "the Court . . . acknowledges its historical disavowal of set formulas [for 'takings'] in almost the same breath as it constructs a rigid per se takings rule"; (2) the Court's "talismanic distinction between a continuous 'occupation' and a transient 'invasion' had 'no basis in either economic logic or Takings clause precedent'"; and (3) "history teaches that takings claims are properly evaluated under a multi-factor balancing test." Under such a "balancing test," the dissenters said, the interference with Mrs. Loretto's use of her apartment building was not "so severe as to constitute a compensable taking in light of the alternative uses of the property." They also noted that Mrs. Loretto "freely admitted that she would have no other use for the cable-occupied space were Teleprompter's equipment not on her building" and that she conceded "not only that owners of other apartment buildings thought that the cable's presence had enhanced the market value of their buildings, . . . but also that her own tenants would have been upset if the cable connections were removed."

In *Property, Utility, and Fairness: Comments on the Ethical Foundations of "Just Compensation" Law*, 80 Harv. L. Rev. 1165 (1967), which is cited in the majority opinion in *Loretto*, Professor Michelman criticizes the "per se taking" rule. He argues that the rule requires compensation "although the invasion is . . . trifling from the owner's point of view" and "the actual harm to . . . [him] is indistinguishable from the noncompensable harm to him which results from activity on the part of the government identical in every respect save that it apparently does not invade 'his' sector of space," and because it makes an arbitrary distinction between "governmental encroachments which take the different forms of affirmative occupancy and negative restraint." *Id.* at 1185–87. Michelman finally concludes that the "per se taking" rule can be justified only "if we are to take a utilitarian rather than an absolute view of fairness." He dismisses the common utilitarian argument that the "per se taking" rule can be justified as isolating situations where the cost of settling property owners' claims for compensation will not be prohibitively high as "rather weak," but suggests, as a possible justification, that the "per se taking" rule allows courts to assuage "the psychological shock, the emotional protest, the symbolic threat to all property and security" arising in cases where "government is an unabashed invader." *Id.* at 1227-28. Reconsider these arguments after you have studied the extension of the per se taking rule in the *Lucas* case, which is reproduced *infra*.

Yee.—The Court limited its holding in *Loretto* in *Yee v. City of Escondito,* 503 U.S. 519 (1992). Plaintiffs were mobile home park owners who rented pads of land to owners of mobile homes. Under state law, a park owner may not require the removal of a mobile home when it is sold or disapprove a purchaser who is able to pay rent. A city ordinance rolled back rents to an earlier level and prohibited rent increases without city approval. The Court held that a taking by physical occupation had not occurred, and that a claim of regulatory taking was not properly before the Court.

The Court rejected an argument that the rent control ordinance authorized a physical taking because, together with the state law's restrictions, it increased the value of a mobile home by giving the owner the right to occupy the pad indefinitely at a sub-market rent. A physical taking occurs only when a law requires an owner to submit to a physical occupation of his land, and here the mobile home park owners voluntarily rented their land to mobile home owners and were not required to do so either by state or local law. These laws merely regulated the landlord-tenant relationship, and a transfer of wealth to mobile home owners does not convert regulation into a physical taking.

Yee seems to limit the physical occupation per se category of takings to actual physical occupation. What was the argument in *Yee* that a physical taking had occurred? That there was a "physical" taking of the intangible possessory interest in property? See *Hall v. City of Santa Barbara,* 833 F.2d 1270 (9th Cir. 1987), *cert. denied,* 485 U.S. 940 (1988), where Judge Kozinski had adopted a similar argument in a case challenging a rent control ordinance requiring landlords in mobile home parks to grant their tenants an indefinite tenancy. *Yee* is a rejection of this decision by a well-known conservative judge.

The rule that a physical occupation of land is a per se taking had an important influence on the Supreme Court's next takings decision, where it considered a case involving a somewhat different kind of land use regulation — an exaction.

NOLLAN v. CALIFORNIA COASTAL COMMISSION

483 U.S. 825 (1987)

JUSTICE SCALIA delivered the opinion of the Court:

James and Marilyn Nollan appealed from a decision of the California court of Appeal ruling that the California Coastal Commission could condition its grant of permission to rebuild their house on their transfer to the public of an easement across their beachfront property. 223 Cal. Rptr. 28 (1986). The California Court rejected their claim that imposition of that condition violates the Takings Clause of the Fifth Amendment, as incorporated against the States by the Fourteenth Amendment. *Ibid.* We noted probable jurisdiction.

I

The Nollans own a beachfront lot in Ventura County, California. A quarter-mile north of their property is Faria County Park, an oceanside public park with a public beach and recreation area. Another public beach area, known locally as "the Cove," lies 1,800 feet south of their lot. A concrete seawall approximately eight feet high separates the beach portion of the Nollans' property from the rest of the lot. The historic mean high tide line determines the lot's oceanside boundary.

The Nollans originally leased their property with an option to buy. The building on the lot was a small bungalow, totaling 504 square feet, which for a time they rented to summer vacationers. After years of rental use, however, the building had fallen into disrepair, and could no longer be rented out.

The Nollans' option to purchase was conditioned on their promise to demolish the bungalow and replace it. In order to do so, under California Public Resources Code §§ 30106, 30212, and 30600, they were required to obtain a coastal development permit from the California Coastal Commission. On February 25, 1982, they submitted a permit application to the Commission in which they proposed to demolish the existing structure and replace it with a three-bedroom house in keeping with the rest of the neighborhood.

The Nollans were informed that their application had been placed on the administrative calendar, and that the Commission staff had recommended [*EXACTION*] that the permit be granted subject to the condition that they allow the public an easement to pass across a portion of their property bounded by the mean high tide line on one side, and their seawall on the other side. This would make it easier for the public to get to Faria County Park and the Cove. The Nollans protested imposition of the condition, but the Commission overruled their objections and granted the permit subject to their recordation of a deed restriction granting the easement.

On June 3, 1982, the Nollans filed a petition for writ of administrative mandamus asking the Ventura County Superior Court to invalidate the access condition. They argued that the condition could not be imposed absent evidence that their proposed development would have a direct adverse impact on public access to the beach. The court agreed, and remanded the case to the Commission for a full evidentiary hearing on that issue.

On remand, the Commission held a public hearing, after which it made further factual findings and reaffirmed its imposition of the condition. It found that the new house would increase blockage of the view of the ocean, thus contributing to the development of "a 'wall' of residential structures" that would prevent the public "psychologically . . . from realizing a stretch of coast-line exists nearby that they have every right to visit." The new house would also increase private use of the shorefront. These effects of construction of the house, along with other area development, would cumulatively "burden the public's ability to traverse to and along the shorefront." Therefore the Commission could properly require the Nollans to offset that burden by providing additional lateral access to the public beaches in the form of an easement across their property. The Commission also noted that it had similarly conditioned 43 out of 60 coastal development permits along the same tract of land, and that of the 17 not so conditioned, 14 had been approved when the Commission did not have administrative regulations in place allowing imposition of the condition, and the remaining 3 had not involved shorefront property.

The Nollans filed a supplemental petition for a writ of administrative mandamus with the Superior Court, in which they argued that imposition of the access condition violated the Takings Clause of the Fifth Amendment, as incorporated against the States by the Fourteenth Amendment. The Superior Court ruled in their favor on statutory grounds,. . . [The court found that the Commission could impose access conditions on development permits for replacement homes only where the proposed development would have an adverse impact on public access to the sea, and that this requirement was not met.] *Access From other Bonches.*

The Commission appealed to the California Court of Appeal. While that appeal was pending, the Nollans satisfied the condition on their option to purchase by tearing down the bungalow and building a new house, and bought the property. They did not notify the Commission that they were taking that action.

The Court of Appeal reversed the Superior Court. 223 Cal. Rptr. 28 (1986). It disagreed with the Superior Court's interpretation of the Coastal Act,. . . It also ruled that that requirement did not violate the Constitution under the reasoning of an earlier case of the Court of Appeal, *Grupe v. California Coastal Comm'n,* 212 Cal. Rptr. 578 (Cal. App. 1985). In that case, the court had found that so long as a project contributed to the need for public access, even if the project standing alone had not created the need for access, and even if there was only an indirect relationship between the access exacted and the need to which the project contributed, imposition of an access condition on a development permit was sufficiently related to burdens created by the project to be constitutional. The Court of Appeal ruled that the record established that case was the situation with respect to the Nollans' house. It ruled that the Nollans' taking claim also failed because, although the condition diminished the value of the Nollans' lot, it did not deprive them of all reasonable use of their property. Since, in the Court of Appeal's view, there was no statutory or constitutional obstacle to imposition of the access condition, the Superior Court erred in granting the writ of mandamus. The Nollans appealed to this Court, raising only the constitutional question.

II

Had California simply required the Nollans to make an easement across their beachfront available to the public on a permanent basis in order to increase public access to the beach, rather than conditioning their permit to rebuild their house on their agreeing to do so, we have no doubt there would have been a taking. To say that the appropriation of a public easement across a landowner's premises does not constitute the taking of a property interest but rather, (as Justice Brennan contends) "a mere restriction on its use," is to use words in a manner that deprives them of all their ordinary meaning. Indeed, one of the principal uses of the eminent domain power is to assure that the government be able to require conveyance of just such interests, so long as it pays for them. Perhaps because the point is so obvious, we have never been confronted with a controversy that required us to rule upon it, but our cases' analysis of the effect of other governmental action leads to the same conclusion. We have repeatedly held that, as to property reserved by its owner for private use, "the right to exclude [others is] one of the most essential sticks in the bundle of rights that are commonly characterized as 'property.'" *Loretto v. Teleprompter Manhattan CATV Corp.*, 458 U.S. 419, 433 (1982), quoting *Kaiser Aetna v. United States*, 444 U.S. 164, 176 (1979). In *Loretto* we observed that where governmental action results in "[a] permanent physical occupation" of the property, by the government itself or by others, see 458 U.S., at 432–433, n.9, "our cases uniformly have found a taking to the extent of the occupation, without regard to whether the action achieves an important public benefit or has only minimal economic impact on the owner," *id.*, at 434–435. We think a "permanent physical occupation" has occurred, for purposes of that rule, where individuals are given a permanent and continuous right to pass to and fro, so that the real property may continuously be traversed, even though no particular individual is permitted presentation himself permanently upon the premises.[1]

Justice Brennan argues that while this might ordinarily be the case, the California Constitution's prohibition on any individual's "exclu[ding] the right of way to [any navigable] water whenever it is required for any public purpose," Article X, § 4, produces a different result here. . . .[2] [The discussion of this issue is omitted.]

---

[1] The holding of *Prune Yard Shopping Center v. Robins,* 447 U.S. 74 (1980), is not inconsistent with this analysis, since there the owner had already opened his property to the general public, and in addition permanent access was not required. The analysis of *Kaiser Aetna v. United States,* 444 U.S. 419 (1979), is not inconsistent because it was affected by traditional doctrines regarding navigational servitudes. Of course neither of those cases involved, as this case does, a classic right-of-way easement.

[2] Justice Brennan also suggests that the Commission's public announcement of its intention to condition the rebuilding of houses on the transfer of easements of access caused the Nollans to have "no reasonable claim to any expectation of being able to exclude members of the public" from walking across their beach. He cites our opinion in *Ruckelshaus v. Monsanto Co., 467 U.S.* 986 (1984) as support for the peculiar proposition that a unilateral claim of entitlement by the government can alter property rights. In *Monsanto,* however, we found merely that the takings clause was not violated by giving effect to the Government's announcement that application for *"the right to [the] valuable Government benefit,"* id., at 1007 (emphasis added), of obtaining registration of an insecticide would confer upon the Government a license to use and disclose the trade secrets contained in the application. *Id.,* at 1007-1008. But the right to build on one's own property —even though its exercise can be subjected to legitimate permitting requirements —cannot remotely be described as a "governmental benefit." And thus the announcement that the application for (or granting of) the permit will entail the yielding of a property interest cannot be regarded as establishing the voluntary "exchange," 467 U.S., at 1007, that we found to have occurred in *Monsanto.* Nor are the Nollans' rights altered because they acquired the land well after the Commission had begun to implement its policy. So long as the Commission could not have deprived the prior owners of the easement without compensating them, the prior owners must be understood to have transferred their full property rights in conveying the lot.

Given, then, that requiring uncompensated conveyance of the easement outright would violate the Fourteenth Amendment, the question becomes whether requiring it to be conveyed as a condition for issuing a land use permit alters the outcome. We have long recognized that land use regulation does not effect a taking if it "substantially advance[s] legitimate state interests" and does not "den[y] an owner economically viable use of his land," *Agins v. Tiburon,* 447 U.S. 255, 260 (1980). See also *Penn Central Transportation Co. v. New York City,* 438 U.S. 104, 127 (1978) ("a use restriction may constitute a 'taking' if not reasonably necessary to the effectuation of a substantial government purpose"). Our cases have not elaborated on the standards for determining what constitutes a "legitimate state interest" or what type of connection between the regulation and the state interest satisfies the requirement that the former "substantially advance" the latter.[3] They have made clear, however, that a broad range of governmental purposes and regulations satisfies these requirements. See *Agins v. Tiburon* (scenic zoning); *Penn Central Transportation Co. v. New York City* (landmark preservation); *Euclid v. Ambler Realty Co.* (residential zoning); Laitos and Westfall, Government Interference with Private Interests in Public Resources, 11 Harv. Envtl. L. Rev. 1, 66 (1987). The Commission argues that among these permissible purposes are protecting the public's ability to see the beach, assisting the public in overcoming the "psychological barrier" to using the beach created by a developed shorefront, and preventing congestion on the public beaches. We assume, without deciding, that this is so —in which case the Commission unquestionably would be able to deny the Nollans their permit outright if their new house (alone, or by reason of the cumulative impact produced in conjunction with other construction)[4] would substantially impede these purposes,

[3] Contrary to Justice Brennan's claim, our opinions do not establish that these standards are the same as those applied to due process or equal-protection claims. To the contrary, our verbal formulations in the takings field have generally been quite different. We have required that the regulation "substantially advance" the "legitimate state interest" sought to be achieved, *Agins v. Tiburon,* 447 U.S. 255, 260 (1980), not that "the States 'could rationally have decided' the measure adopted might achieve the State's objective." [Q]uoting *Minnesota v. Clover Leaf Creamery Co.,* 449 U.S. 456, 466 (1981). Justice Brennan relies principally on an equal protection case, *Minnesota v. Clover Leaf Creamery Co., supra,* and two substantive due process cases, *Williamson v. Lee Optical of Oklahoma, Inc.,* 348 U.S. 483, 487-488 (1955) and *Day-Brite Lighting, Inc. v. Missouri,* 342 U.S. 421, 423 (1952), in support of the standards he would adopt. But there is no reason to believe (and the language of our cases gives some reason to disbelieve) that so long as the regulation of property is at issue the standards for takings challenges, due process challenges, and equal protection challenges are identical; any more than there is any reason to believe that so long as the regulation of speech is at issue the standards for due process challenges, equal protection challenges, and First Amendment challenges are identical. *Goldblatt v. Hempstead,* 369 U.S. 590 (1962), does appear to assume that the inquiries are the same, but that assumption is inconsistent with the formulations of our later cases.

[4] If the Nollans were being singled out to bear the burden of California's attempt to remedy these problems, although they had not contributed to it more than other coastal landowners, the State's action, even if otherwise valid, might violate either the incorporated Takings Clause or the Equal Protection Clause. One of the principal purposes of the Takings Clause is "to bar Government from forcing some people alone to bear public burdens which, in all fairness and justice, should be borne by the public as a whole." *Armstrong v. United States,* 364 U.S. 40, 49 (1960); see also *San Diego Gas & Electric Co. v. San Diego,* 450 U.S. 621, 656 (1981) (Brennan, J., dissenting); *Penn Central Transportation Co. v. New York City,* 438 U.S. 104, 123 (1978). But that is not the basis of the Nollans' challenge here.

unless the denial would interfere so drastically with the Nollans' use of their property as to constitute a taking. See *Penn Central Transportation Co. v. New York City, supra.*

The Commission argues that a permit condition that serves the same legitimate police-power purpose as a refusal to issue the permit should not be found to be a taking if the refusal to issue the permit would not constitute a taking. We agree. Thus, if the Commission attached to the permit some condition that would have protected the public's ability to see the beach notwithstanding construction of a new house —for example, a height limitation, a width restriction, or a ban on fences —so long as the Commission could have exercised its police power (as we have assumed it could) to forbid construction of the house altogether, imposition of the condition would also be constitutional. Moreover (and here we come closer to the facts of the present case), the condition would be constitutional even if it consisted of the requirement that the Nollans provide a viewing spot on their property for passersby with whose sighting of the ocean their new house would interfere. Although such a requirement, constituting a permanent grant of continuous access to the property, would have to be considered a taking if it were not attached to a development permit, the Commission's assumed power to forbid construction of the house in order to protect the public's view of the beach must surely include the power to condition construction upon some concession by the owner, even a concession of property rights, that serves the same end. If a prohibition designed to accomplish that purpose would be a legitimate exercise of the police power rather than a taking, it would be strange to conclude that providing the owner an alternative to that prohibition which accomplishes the same purpose is not.

The evident constitutional propriety disappears, however, if the condition substituted for the prohibition utterly fails to further the end advanced as the justification for the prohibition. When that essential nexus is eliminated, the situation becomes the same as if California law forbade shouting fire in a crowded theater, but granted dispensations to those willing to contribute $100 to the state treasury. While a ban on shouting fire can be a core exercise of the State's police power to protect the public safety, and can thus meet even our stringent standards for regulation of speech, adding the unrelated condition alters the purpose to one which, while it may be legitimate, is inadequate to sustain the ban. Therefore, even though, in a sense, requiring a $100 tax contribution in order to shout fire is a lesser restriction on speech than an outright ban, it would not pass constitutional muster. Similarly here, the lack of nexus between the condition and the original purpose of the building restriction converts that purpose to something other than what it was. The purpose then becomes, quite simply, the obtaining of an easement to serve some valid governmental purpose, but without payment of compensation. Whatever may be the outer limits of "legitimate state interests" in the takings and land use context, this is not one of them. In short, unless the permit condition serves the same governmental purpose as the development ban, the building restriction is not a valid regulation of land use but "an out-and-out plan of extortion." *J. E. D. Associates, Inc. v. Atkinson,* 432 A. 2d 12, 14–15

(N.H. 1981). See also *Loretto v. Teleprompter Manhattan CATV Corp.*, 458 U.S., at 439, n.17.[5]

III

The Commission claims that it concedes as much, and that we may sustain the condition at issue here by finding that it is reasonably related to the public need or burden that the Nollans' new house creates or to which it contributes. We can accept, for purposes of discussion, the Commission's proposed test as to how close a "fit" between the condition and the burden is required, because we find that this case does not meet even the most untailored standards. The Commission's principal contention to the contrary essentially turns on a play on the word "access." The Nollans' new house, the Commission found, will interfere with "visual access" to the beach. That in turn (along with other shorefront development) will interfere with the desire of people who drive past the Nollans' house to use the beach, thus creating a "psychological barrier" to "access." The Nollans' new house will also, by process not altogether clear from the Commission's opinion but presumably potent enough to more than offset the effects of the psychological barrier, increase the use of the public beaches, thus creating the need for more "access." These burdens on "access" would be alleviated by a requirement that the Nollans provide "lateral access" to the beach.

Rewriting the argument to eliminate the play on words makes clear that there is nothing to it. It is quite impossible to understand how a requirement that people already on the public beaches be able to walk across the Nollans' property reduces any obstacles to viewing the beach created by the new house. It is also impossible to understand how it lowers any "psychological barrier" to using the public beaches, or how it helps to remedy any additional congestion on them caused by construction of the Nollans' new house. We therefore find that the Commission's imposition of the permit condition cannot be treated as an exercise of its land use power for any of these purposes.[6] Our conclusion on this point is consistent with the approach taken by every

---

[5] One would expect that a regime in which this kind of leveraging of the police power is allowed would produce stringent land-use regulation which the State then waives to accomplish other purposes, leading to lesser realization of the land-use goals purportedly sought to be served than would result from more lenient (but nontradeable) development restrictions. Thus, the importance of the purpose underlying the prohibition not only does not justify the imposition of unrelated conditions for eliminating the prohibition, but positively militates against the practice.

[6] As Justice Brennan notes, the Commission also argued that the construction of the new house would "'increase private use immediately adjacent to public tidelands,'" which in turn might result in more disputes between the Nollans and the public as to the location of the boundary. That risk of boundary disputes, however, is inherent in the right to exclude others from one's property, and the construction here can no more justify mandatory dedication of a sort of "buffer zone" in order to avoid boundary disputes than can the construction of an addition to a single-family house near a public street. Moreover, a buffer zone has a boundary as well, and unless that zone is a "no-man's land" that is off-limits for both neighbors (which is of course not the case here) its creation achieves nothing except to shift the location of the boundary dispute further on to the private owner's land. It is true that in the distinctive situation of the Nollans' property the sea-wall could be established as a clear demarcation of the public easement. But since not all of the lands to which this land-use condition applies have such a convenient reference point, the avoidance of boundary disputes is, even more obviously than the others, a made-up purpose of the regulation.

other court that has considered the question, with the exception of the California state courts. [At this point the Court cited a number of state and federal court cases that both upheld and struck down subdivision exactions.]

Justice Brennan argues that imposition of the access requirement is not irrational. In his version of the Commission's argument, the reason for the requirement is that in its absence, a person looking toward the beach from the road will see a street of residential structures including the Nollans' new home and conclude that there is no public beach nearby. If, however, that person sees people passing and repassing along the dry sand behind the Nollans' home, he will realize that there is a public beach somewhere in the vicinity. The Commission's action, however, was based on the opposite factual finding that the wall of houses completely blocked the view of the beach and that a person looking from the road would not be able to see it at all.

Even if the Commission had made the finding that Justice Brennan proposes, however, it is not certain that it would suffice. We do not share Justice Brennan's confidence that the Commission "should have little difficulty in the future in utilizing its expertise to demonstrate a specific connection between provisions for access and burdens on access," that will avoid the effect of today's decision. We view the Fifth Amendment's property clause to be more than a pleading requirement, and compliance with it to be more than an exercise in cleverness and imagination. As indicated earlier, our cases describe the condition for abridgement of property rights through the police power as a "substantial advanc[ing]" of a legitimate State interest. We are inclined to be particularly careful about the adjective where the actual conveyance of property is made a condition to the lifting of a land use restriction, since in that context there is a heightened risk that the purpose is avoidance of the compensation requirement, rather than the stated police power objective.

We are left, then, with the Commission's justification for the access requirement unrelated to land use regulation:

> Finally, the Commission notes that there are several existing provisions of pass and repass lateral access benefits already given by past Faria Beach Tract applicants as a result of prior coastal permit decisions. The access required as a condition of this permit is part of a comprehensive program to provide continuous public access along Faria Beach as the lots undergo development or redevelopment.

That is simply an expression of the Commission's belief that the public interest will be served by a continuous strip of publicly accessible beach along the coast. The Commission may well be right that it is a good idea, but that does not establish that the Nollans (and other coastal residents) alone can be compelled to contribute to its realization. Rather, California is free to advance its "comprehensive program," if it wishes, by using its power of eminent domain for this "public purpose," see U.S. Const., Amdt. V; but if it wants an easement across the Nollans' property, it must pay for it.

[Justice Brennan, with whom Justice Marshall joined, dissented. Justice Brennan's views are discussed in the majority opinion and in the Notes that follow. The dissenting opinions of Justices Blackmun and Stevens also are omitted.]

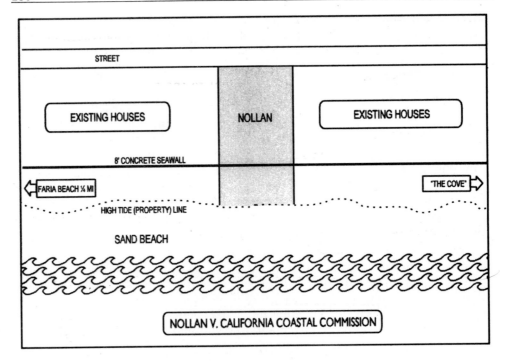

NOLLAN V. CALIFORNIA COASTAL COMMISSION

NOTES AND QUESTIONS

1. *A new class of "takings"?* *Nollan* is a very different type of takings case, if indeed it is properly a takings case at all. The court quoted the two-part *Agins* test, but it is obvious that strangers walking across the Nollan land did not have a serious economic impact on the value of the property. Thus *Nollan* is a case where satisfying the first prong of the *Agins* test, by establishing that the access condition did not serve a legitimate governmental interest, was enough for a taking. Since virtually no court has applied the first prong to find a taking outside the exaction cases, is it possible there is something different in an exactions case that compels this result? There may be something of a hint in the opening sentence in Part II of the opinion, which states there would have been a taking "[h]ad California simply required the Nollans to make an easement across their beachfront available to the public on a permanent basis." Later in *City of Monterey v. Del Monte Dunes*, 526 U.S. 687 (1999), the court held that its rules for exactions apply only to dedications of property for public use.

2. *The nexus test.* Although the *Nollan* opinion doesn't make it clear, the Court was influenced by a nexus test applied in state court cases to determine the validity of "subdivision exactions" imposed on subdivision developers by local governments in order to provide a variety of public facilities such as paved streets, water and sanitary sewer mains, storm drainage, and land for new parks, playgrounds, and school sites. In an omitted part of the opinion, the Court cited many state court cases dealing with challenges to such "subdivision exactions" on constitutional grounds. Some of these cases decide the constitutional validity of such "subdivision exactions" by inquiring whether there is a "rational relationship" (or "nexus") between the exactions and the need for new public facilities generated by the proposed subdivision development. Some of the cases, however, also apply a second test and sustain exactions only if the value of the property (or cash in lieu of property) exacted from the developer is roughly proportional to the benefit conferred on the developer by the provision of new facilities.

The nexus test in the state cases was much easier to satisfy because it was applied to residential subdivisions that created the need for the public facility demanded as an exaction. The special circumstances of *Nollan* made the nexus test more difficult to apply because there is no obvious linkage between construction of a residential dwelling and access to an adjacent beach. In *Dolan v. City of Tigard,* reproduced in Chapter 6, where the subject of exactions is pursued in more detail, the Court considered the related topic of showing that the facility need created by the subdivision justifies the exaction, assuming a nexus is present.

3. *Heightened scrutiny.* Justice Brennan disagreed with the heightened scrutiny standard the Court adopted in footnote 3. He argued that "the Court imposed a standard of precision for the exercise of the State's police power that has been discredited for the better part of this century." Justice Brennan thought that the deferential "minimal rationality" standard of "substantive due process" review was appropriate, rather than the "heightened scrutiny" suggested by the phrase "substantially advance[s] legitimate state interests." Footnote 3 caused quite a stir but has not had many takers. See *South County Sand & Gravel Co. v. Town of South Kingstown,* 160 F.3d 834 (1st Cir. 1998); *Bonnie Briar Syndicate, Inc. v. Town of Mamaroneck,* 721 N.E.2d 971 (N.Y. 1999). Do *Apfel* and *Del Monte Dunes* justify ignoring footnote 3?

Whether courts will require heightened scrutiny depends on whether the Court will continue to hold that inquiry into legitimacy of purpose is proper under the takings clause. Professor Kmiec, assuming that it will, discusses a number of cases in which he believes that heightened scrutiny is necessary. *The "Substantially Advance" Quandary: How Closely Should Courts Examine the Regulatory Means and Ends of Legislative Applications?,* 22 Zoning & Plan. L. Rep. 97 (1999). One of Kmiec's examples is the rezoning of a tract of land from one land use classification to another. This problem is examined in Chapter 5. Can you see the link to the heightened scrutiny issue? See also Wiseman, *When the End Justifies the Means: Understanding Takings Jurisprudence in a Legal System with Integrity,* 63 St. John's L. Rev. 433 (1989).

4. *Physical occupation.* The second test mentioned by the *Nollan* Court, whether the regulation denies the landowner "an economically viable use of his land," is the second *Agins* prong. This inquiry should be irrelevant under *Loretto* because the government has imposed "a permanent physical occupation on an unwilling owner." *Loretto* found a *per se* "taking" of property even though the landowner clearly retained "an economically viable use of his land." Hence it is difficult to understand the *Nollan* Court's statement, *arguendo,* that the California Coastal Commission could constitutionally have required "that the Nollans provide a viewing spot on their property for passersby with whose sighting of the ocean their new house would interfere."

Is it a sufficient answer to say that, although a viewing spot would be a taking if not attached to a permit because it is a permanent grant of access, it is constitutional if attached to a permit because the Commission could prohibit construction of the house to protect the public's view of the beach? If the Coastal Commission had only imposed a restriction on the Nollan's use of their land, it might be constitutionally justified because the Nollans would retain "an economically viable use" of their land; but as we have seen, that is not the test where government imposes "a permanent physical occupation on an unwilling owner."

5. *Average reciprocity of advantage.* Justice Brennan invoked the average reciprocity of advantage principle in his dissent:

> Appellants [the Nollans] have been allowed to replace a one-story 521-square foot beach home with a two-story, 1674-square foot residence and an attached two-car garage, resulting in development covering 2,464 square feet of the lot. Such development obviously significantly increases the value of appellants' property; appellants make no contention that this increase is offset by any diminution in value resulting from the deed restriction, much less that the restriction made the property less valuable than it would have been without the new construction.

Justice Brennan also noted the Nollans gained a new benefit because the deed restrictions on other property in the area allowed them to walk along the beach outside the "confines" of their own property. "Thus, appellants benefit both as private landowners and as members of the public from the fact that new development permit requests are conditioned on preservation of public access."

Is this argument a fair statement of the average reciprocity rule from *Penn Central*? Is it consistent with Justice Rehnquist's reformulation of this rule in his *Penn Central* dissent? Does the failure to invoke this rule in *Nollan* mean it no longer is relevant to land use takings cases?

6. *Investment-backed expectations.* What do you think of Justice Brennan's argument that because "appellants were clearly on notice when requesting a new development permit that a condition of approval would be a provision ensuring public lateral access to the shore . . . they surely could have had no expectation that they could obtain approval of their new development and exercise any right of exclusion afterward"? The majority rejected this argument in footnote 2. This would appear to constitute the death-knell of the "investment-backed expectations" test first set out in *Penn Central* and applied in *Keystone Bituminous,* insofar as that test might have been deemed applicable to cases where ownership of land was acquired with notice of governmental intent to impose an "exaction" at some future time.

The cases, however, have also ignored footnote 2, and refuse to find investment-backed expectations protected by the takings clause if a landowner was on constructive notice of a land use regulation under which a municipality later refused to allow development of the land, even when the regulations was adopted after the landowner purchased the land. *McNulty v. Town of Indialantic,* 727 F. Supp. 604 (M.D. Fla. 1989), where the property owner was prohibited from building under a beach setback ordinance adopted after purchase, is a leading case. A number of cases also refuse to recognize investment-backed expectations when a landowner has actual notice of a regulation under which he was refused development permission. E.g., *Ciampitti v. United States,* 22 Cl. Ct. 310 (1991) (denial of federal permit to develop wetlands). The investment-backed expectations takings factor has become important as an exception to the *per se* taking rule adopted in the *Lucas* case, which is reproduced next, and is considered in a Note following that case.

7. *Sources.* For discussion of *Nollan* see Kayden, *Judges as Planners: Limited or General Partners?,* in Zoning and the American Dream 223 (C. Haar & J. Kayden eds., 1989); Note, *Municipal Development Exactions, The Rational Nexus Test, and The Federal Constitution,* 102 Harv. L. Rev. 992 (1989); Note, *Taking a Step Back: A Reconsideration of the Takings Test of Nollan v. California Coastal Commission,* 102 Harv. L. Rev. 449 (1988). For an article finding that federal and state courts have interpreted *Nollan* in similar ways see Gerry, *Parity Revisited: An Empirical Comparison of State and Lower Federal Court Interpretations of Nollan v. California Coastal Commission,* 23 Harv. J.L. & Pub. Pol'y 233 (1999).

3. THE *LUCAS* CASE: A PER SE TAKINGS RULE

LUCAS v. SOUTH CAROLINA COASTAL COUNCIL

505 U.S. 1003 (1992)

Justice Scalia delivered the opinion of the Court:

In 1986, petitioner David H. Lucas paid $975,000 for two residential lots on the Isle of Palms in Charleston County, South Carolina, on which he intended to build single-family homes. In 1988, however, the South Carolina Legislature enacted the Beachfront Management Act, S.C. Code § 48-39-250 *et seq.* (Supp. 1990) (Act), which had the direct effect of barring petitioner from erecting any permanent habitable structures on his two parcels. See § 48-39-290(A). A state trial court found that this prohibition rendered Lucas's parcels "valueless." This case requires us to decide whether the Act's dramatic effect on the economic value of Lucas's lots accomplished a taking of private property under the Fifth and Fourteenth Amendments requiring the payment of "just compensation." U.S. Const., Amdt. 5.

I

A

South Carolina's expressed interest in intensively managing development activities in the so-called "coastal zone" dates from 1977 when, in the aftermath of Congress's passage of the federal Coastal Zone Management Act of 1972, 16 U.S.C. § 1451 *et seq.,* the legislature enacted a Coastal Zone Management Act of its own. See S.C. Code § 48-39-10 *et seq.* (1987). In its original form, the South Carolina Act required owners of coastal zone land that qualified as a "critical area" (defined in the legislation to include beaches and immediately adjacent sand dunes, § 48-39-10(J)) to obtain a permit from the newly created South Carolina Coastal Council (respondent here) prior to committing the land to a "use other than the use the critical area was devoted to on [September 28, 1977]." § 48-39-130(A).

In the late 1970s, Lucas and others began extensive residential development of the Isle of Palms, a barrier island situated eastward of the City of Charleston. Toward the close of the development cycle for one residential subdivision known as "Beachwood East," Lucas in 1986 purchased the two lots at issue in this litigation for his own account. No portion of the lots, which were located approximately 300 feet from the beach, qualified as a "critical area" under the 1977 Act; accordingly, at the time Lucas acquired these parcels, he was not legally obliged to obtain a permit from the Council in advance of any development activity. His intention with respect to the lots was to do what the owners of the immediately adjacent parcels had already done: erect single-family residences. He commissioned architectural drawings for this purpose.

The Beachfront Management Act brought Lucas's plans to an abrupt end. Under that 1988 legislation, the Council was directed to establish a "baseline" connecting the landward-most "points of erosion . . . during the past forty years" in the region of the Isle of Palms that includes Lucas's lots. § 48-39-280(A)(2) (Supp.1988).[1] In action not challenged here, the Council fixed this baseline landward of Lucas's parcels. That was significant, for under the Act construction of occupiable improvements[2] was flatly prohibited seaward of a line drawn 20 feet landward of, and parallel to, the baseline, § 48-39-290(A) (Supp.1988). The Act provided no exceptions.

B

Lucas promptly filed suit in the South Carolina Court of Common Pleas, contending that the Beachfront Management Act's construction bar effected a taking of his property without just compensation. Lucas did not take issue with the validity of the Act as a lawful exercise of South Carolina's police power, but contended that the Act's complete extinguishment of his property's value entitled him to compensation regardless of whether the legislature had acted in furtherance of legitimate police power objectives. Following a bench trial, the court agreed. Among its factual determinations was the finding that "at the time Lucas purchased the two lots, both were zoned for single-family residential construction and . . . there were no restrictions imposed upon such use of the property by either the State of South Carolina, the County of Charleston, or the Town of the Isle of Palms." The trial court further found

---

[1] This specialized historical method of determining the baseline applied because the Beachwood East subdivision is located adjacent to a so-called "inlet erosion zone" (defined in the Act to mean "a segment of shoreline along or adjacent to tidal inlets which is influenced directly by the inlet and its associated shoals," S.C. Code § 48-39-270(7) (Supp.1988)) that is Anot stabilized by jetties, terminal groins, or other structures," § 48-39-280(A) (2). For areas other than these unstabilized inlet erosion zones, the statute directs that the baseline be established "along the crest of the primary oceanfront sand dune." § 48-39-280(A)(1).

[2] The Act did allow the construction of certain nonhabitable improvements, e.g., "wooden walkways no larger in width than six feet," and "small wooden decks no larger than one hundred forty-four square feet." §§ 48-39-290(A)(1) and (2) (Supp.1988).

that the Beachfront Management Act decreed a permanent ban on construction insofar as Lucas's lots were concerned, and that this prohibition "deprived Lucas of any reasonable economic use of the lots, . . . eliminated the unrestricted right of use, and rendered them valueless." The court thus concluded that Lucas's properties had been "taken" by operation of the Act, and it ordered respondent to pay "just compensation" in the amount of $1,232,387.50.

The Supreme Court of South Carolina reversed. It found dispositive what it described as Lucas's concession "that the Beachfront Management Act [was] properly and validly designed to preserve . . . South Carolina's beaches." 404 S.E.2d 895, 896 (1991). Failing an attack on the validity of the statute as such, the court believed itself bound to accept the "uncontested . . . findings" of the South Carolina legislature that new construction in the coastal zone —such as petitioner intended —threatened this public resource. *Id.*, at 898. The Court ruled that when a regulation respecting the use of property is designed "to prevent serious public harm," *Id.*, at 899, (citing, *inter alia*, *Mugler v. Kansas*, 123 U.S. 623 (1887)), no compensation is owing under the Takings Clause regardless of the regulation's effect on the property's value.

Two justices dissented. They acknowledged that our *Mugler* line of cases recognizes governmental power to prohibit "noxious" uses of property —*i.e.*, uses of property akin to "public nuisances" —without having to pay compensation. But they would not have characterized the Beachfront Management Act's "*primary* purpose [as] the prevention of a nuisance." 404 S.E.2d, at 906 (Harwell, J., dissenting). To the dissenters, the chief purposes of the legislation, among them the promotion of tourism and the creation of a "habitat for indigenous flora and fauna," could not fairly be compared to nuisance abatement. *Id.*, at 906. As a consequence, they would have affirmed the trial court's conclusion that the Act's obliteration of the value of petitioner's lots accomplished a taking.

We granted certiorari.

II

As a threshold matter, we must briefly address the Council's suggestion that this case is inappropriate for plenary review. After briefing and argument before the South Carolina Supreme Court, but prior to issuance of that court's opinion, the Beachfront Management Act was amended to authorize the Council, in certain circumstances, to issue "special permits" for the construction or reconstruction of habitable structures seaward of the baseline. See S.C. Code § 48-39-290(D)(1) (Supp.1991). According to the Council, this amendment renders Lucas's claim of a permanent deprivation unripe, as Lucas may yet be able to secure permission to build on his property. . . . [The Council cited Supreme Court decisions that hold a taking case is not ripe unless the landowner has obtained a final decision, citing *Williamson County Regional Planning Comm'n of Johnson City v. Hamilton Bank*, 473 U.S. 172, 190 (1985), reproduced *infra*.]

We think these considerations would preclude review had the South Carolina Supreme Court rested its judgment on ripeness grounds, as it was (essentially) invited to do by the Council, see Brief for Respondent 9. n.3. The

South Carolina Supreme Court shrugged off the possibility of further administrative and trial proceedings, however, preferring to dispose of Lucas's takings claim on the merits. This unusual disposition does not preclude Lucas from applying for a permit under the 1990 amendment for *future* construction, and challenging, on takings grounds, any denial. But it does preclude, both practically and legally, any takings claim with respect to Lucas's *past* deprivation, *i.e.,* for his having been denied construction rights during the period before the 1990 amendment. . . . [The Court held that Lucas had no need to pursue a temporary taking claim at trial because "as the Act then read, the taking was unconditional and permanent."]

III

A

Prior to Justice Holmes' exposition in *Pennsylvania Coal Co. v. Mahon*, 260 U.S. 393 (1922), it was generally thought that the Takings Clause reached only a "direct appropriation" of property, *Legal Tender Cases*, 12 Wall. 457, 551 (1871), or the functional equivalent of a "practical ouster of [the owner's] possession." *Transportation Co. v. Chicago*, 99 U.S. 635, 642 (1879). Justice Holmes recognized in *Mahon*, however, that if the protection against physical appropriations of private property was to be meaningfully enforced, the government's power to redefine the range of interests included in the ownership of property was necessarily constrained by constitutional limits. 260 U.S., at 414–415. If, instead, the uses of private property were subject to unbridled, uncompensated qualification under the police power, "the natural tendency of human nature [would be] to extend the qualification more and more until at last private property disappeared." *Id.,* at 415. These considerations gave birth in that case to the oft-cited maxim that, "while property may be regulated to a certain extent, if regulation goes too far it will be recognized as a taking." *Ibid.*

Nevertheless, our decision in *Mahon* offered little insight into when, and under what circumstances, a given regulation would be seen as going "too far" for purposes of the Fifth Amendment. In 70-odd years of succeeding "regulatory takings" jurisprudence, we have generally eschewed any "set formula" for determining how far is too far, preferring to "engag[e] in . . . essentially ad hoc, factual inquiries," *Penn Central Transportation Co. v. New York City*, 438 U.S. 104, 124 (1978) (quoting *Goldblatt v. Hempstead*, 369 U.S. 590, 594 (1962)). See Epstein, *Takings: Descent and Resurrection*, 1987 Sup. Ct. Rev. 1, 4. We have, however, described at least two discrete categories of regulatory action as compensable without case-specific inquiry into the public interest advanced in support of the restraint. The first encompasses regulations that compel the property owner to suffer a physical "invasion" of his property. In general (at least with regard to permanent invasions), no matter how minute the intrusion, and no matter how weighty the public purpose behind it, we have required compensation. For example, in *Loretto v. Teleprompter Manhattan CATV Corp.*, 458 U.S. 419 (1982), we determined that New York's law requiring landlords to allow television cable companies to emplace cable facilities in their apartment buildings constituted a taking, *id.*, at 435–440, even though the facilities occupied at most only 12 cubic feet of the landlords' property, see *id.*, at 438, n. 16. See also *United States v. Causby*, 328 U.S. 256, 265, and n. 10 (1946) (physical invasions of airspace); cf. *Kaiser Aetna v. United States*, 444 U.S. 164 (1979) (imposition of navigational servitude upon private marina).

The second situation in which we have found categorical treatment appropriate is where regulation denies all economically beneficial or productive use of land. See *Agins*, 447 U.S., at 260.[6] As we have said on numerous occasions, the Fifth Amendment is violated when land-use regulation "does not substantially advance legitimate state interests *or denies an owner economically viable use of his land.*" *Agins, supra*, at 260 (citations omitted) (emphasis added).[7]

---

[6] We will not attempt to respond to all of Justice Blackmun's mistaken citation of case precedent. Characteristic of its nature is his assertion that the cases we discuss here stand merely for the proposition "that proof that a regulation does not deny an owner economic use of his property is sufficient to defeat a facial taking challenge" and not for the point that "denial of such use is sufficient to establish a taking claim regardless of any other consideration." The cases say, repeatedly and unmistakably, that "'the test to be applied in considering [a] facial [takings] challenge is fairly straightforward. A statute regulating the uses that can be made of property effects a taking if it "denies an owner economically viable use of his land."'" Keystone, 480 U.S., at 495 (quoting Hodel, 452 U.S., at 295–296 (quoting Agins, 447 U.S., at 260)) (emphasis added).

Justice Blackmun describes that rule (which we do not invent but merely apply today) as "altering the long-settled rules of review" by foisting on the State "the burden of showing [its] regulation is not a taking." This is of course wrong. Lucas had to do more than simply file a lawsuit to establish his constitutional entitlement; he had to show that the Beachfront Management Act denied him economically beneficial use of his land. Our analysis presumes the unconstitutionality of state land-use regulation only in the sense that any rule-with-exceptions presumes the invalidity of a law that violates it —for example, the rule generally prohibiting content-based restrictions on speech. Justice Blackmun's real quarrel is with the substantive standard of liability we apply in this case, a long-established standard we see no need to repudiate.

[7] Regrettably, the rhetorical force of our "deprivation of all economically feasible use" rule is greater than its precision, since the rule does not make clear the "property interest" against which the loss of value is to be measured. When, for example, a regulation requires a developer to leave 90% of a rural tract in its natural state, it is unclear whether we would analyze the situation as one in which the owner has been deprived of all economically beneficial use of the burdened portion of the tract, or as one in which the owner has suffered a mere diminution in value of the tract as a whole. (For an extreme —and, we think, unsupportable —view of the relevant calculus, see Penn Central Transportation Co. v. New York City, 366 N. E. 2d 1271, 1276–1277 (N.Y. 1977), aff'd, 438 U.S. 104 (1978), where the state court examined the diminution in a particular parcel's value produced by a municipal ordinance in light of total value of the taking claimant's other holdings in the vicinity.) Unsurprisingly, this uncertainty regarding the composition of the denominator in our "deprivation" fraction has produced inconsistent pronouncements by the Court. Compare Pennsylvania Coal Co. v. Mahon, 260 U.S. 393, 414 (1922) (law restricting subsurface extraction of coal held to effect a taking), with Keystone Bituminous Coal Assn. v. DeBenedictis, 480 U.S. 470, 497-502 (1987) (nearly identical law held not to effect a taking); see also id., at 515–520 (Rehnquist, C.J., dissenting); Rose, Mahon Reconstructed: Why the Takings Issue is Still a Muddle, 57 S. Cal. L. Rev. 561, 566–569 (1984). The answer to this difficult question may lie in how the owner's reasonable expectations have been shaped by the State's law of property —i.e., whether and to what degree the State's law has accorded legal recognition and protection to the particular interest in land with respect to which the takings claimant alleges a diminution in (or elimination of) value. In any event, we avoid this difficulty in the present case, since the "interest in land" that Lucas has pleaded (a fee simple interest) is an estate with a rich tradition of protection at common law, and since the South Carolina Court of Common Pleas found that the Beachfront Management Act left each of Lucas's beachfront lots without economic value.

We have never set forth the justification for this rule. Perhaps it is simply, as Justice Brennan suggested, that total deprivation of beneficial use is, from the landowner's point of view, the equivalent of a physical appropriation. See *San Diego Gas & Electric Co. v. San Diego*, 450 U.S., at 652 (Brennan, J., dissenting). "[F]or what is the land but the profits thereof[?]" 1 E. Coke, Institutes ch. 1, § 1 (1st Am. ed. 1812). Surely, at least, in the extraordinary circumstance when *no* productive or economically beneficial use of land is permitted, it is less realistic to indulge our usual assumption that the legislature is simply "adjusting the benefits and burdens of economic life," *Penn Central Transportation Co.*, 438 U.S., at 124, in a manner that secures an "average reciprocity of advantage" to everyone concerned. *Pennsylvania Coal Co. v. Mahon*, 260 U.S., at 415. And the *functional* basis for permitting the government, by regulation, to affect property values without compensation —that "Government hardly could go on if to some extent values incident to property could not be diminished without paying for every such change in the general law," *id.*, at 413 —does not apply to the relatively rare situations where the government has deprived a landowner of all economically beneficial uses.

On the other side of the balance, affirmatively supporting a compensation requirement, is the fact that regulations that leave the owner of land without economically beneficial or productive options for its use —typically, as here, by requiring land to be left substantially in its natural state —carry with them a heightened risk that private property is being pressed into some form of public service under the guise of mitigating serious public harm. See, *e.g.*, *Annicelli v. South Kingstown*, 463 A.2d 133, 140–141 (R.I. 1983) (prohibition on construction adjacent to beach justified on twin grounds of safety and "conservation of open space"); *Morris County Land Improvement Co. v. Parsippany-Troy Hills Township*, 40 N.J. 539, 552–553, 193 A.2d 232, 240 (1963) (prohibition on filling marshlands imposed in order to preserve region as water detention basin and create wildlife refuge). As Justice Brennan explained: "From the government's point of view, the benefits flowing to the public from preservation of open space through regulation may be equally great as from creating a wildlife refuge through formal condemnation or increasing electricity production through a dam project that floods private property." *San Diego Gas & Elec. Co., supra*, 450 U.S., at 652 (Brennan, J., dissenting). The many statutes on the books, both state and federal, that provide for the use of eminent domain to impose servitudes on private scenic lands preventing developmental uses, or to acquire such lands altogether, suggest the practical equivalence in this setting of negative regulation and appropriation. See, *e.g.*, 16 U.S.C. § 410ff-1(a) (authorizing acquisition of "lands, waters, or interests [within Channel Islands National Park] (including but not limited to scenic easements)"); § 460aa-2(a) (authorizing acquisition of "any lands, or lesser interests therein, including mineral interests and scenic easements" within Sawtooth National Recreation Area); §§ 3921–3923 (authorizing acquisition of wetlands); N.C. Gen. Stat. § 113A-38 (1990) (authorizing acquisition of, *inter alia*, "'scenic easements'" within the North Carolina natural and scenic rivers system); Tenn. Code Ann. §§ 11-15-101— 11-15-108 (1987) (authorizing acquisition of "protective easements" and other rights in real property adjacent to State's historic, architectural, archaeological, or cultural resources).

We think, in short, that there are good reasons for our frequently expressed belief that when the owner of real property has been called upon to sacrifice _all_ economically beneficial uses in the name of the common good, that is, to leave his property economically idle, he has suffered a taking.[8]

B

The trial court found Lucas's two beachfront lots to have been rendered valueless by respondent's enforcement of the coastal-zone construction ban. Under Lucas's theory of the case, which rested upon our "no economically viable use" statements, that finding entitled him to compensation. Lucas believed it unnecessary to take issue with either the purposes behind the Beachfront Management Act, or the means chosen by the South Carolina Legislature to effectuate those purposes. The South Carolina Supreme Court, however, thought otherwise. In its view, the Beachfront Management Act was no ordinary enactment, but involved an exercise of South Carolina's "police powers" to mitigate the harm to the public interest that petitioner's use of his land might occasion. 404 S.E.2d, at 899. By neglecting to dispute the findings enumerated in the Act[10] or otherwise to challenge the legislature's

---

[8] Justice Stevens criticizes the "deprivation of all economically beneficial use" rule as "wholly arbitrary", in that "[the] landowner whose property is diminished in value 95% recovers nothing," while the landowner who suffers a complete elimination of value "recovers the land's full value." This analysis errs in its assumption that the landowner whose deprivation is one step short of complete is not entitled to compensation. Such an owner might not be able to claim the benefit of our categorical formulation, but, as we have acknowledged time and again, "the economic impact of the regulation on the claimant and . . . the extent to which the regulation has interfered with distinct investment-backed expectations" are keenly relevant to takings analysis generally. Penn Central Transportation Co. v. New York City, 438 U.S. 104, 124 (1978). It is true that in at least some cases the landowner with 95% loss will get nothing, while the landowner with total loss will recover in full. But that occasional result is no more strange than the gross disparity between the landowner whose premises are taken for a highway (who recovers in full) and the landowner whose property is reduced to 5% of its former value by the highway (who recovers nothing). Takings law is full of these "all-or-nothing" situations.

Justice Stevens similarly misinterprets our focus on "developmental" uses of property (the uses proscribed by the Beachfront Management Act) as betraying an "assumption that the only uses of property cognizable under the Constitution are developmental uses." We make no such assumption. Though our prior takings cases evince an abiding concern for the productive use of, and economic investment in, land, there are plainly a number of noneconomic interests in land whose impairment will invite exceedingly close scrutiny under the Takings Clause. See, e.g., Loretto v. Teleprompter Manhattan CATV Corp., 458 U.S. 419, 436 (1982) (interest in excluding strangers from one's land).

[10] The legislature's express findings include the following:

"The General Assembly finds that:

"(1) The beach/dune system along the coast of South Carolina is extremely important to the people of this State and serves the following functions:

"(a) protects life and property by serving as a storm barrier which dissipates wave energy and contributes to shoreline stability in an economical and effective manner;

"(b) provides the basis for a tourism industry that generates approximately two-thirds of South Carolina's annual tourism industry revenue which constitutes a significant portion of the state's economy. The tourists who come to the South Carolina coast to enjoy the ocean and dry sand beach contribute significantly to state and local tax revenues;

"(c) provides habitat for numerous species of plants and animals, several of which are threatened or endangered. Waters adjacent to the beach/dune system also provide habitat for many other marine species;

purposes, petitioner "conceded that the beach/dune area of South Carolina's shores is an extremely valuable public resource; that the erection of new construction, *inter alia*, contributes to the erosion and destruction of this public resource; and that discouraging new construction in close proximity to the beach/dune area is necessary to prevent a great public harm." 404 S.E.2d, at 898. In the court's view, these concessions brought petitioner's challenge within a long line of this Court's cases sustaining against Due Process and Takings Clause challenges the State's use of its "police powers" to enjoin a property owner from activities akin to public nuisances. See *Mugler v. Kansas,* 123 U.S. 623 (1887) (law prohibiting manufacture of alcoholic beverages); *Hadacheck v. Sebastian,* 239 U.S. 394 (1915) (law barring operation of brick mill in residential area); *Miller v. Schoene,* 276 U.S. 272 (1928) (order to destroy diseased cedar trees to prevent infection of nearby orchards); *Goldblatt v. Hempstead,* 369 U.S. 590 (1962) (law effectively preventing continued operation of quarry in residential area).

It is correct that many of our prior opinions have suggested that "harmful or noxious uses" of property may be proscribed by government regulation without the requirement of compensation. For a number of reasons, however, we think the South Carolina Supreme Court was too quick to conclude that that principle decides the present case. The "harmful or noxious uses" principle was the Court's early attempt to describe in theoretical terms why government may, consistent with the Takings Clause, affect property values by regulation without incurring an obligation to compensate —a reality we nowadays acknowledge explicitly with respect to the full scope of the State's police power. See, *e.g., Penn Central Transportation Co.,* 438 U.S., at 125

"(d) provides a natural health environment for the citizens of South Carolina to spend leisure time which serves their physical and mental well-being.

"(2) Beach/dune system vegetation is unique and extremely important to the vitality and preservation of the system.

"(3) Many miles of South Carolina's beaches have been identified as critically eroding.

"(4) . . . [D]evelopment unwisely has been sited too close to the [beach/dune] system. This type of development has jeopardized the stability of the [beach/dune] system, accelerated erosion, and endangered adjacent property. It is in both the public and private interests to protect the system from this unwise development.

"(5) The use of armoring in the form of hard erosion control devices such as seawalls, bulkheads, and rip-rap to protect erosion-threatened structures adjacent to the beach has not proven effective. These armoring devices have given a false sense of security to beachfront property owners. In reality, these hard structures, in many instances, have increased the vulnerability of beachfront property to damage from wind and waves while contributing to the deterioration and loss of the dry sand beach which is so important to the tourism industry.

"(6) Erosion is a natural process which becomes a significant problem for man only when structures are erected in close proximity to the beach/dune system. It is in both the public and private interests to afford the beach/dune system space to accrete and erode in its natural cycle. This space can be provided only by discouraging new construction in close proximity to the beach/dune system and encouraging those who have erected structures too close to the system to retreat from it.

" . . . .

"(8) It is in the state's best interest to protect and to promote increased public access to South Carolina's beaches for out-of-state tourists and South Carolina residents alike." S.C. Code §48-39-250 (Supp.1991).

(where State "reasonably conclude[s] that 'the health, safety, morals, or general welfare' would be promoted by prohibiting particular contemplated uses of land," compensation need not accompany prohibition) ("Our cases have not elaborated on the standards for determining what constitutes a 'legitimate state interest[,]' [but] [t]hey have made clear . . . that a broad range of governmental purposes and regulations satisfy these requirements"). We made this very point in *Penn Central Transportation Co.,* where, in the course of sustaining New York City's landmarks preservation program against a takings challenge, we rejected the petitioner's suggestion that *Mugler* and the cases following it were premised on, and thus limited by, some objective conception of "noxiousness":

> "[T]he uses in issue in *Hadacheck, Miller,* and *Goldblatt* were perfectly lawful in themselves. They involved no blameworthiness, . . . moral wrongdoing or conscious act of dangerous risk-taking which induce[d society] to shift the cost to a particular individual.' Sax, Takings and the Police Power, 74 Yale L.J. 36, 50 (1964). These cases are better understood as resting not on any supposed 'noxious' quality of the prohibited uses but rather on the ground that the restrictions were reasonably related to the implementation of a policy —not unlike historic preservation —expected to produce a widespread public benefit and applicable to all similarly situated property." 438 U.S., at 133– 134, n. 30.

"Harmful or noxious use" analysis was, in other words, simply the progenitor of our more contemporary statements that "land-use regulation does not effect a taking if it 'substantially advance[s] legitimate state interests'. . . ." *Nollan, supra,* at 834 (quoting *Agins v. Tiburon,* 447 U.S., at 260).

The transition from our early focus on control of "noxious" uses to our contemporary understanding of the broad realm within which government may regulate without compensation was an easy one, since the distinction between "harm-preventing" and "benefit-conferring" regulation is often in the eye of the beholder. It is quite possible, for example, to describe in *either* fashion the ecological, economic, and aesthetic concerns that inspired the South Carolina legislature in the present case. One could say that imposing a servitude on Lucas's land is necessary in order to prevent his use of it from "harming" South Carolina's ecological resources; or, instead, in order to achieve the "benefits" of an ecological preserve.[11] Compare, *e.g., Claridge v.*

---

[11] In the present case, in fact, some of the "[South Carolina] legislature's 'findings'" to which the South Carolina Supreme Court purported to defer in characterizing the purpose of the Act as "harm-preventing," 404 S.E.2d 895, 896 (1991), seem to us phrased in "benefit-conferring" language instead. For example, they describe the importance of a construction ban in enhancing ASouth Carolina's annual tourism industry revenue," S.C. Code § 48-39-250(1)(b) (Supp.1991), in "provid[ing] habitat for numerous species of plants and animals, several of which are threatened or endangered," § 48-39-250(1)(c), and in "provid[ing] a natural healthy environment for the citizens of South Carolina to spend leisure time which serves their physical and mental well-being." § 48-39-250(1)(d). It would be pointless to make the outcome of this case hang upon this terminology, since the same interests could readily be described in "harm-preventing" fashion.

Justice Blackmun, however, apparently insists that we must make the outcome hinge (exclusively) upon the South Carolina Legislature's other, "harm-preventing" characterizations, focusing on the declaration that "prohibitions on building in front of the setback line are necessary to protect people and property from storms, high tides, and beach erosion." He says "[n]othing

New Hampshire Wetlands Board, 125 N.H. 745, 752, 485 A.2d 287, 292 (1984) (owner may, without compensation, be barred from filling wetlands because landfilling would deprive adjacent coastal habitats and marine fisheries of ecological support), with, *e.g.*, *Bartlett v. Zoning Comm'n of Old Lyme,* 161 Conn. 24, 30, 282 A.2d 907, 910 (1971) (owner barred from filling tidal marshland must be compensated, despite municipality's "laudable" goal of "preserv[ing] marshlands from encroachment or destruction"). Whether one or the other of the competing characterizations will come to one's lips in a particular case depends primarily upon one's evaluation of the worth of competing uses of real estate. See Restatement (Second) of Torts § 822, Comment *g*, p. 112 (1979) ("[p]ractically all human activities unless carried on in a wilderness interfere to some extent with others or involve some risk of interference"). A given restraint will be seen as mitigating "harm" to the adjacent parcels or securing a "benefit" for them, depending upon the observer's evaluation of the relative importance of the use that the restraint favors. See Sax, *Takings and the Police Power*, 74 Yale L.J. 36, 49 (1964) ("[T]he problem [in this area] is not one of noxiousness or harm-creating activity at all; rather it is a problem of inconsistency between perfectly innocent and independently desirable uses"). Whether Lucas's construction of single-family residences on his parcels should be described as bringing "harm" to South Carolina's adjacent ecological resources thus depends principally upon whether the describer believes that the State's use interest in nurturing those resources is so important that *any* competing adjacent use must yield.[12]

When it is understood that "prevention of harmful use" was merely our early formulation of the police power justification necessary to sustain (without compensation) *any* regulatory diminution in value; and that the distinction between regulation that "prevents harmful use" and that which "confers benefits" is difficult, if not impossible, to discern on an objective, value-free basis; it becomes self-evident that noxious-use logic cannot serve as a touchstone to distinguish regulatory "takings" —which require compensation —from regulatory deprivations that do not require compensation. *A fortiori* the legislature's recitation of a noxious-use justification cannot be the basis for departing from our categorical rule that total regulatory takings must be compensated. If it were, departure would virtually always be allowed. The South Carolina Supreme Court's approach would essentially nullify *Mahon's* affirmation of limits to the noncompensable exercise of the police power. Our cases provide no support for this: None of them that employed the logic of "harmful use" prevention to sustain a regulation involved an allegation that

---

in the record undermines [this] assessment," ibid., apparently seeing no significance in the fact that the statute permits owners of existing structures to remain (and even to rebuild if their structures are not "destroyed beyond repair," S.C. Code Ann. § 48-39-290(B)), and in the fact that the 1990 amendment authorizes the Council to issue permits for new construction in violation of the uniform prohibition, see S.C. Code § 48-39-290(D)(1) (Supp.1991).

[12] In Justice Blackmun's view, even with respect to regulations that deprive an owner of all developmental or economically beneficial land uses, the test for required compensation is whether the legislature has recited a harm-preventing justification for its action. Since such a justification can be formulated in practically every case, this amounts to a test of whether the legislature has a stupid staff. We think the Takings Clause requires courts to do more than insist upon artful harm-preventing characterizations.

the regulation wholly eliminated the value of the claimant's land. See *Keystone Bituminous Coal Assn.*, 480 U.S., at 513–514 (Rehnquist, C.J., dissenting).[13]

Where the State seeks to sustain regulation that deprives land of all economically beneficial use, we think it may resist compensation only if the logically antecedent inquiry into the nature of the owner's estate shows that the proscribed use interests were not part of his title to begin with.[14] This accords, we think, with our "takings" jurisprudence, which has traditionally been guided by the understandings of our citizens regarding the content of, and the State's power over, the "bundle of rights" that they acquire when they obtain title to property. It seems to us that the property owner necessarily expects the uses of his property to be restricted, from time to time, by various measures newly enacted by the State in legitimate exercise of its police powers; "[a]s long recognized, some values are enjoyed under an implied limitation and must yield to the police power." *Pennsylvania Coal Co. v. Mahon*, 260 U.S., at 413. And in the case of personal property, by reason of the State's traditionally high degree of control over commercial dealings, he ought to be aware of the possibility that new regulation might even render his property economically worthless (at least if the property's only economically productive use is sale or manufacture for sale), see *Andrus v. Allard*, 444 U.S. 51, 66–67 (1979) (prohibition on sale of eagle feathers). In the case of land, however, we think the notion pressed by the Council that title is somehow held subject to the "implied limitation" that the State may subsequently eliminate all economically valuable use is inconsistent with the historical compact recorded in the Takings Clause that has become part of our constitutional culture.[15]

---

[13] E.g., Mugler v. Kansas, 123 U.S. 623 (1887) (prohibition upon use of a building as a brewery; other uses permitted); Plymouth Coal Co. v. Pennsylvania, 232 U.S. 531 (1914) (requirement that "pillar" of coal be left in ground to safeguard mine workers; mineral rights could otherwise be exploited); Reinman v. Little Rock, 237 U.S. 171 (1915) (declaration that livery stable constituted a public nuisance; other uses of the property permitted); Hadacheck v. Sebastian, 239 U.S. 394 (1915) (prohibition of brick manufacturing in residential area; other uses permitted); Goldblatt v. Hempstead, 369 U.S. 590 (1962) (prohibition on excavation; other uses permitted).

[14] Drawing on our First Amendment jurisprudence, see, e.g., Employment Division, Department of Human Resources of Oregon v. Smith, 494 U.S. 872, 878-879 (1990), Justice Stevens would "loo[k] to the generality of a regulation of property" to determine whether compensation is owing. The Beachfront Management Act is general, in his view, because it "regulates the use of the coastline of the entire state." There may be some validity to the principle Justice Stevens proposes, but it does not properly apply to the present case. The equivalent of a law of general application that inhibits the practice of religion without being aimed at religion, see Oregon v. Smith, supra, is a law that destroys the value of land without being aimed at land. Perhaps such a law —the generally applicable criminal prohibition on the manufacturing of alcoholic beverages challenged in Mugler comes to mind —cannot constitute a compensable taking. See 123 U.S., at 655–656. But a regulation specifically directed to land use no more acquires immunity by plundering landowners generally than does a law specifically directed at religious practice acquire immunity by prohibiting all religions. Justice Stevens' approach renders the Takings Clause little more than a particularized restatement of the Equal Protection Clause.

[15] After accusing us of "launching a missile to kill a mouse," Justice Blackmun expends a good deal of throw-weight of his own upon a noncombatant, arguing that our description of the "understanding" of land ownership that informs the Takings Clause is not supported by early American experience. That is largely true, but entirely irrelevant. The practices of the States prior to incorporation of the Takings and Just Compensation Clauses, see Chicago, B. & Q. R. Co. v. Chicago, 166 U.S. 226 (1897) —which, as Justice Blackmun acknowledges, occasionally included outright physical appropriation of land without compensation —were out of accord with any

Where "permanent physical occupation" of land is concerned, we have refused to allow the government to decree it anew (without compensation), no matter how weighty the asserted "public interests" involved, *Loretto v. Teleprompter Manhattan CATV Corp.*, 458 U.S., at 426 —though we assuredly *would* permit the government to assert a permanent easement that was a pre-existing limitation upon the landowner's title. Compare *Scranton v. Wheeler*, 179 U.S. 141, 163 (1900) (interests of "riparian owner in the submerged lands . . . bordering on a public navigable water" held subject to Government's navigational servitude), with *Kaiser Aetna v. United States*, 444 U.S., at 178–180 (imposition of navigational servitude on marina created and rendered navigable at private expense held to constitute a taking). We believe similar treatment must be accorded confiscatory regulations, *i.e.*, regulations that prohibit all economically beneficial use of land: Any limitation so severe cannot be newly legislated or decreed (without compensation), but must inhere in the title itself, in the restrictions that background principles of the State's law of property and nuisance already place upon land ownership. A law or decree with such an effect must, in other words, do no more than duplicate the result that could have been achieved in the courts —by adjacent landowners (or other uniquely affected persons) under the State's law of private nuisance, or by the State under its complementary power to abate nuisances that affect the public generally, or otherwise. [16]

On this analysis, the owner of a lake bed, for example, would not be entitled to compensation when he is denied the requisite permit to engage in a landfilling operation that would have the effect of flooding others' land. Nor the corporate owner of a nuclear generating plant, when it is directed to remove all improvements from its land upon discovery that the plant sits astride an earthquake fault. Such regulatory action may well have the effect of eliminating the land's only economically productive use, but it does not proscribe a productive use that was previously permissible under relevant property and nuisance principles. The use of these properties for what are now expressly prohibited purposes was *always* unlawful, and (subject to other constitutional limitations) it was open to the State at any point to make the implication of those background principles of nuisance and property law explicit. See Michelman, *Property, Utility, and Fairness, Comments on the Ethical Foundations of "Just Compensation" Law*, 80 Harv. L. Rev. 1165, 1239-1241 (1967). In light of our traditional resort to "existing rules or understandings that stem from an independent source such as state law" to define the

plausible interpretation of those provisions. Justice Blackmun is correct that early constitutional theorists did not believe the Takings Clause embraced regulations of property at all, but even he does not suggest (explicitly, at least) that we renounce the Court's contrary conclusion in Mahon. Since the text of the Clause can be read to encompass regulatory as well as physical deprivations (in contrast to the text originally proposed by Madison, see Speech Proposing Bill of Rights (June 8, 1789), in 12 J. Madison, The Papers of James Madison 201 (C. Hobson, R. Rutland, W. Rachal, & J. Sisson ed. 1979) ("No person shall be . . . obliged to relinquish his property, where it may be necessary for public use, without a just compensation"), we decline to do so as well.

[16] The principal "otherwise" that we have in mind is litigation absolving the State (or private parties) of liability for the destruction of "real and personal property, in cases of actual necessity, to prevent the spreading of a fire" or to forestall other grave threats to the lives and property of others. Bowditch v. Boston, 101 U.S. 16, 18–19 (1880); see United States v. Pacific Railroad, 120 U.S. 227, 238–239 (1887).

range of interests that qualify for protection as "property" under the Fifth (and Fourteenth) amendments, *Board of Regents of State Colleges v. Roth*, 408 U.S. 564, 577 (1972), this recognition that the Takings Clause does not require compensation when an owner is barred from putting land to a use that is proscribed by those "existing rules or understandings" is surely unexceptional. When, however, a regulation that declares "off-limits" all economically produc- tive or beneficial uses of land goes beyond what the relevant background principles would dictate, compensation must be paid to sustain it.

The "total taking" inquiry we require today will ordinarily entail (as the application of state nuisance law ordinarily entails) analysis of, among other things, the degree of harm to public lands and resources, or adjacent private property, posed by the claimant's proposed activities, see, *e.g.*, Restatement (Second) of Torts §§ 826, 827, the social value of the claimant's activities and their suitability to the locality in question, see, *e.g., id.*, §§ 828(a) and (b), 831, and the relative ease with which the alleged harm can be avoided through measures taken by the claimant and the government (or adjacent private landowners) alike, see, *e.g., id.*, §§ 827(e), 828(c), 830. The fact that a particular use has long been engaged in by similarly situated owners ordinar- ily imports a lack of any common-law prohibition (though changed circum- stances or new knowledge may make what was previously permissible no longer so, see Restatement (Second) of Torts, *supra*, § 827, comment *g*. So also does the fact that other landowners, similarly situated, are permitted to continue the use denied to the claimant.

It seems unlikely that common-law principles would have prevented the erection of any habitable or productive improvements on petitioner's land; they rarely support prohibition of the "essential use" of land, *Curtin v. Benson*, 222 U.S. 78, 86 (1911). The question, however, is one of state law to be dealt with on remand. We emphasize that to win its case South Carolina must do more than proffer the legislature's declaration that the uses Lucas desires are inconsistent with the public interest, or the conclusory assertion that they violate a common-law maxim such as *sic utere tuo ut alienum non laedas*. As we have said, a "State, by *ipse dixit*, may not transform private property into public property without compensation . . . ." *Webb's Fabulous Pharmacies, Inc. v. Beckwith*, 449 U.S. 155, 164 (1980). Instead, as it would be required to do if it sought to restrain Lucas in a common-law action for public nuisance, South Carolina must identify background principles of nuisance and property law that prohibit the uses he now intends in the circumstances in which the property is presently found. Only on this showing can the State fairly claim that, in proscribing all such beneficial uses, the Beachfront Management Act is taking nothing[18] . . . .

The judgment is reversed and the cause remanded for proceedings not incon- sistent with this opinion. *So ordered.*

---

[18] Justice Blackmun decries our reliance on background nuisance principles at least in part because he believes those principles to be as manipulable as we find the "harm prevention"/"benefit conferral" dichotomy. There is no doubt some leeway in a court's interpretation of what existing state law permits —but not remotely as much, we think, as in a legislative crafting of the reasons for its confiscatory regulation. We stress that an affirmative decree eliminating all economically beneficial uses may be defended only if an objectively reasonable application of relevant precedents would exclude those beneficial uses in the circumstances in which the land is presently found.

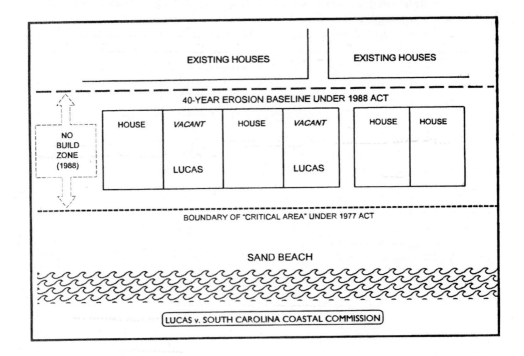

EXISTING HOUSES　　　　　EXISTING HOUSES

40-YEAR EROSION BASELINE UNDER 1988 ACT

NO BUILD ZONE (1988)

HOUSE | VACANT | HOUSE | VACANT | HOUSE | HOUSE

LUCAS　　　　　LUCAS

BOUNDARY OF "CRITICAL AREA" UNDER 1977 ACT

SAND BEACH

LUCAS v. SOUTH CAROLINA COASTAL COMMISSION

NOTES AND QUESTIONS

1. *The several Lucas opinions.* Chief Justice Rehnquist and Justices O'Connor, Thomas, and White joined in Justice Scalia's opinion. Justice Kennedy concurred in the Court's disposition of the case but not in its opinion, and filed a separate opinion in which he adopted a much broader concept of the police power than did the Court. Justice Souter filed a "statement" rejecting both the decision and the reasoning of the Court because he believed the record was so uncertain "that there is little utility in attempting to deal with this case on the merits."

Justices Blackmun and Stevens dissented and filed separate opinions in which they rejected the Court's new "categorical rule" that a regulation depriving land of all "beneficial" or "viable" use effects a compensable "taking" under the Fifth Amendment as made applicable to the States by the Fourteenth Amendment's Due Process clause. The majority opinion discusses some of the arguments in Justice Blackmun's dissent.

Justice Blackmun also criticized the Court for launching "a missile to kill a mouse," noting that Justice Scalia had conceded that the situation assumed to exist in *Lucas* "never has arisen in any of our prior cases" and would arise, in the future, "relatively rarely" or only in "extraordinary circumstances" —a concession apparently based on the belief that land use regulations rarely prohibit *all* economic uses of land.

Justice Stevens, in his dissent, made the following argument not found in Justice Blackmun's dissent:

. . . [D]evelopers and investors may market specialized estates to take advantage of the Court's new rule. The smaller the estate, the more likely that a regulatory change will effect a total taking. Thus, an investor may, for example, purchase the right to build a multi-family home on a specific lot, with the result that a zoning regulation that allows only single-family homes would render the investor's interest "valueless." Either courts will alter the "denominator" in the taking "fraction," rendering the Court's categorical rule meaningless, or investors will manipulate the relevant property interests, giving the Court's rule sweeping effect. To my mind, neither of these results is desirable or appropriate, and both are distortions of our takings jurisprudence.

2. *Disposition of Lucas on remand to the South Carolina Supreme Court.* On remand the South Carolina Supreme Court reversed its original judgment for the Coastal Commission, holding, 424 S.E.2d 484 (1993): (1) that the Council "did not possess the ability under the common law to prohibit the landowner from constructing a habitable structure on his land," and (2) that the landowner "suffered a temporary taking deserving of compensation commencing with the enactment of the act in 1988 and continuing through" the entry of the "instant order" remanding the case to the trial court for "determination of the actual damages Lucas has sustained as a result of his being temporarily deprived of the use of his property." The South Carolina Supreme Court expressly refused to "dictate any specific method of calculating the damages for the temporary nonacquisitory taking." The state later settled with Lucas, acquired the property, and resold it for development.

3. *What constitutes deprivation of "all economic use"?* What does it mean to deprive the owner of all "economically viable" or "economically beneficial or productive" use of the land? Note that the *Lucas* Court rejected the argument that Mr. Lucas' lot, even subject to the prohibition against building a permanent structure, still had some economic value for recreational uses such as camping, swimming, and picnicking. See Justice Blackmun's dissent in *Lucas*, citing state court decisions recognizing economic value in such cases.

As one court pointed out, the "central confusion" in these terms "centers on the relationship between the 'use' of property and its 'value.'" It did not resolve the confusion, but noted that "the economic value of property provides strong evidence of the availability of 'economically beneficial or productive uses.'" *Tahoe-Sierra Preservation Council v. Tahoe Regional Planning Agency,* 216 F.3d 764, 780 (9th Cir. 2000). Is this correct?

Justice Blackmun said that the compensation requirement established in *Lucas* will apply "relatively rarely" or only in "extraordinary circumstances." This statement is almost certainly correct if we consider only ordinary land use regulations adopted by local governments, such as zoning and subdivision regulation. The ordinance will always allow some use and the issue is whether a more intensive use is required. For this reason, cases since *Lucas* have uniformly refused to find a *per se* taking when the regulation allowed some use of the property. See, e.g., *Texas Manufactured Hous. Ass'n v. Nederland,* 101 F.3d 1095 (5th Cir. 1996); *Cannone v. Noey,* 867 P.2d 797 (Alaska 1994) (subdivision denial); *Convent of the Holy Name v. City of Alhambra,* 26 Cal. Rptr.2d 140 (Cal. App. 1993).

4. *Restrictions that "inhere in the title itself" as exceptions to the categorical rule.* Perhaps the most puzzling part of Justice Scalia's *Lucas* opinion is his exception for restrictions that "inhere in the title itself." What are we to make of this? Scalia included two kinds of "background principles" —the State's "law of property" and its "law of nuisance." The first clearly includes the second, but it is much broader in scope; it would include, e.g., the common law of trespass, support, and riparian rights, as well as nuisance. Justice Scalia's further discussion of the "nuisance exception" strongly suggests that he intended to limit the "nuisance exception" to cases where courts could find a common law "private nuisance." Under this doctrine, courts can enjoin only a single use, or a narrow group of related uses, found to interfere unreasonably with the use of adjacent or nearby land, or with the rights of the public generally. Does Justice Scalia's reference, in his discussion of the "nuisance exception," to restrictions that "inhere in the title" apparently "freeze" the scope of the "nuisance exception" to that defined by the state's law of nuisance at the time when a landowner acquires title to his property?

Invocation of "nuisance" doctrines also creates an anomaly. Although Justice Scalia rejects the "balancing" approach adopted where land use regulations deprive the owner of some, but not all, "economically productive uses" of his land, by creating the "nuisance exception" he indirectly reintroduces "balancing" as a basis for decision in cases like *Lucas.* This is because common-law adjudication of "nuisance" cases has always involved, as a primary element, the "balancing" of the "gravity of the harm" suffered by the plaintiff against the "utility of the conduct" of the defendant. See Rest. Torts 2d §§ 826, 827, 828. As the Note that follows indicates, the courts have taken Justice Scalia's exception further than he may intended.

5. *Sources.* For discussion of *Lucas* see Epstein, *Lucas v. South Carolina Coastal Council: A Tangled Web of Expectations,* 45 Stan. L. Rev. 1369 (1993); Lazarus, *Putting the Correct "Spin" on Lucas,* 45 Stan. L. Rev. 1411 (1993); Mandelker, *Of Mice and Missiles: A True Account of Lucas v. South Carolina Coastal Council,* 8 J. Land Use & Envtl. L. 285 (1993); Sax, *Property Rights and the Economy of Nature: Understanding Lucas v. South Carolina Coastal Council,* 45 Stan. L. Rev. 1433 (1993); Washburn, *Land Use Control, the Individual, and Society: Lucas v. South Carolina Coastal Council,* 52 Md. L. Rev. 162 (1993).

A NOTE ON HOW THE COURTS HAVE DRAWN THE TEETH OF THE *LUCAS* DECISION

What Lucas seemed to mean.—The *Lucas* per se rule cast a shadow over land use regulation. It especially threatened environmental land use regulations where total prohibitions on development are necessary. An example is a regulation that prohibits all development in a flood plain. For the most part, however, lower courts have emphasized the exceptions to *Lucas* and have found no takings in cases where *Lucas* might have suggested otherwise. Are these courts misreading Justice Scalia's basic point? Or do the separate opinions in *Lucas* suggest that a majority would confine *Lucas* narrowly. In one important state case narrowing *Lucas, Stevens v. City of Cannon Beach, infra*, Justice Scalia (with Justice O'Connor) felt strongly enough about the denial of certiorari to dissent with full opinion. 510 U.S. 1207, 1209 (1994).

 Parcel as a whole: Segmentation or the denominator rule. —Recall that this rule originated with *Penn Central,* which considered vertical segmentation. *Lucas*, in footnote 7, addresses the more typical instance of horizontal segmentation.

This problem is especially critical in wetland cases, where all development may be prohibited to preserve a wetlands. Since the *Lucas* decision, it has become essential to determine the "whole parcel" or denominator to which the *Lucas* per se taking rule applies. In many of these cases, the parcel includes areas that are not wetlands, on which there is no restriction on development. The owner of the wetland may claim a "conceptual severance," arguing that the wetlands portion should be severed from the rest for takings analysis, and that a per se taking has occurred because no development of the wetlands is permitted.

The same problem can arise under a zoning ordinance when the property is in more than one zone. When the property is under single ownership, the courts tend to treat the entire property as the whole parcel, even though different parts of the property are zoned differently. *Quirk v. Town of New Boston,* 663 A.2d 1328 (N.H. 1995) (part of property zoned as buffer); *Zealy v. City of Waukesha,* 548 N.W.2d 528 (Wis. 1996) (two zones on property). *Contra Twain Harte Assocs. v. County of Tuolumne*, 265 Cal. Rptr. 737 (Cal. App. 1990) (two zones on property).

A flexible approach adopted by the Court of Federal Claims also has influenced the cases. Although the factors given consideration vary, the underlying principle is one of fairness. *Ciampitti v. United States,* 22 Cl. Ct. 310 (1991) (single parcel when lots treated as such for purpose of purchase and financing). The court held it would consider factors such as the degree of contiguity, dates of acquisition, the extent to which the parcel was treated as a single parcel, and the extent to which the regulated lands enhance the value of the remaining lands. The court added that "no doubt many others would enter into the calculus." See also *Tabb Lakes, Ltd. v. United States,* 10 F.3d 796 (Fed. Cir. 1993). For a three-part segmentation problem, see *Palm Beach Isles Assocs. v. United States,* 208 F.3d 1374 (Fed. Cir. 2000) (lake- and ocean-front parcels purchased together but divided by highway are separate despite profitable sale of ocean parcel; lake-front parcel, partially wetlands and partially submerged land, treated as one).

Considering a parcel as a whole avoids the *Lucas* per se takings rule whenever, as is usually the case, the court finds an economically viable use is available on the portion outside the wetlands area. Most of the cases have taken this position. What are the issues here? Consider the suggestion in footnote 7 of *Lucas,* that an "owner's reasonable expectations" as shaped by state property law should be determinative. Is it circular if expectations determine the property interest and also help decide the takings claim? For discussion see Lisker, *Regulatory Takings and the Denominator Problem,* 27 Rutgers L.J. 663 (1996); Mandelker, *New Property Rights Under the Taking Clause,* 81 Marq. L. Review 9 (1997); Note, *Conceptual Severance and Takings in the Federal Circuit,* 85 Cornell L. Rev. 586 (2000).

Background principles that inhere in the title.—When *Lucas* was decided it was generally thought that this exception to the per se takings rule was limited to common law principles, primarily nuisance. Several cases have since held the exception includes other common law principles as well as statutes and local regulations in effect when a landowner purchased the property. A key case is *Kim v. City of New York,* 681 N.E.2d 312 (N.Y.), *cert. denied,* 522 U.S. 809 (1997). The city regraded a public road and placed side fill on the portion of plaintiffs' property abutting the roadway to maintain lateral support between the road and plaintiffs' property. Not surprisingly, since the city had physically occupied their land, plaintiffs sued for a taking. The New York City Charter, codifying common law, required adjacent landowners to provide lateral support.

The court applied the *Lucas* requirement of a "logically antecedent inquiry" to the owner's title to a *Loretto*-type per se claim, and held that a taking had not occurred. To the suggestion that this inquiry should be limited to the common law, it replied:

> Given the theoretical basis of the logically antecedent inquiry— namely, "the State's power over . . . the 'bundle of rights' that [property owners] acquire when they obtain title" [citing *Lucas*]—we can discern no sound reason to isolate the inquiry to some arbitrary earlier time in the evolution of the common law. It would be an illogical and incomplete inquiry if the courts were to look exclusively to common-law principles to identify the preexisting rules of State property law, while ignoring statutory law in force when the owner acquired title. To accept this proposition would elevate common law over statutory law, and would represent a departure from the established understanding that statutory law may trump an inconsistent principle of the common law. [*Id.* at 315.]

Note that *Kim* involves a regulation (the city's Charter) that codifies an older common law rule. The New York court has also applied *Kim* to a modern statute prohibiting development in wetlands, holding a denial of development under the statute was not a taking. *Gazza v. New York State Dep't of Envtl. Conservation,* 679 N.E.2d 1035 (N.Y.), *cert. denied,* 522 U.S. 813 (1997). See also *Hunziker v. State,* 519 N.W.2d 367 (Iowa 1994) (statute requiring buffer around Indian burial ground is a background principle). Other courts have applied the rule that background principles include the common law of a state. *Stevens v. City of Cannon Beach,* 854 P.2d 449, 456 (Or. 1993) (developer had no right to build seawall; "doctrine of custom" use of dry sand was a background principle of property), *cert. denied,* 510 U.S. 1207, 1209 (1994) (Scalia, J., with O'Connor, J., dissenting from denial of certiorari).

Are decisions such as these consistent with *Lucas*? Justice Scalia emphasized common law nuisance, and in that context he warned against allowing the legislature to "declare" a background principle, but he did not explicitly address the broader issues. In his dissent from the denial of certiorari in *Cannon Beach*, he warned against letting judges declare new principles of law, but he seems to have accepted non-nuisance principles, properly found, to fall within his approach. For discussion see Eagle, *The 1997 Regulatory Takings Quartet: Retreating from the "Rule of Law,"* 42 N.Y.L. Sch. L. Rev. 345, 367-70

(1998); Note, *The Lucas Exception: Inclusion, Exclusion, and a Statute of Limitation*, 68 Geo. Wash. L. Rev. 134 (1999).

In any event, does the takings inquiry end if a restrictive land use regulation is a background principle? See *Palm Beach Isles Assocs.*, *supra* ("background" navigation servitude may not apply if government bases denial of permit on environmental concerns instead). The Supreme Court may address this and related takings questions in a case that was before it as this book went to press, Palazzolo v. State, 745 A.2d 707 (R.I. 2000).

Investment-backed expectations.—Recall that in applying this takings factor the Supreme Court adopted a notice rule exception that operates much the same way as the background principles exception in *Lucas*. Landowners who purchased property subject to a land use regulation can have no investment-backed expectations at odds with the restriction because they should have been on notice that they could not develop their land the way they want. Courts have even applied this rule when regulations were adopted after purchase. Justice Scalia's footnote 2 in *Nollan* seemed to sound the end of the notice rule, but that has not happened. Among a substantial number of other cases, *Kim, supra,* expressly rejected Scalia's footnote, holding that "the *Nollan* footnote is readily harmonized with the 'logically antecedent inquiry' subsequently elucidated in *Lucas*." *Id.* at 316 n.3.

Cases in the Court of Federal Claims and its appellate Federal Circuit, which hear takings cases arising out of the wetlands permit program of the Clean Water Act, illustrate how the rule has been applied. In *Good v. United States,* 189 F.3d 1355 (Fed. Cir. 1999), *cert. denied,* 120 S. Ct. 1554 (2000), the statute under which the permit was denied was enacted after the property was purchased. The court held that the landowner should have been aware that increasing concern for environmental protection (a "regulatory climate") affected his property when he bought it, and that regulations could ultimately prevent him from building. Under this approach, time of purchase remains the relevant point of inquiry, but the owner is held to have *present* notice of *prospective* regulations. The court also held that the investment-backed expectations takings factor was relevant even in per se, total destruction of value claims under *Lucas,* and that the failure to show expectations defeated the takings claim. A Federal Court of Claims judge reached a contrary conclusion soon after in *Florida Rock Indus. v. United States,* 45 Fed. Cl. 21 (1999), holding that a federal law enacted after purchase did not destroy investment-backed expectations. A few courts have rejected the notice rule altogether. E.g., *Carpenter v. Tahoe Regional Planning Agency,* 804 F. Supp. 1316 (D. Nev. 1992) ("the court does not accept the analogy to regulated markets").

Mandelker, *Investment-Backed Expectations in Taking Law,* 27 Urb. Law. 215, 236 (1995), suggests a middle-ground approach based on a regulatory risk theory: "If a landowner knows at the time she enters a land market that she is or might be covered by a regulatory program in which government can deny permission to develop her land, it is only fair she should assume the regulatory risk this program creates. . . . The market sends such a signal when there is wide divergence in opinion on whether a landowner will realize her expectations for development." See also Washburn, *"Reasonable Investment-Backed Expectations" as a Factor in Defining Property Interest,* 49 Wash. U.

J. Urb. & Contemp. L. 63 (1996). On the wetlands cases see Meltz, *Wetlands Regulation and the Law of Regulatory Takings,* 30 Envtl. L. Rep. 10468 (2000).

Nuisance.—The nuisance exception to the *Lucas* per se takings rule has had limited application. Justice Scalia's example of damage caused by flooding suggests that this exception might be limited to cases of actual physical invasion. See *Rith Energy, Inc. v. United States,* 44 Fed. Cl. 108 (1999) (relying on state law to hold that mining plan that had high probability of acid mine drainage into water aquifer was a nuisance). In most cases in which a state court would hold that a land use is a nuisance, a zoning ordinance prohibiting that use would allow other viable uses and most likely would escape the per se takings rule.

For additional discussion of the exceptions to *Lucas* see Glicksman, *Making a Nuisance of Takings Law,* 3 Wash. U. J.L. & Pol'y 149 (2000); Sugamelli, *Lucas v. South Carolina Coastal Council: The Categorical and Other "Exceptions" to Liability for Fifth Amendment Takings of Private Property Far Outweigh the "Rule",* 29 Envtl. L. 939 (1999).

4. THE FEDERAL TAKINGS EXECUTIVE ORDER AND FEDERAL AND STATE TAKINGS LEGISLATION

An active property rights movement that seeks greater protection for landowners under the takings clause has so far produced a Presidential Executive Order and a growing number of state takings laws.

Takings Executive Order.—President Reagan issued an Executive Order in 1988 that adopted principles and criteria for federal regulatory programs that cause taking problems, such as the wetlands permit program of the Clean Water Act. Executive Order 12630, 53 Fed. Reg. 8859 (Mar. 15, 1988). The Order says that it is codifying the Supreme Court's 1987 Trilogy of takings cases. For example, the Order states that a taking occurs if a regulation "substantially affects" the value of property, but this statement conflicts with the Supreme Court's holding that a regulation is not a taking unless it denies a landowner all economically viable use of his land. The Order also contains a requirement that a government agency should adopt the least restrictive alternative in their regulatory programs. Is there any support for this requirement in the Supreme Court cases?

The Order requires federal agencies to prepare a Takings Implications Assessment (TIA) that evaluates the takings impacts of their actions. In the summer of 1988 the Attorney General issued Guidelines that further explain and implement the Executive Order. Attorney General's Guidelines for the Evaluation of Risk and Avoidance of Unanticipated Takings (1988). For discussion of the Order see McElfish, *The Takings Executive Order: Constitutional Jurisprudence or Political Philosophy?,* 18 Envtl. L. Rep. 10474 (1988); Pollot, *The Effect of the Federal Takings Executive Order,* 41 Land Use L. & Zoning Dig., No. 5, at 3 (1989). Reports indicate the Order has had limited effect.

State takings legislation.—Over half the states now have takings law. Most are modeled on the federal Executive Order. They require state agencies to do extensive takings reviews of proposed laws and regulations, or require the

state attorney general to establish a process to evaluate the takings implications of proposed regulations. E.g., Ariz. Rev. Stat. Ann. §§ 41-1311 to -1313;
Idaho Code §§ 67-8001 to 67-8004; Ind. Code Ann. § 4-22-2-32; Utah Code
Ann. §§ 63-90-1 to 63-90-4; W. Va. Code §§ 22-1A-1 to 22-1A-6. In some states
these laws include local governments. These laws do not have a substantive
effect.

Only two states have laws that go beyond takings impact analysis and
require compensation for takings. The following excerpt explains how these
laws work:

> *Extreme Substantive Models* go beyond federal and state takings
> case law and provide that any regulatory program that reduces the
> fair market value (FMV) of property to less than fifty percent for the
> uses permitted at the time the owner acquired title to the property
> shall be deemed to have been taken for the use of the public. The
> Models are "extreme" since they consider only the impact on the
> property owner, without regard to other factors (such as the nature
> of the public interest sought to be advanced by governmental restric-
> tion of property) or the potential harm to the public if the property
> owner does what he or she intends to do. . . .
>
> Under an Extreme Substantive Model, the initial —and only —ques-
> tion would be whether the relevant property was diminished in value
> no more than fifty percent. Of course, quite a lot would turn on the
> threshold definition of the relevant property right. Is the relevant
> property right the right to exclude? the right to use? the right to
> develop under existing zoning? [Martinez, *Statutes Enacting Takings
> Law: Flying in the Face of Uncertainty,* 26 Urb. Law. 327, 337 (1994).]

The Texas law requires compensation when governmental action reduces
the value of real property by twenty-five percent or more. Tex. Gov't Code Ann.
§ 2007.002(5)(B). Florida legislation requires compensation when a regulation
places an "inordinate burden" on property. An inordinate burden exists if a
property owner is unable to attain the reasonable investment-backed expectations to an existing or vested use of the property or, in the alternative, if the
owner must permanently bear "a disproportionate share of a burden imposed
for the good of the public, which in fairness should be borne by the public at
large." Fla. Stat. Ann. § 70.001. How would you apply this law to a denial
of a permit for development in a wetlands? The Florida statute requires a
mandatory negotiation process for six months before a takings claim can be
brought into court. In addition, Oregon voters adopted an initiative in the Fall
2000 election that requires compensation when a land use regulation reduces
the "fair market value" of property. The initiative had been challenged in court
as this book went to press.

Critics complain that the compensation laws base a taking solely on
economic loss and do not permit consideration of governmental interests. In
this sense, they resemble the *Lucas* per se takings rule, although the Texas
law goes further. How would you revise these laws to remedy this problem?

For discussion of these laws see Coursen, *Property Rights Legislation: A
Survey of Federal and State Assessment and Compensation Measures,* 26

Envtl. L. Rep. 10,239 (1996); Oswald, *Property Rights Legislation and the Police Power,* 37 Am. Bus. L.J. 527 (2000). For discussion of the property rights movement see H. M. Jacobs, State Property Rights Laws: The Impacts of Those Laws on My Land (1999).

Federal takings legislation.—Federal takings legislation based on the Executive Order was considered but rejected by Congress, but the issue is still alive. See, e.g., The Omnibus Property Rights Act of 1995, S. 605, S. Rep. No. 104–239 (1996). For the history of this legislation see Sax, *Takings Legislation: Where It Stands and What Is Next,* 23 Ecology L.Q. 509 (1996).

A NOTE ON THE TAKINGS CLAUSE LITERATURE

The literature on the takings clause is voluminous. Useful books include S. Eagle, Regulatory Takings (1996); D. Kendall, T. Dowling & A. Schwartz, Takings Litigation Handbook (2000); R. Meltz, D. Merriam & R. Frank, The Takings Issue (1999). Frieden, *Towards a Political Economy of Takings* 3 Wash. U. J.L. & Pol'y 137 (2000), tries to answer the "puzzle" that gives protection under the takings clause to real property but not to other classes of financial assets. References to the periodical literature can be found in the articles cited in this section and in D. Mandelker, Land Use Law 72–75 (1997 & annual supplements).

C. DUE PROCESS AND EQUAL PROTECTION LIMITATIONS UNDER THE FEDERAL CONSTITUTION

Although the takings clause is an important limitation on land use regulation, the due process and equal protection clauses also have significant roles to play. This Note reviews some basic principles in the application of substantive due process and equal protection claims to land use regulation. Chapter 5 considers procedural due process issues.

Substantive due process.—The substantive due process clause requires land use and other government regulations to serve a legitimate governmental purpose. As noted earlier, there is a clear overlap here with a similar requirement the Supreme Court has included as part of its takings clause analysis. As all students of constitutional law also know, substantive due process has been in disrepute since the so-called Lochner Era, named after a Supreme Court decision decided early in the last century. At that time the Supreme Court used substantive due process to strike down socially progressive legislation. See *Lochner v. New York,* 198 U.S. 49 (1905).

Despite the shadow of *Lochner,* substantive due process issues still arise in land use regulation, notably in cases considering exclusionary and aesthetic zoning and other regulations that raise legitimacy of purpose problems. The *Belle Terre* case, reproduced *infra* in Chapter 3, is an example of a substantive due process case in which the Supreme Court considered the facial constitutionality of a zoning ordinance limiting the number of unrelated persons who could live together as a family.

The federal courts are still lukewarm about applying substantive due process. Some hold the substantive due process clause cannot apply when a statute or ordinance can also be attacked under the takings clause. See *Macri v. King County,* 126 F.3d 1125 (9th Cir. 1997). These cases rely on Supreme Court cases holding that a substantive due process claim could not be made when other, more specific, constitutional provisions apply, such as the Fourth Amendment. When the courts do apply substantive due process, their standard of review is deferential. See *County of Sacramento v. Lewis,* 523 U.S. 833 (1998), applying an arbitrary and irrational test to the review of legislative action, and a "shocks the conscience" test to the review of executive action. But see *Welch v. Paicos,* 66 F. Supp. 2d 138 (D. Mass. 1999) ("In the rough-and-tumble politics of land-use planning, very little can shock the constitutional conscience.").

Belle Terre was a facial attack on a zoning ordinance. More difficulties arise when an as-applied substantive due process attack is brought. The major obstacle is the rule, adopted in almost all circuits, that a plaintiff cannot sue in substantive due process unless he has an entitlement to a land use approval. See Mandelker, *Entitlement to Substantive Due Process: Old versus New Property in Land Use Regulation,* 3 Wash. U. J.L. & Pol'y 61 (2000). The constitutional origins of this rule are complex, and need not be spelled out here, but it means a substantive due process claim will not lie when a municipality has the discretion to deny a land use approval, such as a variance. An entitlement exists only if the municipality has a mandatory duty to issue the approval, such as a building permit. The effect of this rule is that a municipality may prevent the creation of an entitlement simply by making its review process discretionary. The entitlement rule thus has the effect of keeping most as-applied substantive due process cases out of court. See also Blaesser, *Substantive Due Process Protection at the Outer Margins of Municipal Behavior,* 3 Wash. U. J.L. & Pol'y 583 (2000).

Suits on what amounts to substantive due process under state constitutions may be handled differently. State courts often apply an "arbitrary and capricious" standard in the review of land use regulations which has the same effect as a substantive due process review. In many state zoning cases, however, it is often difficult to determine whether courts are reviewing under takings clause or substantive due process limitations.

Equal protection.—Equal protection requires fairness in the application of government regulation. It, too, has a facial and as-applied dimension, but the limitations that many courts place on substantive due process do not apply to equal protection cases. The due process clause applies to "property," which is why the courts can insist on entitlements or conclude that the takings clause is the appropriate remedy. The equal protection clause, by contrast, applies to persons.

Federal courts apply (with some fuzziness at the margins) a three-tiered standard of judicial review in equal protection cases. Strict scrutiny equal protection review applies to suspect classifications and when a fundamental constitutional interest is involved. Racial discrimination is an example of a suspect classification in land use regulation. Free speech is a fundamental interest that can be affected by some land use regulation, such as sign regulation. In either case, the regulation must be justified by a compelling governmental interest, which courts seldom find.

Next, there is a level of intermediate scrutiny the Supreme Court applies to discrimination based on certain characteristics, such as gender. This standard of review lies between strict scrutiny and rational relationship review. The Supreme Court considered whether this level of review applies to land use regulation in the *Cleburne* case, reproduced *infra* in Chapter 3, where a municipality denied a special exception for a group home for the mentally disabled.

Finally, the bulk of land use regulation falls under rational relationship review because it affects only economic interests in land. This standard of review is quite relaxed. It requires government only to show some "rational basis" for its regulation, aided by applying a presumption of constitutionality.

Selective enforcement in equal protection cases.—There is a group of equal protection cases that apply different rules when a government selectively enforces a government regulation, such as a land use regulation. The Supreme Court considered this problem in *Village of Wildwood v. Olech,* 120 S. Ct. 1073 (2000) (per curiam). The village refused to supply water to the plaintiffs unless they granted the village an additional easement that it had not required of other property owners. It was alleged that the village did so to retaliate for the plaintiffs having brought (and won) an earlier, unrelated suit against the village.

The district court dismissed the complaint, the court of appeals reversed, and the Supreme Court affirmed. The Court's decision is a puzzle. The question certified to the Court was whether an individual who does not have a suspect classification or fundamental interest claim can nevertheless, as a "class of one," establish an equal protection violation when vindictiveness motivated different treatment. The Court held:

> Our cases have recognized successful equal protection claims brought by a "class of one," where the plaintiff alleges that she has been intentionally treated differently from others similarly situated and that there is no rational basis for the difference in treatment. In so doing, we have explained that "'the purpose of the equal protection clause of the Fourteenth Amendment is to secure every person within the State's jurisdiction against intentional and arbitrary discrimination, whether occasioned by express terms of a statute or by its improper execution through duly constituted agents.'" [*Id.* at 1074 citations omitted.]

The decision is puzzling because in holding that intent and arbitrariness are sufficient, the Court went farther than the petitioner requested. This concerned Justice Breyer, concurring only in the result, who felt that without a subjective element, the floodgates might be opened to constitutionalizing "many ordinary violations of city or state law," merely on a showing that administrative discretion was "honestly (even if ineptly – even if arbitrarily) exercised." The other justices "did not reach" the subjective ill will theory. Might they eventually have to conclude, at least in "ordinary" zoning cases, that erroneous decisions are not arbitrary without vindictiveness or its equivalent?

The contours of *Olech* remain uncertain at this point, but the case raises some interesting questions of constitutional choice in as-applied land use cases.

Assume a landowner has a parcel of land zoned for single family use. She applies for a rezoning to multi-family use. She claims the city approved a similar rezoning on a parcel a block away the previous week. What constitutional clause applies? See Cobb, *Land Use Law: Marred by Public Agency Abuse*, 3 Wash. U. J.L. & Pol'y 195 (2000); Wilson, *Nasty Motives: A Consideration of Recent Federal Damages Claims in Land-Use Cases*, 31 Urb. Law. 937 (1999).

D. FEDERAL REMEDIES FOR CONSTITUTIONAL VIOLATIONS

Bringing a land use action in federal court presents a set of problems very different from bringing a land use action in state court. Because federal court jurisdiction is limited, plaintiffs must overcome barriers created by the ripeness and abstention doctrines to limit that jurisdiction. If these barriers are overcome, plaintiffs must then find a remedy they can use to make their claim. Plaintiffs who wish to bring constitutional claims against municipalities in land use cases must sue under § 1983 of the Civil Rights Act of 1881, and satisfy the complex rules courts have adopted that govern these actions. Inverse condemnation actions claiming a taking are brought directly under the federal constitution, but plaintiffs must also sue under § 1983 if they want an award of attorneys' fees. This section reviews the federal remedies available in land use cases.

1. BARRIERS TO JUDICIAL RELIEF: RIPENESS

Ripeness is a judicial doctrine that determines when a case is ready for adjudication. Ripeness is jurisdictional. A federal court does not have jurisdiction of a case that is not ripe. The Supreme Court adopted ripeness rules for land use cases during a time when landowners were pressing the court to decide whether the federal constitution requires compensation for land use takings. In several of these cases, the Court held the takings claim was not ripe to avoid deciding this question. But, in so doing, the Court set up barriers to the adjudication of takings claims in federal courts that have substantially closed the federal courthouse doors to takings cases. Many federal courts also apply the ripeness rules to due process and equal protection claims.

There are several prongs to the land use ripeness rules: a landowner must make at least one meaningful application for approval of her development, the local land use agency must make a final decision on the application, the landowner must apply for a variance or other available administrative relief from the decision, and must sue in state court for compensation if a state compensation remedy is available.

The Supreme Court adopted the ripeness rules in the following decision:

WILLIAMSON COUNTY REGIONAL PLANNING COMMISSION v. HAMILTON BANK OF JOHNSON CITY

473 U.S. 172 (1985)

Justice Blackmun delivered the opinion of the Court.

Respondent, the owner of a tract of land it was developing as a residential subdivision, sued petitioners, the Williamson County (Tennessee) Regional Planning Commission and its members and staff, in United States District Court, alleging that petitioners' application of various zoning laws and regulations to respondent's property amounted to a "taking" of that property. At trial, the jury agreed and awarded respondent $350,000 as just compensation for the "taking." . . . Petitioners and their amici urge this Court to overturn the jury's award on the ground that a temporary regulatory interference with an investor's profit expectation does not constitute a "taking" within the meaning of the Just Compensation Clause of the Fifth Amendment, or, alternatively, on the ground that even if such interference does constitute a taking, the Just Compensation Clause does not require money damages as recompense. Before we reach those contentions, we examine the procedural posture of respondent's claim.

I

A

[Under Tennessee law, the legislative body is responsible for zoning, while the planning commission is responsible for regulations governing the subdivision of land and must approve a plat for a subdivision before it can be recorded.] [I]n 1973 [the county] adopted a zoning ordinance that allowed "cluster" development of residential areas. Under "cluster" zoning, "both the size and the width of individual residential lots in . . . [a] development may be reduced, provided . . . that the overall density of the entire tract remains constant — provided, that is, that an area equivalent to the total of the areas thus 'saved' from each individual lot is pooled and retained as common open space." 2 N. Williams, American Land Planning Law § 47.01, pp. 212–213 (1974).

Cluster zoning thus allows housing units to be grouped, or "clustered" together, rather than being evenly spaced on uniform lots.

[R]espondent's predecessor-in-interest (developer) in 1973 submitted a preliminary plat for the cluster development of its tract, the Temple Hills Country Club Estates (Temple Hills), to the Williamson County Regional Planning Commission for approval. At that time, the county's zoning ordinance and the Commission's subdivision regulations required developers to seek review and approval of subdivision plats in two steps. The developer first was to submit for approval a preliminary plat, or "initial sketch plan," indicating, among other things, the boundaries and acreage of the site, the number of dwelling units and their basic design, the location of existing and proposed roads, structures, lots, utility layouts, and open space, and the contour of the land. Once approved, the preliminary plat served as a basis for the preparation of a final plat. Under the Commission's regulations, however, approval of a preliminary plat "will not constitute acceptance of the final plat." Approval of a preliminary plat lapsed if a final plat was not submitted within one year of the date of the approval, unless the Commission granted an extension of time, or unless the approval of the preliminary plat was renewed. The final plat, which is the official authenticated document that is recorded, was required to conform substantially to the preliminary plat, and, in addition, to include such details as the lines of all streets, lots, boundaries, and building setbacks.

On May 3, 1973, the Commission approved the developer's preliminary plat for Temple Hills. The plat indicated that the development was to include 676 acres, of which 260 acres would be open space, primarily in the form of a golf course. A notation on the plat indicated that the number of "allowable dwelling units for total development" was 736, but lot lines were drawn in for only 469 units. The areas in which the remaining 276 units were to be placed were left blank and bore the notation "this parcel not to be developed until approved by the planning commission." . . .

Upon approval of the preliminary plat, the developer conveyed to the county a permanent open space easement for the golf course, and began building roads and installing utility lines for the project. The developer spent approximately $3 million building the golf course, and another $500,000 installing sewer and water facilities. Before housing construction was to begin on a particular section, a final plat of that section was submitted for approval. Several sections, containing a total of 212 units, were given final approval by 1979. The preliminary plat, as well, was reapproved four times during that period.

[In 1977, the county changed its zoning ordinance to the disadvantage of the developer, including a decrease in residential density, and in 1979 it decided that the new ordinance would apply to plats submitted for renewal in Temple Hills.] The Commission then renewed the Temple Hills plat under the ordinances and regulations in effect at that time.

In January 1980, the Commission asked the developer to submit a revised preliminary plat before it sought final approval for the remaining sections of the subdivision. . . . [It found surveying errors, some of the land had been condemned by the state] and the areas marked "reserved for future development" had never been platted. A special committee (Temple Hills Committee) was appointed to work with the developer on the revision of the preliminary plat.

The developer submitted a revised preliminary plat for approval in October 1980. Upon review, the Commission's staff and the Temple Hills Committee noted several problems with the revised plat. First, the allowable density under the zoning ordinance and subdivision regulations then in effect was 548 units, rather than the 736 units claimed under the preliminary plat approved in 1973. The difference reflected a decrease in 18.5 acres for the parkway, a decrease of 66 acres for the 10% deduction for roads, and an exclusion of 44 acres for 50% of the land lying on slopes exceeding a 25% grade. Second, two cul-de-sac roads that had become necessary because of the land taken for the parkway exceeded the maximum length allowed for such roads under the subdivision regulations in effect in both 1980 and 1973. Third, approximately 2,000 feet of road would have grades in excess of the maximum allowed by county road regulations. Fourth, the preliminary plat placed units on land that had grades in excess of 25% and thus was considered undevelopable under the zoning ordinance and subdivision regulations. Fifth, the developer had not fulfilled its obligations regarding the construction and maintenance of the main access road. Sixth, there were inadequate fire protection services for the area, as well as inadequate open space for children's recreational activities. Finally, the lots proposed in the preliminary plat had a road frontage that was below the minimum required by the subdivision regulations in effect in 1980. . . .

[The Commission disapproved the plat because it did not comply with density requirements and because required acreage deductions had not been made. The developer appealed to the County Board of Zoning Appeals for an interpretation of the cluster zoning ordinance as it applied to its subdivision. On November 11, 1980, it held the Commission should apply the zoning and subdivision regulations in effect in 1973 in evaluating the density, and required lots with excessive grades to be measured more favorably to the developer.]

On November 26, [1980] respondent, Hamilton Bank of Johnson City, acquired through foreclosure the property in the Temple Hills subdivision that had not yet been developed, a total of 257.65 acres. This included many of the parcels that had been left blank in the preliminary plat approved in 1973. In June 1981, respondent submitted two preliminary plats to the Commission — the plat that had been approved in 1973 and subsequently reapproved several times, and a plat indicating respondent's plans for the undeveloped areas, which was similar to the plat submitted by the developer in 1980. The new plat proposed the development of 688 units; the reduction from 736 units represented respondent's concession that 18.5 acres should be removed from the acreage because that land had been taken for the parkway.

On June 18, the Commission disapproved the plat for eight reasons, including the density and grade problems cited in the October 1980 denial, as well as the objections the Temple Hills Committee had raised in 1980 to the length of two cul-de-sacs, the grade of various roads, the lack of fire protection, the disrepair of the main-access road, and the minimum front-age. . . . The Commission declined to follow the decision of the Board of Zoning Appeals that the plat should be evaluated by the 1973 zoning ordinance and subdivision regulations, stating that the Board lacked jurisdiction to hear appeals from the Commission.

B

Respondent then filed this suit in the United States District Court for the Middle District of Tennessee, pursuant to 42 U.S.C. § 1983, alleging that the Commission had taken its property without just compensation and asserting that the Commission should be estopped under state law from denying approval of the project. Respondent's expert witnesses testified that the design that would meet each of the Commission's eight objections would allow respondent to build only 67 units, 409 fewer than respondent claims it is entitled to build, and that the development of only 67 sites would result in a net loss of over $1 million. Petitioners' expert witness, on the other hand, testified that the Commission's eight objections could be overcome by a design that would allow development of approximately 300 units.

After a 3-week trial, the jury found that respondent had been denied the "economically viable" use of its property in violation of the Just Compensation Clause, and that the Commission was estopped under state law from requiring respondent to comply with the current zoning ordinance and subdivision regulations rather than those in effect in 1973. The jury awarded damages of $350,000 for the temporary taking of respondent's property. The court entered a permanent injunction requiring the Commission to apply the zoning ordinance and subdivision regulations in effect in 1973 to Temple Hills, and to approve the plat submitted in 1981.

The court then granted judgment notwithstanding the verdict in favor of the Commission on the taking claim, reasoning in part that respondent was unable to derive economic benefit from its property on a temporary basis only, and that such a temporary deprivation, as a matter of law, cannot constitute a taking. In addition, the court modified its permanent injunction to require the Commission merely to apply the zoning ordinance and subdivision regulations in effect in 1973 to the project, rather than requiring approval of the plat, in order to allow the parties to resolve "legitimate technical questions of whether plaintiff meets the requirements of the 1973 regulations," through the applicable state and local appeals procedures. . . .

[The Court granted certiorari to determine whether compensation was payable for a temporary taking, but decided the case was premature.]

III

. . . Because respondent has not yet obtained a final decision regarding the application of the zoning ordinance and subdivision regulations to its property, nor utilized the procedures Tennessee provides for obtaining just compensation, respondent's [takings] claim is not ripe.

A

As the Court has made clear in several recent decisions, a claim that the application of government regulations effects a taking of a property interest is not ripe until the government entity charged with implementing the regulations has reached a final decision regarding the application of the regulations to the property at issue. In *Hodel v. Virginia Surface Mining & Reclamation Assn., Inc.*, 452 U.S. 264 (1981), for example, the Court rejected a claim that the Surface Mining Control and Reclamation Act of 1977, 30 U.S.C. § 1201 et seq., effected a taking because:

"There is no indication in the record that appellees have availed themselves of the opportunities provided by the Act to obtain administrative relief by requesting either a variance from the approxi-mate-original-contour requirement of § 515(d) or a waiver from the surface mining restrictions in § 522(e). If [the property owners] were to seek administrative relief under these procedures, a mutually ac-ceptable solution might well be reached with regard to individual prop-erties, thereby obviating any need to address the constitutional questions. The potential for such administrative solutions confirms the conclusion that the taking issue decided by the District Court simply is not ripe for judicial resolution." 452 U.S., at 297 (footnote omitted).

Similarly, in *Agins v. Tiburon,* the Court held that a challenge to the application of a zoning ordinance was not ripe because the property owners had not yet submitted a plan for development of their property. 447 U.S., at 260. . . .

Respondent argues that it "did everything possible to resolve the conflict with the commission," and that the Commission's denial of approval for respondent's plat was equivalent to a denial of variances. The record does not support respondent's claim, however. There is no evidence that respondent applied to the Board of Zoning Appeals for variances from the zoning ordi-nance. As noted, the developer sought a ruling that the ordinance in effect in 1973 should be applied, but neither respondent nor the developer sought a variance from the requirements of either the 1973 or 1980 ordinances. Further, although the subdivision regulations in effect in 1981 required that applications to the Commission for variances be in writing, and that notice of the application be given to owners of adjacent property, the record contains no evidence that respondent ever filed a written request for variances from the cul-de-sac, road-grade, or frontage requirements of the subdivision regula-tions, or that respondent ever gave the required notice.

Indeed, in a letter to the Commission written shortly before its June 18, 1981, meeting to consider the preliminary sketch, respondent took the position that it would not request variances from the Commission until after the Com-mission approved the proposed plat:

"[Respondent] stands ready to work with the Planning Commission concerning the necessary variances. Until the initial sketch is re-newed, however, and the developer has an opportunity to do detailed engineering work it is impossible to determine the exact nature of any variances that may be needed."

The Commission's regulations clearly indicated that unless a developer applied for a variance in writing and upon notice to other property owners, "any condition shown on the plat which would require a variance will constitute grounds for disapproval of the plat." Thus, in the face of respon-dent's refusal to follow the procedures for requesting a variance, and its refusal to provide specific information about the variances it would require, respondent hardly can maintain that the Commission's disapproval of the preliminary plat was equivalent to a final decision that no variances would be granted.

As in *Hodel, Agins,* and *Penn Central* [the Court's discussion of *Penn Central* case is omitted], then, respondent has not yet obtained a final decision regard-ing how it will be allowed to develop its property. Our reluctance to examine taking claims until such a final decision has been made is compelled by the very nature of the inquiry required by the Just Compensation Clause. Although "[the] question of what constitutes a 'taking' for purposes of the Fifth Amendment has proved to be a problem of considerable difficulty," *Penn Central Transp. Co. v. New York City,* 438 U.S., at 123, this Court consistently has indicated that among the factors of particular significance in the inquiry are the economic impact of the challenged action and the extent to which it interferes with reasonable investment-backed expectations. *Id.,* at 124. Those factors simply cannot be evaluated until the administrative agency has arrived at a final, definitive position regarding how it will apply the regulations at issue to the particular land in question.

Here, for example, the jury's verdict indicates only that it found that respondent would be denied the economically feasible use of its property if it were forced to develop the subdivision in a manner that would meet each of the Commission's eight objections. It is not clear whether the jury would have found that the respondent had been denied all reasonable beneficial use of the property had any of the eight objections been met through the grant of a variance. Indeed, the expert witness who testified regarding the economic impact of the Commission's actions did not itemize the effect of each of the eight objections, so the jury would have been unable to discern how a grant of a variance from any one of the regulations at issue would have affected the profitability of the development. Accordingly, until the Commission determines that no variances will be granted, it is impossible for the jury to find, on this record, whether respondent "will be unable to derive economic benefit" from the land.

Respondent asserts that it should not be required to seek variances from the regulations because its suit is predicated upon 42 U.S.C. § 1983, and there is no requirement that a plaintiff exhaust administrative remedies before bringing a § 1983 action. *Patsy v. Florida Board of Regents,* 457 U.S. 496 (1982). The question whether administrative remedies must be exhausted is conceptually distinct, however, from the question whether an administrative action must be final before it is judicially reviewable. While the policies underlying the two concepts often overlap, the finality requirement is concerned with whether the initial decisionmaker has arrived at a definitive position on the issue that inflicts an actual, concrete injury; the exhaustion requirement generally refers to administrative and judicial procedures by which an injured party may seek review of an adverse decision and obtain a remedy if the decision is found to be unlawful or otherwise inappropriate. *Patsy* concerned the latter, not the former.

The difference is best illustrated by comparing the procedure for seeking a variance with the procedures that, under *Patsy,* respondent would not be required to exhaust. While it appears that the State provides procedures by which an aggrieved property owner may seek a declaratory judgment regarding the validity of zoning and planning actions taken by county authorities, see *Fallin v. Knox County Bd. of Comm'rs,* 656 S. W. 2d 338 (Tenn. 1983); Tenn. Code Ann. §§ 27-8-101, 27-9-101 to 27-9-113, and 29-14-101 to 29-14-113 (1980 and Supp. 1984), respondent would not be required to resort to those procedures before bringing its § 1983 action, because those procedures clearly are remedial. Similarly, respondent would not be required to appeal the Commission's rejection of the preliminary plat to the Board of Zoning Appeals, because the Board was empowered, at most, to review that rejection, not to participate in the Commission's decisionmaking.

Resort to those procedures would result in a judgment whether the Commission's actions violated any of respondent's rights. In contrast, resort to the procedure for obtaining variances would result in a conclusive determination by the Commission whether it would allow respondent to develop the subdivision in the manner respondent proposed. The Commission's refusal to approve the preliminary plat does not determine that issue; it prevents respondent from developing its subdivision without obtaining the necessary variances, but leaves open the possibility that respondent may develop the subdivision according to its plat after obtaining the variances. In short, the Commission's denial of approval does not conclusively determine whether respondent will be denied all reasonable beneficial use of its property, and therefore is not a final, reviewable decision.

B

A second reason the taking claim is not yet ripe is that respondent did not seek compensation through the procedures the State has provided for doing so. The Fifth Amendment does not proscribe the taking of property; it proscribes taking without just compensation. Nor does the Fifth Amendment require that just compensation be paid in advance of, or contemporaneously with, the taking; all that is required is that a "'reasonable, certain and adequate provision for obtaining compensation'" exist at the time of the taking. *Regional Rail Reorganization Act Cases,* 419 U.S. 102, 124–125 (1974) (quoting *Cherokee Nation v. Southern Kansas R. Co.,* 135 U.S. 641, 659 (1890)). If the government has provided an adequate process for obtaining compensation, and if resort to that process "[yields] just compensation," then the property owner "has no claim against the Government" for a taking. Thus, we have held that taking claims against the Federal Government are premature until the property owner has availed itself of the process provided by the Tucker Act, 28 U.S.C. § 1491. *[Ruckelshaus v.] Monsanto [Co.],* 467 U.S., [986] at 1016–1020. Similarly, if a State provides an adequate procedure for seeking just compensation, the property owner cannot claim a violation of the Just Compensation Clause until it has used the procedure and been denied just compensation.

The recognition that a property owner has not suffered a violation of the Just Compensation Clause until the owner has unsuccessfully attempted to obtain just compensation through the procedures provided by the State for obtaining such compensation is analogous to the Court's holding in *Parratt v. Taylor,* 451 U.S. 527 (1981). There, the Court ruled that a person deprived of property through a random and unauthorized act by a state employee does not state a claim under the Due Process Clause merely by alleging the deprivation of property. In such a situation, the Constitution does not require predeprivation process because it would be impossible or impracticable to provide a meaningful hearing before the deprivation. Instead, the Constitution is satisfied by the provision of meaningful postdeprivation process. Thus, the

State's action is not "complete" in the sense of causing a constitutional injury "unless or until the state fails to provide an adequate postdeprivation remedy for the property loss." *Hudson v. Palmer,* 468 U.S. 517, 532, n. 12 (1984). Likewise, because the Constitution does not require pretaking compensation, and is instead satisfied by a reasonable and adequate provision for obtaining compensation after the taking, the State's action here is not "complete" until the State fails to provide adequate compensation for the taking.

Under Tennessee law, a property owner may bring an inverse condemnation action to obtain just compensation for an alleged taking of property under certain circumstances. Tenn. Code Ann. § 29-16-123 (1980). The statutory scheme for eminent domain proceedings outlines the procedures by which government entities must exercise the right of eminent domain. §§ 29-16-101 to 29-16-121. The State is prohibited from "[entering] upon [condemned] land" until these procedures have been utilized and compensation has been paid the owner, § 29-16-122, but if a government entity does take possession of the land without following the required procedures, "the owner of such land may petition for a jury of inquest, in which case the same proceedings may be had, as near as may be, as hereinbefore provided; or he may sue for damages in the ordinary way. . . ." § 29-16-123.

The Tennessee state courts have interpreted § 29-16-123 to allow recovery through inverse condemnation where the "taking" is effected by restrictive zoning laws or development regulations. See *Davis v. Metropolitan Govt. of Nashville,* 620 S. W. 2d 532, 533–534 (Tenn. App. 1981); *Speight v. Lockhart,* 524 S. W. 2d 249 (Tenn. App. 1975). Respondent has not shown that the inverse condemnation procedure is unavailable or inadequate, and until it has utilized that procedure, its taking claim is premature. . . .

V

In sum, respondent's claim is premature, whether it is analyzed as a deprivation of property without due process under the Fourteenth Amendment, or as a taking under the Just Compensation Clause of the Fifth Amendment. We therefore reverse the judgment of the Court of Appeals and remand the case for further proceedings consistent with this opinion.

It is so ordered.

NOTES AND QUESTIONS

1. *The ripeness rules. Hamilton Bank* was the first of several cases decided on ripeness grounds during this period of time that allowed the Court to avoid resolving a debate about whether compensation (as opposed to an injunction) was a remedy for a regulatory *taking.* See the *First English* case, reproduced *infra,* requiring compensation. The *Agins* case, reproduced *supra,* had held that at least one application was required in order to make a case ripe. Supreme Court cases after *Hamilton Bank* elaborated on these rules.

2. *The reapplication rule. McDonald, Sommer & Frates v. Yolo County,* 477 U.S. 340 (1986), added a requirement that a second application is necessary after a first application is rejected. The county rejected a subdivision map submitted by plaintiff proposing subdivision of its land into single-family and multi-family residential lots. Plaintiff filed suit in state court and appealed to the Supreme Court after a state appellate court affirmed the dismissal of its complaint. The Supreme Court again held the case was not ripe:

> [The landowner] has submitted one subdivision proposal and has received the Board's response thereto. Nevertheless, [the landowner] still has yet to receive the Board's "final, definitive position regarding how it will apply the regulations at issue to the particular land in question." . . . [T]he holding of both courts below leave open the possibility that some development will be permitted. [*Id.* at 351–52, quoting *Hamilton Bank*.]

3. *More on the final decision requirement.* Notice that the final decision rule is an override of the local decision making process on land use applications. A decision may be final under state law, but not final for purposes of federal jurisdiction. A formal denial is not necessary, however. It is enough if the agency's decision is the functional equivalent of a denial. In *A.A. Profiles, Inc. v. City of Ft. Lauderdale,* 850 F.2d 1483 (11th Cir. 1988), *cert. denied,* 490 U.S. 1020 (1989), the court held there was a final decision when the city stopped a project by suspending project approval and then downzoning the property.

Del Monte Dunes v. City of Monterey, 920 F.2d 1496 (9th Cir. 1990), is a famous case that illustrates the struggles developers must go through before they can satisfy the finality rule. The developer had been seeking permission for a residential development for several years, had repeatedly reduced the size of the project in response to city demands, and obtained the approval of the planning commission before an abrupt change of opinion in the city council produced a denial. The court held the decision was final. This case later went to the Supreme Court on the takings issue.

The federal courts have followed Supreme Court dicta that the submission of "grandiose" plans is not enough. A developer in Hawaii, for example, was required to scale down plans for a beach hotel. *Kaiser Dev. Co. v. City & County of Honolulu,* 649 F. Supp. 926 (D. Haw. 1986), *aff'd,* 898 F.2d 112 (9th Cir. 1990). Must a developer seek to compromise with a city? *Landmark Land Co. v. Buchanan,* 874 F.2d 717 (10th Cir. 1989) (yes, unless this would result in excessive delay).

The Supreme Court has held that the final decision rules do not apply to facial takings claims. *E.g., Lucas v. South Carolina Coastal Council,* 503 U.S. 1003, 1014 n.4 ("Facial challenges are ripe when the act is passed; applied challenges require a final decision on the act's application to the properly in question."). Does this make sense?

4. *Variances and administrative relief. Hamilton Bank* required landowners to seek administrative relief through a variance in order to comply with the ripeness rules. As will be seen in Chapter 5, state courts have long imposed an identical requirement as part of the rule that plaintiffs must exhaust administrative remedies before suing in court. Yet *Hamilton Bank* distinguished the ripeness requirement from exhaustion of remedies, which is not required under § 1983. Does this distinction make sense? A landowner need not apply for a variance if it is not available. *Schulz v. Milne,* 849 F. Supp. 708 (N.D. Cal. 1994). Should he have to appeal a denial of a variance to a court if it is denied? The courts are divided. See *Bannum, Inc. v. City of Ft. Lauderdale,* 906 F. Supp. 1230 (S.D. Fla. 1997), holding no. What about a map amendment to the zoning ordinance or a comprehensive plan? There is some confusion in the courts on this point, and you should reconsider this issue after you study zoning amendments in Chapter 5. See *Tahoe-Sierra Preservation Council v. Tahoe Regional Plan. Agency (II),* 938 F.2d 153 (9th Cir. 1991) (need not apply for amendment to comprehensive plan).

5. *The futility rule.* In *Yolo County* the Supreme Court indicated that repeated "futile" applications need not be made. Some lower federal courts have followed this suggestion. For example, what if a developer's proposal for four dwelling units on 60 acres complies with the zoning ordinance, but is rejected because environmental problems make it inconsistent with the comprehensive plan? The property is then downzoned to require 40 acres for each dwelling unit in order to comply with the plan's environmental policies. The court held that reapplication would be futile in *Hoehne v. County of San Benito,* 870 F.2d 529 (9th Cir.), *cert. denied,* 490 U.S. 1020 (1989). Why didn't the court require reapplication under the new zoning ordinance for one dwelling unit? There is a similar futility exception to the state court requirement that plaintiffs must exhaust administrative remedies before bringing suit. The federal courts are not yet clear on how the futility rule should be applied. It requires federal courts to examine local government attitudes toward a land use application and determine whether it has a chance of approval. A First Circuit rent control case provided one statement of what is required. There must be special circumstances indicating a permit application is not a "viable option," or that the local authority has "dug in its heels" and made it abundantly clear that the permit will not be granted. *Gilbert v. City of Cambridge,* 932 F.2d 51 (1st Cir.), *cert. denied,* 502 U.S. 866 (1991).

The reapplication and futility rules are interconnected. See *Southview Assoc., Ltd. v. Bongartz,* 980 F.2d 84 (2d Cir. 1992), *cert. denied,* 507 U.S. 987 (1993), requiring reapplication when the municipality did not indicate that the landowner's development was effectively barred. How does a landowner know which to choose?

6. *The state compensation remedy. Hamilton Bank* held that plaintiffs must seek compensation in state court if a state remedy is available before suing in federal court. Lower federal courts have seized on this requirement to bar land use claims. Some hold a plaintiff must seek compensation in state court even if the availability of this remedy is not clear, until the state court holds the remedy is not available. Is this a correct interpretation of *Hamilton Bank*? A review of the cases shows that the federal courts have found a compensation remedy available in almost every state. See D. Mandelker, J. Gerard & T. Sullivan, Federal Land Use Law § 4A.02[5][d].

The state compensation remedy requirement became even more complex after the Supreme Court decided in *First English,* reproduced *infra,* that a direct remedy under the federal constitution is available to seek compensation in land use cases. The federal constitution is enforceable in state courts. Should a federal court hold a claim can never be ripe because a plaintiff can always sue for compensation on the federal constitution in state court? Some courts have taken this position, but a Ninth Circuit case held to the contrary, reasoning that otherwise plaintiffs could never bring takings claims in federal court. *Dodd v. Hood River County,* 59 F.3d 852 (9th Cir. 1995).

What if a plaintiff dutifully goes to state court to bring her takings claim, carefully reserving the federal takings claim for a later day and not presenting it in state court. If she attempts to return to federal court after losing her state case, a federal court may well hold her claim precluded. See *Dodd v. Hood River County,* 136 F.3d 1219 (9th Cir. 1998). The reason is that the plaintiff could have raised the takings claim in state court, and so is precluded from raising this claim later in federal court under res judicata principles. This is a fatal Catch-22.

7. *Equal protection and due process claims.* There is language in *Yolo County* indicating that the ripeness rules apply to substantive due process and equal protection claims, and a number of federal courts have taken that position. E.g., *Sameric Corp. v. City of Philadelphia,* 142 F.3d 582 (3d Cir. 1998). A Ninth Circuit panel initially held the ripeness rules do not apply to these claims because they do not require factual inquiries into the economic loss imposed by land use regulations. It then amended its opinion and held the ripeness rules applied. *Herrington v. Sonoma County,* 834 F.2d 1488 (9th Cir. 1987), *amended,* 857 F.2d 567 (9th Cir. 1988), *cert. denied,* 489 U.S. 1090 (1989). Compare *Harris v. County of Riverside,* 904 F.2d 497 (9th Cir. 1990) (contra).

Other circuits have applied the ripeness rules less stringently to equal protection and due process claims. E.g., *Bannum, Inc. v. City of Louisville,* 958 F.2d 1354 (6th Cir. 1992) (proceedings must have reached some sort of "impasse," and position of the parties be defined). Since takings cases require an inquiry into governmental purpose and substantive due process claims require the same inquiry, should the two types of cases be treated differently? See Note, *Determining Ripeness of Substantive Due Process Claims Brought by Landowners Against Local Governments,* 95 Mich. L. Rev. 492 (1996).

8. *A statutory remedy?* The ripeness rules have effectively kept as-applied takings cases out of the federal courts. Concern about this outcome led to congressional legislation, first introduced in 1998, that would modify the ripeness rules. It would eliminate the requirement that takings cases must first be tried in state court. A final decision would exist if an applicant submits a "meaningful" application and it is disapproved. If the application is disapproved, and the "disapproval explains in writing the use, density, or intensity of development that would be approved, with any conditions," the applicant must submit another meaningful application that takes these recommendations "into account" unless reapplication is futile. If a reapplication is disapproved, the decision is final once the applicant files for any available administrative relief that has been disapproved. Are these too many steps?

The bill would also eliminate the requirement that a landowner must sue in state court first for compensation. The constitutionality of this provision has been questioned. Kidalov & Seamon, *The Missing Pieces of the Debate Over Federal Property Rights Legislation,* 27 Hastings Const. L.Q. 1 (1999). The bill passed twice in the House. For discussion see *Testimony of Daniel R. Mandelker on H.R. 1534 Before the House Judiciary Committee,* 31 Urb. Law. 323 (1999).

Model state land use legislation proposed by the American Planning Association makes a decision final after an applicant for development permission has made one meaningful application, which the local government has approved, approved with conditions, or denied. § 10-603(2) (2000 draft). However, the law requires that applications must be "complete," and authorizes local governments to request additional information to make them complete. § 10-203.

The model legislation also adopts a provision from a Florida law that allows a landowner to request a ripeness decision from a local government. §§ 10-204(5), 10-207(10). See Fla. Stat. Ann. § 70.001(5)(a). How would this legislation affect federal ripeness rules? The ripeness requirement is supplemented by another provision that requires land use agencies to make decisions after a designated period of time. § 10-210. Only a few state land use laws have such a requirement. See Cal. Gov't Code § 69590.

9. *Sources.* For additional discussion of ripeness problems see Berger, *Supreme Bait & Switch: The Ripeness Ruse in Regulatory Takings,* 3 Wash. U. J.L. & Pol'y 99 (2000); Delaney & Desisiderio, *Who Will Clean Up the Ripeness Mess? A Call for Reform so Takings Plaintiffs Can Enter the Federal Courthouse,* 31 Urb. Law. 195 (1999); Lyman, *Finality Ripeness in Federal Land Use Cases from Hamilton Bank to Lucas,* 9 J. Land Use & Envtl. L. 101 (1994); Overstreet, *The Ripeness Doctrine of the Taking Clause: A Survey of Decisions Showing Just How Far Federal Courts Will Go to Avoid Adjudicating Land Use Cases,* 10 J. Land Use & Envtl. L. 91 (1995); Overstreet, *Update on the Continuing and Dramatic Effect of the Ripeness Doctrine on Federal Land Use Litigation,* 20 Zoning & Plan. L. Rep. 17, 25 (1997).

2. BARRIERS TO JUDICIAL RELIEF: ABSTENTION

In addition to the ripeness doctrine, the abstention doctrine also limits federal court jurisdiction in land use cases. Like the ripeness doctrine, the abstention doctrine applies when a case is brought in a federal rather than a state court. The principal theme of the abstention doctrine is that state courts should be allowed to decide cases when there are strong reasons for allowing litigation to be tried in a state, rather than a federal, court. The abstention doctrine originated in three United States Supreme Court cases —*Railroad Comm'n v. Pullman Co.,* 312 U.S. 496 (1941), *Burford v. Sun Oil Co.,* 319 U.S. 315 (1943), and *Younger v. Harris,* 401 U.S. 37 (1971).

Pullman abstention.—In *Pullman,* the Supreme Court held that federal courts should abstain from exercising their jurisdiction when resolution of a difficult and unsettled question of state law would make a decision on a federal constitutional issue unnecessary. This would especially be the case if the unsettled state law question "touches a sensitive area of social policy upon which the federal courts ought not to enter unless no alternative to its adjudication is open." 312 U.S. at 498.

In *Hawaii Hous. Auth. v. Midkiff,* 467 U.S. 229 (1984), the Court made it clear that a state or local law must be "fairly subject" to an interpretation that would make a decision of federal constitutional questions unnecessary, and must be uncertain and obviously susceptible of a limiting construction, before the abstention doctrine may be applied. See also *Quackenbush v. Allstate Ins. Co.,* 517 U.S. 706 (1996) (federal question might be obviated if state court can interpret ambiguous state law).

The federal courts have applied the *Pullman* abstention doctrine in a number of land use cases where state law was unsettled. *Kollsman v. City of Los Angeles,* 737 F.2d 830 (9th Cir. 1985) (answer to question whether plaintiff's subdivision should be deemed "approved" depended on interlocking state statutes whose interpretation was unsettled); *C-Y Dev. Co. v. City of Redlands,* 703 F.2d 375 (9th Cir. 1983) (denial of development permit under a growth-management ordinance that awarded permits under a competitive "point" system raised unsettled questions concerning application of the system and justified abstention, even though resolution of the state question would not resolve all federal questions).

The federal courts do not apply the *Pullman* abstention doctrine in land use cases when state law questions are settled. *International College of Surgeons v. City of Chicago,* 153 F.2d 356 (7th Cir. 1998); *Heritage Farms, Inc. v. Solebury Twp.,* 671 F.2d 743 (3d Cir.), *cert. denied,* 456 U.S. 990 (1982) (pointing out that federal as well as state courts can apply state law to difficult facts); *Nasser v. City of Homewood (I),* 671 F.2d 432 (11th Cir. 1982). Courts are less likely to apply the *Pullman* abstention when First Amendment issues are raised in land use cases. *Cinema Arts, Inc. v. Clark County,* 722 F.2d 579 (9th Cir. 1983).

"Mirror image" constitutional problems frequently arise when a defendant asks a federal court to abstain so that a state court can interpret a state constitutional provision that closely parallels a federal constitutional provision —e.g., a state constitutional "taking" clause that closely parallels the Fifth and Fourteenth Amendment "taking" clauses. Although several lower federal courts have invoked the *Pullman* abstention doctrine in such cases, the Supreme Court held in *Midkiff, supra,* that abstention is inappropriate in such a case.

Burford abstention.—In *Burford,* the Supreme Court extended the *Pullman* abstention doctrine to a case challenging a state regulatory program, and held a court should abstain where federal court action would disrupt "state efforts to establish a coherent policy with respect to a matter of substantial state concern." However, the Court has held that the balance "only rarely" favors *Burford* abstention, *Quackenbush v. Allstate Ins. Co.,* 517 U.S. 706 (1996), and federal courts almost universally refuse to apply *Burford* abstention in land use cases because land use regulation is a local function.

Younger abstention.—*Younger* held that federal courts should abstain from enjoining pending criminal court proceedings if the criminal defendant can make an adequate federal defense in the state court proceedings and if abstention does not cause irreparable injury to the criminal defendant. It was later held that even if the federal action was filed first, *Younger* abstention is required if "proceedings of substance" on the merits have not occurred in the federal court at the time a later state action is filed. *Hicks v. Miranda,* 422 U.S. 332 (1975). *Younger* abstention does not often apply in land use cases because criminal prosecution in such cases is uncommon, but examples can be found. See, e.g., *Night Clubs v. City of Fort Smith,* 163 F.3d 475 (8th Cir. 1998) (prosecution of adult uses).

The extension of the *Younger* abstention doctrine to pending state civil proceedings that implicate important state interests, see *Middlesex County Ethics Comm'n v. Garden State Bar Ass'n,* 457 U.S. 423 (1982), and to state administrative proceedings, see *Ohio Civil Rights Comm'n v. Dayton Christian Schools, Inc.,* 477 U.S. 619 (1986), has more potential impact on land use cases. For *Younger* abstention purposes, proceedings by local zoning administrative agencies would seem to qualify as state administrative proceedings. The Supreme Court has often said that abstention should be the exception rather than the rule. How does this statement compare with the Court's attitude in the ripeness cases, where it seems to favor rules making it difficult to make land use cases ripe? Are these two sets of rules based on the same premise?

Sources. For additional discussion of abstention see Blaesser, *Closing the Federal Courthouse Door on Property Owners: The Ripeness and Abstention Doctrines in Section 1983 Land Use Cases,* 2 Hofstra Prop. L.J. 73 (1989). See also Rehnquist, *Taking Comity Seriously: How to Neutralize the Abstention Doctrine,* 46 Stan. L. Rev. 1049 (1994); Staver, *The Abstention Doctrines: Balancing Comity with Federal Court Intervention,* 28 Seton Hall L. Rev. 1102 (1998).

PROBLEM

A client has told you he has a 500-acre tract of land on the edge of an urbanizing area in your county that he wishes to develop as a residential subdivision. He submitted a plan to the county at a density of eight units to the acre. The county rejected the plan because it exceeded the density of six units to the acre allowed by the zoning ordinance, and because the comprehensive plan designated this area as a no-growth area where development should be delayed until necessary public facilities were available. The county has suggested the developer submit a new plan containing affordable housing units, which would entitle him to a density bonus under a state statute and the county ordinance.

The developer does not know whether to proceed with the new submission, which would be costly, or sue in federal court. He is dubious about the county's interest in amending the plan and increasing the zoning density, even if he provides affordable housing, as several county council members are on record as opposing such changes in the area. Moreover, the state court decisions on the state density bonus statute do not clearly indicate density bonuses are available in no-growth areas designated on county plans. What should you advise?

3. INVERSE CONDEMNATION

The case which follows is the third of the 1987 "trilogy" of important takings cases, *Keystone* and *Nollan* being the others:

FIRST ENGLISH EVANGELICAL LUTHERAN
CHURCH OF GLENDALE v. COUNTY OF LOS ANGELES

482 U.S. 304 (1987)

CHIEF JUSTICE REHNQUIST delivered the opinion of the Court:

In this case the California Court of Appeal held that a landowner who claims that his property has been "taken" by a land-use regulation may not recover damages for the time before it is finally determined that the regulation constitutes a "taking" of his property. We disagree, and conclude that in these circumstances the Fifth and Fourteenth Amendments to the United States Constitution would require compensation for that period.

In 1957, appellant First English Evangelical Lutheran Church purchased a 21-acre parcel of land in a canyon along the banks of the Middle Fork of Mill Creek in the Angeles National Forest. The Middle Fork is the natural drainage channel for a watershed area owned by the National Forest Service. Twelve of the acres owned by the church are flat land, and contained a dining hall, two bunkhouses, a caretaker's lodge, an outdoor chapel, and a footbridge across the creek. The church operated on the site a campground, known as "Lutherglen," as a retreat center and a recreational area for handicapped children.

In July 1977, a forest fire denuded the hills upstream from Lutherglen, destroying approximately 3,860 acres of the watershed area and creating a serious flood hazard. Such flooding occurred on February 9 and 10, 1978, when a storm dropped 11 inches of rain in the watershed. The runoff from the storm overflowed the banks of the Mill Creek, flooding Lutherglen and destroying its buildings.

In response to the flooding of the canyon, appellee County of Los Angeles adopted Interim Ordinance No. 11,855 in January 1979. The ordinance provided that "[a] person shall not construct, reconstruct, place or enlarge any building or structure, any portion of which is, or will be, located within the outer boundary lines of the interim flood protection area located in Mill Creek Canyon. . . ." The ordinance was effective immediately because the county determined that it was "required for the immediate preservation of the public health and safety. . . ." The interim flood protection area described by the ordinance included the flat areas on either side of Mill Creek on which Lutherglen had stood.

The church filed a complaint in the Superior Court of California a little more than a month after the ordinance was adopted. As subsequently amended, the complaint alleged two claims against the county and the Los Angeles County Flood Control District. The first alleged that the defendants were liable under Cal. Gov't Code Ann. § 835 (West 1980)[1] for dangerous conditions on their upstream properties that contributed to the flooding of Lutherglen. As a part of this claim, appellant also alleged that "Ordinance No. 11,855 denies [appellant] all use of Lutherglen." The second claim sought to recover

---

[1] Section 835 of the California Government Code establishes conditions under which a public entity may be liable "for injury caused by a dangerous condition of its property. . . ."

from the Flood District in inverse condemnation and in tort for engaging in cloud seeding during the storm that flooded Lutherglen. Appellant sought damages under each count for loss of use of Lutherglen. The defendants moved to strike the portions of the complaint alleging that the county's ordinance denied all use of Lutherglen, on the view that the California Supreme Court's decision in *Agins v. Tiburon,* 598 P. 2d 25 (Cal. 1979), aff'd on other grounds, 447 U.S. 255 (1980), rendered the allegation "entirely immaterial and irrelevant, [with] no bearing upon any conceivable cause of action herein." See Cal. Civ. Proc. Code Ann. § 436 (West Supp. 1987) ("The court may . . . strike out any irrelevant, false, or improper matter inserted in any pleading").

In *Agins v. Tiburon, supra,* the Supreme Court of California decided that a landowner may not maintain an inverse condemnation suit in the courts of that State based upon a "regulatory" taking. In the court's view, maintenance of such a suit would allow a landowner to force the legislature to exercise its power of eminent domain. Under this decision, then, compensation is not required until the challenged regulation or ordinance has been held excessive in an action for declaratory relief or a writ of mandamus and the government has nevertheless decided to continue the regulation in effect. Based on this decision, the trial court in the present case granted the motion to strike the allegation that the church had been denied all use of Lutherglen. It explained that "a careful re-reading of the *Agins* case persuades the Court that when an ordinance, even a non-zoning ordinance, deprives a person of the total use of his lands, his challenge to the ordinance is by way of declaratory relief or possibly mandamus." Because the appellant alleged a regulatory taking and sought only damages, the allegation that the ordinance denied all use of Lutherglen was deemed irrelevant.[2]

On appeal, the California Court of Appeal read the complaint as one seeking "damages for the uncompensated taking of all use of Lutherglen by County Ordinance No. 11,855. . . ." It too relied on the California Supreme Court's decision in *Agins* in rejecting the cause of action, declining appellant's invitation to reevaluate *Agins* in light of this Court's opinions in *San Diego Gas & Electric Co. v. San Diego,* 450 U.S. 621 (1981). The court found itself obligated to follow *Agins* "because the United States Supreme Court has not yet ruled on the question of whether a state may constitutionally limit the remedy for a taking to nonmonetary relief. . . ." It accordingly affirmed the trial court's decision to strike the allegations concerning appellee's ordinance.[3] The Supreme Court of California denied review.

---

[2] The trial court also granted defendants' motion for judgment on the pleadings on the second cause of action, based on cloud seeding. It limited trial on the first cause of action for damages under Cal. Gov't Code Ann. § 835 (West 1980), rejecting the inverse condemnation claim. At the close of plaintiff's evidence, the trial court granted a nonsuit on behalf of defendants, dismissing the entire complaint.

[3] The California Court of Appeal also affirmed the lower court's orders limiting the issues for trial on the first cause of action, granting a nonsuit on the issues that proceeded to trial, and dismissing the second cause of action —based on cloud seeding —to the extent it was founded on a theory of strict liability in tort. The court reversed the trial court's ruling that the second cause of action could not be maintained against the Flood Control District under the theory of inverse condemnation. The case was remanded for further proceedings on this claim. These circumstances alone, apart from the more particular issues presented in takings cases and discussed in the text, require us to consider whether the pending resolution of further liability

This appeal followed, and we noted probable jurisdiction. Appellant asks us to hold that the Supreme Court of California erred in *Agins v. Tiburon* in determining that the Fifth Amendment, as made applicable to the States through the Fourteenth Amendment, does not require compensation as a remedy for "temporary" regulatory takings —those regulatory takings which are ultimately invalidated by the courts. Four times this decade, we have considered similar claims and have found ourselves for one reason or another unable to consider the merits of the *Agins* rule. For the reasons explained below, however, we find the constitutional claim properly presented in this case, and hold that on these facts the California courts have decided the compensation question inconsistently with the requirements of the Fifth Amendment.

I

Concerns with finality left us unable to reach the remedial question in the earlier cases where we have been asked to consider the rule of *Agins*. In each of these cases, we concluded either that regulations considered to be in issue by the state court did not effect a taking, or that the factual disputes yet to be resolved by state authorities might still lead to the conclusion that no taking had occurred. Consideration of the remedial question in those circumstances, we concluded, would be premature.

The posture of the present case is quite different. Appellant's complaint alleged that "Ordinance No. 11,855 denies [it] all use of Lutherglen," and sought damages for this deprivation. In affirming the decision to strike this allegation, the Court of Appeal assumed that the complaint sought "damages for the uncompensated *taking* of all use of Lutherglen by County Ordinance No. 11,855." (emphasis added). It relied on the California Supreme Court's *Agins* decision for the conclusion that "the remedy for a taking [is limited] to nonmonetary relief. . . ." (emphasis added). The disposition of the case on these grounds isolates the remedial question for our consideration. The rejection of appellant's allegations did not rest on the view that they were false. Nor did the court rely on the theory that regulatory measures such as Ordinance No. 11,855 may never constitute a taking in the constitutional sense. Instead, the claims were deemed irrelevant solely because of the California Supreme Court's decision in *Agins* that damages are unavailable to redress a "temporary" regulatory taking. The California Court of Appeal has thus held that regardless of the correctness of appellants' claim that the challenged ordinance denies it "all use of Lutherglen" appellant may not recover damages until the ordinance is finally declared unconstitutional, and then only for any period after that declaration for which the county seeks to

questions deprives us of jurisdiction because we are not presented with a "final judgmen[t] or decre[e]" within the meaning of 28 U.S.C. § 1257. We think that this case is fairly characterized as one "in which the federal issue, finally decided by the highest court in the State [in which a decision could be had], will survive regardless of the outcome of future state-court proceedings." Cox Broadcasting Corp. v. Cohn, 420 U.S. 469, 480 (1975). As we explain infra, the California Court of Appeal rejected appellant's federal claim that it was entitled to just compensation from the county for the taking of its property; this distinct issue of federal law will survive and require decision no matter how further proceedings resolve the issues concerning the liability of the flood control district for its cloud seeding operation.

enforce it. The constitutional question pretermitted in our earlier cases is therefore squarely presented here.[6]

We reject appellee's suggestion that, regardless of the state court's treatment of the question, we must independently evaluate the adequacy of the complaint and resolve the takings claim on the merits before we can reach the remedial question. However "cryptic" —to use appellee's description —the allegations with respect to the taking were, the California courts deemed them sufficient to present the issue. We accordingly have no occasion to decide whether the ordinance at issue actually denied appellant all use of its property[7] or whether the county might avoid the conclusion that a compensable taking had occurred by establishing that the denial of all use was insulated as a part of the State's authority to enact safety regulations. These questions, of course, remain open for decision on the remand we direct today. We now turn to the question of whether the Just Compensation Clause requires the government to pay for "temporary" regulatory takings.

II

Consideration of the compensation question must begin with direct reference to the language of the Fifth Amendment, which provides in relevant part that "private property [shall not] be taken for public use, without just compensation." As its language indicates, and as the Court has frequently noted, this provision does not prohibit the taking of private property, but instead places a condition on the exercise of the power. This basic understanding of the Amendment makes clear that it is designed not to limit the governmental interference with property rights per se, but rather to secure compensation in the event of otherwise proper interference amounting to a taking. Thus, government action that works a taking of property rights necessarily implicates the "constitutional obligation to pay just compensation." *Armstrong v. United States,* 364 U.S. 40, 49 (1960).

We have recognized that a landowner is entitled to bring an action in inverse condemnation as a result of "'the self-executing character of the constitutional provision with respect to compensation. . . .'" *United States v. Clarke,* 445 U.S. 253, 257 (1980), quoting 6 P. Nichols, Eminent Domain § 25.41 (3d rev. ed. 1972). As noted in Justice Brennan's dissent in *San Diego Gas & Electric Co.,*

---

[6] Our cases have also required that one seeking compensation must "seek compensation through the procedures the State has provided for doing so" before the claim is ripe for review. Williamson County Regional Planning Comm'n v. Hamilton Bank, 473 U.S. 172, 194 (1985). It is clear that appellant met this requirement. Having assumed that a taking occurred, the California court's dismissal of the action establishes that "the inverse condemnation procedure is unavailable. . . ." Id., at 197. The compensation claim is accordingly ripe for our consideration.

[7] Because the issue was not raised in the complaint or considered relevant by the California courts in their assumption that a taking had occurred, we also do not consider the effect of the county's permanent ordinance on the conclusions of the courts below. That ordinance, adopted in 1981 . . ., provides that "[a] person shall not use, erect, construct, move onto, or . . . alter, modify, enlarge or reconstruct any building or structure within the boundaries of a flood protection district except . . . [a]ccessory buildings and structures that will not substantially impede the flow of water, including sewer, gas, electrical, and water systems, approved by the county engineer . . . [a]utomobile parking facilities incidental to a lawfully established use . . . [and] [f]lood-control structures approved by the chief engineer of the Los Angeles County Flood Control District." County Code § 22.44.220.

450 U.S., at 654–655, it has been established at least since *Jacobs v. United States,* 290 U.S. 13 (1933), that claims for just compensation are grounded in the Constitution itself:

> "The suits were based on the right to recover just compensation for property taken by the United States for public use in the exercise of its power of eminent domain. *That right was guaranteed by the Constitution.* The fact that condemnation proceedings were not instituted and that the right was asserted in suits by the owners did not change the essential nature of the claim. The form of the remedy did not qualify the right. It rested upon the Fifth Amendment. Statutory recognition was not necessary. A promise to pay was not necessary. Such a promise was implied because of the duty imposed by the Amendment. *The suits were thus founded upon the Constitution of the United States." Id.,* at 16. (Emphasis added.)

Jacobs, moreover, does not stand alone, for the Court has frequently repeated the view that, in the event of a taking, the compensation remedy is required by the Constitution. See e.g., *Kirby Forest Industries, Inc. v. United States,* 467 U.S. 1, 5 (1984). [Other citations omitted.][9]

It has also been established doctrine at least since Justice Holmes' opinion for the Court in *Pennsylvania Coal Co. v. Mahon,* 260 U.S. 393 (1922) that "[t]he general rule at least is, that while property may be regulated to a certain extent, if regulation goes too far it will be recognized as a taking." *Id.,* at 415. While the typical taking occurs when the government acts to condemn property in the exercise of its power of eminent domain, the entire doctrine of inverse condemnation is predicated on the proposition that a taking may occur without such formal proceedings. In *Pumpelly v. Green Bay Co.,* 13 Wall. 166, 177-178 (1872), construing a provision in the Wisconsin Constitution identical to the Just Compensation Clause, this Court said:

> "It would be a very curious and unsatisfactory result if . . . it shall be held that if the government refrains from the absolute conversion of real property to the uses of the public it can destroy its value entirely, can inflict irreparable and permanent injury to any extent, can, in effect, subject it to total destruction without making any compensation, because, in the narrowest sense of that word, it is not *taken* for the public use."

Later cases have unhesitatingly applied this principle. See, e.g., *Kaiser Aetna v. United States,* 444 U.S. 164 (1979). [Other citations omitted.]

While the Supreme Court of California may not have actually disavowed this general rule in *Agins,* we believe that it has truncated the rule by

---

[9] The Solicitor General urges that the prohibitory nature of the Fifth Amendment, combined with principles of sovereign immunity, establishes that the Amendment itself is only a limitation on the power of the Government to act, not a remedial provision. The cases cited in the text, we think, refute the argument of the United States that "the Constitution does not, of its own force, furnish a basis for a court to award money damages against the government." Though arising in various factual and jurisdictional settings, these cases make clear that it is the Constitution that dictates the remedy for interference with property rights amounting to a taking. See San Diego Gas & Electric Co. v. San Diego, 450 U.S. 621, 655, n. 21 (1981) (Brennan, J., dissenting), quoting United States v. Dickinson, 331 U.S. 745, 748 (1947).

disallowing damages that occurred prior to the ultimate invalidation of the challenged regulation. The Supreme Court of California justified its conclusion at length in the *Agins* opinion, concluding that:

> "In combination, the need for preserving a degree of freedom in the land-use planning function, and the inhibiting financial force which inheres in the inverse condemnation remedy, persuade us that on balance mandamus or declaratory relief rather than inverse condemnation is the appropriate relief under the circumstances." *Agins v. Tiburon,* 598 P. 2d, at 31.

We, of course, are not unmindful of these considerations, but they must be evaluated in the light of the command of the Just Compensation Clause of the Fifth Amendment. The Court has recognized in more than one case that the government may elect to abandon its intrusion or discontinue regulations. See, e.g., *Kirby Forest Industries, Inc. v. United States,* 467 U.S. 1 (1984); *United States v. Dow,* 357 U.S. 17, 26 (1958). Similarly, a governmental body may acquiesce in a judicial declaration that one of its ordinances has affected an unconstitutional taking of property; the landowner has no right under the Just Compensation Clause to insist that a "temporary" taking be deemed a permanent taking. But we have not resolved whether abandonment by the government requires payment of compensation for the period of time during which regulations deny a landowner all use of his land.

In considering this question, we find substantial guidance in cases where the government has only temporarily exercised its right to use private property. In *United States v. Dow, supra,* at 26, though rejecting a claim that the Government may not abandon condemnation proceedings, the Court observed that abandonment "results in an alteration in the property interest taken —from [one of] full ownership to one of temporary use and occupation. . . . In such cases compensation would be measured by the principles normally governing the taking of a right to use property temporarily. See *Kimball Laundry Co. v. United States,* 338 U.S. 1 [1949]; *United States v. Petty Motor Co.,* 327 U.S. 372 [1946]; *United States v. General Motors Corp.,* 323 U.S. 373 [1945]." Each of the cases cited by the Dow Court involved appropriation of private property by the United States for use during World War II. Though the takings were in fact "temporary," there was no question that compensation would be required for the Government's interference with the use of the property; the Court was concerned in each case with determining the proper measure of the monetary relief to which the property holders were entitled.

These cases reflect the fact that "temporary" takings which, as here, deny a landowner all use of his property, are not different in kind from permanent takings, for which the Constitution clearly requires compensation. Cf. *San Diego Gas & Electric Co.,* 450 U.S., at 657 (Brennan, J., dissenting) ("Nothing in the Just Compensation Clause suggests that 'takings' must be permanent and irrevocable"). It is axiomatic that the Fifth Amendment's just compensation provision is "designed to bar Government from forcing some people alone to bear public burdens which, in all fairness and justice, should be borne by the public as a whole." *Armstrong v. United States,* 364 U.S., at 49. In the present case the interim ordinance was adopted by the county of Los Angeles in January 1979, and became effective immediately. Appellant filed suit within a month after the effective date of the ordinance and yet when the Supreme Court of California denied a hearing in the case on October 17, 1985, the merits of appellant's claim had yet to be determined. The United States has been required to pay compensation for leasehold interests of shorter duration than this. The value of a leasehold interest in property for a period of years may be substantial, and the burden on the property owner in extinguishing such an interest for a period of years may be great indeed. See, e.g., *United States v. General Motors, supra.* Where this burden results from governmental action that amounted to a taking, the Just Compensation Clause of the Fifth Amendment requires that the government pay the landowner for the value of the use of the land during this period. Cf. *United States v. Causby,* 328 U.S., at 261 ("It is the owner's loss, not the taker's gain, which is the measure of the value of the property taken"). Invalidation of the ordinance or its successor ordinance after this period of time, though converting the taking into a "temporary" one, is not a sufficient remedy to meet the demands of the Just Compensation Clause.

Appellee argues that requiring compensation for denial of all use of land prior to invalidation is inconsistent with this Court's decisions in *Danforth v. United States,* 308 U.S. 271 (1939), and *Agins v. Tiburon,* 447 U.S. 255 (1980). In *Danforth,* the landowner contended that the "taking" of his property had occurred prior to the institution of condemnation proceedings, by reason of the enactment of the Flood Control Act itself. He claimed that the passage of that Act had diminished the value of his property because the plan embodied in the Act required condemnation of a flowage easement across his property. The Court held that in the context of condemnation proceedings a taking does not occur until compensation is determined and paid, and went on to say that "[a] reduction or increase in the value of property may occur by reason of legislation for or the beginning or completion of a project," but "[s]uch changes in value are incidents of ownership. They cannot be considered as a 'taking' in the constitutional sense." *Danforth, supra,* at 285. *Agins* likewise rejected a claim that the city's preliminary activities constituted a taking, saying that "[m]ere fluctuations in value during the process of governmental decisionmaking, absent extraordinary delay, are 'incidents of ownership.'" See 447 U.S., at 263, n. 9.

But these cases merely stand for the unexceptional proposition that the valuation of property which has been taken must be calculated as of the time of the taking, and that depreciation in value of the property by reason of preliminary activity is not chargeable to the government. Thus, in *Agins,* we concluded that the preliminary activity did not work a taking. It would require a considerable extension of these decisions to say that no compensable regulatory taking may occur until a challenged ordinance has ultimately been held invalid.[10]

---

[10] Williamson County Regional Planning Comm'n, is not to the contrary. There, we noted that "no constitutional violation occurs until just compensation has been denied." 473 U.S., at 194, n. 13. This statement, however, was addressed to the issue of whether the constitutional claim was ripe for review and did not establish that compensation is unavailable for government activity occurring before compensation is actually denied. Though, as a matter of law, an illegitimate taking might not occur until the government refuses to pay, the interference that effects a taking

Nothing we say today is intended to abrogate the principle that the decision to exercise the power of eminent domain is a legislative function, "'for Congress and Congress alone to determine.'" *Hawaii Housing Authority v. Midkiff,* 467 U.S. 229, 240 (1984), quoting *Berman v. Parker,* 348 U.S. 26, 33 (1954). Once a court determines that a taking has occurred, the government retains the whole range of options already available — amendment of the regulation, withdrawal of the invalidated regulation, or exercise of eminent domain. Thus we do not, as the Solicitor General suggests, "permit a court, at the behest of a private person, to require the . . . Government to exercise the power of eminent domain. . . ." Brief for United States as "Amicus Curiae 22. We merely hold that where the government's activities have already worked a taking of all use of property, no subsequent action by the government can relieve it of the duty to provide compensation for the period during which the taking was effective.

We also point out that the allegation of the complaint which we treat as true for purposes of our decision was that the ordinance in question denied appellant all use of its property. We limit our holding to the facts presented, and of course do not deal with the quite different questions that would arise in the case of normal delays in obtaining building permits, changes in zoning ordinances, variances, and the like which are not before us. We realize that even our present holding will undoubtedly lessen to some extent the freedom and flexibility of land-use planners and governing bodies of municipal corporations when enacting land-use regulations. But such consequences necessarily flow from any decision upholding a claim of constitutional right; many of the provisions of the Constitution are designed to limit the flexibility and freedom of governmental authorities and the Just Compensation Clause of the Fifth Amendment is one of them. As Justice Holmes aptly noted more than 50 years ago, "a strong public desire to improve the public condition is not enough to warrant achieving the desire by a shorter cut than the constitutional way of paying for the change." *Pennsylvania Coal Co. v. Mahon,* 260 U.S., at 416.

Here we must assume that the Los Angeles County ordinances have denied appellant all use of its property for a considerable period of years, and we hold that invalidation of the ordinance without payment of fair value for the use of the property during this period of time would be a constitutionally insufficient remedy. The judgment of the California Court of Appeals is therefore reversed, and the case is remanded for further proceedings not inconsistent with this opinion.

It is so ordered.

JUSTICE STEVENS, with whom JUSTICE BLACKMUN and JUSTICE O'CONNOR join as to Parts I and III, dissenting. [Most of Justice Stevens' dissent is omitted, but his comments on the notion that a normal delay in decision making is not a taking are of interest:]

---

might begin much earlier, and compensation is measured from that time. See Kirby Forest Industries, Inc. v. United States, 467 U.S. 1, 5 (1984) (Where Government physically occupies land without condemnation proceedings, "the owner has a right to bring an 'inverse condemnation' suit to recover the value of the land on the date of the intrusion by the Government").

The Court's reasoning also suffers from severe internal inconsistency. Although it purports to put to one side "normal delays in obtaining building permits, changes in zoning ordinances, variances and the like," the Court does not explain why there is a constitutional distinction between a total denial of all use of property during such "normal delays" and an equally total denial for the same length of time in order to determine whether a regulation has "gone too far" to be sustained unless the Government is prepared to condemn the property. Precisely the same interference with a real estate developer's plans may be occasioned by protracted proceedings which terminate with a zoning board's decision that the public interest would be served by modification of its regulation and equally protracted litigation which ends with a judicial determination that the existing zoning restraint has "gone too far," and that the board must therefore grant the developer a variance. The Court's analysis takes no cognizance of these realities. Instead, it appears to erect an artificial distinction between "normal delays" and the delays involved in obtaining a court declaration that the regulation constitutes a taking.

NOTES AND QUESTIONS

1. *All use?* Note Chief Justice Rehnquist's statement in *First English* that he "treated as true" the allegations in the complaint that the ordinance denied "all use" of the property and that he limited the holding to "the facts presented." Does this statement mean that compensation for a temporary taking is available only in this circumstance? Assume an owner's land is zoned single-family, that he wants to build a multifamily development, and that he successfully brings an action in federal court claiming the single family zoning is a taking. Is he entitled to compensation for a temporary taking under *First English*?

Some cases hold not, a result which if generally applied would seriously limit compensation in land use cases. E.g., *Cobb County v. McColister,* 413 S.E.2d 441 (Ga. 1992); *Lake Forest Chateau v. City of Lake Forest,* 549 N.E.2d 336 (Ill. 1990); *Staubes v. City of Folly Beach,* 500 S.E.2d 160 (S.C. 1998). But see *Cannone v. Noey,* 867 P.2d 797 (Alaska 1994) (contra); *Whitehead Oil Co. v. City of Lincoln (III),* 515 N.W.2d 401 (Neb. 1994).

2. *The property interest taken.* Is an award of monetary compensation necessarily required by the Fifth and Fourteenth Amendments once a state court determines that a *"temporary regulatory taking"* has occurred? If so, will it not be necessary to define the property interest "taken"? *Florida Rock, Inc. v. United States,* 45 Fed. Cl. 21, 43 n. 13 held that "[i]f it is necessary to name the government's interest post taking, the court would suggest the government now owns a negative easement." How easy is this to accomplish? The court did not actually suggest that an easement be conveyed to the government. What if the property owner, after he receives compensation, applies again for permission? Does payment of compensation preclude this?

How should the duration of the "negative easement" be determined? In *Hernandez v. City of Lafayette,* 643 F.2d 1188 (5th Cir. 1981), *cert. denied,* 455 U.S. 907 (1982), the court stated that the "regulatory taking" should not be deemed to begin (1) until the time when, "due to changing circumstances," a previously valid "general zoning ordinance" becomes so restrictive as to deny a landowner any "economically viable use of his land," or (2) until expiration of a reasonable time after a landowner questions the validity of a new zoning classification that denies him any "economically viable use of his land." The second alternative is designed to give the local governing body "a realistic time within which to review its zoning legislation vis-à-vis the particular property and to correct the inequity." Under *First English* the "*temporary* regulatory taking" period should end either when, prior to a judicial declaration of unconstitutionality, the offending regulation is repealed (or, presumably, amended so as to make it clearly constitutional), or when the court holds the regulation to be unconstitutional.

3. *The measure of compensation.* How should the amount of monetary compensation be determined? In formal eminent domain proceedings, the courts have held that the landowner, as a general rule, is entitled to receive the "market value" of the land "taken" for public use, but other modes of valuation have been approved in cases where the "market value" formula cannot be easily applied. Thus, in "*temporary* regulatory taking" cases, a court might hold that the required amount of compensation should be either (1) the rental value of the land during the "temporary taking" period, (2) the value of an option on the land for such period, or (3) the difference between the value of the land at the beginning and at the end of such period, in cases where the value of the land decreases during the period.

None of these compensation formulas may be appropriate in the typical situation where a developer has bought or obtained an option to buy land and is then precluded from developing the land by land use regulations that do not permit any "viable economic use" of the land. The first compensation formula would be inappropriate where the developer did not intend to rent the land but to develop it. The second compensation formula would be inappropriate where the developer has actually purchased the land rather than merely obtaining an option on it. And the third formula would obviously be inappropriate where the land has increased in value during the "temporary taking" period because of inflation and is worth more at the end of such period than at the beginning.

Moreover, none of the suggested formulas would be appropriate where, as in *Hamilton Bank,* the developer actually completes a substantial part of his proposed project and then suffers substantial "business losses" because completion of the project according to plan is prevented by enactment of a "downzoning" amendment or a substantial change in the applicable subdivision regulations. In cases of the latter type, the developer will often have installed the required "infrastructure" (streets, sewer and water lines, etc.) for the entire project. But the substantial "business losses" that may result in such a case are generally not recoverable as "just compensation" under the rules usually applied in formal eminent domain proceedings.

The few cases that have considered the compensation issue in zoning cases have been downzoning cases. In *Wheeler v. City of Pleasant Grove (III),* 833 F.2d 267 (11th Cir. 1987), for example, the court found a taking when the city adopted an ordinance prohibiting plaintiff's proposed apartment development after community opposition arose. The court held that compensation should be based on the property's potential for producing income or profit, measured by the rate of return on the amount by which the ordinance reduced the market value of the property. The court refused to award compensation for lost profits or increased development costs, but held that compensation was payable even though the property increased in value during the time the ordinance was in force. Does this make sense?

The Court of Appeals affirmed this holding in a later appeal after the district court refused to award compensation on remand. 896 F.2d 1347 (11th Cir. 1990). It awarded compensation at the market rate of return for the temporary taking period on plaintiff's 25 percent equity in the project. Accord *Nemmers v. City of Dubuque (II),* 764 F.2d 502 (8th Cir. 1985). *Wheeler* did not consider the uncertainty that the project might not have been built. Is this correct?

Does the compensation issue change when a court holds that a refusal to upzone is a taking? In this case the court must value the "highest and best" use that is available to the property owner in order to determine the difference in value on which rate of return is calculated. How is the court to carry out this hypothetical exercise? Will it have to second-guess the municipality? Is this judicial zoning?

A comparison of the market value of property before and after a regulatory restriction is another accepted measure of value. Market value is usually determined through an examination of sales of comparable property. *Florida Rock Indus., Inc. v. United States,* 45 Fed. Cl. 21 (1999), used this measure of damages and awarded compensation when a denial of a permit for mining in a wetlands deprived the landowner of 73.1% of the value of its property. Should this measure of damages apply in zoning cases?

4. *Uncertainty and speculative value.* Other courts have followed the *Wheeler* formula for determining compensation, but have criticized that case for awarding compensation based on a property's potential for producing income because lost profits are not usually compensable in eminent domain. *Corn v. City of Lauderdale Lakes,* 771 F. Supp. 1557 (S.D. Fla. 1991). Uncertainty is another problem, because it was not certain that the project in *Wheeler* would actually be built after the downzoning was invalidated.

In *City of Austin v. Teague,* 570 S.W.2d 389 (Tex. 1978), the court refused to award plaintiffs compensation for loss of rental value when the city denied them a development permit. It held the award was improper because anticipated rentals were as speculative as lost profits, the landowners had no "kind of plan" for the property, and had not shown they would have earned any return at all. This holding reflects the rule in some states that only actual loss will be compensated. *Corrigan v. City of Scottsdale,* 720 P.2d 513 (Ariz. 1986) (invalidating hillside protection ordinance).

A court could award a landowner damages based upon proof of his "actual loss" in a "constitutional tort action" under 42 U.S.C. § 1983. It has been assumed in several lower federal court cases that such an action is available to a landowner as an alternative to a direct "inverse condemnation" action under the Fifth and Fourteenth Amendments. See, e.g., *Hernandez v. City of Lafayette, supra* Note 2. But it is not clear whether the Court's holding in *First English* will permit the use of a § 1983 action in lieu of a direct action under the Fifth and Fourteenth Amendments in view of the Court's assertion that the legal consequences of a "temporary regulatory taking" are the same as the legal consequences of any other "temporary taking" — e.g., one effected by the condemnation of a leasehold estate.

If a § 1983 action is held to be available to the landowner in "temporary regulatory taking" cases, an award of damages based on proof of "actual loss" may in many, if not most, cases be preferable to an award of compensation based on some formula for valuing the "negative easement" that was "temporarily taken" from the landowner. In a § 1983 action it would be unnecessary for the court to define the property interest "taken," and "business losses" caused by the application of the invalid land use regulation would clearly be recoverable by the landowner.

5. *Delay as a taking.* What about the "different questions" Chief Justice Rehnquist raises concerning "normal delays" in obtaining zoning changes and the like? Do you agree with Justice Stevens' criticism of this distinction. Most courts have applied this dictum to hold that even prolonged decision making by government agencies on land use applications is not a taking during the decision making period. *Tabb Lakes v. United States,* 10 F.3d 796 (D.C. Cir. 1993), is a leading case. The key issue is whether the delay was reasonable, but most courts are willing to assume that local officials are carrying out their duties in good faith. See *Dufau v. United States,* 22 Cl. Ct. 156 (1990) (16-month delay in considering permit application held reasonable). See also *Hills Dev. Co. v. Bernards Twp.*, 510 A.2d 621,650 (N.J.1986) ("No builder with the slightest amount of experience can be surprised by extended delays").

A somewhat different problem arises if a municipality improperly denies a rezoning, variance or some other approval for the use of land, the landowner appeals and the court holds the denial was invalid but was not a taking. Most courts do not find a temporary taking occurred during the time the case was litigated. *Landgate, Inc. v. California Coastal Comm'n,* 953 P.2d 1188 (Cal.), *cert. denied,* 525 U.S. 876 (1998). *Eberle v. Dane County Bd. of Adjustment,* 595 N.W.2d 730 (Wis. 1999), held the other way in a case in which the court found the board had improperly denied access to two residential lots. It held that a "complete lack of access" was a denial of all or substantially all practicable uses during the time the case was litigated. The dissent argued the landowner's eventual receipt of a permit after the court reversed the board's decision made the case one of temporary delay and not a temporary taking. Whether a moratorium on the use of property is a noncompensable normal delay is considered in Chapter 7, *infra.*

6. *Subsequent proceedings in First English.* On remand from the Supreme Court, the California Court of Appeal, without returning *First English* to the trial court for a hearing and a determination whether the facts established at the hearing effected a *de facto* taking, made its own determination that the complaint failed to state a cause of action, because the interim ordinance substantially advanced a legitimate state purpose and did not deny plaintiff all use of its property. 258 Cal. Rptr. 893 (1989). Of course, moratoria of this kind are now suspect as a per se taking under *Lucas* if they deny a landowner "all use" of his property.

7. *Sources.* For discussion of *First English* see Cooperstein, *Sensing Leave for One's Takings: Interim Damages and Land Use Regulation,* 7 Stan. Envtl. L.J. 49 (1987–88); White & Barkhordari, *The First English Evangelical Lutheran Church Case: What Did It Actually Decide?,* 7 UCLA J. Envtl. L. & Pol'y, 155 (1988) (co-author argued case in Supreme Court).

4. RELIEF UNDER SECTION 1983 OF THE FEDERAL CIVIL RIGHTS ACT

First English, supra, approved an action brought directly under the Constitution claiming a violation of the taking clause and asking for an inverse condemnation award. A Reconstruction-era Statute, now 42 U.S.C. § 1983, originally enacted in 1871, provides an alternative remedy for land use plaintiffs in federal courts. Section 1983 provides:

> Every person who, under color of any statute, ordinance, custom or usage, of any State or Territory, subjects, or causes to be subjected, any citizen of the United States or other person within the jurisdiction thereof to the deprivation of any rights, privileges, or immunities secured by the Constitution and laws, shall be liable to the party injured in an action at law or suit in equity, or other proper proceeding for redress.

Section 1983 remedies against municipalities were barred for decades by a Supreme Court decision holding that municipalities were not "persons" under the act, but as will be seen in the next section the Court reversed this ruling in 1978. Since then there has been a substantial increase in land use litigation in federal courts. The availability of § 1983 as the basis for a federal action requires land use lawyers to make an important and often critical choice between bringing a federal or state court action.

The world of § 1983 jurisprudence is a labyrinth that requires extensive study. The following sections raise some of the more important issues as they apply to land use litigation.

a. The General Scope of Section 1983

Section 1983 creates a cause of action for any person whose federal constitutional or statutory rights are violated, "under color of" state law, by any other "person." The "color of law" requirement is usually not troublesome in § 1983 land use actions, since most § 1983 actions arise out of the conduct of state or local land use control agencies or officials. The "persons" who may be liable under § 1983 include natural persons, citizens' groups, corporations and other business entities, and — under *Monell v. Department of Social Servs.,* 436 U.S. 658 (1978) — local government units. States, however, are not "persons" and therefore are not subject to liability under § 1983. *Quern v. Jordan,* 440 U.S. 332 (1980).

Custom and policy.—*Monell* refused to adopt the respondeat superior theory of municipal liability under § 1983. Instead it interpreted the "custom and usage" requirement to mean that local governments are liable only for actions that are "official policy" or "visited pursuant to governmental custom," but did not fully explain these terms. The "official policy" or "governmental custom" requirement is not a problem in most land use cases because a governmental body is usually responsible for the action which is the basis of a § 1983 action. But cases may arise in which a § 1983 action is based on a single act by a local government official, such as a zoning administrator. A partial answer to the question whether such a single act is "pursuant to governmental custom" was provided in *Pembaur v. City of Cincinnati*, 475 U.S. 469 (1986) — not a land use case — where the Court held that "municipal liability may be imposed for a single decision by municipal policymakers under appropriate circumstances," although only a plurality of the Justices agreed on a standard for imposing liability in such cases. The plurality said that

> municipal liability under § 1983 attaches where — and only where — a deliberate choice to follow a course of action is made from among various alternatives by the official or officials responsible for establishing a final policy with respect to the subject matter in question. [*Id.* at 482.]

The Court has not really clarified this question. *City of St. Louis v. Praprotnik*, 485 U.S. 112 (1988), an employee discharge case, was again a plurality decision. It confirmed a statement in *Pembaur* that the identification of policymaking officials was a matter of state law. An excessive force case, *Board of County Comm'rs v. Brown*, 520 U.S. 397 (1997), summarized the rules it had adopted in these two cases in a majority decision. It held that proof that an action taken or directed by a municipality or authorized decisionmaker itself violates federal law will determine "that the municipal action was the moving force behind the injury of which the plaintiff complains."

The "custom and policy" question is not a problem in many land use cases because a formal action by the city council or a zoning board often triggers the litigation. *Discovery House, Inc. v. Consolidated City of Indianapolis*, 43 F. Supp. 2d 997 (N.D. Ind. 1999) (zoning board). Actions by individual officers or employees may not constitute a municipal custom or policy. E.g., *Zahra v. Town of Southfold*, 48 F.3d 674 (2d Cir. 1995) (no proof of municipal policy on enforcement). Uncertainties in the definition of what constitutes custom and policy put municipalities at risk in land use cases.

In the field of land use control, most of the § 1983 actions have been based on the Fourteenth Amendment, alleging violations of the due process or equal protection clause, although the First Amendment and the federal antitrust laws may also provide a basis for § 1983 actions. Under the Fourteenth Amendment, § 1983 actions may be based on claims that plaintiff was deprived of property without substantive due process of law or without procedural due process of law. Since the Fourteenth Amendment's due process clause makes the Fifth Amendment's takings clause applicable to the states, § 1983 can also provide a basis for a "regulatory taking" claim.

When plaintiffs in § 1983 actions attempt to transmute what are essentially state law violations into deprivations of federal constitutional rights they are generally unsuccessful. The following case illustrates the problem.

CLOUTIER v. TOWN OF EPPING

714 F.2d 1184 (1st Cir. 1983)

CAMPBELL, CHIEF JUDGE:

This "Epic of Epping" concerns a dispute over the development of a mobile home park in Epping, New Hampshire. Wilfred and Mary Cloutier, and Pine & Pond, Inc. are developers who brought the present action in the district court claiming that Epping and several of its officers violated their civil rights by revoking a sewage connection permit, denying them other permits, and engaging in a pattern of harassment aimed at retarding or destroying their development plans. Concluding that plaintiffs had failed to raise a substantial federal question, the court below dismissed the case for lack of jurisdiction. Although we cannot say that the court lacked jurisdiction, we affirm the dismissal.

I

We present the facts in a light most favorable to appellants. Epping, New Hampshire is a town with a population of about 3,000. Zoning, land use, and development have long been heated issues in the town. In the mid-1960s the Cloutiers began making plans to develop a large mobile home park in Epping. They obtained a road entrance permit in 1965 and approval from the Planning Board in 1968.

On April 27, 1972 the Cloutiers applied for and received from one of the three sewer commissioners a permit to connect the mobile home park to the town's newly constructed sewage system. On May 4, 1972 the other two sewer commissioners, defendants Robert Chamberlain and Brendan Splaine, met informally and revoked this permit. The Cloutiers were invited to discuss the revocation at the commission's next meeting several days later.

Following revocation, the Cloutiers filed an action in Rockingham County Superior Court for a writ of mandamus. Plaintiffs contend that it was only in the course of the litigation that they learned the commission's real reasons for revoking the permit: a 1968 zoning ordinance prohibiting mobile homes in the town's "sewered zone," and commission regulations forbidding the connection of structures more than 200 feet from the sewer main. Plaintiffs further allege that defendants gave erroneous and perjured testimony at the trial before the Superior Court. The court found for the town, and plaintiffs appealed.

While their appeal was pending before the New Hampshire Supreme Court, plaintiffs continued to attempt to obtain the permit from defendants. . . . [A March, 1975 town meeting passed an article requiring connections of the Cloutier park to the system and defeated a zoning amendment proposed by the planning board that would have limited the number of mobile homes in the town.]

Despite the Cloutiers' victories before the town meeting, defendants continued to oppose the connection of Pine & Pond to the sewer system. The sewer commission told plaintiffs that another town meeting vote would be required before the permit would be granted and that Planning Board approval would also be necessary. The Planning Board, meanwhile, posted another amendment to the town's zoning laws that was similar to the one that had just been defeated by the meeting.

On May 29, 1976 the New Hampshire Supreme Court rendered its decision. *Cloutier v. Epping Water and Sewer Commission,* 116 N.H. 276, 360 A.2d 892 (1976). The court ruled that the 1968 zoning ordinance forbidding mobile homes within the town's sewered zone was invalid because the zone had not been adequately defined. The court held that the town had to connect the mobile homes that were within 200 feet of the sewer system. *Id.* at 279, 360 A.2d at 895. But it also held that the sewer commission regulation barring the connection of structures beyond 200 feet from the main was valid and that the town meeting lacked authority to override the commission. *Id.* at 280, 360 A.2d at 896. The court refused to decide whether or not zoning was ever validly enacted in Epping, finding that there was no reason why the "newly discovered evidence" put forward by the Cloutiers could not have been presented to the Superior Court. *Id.* at 278.

Following the New Hampshire Supreme Court's decision, the dispute continued to heat up and expand in several new directions. First, the Cloutiers again brought the issue before the town meeting which once again voted in favor of their position. Defendants, however, still refused to grant the permit. Then, on August 3, 1976, defendants sought an injunction from the Rockingham County Superior Court against the Cloutiers' development of a second mobile home park in Epping on the ground that the lot was substandard. Following the filing of the state action, Wilfred Cloutier commenced the present case in federal district court, charging that the state action and the previous denials of the sewer permit for Pine & Pond constituted a deprivation of property without due process, a denial of equal protection, and a violation of the Privileges and Immunities Clause of the Fourteenth Amendment. The complaint sought damages and an injunction against the Superior Court action. On November 3, 1976 the district court, citing the *Younger* doctrine, 401 U.S. 37 (1971), denied Cloutier's request for a preliminary injunction. The Superior Court action was dismissed in 1978 by a subsequent board of selectmen.

The election of new town officials in 1978 led to the Cloutiers' finally obtaining a sewer connection permit and a water connection permit. The day after the permits were issued defendant Roger Gauthier filed a lawsuit to invalidate the appointment of the new commissioner. This action was dismissed by the state court.

After receiving the sewer connection permit, the Cloutiers still had to obtain a discharge permit from the New Hampshire Water Supply and Pollution Control Commission (WSPCC). According to plaintiffs, defendants gave false information to the WSPCC, delaying its approval of the permit until July 1981. . . .

On July 20, 1982, defendants moved for summary judgment. . . . On September 16, 1982 the district court dismissed the complaint for lack of federal jurisdiction.

II

Jurisdiction

While we agree with the substance of the district court's analysis, we are not sure that the claims are all so patently frivolous as to warrant dismissal for lack of federal jurisdiction. . . .

Still, looking at the record — which besides the pleadings includes affidavits, depositions and other supporting papers — in the light most favorable to appellants, we are satisfied . . . that there is no genuine issue as to any material fact and that defendants are entitled to judgment as a matter of law. Because defendants moved below for summary judgment, and plaintiffs had a full opportunity to respond to those motions, we think it proper to affirm the dismissal on that basis.

III

Zoning Disputes, Due Process and Equal Protection

Plaintiffs contend that zoning was never validly enacted in Epping, that the New Hampshire Supreme Court held the zoning scheme unenforceable, and that defendants' continued reliance on the zoning laws violated 42 U.S.C. § 1983 by depriving plaintiffs of due process and equal protection of the laws. . . .

Plaintiffs further contend that defendants engaged in a number of malicious delaying tactics which impeded plaintiffs' ability to proceed with their development plans. While plaintiffs ultimately achieved many of their goals, they say that defendants deprived them of their property without due process by adding years of delay and extra costs.

This is not the first time we have considered claims of this type. In *Creative Environments, Inc. v. Estabrook,* 680 F.2d 822 (1st Cir.), *cert. denied,* 459 U.S. 989 (1982), we refused to entertain under section 1983 a claim that local officials had misapplied zoning laws in order to thwart a development project. We assumed that defendants might have engaged in "adversary and even arbitrary tactics," in order to stop plaintiffs' development plans. *Id.* at 829. We said, however, that "'[t]he violation of a state statute does not automatically give rise to a violation of rights secured by the Constitution.'" *Id.* at 833, *quoting Crocker v. Hakes,* 616 F.2d 237, 239 (5th Cir. 1980) (per curiam), and that

> [e]*very* appeal by a disappointed developer from an adverse ruling by a local . . . planning board necessarily involves some claim that the board exceeded, abused or "distorted" its legal authority in some manner, often for some allegedly perverse (from the developer's point of view) reason. It is not enough simply to give these state law claims constitutional labels such as "due process" or "equal protection" in order to raise a substantial federal question under section 1983. [*Id.* at 833.]

We recently reaffirmed these principles. . . .

Plaintiffs attempt to distinguish *Creative Environments* and its successors. First, they say the issue here is not the mere misapplication of valid zoning laws, as was the case in *Creative Environments* . . ., but instead the blatant application of ordinances which defendants knew were totally void. Second, plaintiffs argue, defendants engaged in numerous unlawful tactics that independently violated the Constitution. Among the unlawful actions alleged are the abuse of process, perjury, failing to come forward with material evidence, and giving false information to a state agency about the plaintiffs.

The contention that the Epping zoning laws were totally invalid fails to withstand scrutiny. In *Cloutier* the New Hampshire Supreme Court held that Article II(A) of the Epping zoning regulations, which prohibited placing mobile homes in the sewered zone, was unenforceable because the zone had never been adequately defined. The court never addressed the validity of the remaining provisions of the zoning ordinance. As the ordinance had a severability clause and as severability is the general rule when construing zoning ordinances in New Hampshire, it was scarcely an act of lawlessness for defendants to continue relying upon the ordinance's remaining provisions. Moreover, the state court in *Cloutier* specifically approved of the revocation of plaintiffs' sewer connection permit, and found that the sewer commission was not bound to connect the Cloutiers' park on the basis of the town meeting votes. Thus the state court did not unambiguously reject defendants' positions; defendants' actions taken to enforce their interpretations of the governing laws cannot be seen as a gross abuse of power.

Similarly, plaintiffs' long list of harassing actions reveals not the type of egregious behavior that might violate the due process clause, but rather, for the most part, further disputes over the interpretation of the state and town zoning laws. Plaintiffs contend that defendants maliciously abused state process by commencing an action in Rockingham County Superior Court to enjoin the Cloutiers' development of a second mobile home park in Epping. However, as the Fifth Circuit has stated,

> "[n]either the Fourteenth Amendment nor the Civil Rights Acts purported to secure a person against unfounded or even malicious claims or suits in state courts, especially so when the laws of the state are available and furnished adequate remedies to a person aggrieved." [*Beker Phosphate Corp. v. Muirhead,* 581 F.2d 1187, 1189 (5th Cir. 1978), *quoting Curry v. Ragan,* 257 F.2d 449, 450 (5th Cir.), *cert. denied,* 358 U.S. 851 (1958).]

Here, plaintiffs made no effort to seek state remedies for the alleged abuse of process. Moreover, because the suit was brought to enforce the zoning laws, the question whether the prosecution was malicious depends upon the proper interpretation of the state's zoning laws. Thus the malicious prosecution claim is nothing more than a reformulation of plaintiffs' general claim of misapplication of the zoning laws — the very question that we have held not to be cognizable under section 1983.

Plaintiffs' charge that defendants gave false information to the New Hampshire WSPCC is similarly a mere rephrasing of the overall zoning law issue.

Plaintiffs claim that the defendants falsely told the commission that the Cloutiers' plans did not conform to local zoning regulations and required Planning Board approval prior to obtaining the state permit. Whether or not such statements were false, however, obviously depends upon the validity of defendants' interpretation of the zoning laws. Thus we see no distinction from *Creative Environments*. . . .

The fact that plaintiffs allege many claims does not change the foregoing. It is the nature of the allegations, not their quantity, which is significant. Here, although plaintiffs raise numerous charges, the vast majority merely concern disputes over the town's zoning laws. The rest of the charges either fail to state a federal claim or concern matters for which damages are unavailable.

IV

Procedural Due Process

Plaintiffs also seem to contend that defendants deprived them of procedural due process by revoking the original sewer permit without first granting them a hearing.[5]

The due process clause of the fourteenth amendment requires that states provide individuals with procedural protections when they are deprived of either their property or their liberty. The type of process that must be afforded varies, however, depending upon the particular situation. See *Mathews v. Eldridge*, 424 U.S. 319, 334 (1972). Even if we assume that plaintiffs acquired a property right in the sewer connection permit once it was issued, and thus a right to some procedural protections before its revocation, they received here all of the process the Constitution required.

Plaintiffs received a written notification of the revocation which invited them to discuss the situation with the commission at its next meeting only three days later. And whether or not the Cloutiers attended that meeting, there are indications in the record that the Cloutiers and their attorney did at some later time discuss the matter with the commission. Following that discussion, the sewer commission reviewed and affirmed the revocation. The Cloutiers then brought an action in state court for a writ of mandamus.

These procedures were adequate. Full judicial-type hearings are not required when local boards engage in the quasi-legislative task of granting or revoking zoning or similar types of permits. Moreover, the permit here had been in plaintiffs' possession only a few days before it was revoked. And plaintiffs were not shown to have acted in reliance on it. Cf. *Henry & Murphy, Inc. v. Town of Allenstown*, 424 A.2d 1132 (N.H. 1980) (zoning rules may be changed to developer's detriment except where the developer has made substantial construction in reliance upon old rules). Given plaintiffs' limited interest and the risk they might act in reliance upon the permit and thus gain a greater interest in it as time went on, defendants were entitled to revoke

---

[5] To the extent that plaintiffs argue that the revocation violated the substantive requirements of the due process clause, they do not state a federal claim. See *Creative Environments*.

without the delay of a prerevocation hearing. The prompt, informal proceedings offered by the town coupled with the judicial review provided by the state courts satisfied the requirements of the due process clause. . . .

NOTES AND QUESTIONS

1. In *Estabrook,* the court also characterized the claim as "too typical of the run of the mill dispute between a developer and a town planning agency" to constitute a due process violation, but said that it would hold differently in cases of "egregious" behavior or where there was a "gross abuse of power, invidious discrimination, or fundamentally unfair procedures." The First Circuit decisions refusing jurisdiction in § 1983 land use cases have been followed in other circuits. See *Norton v. Village of Corrales,* 103 F.3d 928 (10th Cir. 1996); *Burrell v. City of Kankakee,* 815 F.2d 1127 (7th Cir. 1987) (rezoning); *Hynes v. Pasco County,* 801 F.2d 1269 (11th Cir. 1986) (revocation of building permit). Review the *Olech* case, discussed *supra,* and decide whether that case is actionable under the *Cloutier* decision.

2. *Procedural due process actions.* A set of complicated rules the Supreme Court has adopted for procedural due process actions under § 1983 create additional barriers for these lawsuits. These rules hold a violation of procedural due process cannot be litigated in federal court if state procedures are available to correct the violation after it has occurred. See *Zinermon v. Burch,* 494 U.S. 113 (1990); *Parratt v. Taylor,* 451 U.S. 527 (1981). To decide this question, courts must apply a balancing test that identifies the risk of not providing procedural safeguards before decisions are made, and then evaluates the effectiveness of predeprivation safeguards in relationship to that risk. The revocation of a building permit is an example in a land use setting. *Landmar Corp. v. Rendine,* 811 F. Supp. 47 (D.R.I. 1993), held a hearing had to be provided in such cases before a permit could be revoked.

3. *Causation.* The Supreme Court's holding in *Monroe v. Pape,* 365 U.S. 167, 187 (1961), that courts should interpret § 1983 against a "background of tort liability," requires a § 1983 plaintiff to show that the "deprivation" complained of was "caused" by official action. The "causation" requirement is usually not a problem in land use cases because legislative or administrative action is ordinarily responsible for the "deprivation," although "causation" problems may occasionally arise. See *Bateson v. Geisse,* 857 F.2d 1300 (9th Cir. 1988) (wrongful withholding of building permit was moving force behind damage to plaintiff).

4. *State tort liability.* The Supreme Court has said that § 1983 provides a remedy for a constitutional tort. Under tort law doctrine in most states, a local government is liable in tort for the exercise of a ministerial function but not a governmental function, but many functions in the land use control process are classified as discretionary. See *City of Seymour v. Onyx Paving Co.,* 541 N.E.2d 951 (Ind. App. 1989) (enforcement of zoning ordinance); *Veling v. Borough of Ramsey,* 228 A.2d 873 (N.J. App. Div. 1967) (zoning amendment). A municipality may still be liable for the negligent exercise of a discretionary function.

A recurring problem is the case where a municipality mistakenly issues and then revokes a building permit after construction has started. Most courts conclude there is no liability under a "public duty" rule holding that officials owe a "public duty" to preserve the integrity of the land use regulations in this situation. See *Allen v. City of Honolulu,* 571 P.2d 328 (Hawaii 1977) (no liability). Does the landowner have a vested right to continue construction, however? See Chapter 5, *infra.*

b. Immunity from Section 1983 Liability

Immunity of the municipal body.—After the Supreme Court's decision in *Monell,* it was generally expected that municipalities would enjoy complete immunity from § 1983 liability if the governmental officials responsible for depriving a plaintiff of his or her federal rights acted in good faith. But the Court refused, in *Owen v. City of Independence,* 445 U.S. 622 (1980), to recognize any official immunity in such a case. Moreover, the Court refused to recognize any distinction, with respect to § 1983 liability, between either the "governmental" and "proprietary" functions or the "discretionary" and "ministerial functions" of municipalities. But *Owen* did not hold that municipalities are absolutely liable for violations of federal rights; constitution-violating municipal conduct is still required. "Municipalities" in their corporate sense are responsible for the actions of their constituent bodies, such as a legislature or a planning board.

Immunity of individuals.—Although individuals employed by, or acting on behalf of, the corporate municipal body often will not be financially attractive defendants, that is not always the case. The question is whether they enjoy an absolute or qualified immunity from liability in § 1983 actions.

Legislators.—The Supreme Court held that local legislators are entitled to absolute immunity in § 1983 cases in *Bogan v. Scott-Harris,* 523 U.S. 44 (1998), in which a city council adopted a budget that eliminated a temporary employee. The Court held it was the "pervasive view" at common law, at the time § 1983 was adopted, that local legislators were absolutely immune from liability. Judicial interference, distorted by the fear of personal liability, should not be allowed to inhibit the exercise of legislative discretion. At the local level, the Court noted, the time and energy necessary to defend against a lawsuit were of particular concern because part-time legislators are common. In addition, deterrents to legislative abuse are greater at the local level because municipalities are liable for constitutional violations, and there is the electoral check on governmental abuse.

The Court then held whether an act is legislative turns, not on the motive of the legislators, but on whether the act was "formally legislative" and within the "traditional sphere of legislative activity." In this case the act was legislative because it was a "discretionary, policymaking decision" that could well have prospective effect. Reconsider this holding after you have studied the zoning process in Chapter 5.

Judges.—Judges are absolutely immune from § 1983 liability. As a result, land use regulatory agencies and officials also are absolutely immune if they exercise adjudicatory functions. *Butz v. Economou,* 438 U.S. 478 (1978) (adjudication by agencies is "functionally comparable" to adjudication by judges and should enjoy the same absolute immunity judges enjoy). Note that the municipality in its corporate capacity cannot be liable for decisions of judge-like officials. But the applicability of *Butz* to zoning and planning agencies and officials is problematic because the zoning and planning process may not be deemed adjudicatory (quasi-judicial). A court may refuse to extend absolute immunity to the decisionmaking procedures of a planning board or board of adjustment. *Cutting v. Mazzey,* 724 F.2d 259 (1st Cir. 1984).

Administrators.—Absolute immunity is not available when a body or individual acts in an administrative capacity. *Crymes v. DeKalb County,* 923 F.2d 1482 (11th Cir. 1991) (permit denial). When a local governing body adopts an ordinance or resolution establishing a general policy, it is acting legislatively, but when it singles out specific individuals and treats them differently from others, it is acting administratively. The *Bogan* case, *supra,* provided a test on when a governing body's action is legislative. See also *Haskell v. Washington Twp.,* 864 F.2d 1266 (6th Cir. 1988) (stating that even if an action is legislative, it will provide a basis for imposing § 1983 liability if the governing body acted corruptly, in bad faith, or in furtherance of a personal rather than a public interest). However, if the action can be classified as adjudicative, it would presumably be immune to § 1983 liability for the same reasons that the adjudicative actions of an administrative agency are immune. See discussion of this point *infra.*

Municipal mayors may perform both legislative and administrative functions and thus qualify for absolute § 1983 immunity. In *Hernandez v. City of Lafayette,* 643 F.2d 1188 (5th Cir. 1982), *cert. denied,* 455 U.S. 907 (1982), the court concluded that a mayor, in vetoing a zoning ordinance adopted by the city council, performed "a legislative function and is entitled to absolute immunity from a civil suit complaining about actions taken in his legislative capacity." *Id.* at 1194.

Qualified immunity.—Planning and zoning officials enjoy a qualified good faith immunity if they do not enjoy an absolute immunity in a particular case. The land use cases apply a good faith immunity rule developed in several Supreme Court cases not involving land use. *Scheuer v. Rhodes,* 416 U.S. 232 (1974); *Harlow v. Fitzgerald,* 457 U.S. 800 (1982); *Davis v. Scherer,* 468 U.S. 183 (1984); and *Anderson v. Creighton,* 483 U.S. 635 (1987), noted, *The Supreme Court: 1986 Term: Leading Cases,* 101 Harv. L. Rev. 101, 220 (1987).

In *Davis,* the Court held that good faith immunity is defeated only if the public official has violated a clearly established federal right. *Anderson, supra,* held that whether the defendant acted reasonably is determined by the "contours" of a constitutional right, and these contours must be sufficiently clear so that "a reasonable official would understand that what he is doing violates that right." The Court added that the action in question need not have been held unlawful, but that "in light of preexisting law the unlawfulness must be apparent."

Decisions on qualified immunity depend on how well the right was established when the official decision was made. Compare *Natale v. Town of Ridgefield,* 927 F.2d 101 (2d Cir. 1991) (official could reasonably believe that plaintiff's "grandparented" status under zoning ordinance was in doubt), with *R.S.S.W., Inc. v. City of Keego Harbor,* 18 F. Supp.2d 738 (E.D. Mich. 1998) (city violated clearly established right to operate a business). An interesting question is whether a constitutional right can be clearly established by a case in another circuit. The cases are divided. See *Marks v. City of Chesapeake*, 883 F.2d 308 (4th Cir. 1989) (holding no).

In *Anderson*, which was a § 1983 action against police officers who conducted a warrantless search, the Supreme Court also held that a "fact-specific" inquiry is required and that the trial court must determine whether a reasonable officer could have believed that a warrantless search was constitutional in light of the clearly established law and the available facts. It would seem, since land use actions are so often "fact-specific," that *Anderson* could lead to an expansion of official good faith immunity in § 1983 land use cases. Notice, however, that a plaintiff cannot recover from the municipality if there is no municipal "custom or policy" that makes the municipality liable for the official's action.

c. Remedies in Section 1983 Actions

In appropriate cases, declaratory and injunctive relief, damages, and attorney's fees may be awarded in § 1983 actions. Recovery of damages must be sought under § 1983 for due process and equal protection violations; it is not clear whether § 1983 may be used in temporary takings cases, though these cases are regularly sued as § 1983 actions. A § 1983 action has several advantages:

(1) A court that is hesitant to award compensation on an "inverse condemnation" theory, because of the difficulty of defining the interest "taken" by the government and the difficulty of valuing that interest, may be more willing to award damages measured by "actual loss" on a "constitutional tort" theory.

(2) A court may be willing to award "consequential damages" in a § 1983 action, although such damages are clearly not available in an "inverse condemnation" action based directly on the Fourteenth and Fifth Amendments.

(3) The plaintiff in a § 1983 action can recover attorney's fees by virtue of Civil Rights Attorney's Fees Award Act of 1976, 42 U.S.C. § 1988. The cases have adopted a generous view of the circumstances under which plaintiffs can recover attorney's fees in § 1983 cases. In *Hensley v. Eckerhart*, 461 U.S. 461 (1983), the Court held that plaintiffs can recover attorney's fees as prevailing parties if they "succeed on a significant issue in litigation which achieves some of the benefits" the plaintiffs sought in bringing suit. See also *Maher v. Gagne*, 448 U.S. 112 (1980) (can recover fees even if favorable settlement obtained).

(4) *Cary v. Piphus*, 435 U.S. 247 (1978), established that nominal damages may be awarded under § 1983 for "presumed injury" and that the court may then award punitive damages against municipal officials for serious violations of constitutional rights, even though the plaintiff cannot prove actual damages. This was a procedural due process case in which it was not shown that following due process procedures would have produced a different result. The rule also applies in substantive due process cases. But punitive damages are not available against municipalities. *City of Newport v. Fact Concerts, Inc.*, 458 U.S. 247 (1981).

As noted earlier, the rules for damage awards in § 1983 cases differ from the rules for awarding compensation in temporary takings cases. The Supreme Court in *Cary* held that common law tort damage rules provide a helpful analogy in § 1983 cases, but cautioned that common law principles must be carefully adapted when a constitutional right protected under § 1983 does not have a tort analogy. *Memphis Community School Dist. v. Stachura,* 477 U.S. 299 (1986), added that damages in § 1983 cases are awarded for actual losses caused by a defendant's breach of duty. This rule is the same as the rule in some state courts that awards compensation only for actual losses in temporary takings cases.

NOTES AND QUESTIONS

1. *A damages formula.* Assume your client was denied zoning approval for a residential project. You sued for her in federal court under § 1983 and the court held the zoning denial violated substantive due process and equal protection. What do you think of the following formula for awarding damages?

[(aX + bY) − Y] Rt + ac = damages, where *a* is the probability of approval, *b* is the probability of disapproval, X is the value of the land with approval, Y is the value of the land without approval, (aX + bY) is the weighted probability of approval, R is the rate of interest, *t* is the duration of the delay after denial, and *c* is the increased cost of development resulting from the delay.

Probabilities of approval and disapproval are in the equation because the decision invalidating the denial does just that: it does not guarantee an approval, and it is possible the municipality could deny approval later in a way that would withstand a court challenge. Try this formula out on a number of hypotheticals. For the case approving this formula see *Herrington v. County of Sonoma,* 790 F. Supp. 909 (N.D. Cal. 1991), *aff'd,* 12 F.3d 901 (9th Cir. 1993).

2. For discussion of § 1983 see S. Nahmod, Civil Rights and Civil Liberties Litigation: A Guide to § 1983 (3d ed. 1991); M. Schwartz & J. Kirlin, Section 1983 Litigation: Claims, Defenses and Remedies (2d ed. 1981).

PROBLEM

Your client is a developer who had planned to build a convenience store on a major highway in a developing area of your county. The county ordinance required submission of a site plan, which your client submitted, and which the county council then reviewed under the zoning ordinance. This ordinance contains a number of criteria for site plan approval, all of which require a considerable exercise of judgment by the council. The council, following its rules, did not hold a hearing on the site plan but considered the plan in executive session. Your client was not present. The council denied approval of the plan and notified your client of its decision.

Similar stores are located in this area, and your client claims the council denied the plan because of a dispute he had earlier with one of the council members concerning another development. Your client also claims his project

meets all the criteria of the site plan review ordinance, and that the council
should have given its approval. It is now two years since the council denied
the project, and your client admits the market environment is no longer as
favorable for his project as it was then. Would you advise suing the city under
§ 1983? The city council members? What defenses might the council members
raise?

NUISANCE Common Law / Public at Large / Private one (58) Reciprocity Co existance w/ neig
Bove v Hanna Coke (54) Private Nuisance Rule Use property not to injure that of anot
provided Does not violate ordinance on statue. Boomer v Atlantic Cement (6)
Econ. consequences of stopping Cement plant. Disparity Between Nuisance + t
SPUR v WEBB (64) Private Nuisance Develop encroached on Feed Lot. Webb paid Spur
Problems with Nuisance (27) created need for Zoning to segregate uses
/ Taking inherent power of sovereignty / Power of Eminent Domain / Take private land for public use
States Police process regulation - Police power to protect Public Health, Safety morals or General welfare
Compensation by 5th + 14th amend (73) Taking Substantive issue - what property take low / nominal
invalidate constitutional violation on compensate property owner, MUGLER v KANSAS (74) All property
held under implied obligation that owners use not injurious to community, must be Police power.
Lawton Test for Substantive Due Process 14th / Interest of public requires interference / reasonable
accomplishment of purpose / not oppressive on owner (78) HADACHECK v SEBASTIAN (79) Brick making
yard Forced to close without compensation Private Interest must yield to good of community.
L.A. Ordinance intended to Protect Health and Comfort of Residences, still Had economic use of land
PENN Coal v Mahon (80) Taking Rule Property Regulated to certain extent; to far considered Taking. % of t
Taking can not be greater than the whole, buena e reciprocity of Advantage (82) denomination problem.
Euclid vs Ambler (85) 1st modern zoning challenge; Ambler challenged Police power to zone e
public right to regulate use for Health safety convenience welfare. Penn Central v
Cities may enact land use restrictions to enhance quality of Life / No segmentation view as
whole. Balancing Test Factors / economic impact of regulation; interference with investment backed
expectations; character of Gov Action (103) AGINS v TIBURON (115) 1st apply ripeness Two Part Test (118)
Taking if ordinance does not advance state interest, denies owner economically viable use
of land, Keystone v Debenedictis (119) Used AGINS state interest to protect public whole Parcel e
Loretto v CATV (120) Per Se Taking physical invasion of Property to promote common good;
NOLLAN v Calif (123) EXACTION Provide Easement as condition to build; right to exclude
essential in Bundle of Property rights, Lacked essential nexus (Link) to public good (127) Use
eminent domain / compensate. Heighten Scrutiny. LUCAS v SC (133) Per Se Taking Rule Two Categories
of regulatory Action Physical invasion + denial of all economic Beneficial Productive use (137) SC Beach Front
To mitigate Harm to Public Interest Protect Beach. Total Taking, inquiry (149) degree of Harm to
Public Lands + Resources on Adjacent Private Property / social value and suitability to Location / ease
eliminating Harm. Categorical rule Regulation depriving land of All Beneficial or viable use
Based on extraordinary belief land regulation merely Prohibits all economic use; Confusion
About use and value (147) Restrictions inherent in Title, Law of Property / Law of Nuisance 148
Notice rule to investment Backed Expectations (151) Nuisance Exception to Takings Rule
RIPENESS, At least one application / Final Decision / Apply for variance or admin relief /
Sue in State court if Available. (58) Williamson County v Hamilton Bank (159) Ripeness
Similar to Agins, Penn Central. Facial Claims ripe when Act Passed / As Applied
requires Final Decision out of Fed Court. Because of Ripeness (166) Futility Rule (167)

PENN Central	AGINS	LUCAS (Due Process claim) w	1st English
Ad Hoc Balancing	Disjunctive	Denial of Use	Inverse Condemnation
whole Parcel rule	Two Part Test Test	Per Se Taking	Land condemned +
effect on Property	invalidates regulation	Except if nuisance/	Temporary Taking
Investment Backed	Facial or	Property law use.	regulation (172)
Expectations	Compensate		
Balancing Test		whole Parcel rule (149)	
Nature of Gov't Action	NOLLAN (Due Process)		
Benefits, Burdens Singling	Essential Nexus	PALAZZOLO v RI	
out Property owners to	Taking Property as	NOTICE - can not be thought to stop claim	
Bear Public Burden	Condition of Permit	- applies to Balance Factors	
	right to exclude.	- Investment Backed Expectations	
Facial	Heighten Scrutiny	Due Process can't be used as applied cla	
TDR	As Applied	Need Property right	

ONING STANDING (213)
EXHAUSTION of Romodios (219)
SECURS JUDICIAL REVIEW (225)

ROMODY (228)
INJUNCTIONS
Declaratory Judgment
Mamdamus

Chapter 3

CONTROL OF LAND USE BY ZONING

Property rights — Right to Exclude
Right to Earn Profits

A. THE HISTORY AND STRUCTURE OF THE ZONING SYSTEM

1. SOME HISTORY

The origins of modern zoning.—The most important form of land use control in urban areas has been zoning, defined by Edward M. Bassett, the "father of zoning," as "the division of land into districts having different regulations." E. Bassett, Zoning 9 (1940). Early examples of zoning may be found in Boston and Los Angeles. But New York City was the first American municipality to adopt a comprehensive zoning ordinance of the modern type.* The New York City Building Zone Resolution of 1916, authorized by a 1914 special act of the New York legislature, was based on three years of painstaking research and investigation by a committee of which Bassett was a member.

The Building Zone Resolution of 1916 embodied a complete and comprehensive system of building and land use control for all the five boroughs of New York City. It established three separate classes of districts to regulate, respectively, the use of land and buildings, the height of buildings, and the percentage of a lot that could be occupied by buildings, with a separate set of maps for each class. There were three "use" districts: residential, business, and unrestricted. In the residence districts, business and industry of all types were prohibited. In business districts, specified businesses and industries — mainly nuisance-creating manufacturing businesses such as boiler making, ammonia manufacturing, and paint manufacturing — were prohibited, and all other uses were permitted. In unrestricted districts, all kinds of residential, business, and industrial uses were permitted.

The New York City Building Zone Resolution of 1916 did not apply retroactively to existing, lawfully established uses of land or buildings. As one early commentator stated, "[i]t did not attempt to cure past and existing evils by ordering the demolition of particular types of buildings or removal of certain types of businesses to other areas. But it did prescribe a rational plan for future building in the city." J. McGoldrick, S. Graubard & R. Horowitz, Building Regulation in New York City 93 (1944). (For a more detailed

---

* The Massachusetts legislature enacted height regulations for the entire city of Boston in 1904-05. These restrictions embodied the "zoning" principle, since there were different maximum heights in different districts. The Boston height restrictions were sustained against constitutional attack in *Welch v. Swasey,* 214 U.S. 91 (1909). In 1909, Los Angeles adopted an ordinance dividing the city into industrial and residential districts. The exclusion of laundries from a residential district was upheld by the California court in *Ex parte Quong Wo,* 118 P. 714 (Cal. 1911). In 1910, Los Angeles adopted an ordinance excluding brick factories from one or two of the industrial districts. The 1910 ordinance was sustained against constitutional attack in *Hadacheck v. Sebastian, supra.*

Nollan - Houghton Scrutiny (126)

TAKINGS — Due Process — Equall Protection
ARE IDENTICAL

LUCAS — No fed Property Law
STATES Defins Property

discussion of the background and drafting of the New York City Building Zone Resolution of 1916, see S. Toll, Zoned America 78–187 (1969)).

Zoning in the Supreme Court.—Zoning spread rapidly after the New York City Building Zone Resolution was sustained against constitutional attack by the New York court in 1920, *Lincoln Trust Co. v. Williams Bldg. Corp.,* 128 N.E. 209 (N.Y. 1920). In 1922, it was reported that some twenty state zoning enabling acts and fifty municipal zoning ordinances were in force or in process of formulation. Some municipalities proceeded to adopt zoning ordinances without waiting for enactment of enabling legislation, but it was generally believed, and occasionally held, that the broad grant of police power by state legislatures to local units of government, even under home rule constitutional provisions, was insufficient to empower local governments to regulate land use by means of zoning. Hence, in the states where interest in zoning was greatest, new enabling legislation was generally enacted.

By 1926, all but five of the then forty-eight states had adopted zoning enabling acts; some 420 municipalities with a total population of more than 27,000,000 had adopted zoning ordinances; and hundreds of other municipalities were engaged in preparing zoning ordinances. But judicial acceptance of zoning was far from unanimous in 1926. Decisions favorable to the constitutionality of zoning had been rendered by the highest courts of California, Illinois, Kansas, Louisiana, Massachusetts, Minnesota, New York, Ohio, Oregon, and Wisconsin. Adverse decisions had been rendered by the highest courts of Delaware, Georgia, Maryland, Missouri, and New Jersey. Thus the future of the zoning technique as a means of governmental control of private land use was not assured until the Supreme Court, in *Village of Euclid v. Ambler Realty Co.,* reprinted *supra* as a principal case, held that the new zoning technique, in its general aspects, does not violate the Fourteenth Amendment's due process clause. Although state courts were still free, after *Euclid*, to find that zoning violated *state* constitutional provisions, judicial attention shifted from the concept of zoning to the details of its implementation.

The Nectow Decision.—In disposing of the facial attack against zoning, the *Euclid* court included the following caveat:

> It is true that when, if ever, the provisions set forth in the ordinance in tedious and minute detail, come to be concretely applied to particular premises, including those of the appellee, or to particular conditions, or to be considered in connection with specific complaints, some of them, or even many of them, may be found to be clearly arbitrary and unreasonable. [272 U.S. at 395.]

In *Nectow v. City of Cambridge,* 277 U.S. 183 (1928), the Court had before it a comprehensive zoning ordinance that, in its general scope, was conceded to be constitutional under the decision in *Euclid v. Ambler Realty Co.* Plaintiff landowner attacked the ordinance, however, on the ground that, as specifically applied to him, it deprived him of his property without due process of law in contravention of the Fourteenth Amendment. The Supreme Court held the residential-use classification of plaintiff's property to be invalid. In his opinion for the court, Justice Sutherland stated:

Here, the express finding of the master, already quoted, confirmed by the court below, is that the health, safety, convenience and general welfare of the inhabitants of the part of the city affected will not be promoted by the disposition made by the ordinance of the locus in question. This finding of the master, after a hearing and an inspection of the entire area affected, supported, as we think it is, by other findings of fact, is determinative of the case. That the invasion of the property of plaintiff in error was serious and highly injurious is clearly established; and, since a necessary basis for the support of that invasion is wanting, the action of the zoning authorities comes within the ban of the Fourteenth Amendment and cannot be sustained. [277 U.S. at 188–89.]

Although the record in the *Nectow* case "made it pretty clear that because of the industrial and railroad purposes to which the immediately adjoining lands to the south and east have been devoted and for which they are zoned, the locus is of comparatively little value for the limited uses permitted by the ordinance," the Court did not hold that the zoning ordinance, as applied to the locus, amounted to a de facto taking. *Id.* at 187.

The shift to state law.—In *Nectow* the United States Supreme Court seemed to have embarked on a course foreshadowed by its *Euclid* caveat: close supervision of the exercise of the zoning power "concretely applied to particular premises." However, after 1928, the Supreme Court consistently refused to review any cases raising legal issues in the planning and zoning field until it decided *Goldblatt v. Town of Hempstead,* 369 U.S. 590 (1962), where the Court sustained what was essentially a zoning ordinance enacted under the town's general police power, prohibiting the mining of sand and gravel to a depth below the water table and requiring the backfilling of any existing excavation below that level.

Having established the basic constitutionality of zoning, the Supreme Court left to the state courts the task of applying the constitutional test of reasonableness and/or the constitutional "taking" test to individual cases in which the exercise of the zoning power was challenged, "as concretely applied to particular premises," for almost four decades. Thus, the "American law of zoning" was largely (though not entirely) developed by the decisions of the state courts, with decided differences in legal doctrine and judicial approach in different jurisdictions.

The Supreme Court reentered the land use field with a 1974 decision on family zoning, its 1987 trilogy of taking decisions, and it has continued to decide cases with land use issues, including free speech decisions on sign ordinances and "adult" uses. The resulting interplay between state and Supreme Court zoning law is very important. Since the federal constitution is directly enforceable in state courts, however, they must of course apply federal law in areas such as takings and free speech.

State appellate court jurisdiction.—In states in which there is an intermediate appellate court, and in which appeals to the highest appellate court as a matter of right are limited to cases involving, e.g., constitutional claims, zoning appeals may be restricted. Noting the "familiar due process and equal protection" arguments, one court reasoned this way:

While [the] statutory prerequisites [claimed to be violated] have loose constitutional connotations, the fundamental question here resolves itself into a matter of application of statutory standards to a particular factual situation under long established principles. At this relatively advanced stage of the law of land use regulation, it will be the rare case concerned with the validity of use classification which will present an issue of sufficient constitutional involvement for purposes of [an appeal as of right]. . . . [*Tidewater Oil Co. v. Mayor & Council*, 209 A.2d 105, 108 (N.J. 1965).]

New York, Pennsylvania, Illinois and California have similar procedures. As a result, conflicts in decisions are possible in states where intermediate appellate courts are designated for geographic regions. Of course, the high court has the discretionary power to take these cases to resolve conflicting decisions when a recurring fact pattern appears. Recall also the federal Court of Appeals distaste for reviewing "ordinary" zoning cases in *Cloutier v. Town of Epping, supra* ch. 2.

2. ZONING ENABLING LEGISLATION

At the present time, all of the fifty states have zoning enabling legislation for municipalities, and many states also have zoning enabling legislation for counties. Most of the zoning enabling legislation originally adopted prior to 1924 was based on the New York general city enabling act of 1917. Most of the zoning enabling acts adopted after 1924, however, were modeled on the Standard State Zoning Enabling Act, which was prepared under the aegis of the United States Department of Commerce and first published in mimeographed form in 1923. The Standard Act, revised and printed for the first time in 1924, and reprinted in 1926, was itself based on the New York general city enabling act, but departed substantially in some respects from the New York model. Although many current zoning enabling acts embody even more substantial changes from the Standard Act, most state legislation still retains the substance of the Standard Act.

We reprint here the most important sections from the Standard State Zoning Enabling Act:

A STANDARD STATE ZONING ENABLING ACT [*]

Section 1. *Grant of Power.* For the purpose of promoting health, safety, morals, or the general welfare of the community, the legislative body of cities and incorporated villages is hereby empowered to regulate and restrict the height, number of stories, and size of buildings and other structures, the percentage of lot that may be occupied, the size of yards, courts, and other open spaces, the density of population, and the location and use of buildings, structures, and land for trade, industry, residence, or other purposes.

---

[*] The drafter's footnotes have been omitted. The Standard State Zoning Enabling Act is no longer in print in its original form as a publication of the U.S. Department of Commerce, but it is reprinted in full, with the drafter's footnotes as appendix A, in American Law Institute, A Model Land Development Code, Tentative Draft No. 1, at p. 210 (1968).

Sec. 2. *Districts.* For any or all of said purposes the local legislative body may divide the municipality into districts of such number, shape, and area as may be deemed best suited to carry out the purposes of this act; and within such districts it may regulate and restrict the erection, construction, reconstruction, alteration, repair, or use of buildings, structures, or land. All such regulations shall be uniform for each class or kind of building throughout each district, but the regulations in one district may differ from those in other districts.

Sec. 3. *Purposes in View.* Such regulations shall be made in accordance with a comprehensive plan and designed to lessen congestion in the streets; to secure safety from fire, panic, and other dangers; to promote health and the general welfare; to provide adequate light and air; to prevent the overcrowding of land; to avoid undue concentration of population; to facilitate the adequate provision of transportation, water, sewerage, schools, parks, and other public requirements. Such regulations shall be made with reasonable consideration, among other things, to the character of the district and its peculiar suitability for particular uses, and with a view to conserving the value of buildings and encouraging the most appropriate use of land throughout such municipality.

[Sections 4 and 5 dealt with procedures for adopting and changing a zoning ordinance. A "change" is now called an amendment. No standards are provided for amendments. Three-fourths of the members of the legislative body must vote for an amendment if 20% of the owners of the lots included in an amendment or 20% of the owners of adjacent lots protest. Section 6 provided for the establishment of a Zoning Commission, an anachronism that today is almost always replaced by a Planning Commission or Planning Board.—Eds.]

Sec. 7. *Board of Adjustment.* Such local legislative body may provide for the appointment of a board of adjustment, and in the regulations and restrictions adopted pursuant to the authority of this act may provide that the said board of adjustment may, in appropriate cases and subject to appropriate conditions and safeguards, make special exceptions to the terms of the ordinance in harmony with its general purpose and intent and in accordance with general or specific rules therein contained. [Procedures are specified.—Eds.]

The board of adjustment shall have the following powers:

1. To hear and decide appeals where it is alleged there is error in any order, requirement, decision, or determination made by an administrative official in the enforcement of this act or of any ordinance adopted pursuant thereto.

2. To hear and decide special exceptions to the terms of the ordinance upon which such board is required to pass under such ordinance.

3. To authorize upon appeal in specific cases such variance from the terms of the ordinance as will not be contrary to the public interest, where, owing to special conditions, a literal enforcement of the provisions of the ordinance will result in unnecessary hardship, and so that the spirit of the ordinance shall be observed and substantial justice done.

[The remainder of Section 7 specified voting procedures and a method of appeal, Section 8 provided for enforcement and remedies, and Section 9 provided for conflicts between this and other regulations. The statutory provisions for the judicial review of board decisions are reproduced *infra*, in Section B.3.—Eds.]

NOTES AND QUESTIONS

1. *Zoning powers.* Read the first two sections of the act carefully. What is the "zoning" power that these sections confer? What is the power to adopt "districts"? Do you read § 1 of the Standard Act as requiring the local legislative body to divide the municipality into two or more districts? Would a "bedroom suburb" be required to zone at least some land for non-residential uses? See *Village of Belle Terre v. Boraas, infra.*

2. *The comprehensive plan.* What is the "comprehensive plan" mentioned in § 3 of the Standard State Zoning Enabling Act (hereafter SSZEA)? Can "comprehensive plan" be deemed to refer to the "master plan" authorized by § 6 of the Standard City Planning Enabling Act reproduced in Ch. 1, *supra*? If not, what does the term "comprehensive plan" mean? Must it be a document prepared by the municipal planning commission and adopted by the planning commission and/or the local governing body? See Ch. 5, sec. G, *infra*.

3. *Amendments and administrative relief.* Sections 5 and 7 contain the provisions for amendments and administrative relief. What do these sections indicate about these methods for change and the regulations contained in zoning district regulations. Section 7, including the parts omitted, is longer than all the rest of the SSZEA put together. Do the drafters imply that "special exceptions" and "variances" are where the real work of zoning is done? Read on.

A NOTE ON CONTEMPORARY ZONING ENABLING LEGISLATION

Until about thirty years ago, most of the state zoning enabling acts still contained essentially the provisions of the SSZEA or the earlier New York zoning enabling legislation on which the SSZEA was based. During the last three decades, however, the zoning enabling acts of many states have been substantially changed by legislative amendment. Here are excerpts from the recent zoning act revisions in Rhode Island:

> § 45-24-30 **General purposes of zoning ordinances.** Zoning regulations shall be developed and maintained in accordance with a comprehensive plan . . . [and] shall be designed to address the following purposes: [There are 16 purposes. Here are some of the more important ones:] (2) Providing for a range of uses and intensities of use appropriate to the character of the city or town and reflecting current and expected future needs. (3) Providing for orderly growth and development . . .

> § 45-24-33 **Standard provisions.** (a) A zoning ordinance addresses each of the purposes stated in § 45-24-30 and addresses the following general provisions . . . [There are 23 provisions. Here are some of the most important:]

(1) Permitting, prohibiting, limiting, and restricting the development of land and structures in zoning districts, and regulating those land and structures according to their type, and the nature and extent of their use;

(2) Regulating the nature and extent of the use of land for residential, commercial, industrial, institutional, recreational, agricultural, open space, or other use or combination of uses, as the need for land for those purposes is determined by the city or town's comprehensive plan;

(3) Permitting, prohibiting, limiting, and restricting buildings, structures, land uses, and other development by performance standards, or other requirements, related to air and water and groundwater quality, noise and glare, energy consumption, soil erosion and sedimentation, and/or the availability and capacity of existing and planned public or private services;

(4) Regulating within each district and designating requirements for:

(i) The height, number of stories, and size of buildings;

(ii) The dimensions, size, lot coverage, floor area ratios, and layout of lots or development areas;

(iii) The density and intensity of use;

(iv) Access to air and light, views, and solar access;

(v) Open space, yards, courts, and buffers;

(vi) Parking areas, road design, and, where appropriate, pedestrian, bicycle, and other circulator systems;

(vii) Landscaping, fencing, and lighting;

(viii) Appropriate drainage requirements and methods to manage stormwater runoff;

(ix) Public access to waterbodies, rivers, and streams; and

(x) Other requirements in connection with any use of land or structure; . . .

(8) Providing for adequate, safe, and efficient transportation systems; and avoiding congestion by relating types and levels of development to the capacity of the circulation system, and maintaining a safe level of service of the system; . . . [This provision authorizes adequate public facilities ordinances, which are discussed in Chapter 7.]

(19) Providing standards and requirements for the regulation, review, and approval of any proposed development in connection with those uses of land, buildings, or structures specifically designated as subject to development plan review in a zoning ordinance; . . . [This provision authorizes site plan review, which is discussed in Chapter 5.]

[Provisions are also required for regulating development in floodplains, hazardous and historic areas; promoting energy conservation; protecting drinking water; and the application of state and federal fair housing acts. The statute also authorizes "special provisions," including incentive zoning provisions, which are discussed in this chapter, *infra*.]

NOTES AND QUESTIONS

The Rhode Island statute authorizes many land use control techniques that were unknown when the SSZEA was promulgated in 1923. Look back at the SSZEA and identify the differences. Does the Standard Act authorize by implication the measures that are explicitly authorized in the Rhode Island legislation? As discussed in chapter 1, a very important provision in this modern statute is that the zoning ordinance must be consistent with an *adopted* comprehensive plan. This is a departure from the much more permissive way the Standard Act's "in accordance with a comprehensive plan" language had generally been interpreted. Most states still do not specifically require consistency with the plan in their zoning legislation because most are still based on the Standard Act. This requirement will be considered in some detail later in this casebook.

3. THE ZONING ORDINANCE

All states delegate to local governments the power to enact and enforce zoning regulations. These regulations are almost invariably embodied in a zoning ordinance. Local zoning ordinances of the type adopted in New York City in 1916, with different classes of regulations for "use," "height," and "land coverage," are no longer common. There are, of course, vast differences between the zoning ordinances adopted in different municipalities and counties. The zoning ordinance that follows includes examples of regulations contained in most zoning ordinances, although it is a very simple ordinance intended for a small and essentially residential community. A zoning ordinance for a large city would invariably be much longer and more complex. Even so, some details are omitted or summarized. Is there a rationale for allowing local governments to make the major zoning decisions? Should a market-oriented policymaker prefer state or local decision making on land use issues? Does it matter what kind of land use issue is involved? Problems of this type are pursued in Ch. 4 with respect to exclusionary zoning.

A TYPICAL ZONING ORDINANCE

Article I. Purposes

[Zoning ordinances often include a statement of purpose, which helps ensure favorable judicial interpretation by stating the zoning policy of the community, although many ordinances for small communities squander this opportunity by merely repeating as "boilerplate" the "purpose" language from the state enabling act.]

Article II. Definitions

Building. A structure having a roof supported by columns or walls for the shelter, support or enclosure of persons or property.

Dwelling. A house or other building designed for occupancy by one family.

Family. An individual, or two or more persons related by blood, marriage, or adoption, or a group of not more than 6 unrelated persons living together as a single housekeeping unit in a dwelling. [Do you see any constitutional problems with this definition?—Eds.]

Home Occupation. An accessory occupational use conducted entirely within a dwelling which is clearly incidental to the use of the dwelling for residential purposes and does not change the residential character of the use.

Lot. A piece or parcel of land in one undivided ownership.

Nonconforming Use. A lawful use of any building, lot or sign that does not conform with the currently applicable regulations of this ordinance but which complied with these regulations at the time the use was established.

Parking Space. An area on the same lot as the principal use which is used or intended for use for parking a motor vehicle and which has permanent access to and from a public street or alley.

Sign. Any device or free-standing structure used for purposes of advertising or display. [Refer back to this definition when you consider sign regulation later in the casebook.]

Yard. A space on the same lot with a principal building which is open, unoccupied and unobstructed by buildings or structures from 30 inches above the ground level upwards.

[Are there too many definitions? Too few? What other words might be defined? — Eds.]

Article III. Establishment of Districts

Section 1. Types of Districts.

The Village of _____ is divided into the following three districts:

   A.   A Residential District

   B.   A Multi-Family District

   C.   A Neighborhood Retail District

[Sections 2 and 3 require a zoning map and state rules for determining district boundaries at street and lot lines.]

Article IV. District Regulations

Section 1. Application of Regulations.

A. No building, structure, or land shall hereafter be used or occupied, and no building or structure or part thereof shall hereafter be erected, constructed, moved, or altered unless in compliance with all of the regulations applicable to the district in which it is located. All other uses, buildings, and structures are prohibited.

B. No building or other structure shall hereafter be erected or altered:

1. to exceed the height; or

2. to accommodate or house a greater number of families; or

3. to occupy a greater percentage of lot area; or

4. to have narrower or smaller rear yards, front yards or side yards than required by the provisions of this ordinance.

Section 2. Residential District. [This is a typical text that would be used for the SR-3 district in the zoning format reproduced *infra,* or for the SR district on the zoning map, also reproduced *infra.*]

A. *Principal Uses.*

1. Single-family dwelling.

2. Parks, playgrounds and parking areas, if publicly owned.

B. *The Following Accessory Uses,* if located in the same lot with the permitted principal use.

1. Private garage with capacity for not more than two (2) motor vehicles.

2. Home occupations.

3. Other customary accessory uses and buildings incidental to the principal use.

C. *Advertising Signs.* One sign advertising the sale or rent of the land or buildings upon which it is located not to exceed three (3) square feet in area. [Is this provision constitutional?]

D. *Conditional Uses,* if authorized by a conditional use permit as provided in Section 6, Article IV.

1. Churches, synagogues or similar places of worship; rectories and parish houses.

2. Community meeting halls and lodges and private clubs not conducted primarily for profit.

3. Nurseries and day care centers for pre-school children, if not conducted in a dwelling.

E. *Lot Area and Width.* Lots must be not less than 6000 square feet in area and not less than 75 feet in width.

F. *Percentage of Lot Coverage.* All buildings including accessory buildings, porches, breezeways and roof projections shall cover not more than 30 per cent of the area of the lot.

G. *Building Height.*

1. Two and one-half stories, but not exceeding 35 feet, for single-family dwellings.

2. The maximum height for accessory buildings is 18 feet.

H. *Minimum Ground Floor Area Per Dwelling.*

1. One-story dwellings: 1200 square feet.

2. Dwellings having more than one story: 700 square feet on each story.

I. *Yards for Single-Family Dwellings.*

1. Front yard depth: 35 feet.

2. Side yard width: 5 feet.

Section 3. Multi-Family District.

[If a separate district for apartment development is provided, the regulations may look very much like the regulations for the single-family residential district except that the numbers may be changed. Just how they will be changed is another matter. The zoning format, reproduced *infra,* provides some examples. The minimum lot area required for the apartment site may be increased, while an area requirement for each dwelling unit in the apartment complex may be added but will probably be less than the area requirement for dwelling units in the single-family districts. Side and other perimeter requirements for apartment developments may be increased.

[This approach is the conventional treatment. It implies a separation of single-family and apartment developments into separate "use" districts. We cannot explore all of the complexities here, but several problems come to mind. Why treat apartments and single-family dwellings as separate uses? Since, as we have suggested (see Note 7 following *Euclid* in Ch. 2), the real problem is density and site control, why not write the ordinance in these terms? Is the zoning envelope treatment for single-family dwellings, which contemplates one dwelling unit for each lot, really adaptable to apartment developments? — Eds.]

Section 4. Neighborhood Commercial District. [This is a typical text that would be used for the NC district in the zoning format reproduced *infra,* or for the NC district on the zoning map, also reproduced *infra.*]

A. *Principal Uses.*

1. Retail stores, including but not limited to bakeries, florists, gift shops, stationery stores, and liquor stores.

2. Restaurants, other than drive-in establishments. [Is this a legally acceptable distinction?]

3. Offices for individual businesses and services, including but not limited to attorneys, dentists, barbers and beauticians, travel and insurance agencies, and real estate and investment brokers.

B. *Accessory Uses.* Uses and structures customarily incidental and accessory to principal uses and structures.

C. *Conditional Uses,* if authorized by a conditional use permit as provided in Section 6, Article IV.

1. Gasoline filling stations.

2. Car wash facilities.

3. Convenience grocery stores if less than 5000 square feet in area. [Is this conditional use permissible? This question is considered in Chapter 5.]

D. *Advertising Signs.*

1. One non-illuminated wall sign, not to exceed one square foot of sign area for each lineal front foot of building frontage, but not in excess of 100 square feet in sign area. [Is this good aesthetic control?]

2. One non-illuminated ground sign, not to exceed 12 square feet in sign area, and to be set back a minimum of 50 feet from the property line.

[The ordinance also requires a minimum lot area of 5000 square feet and a minimum lot width of 50 feet, but does not contain setback requirements except for a minimum setback of ten feet adjacent to any street.]

Section 5. Off-street Parking.

A. *Requirements.*

1. Dwelling (Residential). A minimum of one parking space for each dwelling.

2. Multi-family residential. A minimum of two parking spaces for each dwelling unit, except that for age-restricted developments (minimum age 65) a minimum of one parking space for each dwelling unit.

2. Restaurant. A minimum of one parking space for each five seats in accordance with designed capacity.

3. Retail stores. At least one parking space for each sixty square feet of floor area.

B. *Parking Space Standards.*

1. Parking spaces must be surfaced with an all-weather, dustfree material and located on the same lot with the building or in a dedicated but unaccepted roadway.

2. An off-street parking space must include an area of not less than nine by twenty square feet.

C. *Prohibited Parking.* A parking space may not be provided or maintained for a mobile home. [Why not?]

Section 6. Conditional Use Permits.

A. *Procedure.*

1. An applicant for a conditional use permit shall submit a plan to the Plan Commission which shall indicate the location of all buildings, parking areas, traffic access and circulation drives, open spaces, landscaping, and storm and sewage drainage facilities.

2. The Plan Commission shall give notice of a public hearing to be held on an application for a conditional use permit within 60 days after its receipt.

3. Within 30 days after the public hearing, the Plan Commission may grant or deny the conditional use permit and shall state reasons for its decision. In granting the conditional permit, the Plan Commission may permit the use subject to such reasonable conditions as it may impose. These conditions may contain such requirements for improving, maintaining, operating, and screening the conditional use as will protect the character of the surrounding property.

B. *Standards Applicable to Conditional Uses.* The Plan Commission shall apply the following standards when it decides whether to grant or deny a conditional use:

1. Compatibility with existing or permitted adjacent uses.

2. The effect of the conditional use on vehicular and pedestrian traffic in the vicinity.

3. The adequacy of adjacent sewer, water and other community facilities to serve the conditional use.

4. The adequacy and convenience of off-street parking and loading facilities.

[Do you see a difference between the fourth standard and the other three? What do you suppose is the justification for regulating the external impacts of a conditional use? Internal design?]

Section 7. Nonconforming Uses.

A. A nonconforming use may not be changed except to a use permitted in the district in which it is located. A nonconforming use may be repaired or maintained in an amount not exceeding twenty percent of the value of the nonconforming use.

B. If a nonconforming use is destroyed in an amount in excess of fifty percent of its value at the time of destruction it may not be reconstructed except in compliance with the provisions of this ordinance.

C. If a nonconforming use is discontinued for six consecutive months it may not be resumed except in compliance with the provisions of this ordinance.

D. A nonconforming use must be discontinued within five years of the date on which it became a nonconforming use.

[What is the effect of these provisions on nonconforming uses? Do you see any problems with Paragraph D? As applied to a sign? As applied to a nonconforming grocery store in a residential district?]

Article V. Administration and Enforcement

Section 1. Administration.

A. *Zoning Commissioner.* The Village Council shall appoint a Zoning Commissioner, who shall enforce this ordinance.

B. *Improvement Location Permit.* No person shall erect or structurally alter a building unless the Zoning Commissioner has issued an Improvement Location Permit which states that the building and its proposed use complies with the provisions of this ordinance.

C. *Certificate of Occupancy.* No person shall use or occupy any land or building until the Zoning Commissioner has issued a Certificate of Occupancy which states that the use or occupancy complies with the provisions of this ordinance. [The permit and certificate provide a method of enforcing compliance with the ordinance.]

D. *Forms.* [Omitted.]

Section 2. Board of Zoning Appeals.

A. *Creation.* A Board of Zoning Appeals is hereby established, which shall consist of five (5) members to be appointed by the Village Council as prescribed by statute.

B. *Procedure.* Reference is hereby made to the applicable sections of the Zoning Act for the provisions governing procedures before the Board of Zoning Appeals. The Board shall adopt any additional rules necessary to the conduct of its affairs.

C. *Interpretation.* On an appeal by the Zoning Commissioner, the Plan Commission, the Village Council, or any other person aggrieved, the Board of Zoning Appeals shall decide any question involving the interpretation or administration of this ordinance.

D. *Variances.* The Board of Zoning Appeals may vary or adapt any provisions of this ordinance. The Board shall not grant a variance to allow a use not permitted by the terms of this ordinance. The Board shall not grant a variance unless it makes positive findings of fact on all of the following:

1. That the lot is exceptionally irregular, narrow, shallow, or steep, or that the land, or building, or structure is subject to other exceptional physical conditions peculiar to it;

2. That the application of the provisions of this ordinance to the land, building, or structure would result in practical difficulty or unnecessary hardship that would deprive the owner of the reasonable use of the land, building, or structure;

3. That the granting of the variance will be in harmony with the general purposes and intent of this ordinance, and will not be injurious to the neighborhood or otherwise detrimental to the public welfare.

E. *Conditions.* When allowing any appeal, or when granting any variance, the Board of Zoning Appeals may prescribe any conditions that it considers necessary or desirable.

[Is the prohibition of "a variance to allow a use not permitted by the terms of this ordinance" consistent with the provision as to variances in § 7 of the Standard Zoning Act? If not, can the village adopt it in a state using SSZEA?]

Section 3. Enforcement. [Omitted.]

NOTES AND QUESTIONS

1. The zoning ordinance contains a limited number of districts because it was drafted for a small residential community. Most communities have substantially more districts, and divide the basic triad of residential, commercial and industrial uses between a number of subdistricts. The following zoning format illustrates a typical schedule of zoning districts:

A Standard Zoning Format

SR-1, Single-Family Large Lot	One-Acre Lots
SR-2, Single-Family Medium	Half-Acre Lots
SR-3, Single-Family Standard	6,000 Sq. Ft. Lot Minimum

MR-1, Multifamily Low Density	18–26 Units/Acre
MR-2, Multifamily Medium Density	24-29 Units/Acre
MR-3, Multifamily High Density	37–44 Units/Acre
GO, General Office	Offices and Limited Uses Serving Community and City-Wide Needs
NC, Neighborhood Commercial	Neighborhood Retail and Office Facilities
GC, General Community Commercial	Shopping Centers Providing Sub-Regional and Regional Retail and Office Facilities
SC, Service Commercial	Commercial Service Facilities in Central Business Area CBD, Central Business District Office and Commercial Facilities in Central Business Area
LM, Limited Industrial	Light Manufacturing
HM, Heavy Industrial	Heavy Manufacturing
PA, Public Activity	Public Facilities such as Schools, Hospitals and Cemeteries

[Adapted from D. Mandelker, Land Use Law 145 (4th ed. 1997).]

2. The map that follows is a part of a zoning map from a small suburban community in the St. Louis, Missouri, metropolitan area, and accompanies a zoning ordinance which employs a simplified adaptation of the zoning format reproduced above. The SR (Single-Family Residential) District on the map is the equivalent of the SR-3 District in the zoning format. The MR (Multifamily Residential), NC (Neighborhood Commercial) and GC (General Community Commercial) Districts on the zoning map are the equivalent of the MR-3, NC and GC Districts in the zoning format. What does this tell you about the character of this community?

Note the large number of zoning districts in a relatively small geographic area. There usually are two reasons for this. First, most zoning plans, most of the time, try to follow established existing uses, unless a conscious planning decision has been made to encourage a use change in the district. Second, the Standard Zoning Act requires that uses be uniform within districts. This makes it difficult to adopt a single district for an area where land uses are mixed, such as in the example. Even before you begin reading the cases in this chapter, consider what legal problems this map might present. Does this approach to land use control complicate zoning administration? Is it consistent with the "market failure" theory of land use controls to use the zoning map to "freeze" privately determined land uses?

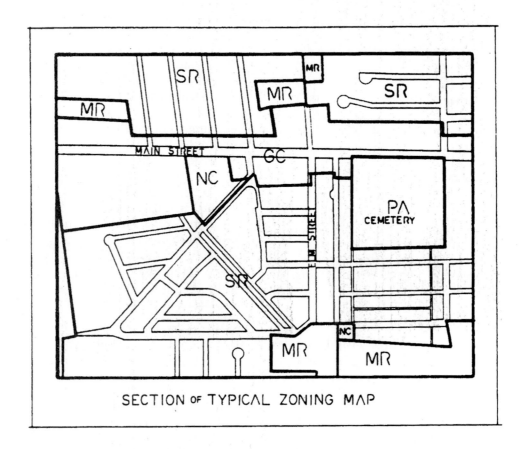

SECTION OF TYPICAL ZONING MAP

PROBLEM

It will help in understanding how the zoning ordinance works to imagine a case in which your client wants a zoning change on a lot in the area covered by this map. Assume she owns a vacant 6000-square-foot lot in the Multifamily Residential (MR) District on the west side of Elm Street north of Main Street. The lot is adjacent to the General Commercial (GC) District. Your client would like to use this lot for a use permitted in the GC District. This type of zoning change is known as an upzoning. One way of making this change is for the municipality to amend the zoning map to move your client's lot from the MR to the GC district. We will consider zoning map amendments in Chapter 5.

Assume, however, that your client applied for a zoning map amendment but the municipality refused to make it. One option at this point is to sue the municipality. It is unlikely your client can claim a taking of her property because she can still use it for a multi-family use. However, she can claim that the existing zoning is arbitrary. Consider how your client can get this case into court, how she can show that the existing zoning is arbitrary, and what remedy she can get if she wins her case. These issues are all considered later in this chapter.

B. HOW A ZONING CASE GETS TO STATE COURT

Most zoning litigation is brought in state courts, and the way in which courts structure zoning litigation has a critical influence on zoning law. Not just anyone can sue in a zoning case, for example. The special rules applicable to standing to sue determine the kinds of zoning cases courts are willing to decide. Exhaustion of remedies is another doctrine that affects zoning litigation. Zoning ordinances provide a number of opportunities for administrative and legislative decision making on land use proposals. The courts hold that litigants must exhaust these remedies before bringing suit.

Neither may a zoning litigant invoke the jurisdiction of a court simply by drafting a complaint and asking a court to consider his case. Local governments and the local government agencies that administer zoning ordinances may be sued only if a litigant is entitled to bring one of the special causes of action that all litigants must rely on when they sue local governments and their agencies, unless a statutory appeal is available. This problem is not usually serious because of the widespread availability of the injunction to litigate zoning claims, but some problems do arise. One problem is that the discretionary nature of local zoning administration limits the courts in their ability to provide judicial relief that will allow the plaintiff to proceed with his land use project.

This section discusses standing, exhaustion of remedies and judicial relief questions. They determine the way in which a zoning case gets to court and the extent to which a court can provide effective remedial relief.

PROBLEM

The Willow Hill Neighborhood Association, a group representing a subdivision of attractive single-family homes, is upset by a decision of the city council rezoning land on one edge and across the street from the subdivision for a multifamily residential development. The land previously was zoned for single-family development on three-acre lots. The homes in the Willow Creek subdivision are on half-acre lots. They wish to bring a lawsuit claiming the rezoning is invalid. Can they bring suit? What kind of action should they bring? If they win, what kind of relief can they get from the court? Will it solve all their problems with this tract of land? Does the size of the Willow Hill subdivision and the new multifamily development make a difference?

1. STANDING

Landowners normally have standing to challenge the zoning of their own property, but standing can be a serious problem when a third party brings suit, either to challenge a zoning approval or an exclusionary zoning ordinance. Third-party standing in exclusionary zoning cases is discussed in ch. 4, *infra*. This section discusses the third-party-standing problems that arise when a third party challenges a zoning approval, such as a rezoning, in a state court.

Third-party standing is critical when a local government agency approves a land use project proposed by the owner. If third-party litigation is not allowed, the zoning approval cannot be challenged. Third-party standing law in state courts differs from third-party-standing law in federal courts. Standing in federal courts is governed by the "case and controversy" requirement of the federal constitution and by "prudential" standing rules adopted by the Supreme Court that also limit standing to sue. State constitutions do not usually have "case and controversy" limitations on state-court jurisdiction. State courts do limit standing to sue by limiting their jurisdiction to justiciable controversies.

Third-party standing in state zoning cases is limited by the rule usually applied that the plaintiff must show some "special" damage flowing from the zoning approval that is different from the damage suffered by the general public. *Palmer v. St. Louis County,* 591 S.W.2d 39 (Mo. App. 1980). A concrete and "special" injury assures the court that the controversy is justiciable. The rule may also stem from the nuisance basis of zoning law, which bases the constitutionality of zoning on the role of the zoning ordinance in separating incompatible uses to prevent injury to adjacent property. How the adjacency and "special" injury rules affect third-party standing is indicated by the following case, which adopts an unusually strict rule.

222 EAST CHESTNUT STREET CORP. v. BOARD OF APPEALS

14 Ill. 2d 190, 152 N.E.2d 465 (1956)

DAILY, JUSTICE:

Based upon a finding of necessity for the public convenience, the Chicago zoning board of appeals granted an application of 199 Lake Shore Drive, Inc., for a special use of certain real property as a parking lot for private passenger automobiles. The property, a vacant lot at the northeast corner of Chestnut Street and DeWitt Place, is situated in an area zoned as an apartment house district, a classification which does not permit use as a parking lot. The 222 East Chestnut Street Corporation, owner of a 19-story apartment building on an adjoining lot, was an objector to the application and thereafter filed a complaint for administrative review in the circuit court of Cook County, wherein it prayed for a reversal of the board's decision. The court, however, affirmed such decision and plaintiff has prosecuted a direct appeal to this court on the ground that the validity of a statute is involved.

Under the circumstances of the case our first consideration must be given to the question of whether the plaintiff may maintain an action under the Administrative Review Act. The law is well settled that the right to review a final administrative decision is limited to those parties to the proceeding before the administrative agency whose rights, privileges or duties are affected by the decision. In recently applying this principle in zoning litigation to which the present plaintiff was also a party, we held it is incumbent upon the party seeking review to both allege and prove that the board's decision would in fact adversely affect such party. This is in accord with the majority view which holds that the right to maintain a suit in such cases depends upon whether the zoning inflicts a special or peculiar injury upon the party bringing the suit.

The complaint for administrative review clearly alleges that the effect of the board's decision will be to cause injury, damage and depreciation in value to the plaintiff's property, thus the problem of its right to maintain the action resolves itself into a question of whether such allegations find support in the proof.

With regard to physical facts the proof reveals that it is the east side of plaintiff's building which adjoins the proposed parking lot. On this side is a tier of eighteen apartments, each having six rooms, and in each apartment the windows in the kitchen, pantry, dining room, bath room and two bedrooms overlook the lot in controversy. The latter property is a rectangle, 110 x 135 feet, and the owner proposed to surface it with blacktop, to outline stalls for 51 vehicles, to rent such stalls to apartment dwellers in the area, and to control ingress and egress by means of a locked gate for which those using the lot will have keys.

In support of the claim that it would suffer special injury and damage, the plaintiff introduced the testimony of Edith Wyatt, a tenant occupying an apartment on the east side of its building, and that of Patricia DeBoisen, a resident of still another apartment building that will face the parking lot. Both witnesses testified they "felt" that carbon monoxide fumes from the cars using the lot would be injurious, and the first named witness expressed an opinion that noise, air pollution and dust emanating from the special use would make her apartment less comfortable and less desirable. It was stipulated that seventeen other witnesses, all occupants of apartments on the east side of plaintiff's structure, would give testimony substantially the same as that of Edith Wyatt, viz., that the parking lot was objectionable to them and that it would render their apartments less desirable. To complete its burden of proof, plaintiff asks this court to take judicial notice, first, that the fumes, noise and dust contemplated by the witnesses would in fact cause such injury as to render plaintiff's apartments less desirable and, second, that their effect will extend to a depreciation of the rental and sale value of plaintiff's property. It is our opinion, however, that such elements of special damage are matters of affirmative proof, not judicial notice.

To say that a court will take judicial notice of a fact is merely another way of saying that the usual forms of evidence will be dispensed with if the fact is one of public concern and notoriety which is known generally by all well-informed persons. While it is perhaps common knowledge that the operation of motor vehicles is attended by noise and fumes, it is equally well known in this automotive age that such by-products of the automobile become injurious to health and safety only under extreme or unusual conditions. Here there is no proof that the parking lot in question will create fumes, dust or noise in such concentrations as to be injurious or dangerous, but only an expressed "feeling" of inexpert witnesses that such will be the case. The operation of a great number of motor vehicles and the maintenance of parking lots in inhabited areas, all without injury from resulting fumes and noises, are commonplace features in our daily existence. Considering these factors, together with the meager evidence produced by the plaintiff, we cannot say that special injury in the respect claimed may be assumed, or that proof thereof may be dispensed with, in this case.

Nor do we believe that the testimony of present tenants, to the effect that the parking lot will render their apartments less desirable, permits us to take judicial notice that plaintiff's building will be depreciated in sale and rental value. None of the witnesses testified they would move from the premises, or demand lower rentals, and even if they should, it does not follow that the value of plaintiff's property will be adversely affected. In the complete absence of affirmative proof it is just as reasonable to assume that less sensitive apartment seekers, perhaps attracted by the convenient off-street parking to be afforded by the lot, would find plaintiff's apartments to be completely desirable at the same rental prices. Apart from this we find the well-defined rule to be that courts will not take judicial notice of the value of specific realty and improvements, inasmuch as innumerable factors affect their value. Here there is a complete absence of proof relating to the value of plaintiff's property and of the effect the parking lot will have on such values. It is true, as plaintiff suggests, that the proximity of certain uses will depreciate the rental value of nearby property, but we have found no authority holding that a mere showing of the existence of such use relieves a party from affirmatively proving alleged damage to his property. We conclude, therefore, that we may not take judicial notice of the matters prayed and that there is a complete failure of the proof to support the allegations of special injury made in the plaintiff's complaint. . . .

It is our opinion that the proof fails to show that plaintiff is a party whose rights, privileges or duties were adversely affected by the administrative decision sought to be reviewed. Accordingly, the judgment below is affirmed.

Judgment affirmed.

BRISTOW, JUSTICE (specially concurring):

Although I concur in the ultimate result reached by the majority of the court in affirming the judgment below, I cannot concur in the view taken by the majority that plaintiff failed to prove damages to give him standing as a proper party plaintiff.

The holdings of this court merely require a party seeking review to both allege and prove that the decision would adversely affect such party in a special manner peculiar to such party and different in degree than that suffered by the public in general. Nowhere do such cases require an allegation and proof of pecuniary damage in a positive dollar-and-cents amount. The direct testimony of plaintiff's witnesses as set forth in the majority opinion, and the defense stipulation that seventeen other witnesses would testify to the same effect, provides ample basis to establish special damage to plaintiff peculiar to it and different from that suffered by the general public. The degree of damage required to be shown in such cases as this is comparable to that required in injunction suits against a public nuisance, and is in no way comparable to the proof required in suits *in personam* for monetary damages.

There is a rank difference in the facts found in the cases relied upon by the majority and those appearing in this record. To find any similarity, one's mental plow must be clear out of focus.

SCHAEFER, J., is also of the opinion that there was a sufficient showing of special damages to call for a decision of the merits.

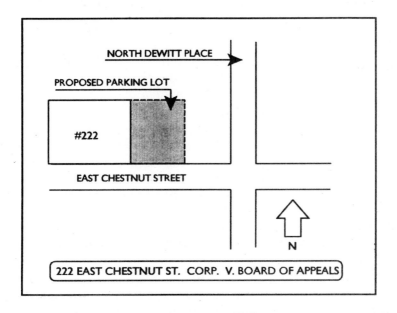

NOTES AND QUESTIONS

1. *Standing for neighbors.* The principal case goes contrary to the usual tendency to grant standing to adjacent property owners. See *Mings v. City of Ft. Smith,* 701 S.W.2d 705 (Ark. 1986); *Hoke v. Moyer,* 865 P.2d 624 (Wyo. 1993) (zoning change doubled density on adjacent land). Was the problem in the principal case an absence of injury? If so why? Reread the Model Zoning Ordinance, *supra,* and note the requirements for on-site off-street parking. What does this suggest?

Courts often apply a presumption that neighbors have standing, or take a lenient view toward their standing claims. *Christy's Realty Ltd. Partnership v. Town of Kittery,* 663 A.2d 59 (Me. 1995); but see *Foran v. Zoning Bd. of Appeals,* 260 A.2d 609 (Conn. 1969) ("mere fact" of proximity not enough to confer standing). There must be an injury different from that suffered by the general public. What this must be is not always clear. Intangible damage, like that in the principal case, may not be enough. See *Gulf House Ass'n v. Town of Gulf Shores,* 484 So. 2d 1061 (Ala. 1985) (loss of view does not confer standing). But see *AT&T Wireless PCS, Inc. v. Leafmore Forest Condo. Ass'n of Owners,* 509 S.E.2d 374 (Ga. App. 1998) (visibility of communication tower and decline in property values enough to confer standing).

2. *Proving standing by neighbors.* Standing is easier to show when the use that is challenged has physical impacts on the plaintiff's property, such as littering and fire and health hazards. See *Buckelew v. Town of Parker,* 937 P.2d 368 (Ariz. App. 1996). Many courts will not base standing on an increase in traffic from the challenged development, viewing it as part of urban development. *Macon-Bibb County Planning & Zoning Comm'n v. Vineville Neighborhood Ass'n,* 462 S.E.2d 764 (Ga. App. 1995). The cases are reviewed in *Sanitary & Improvement Dist. No. 347 v. City of Omaha,* 589 N.W.2d 160 (Neb. App. 1999).

Some courts apply a multi-factor balancing test to determine standing. See *Reynolds v. Dittmer,* 312 N.W.2d 75 (Iowa 1981) (proximity, character of neighborhood, type of zoning change, right to notice). And courts will only confer standing if the plaintiff is within the zone of interest protected by the ordinance. *Sun-Brite Car Wash, Inc. v. Board of Zoning & Appeals,* 508 N.E.2d 130 (N.Y. 1987) (standing cannot be based on right to be free of competition).

The application in the principal case was for a special use, also called a special exception. A special use must be approved by one of the local zoning agencies, in this case the board of appeals. See § 7 of the Standard Act, in sec. A of this chapter, *supra.* The plaintiff was a party to the board proceedings. Some courts hold that a plaintiff who did not participate in the agency proceedings may not appeal. See *Bryniarski v. Montgomery County Bd. of Appeals,* 230 A.2d 289 (Md. 1967). Standing for neighbors is an important issue because they are the ones who can challenge a zoning action that benefits a nearby landowner, such as the special use in this case. See Chapter 5.

3. *Aggrievement.* The appeal in the principal case was taken under the state's administrative procedure act, which the court interpreted to require an "adverse effect" as the basis for standing. In most states the applicable provision for appeals from a board of zoning appeals is the provision modeled on § 7 of the Standard Zoning Act that authorizes appeals by "persons aggrieved," which is a similar standing requirement.

The Standard Act also authorizes appeals by "any taxpayer," but only a minority of states have enacted this provision. In the absence of a statutory provision, most states deny standing to taxpayers or citizens who do not own property affected by the zoning action. See *Citizens Growth Mgt. Coalition of W. Palm Beach, Inc. v. City of W. Palm Beach, Inc.,* 450 So. 2d 204 (Fla. 1984) (no standing to challenge consistency of zoning with comprehensive plan).

4. *Nonresident landowners.* What about residents of one municipality who own land contiguous with or near the land affected by a zoning change in another municipality? Should municipal boundaries make a difference? Most courts now think not. A leading case is *Scott v. City of Indian Wells,* 492 P.2d 1137 (Cal. 1972). The court held that denying standing would "'make a fetish out of invisible boundary lines and mockery of the principles of zoning.'" Accord *Stokes v. City of Mishawaka,* 441 N.E.2d 24 (Ind. Ct. App. 1982) (reviewing cases).

5. *Neighbors and organizations.* Even when the courts give them standing, neighbors are at a disadvantage when they attempt to challenge zoning decisions to which they object. Zoning litigation is costly, and mobilizing to provide the necessary funding, expertise and legal counsel can be difficult. One way out of these difficulties is to grant standing to neighborhood organizations that can more effectively handle zoning litigation and arrange the necessary funding. Is this consistent with the "market failure" theory of zoning?

The U.S. Supreme Court has granted standing to organizations, but only where actual injury to the organization or its members is alleged. Compare *U.S. v. SCRAP*, 412 U.S. 669 (1973) (injury to members alleged; standing) with *Sierra Club v. Morton*, 405 U.S. 727 (1972) (injury to public interest alleged; no standing). *Warth v. Seldin, infra* Ch. 4, sec. C1, recognized the principle of organizational standing in an exclusionary zoning case, but applied the rules stringently and denied standing to all of the organizational plaintiffs.

The state courts divide on this issue, although the trend is toward granting standing. *Douglaston Civic Ass'n v. Galvin,* 324 N.E.2d 317 (N.Y. 1974), is a leading affirmative case. The court relied on the realities of zoning litigation. "By granting the neighborhood and civic associations standing . . ., the expense can be spread out over a number of property owners putting them on an economic parity with the developer." The court adopted a set of factors to determine whether an organization should have standing, including the ability of the organization to take an adversary position and the extent to which it represented neighborhood interests. For more recent cases on this issue compare *Lindsey Creek Area Civic Ass'n v. Consolidated Gov't,* 292 S.E.2d 61 (Ga. 1982) (standing denied), with *Timber Trails Corp. v. Planning & Zoning Comm'n,* 610 A.2d 620 (Conn. 1992) *(contra).*

6. *Municipalities.* What about municipalities? The courts allow municipalities to challenge actions by their zoning agencies, but are divided in allowing municipalities to challenge zoning approvals by adjacent municipalities. A leading case granting standing is *Village of Barrington Hills v. Village of Hoffman Estates,* 410 N.E.2d 37 (Ill. 1980), *cert. denied,* 449 U.S. 1126 (1981). The court granted standing to challenge the approval of an open-air theater in an adjacent municipality. The court noted that the plaintiff municipality would suffer special "corporate" damages from a decline in property values, increased traffic control costs and air quality degradation caused by motor vehicle traffic attracted by the theater. How does a municipality compare to a civic association as a representative of the collective interest?

7. *Sources.* Standing questions in zoning litigation have not received as much attention in the literature as they deserve. For two helpful early articles, see Ayer, *The Primitive Law of Standing in Land Use Disputes: Some Notes From a Dark Continent,* 55 Iowa L. Rev. 344 (1969); Note, *The "Aggrieved Person" Requirement in Zoning,* 8 Wm. & Mary L. Rev. 294 (1967). See also Bobrowski, *The Zoning Act's "Person Aggrieved" Standard: From Barvenik to Marashlian,* 18 W. New Eng. L. Rev. 385 (1996) (reviewing changing views in Massachusetts).

2. EXHAUSTION OF REMEDIES

The widely applied rule that plaintiffs may not sue to challenge the validity of a statute or ordinance unless they have exhausted their administrative remedies applies to zoning litigation. The exhaustion of remedies doctrine must be distinguished from the ripeness doctrine, which is similar and is discussed in Chapter 2. The following case indicates how the exhaustion rule applies in zoning litigation.

BEN LOMOND, INC. v. MUNICIPALITY OF ANCHORAGE

761 P.2d 119 (Alaska 1988)

COMPTON, JUSTICE:

The case arises from the revocation of building permits for the renovation of the S & S Apartments in Anchorage. The building's owner, Ben Lomond, Inc. (Ben Lomond), chose not to appeal the revocation or seek a variance. Ben Lomond claims that the Municipality unconstitutionally revoked its permits and, therefore, is liable in damages to Ben Lomond. The trial court denied Ben Lomond compensation reasoning that the Municipality of Anchorage (Municipality) was immune from an action for damages. We affirm the judgment on different grounds.

I. Factual and Procedural Background

The S & S Apartments are a group of eight wooden, two-story buildings constructed in 1952. The buildings have had several owners. In 1977 Glen Cassity of New Alaska Development Corporation purchased the property from the Alaska Housing Corporation. In 1983 the United States Department of Housing and Urban Development (HUD), which insured the mortgage on the apartments, determined that the buildings had been vacant for over four years and the property was "in very poor, abandoned and condemned condition."
. . .

On March 14, 1983, Ben Lomond purchased Cassity's interest in the apartments. . . . Sometime before May 3, 1983, Ben Lomond took possession of the property and started to strip the buildings down to the bare framing. [Eventually, the United States foreclosed on Cassity's interest and Ben Lomond was the successful bidder at the foreclosure sale. It tendered $218,000 to HUD as a 10% down payment with the remaining 90% due August 26, 1983.]

On May 13, 1983 Ben Lomond applied for the first time to the Municipality for building and demolition permits. The permits indicated Ben Lomond intended to demolish the interior of and then renovate building #4. Shortly thereafter Ben Lomond's architect prepared a report for the entire project showing that the apartment complex then contained 224 units and that when all the buildings were renovated there would be a total of 280 apartment units. The record does not indicate when the city received a copy of that report.

On June 8, 1983, Ben Lomond applied to the city for building permits to renovate the other seven buildings. Taken together the applications show an intent to renovate 264 apartment units. However, as required by the building code, Thompson [president of Ben Lomond] submitted architectural plans with the applications; those plans showed a total of 280 proposed units. At that time the site was zoned R-3, which allowed only 234 units.

On June 28, 1983 the Municipality's building official, John Bishop, met with Thompson to discuss the size of the apartment complex's parking lot. The number of parking spaces shown on the plans for 280 units did not meet the parking requirements of Anchorage Municipal Code (AMC) Title 21. However,

Bishop thought Ben Lomond had grandfather rights to maintain a parking deficiency. After consulting a city attorney, Bishop decided to issue the permits. When Bishop issued the permits he was unaware the R-3 zoning limited the number of units to 234. . . .

Sometime during late July or early August, the Municipality's executive manager for public services Chip Dennerlein received numerous complaints from persons in the Fairview community regarding Ben Lomond's proposed project. Dennerlein then had several conferences with various city officials to review the validity of the complaints. Dennerlein concluded that the zoning designation allowed only 234 units and that Ben Lomond could not be allowed to build 280 units. See AMC 21.40.050(f). Consequently, Bishop notified Ben Lomond that the building permits for the project were revoked. In a letter dated August 19, 1983 Bishop explained that the project did not enjoy non-conforming use status, see AMC 21.55.030(c), and that it therefore had to meet the current zoning code. Bishop wrote:

> Based on the current R-3 zoning and the size of property, a maximum of 234 dwelling units may be permitted. For that number of dwelling units, you would need to provide 351 parking spaces.

The letter indicated new permits would be issued if Ben Lomond submitted a revised site plan that complied with the code.

After sending the August 19 letter, Dennerlein met with Thompson regarding possible options for Ben Lomond. Over the course of several meetings they discussed the following options: Ben Lomond could (1) appeal the Municipality's action denying the 280 unit project to the Zoning Board of Examiners and Appeals (Zoning Board); (2) apply to the Zoning Board for a variance from the 234 unit limit; or (3) build the project with 234 units. Thompson responded that he did not wish to pursue any remedies before the Zoning Board that would involve a public hearing. Accordingly Ben Lomond did not appeal the revocation of the permits.

In light of the August 19 letter Ben Lomond did not tender the remainder of the sale price by August 26, 1983 and thereby forfeited its right to purchase the S & S Apartments from HUD. On September 30, 1983 the United States Marshall conducted a second foreclosure sale. Ben Lomond did not bid at the second sale and HUD obtained title to the property. In February 1984 Ben Lomond filed suit against the Municipality requesting over $3 million in damages resulting from the permit revocations. In March 1984, the Municipality purchased the property from HUD.

Almost a year later Ben Lomond learned through the newspaper that the Municipality planned to demolish the buildings. Ben Lomond moved for, but was denied, a temporary restraining order to halt the demolition. The Municipality demolished the buildings and built a park.

Ben Lomond then moved for a summary judgment on the issue that it was deprived of property without due process. The Municipality also moved for partial summary judgment to dismiss all causes of action for damages arguing that it was immune under AS 09.65.070. The superior court granted the Municipality's motion for summary judgment. The parties stipulated to an entry of final judgment. Ben Lomond appeals.

II. Discussion

This case was decided upon cross-motions for summary judgment. The moving party must show that there is no genuine issue as to any material fact and that the moving party is entitled to judgment as a matter of law. All factual matters are to be resolved in favor of the non-moving party.

The parties to this appeal raise two major issues. First, whether the permits were unconstitutionally revoked and second, whether the Municipality was immune from suit for such actions. We need not reach these issues because we decide the case on other grounds. We believe the trial court improperly reached the merits in this case because Ben Lomond failed to exhaust its administrative remedies.

"The doctrine of exhaustion of administrative remedies is an expression of administrative autonomy and a rule of sound judicial administration." *State Dep't of Labor v. University of Alaska,* 664 P.2d 575, 581 (Alaska 1983) (citing B. Schwartz, Administrative Law § 172, at 498 (1976)). Whether a court will require exhaustion of remedies turns on an assessment of the benefits obtained through affording an agency an opportunity to review the particular action in dispute. In particular we have observed that "[t]he basic purpose of the exhaustion doctrine is to allow an administrative agency to perform functions within its special competence — to make a factual record, to apply its expertise, and to correct its own errors so as to moot judicial controversies." *Van Hyning v. University of Alaska,* 621 P.2d 1354, 1355-56 (Alaska) (quoting *Parisi v. Davidson,* 405 U.S. 34, 37 (1972)), *cert. denied,* 454 U.S. 958 (1981).

We have not articulated a principle governing when a regulatory scheme's constitutionality may be challenged without exhausting administrative remedies. According to Professor Davis, exhaustion, generally, is not required when the constitutionality of the statute is the only issue raised in a case. See 4 K. Davis, Administrative Law Treatise § 26:6 (2d ed. 1983). Davis concludes that exhaustion may be required when non-constitutional issues are present or when a factual context is needed for deciding the constitutional issue. *Id.* We believe that requiring exhaustion is particularly appropriate where a complainant raises both constitutional and non-constitutional issues. This is because successful pursuit of a claim through the administrative process could obviate the need for judicial review of the constitutional issues. We further believe that it is axiomatic to our system of justice that we have a factual context within which to review a case. Applying these principles to the instant case we conclude that the benefits that could have been obtained from allowing the agency to review this case justify application of the exhaustion doctrine.

When the Municipality revoked Ben Lomond's permits, Ben Lomond could have promptly appealed the revocation to the Zoning Board of Examiners and Appeals. AMC 21.30.110. At that time Ben Lomond could have presented its interpretation of various Building and Zoning Code provisions as applied to the apartment site. In addition, Ben Lomond could have argued to the Zoning Board that the Municipality was estopped to revoke the permits. By failing to take even the first step in the administrative appeal process Ben Lomond deprived the Municipality of the opportunity to make a factual record and correct its own errors.

The record indicates that the Municipality erroneously issued Ben Lomond's building permits for 264 apartments. The record also indicates that if given the opportunity the Zoning Board could have corrected the Municipality's error and directed that building permits be issued for 234 units. Alternatively, the Zoning Board could have accepted Ben Lomond's estoppel argument and reinstated the permit for 280 units. As another alternative, the Zoning Board could have determined it was appropriate to issue building permits for any number of units between 234 and 280. Had Ben Lomond pursued and obtained relief from the Zoning Board we might not now be faced with a constitutional challenge to the Building and Zoning Codes. For the foregoing reasons we hold that Ben Lomond has waived its right to pursue its claim because it failed to exhaust its administrative remedies.

NOTES AND QUESTIONS

1. *Understanding exhaustion.* What was the basis for plaintiff's claim in the principal case? Was it constitutional or was it based on an interpretation of the zoning ordinance? Does it make a difference? Compare *Northwestern Univ. v. City of Evanston,* 383 N.E.2d 964 (Ill. 1978), holding that exhaustion was required when the plaintiff attacked the distinction between commercial and noncommercial uses in a zoning ordinance as "inherently arbitrary." Why do you suppose exhaustion was required in this situation?

A common case in which exhaustion is required is the case in which a landowner claims a zoning ordinance is a taking of his property. The landowner can claim a facial taking or can claim a taking "as applied" to his property. Do you see the difference? *Poe v. City of Baltimore,* 216 A.2d 707 (Md. 1966), reviews the exhaustion rules applicable to taking claims and holds that exhaustion is required when a plaintiff makes an "as applied" attack on a zoning ordinance but is not required when a plaintiff makes a "facial" attack. The zoning variance, discussed in Chapter 5, is an important alternative to a takings claim.

Compare *Grimpel Assocs. v. Cohalan,* 361 N.E.2d 1022 (N.Y. 1977). The plaintiff attacked a downzoning of its land to a less intensive use. The court did not require exhaustion because the ordinance "absolutely prohibited" the plaintiff's use and plaintiff claimed that the ordinance was confiscatory. Is this an "as applied" attack?

The exhaustion rule requires the plaintiff to go before the administrative board to make his constitutional claim. Is this practicable? Does the board have jurisdiction to hear the constitutional claim? Consult § 7 of the Standard Act, in sec. A of this chapter, *supra,* on this point. What kind of a record do you think a plaintiff could make on the constitutional claim before the board? Is the board hearing adversarial?

2. *Adequacy of the administrative remedy.* It is clear that administrative remedies provided by statute must be exhausted. See *Shors v. Johnson,* 581 N.W.2d 648 (Iowa 1998), holding that a neighbor had to exhaust an administrative remedy allowing the board of adjustment to interpret the zoning ordinance before she could challenge the issuance of a building permit that violated setback requirements. This remedy comes from § 7 of the Standard

Zoning Act. Exhaustion is not required when administrative remedies are inadequate. See *Smoke v. City of Seattle,* 937 P.2d 186 (Wash. 1997), reviewing the cases on adequacy and holding that an interpretation of the zoning ordinance could not reverse a permit denial.

3. *The futility rule.* An important exception to the exhaustion doctrine is the futility rule: The plaintiff need not exhaust an administrative remedy when to do so would be futile. The rule applies when the agency does not have the authority to grant the requested relief. See *Sinclair Pipe Line Co. v. Village of Richton Park,* 167 N.E.2d 406 (Ill. 1960) (need not apply for variance because no authority to grant for change in use).

The futility rule also applies when it is clear that administrative relief will not be granted. *League of Women Voters of Appleton, Inc. v. Outagamie County,* 334 N.W.2d 887 (Wis. 1983) illustrates this application of the futility rule. The League appealed the issuance of a use permit for a shopping mall. The court held no exhaustion was required:

> [A]ssuming that the plaintiffs had a right to appeal to the board of adjustment, such an appeal would have been futile. The attorney for the county and the board of adjustment had made very clear, on the record of this case, his clients' position that no appeal to the board of adjustment would be entertained. [*Id.* at 890.]

How much opposition must a plaintiff show before he can invoke the futility rule? What if he claims that relief probably will not be granted, but there is no history as in the *League of Women Voters* case indicating relief will be denied? *Northwestern Univ., supra,* is a case refusing to apply the futility rule in these circumstances. A court may apply a presumption that a zoning agency is not biased, and hold that a plaintiff must demonstrate actual rather than potential bias. See *O & G Indus. v. Planning & Zoning Comm'n,* 655 A.2d 1121 (Conn. 1995) (bias not found).

4. *Amendments.* Does the exhaustion doctrine require a plaintiff to apply for a zoning amendment that would allow his land use? The answer to this question usually turns on whether the amendment is a legislative or quasi-judicial act. See Ch. 5, sec. D3 *infra.* Exhaustion usually is required only when the amendment is considered quasi-judicial, which is the characterization the courts give to it in several states. See *Fifth Ave. Corp. v. Washington County,* 581 P.2d 50 (Or. 1978). Can you see why this is so?

5. *The ripeness alternative.* Recall that the ripeness rule adopted by the federal courts and discussed in Ch. 2 requires plaintiffs to obtain a final decision from local agencies before bringing a taking claim in federal court. Is this rule the equivalent of the exhaustion of remedies rule? The Supreme Court thought not in *Hamilton Bank, supra,* where the plaintiff claimed a taking based on a denial of a subdivision plat and the subdivision ordinance contained variance provisions. The Court drew a distinction between finality ("whether the initial decision maker has arrived at a definitive position on the issue that inflicts an actual, concrete injury") and exhaustion ("administrative and judicial procedures by which an injured party may seek review of an adverse decision and obtain a remedy if the decision is found to be unlawful or otherwise inappropriate"). [473 U.S. at 192-93.]

Can you see the difference? A number of states now apply the federal ripeness rules, such as the finality rule, to takings claims in state courts. See *Paragron Props. Co. v. City of Novi,* 550 N.W.2d 772 (Mich. 1996); *Beverly Bank v. Illinois Dep't of Transp.,* 579 N.E.2d 815 (Ill. 1991); *Ward v. Bennett,* 592 N.E.2d 787 (N.Y. 1992); *Estate of Friedman v. Pierce County,* 768 P.2d 462 (Wash. 1989). Does it make sense to apply rules concerning the limited jurisdiction of federal courts to takings claims in state courts that do not have comparable jurisdictional limitations?

6. *Sources.* For additional discussion of the exhaustion doctrine, see Note, *Exhaustion of Remedies in Zoning Cases,* 1964 Wash. U. L.Q. 368; Comment, *Exhausting Administrative and Legislative Remedies in Zoning Cases,* 48 Tul. L. Rev. 665 (1974).

3. SECURING JUDICIAL REVIEW

The problem.—Securing judicial review of zoning ordinances and decisions is complicated in several ways. First, civil procedure is usually an intricate body of law in each state, and jurisdictions vary widely in how litigation is structured, including the labels used to denominate actions. Thus, in this casebook, we can do no more than sketch the broadest outlines of the topic. You are encouraged to consult your own state's statutes and caselaw to acquire more specific insight into these matters.

Another complication is that some of the land use decisions that a party might wish to challenge will be characterized as "legislative" decisions and others will be characterized as "administrative," (or, sometimes, "quasi-judicial"). Adoption of a revised zoning ordinance, downzoning (or upzoning) a belt of farmland at the edge of the community, is an example of the first type of action; denying (or granting) a variance for a specific parcel of land in a suburban residential neighborhood is an example of the second. This complication is further complicated because legislative bodies may sometimes act administratively and bodies that nominally have only advisory functions, planning commissions under the SSZEA, for example, may in fact have operational duties assigned to them as well. The authority to issue special-use permits illustrates both points, this duty sometimes being lodged in the legislative body that also adopts the underlying ordinance, and sometimes in bodies such as the planning commission.

Certiorari.—The labels matter here, because, generally speaking, different procedures will be specified for questioning "legislative" and non-legislative acts (different substantive standards of review may also apply). The Standard Zoning Act on which most states have modeled their zoning legislation provides little guidance. Section 7 of the Act provides that persons "aggrieved" by a decision of the board of adjustment may obtain review by way of a writ of certiorari, an extraordinary remedy to review administrative agency decisions for jurisdictional defects or illegality in the exercise of jurisdiction. Most states have adopted this Standard Act provision. It is important to note that review by way of certiorari is on the record made before the board, although § 7 allows a court to take additional evidence if "testimony is necessary for the proper disposition of the matter." But see *Bentley v.*

Chastain, 249 S.E.2d 38 (Ga. 1978) (de novo trial unconstitutional). Certiorari is thus the typical method for reviewing zoning board decisions on variances and conditional uses.

But the SSZEA says nothing about decisions of other bodies, nor does it address the administrative/legislative distinction. The following case provides one answer:

COPPLE v. CITY OF LINCOLN

210 Neb. 504, 315 N.W.2d 628 (1982)

CLINTON, JUSTICE:

This action originates by a "petition on appeal" filed in the District Court for Lancaster County by the plaintiff Copple against the City of Lincoln, its mayor, the members of its city council, and Old Cheney Road, Inc. The plaintiff's petition alleges the action is an appeal under the provisions of Neb. Rev. Stat. § 15–1202 from an amendment to a zoning ordinance of the City. It further alleges, among other things, that on May 9, 1977, the council approved ordinance No. 11976 which changed the zoning classification of a tract of land in the southwest quarter of Section 9, Township 9 North, Range 7 East, Lancaster County, from "G-Local Business District Zoning and A-1 Single Family Dwelling District Zoning to J-1 Planned Regional Commercial District Zoning." The plaintiff alleges he is a citizen, resident, and taxpayer of Lincoln and Lancaster County, and he is owner of a tract of land described as the northeast quarter of Section 18, Township 9 North, Range 7 East of the 6th P. M., Lancaster County, Nebraska. He further alleges the zone change "will have a detrimental affect [sic] on plaintiff and his real property, in that plaintiff wishes to build a regional shopping center in close proximity to the area here involved, specifically at 40th Street and Old Cheney Road and currently has pending applications for said regional shopping center and a lawsuit to determine plaintiff's right to build said regional shopping center. The decision of the City Council herein would cause undue hardship on the plaintiff if in fact a shopping center is allowed to be built on the rezoned tract in said close proximity to plaintiff's proposed shopping center site."

The petition further alleges the city council of the City of Lincoln acted arbitrarily and capriciously in enacting the amendment to the zoning ordinance and sets forth various reasons for the conclusion.

The District Court, after a hearing on the merits of the plaintiff's petition, found that the plaintiff was not a person aggrieved within the meaning of Neb. Rev. Stat. § 15-1201; that he did not have standing to sue; and that even if he had legal standing, he had failed to prove he suffered some special injury peculiar to himself as required by law to have standing to appeal the action of the council. It further found: "That if it should be determined that the plaintiff possesses legal standing to appeal this action, the plaintiff still has the burden of proving that the action of the defendant, City of Lincoln, was arbitrary, unreasonable, and without substantial relation to the public safety, health, morals, or the general welfare." The court then made findings indicating a lack of merit in each of the plaintiff's specific claims of invalidity of the ordinance. It ordered the plaintiff's appeal dismissed.

We affirm on two alternative grounds. The first ground is that the enactment of a zoning ordinance by a municipal governing body is an exercise of legislative authority from which no direct appeal lies. An appeal or error proceeding does not lie from a purely legislative act by a public body to which legislative authority has been delegated. The only remedy in such cases is by collateral attack, that is, by injunction or other suitable actions. . . .

Section 15-1201 provides: "Any person or persons, jointly or severally aggrieved by any final administrative or judicial order or decision of the board of zoning appeals, the board of equalization, the city council, or any officer or department or board of a city of the primary class, shall, except as provided for claims in sections 15-840 to 15-842.01, appeal from such order or decision to the district court in the manner herein prescribed." The above statute applies only where the bodies mentioned act judicially or quasi-judicially. Any other construction would render the statute unconstitutional. The Legislature may not delegate legislative power to the courts. A delegation of legislative power to the courts is violative of article II, § 1, of the Constitution of Nebraska.

The alternative ground of our decision is that the plaintiff has not shown that he is an "aggrieved" person within the meaning of § 15-1201. In order to have standing as an aggrieved person for the purpose of attacking a change of zone, the plaintiff must demonstrate that he suffers a special injury different in kind from that suffered by the general public. The possibility that zone changes may afford competition for businesses which the plaintiff hopes will be established on his property if it is rezoned is not sufficient to give standing. An increase in business competition is not sufficient to confer standing to challenge a change of zone.

Affirmed.

NOTES AND QUESTIONS

1. Note that the Nebraska statute authorized actions to appeal decisions by the city council, but that the court held that an injunction must be brought. Do you see why? Certiorari also is available if the court holds that the council acts quasi-judicially, *Snyder v. City of Lakewood,* 542 P.2d 371 (Colo. 1975), but not if it acts legislatively. *Leavitt v. Jefferson County,* 875 P.2d 681 (Wash. App. 1994) (adoption of countywide development code). Note also the holding in *Copple* on the standing question. For more on the status of competitive injury in zoning, see sec. C3 *infra.*

2. The courts are divided on whether they can consider the constitutionality of a zoning ordinance when a variance is appealed, see *City of Cherokee v. Tatro,* 636 P.2d 337 (Okla. 1981) (may consider if facially unconstitutional). How does a decision on this issue affect the exhaustion doctrine requirement that a plaintiff must apply for a zoning variance before bringing suit? See sec. 2 *supra.*

3. Legislation in some states provides for a statutory appeal of zoning decisions and regulations to the courts, and some of this legislation applies to the governing body as well as zoning boards and planning commissions. Alaska Stat. § 29.40.060 (local governing body may provide for appeal); Conn. Gen. Stat. § 8-8 (boards and commissions).

4. FORMS OF REMEDY

A PRELIMINARY NOTE ON REMEDIES IN LAND USE CASES

In *Copple, supra,* the form of action, injunction, determined the form of remedy as well. But there can be other forms of remedies in land use cases. We survey the most typical ones in this Note.

Injunctions.—An injunction is the standard remedy to challenge zoning actions by the governing body in states where the zoning process is legislative. An injunction lies because an alternative legal remedy is not available. Appeal and certiorari are not available, for instance, to review zoning actions by the governing body if these actions are legislative. Note that the injunction is a negative, not an affirmative, remedy. The landowner argues that a zoning restriction as applied to her property is unconstitutional or illegal, and that its enforcement by the municipality should be enjoined.

The courts in zoning injunction cases follow the usual rule, that an injunction may be granted only on a showing of irreparable injury and may not be granted if the harm is only threatened. For example, in *Citizens for Orderly Dev. & Env't v. City of Phoenix,* 540 P.2d 1239 (Ariz. 1975), the plaintiff was denied an injunction against a rezoning ordinance that had only been conditionally approved. No final action had been taken by the governing body. See also *Tahoe Keys Prop. Owners' Ass'n v. State Water Resources Bd.,* 28 Cal. Rptr. 2d 734 (Cal. App. 1994) (denying preliminary injunction when damages would compensate plaintiffs and injunction would cause serious harm).

Injunctions are commonly used in the enforcement of zoning ordinances. See the Standard Act, § 8, authorizing municipalities to bring "any appropriate action or proceedings" to prevent a violation of the Act or a zoning ordinance. The courts do not require an irreparable injury as the basis for an enforcement injunction. See *Johnson v. Murzyn,* 469 A.2d 1227 (Conn. App. 1984). Neither do the courts apply the rule that an injunction is not available to enjoin the violation of a crime. This exception is necessary because the Standard Act also makes the violation of a zoning ordinance a misdemeanor. What policy reasons are there for adopting these exceptions when the municipality uses the injunction for enforcement?

Declaratory judgment.—Plaintiffs in zoning cases may also seek a declaratory judgment, which is authorized under the Uniform Declaratory Judgment Act adopted in most states. The declaratory judgment is a helpful alternative to an injunction because it authorizes the court to make a declaration of rights even though the plaintiff has not suffered actual harm. In many zoning actions, the plaintiff asks for both an injunction and a declaratory judgment. Relief through declaratory judgment is still limited because the courts usually insist that a justiciable controversy be present. They may not provide declaratory relief if the plaintiff has not been adversely affected by the zoning ordinance, although they may apply this requirement liberally.

One example of a case where a declaratory judgment is useful is when a land use action, such as the adoption of a comprehensive plan, is imminent but has not yet occurred. Adjudication of the plaintiff's rights in advance of adoption can forestall an adverse action. See *County Comm'rs v. Days Cove Reclamation Co.,* 713 A.2d 351 (Md. App. 1998) (imminent adoption of comprehensive plan excluding plaintiff's use). A plaintiff may also bring a declaratory judgment to test the legality of a procedure to avoid going through the time and expense of applying for a land use approval the procedure requires. See *Board of Supvrs. v. Southland Corp.,* 297 S.E.2d 718 (Va. 1982), *infra,* ch. 5 where the court allowed a plaintiff to challenge the validity of a conditional use procedure without applying for a conditional use. It noted that the plaintiff was engaged in the business of obtaining sites for its stores, and that it was injured in conducting its business by being compelled to go through the special-use process.

Another example is a declaratory judgment action brought to obtain an interpretation of a zoning ordinance to clarify zoning requirements that might impede the sale or use of a property. *ML Plainsboro Ltd. Pshp. v. Township of Plainsboro,* 719 A.2d 1285 (N.J. App. Div. 1998). However, a declaratory judgment will not lie when another remedy is available. *Farmer's Stone Prods. Co. v. Hoyt,* 950 S.W.2d 673 (Mo. App. 1997) (certiorari available to appeal decision of zoning board).

Mandamus.—Mandamus is another extraordinary remedy that can sometimes be useful in zoning litigation. Mandamus lies to compel a public official or agency to do a ministerial act. *Clark v. City of Shreveport,* 655 So. 2d 617 (La. App. 1995) (issuance of variance). It does not lie to compel the performance of a discretionary act, although a court will allow a writ of mandamus to compel an official to make a discretionary decision or to set aside an exercise of discretion when it is arbitrary. *Nova Horizon, Inc. v. City Council,* 769 P.2d 721 (Nev. 1989). See *Allen v. St. Tammany Parish Police Jury,* 690 So. 2d 150 (La. App. 1997), for a discussion of when provisions for approval in a subdivision ordinance are mandatory or discretionary. But a court will not issue a writ of mandamus if a statutory appeal is available, such as an appeal from a decision of a board of adjustment.

Mandamus can be a useful remedy in zoning litigation because it can compel the exercise of an official act that provides the plaintiff with necessary judicial relief. *Schrader v. Guildford Planning & Zoning Comm'n,* 418 A.2d 93 (Conn. Super. 1980) is an example. The court held a nine-month development moratorium was invalid. It granted a writ of mandamus to compel the commission to accept an application that had been barred by the moratorium. See also *Petition of Fairchild,* 616 A.2d 228 (Vt. 1992) (mandamus available to enforce ministerial duties of executive officer).

The rule that mandamus will not issue to compel the exercise of discretionary authority often limits its availability because so much of zoning administration is discretionary. See *Big Train Constr. Co. v. Parish of St. Tammany,*

446 So. 2d 889 (La. App. 1984) (issuance of building permit held discretionary); *Teed v. King County,* 677 P.2d 179 (Wash. App. 1984) (rezoning).

For general discussion of the judicial remedies available against local government, see D. Mandelker, D. Netsch, P. Salsich & J. Wegner, State and Local Government in a Federal System, ch. 12 (4th ed. 1996); O. Reynolds, Handbook of Local Government Law, ch. 31 (1982).

————

Specific relief of some kind is generally available to a landowner when land use controls are found to have violated his constitutional rights. Specific relief may be granted in the form of a declaratory judgment, or by enjoining the enforcement of specified land use regulations, or by issuing an order ("mandamus") directing a local official (often the building inspector) to issue a permit for land development that he has no authority to issue if specified land use regulations are valid. Although a declaratory judgment may be the most common form of relief, some form of coercive or "further" relief often is demanded by way of injunction or mandamus. Site-specific relief is obviously important to a developer, so that it can proceed with the land use project that the municipality or the neighbors opposed. But the courts face obstacles when they attempt to provide specific judicial relief in these actions, as the following case illustrates.

CITY OF RICHMOND v. RANDALL

215 Va. 506, 211 S.E.2d 56 (1975)

POFF, JUSTICE:

Dr. Russell E. Randall, Jr., and J. W. Keith (landowners) filed a motion for declaratory judgment against City of Richmond (City) asking the chancellor to declare that "(1) the R-2 (single family residence on minimum 12,500 square foot lot) zoning classification as it applies to their 3.24 acres of vacant land . . . is invalid; (2) the refusal . . . to grant their Special Use request . . . is unreasonable, arbitrary and capricious; and (3) the Court order the City Council to issue the Special Use permit. . . ." By letter opinion dated October 12, 1973, and final decree entered November 9, 1973, the chancellor made extensive findings of fact and ruled, *inter alia,* that the "existing ordinance . . . in its application to Plaintiffs' property is unreasonable and confiscatory and therefore unconstitutional"; that since "the unchallenged *evidence* before Council established that Council's action [denying the special use permit] would result in completely depriving the plaintiffs of the beneficial use of their property by precluding all practical uses, Council's action was unreasonable, confiscatory and arbitrary" and "bears no substantial relationship . . . [to] the public health, safety, morals or general welfare"; and that "Council of the City of Richmond within thirty (30) days from the entry of this Decree shall either adopt Ordinance 73-112 [granting the special use permit] or rezone the land to a zoning category which will permit construction of the proposed building". . .

[The plaintiffs, who planned to build a three-story building for medical and general office purposes, requested a change from R-2 residential zoning to RO-1, a Residential-Office District. They also requested a special use permit. The city council rejected the special use permit. At the trial court level, the chancellor held that the R-2 zoning was unreasonable as applied to plaintiffs' property. He also held that the special use permit was improperly rejected.]

Having made these two adjudications of invalidity, the chancellor proceeded to determine what definitive relief would be appropriate. It was apparent that entry of a simple adjudicatory decree granting no definitive relief would work a legal absurdity; the governing body might be left with an island of unzoned land, and the landowners might be left free to put their land to any use, short of a nuisance, they saw fit. Left in that posture, the governing body would be constrained to act hurriedly to zone the unzoned island to a new category. In the rush, and absent definitive guidelines from the court, it might select a category that did not allow the one use shown by the record to be reasonable. In such case, new litigation would ensue. If the new court decree declared the new category unreasonable but again granted no definitive relief, the process of re-zoning and re-litigation could continue *ad infinitum*. The law eschews multiplicity of litigation. When the property rights of an individual and the interests of the community collide, the conflict must be resolved. To expedite a full and final resolution, a court confronted with the conflict must have the power not only to adjudicate the dispute but also to order action not inconsistent with its adjudication.

In the exercise of its power to order such action, a court may not usurp the legislative prerogative. "Zoning is properly a legislative function" and "this court will not substitute its judgment for that of the Board. . . ." But when the evidence shows that the existing zoning ordinance is invalid and the requested use reasonable, and when, as here, the legislative body produces no evidence that an alternative reasonable use exists, then no legislative options exist and a court decree enjoining the legislative body from taking any action which would disallow the one use shown to be reasonable is not judicial usurpation of the legislative prerogative.[3]

This Court has no power to re-zone land to any classification or to order a legislative body to do so. See *Board of Supervisors v. Allman,* [Va.], 211 S.E.2d 48 (1975), this day decided. It follows that trial courts have no such power.

Nor does this Court or any court have power, even when it finds the existing zoning ordinance invalid and a requested use reasonable, to order approval of a special use permit, where, as here, a legislative body is vested by law with jurisdiction over such permits, including legislative discretion to amend

[3] Courts in Illinois have held that a court has power to grant a requested use after it has found the existing zoning ordinance void and the requested use reasonable. See Sinclair Pipe Line Co. v. Village of Richton Park, 167 N.E.2d 406, 411 (Ill. 1960). We believe these holdings, which compel affirmative action by legislative bodies, go too far. The injunction is a more traditional remedy and one less offensive to the concept of separation of powers. Concerning use of an injunction as definitive relief in resolving land use disputes, see City of Miami Beach v. Weiss, 217 So. 2d 836, 837 (Fla. 1969).

the permit ordinance and impose conditions upon the use requested.[4] The power to amend is part of the legislative prerogative.

Here, the chancellor ordered City Council to either enact a new zoning classification for the property which would allow construction of "the proposed building," or to enact Ordinance 73-112, the specific permit ordinance proposed. The order restricts Council to two alternatives. As to the first, the order transgresses the legislative prerogative. As to the second, by foreclosing Council's right under its charter to amend the permit ordinance and impose conditions upon the requested use, the order infringes legislative discretion. For these reasons, the decree must be reversed in part.

As to the chancellor's two adjudications of invalidity, we affirm the decree. As to the chancellor's directions to City Council, we reverse the decree and remand the cause with instructions to modify the decree. The new decree will suspend the adjudications of invalidity for a prescribed period of time and remand the cause to City Council for further legislative action. Since City made no showing of an alternative reasonable use, the new decree will enjoin Council during that period from taking any action which would disallow the one use shown by the record to be reasonable, subject to Council's right under its charter to amend a permit ordinance and impose reasonable conditions not inconsistent with such use. The new decree will further provide that if Council fails to comply within the time prescribed, the adjudications of invalidity will become operative and the injunction will become permanent, provided that landowners shall not put their property to any use other than the use shown by the record to be reasonable.

Affirmed in part, reversed in part and remanded.

NOTES AND QUESTIONS

1. *Specific relief not available.* Despite the principal case and the cases discussed in the following Note, the majority rule still is that specific affirmative relief is not available in zoning actions. The rationale for the majority view was stated in *City of Conway v. Housing Auth.,* 584 S.W.2d 10 (Ark. 1979):

> [I]t follows that the power of the court to review the action of the municipalities is limited to determining whether or not such action was arbitrary, capricious, or wholly inequitable. The judiciary has no right or authority to substitute its judgment for that of the legislative branch of government. . . . Courts are not super zoning commissions and have no authority to classify property according to zones. [*Id.* at 13.]

The rule, that specific affirmative relief is not available in zoning actions, has been substantially modified in the exclusionary zoning cases. See Ch. 4 sec. B *infra.*

---

[4] City's charter § 17.11(b) (Acts 1960, c. 7, pp. 12, 13; Acts 1968, c. 644, pp. 972, 980) vests Council with jurisdiction over special use permits and provides in part that "the council may impose such conditions upon the use of the land, buildings and structures as will, in its opinion, protect the community and area involved and the public from adverse effects and detriments that may result therefrom." Like other legislative zoning actions, conditions imposed by such amendments must meet the test of reasonableness.

2. *Specific relief available. Sinclair Pipe Line,* which is cited in footnote 3 of the principal case, suggests the rationale for specific relief. In *Sinclair,* the trial court granted the plaintiff a "variation" from the applicable zoning restriction and ordered the issuance of all permits. The supreme court affirmed the order. It held that it was "appropriate" to frame the decree with reference to the record and the evidence developed at trial. This type of relief "did not go beyond the realm of adjudication" but was simply a form of specific relief comparable to the relief available in mandamus and administrative review actions. Accord *Schwartz v. City of Flint,* 395 N.W.2d 678 (Mich. 1986).

Justice Hoff, in the principal case, seems to appreciate the rationale for specific relief, but he nonetheless is concerned about courts going "too far," and he rejects *Sinclair Pipe.* Do you see any real difference between the chancellor's order and the state supreme court's modification of that order? Will the plaintiffs get what they want under the supreme court's modified order? Note the court's limitation of specific relief to a case in which the "evidence shows that . . . the requested use [is] reasonable" and that there is no "alternative reasonable use." Why is this limitation necessary?

In *Weiss,* also cited in footnote 3 of the principal case, the decree "directed" the rezoning of the property. The court held this was improper. The proper form of relief was "a decree enjoining the enforcement of a classification more restrictive than that named in the decree." Is there a difference?

3. *Alternatives to specific relief.* Some courts have approved other alternatives that provide some form of specific affirmative relief in zoning actions:

(a) Occasionally, a court will invalidate the current zoning and leave the land unzoned. See *State ex rel. Nagawicka Island Corp. v. City of Delafield,* 343 N.W.2d 816 (Wis. App. 1983) (use subject only to Building Code requirements); *City of Cherokee v. Tatro,* 636 P.2d 337 (Okla. 1981). Generally, however, the courts are agreed that leaving the land unzoned is an unacceptable remedy, although they may invalidate the zoning regulations as applied to the plaintiff's land and threaten to leave it unregulated unless the municipality rezones within a specified period of time. See *City of Atlanta v. McLennan,* 226 S.E.2d 732 (Ga. 1976). How did the court in the principal case address this possibility?

(b) The municipality downzones the plaintiff's land to a more restrictive use. The court may invalidate the downzoning. It may then order the reinstatement of the prior zoning classification. *H. Dev. Corp. v. City of Yonkers,* 407 N.Y.S.2d 573 (App. Div. 1978).

4. In an appeal from the board of adjustment, the Standard Act, § 7, provides that "[t]he court may reverse or affirm, wholly or partly, or may modify the decision brought up for review." A remand is appropriate when the right to judicial relief has not been clearly shown. See *Bogue v. Zoning Bd. of Appeals,* 345 A.2d 9 (Conn. 1975).

5. For additional discussion of judicial relief in zoning cases, see Krasnowiecki, *Zoning Litigation — How to Win Without Really Losing,* 1976 Inst. on Plan. Zoning & Eminent Domain 1 (1976); Note, *Beyond Invalidation: The Judicial Power to Zone,* 9 Urb. L. Ann. 159 (1975).

C. THE BASIC ZONING TECHNIQUES: USE, BULK, AND DENSITY CONTROLS

1. DISTRICTING AND NONCONFORMING USES

Section 2 of the Standard State Zoning Enabling Act, and a similar provision in each of the state zoning enabling acts now in force, authorizes but does not require the local governing body to divide the municipality or other unit of local government "into districts of such number, shape, and area as may be deemed best suited to carry out the purposes of" the act. As previously indicated, the New York City Zoning Resolution of 1916 divided New York City into three classes of districts designed to regulate, respectively, the use of land and buildings, the height of buildings, and the percentage of a lot that could be occupied by buildings, with a separate set of maps for each class. Only three use districts were provided: residential, business, and unrestricted. The Euclid, Ohio zoning ordinance sustained in the *Euclid* case, on the other hand, provided for six use districts, three height districts, and four area districts, although Euclid was only a small suburban village. The Model Zoning Ordinance reproduced (in part) in sec. A of this chapter provides for only three use districts; and it includes, as a part of the regulations applicable in each use district, regulations as to maximum building height, maximum percentage of each lot that may be covered by structures, minimum lot size, minimum ground floor area of buildings, and — in residential and multi-family districts — the maximum number of families that may occupy a dwelling and the distance that each building must be set back from the lot lines. Regulations other than those relating to the permitted uses of land and buildings within a district are generally termed "bulk and density" regulations. As we shall see, the distinction between "use" regulations and "bulk" regulations can be legally important, such as when a variance is requested. This problem is taken up in Ch. 5.

The nonconforming use problem.—When a zoning ordinance is enacted for the first time in a municipality or other local government unit, undeveloped areas can be divided into districts in which, initially at least, all new development will be required to conform to the district regulations. But this may be impossible when a zoning ordinance is enacted for the first time in an area that is already substantially or entirely developed. As one of our most perceptive zoning commentators has observed:

> One of the most troublesome problems which faces the planners and administrators of zoning ordinances is where to draw the boundary lines of use districts. The haphazard growth of our cities and villages has resulted in an inter-larding of strips of residential areas with stores, gas stations, and even heavy industrial properties. To superimpose a use map upon an established urban area must inevitably result in creating large numbers of nonconforming uses and, in many cases, in establishing dividing lines between use districts which will offend those who own property on or near the border line. [Babcock, *The Illinois Supreme Court and Zoning: A Study in Uncertainty,* 15 U. Chi. L. Rev. 87, 94 (1947).]

Whether a zoning ordinance will create nonconforming uses often becomes a strategic question that affects the drawing of district boundaries. This point is often overlooked in discussions of the nonconforming use problem, which typically start with the assumption that land use mixtures are evil and should be eliminated. Look again at the sample zoning map and accompanying text in § A, *supra*.

The drafters of the Standard State Zoning Enabling Act omitted any reference to nonconforming uses, and most of the early zoning legislation (including the pioneering New York legislation) was as silent as the Standard Act on this point. The omission of any reference to the problem of nonconforming uses was apparently largely based on political considerations; the drafters of the early enabling statutes feared that state legislatures would not enact them if they expressly authorized the elimination of nonconforming uses without payment of compensation. Thus, Bassett states that

> [d]uring the preparatory work for the zoning of Greater New York fears were constantly expressed by property owners that existing nonconforming buildings would be ousted. The demand was general that this should not be done. The Zoning Commission went as far as it could to explain that existing nonconforming uses could continue, that zoning looked to the future, and that if orderliness could be brought about in the future the nonconforming buildings would to a considerable extent be changed by natural causes as time went on. It was also stated by the Commission that the purpose of zoning was to stabilize and protect lawful investments and not to injure assessed valuations or existing uses. This has always been the view in New York. No steps have been taken to oust existing nonconforming uses. Consideration for investments made in accordance with the earlier laws has been one of the strong supports of zoning in that city. [E. Bassett, Zoning 113 (rev. ed. 1940).]

Whether the United States Supreme Court, in the 1920s, would have upheld zoning regulations requiring termination of lawfully established nonconforming uses without compensation is far from clear. *Hadacheck* and *Reinman, supra,* would certainly have supported termination requirements applicable to "nuisance" types of land use, but would not necessarily have supported termination requirements where the nonconforming use, though "incompatible" with surrounding land uses, was not close to being a "nuisance." Moreover, the *Pennsylvania Coal Co.* case, *supra,* could have been adduced against any termination requirement in cases where the capital value of the nonconforming use was substantial. In any case, many state courts could have been expected to take a strict view of the limits of the police power and to hold that elimination of nonconforming uses without compensation was an unconstitutional "taking" of private property. That is in fact the position that state courts generally take today. An early leading case is *Jones v. City of Los Angeles,* 295 P. 14 (Cal. 1930).

A number of states prohibit the termination of nonconforming uses. E.g., Ky. Rev. Stat. § 100.253; Utah Code Ann. § 10-9-408. When a state's zoning enabling act was silent on the subject of nonconforming uses, the early zoning ordinances almost invariably provided expressly that lawfully established nonconforming uses might continue, although many ordinances contained a wide variety of restrictive regulations which were meant to hasten their disappearance. Such provisions are still a feature of almost all local zoning ordinances. Typically, they prohibit or severely restrict the physical extension of nonconforming uses, impose limitations on the repair, alteration, or reconstruction of nonconforming structures, and prohibit the resumption of nonconforming uses after "abandonment" or "discontinuance." See the Model Zoning Ordinance, *supra*.

Two competing philosophies dominate the cases on the validity of these restrictions. One is based on an expansive view of the police power that favors the gradual elimination of nonconforming uses. The other is more restrictive and views restrictions on nonconforming uses as a "taking" of rights vested under the zoning ordinance.

Expansion and change of nonconforming use.—Expansion and change in nonconforming businesses occur all the time. The question is whether this results in a loss of nonconforming use status. A court may be strict. In *Stuckman v. Kosciusko County Bd. of Zoning Appeals,* 506 N.E.2d 1079 (Ind. 1987), the plaintiffs owned a nonconforming automobile graveyard and expanded the business after the zoning ordinance was adopted by clearing and smoothing some of their lots and increasing the number of cars stored and sold. The court held the nonconforming use was limited to the area in which it was conducted when the zoning ordinance was adopted. Which view of nonconforming uses did these courts adopt? Compare *Conway v. City of Greenville,* 173 S.E.2d 648 (S.C. 1970). Part of a large tract had been used for commercial purposes — the operation of a construction business — and the court held that this prior nonconforming use justified the use of the entire property for construction of a shopping center.

A change of use within a building also can present problems. Compare *DiBlasi v. Zoning Bd. of Appeals,* 624 A.2d 372 (Conn. 1993) (change of use to probation office does not change nonconforming status), with *Philm Corp. v. Washington Township,* 638 A.2d 388 (Pa. Commw. 1994) (addition of go-go dancers to restaurant changes nonconforming status). Physical changes may lead to a loss of nonconforming use status. An example is the addition of an automated car wash to a nonconforming filling station. *Anderson v. Board of Adjustment,* 931 P.2d 517 (Colo. App. 1996). *Baxter v. City of Preston,* 768 P.2d 1340 (Idaho 1989), provides an extensive review of the case law on the change and expansion of nonconforming uses and adopts a flexible, case-by-case approach in holding that a nonconforming use of land for grazing livestock could not be converted to a year-round feed lot.

Note how the rules on change and expansion of nonconforming uses can "solve" the nonconforming use problem if the use loses nonconforming status. This can be considered an alternative to amortization, which is considered *infra.*

Repair, alteration, and reconstruction.—The relationship between the zoning ordinance, governing land use, and building codes, governing safety, can be difficult. In *In re O'Neal,* 92 S.E.2d 189 (N.C. 1956), the nonconforming use was a small nursing home. Its owners were notified that the building must be torn down because it was not fireproof and because it violated the institutional provisions of the building code. The owners wished to reconstruct a fireproof nursing home on their premises. The court noted that the new home could not exceed the capacity of the old, but held that the applicants were entitled to rebuild their building. The protection of preexisting "lawful" uses referred to the zoning ordinance and not the building code, and protected any use that was lawful under the zoning regulations. A reasonable construction of the zoning regulations required that a balance be struck between the impairment of neighborhood character and the restriction of an existing use of land by means of new regulations. This ordinance did not contain a prohibition on "structural alterations" and, in addition, the new construction was imposed involuntarily under the building code.

In *Granger v. Board of Adjustment,* 44 N.W.2d 399 (Iowa 1950), a manufacturer of burial vaults was allowed to replace the brick and frame walls and roof of his nonconforming building with concrete and steel. The court held that the work could be categorized as a reasonable repair rather than as a structural alteration. Contra *Selligman v. Von Allmen Bros.,* 179 S.W.2d 207 (Ky. 1944). Ky. Rev. Stat. § 100.253 restricts the enlargement or extension of nonconforming use "beyond the scope and area of its operation at the time of the regulation."

Abandonment and discontinuance.—Zoning ordinances often provide that a nonconforming use that has been discontinued may not be resumed, and have usually been interpreted to require an abandonment of the nonconforming use before the right to continue will be terminated. The effectiveness of these provisions is limited by the requirement that an actual intent to abandon must be shown. See *Boles v. City of Chattanooga,* 892 S.W.2d 416 (Tenn. App. 1994) (reviewing cases and finding clear majority require intent). This holding avoids constitutional problems.

The intent rule can be nullified by an ordinance provision specifying a time limit on the failure to exercise a nonconforming use; under these provisions, mere nonuse for the stated period of time is sufficient to terminate the nonconforming use. See, e.g., *Hartley v. City of Colorado Springs,* 764 P.2d 1216 (Colo. 1988) (noting that "intent to abandon" rule makes it difficult to remove nonconforming uses). Numerous problems arise if disaster, e.g., a fire, strikes the non-conforming use, and the owner seeks to rebuild, immediately or after some delay. See *Bruce L. Rothrock Charitable Foundation v. Zoning Hear'g Bd.,* 651 A.2d 587 (Pa. Comm. 1994).

Some statutes deal with these problems. Neb. Rev. Stat. § 19-904.01 (nonconforming use terminates if "discontinued" for 12 months); R. I. Gen. Laws § 45-24-39 (overt act or failure to act required; involuntary interruption such as by fire or catastrophe does not terminate nonconforming use).

Nonconforming signs will more easily disappear if the municipality can remove them once a business the nonconforming sign advertised has closed. The question is whether the abandonment of the business is an abandonment of the nonconforming sign. See *Camara v. Board of Adjustment,* 570 A.2d 1012 (N.J. App. Div. 1990) (holding yes), though the cases are divided. Compare *contra, Motel 6 Operating Ltd. Partnership v. City of Flagstaff,* 991 P.2d 272 (Ariz. App. 1999), where the businesses did not close but wanted to replace nonconforming signs with new sign faces. See Strauss & Geise, *Elimination of Nonconformities: The Case for Voluntary Discontinuance,* 25 Urb. Law. 159 (1993).

Change of ownership or development of land.—In *Village of Valatie v. Smith,* 632 N.E.2d 1264 (N.Y. 1994) the New York court held that a municipality can terminate a nonconforming mobile home when there is a change of ownership, a result somewhat contrary to the usual assumption that nonconforming uses "run with the land." The owner of the nonconforming use argued that the length of an amortization period must be related to land use objectives or the owner's financial recoupment needs. She also argued that the law violated the principle that zoning can only regulate land use, not ownership.

The court held that amortization periods need not be based solely on a municipality's land use objectives but require a balancing of the interests of the nonconforming use with those of the public. It was not irrational for the village to consider the nonfinancial interest of individual owners of nonconforming uses by protecting them from forced relocation at the end of a predetermined amortization period, even though they were still in possession. The court cited, but did not discuss, the contrary case of *O'Connor v. City of Moscow,* 202 P.2d 401 (Idaho 1949).

Outdoor Systems, Inc. v. City of Mesa, 997 F.2d 604 (9th Cir. 1993), upheld ordinances requiring the removal of nonconforming signs when vacant land is developed. The court held there was a "simple and clear" nexus between this requirement and the interest of the cities in removing nonconforming signs.

Defining a nonconforming use.—The term "nonconforming use" is imprecise. It may include any of the following: (a) various types of open land use such as junkyards, lumber yards, and storage yards for heavy machinery; (b) small structures of a nonconforming type such as a shed or a billboard; (c) buildings designed for a conforming use, or at least capable of such use, which have in fact been devoted to some nonconforming use — e.g., an office or store on the ground floor of a residential building; (d) buildings designed, and really only usable, for nonconforming purposes — e.g., a factory building; (e) the use of a building of a generally conforming type for a conforming use, but with some nonconformity as to lot size, lot frontage, setbacks, height, or bulk. Moreover, a zoning nonconformity also occurs when an undeveloped tract of land does not conform to minimum lot area or frontage regulations, although in such a case there is no "use" of the land.

It is not always easy to determine when a nonconforming use has been lawfully established. Where the "use" itself — whether of open land or of a structure — rather than the structure (if any) with which it is associated is nonconforming, most courts seem to require a qualitatively substantial devotion of the property to that use prior to the date when the zoning regulation prohibiting the use becomes effective. See, e.g., *Township of Fruitport v. Baxter,* 148 N.W.2d 888 (Mich. App. 1967), holding that it was not sufficient that several truckloads of junked cars were moved onto the tract just before the effective date of the zoning regulation. But see *Kubby v. Hammond,* 198 P.2d 134 (Ariz. 1948) (nonconforming junkyard was established by a show of intent to establish such a use — building a fence and placing a few junked cars on the tract); *County of DuPage v. Gary-Wheaton Bank,* 192 N.E.2d 311

(Ill. App. 1963) (nonconforming gravel pit was established by one day's work thereon).

Where a developer undertakes a building project that becomes nonconforming under new lot area, frontage, setback, height, bulk, density or building type regulations before construction is completed, a more difficult problem is presented. The developer may then be able to argue she has a vested right to complete the development, or that the municipality is estopped to enforce the new ordinance. For discussion of estoppel see Chapter 5 sec. D1, *infra*.

———

The most controversial technique for eliminating nonconforming uses and structures is "amortization" — a technique considered in the next principal case.

CITY OF LOS ANGELES v. GAGE

127 Cal. App. 2d 442, 274 P.2d 34 (1954)

VALLEE, JUSTICE:

This appeal involves the constitutionality of the provisions of a zoning ordinance which require that certain nonconforming existing uses shall be discontinued within five years after its passage, as they apply to defendants' property.

Plaintiff brought this suit for an injunction to command defendants to discontinue their use of certain property for the conduct of a plumbing business and to remove various materials therefrom, and to restrain them from using the property for any purpose not permitted by the comprehensive zoning plan provisions of the Los Angeles Municipal Code. The cause was submitted to the trial court on admissions in the pleadings and a stipulation of facts. Defendants will be referred to as "Gage."

In 1930 Gage acquired adjoining lots 220 and 221 located on Cochran Avenue in Los Angeles. He constructed a two-family residential building on lot 221 and rented the upper half solely for residential purposes. He established a wholesale and retail plumbing supply business on the property. He used a room in the lower half of the residential building on lot 221 as the office for the conduct of the business, and the rest of the lower half for residential purposes for himself and his family; he used a garage on lot 221 for the storage of plumbing supplies and materials; and he constructed and used racks, bins, and stalls for the storage of such supplies and materials on lot 220. Later Gage incorporated defendant company. . . .

In 1930 the two lots and other property facing on Cochran Avenue in their vicinity were classified in "C" zone by the zoning ordinance then in effect. Under this classification the use to which Gage put the property was permitted. Shortly after Gage acquired lots 220 and 221, they were classified "C-3" zone and the use to which he put the property was expressly permitted. In 1936 the city council of the city passed Ordinance 77,000 which contained a comprehensive zoning plan for the city. Ordinance 77,000 re-enacted the prior ordinances with respect to the use of lots 220 and 221. In 1941 the city council passed Ordinance 85,015 by the terms of which the use of a residential building for the conduct of an office in connection with the plumbing supply business was permitted. Ordinance 85,015 prohibited the open storage of materials in zone "C-3" but permitted such uses as had been established to continue as nonconforming uses. The use to which lots 220 and 221 were put by defendants was a nonconforming use that might be continued. In 1946 the city council passed Ordinance 90,500. This ordinance reclassified lots 220 and 221 and other property fronting on Cochran Avenue in their vicinity from zone "C-3" to zone "R-4" (Multiple dwelling zone). Use of lots 220 and 221 for the conduct of a plumbing business was not permitted in zone "R-4." At the time Ordinance 90,500 was passed, and at all times since, the Los Angeles Municipal Code (§ 12.23 B & C) provided:

> "(a) The nonconforming use of a conforming building or structure may be continued, except that in the 'R' Zones any nonconforming commercial or industrial use of a residential building or residential accessory building shall be discontinued within five (5) years from June 1, 1946, or five (5) years from the date the use becomes nonconforming, whichever date is later. . . .

> "(b) The nonconforming use of land shall be discontinued within five (5) years from June 1, 1946, or within five (5) years from the date the use became nonconforming, in each of the following cases: (1) where no buildings are employed in connection with such use; (2) where the only buildings employed are accessory or incidental to such use; (3) where such use is maintained in connection with a conforming building."

Prior to the passage of Ordinance 90,500 about 50% of the city had been zoned. It was the first ordinance which "attempted to zone the entire corporate limits of the city." Prior to its passage, several thousand exceptions and variances were granted from restrictive provisions of prior ordinances, some of which permitted commercial use of property zoned for residential use, "and in some cases permitted the use of land for particular purposes like or similar to use of subject property which otherwise would have been prohibited." Under Ordinance 90,500, the uses permitted by these exceptions and variances that did not carry a time limit may be continued indefinitely.

The business conducted by Gage on the property has produced a gross revenue varying between $125,000 and $350,000 a year. If he is required to abandon the use of the property for his business, he will be put to the following expenses: "(1) The value of a suitable site for the conduct of its business would be about $10,000; which would be offset by the value of $7,500 of the lot now used. (2) The cost incident to removing of supplies to another location and construction of the necessary racks, sheds, bins and stalls which would be about $2,500. (3) The cost necessary to expend to advertise a new location. (4) The risk of a gain or a loss of business while moving, and the cost necessary to reestablish the business at a new location, the amount of which is uncertain."

The noise and disturbance caused by the loading and unloading of supplies, trucking, and the going and coming of workmen in connection with the operation of a plumbing business with an open storage yard is greater than the noise and disturbance that is normal in a district used solely for residential purposes. . . .

The [trial] court concluded: Gage became vested with the right to use the property for the purpose that it was used; insofar as the Los Angeles Municipal Code purports to require the abandonment of the use of the building on Lot 221 as an office for the plumbing and plumbing supply business or the use of Lot 220 for the open storage of plumbing supplies in the manner that it has been and is being used by Gage, it is void and of no legal effect . . . in that it deprives him of a vested right to use the property for the purpose it has been used continuously since 1930 and deprives him of property without due process of law. Judgment was that plaintiff take nothing. Plaintiff appeals. . . .

The fact that various exceptions and variances were granted under zoning ordinances prior to Ordinance 90,500, and that some of them permitted the use of land for particular purposes like or similar to the use of defendants' property which otherwise would have been prohibited, presents a question for the zoning authorities of the city. They are the persons charged with the duty of deciding whether the conditions in other parts of the city require like prohibition. The mere fact that a prior ordinance excepts a parcel of land in a residential district does not give the owner thereof a vested right to have the exception continued so as to entitle him, on that ground, to attack the validity of a later ordinance repealing the former. . . .

The right of a city council, in the exercise of the police power, to regulate or, in proper cases, to prohibit the conduct of a given business, is not limited by the fact that the value of investments made in the business prior to any legislative actions will be greatly diminished. A business which, when established, was entirely unobjectionable, may, by the growth or change in the character of the neighborhood, become a source of danger to the public health, morals, safety, or general welfare of those who have come to be occupants of the surrounding territory. . . .

No case seems to have been decided in this state squarely involving the precise question presented in the case at bar. Until recently zoning ordinances have made no provision for any systematic and comprehensive elimination of the nonconforming use. The expectation seems to have been that existing nonconforming uses would be of little consequence and that they would eventually disappear. It is said that the fundamental problem facing zoning is the inability to eliminate the nonconforming use. The general purpose of present-day zoning ordinances is to eventually end all nonconforming uses. There is a growing tendency to guard against the indefinite continuance of nonconforming uses by providing for their liquidation within a prescribed period. It is said, "The only positive method of getting rid of nonconforming uses yet devised is to amortize a nonconforming building. That is, to determine the normal useful remaining life of the building and prohibit the owner from maintaining it after the expiration of that time." Crolly and Norton, Termination of Nonconforming Uses, 62 Zoning Bulletin 1, Regional Plan Assn., June 1952.

Amortization of nonconforming uses has been expressly authorized by recent amendments to zoning enabling laws in a number of states. Ordinances providing for amortization of nonconforming uses have been passed in a number of large cities. The length of time given the owner to eliminate his nonconforming use or building varies with the city and with the type of structure. . . . [The court discussed cases from other states that upheld amortization.]

The theory in zoning is that each district is an appropriate area for the location of the uses which the zone plan permits in that area, and that the existence or entrance of other uses will tend to impair the development and stability of the area for the appropriate uses. . . . The presence of any nonconforming use endangers the benefits to be derived from a comprehensive zoning plan. Having the undoubted power to establish residential districts, the legislative body has the power to make such classification really effective by adopting such reasonable regulations as would be conducive to the welfare, health, and safety of those desiring to live in such district and enjoy the benefits thereof. There would be no object in creating a residential district unless there were to be secured to those dwelling therein the advantages which are ordinarily considered the benefits of such residence. It would seem to be the logical and reasonable method of approach to place a time limit upon the continuance of existing nonconforming uses, commensurate with the investment involved and based on the nature of the use; and in cases of nonconforming structures, on their character, age, and other relevant factors.

Exercise of the police power frequently impairs rights in property because the exercise of those rights is detrimental to the public interest. Every zoning ordinance effects some impairment of vested rights either by restricting prospective uses or by prohibiting the continuation of existing uses, because it affects property already owned by individuals at the time of its enactment. In essence there is no distinction between requiring the discontinuance of a nonconforming use within a reasonable period and provisions which deny the right to add to or extend or enlarge an existing nonconforming use, or which deny the right to substitute new buildings for those devoted to an existing nonconforming use — all of which have been held to be valid exercises of the police power.

The distinction between an ordinance restricting future uses and one requiring the termination of present uses within a reasonable period of time is merely one of degree, and constitutionality depends on the relative importance to be given to the public gain and to the private loss. Zoning as it affects every piece of property is to some extent retroactive in that it applies to property already owned at the time of the effective date of the ordinance. The elimination of existing uses within a reasonable time does not amount to a taking of property nor does it necessarily restrict the use of property so that it cannot be used for any reasonable purpose. Use of a reasonable amortization scheme provides an equitable means of reconciliation of the conflicting interests in satisfaction of due process requirements. As a method of eliminating existing nonconforming uses it allows the owner of the nonconforming use, by affording an opportunity to make new plans, at least partially to offset any loss he might suffer. The loss he suffers, if any, is spread out over a period

Facial
+ Applied

of years, and he enjoys a monopolistic position by virtue of the zoning ordinance as long as he remains. If the amortization period is reasonable the loss to the owner may be small when compared with the benefit to the public. Nonconforming uses will eventually be eliminated. A legislative body may well conclude that the beneficial effect on the community of the eventual elimination of all nonconforming uses by a reasonable amortization plan more than offsets individual losses.

The ordinance in question provides, according to a graduated periodic schedule, for the gradual and ultimate elimination of all commercial and industrial uses in residential zones. These provisions require the discontinuance of nonconforming uses of land within a five-year period, and the discontinuance of nonconforming commercial and industrial uses of residential buildings in the "R" zones within the same five-year period. These provisions are the only ones pertinent to the decision in this case. However, it may be noted that other provisions of the ordinance require the discontinuance of nonconforming billboards and, in residential zones, the discontinuance of nonconforming buildings and of nonconforming uses of nonconforming buildings, within specified periods running from 20 to 40 years according to the type of building construction.

We have no doubt that Ordinance 90,500, in compelling the discontinuance of the use of defendants' property for a wholesale and retail plumbing and plumbing supply business, and for the open storage of plumbing supplies within five years after its passage, is a valid exercise of the police power. Lots 220 and 221 are several blocks from a business center and it appears that they are not within any reasonable or logical extension of such a center. The ordinance does not prevent the operation of defendants' business; it merely restricts its location. Discontinuance of the nonconforming use requires only that Gage move his plumbing business to property that is zoned for it. Such property can be found within a half mile of Gage's property. The cost of moving is $5,000, or less than 1% of Gage's minimum gross business for five years, or less than half of 1% of the mean of his gross business for five years. He has had eight years within which to move. The property is usable for residential purpose. Since 1930 lot 221 has been used for residential purposes. All of the land within 500 feet of Gage's property is now improved and used for such purposes. Lot 220, now unimproved, can be improved for the same purposes.

We think it apparent that none of the agreed facts and none of the ultimate facts found by the court justify the conclusion that Ordinance 90,500, as applied to Gage's property, is clearly arbitrary or unreasonable, or has no substantial relation to the public's health, safety, morals, or general welfare, or that it is an unconstitutional impairment of his property rights. . . .

The judgment is reversed. . . .

NOTES AND QUESTIONS

1. *Constitutional issues. Gage* held that a zoning ordinance that amortizes nonconforming uses is facially constitutional, and also held the amortization period constitutional as applied to the property. An overwhelming majority of the courts now uphold amortization as a constitutional zoning technique, although the courts so holding do not always accept the *Gage* rationale that the distinction between prospective zoning and elimination of lawfully established nonconforming uses is only a matter of degree. See D. Mandelker, Land Use Law § 5.74 n.289 (4th ed. 1997) (citing cases). Are these due process or taking cases? To the extent that taking law is involved, is *Lucas* or *Penn Central* the relevant starting point?

Some courts take a middle ground and hold amortization constitutional only if applied to nonconforming uses that constitute nuisances. E.g., *Loundsbury v. City of Keene,* 453 A.2d 1278 (N.H. 1982); *Northern Ohio Sign Contrs. Ass'n v. City of Lakewood,* 513 N.E.2d 324 (Ohio 1987). See also *Stoner McCray Sys. v. City of Des Moines,* 78 N.W.2d 843 (Iowa 1956) (indicating it would uphold amortization if period reasonable and nonconforming use endangered health, safety and welfare). *Sed quaere* why nonconforming uses that amount to nuisances or endanger health and safety cannot be summarily terminated, without allowing any "amortization" period. In Missouri, the supreme court held that "amortization" is unconstitutional as applied to open land storage uses, but later held that "amortization" of billboards was constitutional. *Hoffman v. Kinealy,* 389 S.W.2d 745 (Mo. 1965) (open land storage); *University City v. Diveley Auto Body Co.,* 417 S.W.2d 107 (Mo. 1967).

2. *Unconstitutional.* In *Harbison v. City of Buffalo,* 152 N.E.2d 42 (N.Y. 1958), where two judges embraced the "amortization" theory but the other two judges who joined to make up a majority only concurred in the result, Judge Van Voorhis, in dissent, said:

> This theory [amortization] to justify extinguishing nonconforming uses means less the more one thinks about it. . . . [T]he term "amortization," as thus employed, has not the same meaning which it carries in law or accounting. . . . It is just a catch phrase, and the reasoning is reduced to argument by metaphor. Not only has no effort been made in the reported cases . . . to determine what is the useful life of the structure, but almost all were decided under ordinances or statutes which prescribe the same time limit for many different kinds of improvements. This demonstrates that it is not attempted to measure the life of the particular building or type of building, and that the word "amortization" is used as an empty shibboleth. . . . [*Id.* at 54.]

Until recently, this view was a minority, but Georgia and Pennsylvania have now held that amortization is an unconstitutional zoning technique. *Lamar Advertising of South Georgia, Inc. v. Albany,* 389 S.E.2d 216 (Ga. 1990); *PA Northwest Distribs., Inc. v. Zoning Hearing Board,* 584 A.2d 1372 (Pa. 1991). These courts took the absolutist position that property is property and cannot be "taken" without compensation. As the Pennsylvania court said, "[i]t is clear that if we were to permit the amortization of nonconforming uses in this Commonwealth, any use could be amortized out of existence without just compensation."

3. *The takings question.* The courts rarely make it clear just what is being "amortized" when they consider the validity of zoning ordinance provisions authorizing the "amortization" of nonconforming uses. This makes it difficult for courts to formulate a test for determining the reasonableness of "amortization" provisions. Some zoning ordinances set out the factors to be considered in determining the length of the "amortization" period.

In *Metromedia, Inc. v. City of San Diego,* 610 P.2d 407 (Cal. 1980), *rev'd on other grounds,* 453 U.S. 490 (1981), the court upheld a provision requiring "amortization" of nonconforming signs in one to four years, depending on the "adjusted market value" of a particular sign, defined as the sign's original cost less ten percent of the original cost for each year the sign was in place prior to the effective date of the ordinance. But what is the rational basis for assuming that the market value of all signs decreased at the rate of ten percent of original cost per year?

In *Metromedia, supra,* the court said that the constitutionality of "amortization" provisions as applied to nonconforming structures depends in part on facts peculiar to particular structures, including, in the case of billboards, "the cost of the billboard, its depreciated value, remaining useful life, the length and remaining term of the lease under which it is maintained, and the harm to the public if the structure remains standing beyond the prescribed amortization period." The highest New York court approved similar factors in *Modjeska Sign Studios, Inc. v. Berle,* 373 N.E.2d 255 (N.Y. 1977), *appeal dismissed,* 439 U.S. 809 (1978), where the court said:

> . . . Whether an amortization period is reasonable is a question that must be answered in the light of the facts of each particular case. Certainly, a critical factor is the length of the amortization period in relation to the investment. Similarly, another factor considered significant by some courts is the nature of the nonconforming activity prohibited; generally a shorter period may be provided for a nonconforming use as opposed to a nonconforming structure. The critical question, however, . . . is whether the public gain achieved by the exercise of the police power outweighs the private loss suffered by the owners of nonconforming uses. While an owner need not be given that period of time necessary to recoup his investment entirely, the amortization period should not be so short as to result in a substantial loss. In determining what constitutes a substantial loss, the court should look to, for example, such factors as: initial capital investment, investment realization to date, life expectancy of the investment, and the existence or nonexistence of a lease obligation as well as a contingency clause permitting termination of the lease. Generally, most regulations requiring the removal of nonconforming billboards and providing a reasonable amortization period should pass constitutional muster. [*Id.* at 262.]

This approach has survived the 1987 Supreme Court takings trilogy. For example, in *Outdoor Graphics v. City of Burlington,* 103 F.3d 690 (8th Cir. 1996), the court upheld a five-year amortization period for a nonconforming sign, "weighing such factors as whether the land has any other economic use, the depreciation and life expectancy of the billboards, the income from the billboards during the amortization or grace period, the salvage value of the billboards and whether any amortization period is reasonable." See also *Georgia Outdoor Advertising, Inc. v. City of Waynesville (II),* 900 F.2d 783 (4th

Cir. 1990) (amortization clause one factor to consider in deciding taking objection to sign ordinance).

Courts sometimes place emphasis on particular factors, such as whether the nonconforming use has been amortized for tax purposes. *National Adv. Co. v. Monterey County,* 464 P.2d 33 (Cal. 1970) (billboards deemed "fully amortized" on basis of Internal Revenue Service rules as to "amortization" for tax purposes). Another question is whether courts should consider whether a nonconforming use has remaining physical life. See *La Mesa v. Tweed & Gambrell Planing Mill,* 304 P.2d 803 (Cal. App. 1957) (5-year "amortization" period invalid as applied to 20-year-old building with remaining useful life of 21 years). However, in *AVR, Inc. v. City of St. Louis Park,* 585 N.W.2d 411 (Minn. App. 1998), *cert denied,* 526 U.S. 1114 (1999), the court refused to consider whether a nonconforming cement mixing plant had a remaining "economic" life because its owners had recovered 560% on their investment and it was fully depreciated for tax purposes. Otherwise, the court said, the owner of a nonconforming use could extend its life by replacements or improvements. See accord, e.g., *City of University Park v. Benners,* 485 S.W.2d 773, 777 (Tex. 1972).

4. *Statutory authority.* Statutory authority is another major problem. Most courts have found an implied authority to amortize when express authority is not provided. See *Mayor & Council v. Rollins Outdoor Adv., Inc.,* 475 A.2d 355 (Del. 1975). Many states now prohibit amortization for billboards located on federal highways to comply with provisions in the federal Highway Beautification Act that require compensation for their removal. See Chapter 8. Other states prohibit amortization for all nonconforming uses. See Minn. Stat. Ann. § 394.21(1a), adopted in reaction to the *AVR* case, supra.

5. *Does amortization work?* In 1971, the American Society of Planning Officials polled its membership to determine the extent to which amortization was being used to eliminate nonconforming uses. Out of 489 cities and counties responding, 159 reported that they had zoning ordinances providing for amortization, but only 27 municipalities reported use of the amortization technique against buildings. The report indicated that amortization has most frequently been used against billboards and other uses involving a small capital investment. Most of the zoning administrators who responded expressed dissatisfaction with the amortization technique. R. Scott, The Effect of Nonconforming Land-Use Amortization (American Soc'y of Planning Officials, Planning Advisory Service Rep. No. 280, May 1972).

The American Planning Association's model legislation authorizes amortization in a zoning ordinance. § 8-502(4) (draft 2000). It does not attempt to specify the factors that should govern amortization but provides two alternative methods. A zoning ordinance may "state a period of time after which nonconforming land uses or structures, or designated classes of nonconforming land uses or structures, must terminate." In the alternative, it may provide "criteria" that the local planning or code enforcement agency "may apply to provide a period of time after which a nonconforming land use or structure must terminate." Do you see the advantage of this approach? The *AVR* case, *supra,* held that the adoption of an amortization period by applying criteria was not a quasi-judicial action.

The model legislation also authorizes amortization only if a local government adopts a comprehensive plan and amortization "implements an express policy contained in the plan." § 8-502(5). The requirement will compel municipalities to decide where amortization can be useful, and should support its constitutionality by specifying the benefits that amortization can bring.

6. For further discussion of amortization see Cobb, *Amortizing Nonconforming Uses,* Land Use L. & Zoning Dig., Vol. 37, No. 1, at 3 (1985); Peterson & McCarthy, *Amortization of Legal Land Use Nonconformities as Regulatory Takings: An Uncertain Future,* 35 Wash. U. J. Urb. & Contemp. L. 37 (1989); Reynolds, *The Reasonableness of Amortization Periods for Nonconforming Uses — Balancing the Private Interest and the Public Welfare,* 34 *id.,* at 99 (1988).

2. RESIDENTIAL USE CLASSIFICATIONS

a. Separation of Residential from Non-Residential Use

"As-applied" problems.—Although the constitutionality of zoning regulations separating "residential" from "non-residential" land uses was established, as a matter of general principle, in *Euclid,* the Supreme Court warned that such regulations might be found to be unreasonable and therefore invalid when "concretely applied to particular premises." Indeed, as has already been pointed out, the Supreme Court held a "residential use" classification, as applied to part of a larger tract, invalid in *Nectow v. City of Cambridge,* 277 U.S. 183 (1928), because it did not promote "the health, safety, convenience and general welfare of the inhabitants of the part of the city affected." In *Nectow,* the Court accepted, as a basis for its decision, the findings of the master appointed by the Massachusetts court, as follows:

> When the zoning ordinance was enacted, plaintiff in error was and still is the owner of a tract of land containing 140,000 square feet, of which the locus here in question is a part. The locus contains 29,000 square feet, with a frontage on Brookline street, lying west, of 304.75 feet, on Henry street, lying north, of 100 feet, on other land of the plaintiff in error, lying east, of 264 feet, and on land of the Ford Motor Company, lying southerly, of 75 feet. The territory lying east and south is unrestricted. The lands beyond Henry street to the north and beyond Brookline street to the west are within a residential district. The effect of the zoning is to separate from the west end of plaintiff in error's tract a strip 100 feet in width. The Ford Motor Company has a large auto assembling factory south of the locus; and a soap factory and the tracks of the Boston & Albany Railroad lie near. Opposite the locus, on Brookline street, and included in the same district, there are some residences; and opposite the locus, on Henry street, and in the same district, are other residences. The locus is now vacant, although it was once occupied by a mansion house. Before the passage of the ordinance in question, plaintiff in error had outstanding a contract for the sale of the greater part of his entire tract of land for the sum of $63,000. Because of the zoning restrictions the purchaser refused to comply with the contract. Under the ordinance, business and industry of all

sorts are excluded from the locus, while the remainder of the tract is unrestricted. It further appears that provision has been made for widening Brookline street, the effect of which, if carried out, will be to reduce the depth of the locus to 65 feet. [*Id.* at 186–87.]

These findings clearly illustrate the grounds on which courts have invalidated "residential use" classifications in a substantial number of cases: the land in question is — for various reasons — unsuitable for residential development, and this lack of suitability leads to the conclusion reached by the master in the *Nectow* case — that "no practical use can be made of the land . . . for residential purposes."

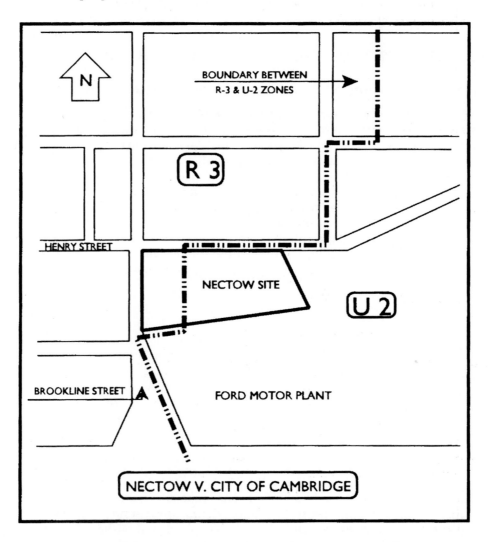

Arverne Bay Constr. Co. v. Thatcher, 15 N.E.2d 587 (N.Y. 1938), is another early case holding a residential use classification invalid as applied to a particular tract. The record in *Arverne Bay* established the following facts:

> There are only three buildings on Linden Avenue . . . [in the vicinity
> of plaintiff's tract]. One of these buildings is a cow stable and a second
> building is used as an office in connection with a dairy business
> conducted there. . . . [I]n the vicinity of the plaintiff's premises the
> city operates an incinerator which "gives off offensive fumes and odors
> which permeate plaintiff's premises." About 1,200 or 1,500 feet from
> plaintiff's land, "a trunk sewer carrying both storm and sanitary
> sewage empties into an open creek. . . . The said creek runs to the
> south of plaintiff's premises and gives off nauseating odors which per-
> meate the said property." [*Id.* at 590–91.]

The New York Court of Appeals assumed that "the zoning ordinance is the
product of farsighted planning calculated to promote the general welfare of
the city at some future time," but it held the residential use classification
unconstitutional as applied to plaintiff's tract because it "cannot at present
or in the immediate future be profitably or reasonably used without violation
of the restriction," and "no inference is permissible that within a reasonable
time the property can be put to a profitable use or that the present inconvenience and hardship imposed upon the plaintiff is temporary." Hence, the
court said, the "residential use" classification was "in substance a taking of
the land prohibited by the Constitution of the United States and by the
Constitution of the State."

The New York court, in so holding, relied heavily upon *Pennsylvania Coal
Co. v. Mahon, supra.* However, in *Nectow* the Court noted that "[t]he attack
upon the ordinance is that, as specifically applied to plaintiff in error, it
deprived him of his property without due process of law in contravention of
the Fourteenth Amendment."

b. Separation of Single-Family and Multifamily Uses

Basis for single-family zoning.—Although the New York City Zoning Resolution of 1916 did not do so, most municipal zoning ordinances, from the earliest
days of zoning, provided for two or more residential use classifications, one
of which was a "single-family residential use" classification. Indeed, the
Euclid, Ohio zoning ordinance provided for a single-family residential use
classification. But the *Euclid* opinion did not expressly discuss the validity
of such a classification; and the "nuisance prevention" rationale of *Euclid* with
respect to segregation of apartments from other dwellings would not necessarily have justified the exclusion of two-family dwellings as well as apartment
houses from a single-family residential use district. But in *Brett v. Building
Comm'r,* 145 N.E. 269 (Mass. 1924), some two years before *Euclid,* the court
sustained an exclusive single-family residential use classification against a
constitutional challenge. The rationale of *Brett* was as follows:

> Restriction of the use of land to buildings each to be occupied as
> a residence for a single family may be viewed at least in two aspects.
> It may be regarded as preventive of fire. It seems to us manifest that,
> other circumstances being the same, there is less danger of a building
> becoming ignited if occupied by one family than if occupied by two or
> more families. Any increase in the number of persons or of stoves or
> lights under a single roof increases the risk of fire. A regulation

designed to decrease the number of families in one house may reason-ably be thought to diminish that risk. The space between buildings likely to arise from the separation of people into a single family under one roof may rationally be thought also to diminish the hazard of conflagration in a neighborhood. Statutes designed to minimize this hazard by regulations as to mechanical construction, air spaces and similar contrivances are familiar and have been upheld. . . . We can-not say that it may not be a rational means to the same end to require that no more than one family inhabit one house, where conditions as to population permit.

It may be a reasonable view that the health and general physical and mental welfare of society would be promoted by each family dwelling in a house by itself. Increase in fresh air, freedom for the play of children and of movement for adults, the opportunity to cultivate a bit of land, and the reduction in the spread of contagious diseases may be thought to be advanced by a general custom that each family live in a house standing by itself with its own curtilage. These features of family life are equally essential or equally advantageous for all inhabitants, whatever may be their social standing or material prosperity. There is nothing on the face of this by-law to indicate that it will not operate indifferently for the general benefit. It is matter of common knowledge that there are in numerous districts plans for real estate development involving modest single-family dwellings within the reach as to price of the thrifty and economical of moderate wage earning capacity.

This provision of the by-law does not extend to the entire territory of the town. That is not such inequality as denies equal protection of the laws to those within the restricted area. Reasonable classification as to the designation of areas as well as in other respects must be permitted to the law-making power. . . . That is a necessary corollary of a zoning law of any kind.

The question to be decided is not whether we approve such a by-law. It is whether we can pronounce it an unreasonable exercise of power having no rational relation to the public safety, public health or public morals. We do not see our way clear to do that. In reaching this conclusion we are not unmindful of decisions either reaching the opposite conclusion or having a contrary appearance. . . . We think the sounder reasoning and the weight of authority supports the conclusion we have reached. [*Id.* at 271.]

The reasoning of the Massachusetts court in *Brett* is obviously similar to the reasoning of the United States Supreme Court in *Euclid* in regard to the exclusion of apartments from a "one-and-two-family residential use" district. Since the 1920s, it seems generally to have been assumed that exclusive one-family residential districts are constitutionally permissible.

Both *Euclid* and *Brett* purport to furnish a rationale for segregating residential buildings by building type. A more complete summary of the reasons advanced by courts to justify such segregation would include the following:

(a) More restrictive building-type districts tend to have a lower density, i.e., a single-family district usually has a lower density than a two-family or a multiple-family district. This results in the following benefits: (i) limitation on the resulting traffic in the area; (ii) protection of peace and quiet, and reduction in the amount of noise in the area; (iii) protection of access to light, air, and sunlight; (iv) protection of public health, by wider spacing between dwelling units, with correspondingly greater protection against contagious diseases; (v) increased safety from fire, primarily also as a result of increased space between dwelling units; (vi) limitation of the burden on public services such as sewerage, water supply, police and fire protection, and consequent limitation of the burden of property taxes.

(b) Multiple-family dwellings are incompatible with the residential character of the area for aesthetic reasons, and also because their occupancy is more transient than that of single-family dwellings.

(c) Because of the factors listed in (a) and (b), above, multiple-family dwellings lower the value of single-family homes in the same area and start a trend toward blight and the development of slums.

(d) Segregation of residential structures by building type provides for a more "orderly" and "balanced" pattern of development.

Lees, *Preserving Property Values? Preserving Proper Homes? Preserving Privilege?: The Pre-Euclid Debate over Zoning for Exclusively Private Residential Areas, 1916–1926,* 56 U. Pitt. L. Rev. 367 (1994), reviews these and other justifications for exclusive residential zoning in the days before *Euclid.*

The arguments based upon "density" clearly are no longer always valid. Many modern "garden apartment" developments have comparatively modest densities and may have landscaping and other features that enhance the attractiveness of the project. Indeed, some of these developments arguably are more attractive than many older single-family residential areas where homes are built on small lots lined up along streets. Is the basis for single-family zoning really aesthetic?

Judicial review standards.—Although the separation of single-family and multi-family uses, like other zoning restrictions, raises an "as applied" taking problem, state court handling of these cases is not always clear. Some courts do not explicitly consider the taking question, but examine zoning and existing development in the surrounding area to determine if the zoning restriction is "arbitrary and capricious." This inquiry reflects the nuisance basis of zoning law. When the taking issue is considered, the majority of state courts hold that a taking occurs only if the restriction does not allow any economically viable use of the land. The Supreme Court's *Lucas* case holds a per se taking occurs in this situation. The following is a typical pre-*Lucas* decision indicating how state courts handle the taking problem when a claim is made that a property is improperly restricted to single-family rather than multi-family use:

KRAUSE v. CITY OF ROYAL OAK

11 Mich. App. 183, 160 N.W.2d 769 (1968)

BURNS, JUDGE:

The city of Royal Oak appeals from a judgment restraining it from enforcing a zoning ordinance which places plaintiffs' property in a one-family residential use classification. The judgment permits plaintiffs to use their land for multiple-family residential purposes.

Plaintiffs' property is located in the city of Royal Oak and consists of approximately 3.5 acres of land, which, for purposes of this opinion, can be described in terms of a geometrically imperfect right triangle. The Grand Trunk Western railroad, which is elevated and runs in a northwesterly and southeasterly direction, forms the hypotenuse of this triangle. Starr road, which runs roughly east and west, provides a southern base for the triangle. The remaining part of the triangle, the western border of plaintiffs' property, is composed of one lot which fronts on the north side of Starr road and other lots which front on the east side of Benjamin avenue, a north-south thoroughfare. Within this area are 14 subdivided lots surrounding a 350 foot, undeveloped cul-de-sac.

The territory bounded by the railroad, Starr road and Benjamin avenue has been zoned for one-family residential use since 1957. Other than one nonconforming 3-family multiple dwelling, which was erected prior to 1957 when multiple dwellings were permissible, the east side of Benjamin avenue and the first 2 lots on the north side of Starr avenue, east of Benjamin, are developed with single-family residences. Located upon the subject property itself are 2 comparatively old one-family homes which, all parties agree, will be removed for purposes of replatting, regardless of the course of future development.

The neighborhood surrounding the area bounded by Starr road, Benjamin avenue and the railroad is of a mixed character. The Royal Oak municipal golf course is on the west side of Benjamin (across the street from the lots which back up to the subject property). The area north and east of the railroad is zoned for one-family residences, and improvements exist on a number of those lots. The property south of Starr road is zoned for and has been developed with multiple-family dwellings. This property also fronts upon heavily traveled 13 Mile road which is exclusively bounded by multiple-family complexes from the Grand Trunk Western railroad tracks west to one of the main arteries of the Detroit metropolitan area, Woodward avenue (US-10), where nonresidential uses are permitted.

Since 1961, owners of part of the subject property have made unsuccessful applications for a zoning change, but it was not until 1966 that plaintiffs commenced this action to enjoin the defendant from enforcing the zoning ordinance as it affects their land. The trial judge listened to the proofs, viewed the premises, and held that the one-family zoning classification was void because it constituted an unreasonable and arbitrary exercise of the police power of the city of Royal Oak and was confiscatory in that it deprived plaintiffs of their property without due process of law.

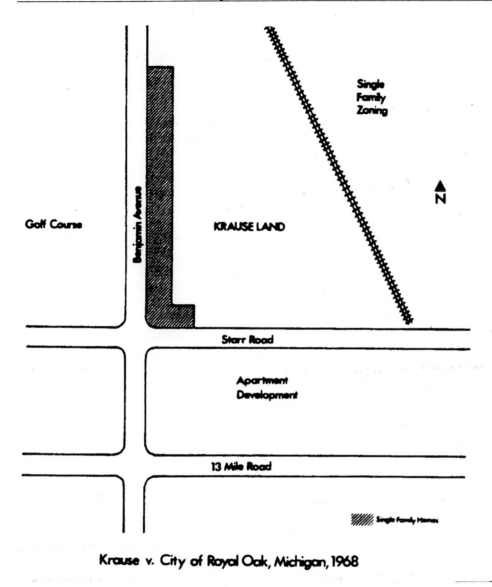

Golf Course

Benjamin Avenue

KRAUSE LAND

Single
Family
Zoning

N

Starr Road

Apartment
Development

13 Mile Road

////// Single Family Homes

Krause v. City of Royal Oak, Michigan, 1968

Our review of this judgment is guided by certain elementary principles. . . .

The propositions that an "ordinance is presumed valid" and that it is plaintiff's burden to overcome that presumption "by clear and satisfactory proof" are of critical importance in this case. . . .

To place this case in its proper perspective, we should note that plaintiff did not claim that any depreciation in property value resulted from the adoption of the zoning ordinance imposing the restriction to which the property was not previously subject. Rather, it appears that the essence of plaintiffs' objection is that their land should be freed of the restriction imposed by the ordinance of 1957 to the end that they might have the benefit of appreciated value. Although one witness, a home builder testifying on behalf of plaintiffs, stated the land was unsuited for single-residential use, another one of the plaintiffs' witnesses, an appraiser who was more familiar with property values, testified that the land was not without value as zoned but that it would be more valuable for multiple-family use. Defendant conceded that such was the case but disputed the ratio of difference in valuations as computed by plaintiffs' witnesses.

According to the plaintiffs' witnesses, the marketability of the property for one-family residences was impaired by the presence of the railroad. The proximity of the tracks to the lots made it impossible to obtain Federal Housing Administration financing, thereby eliminating a good percentage of prospective buyers who could not secure Veterans Administration or conventional loans. In addition, plaintiffs' witnesses pointed out the undesirability of constructing one-family residences next to a railroad because of the vibration, noise, possible danger to children, and the smell. Yet, by plaintiffs' proposal to build multiple dwellings (40 one-bed units and 40 two-bed units) they would invite many more persons (than the 14 one-family houses would accommodate) to share in this feigned misery. The alleged adverse effect the railroad may have on marketability of single-family homes is at best dubious because of plaintiffs' own appraiser's acknowledgment upon cross-examination that a number of single-family homes in Royal Oak lie adjacent to the railroad although these areas located next to the tracks have been the last to develop for residential purposes. The proximity of a railroad does not render zoning for one-family residential purposes arbitrary and unreasonable.

This is not to say, however, that the value of the property and the effect, if any, a railroad has on that value, plays no role in our deliberations. The Supreme Court of Michigan has repeatedly recognized that "the mere fact that land may have a greater selling value for a possible use of different character than that for which it is zoned is not a sufficient basis for holding the ordinance invalid, as applied to such property, although, of course, it is a matter to be considered with other elements affecting the situation." *Paka Corp. v. City of Jackson,* 110 N.W.2d 620, 623 (Mich. 1961).

The disparity of valuations in the cases cited by the plaintiffs wherein zoning ordinances have been held for naught are invariably accompanied by other factors which clearly affect the public health, safety or general welfare of the people. For instance, in *Smith v. Village of Wood Creek Farms,* [123 N.W.2d 210 (Mich. 1963)], the disparity of value of 3 lots and the presence of 2 busy highways and nearby commercial locations were sufficient to invalidate an ordinance restricting those lots to residential purposes, whereas the disparity of value of a fourth lot, which was bordered on but one side by a highway, was insufficient to negate the zoning ordinance.

In the present case the difference in value is accompanied by no convincing evidence bearing on the improper use of the police power. The most positive evidence tendered by plaintiffs was the testimony of the city's planning director who said that no question of public health is involved. Other than this, plaintiffs' proofs fail to adequately cope with most of the public interest considerations which we must assume prompted the adoption of the zoning ordinance.

In this respect, however, there was some testimony introduced regarding the impact that a multiple dwelling development would have upon the people whose backyards abut the subject property. During plaintiffs' case in chief, plaintiffs' appraiser testified that the presence of multiple dwellings would have no adverse effect on the immediate neighborhood, but the adverse effect to which he referred was in terms of price not people. Plaintiffs' home building witness also testified as to this problem, but his concept of adverse effect was his personal opinion of whether or not he would purchase a house completely surrounded with multiple dwellings. Both of plaintiffs' witnesses who spoke on this issue approached the problem as one of basic economics. Contrary to this dollars and cents approach, we have the defendant's planning director's testimony which probably explains a portion of the rationale for having the subject property zoned as it is.

" Q: *[Counsel for defendant]* In your professional opinion, as a person who works in the field of zoning and community planning, does the existing one-family zoning of the subject property tend to promote the public peace, safety and general welfare?

" A: *[City planning director]* In my opinion it does, yes.

" Q: Will you tell us why?

" A: Well, I might preface my comments to the fact that in this specific area the public involved would be the public that would be in the triangle for the immediate vicinity of the lots in question. This would be from 13 Mile road on the south, Benjamin on the west, and essentially the Grand Trunk on the easterly boundary. They would be the immediate public involved. The area is predominantly single-family north of Starr road and these people would be forced to experience the increased confusion and congestion, noise, *et cetera* that would accompany a development other than single-family, a development that would allow a drastic increase in the total number of people that would live in the three acres more or less in question. The single-family zoning in the area would promote a 13-family development, at least 13 families, would generate at best 26 cars so there would not be a traffic problem coming into or off of Benjamin from Starr road. Also the nature of the residential amenities that accrue to other residential properties from single-family developments would tend to go along with the type of development that is already north of Starr road. Also, we feel that this type of zoning does allow for the natural growth of single-family development with the schools and the other residential amenities [which] are in the area. . . .

" Q: Mr. Bowman, as a professional in the field of planning and zoning, what is your opinion as to the comparative desirability of having multiple-family residences back up to single-family residences, compared to facing multiple-family to single-family with a street in between, sir?

" A: Well, it's my opinion, based upon the experiences we have had in the recent past, over the past 2 or 3 years, with the rapid development of apartments in Royal Oak and in our surrounding communities, that due to the general demand of the occupants of apartments for parking, for the use of a swimming pool, other recreational facilities, the high density of people living in these developments, that it is far better to face the apartment development across a street which is 50 or 60 feet in width to the single-family development rather than having it abut to the rear yards where all of the service parking and all of the congestion takes place; that we have found that we have more and more of our abutting property owners object where it is a rear yard situation rather than a face to face situation."

We think it is fair to conclude, therefore, that the municipal authority enacting this ordinance was trying to avoid the situation described in *Euclid v. Ambler Realty Company* [Here the court quoted the paragraph in the *Euclid* case which held, in effect, that apartment development was parasitical in single-family residential areas. — Eds.]

Not to be overlooked is plaintiffs' evidence which, we surmise, was directed to the claim that the city's zoning practice in this instance was arbitrary and capricious. In 1964 a triangular-shaped parcel of property, which is also situated next to the Grand Trunk Western railroad and directly northwest of the subject property, was rezoned from one-family to multiple-family residential. We gather from the city planning director's testimony, however, that there were no existing one-family houses on the rezoned land and there are on the subject property. Furthermore, it is important to note that the area catercorner from this parcel is zoned for heavy industry purposes and that it is bordered predominantly with multiple-family or non-residential zoning classifications. The 1964 rezoning was completely reasonable in our opinion and bears no relation to the alleged unreasonable characterization of plaintiffs' property.

Plaintiffs' case, amounting to substantially nothing more than a partial deprivation of the best economic use of their property, does not persuade us to subvert the interests of the public as expressed by the legislative body which enacted the zoning ordinance in question. The evidence introduced by plaintiffs is alarmingly insufficient to rebut the ordinance's presumption of validity. At best, plaintiffs' evidence presents nothing more than a debatable question.

Judgment vacated. No costs, a public question being involved.

LEVIN, PRESIDING JUDGE (dissenting):

The plaintiffs challenged their property's present zoning both on the ground that it bears no substantial relationship to public health, morals, safety, or general welfare and on the ground that it deprives the property of any reasonable use. Holding for the plaintiffs on both grounds, the trial judge found the zoning both irrational and confiscatory.

Concluding that at best plaintiffs' evidence presented nothing more than a "debatable question" on the rationality of present zoning, the majority reverses the trial judge. However, even if zoning is entirely reasonable in the sense it bears a substantial relationship to public health, morals, safety, or general welfare, it may nonetheless be unreasonable in its application to particular property if that property cannot reasonably be used as zoned. Zoning which prevents any reasonable use of property is confiscatory and, for that reason, invalid.

While the trial judge and we must find for the municipality if we find there is a debatable question concerning the rationality of the zoning, i.e., zoning is not irrational if, on the evidence presented, its rationality remains debatable, a "debatable question" rule has not been established where the question presented is whether the zoning is unreasonable because it is confiscatory. Whether zoning is confiscatory is more a question of fact than of judgment. That fact may be proved like any other fact. It is not necessary for one claiming confiscation to prove it beyond dispute.

The evidence presented here concerning the confiscation issue was in conflict. The trial judge correctly went about resolving that factual dispute in the same manner he would approach decision of any disputed factual issue in a case tried to him. Merely because all reasonable men would not necessarily have reached the same decision did not oblige the trial judge to decide the issue of confiscation for the municipality. . . .

On the entire evidence I am not left with the *definite and firm conviction* that a mistake was committed by the trial judge. The trial judge stated that the plaintiffs' house builder witness "made the greatest impression on the court. A home builder with considerable experience in Royal Oak, he testified that plaintiff's land was totally unsuited to single residence development and that at least to him the land had no value for that purpose. Based on his own experience he said that lots adjacent to the unsightly and noisy railroad tracks were not readily salable for single residence purposes. He has owned 2 comparable lots for some time and has been unable to dispose of them. Furthermore, again based on his own experience, he said that adequate home financing could not be obtained on land adjacent to railroad tracks."

The trial judge thereby indicated he chose to adopt the testimony offered in behalf of the plaintiffs in preference to testimony offered in behalf of the defendant.

There is no reason to reject the trial judge's evaluation of the conflicting testimony. The testimony of plaintiffs' house builder witness so adopted by the trial judge was not incredible. It was supported by the testimony of plaintiffs' appraisal witness who, while he valued the property at $11,500, stated that a prudent developer would not buy it. I interpret that to mean a speculator could be found to buy the property, but not a developer. The question before the trial judge and us, on the issue of confiscation, is whether the property can reasonably be *used* as zoned, not whether it has an exchange value. That a buyer could be found for it, that it has a buying and selling value, does not establish that anyone could be found who would develop and use the property.

Passage of time and accompanying changes in controlling facts, a change in zoning itself, might make the property more valuable and justify a speculator's investment. And then again the property might become worth less. The judicial inquiry is not concerned with the speculative possibilities of the property, but rather seeks to determine whether it can now be reasonably *used* as now zoned.

That the 12 home owners between plaintiffs' property and Benjamin avenue foresee damage to their property from further multiple development, bears out plaintiffs' expert testimony that it would be difficult to find home buyers willing to make an investment in single-family residences constructed on plaintiffs' property located, as it is, alongside extensive multiple development to the south. It is entirely believable that, with the location disadvantages of both adjoining multiple dwellings to the south and adjoining railroad tracks to the east, plaintiffs' property could not prudently be developed consistent with present zoning.

The defendant acknowledges that the property could not be developed for single family use until the existing structures are removed, the property platted and utilities and other land improvements installed. On the record before him, the trial judge was entirely justified in concluding it would be so difficult to find a land developer or house builder willing to speculate in the improvement of this land in preference to land which does not have the location disadvantages which this land has, that this land was not suitable for *development* with single-family residences, and that, accordingly, present zoning was confiscatory. Such finding not being clearly erroneous, I would affirm on that issue.

NOTES AND QUESTIONS

1. *Which law governs?* Is *Krause* a "substantive due process" case or a "regulatory taking" case? (For that matter, is the court deciding the case under federal or state law? Note how few citations of authority the majority opinion uses.) Is the court blending the two doctrinal approaches? Consider the following:

2. *Arbitrary or reasonable?* In *Krause* the court seemed to assume the incompatibility of single-family residential and multiple family dwelling zoning classifications. Such an assumption, of course, was the basis of that part of the *Euclid* opinion in which the Court sustained the exclusion of apartments from the one-and two-family districts. But, as pointed out in a Note following the *Euclid* case reprinted *supra*, this part of the *Euclid* opinion is based upon an unwarranted assumption that apartments must always be built at high density and have those noxious attributes so graphically described by Justice Sutherland. Modern "garden" apartments are often built at relatively low densities, with ample open space around the buildings, and are therefore not really incompatible with nearby "single-family residential" zoning. In a case where a challenge was brought to a rezoning for apartments, the North Carolina court rejected the *Euclid* analysis of an apartment's detrimental impact. *Allred v. City of Raleigh,* 173 S.E.2d 533 (N.C. App. 1970), *rev'd on other grounds,* 178 S.E.2d 432 (N.C. 1971). It pointed out that "Many modern and luxurious apartment buildings tend to complement the area where they are located." *Id.* at 538.

Another successful attack by an apartment developer on single-family zoning is *Socha v. Smith,* 306 N.Y.S.2d 551 (N.Y. App. Div. 1969), *aff'd,* 259 N.E.2d 738 (N.Y. 1970). Here the tract was surrounded by single-family residences. However, the developer's tract was swampy and so there was evidence that to make a profit for single-family uses he would have to develop it for expensive homes, for which there was no market. See also *Bartlett v. City of Chicago,* 204 N.E.2d 780 (Ill. App. 1965), where the court invalidated the application of single-family residential zoning to a tract of land virtually surrounded by high-rise apartments.

3. *Confiscatory?* What do the majority and the dissenting opinions mean by "confiscatory" with respect to a zoning classification? Is it fair to assume that they mean "amounting to a taking of private property without compensation"? If so, do you agree with Judge Levin that "whether zoning is confiscatory is more a question of fact than of judgment" and that the "debatable question" test is not applicable "where the question presented is whether the zoning is unreasonable because it is confiscatory"? Would it be accurate to conclude that the majority implicitly applies a "balancing" test when zoning is claimed to be "confiscatory," while Judge Levin's test is simply whether the economic impact of the landowner or developer is too severe, regardless of the "reasonableness" of the zoning when the economic impact is not considered? Can you tell, by the way, whether they are applying federal or state taking rules?

4. *Post-Lucas.* If *Krause* had been decided after *Lucas,* would this decision be relevant to any issue in *Krause*? It seems clear a court after *Lucas* would hold the residential zoning unconstitutional if it equated the trial court's finding that the zoning was confiscatory with a finding that it denied all economically viable use of the property. This seems to be the teaching of similar cases decided post-*Lucas.*

Tim Thompson, Inc. v. Village of Hinsdale, 617 N.E.2d 1227 (Ill. App. 1993), is a typical post-*Lucas* residential zoning case. The court held a taking did not occur when the village downzoned the property to a residential density half that in the surrounding area. The court noted the landowner could still develop the property at a lower density. Is this likely to be the holding in most post-*Lucas* cases where a landowner claims residential zoning improperly restricts him from building a multifamily project? [7]

Note the argument of the dissent, that property must be able to be reasonably used as zoned, not that it has an "exchange value." *Del Monte Dunes* discussed this issue. *Tahoe-Sierra Preservation Council, Inc. v. Tahoe Regional Planning Agency,* 216 F.3d 764, 781 n.25 (9th Cir. 2000), interpreted that case to mean that an absence of a "competitive market" was only some evidence that could support a finding of an "absence of value." To defeat plaintiff's claim that a taking had occurred, it was not necessary to affirmatively prove, however, that a "competitive market" existed. Is this holding consistent with the dissent?

c. Single-Family Residential Use: The Non-Traditional "Family"

When a zoning ordinance creates a single-family residential use classification, it is necessary, of course, to define the meaning of the term "family" as used in the ordinance. Until the late 1960s, most zoning ordinances appear to have defined a family in pretty much the way it is defined in the Model Zoning Ordinance reprinted *supra:* "One or more persons occupying a single dwelling and using common cooking facilities, provided that no family shall contain more than five adult persons." The numerical limit on adult persons might vary substantially from one ordinance to another, but the "family" definitions commonly employed generally did not require that the persons comprising a family be related by blood, marriage, or adoption.

In a number of cases the state courts had to interpret such definitions of family in local zoning ordinances. Fraternities, sororities, and retirement homes for the elderly did not fare well when they claimed to be families for zoning purposes. State court decisions were more evenly divided, however, with respect to group homes for juvenile offenders or mentally retarded adults and residential drug treatment centers. And the state courts were generally favorable toward claims that religious groups living together in single-family residences were families for zoning purposes. See, e.g., *Carroll v. City of Miami Beach,* 198 So. 2d 643 (Fla. App. 1967) (group of novices living with a Mother Superior as a single housekeeping unit); *Missionaries of Our Lady of LaSallette v. Village of Whitefish Bay,* 66 N.W.2d 627 (Wis. 1954) (group of eight priests and lay brothers living together as a single housekeeping unit); *Laporte v. City of New Rochelle,* 152 N.Y.S.2d 916 (App. Div. 1956), *aff'd,* 141 N.E.2d 917 (N.Y. 1957) (proposed dormitory for sixty students in a Roman Catholic college would constitute a family within definition of family as "one or more persons occupying a dwelling unit as a single, non-profit housekeeping unit," and the dormitory would be a "single dwelling unit").

Beginning in the 1960s, however, many municipalities began to change the definition of a family in their zoning ordinances to exclude or limit the number of persons unrelated by blood, marriage or adoption who might constitute a family for zoning purposes. This was almost certainly motivated by the desire of local authorities to prevent establishment of "counter-culture" or "hippy" communes in single-family residential neighborhoods. As might be expected, such zoning ordinance restrictions on family composition led to court challenges on constitutional grounds. The first case to reach the Supreme Court of the United States is reprinted as the next principal case.

VILLAGE OF BELLE TERRE v. BORAAS

416 U.S. 1 (1974)

JUSTICE DOUGLAS delivered the opinion of the Court:

Belle Terre is a village on Long Island's north shore of about 220 homes inhabited by 700 people. Its total land area is less than one square mile. It has restricted land use to one-family dwellings excluding lodging houses, boarding houses, fraternity houses, or multiple dwelling houses. The word "Family" as used in the ordinance means, "One or more persons related by blood, adoption, or marriage, living and cooking together as a single housekeeping unit, exclusive of household servants. A number of persons but not exceeding two (2) living and cooking together as a single housekeeping unit though not related by blood, adoption, or marriage shall be deemed to constitute a family."

Appellees (Dickmans) are owners of a house in the village and leased it in December, 1971 for a term of 18 months to Michael Truman. Later Bruce

Boraas became a colessee. Then Anne Parish moved into the house along with three others. These six are students at nearby State University at Stony Brook and none is related to the other by blood, adoption, or marriage. When the village served the Dickmans with an "Order to Remedy Violations" of the ordinance, the owners plus three tenants thereupon brought this action under 42 U.S.C. § 1983 for an injunction declaring the ordinance unconstitutional. The District Court held the ordinance constitutional and the Court of Appeals reversed, one judge dissenting. The case is here by appeal, 28 U.S.C. § 1254(2); and we noted probable jurisdiction.

This case brings to this Court a different phase of local zoning regulations than we have previously reviewed. [The court summarized the facts in *Euclid*.] . . .

The Court [in *Euclid*] sustained the zoning ordinance under the police power of the State, saying that the line "which in this field separates the legitimate from the illegitimate assumption of power is not capable of precise delimitation. It varies with circumstances and conditions." 272 U.S., at 387. And the Court added "A nuisance may be merely a right thing in the wrong place, like a pig in the parlor instead of the barnyard. If the validity of the legislative classification for zoning purposes be fairly debatable, the legislative judgment must be allowed to control." *Id.,* at 388. The Court listed as considerations bearing on the constitutionality of zoning ordinances the danger of fire or collapse of buildings, the evils of overcrowding people, and the possibility that "offensive trades, industries, and structures" might "create nuisance" to residential sections. *Ibid.* But even those historic police power problems need not loom large or actually be existent in a given case. For the exclusion of "all industrial establishments" does not mean that "only offensive or dangerous industries will be excluded." *Ibid.* That fact does not invalidate the ordinance; the Court held:

> "The inclusion of a reasonable margin to insure effective enforcement, will not put upon a law, otherwise valid, the stamp of invalidity. Such laws may also find their justification in the fact that, in some fields, the bad fades into the good by such insensible degrees that the two are not capable of being readily distinguished and separated in terms of legislation." *Id.,* 388–389.

The main thrust of the case in the mind of the Court was in the exclusion of industries and apartments and as respects that it commented on the desire to keep residential areas free of "disturbing noises"; "increased traffic"; the hazard of "moving and parked automobiles"; the "depriving children of the privilege of quiet and open spaces for play, enjoyed by those in more favored localities." *Id.,* at 394. The ordinance was sanctioned because the validity of the legislative classification was "fairly debatable" and therefore could not be said to be wholly arbitrary. *Id.,* at 388.

Our decision in *Berman v. Parker,* 348 U.S. 26, sustained a land use project in the District of Columbia against a land owner's claim that the taking violated the Due Process Clause and the Just Compensation Clause of the Fifth Amendment. The essence of the argument against the law was, while taking property for ridding an area of slums was permissible, taking it "merely to develop a better balanced, more attractive community" was not, 348 U.S., at 31. We refused to limit the concept of public welfare that may be enhanced by zoning regulations. We said:

> "Miserable and disreputable housing conditions may do more than spread disease and crime and immorality. They may also suffocate the spirit by reducing the people who live there to the status of cattle. They may indeed make living an almost unsufferable burden. They may also be an ugly sore, a blight on the community which robs it of charm, which makes it a place from which men turn. The misery of housing may despoil a community as an open sewer may ruin a river.

> "We do not sit to determine whether a particular housing project is or is not desirable. The concept of the public welfare is broad and inclusive. . . . The values it represents are spiritual as well as physical, aesthetic as well as monetary. It is within the power of the legislature to determine that the community should be beautiful as well as healthy, spacious as well as clean, well-balanced as well as carefully patrolled." *Id.,* 32–33.

If the ordinance segregated one area only for one race, it would immediately be suspect under the reasoning of *Buchanan v. Warley,* 245 U.S. 60, where the Court invalidated a city ordinance barring a Black from acquiring real property in a white residential area by reason of an 1866 Act of Congress, 42 U.S.C. § 1982 and an 1870 Act, 16 Stat. 144, both enforcing the Fourteenth Amendment. *Id.,* 78–82.

In *Seattle Title Trust Co. v. Roberge,* 278 U.S. 116, Seattle had a zoning ordinance that permitted a "philanthropic home for children or for old people" in a particular district "when the written consent shall have been obtained of the owners of two thirds of the property within four hundred (400) feet of the proposed building." *Id.,* at 118. The Court held that provision of the ordinance unconstitutional saying that the existing owners could "withhold consent for selfish reasons or arbitrarily and may subject the trustee [owner] to their will or caprice." *Id.,* at 122. Unlike the billboard cases (*Cusack Co. v. City of Chicago,* 242 U.S. 526), the Court concluded that the Seattle ordinance was invalid since the proposed home for the aged poor was not shown by its maintenance and construction "to work any injury, inconvenience or annoyance to the community, the district or any person." *Id.,* 278 U.S., at 122.

The present ordinance is challenged on several grounds: that it interferes with a person's right to travel; that it interferes with the right to migrate to and settle within a State; that it bars people who are uncongenial to the present residents; that the ordinance expresses the social preferences of the residents for groups that will be congenial to them; that social homogeneity is not a legitimate interest of government; that the restriction of those whom the neighbors do not like trenches on the newcomers' rights of privacy; that it is of no rightful concern to villagers whether the residents are married or unmarried; that the ordinance is antithetical to the Nation's experience, ideology and self-perception as an open, egalitarian, and integrated society.

We find none of these reasons in the record before us. It is not aimed at transients. Cf. *Shapiro v. Thompson,* 394 U.S. 618. It involves no procedural disparity inflicted on some but not on others such as was presented by *Griffin v. Illinois,* 351 U.S. 12. It involves no "fundamental" right guaranteed by the Constitution, such as voting, *Harper v. Virginia State Board,* 383 U.S. 663; the right of association, *NAACP v. Alabama ex rel. Patterson,* 357 U.S. 449; the right of access to the courts, *NAACP v. Button,* 371 U.S. 415; or any rights of privacy, cf. *Griswold v. Connecticut,* 381 U.S. 479; *Eisenstadt v. Baird,* 405 U.S. 438, 453–454. We deal with economic and social legislation where legislatures have historically drawn lines which we respect against the charge of violation of the Equal Protection Clause if the law be "reasonable, not arbitrary" (quoting *F. S. Royster Guano Co. v. Virginia,* 253 U.S. 412, 415) and bears "a rational relationship to a [permissible] state objective." *Reed v. Reed,* 404 U.S. 71, 76.

It is said, however, that if two unmarried people can constitute a "family," there is no reason why three or four may not. But every line drawn by a legislature leaves some out that might well have been included. That exercise of discretion, however, is a legislative not a judicial function.

It is said that the Belle Terre ordinance reeks with an animosity to unmarried couples who live together. There is no evidence to support it; and the provision of the ordinance bringing within the definition of a "family" two unmarried people belies the charge.

The ordinance places no ban on other forms of association, for a "family" may, so far as the ordinance is concerned, entertain whomever they like.

The regimes of boarding houses, fraternity houses, and the like present urban problems. More people occupy a given space; more cars rather continuously pass by; more cars are parked; noise travels with crowds.

A quiet place where yards are wide, people few, and motor vehicles restricted are legitimate guidelines in a land use project addressed to family needs. This goal is a permissible one within *Berman v. Parker, supra.* The police power is not confined to elimination of filth, stench, and unhealthy places. It is ample to lay out zones where family values, youth values, and the blessings of quiet seclusion, and clean air make the area a sanctuary for people.

The suggestion that the case may be moot need not detain us. A zoning ordinance usually has an impact on the value of the property which it regulates. But in spite of the fact that the precise impact of the ordinance sustained in *Euclid* on a given piece of property was not known, 272 U.S., at 397, the Court, considering the matter a controversy in the realm of city planning, sustained the ordinance. Here we are a step closer to the impact of the ordinance on the value of the lessor's property. He has not only lost six tenants and acquired only two in their place; it is obvious that the scale of rental values rides on what we decide today. When *Berman* reached us it was not certain whether an entire tract would be taken or only the buildings on it and a scenic easement. 348 U.S., at 36. But that did not make the case any the less a controversy in the constitutional sense. When Mr. Justice Holmes said for the Court in *Block v. Hirsh,* 256 U.S. 135, 155, "property rights may be cut down, and to that extent taken, without pay," he stated the issue here. As is true in most zoning cases, the precise impact on value may, at the threshold of litigation over validity, not yet be known.

Reversed.

JUSTICE BRENNAN, dissenting. [Justice Brennan found that no case or controversy existed. The tenants had moved out, and he would hold that the landlord does not have standing to assert the rights of his tenants.]

JUSTICE MARSHALL, dissenting. . . . In my view, the disputed classification burdens the students' fundamental rights of association and privacy guaranteed by the First and Fourteenth Amendments. Because the application of strict equal protection scrutiny is therefore required, I am at odds with my brethren's conclusion that the ordinance may be sustained on a showing that it bears a rational relationship to the accomplishment of legitimate governmental objectives. . . .

My disagreement with the Court today is based upon my view that the ordinance in this case unnecessarily burdens appellees' First Amendment freedom of association and their constitutionally guaranteed right to privacy. Our decisions establish that the First and Fourteenth Amendments protect the freedom to choose one's associates. Constitutional protection is extended not only to modes of association that are political in the usual sense, but also to those that pertain to the social and economic benefit of the members. The selection of one's living companions involves similar choices as to the emotional, social, or economic benefits to be derived from alternative living arrangements.

[The remainder of Justice Marshall's dissent is omitted. Justice Marshall concluded that the Belle Terre ordinance discriminated on the basis of "personal lifestyle choice as to household companions." It imposed "significantly greater restrictions" on "those who deviate from the community norm in their choice of living companions." He noted that this was not a case "where the Court is being asked to nullify a township's sincere efforts to maintain its residential character." He saw "no constitutional infirmity in a town limiting the density of use in residential areas by zoning regulations which do not discriminate on the basis of constitutionally suspect criteria." But this ordinance limited "the density of occupancy of only those homes occupied by unrelated persons." The means chosen to achieve legitimate zoning goals were both over-inclusive and under-inclusive.

[JUSTICE MARSHALL noted that "[t]he village is justifiably concerned with density of population and the related problems of noise, traffic, and the like." He suggested the village could deal with these problems by limiting each household to a specified number of adults, without limiting the number of dependents; by adopting rent control; and by placing limits on the number of vehicles per household.]

NOTES AND QUESTIONS

Belle Terre was the first zoning case to be reviewed by the United States Supreme Court since the late 1920s. The District Court had upheld Belle Terre's definition of "family" on the ground that the interest of conventional "families" in limiting residential areas to occupancy by their own kind was a "legally protectable affirmative interest," and thus was by itself a legitimate goal of zoning. The Second Circuit's majority explicitly repudiated that ground, stating:

> [W]e start by examination of the sole ground upon which it was upheld by the district court, namely the interest of the local community in the protection and maintenance of the prevailing traditional family pattern which consists of occupancy of one-family houses by families based on consanguinity or legal affinity. In our view such a goal fails to fall within the proper exercise of state police power. It can hardly be disputed — and the district court so found — that the ordinance has the purpose and effect of permitting existing inhabitants to compel all others who would take up residence in the community to conform to its prevailing ideas of life-style, thus insuring that the community will be structured socially on a fairly homogeneous basis. Such social preferences, however, while permissible in a private club, have no relevance to public health, safety or welfare.
>
> The effect of the Belle Terre ordinance would be to exclude from the community, without any rational basis, unmarried groups seeking to live together, whether they be three college students, three single nurses, three priests, or three single judges. Although local communities are given wide latitude in achieving legitimate zoning needs, they cannot under the mask of zoning ordinances impose social preferences of this character upon their fellow citizens. [476 F.2d 806, at 815.]

For an extended critique of *Belle Terre*, see 3 N. Williams, American Land Planning Law § 66.90 (Rev. ed. 1985).

One might have expected that state courts would "fall in line" after the Supreme Court's decision in *Belle Terre* and sustain local zoning ordinances severely restricting the number of unrelated persons who might comprise a family for zoning purposes. Most have, but a few statute courts have held that such restrictive definitions violate state constitutional guarantees of due process and/or privacy, as did the next principal case.

STATE v. BAKER

81 N.J. 99, 405 A.2d 368 (1979)

PASHMAN, J:

The issue presented by this appeal is whether a municipality may utilize criteria based upon biological or legal relationships in order to limit the types of groups that may live within its borders. Specifically, we must determine the validity of § 17:3-1(a) (17) of the Plainfield Zoning Ordinance which seeks to preserve the "family" character of the municipality's neighborhoods by prohibiting more than four unrelated individuals from sharing a single housing unit. For the reasons to be given below, we conclude that although the goal sought to be furthered by that provision is entirely legitimate, the means chosen do not bear a substantial relationship to the effectuation of that goal. Hence, the regulation violates *N.J. Const.* (1947) Art. I, par. 1 and Art. IV, § 6, par. 2, and cannot stand.

Defendant Dennis Baker is the owner of a house located at 715 Sheridan Avenue, Plainfield. This dwelling is situated in a zone restricted to single family use. On three separate occasions during the fall of 1976 defendant was charged with allowing more than one family to reside in his home in violation of section 17:11-2 of the Plainfield Zoning Ordinance. "Family" is defined in the ordinance as:

> One (1) or more persons occupying a dwelling unit as a single non-profit housekeeping unit. More than four (4) persons . . . not related by blood, marriage, or adoption shall not be considered to constitute a family. [City of Plainfield Zoning Ordinance § 17: 3-1(a) (17)]

A trial as to all three charges was held in Plainfield Municipal Court. The evidence presented indicated that the home was generally shared by nine individuals: Mr. and Mrs. Baker, their three daughters, Mrs. Conata and her three children. Several other persons also apparently resided within the household for indeterminate periods of time.

The Bakers and Conatas lived together in what a defendant termed an "extended family." The two groups view each other as part of one large family and have no desire to reside in separate homes. Defendant, an ordained minister of the Presbyterian Church, testified that the living arrangement arose out of the individuals' religious beliefs and resultant desire to go through life as "brothers and sisters." The Bakers and Conatas ate together, shared common areas and held communal prayer sessions. Each occupant contributed a fixed amount per week to defray household expenses.

Defendant was found guilty of all three charges and fines were imposed. After a trial *de novo* in the Union County Court — based upon the Municipal Court transcript, *see R* 3:23-8(a) — defendant was again found in violation of the ordinance. The County Court judge concluded that defendant's religious beliefs regarding his lifestyle were sincere and that the household resembled a traditional extended family, thus constituting a "single non-profit housekeeping unit" within the meaning of the zoning ordinance. Nevertheless, he found both that the living arrangement of the Bakers and Conatas violated the numerical restriction of § 17:3-1(a) (17) and that the provision was a valid exercise of the municipality's police powers. Accordingly, he imposed the same penalties as had the Municipal Court. He ordered, however, that the fines for the first and third violations be suspended.

Defendant filed a notice of appeal to the Appellate Division. The appellate judges concluded that "the Plainfield ordinance . . . 'so narrowly delimits the persons who may occupy a single family dwelling as to prohibit numerous potential occupants who pose no threat to the style of family living sought to be preserved[.]'" Consequently, they held the ordinance invalid insofar as it classified permissible uses according to occupants' biological or legal relationships. The judges also ruled, however, that the "single non-profit housekeeping unit" criterion used in the ordinance was valid. After concluding that the County Court's finding that the Baker household constituted such a unit "could reasonably have been reached on sufficient credible evidence present in the record, considering the proofs as a whole . . .," they reversed defendant's convictions and vacated the fines.

We granted the State's petition for certification. The Public Advocate was permitted to appear as *amicus curiae*. We now affirm.

I

A municipality's zoning power, although broad, is not without limits. In order to be valid, a zoning regulation must both represent a reasonable exercise of the police power and bear a real and substantial relation to a legitimate municipal goal. Moreover, the regulation may "not exceed the public need or substantially affect uses which do not partake of the offensive character of those which cause the problem sought to be ameliorated." . . . Under this test the numerical limitations of § 17:3-1(a) (17) must fall.

We have no quarrel with the legitimacy of Plainfield's goal. Local governments are free to designate certain areas as exclusively residential and may act to preserve a family style of living. A municipality is validly concerned with maintaining the stability and permanence generally associated with single family occupancy and preventing uses resembling boarding houses or other institutional living arrangements. *See Berger v. State,* [364 A.2d 993 (N.J. 1976)]. Moreover, a municipality has a strong interest in regulating the intensity of land use so as to minimize congestion and overcrowding. As we stated in *Berger,* a municipality may endeavor in every legitimate way to "secure and maintain 'the blessings of quiet seclusion' and to make available to its inhabitants the refreshment of repose and the tranquility of solitude."

Nevertheless, the power to attain these goals is not without limits. A municipality may not, for example, zone so as to exclude from its borders the poor or other unwanted minorities. Nor may zoning be used as a tool to regulate the internal composition of housekeeping units. A municipality must draw a careful balance between preserving family life and prohibiting social diversity.

The fatal flaw in attempting to maintain a stable residential neighborhood through the use of criteria based upon biological or legal relationships is that such classifications operate to prohibit a plethora of uses which pose no threat to the accomplishment of the end sought to be achieved. Moreover, such a classification system legitimizes many uses which defeat that goal. Plainfield's ordinance, for example, would prohibit a group of five unrelated "widows, widowers, older spinsters or bachelors — or even of judges" from residing in a single unit within the municipality. *Kirsch Holding Co. v. Borough of Manasquan,* [281 A.2d 513 (N.J. 1971).] On the other hand, a group consisting of 10 distant cousins could so reside without violating the ordinance.[1] Thus the ordinance distinguishes between acceptable and prohibited uses on grounds which may, in many cases, have no rational relationship to the problem sought to be ameliorated.

---

[1] These examples are not, as our dissenting colleagues contend, intended to suggest the possibility of "invasions by swarms of country cousins." Rather, they are set forth merely to demonstrate that the distinctions utilized by the ordinance are not closely related to the municipality's valid concerns. Although some arbitrariness in line-drawing may be countenanced when necessary to achieve a legitimate goal, it is not to be tolerated where, as here, more precise methods of reaching the desired end are available.

Regulations based upon biological traits or legal relationships necessarily reflect generalized assumptions about the stability and social desirability of households comprised of unrelated individuals — assumptions which in many cases do not reflect the real world. Justice Schaefer, writing for the Supreme Court of Illinois, has noted that

> a group of persons bound together only by their common desire to operate a single housekeeping unit, might be thought to have a transient quality that would affect adversely the stability of the neighborhood,. . . . And it might be considered that a group of unrelated persons would be more likely to generate traffic and parking problems than would an equal number of related persons.
>
> *But none of these observations reflects a universal truth.* Family groups are mobile today, and not all family units are internally stable and well-disciplined. Family groups with two or more cars are not unfamiliar. [*City of Des Plaines v. Trottner,* 216 N.E.2d 116, 119 (Ill. 1966) (emphasis supplied).]

Accordingly, that court held a municipality without power to adopt a zoning ordinance which would "penetrate so deeply . . . into the internal composition of a single housekeeping unit."[2] *Id.* at 120.

Nevertheless, despite the inexactitude and overinclusiveness of such regulations, we would be reluctant to condemn them in the absence of less restrictive alternatives. Such options do, however, exist.

The courts of this and other states have often noted that the core concept underlying single family living is not biological or legal relationship but, rather, its character as a single housekeeping unit. As long as a group bears the "generic character of a family unit as a relatively permanent household," it should be equally as entitled to occupy a single family dwelling as its biologically related neighbors.

Plainfield has a legitimate interest in preserving a "family" style of living in certain residential neighborhoods. Such a goal may be achieved, perhaps more sensibly, by the single-housekeeping unit requirement, as well as the exclusion of incompatible residential uses such as commercial residences, nonfamilial institutional uses, boarding homes and other such occupancies without infringing unnecessarily upon the freedom and privacy of unrelated individuals.[3]

In addition to preserving a "family" style of living, the municipality also defends its ordinance as necessary to prevent overcrowding and congestion. The instant regulation, however, is too tenuously related to these goals to

---

[2] The dissent notes that *Des Plaines* has in fact been superseded by statute. It is cited here, however, not for its result but rather for its reasoning which, in our view, remains as valid today as when it was written. See *Kirsch Holding Co., supra,* (citing *Des Plaines* with approval).

[3] The dissent suggests that today's opinion will allow multi-family occupancy in single family homes. This ignores the fact that municipalities are empowered to restrict residences to groups which actually constitute *bona fide* single-housekeeping units — the true criterion of single residence dwellings. Municipal officials remain free to define in a reasonable manner what constitutes such a unit. Moreover, space-related occupancy limitations, discussed *infra,* may be used to preclude the possibility of household groups of "unrestricted" size. Thus, only groups compatible with a residential area will benefit by today's opinion.

justify its impingement upon the internal makeup of the housekeeping entity. The Plainfield Ordinance is both underinclusive and overinclusive. It is over-inclusive because it prohibits single housekeeping units which may not, in fact, be overcrowded or cause congestion; it is underinclusive because it fails to prohibit certain housekeeping units — composed of related individuals — which do present such problems. Thus, for example, five unrelated retired gentlemen could not share a large eight bedroom estate situated upon five acres of land, whereas a large extended family including aunts, uncles and cousins, could share a small two bedroom apartment without violating this ordinance.

An appropriate method to prevent overcrowding and congestion was suggested by this Court in *Kirsch Holding Co. v. Borough of Manasquan, supra*. We there stated that

> [w]hen intensity of use, *i.e.,* overcrowding of dwelling units and facilities [presents a problem], consideration might quite properly be given to zoning or housing code provisions, which would have to be of general application, *limiting the number of occupants in reasonable relation to available sleeping and bathroom facilities or requiring a minimum amount of habitable floor area per occupant.* [Emphasis supplied.] [4]

Area or facility-related ordinances not only bear a much greater relation to the problem of overcrowding than do legal or biologically based classifications, they also do not impact upon the composition of the household. They thus constitute a more reasoned manner of protecting the public health. [5]

Other legitimate municipal concerns can be dealt with similarly. Traffic congestion can appropriately be remedied by reasonable, evenhanded limitations upon the number of cars which may be maintained at a given residence. Moreover, area-related occupancy restrictions will, by decreasing density, tend by themselves to reduce traffic problems. Disruptive behavior — which, of course, is not limited to unrelated households — may properly be controlled through the use of the general police power. As we stated in *Kirsch v. Borough of Manasquan, supra*:

> Ordinarily obnoxious personal behavior can best be dealt with officially by vigorous and persistent enforcement of general police power ordinances and criminal statutes . . . . Zoning ordinances are not intended and cannot be expected to cure or prevent most anti-social conduct in dwelling situations.

Restrictions based upon legal or biological relationships such as Plainfield's impact only remotely upon such problems and hence cannot withstand judicial scrutiny.

---

[4] We have, in fact, today reaffirmed the appropriateness of such restrictions as a solution to density-related problems. *Home Builders League of So. Jersey, Inc. v. Tp. of Berlin,* 405 A.2d 381 (N.J. 1979).

[5] We note that Plainfield does in fact have a minimum space per occupant requirement, although the zoning officer who testified at trial did not know if the Baker household was in violation thereof.

Plainfield, in attempting to justify its regulation, relies upon *Village of Belle Terre v. Boraas,* 416 U.S. (1974). In that case the United States Supreme Court upheld an ordinance which limited to two the number of unrelated individuals who could reside in a single-family dwelling. *Belle Terre* has been widely criticized by the commentators[6] and its rationale appears to have been undermined in part by the more recent case of *Moore v. City of E. Cleveland,* 431 U.S. 494 (1977).[7] In any event, *Belle Terre* is at most-dispositive of any federal constitutional question here involved. We, of course, remain free to interpret our constitution and statutes more stringently. *See generally* Brennan, "State Constitutions and the Protection of Individual Rights," 90 Harv. L. Rev. 489 (1977).[8] We find the reasoning of *Belle Terre* to be both unpersuasive and inconsistent with the results reached by this Court in *Kirsch Holding Co. v. Borough of Manasquan, supra,* and *Berger v. State, supra.* Hence we do not choose to follow it. . . .

Accordingly, we hold that zoning regulations which attempt to limit residency based upon the number of unrelated individuals present in a single non-profit housekeeping unit cannot pass constitutional muster. Although we recognize that we are under a constitutional duty to construe municipal powers liberally, *see N.J. Const.* (1947), Art. IV, § 7, par. 11, municipalities cannot enact zoning ordinances which violate due process. *N.J. Const.* (1947), Art. I, par. 1; Art. IV, § 6, par. 2.[10]

II

Having concluded that Plainfield's numerical requirement is invalid, we must determine whether the Baker household fulfilled the remaining municipal criterion of a "single non-profit housekeeping unit." We conclude that the

---

[6] *See, e.g.,* Williams and Doughty, *"Studies in Legal Realism: Mount Laurel, Belle Terre and Berman,"* 29 Rutgers L. Rev. 73, 76–82 (1975); Hartman, *"Village of Belle Terre v. Boraas: Belle Terre Is a Nice Place to Visit — But Only 'Families' May Live There,"* 8 Urb. L. Ann. 193 (1974); Note, *"Village of Belle Terre v. Boraas: 'A Sanctuary for People,'"* 9 U.S.F. L. Rev. 391 (1974).

[7] *See, e.g.,* "Developments in the Law—Zoning," 91 Harv. L. Rev. 1427, 1568–1574 (1978); *"Moore v. City of East Cleveland, Ohio: The Emergence of the Right of Family Choice in Zoning,"* 5 Pepperdine L. Rev. 547 (1978).

[8] As Justice Brennan aptly remarked, "state courts cannot rest when they have afforded their citizens the full protections of the federal Constitution. State Constitutions, too, are a font of individual liberties, their protections often extending beyond those required by the [United States] Supreme Court's interpretation of federal law." *Id.* at 491. Constitutional decisions by federal courts, he declared, should only be considered as "guideposts" in interpreting state constitutional provisions "if they are found to be logically persuasive and well-reasoned, paying due regard to precedent and the policies underlying specific constitutional guarantees. . . ." *Id.* at 502.

[10] Article I, par. 1 of our Constitution ensures the natural and unalienable right of individuals to pursue and obtain safety and happiness. Encompassed within its strictures is the requirement of due process upon which today's analysis is based. In addition, we would be remiss if we did not note that the right of privacy is also included within the protection offered by that provision. *See, e.g., State v. Saunders,* 381 A.2d 333 (N.J. 1977). Although this right is not absolute, it may be restricted only when necessary to promote a compelling government interest. Article IV, § 6, par. 2 expressly provides that the power to zone shall be deemed to be within the police power of the State. We have, however, interpreted that provision as mandating that zoning regulations reasonably promote the welfare of the public as a whole. These provisions, when read together, require that zoning restrictions be accomplished in the manner which least impacts upon the right of individuals to order their lives as they see fit. For the reasons contained herein, the Plainfield regulation fails this test. Thus, it violates the right of privacy and due process.

Baker-Conata alliance was of sufficient permanence so as to resemble a more traditional extended family. Thus, the County Court judge's finding that the Baker household constituted a "single non-profit housekeeping unit" within the intendment of § 17:3-1(a) (17) is adequately based on the record.

Today we hold that municipalities may not condition residence upon the number of unrelated persons present within the household. Given the availability of less restrictive alternatives, such regulations are insufficiently related to the perceived social ills which they were intended to ameliorate. Although we do not doubt Plainfield's good faith, the means it chose to further its legitimate goals were overreaching in their scope and hence cannot be permitted to stand.

For the foregoing reasons, the judgment of the Appellate Division is affirmed.

MOUNTAIN, J., dissenting. . . .

[Some of the arguments made in the dissenting opinion are discussed in the footnotes to the majority opinion. Justice Mountain was particularly concerned that the majority had placed the decision on constitutional grounds, thus making it impossible for the legislature to remedy the deficiencies the majority found in the ordinance. He concluded that the majority "has agreed and in so doing has deplorably denigrated one of the greatest and finest of our institutions — the family. The family should be entitled — as until now it has been — to stand on its own in a distinctly *preferred* position. There is no support in our *mores* as there should be none in our law, to justify the elevation of any group of unrelated persons to a position of parity with a family. . . ."]

NOTES AND QUESTIONS

1. *Basis for the decision.* Does the *Baker* decision really reject the concept of a family or simply redefine it? The latest data at this time shows that only 40% of American families are nuclear families consisting of two parents and children. What is the basis on which the court finds the definition of "family" unacceptable? Could you say that the holding of the case is represented by the phrase, "zoning protects the use, not the users"?

In footnote 10 in the majority opinion, Justice Pashman says that the decision in the principal case is based on "the requirement of due process" encompassed within Art. I, par. 1 of the New Jersey Constitution. Should the majority opinion be read as holding that the Plainfield zoning ordinance's definition of "family" failed to meet the usual substantive due process test of minimum rationality? Or is the court applying a stricter test — e.g., "strict scrutiny," or some middle-level test? And what do you make of the statement in footnote 10 that "the right of privacy is also included within the protection offered by" Art. I, par. 1, and that, "although this right is not absolute, it may be restricted only when necessary to promote a compelling government interest"? Art. I, par. 1 of the New Jersey Constitution does not expressly mention either "due process" or "privacy."

2. *Limiting family size.* The majority opinion in the principal case states that "area or facility-related ordinances not only bear a much greater relation to the problem of overcrowding than do legal or biologically based classifications, they also do not impact upon the composition of the household" and "thus constitute a more reasoned manner of protecting the public health." Later, the majority opinion interprets the earlier case of *Berger v. State* as legitimizing "space-related restrictions of general application." Does this mean that the majority believes it would be constitutional to impose a "reasonable space-related restriction" upon the number of persons who may compose a "family" for zoning purposes, regardless of whether the members of the "family" are, or are not, related by blood, marriage, or adoption? If such a restriction were imposed, would the court enforce the restriction in a case where the birth of additional children so enlarges a traditional biologically based family as to render its continued occupation of a "single-family" house unlawful? In considering this question, is *Moore v. East Cleveland,* summarized *infra,* relevant? See *Borough of Glassboro v. Vallorosi,* 568 A.2d 888 (N.J. 1990), where the court held on the facts that ten unrelated male college students were a "family" under a zoning ordinance limiting the occupancy of dwellings in residential districts to families only.

3. *The California approach.* In a case rather similar to the principal case on its facts, the California Supreme Court followed New Jersey in holding that a local zoning ordinance allowing only five persons unrelated by blood, marriage, or adoption to constitute a "family" for zoning purposes violated that state's constitution. *City of Santa Barbara v. Adamson,* 610 P.2d 436 (Cal. 1980). But the *Adamson* decision was premised on the California Constitution's protection of "privacy" rather than on substantive due process. The constitutional provision relied on in *Adamson* was practically identical with the provision relied on in *Baker,* except that, in California, a 1972 amendment added "privacy" to the list of rights entitled to constitutional protection.

The Santa Barbara zoning ordinance definition of family, invalidated in *Adamson,* allowed "a group of not to exceed five persons, excluding servants, living together as a single housekeeping unit in a dwelling unit," as an alternative to the traditional family, defined as "an individual, or two or more persons related by blood, marriage or legal adoption living together as a single housekeeping unit in a dwelling unit." The group challenging the zoning ordinance definition of "family" were "a group of 12 adults who live in a 24-room, 10-bedroom, 6-bathroom house . . . not related by blood, marriage, or adoption," who shared expenses, rotated chores, and ate evening meals together. Some of them had children who regularly visited. They alleged that they had become "a close group with social, economic, and psychological commitments to each other" which provided them with "emotional support and stability." As the court construed the Santa Barbara zoning ordinance, this group of unrelated persons was barred from residing, as of right, anywhere in the city, not just in "one-family zones."

The court held that Santa Barbara had failed to establish that any "compelling [public] interest" justified the infringement on the fundamental constitutional right of privacy resulting from the restrictive definition of family in the zoning ordinance. In so holding, the California court rejected the city's arguments that (1) transiency results from "lack of any biological or marriage relation among the residents" of a dwelling; and (2) that the restrictive definition of family was necessary to maintain low density, "the essential characteristics of the [residential] districts," and "a suitable environment for family life where children are members of most families." With respect to the last argument, the court went on to say that the implied goal of protecting children from "an immoral environment" by prohibiting residence by large groups of unrelated persons "would not be legitimate," citing one of its earlier decisions holding invalid an irrebuttable presumption in a public housing regulation that unmarried cohabitation is immoral, irresponsible, or demoralizing to tenant relations. The California court split 4-3 in the *Adamson* case.

4. *Belle Terre's shadow.* Other cases rejecting *Belle Terre* and holding that limitations on the size of unrelated families are invalid include *Kirsch v. Prince George's County,* (Md.), 626 A.2d 372, *cert. denied,* 114 S. Ct. 600 (1993); *Charter Twp. of Delta v. Dinolfo,* 351 N.W.2d 831 (Mich. 1984); *Baer v. Town of Brookhaven,* 537 N.E.2d 619 (N.Y. 1989) — all holding that there was no rational relationship between the restrictive definition of family and the purported state interest in controlling population density and/or maintenance of property values.

Fifteen states have followed *Belle Terre.* Two recent cases that have done so are *City of Brookings v. Winker,* 554 N.W.2d 827 (S.D. 1996), and *State v. Champoux,* 555 N.W.2d 69 (Neb. App. 1996). This case applied a presumption of constitutionality to uphold a restrictive family definition, but *Brookings* upheld an ordinance limiting occupancy to three unrelated persons. The case was brought by a landlord who rented to four college students. The court applied a more rigid test than the federal test, holding a statute must have "a real and substantial relation to the objects sought to be attained." However, the court concluded that the ordinance had a reasonable relationship to the city's zoning goals because Brookings was a college town with unavoidable population density problems. In South Dakota?

5. For discussion of the family definition problem in zoning, see Scott, *A Psycho-Social Analysis of the Concept of Family as Used in Zoning Laws,* 88 Dick. L. Rev. 368 (1984); Note, *Single-family Zoning: Ramifications of State Court Rejection of Belle Terre on Use and Density Controls,* 32 Hastings L.J. 1687 (1981); Scott, *Restricting the Definitions of "Single Family,"* 36 Land Use L. & Zoning Dig., No. 10, at 7 (1984), Note, *Belle Terre and Single-Family Home Ordinances: Judicial Perceptions of Local Government and the Presumption of Validity,* 74 N.Y.U. L. Rev. 447 (1999).

A NOTE ON SUBSEQUENT TREATMENT OF "FAMILY" ZONING IN THE SUPREME COURT: MOORE v. CITY OF EAST CLEVELAND

In *Moore v. City of E. Cleveland,* 431 U.S. 494 (1977), the Supreme Court made it clear that the definition of family in a local zoning or housing ordinance may violate substantive due process even when it would satisfy the deferential, "minimum rationality" standard for judicial review employed in *Euclid* and *Belle Terre.* The East Cleveland ordinance defined a family as follows:

"Family" means a number of individuals related to the nominal head of the household or to the spouse of the nominal head of the household living as a single housekeeping unit in a single dwelling unit, but limited to the following:

(a) Husband or wife of the nominal head of the household.

(b) Unmarried children of the nominal head of the household or of the spouse of the nominal head of the household, provided, however, that such unmarried children have no children residing with them.

(c) Father or mother of the nominal head of the household or of the spouse of the nominal head of the household.

(d) Notwithstanding the provisions of subsection (b) hereof, a family may include not more than one dependent married or unmarried child of the nominal head of the household or of the spouse of the nominal head of the household and the spouse and dependent children of such dependent child. For the purpose of this subsection, a dependent person is one who has more than fifty percent of his total support furnished for him by the nominal head of the household and the spouse of the nominal head of the household.

(e) A family may consist of one individual.

By a five-to-four vote, the Supreme Court invalidated the East Cleveland ordinance's restrictive definition of family. But only Justices Brennan, Marshall, and Blackmun joined in the plurality opinion by Justice Powell who advanced the following rationale for invalidation:

When a city undertakes such intrusive regulation of the family, neither *Belle Terre* nor *Euclid* governs; the usual judicial deference to the legislature is inappropriate. "This Court has long recognized that freedom of personal choice in matters of marriage and family life is one of the liberties protected by the Due Process Clause of the Fourteenth Amendment." *Cleveland Board of Education v. LaFleur,* 414 U.S. 632, 639–640 (1974). A host of cases, tracing their lineage to *Meyer v. Nebraska,* 262 U.S. 390, 399–401 (1923), and *Pierce v. Society of Sisters,* 268 U.S. 510, 534–535 (1925), have consistently acknowledged a "private realm of family life which the state cannot enter." *Prince v. Massachusetts,* 321 U.S. 158, 166 (1944). Of course, the family is not beyond regulation. But when the government intrudes on choices concerning family living arrangements, this Court must examine carefully the importance of the governmental interests advanced and the extent to which they are served by the challenged regulation.

When thus examined, this ordinance cannot survive. The city seeks to justify it as a means of preventing overcrowding, minimizing traffic and parking congestion, and avoiding an undue financial burden on East Cleveland's school system. Although these are legitimate goals, the ordinance before us serves them marginally, at best. For example, the ordinance permits any family consisting only of husband, wife, and unmarried children to live together, even if the family contains a half-dozen licensed drivers, each with his or her own car. At the same time it forbids an adult brother and sister to share a household, even if both faithfully use public transportation. The ordinance would permit a grandmother to live with a single dependent son and children, even if his school-age children number a dozen, yet it forces Mrs. Moore to find another dwelling for her grandson John, simply because of the presence of his uncle and cousin in the same household. We need not labor the point. Section 1341.08 has but a tenuous relation to alleviation of the conditions mentioned by the city. . . .

Substantive due process has at times been a treacherous field for this Court. There *are* risks when the judicial branch gives enhanced protection to certain substantive liberties without the guidance of the more specific provisions of the Bill of Rights. As the history of the *Lochner* era demonstrates, there is reason for concern lest the only limits to such judicial intervention become the predilections of those who happen at the time to be Members of this Court. That history counsels caution and restraint. But it does not counsel abandonment, nor does it require what the city urges here: cutting off any protection of family rights at the first convenient, if arbitrary boundary — the boundary of the nuclear family.

Appropriate limits on substantive due process come not from drawing arbitrary lines but rather from careful "respect for the teachings of history [and] solid recognition of the basic values that underlie our society." *Griswold v. Connecticut*, 381 U.S., at 501 (Harlan, J., concurring). Our decisions establish that the Constitution protects the sanctity of the family precisely because the institution of the family is deeply rooted in this Nation's history and tradition. It is through the family that we inculcate and pass down many of our most cherished values, moral and cultural.

Ours is by no means a tradition limited to respect for the bonds uniting the members of the nuclear family. The tradition of uncles, aunts, cousins, and especially grandparents sharing a household along with parents and children has roots equally venerable and equally deserving of constitutional recognition. Over the years millions of our citizens have grown up in just such an environment, and most, surely, have profited from it. Even if conditions of modern society have brought about a decline in extended family households, they have not erased the accumulated wisdom of civilization, gained over the centuries and honored throughout our history, that supports a larger conception of the family. Out of choice, necessity, or a sense of family responsibility, it has been common for close relatives to draw together and participate in the duties and the satisfactions of a common home. . . . Especially in times of adversity, such as the death of a spouse or economic need, the broader family has tended to come together for mutual sustenance and to maintain or rebuild a secure home life. This is apparently what happened here.

Whether or not such a household is established because of personal tragedy, the choice of relatives in this degree of kinship to live together may not lightly be denied by the State. *Pierce* struck down an Oregon law requiring all children to attend the State's public schools, holding that the Constitution "excludes any general power of the State to standardize its children by forcing them to accept instruction from public teachers only." 268 U.S., at 535. By the same token the Constitution prevents East Cleveland from standardizing its children — and its adults — by forcing all to live in certain narrowly defined family patterns. [*Id.* at 499–500, 502–06.]

Justices Brennan and Marshall joined in a separate concurring opinion written by Justice Brennan, who noted that "[t]he Court's opinion conclusively demonstrates that classifying family patterns in this eccentric way is not a rational means of achieving the ends East Cleveland claims for its ordinance," and then went on to emphasize the significant impact the East Cleveland ordinance could be expected to have on "ethnic and minority groups" — especially blacks — because of the prevalence of the "extended family" pattern among such groups. Chief Justice Burger dissented because appellants had not exhausted their administrative remedies. Justices Stewart, Rehnquist, and White all dissented and held that the East Cleveland ordinance had not violated appellants' substantive due process rights.

Justice Stevens concurred and cast the deciding vote but did not accept Justice Powell's rationale. Instead, he wrote a brief, cryptic opinion arguing that the East Cleveland ordinance constituted "a taking of property without due process and without just compensation." In what sense could Justice Stevens be applying the taking rationale? While *Moore* has been cited frequently by the court in later opinions, the lack of a full consensus among the justices has left constitutional doctrine in this area somewhat unsettled, particularly in light of the obvious tension between *Moore* and *Belle Terre*.

This "tension" between the *Moore* and *Belle Terre* perspectives is reflected also in the next principal case, in which the Supreme Court took up another type of non-traditional "family," group homes for the mentally handicapped, mentally disabled and other disadvantaged groups. Many municipalities exclude or restrict these group homes, and the Supreme Court took an opportunity to review a group home restriction when a city in Texas denied a special use permit for a group home for the mentally disabled. The case raised the important issue of whether exclusions of this kind required a stricter standard of judicial review than the traditional "rational relationship" standard the courts used in equal protection cases.

CITY OF CLEBURNE v. CLEBURNE LIVING CENTER

473 U.S. 432 (1985)

JUSTICE WHITE delivered the opinion of the Court:

A Texas city denied a special use permit for the operation of a group home for the mentally retarded, acting pursuant to a municipal zoning ordinance requiring permits for such homes. The Court of Appeals for the Fifth Circuit held that mental retardation is a "quasi-suspect" classification and that the ordinance violated the Equal Protection Clause because it did not substantially further an important governmental purpose. We hold that a lesser standard of scrutiny is appropriate, but conclude that under that standard the ordinance is invalid as applied in this case.

I

In July 1980, respondent Jan Hannah purchased a building at 201 Featherston Street in the city of Cleburne, Texas, with the intention of leasing it to Cleburne Living Center, Inc. (CLC), for the operation of a group home for the mentally retarded. It was anticipated that the home would house 13 retarded men and women, who would be under the constant supervision of CLC staff members. The house had four bedrooms and two baths, with a half bath to be added. CLC planned to comply with all applicable state and federal regulations.[2]

The city informed CLC that a special use permit would be required for the operation of a group home at the site, and CLC accordingly submitted a permit application. In response to a subsequent inquiry from CLC, the city explained that under the zoning regulations applicable to the site, a special use permit, renewable annually, was required for the construction of "[h]ospitals for the insane or feeble-minded, or alcoholic [sic] or drug addicts, or penal or correctional institutions."[3] The city had determined that the proposed group home should be classified as a "hospital for the feebleminded." After holding a public

---

[2] It was anticipated that the home would be operated as a private Level I Intermediate Care Facility for the Mentally Retarded, or ICF-MR, under a program providing for joint federal-state reimbursement for residential services for mentally retarded clients. See 42 U.S.C. § 1396d(a) (15); Tex. Human Resources Code Ann. § 32.001 et seq. (1980 and Supp. 1985). ICF-MR's are covered by extensive regulations and guidelines established by the United States Department of Health and Human Services and the Texas Departments of Human Resources, Mental Health and Mental Retardation, and Health. See also 42 CFR § 442.1 et seq. (1984); 40 Tex. Adm. Code § 27.101 et seq. (1981).

[3] The site of the home is in an area zoned "R-3," an "Apartment House District." Section 8 of the Cleburne zoning ordinance, in pertinent part, allows the following uses in an R-3 district:

"1. Any use permitted in District R-2.

"2. Apartment houses, or multiple dwellings.

"3. Boarding and lodging houses.

"4. Fraternity or sorority houses and dormitories.

"5. Apartment hotels.

"6. Hospitals, sanitariums, nursing homes or homes for convalescents or aged, *other than for the* insane or *feeble-minded* or alcoholics or drug addicts.

"7. Private clubs or fraternal orders, except those whose chief activity is carried on as a business.

"8. Philanthropic or eleemosynary institutions, other than penal institutions.

"9. Accessory uses customarily incident to any of the above uses . . . ." (emphasis added).

Section 16 of the ordinance specifies the uses for which a special use permit is required. These include "[h]ospitals for the insane or feebleminded, or alcoholic [sic] or drug addicts, or penal or correctional institutions." Section 16 provides that a permit for such a use may be issued by "the Governing Body, after public hearing, and after recommendation of the Planning Commission." All special use permits are limited to one year, and each applicant is required "to obtain the signatures of the property owners within two hundred (200) feet of the property to be used."

hearing on CLC's application, the City Council voted 3 to 1 to deny a special use permit.[4]

CLC then filed suit in Federal District Court against the city and a number of its officials, alleging, inter alia, that the zoning ordinance was invalid on its face and as applied because it discriminated against the mentally retarded in violation of the equal protection rights of CLC and its potential residents. . . . [T]he District Court held the ordinance and its application constitutional. . . .

The Court of Appeals for the Fifth Circuit reversed, determining that mental retardation was a quasi-suspect classification and that it should assess the validity of the ordinance under intermediate-level scrutiny. . . .[8]

II

The Equal Protection Clause of the Fourteenth Amendment commands that no State shall "deny to any person within its jurisdiction the equal protection of the laws," which is essentially a direction that all persons similarly situated should be treated alike. Section 5 of the Amendment empowers Congress to enforce this mandate, but absent controlling congressional direction, the courts have themselves devised standards for determining the validity of state legislation or other official action that is challenged as denying equal protection. The general rule is that legislation is presumed to be valid and will be sustained if the classification drawn by the statute is rationally related to a legitimate state interest. When social or economic legislation is at issue, the Equal Protection Clause allows the States wide latitude, and the Constitution presumes that even improvident decisions will eventually be rectified by the democratic processes.

The general rule gives way, however, when a statute classifies by race, alienage, or national origin. These factors are so seldom relevant to the achievement of any legitimate state interest that laws grounded in such considerations are deemed to reflect prejudice and antipathy — a view that those in the burdened class are not as worthy or deserving as others. For these reasons and because such discrimination is unlikely to be soon rectified by legislative means, these laws are subjected to strict scrutiny and will be sustained only if they are suitably tailored to serve a compelling state interest. Similar oversight by the courts is due when state laws impinge on personal rights protected by the Constitution.

Legislative classifications based on gender also call for a heightened standard of review. That factor generally provides no sensible ground for

---

[4] The city's Planning and Zoning Commission had earlier held a hearing and voted to deny the permit.

[8] *Macon Assn. for Retarded Citizens v. Macon-Bibb County Planning and Zoning Comm'n,* 252 Ga. 484, 314 S.E.2d 218 (1984), dism'd for want of a substantial federal question, 469 U.S. 802 (1984), has no controlling effect on this case. *Macon Assn. for Retarded Citizens* involved an ordinance that had the effect of excluding a group home for the retarded only because it restricted dwelling units to those occupied by a single family, defined as no more than four unrelated persons. In *Village of Belle Terre v. Boraas,* 416 U.S. 1 (1974), we upheld the constitutionality of a similar ordinance, and the Georgia Supreme Court in *Macon Assn.* specifically held that the ordinance did not discriminate against the retarded. 252 Ga., at 487, 314 S.E.2d, at 221.

differential treatment. "[W]hat differentiates sex from such nonsuspect statuses as intelligence or physical disability . . . is that the sex characteristic frequently bears no relation to ability to perform or contribute to society." *Frontiero v. Richardson,* 411 U.S. 677, 686 (1973) (plurality opinion). Rather than resting on meaningful considerations, statutes distributing benefits and burdens between the sexes in different ways very likely reflect outmoded notions of the relative capabilities of men and women. A gender classification fails unless it is substantially related to a sufficiently important governmental interest. Because illegitimacy is beyond the individual's control and bears "no relation to the individual's ability to participate in and contribute to society," *Mathews v. Lucas,* 427 U.S. 495, 505 (1976), official discriminations resting on that characteristic are also subject to somewhat heightened review. Those restrictions "will survive equal protection scrutiny to the extent they are substantially related to a legitimate state interest." *Mills v. Habluetzel,* 456 U.S. 91, 99 (1982).

We have declined, however, to extend heightened review to differential treatment based on age:

> "While the treatment of the aged in this Nation has not been wholly free of discrimination, such persons, unlike, say, those who have been discriminated against on the basis of race or national origin, have not experienced a 'history of purposeful unequal treatment' or been subjected to unique disabilities on the basis of stereotyped characteristics not truly indicative of their abilities." *Massachusetts Board of Retirement v. Murgia,* 427 U.S. 307, 313 (1976).

The lesson of *Murgia* is that where individuals in the group affected by a law have distinguishing characteristics relevant to interests the State has the authority to implement, the courts have been very reluctant, as they should be in our federal system and with our respect for the separation of powers, to closely scrutinize legislative choices as to whether, how, and to what extent those interests should be pursued. In such cases, the Equal Protection Clause requires only a rational means to serve a legitimate end.

III

Against this background, we conclude for several reasons that the Court of Appeals erred in holding mental retardation a quasi-suspect classification calling for a more exacting standard of judicial review than is normally accorded economic and social legislation. First, it is undeniable, and it is not argued otherwise here, that those who are mentally retarded have a reduced ability to cope with and function in the everyday world. Nor are they all cut from the same pattern: as the testimony in this record indicates, they range from those whose disability is not immediately evident to those who must be constantly cared for.[9] They are thus different, immutably so, in relevant

---

[9] Mentally retarded individuals fall into four distinct categories. The vast majority — approximately 89% — are classified as "mildly" retarded, meaning that their IQ is between 50 and 70. Approximately 6% are "moderately" retarded, with IQs between 35 and 50. The remaining two categories are "severe" (IQs of 20 to 35) and "profound" (IQs below 20). These last two categories together account for about 5% of the mentally retarded population. (testimony of Dr. Philip Roos).

respects, and the States' interest in dealing with and providing for them is
plainly a legitimate one.[10] How this large and diversified group is to be treated
under the law is a difficult and often a technical matter, very much a task
for legislators guided by qualified professionals and not by the perhaps ill-
informed opinions of the judiciary. Heightened scrutiny inevitably involves
substantive judgments about legislative decisions, and we doubt that the predicate for such judicial oversight is present where the classification deals with
mental retardation. *Defer to Legislature*

Second, the distinctive legislative response, both national and state, to the
plight of those who are mentally retarded demonstrates not only that they
have unique problems, but also that the lawmakers have been addressing
their difficulties in a manner that belies a continuing antipathy or prejudice
and a corresponding need for more intrusive oversight by the judiciary. [The
Court noted the federal government had prohibited discrimination against the
mentally retarded in federally funded programs, had guaranteed the right to
appropriate treatment, had conditioned federal education funds on assurances
from states that they would receive an education that is integrated with
nonmentally retarded children "to the maximum extent appropriate," and had
facilitated their employment by exempting them from competitive examina-
tions.]. . .The State of Texas has similarly enacted legislation that acknowledges the special status of the mentally retarded by conferring certain rights
upon them, such as "the right to live in the least restrictive setting appropriate
to [their] individual needs and abilities," including "the right to live. . . in
a group home." Mentally Retarded Persons Act of 1977, Tex. Rev. Civ. Stat.
Ann., Art. 5547–300, § 7 (Vernon Supp. 1985).[11]

Such legislation thus singling out the retarded for special treatment reflects
the real and undeniable differences between the retarded and others. That
a civilized and decent society expects and approves such legislation indicates

---

Mental retardation is not defined by reference to intelligence or IQ alone, however. The
American Association on Mental Deficiency (AAMD) has defined mental retardation as "'significantly subaverage general intellectual functioning existing concurrently with deficits in adaptive
behavior and manifested during the developmental period.'" Brief for AAMD et al. as *Amici Curiae*
3 (quoting AAMD, Classification in Mental Retardation 1 (H. Grossman ed., 1983)). "Deficits in
adaptive behavior" are limitations on general ability to meet the standards of maturation,
learning, personal independence, and social responsibility expected for an individual's age level
and cultural group. Brief for AAMD et al. as *Amici Curiae* 4, n. 1. Mental retardation is caused
by a variety of factors, some genetic, some environmental, and some unknown. *Id.,* at 4.

[10] As Dean Ely has observed:

"Surely one has to feel sorry for a person disabled by something he or she can't do
anything about, but I'm not aware of any reason to suppose that elected officials are
unusually unlikely to share that feeling. Moreover, classifications based on physical
disability and intelligence are typically accepted as legitimate, even by judges and
commentators who assert that immutability is relevant. The explanation, when one is
given, is that those characteristics (unlike the one the commentator is trying to render
suspect) are often relevant to legitimate purposes. At that point there's not much left
of the immutability theory, is there?" J. Ely, Democracy and Distrust 150 (1980)
(footnote omitted). See also *id.,* at 154–155.

[11] . . .A number of States have passed legislation prohibiting zoning that excludes the retarded.
See, e.g., Cal. Health & Safety Code Ann. § 1566 et seq. (West 1979 and Supp. 1985); Conn. Gen.
Stat. § 8-3e (Supp. 1985); N.D. Cent. Code § 25-16-14(2) (Supp. 1983); R.I. Gen. Laws. § 45-24-22
(1980). See also Md. Health Code Ann. § 7-102 (Supp. 1984).

that governmental consideration of those differences in the vast majority of situations is not only legitimate but also desirable. . . . .

Third, the legislative response, which could hardly have occurred and survived without public support, negates any claim that the mentally retarded are politically powerless in the sense that they have no ability to attract the attention of the lawmakers. Any minority can be said to be powerless to assert direct control over the legislature, but if that were a criterion for higher level scrutiny by the courts, much economic and social legislation would now be suspect.

Fourth, if the large and amorphous class of the mentally retarded were deemed quasi-suspect for the reasons given by the Court of Appeals, it would be difficult to find a principled way to distinguish a variety of other groups who have perhaps immutable disabilities setting them off from others, who cannot themselves mandate the desired legislative responses, and who can claim some degree of prejudice from at least part of the public at large. One need mention in this respect only the aging, the disabled, the mentally ill, and the infirm. We are reluctant to set out on that course, and we decline to do so.

Doubtless, there have been and there will continue to be instances of discrimination against the retarded that are in fact invidious, and that are properly subject to judicial correction under constitutional norms. But the appropriate method of reaching such instances is not to create a new quasi-suspect classification and subject all governmental action based on that classification to more searching evaluation. Rather, we should look to the likelihood that governmental action premised on a particular classification is valid as a general matter, not merely to the specifics of the case before us. Because mental retardation is a characteristic that the government may legitimately take into account in a wide range of decisions, and because both State and Federal Governments have recently committed themselves to assisting the retarded, we will not presume that any given legislative action, even one that disadvantages retarded individuals, is rooted in considerations that the Constitution will not tolerate.

Our refusal to recognize the retarded as a quasi-suspect class does not leave them entirely unprotected from invidious discrimination. To withstand equal protection review, legislation that distinguishes between the mentally retarded and others must be rationally related to a legitimate governmental purpose. This standard, we believe, affords government the latitude necessary both to pursue policies designed to assist the retarded in realizing their full potential, and to freely and efficiently engage in activities that burden the retarded in what is essentially an incidental manner. The State may not rely on a classification whose relationship to an asserted goal is so attenuated as to render the distinction arbitrary or irrational. See *Zobel v. Williams,* 457 U.S. 55, 61–63 (1982); *United States Dept. of Agriculture v. Moreno,* 413 U.S. 528, 535 (1973). Furthermore, some objectives — such as "a bare . . . desire to harm a politically unpopular group," *id.,* at 534 — are not legitimate state interests. See also *Zobel, supra,* at 63. Beyond that, the mentally retarded, like others, have and retain their substantive constitutional rights in addition to the right to be treated equally by the law.

IV

We turn to the issue of the validity of the zoning ordinance insofar as it requires a special use permit for homes for the mentally retarded.[14] We inquire first whether requiring a special use permit for the Featherston home in the circumstances here deprives respondents of the equal protection of the laws. If it does, there will be no occasion to decide whether the special use permit provision is facially invalid where the mentally retarded are involved, or to put it another way, whether the city may never insist on a special use permit for a home for the mentally retarded in an R-3 zone. This is the preferred course of adjudication since it enables courts to avoid making unnecessarily broad constitutional judgments.

The constitutional issue is clearly posed. The city does not require a special use permit in an R-3 zone for apartment houses, multiple dwellings, boarding and lodging houses, fraternity or sorority houses, dormitories, apartment hotels, hospitals, sanitariums, nursing homes for convalescents or the aged (other than for the insane or feebleminded or alcoholics or drug addicts), private clubs or fraternal orders, and other specified uses. It does, however, insist on a special permit for the Featherston home, and it does so, as the District Court found, because it would be a facility for the mentally retarded. May the city require the permit for this facility when other care and multiple-dwelling facilities are freely permitted?

It is true, as already pointed out, that the mentally retarded as a group are indeed different from others not sharing their misfortune, and in this respect they may be different from those who would occupy other facilities that would be permitted in an R-3 zone without a special permit. But this difference is largely irrelevant unless the Featherston home and those who would occupy it would threaten legitimate interests of the city in a way that other permitted uses such as boarding houses and hospitals would not. Because in our view the record does not reveal any rational basis for believing that the Featherston home would pose any special threat to the city's legitimate interests, we affirm the judgment below insofar as it holds the ordinance invalid as applied in this case.

The District Court found that the City Council's insistence on the permit rested on several factors. First, the Council was concerned with the negative attitude of the majority of property owners located within 200 feet of the Featherston facility, as well as with the fears of elderly residents of the neighborhood. But mere negative attitudes, or fear, unsubstantiated by factors which are properly cognizable in a zoning proceeding, are not permissible bases for treating a home for the mentally retarded differently from apartment houses, multiple dwellings, and the like. It is plain that the electorate as a whole, whether by referendum or otherwise, could not order city action violative of the Equal Protection Clause, *Lucas v. Forty-Fourth General Assembly of Colorado*, 377 U.S. 713, 736–737 (1964), and the city may not avoid the strictures of that Clause by deferring to the wishes or objections of some fraction of the body politic. "Private biases may be outside the reach of the

---

[14] It goes without saying that there is nothing before us with respect to the validity of requiring a special use permit for the other uses listed in the ordinance. See n. 3, *supra.*

law, but the law cannot, directly or indirectly, give them effect." *Palmore v. Sidoti,* 466 U.S. 429, 433 (1984).

Second, the Council had two objections to the location of the facility. It was concerned that the facility was across the street from a junior high school, and it feared that the students might harass the occupants of the Featherston home. But the school itself is attended by about 30 mentally retarded students, and denying a permit based on such vague, undifferentiated fears is again permitting some portion of the community to validate what would otherwise be an equal protection violation. The other objection to the home's location was that it was located on "a five hundred year flood plain." This concern with the possibility of a flood, however, can hardly be based on a distinction between the Featherston home and, for example, nursing homes, homes for convalescents or the aged, or sanitariums or hospitals, any of which could be located on the Featherston site without obtaining a special use permit. The same may be said of another concern of the Council — doubts about the legal responsibility for actions which the mentally retarded might take. If there is no concern about legal responsibility with respect to other uses that would be permitted in the area, such as boarding and fraternity houses, it is difficult to believe that the groups of mildly or moderately mentally retarded individuals who would live at 201 Featherston would present any different or special hazard.

Fourth, the Council was concerned with the size of the home and the number of people that would occupy it. The District Court found, and the Court of Appeals repeated, that "[i]f the potential residents of the Featherston Street home were not mentally retarded, but the home was the same in all other respects, its use would be permitted under the city's zoning ordinance." 726 F.2d, at 200. Given this finding, there would be no restrictions on the number of people who could occupy this home as a boarding house, nursing home, family dwelling, fraternity house, or dormitory. The question is whether it is rational to treat the mentally retarded differently. It is true that they suffer disability not shared by others; but why this difference warrants a density regulation that others need not observe is not at all apparent. At least this record does not clarify how, in this connection, the characteristics of the intended occupants of the Featherston home rationally justify denying to those occupants what would be permitted to groups occupying the same site for different purposes. Those who would live in the Featherston home are the type of individuals who, with supporting staff, satisfy federal and state standards for group housing in the community; and there is no dispute that the home would meet the federal square-footage-per-resident requirement for facilities of this type. See 42 CFR § 442.447 (1984). In the words of the Court of Appeals, "[t]he City never justifies its apparent view that other people can live under such 'crowded' conditions when mentally retarded persons cannot." 726 F.2d, at 202.

In the courts below the city also urged that the ordinance is aimed at avoiding concentration of population and at lessening congestion of the streets. These concerns obviously fail to explain why apartment houses, fraternity and sorority houses, hospitals and the like, may freely locate in the area without a permit. So, too, the expressed worry about fire hazards, the serenity of the neighborhood, and the avoidance of danger to other residents fail rationally to justify singling out a home such as 201 Featherston for the special use permit, yet imposing no such restrictions on the many other uses freely permitted in the neighborhood.

The short of it is that requiring the permit in this case appears to us to rest on an irrational prejudice against the mentally retarded, including those who would occupy the Featherston facility and who would live under the closely supervised and highly regulated conditions expressly provided for by state and federal law.

The judgment of the Court of Appeals is affirmed insofar as it invalidates the zoning ordinance as applied to the Featherston home. The judgment is otherwise vacated.

It is so ordered.

[Most of the discussion in the concurring and dissenting opinions is omitted, but Justice Marshall's arguments in his concurring and dissenting opinion are of interest:]

JUSTICE MARSHALL, with whom JUSTICE BRENNAN and JUSTICE BLACKMUN join, concurring in the judgment in part and dissenting in part:

The Court holds that all retarded individuals cannot be grouped together as the "feebleminded" and deemed presumptively unfit to live in a community. Underlying this holding is the principle that mental retardation per se cannot be a proxy for depriving retarded people of their rights and interests without regard to variations in individual ability. With this holding and principle I agree. The Equal Protection Clause requires attention to the capacities and needs of retarded people as individuals.

I cannot agree, however, with the way in which the Court reaches its result or with the narrow, as-applied remedy it provides for the city of Cleburne's equal protection violation. The Court holds the ordinance invalid on rational-basis grounds and disclaims that anything special, in the form of heightened scrutiny, is taking place. Yet Cleburne's ordinance surely would be valid under the traditional rational-basis test applicable to economic and commercial regulation. In my view, it is important to articulate, as the Court does not, the facts and principles that justify subjecting this zoning ordinance to the searching review — the heightened scrutiny — that actually leads to its invalidation. Moreover, in invalidating Cleburne's exclusion of the "feebleminded" only as applied to respondents, rather than on its face, the Court radically departs from our equal protection precedents. Because I dissent from this novel and truncated remedy, and because I cannot accept the Court's disclaimer that no "more exacting standard" than ordinary rational-basis review is being applied, I write separately. [The dissenting opinion argued that the Court should have invalidated the special permit requirement under "second-order" heightened scrutiny review.]

NOTES AND QUESTIONS

1. *Disadvantaged groups in the zoning process. Cleburne* is an important case because it again deals with the legal status of disadvantaged groups in the zoning process. You should compare the way in which the Court handled the denial of the special use permit with the way in which the Court rejected a facial attack on an ordinance limiting the number of persons who can live together in *Belle Terre*. Are the groups distinguishable? The question of how disadvantaged groups should be treated in the zoning process is picked up again in Chapter 4, *infra*. Note, however, that strict scrutiny applies to laws that discriminate on the basis of race, and this includes zoning ordinances.

Commentators criticized the Court's handling of the quasi-suspect issue in *Cleburne*. Comment, *City of Cleburne v. Cleburne Living Center: Equal Protection for the Mentally Retarded?*, 9 Harv. J.L. & Pub. Pol'y 231 (1986); Comment, *Cleburne: An Evolutionary Step in Equal Protection Analysis*, 46 Md. L. Rev. 163 (1986). They argued that the Court did not provide a principled basis for determining when the quasi-suspect category applies and that it was incorrect in holding that legislative recognition of the interests of the mentally retarded was a reason not to characterize them as quasi-suspect. See also Jaffe, *Coping with Cleburne*, Land Use L. & Zoning Dig., Vol. 38, No. 2, at 5 (1986); Mandelker, *Group Homes: The Supreme Court Revives the Equal Protection Clause in Land Use Cases*, in 1986 Inst. on Plan. Zoning & Eminent Domain, ch. 3.

2. *What was unconstitutional?* The majority makes it clear that it is undertaking an as-applied analysis of Cleburne's zoning ordinance:

> We inquire first whether requiring a special use permit for the Featherston home in the circumstances here deprives respondents of the equal protection of the laws. If it does, there will be no occasion to decide whether the special use permit provision is facially invalid where the mentally retarded are involved, or to put it another way, whether the city may never insist on a special use permit for a home for the mentally retarded in an R-3 zone.

But even within this as-applied context, is it the specific decision to deny CLC's permit that is invalid, or the broader decision to single out group homes for the mentally retarded for the special permit requirement? Wasn't the language of the permit requirement in *Cleburne* facially unconstitutional as the dissent suggested?

Although the Court applied rational relationship equal protection review in *Cleburne,* its reasoning in striking down the special permit denial echoed the intermediate, means-focused judicial review it said it rejected. This holding could mean that federal and possibly state courts should be more willing to strike down land use regulation under the rational relationship test. The court in *Cleburne* seems to find "irrationality" in the city's failure to apply the special permit requirement evenhandedly to similar types of facilities. But what is "evenhanded"? Recall cases such as *Hadacheck, supra* ch. 2, where the court held that Los Angeles could prohibit brickmaking from some residential districts without applying the prohibition to all similar residential districts. Is the familiar "one step at a time" rule of equal protection law called into question by *Cleburne*?

3. *Post-Cleburne cases.* The cases since *Cleburne* have divided on whether a municipality can constitutionally require a conditional use permit for a group home. See *Bannum, Inc. v. City of Louisville,* 958 F.2d 1354 (6th Cir. 1992) (invalidating requirement). *Bannum, Inc. v. City of St. Charles,* 2 F.3d 267 (8th Cir. 1993) upheld a conditional use requirement for a group home for prisoners in the last stages of their sentence before release. In distinguishing *Cleburne* the court said:

> Here, the classification in the amended ordinance is addressed to halfway houses which serve any prisoner, ex-prisoner, or juvenile offender. The City could rationally believe that some groups in this classification could pose a threat to the public welfare. Such concerns are not based on irrational prejudice, but rather on a realistic view that some members of these groups could pose a threat in some locations. It is not irrational for the City to believe that recidivism could be a problem with some persons served by half-way houses. This is a legitimate concern which can be addressed on a case-by-case basis through application for conditional permits. [*Id.* at 272.]

Do you agree? Accord in distinguishing *Cleburne,* see *Bannum, Inc. v. City of Fort Lauderdale,* 157 F.3d 819 (11th Cir. 1998), *cert. denied,* 120 S. Ct. 67 (1999).

In *Doe v. City of Butler,* 892 F.2d 315 (3d Cir. 1989), the court upheld a requirement for conditional uses for group homes in single-family residential districts, the denial of a permit for a group home for battered women, and a provision limiting occupancy in group homes to six persons. The court relied on *Belle Terre* to hold that the occupancy restriction was a reasonable density limitation in an R-2 (two-family) residential district. The court distinguished *Cleburne* because it said that the "vice" in that case was that group homes for the mentally retarded required a special use permit while other group homes did not. Is this a correct reading? The court in *Doe* then remanded the case to determine whether the occupancy limitation was reasonable in apartment building residential districts.

State courts are quite capable of striking down a denial of a conditional use for a group home when the denial was based on opposition by neighbors unsupported by evidence, and can do so without the help of *Cleburne.* See *Wilson County Youth Emergency Shelter, Inc. v. Wilson County,* 13 S.W.2d 338 (Tenn. App. 2000). The board denied the group home because of a vague reference to "location," a lack of fire protection and the number of people living in the home. Accord *Bannum, Inc. v. City of Columbia,* 516 S.E.2d 439 (S.C. 1999). Conditional uses are reviewed in Chapter 5, *infra.*

4. *The Macon case.* In considering the foregoing, reexamine footnote eight of the majority opinion, in which Justice White distinguishes *Macon Ass'n for Retarded Citizens v. Macon-Bibb County Planning & Zoning Comm'n.* In *Macon,* a state case rejecting a challenge to a zoning ordinance excluding group homes, the Court explained that the group home exclusion was acceptable because it was produced by a zoning ordinance restricting dwelling units to families of no more than four unrelated persons. The Court noted it had upheld a similar ordinance in *Belle Terre* and that the ordinance in *Macon* did not discriminate against the retarded. Does this shed any light on the questions raised in the preceding note?

"GROUP HOMES ARE A REAL PROBLEM IN OUR COMMUNITY"

5. *Defining "family."* A number of state cases have interpreted the definition of "family" or "accessory use" in zoning ordinances to include group homes. They sometimes stress that a zoning ordinance may regulate only uses, not users, and that a regulation based on users would violate substantive due process. Some cases have adopted a "functional equivalence" rule as the basis for bringing group homes within the definition of "family." In *City of White Plains v. Ferraioli*, 313 N.E.2d 756 (N.Y. 1974), for example, the court distinguished *Belle Terre* and held that a foster home was a "relatively normal, stable, and permanent family unit." If a zoning ordinance adopted this definition, would it be constitutional under *Cleburne*?

6. *State and federal legislation.* All states now have legislation that governs zoning for group homes and that determines how group homes are handled in local zoning ordinances. The statutes vary in defining the protected groups that are covered by the statute. They also vary in indicating where group homes can locate. Some permit group homes in "all zones," while others limit them to single-family or multi-family districts. All the statutes have occupancy limits, some limit the number of staff, and some require supervision. Other statutes require the dispersal of group homes throughout residential areas, through spacing or other requirements, to avoid excessive concentration. For discussion see Davis & Gaus, *Protecting Group Homes for the Non-Handicapped: Zoning in the Post-Edmonds Era*, 46 Kan. L. Rev. 777, 789–96 (1998). See, e.g., Ariz. Rev. Stat. Ann. §§ 36-581, 36-582; Kan. Stat. Ann. § 12-736. Are these statutes constitutional?

The federal Fair Housing Act, 42 U.S.C. § 3601 et seq., was amended in 1988 to prohibit discrimination against group homes for the mentally handicapped, including discrimination through zoning. Note however, that the Act's "handicap" basis limits its scope in comparison to *Cleburne*. This statute is discussed in Chapter 4. Do any provisions of the state statutes described above violate the federal Fair Housing Amendments Act of 1988, insofar as they cover the same classes of people?

A NOTE ON ALTERNATIVES TO SINGLE-FAMILY ZONING: THE ACCESSORY APARTMENT

Two leading land use commentators argued some time ago that single-family zoning is no longer defensible as a land use strategy. Babcock, *The Egregious Invalidity of the Exclusive Single-Family Zone*, 35 Land Use L. & Zoning Dig., No. 7, at 4 (1983); Ziegler, *The Twilight of Single-Family Zoning*, 3 UCLA J. Envtl. L. & Pol'y 161 (1983). Both noted that single-family houses all across the nation are increasingly being converted into two-unit dwellings by internal subdivision to create an "accessory apartment," often for elderly parents. This kind of housing is even more important today, as the population ages and housing costs escalate.

Although accessory housing units can help with the affordable housing problem, some commentators argue they can also create parking and traffic congestion problems for residential neighborhoods, and can change the character of residential neighborhoods by increasing density and by creating rental units in the midst of owner-occupied homes. See Weinberg & McGuire, *"Granny Flats" and Second Unit Housing: Who Speaks for the Neighborhood?*, 23 Zoning & Plan. L. Rep. 25 (2000). However, although accessory apartment conversions violate single-family zoning restrictions, most communities overlook them unless there are complaints by neighbors because they do not usually cause significant noise or traffic problems. Some communities are also responding to the new realities by authorizing accessory housing, though with some restrictions. Owners usually must occupy such housing, and ordinances usually restrict eligible tenants, lot and apartment size, exterior appearance, and parking.

Are these ordinances constitutional? *Kasper v. Brookhaven*, 535 N.Y.S.2d 621 (App. Div. 1988), upheld an ordinance allowing residents who occupied their homes to secure permits for accessory rental apartments but denying permits to nonresidents. The ordinance also provided that no permit could be issued for an accessory apartment if five percent or more of the lots within a one-half-mile radius of the subject parcel contained accessory apartments. The court held the ownership limitation was reasonable because, otherwise, the quota for accessory apartments could be exhausted by nonresidents. The court also held the ordinance was not unconstitutional because it regulated the users, not the use, noting a case upholding an ordinance creating a district for housing for the elderly. What has home ownership got to do with land use issues? A quota?

A California statute authorizes local governments to adopt ordinances authorizing special use permits for accessory second residential units. Cal. Govt. Code § 65852.2. The ordinance may designate areas of the city where these residences can be located, and may include parking, height, setback, lot coverage, architectural review, and maximum size standards. It may also provide that a second unit cannot exceed the allowable density for the lot upon which it is located, and that it is a residential use consistent with the existing general plan and zoning designation for the lot. The statute authorizes an owner occupancy requirement. See *Sounhein v. City of San Dimas*, 55 Cal. Rptr. 2d 290 (Cal. App. 1996) (owner occupancy requirement runs with the land). On what basis could a special use permit be denied? See *Kisil v. City of Sandusky,* 465 N.E.2d 848 (Ohio 1984) (reversing denial of lot area variance to allow conversion of single-family residence into two-family residence when much of surrounding area had been converted to such residences).

Compare Vt. Stat. Ann. tit. 24, § 4406(4)(D). The statute authorizes second units as a conditional use. It has an owner occupancy requirement and also restricts occupancy to not more than two persons, "one of whom is related by blood or marriage to the owner of the single family residence, is disabled . . . or is at least 55 years of age." In addition, "floor space shall not exceed 30 percent of the floor space of the existing living area of the single family residence or 400 square feet, whichever is greater." How would you evaluate the constitutionality of this statute under *Belle Terre, Baker* and *East Cleveland*? Would you recommend repealing or revising the provisions on relationships or floor space?

For a discussion of zoning ordinance provisions for accessory apartments, see P. Hare, Accessory Apartment's: Using Surplus Space in Single-Family Houses (Am. Plan. Ass'n, Plan. Advisory Serv. Rep. No. 365, 1981). See also M. Gellen, Accessory Apartments in Single-Family Housing (1985). Exclusionary zoning is discussed in Chapter 4, and zoning for the aged is discussed *infra* in this chapter.

d. Manufactured Housing

So-called mobile or manufactured housing is an important part of the affordable housing supply. Mobile homes are now more commonly referred to as manufactured housing, but the term "mobile home" is retained in this discussion because manufactured housing can also mean housing built in modular sections at a factory and assembled on-site. A mobile home is built in its entirety at the factory, shipped to its site and placed on a base. Mobile homes can make up as much as one-third of all housing starts nationally in any one year. They are more common in some sections of the country than others, such as the south, and are more common in rural areas.

Local resistance to mobile homes remains strong. Objections include health problems that can arise from a lack of proper facilities, the usual concerns about high density development, the association of mobile homes with low-income status, and lack of neighborhood stability because mobile home residents are transient. A number of these objections may not be valid, such as the transiency problem, and some can be solved, such as the facility problem. Claims that mobile homes do not last as long as conventionally built housing have been disproved by studies.

An implicit objection may often be aesthetic. When people think about mobile homes they usually envision the narrow "single-wides," which can have a flat roof and unattractive corrugated metal siding. Today, only about 10% of all mobile home production is in this form. The "double-wide," a mobile home that consist of two single sections and can be as attractive as any conventionally built home, is more common. Two-story mobile homes are possible, and mobile home developments can be as attractive as any conventionally built housing.

Total exclusions.—Municipalities may try to exclude mobile homes completely. Although an early New Jersey case upheld this tactic, *Vickers v.*

Township Comm., 181 A.2d 129, *cert. denied,* 371 U.S. 233 (1963), more recent cases have held the total exclusion of mobile homes invalid or highly suspect. See, e.g., *Town of Glocester v. Olivo's Mobile Home Court, Inc.,* 300 A.2d 465 (R.I. 1973); *Town of Pompey v. Parker,* 377 N.E.2d 741 (N.Y. 1978) (challenged law does not exclude all mobile homes; validity of total exclusion reserved); *Oak Forest Mobile Home Park, Inc. v. City of Oak Forest,* 326 N.E.2d 473 (Ill. App. 1975).

Mobile home parks.—When a local government does not totally exclude mobile homes, it often tries to minimize their supposed negative impact upon the community by requiring them to be located in "mobile home parks," which are often subject to a special licensing requirement. Most courts have upheld these ordinances. See, e.g., *Texas Manufactured Hous. Ass'n v. City of Nederland,* 101 F.3d 1095 (5th Cir. 1996), *cert. denied,* 521 U.S. 1112 (1997); *People of Village of Cahokia v. Wright,* 311 N.E.2d 153 (Ill. 1974); *Town of Granby v. Landry,* 170 N.E.2d 364 (Mass. 1960); *State v. Larson,* 195 N.W.2d 180 (Minn. 1972); *City of Brookside Village v. Comeau,* 633 S.W.2d 790 (Tex.), *cert. denied,* 459 U.S. 1087 (1982).

The leading case invalidating an ordinance limiting mobile homes to mobile home parks is *Robinson Twp. v. Knoll,* 302 N.W.2d 146 (Mich. 1981). The court noted that changes in mobile home construction made them as attractive as conventional single-family dwellings. Aesthetic objections to mobile homes were no longer justified, and the investment required for a modern mobile home precluded any objections based on transient occupancy. More appropriate regulations, such as local plumbing codes and a regulation requiring attachment to a solid foundation, could handle health and safety problems.

The Mississippi court reached the same conclusion in *Carpenter v. City of Petal,* 699 So. 2d 928 (Miss. 1997). It noted that most of the cases upholding such restrictions predated federal statutory requirements for mobile homes, discussed *infra,* and said:

> Prohibiting individual mobile home or even modular home sites in any area other than designated mobile home parks, however, bears no relationship to the goal of preserving surrounding residential property values. In the Rural Fringe District, where Carpenter's property is located, permitted land uses include agriculture, farming, forestry and livestock production; nurseries and truck gardens; public or commercial stables and kennels; poultry, livestock and small animal raising; single-family dwellings; two-family dwellings; and accessory uses including signs and incidental home occupations. [*Id.* at 933.]

The Court also quoted the Mississippi Manufactured Housing Association, whose *amicus* brief pointed out that

> [i]n the Rural Fringe District, Petal will allow commercial stables, dog runs, pig pens and chicken yards within 100 feet of a property line, but have [sic] refused to allow Mr. Carpenter to locate his manufactured home 550 feet from the street on a 100 by 200 foot tract in the middle of his 92 acres.[*Id.*]

Accord *Cannon v. Coweta County,* 389 S.E.2d 329 (Ga. 1990); *Luczynski v. Temple,* 497 A.2d 211 (N.J. Ch. Div. 1985).

However, *Barre Mobile Home Park v. Town of Petersham,* 592 F. Supp. 633 (D. Mass. 1984), upheld an ordinance prohibiting a mobile home park anywhere in the community. This court said:

> The evidence justifies Petersham's prohibition of mobile home parks. It has a right to assure the orderly development of the entire community and avoid concentrations of populations such as mobile home parks unquestionably bring. The town could reasonably foresee a demand for additional municipal services which it is not prepared to provide. Its experience with its existing sewage and waste disposal systems alerted the town to the need to avoid concentrations of dwellings. Finally, no matter how improved mobile homes have become, they are out of character for the large, well-maintained colonial homes typical of Petersham. [*Id.* at 636.]

count all over no consonus

Go to a mobile home sales lot and try to decide which court is right.

Residential district exclusion.—Sometimes zoning ordinances do not require mobile homes to be located in mobile home parks but exclude them from any of the traditional residential districts. This exclusion has generally been sustained. See, e.g., *Jensen's Inc. v. Town of Plainville,* 150 A.2d 297 (Conn. 1959); *City of Raleigh v. Morand,* 100 S.E.2d 870 (N.C. 1957), *appeal dismissed,* 357 U.S. 343 (1958); *Corning v. Town of Ontario,* 121 N.Y.S.2d 288 (Sup. Ct. 1953); *Duckworth v. City of Bonney Lake,* 586 P.2d 860 (Wash. 1978). The exclusion of mobile homes from industrial and commercial districts and from rural and agricultural areas has also been sustained. See, e.g., *Camboni's, Inc. v. County of Du Page,* 187 N.E.2d 212 (Ill. 1962) (industrial zone). See also 42 A.L.R.3d 598 (1972).

What about an ordinance that permitted modular factory-built homes in residential districts that are assembled on-site, but prohibited mobile homes transported to sites on their own wheels. *Bourgeois v. Parish of St. Tamany,* 628 F. Supp. 159 (E.D. La. 1986) held such an ordinance violated equal protection because it had no aesthetic justification. Is this result compelled by *Cleburne*? (*Bourgeois* does not cite *Cleburne*.) The parish admitted the ordinance would permit a tar paper shack in a residential district if it was site-built.

Conditional uses.—Another common way of regulating the location of mobile homes is to treat them as special exceptions or conditional uses that must be approved by the zoning board of adjustment (or appeals). Special exceptions or conditional uses in a zoning ordinance may, of course, be administered in such a way as to effect a practically complete exclusion of mobile homes from the community. For cases striking down vaguely drafted special exception or conditional use provisions such as those requiring proof of "necessity," see *Pioneer Trust & Sav. Bank v. County of McHenry,* 241 N.E.2d 454 (Ill. 1968) (necessity requirement invalid); *Lakewood Estates, Inc. v. Deerfield Twp. Zoning Bd. of Appeals,* 194 N.W.2d 511 (Mich. App. 1971) (vague standards invalid); *Walworth Leasing Corp. v. Sterni,* 316 N.Y.S.2d 851 (Sup. Ct.1970). But see *Jensen's, Inc. v. City of Dover,* 547 A.2d 277 (N.H. 1988), where the court held that increased density justified a conditional use classification for mobile homes; the mobile home density would have been three times the density allowed by the "as of right" zoning classification. Courts can, of course, reverse a denial of a conditional use if they believe it was improper. *Clark v. City of Asheboro,* 524 S.E.2d 46 (N.C. App. 1999).

Appearance codes.—Another form of zoning that affects mobile homes is the appearance code. This type of code attempts to make mobile homes conform to conventional housing in appearance and size. For example, a Nebraska statute provides:

> (i) The home shall have no less than nine hundred square feet of floor area; (ii) The home shall have no less than an eighteen-foot exterior width; (iii) The roof shall be pitched with a minimum vertical rise of two and one-half inches for each twelve inches of horizontal run; (iv) The exterior material shall be of a color, material, and scale comparable with those existing in residential site-built, single-family construction; (v) The home shall have a nonreflective roof material which is or simulates asphalt or wood shingles, tile, or rock; and (vi) The home shall have wheels, axles, transporting lights, and removable towing apparatus removed. [Neb. Rev. Stat. § 14-402(2)(a).]

One of the purposes of a statute like this is to prevent the use of metal roofs and sides, which are not used on conventionally built housing. The roof pitch requirement is intended to prevent flat roofs, but once had the effect of precluding shipment of the mobile home if the roof pitch was so high that the mobile home truck could not get under bridges. This problem has apparently been solved by the manufacturers. Local ordinances may have similar requirements.

The courts have upheld these requirements, noting that "the County could have been pursuing the goal of 'aesthetic compatibility,' seeking to reduce friction between the appearance of site-built homes and manufactured homes by requiring manufactured homes to conform with standard characteristics of site-built homes, such as roof pitch and foundation. The goal of aesthetic compatibility is a legitimate government purpose." *Georgia Manufactured Hous. v. Spalding County,* 148 F.3d 1304 (11th Cir. 1998). Accord *CMH Mfg. v. Catawba County,* 994 F. Supp. 697 (W.D.N.C. 1998). What about the impact of these requirements on the cost of the mobile home? Aesthetic zoning is considered in Chapter 8.

State legislation.—There are many state statutes authorizing the licensing of mobile homes. The courts have generally not held that these statutes preempt local zoning control over mobile homes. E.g., *Adams v. Cowart,* 160 S.E.2d 805 (Ga. 1968). Some states have enacted statutes providing for state certification of mobile homes that meet state construction standards. These statutes preempt local regulation of local homes under building codes and, in some cases, under zoning ordinances. E.g., *Warren v. Municipal Officers,* 431 A.2d 624 (Me. 1981).

States have enacted statutes that prohibit discriminatory treatment of mobile homes in zoning ordinances. Some of this legislation deals with the mobile home exclusion problem by prohibiting exclusion "except upon the same terms and conditions as conventional housing is excluded." Vt. Stat. Ann. tit.24, § 4406(4)(A). See also Idaho Code § 67-6509B. *In re Lunde,* 688 A.2d 1312 (Vt. 1997), held that the statute invalidated an ordinance that restricted mobile homes to mobile home parks. See Bredin, *Manufactured Housing Statutes,* Am. Plan. Ass'n News, June 2000.

Federal legislation.—Federal legislation requires mobile home manufacturers to comply with federal construction and safety standards. 43 U.S.C. § 5415. *City of Brookside Village v. Comeau,* 633 S.W.2d 790 (Tex.), *cert. denied,* 459 U.S. 1087 (1982), held that the federal legislation did not preempt local zoning. The *Nederland* case, *supra,* held it did not preempt a zoning ordinance limiting mobile homes to mobile home parks. But in *Scurlock v. City of Lynn Haven,* 858 F.2d 1521 (11th Cir. 1988), the court invalidated an ordinance provision that allowed mobile homes certified under federal law in residential districts only if they met additional safety requirements, because (1) the federal legislation preempted state law on this point and (2) the provision was also invalid under state law. Some states have enacted legislation that prohibits municipalities from adopting restrictive zoning applicable to manufactured housing certified under the federal legislation. E.g., Iowa Code Ann. § 414.28. The *Spaulding* and *Catawba* cases, *supra,* held the federal statute did not preempt appearance codes.

Sources.—See W. Sanders, *Manufactured Housing: Regulation, Design Innovations, with Development Options,* American Planning Association, Planning Advisory Serv. Rep. No. 478 (1998); Jaffe, *Mobile Homes in Single-Family Neighborhoods,* 35 Land Use L. & Zoning Dig., No. 6, at 4 (1983); Kmiec, *Manufactured Home Siting: A Statutory and Judicial Overview,* 6 Zoning & Plan. L. Rep. 105, 113 (1983); Note, *Rescuing Manufactured Housing From the Perils of Municipal Zoning Laws,* 37 Wash. U. J. Urb. & Contemp. L. 189 (1990).

PROBLEM

You are the attorney for a suburban municipality on the edge of a metropolitan area of one million people. The municipality is about 15 miles square, is largely residential, and has a substantial amount of undeveloped land on its edges. Some of this consists of farms that are threatened by urban growth, and their owners have been talking to developers about selling their land for mobile home park subdivisions. All the homes in the parks would be double-wides situated on paved residential streets, and the subdivisions would meet all county requirements. Several owners of individual lots in these areas are considering the placement of mobile homes on their properties.

There presently are no regulations for mobile homes and mobile home parks in the zoning ordinance. There is no state statute, except the usual statute prohibiting the exclusion of a mobile home that meets federal standards. In light of these materials, what kind of an ordinance would you propose for mobile home development?

A NOTE ON ZONING AND THE ELDERLY

The over-65 age group is growing rapidly as a proportion of the total population. In 1900 only five percent of the population was over 65, but by 2050 it is estimated that 20 percent will be over 65. Edmonds & Merriam, *Zoning and the Elderly: Issues for the 21st Century,* Land Use L. & Zoning

Dig., Vol. 47, No. 3, at 3 (1995). A number of zoning measures can provide for elderly housing needs, such as zoning ordinances that allow accessory apartments and shared housing. See the Note on the Future of Single-Family Residential Zoning, *supra.*

Age-restrictive zoning.—Age-restrictive zoning is another option. This type of zoning is intended to encourage the establishment of retirement communities designed especially for the elderly that can contain a variety of building types, living arrangements and supporting facilities. The legal question is whether a zoning ordinance may classify the elderly for special treatment by adopting an exclusive age-restricted zone.

One of the leading cases sustaining age-restrictive zoning is *Taxpayers Ass'n v. Weymouth Twp.,* 364 A.2d 1016 (N.J. 1976), *appeal dismissed* and *cert. denied,* 430 U.S. 977 (1977). On the issue of authority to adopt age-restrictive zoning regulations, the New Jersey court held that "the concept of the 'general welfare' in land use regulation is quite expansive, and encompasses the provision of housing for *all categories of people,* including the elderly"; and that age-restrictive zoning may advance the general welfare by "bringing about 'the greatest good of the greatest number.'" Moreover, the court concluded, "ordinances which regulate use by regulating identified users are not inherently objectionable" so long as they bear "a real and substantial relationship to the regulation of land within the community."

The court then continued with the most elaborate equal protection analysis in any zoning case dealing with age-restrictive regulations. Noting that housing has not been deemed a fundamental right under the Fourteenth Amendment — see *Lindsey v. Normet,* 405 U.S. 56 (1972) — the court moved on to the question whether the Weymouth zoning ordinance involved a suspect classification that would require strict scrutiny. The court concluded that age is not a suspect classification. The court then applied the traditional rational relationship test and held that the plaintiffs had failed to carry the burden of proving that the age-restrictive zoning regulations lacked a rational relationship to a legitimate state objective. Although it recognized that the choice of fifty-two as the minimum age for residency in the age-restrictive mobile park district might be suspect, the court characterized the choice of a minimum age as a legislative question "which ought not to be disturbed by the judiciary unless it exceeds the bounds of reasonable choice." Finally, the court analyzed the age-restrictive regulations under the New Jersey equal protection principle said to be embodied in the state constitution and concluded that these regulations would survive even close scrutiny because the legislative classification was "based upon real factual distinctions, and also [bore] a real and substantial relationship to the ends which the municipality [sought] to accomplish by that classification."

In a companion case to *Weymouth, Shepard v. Woodland Twp. Comm. & Planning Bd.,* 364 A.2d 1005 (N.J. 1976), the New Jersey court made it clear that it wished to circumscribe judicial review of age-restrictive zoning classifications: "[I]t is a major question whether the aged should live in special segregated areas, or scattered among the general population; a decision on this is likely to be phrased in terms of a land use decision. Why should the courts invoke judge-made policy to preclude responsible local officials from implementing such policies?" [*Id.* at 1015–16.] Age-restrictive zoning also was sustained in *Maldini v. Ambro,* 330 N.E.2d 403 (N.Y.), *cert. denied,* 423 U.S. 993 (1975). Is the New Jersey court's analysis sufficiently persuasive to withstand a challenge under *Cleburne*?

Federal Fair Housing Act.—In 1988 Congress added discrimination against "familial status" as another type of discrimination covered by the Fair Housing Act. 42 U.S.C. § 3602(k). Congress adopted this amendment to prohibit discrimination against families with children in the sale and rental of housing, but after intensive lobbying by developers and senior citizens' groups, Congress added an exemption for "housing for older persons," which includes housing projects specially designated by the Department of Housing and Urban Development for the elderly, and housing primarily occupied by persons over designated age limits or providing specific services for the elderly. 42 U.S.C. § 3607(b)(2). Do you see why, in the absence of this amendment, zoning such as that approved in *Weymouth* might violate the 1988 amendments? Although the exemption was intended to apply to private owners of elderly housing, not age-restricted zoning, it presumably preempts zoning that establishes a younger age cut-off than does the federal law. For additional discussion of the 1988 amendments see Chapter 4, *infra.* See, generally, Weinstein, *The Challenge of Providing Adequate Housing for the Elderly . . . Along With Everyone Else,* 11 J.L. & Health 133 (1996–97).

PROBLEM

Your city council is concerned about recent case law on allowable uses in single-family districts and has asked you as city attorney for an opinion on the following proposed single-family zoning district ordinance: The ordinance defines a "single-family dwelling" as a "housekeeping unit" in which individuals share common living quarters, cooking and other facilities. The council also is considering a requirement that no more than four unrelated persons be allowed to live together, but is unsure about its constitutionality.

There is a separate provision for group homes. How would you draft the group home definition? Group homes with no more than six unrelated persons living together are allowed in single-family districts. Group homes with seven or more persons living together or that provide on-site medical treatment facilities are allowed in single-family districts only as conditional uses. Reconsider this problem when you study the group home provisions of the federal Fair Housing Act in Chapter 4.

e. Density Restrictions: Large Lot Zoning

One of the most important trends in residential development has been the decline in residential densities in the last half-century. All metropolitan areas show a sloping density gradient, with the highest densities at the core and the lowest at the suburban fringe. It is customary to specify density in terms of a specified number of dwelling units to the acre, but low suburban densities are maintained by large lot zoning at one dwelling unit to the acre or more. The next case considers the constitutional issues raised by large lot zoning, which is a major land use strategy in suburban areas:

JOHNSON v. TOWN OF EDGARTOWN

425 Mass. 117, 680 N.E.2d 37 (1997)

WILKINS, C.J. This case concerns a challenge to a three-acre minimum area requirement for residential lots in the RA-120 Residential/Agricultural zoning district (RA-120 district) in Edgartown on the island of Martha's Vineyard. The plaintiff landowners, trustees of the Herring Creek Farm Trust, whom we shall refer to as the trust, sought a declaratory judgment, pursuant to G. L. c. 240, § 14A, that the three-acre requirement is arbitrary and unreasonable because it does not advance any valid zoning objective.

A judge of the Land Court entered a judgment that the challenged by-law serves a permissible public purpose and does not violate any constitutional or statutory provision. We granted direct appellate review of the trust's appeal. Before us, the trust asserts that the challenged by-law bears no substantial relation to any legitimate public interest. We affirm the judgment of the Land Court.

We summarize relevant parts of the judge's decision. Edgartown adopted a revised zoning by-law in 1973, establishing zoning districts with minimum lot requirements then ranging from 5,000 square feet to three acres. The RA-120 district boundaries are consistent with a plan prepared by the engineering firm of Metcalf & Eddy designating certain areas as "open space" due to the "fragile" nature of the environment. Now, about one-half the town (8,736 of 17,181 acres) is zoned for three-acre lots; about 4,900 acres are zoned for one-half acre or one acre lots; and about 3,200 acres are zoned for one and one-half acre lots.[4] During the early 1970s, other Martha's Vineyard towns (Tisbury, West Tisbury, and Chilmark on their south shores) as well as Nantucket adopted three-acre zoning for portions of their towns.

The trust owns 215 acres in the RA-120 district abutting the Atlantic Ocean on the south and Edgartown Great Pond on the west. A farm on the locus is devoted to horticultural uses and has received a special assessment and tax rate under G. L. c. 61A, § 4. Earlier in this decade, the trust submitted to the town's planning board a fifty-four lot subdivision plan for the locus, each lot having in excess of three acres and twenty-five acres dedicated to open space. That plan was referred to the Martha's Vineyard Commission. See St. 1977, c. 831. On February 10, 1994, the commission voted to deny permission to grant the necessary development permits. [The Court noted in a footnote that "the trust has appealed from the commission's decision. That appeal is not before us."]

The judge considered extensive expert testimony from both sides in relation to the permissible statutory objectives of zoning and concluded that there was a substantial relation between the by-law and the permissible objectives of zoning. He stated that the by-law "facilitates the provision of open space, conserves the value of land, promotes the conservation of natural resources, prevents blight and pollution of the environment, and preserves the Island's

---

[4] In 1990 a master plan indicated that there was a significant amount of vacant land in the one-half acre zone. There was evidence that Edgartown had more half-acre or smaller lots than any other town on the Vineyard.

unique natural, ecological and other values." The judge credited the testimony of the town's expert, a marine ecologist specializing in coastal areas, to conclude that the effect of nitrate loading on drinking water and on Edgartown Great Pond justified three-acre zoning in the RA-120 district to protect the public health, water, water supply, and water resources. He also concluded that the three-acre requirement allowed a reasonable margin to provide for future problems. The judge identified an independent justification in the "unique ecological integrity of the area including coastal waters, embayments, plant and animal life."

The judge considered the trust's claim that the area requirement of the RA-120 district excluded certain people from the town. He said: "Edgartown is located on a relatively small island with limited accessibility and with inherent resulting economic issues including those of supply and demand. In addition, it is apparent that the setting, topography, weather and natural resources make the entire island highly desirable as a vacation and retirement area. One would reasonably expect such factors to exert an increasingly upward pressure on the price of real estate. Zoning most likely makes some contribution to such pressures, but there is herein a lack of credible evidence as to how and to what extent if any, zoning factors contribute to the availability (or unavailability) of real estate, and more importantly, whether or not the determinative factor of the equation is large lot zoning. I note further the lack of evidence of any person being denied housing because of, or largely because of, such zoning constraints."

We turn first to general principles that guide our decision. In a sense, insular thinking is appropriate here. The values that the town seeks to protect are not simply local ones. The Legislature has recognized "a regional and statewide interest in preserving and enhancing" Martha's Vineyard's "unique natural, historical, ecological, scientific, cultural, and other values," values that may be irreversibly damaged by inappropriate uses of land. St. 1977, c. 831, § 1. In a challenge to an Edgartown zoning by-law, the Legislature's expression of public interest in the preservation of the qualities of Martha's Vineyard is a relevant factor. See *Sturges v. Chilmark*, 402 N.E.2d 1346 (Mass. 1980). The Legislature's proclamation also blunts any claim that, in purporting to act to protect its environment, Edgartown is doing so only in support of its parochial interests.

The fact that Edgartown is on an island is important in another respect. Edgartown is not a rural or suburban municipality lying in the path of suburban growth. The trust's claim that large lot zoning is exclusionary, and thus particularly suspect, lacks the force it might have in many other situations. The trust did not establish, nor indeed did it seek to prove by direct evidence, that people were excluded from settling in Edgartown because of three-acre zoning in approximately half the town. In discussing a challenge to a zoning provision of another Martha's Vineyard town, we said that "in a rural, as opposed to a suburban, setting, where no showing has been made of regional demand for primary housing, the public interest in preserving the environment and protecting a way of life may outweigh whatever undesirable economic and social consequences inhere in partly 'closing the doors' to affluent outsiders primarily seeking vacation homes" (citation omitted). *Sturges v. Chilmark,* supra at 255. We reject any suggestion that Edgartown's three-acre zoning is presumptively exclusionary and that, therefore, the town should have the burden of proving the reasonableness of the zoning regulation.

Apart from its argument that the burden falls on a municipality to justify its large lot zoning because it is exclusionary, the trust argues, in any event, that the traditional, heavy burden on one challenging the constitutionality of a zoning law should not be imposed in a challenge to large lot zoning. We do not agree. The general rule is that a zoning by-law whose reasonableness is fairly debatable will be sustained. On occasion the court has adopted the criminal law concept of proof "beyond reasonable doubt" to describe the burden that is placed on one challenging the validity of a zoning provision. The characterization of a challenger's burden as one of proof beyond reasonable doubt may not be instructive. A better characterization is that the challenger must prove by a preponderance of the evidence that the zoning regulation is arbitrary and unreasonable, or substantially unrelated to the public health, safety, morals, or general welfare.

As residential lot size requirements increase, it becomes more difficult to justify the requirements. See *Aronson v. [Town of] Sharon,* [195 N.E.2d 341 (Mass. 1964)] (in such situations, "the law of diminishing returns will set in at some point"). In *Simon v. [Town of] Needham,* [42 N.E.2d 516 (Mass. 1942)], although skeptical of the town's position, this court rejected a challenge to a zoning requirement of one acre for each house lot, concluding that the town could fairly decide that such a requirement would enhance the public interest. The case appears to have been decided on the classical standard of what the town's legislative body could rationally have concluded. The court intimated that the result would have been different if a landowner had proved that the one-acre requirement created "a barrier against the influx of thrifty and respectable citizens who desire to live there and who are able and willing to erect homes upon lots upon which fair and reasonable restrictions have been imposed."

Twenty-two years later, in *Aronson v. [Town of] Sharon,* this court held invalid a town zoning by-law requiring house lots of 100,000 square feet. The court decided that the zoning provision exceeded the town's statutory authority and suggested that the operation of the by-law was confiscatory. The town sought to justify the large lot requirement on the ground that it would encourage the retention of land in its natural state for the benefit of the community. The court concluded that the permissible and judicially assumed advantages that justified one-acre zoning in *Simon v. [Town of] Needham,* would not justify 100,000 square foot house lots.

Although an objecting landowner has the burden of proving that large lot zoning is unjustified, the *Aronson* opinion indicates that a municipality's reliance on generalities concerning the public benefit of large lot zoning will not carry the day. In such a case, the municipality has the burden of coming forward with something tangible to justify its action. Thus, in 1975, in deciding a challenge to two-acre zoning in a portion of Sherborn, the Appeals Court stated that the record must show that there is a reasonable basis for concluding "that there are special needs that are met by two-acre zoning." *Wilson v. [Town of] Sherborn,* 326 N.E.2d 922 (Mass. App. 1975). The town successfully justified its two-acre zoning as an appropriate health protection measure based on an established and reasonable relationship between two-acre zoning and sewage and water conditions in the two-acre zone.

We are now in a position to move from general considerations to the specifics of the record in this case to see whether the judge was warranted in finding that the evidence justified his conclusion that the three-acre zoning requirement served a permissible public purpose authorized by The Zoning Act. Not every beneficial effect of the three-acre zoning requirement in the RA-120 district that the judge noted would, standing alone, justify the restriction. Neither the provision of open space nor the protection of plant and animal life, for example, would singly justify large lot zoning. That benefits of this character incidentally may flow from large lot zoning does not, however, detract from those justifications that do support large lot zoning. We, therefore, need not dwell on the trust's persuasive argument that the record does not support any claim that three-acre zoning in the RA-120 district is partially justified by a need to preserve animal and plant life. We turn, therefore, to other reasons advanced by the town in support of the area requirements of the RA-120 district.

The parties substantially agree that a lot of two acres in the RA-120 district would be sufficient to provide a safe on-site source of water on a lot having its own septic system. We need not decide whether there is any justification for adding an acre as a margin of safety for on-site drinking water, a concept whose reasonableness was not explained in the record. Nor need we reach the trust's doubtful argument that the State's requirements for septic systems somehow make inappropriate zoning requirements founded on considerations of safe drinking water and pollution from sewage. We need not decide these points because there is an independent ground for concluding that the town has come forward with sufficient proof of a reasonable basis for the need of three-acre zoning in the RA-120 district.

The town produced evidence, credited by the judge, that house lots of three acres or more were required in order to protect the ecology of Edgartown Great Pond. The pond, which consists of 890 acres, is a coastal and marine water formed in the sandy soil of the outwash plain of the melting glacier that created Martha's Vineyard. The pond, which the town opens to the ocean periodically and which opens naturally as well from time to time, is brackish (its water being between saline and fresh). It is vulnerable to nutrient pollution from excess nitrogen which would encourage plant growth that periodically deprives the water of oxygen. This anoxia kills shellfish and other organisms on the bottom of the pond and kills finfish. Without oxygen, sulfates in the water will produce hydrogen sulfide gas, "a sewer gas smell." The pond is on the brink of, and sometimes crosses the line of, becoming unhealthy.

The town's evidence concerning the need to protect the ecology of Edgartown Great Pond, evidence of the need for pollution control that the judge accepted, was sufficient to meet its burden of going forward with a demonstration of why three-acre zoning in the RA-120 district is rational and related to the public welfare. The town's expert testified that the nitrogen carrying capacity of the pond was five grams per square meter each year and that the appropriate average minimum lot size in the RA-120 district, to limit properly the nitrogen entering the pond, was three to three and one-half acres.[7] An expert presented by the trust had testified before the Martha's Vineyard Commission that his nutrient loading study validated "the density allowed by current zoning of one unit at three acres."

The judge's ruling is bolstered by the need to protect the amenities and character of a rural resort, such as the Vineyard, in order to assist its economic stability, including its shellfish industry and tourism. As one of the trust's experts testified, the quality of the Vineyard's landscape is important to the quality of life and the promotion of tourism. As we noted earlier, there are regional and Statewide interests in the preservation of the unique quality of Martha's Vineyard. Those interests justify the making of conservative assumptions about the consequences of land uses, even if standing alone protection of those interests might not support the imposition of three-acre zoning.

The trust makes much of the fact that part of its land is not within the watershed of Edgartown Great Pond. The burden was on the trust to prove that the zoning restriction was unlawful, and not on the town to prove its validity. The trust's land not within the watershed of the great pond is generally in the watershed of another coastal pond, and the trust did not prove that the circumstances of any other watershed were significantly different from the conditions in the watershed of Edgartown Great Pond.

This opinion should not be read as an endorsement of three-acre zoning. We have upheld the challenged zoning provision because of the special circumstances of this case, particularly the proximity of the restricted land to a coastal great pond. We are confident in the special circumstances of this case that the three-acre zoning provision has not been shown to be arbitrary and unreasonable or substantially unrelated to the public health, safety, and general welfare.

NOTES AND QUESTIONS

1. *Justifying large lot zoning.* The most striking and unusual features of the *Johnson* case are its skepticism about large lot zoning and its concern about exclusionary impacts. Why should this be so? Although large lot zoning requires more land for a dwelling, only one dwelling may be built on the lot, so the price per square foot may decrease enough to offset the increase in lot size. However, studies (though dated) indicate that increasing lot size increases lot price. See W. McEachern, *Large-Lot Zoning in Connecticut: Incentives and Effects,* U. Conn. Center for Real Est. & Urb. Econ. Studies (1979). If this is so, and if the ratio between dwelling costs and lot costs is fixed (which may be the case), the price of a dwelling built on the lot will increase proportionately.

There appear to be two major justifications for the large lot zoning in *Johnson*: environmental problems and the need to preserve the character of the island. Are these acceptable justifications? The environmental issue raises

---

[7] He assumed that the town would operate its wastewater plant so as to produce effluent only within permitted limits. In his calculation he also excluded as a source of nitrates in the pond's watershed land that is protected from development.

what can be called the "upland" problem. The trust's land apparently presented no environmental problems, but its development could endanger the nearby pond. Why not provide public sewerage or enforce sanitary regulations? If the trust land had been a wetlands, development could have been prevented entirely. See Section D *infra*. Notice, however, that the court did not decide whether a margin of safety for on-site drinking water justified the large lot zoning. It was doubtful about the argument that the state's septic system requirements made large lots unnecessary. But see the Pennsylvania cases, discussed in Note 7.

Although the special quality of Martha's Vineyard helped the court in finding that large lot zoning protected its character and amenities, the same issues arise in large lot zoning for mainland suburbs. For example, in the *Simon* case the court said:

> The advantages enjoyed by those living in one-family dwellings located upon an acre lot might be thought to exceed those possessed by persons living upon a lot of ten thousand square feet. More freedom from noise and traffic might result. The danger from fire from outside sources might be reduced. A better opportunity for rest and relaxation might be afforded. Greater facilities for children to play on the premises and not in the streets would be available. There may perhaps be more inducement for one to attempt something in the way of the cultivation of flowers, shrubs and vegetables. [42 N.E.2d at 562–63.]

The justifications used in *Simon* can be found in many cases upholding large lot zoning. However, the question is whether oversized lots are needed to obtain these objectives, and why the separation of residential from nonresidential uses isn't enough to achieve these objectives. Notice that the *Johnson* court rejected the provision of open space and the protection of plant and animal life as justifications for the large lot zoning.

2. The *Aronson* case, discussed in the principal opinion, indicated there are limits on how far these justifications will carry, at least in Massachusetts. The large lot requirement in that case was about 2.3 acres. The court also said:

> While initially an increase in lot size might have the effects there noted, the law of diminishing returns will set in at some point. As applied to the petitioners' property, the attainment of such advantages does not reasonably require lots of 100,000 square feet. Nor would they be attained by keeping the rural district undeveloped, even though this might contribute to the welfare of each inhabitant. Granting the value of recreational areas to the community as a whole, the burden of providing them should not be borne by the individual property owner unless he is compensated. [195 N.E.2d at 345.]

Does the *Johnson* case discredit the "diminishing returns" holding?

3. *Additional justifications.* Despite the skepticism in the principal case, most courts uphold large lot zoning. Here are some of the most common justifications:

(a) Preservation of the semi-rural character and appearance of a suburban community by assuring sufficient open space around buildings to create a dominant visual impression of open space rather than structures. *Gignoux v. Village of Kings Point,* 99 N.Y.S.2d 280 (Sup. Ct. 1950) (one acre). See also *Levitt v. Village of Sands Point,* 160 N.E.2d 501 (N.Y. 1959) (two acres); *Senior v. Zoning Comm'n,* 153 A.2d 415 (Conn. 1959), *appeal dismissed,* 363 U.S. 143 (1960) (four acres); *Flora Realty & Inv. Co. v. City of Ladue,* 246 S.W.2d 771 (Mo.), *appeal dismissed,* 344 U.S. 802 (1952) (three acres); Mayhew v. Town of Sunnyvale, 964 S.W.2d 922 (Tex. 1998), *cert. denied,* 526 U.S. 1144 (1999) (upholding denial of high density planned development in low density rural community).

(b) Preservation of specific historic sites and buildings in their historic settings. *County Comm'rs v. Miles,* 228 A.2d 450 (Md. 1967) (five acres).

(c) Preservation for low density development of sites which, because of their topography, are not easily buildable for higher density development. *Metropolitan Homes, Inc. v. Town Planning & Zoning Comm'n,* 202 A.2d 241 (Conn. 1964) (30,000 sq. ft.). See also *Senior v. Zoning Comm'n, supra* para. (a); *Larsen v. Zoning Comm'n,* 217 A.2d 715 (Conn. 1966) (one acre); *Bogert v. Washington Twp.,* 135 A.2d 1 (N.J. 1957) (one acre); *Honeck v. County of Cook,* 146 N.E.2d 35 (Ill. 1957) (five acres); *Flora Realty & Inv. Co. v. City of Ladue, supra* para. (a).

(d) Provision of large enough building sites to assure a safe water supply and safe sewage disposal in areas without a public water supply and/or without public sanitary sewers. *Zygmont v. Planning & Zoning Comm'n,* 210 A.2d 172 (Conn. 1965) (four acres); *De Mars v. Zoning Comm'n,* 115 A.2d 653 (Conn. 1955) (one acre); *Carruthers v. Board of Adjustment,* 290 S.W.2d 340 (Tex. Civ. App. 1956) (one acre); *Salamar Bldrs. Corp. v. Tuttle,* 275 N.E.2d 585 (N.Y. 1971) (two acres). See also *Albano v. Mayor & Twp. Comm.,* 476 A.2d 852 (N.J. App. Div. 1984) (three acres; to prevent pollution of lake).

(e) Preservation of the natural capacity of the soil to absorb rainfall by limiting the area built upon, and thus to provide protection against flooding and soil erosion after heavy rains. *Bogert v. Washington Twp., supra* para. (c).

(f) Regulation of the rate and pattern of suburban growth to assure orderly, efficient, and economical expansion of necessary public facilities. *Rockaway Estates v. Rockaway Twp.,* 119 A.2d 461 (N.J. App. Div. 1955); *Flora Realty & Inv. Co. v. City of Ladue, supra* at para. (a). See also *Security Management Corp. v. Baltimore County,* 655 A.2d 1326, (Md. App. 1995) (providing for orderly development and the protection of natural resources), *cert. denied,* 516 U.S. 1115 (1996).

(g) Implementation of specific planning principles as to proper organization of residential areas. *Padover v. Farmington Twp.,* 132 N.W.2d 687 (Mich. 1965) (20,000 sq. ft., based on "neighborhoods of the optimum size" to "support an elementary school of an ideal size and . . . location").

(h) Preservation of community identity by providing predominantly open areas ("green belts") between communities. *Norbeck Village Joint Venture v. Montgomery County Council,* 254 A.2d 700 (Md. 1969) (two acres). See also *Morse v. County of San Luis Obispo,* 55 Cal. Rptr. 710 (Cal. App. 1967).

(i) Provision of some "high class" low-density residential areas, viewed as essential to the local economy, and prevention of the "blanketing" of the community with small, low-cost houses. *Clary v. Borough of Eatontown*, 124 A.2d 54 (N.J. App. Div. 1956) (half an acre).

(j) Protection of the value of houses previously constructed on large lots against the depreciation that would result "if sections here and there are developed with smaller lots." *Flora Realty & Inv. Co. v. City of Ladue, supra* para. (a).

4. *Standards of review.* A student article reviewing the early large-lot zoning cases concluded they had adopted an unspoken rule of reason leading to a "gentle" judicial treatment of large-lot zoning restrictions. Comment, *Large Lot Zoning*, 78 Yale L.J. 1418, 1436, 1437 (1969). To what extent does the principal case support this conclusion? The cases discussed in the Notes? See Note, *Judicial Acquiescence in Large Lot Zoning: Is It Time to Rethink the Trend?*, 16 Colum. J. Envtl. L. 183 (1991).

5. *Taking problems.* These are usually not serious in large-lot zoning cases. The landowner may develop her land for residential use, although at lower densities. *Security Management, supra* Note 3, paragraph (f), easily dismissed a takings challenge post-*Lucas.* There may be cases, of course, where special circumstances result in a taking. See *Zeltig Land Dev. Corp. v. Bainbridge Township Bd. of Trustees,* 599 N.E.2d 383 (Ohio App. 1991) (bedrock made public sewers necessary but development then not economically feasible at required five-acre size); *State ex rel. Nagawicka Island Corp. v. City of Delafield*, 343 N.W.2d 816 (Wis. App. 1983) (three-acre zoning applied to two-acre island).

6. *Fiscal reasons.* In *Simon v. Needham,* the court indicated that large lot zoning could not be justified by fiscal reasons. The courts have primarily considered the exclusionary effects of large-lot zoning in cases that reviewed a number of suburban zoning exclusionary techniques. See Chapter 4 *infra.* A few courts have also considered the exclusionary effects of large-lot zoning in cases limited to a challenge of a large-lot zoning restriction. In *Board of County Supvrs. v. Carper*, 107 S.E.2d 390 (Va. 1959), the court invalidated two-acre zoning applied to the undeveloped western two-thirds of Fairfax County, which is located in the Washington, D.C., metropolitan area and which was rapidly urbanizing at that time. The court rejected environmental and growth-management justifications for the two-acre zoning, holding that it prevented lower income people from living in the western two-thirds of the county.

7. *Held invalid.* The leading case invalidating large-lot zoning is *National Land & Inv. Co. v. Kohn*, 215 A.2d 597 (Pa. 1965). A four-acre zoning restriction applied to thirty percent of a municipality that was in the path of development in the Philadelphia area. The court concluded that the reasons advanced for the four-acre zoning did not justify the loss in value it would impose on the property owner. The court rejected drainage and sewer problems as a reason for the zoning, holding that the municipality could handle these problems through sanitary regulations. Neither was four-acre zoning a "necessary" or "reasonable" method to protect the community from pollution. The court rejected an argument that inadequate fire and road services justified the four-acre zoning. In an important dictum, it stated that zoning "may not be used . . . to avoid the increased responsibilities and economic burdens which time and natural growth inevitably bring." *Id.* at 612. Finally, the court rejected an argument that the four-acre zoning was necessary to preserve the "character" of the community by creating a green belt.

Later, in what amounted to a plurality opinion, the Pennsylvania court relied on *National Land* to invalidate two-acre and three-acre zoning. *In re Concord Twp. Appeal (Kit-Mar)*, 268 A.2d 765 (Pa. 1970). The court held that large-lot zoning of this size was invalid absent "extraordinary justification," and that the difference in size between a three-acre and one-acre lot was "irrelevant to the problem of sewage disposal." The court had upheld one-acre zoning pre-*National Land*, relying on the usual presumption of constitutionality and holding that the plaintiff had not introduced evidence sufficient to rebut the presumption. *Bilbar Constr. Co. v. Easttown Twp. Bd. of Adjustment*, 141 A.2d 851 (Pa. 1958). The subsequent history of large-lot zoning in Pennsylvania is best told as part of that state's efforts to deal more comprehensively with exclusionary zoning problems. See Chapter 4.

3. COMMERCIAL AND INDUSTRIAL USES

a. In the Zoning Ordinance

This introductory section discusses some of the common zoning problems raised by industrial and commercial uses. The sections that follow discuss zoning problems raised by the use of zoning to control competition in land use and by application of the federal antitrust laws to anticompetitive zoning.

Districting problems.—Zoning districts for commercial and industrial uses present the usual land use classification problems. Courts uphold commercial and industrial districts if they find the distinctions between uses excluded and included defensible. *Tidewater Oil Co. v. Mayor & Council*, 209 A.2d 105 (N.J. 1965) (industrial zoning); *State ex rel. American Oil Co. v. Bessent*, 135 N.W.2d 317 (Wis. 1966) (filling stations excluded from retail commercial district).

A more difficult problem arises if a community attempts to determine the retail character of a district by excluding certain types of retail uses. One example is the exclusion of drive-in businesses to encourage walk-in trade. In *Board of Supvrs. v. Rowe*, 216 S.E.2d 199 (Va. 1975), the court held unconstitutional a commercial district that permitted hotels but not banks and that permitted restaurants but not drive-in restaurants. The court held that the excluded commercial uses were legitimate and no more detrimental than the uses included. This seems sensible, but on what constitutional basis do you suppose the court relied? Compare *Manalapan Realty, L.P. v. Township Comm.*, 658 A.2d 1230 (N.J. 1995) (upholding ordinance excluding unenclosed uses from shopping center).

What if a zoning ordinance prohibits a convenience store from selling liquor on the premises. The court thought this restriction had no reasonable relationship to zoning purposes in *Gas 'N Shop, Inc. v. City of Kearney*, 539 N.W.2d 423 (Neb. 1995). What do you suppose was the purpose behind these ordinances?

Ribbon development is a nagging commercial-use problem. One commercial use on a busy thoroughfare usually leads to others and a commercial strip is the result. What if a municipality attempts to stop ribbon development by limiting commercial uses on thoroughfares to intersections? See *City of Phoenix v. Fehlner,* 363 P.2d 607 (Ariz. 1961) (held constitutional under fairly debatable rule).

Big box retail.—Some consider the new big box stores, like Wal-Mart and K Mart, ugly and a threat to smaller business enterprises. What if a municipality tries to exclude them by limiting the size of retail stores? A district court refused to dismiss a complaint claiming that the distinction between size of store served no zoning purpose, that it restricted "the public's ability to take advantage of the product selection and price advantages offered by super-stores," and that it served the economic interests of existing businesses by protecting them from competition. *A&P v. Town of E. Hampton,* 997 F. Supp. 340 (E.D.N.Y. 1998). Contra *Loreto Dev. Co. v. Village of Chardon,* 695 N.E.2d 1151 (Ohio App. 1996), holding that an ordinance restricting the size of business was intended to prevent traffic congestion, excessive noise and "other objectionable influences." Sites were available for large stores elsewhere in the village, which wanted to preserve the residential, small town character of that part of town.

Compare this case with the *Baker* case, reproduced *supra,* which invalidated a restriction on the number of unrelated people who could live together and suggested other means of dealing with the problem they might present. Are there other ways to deal with the big box problem?

Non-cumulative or "exclusive" zoning.—The first zoning ordinances were cumulative: any less restrictive use was allowed in a more restrictive zoning district. Some cities still have cumulative zoning. This practice makes development difficult to control. Multi-family development is permitted as-of-right in a commercial district, for example. Modern zoning ordinances are non-cumulative, or exclusive. Each district is limited to the uses permitted as-of-right or as a conditional use.

An argument can be made that non-cumulative zoning, especially for the more intensive uses such as commercial and industrial uses, is unconstitutional. It does not recognize the hierarchical "compatibility" principle established by the *Euclid* case. This principle would seem to authorize restrictions on land use only to protect the less intensive from the more intensive uses. Do industrial uses need protection from residential uses?

Non-cumulative zoning was held constitutional in a leading case, *People ex rel. Skokie Town House Bldrs., Inc. v. Village of Morton Grove,* 157 N.E.2d 33 (Ill. 1959). The court held that the compatibility principle cuts both ways, and that the exclusion of incompatible uses from all zoning districts would ensure a "better and more economical use of municipal services." The developer planned to build townhouses in a non-cumulative industrial district. The court noted that spotty residential development in the district "may make industrial or commercial expansion impossible or prohibitively expensive." The court indicated that excessive non-cumulative zoning for industrial uses might be unconstitutional. See also *Corthouts v. Town of Newington,* 99 A.2d 112 (Conn. 1953). Why is this so? See *Kozesnik v. Township of Montgomery,*

131 A.2d 1 (N.J. 1957) (upholding industrial district restricted to single use). But see *Katobimar Realty Co. v. Webster,* 118 A.2d 824 (N.J. 1955) (invalidating light industrial district excluding all retail uses because uses held not incompatible). See Note, *Industrial Zoning to Exclude Higher Uses,* 32 N.Y.U. L. Rev. 1261 (1957).

Total exclusion.—Some courts have invalidated residential exclusionary zoning in suburban municipalities. See Ch. 4. Most courts have not invalidated commercial and industrial exclusions. *Town of Los Altos Hills v. Adobe Creek Properties, Inc.,* 108 Cal. Rptr. 271 (Cal. App. 1973) (commercial); *Town of Beacon Falls v. Posick,* 563 A.2d 285 (Conn. 1989) (exclusion of landfill); *Duffcon Prods., Inc. v. Borough of Cresskill,* 64 A.2d 347 (N.J. 1949) (upholding industrial exclusion because other industrial sites available in region).

Pennsylvania has long held that a total exclusion of a commercial use shifts the burden to justify the exclusion to the municipality. See *Borough Council v. Pagal, Inc.,* 460 A.2d 1214 (Pa. Commw. 1983). The court held invalid the total exclusion of restaurants from a municipality. It refused to accept arguments in support of the exclusion that the community was historically residential and that surrounding communities had readily accessible restaurants. The Michigan courts also have struck down total exclusions of nonresidential uses. See *Ottawa County Farms, Inc. v. Township of Polkton,* 345 N.W.2d 672 (Mich. App. 1983) (sanitary landfill). Compare *Wrigley Properties, Inc. v. City of Ladue,* 369 S.W.2d 397 (Mo. 1963) (regional shopping needs do not invalidate residential zoning prohibiting commercial use).

NOTES AND QUESTIONS

1. *Regional needs.* As the text notes, some courts consider the availability in the region of uses excluded by a municipality. A few cases have given more explicit attention to regional land use needs in nonresidential zoning cases. In *Save a Valuable Env't v. City of Bothell,* 576 P.2d 401, 405 (Wash. 1978), the court invalidated a rezoning for a major regional shopping center. The court held that the shopping center would have serious detrimental effects on areas outside the city:

> [A]gricultural and low density residential uses of land around the center could not be maintained. Pressures for secondary business growth would be severe. Not only would desirable agricultural land be lost, but intensified commercial uses would require substantial investments in highways, sewers, and other services and utilities. The economic and aesthetic values of the essentially rural character of the Valley would be lost.

The court added that in cases like this "the zoning body must serve the welfare of the entire affected community." What can the city now do to validate the rezoning?

Is the court's decision in *City of Bothell* consistent with the market failure theory of zoning? Note that, in the Court's view, it is the political "market" that has failed, in that the City, serving its own interests, has not expressed the interest of "the entire affected community." How does the court know this?

Is an implicit aspect of the court's holding that major regional decisions must be made by a body that internalizes the regional interest?

2. *Buffers.* One way of handling the problem of incompatible uses in close proximity is to provide for a buffer zone. A general residential district in which apartments are permitted is often used as a buffer between single-family districts and commercial districts. See, e.g., *Evanston Best & Co. v. Goodman,* 16 N.E.2d 131, 132 (Ill. 1938), approving the use of this technique "to prevent an impact between the intensity of the use to which commercial areas are put with the quiet and cleanliness which are essential to property devoted to higher type residential uses." Accord *Stampfl v. Zoning Board of Appeals,* 599 N.E.2d 646 (Mass. App. 1992) (upholding 75 foot buffer between industrial and residential use); *Carlson v. City of Bellevue,* 435 P.2d 957 (Wash. 1968) (district allowing multifamily housing and nonretail business may be used as buffer between "prime residential" and industrial areas). But cf. Hagman's criticism: "[i]f zoning is in the interest of the poor, why is it that apartment buildings are the buffer zone between industrial-commercial zones and single-family residential zones, rather than the single-family zones, with fewer people, being the neighbor of the undesirable commercial and industrial uses?" D. Hagman, Urban Planning and Land Development Control Law 474 (1971).

Sometimes a landscaped strip must be provided as a buffer between residential and nonresidential use districts. See, e.g., *State v. Gallop Bldg.,* 247 A.2d 350 (N.J. App. Div. 1968), where a twenty-foot screen belt of trees was required for every business use adjacent to a residential district. An objection was made that requiring a strip this wide was unconstitutional. The court appeared to think not, and approved the buffer concept implicit in the ordinance. Why would the business property owner object to this requirement? Streets may also be used as dividing lines between zoning districts. See *Perron v. Village of New Brighton,* 145 N.W.2d 425 (Minn. 1966), and *Carlson, supra.*

3. *As-applied problems.* Commercial developers prohibited from developing their property by residential zoning may make the usual claim that the residential zoning is unconstitutional "as applied." In many of these cases, the residential area already has been invaded by commercial uses. What if the commercial uses already in the residential area were allowed by the municipality? Although most courts do not hold municipalities bound by their prior zoning actions, a court occasionally takes the opposite view. *City of Birmingham v. Morris,* 396 So. 2d 53 (Ala. 1981).

4. *Industrial performance zoning.* This is a zoning technique that became popular in the 1960s. It is intended to provide an alternative or a supplement to traditional zoning for industrial uses. The zoning ordinance adopts performance standards applicable to noise, vibrations, smoke, odors, and air pollutants. The idea has caught on to some extent, although the adoption of strict pollution standards in the national Clean Air Act of 1970 has somewhat undercut industrial zoning performance standards.

In *DeCoals, Inc. v. Board of Zoning Appeals,* 284 S.E.2d 856 (W. Va. 1981), the court upheld an industrial performance zoning ordinance that included an absolute "no dust" prohibition. It cited air pollution cases to hold that the technology-forcing "no dust" standard was valid and that any technical infeasibility or economic hardship in complying with the standard need not be considered. See also *State v. Zack,* 674 P.2d 329 (Ariz. App. 1983) (ordinance prohibiting "offensive vibration" not unconstitutionally vague). Contra, *Lithonia Asphalt Co. v. Hall County Planning Comm'n,* 364 S.E.2d 860 (Ga. 1988). For discussion, see J. Schwab, *Industrial Performance Standards for a New Century,* American Planning Association, Planning Advisory Serv. Rep. No. 444 (1993); Duerksen, *Modern Industrial Performance Standards: Key Implementation and Legal Issues,* 18 Zoning & Plan. L. Rep. 33 (1995).

5. *Design issues.* Bulk and density controls in commercial areas can have a major effect on building design. In *La Salle Nat'l Bank v. City of Evanston,* 312 N.E.2d 625 (Ill. 1974), for example, a landowner challenged a zoning district reducing height limitations and the percentage of lot that could be occupied on the edge of a central business district in order to provide a "tapering effect." The court upheld the ordinance. It noted that the property owner's proposed multi-family building would alter the character of the area and would disrupt the city's attempt "to have a gradual tapering of building heights toward an open lakefront and park area." See also *Chicago City Bank & Trust Co. v. City of Highland Park,* 137 N.E.2d 835 (Ill. 1956) (approving height and lot size requirements in central business areas).

Manhattan is a major example of bulk and density controls affecting building design. The first New York City ordinance in 1916, for example, established height and lot coverage regulations for midtown Manhattan that created an ugly and inefficient type of architecture for office buildings and apartment houses called the wedding cake or ziggurat style. Only by using this shape could a builder achieve the maximum rentable floor space on his site, except in the relatively rare case when he could utilize a "tower privilege" permitting unlimited height for a tower covering no more than twenty-five percent of the lot area. See generally Planning and Zoning in New York City (T. Bressi ed., 1993).

Zoning ordinances in other cities can also create ziggurats. See *Texans to Save the Capitol, Inc. v. Board of Adjustment,* 647 S.W.2d 773 (Tex. App. 1983). The Austin zoning ordinance contained a 200-foot height limit on downtown buildings. The court allowed a developer to build a 398-foot building by relying on a provision in the ordinance that allowed three additional feet of height for each foot of setback from the street line. This exception is common in zoning ordinances. The court held the height bonus was allowable for any setback on any part of the building, and achieved the additional height through a ziggurat style. The court noted that this "interpretation encourages dissimilar and unique architecture in downtown Austin and dissuades builders from constructing box-like structures which create a 'crayon' effect on the street below."

A revision of the New York City ordinance in 1960–1961 enacted an entirely new set of bulk and density controls, producing the tower block design typical of office and apartment construction that now dominates much of midtown Manhattan. The 1982 revision of the New York zoning ordinance enacted new performance criteria for preventing the obstruction of sunlight that allows but does not require a return of the ziggurat style. "Rather than having to conform to a setback curve that relates buildings to angles of visibility from the street, a structure is gauged according to the amount of 'sky' left unobstructed" by the building mass. T. Lassar, Carrots and Sticks: New Zoning Downtown 90 (1989). This "performance" approach allowed for greater design variety. A new planned revision of the zoning ordinance would impose new and lower height controls.

A NOTE ON INCENTIVE ZONING

Incentive zoning is a land use regulatory technique through which cities grant private real estate developers the legal right to disregard otherwise applicable zoning restrictions in return for providing environmental amenities such as public parks and plazas and, most recently, social facilities and services such as affordable housing, day care centers, and job training. Command-and-control gives way to a bargaining process between local government and private developer.

Incentive zoning expressly enlists market forces by offering developers a choice of regulatory incentives that either increase revenue or reduce costs. The most popular incentive, the floor area bonus, grants developers the right to build additional rentable space [see illustration below]. Other incentives may exempt development from height and setback requirements or reduce the required parking ratio and thereby significantly reduce construction costs. When the value of an incentive exceeds the cost of providing an amenity, then developers may find it in their self-interest to engage in such public-private transactions. [Kayden, *Market-Based Regulatory Approaches: A Comparative Discussion of Environmental and Land Use Techniques in the United States,* 19 B.C. Envtl. Aff. L. Rev. 565, 568 (1992).]

FLOOR AREA BONUS CONCEPT

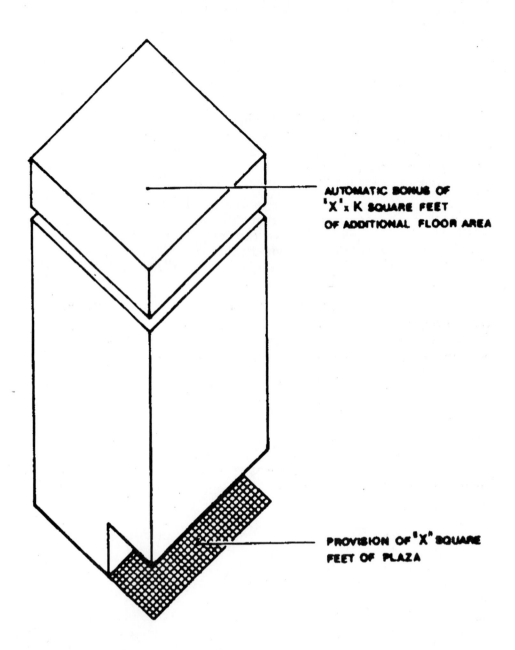

This diagram illustrates the density bonus concept that adds floor area in return for a ground-level plaza.

Professor Kayden lists a number of problems that can arise in incentive zoning programs. One is necessity. Since many on-site amenities pay for themselves in higher rents, there is an argument the private market would provide them without a bonus. Pricing is another problem. Kayden believes "the experience in many United States cities shows a consistent pattern of underpricing incentives by granting more of them than is necessary to encourage the desired private behavior." *Id.* at 571. See Office of the New York State Comptroller, New York City Planning Commission — Granting Special Permits for Bonus Floor Area (1988). Can underpricing or lack of necessity be challenged on legal grounds?

There are also equity problems. Incentive zoning can create social costs that are unfairly distributed. "For example, the tenants of a building adjacent to an incentive building substantially larger than otherwise permitted will not be happy with the enlarged shadow cast over their residences or with the greater street and sidewalk congestion." *Id.* at 572.

Corruption of the zoning system is another issue. Kayden believes "regulators will fall prey to the corruption of the transaction and give the 'green light' to otherwise undesirable projects solely to obtain the benefits."

In *Municipal Art Soc'y v. City of New York,* 522 N.Y.S.2d 800 (N.Y. 1987), the city agreed to convey the site of the city's Coliseum to a developer and to grant permission to exceed existing zoning by 20 percent. The developer agreed to a sales price in addition to a commitment to pay a substantial sum for improvements to a nearby subway station. In addition, the parties agreed that the price of the property would be cut by over 10 percent if the city withheld the density bonus. The court held that this provision violated the incentive zoning ordinance because it effectively exchanged a density bonus for a substantial sum of money available for citywide use and not one of the amenities specified in the ordinance as the basis for density increases. Does this case affect the validity of the density bonus incentive program in cases where a sale of city property is not involved? See Kayden, *Zoning for Dollars: New Rules for an Old Game? Comments on the Municipal Art Society and Nollan Cases,* 39 Wash. U. J. Urb. & Contemp. L. 3 (1991).

The property rights baseline.—A city may have to adopt restrictive density and bulk requirements in the city core to make an incentive zoning system attractive to developers. Developers may then claim that the existing zoning without the density bonus is so limiting that it is a taking of property. The court rejected this contention in *Montgomery County v. Woodward & Lothrop, Inc.,* 376 A.2d 483 (Md. 1977). It held the record did not support a developer's claim that she had to obtain a density bonus to make a reasonable use of her land.

What other legal objections could developers make to this practice? What if a municipality gradually confers so many density bonuses that few parcels in the central business district are subject to the more restrictive bulk and density requirements? Could an owner of one of these remaining non-bonused parcels argue that he is legally entitled to a density bonus as-of-right?

How has it worked?—Incentive zoning is only one of many zoning techniques that substitute bargaining between the public agency and private developer for the more typical "command and control" land use regulation. Other examples are the development agreement, discussed in Chapter 5, *infra,* and planned unit developments, discussed in Chapter 6, *infra.* To this extent, incentive zoning is an attempt to introduce market bargaining into the zoning process. See Chapter 1, *supra.*

Whether incentive zoning has worked as planned is another question. This Note has raised some of the legal and policy questions, but design outcomes are another issue. Professor Kayden carried out an extensive study of the incentive zoning program in New York City and found mixed results. Privately Owned Public Space: The New York Experience (2000). In an article on his study he noted that adequate legal standards were initially a problem, but that enforcement of the law was now a major issue. *Plaza Suites,* Planning, Vol. 66, No. 3, at 16 (2000).

Public use of the private spaces has increased now that quality has improved, so some owners are locking the public out! Yet Kayden wonders whether enforcement will ever be adequate. New York now plans to repeal its incentive zoning for plazas except in certain business districts, including Manhattan and Brooklyn. For additional reading see J. Getzels & M. Jaffe, *Zoning Bonuses in Central Cities,* American Planning Association, Planning Advisory Rep. No. 410, 1988; M. Morris, Incentive Zoning: Meeting Urban Design and Affordable Housing Objectives, American Planning Association, Planning Advisory Rep. No. 494, 2000; Morris, *Using Zoning Bonuses for Smart Growth Development*, Am. Plan. Ass'n Zoning News, July 2000 (discusses programs in several cities).

b. Control of Competition as a Zoning Purpose

Unlike residential zoning, commercial zoning can raise legitimacy of purpose issues because a zoning decision can favor one competitor over another. This section considers this problem as it is handled in state law, and the next section considers whether and how federal antitrust law applies.

ENSIGN BICKFORD REALTY CORP. v. CITY COUNCIL

68 Cal. App. 3d 467, 137 Cal. Rptr. 304 (1977)

SCOTT, ASSOCIATE JUSTICE:

The City of Livermore appeals from a judgment granting Ensign Bickford Realty Corporation's petition for a writ of mandamus directing appellant City to reconsider Bickford's rezoning application.

Respondent Bickford is the owner of a parcel of real property located in the northeast section of the City of Livermore. The property was annexed by the City in 1968, and shortly thereafter was zoned "CN," a classification permitting neighborhood commercial facilities. The CN zoning of the property was at all times consistent with the City's General Plan and was retained until June 3, 1974, when the City rezoned the property "RS-4," for residential use only. In 1975 Bickford applied to the City Council for rezoning to CN, stating that a neighborhood shopping center would presently be constructed on its property and that Tradewell Stores, Inc., a grocery store chain, would be the major tenant. The City Planning Commission, by a resolution adopted on May 6, 1975, recommended against the CN zoning. Its recommendation was based upon the following factors: "1. That although the proposed rezoning is in conformance with the General Plan, the public necessity, convenience, and general welfare does not require the adoption of 'CN' zoning of this property at this time. 2. That the population base to support a Neighborhood Commercial area, as outlined in the General Plan, is not adequate at this time, nor is it anticipated that the neighborhood population will become large enough in the immediate future to justify rezoning at this time. 3. Inasmuch as the principal use proposed for the subject site is one intended to serve the 'community,' the intent of the proposed rezoning to 'CN' would not be served (provision of day to day shopping convenience to the surrounding neighborhood). 4. That current lack of sewer capacity makes it unlikely that necessary supporting population will develop in the near future."

On July 28, 1975, following a public hearing, the City Council denied Bickford's application by a vote of three to one. The City Council hearing was recorded and a transcript thereof was introduced into evidence and considered by the court below. It appears from the discussion at the public hearing that a portion of the northeast section of Livermore, in the so-called Springtown area, had already been zoned CN. The council wanted to develop this area before permitting commercial development elsewhere in the northeast section of Livermore. Various members of the council expressed the view that although there was a sufficient population base in the area to support one shopping center, the population was insufficient to sustain two such centers and the commercial development should be located in Springtown. Three of the four council members present felt that to allow the development of a shopping center on Bickford's property would frustrate the announced policy of promoting development of the Springtown area where land had already been zoned CN for a neighborhood commercial center.

Thereafter, at the request of the City Council, the city manager wrote to Tradewell Stores, Inc., urging that Tradewell consider locating its store in the proposed Springtown shopping complex. The letter expressed the unanimous view of the City Council that the northeast sector of Livermore (wherein respondent's property is located) needed neighborhood shopping accommodations.

The trial court found . . . that the purpose in denying respondent's application was to encourage development of the Springtown CN zoned property by eliminating a competitive economic threat to such property, and that the council's decision was not predicated upon considerations of public health, welfare, safety or morals. The court concluded that the refusal of the City to rezone its property was arbitrary and capricious, unconstitutionally discriminatory against Bickford, and denied it equal protection of the laws.

Appellant contends that the decision of the City Council in refusing to rezone respondent's property from a residential to a commercial classification was a valid exercise of the police power, and hence did not constitute an abuse of discretion or a denial of equal protection. We agree. . . . We have concluded that the City Council acted reasonably in denying respondent's rezoning application and that the writ of mandamus should have been denied. . . .

[The court first restated the usual rules applicable to the judicial review of zoning ordinances. The sole purpose of judicial review is to determine whether the ordinance "reasonably relates to a legitimate governmental purpose." The ordinance enjoys a presumption of constitutionality. "The sole issue here is whether there is any reasonable basis in fact to support the legislative determination of the City Council."]

At the public hearing held on the matter, it was generally agreed that the northeastern section of the City needed a shopping center, and that the population base in that area would support one, but not two such centers. The issue, then, was where the shopping center should be located. The council members, after discussing the issue among themselves and hearing the views of residents in the community, determined that it would be in the best interests of the City to attract new residents to Springtown, and hence decided to encourage the development of a commercial complex in that area. Thus it was determined that the CN zoning would be limited to Springtown, already zoned for such use, and the surrounding area would remain residential.

Bickford contends that the purpose of the City Council in making the above decision was to restrict competition, and that inasmuch as the restriction of competition or the protection of monopolies is an impermissible zoning objective, the City Council's decision cannot stand. Where the sole purpose of a zoning ordinance or decision is to regulate or restrict business competition, the regulation is subject to challenge. It is not the proper function of a zoning ordinance to restrict competition or to protect an enterprise which may have been encouraged by a prior zoning classification.

Despite the principle that cities may not directly restrict competition under the guise of the zoning power, it must be recognized that land use and planning decisions cannot be made in a vacuum, and all such decisions must necessarily have some impact on the economy of the community. In *Van Sicklen v. Browne* 92 Cal. Rptr. 786 (Cal. App. 1971), a conditional use permit for a gas station was denied on the ground, inter alia, that "Approval would create a further proliferation of this type of land use in a neighborhood already adequately served by service stations. . . . There is no demonstrated need for an additional service station in this neighborhood at this time." The court stated: "Although cities may not use zoning powers to regulate economic competition [citations], it is also recognized that land use and planning decisions cannot be made in any community without some impact on the economy of the community. As stated in *Metromedia, Inc. v. City of Pasadena*, 216 Cal. App. 2d 270, 273 [30 Cal. Rptr. 731], 'Today, economic and aesthetic considerations together constitute the nearly inseparable warp and woof of the fabric upon which the modern city must design its future.' Taking cognizance of this concept we perceive that planning and zoning ordinances traditionally seek to maintain property values, protect tax revenues, provide neighborhood social and economic stability, attract business and industry and encourage conditions which make a community a pleasant place to live and work. Whether these be classified as 'planning considerations' or 'economic considerations,' *we hold that so long as the primary purpose of the zoning ordinance is not to regulate economic competition, but to subserve a valid objective pursuant to a city's police powers, such ordinance is not invalid even though it might have an indirect impact on economic competition.*" (Emphasis added.) Bickford urges that *Van Sicklen* should be read as permitting the restricting of competition only when the business activity is hazardous. The court did discuss the legislative right to regulate overconcentration of gas stations because they "use products which are highly inflammable and explosive," and an increase in their number in a small area "increases the danger to the public." We view this as a supplemental rationale for the upholding of the city's determination.

Here, the City Council determined that the area needed and would support one shopping center, and that to further the long-range development plan for the City, the shopping center should not be located on Bickford's property, but in Springtown. This would have the effect of encouraging residential and commercial development in that area. It would also undoubtedly have the effect of decreasing the market or lease value of respondent's property. By its very nature, a zoning ordinance may be expected to depress the value of some land while it operates, in its total effect, to achieve an end which will benefit the whole community. An ordinance is not constitutionally defective where it classifies for residential use land which would yield a greater profit if used for business purposes. Nor does the fact that two parcels of property which are similar in nature but zoned differently make the zoning unreasonable.

The cases cited by respondent in support of its contention that appellant was unlawfully attempting to restrict competition are distinguishable. . . . Here, the City is attempting to regulate *where*, within the City, business will be developed. In furtherance of this legitimate end, it is necessary to permit business development in one area before allowing commercial development in another. The economic impact upon the property involved is only incidental. The primary purpose is clearly the reasonable regulation of land use. There is no evidence, nor can it be inferred, that the City Council was attempting to permit commercial development on one parcel and deny it as to another for the purpose of creating a business monopoly or to unreasonably regulate the commercial development of the City. To the contrary, the council was regulating the commercial growth of the City as it related to the needs of the residential areas for that commercial development.

Contrary to respondent's assertions, the motive of the City Council in declining to amend its zoning ordinance is irrelevant to any inquiry concerning its reasonableness. The reasonableness of its action is to be judged on the objective results of the decision. If there is any rational basis for a zoning decision from the objective facts, the actual motive for the decision becomes immaterial. Here, the record is replete with objective facts to support the denial of respondent's rezoning application. Respondent's property had been zoned CN at one time, then rezoned to residential. There is no suggestion that such rezoning was improper. It was, in fact, a decision made consistent with the City's General Plan.

The effect of the council's decision here was to maintain the zoning status quo. There was testimony at the hearing from residents within the affected area that rezoning would have a deleterious impact on the surrounding property and the general neighborhood. The court erred in concluding that the council's action was improperly motivated solely from economic considerations relating to competition. In *Village of Arlington Heights v. Metropolitan Housing Development Corp.* (1977) 429 U.S. 252, the United States Supreme Court discussed with approval the general principle that motivation for legislative acts is not material, noting: "Rarely can it be said that a legislature or administrative body operating under a broad mandate made a decision motivated solely by a single concern, or even that a particular purpose was the 'dominant' or 'primary' one." However, the court stated, "When there is a proof that a [racially] discriminatory purpose has been a motivating factor in the decision, this judicial deference is no longer justified." No racial motivation is suggested in the instant case; therefore, judicial deference must be given to the legislative act.

At oral argument respondent conceded, as indeed it must, that inquiry into the motives of the councilmen to determine their reasons for denying the rezoning would be improper. Respondent argues, however, that when a record is made, as in the instant case, wherein various councilmen in fact state their reasons, the court must consider those reasons in determining whether the decision was arbitrary or unreasonable. Based upon this analysis, respondent argues that the record demonstrates that the councilmen were motivated by economic and business competition factors and not by reasons based upon the public health, safety and welfare. To accept respondent's argument would place an onerous burden on legislators to carefully articulate for the record all of the reasons and motives behind their decisions. To fail to do so would put their action in peril. As often as not, members of administrative bodies make decisions for unarticulated reasons. Often the discussions at a public hearing are guided by the direction taken by members of the public who speak. These discussions may or may not include what is significant to a given member of the agency. There are a host of reasons why the utterances of councilmen at public hearings cannot be said to encompass the totality of their thought processes. It would be manifestly burdensome and unproductive to require that once a councilman started discussing the merits of a decision he was being called upon to make, he must set forth all of his opinions on the subject under discussion. Such an inhibiting factor would lead inevitably to silent council meetings. The members of the public would lose the benefit of open discussion of the public business. Conversely, public statements by members of the City Council to the effect that their decision is based upon considerations of public health, safety or welfare cannot make the decision valid if it is in fact arbitrary or unreasonable. The decision of the City Council must be found reasonable or unreasonable based upon its effect in light of the facts as they exist relevant to that decision.

We conclude that the denial of Bickford's zoning application was not unreasonable nor a denial of its right to equal protection under the law. The record clearly establishes a rational basis for the City's action as a proper exercise of its police power.

The judgment is reversed, with directions that judgment be entered in favor of appellant.

NOTES AND QUESTIONS

1. *Control of competition.* Why does the principal case present a "control of competition" problem? What if the council denied the shopping center rezoning because it was inconsistent with adjacent residential uses? This is a standard reason for denying commercial rezonings. See the *Krause* case,

supra. Would this raise a control of competition problem? What if the proposed rezoning had been for a multi-family development in a residential area and the council denied it? Would this raise a control of competition problem? Why might motive be an issue in a "control of competition" zoning case but not in other zoning cases? The *Arlington Heights* case cited and discussed in the principal case is reproduced and discussed in Ch. 4, sec. C2 *infra.*

Does the statement quoted in the principal case, that zoning is not invalid so long as its primary purpose is not the control of competition, help? How do you make this distinction? See also *In re Lieb,* 116 A.2d 860 (Pa. 1955) (the purpose of zoning may not be the restriction of competition).

2. *Applying the rule.* The rule that zoning may not be used to control competition is well established in zoning law although, as the principal case indicates, it has its exceptions. One function of the rule is to limit standing in zoning litigation. See sec. B1 *supra.* The basis for the rule, and its role in standing cases, is illustrated by *Circle Lounge & Grille, Inc. v. Board of Appeal,* 86 N.E.2d 920 (Mass. 1949). Circle Lounge sued to challenge a variance that permitted the construction of a Howard Johnson restaurant across the street in a residential zoning district. The court held that competition from the new restaurant did not give the Circle Lounge standing to challenge the variance. The purpose of zoning is to ensure the compatibility of uses. Residential owners in the residential zone could challenge the variance. A commercial use in an adjacent commercial zone could not, even though the commercial use was located in a residential zone. Accord *Nautilus of Exeter v. Town of Exeter,* 656 A.2d 407 (N.H. 1995); *Sun-Brite Car Wash, Inc. v. Board of Zoning & Appeals,* 508 N.E.2d 130 (N.Y. 1987).

See also *Swain v. County of Winnebago,* 250 N.E.2d 439 (Ill. App. 1969). Downtown business merchants were denied standing to challenge a regional shopping center rezoning some distance from the downtown in the adjacent county. The court found that competition from the new shopping center was the only damage suffered by the downtown merchants:

> Free and open competition has always been a strong pillar in the foundation of our society. A person can have no vested or special property right in either the monopoly or competitive advantage accorded by zoning restrictions at a given time. [*Id.* at 444.]

The facts in *Swain* were somewhat similar to the facts in the principal case. Then why wasn't standing an issue in the principal case? Does it make a difference whether a municipality is defending a refusal to rezone or whether a competitor is attempting to invalidate a rezoning?

3. *Examples of control of competition problems.*

(a) *Distance requirements.* Municipalities commonly adopt distance requirements for gasoline filling stations, liquor stores and other similar uses, requiring that they be separated by a minimum distance. The justification, in the case of filling stations, is that close proximity will increase fire and other hazards, but some courts have rejected these reasons. See *Chicago Title & Trust Co. v. Village of Lombard,* 166 N.E.2d 41 (Ill. App. 1961) (also noting that the effect of a 650 foot distance requirement was to protect existing stations violating that requirement from new competition). Compare *Stone v.*

City of Maitland, 446 F.2d 83 (5th Cir. 1971) (upholding a 350 foot distance requirement). The court noted that "[a]bsent these requirements, the probability of business failure in this highly competitive area is high. The result is abandoned stations." *Id.* at 89. The court added that abandoned stations detract from the quality of the aesthetic environment. What is the primary zoning purpose in the distance cases? See also the reference to the hazards of filling stations in the principal case. When commercial uses enjoy First Amendment protection, distance requirements require additional analysis. See sec. 4, *infra.*

(b) *The "need" cases.* In *Van Sicklen,* discussed in the principal case, the court upheld the denial of a filling station as a conditional use because no need for the station was shown. For discussion of conditional uses, see Ch. 5, sec. C *infra.* Need is not usually a criterion for the approval of conditional uses, which are uses similar to those permitted in the zoning district that require individual review. Filling stations are an example. See also *Technical & Prof. Serv., Inc. v. Board of Zoning Adjustment,* 558 S.W.2d 798 (Mo. App. 1977). The court upheld a board decision denying a conditional use for a cemetery. The ordinance required, inter alia, that the board find that the use would not "seriously injure the appropriate use of neighboring property." The court held that the board weighed this factor with the need for a cemetery "and concluded that the scales tipped heavily in favor of the latter." *Id.* at 802. Compare *Cardinal Props. v. Borough of Westwood,* 547 A.2d 316 (N.J. App. Div. 1988) (invalidating need standard for storage yards as improper.)

(c) *Protection of existing businesses.* In *Zahring v. Long Beach Twp.,* 151 A.2d 425 (N.J.L. Div. 1959), the municipality zoned as marine commercial all lots in residential districts on which nonconforming marine commercial uses existed. The effect of the rezoning was to allow these uses to expand without restrictions; had they remained as nonconforming uses, a variance would have been required for them to expand. Other lots suitable for marine commercial use were not rezoned for this use. The court struck down the rezoning, noting it was "adopted to solve the economic and competitive problems of particular individuals." *Id.* at 430.

See also *Fogg v. City of S. Miami,* 183 So. 2d 219 (Fla. App. 1966). The court invalidated a zoning ordinance prohibiting drive-in retail businesses in a commercial district. It stated that a "benefit or anticipated benefit to a special group" is not enough to sustain a zoning restriction. The court admitted the city could prohibit drive-in businesses that create excess noise or traffic or the "gathering of unsavory elements," but concluded that the drive-in store excluded by the ordinance was not in this category. Accord *Frost v. Borough of Glen Ellyn,* 195 N.E.2d 616 (Ill. App. 1964) (drive-in restaurant).

(d) *Protection of existing business districts and downtown areas.* As *Ensign Bickford* indicates, the courts may take a different view when a commercial rezoning is denied to protect an existing business district. See also *Chevron Oil Co. v. Beaver County,* 449 P.2d 989 (Utah 1969) (upholding denial of rural gasoline filling station zoning to protect business district in center of county). What distinguishes these cases from cases like *Fogg, supra?*

Restrictive commercial zoning to protect a downtown business district was upheld in *Forte v. Borough of Tenafly,* 255 A.2d 804 (N.J. App. Div.), *petition for certification denied,* 258 A.2d 13 (N.J. 1969). To protect a deteriorating downtown business district, a municipality adopted a commercial zoning district limiting commercial uses to neighborhood retail stores in areas outside the central business district. About ninety-three percent of all the retail business in the municipality was in the central business district.

The limited commercial classification was the basis for prohibiting plaintiffs from building a supermarket outside the downtown business district. They claimed this district was unconstitutional because it was adopted for the sole benefit of the downtown merchants. The court disagreed. It held that zoning could be used to maintain and revitalize a downtown business district even though it gave the district a "virtual monopoly over retail business." Plaintiffs also claimed the limited commercial district was unconstitutional as applied because similar retail uses were located in the vicinity of their lot. The court held that these uses were not so numerous that the restrictions applicable in the district were unreasonable. What if several supermarkets were already located nearby?

For a case requiring an environmental impact statement prepared under a state environmental policy act to consider the impact of a regional shopping center on a downtown business district, see *Barrie v. Kitsap County,* 613 P.2d 1148 (Wash. 1980).

4. *Providing a conceptual basis for the control of competition cases.* Mandelker, *Control of Competition as a Proper Purpose in Zoning,* 14 Zoning Dig. 33, 34 (1962), suggests that these cases can be divided into proximity and market-demand cases. Another commentator notes that both questions are present in many cases. In a proximity case, an existing entrepreneur objects to a new market entrant because his market share is threatened. In a market-demand case, the argument is "that entrants must be regulated because the market cannot absorb them." Existing entrepreneurs argue that a failure to regulate will cause severe economic dislocations, such as bankruptcies and property tax losses caused by underutilized or abandoned land. "The sophisticated protectionist may even argue that regulation of market entry . . . [prevents] one decision maker from shifting external costs to non-decision makers — the most traditional basis for public regulation of land use." Tarlock, *Not in Accordance With a Comprehensive Plan: A Case Study of Regional Shopping Center Location Conflicts in Lexington, Kentucky,* 1970 Urb. L. Ann. 133, 175. Do you agree with this "sophisticated" argument?

5. For additional reading, see Strom, *Land Use Controls: Effects on Business Competition I,* 3 Zoning & Plan. L. Rep. 33 (1980); *II, id.,* at 41; Weaver & Duerksen, *Central Business District Planning and the Control of Outlying Shopping Centers,* 14 Urb. L. Ann. 57 (1977).

PROBLEM

You are the city attorney for the town of Rustic Hills, a small rural town that is a shopping center for surrounding agricultural areas. However, the town's business district has been declining. A city council member received a call from a friend of his who is in real estate advising that a Big Box retail company was planning to buy a large site on the edge of town for a Big Box store. The site is zoned residential but is adjacent to a state highway.

What would you recommend? (1) A ten-month moratorium on all commercial retail development so the town can study the problem? (2) Stringent design standards for the Big Box retail store? (3) A cap of 10,000 square feet on all new retail stores? The cap would not affect existing stores, all of which are under this size. (4) A quota relating commercial retail space to population? The quota would be set low enough so that it would exclude any new Big Box stores. (5) A requirement that all new Big Box stores prepare an economic statement detailing the effect they would have on existing retail stores in the town? Any legal problems? See Walters, *Blocking the Big Box,* Governing, July, 2000, at 48.

c. Antitrust Problems

Reconsider the facts in the *Ensign Bickford* case, reproduced *supra.* Do they raise a possibility of municipal liability under the Sherman Antitrust Act? Section 1 of the Act, 15 U.S.C. § 1, provides:

> Every . . . conspiracy, in restraint of trade or commerce among the several States, . . . is hereby declared to be illegal.

Section 2, 15 U.S.C. § 2, provides:

> Every person who shall monopolize, or attempt to monopolize, or combine or conspire with any other person or persons, to monopolize any part of the trade or commerce among the several States . . . shall be deemed guilty of a felony.

In *Parker v. Brown,* 317 U.S. 341 (1943), the Court construed the Sherman Act to contain a "state action" exemption that excused, on principles of intergovernmental comity, *state*-approved anticompetitive behavior. It was assumed that the *Parker v. Brown* exemption also applied to local governments, until the Court held that it did not in *City of Lafayette v. Louisiana Power & Light Co.,* 435 U.S. 389 (1978). In a series of subsequent cases, the Supreme Court applied antitrust liability to local governments but it then effectively restored the exemption for land use cases. Here are the important cases:

Community Communications Co. v. City of Boulder, 455 U.S. 405 (1982). In a case challenging a moratorium on new cable television licenses, the Court held a city's home rule status did not afford it immunity under the state action doctrine. The Court confirmed the rule adopted in *Lafayette* that municipal immunity from the antitrust law requires clearly and affirmatively expressed state policy to displace competition. The Court held the constitutional home rule authority under which the city adopted the moratorium did not confer immunity under this test.

Town of Hallie v. City of Eau Claire, 471 U.S. 34 (1985). Four unincorporated townships adjacent to the city brought an antitrust action against the city. They claimed they were potential competitors of the city and that the city used its monopoly power over sewage treatment to gain an unlawful monopoly over the provision of sewage collection and transportation services. The Court upheld the district court's dismissal of the complaint.

Wisconsin statutes gave cities the authority to construct sewerage systems and to determine the area to be served. The Court held that the statutes evidenced "a 'clearly articulated and affirmatively expressed' state policy to displace competition with regulation in the area of municipal provision of sewerage services." The Court held it was enough if these statutes contemplated that the city might engage in anticompetitive conduct, and that such conduct was "a foreseeable result of empowering the City to refuse to serve unannexed areas." It was not necessary for the state legislature to state explicitly that it expected the City to engage in anticompetitive conduct. *Lafayette* means only it is enough if "the statutes authorized the City to provide sewage services and also to determine the areas to be served. We think it is clear that anticompetitive effects logically would result from this broad authority to regulate." *Id.* at 42. The Court also held it was not necessary that the state "compelled" the city to act.

City of Columbia v. Omni Outdoor Advertising Co., 499 U.S. 365 (1991). The Court held that state action immunity protected a municipality from antitrust liability claimed to arise from an ordinance restricting the size, location and spacing of billboards. These restrictions, especially those on spacing, benefitted an existing billboard company that controlled 95% of the local market, because they already had billboards in place, and severely hindered a potential competitor that was trying to enter the market.

The Court held that state action immunity was conferred by the city's "unquestioned zoning power over the size, location and spacing of billboards" that the state zoning act, which was based on the Standard Act, authorized. The Court rejected a defense that state action immunity did not apply if a municipality exercises its delegated authority in a substantively or procedurally defective manner. This defense would undercut the "very interests of federalism" the state action doctrine was designed to protect. This holding means immunity is available even if a state court holds a zoning regulation invalid because it is an improper control of competition.

The Court next held the "clear articulation" rule was "amply met here" because "[t]he very purpose of zoning regulation is to displace unfettered business freedom in a manner that regularly has the effect of preventing normal acts of competition, particularly on the part of new entrants." An ordinance restricting the size, location and spacing of billboards, which the Court characterized as "a common form of zoning," necessarily protects existing billboards from new competition. The Court also rejected a conspiracy exception to state action immunity and held that bribery and misconduct would not make state action immunity unavailable.

NOTES AND QUESTIONS

1. *Local government liability today.* The Court's decision in *Omni* almost totally protects local government land use actions from antitrust liability. See also *Jacobs, Visconsi & Jacobs Co. v. City of Lawrence,* 927 F.2d 1111 (10th Cir. 1991) (immunity found when city refused suburban shopping center zoning to implement plan designating downtown as primary retail area).

What about home rule municipalities? *Omni* did not discuss *Boulder,* which held that state action immunity does not apply to a home rule municipality. Can a home rule municipality claim antitrust immunity by relying on statutory rather than home rule powers to carry out land use controls?

2. *Noerr-Pennington doctrine.* This doctrine, which is based on two Supreme Court cases, provides a First Amendment antitrust defense for competitors who petition to influence governmental action. *United Mine Workers v. Pennington,* 381 U.S. 657 (1965); *Eastern R.R. Presidents Conference v. Noerr Motor Freight Co.,* 365 U.S. 127 (1961). The doctrine is important in land use cases, like *Omni,* where an entity uses political advocacy to influence the adoption of a regulation that hinders a competitor. The Court held in *Omni* that there is no conspiracy exception to the *Noerr-Pennington* doctrine.

There is also a "sham" exception to the doctrine, but in *Professional Real Estate Investors, Inc. v. Columbia Pictures Indus., Inc.,* 508 U.S. 49 (1993), the Court held the sham exception requires objective proof and cannot be based on the subjective intent of the parties. *Columbia Pictures* substantially restricts opportunities to prove a sham exception. See *VIM, Inc. v. Somerset Hotel Ass'n,* 19 F. Supp. 2d 422 (W.D. Pa. 1998), *aff'd without opinion,* 187 F.3d 627 (3d Cir. 1999). Defendants defeated a claim that they had impeded the construction of plaintiff's hotel, which eventually was built, by interposing patently meritless legal challenges to plaintiffs' positions before the local zoning and planning commissions, and before the courts.

3. *Private liability.* What is left of antitrust liability after *Omni*? Private party liability in land use cases is still a possibility. Consider, for example, how private party liability might arise on the facts of the *Omni* case. The Court addressed private party liability under the antitrust laws in *FTC v. Ticor Title,* 504 U.S. 621 (1992), in which six large title insurance companies were charged with price-fixing. For private entities to claim antitrust immunity under the state action doctrine, the Court held, they must show that the state "has played a substantial role in determining the specifics of supervision." The mere potential for state supervision is not enough. Nor is it enough, as in *Ticor,* that the state retained the right to reject proposed rates for thirty days, after which rates become final. Land use regulation does not meet the *Ticor* test except in states which have active state land use control programs. Thus, private antitrust liability remains a possibility.

4. *The Local Government Antitrust Act of 1984.* Even before *Omni,* this statute had taken much of the sting out of antitrust actions against local governments by prohibiting awards of damages and attorney's fees against municipalities. 15 U.S.C. § 34-36. Had the antitrust laws otherwise remained an attractive source of law for plaintiffs, it is unclear whether the limitation of remedies would have diminished the incentive to bring such suits. It is likely that it would have diminished the incentive for municipalities to settle antitrust cases. (Consider the parallel to the "damages" issue in *First English, supra* ch. 2.)

5. *State immunity legislation.* Some states have granted their local governments an exemption from federal antitrust liability. Some of this legislation is limited to specific functions, such as public transportation and water and sewage systems, but some statutes are broad enough to cover zoning. Consider the following:

> All immunity of the state from the provisions of the Sherman Antitrust Act . . . is hereby extended to any city or city governing body acting

within the scope of the grants of authority [contained in statutes grant-ing authority to municipalities]. When acting within the scope of the grants of authority . . . a city or city governing body shall be presumed to be acting in furtherance of state policy. [N.D. Cent. Code § 40-01-22.]

Can a *state* alter the meaning of federal law this way? Remember that the state action exemption is the result of the *federal court's* construction of *Congress'* intent. There are no cases.

6. For discussion of *Omni*, see The Supreme Court, 1990 Term: Leading Cases, 105 Harv. L. Rev. 177, 361 (1991); Note, *Municipal Antitrust Immunity After City of Columbia v. Omni Outdoor Advertising, Inc.,* 67 Wash. L. Rev. 479 (1992). See also Sullivan, *Antitrust Regulation of Land Use: Federalism's Triumph Over Competition, The Last Fifty Years,* 3 Wash. U. J.L. & Pol'y 473 (2000).

4. USES ENTITLED TO SPECIAL PROTECTION

a. Free Speech-Protected Uses: Adult Businesses

Supreme Court decisions in the mid-1970s made free speech doctrine applicable to zoning ordinances regulating land uses that affect free speech. This change occurred because the Court brought commercial speech within the protection of the free speech clause. See *Bigelow v. Virginia,* 421 U.S. 809 (1975) (newspaper advertisement for abortion services). Free speech review of zoning ordinances applies to a limited number of land uses. It applies to zoning for adult sex businesses, such as adult book stores and cinemas. This problem is discussed in this section. Sign regulation is also entitled to free speech protection. See Ch. 8, *infra.* Free speech protection has produced a revolution in the judicial review of land use controls. The courts substantially reverse the usual presumption of constitutionality and review more inten-sively the justifications for zoning restrictions.

How much is commercial speech protected?—The Supreme Court stated its tests for the review of commercial speech in *Central Hudson Gas & Elec. Corp. v. Public Serv. Comm'n,* 447 U.S. 557 (1980) (invalidating regulation prohibit-ing electricity promotion advertising). The Court adopted a four-part test for commercial free speech review; this is the test now applied to adult businesses. The *Central Hudson* tests require the court to determine: whether the "asserted governmental interest" in regulation is "substantial," whether the regulation "directly advances the governmental interest asserted," and whether "it is not more extensive than is necessary" to serve that interest. *Id.* at 563. The Court has moderated the last requirement of the *Central Hudson* test to permit more extensive regulation so long as there is a reasonable "fit" between the legislature's ends and the means chosen to accomplish them. See *Board of Trustees v. Fox,* 492 U.S. 469 (1989).

Another principle in free speech law that affects land use regulation is the requirement that regulation of speech must be content-neutral, not content-based. One example of a content-neutral regulation is a time, place and manner regulation, such as a zoning ordinance that regulates adult busi-nesses. These principles are explained as applied to adult use regulation in the Supreme Court's *Renton* case, which is reproduced *infra,* and there is additional discussion in the section on sign regulation in Chapter 8. First, it is necessary to look at Supreme Court adult use regulation cases that precede *Renton.*

The Supreme Court adult business cases.—The first two Supreme Court adult business decisions, *Young v. American Mini Theatres, Inc.,* 427 U.S. 50 (1976), and *Schad v. Borough of Mt. Ephraim,* 452 U.S. 61 (1981), provided some guidance on how free speech doctrine applies to zoning regulations affecting these businesses, but they were plurality decisions that left many questions unanswered. *Young v. American Mini Theatres, Inc.,* considered the constitutionality of a deconcentration zoning strategy adopted by the City of Detroit. The zoning ordinance required a distance of 1000 feet between adult businesses. This requirement applied to a number of other businesses, such as hotels and bars. The ordinance also prohibited any of these businesses from locating within 500 feet of a residential area. Operators of two adult movie theaters brought an action challenging the constitutionality of both requirements on free speech grounds. Justice Stevens wrote a plurality opinion upholding the ordinance, in which Justice Powell concurred.

Justice Stevens first noted that the free-speech clause did not absolutely prohibit the deconcentration ordinance. The ordinance did not regulate free speech because of its point of view, and he would not give adult sexual expression the same protection under the free-speech clause that he would give to political debate. He then found a factual basis for concluding that the zoning ordinance would have its desired effect of preserving the character of city neighborhoods. "[T]he city's interest in attempting to preserve the quality of urban life is one that must be accorded high respect."

Justice Powell agreed with the plurality, although he would give adult sexual expression the same protected status as political debate. He upheld the ordinance as an "incidental" interference with First Amendment concerns. Noting that the Court had upheld innovative zoning techniques, he indicated that the Detroit ordinance was constitutional because it only controlled the "secondary effects" of "adult" expression on neighborhoods.

The plurality and concurring opinions in *Mini Theatres* do not indicate how far a municipality may go in restricting adult businesses within a city. In an important footnote, Justice Stevens indicated that the situation "would be quite different" if the ordinance had suppressed or greatly restricted access to lawful speech. In *Schad v. Borough of Mount Ephraim,* a suburban municipality in New Jersey adopted a zoning ordinance that the court interpreted to exclude all live entertainment, including nude dancing. An adult book store owner installed glass booths in which customers could observe nude dancers perform. He brought an action challenging the ordinance as a violation of free speech.

The actual holding in the case was quite narrow. The Court wrote five opinions, including a plurality opinion signed by three Justices. The seven Justices whose opinions made up a majority could only agree that the ordinance was facially overbroad and that the municipality had not justified it. The municipality claimed that the exclusion of the adult business was justified because the ordinance allowed businesses that met only local needs.

The plurality rejected this justification, noting that the ordinance did allow other businesses that met nonlocal needs. The plurality also held that the live entertainment businesses excluded by the ordinance did not present any more parking, police or other problems than the businesses the ordinance permitted.

The borough also claimed that the ordinance was a reasonable "time, place and manner" regulation of free speech. This refers to First Amendment doctrine that permits regulation that advances a governmental interest and does not have as its primary purpose the suppression of free speech. The court rejected this justification because the borough did not offer evidence that live entertainment was basically incompatible with normal uses in commercial districts. It was on this point that five of the Justices in other concurring opinions disagreed, so a majority of the court actually held that a community could ban adult businesses under appropriate circumstances.

The issues left unresolved in *Mini-Theatres* and *Schad* were resolved to a considerable extent in the *Renton* decision, which follows. You may note that the Court relies for its free speech doctrine on the Supreme Court's decision in *O'Brien v. United States* rather than *Central Hudson*. However, the principles adopted in the two cases are, for all practical purposes, identical.

CITY OF RENTON v. PLAYTIME THEATRES, INC.

475 U.S. 41 (1986)

JUSTICE REHNQUIST delivered the opinion of the Court:

This case involves a constitutional challenge to a zoning ordinance, enacted by appellant, the city of Renton, Washington, that prohibits adult motion picture theaters from locating within 1,000 feet of any residential zone, single-or multiple-family dwelling, church, park, or school. Appellees, Playtime Theatres, Inc., and Sea-First Properties, Inc., filed an action in the United States District Court for the Western District of Washington seeking a declaratory judgment that the Renton ordinance violated the First and Fourteenth Amendments and a permanent injunction against its enforcement. The District Court ruled in favor of Renton and denied the permanent injunction, but the Court of Appeals for the Ninth Circuit reversed and remanded for reconsideration. 748 F.2d 527 (1984). We noted probable jurisdiction, and now reverse the judgment of the Ninth Circuit.

In May 1980, the Mayor of Renton, a city of approximately 32,000 people located just south of Seattle, suggested to the Renton City Council that it consider the advisability of enacting zoning legislation dealing with adult entertainment uses. No such uses existed in the city at that time. Upon the Mayor's suggestion, the City Council referred the matter to the city's Planning and Development Committee. The committee held public hearings, reviewed the experiences of Seattle and other cities, and received a report from the City Attorney's Office advising as to developments in other cities. The City Council, meanwhile, adopted Resolution No. 2368, which imposed a moratorium on the licensing of "any business . . . which . . . has as its primary purpose the selling, renting or showing of sexually explicit materials." The resolution contained a clause explaining that such businesses "would have a severe impact upon surrounding businesses and residences."

In April 1981, acting on the basis of the Planning and Development Committee's recommendation, the City Council enacted Ordinance No. 3526. The ordinance prohibited any "adult motion picture theater" from locating within 1,000 feet of any residential zone, single-or multiple-family dwelling, church, or park, and within one mile of any school. The term "adult motion picture theater" was defined as "[a]n enclosed building used for presenting motion picture films, video cassettes, cable television, or any other such visual media, distinguished or characteri[zed] by an emphasis on matter depicting, describing or relating to 'specified sexual activities' or 'specified anatomical areas' . . . for observation by patrons therein."

In early 1982, respondents acquired two existing theaters in downtown Renton, with the intention of using them to exhibit feature-length adult films. The theaters were located within the area proscribed by Ordinance No. 3526. At about the same time, respondents filed the previously mentioned lawsuit challenging the ordinance on First and Fourteenth Amendment grounds, and seeking declaratory and injunctive relief. While the federal action was pending, the City Council amended the ordinance in several respects, adding a statement of reasons for its enactment and reducing the minimum distance from any school to 1,000 feet. In November 1982, the Federal Magistrate to whom respondents' action had been referred recommended the entry of a preliminary injunction against enforcement of the Renton ordinance and the denial of Renton's motions to dismiss and for summary judgment. The District Court adopted the Magistrate's recommendations and entered the preliminary injunction, and respondents began showing adult films at their two theaters in Renton. Shortly thereafter, the parties agreed to submit the case for a final decision on whether a permanent injunction should issue on the basis of the record as already developed.

The District Court then vacated the preliminary injunction, denied respondents' requested permanent injunction, and entered summary judgment in favor of Renton. The court found that the Renton ordinance did not substantially restrict First Amendment interests, that Renton was not required to show specific adverse impact on Renton from the operation of adult theaters but could rely on the experiences of other cities, that the purposes of the ordinance were unrelated to the suppression of speech, and that the restrictions on speech imposed by the ordinance were no greater than necessary to further the governmental interests involved. Relying on *Young v. American Mini Theatres, Inc.,* 427 U.S. 50 (1976), and *United States v. O'Brien,* 391 U.S. 367 (1968), the court held that the Renton ordinance did not violate the First Amendment.

The Court of Appeals for the Ninth Circuit reversed. The Court of Appeals first concluded, contrary to the finding of the District Court, that the Renton ordinance constituted a substantial restriction on First Amendment interests. Then, using the standards set forth in *United States v. O'Brien, supra,* the Court of Appeals held that Renton had improperly relied on the experiences of other cities in lieu of evidence about the effects of adult theaters on Renton, that Renton had thus failed to establish adequately the existence of a substantial governmental interest in support of its ordinance, and that in any event Renton's asserted interests had not been shown to be unrelated to the suppression of expression. The Court of Appeals remanded the case to the District Court for reconsideration of Renton's asserted interests.

In our view, the resolution of this case is largely dictated by our decision in *Young v. American Mini Theatres, Inc., supra.* There, although five Members of the Court did not agree on a single rationale for the decision, we held that the city of Detroit's zoning ordinance, which prohibited locating an adult theater within 1,000 feet of any two other "regulated uses" or within 500 feet of any residential zone, did not violate the First and Fourteenth Amendments. 427 U.S., at 72–73 (plurality opinion of Stevens, J., joined by Burger, C.J., and White and Rehnquist, JJ.); *id.,* at 84 (Powell, J., concurring). The Renton ordinance, like the one in *American Mini Theatres,* does not ban adult theaters altogether, but merely provides that such theaters may not be located within 1,000 feet of any residential zone, single-or multiple-family dwelling, church, park, or school. The ordinance is therefore properly analyzed as a form of time, place, and manner regulation. *Id.,* at 63, and n.18; *id.,* at 78–79 (Powell, J., concurring). Describing the ordinance as a time, place, and manner regulation is, of course, only the first step in our inquiry. This Court has long held that regulations enacted for the purpose of restraining speech on the basis of its content presumptively violate the First Amendment. See *Carey v. Brown,* 447 U.S. 455, 462–463, and n.7 (1980); *Police Dept. of Chicago v. Mosley,* 408 U.S. 92, 95, 98–99 (1972). On the other hand, so-called "content-neutral" time, place, and manner regulations are acceptable so long as they are designed to serve a substantial governmental interest and do not unreasonably limit alternative avenues of communication.

At first glance, the Renton ordinance, like the ordinance in *American Mini Theatres,* does not appear to fit neatly into either the "content-based" or the "content-neutral" category. To be sure, the ordinance treats theaters that specialize in adult films differently from other kinds of theaters. Nevertheless, as the District Court concluded, the Renton ordinance is aimed not at the *content* of the films shown at "adult motion picture theatres," but rather at the *secondary effects* of such theaters on the surrounding community. The District Court found that the City Council's *"predominate* concerns" were with the secondary effects of adult theaters, and not with the content of adult films themselves (emphasis added). But the Court of Appeals, relying on its decision in *Tovar v. Billmeyer,* 721 F.2d 1260, 1266 (CA9 1983), held that this was not enough to sustain the ordinance. According to the Court of Appeals, if *"a motivating factor"* in enacting the ordinance was to restrict respondents' exercise of First Amendment rights the ordinance would be invalid, apparently no matter how small a part this motivating factor may have played in the City Council's decision. 748 F.2d, at 537 (emphasis in original). This view of the law was rejected in *United States v. O'Brien,* 391 U.S. 367, 382–386 (1968), the very case that the Court of Appeals said it was applying:

> "It is a familiar principle of constitutional law that this Court will not strike down an otherwise constitutional statute on the basis of an alleged illicit legislative motive. What motivates one legislator to make a speech about a statute is not necessarily what motivates scores of

others to enact it, and the stakes are sufficiently high for us to eschew guesswork." *Id.,* at 383–384.

The District Court's finding as to "predominate" intent, left undisturbed by the Court of Appeals, is more than adequate to establish that the city's pursuit of its zoning interests here was unrelated to the suppression of free expression. The ordinance by its terms is designed to prevent crime, protect the city's retail trade, maintain property values, and generally "protec[t] and preserv[e] the quality of [the city's] neighborhoods, commercial districts, and the quality of urban life," not to suppress the expression of unpopular views. As Justice Powell observed in *American Mini Theatres,* "[i]f [the city] had been concerned with restricting the message purveyed by adult theaters, it would have tried to close them or restrict their number rather than circumscribe their choice as to location." 427 U.S., at 82, n.4.

In short, the Renton ordinance is completely consistent with our definition of "content-neutral" speech regulations as those that "are *justified* without reference to the content of the regulated speech." *Virginia Pharmacy Board v. Virginia Citizens Consumer Council, Inc.,* 425 U.S. 748, 771 (1976) (emphasis added). The ordinance does not contravene the fundamental principle that underlies our concern about "content-based" speech regulations: that "government may not grant the use of a forum to people whose views it finds acceptable, but deny use to those wishing to express less favored or more controversial views." *Mosley, supra,* at 95–96. It was with this understanding in mind that, in *American Mini Theatres*, a majority of this Court decided that, at least with respect to businesses that purvey sexually explicit materials, zoning ordinances designed to combat the undesirable secondary effects of such businesses are to be reviewed under the standards applicable to "content-neutral" time, place, and manner regulations. Justice Stevens, writing for the plurality, concluded that the city of Detroit was entitled to draw a distinction between adult theaters and other kinds of theaters "without violating the government's paramount obligation of neutrality in its regulation of protected communication," 427 U.S., at 70, noting that "[i]t is th[e] secondary effect which these zoning ordinances attempt to avoid, not the dissemination of 'offensive' speech," *id.,* at 71, n.34. Justice Powell, in concurrence, elaborated:

> "[The] dissent misconceives the issue in this case by insisting that it involves an impermissible time, place, and manner restriction based on the content of expression. It involves nothing of the kind. We have here merely a decision by the city to treat certain movie theaters differently because they have markedly different effects upon their surroundings. . . . Moreover, even if this were a case involving a special governmental response to the content of one type of movie, it is possible that the result would be supported by a line of cases recognizing that the government can tailor its reaction to different types of speech according to the degree to which its special and overriding interests are implicated." *Id.,* at 82, n.6.

The appropriate inquiry in this case, then, is whether the Renton ordinance is designed to serve a substantial governmental interest and allows for reasonable alternative avenues of communication. It is clear that the ordinance meets such a standard. As a majority of this Court recognized in

American Mini Theatres, a city's "interest in attempting to preserve the quality of urban life is one that must be accorded high respect." 427 U.S., at 71 (plurality opinion); see *id.,* at 80 (Powell, J., concurring) ("Nor is there doubt that the interests furthered by this ordinance are both important and substantial"). Exactly the same vital governmental interests are at stake here.

The Court of Appeals ruled, however, that because the Renton ordinance was enacted without the benefit of studies specifically relating to "the particular problems or needs of Renton," the city's justifications for the ordinance were "conclusory and speculative." 748 F.2d, at 537. We think the Court of Appeals imposed on the city an unnecessarily rigid burden of proof. The record in this case reveals that Renton relied heavily on the experience of, and studies produced by, the city of Seattle. In Seattle, as in Renton, the adult theater zoning ordinance was aimed at preventing the secondary effects caused by the presence of even one such theater in a given neighborhood. See *Northend Cinema, Inc. v. Seattle,* 585 P.2d 1153 (Wash. 1978). The opinion of the Supreme Court of Washington in *Northend Cinema,* which was before the Renton City Council when it enacted the ordinance in question here, described Seattle's experience as follows:

> "The amendments to the City's zoning Code which are at issue here are the culmination of a long period of study and discussion of the problems of adult movie theaters in residential areas of the City. . . . [T]he City's Department of Community Development made a study of the need for zoning controls of adult theaters . . . . The study analyzed the City's zoning scheme, comprehensive plan, and land uses around existing adult motion picture theaters. . . ." *Id.,* at 1155.

> "[T]he [trial] court heard extensive testimony regarding the history and purpose of these ordinances. It heard expert testimony on the adverse effects of the presence of adult motion picture theaters on neighborhood children and community improvement efforts. The court's detailed findings, which include a finding that the location of adult theaters has a harmful effect on the area and contribute to neighborhood blight, are supported by substantial evidence in the record." *Id.,* at 1156.

> "The record is replete with testimony regarding the effects of adult movie theater locations in residential neighborhoods." *Id.,* at 1159.

We hold that Renton was entitled to rely on the experiences of Seattle and other cities, and in particular on the "detailed findings" summarized in the Washington Supreme Court's *Northend Cinema* opinion, in enacting its adult theater zoning ordinance. The First Amendment does not require a city, before enacting such an ordinance, to conduct new studies or produce evidence independent of that already generated by other cities, so long as whatever evidence the city relies upon is reasonably believed to be relevant to the problem that the city addresses. That was the case here. Nor is our holding affected by the fact that Seattle ultimately chose a different method of adult theater zoning than that chosen by Renton, since Seattle's choice of a different remedy to combat the secondary effects of adult theaters does not call into question either Seattle's identification of those secondary effects or the relevance of Seattle's experience to Renton.

We also find no constitutional defect in the method chosen by Renton to further its substantial interests. Cities may regulate adult theaters by dispersing them, as in Detroit, or by effectively concentrating them, as in Renton. "It is not our function to appraise the wisdom of [the city's] decision to require adult theaters to be separated rather than concentrated in the same areas. . . . [T]he city must be allowed a reasonable opportunity to experiment with solutions to admittedly serious problems." *American Mini Theatres, supra,* at 71 (plurality opinion). Moreover, the Renton ordinance is "narrowly tailored" to affect only that category of theaters shown to produce the unwanted secondary effects, thus avoiding the flaw that proved fatal to the regulations in *Schad v. Mount Ephraim,* 452 U.S. 61 (1981), and *Erznoznik v. City of Jacksonville,* 422 U.S. 205 (1975).

Respondents contend that the Renton ordinance is "under-inclusive," in that it fails to regulate other kinds of adult businesses that are likely to produce secondary effects similar to those produced by adult theaters. On this record the contention must fail. There is no evidence that, at the time the Renton ordinance was enacted, any other adult business was located in, or was contemplating moving into, Renton. In fact, Resolution No. 2368, enacted in October 1980, states that "the City of Renton does not, at the present time, have any business whose primary purpose is the sale, rental, or showing of sexually explicit materials." That Renton chose first to address the potential problems created by one particular kind of adult business in no way suggests that the city has "singled out" adult theaters for discriminatory treatment. We simply have no basis on this record for assuming that Renton will not, in the future, amend its ordinance to include other kinds of adult businesses that have been shown to produce the same kinds of secondary effects as adult theaters. See *Williamson v. Lee Optical Co.,* 348 U.S. 483, 488–489 (1955).

Finally, turning to the question whether the Renton ordinance allows for reasonable alternative avenues of communication, we note that the ordinance leaves some 520 acres, or more than five percent of the entire land area of Renton, open to use as adult theater sites. The District Court found, and the Court of Appeals did not dispute the finding, that the 520 acres of land consists of "[a]mple, accessible real estate," including "acreage in all stages of development from raw land to developed, industrial, warehouse, office, and shopping space that is criss-crossed by freeways, highways, and roads."

Respondents argue, however, that some of the land in question is already occupied by existing businesses, that "practically none" of the undeveloped land is currently for sale or lease, and that in general there are no "commercially viable" adult theater sites within the 520 acres left open by the Renton ordinance. The Court of Appeals accepted these arguments,[3] concluded that the 520 acres was not truly "available" land, and therefore held that the

---

[3] The Court of Appeals' rejection of the District Court's findings on this issue may have stemmed in part from the belief, expressed elsewhere in the Court of Appeals' opinion, that, under *Bose Corp. v. Consumers Union of United States, Inc.,* 466 U.S. 485 (1984), appellate courts have a duty to review *de novo* all mixed findings of law and fact relevant to the application of First Amendment principles. See 748 F.2d 527, 535 (CA9 1984). We need not review the correctness of the Court of Appeals' interpretation of *Bose Corp.,* since we determine that, under any standard of review, the District Court's findings should not have been disturbed.

Renton ordinance "would result in a substantial restriction" on speech. 748 F.2d, at 534.

We disagree with both the reasoning and the conclusion of the Court of Appeals. That respondents must fend for themselves in the real estate market, on an equal footing with other prospective purchasers and lessees, does not give rise to a First Amendment violation. And although we have cautioned against the enactment of zoning regulations that have "the effect of suppressing, or greatly restricting access to, lawful speech," *American Theatres,* 427 U.S., at 71, n.35 (plurality opinion), we have never suggested that the First Amendment compels the Government to ensure that adult theaters, or any other kinds of speech-related businesses for that matter, will be able to obtain sites at bargain prices. See *id.,* at 78 (Powell, J., concurring) ("The inquiry for First Amendment purposes is not concerned with economic impact"). In our view, the First Amendment requires only that Renton refrain from effectively denying respondents a reasonable opportunity to open and operate an adult theater within the city, and the ordinance before us easily meets this requirement.

In sum, we find that the Renton ordinance represents a valid governmental response to the "admittedly serious problems" created by adult theaters. See *id.,* at 71 (plurality opinion). Renton has not used "the power to zone as a pretext for suppressing expression," *id.,* at 84 (Powell, J., concurring), but rather has sought to make some areas available for adult theaters and their patrons, while at the same time preserving the quality of life in the community at large by preventing those theaters from locating in other areas. This, after all, is the essence of zoning. Here, as in *American Mini Theatres,* the city has enacted a zoning ordinance that meets the goals while also satisfying the dictates of the First Amendment. The judgment of the Court of Appeals is therefore

Reversed.

Ronton wins

Justice Blackmun concurs in the result.

Justice Brennan joined by Justice Marshall, dissenting:

Renton's zoning ordinance selectively imposes limitations on the location of a movie theater based exclusively on the content of the films shown there. The constitutionality of the ordinance is therefore not correctly analyzed under standards applied to content-neutral time, place, and manner restrictions. But even assuming that the ordinance may fairly be characterized as content-neutral, it is plainly unconstitutional under the standards established by the decisions of this Court. Although the Court's analysis is limited to cases involving "businesses that purvey sexually explicit materials," and thus does not affect our holdings in cases involving state regulation of other kinds of speech, I dissent. . . . [Most of Justice Brennan's dissent is omitted, but the following paragraphs illustrate his views on the impact of the free speech clause on the allocation of land for adult businesses under zoning ordinances:]

Finally, the ordinance is invalid because it does not provide for reasonable alternative avenues of communication. The District Court found that the ordinance left 520 acres in Renton available for adult theater sites, an area comprising about five percent of the city. However, the Court of Appeals found that because much of this land was already occupied, "[l]imiting adult theater uses to these areas is a substantial restriction on speech." 748 F.2d, at 534. Many "available" sites are also largely unsuited for use by movie theaters. Again, these facts serve to distinguish this case from *American Mini Theatres,* where there was no indication that the Detroit zoning ordinance seriously limited the locations available for adult businesses. See *American Mini Theaters, supra,* at 71 n.35 (plurality opinion) ("The situation would be quite different if the ordinance had the effect of . . . greatly restricting access to, lawful speech"); see also *Basiardanes v. City of Galveston,* 682 F.2d 1203, 1214 (CA5 1982) (ordinance effectively banned adult theaters by restricting them to "'the most unattractive, inaccessible, and inconvenient areas of a city'"); *Purple Onion, Inc. v. Jackson,* 511 F. Supp. 1207, 1217 (N.D. Ga. 1981) (proposed sites for adult entertainment uses were either "unavailable, unusable, or so inaccessible to the public that . . . they amount to no locations").

Despite the evidence in the record, the Court reasons that the fact "that respondents must fend for themselves in the real estate market, on an equal footing with other prospective purchasers and lessees, does not give rise to a First Amendment violation." However, respondents are not on equal footing with other prospective purchasers and lessees, but must conduct business under severe restrictions not imposed upon other establishments. The Court also argues that the First Amendment does not compel "the government to ensure that adult theatres, or any other kinds of speech-related businesses for that matter, will be able to obtain sites at bargain prices." However, respondents do not ask Renton to guarantee low-price sites for their businesses, but seek only a reasonable opportunity to operate adult theaters in the city. By denying them this opportunity, Renton can effectively ban a form of protected speech from its borders. The ordinance "greatly restrict[s] access to lawful speech," *American Mini Theatres, supra,* at 71, n.35 (plurality opinion), and is plainly unconstitutional.

NOTES AND QUESTIONS

1. *Renton* resolved many of the questions left open by earlier Supreme Court adult business zoning cases, but commentators have criticized the Court's handling of the free speech issues:

> The Renton ordinance was content-based regulation of the first order. The ordinance identified speech of a certain content and, on the theory that such speech caused undesirable effects, restricted its exercise. Precisely this sort of content-regarding ordinance, under the Court's prior holdings, demands the strictest scrutiny. . . .
>
> The Court's analysis of the facial underinclusiveness of the ordinance also departed from precedent. [The Court held that the ordinance was constitutional even though it singled out adult theaters for regulation but not businesses causing similar problems].
>
> This reasoning marks a startling break with traditional first amendment jurisprudence. Although the Court has held that, in the field of economic regulation, a legislature can address one evil at a time

without offending the equal protection clause, the Court's underinclusiveness doctrine has not been so permissive when the first amendment is involved. [*The Supreme Court, 1985 Term*, 100 Harv. L. Rev. 1, 195, 196 (1986).]

Nevertheless, the Court's treatment of what is essentially a hybrid regulation — one that regulates content while at the same time regulating the secondary effects of a business — stands.

For additional commentary on *Renton*, see Stein, *Regulation of Adult Businesses Through Zoning After Renton*, 18 Pac. L.J. 351 (1987); Ziegler, *City of Renton v. Playtime Theatres, Inc.: Supreme Court Reopens the Door for Zoning of Sexually Oriented Businesses*, 9 Zoning & Plan. L. Rep. 33 (1986).

A plurality of the Supreme Court has now extended *Renton's* holding that a city may rely on studies done elsewhere in a case upholding an ordinance banning nude dancing. *City of Erie v. Pap's A.M.*, 120 S. Ct. 1382 (2000). The plurality relied on the facts of earlier Court decisions, recitals in the ordinance preamble and on evidence that members of the council had relied on their own familiarity with problems in the downtown area when they adopted the ordinance.

2. *Current practice.* So-called concentration ordinances, that concentrate adult uses in one area of a community, are no longer common. The "Boston Combat Zone," for example, is practically gone. See Gilmore, *Zoned Out: A New Take on Regulating Adult Businesses*, Planning, Vol. 65, No. 2, at 15 (1999). Some ordinances also set a minimum distance between adult businesses, as well as a minimum distance between adult uses and vulnerable areas and uses, such as residential areas. Which methods of control are used has an important effect on the courts' decisions.

3. *Availability of sites in a relevant market.* Renton caused a revolution by requiring courts to consider the adequacy of alternative sites for adult businesses. This is a market share approach unknown in other areas of land use regulation. The inquiry first requires consideration of the relevant market. Most courts have followed *Renton's* holding and have excluded economic considerations from the test. *Woodall v. City of El Paso (II)*, 959 F.2d 1305 (5th Cir.) (per curiam), *cert. denied*, 506 U.S. 908 (1992) is typical of the narrow rule of invalidity that is applied: "Cities that allocate only land that is completely unsuitable from a legal or physical standpoint for adult business use do exactly what the court proscribed in *Renton*: effectively suppress protected speech." *Id.* at 1306.

Just what does availability mean? *Hickerson v. City of New York*, 146 F.3d 99 (2d Cir. 1998), held that municipalities need only identify general areas, not exact sites. Nor is there a free speech violation even if the cost of relocating puts the adult use out of business. *Holmberg v. City of Ramsey*, 12 F.3d 140 (8th Cir. 1993). *Vincent v. Broward County*, 200 F.3d 1325 (11th Cir. 2000), reviews the cases and summarizes the rules. The court added that a site is not unavailable even though some development is required before a site can accommodate an adult business, such as having to build a new building or comply with parking requirements. A lot need not be ideal, and a business may have to put up with a smaller building or purchase a larger lot than needed.

The courts have applied the rule that adult businesses must fend for themselves in the real estate market. *Vincent, supra,* for example, held that it does not matter "that the real estate market may be tight and sites currently unavailable for sale or lease, or that property owners may be reluctant to sell to an adult venue." A California case upheld an ordinance requiring location in a shopping center to escape a distance requirement, even though the three existing shopping centers might not accommodate or be feasible for adult businesses. *City of National City v. Wiener,* 12 Cal. Rptr.2d 701 (Cal. App. 1992). Do these cases stretch *Renton* too far? How would you advise a city to comply with these decisions?

4. *Adequacy of sites.* As one case pointed out, courts have looked to a variety of factors on a case-by-case basis to determine whether there is a sufficient number of available sites. These include the percentage of land theoretically available to adult businesses; the number of sites potentially available in relation to the population of the city, the number of sites compared with the existing number of adult businesses, and the number of businesses desiring to offer adult entertainment. *Diamond v. City of Taft,* 29 F. Supp.2d 633, 645 (E.D. Cal. 1998). There is no requirement that a specific proportion of a municipality be available for adult businesses. *D.H.L. Assocs., Inc. v. O'Gorman,* 199 F.3d 50 (1st Cir. 1999).

These factors seem to be based in part on the demand for adult entertainment, not solely on the availability of sites based on some arithmetic percentage. A number of Florida cases have relied on the ratio of sites to population, which arguably is one estimate of demand. See *Centerfold Club v. City of St. Petersburg,* 969 F. Supp. 1288 (M.D. Fla. 1997) (striking down one site per 12,516 residents, and noting that Florida cases have upheld ratios of about 1/6000). A court of appeal upheld a local ordinance because 22 to 56 sites were available when the complaining adult business opened, because the city received only a few requests each year about possible locations and because 35 adult businesses already operated in the city. *North Avenue Novelties, Inc. v. City of Chicago,* 88 F.3d 441 (7th Cir. 1996). Doesn't shifting the inquiry to the demand side ignore the "chilling" effect of regulation on free speech?

There was a suggestion in *Schad* that the availability of sites in nearby areas outside the city might be sufficient. New Jersey municipalities can consider locations in other municipalities under a statute authorizing buffer zones around adult uses. *Township of Saddle Brook v. A.B. Family Center,* 722 A.2d 530 (N.J. 1999). The issue is not settled under the free speech clause. *Boss Capital, Inc. v. City of Casselberry,* 187 F.3d 1251 (11th Cir. 1999), *cert. denied,* 120 S. Ct. 1423 (2000). Certainly courts should be lenient when a municipality is small in area and has a small population. See *421 Northlake Blvd. Corp. v. Village of North Palm Beach,* 753 So.2d 754 (Fla. App. 2000) (two sites and population ratio of 1/6100). See also Cal. Gov't Code § 65850.4 (authorizing local governments to cooperate in the regulation of adult businesses).

5. *Amortization.* The plurality opinion in *Mini-Theatres* left open the constitutionality of an amortization period for adult businesses. 427 U.S. 50 at 71 n.35. However, most courts have held that zoning provisions amortizing adult businesses are constitutional. See *Lydo Enters. v. City of Las Vegas,* 745

F.2d 1211 (9th Cir. 1986); *Ambassador Books & Video, Inc. v. City of Little Rock*, 20 F.3d 858 (8th Cir. 1994).

6. *The prior restraint problem.* It is usual, as Chapter 5 explains, for zoning ordinances to authorize some uses as "conditional" uses in their districts; these are uses that, even though permitted by the ordinance, require the site-specific approval of a zoning agency. Conditional use provisions often contain broad criteria that authorize the approval of a conditional use if it is compatible with existing uses in the neighborhood. One way of handling adult businesses is to authorize them as conditional uses, which gives municipalities more individualized control. Under traditional First Amendment rules, however, speech usually cannot be subjected to "prior restraints." Vague standards which would allow decision makers to make arbitrary decisions on applications for conditional use approval can run afoul of the prior restraint doctrine. See *FW/PBS, Inc. v. City of Dallas*, 493 U.S. 215 (1990), an adult business licensing case. *Diamond v. City of Taft, supra,* reviews the lower court cases dealing with adult use zoning. To avoid this problem, more clearly defined standards for the review of conditional uses for adult businesses must be established.

There are also procedural requirements in conditional use cases that apply only to uses protected by the free speech clause. A decision must be made within a brief, specified and reasonably prompt period of time. If an application is denied, there must be provisions for prompt judicial review, and the administrative agency denying the use has the burden of going to court and justifying the denial. *Baby Tam & Co., Inc. v. City of Las Vegas,* 154 F.3d 1097 (9th Cir. 1998), held that a provision in an ordinance authorizing an applicant denied a license to petition for a writ of mandamus to a state court did not satisfy the "prompt judicial review" requirement because the petition did not have to be heard within any prescribed period of time. Contra *Boss Capital, supra.* How can a municipality provide for prompt judicial review in a state court?

The prior restraint doctrine mandates these same requirements, including adequate standards, for sign regulations and for the licensing of adult uses. The "prompt judicial decision" requirement was held satisfied with respect to an adult business license by an administrative review procedure in *City News and Novelty, Inc. v. Waukesha, Wis.*, 604 N.W. 2d 870 (Wis. App. 1999), *cert. granted,* 2000 U.S. Lexis 4158.

7. *Statutory regulation.* Legislation in some states authorizes the regulation of adult businesses. California, for example, authorizes ordinances that advance a substantial governmental interest, and that do not unreasonably restrict avenues of communication. Cal. Gov't Code § 65850(g). See also N.C. Gen. Stat. § 160A-1801.1 (authorizing regulation); Tex. Local Gov't Code § 243.002 (same).

8. *Video games.* What about those video games we all like to play? Most courts deny First Amendment protections to video games subject to zoning and licensing restrictions. See *America's Best Family Showplace Corp. v. City of N.Y.,* 536 F. Supp. 170 (E.D.N.Y. 1982) (not a protected free speech category); *Marshfield Family Skateland, Inc. v. Town of Marshfield,* 450 N.E.2d 605 (Mass.), *appeal dismissed,* 464 U.S. 987 (1983) (expression of ideas during video game held inconsequential). For discussion, see Ziegler, *Trouble in Outer Galactica: The Police Power, Zoning, and Coin-Operated Videogames,* 24 Syracuse L. Rev. 453 (1983); Note, *The First Amendment Side Effects of Curing Pac-Man Fever,* 84 Colum. L. Rev. 744 (1984).

9. For additional reading see J. Gerard, Local Regulation of Adult Businesses (2000); Gerard, *New Developments in the Effective Preclusion of Adult Businesses by Zoning Ordinances,* 17 Zoning & Plan. L. Rep. 26 (1994); Kelly, *Local Regulation of Lawful Sex Businesses,* Land Use L. & Zoning Dig., Vol. 51, No. 9, at 3 (1999); Weinstein, *Courts Take Close Look at Adult Use Regs,* Land Use L. & Zoning Dig., Vol. 46, No. 5, at 3 (1994); Note, *Adult Uses and the First Amendment: The Stringfellows Decision and Its Impact on Municipal Control of Adult Businesses,* 15 Touro L. Rev. 241 (1998).

b. Religious Uses

The conflict between the demands of religious institutions enjoying constitutional protection to carry out their institutional activities without restraint by the zoning ordinance, and zoning ordinances that limit religious activities to protect community well-being have raised important state and federal constitutional issues. The exclusion of religious institutions by zoning ordinances from residential areas is a common problem. This section examines state and federal court approaches to the religious use problem.

The problem.—Churches and their accessory uses often face substantial opposition when they attempt to get necessary approvals in the zoning process. This opposition is concentrated on small and fundamentalist denominations, not part of the mainstream religious community. One study found, for example, that while minority religions constitute about nine percent of the general population, they were litigants in over forty-nine percent of the cases concerning the location of a religious building, and over thirty-three percent of the cases where approval of accessory uses was the issue. Keetch & Richards, *The Need for Legislation to Enshrine Free Exercise in the Land Use Context,* 32 U.C. Davis L. Rev. 725 (1999).

These findings suggest that religious discrimination is a factor in much of the opposition to zoning for religious uses. Consider that one group of cases holds that churches should not be allowed in residential areas because they generate traffic, see *State v. Cameron,* 445 A.2d 75, 80 (N.J.L. Div. 1982) (collecting cases on traffic problems associated with churches), *rev'd on other grounds,* 498 A.2d 1217 (N.J. 1985), while another group holds they should not be allowed in commercial areas because they don't generate enough traffic, see *International Church of the Foursquare Gospel v. City of Chicago Heights,* 955 F. Supp. 878, 881 (N.D. Ill. 1996). The question is whether the law as it now stands strikes a proper balance between religious and community needs, as expressed through zoning restrictions.

State cases.—State courts traditionally apply a substantive due process analysis to zoning restrictions, but the cases are divided. The majority-view cases accord special protection to religious uses and frequently reverse the presumption of constitutionality accorded to zoning ordinances. See *Jehovah's Witnesses Assembly Hall v. Woolwich Twp.,* 532 A.2d 275 (N.J.L. Div. 1987) (citing cases); *State ex rel. Lake Shore Drive Baptist Church v. Village of Bayside Bd. of Trustees,* 108 N.W.2d 288 (Wis. 1961). Courts in these states strike down zoning ordinances excluding churches from residential districts. Courts following the majority view may uphold site development regulations with which a church can reasonably comply. See *Board of Zoning Appeals v. Decatur, Ind. Congregation of Jehovah's Witnesses,* 117 N.E.2d 115 (Ind. 1954) (invalidating parking requirement but upholding setback requirement).

A minority of courts take an opposite view. California leads this group. In *Corporation of Presiding Bishop of Church of Jesus Christ of Latter-Day Saints v. City of Porterville,* 203 P.2d 823 (Cal.), *appeal dismissed,* 338 U.S. 805 (1949), the court accepted traffic congestion and property value arguments to uphold the exclusion of churches from residential districts. Accord *Seward Chapel, Inc. v. City of Seward,* 655 P.2d 1293 (Alaska 1982).

New York, which was once a leading state adopting the majority view, no longer follows it. The highest New York court in *Cornell Univ. v. Bagnardi,* 503 N.E.2d 509 (N.Y. 1986), adopted a balancing approach that illustrates the difficulties of reconciling the conflicting claims of religious institutions and zoning objectives. The case actually considered the zoning problems of educational as well as religious institutions. The following paragraphs summarize the court's views on how to handle zoning disputes:

> On a broader level, the courts held that schools, public, parochial and private, by their very nature, singularly serve the public's welfare and morals. . . . Because of the inherently beneficial nature of churches and schools to the public, we held that the total exclusion of such institutions from a residential district serves no end that is reasonably related to the morals, health, welfare and safety of the community. Since a municipality's power to regulate land use is derived solely from its right to use its police powers to promote these goals, such total exclusion is beyond the scope of the localities' zoning authority.

> These general rules, however, were interpreted by some courts to demand a full exemption from zoning rules for all educational and church uses. The result has been to render municipalities powerless in the face of a religious or educational institution's proposed expansion, no matter how offensive, overpowering or unsafe to a residential neighborhood the use might be. Such an interpretation, however, is mandated neither by the case law of our State nor common sense. . . .

> The controlling consideration in reviewing the request of a school or church for permission to expand into a residential area must always be the over-all impact on the public's welfare. Although the special treatment afforded schools and churches stems from their presumed beneficial effect on the community, there are many instances in which a particular educational or religious use may actually detract from the public's health, safety, welfare or morals. In those instances, the institution may be properly denied. There is simply no conclusive presumption that any religious or educational use automatically outweighs its ill effects. The presumed beneficial effect may be rebutted

with evidence of a significant impact on traffic congestion, property values, municipal services and the like.

Thus, educational and religious uses which would unarguably be contrary to the public's health, safety or welfare need not be permitted at all. A community that resides in close proximity to a college should not be obliged to stand helpless in the face of proposed uses that are dangerous to the surrounding area. Such uses, which are clearly not what the court had in mind when it stated that traffic and similar problems are outweighed by the benefits a church or school brings, are unquestionably within the municipality's police power to exclude altogether. "[Even] religious [and educational] institutions [must] accommodate to factors directly relevant to public health, safety or welfare, inclusive of fire and similar emergency risks, and traffic conditions insofar as they involve public safety [citations omitted]" [case citation omitted.]

Less extreme forms of expansion that are nonetheless obnoxious to the community's residents, of course, require a more balanced approach than total exclusion. . . . A special permit may be required and reasonable conditions directly related to the public's health, safety and welfare may be imposed to the same extent that they may be imposed on noneducational applicants. Thus, a zoning ordinance may properly provide that the granting of a special permit to churches or schools may be conditioned on the effect the use would have on traffic congestion, property values, municipal services, the general plan for development of the community, etc. The requirement of a special permit application, which entails disclosure of site plans, parking facilities, and other features of the institution's proposed use, is beneficial in that it affords zoning boards an opportunity to weigh the proposed use in relation to neighboring land uses and to cushion any adverse effects by the imposition of conditions designed to mitigate them. These conditions, if reasonably designed to counteract the deleterious effects on the public's welfare of a proposed religious or educational use should be upheld by the courts, provided they do not, by their cost, magnitude or volume, operate indirectly to exclude such uses altogether. [*Id.* at 514–516.]

Why is a conditional use permit a "more balanced approach than total exclusion"? States that have adopted the preferred status rule rely on this rule or on a finding that a religious use would not substantially increase traffic congestion to reverse denials of conditional uses. States that do not follow the preferred status rule have upheld conditional use denials when there would be an increase in traffic congestion. The facts, of course, may be influential. Compare *Kali Bari Temple v. Board of Adjustment,* 638 A.2d 839 (N.J. App. Div. 1994) (use of home in residential area; any adverse effect on neighborhood reduced by conditions), with *Macedonian Orthodox Church v. Planning Bd.,* 636 A.2d 96 (N.J. App. Div. 1994). For more on conditional uses see Chapter 5, *infra.* For the difficult problem of applying historic preservation laws to religious structures, see Chapter 8, *infra.*

The courts have recognized that a wide variety of uses are acceptable as accessory uses to religious institutions. *City of Richmond Heights v. Richmond*

Heights Presbyterian Church, 764 S.W.2d 647 (Mo. 1989) (day care center); *Slevin v. Long Island Jewish Medical Center,* 319 N.Y.S.2d 937 (Misc. 1971) (center for counseling drug users).

Land use restrictions on religious uses also are subject to attack under the free exercise clause of the federal constitution. The following case illustrates the prevailing approach:

FIRST ASSEMBLY OF GOD OF NAPLES v. COLLIER COUNTY

20 F.3d 419 (11th Cir. 1994), *cert. denied,* 513 U.S. 1080 (1995)

DUBINA, CIRCUIT JUDGE:

. . . .

First Assembly is a Christian church affiliated with the Assemblies of God of the United States, and located in Naples, Florida. First Assembly was established in 1956 when unincorporated Collier County imposed no zoning ordinances. In 1982, Collier County adopted Zoning Ordinance 82-2, which imposed zoning regulation on all of the unincorporated County. Pursuant to Ordinance 82-2, First Assembly was zoned RMF-6. An RMF-6 district is a multi-family residential district that also permits a number of community uses, including churches and their "customary accessory uses."

In 1985, First Assembly decided to build a new structure on its property, and received permission for the construction. The new building was primarily used as a day care center. In 1989, due to community need, First Assembly converted the building into a homeless shelter. Subsequently, the people of Naples became concerned about the problem of the homeless in their community. The record indicates that homeless people had taken up residence in vacant lots, where the living conditions were unsanitary. As a result, there was great community distress over both health and safety concerns. First Assembly's shelter was, no doubt, seen as part of the problem.

In April of 1991, a county official charged that First Assembly's homeless shelter violated several zoning ordinances. . . . [The Collier County Code Enforcement Board adjudicated these violations. It determined the shelter was not a "customary accessory use" of the church and that it violated the zoning ordinance. The Board also found the church had not applied for a provisional permit to maintain a homeless shelter on its premises. The church closed the shelter rather than pay a fine. The district court granted summary judgment for the county.]

. . . .

First Assembly contends that the enforcement of Naples' zoning ordinances violates the Free Exercise Clause of the First Amendment because it prevents the church from practicing its religion. First Assembly claims that sheltering the homeless is an essential aspect of the Christian religion; thus, the forced closing of the homeless shelter interferes with First Assembly's free exercise of religion.

The most recent Supreme Court case interpreting the Free Exercise Clause is *Church of the Lukumi Babalu Aye v. City of Hialeah,* 113 S. Ct. 2217 (1993). In that case, the Court held that a local law targeting the use of animal sacrifice for religious purposes violated the Free Exercise Clause. In so holding, the Court reversed this court which had affirmed the district court's upholding of the local ordinance.

The Supreme Court explained that "a law that is neutral and of general applicability need not be justified by a compelling governmental interest even if the law has the incidental effect of burdening a particular religious practice." *Id.* at 2226. A law that does not meet these requirements, however, must be justified by a compelling state interest and must be narrowly tailored to meet that interest. *Id.* Thus, the threshold questions in analyzing a law challenged under the Free Exercise Clause are (1) is the law neutral, and (2) is the law of general applicability?

The Court applied these requirements in *Hialeah,* and determined that the ordinances, which were enacted only when the community realized that the Santerians were planning to build a church in their community, and which explicitly targeted the religious conduct of animal sacrifice, were not neutral. In addition, the Court found that the laws were not of general applicability, but rather applied "only against conduct motivated by religious belief." *Id.* at 2233. Therefore, the ordinance at issue in *Hialeah* had to endure strict scrutiny — an obstacle it could not overcome.

First Assembly relies on *Hialeah,* in the mistaken belief that the present case is analogous. Clearly, the present case is distinguishable from *Hialeah.* Even if it is assumed for the sake of argument that sheltering the homeless is a central, essential element of the Christian religion, the fact still remains that the Naples ordinances are neutral and of general applicability. The first zoning ordinance, 82-2, simply does not implicate the Free Exercise Clause. This ordinance, as passed, zones an entire residential area and makes a special exception for churches. It is neutral on its face and is of general applicability. Thus, it is only the second ordinance, 91–34, which is really in question here.

Ordinance 91-34 was passed subsequent to the opening of the shelter, amid much consternation over the problem of the homeless in the Naples community. This ordinance identifies a homeless shelter as a group home and provides regulations for its operation. The ordinance is also facially neutral — it applies to any homeless shelter, regardless of who operates it. More importantly, Naples has not prohibited the operation of homeless shelters. On the contrary, it has defined areas in which the shelters may operate and provided regulations for such. These regulations apply to all group homes, once again regardless of their ownership or affiliation, and were motivated by wholly secular concerns. The intent of the ordinance was not to inhibit or oppress any religion; rather, the Commission was motivated to address a general problem of health and safety concerns. The fact that First Assembly was affected was incidental. Thus, this ordinance is of general applicability.

Another case which aids our analysis is this court's decision in *Grosz v. City of Miami Beach,* 721 F.2d 729 (11th Cir.1983), cert. denied, 469 U.S. 827 (1984). *Grosz* is particularly helpful in this case because it is so closely analogous. The plaintiff in *Grosz* was a Jewish Rabbi who began conducting orthodox worship services at his home. His religion required that at least ten adult males be present at the ceremony. Word spread of the services, and sometimes as many as fifty people would worship in his remodeled garage. *Id.* at 731–732. Unfortunately, these services were in violation of Miami Beach zoning ordinances. Following complaints from neighbors, the city notified Grosz that he was in violation of the zoning laws. *Id.*

In deciding that the zoning laws did not violate Grosz's right to free exercise of religion, this court established a three part test. First, the government regulation must regulate religious conduct, not belief. Second, the law must have a secular purpose and a secular effect. Third, once these two thresholds are crossed, the court engages in a balancing of competing governmental and religious interests. 721 F.2d at 733. In *Grosz,* as in the instant case, the two thresholds are easily met. The focus is thus on the balancing of interests.

In balancing those interests in *Grosz,* this court explained:

> On the free exercise side of the balance weighs the burden that Appellees bear of conducting their services in compliance with applicable zoning restrictions or relocating in a suitably zoned district. Countering on the government's side is the substantial infringement of the City's zoning policy that would occur were the conduct allowed to continue. . . . The relative weights of the burdens favor the government.

Id. at 741. The same could be said for the present case. The burden on First Assembly to either conform its shelter to the zoning laws, or to move the shelter to an appropriately zoned area, is less than the burden on the County were it to be forced to allow the zoning violation. Thus, under the *Grosz* test, First Assembly's right to free exercise of religion is not violated by the County's zoning ordinances.

The Naples ordinances pass the threshold tests under the Supreme Court's Free Exercise Clause analysis, as well as this court's test as articulated in the *Grosz* case. Thus, the district court did not err in granting summary judgment in favor of the County on this issue. . . .

NOTES AND QUESTIONS

1. *Free exercise law.* The principal case sums up free exercise law in the Supreme Court, although the principles are not quite as clear as the case would suggest. The rule that the compelling interest standard does not apply to a law of "general applicability" comes from *Employment Division v. Smith,* 494 U.S. 872 (1990). In *Smith,* the Court upheld the firing of a drug counselor for using a controlled substance as part of a Native American ritual. No Supreme Court case has considered a land use regulation, although a zoning ordinance contained some of the restrictions invalidated in *Hialeah.* Why is the principal case distinguishable from *Hialeah*?

Is the free exercise clause violated only when government compels someone to act in violation of her religious beliefs, not when a government regulation has only an incidental effect on a religious belief? *Lyng v. Northwest Cemetery Protective Ass'n,* 455 U.S. 439 (1988), which closely resembles a land use case, illustrates this point. This was a suit to prevent the government from building a road through, and allowing logging in, a sacred Indian area. The Court did not find a violation. The government had not coerced individuals into violating their beliefs, nor would they be penalized for their beliefs. The free exercise clause "is written in terms of what the government cannot do to the individual, not in terms of what the individual can exact from government." *Id.* at 451.

How does the government's justification burden in the free exercise cases compare with its justification burden in the free speech adult use cases? And with government's justification burden in the family definition cases, such as *Belle Terre*? Why do the courts shift the justification burden to government in these cases?

2. *The exclusion problem.* The court also adopted a balancing approach to the exclusion problem in *Lakewood, Ohio Congregation of Jehovah's Witnesses, Inc. v. City of Lakewood,* 699 F.2d 303 (6th Cir. 1983), upholding a zoning ordinance prohibiting churches in residential districts as applied to a congregation that planned to build a church. The court first considered whether building a church fell within the protection of the free exercise clause. The court held that it did not because the right to build a church was not a "fundamental tenet" or "cardinal principle" of the religion's faith. The ordinance prohibited only "the purely secular act of building." In addition, the burdens imposed by the zoning restriction on the church were only "an indirect financial burden and a subjective aesthetic burden." The zoning ordinance permitted churches in nonresidential districts covering ten percent of the city. The church could build in these districts, even though this would be more expensive and "less conducive to worship."

Because the free exercise clause did not apply, the court held that the compelling interest the Supreme Court requires to justify an infringement on that clause was not required. The *Lakewood* court turned instead to the substantive due process clause. It upheld the zoning restriction under that clause by relying on Supreme Court cases recognizing the right of a municipality to create exclusive residential districts. How does the balancing test in this case compare with the balancing test of *Grosz,* adopted and applied in the principal case? With the balancing test adopted in *Cornell University*? What is the basis for applying a balancing test to the exclusion problem? The next chapter considers the exclusion of lower income groups by zoning ordinances. Is this the same problem?

Courts will, of course, strike down the exclusion of a religious edifice when there is blatant discrimination. *Islamic Center of Mississippi, Inc. v. City of Starkville,* 840 F.2d 293 (5th Cir. 1988) (Muslims only worshipers denied exception to prohibition of churches in residential zone). But see *Christian Gospel Church, Inc. v. San Francisco,* 896 F.2d 1221 (9th Cir.) (following *Grosz*), *cert. denied,* 498 U.S. 999 (1990).

3. *Religious Freedom Restoration Acts.* Critics who are concerned that free exercise law does not provide enough protection for religious uses have long campaigned for legislative relief. The campaign paid off when a Religious Freedom Restoration Act adopted by Congress in 1993 restored the "compelling governmental interest" test the Supreme Court previously required to justify governmental action affecting the free exercise of religion. The Act did not mention zoning, but it was clear from the legislative history that Congress intended the Act to apply to zoning actions.

The Supreme Court held the Act unconstitutional in *City of Boerne v. Flores,* 521 U.S. 507 (1997), because it exceeded the powers of Congress. However, a number of states have since enacted similar statutes patterned on the federal legislation. *E.g.,* Fla. Stat. Ann. § 761.03; 775 Ill. Comp. Stat. 35/15 to 35/25; R.I. Gen. Laws. §§ 42-80.1-1 to 42-80.1-4; S.C. Code §§ 1-32-10 to 1-32-60; Tex. Civ. Practice & Remedies Code §§ 110.001-110.012. Like the federal act, the state acts could apply to land use regulations that affect religious uses and could provide more protection than the federal constitution. But see *City of Chicago Heights v. Living Word Outreach Full Gospel Church & Ministries, Inc.,* 707 N.E.2d 53 (Ill. App. 1999) (upholding special use requirement for church under act). See Laycock, *State RFRAs and Land Use Regulation,* 32 U.C. Davis L. Rev. 755 (1999).

Congress enacted a new religious freedom act in August 2000 that applies specifically to land use regulation. A constitutional challenge to the act is expected.

4. For discussion of free exercise and land use problems see Saxer, *When Religion Becomes a Nuisance: Balancing Land Use and Religious Freedom When Activities of Religious Institutions Bring Outsiders into the Neighborhood,* 84 Ky. L.J. 507 (1995/96); Note, *Religion, Zoning, and the Free Exercise Clause: The Impact of Employment Division v. Smith,* 7 B.Y.U. J. Pub. L. 395 (1993); Comment, *Why Free Exercise Jurisprudence in Relation to Zoning Restrictions Remains Unsettled After Boerne v. Flores,* 52 SMU L. Rev. 305 (1999).

5. *The "establishment" clause.* This is the converse of the "free exercise" problem. The Establishment Clause provides that "Congress shall make no law respecting the establishment of religion." U.S. Const. Amend. I. An Establishment Clause problem can arise when a zoning ordinance gives a preferred status to a religious use.

Larkin v. Grendel's Den, Inc., 459 U.S. 116 (1982), *noted,* 28 Vill. L. Rev. 1000 (1982–83), upheld a claim that a Massachusetts statute providing that liquor licenses could not be issued if vetoed by a church or school located within 500 feet of the licensed premises violated the Establishment Clause. A church vetoed a liquor license under this provision. The Court held that the statutory veto violated the establishment of religion clause of the federal constitution. Similar veto provisions are contained in many zoning regulations.

The Court applied its separation of church and state line of authority. It held that the usual deference due zoning ordinances was not warranted because the delegation was to a private entity. The veto violated the three establishment clause criteria adopted in *Lemon v. Kurtzman,* 403 U.S. 602 (1971). The regulation must have a secular purpose. The purpose was secular here because the veto would protect churches and schools from disturbances from liquor outlets. The regulation also must not primarily advance or inhibit religion. This test was not met because the standardless veto authorized by the statute could be used by churches for religious purposes. Finally, the regulation must not foster excessive government entanglement with religion. This test was not met because the statute "enmeshes churches in the process of government" and could create political fragmentation on religious lines. *Id.* at 127.

Justice Rehnquist dissented. He would have upheld the statute as "a quite sensible Massachusetts liquor zoning law." *Id.* at 128. He noted that a flat ban on liquor stores within a certain radius of churches, "which the majority concedes is valid, is more protective of churches and more restrictive of liquor sales than the present [statute]." *Id.* He concluded that "[t]he State can constitutionally protect churches from liquor for the same reasons it can protect them from fire, noise, and other harm." *Id.* at 130.

Establishment clause issues may become more important as states and municipalities seek to provide favorable treatment for religious uses. See Colo. Rev. Stat. § 29-1-1202, prohibiting local governments from limiting when or how frequently individuals may meet in private residences to pray or worship. In *Concerned Citizens v. Hubbard,* 84 F. Supp. 2d 668 (D. Md. 2000), a county granted a number of exemptions from conditional use permits to a number of uses, including religious uses. The court found the Establishment Clause not violated because the ordinance was a neutral measure that had a sectarian purpose in encouraging development that was harmonious and compatible with single family residential use. The court distinguished *Renzi v. Connelly School of the Holy Child,* 61 F. Supp. 2d 440 (D. Md. 1999), where the court held unconstitutional an ordinance specifically exempting religious uses from the conditional use requirement.

5. SITE DEVELOPMENT REQUIREMENTS

In addition to regulating the use of land, zoning ordinances also include controls on building bulk and density. These controls are a critical part of the zoning ordinance because they regulate the intensity of land use. Yet they have received little attention in the cases except in the cases invalidating density controls as a form of exclusionary zoning. See Chapter 4, *infra.* The following bulk and density controls are commonly included in zoning ordinances:

Yard and setback regulations.—Zoning ordinances typically require front yards by requiring minimum setbacks from the street. They also usually include side and back yard setbacks. The constitutionality of these requirements was upheld in *Gorieb v. Fox,* 274 U.S. 603 (1927), an early case decided a year after the Court's *Euclid* decision upheld the constitutionality of zoning. The Court upheld street setbacks as a proper police power measure that would provide separation from street noise, improve the attractiveness of residential environments, and ensure the availability of light and air. As one court put it recently, the constitutionality of setbacks was decided "long ago." *In re Letourneau,* 726 A.2d 31 (Vt. 1998).

Frontage requirements.—Zoning ordinances also usually require that lots have a minimum street frontage. The reasons that led the Court in *Gorieb* to uphold setbacks also apply to frontage requirements. Courts may also uphold these requirements as a control on density. *Di Salle v. Giggal,* 261 P.2d 499 (Colo. 1953).

Height limitations.—Maximum height limitations also limit building bulk. Another early U.S. Supreme Court case, *Welch v. Swasey,* 214 U.S. 91 (1909), upheld height limitations that were imposed under a state statute. The Court upheld the statute on traditional due process grounds, taking special note of the aesthetic basis for the height limitation.

Site ratio.—Some zoning ordinances also control density and building bulk by limiting the percentage of a lot that can be occupied by a building. This control is called a site ratio. In *La Salle Nat'l Bank v. City of Chicago,* 125 N.E.2d 609 (Ill. 1955), the court upheld a site ratio as applied to multi-family dwellings and applied the usual presumption of constitutionality. It found no evidence indicating that the site ratio was unreasonable.

Floor area ratio.—Some communities, especially in downtown office and multi-family districts, regulate building bulk through a floor area ratio (FAR). The FAR specifies a ratio between the square footage allowable in a building and the square footage of the building lot. A FAR of 2:1, for example, allows two square feet of building for each square foot of the lot. The FAR encourages innovative building design because the developer may utilize the FAR any way it wishes subject to height and other limitations on the site, such as setbacks. Under a FAR of 2:1, for example, the developer could construct a four-story building on half the lot if a building height of four stories was permitted. No case has considered the validity of floor area ratios. But see *Broadway, Laguna, Vallejo Ass'n v. Board of Permit Appeals,* 427 P.2d 810 (Cal. 1967) (stressing the importance of the FAR as a zoning control).

Due Process

facts + reasonable in content as well as application

FLOOR AREA RATIO (F.A.R.) CONCEPT

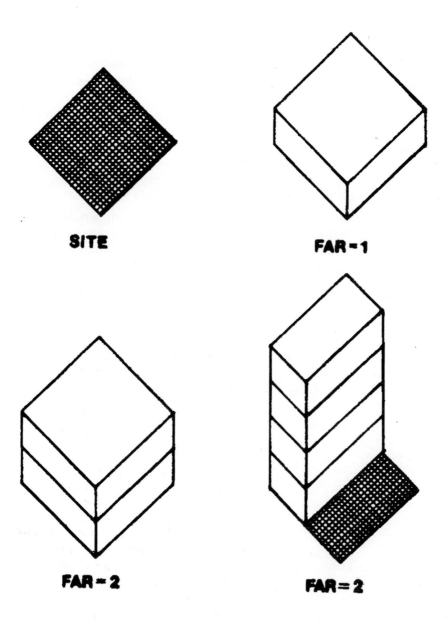

Minimum lot size requirements.—Density is usually expressed in residential districts in terms of how many dwelling units are allowed per acre. It is also common to specify minimum lot sizes. See *Johnson v. Town of Edgartown, supra,* and Notes following, that discuss minimum lot size requirements. A zoning ordinance might also require minimum lot sizes for industrial and multifamily uses.

Off-street parking.—The buildable area available on a lot also is limited by off-street parking requirements. The number of required parking spaces is based on the number of dwelling units in multifamily residential projects. For commercial, office, and industrial development the required number of spaces may be based on square footage or on the type of use. In the only case directly addressing the issue, the court held off-street parking requirements constitutional. *Stroud v. City of Aspen*, 532 P.2d 720 (Colo. 1975) ("cannot believe" ordinance unconstitutional in "these days of environmental concerns").

Open space requirements.—Because parking areas are paved, communities that want to ensure that part of the lot is left in its natural state may also include a usable open space requirement. This requirement specifies a percentage of the lot that must be left in its natural condition.

NOTES AND QUESTIONS

As-applied constitutional problems can still arise under site development standards:

1. *Setbacks.* In *Miller & Son Paving, Inc. v. Wrightstown Twp.*, 451 A.2d 1002 (Pa. 1982), a quarry owner claimed that setback regulations were a taking of property because they prevented it from quarrying over two million tons of stone that lay within the setback area. The court rejected this contention, noting that to adopt the owner's argument would make all setbacks per se unreasonable. The quarry owner had not met its burden of showing that the setback was "patently unreasonable" or that it did not serve the community's general welfare. Compare *Board of Supvrs. v. Rowe*, 216 S.E.2d 199 (Va. 1975) (invalidating setback eliminating twenty-nine percent of the buildable area of a lot). Can the cases be distinguished? See also *Giambrone v. City of Aurora*, 621 N.E.2d 475 (Ohio App. 1993) (setback held excessive); *Schmalz v. Buckingham Twp. Zoning Bd. of Adjustment*, 132 A.2d 233 (Pa. 1957) (reasons justifying setbacks in urban areas do not apply in rural areas).

2. *Frontage requirements.* The courts have considered "as applied" objections to frontage requirements. In *MacNeil v. Town of Avon*, 435 N.E.2d 1043 (Mass. 1982), a lot was ten feet short of a required 200-foot frontage. The court upheld the frontage requirement as applied to the lot, noting that the requirement would reduce the number of dwelling units and thus the amount and size of firefighting equipment needed to respond to fires. The requirement was valid even though the lot was only marginally short of the required frontage, the court noting that lines must be drawn somewhere in zoning ordinances. There was no taking of property because the lot could be put to uses allowed by the zoning ordinance. Contra under similar facts, *Metzger v. Town of Brentwood (II)*, 374 A.2d 954 (N.H. 1977). The court noted that "frontage requirements can be justified . . . [as] a method of determining lot size to prevent overcrowding," but that the lot size far exceeded the lot size implicitly contemplated by the frontage requirement. Neither was access by fire trucks and other vehicles restricted by the shorter frontage. Are the cases distinguishable?

3. *Height limitations.* Height limitations also are subject to "as applied" taking claims. In *Williams C. Haas & Co. v. City & County of San Francisco*,

605 F.2d 1117 (9th Cir. 1979), the city, in order to implement an urban design plan, downzoned the height limitation on a tract of land on which the owner had planned a high-rise building. The court rejected the taking claim even though the owner argued that the downzoning imposed a $1.9 million dollar loss on a $2 million dollar investment in the property. The court also rejected a reverse spot zoning argument, holding that the downzoning was part of a comprehensive plan that affected all of the property owners in the area. For additional favorable height limitation cases, see *City of St. Paul v. Chicago, St. P., M. & O. Ry.*, 413 F.2d 762 (8th Cir. 1969) (applied to single property owner); *State v. Pacesetter Constr. Co.*, 571 P.2d 196 (Wash. 1977) (residential height limitation contained in shoreline management act). However, these cases were decided before the Supreme Court adopted a categorical per se takings rule in *Lucas*. How would *Lucas* affect these decisions?

6. ZONING INNOVATIONS

This chapter has discussed the conventional zoning system based on a zoning district concept and has examined how that system works. But there has been active criticism of the conventional system. One argument is that the separation of uses that zoning demands is no longer required. Another is that the restrictions that zoning ordinances contain are either overinclusive or underinclusive: they either demand too much or too little. Also, there is the argument that zoning is quality-neutral. Nothing in the zoning ordinance ensures that it will produce good quality development. The zoning innovations discussed here attempt to remedy these problems and provide a new format for land use regulation.

a. Mixed Use Development (MXD)

Mixed use development, or MXD, is a type of development, begun in the 1960s, which can range from individual buildings with mixed uses to coordinated large-scale developments with a variety of use types. MXD usually occurs in downtown or suburban centers, and typically includes high density housing. Transit-oriented development, which is discussed in detail in Chapter 7, *infra*, is an example. MXD is also possible as infill in existing neighborhoods.

MXD requires special treatment in the zoning ordinance. One approach is discretionary review, usually done through the approval of a planned unit development for an MXD. Planned unit developments are discussed in Chapter 6, *infra*. An alternative is to provide specially tailored zoning districts. Tacoma, Washington developed a set of districts for its development program in downtown:

> Four districts were eventually established, each allowing a broad mix of uses, but each with a somewhat different emphasis. The district called "commercial core" emphasized high-rise commercial development. The downtown residential district focused on mid-rise housing. The downtown mixed-use district stressed public and civic uses, but allowed housing and commercial development. And the warehouse residential district emphasized the conversion of old factory and

warehouse buildings into housing. [Hinshaw, *Rezone or Dezone?,* Planning, Vol. 66, No. 6, at 12, 15 (2000).]

MXD districts may require land use regulations not typically found in zoning ordinances. What is required may depend upon the purpose of the MXD. The ordinance may require minimum densities and floor area ratios in order to achieve desired residential and commercial densities for a high-density MXD. At the other end of the spectrum, for a mid-scale MXD in an existing downtown or other center the MXD ordinance may impose maximum parking ratios and limitations on square footage to keep out Big Box retail and other large developments that might overwhelm the neighborhood. See Tillett, *Retrofitting the Suburbs: The Gresham Civic Neighborhood,* American Plan. Ass'n, PAS Memo, Nov., 1995. What legal problems do you see?

For discussion of MXD see Urban Land Inst., Mixed-Use Development Handbook (1987); Baers, *Zoning Code Revisions to Permit Mixed Use Development,* 7 Zoning & Plan. L. Rep. 81 (1984); Gosling, *Patterns of Association,* Urb. Land, Vol. 57, No. 10, at 42 (1998) (discussing MXDs in various cities). For an example of a large-scale MXD see Gosling, *Addison Circle: Beyond New Urbanism,* Urb. Land, Vol. 55, No. 3, at 19 (1996) (3000-unit MXD in Dallas, Texas suburb with supporting retail and employment). In the days of telecommuting, MXD can be used to develop live/work neighborhoods. See Jenkins, *Housing That Works,* Builder, Sep. 1998, at 133.

b. Overlay Zones

An overlay is a zone that is placed on the zoning map "over" traditional zoning districts. Overlay zoning was born of the necessity to add an additional dimension to land use control to the zoning map for some special public purpose that does not coincide with the boundaries of the current zoning. Overlay zoning has been in use since the 1960s, although its application to a wide variety of public interests, particularly protection of environmentally sensitive areas, historic sites, . . . and viewshed protection, are of more recent origin. [Maryland Office of Planning, Overlay Zones 2 (1995).]

The effect of an overlay zone is to add additional requirements to the underlying zoning ordinance to implement the purposes of the zone. Overlay zones are often used for floodplain and historic area districts. The Maryland report provides several examples of overlay zones, including a Residential Conservation and Highway Corridor overlay zone. Each zone contains a statement of purpose and standards to be applied within the zone through discretionary review development applications. For example, the statement of purpose for the Annapolis, Maryland Residential Conservation Overlay District provides:

The purpose of the . . . district is to preserve patterns of design and development in residential neighborhoods characterized by a diversity of styles and to ensure the preservation of a diversity of land uses, together with the protection of buildings, structures or areas the destruction or alteration of which would disrupt the existing scale and architectural character of the neighborhood. [*Id.* at 19–20.]

Four additional standards are then provided, directed to preservation of architectural and neighborhood scale, compatibility and encouragement of existing land uses. In a variant of this approach, the ordinance may provide for the adoption of a neighborhood plan, which then becomes the basis on which new development is reviewed.

Coordination between the review standards in the overlay district and the underlying ordinance is essential. See *Dallen v. Kansas City,* 822 S.W.2d 429 (Mo. App. 1991), holding that a setback requirement in a Main Street Special Review District was a modification of the underlying zoning that violated a provision in the city's zoning ordinance that prohibited such modifications. The decision contains the text of the special district ordinance.

c. Special Districts

A special district is similar to an overlay zone, except that it takes the place of the underlying zoning regulations. Like the overlay zone, the special district can include area-specific land use regulations and standards, and can also use the discretionary review of new development to ensure that district requirements will be met. New York has an extensive special district program in Manhattan. *Franchise Developers, Inc. v. City of Cincinnati,* 505 N.E.2d 966 (1987), held that standards contained in an Environmental Quality District were not unconstitutionally vague. See also *Bell v. City of Waco,* 835 S.W.2d 211 (Tex. App. 1992), holding the standards contained in a Neighborhood Conservation District were reasonable, and that the district was authorized by the zoning statute.

For discussion see R. Babcock & W. Larsen, Special Districts (1990); Ziegler, *Shaping Megalopolis: The Transformation of Euclidean Zoning by Special Zoning Districts and Site-Specific Development Review Techniques,* 15 Zoning & Plan. L. Rep. 57 (1992).

d. Performance Zoning

The conceptual heart of performance standards is that regulation of land uses is based not on use categories determined at the time zoning ordinances are adopted but on their actual physical characteristics and functions — their "performance" — measured against predetermined criteria and standards. Performance factors can include traffic generation, noise, lighting levels, stormwater runoff, loss of wildlife or vegetation, or even architectural style. Theoretically, in a regulatory system based solely on performance standards, any use could locate adjacent to any other use, provided that it could satisfy the criteria and standards contained in the ordinance. Questions of potential use are wide open, whereas site planning, building design, and facility operation, among other factors, may be strictly controlled. [D. Porter, P. Phillips & T. Lassar, Flexible Zoning: How It Works 11, 12, 112, 113 (1988).]

Performance zoning requires the review of individual developments in a discretionary review process, and some of these ordinances include a point system. Each performance standard is assigned a number of points, and developments acquire points depending on how well they satisfy the standard and must acquire a minimum number of points in order to be approved.

Animal Shelter League, Inc. v. Christian County Bd. of Adjustment, 995 S.W.2d 533 (Mo. App. 1999), upheld a decision by a zoning board finding that a request to construct and operate a small animal shelter failed the county's performance standards because the shelter was assigned minus points on three "relative criteria." It credited evidence that the board was correct making this decision. The case quotes and explains the performance zoning system in detail.

A recent survey by Douglas Porter found that the use of performance zoning is waning, and that some communities that had adopted it have dropped it. Porter, *Flexible Zoning: A Status Report on Performance Standards,* Am. Plan. Ass'n, Zoning News, Jan. 1998. Reasons are that this type of zoning creates uncertainties in the development review process and complexities in administration. For example, a performance-based ordinance adopted in Queen Anne's County, Maryland, contained floor area ratios, impervious service ratios, open space multipliers and natural resource multipliers.

> County planners found that a typical subdivision plat might require two or three pages of mathematical formulas to determine appropriate densities and open space provisions. [They] also required a considerable amount of day-to-day interpretation which, if not rigorously recorded, led to varying results and inevitable conflicts. The system was difficult to explain to developers, citizens, and county officials. [*Id.* at 2.]

What does this experience say about the advantages of conventional zoning? Chapter 5 looks at discretionary review techniques in zoning ordinances, such as site plan review. After studying that chapter, try to decide whether performance zoning is any more uncertain or complex. Mr. Porter points out, however, that performance standards like those used in performance zoning are increasingly being incorporated into conventional zoning ordinances. He also notes that innovations such as MXD, overlay and special districts are also examples of the performance approach.

For a book explaining the performance zoning idea and including a model ordinance see L. Kendig, Performance Zoning (1981). For a critique of the Kendig model see Note, *Performance Zoning,* 67 Notre Dame L. Rev. 363 (1991).

D. ENVIRONMENTAL LAND USE REGULATION

The environmental movement has introduced a new set of land use controls, directed at the preservation of natural resource areas such as wetlands and floodplains. These controls are outside of and not integrated with local land use planning and regulation. The emergence of a separate regulatory structure is not surprising. As one early study indicated, planners were slow to incorporate environmental values in local comprehensive planning. E. Kaiser, Promoting Environmental Quality Through Urban Planning and Controls 430 (1977). Zoning also has had much narrower objectives for regulating land use than the environmental movement has thought necessary. Although zoning often addresses the preservation of natural areas, it has essentially accepted the inevitability of converting land to development and has sought only to manage the process.

Environmental land use regulation has a number of features that distinguish it from conventional zoning. One is an important federal and state presence. Federal legislation often encourages and may even mandate environmental land use regulation, as may state legislation. Another important difference is that environmental land use regulation is resource-driven, and is intended to protect defined natural resource areas that are vulnerable to development. These regulations do not usually rely on a zoning system based on a comprehensive plan, but usually require the issuance of permits for development that satisfy specified regulatory standards.

There is an erratic distribution of governmental responsibility in environmental land use regulation programs. They do not provide a coordinated response to the problems of environmental land use protection, but were enacted piecemeal as environmental land use issues attracted public attention. Also, environmental land use regulations usually place constraints on development, rather than permitting development. This distinguishes them from zoning regulations, and limits development opportunities in areas where environmental land use controls are in place.

This section will introduce you to some of the important environmental land use regulations. Its purpose is to outline how they work, and to highlight the differences between these controls and traditional zoning regulations.

NOTES AND QUESTIONS

1. *Environmental elements in plans.* Some state land use planning statutes now include requirements for environmental planning. The California statute, for example, requires

> A conservation element for the conservation, development, and utilization of natural resources including water and its hydraulic force, forests, soils, rivers and other waters, harbors, fisheries, wildlife, minerals, and other natural resources. [Cal. Gov't Code § 65302(d).]

The statute also authorizes the conservation element to include other measures, such as the regulation of land use in stream channels; the prevention, control, and correction of the erosion of soils, beaches, and shores; and the protection of watersheds, and flood control. See also Fla. Stat. Ann. § 163.3177(6)(d) (conservation element). The conservation element in California and Florida is implemented through zoning and other land use controls, which must be consistent with the comprehensive plan.

2. *Environmental evaluation.* Model legislation proposed by the American Planning Association would require the local planning agency to prepare an "environmental evaluation" in which it considers and evaluates the significant environmental effects of the land use, housing, transportation and community facilities elements of a comprehensive plan. Legislative Guidebook Phases I & II, Interim Edition, § 12-101(1) (1998). The purpose of the evaluation is

"to ensure that an assessment is made of the significant effects, both beneficial and detrimental, of these elements on the environment, and that alternatives to these environmental effects are adequately identified." § 12-101(2). However, the local planning agency is not required to modify a comprehensive plan as a result of the environmental evaluation. What are the advantages of this proposal as compared with simply requiring an environmental element in comprehensive plans?

1. WETLANDS

a. Why Wetlands Are Important

Wetlands, the wet areas between land and bodies of water, have important ecological functions. Wetlands can be either coastal or inland. They include salt and freshwater marshes, swamps, wet meadows, bogs, fens, and potholes. Many wetlands, both coastal and inland, are in attractive locations, which makes them ideal for residential and recreational development. Coastal wetlands also attract development that is water-dependent, such as port and industrial uses.

Wetlands can reduce floodpeaks by storing and conveying stormwater, they are important in groundwater recharge, and are essential to fish and wildlife that are wetland-dependent. Wetlands also improve the quality of water that flows over and through them by temporarily retaining pollutants, such as toxic chemicals, and disease-causing micro-organisms.

The loss of wetlands through land development has been dramatic. Development in wetlands usually entails the use of a process known as "dredging and filling." Wetlands are dredged to provide artificial waterways, and soil removed in the dredging process or brought in from elsewhere is used to build up the wetlands so they can be developed. Regulatory programs in wetland areas attempt to control this process by prohibiting or limiting dredge and fill activities.

b. The Federal Wetlands Protection Program of the Clean Water Act

Wetlands are the only natural resource area protected by a federal statutory permit program. The regulation of development under this program is backhanded. Section 404 of the Clean Water Act, 33 U.S.C. § 1344, requires permits for the discharge of pollutants into the "waters of the United States," which include wetlands. Dredge and fill material is defined as the "discharge" of a pollutant, which means that development in wetlands is regulated under Section 404 when — and only when — dredging and filling occurs. See also Smith, *Western Wetlands: The Backwater of Wetlands Regulation,* 39 Nat. Resources J. 357 (1999) (discussing wetlands not covered). *United States v. Riverside Bayview Homes, Inc.,* 474 U.S. 121 (1986), upheld the constitutionality of the statute under the commerce clause.

Obtaining a permit under Section 404 also requires an environmental analysis under the National Environmental Protection Act. 42 U.S.C. § 4332. This Act adds another layer of environmental review but requires only an assessment of environmental impacts rather than a decision on whether a development should be permitted.

Authority to regulate under the § 404 program.—Section 404 provides for a complex sharing of authority between the Environmental Protection Agency (EPA), which is responsible for the administration of the Clean Water Act, and the U.S. Army Corps of Engineers. Section 404(a) states that the Corps "may issue permits . . . for the discharge of dredged or fill material . . . at specified disposal sites." Note that there are no standards for the issuance of permits. Section 404(b) (1) provides that substantive criteria that must be met by permit applicants are to be set forth in guidelines adopted by EPA in conjunction with the Corps. Finally, § 404(c) authorizes the EPA to veto a permit for any disposal site whenever

> the discharge of such materials into such area will have an unaccept-able adverse effect on municipal water supplies, shellfish beds, and fishery areas (including spawning and breeding areas), wildlife, or recreational areas.

Although EPA has not exercised its veto authority frequently, it has become a highly controversial element of the program. As you might expect, the two agencies have often been at odds over how the program should be administered.

Criteria for permits; the water dependency rule.—The Corps has imple-mented its permit authority by adopting regulations authorizing it to consider whether granting a permit would be in the "public interest." Corps regulations state:

> The decision whether to issue a permit will be based on an evaluation of the probable impacts, including cumulative impacts, of the proposed activity and its intended use on the public interest. Evaluation of the probable impact which the proposed activity may have on the public interest requires a careful weighing of all those factors which become relevant in each particular case. The benefits which reasonably may be expected to accrue from the proposal must be balanced against its reasonably foreseeable detriments. The decision whether to authorize a proposal, and if so, the conditions under which it will be allowed to occur, are therefore determined by the outcome of this general balancing process. [33 C.F.R. § 320.4(a) (1).]

This wide-ranging balancing test is quite different from the decision criteria applied to most land development proposals, and the EPA guidelines provide an even more restrictive rule that requires the consideration of alternatives:

> [N]o discharge of dredged or fill material shall be permitted if there is a practicable alternative to the proposed discharge which would have less adverse impact on the aquatic system, so long as the alternative does not have other significant adverse environmental consequences. [40 C.F.R. § 230.10(a).]

A requirement that agencies must consider alternatives to a development proposal is an important new element in decision making for land use that the wetlands and other environmental programs have introduced. A consider-ation of alternatives has no place in traditional zoning controls.

An even more stringent "water dependency" rule that affects the application of the alternatives rule applies to development in wetlands:

> Where the activity associated with a discharge which is proposed for a special aquatic site . . . [such as wetlands] does not require access or proximity to or siting within the special aquatic site in question to fulfill its basic purpose (i.e., is not "water dependent"), practicable alternatives that do not involve special aquatic sites are presumed to be available unless clearly demonstrated otherwise. [40 C.F.R. § 230.10(a) (3).]

Residential development is not water-dependent, but developers argue that the construction of riverfront boat docking and storage facilities makes residential development in wetlands water-dependent. The courts have rejected this kind of bootstrapping. See *National Wildlife Fed'n v. Whistler,* 27 F.3d 1341 (8th Cir. 1994).

Applying the "practicable alternatives" rule.—*Bersani v. Robichard,* 850 F.2d 36 (2d Cir. 1988), *cert. denied,* 489 U.S. 1089 (1989), is the most important case applying the "practicable alternatives" rule. This case considered a challenge to a permit veto by EPA in a wetlands known as Sweeden's Swamp, near Attleboro, Massachusetts. This was one of the few times EPA has vetoed a Corps permit and the Sweeden's Swamp controversy generated intense national interest.

A development corporation purchased an 80-acre site with about 50 acres of wetlands sometime before 1982 to construct a regional shopping center but sold the site to the Pyramid Company in 1983. An alternative upland site was available until July of that year but was then purchased by a competitor. There was some evidence that both centers could not succeed in this area. The Corps granted a permit because the alternative site was no longer in the market, but EPA vetoed the permit because Pyramid had not overcome the presumption that an alternative site was available.

EPA concluded that its regulation required alternatives to be evaluated at the time a developer entered the market, not at the time of the permit application. Under EPA's theory, the upland site was available in this case. Pyramid argued that the market entry theory was an incorrect interpretation of the regulation but the Court of Appeals disagreed:

> [A]s EPA has pointed out, the preamble to the 404(b) (1) guidelines states that the purpose of the "practicable alternatives" analysis is "to recognize the special value of wetlands and to avoid their unnecessary destruction, particularly where practicable alternatives *were* available in non-aquatic areas to achieve the basic purpose of the proposal." 45 Fed. Reg. 85,338 (1980) (emphasis added). . . . If the practicable alternatives analysis were applied to the time of the application for a permit, the developer would have little incentive to search for alternatives, especially if it were confident that alternatives soon would disappear. Conversely, in a case in which alternatives were not available at the time the developer made its selection, but became available by the time of application, the developer's application would be denied even though it could not have explored the alternative site at the time of its decision. [*Id.* at 43–44.]

NOTES AND QUESTIONS

1. *Market entry.* Do you agree with EPA's "market entry" requirement as approved by the court? Or is this requirement opposed to good planning because it allows the Corps, EPA and the courts to determine the location of major developments on a case-by-case basis? If so, how would you interpret the alternatives requirement for wetlands development which is not water-dependent? For a critical analysis of the *Bersani* case see Bosselman, *Sweeden's Swamp: The Morass of Wetland Regulation,* 49 Land Use L. & Zoning Dig., No. 3, at 3 (1989).

2. *The "public interest" review.* This review is wide-ranging. Are there any limits to the development impacts the Corps may consider? In *Mall Props., Inc. v. Marsh,* 672 F. Supp. 561 (D. Mass. 1987), *aff'd,* 841 F.2d 440 (1st Cir.), *cert. denied,* 488 U.S. 848 (1988), the court held the Corps need not deny a permit for a suburban shopping center to protect the economy of a nearby older city. The Corps is required to consider economic factors only when they have a "reasonably close causal relationship" with a change in the physical environment. The court relied on cases reaching the same conclusion under the National Environmental Policy Act. How does this decision compare with the "control of competition" rule in zoning? Is there a difference between judging alternatives at the time of market entry and denying a permit because of market protection?

3. *The takings issue.* The taking problem is especially troublesome since the Supreme Court's *Lucas* decision, reproduced *supra* in Chapter 2, held a taking per se occurs when a landowner is denied all economically viable use of her land. However, as a Note in Chapter 2 indicates, the court have so far applied exceptions to the *Lucas* decision in many cases to avoid a holding that a taking occurred when a permit for development in a wetlands was denied under § 404.

4. *Mitigation.* As in many environmental land use programs, mitigation is an important part of the § 404 permitting process. Mitigation through the creation or restoration of wetlands is controversial because of doubts about the viability of restoration or creation measures. The public purchase of existing wetlands does not increase wetlands acreage. Mitigation banks are another innovation. They are created by developers, either singly or jointly, to create or restore wetlands and "bank" them for future projects. For discussion of mitigation see D. Salvesen, Wetland Mitigation (2d ed. 1994); Mitigation Banking: Theory and Practice (L. Marsh, D. Porter & D. Salvesen eds., 1995); Comment, *Paving the Road to Wetlands Mitigation Banking,* 27 B.C. Envtl. Aff. L. Rev. 161 (1999).

5. *Wetlands Executive Order.* President Carter issued Executive Order 11,990 in 1977, 13 Weekly Comp. Pres. Doc. 806 (May 24, 1977), which applies to federal and federally assisted activities and projects in wetlands but exempts the § 404 dredge and fill permit program. Federal agencies carrying out these activities are to consider their effect on "the survival and quality" of wetlands, § 5. New construction in wetlands is not allowed unless there is no practicable alternative and all practicable mitigation measures have been taken, § 2(a). See *City of Carmel-by-the-Sea v. United States Dep't of Transp.,* 123 F.3d 1142 (9th Cir. 1997) (proposed highway complied with Order).

6. *Sources.* See W. Want, Law of Wetlands Regulation; *Guttery et al., Federal Wetlands Regulation: Restrictions on the Nationwide Permit Program and the Implications for Residential Property Owners,* 37 Am. Bus. L.J. 299 (2000) (finding negative impacts on property values); Mortimer, *Irregular Regulation under Section 404 of the Clean Water Act: Is the Congress or the Corps of Engineers to Blame?,* 13 J. Envtl. L. & Litig. 445 (1998). The site of the American Society of Wetlands Managers at www.aswm.org is an excellent source of material on wetlands regulation.

PROBLEM

Assume you are a residential developer, and that you have just been offered an attractive development site in a wetlands. The wetlands is known as a nesting habitat for a variety of bird species. There are alternative sites in your market, but some of them are located in other environmentally threatened areas, such as hillsides. What are your chances for permit approval under the § 404 permit program?

c. State and Local Wetlands Protection Programs

The regulatory framework.—Most of the coastal states have legislation that protects coastal wetlands and some also regulate inland wetlands. A few non-coastal states have also adopted wetlands statutes. Some state statutes are modeled on the federal program, but some go beyond it by regulating more than dredge and fill activities and by covering a buffer strip around wetlands as well as wetlands areas. Activities that are not harmful to wetlands may be permitted, such as recreation, grazing, and farming.

Like the federal law, state wetlands statutes usually provide for the direct regulation of development in wetlands through permit powers. Some statutes also authorize the adoption of "land use regulations" in wetlands areas specifying permitted uses. See N.Y. Envtl. Conserv. Law § 25-0302. An alternative but similar regulatory technique authorizes the state agency to adopt orders "regulating, restricting or prohibiting dredging, filling, removing or otherwise altering, or polluting" coastal wetlands. N.J. Stat. Ann. § 13:9A-2.

State wetlands statutes may also provide standards for the issuance of permits. Some of the statutes contain general standards authorizing consideration of the "public interest" or the "policy" of the proposed act. These statutes may also contain more specific "factors" for consideration in permit review, such as the environmental impact of the proposed development and its suitability for the area in which it is proposed. For example, the Florida statute requires consideration of the following "criteria" to determine whether the "public interest" standard is met:

1. Whether the activity will adversely affect the public health, safety, or welfare or the property of others;

2. Whether the activity will adversely affect the conservation of fish and wildlife, including endangered or threatened species, or their habitats;

3. Whether the activity will adversely affect navigation or the flow of water or cause harmful erosion or shoaling;

4. Whether the activity will adversely affect the fishing or recreational values or marine productivity in the vicinity of the activity;

5. Whether the activity will be of a temporary or permanent nature;

6. Whether the activity will adversely affect or will enhance significant historical and archaeological resources . . . ; and

7. The current condition and relative value of functions being performed by areas affected by the proposed activity. [Fla. Stat. Ann. § 373.414(1)(a).]

Compare these criteria with the balancing test contained in Corps regulations for the § 404 permit program. Are these criteria different because they contain substantive standards? Would the developer in the Problem, *supra,* get approval under this statute?

A number of the state wetlands statutes provide a role for local government. Local governments are required to adopt wetlands regulations consistent with the state statute and subject to the approval of the state agency. The state agency may adopt regulations for the local government if it fails to enact them. See N.Y. Envtl. Conserv. Law § 24-0903(4). Some state legislation in the Midwest requires local regulation of shoreland areas, which include wetlands, and also requires local adoption of regulatory programs subject to state approval.

The takings issue.—The regulatory framework of state wetlands legislation sets the stage for consideration of the takings issue. Some state statutes specifically provide for judicial consideration of taking problems in judicial appeals from wetlands permit denials. The New Jersey legislation authorizing judicial appeal of a wetlands permit or order provides: "If a court finds the order or permit to be an unreasonable exercise of the police power, the court shall enter a finding that such order or permit shall not apply to the land of the plaintiff." N.J. Stat. Ann. § 13:9A-6.

The courts have applied exceptions to the *Lucas* decision to hold that permit denials under state wetlands laws were not takings, just as they have applied these exceptions to reach the same conclusion under the federal wetlands program. State takings law can still present an obstacle. Early cases held that restrictions in wetlands regulations were a taking of property. See *State v. Johnson,* 265 A.2d 711 (Me. 1970) (denial of permit to fill wetland held a taking). Judicial attitudes shifted with the leading decision in *Just v. Marinette County,* 201 N.W.2d 761 (Wis. 1972), which applied the harm-benefit rule of the takings clause to uphold a wetlands law as means of preventing development that could harm the wetlands environment. Whether the reasoning of this case survives the rejection of the harm-benefit rule in the *Lucas* case is not yet clear.

2. FLOODPLAIN REGULATION

Between seven and ten percent of our land is located in floodplains. About 90 percent of all losses from natural disasters are caused by floods, and economic losses from floods are astronomic. These facts provide strong support for programs that can avoid flood losses. Although flood losses can be avoided through dams, reservoirs, river channeling, and similar structural measures, land use regulation in floodplains is an important alternative loss avoidance technique.

Floodplains are natural flood overflow areas adjacent to stream channels. The floodplain is defined as an area subject to a 100-year flood, which means that the statistical chance that a flood will occur is one percent in any one year. A floodplain includes the stream channel and its overbank area, as well as the adjacent floodway fringe. Land use regulation in floodplains applies different types of controls to these two areas. All structural development in the floodplain channel is usually prohibited. Structural uses are allowed in the floodway fringe subject to requirements that help avoid flood losses, such as requirements that structures be elevated or floodproofed. The figure illustrates a typical floodplain and the land use regulations usually applied.

FLOODPLAIN DISTRICT REGULATION

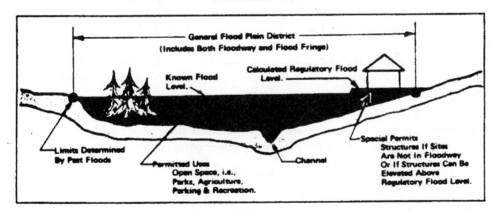

Source: American Soc'y of Planning Officials, Regulations for Flood Plains, Fig. 17, p. 45 (Planning Advisory Service Rep. No. 277 (1972).

a. The Federal Role and the Federal Flood Insurance Program

The federal role in flood management is substantial, and includes participation by many federal agencies. Dam and levee construction by the Corps of Engineers to contain flooding and prevent flood damage is an important part of federal efforts at flood management. Federal efforts are uncoordinated, however, and the massive midwest flood of 1993 called into question the federal strategy of flood containment. The report of a federal committee established after the flood recommends an improved federal flood management strategy that includes measures for reducing flood loss by avoiding inappropriate uses of floodplains. Sharing the Challenge: Floodplain Management Into the 21st Century, Report of the Interagency Floodplain Management Review Committee (1994).

   The Flood Insurance Program.—Congress enacted a federal Flood Insurance Program (FIP) in 1968 to make flood insurance more affordable and increase the number of insured structures. Insurance can be issued by the Federal Emergency Management Agency (FEMA), which administers the program, or from private "Write Your Own" insurers which are reimbursed by FEMA. Participation in the program was originally voluntary, but in 1973 Congress amended the program to include a "Mandatory Purchase Requirement" which makes flood insurance mandatory on loans from private financial institutions regulated or insured by the federal government and for the receipt of direct federal financial assistance. 42 U.S.C. § 4012a. Participation in the program is low despite these requirements, as fewer than 25% of eligible structures in floodplains are covered by policies under the program. Amendments to the program in 1994 strengthened the requirements for participation and should lead to greater coverage. See Bernstein, Myers, & Steen, *Flood Insurance "Reform" Act Engulfs Mortgage Lenders,* 48 Consumer Fin. L.Q. Rep. 304 (1994).

   The FIP is not subsidized and is substantially in debt because of low participation rates. Repetitive claims, and the rebuilding of properties in floodplains despite a federal rule prohibiting rebuilding when a property incurs a 50% loss, are other major problems. See National Wildlife Fed'n, Higher Ground — A Report on Voluntary Buyouts in the Nation's Floodplains (1998); Warrick, *Seeking an End to a Flood of Claims,* Nat'l Wildlife, June-July 1999.

   The FIP requires communities to adopt floodplain regulations to make landowners in the community eligible for federal flood insurance. As administrator of the federal program, FEMA is to adopt "comprehensive criteria" for

   the adoption of adequate State and local measures which, to the maximum extent feasible, will —

   (1)   constrict the development of land which is exposed to flood damage where appropriate,

   (2)   guide the development of proposed construction away from locations which are threatened by flood hazards,

   (3)   assist in reducing damage by floods, and

   (4)   otherwise improve the long-range land management and use of floodprone areas. . . . [42 U.S.C. § 4102(c).]

For a summary of FEMA regulatory and design standards for floodplain regulation see Floodplain Management in the United States: An Assessment Report ch. 8 (Federal Interagency Floodplain Management Task Force 1992).

   Almost all eligible communities participate in the program, and the amount of insurance has doubled in recent years. Whether the insurance program has helped to prevent flood loss is another question. Some critics claim the availability of insurance in floodplain areas has encouraged development by providing an assurance that losses will be paid if flooding occurs. Furthermore, federal regulations have not served as a barrier to development in floodprone areas, since development is allowed when structure elevation or other protective measures can avoid or mitigate flood damage. Existing development in areas where it is prohibited under the regulations also has been a problem. The courts have rejected takings claims against the program. See *Adolph v. Federal Emergency Mgt. Agency*, 854 F.2d 732 (5th Cir. 1988).

Floodplain Executive Order.—President Carter issued a Floodplain Management Order, Exec. Order No. 11,988, 13 Weekly Comp. Pres. Doc. 803 (May 24, 1977), which is similar to the Executive Order for wetlands. The order requires federal agencies to "provide leadership and . . . take actions to reduce the risk of flood losses, to minimize the impact of floods on human safety, health and welfare, and to restore and preserve the natural and beneficial values served by floodplains." Federal agencies proposing actions in floodplains must consider "alternatives to avoid adverse effects and incompatible development in the floodplains." Federal structures and facilities constructed in floodplains must also be consistent with criteria imposed by the flood insurance program.

b. State and Local Floodplain Regulation

Local floodplain ordinances are quite common because of the requirements in the FIP. They are usually adopted as overlay zoning. As the graphic reproduced above indicates, limitations on development in the floodplain are quite restrictive. Only nonstructural uses are allowed, such as boat docks, farming and golf courses. Additional nonstructural uses may be authorized by a special permit.

A number of states have legislation requiring state or local regulation of floodplains. One type of statute provides for direct state control by a state agency authorized to issue permits for development in floodplains. E.g., Iowa Code Ann. §§ 455B.264 -455B.269. Other statutes provide for local administration under ordinances that receive state approval. E.g., Minn. Stat. Ann. § 103F.121.

Unlike wetlands legislation, which may be limited to dredge and fill and related activities, state floodplain legislation may authorize more extensive control over existing uses and new development. Some statutes also authorize the review of new subdivisions. The New Jersey legislation is typical. It authorizes the state agency

> to adopt . . . rules and regulations and to issue orders concerning the development and use of land in any delineated floodway which shall be designed to preserve its flood carrying capacity and to minimize the threat to the public safety, health and general welfare. [N.J. Stat. Ann. § 58:16A-55(a).]

c. The Takings Issue

Pre-Lucas cases.—Although there was no landmark state floodplain case comparable to the *Just* decision upholding wetlands regulation, a number of significant decisions upheld floodplain regulations prior to the Supreme Court's *Lucas* decision, whose per se takings rule could conceivably threaten floodplain regulation. *Maple Leaf Investors, Inc. v. State,* 565 P.2d 1162 (Wash. 1977), is a leading case. Other leading cases upholding floodplain regulation included *Turner v. County of Del Norte,* 101 Cal. Rptr. 93 (Cal. App. 1972), and *Turnpike Realty Co. v. Town of Dedham,* 284 N.E.2d 891 (Mass. 1972), *cert. denied,* 409 U.S. 1108 (1973).

Post-Lucas.—Floodplain regulation could constitute a per se taking under *Lucas* when it prevents any economically viable use of the land. The Court did indicate in *Lucas* that a restriction on the use of land to prevent flooding *others'* land would fall within the nuisance exception to the per se taking rule, but it is not clear how this rule would apply when it is the land under development that is primarily at risk. See, however, *Leonard v. Town of Broomfield,* 666 N.E.2d 1300 (Mass.), *cert. denied,* 519 U.S. 1028 (1996) (no taking when not all of land within floodplain and owner had constructive notice of regulation when property purchased).

Taking attacks on floodplain regulations also are offset to some extent in floodway fringe areas because regulations in these areas do not prohibit development absolutely; development above flood height elevations usually is allowed. This option substantially mitigates the regulatory burden, and may prevent facial taking attacks by landowners who have not exhausted the possibilities for development that does not interfere with floodway flow. See *Vartelas v. Water Resources Comm'n,* 153 A.2d 822 (Conn. 1959).

Sources.—The web site of the Association of State Floodplain Managers, www.floods.org, contains useful publications and information on floodplain regulation and the FIP. See also Burby et al., *Unleashing the Power of Planning to Create Disaster-Resistant Communities,* 65 J. Am. Plan. Ass'n 247 (1999).

PROBLEM

Consider the differences between wetlands and floodplain regulation. Floodplain regulation is quite restrictive and is driven by the location of a building site in relation to the floodway. The balancing that occurs in wetlands regulation is more permissive. Why the difference? Go back to the Problem, *supra,* in which a developer was offered an attractive site in a wetlands, and consider under what circumstances she would be allowed to build in a floodplain.

3. GROUNDWATER PROTECTION

Groundwater quality protection is a major environmental issue, but a fully coordinated intergovernmental groundwater protection strategy is yet to emerge. A number of federal, state and local programs include groundwater protection elements.

Federal legislation.—Federal controls are fragmented and a large number of statutes apply to groundwater. The courts are split on whether the Clean Water Act applies to sources that pollute groundwater. See *Umatilla Water*

Quality Protective Ass'n v. Smith Frozen Foods, 962 F. Supp. 1312 (D. Ore. 1997), summarizing the cases, and Quatrochi, *Groundwater Jurisdiction Under the Clean Water Act: The Tributary Groundwater Dilemma,* 23 B.C. Envtl. Aff. L. Rev. 603 (1996).

EPA has followed cases holding it does not have jurisdiction and has relied on other statutes, such as the Resource Conservation and Recovery Act, 42 U.S.C. §§ 6901-6991i, which protects groundwater that is threatened by waste disposal facilities. The Safe Drinking Water Act has a program for the protection of underground water aquifers, but it is limited to prohibitions on federal assistance for development over groundwater sources. 42 U.S.C. § 300h-3(e). Amendments to this statute in 1996 substantially expanded its water source protection program, and EPA now relies on it to implement its groundwater policy. See EPA, A Ground-Water Protection Strategy for the Environmental Protection Agency (1984). A key program provides federal assistance to the states for a Comprehensive Ground Water Protection program. It authorizes federal assistance to states "for the development and implementation of a State program to ensure the coordinated and comprehensive protection of ground water resources within the State." *Id.,* § 300h-8(a).

In addition, states must conduct a Source Water Assessment Program to determine the boundaries of source waters and identify origins of contaminants within these areas that require monitoring under the statute. *Id.,* § 300j-14. For discussion see Cox, *Evolution of the Safe Drinking Water Act: A Search for Effective Quality Assurance Strategies and Workable Concepts of Federalism,* 21 Wm. & Mary Envtl. L. & Pol'y Rev. 69 (1997).

State programs.—State programs vary widely and include controls on discharges to groundwater and the adoption of groundwater quality standards. See Vance, *Total Aquifer Management: A New Approach to Groundwater Protection,* 30 U.S.F.L. Rev. 803 (1996). They do not usually include land use controls. For examples of state legislation authorizing the consideration of local groundwater protection in planning and zoning see Conn. Gen. Stat. §§ 8-2, 8-25 (local development plans and zoning to consider protection of drinking water supplies); Fla. Stat. Ann. § 163.3177(6) (c) (local comprehensive plan to include groundwater recharge element and protection requirements). For a critique of groundwater control strategies see George, *Is Groundwater Regulation Blindman's Bluff?,* 3 J. Plan. Lit. 231 (1988).

Local programs.—Local governments have adopted controls for the regulation of land use that considers its impact on groundwater. The following article explains how they work:

> The regulated area is typically depicted with overlay mapping. After the resource area is delineated, it is laid over the zoning districts. This is the recommended approach because it would be extremely difficult to conform underlying zoning districts to the haphazard shapes of watershed and water resources. . . .
>
> The text establishing the rules for the overlay district varies depending upon the resource being protected: Some regulations prohibit most uses deemed a threat to water resources, others use "performance based" criteria. Most water resource protection regulations list uses

that are prohibited because they are deemed a threat to water systems. In some cases, this list is extensive, in others only the allowed uses are listed. [Witten, *Water Resource Protection and the Takings Issue,* Land Use L. & Zoning Dig., Vol. 50, No. 5, at 3 (1998).]

Some ordinances also provide for conditional uses. *Id.* at 3–4. See also Tarlock, *Prevention of Groundwater Contamination,* 8 Zoning and Planning Law Report 121, 125–126 (1985).

NOTES AND QUESTIONS

1. *Zoning strategies.* The strategy suggested in the Tarlock article often is implemented through the adoption of a series of concentric zones surrounding a groundwater resource, such as a stream. A three-tier system to protect streams that feed groundwater sources is typical. For example, development is prohibited in streamside areas up to 40 feet wide adjacent to streams. Buffer zones are adjacent to the critical areas and may extend up to 700 feet. Development in these zones is severely restricted. Average densities may be as low as 0.33 units per acre, and commercial development is prohibited. Upland zones are the furthest away from streamside, and controls in these areas are the least restrictive. They can act as receiving areas for development rights transferred from the more restrictive zones. Transfer of development rights programs are discussed in Chapter 8. For discussion of a system of this type adopted in Austin, Texas and still in effect see DiNovo & Jaffe, *Local Regulations for Groundwater Protection Part I: Sensitive-Area Controls,* 36 Land Use L. & Zoning Dig., No. 5, at 6, 12, 13 (1984). See also M. Jaffe & F. DiNovo, Local Groundwater Protection 49–54 (1987); Marsh & Hill-Rowley, *Water Quality, Stormwater Management, and Development Planning in the Urban Fringe,* 36 Wash. U.J. Urb. & Contemp. L. 3 (1989) (discussing Austin). On hydrology problems see R. Hughto, M. Nelson & J. Witten, Environmental Science and Engineering for Lawyers § 9 (2000).

2. *The overlap problem.* Notice that land use controls for water resources are adopted as an overlay zone, and that the three-tier strategy described in the previous Note can overlap floodplain and wetlands regulation. Floodplain regulations are usually adopted as overlay zones, and wetland permit programs often act as overlays on the zoning ordinance. It is this kind of overlap that creates multiple vetoes and a series of decision points for developers. A failure to get approval under any of these regulations can stop a project. See discussion of permit simplification, *supra,* in this chapter.

3. *The takings issue.* In *Moviematic Industries Corp. v. Board of County Commissioners of Metropolitan Dade County,* 349 So. 2d 667 (Fla. App. 1977), Dade County (which includes Miami) imposed a building moratorium on an area of 323 square miles to study groundwater protection measures. When the study was completed the county downzoned the Moviematic property from industrial to single-family residential zoning with a five-acre minimum lot size requirement. The court stated that the "preservation of the ecological balance of a particular area is a valid exercise of the police power as it relates to the general welfare." *Id.* at 669. It held that a taking had not occurred because the developer could develop his property in accordance with the uses permitted

by the ordinance. Accord *New Jersey Bldrs. Ass'n v. Department of Envtl. Protection,* 404 A.2d 320 (N.J. App. Div.), (upholding restrictive land use regulation adopted to protect water aquifer underlying New Jersey Pine Barrens), *cert. denied,* 408 A.2d 796 (N.J. 1979).

The Supreme Court's *Lucas* case does not seem to be a problem because most groundwater protection ordinances allow some beneficial use of the land. See Fahey & Roznoy, *Aquifer Protection in Connecticut: Environmental Land Use Restrictions Run Deep,* 68 Conn. B.J. 98 (1994). In *Security Mgt. Corp. v. Baltimore County,* 655 A.2d 1326 (Md. App. 1995), the court held a resource conservation zone requiring five acres for each dwelling, and adopted to prevent unsuitable development that would contaminate a watershed, was not a taking. It considered *Lucas* but held the ordinance did not deny "all" economically beneficial or productive use of the land.

4. PROTECTING HILLSIDES

As discussed above, wetlands and floodplains are flat areas that present certain kinds of environmental problems. Hillsides and hilly areas present different environmental problems. For example, building sites on steep slopes are attractive for development and command high prices because people like home sites with vistas. But steep slope development presents a number of problems. Landslides are one. See Andrews, *Shifting Sands, Sliding Land,* Planning, Vol. 65, No. 6, at 4 (1999) (discussing landslides in Laguna Beach, California).

Hillside development can also increase the risk of fire hazards as fires beginning in remote areas of a hill can be fanned uphill by winds and spread out of control. Erosion and drainage problems can be intensified because the removal of vegetation for development can accelerate water runoff. These dangers are not the only reason for hillside regulation. A substantial number of communities also regulate hillside development for aesthetic reasons, as many hillsides contain unique environmental features, such as river corridors and uncommon vegetation.

The first attempt to regulate hillside development was through grading ordinances, which are now included in all model building codes. These were followed by slope/density ordinances, which relate the density of development to hillside slope based on the ability of a site to handle physical pressures caused by new development. Hillside development regulations today utilize a variety of approaches:

> A jurisdiction might choose to encourage development while emphasizing public safety, thus requiring extensive mass regrading and re-engineering of hillsides to provide high-quality roadways that allow quick access for public safety vehicles. Or a jurisdiction might require selective grading and improvements of hillsides for safety concerns, while imposing development standards (e.g., setbacks from ridgelines, restrictions on removal of native vegetation) to protect important natural features. A third approach could be to prohibit hillside development altogether. [C. Duerksen & M. Goebel, *Aesthetics, Community*

Character, and the Law 47, American Planning Association, Planning Advisory Service Rep. Nos. 489–490 (1999).]

The important lesson here is that building on steep slopes requires a substantial modification of traditional zoning controls.

Often the hillside protection ordinance is contained in an overlay zone, such as the Foothills and Canyons Overlay Zoning District adopted in Salt Lake County, Utah. One feature of this district is the establishment of "limits of disturbance" that indicate the areas of a site on which development can occur. *Id.* at 48–49. The article by Andrews, cited above, discussed the hillside protection program in Seattle, Washington. For a detailed review see R. Olshansky, *Planning for Hillside Development,* American Planning Association, Planning Advisory Service Rep. No. 466 (1996).

Hillside controls can create takings problems if they prohibit or severely restrict development. Although the Arizona court has held that hillside controls were a taking, *Corrigan v. City of Scottsdale,* 720 P.2d 513 (Ariz. 1986), later cases upheld these controls under reasoning similar to that used in floodplain control cases. *Sellon v. City of Manitou Springs,* 745 P.2d 229 (Colo. 1987); *Jones v. Zoning Hearing Board of McCandless,* 578 A.2d 1369 (Pa. 1990). These cases were pre-*Lucas,* which may require a holding that prohibitive or restrictive controls are a per se taking unless the propensity of hillside developments to trigger mudslides or other dangerous conditions could bring them within the nuisance exception. Are there any other exceptions that might make *Lucas* inapplicable?

5. COASTAL ZONE MANAGEMENT

a. The National Coastal Zone Management Act

The nation's coastal areas are a valuable but threatened environmental resource. More than 75 percent of the population now lives in coastal areas or nearby, and this proportion is increasing.

Like the other environmental land use regulation programs discussed in this section, coastal management is resource-driven, but with a difference. Coastal areas differ widely in character, and can include developed urban as well as natural areas, such as wetlands and agricultural areas.

Congress responded to concern about the coastal zone by enacting the national Coastal Zone Management Act of 1972 (CZMA), which established a program of federal assistance to the states for the development of coastal management programs.

The primary motivation behind the CZMA was that proximity to the coast presents a special land use management challenge, and that state intervention guided by national requirements was necessary to guide local regulation that might otherwise not respect coastal resources in advancing local interests. For this reason, the CZMA and the state programs are as much about process as they are about substance, and in this respect resemble the statutory structure created by the standard planning and zoning acts.

State participation in the program is voluntary, but the CZMA provides an incentive for state participation by requiring federal projects and funded activities in the coastal zone to be consistent with approved state coastal programs. Most of the states in the coastal zone, which includes the Great Lakes states, participate. The CZMA authorizes more than just land use controls, as it includes a grant program for the acquisition of National Estuarine Reserves, but this section concentrates on the land use control elements of the program.

The national legislation.—From the beginning, the CZMA has had an ambiguous charter, and its original statutory purpose did not describe it as a program intended to protect coastal zones from development. Amendments adopted by Congress in 1980 enacted a set of protective statutory policies for state coastal management that to some extent answered claims that the program lacked an articulate purpose, but the state coastal programs were developed before the 1980 amendments were adopted.

The CZMA may be found at 16 U.S.C. §§ 1451–1474. References in this discussion are to the section numbers of the original legislation as adopted by Congress.

The coastal zone.—The CZMA defines the coastal zone as "the coastal waters . . . and the adjacent shorelands . . . strongly influenced by each other"; the statute also provides that the coastal zone "extends inland from the shorelines only to the extent necessary to control shorelands, the uses of which have a direct and significant impact on the coastal waters." § 304(1). In some states, like California, the coastal zone is a narrow strip of land along the coast. Elsewhere, as in North Carolina, the coastal zone includes all coastal counties.

The coastal management program.—The CZMA authorizes funding for a "management program," which is vaguely defined by the statute (§ 305). The program includes a definition of "permissible land uses and water uses" and identifies the "means" by which the states are to exercise control in the coastal zone. The statutory definition of a "management program" also suggests that something like a comprehensive plan is required (§ 304(12)). In practice, the national coastal office does not require a conventional planning program. State coastal "plans" are not plans in the conventional sense but a combination of policy elements and implementation programs for the state coastal effort.

A separate section of the CZMA, revised and revived in 1990, provides for "administrative" grants and requires specific state "means" of control in the coastal zone (§ 306). The effect of these requirements is complicated by a statutory provision that requires a lead coastal agency in each state, but does not require that agency to have and to exercise the required "means" of state control. The state agency may completely delegate the administration of the program to local governments and share it with them, which has happened in some states.

The three "means" of control include, either separately or in combination: (1) state criteria and standards for local implementation, subject to state review; (2) direct state planning and regulation; or (3) state administrative review of state and local plans, projects, and regulations to determine consistency with the state coastal program. There must also be a method for assuring that state and local coastal zone regulations "do not unreasonably restrict or exclude land and water uses of regional benefit." Another related section affecting state review of land development requires "adequate consideration of the national interest" in the planning and siting of facilities, including energy facilities, that "meet requirements which are other than local in nature." § 306(d) (12).

States do not have to adopt entirely new programs to satisfy these statutory requirements, as they can "network" existing statutory programs covering the coastal zone. Coastal wetlands and related legislation are usually included in the network. Another concession from the national coastal office allows the state to supervise local land use actions in the coastal zone through judicial review.

The national coastal policies adopted in the 1980 amendments, see § 303(2), also influence the state coastal programs. These policies require the "protection of natural resources," including floodplains and wetlands. They also require "the management of coastal development to minimize the loss of life and property caused by improper development" in flood-prone and similar areas and by the destruction of "natural protective features," such as wetlands and barrier islands. "Priority consideration" must be given to coastal-dependent uses.

The 1980 amendments added a provision that encourages the preparation of special area management plans to provide "increased specificity in protecting significant natural resources, reasonable coastal-dependent economic growth, [and] improved protection of life and property in hazardous areas. . . ." § 303(3). A similar provision in § 306 authorizes the designation of "areas of particular concern."

NOTES AND QUESTIONS

1. *Intergovernmental relationships.* The CZMA sets up a three-tiered system of intergovernmental relationships based on a federal program of financial assistance that is unique in the programs discussed in this section. The federal statute contains program criteria that the states must meet in order to receive federal funding. A national coastal zone office in the National Oceanic and Atmospheric Administration (NOAA) administers the federal program, but the only recourse it has if states do not comply with federal requirements is to disqualify the state program and refuse any more federal assistance.

There are additional intergovernmental tensions at the state level if the administration of all or a part of the coastal management program is delegated to local governments, which may be jealous of any usurpation of local authority by state agencies, especially when it comes to land use matters. *Gherini v. California Coastal Comm'n,* 251 Cal. Rptr. 426 (Cal. App. 1988), is an example of a case upholding a state agency's disapproval of a local coastal plan. You should look for evidence of these intergovernmental tensions in the materials that follow.

2. *The role of state coastal plans. American Petr. Inst. v. Knecht,* 456 F. Supp. 889 (C.D. Cal. 1978), *aff'd,* 609 F.2d 1306 (9th Cir. 1979), interpreted the federal statutory requirements that determine the content of state coastal plans. The question was whether the California coastal management plan lacked the specificity Congress intended to enable landowners in the coastal

zone to "predict with reasonable certainty" whether their activities were consistent with the management plan. The court held that Congress did not intend states to

> establish such detailed criteria that private users [will] be able to rely on them as predictive devices for determining the fate of projects without interaction between the relevant state agencies and the user. [456 F. Supp. at 919.]

3. *Federal consistency.* The CZMA includes a federal consistency requirement in § 307, which is an important incentive to state participation. Federal agency activities and private activities that require federal licenses and permits must be consistent with approved state coastal programs. States are given the authority to limit federal and federally approved land uses when they conflict with their coastal programs. Thus, for example, states like Alaska and California have used the consistency requirement to block offshore exploration for oil and gas. See *Trustees for Alaska v. State of Alaska Dep't of Natural Resources,* 851 P.2d 1340 (Alaska 1993) (remanding finding that offshore lease sale was consistent with state coastal program); Note, *Managing Alaska's Coastal Development: State Review of Federal Oil and Gas Lease Sales,* 11 Alaska L. Rev. 377 (1994). See also *California Coastal Comm'n v. United States,* 5 F. Supp.2d 1106 (S.D. Cal. 1998) (granting preliminary injunction against Corps permit for beach replenishment project in coastal zone to allow Commission to consider alternatives).

4. *The Coastal Barrier Resource Act.* Another important federal act that affects land use and development in the coastal zone is the Coastal Barrier Resources Act, 16 U.S.C. §§ 3501–3510. Coastal barriers are sediment-composed landforms, such as islands and wetlands, that line the perimeter of the continent and the Great Lake shores. Substantial development has occurred in barrier systems since World War II, and federal subsidies are partly responsible. The Act is intended to prevent development in these barrier systems.

With certain exceptions, such as federal navigation channel maintenance and wildlife management, the Act prohibits federal assistance for (1) the construction or purchase of any structure, appurtenance, facility, or related infrastructure; (2) the construction or purchase of any road, airport, boat landing facility, or other facility on, or bridge or causeway to, any System unit; and (3) the carrying out of any project to prevent the erosion of, or to otherwise stabilize, any inlet, shoreline, or inshore area. 16 U.S.C. § 3504(a).

The legislation has a limited effect, because the Department of Interior, which administers the Act, does not have a veto power over decisions of other federal agencies, which may ignore (and have ignored) the statute. A 1990 amendment requires agencies to ensure compliance directly with the Department of Interior and appropriate congressional committees. There are also problems with the statutory exemptions, which agencies have interpreted generously. Neither is the Act clear on whether it prohibits federal assistance for projects outside the barrier system that encourage construction within it, such as roads and bridges.

5. *Sources.* For discussion of coastal management statutes see T. Beatley, D. Brower & A. Schwab, An Introduction to Coastal Zone Management (1994);

Jones, *Economic Incentives for Environmental Protection: The Coastal Barrier Resources Act: A Common Cents Approach to Coastal Protection*, 21 Envtl. L. 1015 (1991); Rychlak, *Coastal Zone Management and the Search for Integration*, 40 DePaul L. Rev. 981 (1991).

b. State Coastal Management Programs

Coastal management programs vary widely. Some jurisdictions have a limited program expressly designed for the control of development in coastal areas. See V.I. Code Ann. tit. 12 §§ 901–914. Most states delegate all or most program administration to local governments. Connecticut's program is based on case-by-case review of development proposals. Developers must submit a coastal site plan for development projects. Local governing bodies review site plans to "ensure that the potential adverse impacts of the proposed activity on both coastal resources and water-dependent development activities are acceptable." Conn. Gen. Stat. § 22a-105(e).

Washington state has a permit program based on local plans. Its Shoreline Management Act, adopted by popular initiative before the enactment of the CZMA, requires the adoption of local "master programs" for shoreline areas, which must be approved by the state environmental agency. The programs, which are a form of land use plan for the shoreline area, are implemented through a permit system for coastal development which is administered by local governments. Appeals from these decisions may be taken to a Shoreline Management Hearings Board, and then to the courts. Wash. Rev. Code Ann. §§ 90.58.010-90.58.920.

The showpiece of the national coastal program is the California Coastal Act of 1976, adopted to replace an interim coastal act adopted by popular initiative in 1972. The *Nollan* beach access case, reproduced *supra* in Chapter 2, arose under the California program. The 1972 initiative required the preparation of a state coastal plan, which contained a set of state coastal policies, many of which were included in legislation adopted in 1976. These policies provide guidelines for local coastal plans, which the act requires local governments to adopt for coastal areas. After these plans are approved by the state coastal commission, local governments administer a permit program for development in the coastal zone. Local permit decisions may be appealed to the state coastal commission on a limited basis.

Prior to the approval of local coastal plans, the statute provides for a state development permit program in the coastal zone administered by the coastal commission.

Coastal dependency.—An important coastal policy added to the national CZMA by the 1980 amendments requires priority for coastal-dependent uses. Many state coastal acts have a similar provision, which is intended to restrict coastal development to uses that need to be near the water. Recall that a similar water dependency requirement is included in regulations that implement the federal wetlands permit program.

What does coastal dependency mean? *Hayes v. Yount*, 552 P.2d 1038 (Wash. 1976), decided under the Washington state Shoreline Management Act, provides one interpretation. A local government granted a permit allowing a

PLANNING MAP FOR AREAS SUBJECT TO NEW JERSEY COASTAL LAW (CAFRA)

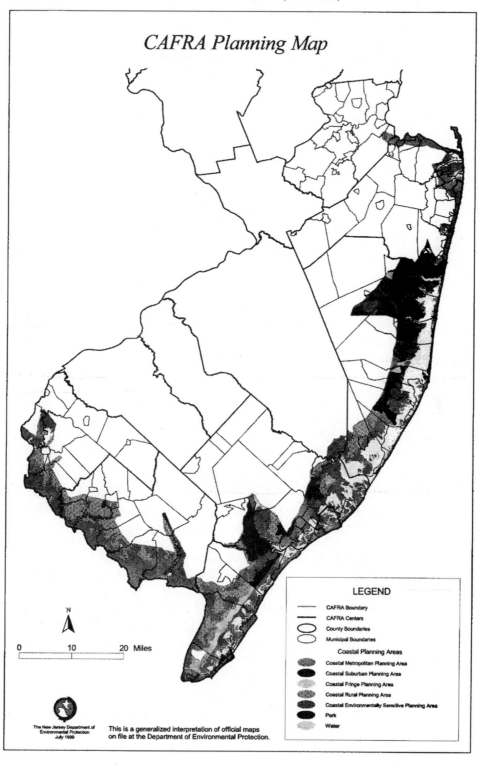

landowner to fill a wetland. The supreme court remanded the case for further proceedings but adopted an "intrinsic" suitability test for coastal dependency in an explanatory dictum: "The policy builds on the fundamental notions that the use of land should depend to a great extent on the suitability of a site for the particular use and that land may possess 'intrinsic suitability' for certain uses." *Id.* at 1057. The court then quoted from a leading environmental management text, which noted that even these uses should be limited to "those which do not diminish the present or prospective value of surface water for supply, recreation or amenity."

Has the court provided an adequate definition of "coastal dependency"? Can you develop a definition of what is and what is not "intrinsically suitable" for a coastal location? What about housing? Will the coastal dependency rule provide a net environmental benefit if a proposed development is required to move inland, where it may cause as much if not more environmental damage?

Implementing coastal plans.—Coastal plans, like any land use plan, must be implemented, and in coastal programs this may be done, as in Washington state, through a permit requirement so that consistency with the local plan can be ensured. How is this to be done?

In *Jefferson County v. Seattle Yacht Club,* 870 P.2d 987 (Wash. App. 1994), the county denied a permit for a docking facility under the state's Shoreline Management Act, the Shorelines Hearings Board reversed, and the court upheld the county. One of the issues was whether the facility complied with the Shoreline Management Program, which required the project to be compatible with other uses in the area. The surrounding area was undeveloped except for a similar nonconforming use, which the court held could not be considered, noting that nonconforming uses were expected to disappear. The court also held it was improper to determine compatibility on an areawide base rather than by considering only uses in the immediate vicinity of the project because otherwise "any project can be justified." The management program required "projects to be compatible with the area where the development is to be located."

Professor Houck has stated:

> [D]evelopment is cumulative and case-by-case. And this is exactly why the regulatory programs fail. Each proposal seems reasonable. How can a development proposal be denied on the grounds of what has already been done, by entirely different parties, sometime before? Even more problematic, how can it be denied on the basis of what others will do, or may do, in the future? [*Ending the War: A Strategy to Save America's Coastal Zone,* 47 Md. L. Rev. 358, 361 (1988).]

How can this problem be remedied? Would it have helped in the Washington cases if the cumulative impact of a new development project had to be considered?

Intergovernmental tensions in state coastal programs are evident in *Overlake Fund v. Shoreline Hearings Bd.,* 954 P.2d 304 (Wash. App. 1998). A Seattle suburb approved a hotel development under its zoning ordinance and decided it complied with its management plan. An appeal was taken to the state hearings board, which reversed, but the court reversed the board on appeal. The court noted that the development had received an extensive review under the city's land use regulations, and that the board really overturned the project because it thought it was not reasonable.

NOTES AND QUESTIONS

1. *Do the state programs work?* Between 1995 and 1997, the national coastal office conducted a study of the effectiveness of the CZMA based on five criteria: protection of estuaries and coastal wetlands; protection of beaches, dunes, bluffs, and rocky shores; public access to the shore; revitalization of urban waterfronts; and the accommodation of seaport development. The study concluded that the state programs were effectively implementing the national goals. Hershman et al., *The Effectiveness of Coastal Zone Management in the United States,* 27 Coast. Mgt. 113 (1999). A previous survey of coastal user groups, coastal zone managers, and academics done by the Center for the Study of Marine Policy found that the North Atlantic region's coastal zone management programs were best in the protection of coastal resources, the management of coastal development, and the management of coastal hazards. The Great Lakes region states excelled in providing public access to the shore. Knecht et al., *Perceptions of the Performance of State Coastal Zone Management Programs in the United States,* 25 Coast. Mgt. 141 (1996); Knecht et al., *Perceptions of the Performance of State Coastal Zone Management Programs in the United States: Regional and State Comparisons,* 25 Coastal Mgt. 325 (1997).

2. *Coastal erosion and setbacks.* Substantial erosion of coastal shorelines is a major environmental problem. The national CZMA states that one of its policies is to minimize loss of life and property in erosion-prone areas, and the coastal states have adopted erosion control and coastal setback legislation. A Michigan statute, for example, requires the state environmental agency to identify high risk coastal erosion areas and requires commission approval of local zoning ordinances that regulate coastal erosion. Mich. Comp. Laws § 34.3211. In California, one of the statutory coastal policies requires new development to minimize risks to "assure stability and structural integrity, and neither create nor significantly contribute to erosion." Cal. Pub. Res. Code § 30253(2). See Nat'l Research Council, Managing Coastal Erosion (1990); Houlahan, *Comparison of State Construction Setbacks to Manage Development in Coastal Hazard Areas,* 17 Coastal Mgt. 219 (1989).

The Supreme Court held the denial of a development permit under the South Carolina coastal setback law was a per se taking in the *Lucas* case, reproduced in Chapter 2. One of the factors in the decision was the absence of a variance or exception provision in the law. Lucas also owned two small residential lots. Opportunities for internal density tradeoffs exist when the property is larger and some of it is outside the setback area. See *City of Hollywood v. Hollywood, Inc.,* 432 So. 2d 1332 (Fla. App. 1985). What else would you recommend?

3. *The critical area concept.* Recall that the CZMA authorizes states to designate areas of particular concern in coastal areas. This is an adaptation of the critical area concept, an idea first proposed in the American Law

Institute's 1976 Model Land Development Code. See § 7-201. The code authorized the state planning agency to designate critical areas. Once designated, the agency was to state by rule the "dangers that might result from uncontrolled or inadequate development of the area" and "general principles for guiding development of the area." The state planning agency could review and modify local development controls that were inconsistent with state policies for the critical area, and adopt development controls in critical areas for local governments that did not have them. Development in critical areas had to be consistent with the local controls. See Berry, *Areas of Critical State Concern in Modernizing State Planning Legislation: The Growing Smart Papers,* Vol. 1, at 105, American Planning Association, Planning Advisory Serv. Rept. Nos. 462-463 (1996).

Several states have adopted legislation authorizing critical areas. Florida has one of the most successful programs. It closely follows the ALI Code and has been successfully applied in the Florida Keys and other coastal and environmental areas. Fla. Stat. Ann. § 390.05. For discussion see DeGrove, *Critical Area Programs in Florida: Creative Balancing of Growth and the Environment,* 34 Wash. U. J. Urb. & Contemp. L. 51 (1988). Maryland also has a successful critical area program that protects Chesapeake Bay. Note, *The Chesapeake Bay Preservation Act: Does State Land Use Regulation Protect Interstate Resources?,* 31 Wm. & Mary L. Rev. 735 (1990). Washington state requires local governments to designate critical areas and protect their functions and values. Wash. Rev. Code §§ 36.70.060, 36.70.172, 36.70A.170.

Model legislation proposed by the American Planning Association includes authority for state designation of critical areas that improves on the ALI Code model, particularly by requiring the integration of critical area planning and controls with local comprehensive plans. Legislative Guidebook Phases I & II, Interim Edition, 5-24 to 5-44 (1998). The Guidebook also authorizes local governments to include a Critical and Sensitive Areas Element in their comprehensive plans. *Id.* at 7-134 to 7-141.

4. *Carrying capacity analysis.* Mention should be made of this planning concept, which is a method for evaluating the capacity of environmental resources to accept new development, and is an analytic technique often used in planning for environmental areas. The American Planning Association Guidebook recommends using carrying capacity analysis as a tool for evaluating the development capacity of critical areas:

> [Carrying capacity] analysis is an assessment of the ability of a natural system to absorb population growth as well as other physical development with substantial degradation. Understanding the carrying capacity or constraints of natural resources (particularly ground and surface water systems) provides local governments with an effective method for identifying which portions of the community or region are most suitable sites for new and expanded development . . . and allows local government, residents and officials to make more rational and defensible decisions regarding how and where development may occur in critical and sensitive areas. [*Id.* at 7-135.]

Some object to a planning approach that relies on physical determinants:

The danger lies in not recognizing the tenuousness of carrying capacity conclusions and mistaking them for finite limits or thresholds rather than estimates or ranges. People who are unfamiliar with carrying capacity analyses can be misled, either innocently or deliberately, into thinking that the results of carrying capacity analyses are more concrete than they are. One possible abuse of carrying capacity analysis in this vein is its use for exclusionary purposes. [D. Schneider, D. Godschalk & N. Axler, *The Carrying Capacity Concept as a Planning Tool* 9, American Planning Association, Planning Advisory Serv. Rep. No. 338, 1978.]

Consider how, and whether, carrying capacity analysis can be useful in the environmental programs discussed in this section, and whether it has any place in the administration of zoning ordinances.

5. *Sources.* For additional discussion of state coastal programs see D. Beatley, D. Brower & A. Schwab, An Introduction to Coastal Zone Management, ch. 2 (1994); Dennison, *State and Local Authority to Regulate Coastal Land Use Practices Under the Coastal Zone Management Act,* 15 Zoning & Plan. L. Rep. 65 (1992).

PROBLEM

This is a good place to ask some questions about environmental land use controls and how they work. The important issue to note is how they place constraints on land development that go beyond restrictions contained in a zoning ordinance. As noted at the beginning of this section, these constraints can place substantial limitations on development opportunities. Review this section again as you study growth management programs in Chapter 7, and decide whether and how they can implement these programs.

Now examine the natural resource areas in your region, decide what they are, and consider what environmental land use regulations would be appropriate to protect them. It might be helpful to prepare a matrix of these controls to see what they accomplish, whether they overlap, and whether they provide a coordinated system of environmental protection.

Chapter 4

EQUITY ISSUES IN LAND USE: "EXCLUSIONARY ZONING" AND FAIR HOUSING

A. INTRODUCTION

"Exclusionary zoning" is the use of zoning ordinances by (primarily) suburban municipalities to exclude housing that is affordable to lower-income households. A related issue is the persistence of discrimination — racial and otherwise — in land use matters. As a rough generalization, "affordable housing" and other income-related land use issues have been dealt with (if at all) primarily by state courts and legislatures, and other forms of discrimination have been best addressed under federal law although, as you will see, these categories are far from mutually exclusive. Section B will consider these problems of equity in land use from the state law perspective, and then Section C will cover some of the same ground from the federal perspective, and introduce new issues under federal law.

B. EXCLUSIONARY ZONING AND AFFORDABLE HOUSING: STATE LAW

1. THE PROBLEM

The statement of facts which follows is taken from the first *Mount Laurel* case. It describes the conditions which, collectively, have come to be known as "exclusionary zoning." Various techniques for dealing with the problems described by Justice Hall will be set out later in this chapter. (Some details have been omitted from the statement of the facts without noting each omission separately, and some relevant footnote material has been incorporated into the text.) Keep in mind that townships have been given planning and land use powers by statute.

SOUTHERN BURLINGTON COUNTY NAACP v. TOWNSHIP OF MOUNT LAUREL (I)

67 N.J. 151, 336 A.2d 713 (1975)
appeal dismissed & cert. denied, 423 U.S. 808 (1975)

HALL, J.

Mount Laurel is a flat, sprawling township, 22 square miles in area, on the west central edge of Burlington County. It is about seven miles from the boundary line of the city of Camden and not more than 10 miles from the

Benjamin Franklin Bridge crossing the river to Philadelphia. In 1950, the township had a population of 2817, only about 600 more people than it had in 1940. It was then, as it had been for decades, primarily a rural agricultural area with no sizeable settlements or commercial or industrial enterprises. [The court described the growth of the township to a population of 11,221 by 1970. Although 4,121 acres had been zoned for business, only 100 had been developed. There was a small commercial area, but no downtown. The court then described the residential zoning:]

The R-1 zone requires a minimum lot area of 9,375 square feet, minimum lot width of 75 feet at the building line, and a minimum dwelling floor area of 1,100 square feet if a one-story building and 1,300 square feet if one and one-half stories or higher. Most of the subdivisions have been constructed within it so that only a few hundred acres remain. The R-2 zone, comprising a single district of 141 acres in the northeasterly corner, has been completely developed. While it only required a minimum floor area of 900 square feet for a one-story dwelling, the minimum lot size was 11,000 square feet; otherwise the requisites were the same as in the R-1 zone.

The general ordinance places the remainder of the township, outside of the industrial and commercial zones and the R-1D district (to be mentioned shortly), in the R-3 zone. This zone comprises over 7,000 acres — slightly more than half of the total municipal area — practically all of which is located in the central part of the township extending southeasterly to the apex of the triangle. The testimony was that about 4,600 acres of it then remained available for housing development. Ordinance requirements are substantially higher, however, in that the minimum lot size is increased to about one-half acre (20,000 square feet). . . . Lot width at the building line must be 100 feet. Minimum dwelling floor area is as in the R-1 zone. Presently this section is primarily in agricultural use; it contains as well most of the municipality's substandard housing.

[The Court described the R-1D District, which permitted clustering on smaller lots but with overall low density requirements roughly comparable to the R-3 zone. The court then described a procedure to allow planned unit developments within the township that could include multi-family housing, but noted that it was not available to lower income groups. This was also true of housing allowed in a Planned Retirement Zone. The court noted "the lack of action, and indeed hostility, with respect to affording any opportunity for decent housing for the township's own poor living in substandard accommodations." The township had also refused to approve a subsidized, multi-family housing project.]

There cannot be the slightest doubt that the reason for this course of conduct has been to keep down local taxes on property (Mount Laurel is not a high tax municipality) and that the policy was carried out without regard for nonfiscal considerations with respect to people, either within or without its boundaries. This policy of land use regulation for a fiscal end derives from New Jersey's tax structure, which has imposed on local real estate most of the cost of municipal and county government and of the primary and secondary education of the municipality's children. . .

[Justice Hall then noted the postwar exodus of population and jobs from the inner cities, such as Camden, and noted that low-income employees could not reach outlying centers of employment and needed cheaper housing than the suburbs provided.]

NOTES AND QUESTIONS

1. *Some history.* The *Mount Laurel* decision had some important historical background. Nationally, the Supreme Court changed directions in the mid-1970s, and disappointed hopes that it would treat housing as a fundamental right that would demand strict scrutiny of restrictive regulation. *Lindsey v. Normet*, 405 U.S. 56 (1972). In New Jersey, a 5-2 Supreme Court decision about a decade before, upholding a prohibition on mobile homes throughout a township, had drawn a vigorous dissent from Justice Hall. *Vickers v. Gloucester Township*, 181 A.2d 129 (N.J., 1962). Several years later, an influential article documented exclusionary zoning practices in the northern New Jersey suburbs. Williams & Norman, *Exclusionary Land Use Controls: The Case of North-Eastern New Jersey*, 22 Syracuse L. Rev. 475, 486–487 (1971). *Mount Laurel* followed.

2. *Exclusionary effects.* All zoning restrictions have some exclusionary effects. Indeed, the essence of any zoning ordinance is the exclusion of certain uses, densities, and building types from particular districts. But the term "exclusionary zoning" describes local land use controls that exclude most low-income and many moderate-income households from suburban communities and, indirectly, most members of minority groups as well. The generally accepted approach is to define low-income households as earning less than 50% of the regional median income and moderate-income groups as earning between 50-80% of median. To be nonexclusionary, there must be housing opportunities for each group.

The most important land use controls that may have this effect are, of course, zoning regulations, but other land use controls, such as subdivision regulations, may also operate in an exclusionary manner, particularly in combination with a zoning ordinance. Standing alone, each of these regulations may have relatively little impact on the cost of housing. The real issue is whether they have a significant exclusionary effect on housing costs when taken together. It is generally assumed that they do, and some empirical studies support this assumption. See, e.g., L. Sagalyn & G. Sternlieb, Zoning and Housing Costs: The Impact of Land Use Controls on Housing Price (Center for Urban Policy Research, Rutgers Univ. 1972); Pollakowski & Wachter, *The Effects of Land-Use Constraints on Housing Prices,* 66 Land Econ. 31 (1990). One commentator has added that exclusionary zoning segregates the tax base into wealthy suburban and poor urban components, and encourages the concentration of poverty. Dietderich, *An Egalitarian's Market: The Economics of Inclusionary Zoning Reclaimed*, 24 Fordham Urb. L.J. 23, 31–33 (1996).

3. *Redistribution of wealth.* Opponents of exclusionary zoning argue that opening up the suburbs is justified because it positively redistributes wealth to the lower-income households that move to suburban areas, for instance, by providing better housing and better schools. An influential statement of the general argument is A. Downs, Opening Up the Suburbs (1973). Metzger bitterly attacked Downs and other advocates of "deconcentration" strategies, however, contending that such policies (and even the advocacy of such policies) hastens the decline of potentially viable urban neighborhoods and worsens the plight of those left behind. He advocates community reinvestment and other neighborhood revitalization strategies. Metzger, *Planned Abandonment: The Neighborhood Life-Cycle Theory and National Urban Policy,* 11 Hous. Pol. Debate 7 (2000); see also Downs, *Comment on John T. Metzger's "Planned Abandonment: The Neighborhood Life-Cycle Theory and National Urban Policy," id.* at 41 (2000); D. Troutt, *Mount Laurel and Urban Possibility: What Social Science Research Might Tell the Narratives of Futility,* 27 Seton Hall L. Rev. 1471 (1997) (linking Mount Laurel Doctrine to urban revitalization).

4. *Jobs and housing.* The spatial mismatch between jobs and housing has figured prominently in arguments about exclusionary zoning. Early commentators claimed that jobs were in the suburbs, the poor were in the older central cities, public transportation to suburban jobs was nonexistent, and that an end to exclusionary zoning would end these problems. M. Danielson, The Politics of Exclusion 23–24 (1976). See especially Kain, *The Spatial Mismatch Hypothesis: Three Decades Later,* 3 Hous. Pol. Debate 371 (1994).

Today these issues are much more complicated. Locating jobs close to housing is an important strategy in growth management programs, where it figures as a method of improving commuting times, traffic congestion and air quality. See Chapter 7. One study showed, however, that this strategy may not necessarily have these effects but that affordable housing at higher densities would be attractive to low-to medium-income single worker households. See Levine, *Rethinking Accessibility and Jobs-Housing Balance,* 65 J. Am. Plan. Ass'n 133 (1998). But see Arnott, *Economic Theory and the Spatial Mismatch Hypothesis,* 35 Urb. Studies 1171 (1998) (questioning theory and assumption that job dispersal to suburbs causes low rates of employment and wages for African-Americans in inner cities).

5. *Efficiency or monopoly?* Dietderich's analysis, *supra,* turns in significant part on exclusionary zoning as an improper use of a monopoly zoning power. This argument claims that suburbs impose random, arbitrary zoning restrictions on housing markets that impede their ability to meet lower-income housing needs. Does the monopoly argument stand up? One study supported a hypothesis that when fiscal community costs are proportional to the density of development, a community does have an incentive to adopt a zoning monopoly. This incentive decreases in jurisdictions where suburban governments are geographically small because no single jurisdiction can capture the benefits of monopoly zoning power. Hamilton, *Zoning and the Exercise of Monopoly Power,* 5 J. Urb. Econ. 116 (1978). Another study found that towns with monopoly power tend to have higher housing prices, but that there is no evidence they used their power to limit the production of new housing. Thorson, *An Examination of the Monopoly Zoning Hypothesis,* 72 Land Econ. 43 (1996). For an argument that price levels for housing in suburbs are a function of the degree of competition in the local housing market and that this is determined by the extent to which the market erects barriers to entry through land use controls see Landis, *Land Regulation and the Price of New Housing: Lessons From Three California Cities,* 52 J. Am. Plan. Ass'n 9 (1986).

6. *Exclusionary zoning and race.* The litigation against Mount Laurel Township was brought on behalf of minority plaintiffs by the NAACP. There are many more poor white households in New Jersey than there are non-white, even though non-white households are disproportionately poor, creating a risk that white families would dominate any relief efforts, particularly if the number of new affordable units fell far short of the need (as indeed was to be the case). Before too long, the minority community began sounding the alarm. See Holmes, *A Black Perspective on Mount Laurel II: Toward a Black "Fair Share,"* 14 Seton Hall L. Rev. 944 (1984). See also Boger, *Toward Ending Residential Segregation: A Fair Share Proposal for the Next Reconstruction,* 71 N.C. L. Rev. 1573 (1993). In addition, many minority politicians regard the attack on exclusionary zoning as a threat to their hard-won ascendance in urban city halls, seeing a dilution of their constituent base and a diminution of their ability to "bargain" politically for that constituency, as public choice theory would have them do.

2. REDRESSING EXCLUSIONARY ZONING: DIFFERENT APPROACHES

Mount Laurel I.—After reciting the facts set out above, the New Jersey Supreme Court concluded that the Mount Laurel zoning ordinance was unconstitutional. It held that if a "developing community" regulates land uses (as, of course, all developing communities do), it must use its delegated zoning power so as to afford a "realistic opportunity for the construction of its fair share of the present and prospective regional need for low and moderate income housing." The subsequent history of *"Mount Laurel"* is considered below. The social history of the *Mount Laurel* litigation is engagingly told in David L. Kirp et al., Our Town: Race, Housing and the Soul of Suburbia (1995).

The first *Mount Laurel* decision gave no attention to remedies for exclusionary zoning and simply ordered the municipality to comply. In later cases the Court approved weak remedies that inadvertently encouraged municipal intransigence. Finally, in 1980, the Court assembled six appeals that presented a full range of remedial issues, heard four full days of oral argument, and then retired to ponder the problem for more than two years before issuing *Mount Laurel II*. The story is told in Payne, *Housing Rights and Remedies: A "Legislative" History of Mount Laurel II*, 14 Seton Hall L. Rev. 889 (1984). The court helpfully supplied its own summary of the key rulings, which is presented here.

SOUTHERN BURLINGTON COUNTY NAACP v. TOWNSHIP OF MT. LAUREL (II)

92 N.J. 158, 456 A.2d 390 (1983)

The opinion of the Court was delivered by WILENTZ, C.J.:

This is the return, eight years later, of *Southern Burlington County N.A.A.C.P. v. Township of Mount Laurel (Mount Laurel I)*. We set forth in that case, for the first time, the doctrine requiring that municipalities' land use regulations provide a realistic opportunity for low and moderate income housing. The doctrine has become famous. The *Mount Laurel* case itself threatens to become infamous. After all this time, ten years after the trial court's initial order invalidating its zoning ordinance, Mount Laurel remains afflicted with a blatantly exclusionary ordinance. Papered over with studies, rationalized by hired experts, the ordinance at its core is true to nothing but Mount Laurel's determination to exclude the poor. Mount Laurel is not alone; we believe that there is widespread non-compliance with the constitutional mandate of the original opinion in this case. . . .

This case is accompanied by five others, heard together and decided in this opinion. All involve questions arising from the *Mount Laurel* doctrine. They demonstrate the need to put some steel into that doctrine. The deficiencies in its application range from uncertainty and inconsistency at the trial level to inflexible review criteria at the appellate level. The waste of judicial energy involved at every level is substantial and is matched only by the often needless expenditure of talent on the part of lawyers and experts.

. . . .

The following is a summary of the more significant rulings of these cases:

(1) *Every* municipality's land use regulations should provide a realistic opportunity for decent housing for at least some part of its resident poor who now occupy dilapidated housing. The zoning power is no more abused by keeping out the region's poor than by forcing out the resident poor. In other words, each municipality must provide a realistic opportunity for decent housing for its indigenous poor except where they represent a disproportionately large segment of the population as compared with the rest of the region. This is the case in many of our urban areas.

(2) The existence of a municipal obligation to provide a realistic opportunity for a fair share of the region's present and prospective low and moderate income housing need will no longer be determined by whether or not a municipality is "developing." The obligation extends, instead, to every municipality, any portion of which is designated by the State, through the SDGP [the State Development Guide Plan] as a "growth area." This obligation, imposed as a remedial measure, does not extend to those areas where the SDGP discourages growth — namely, open spaces, rural areas, prime farmland, conservation areas, limited growth areas, parts of the Pinelands and certain Coastal Zone areas. The SDGP represents the conscious determination of the State, through the executive and legislative branches, on how best to plan its future. It appropriately serves as a judicial remedial tool. The obligation to encourage lower income housing, therefore, will hereafter depend on rational long-range land use planning (incorporated into the SDGP) rather than upon the sheer economic forces that have dictated whether a municipality is "developing." Moreover, the fact that a municipality is fully developed does not eliminate this obligation although, obviously, it may affect the extent of the obligation and the timing of its satisfaction. The remedial obligation of municipalities that consist of both "growth areas" and other areas may be reduced based on many factors, as compared to a municipality completely within a "growth area."

There shall be a heavy burden on any party seeking to vary the foregoing remedial consequences of the SDGP designations.

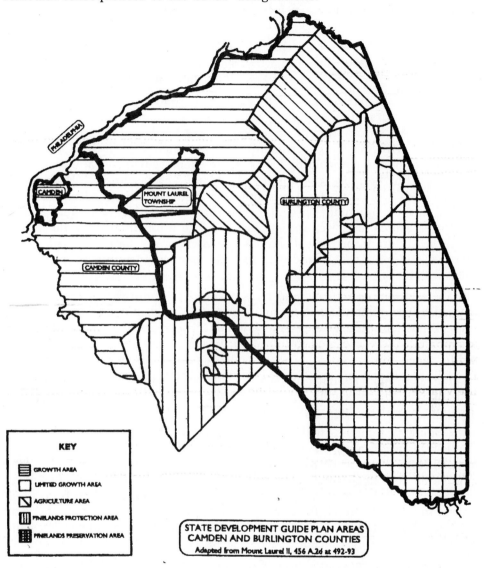

KEY

- GROWTH AREA
- LIMITED GROWTH AREA
- AGRICULTURE AREA
- PINELANDS PROTECTION AREA
- PINELANDS PRESERVATION AREA

STATE DEVELOPMENT GUIDE PLAN AREAS
CAMDEN AND BURLINGTON COUNTIES
Adapted from Mount Laurel II, 456 A.2d at 492-93

(3) *Mount Laurel* litigation will ordinarily include proof of the municipality's fair share of low and moderate income housing in terms of the number of units needed immediately, as well as the number needed for a reasonable period of time in the future. "Numberless" resolution of the issue based upon a conclusion that the ordinance provides a realistic opportunity for *some* low and moderate income housing will be insufficient. Plaintiffs, however, will still be able to prove a *prima facie* case, without proving the precise fair share of the municipality, by proving that the zoning ordinance is substantially affected by restrictive devices, that proof creating a presumption that the ordinance is invalid.

The municipal obligation to provide a realistic opportunity for low and moderate income housing is not satisfied by a good faith attempt. The housing opportunity provided must, in fact, be the substantial equivalent of the fair share.

(4). . . [The court directed that *Mount Laurel* litigation be assigned to a panel of three judges, designated by region. The panel was appointed and served until replaced by legislation adopted later which is discussed *infra*.]

(5) The municipal obligation to provide a realistic opportunity for the construction of its fair share of low and moderate income housing may require more than the elimination of unnecessary cost-producing requirements and restrictions. Affirmative governmental devices should be used to make that opportunity realistic, including lower-income density bonuses and mandatory set-asides. Furthermore, the municipality should cooperate with the developer's attempts to obtain federal subsidies. For instance, where federal subsidies depend on the municipality providing certain municipal tax treatment allowed by state statutes for lower income housing, the municipality should make a good faith effort to provide it. Mobile homes may not be prohibited, unless there is solid proof that sound planning in a particular municipality requires such prohibition.

(6) The lower income regional housing need is comprised of both low and moderate income housing. A municipality's fair share should include both in such proportion as reflects consideration of all relevant factors, including the proportion of low and moderate income housing that make up the regional need.

(7) Providing a realistic opportunity for the construction of least-cost housing will satisfy a municipality's *Mount Laurel* obligation if, and only if, it cannot otherwise be satisfied. . . .

(8) Builder's remedies will be afforded to plaintiffs in *Mount Laurel* litigation where appropriate, on a case-by-case basis. Where the plaintiff has acted in good faith, attempted to obtain relief without litigation, and thereafter vindicates the constitutional obligation in *Mount Laurel*-type litigation, ordinarily a builder's remedy will be granted, provided that the proposed project includes an appropriate portion of low and moderate income housing, and provided further that it is located and designed in accordance with sound zoning and planning concepts, including its environmental impact. . . .

We reassure all concerned that *Mount Laurel* is not designed to sweep away all land use restrictions or leave our open spaces and natural resources prey to speculators. Municipalities consisting largely of conservation, agricultural, or environmentally sensitive areas will not be required to grow because of *Mount Laurel*. No forests or small towns need be paved over and covered with high-rise apartments as a result of today's decision.

As for those municipalities that may have to make adjustments in their lifestyles to provide for their fair share of low and moderate income housing, they should remember that they are not being required to provide more than their *fair* share. No one community need be concerned that it will be radically transformed by a deluge of low and moderate income developments. [The Court held that trial judges could phase new housing over a period of years to avoid too-rapid change.] Nor should any community conclude that its residents will move to other suburbs as a result of this decision, for those "other suburbs" may very well be required to do their part to provide the same housing. Finally, once a community has satisfied its fair share obligation, the *Mount Laurel* doctrine will not restrict other measures, including large-lot and open area zoning, that would maintain its beauty and communal character.

. . . .[A]ny changes brought about by this opinion need not be drastic or destructive. Our scenic and rural areas will remain essentially scenic and rural, and our suburban communities will retain their basic suburban character. But there will be *some* change, as there must be if the constitutional rights of our lower income citizens are ever to be protected. That change will be much less painful for us than the status quo has been for them. . . .

III.

Resolution of the Cases

A. Mount Laurel II

Nothing has really changed since the date of our first opinion, either in Mount Laurel or in its land use regulations. The record indicates that the Township continues to thrive with added industry, some new businesses, and continued growth of middle, upper middle, and upper income housing. As far as lower income housing is concerned, from the date of that opinion to today (as far as the record before us shows) no one has yet constructed one unit of lower income housing — nor has anyone even tried to. Mount Laurel's lower income housing effort has been either a total failure or a total success — depending on its intention. . . .

[Mt. Laurel rezoned only about one-fourth of one percent of its land. The R-5 zone, consisting of 13 acres, allowed multifamily housing at a density of 10 units per acre, but it was surrounded by industrially zoned land and completely unsuitable for residential development. The R-6 zone permitted detached single family residences on relatively small 6,000 square foot lots, but the site had severe environmental constraints and was so small that development of lower income housing would have been prohibitively expensive. The R-7 zone permitted, but did not require, lower income housing in a portion of an already approved PUD and the court found that there were no incentives that would induce the developer to voluntarily relinquish its right to build more profitable market rate housing. The court then held that its fair share study was inaccurate, primarily in its "self-serving" allocation of housing need among the municipalities in the county.]

2. The Builder's Remedy . . .

[Davis Enterprises, which was permitted to intervene as plaintiff in the case, proposed a 535 unit, 107 acre mobile home park for the Township. The lower court awarded Davis a builder's remedy that would allow it to construct its project.]

We affirm the grant of a builder's remedy. It is clearly appropriate in this case under the new standard enunciated in this opinion. First, the Davis

project will provide lower income housing for Mount Laurel. Beside the fact
that mobile homes are generally much less costly than site-built housing, the
trial court's decision requires that Davis construct at least 20 percent of its
units for lower income persons. In addition, the site chosen by Davis is plainly
suited for mobile home development and Mount Laurel has presented no real
evidence to the contrary. Finally, we feel that after ten years of litigation it
is time that something be built for the resident and non-resident lower income
plaintiffs in this case who have borne the brunt of Mount Laurel's unconstitutional policy of exclusion. . . .

NOTES AND QUESTIONS

1. *Remedies. Mount Laurel II* is a case about remedies. Most important was
the decision to encourage the "builder's remedy," which Charles Haar described as "one of the court's bolder and most politically savvy moves." Haar,
Suburbs Under Siege: Race, Space and Audacious Judges 44–45 (1996). The
remedy was especially bold because, as noted in Chapter 3, *infra*, courts do
not usually give specific relief in zoning cases. The builders remedy was
heavily used, see Mallach, *The Tortured Reality of Suburban Exclusion:
Zoning, Economics and the Future of the Berenson Decision*, 4 Pace Envtl. L.
Rev. 37, 119 (1986) (more than 100 builders suits against 70 municipalities
between 1983 and 1986). Adoption of the Fair Housing Act, discussed *infra,*
has displaced the builder's remedy.

2. *Regional need and fair share. Mount Laurel I* had offered virtually no
guidance on how to determine regional need or fair share, and two years later,
in *Oakwood at Madison v. Madison Township,* 371 A.2d 1192 (N.J. 1977), the
court approved a "numberless" approach, leaving litigants to slug it out in
endless trial proceedings. To "put some steel" into the *Mount Laurel* doctrine,
Mount Laurel II reversed course and required the three specially appointed
trial judges to develop an objective methodology that would result in each
municipality knowing, in advance of litigation, exactly what its presumptive
fair share number was. See *AMG Realty Co. v. Warren Township,* 504 A.2d
692 (N.J.L.Div. 1984), defining housing regions, accepting an estimate of
present and prospective housing need, and approving a fair share allocation
formula.

3. *The State Development Guide Plan (SDGP).* Another of *Mount Laurel II's*
bold innovations was to rescue from obscurity a document called the State
Development Guide Plan and use it as the basis for allocating fair share
obligations. In 1986, the legislature mandated the creation of a completely
new State Development and Redevelopment Plan (SDRP), described *infra*,
which has now replaced the older plan as a guide for *Mount Laurel* allocations.

4. *Presumption of validity.* As we have seen elsewhere, courts normally give
substantial deference to governmental decision making in land use matters.
See, e.g., *Krause v. Royal Oak,* reproduced *supra* in Chapter 3. This is what
the *Mount Laurel II* court had to say about the presumption of validity:

> Mount Laurel's actions in this matter, . . . require a modification
> of the rule that attaches presumptive validity to municipal ordinances.
> Its actions not only make such a presumption inappropriate, but, given

the importance of the constitutional obligation, require just the
reverse, namely, that the burden be cast on Mount Laurel to prove
that its ordinances are valid.

What is the relationship between the presumption reversal and the substantive obligations of *Mount Laurel?*

5. *Following New Jersey's lead.* The *Mount Laurel II* opinion is a leading
case without a following. New Hampshire came closer than any other state,
in *Britton v. Town of Chester,* 595 A.2d. 492 (1991), but ultimately it stopped
short. The court held that Chester's ordinance was exclusionary, relying in
part on *Mount Laurel I,* but without delineation of housing regions, explicit
rejection of a numerical fair share, and on statutory rather than constitutional
grounds. It permitted a "builder's remedy," following a conventional rule
followed in some other states, rather than the expansive remedy announced
in *Mount Laurel II.* See the discussion of zoning remedies in Chapter 3, *supra.*
Payne, *From the Courts: Exclusionary Zoning and the "Chester Doctrine",* 20
Real Est. L.J. 366, 370–72 (1992) argues that *Chester* may be an astute
repackaging of *Mount Laurel,* noting that the court relied on an existing state
plan that assigned the town a "fair share" of 90 lower-income units. See
Blaesser, et al., *Advocating Affordable Housing in New Hampshire,* 40 Wash.
U. J. Urb. & Contemp. L. 3, 20 n.50 (1991).

6. *Standing to sue.* New Jersey has taken a liberal approach to standing
to sue, relying in part on a statute granting standing in land use cases to
nonresidents, N.J. Stat. Ann. § 40:55D-4. The court has at various times
granted standing to a trade organization, "the public," represented by the New
Jersey Public Advocate, and several advocacy organizations. It found they had
"a sufficient stake and real adversariness" to achieve "individual justice, along
with the public interest," without "procedural frustrations." See, e.g., *Home
Bldrs. League v. Township of Berlin,* 405 A.2d 381, 384 (N.J. 1979), *Urban
League v. Mayor & Council,* 359 A.2d 526 (N.J. Ch. Div. 1977); *Urban League
v. Township of Mahwah,* 370 A.2d 521 (N.J. App. Div. 1977). New York has
also granted standing to a wide variety of individuals and groups. See *Suffolk
Hous. Serv. v. Town of Brookhaven,* 397 N.Y.S.2d 302 (Sup. Ct.), *aff'd as
modified,* 405 N.Y.S.2d 302 (App. Div. 1978).

A NOTE ON POLICY AND PLANNING ISSUES

The constitutional basis for Mount Laurel II.—Art. I, par. 1, of the New
Jersey Constitution, in language similar to most state constitutions, provides
that "All persons are by nature free and independent, and have certain natural
and unalienable rights, among which are those of enjoying and defending life
and liberty, *of acquiring, possessing, and protecting property,* and of pursuing
and obtaining safety and happiness." (Emphasis added.) The *Mount Laurel
I* court reasoned that this provision guarantees substantive due process and
equal protection of the laws, and operates as a restriction on the police power
of the state to legislate.

However, the court in *Mount Laurel II* accomplished a major shift from the
passive remedies of *Mount Laurel I* to the mandatory use of inclusionary
zoning. Professor Payne has suggested three justifications for the shift: that

affirmative remedies were necessary to undo past discrimination, that the state's monopoly over control of land imposes an obligation of fairness on it, and that individuals have a "right to shelter" that gives them a claim to public assistance. See Payne, *Reconstructing the Constitutional Theory of* Mount Laurel II, 3 Wash. U. J.L. & Policy 555 (2000). The first justification is inconsistent with the requirement that *all* municipalities implement the *Mount Laurel* doctrine, the second is plausible but doesn't distinguish land use controls from the many other fields in which regulation interferes with the private market, leaving the third, which adequately explains the case even if it flies in the face of conventional wisdom about social welfare rights.

The state plan.—Partly in response to the *Mount Laurel II* decision, the legislature adopted a State Planning Act authorizing a State Planning Commission to prepare a new State Development and Redevelopment Plan (SDRP). N.J. Stat. Ann. §§ 52:18A-196 to 52:18A-207. The Plan is to provide a coordinated, integrated and comprehensive plan for the growth, development, renewal and conservation of the State and its regions and which shall identify areas for growth, agriculture, open space conservation and other appropriate designations. § 52:18A-199(a). The SDRP, adopted in the early 1990s after an extensive "cross acceptance" process of negotiation with local communities, adopts a weak form of Oregon's growth boundary approach, see Chapter 7, *infra*, by encouraging higher density growth where development and infrastructure already exist and setting aside extensive agricultural and conservation areas, but also permitting new centers of compact growth in rural areas. See Payne, *General Welfare and Regional Planning: How the Law of Unintended Consequences Gave New Jersey a Modern State Plan*, 73 St. John's L. Rev. 1103, 1117–21 (1999). How are these policies, if followed (compliance with the Plan is not mandatory), likely to affect the *Mount Laurel* process, which has relied so heavily on large-scale inclusionary developments?

Growth share.—Could the *Mount Laurel* process be simplified? One way is to adopt a flat 10% affordable housing obligation, eliminating the need for complex "fair share" calculations. Another, described as "growth share," would permit municipalities to establish whatever growth (or no-growth) policies they choose, subject only to whatever constraints are imposed on them by general state planning statutes or other sources of law. Then, periodically, actual growth (both residential and nonresidential) would be measured and the municipality's "fair share" would be calculated as some "share" of what had actually occurred. Since both growth and the growth share would be known at all times, the municipality would be expected to comply with *Mount Laurel* as it went along, or suffer serious restrictions on future growth until the deficit was made up. This idea is explored in Payne, *Rethinking Fair Share*, 16 Real Est. L.J. 20 (1987) and *id.*, *Remedies for Affordable Housing: From Fair Share to Growth Share*, 49 Land Use & Zon. L. Dig. No. 6 at 3 (1997).

Sources.—Additional commentary on *Mount Laurel II* includes Anglin, *Searching for Justice: Court-Inspired Housing Policy as a Mechanism for Social and Economic Mobility,* 29 Urb. Aff. Quarterly 432 (1994) (negative appraisal); Mount Laurel Housing Symposium, 27 Seton Hall L. Rev. 1268 (1997); Patrick, Gilbert & Wheeler, *Trading the Poor: Intermunicipal Housing Negotiation in New Jersey,* 2 Harv. Negotiation L. Rev. 1 (1997)

A NOTE ON EXCLUSIONARY ZONING DECISIONS IN OTHER STATES

Pennsylvania.—Nationally, the first significant limitation on exclusionary land use practices came in *National Land & Investment Co., Inc. v. Kohn*, 215 A.2d 597 (Pa. 1965), which held invalid a four-acre minimum lot size requirement. See also *Appeal of Kit-Mar Builders*, 268 A.2d 765 (Pa. 1970) (same, 2–3 acre zoning). Five years later, the same court held in *Appeal of Girsch*, 263 A.2d 395 (Pa. 1970), every municipality must zone at least some of its land for multi-family dwellings. In the middle 1970s, the Pennsylvania Supreme Court seemed to be aligning itself with the "fair share" approach to lower income housing that was evolving next door in New Jersey, see *Township of Williston v. Chesterdale Farms*, 341 A.2d 466 (Pa. 1975), but in *Surrick v. Zoning Hearing Board*, 382 A.2d 105 (Pa. 1977), the Court reduced any "fair share" concept to the status of a non-binding "general precept."

Finally, in *BAC, Inc. v. Millcreek Township*, 633 A.2d 144, 147 (Pa. 1993), the Court held that only restrictions on uses of property, not classes of people, were covered by the Pennsylvania rules. It concluded that the unmet needs of lower-income households in the community were irrelevant to whether adequate provision for mobile homes had been made. The *BAC* case would seem to erode the modest holding of *Fernley v. Board of Supervisors*, 502 A.2d 585 (Pa. 1985), which held invalid a total exclusion of multi-family housing, placing it squarely on "use" rather than "user" grounds. For an evaluation of the Pennsylvania cases prior to *Fernley* that questions the simplicity of the Pennsylvania rules see Hyson, *Pennsylvania Exclusionary Zoning Law: A Simple Alternative to Mount Laurel II?*, 36 Land Use L. & Zoning Dig., No. 9, at 3 (1984).

New York.—In 1975, the same year as New Jersey's *Mount Laurel I* and Pennsylvania's *Williston* decisions, New York jumped into the fray with *Berenson v. Town of New Castle*, 341 N.E.2d 236 (N.Y. 1975), involving a total exclusion of multiple dwelling units. Denying the Town's motion for summary judgment, the Court of Appeals established a two-part test that the municipality would have to satisfy in order to prevail:

> The first branch of the test, then, is simply whether the board has provided a properly balanced and well ordered plan for the community. . . . Secondly, in enacting a zoning ordinance, consideration must be given to regional needs and requirements. . . . [New Castle may have enough multi-family units to satisfy its present and future population, but] residents of [surrounding] Westchester County, as well as the larger New York City metropolitan region, may be searching for multiple-family housing in the area to be near their employment or for a variety of other social and economic reasons. There must be a balancing of the local desire to maintain the status quo within the community and the greater public interest that regional needs be met. [*Id.* at 249.]

Although the New York court has never expressly repudiated the more adventurous implications of *Berenson*, neither has it found an opportunity to pursue them. The *New Castle* case itself was resolved without building low income housing. See *Blitz v. Town of New Castle*, 463 N.Y.S.2d 832 (1983). Subsequently, in *Suffolk Housing Services v. Town of Brookhaven*, 511 N.E.2d 67 (N.Y. 1987), brought by a low-income advocacy organization specifically to test the implications of *Berenson*, the Court of Appeals denied relief, emphasizing that no identified lower-income households had been shown to have been denied housing, and expressing concern that to order a broad rezoning of the Town would be to invade the province of the legislature. In effect, the court limited *Berenson* to site-specific challenges brought by developers. See also *Asian Americans for Equality v. Koch,* 527 N.E.2d 265 (N.Y. 1988) (no *Berenson* issue in claim that a special New York City zoning district adopted for Chinatown would displace lower-income housing, because lower-income housing was available elsewhere in the entire city). For a contemporaneous comment on the New York cases, see Mallach, *The Tortured Reality of Suburban Exclusion: Zoning, Economics and the Future of the Berenson Doctrine,* 4 Pace Envtl. L. Rev. 37 (1986).

3.   AFFORDABLE HOUSING LEGISLATION

a.   The New Jersey Fair Housing Act

The Fair Housing Act of 1985, N.J. Stat. §§ 52:27D-301 *et seq.* was adopted as a legislative response to *Mount Laurel II*. The Act explicitly confirms the "fair share" concept as legislative policy, but provides new procedures. A state agency was established, the Council on Affordable Housing (COAH), with "primary jurisdiction for the administration of housing obligations in accordance with sound regional planning considerations." *Id.* § 304. Before being sued by a developer seeking a builder's remedy, a municipality can voluntarily present a *Mount Laurel* compliance plan to COAH and, if COAH finds that the plan "make[s] the achievement of the municipality's fair share of low and moderate income housing realistically possible," it can grant "substantive certification." *Id.* §§ 313, 314. If there is objection to the plan, a "mediation and review process" is provided for, rather than litigation. *Id.* § 315. Once "substantively certified," a municipality's fair share plan is presumed constitutional if there is subsequent litigation, rebuttable only on a "clear and convincing evidence" standard. The New Jersey Supreme Court held the Act constitutional in *Hills Dev. Co. v. Township of Bernards,* 510 A.2d 621 (N.J. 1986).

The Act contained one novel feature, authorization for "regional contribution agreements," or RCAs. Over 100 million dollars has been transferred through RCAs, and one commentator endorses them as an effective and practical means of distributing regional expenses. Poindexter, *Towards a Legal Framework for Regional Redistribution of Poverty-Related Expenses*, 47 Wash. U. J. Urb. & Contemp. L. 3 (1995). But see McDougall, *Regional Contribution Agreements: Compensation for Exclusionary Zoning,* 60 Temple L.Q. 665 (1987) ("regional contribution agreements" may well prove ineffective in correcting inequities as between suburbs and central cities).

There has been surprisingly little systematic study of the actual results of *Mount Laurel II* and the New Jersey Fair Housing Act. Earlier work is summarized in Payne, *Norman Williams, Exclusionary Zoning and the Mount*

Laurel Doctrine: Making the Theory Fit the Facts, 20 Vt. L. Rev. 665, 669–673 (1996). After roughly ten years of implementation of *Mount Laurel II*, it was estimated that about 13,500 low and moderate income housing units had been constructed or rehabilitated, a number which has continued to grow. A more recent study focuses on the occupants of *Mount Laurel* housing, rather than on the number of units. See Wish & Eisdorfer, *The Impact of Mount Laurel Initiatives: An Analysis of Applicants and Occupants*, 27 Seton Hall L. Rev. 1268 (1997). They concluded that most of the beneficiaries of the *Mount Laurel* process already lived in the suburbs, that whites were more successful than minorities in obtaining a *Mount Laurel* unit, and that in order to obtain a unit, some minority households relocated from a suburb to an urban location.

b. Housing Elements in Comprehensive Plans

Half the states have legislation requiring a housing element in comprehensive plans. See, e.g., Conn. Gen. Stat. § 8-23; Fla. Stat. Ann. § 163.3177(6); N.Y. Town Law § 277-a(3)(h); R.I. Gen. Laws § 45-22.2-6(C); Vt. Stat. Ann. tit. 24, § 4302(C)(11). Some of these statutes are brief and may only require provision for the housing needs of their residents. See the Pennsylvania planning law reproduced *supra* in Chapter 1. Housing elements in comprehensive plans are especially helpful in states that require land use controls to be consistent with the comprehensive plan.

California.—The California legislation is an example of statutory direction for a detailed housing element. See Cal. Gov't Code §§ 65580-65589.8. The housing element must include—

— an "assessment of housing needs, including 'the locality's share of the regional housing need,' and an inventory of resources and constraints relevant to the meeting of these needs."

— an analysis of "potential and actual government constraints" on "development of housing for all income levels, including land use controls";

— an analysis of the "availability of financing, the price of land, and the cost of construction";

— a five-year housing program which must identify "adequate sites which will be made available through appropriate zoning and development standards and with public services and facilities needed" for "the development of a variety of types of housing for all income levels" and must "[a]ddress and, where appropriate and legally possible, remove governmental constraints to the . . . development of housing."

— the zoning of "sufficient vacant land for residential use with appropriate standards . . . to meet housing needs as identified in the general plan," *Id.* § 65913.1.

Local governments submit their comprehensive plans, including the housing element, to the state Department of Housing and Community Development (HCD), which reviews it for compliance with the statute. *Id.* § 65585. However, a local government may adopt a housing element despite HCD's objections if it makes findings that the element is in compliance. *Id.* § 65583(f)(2). HCD has no powers of enforcement, and this has limited the effectiveness of the statute. Enforcement is through private litigation, which can be effective because the statute authorizes a hold on the issuance of building permits until an approved housing element is produced. *Id.* § 65587.

The issue in litigation is whether there has been substantial compliance with the statute; the court does not consider the merits of the plan. The usual presumptions would seem to protect most plans. See *Hernandez v. City of Encinitas,* 33 Cal. Rptr. 2d 875 (Cal. App. 1994) (rejecting plaintiff's argument as an attack on the merits where housing element appeared to contain all statutorily required elements). Note how this decision confers considerable discretion on the local government in deciding how to comply with the statute. Even so, the threat of litigation has encouraged local governments to adopt inclusionary housing programs, discussed *infra.*

In an important exception, the provision of the law requiring identification of "adequate" sites can be judicially enforced if the court finds that the sites provided do not meet statutory requirements. *Hoffmaster v. City of San Diego,* 64 Cal. Rptr. 2d 684 (Cal. App. 1997) (sites not "adequate" because development standards constrained their potential for development).

What remedies are available to a developer if sites are adequately specified? Recall from Chapter 3 that most courts will not require the rezoning of land to a more intensive use to comply with the policies in a comprehensive plan. Does this rule apply to the "adequate sites" policy? Would it help if the statute required the housing element to designate "a sufficient supply of sites in the housing element that will be zoned at densities that may accommodate low- and moderate-income housing," as required by a proposed model law? See American Planning Association, Growing Smart Legislative Guidebook: Model Statutes for Planning and the Management of Change § 4-208.9 (Interim Ed. 1998). The American Planning Association model provides for review with powers of enforcement by a state or regional agency.

For an article suggesting statutory changes in the California law see Comment, *Building Houses From the Ground Up: Strengthening California Law to Ensure Adequate Locations for Affordable Housing,* 39 Santa Clara L. Rev. 503 (1999). See also Landis & LeGates, Housing Planning and Policy in the Practice of Local Government Planning ch. 10 (C. Hoch, L. Dalton & F. So eds., 3d ed. 2000); Calavita *et al., Inclusionary Housing in California and New Jersey: A Comparative Analysis,* 8 Hous. Pol. Debate 109 (1997). Oregon has affordable housing legislation in its state land use program, which is discussed in Chapter 7, *infra.*

c. Inclusionary Zoning

The "mandatory set-aside" referred to by the *Mount Laurel* court is a form of "inclusionary zoning." The New Jersey court did not invent this technique, but by endorsing it and insuring that it would be widely used under court order, *Mount Laurel II* stimulated wider use elsewhere. See, e.g., Cal. Gov't Code §§ 65915, 65915.5; Md. Ann. Code Art. 66B, §12.01; N.H. Rev. Stat. §674:21; N.Y. Town Law §261-b. The premise of inclusionary zoning is simple: in exchange for a profitable increase in allowable density of residential development, the builder is required to "set aside" a portion of the units to be sold or rented to low-and moderate-income households with deed restrictions requiring controlled, "affordable" prices for a period of years. The ordinance can also relax site development requirements, provide for the provision of affordable housing off-site or in-lieu cash payments, and it may give a public agency an option to purchase units to operate as "public housing." *Mount Laurel II* held that a "minimum" of 20% of the units had to be "affordable" for the project to be considered "inclusionary." It is generally agreed that inclusionary zoning programs must be mandatory to work under most circumstances. The most comprehensive discussion of these programs is A. Mallach, Inclusionary Housing Programs: Policies and Practices (1984). See also Note, *Breaking the Exclusionary Land Use Regulation Barrier: Policies to Promote Affordable Housing in the Suburbs,* 82 Geo. L.J. 2039 (1994).

An early Virginia case invalidated a mandatory set-aside ordinance as "socio-economic zoning," *Board of Supvrs. v. DeGroff Enters.,* 198 S.E.2d 600 (Va. 1973), but the New Jersey court disagreed in *Mount Laurel II:*

> It is nonsense to single out inclusionary zoning (providing a realistic opportunity for the construction of lower income housing) and label it "socio-economic" if that is meant to imply that other aspects of zoning are not. It would be ironic if inclusionary zoning to encourage the construction of lower income housing were ruled beyond the power of a municipality because it is "socio-economic" when its need has arisen from the socio-economic zoning of the past that excluded it. [456 A.2d at 449.]

Reconsider large lot zoning, which was discussed in Chapter 3, *supra.* Is that proper or improper "socioeconomic" zoning?

Another method of obtaining affordable housing is to charge a housing "linkage" fee on new development. The New Jersey Supreme Court has also held that mandatory development fees for affordable housing imposed on commercial and non-inclusionary residential development are authorized by the Fair Housing Act and the zoning enabling act. *Holmdel Bldrs. Ass'n v. Township of Holmdel,* 583 A.2d 277 (N.J. 1990). Because this is an exaction, it raises a different set of problems, discussed in Chapter 6, *infra.*

Inclusionary housing programs have been adopted in a number of communities and are reviewed in Calavita & Grimes, *Inclusionary Housing in California: The Experience of Two Decades,* 64 J. Am. Plan. Ass'n 159 (1998) (reporting 24,000 units built). Swope, *The Little House in the Suburbs,* Governing, Vol. 13, No. 7, at 18 (2000), reports a successful program in Montgomery County, Maryland, that has produced 10,000 affordable dwellings. The program requires 15% of all homes in every development to be affordable and provides a 20% density bonus to developers. The article reports that affordable dwellings must be scattered throughout each development and are not distinguishable from other units. See also Padilla, *Reflections on Inclusionary Zoning and a Renewed Look at its Viability,* 23 Hofstra L. Rev. 539 (1995).

A dated critique of inclusionary zoning argued that inclusionary zoning is an "irony" because it provides very few "winners," while inefficiently raising housing prices everywhere else in the community, which makes it even more impossible for the far larger group of low-income "losers" to find affordable shelter. Ellickson, *The Irony of Inclusionary Zoning*, 54 S. Cal. L. Rev. 1167 (1981). For a convincing rebuttal of this argument see the article by Diet-derich, *supra. See also* M. Morris, Incentive Zoning: Meeting Urban Design and Affordable Housing Objectives Pt. 3, American Planning Association, Planning Advisory Rep. No. 494 (2000).

d. Housing Appeals Boards

A few New England states have experimented with housing appeals boards as a technique for providing affordable housing. A Connecticut statute permits direct appeals to specially designated trial judges if affordable housing is denied or approved with restrictions that have a substantial adverse impact on its viability or affordability. The municipality must justify its decision and has the burden to show that:

> (A) the decision from which such appeal is taken and the reasons cited for such decision are supported by sufficient evidence in the record; (B) the decision is necessary to protect substantial public interests in health, safety, or other matters which the commission may legally consider; (C) such public interests clearly outweigh the need for affordable housing; and (D) such public interests cannot be protected by reasonable changes to the affordable housing development. [Conn. Gen. Stat. § 8-30g(c).]

In *West Hartford Interfaith Coalition, Inc. v. Town of West Hartford*, 636 A.2d 1342 (1994), a case of first impression, the court gave the statute a sympathetic reading. It held that under the statute, the trial court could order a requested zone change and approve a special development district designation. Later decisions held that a court can approve an affordable housing application even though it does not comply with local zoning, *Wisniowski v. Planning Comm'n*, 655 A.2d 1146 (Conn. 1995), and that traffic and environmental problems did not justify denial of an affordable housing application, *Kaufman v. Zoning Comm'n*, 653 A.2d 798 (Conn. 1995).

However, *Christian Activities Council, Congregational v. Town of Glastonbury*, 735 A.2d 231 (1999), upheld the town's denial of an affordable housing developer's application to rezone based on the need to preserve open space. The court rejected the plaintiff's claim that a "preponderance of the evidence" standard should be used, accepting instead a weaker "sufficiency of the evidence" approach derived from traditional land use cases. It also held that in striking the balance required by paragraph (C) quoted above, the focus should be on the *local* need for affordable housing, rather than a regional or statewide need. The dissenting justice lamented that the majority opinion "rips the soul out of affordable housing in Connecticut." Do you see why? As of this writing, the Connecticut statute is under review. For discussion of experience under the law see Vodola, *Connecticut's Affordable Housing Appeals Procedure Law in Practice,* 29 Conn. L. Rev. 1235 (1997).

Rhode Island has a similar law that provides for an appeal to a state appeals board. R.I. Gen. Laws § 45-53-1 to 45-53-8. See *Curran v. Church Community Hous. Corp.*, 672 A.2d 453 (R.I. 1996) (upholding grant of approval). A pioneering Massachusetts law, Mass. Gen. L. ch. 40B (1969), serves as a model for Rhode Island and Connecticut, but has a somewhat different set of criteria for review and applies only to government-subsidized dwellings. All three statutes (plus New Jersey) are surveyed, with data, in Symposium: *Increasing Affordable Housing and Regional Housing Opportunities in New England,* 23 W. New Eng. L. Rev. (Mar. 2001).

C. EXCLUSIONARY ZONING LITIGATION IN THE FEDERAL COURTS

1. FEDERAL "STANDING" RULES

It is now clear that the only private plaintiffs who have standing to challenge allegedly exclusionary land use control in federal court are developers of subsidized housing seeking site-specific relief from zoning and/or other land use restrictions. Any broad challenge by civil rights organizations or low-income housing sponsors on the ground that the general, overall effect of the land use restrictions is exclusionary is practically foreclosed by the decision of the United States Supreme Court in *Warth v. Seldin,* 422 U.S. 490 (1975).

In *Warth,* suit was brought in Federal District Court against Penfield, a suburb of Rochester, New York, alleging that its zoning ordinance, by its terms and as enforced, effectively excluded persons of low and moderate income from living in the town, in violation of petitioners' constitutional rights and of 42 U.S.C. §§ 1981, 1982, and 1983. Plaintiffs and intervenors included local housing advocacy groups, individual Rochester taxpayers, several Rochester area residents with low or moderate incomes who are also members of minority racial or ethnic groups, and the Rochester Home Builders Association. The Supreme Court affirmed holdings below that none of these parties had standing under Article III's "case and controversy" doctrine.

The taxpayers and advocacy groups were denied standing on prudential grounds, in that they suffered little or no direct injury and thus were within the "normal" rule barring third party standing to assert the rights of others. The builder's organization lacked standing because it also suffered no injury, and the possible injury to its members would be peculiar to each case, requiring in effect that an actual builder with an actual project be in court before a claim could be evaluated. Why might a developer, even one with a relatively strong claim, prefer to have the Builder's Association conduct the litigation? Might there be a "free rider" problem in going it alone?

Given the Court's reluctance to let third parties, even those with some stake in the outcome, represent the interests of the lower income persons with the primary constitutional and statutory claims, the most surprising aspect of *Warth* is its holding that these plaintiffs also lacked standing. Their problem, the Court held, was that they might not actually benefit from a revision of Penfield's ordinance, because they still might not find or be able to afford a home or apartment in Penfield. Justice Powell described one plaintiff, Ms. Reyes, who earned $14,000 per year, which put her over the eligibility limit for a subsidized development that Penfield had turned down. "There is no indication that in nonsubsidized projects, removal of the challenged zoning restrictions—in 1971—would have reduced the price on new single-family residences to a level that petitioner Reyes thought she could afford." 422 U.S. at 507, n.17. Inclusionary zoning is not mentioned in *Warth*. Especially after *Mount Laurel II,* how might Ms. Reyes have answered Justice Powell's disposition of her standing claim? For commentary on *Warth v. Seldin,* see Note, *Alternatives to Warth v. Seldin: The Potential Resident Challenger of an Exclusionary Zoning Scheme,* 11 Urb. L. Ann. 223 (1976). See also *Hope, Inc. v. County of DuPage,* 738 F.2d 797 (7th Cir. 1984) (denying standing to nonresident individuals and a low-cost housing sponsor who had not formulated a concrete, site-specific low-cost housing project).

Where a federal statute expressly authorizes the United States to bring a particular kind of action, see, e.g., *U.S. v. Luebke,* 345 F. Supp. 179 (D.Colo. 1972) (Civil Rights Act of 1968), it is clear, of course, that the United States has standing. The Court has also indicated that "private attorneys general" provisions in such a statute merit generous interpretation with respect to the standing of individuals. See *Trafficante v. Metropolitan Life Ins. Co.,* 409 U.S. 205 (1972) (standing of white tenants in development that allegedly discriminated against minorities).

2. THE FEDERAL COURT FOCUS ON RACIAL DISCRIMINATION

a. The Constitution

Zoning is "state action," but federal constitutional doctrine is not hospitable to the economic discrimination theory used in *Mount Laurel II,* see *San Antonio Independent School District v. Rodriguez,* 411 U.S. 1 (1973), nor to housing as a "fundamental right," see *Lindsey v. Normet,* 405 U.S. 56 (1972). Where exclusionary zoning claims have been successful in the federal courts it has been on the theory that restrictive land use controls violate equal protection by indirectly discriminating against blacks and other minorities by excluding low-income and moderate-income households from the suburbs.

The first barrier to implementing this approach originates in *Washington v. Davis,* 426 U.S. 229 (1976), an employment discrimination case where the Court held that proof of discriminatory intent is essential to the success of a racial discrimination claim under the Fourteenth Amendment. In the course of its opinion, the Court said:

> [V]arious Courts of Appeals have held in several contexts . . . that the substantially disproportionate impact of a statute or official practice standing alone and without regard to discriminatory purpose, suffices to prove racial discrimination violating the Equal Protection Clause absent some justification going substantially beyond what would be necessary to validate most other legislative classifications. . . . [T]o the extent that those cases rested on or expressed the view that proof of discriminatory racial purpose is unnecessary in making out an equal protection violation, we are in disagreement. [*Id.* at 244–45.]

In a footnote to this passage the Court cited, among other cases, the Seventh Circuit decision in *Arlington Heights*, an exclusionary zoning case in which it had recently granted certiorari. With this daunting preview, counsel for the low income housing developer then tried to convince the Court that Arlington Heights' disapproval of a subsidized, racially integrated housing development was racially motivated.

VILLAGE OF ARLINGTON HEIGHTS v. METROPOLITAN HOUSING DEVELOPMENT CORP.

429 U.S. 252 (1977)

JUSTICE POWELL delivered the opinion of the Court

In 1971 respondent Metropolitan Housing Development Corporation (MHDC) applied to petitioner, the Village of Arlington Heights, Ill., for the rezoning of a 15-acre parcel from single-family to multiple-family classification. Using federal financial assistance, MHDC planned to build 190 clustered townhouse units for low and moderate income tenants. The Village denied the rezoning request. [MHDC, joined by other plaintiffs, sued in district court. The court found for the village after a bench trial, and the plaintiffs appealed. The Seventh Circuit reversed, finding that the "ultimate effect" of the denial was racially discriminatory and a violation of the Fourteenth Amendment.]

I

Arlington Heights is a suburb of Chicago, located about 26 miles northwest of the downtown Loop area. Most of the land in Arlington Heights is zoned for detached single-family homes, and this is in fact the prevailing land use. The Village experienced substantial growth during the 1960s, but, like other communities in northwest Cook County, its population of racial minority groups remained quite low. According to the 1970 census, only 27 of the Village's 64,000 residents were black.

The Clerics of St. Viator, a religious order (the Order), own an 80-acre parcel just east of the center of Arlington Heights. Part of the site is occupied by the Viatorian high school, and part by the Order's three-story novitiate building, which houses dormitories and a Montessori school. Much of the site, however, remains vacant. Since 1959, when the Village first adopted a zoning ordinance, all the land surrounding the Viatorian property has been zoned R-3, a single-family specification with relatively small minimum lot size requirements. On three sides of the Viatorian land there are single-family homes just across a street; to the east the Viatorian property directly adjoins the back yards of other single-family homes. . . . [MHDC and the Order entered into a 99-year lease and contract of sale covering a 15-acre site in the southeast corner of the Viatorian property, contingent upon obtaining zoning clearances from the Village and § 236 housing assistance from the federal government.]

MHDC engaged an architect and proceeded with the project, to be known as Lincoln Green. The plans called for 20 two-story buildings with a total of

190 units, each unit having its own private entrance from outside. One hundred of the units would have a single bedroom, thought likely to attract elderly citizens. The remainder would have two, three or four bedrooms. A large portion of the site would remain open, with shrubs and trees to screen the homes abutting the property to the east. . . .MHDC consulted with the Village staff for preliminary review of the development. The parties have stipulated that every change recommended during such consultations was incorporated into the plans.

During the Spring of 1971, the Plan Commission considered the proposal at a series of three public meetings, which drew large crowds. Although many of those attending were quite vocal and demonstrative in opposition to Lincoln Green, a number of individuals and representatives of community groups spoke in support of rezoning. Some of the comments, both from opponents and supporters, addressed what was referred to as the "social issue" — the desirability or undesirability of introducing at this location in Arlington Heights low and moderate income housing, housing that would probably be racially integrated.

Many of the opponents, however, focused on the zoning aspects of the petition, stressing two arguments. First, the area always had been zoned single-family, and the neighboring citizens had built or purchased there in reliance on that classification. Rezoning [to R-5] threatened to cause a measurable drop in property value for neighboring sites. Second, the Village's apartment policy, adopted by the Village Board in 1962 and amended in 1970, called for R-5 zoning primarily to serve as a buffer between single-family development and land uses thought incompatible, such as commercial or manufacturing districts. Lincoln Green did not meet this requirement, as it adjoined no commercial or manufacturing district.

At the close of the third meeting, the Plan Commission adopted a motion to recommend to the Village's Board of Trustees that it deny the request. The motion stated: "While the need for low and moderate income housing may exist in Arlington Heights or its environs, the Plan Commission would be derelict in recommending it at the proposed location." Two members voted against the motion and submitted a minority report, stressing that in their view the change to accommodate Lincoln Green represented "good zoning." The Village Board. . .denied the rezoning by a 6-1 vote. . . .

A divided Court of Appeals reversed [a holding in favor of the village]. It first approved the District Court's finding that the defendants were motivated by a concern for the integrity of the zoning plan, rather than by racial discrimination. Deciding whether their refusal to rezone would have discriminatory effects was more complex. The court observed that the refusal would have a disproportionate impact on blacks. Based upon family income, blacks constituted 40% of those Chicago area residents who were eligible to become tenants of Lincoln Green, although they comprised a far lower percentage of total area population. The court reasoned, however, that under our decision in *James v. Valtierra,* 402 U.S. 137 (1971), such a disparity in racial impact alone does not call for strict scrutiny of a municipality's decision that prevents the construction of the low-cost housing.

There was another level to the court's analysis of allegedly discriminatory results. Invoking language from *Kennedy Park Homes Association v. City of Lackawanna,* 436 F.2d 108, 112 (C.A.2 1970), *cert. denied,* 401 U.S. 1010 (1970), the Court of Appeals ruled that the denial of rezoning must be examined in light of its "historical context and ultimate effect."[6] Northwest Cook County was enjoying rapid growth in employment opportunities and population, but it continued to exhibit a high degree of residential segregation. The court held that Arlington Heights could not simply ignore this problem. Indeed, it found that the Village had been "exploiting" the situation by allowing itself to become a nearly all white community. The Village had no other current plans for building low and moderate income housing, and no other R-5 parcels in the Village were available to MHDC at an economically feasible price.

Against this background, the Court of Appeals ruled that the denial of the Lincoln Green proposal had racially discriminatory effects and could be tolerated only if it served compelling interests. Neither the buffer policy nor the desire to protect property values met this exacting standard. The court therefore concluded that the denial violated the Equal Protection Clause of the Fourteenth Amendment.

II

At the outset, petitioners challenge the respondents' standing to bring the suit. It is not clear that this challenge was pressed in the Court of Appeals, but since our jurisdiction to decide the case is implicated, we shall consider it. . . .

A

[The Court held that MHDC had standing because its proposed project was "detailed and specific." Even though the contingent nature of its lease spared it from major economic loss, it had expended a considerable amount of money pursuing its application, and it had also suffered non-economic harm to its social objectives.]

B

Clearly MHDC has met the constitutional requirements and it therefore has standing to assert its own rights. Foremost among them is MHDC's right to be free of arbitrary or irrational zoning actions. [Citing *Euclid, Nectow and Belle Terre.*] But the heart of this litigation has never been the claim that the Village's decision fails the generous *Euclid* test, recently reaffirmed in *Belle Terre.* Instead it has been the claim that the Village's refusal to rezone discriminates against racial minorities in violation of the Fourteenth Amendment. As a corporation, MHDC has no racial identity and cannot be the direct target of the petitioners' alleged discrimination. In the ordinary case, a party is denied standing to assert the rights of third persons. *Warth v. Seldin,* 422

---

[6] This language apparently derived from our decision in *Reitman v. Mulkey,* 387 U.S. 369, 373 (1967) (quoting from the opinion of the California Supreme Court in the case then under review).

U.S., at 499. But we need not decide whether the circumstances of this case would justify departure from that prudential limitation and permit MHDC to assert the constitutional rights of its prospective minority tenants. For we have at least one individual plaintiff who has demonstrated standing to assert these rights as his own.[9]

Respondent Ransom, a Negro, works at the Honeywell factory in Arlington Heights and lives approximately 20 miles away in Evanston in a 5-room house with his mother and his son. The complaint alleged that he seeks and would qualify for the housing MHDC wants to build in Arlington Heights. Ransom testified at trial that if Lincoln Green were built he would probably move there, since it is closer to his job.

The injury Ransom asserts is that his quest for housing nearer his employment has been thwarted by official action that is racially discriminatory. If a court grants the relief he seeks, there is at least a "substantial probability," *Warth v. Seldin,* 422 U.S., at 504, that the Lincoln Green project will materialize, affording Ransom the housing opportunity he desires in Arlington Heights. His is not a generalized grievance. Instead, as we suggested in *Warth, id.,* at 507, 508 n.18, it focuses on a particular project and is not dependent on speculation about the possible actions of third parties not before the court. See *id.,* at 505; *Simon v. Eastern Kentucky Welfare Rights Org.,* 426 U.S., at 41–42. Unlike the individual plaintiffs in *Warth,* Ransom has adequately averred an "actionable causal relationship" between Arlington Heights' zoning practices and his asserted injury. *Warth v. Seldin,* 422 U.S., at 507. We therefore proceed to the merits.

III

Our decision last Term in *Washington v. Davis,* 426 U.S. 229 (1976), made it clear that official action will not be held unconstitutional solely because it results in a racially disproportionate impact. "Disproportionate impact is not irrelevant, but it is not the sole touchstone of an invidious racial discrimination." *Id.,* at 242. Proof of racially discriminatory intent or purpose is required to show a violation of the Equal Protection Clause. Although some contrary indications may be drawn from some of our cases, the holding in *Davis* reaffirmed a principle well established in a variety of contexts.

Davis does not require a plaintiff to prove that the challenged action rested solely on racially discriminatory purposes. Rarely can it be said that a legislature or administrative body operating under a broad mandate made a decision motivated solely by a single concern, or even that a particular purpose was the "dominant" or "primary" one. In fact, it is because legislators and administrators are properly concerned with balancing numerous competing considerations that courts refrain from reviewing the merits of their decisions, absent a showing of arbitrariness or irrationality. But racial discrimination is not just another competing consideration. When there is proof that a discriminatory purpose has been a motivating factor in the decision, this judicial deference is no longer justified.

---

[9] Because of the presence of this plaintiff, we need not consider whether the other individual and corporate plaintiffs have standing to maintain the suit.

Determining whether invidious discriminatory purpose was a motivating factor demands a sensitive inquiry into such circumstantial and direct evidence of intent as may be available. The impact of the official action — whether it "bears more heavily on one race than another," *Washington v. Davis,* 426 U.S., at 242 — may provide an important starting point. Sometimes a clear pattern, unexplainable on grounds other than race, emerges from the effect of the state action even when the governing legislation appears neutral on its face. The evidentiary inquiry is then relatively easy. But such cases are rare. Absent a pattern as stark as that in *Gomillion* [364 U.S. 339 (1960)] or *Yick Wo* [118 U.S. 356 (1886)] impact alone is not determinative, and the Court must look to other evidence. [15]

The historical background of the decision is one evidentiary source, particularly if it reveals a series of official actions taken for invidious purposes. The specific sequence of events leading up to the challenged decision also may shed some light on the decisionmaker's purposes. For example, if the property involved here always had been zoned R-5 but suddenly was changed to R-3 when the town learned of MHDC's plans to erect integrated housing, [16] we would have a far different case. Departures from the normal procedural sequence also might afford evidence that improper purposes are playing a role. Substantive departures too may be relevant, particularly if the factors usually considered important by the decisionmaker strongly favor a decision contrary to the one reached. [17]

The legislative or administrative history may be highly relevant, especially where there are contemporary statements by members of the decisionmaking body, minutes of its meetings, or reports. In some extraordinary instances the members might be called to the stand at trial to testify concerning the purpose of the official action, although even then such testimony frequently will be barred by privilege.

The foregoing summary identifies, without purporting to be exhaustive, subjects of proper inquiry in determining whether racially discriminatory intent existed. With these in mind, we now address the case before us.

IV

[The Court discussed the decisions below.] . . .

We also have reviewed the evidence. The impact of the Village's decision does arguably bear more heavily on racial minorities. Minorities comprise 18% of the Chicago area population, and 40% of the income groups said to be

---

[15] In many instances, to recognize the limited probative value of disproportionate impact is merely to acknowledge the "heterogeneity" of the nation's population.

[16] See, *e.g., Progress Development Corp. v. Mitchell,* 286 F.2d 222 (C.A.7 1961) (park board allegedly condemned plaintiffs' land for a park upon learning that the homes plaintiffs were erecting there would be sold under a marketing plan designed to assure integration); *Kennedy Park Homes Association, Inc. v. City of Lackawanna,* 436 F.2d 108 (C.A.2 1970), cert. denied, 401 U.S. 1010 (1971) (town declared moratorium on new subdivisions and rezoned area for park land shortly after learning of plaintiffs' plans to build low income housing). To the extent that the decision in *Kennedy Park Homes* rested solely on a finding of discriminatory impact, we have indicated our disagreement. *Washington v. Davis,* 426 U.S., at 244–245.

[17] See *Daily v. City of Lawton,* 425 F.2d 1037 (C.A.10 1970). . . .

eligible for Lincoln Green. But there is little about the sequence of events leading up to the decision that would spark suspicion. The area around the Viatorian property has been zoned R-3 since 1959, the year when Arlington Heights first adopted a zoning map. Single-family homes surround the 80-acre site, and the Village is undeniably committed to single-family homes as its dominant residential land use. The rezoning request progressed according to the usual procedures.[19] The Plan Commission even scheduled two additional hearings, at least in part to accommodate MHDC and permit it to supplement its presentation with answers to questions generated at the first hearing.

The statements by the Plan Commission and Village Board members, as reflected in the official minutes, focused almost exclusively on the zoning aspects of the MHDC petition, and the zoning factors on which they relied are not novel criteria in the Village's rezoning decisions. There is no reason to doubt that there has been reliance by some neighboring property owners on the maintenance of single-family zoning in the vicinity. The Village originally adopted its buffer policy long before MHDC entered the picture and has applied the policy too consistently for us to infer discriminatory purpose from its application in this case. Finally, MHDC called one member of the Village Board to the stand at trial. Nothing in her testimony supports an inference of invidious purpose.[20]

In sum, the evidence does not warrant overturning the concurrent findings of both courts below. Respondents simply failed to carry their burden of proving that discriminatory purpose was a motivating factor in the Village's decision.[21] This conclusion ends the constitutional inquiry. The Court of Appeals' further finding that the Village's decision carried a discriminatory "ultimate effect" is without independent constitutional significance.

---

[19] Respondents have made much of one apparent procedural departure. The parties stipulated that the Village Planner, the staff member whose primary responsibility covered zoning and planning matters, was never asked for his written or oral opinion of the rezoning request. The omission does seem curious, but respondents failed to prove at trial what role the Planner customarily played in rezoning decisions, or whether his opinion would be relevant to respondents' claims.

[20] Respondents complain that the District Court unduly limited their efforts to prove that the Village Board acted for discriminatory purposes, since it forbade questioning Board members about their motivation at the time they cast their votes. We perceive no abuse of discretion in the circumstances of this case, even if such an inquiry into motivation would otherwise have been proper. Respondents were allowed, both during the discovery phase and at trial, to question Board members fully about materials and information available to them at the time of decision. In light of respondents' repeated insistence that it was effect and not motivation which would make out a constitutional violation, the District Court's action was not improper.

[21] Proof that the decision by the Village was motivated in part by a racially discriminatory purpose would not necessarily have required invalidation of the challenged decision. Such proof would, however, have shifted to the Village the burden of establishing that the same decision would have resulted even had the impermissible purpose not been considered. If this were established, the complaining party in a case of this kind no longer fairly could attribute the injury complained of to improper consideration of a discriminatory purpose. In such circumstances, there would be no justification for judicial interference with the challenged decision. But in this case respondents failed to make the required threshold showing. See *Mt. Healthy City School Dist. Bd. of Education v. Doyle,* 429 U.S. 274.

V. . .

[The Court remanded the case to the Court of Appeals to consider a statutory claim under the Fair Housing Act, which it had not considered.]

Reversed and remanded.

[The opinion of Justice Marshall, joined by Justice Brennan, concurring in part and dissenting in part, is omitted, as is the dissenting opinion of Justice White. Justice Stevens took no part in the consideration or decision of this case. — Eds.]

NOTES AND QUESTIONS

1. *Is proof of intent realistically possible?* The implicit holding of the case is that a zoning decision is not racially discriminatory if it is supported by "normal" zoning factors. Professor Mandelker offers this critique:

> The Supreme Court's decision in *Arlington Heights* has foreclosed a finding of racially discriminatory intent in all but the most blatant cases. Unless a municipality has historically discriminated against zoning proposals for subsidized housing, or unless the municipality abruptly changes a zoning classification or otherwise acts affirmatively to frustrate the construction of a subsidized housing development, no opportunity for proving the existence of racially discriminatory intent appears present. Moreover, none of these events is likely to surface. Developers facing a hostile municipality are unlikely to challenge that municipality's zoning to any great extent, so that no "clear pattern" of discrimination is likely to emerge. [Mandelker, *Racial Discrimination and Exclusionary Zoning: A Perspective on Arlington Heights,* 55 Tex. L. Rev. 1217, 1239 (1977).]

Reconsider the "but for" test explained by the Court in footnote 21. How does this test make proof of racial discrimination in zoning difficult? Since the Court said that "[s]ometimes a clear pattern, unexplainable on grounds other than race," will support a finding of racial discrimination, why wasn't the refusal to zone racially discriminatory considering the nearly all-white character of the village's population?

2. *Segregative intent.* Most cities, unlike most suburbs, do not totally exclude subsidized housing, but they often handle siting and occupancy in a racially discriminatory way, as a number of courts have found. The best known case finding intentional discrimination is *United States v. Yonkers Bd. of Educ.,* 624 F. Supp. 1276 (S.D.N.Y. 1985) (extensive findings of fact). These cases are relevant to *Arlington Heights* because the remedy typically involves construction of racially integrated subsidized housing in white areas. The different fact pattern in these urban discrimination cases underscores Professor Mandelker's conclusion about the unlikelihood of proving intent in suburban zoning cases. The *Yonkers* case reached the Supreme Court in *Spallone v. United States,* 493 U.S. 265 (1990), where the issue was the scope of the district court's contempt power, rather than the merits of the housing claims.

3. *Lower court cases.* The cases since *Arlington Heights* have not found equal protection violations when zoning has been challenged on constitutional grounds as racially discriminatory. Proof of racial discrimination has become more difficult with the termination of federal construction subsidies for housing. Minorities are less likely to be able to afford unsubsidized developments. *Orange Lake Assocs. v. Kirkpatrick,* 21 F.3d 1214 (2d Cir. 1994) (no racial discrimination when downzoning prevented construction of high-priced dwellings.) However, courts have refused to dismiss complaints that arguably made a case for zoning discrimination. E.g., *Barnes Foundation v. Township of Lower Merion,* 982 F. Supp. 970 (E.D. Pa. 1997) (claim of discrimination because some of plaintiff's trustees were African-American).

4. *Standing.* Is the Court's holding on standing in *Arlington Heights* consistent with its holding in *Warth,* discussed in sec. C1 *supra?* How likely is it that the black plaintiff in *Arlington Heights* would actually be offered a dwelling unit in the project if it were built? Professor Sager claims that

> In adjudging [the private plaintiff's] injury [in Arlington Heights] to be sufficient under the Warth test, the Court ignored both the possibility that the housing might not in fact be constructed and the remoteness of the likelihood that any one applicant would obtain housing amid the brisk competition for the units which would develop if they were completed. [Sager, *Questions I Wish I Had Never Asked: The Burger Court in Exclusionary Zoning,* 11 S.W.2d. U. L. Rev. 509, 517 n.25 (1979).]

Cases since *Arlington Heights* have granted standing to developers to challenge zoning claimed to be racially discriminatory. See *Scott v. Greenville County,* 716 F.2d 1409 (4th Cir. 1983) (if standing not granted to developer, local officials could destroy a project at an early stage before occupancy could be determined).

5. For additional discussion of the constitutional and standing issues raised by *Arlington Heights* see D. Mandelker, J. Gerard & T. Sullivan, Federal Land Use Law §§ 3.02[2], 3.03; Daye, *The Race, Class and Housing Conundrum: A Rationale and a Proposal for a Legislative Policy of Suburban Inclusion,* 9 N.C. Cent. L.J. 37 (1977); *Developments in the Laws — Zoning,* 91 Harv. L. Rev. 1427, 1666–79 (1978).

b. Fair Housing Legislation

The Federal Fair Housing Act, 42 U.S.C. §§ 3601-3617, generally forbids racial discrimination in housing. 42 U.S.C. § 3604(a) provides in part that "it shall be unlawful . . . [t]o make unavailable or deny . . . a dwelling to any person because of race, color, religion, or national origin." Although the statute does not explicitly mention zoning, the courts have held that discrimination in zoning ordinances makes housing "unavailable" under the statute. Much of the exclusionary zoning litigation in the federal courts has been based on allegations that local land use controls, as applied, violate the Fair Housing Act.

Arlington Heights after remand.—Upon the Supreme Court's remand in *Arlington Heights,* the court of appeals held that "at least under some circumstances a violation of section 3604(a) can be established by a showing of discriminatory effect without a showing of discriminatory intent." 558 F.2d 1283 (7th Cir. 1977), *cert. denied,* 434 U.S. 1025 (1978). The rationale of this holding is stated in the following excerpt from the court's opinion:

> The major obstacle to concluding that action taken without discriminatory intent can violate section 3604(a) is the phrase "because of race" contained in the statutory provision. The narrow view of the phrase is that a party cannot commit an act "because of race" unless he intends to discriminate between races. By hypothesis, this approach would excuse the Village from liability because it acted without discriminatory intent. The broad view is that a party commits an act "because of race" whenever the natural and foreseeable consequence of that act is to discriminate between races, regardless of his intent. Under this statistical, effect-oriented view of causality, the Village could be liable since the natural and foreseeable consequence of its failure to rezone was to adversely affect black people seeking low-cost housing and to perpetuate segregation in Arlington Heights. [*Id.* at 1288.]

In order to determine whether Arlington Heights had violated § 3604(a), the Seventh Circuit panel said that four factors must be weighed: (1) "how strong is the plaintiff's evidence of discriminatory effect"? (2) "is there evidence of discriminatory intent, though not enough to satisfy the constitutional standard of *Washington v. Davis*"? (3) "what is the defendant's interest in taking the action complained of"? (4) "does the plaintiff seek to compel the defendant to affirmatively provide housing for minority groups or merely to restrain the defendant from interfering with individual property owners who wish to provide such housing"? Consideration of these factors led the court to conclude that "this is a close case" and that "whether the Village's refusal to rezone has a strong discriminatory effect because it effectively assures that Arlington Heights will remain a segregated community is unclear from the record."

The court then remanded the case to the district court with directions to determine whether the case was moot; whether, absent a subsidy under § 236 of the National Housing Act, alternative subsidies would be available, and whether the project would be racially integrated. The court also put on the defendant

> the burden of identifying a parcel of land within Arlington Heights which is both properly zoned and suitable for low-cost housing under federal standards. If defendant fails to satisfy this burden, the district court should conclude that the Village's refusal to rezone effectively precluded plaintiffs from constructing low-cost housing within Arlington Heights, and should grant plaintiffs the relief they seek. [*Id.* at 1295.]

The settlement in Arlington Heights.—The district court never resolved the question whether Arlington Heights had violated the Civil Rights Act of 1968. After the case was remanded, Arlington Heights annexed an unincorporated tract — presumably owned or controlled by MHDC — abutting the nearby

Village of Mount Prospect, and then agreed both to rezone this tract to allow multi-family and commercial uses and to exempt it from most subdivision exactions. MHDC agreed to build 190 units of subsidized rental housing on the tract, and to give residents of Arlington Heights preference in renting these units to the extent permitted by federal law. Both the Village of Mount Prospect and nearby landowners intervened and objected to this proposed resolution of the suit against Arlington Heights, but the district court approved it and entered a consent judgment dismissing the suit. 469 F. Supp. 836 (E.D. Ill. 1979), aff'd, 616 F.2d 1006 (7th Cir. 1980).

In a footnote, the Seventh Circuit panel observed "that Lincoln Green would conform with the standard set by the Village's multiple zoning classification," and hence that it "need not reach the question of whether plaintiffs would have been entitled to relief if Lincoln Green had been out of conformance with the Village's multiple family zoning classification as well as its single family zoning classification." Suppose the latter had been the case, but that the Village's multi-family zoning classification required a density so low as to preclude construction of any low-cost housing?

Why should it be relevant, in a case where discriminatory intent need not be proved, to determine whether there is "evidence of discriminatory intent"? Did the final settlement of the *Arlington Heights* case result in satisfaction of the Village's obligation under 42 U.S.C. § 3604(a) not to "make unavailable or deny . . . a dwelling to any person because of race, color, religion, or national origin"?

For a critical analysis of the Seventh Circuit's formula, see Clamore, *Fair Housing and the Black Poor,* 18 Clearinghouse Rev. 606, 646–50 (1984).

There have been several other cases applying the Fair Housing Act to claims of racial discrimination. The following case is one of the most important of these decisions. Note how it modifies the *Arlington Heights* test.

HUNTINGTON BRANCH, NAACP v. TOWN OF HUNTINGTON

844 F.2d 926 (2d Cir. 1988)
Noted, 37 Wash. U.J. Urb. & Contemp. L. 257 (1990)

KAUFMAN, CIRCUIT JUDGE:

. . . .

The Huntington Branch of the National Association for the Advancement of Colored People (NAACP), Housing Help, Inc. (HHI), and two black, low-income residents of Huntington appeal from an adverse judgment of the United States District Court for the Eastern District of New York (Glasser, J.), following a bench trial, in their suit against the Town of Huntington (the Town) and members of its Town Board. Appellants allege that the Town violated Title VIII by restricting private construction of multi-family housing to a narrow urban renewal area and by refusing to rezone the parcel outside this area where appellants wished to build multi-family housing. Specifically, appellants sought to construct an integrated, multi-family subsidized apartment complex in Greenlawn/East Northport, a virtually all-white neighborhood. The Town's zoning ordinance, however, prohibited private construction of multi-family housing outside a small urban renewal zone in the Huntington Station neighborhood, which is 52% minority. Thus, appellants petitioned the Town to revise its code to accommodate the project. When the Town refused, appellants brought this class-action to compel the change under Title VIII. . . . [The court reversed the district court and granted site-specific relief.]

Huntington is a town of approximately 200,000 people located in the northwest corner of Suffolk County, New York. In 1980, 95% of its residents were white. Blacks comprised only 3.35% of the Town's population and were concentrated in areas known as Huntington Station and South Greenlawn. [Additional racial data is repeated later in the opinion.]. . .

Although a disproportionate number of minorities need low-cost housing, the Town has attempted to limit minority occupancy in subsidized housing projects. . . .

In response to the great need for subsidized housing in the Town, HHI decided to sponsor an integrated housing project for low-income families. HHI determined that the project could foster racial integration only if it were located in a white neighborhood outside the Huntington Station and South Greenlawn areas. . . .[T]he only vacant R-3M property [is] located in the urban renewal area. . . .

After a lengthy search, HHI determined that a 14.8 acre parcel located at the corner of Elwood and Pulaski roads in the Town was well suited for a 162-unit housing project. This flat, largely cleared and well-drained property was near public transportation, shopping and other services, and immediately adjacent to schools.

Ninety-eight percent of the population within a one-mile radius of the site is white. HHI set a goal of 25% minority occupants. The district court found that "a significant percentage of the tenants [at Matinecock Court] would have belonged to minority groups." *Huntington*, 668 F. Supp. at 785. HHI officials determined that the property was economically feasible and offered a lengthy option period. . . .

[Miness, a local planning official, assured HHI that zoning would not be an obstacle if the town supported the project. HHI obtained an option to purchase the Elwood-Pulaski parcel on January 23, 1980. Miness stated, when asked, that he was familiar with the property and believed it was a good location for development.]

Throughout 1980, HHI sought to advance its project by gaining the approval of the Town Board to rezone the property to R-3M from its R-40 designation. . . .

When the proposal became public, substantial community opposition developed. . . [A petition with 4,100 signatures was submitted to the Town Board, and a protest meeting drew 2,000 persons.] Matinecock Court came before the Town Board at a meeting on January 6, 1981. The Board rejected the proposed zoning change and adopted the following resolution [which concluded that]:. . .

THE TOWN BOARD finds that although favoring housing for the senior citizens and others, in appropriate areas, that the location referred to herein is not an appropriate location due to lack of transportation, traffic hazard and disruption of the existing residential patterns in the Elwood area and requests that the Department of Housing and Urban Development (HUD) reject the application by HOUSING HELP, INC.

The district court based its refusal to order rezoning on three alternative grounds: (1) appellants never formally applied for rezoning; (2) even if they had applied, they failed to make the requisite prima facie showing of discriminatory effect; and (3) even if they had demonstrated discriminatory effect, the city had rebutted it by articulating legitimate, non-pretextual justifications. We now consider each ground separately. . . .

[The court held that exhaustion of remedies was not required.]

In its second holding, the court adopted the four-prong disparate impact test set out in [the Seventh Circuit's decision in *Arlington Heights* on remand from the Supreme Court, which is discussed *supra*,] and concluded that, even if appellants applied for a rezoning change, they had failed to make out a prima facie case. . . . [The court quoted the "four-prong" test adopted by the Seventh Circuit and discussed the district court's holding.]

In its third rationale, the court applied the test set forth in *McDonnell Douglas Corp. v. Green,* 411 U.S. 792 (1973), as a final determination on the merits for Title VII disparate treatment cases. . . .

We find it convenient to discuss Judge Glasser's second and third holdings together. In considering them, we start by pointing out that this case requires what has been called "disparate impact" or "disparate effects" analysis, not "disparate treatment" analysis. A disparate impact analysis examines a facially-neutral policy or practice, such as a hiring test or zoning law, for its differential impact or effect on a particular group. Disparate treatment analysis, on the other hand, involves differential treatment of similarly situated persons or groups. The line is not always a bright one, but does adequately delineate two very different kinds of discrimination claims. . . .

Under disparate impact analysis, as other circuits have recognized, a prima facie case is established by showing that the challenged practice of the defendant "actually or predictably results in racial discrimination; in other words that it has a discriminatory effect." *United States v. City of Black Jack,* 508 F.2d 1179, 1184–85 (8th Cir. 1974), *cert. denied,* 422 U.S. 1042 (1975). The plaintiff need not show that the decision complained of was made with discriminatory intent. Refusal to require intent in disparate impact cases is entirely consistent with our prior decisions. In determining whether discriminatory effect is sufficient, we look to congressional purpose, as gleaned from the legislative history of Title VIII, related Title VII jurisprudence, and practical concerns. Although none of these considerations is alone determinative, taken together they strongly suggest that discriminatory impact alone violates Title VIII . . . . [The court held that the purpose of the act, legislative history and the parallel between Title VII and Title VIII supported their conclusion that "a Title VIII violation can be established without proof of discriminatory intent."]

Once a prima facie case of adverse impact is presented, as occurred here, the inquiry turns to the standard to be applied in determining whether the defendant can nonetheless avoid liability under Title VIII. [The court decided to "refine" the standard adopted in *Arlington Heights* and in *Resident Advisory Bd. v. Rizzo,* 564 F.2d 126 (3d Cir. 1977), *cert. denied,* 453 U.S. 908 (1978).]

In considering the defendant's justification, we start with the framework of Title VII analysis. When an employer's facially neutral rule is shown to have a racially disproportionate effect on job applicants, that rule must be shown to be substantially related to job performance. In a zoning case, the facially neutral rule is the provision of the zoning ordinance that bars the applicant and, in doing so, exerts a racially disproportionate effect on minorities. The difficulty, however, is that in Title VIII cases there is no single objective like job performance to which the legitimacy of the facially neutral rule may be related. A town's preference to maintain a particular zoning category for particular sections of the community is normally based on a variety of circumstances. The complexity of the considerations, however, does not relieve a court of the obligation to assess whatever justifications the town advances and weigh them carefully against the degree of adverse effect the plaintiff has shown. Though a town's interests in zoning requirements are substantial, they cannot, consistently with Title VIII, automatically outweigh significant disparate effects. . . .

A district court's findings of fact may not be set aside "unless clearly erroneous." Fed. R. Civ. P. 52(a). . . . We review Judge Glasser's findings in two areas: the strength of the discriminatory effect and the import of the Town's justifications.

The discriminatory effect of a rule arises in two contexts: adverse impact on a particular minority group and harm to the community generally by the perpetuation of segregation. In analyzing Huntington's restrictive zoning, however, the lower court concentrated on the harm to blacks as a group, and failed to consider the segregative effect of maintaining a zoning ordinance that restricts private multi-family housing to an area with a high minority concentration. Yet, recognizing this second form of effect advances the principal purpose of Title VIII to promote, "open, integrated residential housing patterns." *Otero v. New York Housing Authority,* 484 F.2d 1122, 1134 (2d Cir. 1973).

Seventy percent of Huntington's black population reside in Huntington Station and South Greenlawn. Matinecock Court, with its goal of 25% minorities, would begin desegregating a neighborhood which is currently 98% white. Indeed, the district court found that a "significant percentage of the tenants" at Matinecock Court would belong to minority groups. The court, however, failed to take the logical next step and find that the refusal to permit projects outside the urban renewal area with its high concentration of minorities reinforced racial segregation in housing. This was erroneous. Similarly, the district court found that the Town has a shortage of rental housing affordable for low and moderate-income households, that a "disproportionately" large percentage of the households using subsidized rental units are minority citizens, and that a disproportionately large number of minorities are on the waiting lists for subsidized housing and existing Section 8 certificates. [The certificates are a federal subsidy. — Eds.] But it failed to recognize that Huntington's zoning ordinance, which restricts private construction of multi-family housing to the largely minority urban renewal area, impeded integration by restricting low-income housing needed by minorities to an area already 52% minority. We thus find that Huntington's refusal to amend the restrictive zoning ordinance to permit privately-built multi-family housing outside the urban renewal area significantly perpetuated segregation in the Town.

On the question of harm to blacks as a group, the district court emphasized that 22,160 whites and 3,671 minorities had incomes below 200% of the poverty line, a cutoff close to the Huntington Housing Authority's qualification standards. Thus, the district court focussed on the greater absolute number of poor whites compared with indigent minorities in Huntington. The district court, however, did not analyze the disproportionate burden on minorities as required by *Griggs v. Duke Power Co.,* 401 U.S. 424 (1971). By relying on absolute numbers rather than on proportional statistics, the district court significantly underestimated the disproportionate impact of the Town's policy. Thus, the district court perceived facts through a misapprehension of the applicable law and we must make our own findings at least as to the significance of the undisputed underlying facts.

The parties have stipulated that 28% of minorities in Huntington and 11% of whites have incomes below 200% of the poverty line. What they dispute is the meaning of these statistics. Judge Glasser found that, as the Town contends, there is no showing of discriminatory effect because a majority of the victims are white. We disagree for reasons analogous to those the Supreme Court enumerated in *Griggs.* The disparity is of a magnitude similar to that in *Griggs,* where the Court found discriminatory an employer's policy of hiring only high school graduates because 12% of black males in North Carolina had high school diplomas while 24% of white males were high school graduates. But the plaintiffs presented even stronger evidence reflecting the disparate impact of preventing the project from proceeding. Under the Huntington HAP for 1982-1985, 7% of all Huntington families needed subsidized housing, while 24% of the black families needed such housing. In addition, minorities constitute a far greater percentage of those currently occupying subsidized rental projects compared to their percentage in the Town's population. Similarly, a disproportionately high percentage (60%) of families holding Section 8 certificates from the Housing Authority to supplement their rents are minorities, and an equally disproportionate percentage (61%) of those on the waiting list for such certificates are minorities. Therefore, we conclude that the failure to rezone the Matinecock Court site had a substantial adverse impact on minorities.

In sum, we find that the disproportionate harm to blacks and the segregative impact on the entire community resulting from the refusal to rezone create a strong prima facie showing of discriminatory effect . . . . Thus, we must consider the Town's asserted justifications.

The *Rizzo* approach has two components: (1) whether the reasons are bona fide and legitimate; and (2) whether any less discriminatory alternative can serve those ends. For analytical ease, the second prong should be considered first. Concerns can usually be divided between "plan-specific" justifications and those which are "site-specific." "Plan-specific" problems can be resolved by the less discriminatory alternative of requiring reasonable design modifications. "Site-specific" justifications, however, would usually survive this prong of the test. Those remaining reasons are then scrutinized to determine if they are legitimate and bona fide. By that, we do not intend to devise a search for pretext. Rather, the inquiry is whether the proffered justification is of substantial concern such that it would justify a reasonable official in making this determination. Of course, a concern may be non-frivolous, but may not be sufficient because it is not reflected in the record.

Appellants challenge both the ordinance which restricts privately-built multi-family housing to the urban renewal area and the Town Board's decision to refuse to rezone the Elwood-Pulaski site. All the parties and the district court judge, however, focussed on the latter issue. Indeed, appellees below simply relied on the existence of the Housing Assistance Plan and the zoning ordinance and failed to present any substantial evidence indicating a significant interest in limiting private developers to the urban renewal area. On appeal, appellees now contend that the ordinance is designed to encourage private developers to build in the deteriorated area of Huntington Station. Although we believe that the Town's failure to raise this argument below precludes its consideration here, we briefly address this contention. The Town asserts that limiting multi-family development to the urban renewal area will encourage restoration of the neighborhood because, otherwise, developers will choose to build in the outlying areas and will by-pass the zone. The Town's goal, however, can be achieved by less discriminatory means, by encouraging development in the urban renewal area with tax incentives or abatements. The Town may assert that this is less effective, but it may actually be more so.

Developers are not wed to building in Huntington; they are filling a perceived economic void. Developments inside the urban renewal area and outside it are not fungible. Rather, developers prevented from building outside the urban renewal area will more likely build in another town, not the urban renewal area. Huntington incorrectly assumes that developers limit their area of interest by political subdivision. In fact, the decision where to build is much more complex. Hence, if the Town wishes to encourage growth in the urban renewal area, it should do so directly through incentives which would have a less discriminatory impact on the Town.

We turn next to the Town's reasons rejecting the Elwood-Pulaski site. . . . [The court held that only the traffic and health hazard issues were site-specific.]

At trial, however, none of Huntington's officials supported these objections. Butterfield, for example, was primarily concerned that the Matinecock Court project would "torpedo" the Town's plan to develop the site at Broadway and New York Avenue in the urban renewal area in Huntington Station. (Testimony of Kenneth C. Butterfield.) Moreover, Huntington's only expert, planner David Portman, set forth entirely different problems than were contained in Butterfield's letters. Specifically, he noted sewage concerns, lack of conformity with the low density of the surrounding neighborhood, and inaccessibility of the site to public transportation (Testimony of David J. Portman.) Once during his testimony, he did mention "the relationship [of the site] to the power station." Never, however, did he raise any concern about a health hazard from the proximity to the substation. Indeed, appellees do not broach this issue in their brief to this court. Accordingly, we find the reasons asserted are entirely insubstantial.

The sewage problem was first raised at trial by appellees' expert Portman. Appellees now advance it as an additional concern. The district court, however, chose not to consider it. We agree. Post hoc rationalizations by administrative agencies should be afforded "little deference" by the courts, and therefore cannot be a bona fide reason for the Town's action. Moreover, the sewage concern could hardly have been significant if municipal officials only thought of it after the litigation began. If it did not impress itself on the Town Board at the time of rejection, it was obviously not a legitimate problem. In sum, the only factor in the town's favor was that it was acting within the scope of its zoning authority, and thus we conclude that the Town's justifications were weak and inadequate. . . .

Appellees argue that we should deny site-specific relief because there are 64 "community development" sites available for low-cost multi-family housing in Huntington. [The court rejected this argument and held that "there is only one site, not 64 sites, zoned and available for private low-cost multi-family housing."] However, even as to the one site — the MIA site in Huntington Station — by the time of trial, HUD had determined it was in an area with a high concentration of minorities and therefore an inappropriate location for a federally subsidized housing development.

Ordinarily, HHI would not be automatically entitled to construct its project at its preferred site. The Town might well have legitimate reasons for preferring some alternative site to the one preferred by HHI. On the other hand, the Town would not be permitted to select a site that suits the Town's preference if that site imposed undue hardships on the applicant, such as distance from public transportation or other services. Thus, we would ordinarily remand this case to the district court to afford the appellees an opportunity to identify an alternative site, outside the urban renewal area, that would be appropriate for HHI's project and eligible for the same financial arrangements and assistance available at the Matinecock Court site. If the Town identified such a site, it would then have the burden of persuading the district court that there were substantial reasons for using its preferred site and that those reasons did not impose undue hardships on the appellants. If the district court was not persuaded on balance of the benefits of an alternative site, it would then enter an appropriate judgment to enable HHI to proceed with its project at the Matinecock Court site. . . .

This case, however, is not ordinary. [The court granted site-specific relief to rezone the plaintiff's property to R-3M zoning because of the protracted nature of the litigation, because the Town had demonstrated little good faith, and because "the other 63 parcels outside the urban renewal area are not presently zoned for multi-family housing."]

NOTES AND QUESTIONS

1. *How settled is the effects standard?* The judgment of the Court of Appeals in the principal case was affirmed (per curiam), 488 U.S. 15 (1988), but by taking a somewhat strained view of the procedural posture of the case, the Supreme Court was able to avoid deciding whether proof of "disparate impact," without proof of "discriminatory intent," satisfies the Fair Housing Act. The Court's entire discussion of the question was as follows: "Without endorsing the precise analysis of the Court of Appeals, we are satisfied on this record that disparate impact was shown, and that the sole justification proffered to rebut the prima facie case was inadequate." 488 U.S. at 18. When Congress substantially amended the Fair Housing Act in 1988, it did not address the discriminatory impact question, but President Reagan, in signing the bill into law, asserted his understanding ("executive history?") that it embodied an intent standard. Senator Kennedy, the Act's principal sponsor, promptly replied, noting that all of the federal courts of appeals had accepted the impact test. 134 Cong. Rec. S12449 (Sept. 14, 1988). Thus the matter stands.

The *Black Jack* decision, discussed in the principal case, held that once a discriminatory effect was shown, the government must defend the challenged zoning (exclusion of multi-family housing, in a community in the heavily segregated St. Louis metropolitan area) by showing a "compelling" interest. How does this differ from *Huntington*? Which approach is preferable?

2. *Later cases.* The effects test applied under the Fair Housing Act has allowed courts to grant summary judgment or refuse to dismiss complaints in cases claiming discrimination under zoning ordinances. *Summerchase Ltd. Partnership I v. City of Gonzales,* 970 F. Supp. 522 (M.D. La. 1997) (granting summary judgment); *Homeowner/Contractor Consultants, Inc. v. Ascension Parish Planning & Zoning Comm'n,* 32 F. Supp.2d 384 (M.D. La. 1999) (refusing to grant motion to dismiss). Other cases refused to find violations of the statute when developers claimed a denial of zoning approval was discriminatory. E.g., *Jackson v. City of Auburn,* 41 F. Supp.2d 1300 (M.D. Ala. 1999) (denial of conditional use permit).

For example, in *Housing Investors, Inc. v. City of Clanton,* 68 F. Supp. 2d 1287 (M.D. Ala. 1999), the city denied approval of a housing project for low-and moderate-income persons. To show that the city was a segregated enclave within the county, the plaintiff quoted statistics indicating higher median monthly rents and a significantly higher concentration of nonwhites in the city as compared with the county. The court held this was not enough, and that the plaintiff must show "such indicia of segregation as localized concentrations of minority groups within the municipality; comparisons of the racial composition of the areas inside and outside the municipality, showing that minority groups have been excluded from the municipality; and historical practices of segregation, the effects of which linger in the present," citing the Supreme Court decision in *Huntington.* In view of the actual Supreme Court language, note 1 *supra,* is this holding defensible?

3. *The federal role.* A 1991 Report by an Advisory Commission on Regulatory Barriers to Affordable Housing, *"Not in My Back Yard:" Removing Barriers to Affordable Housing,* examined a variety of land use issues and made a number of proposals for reform. The Commission identified growth controls, exclusionary zoning, impact fees, and environmental regulations as among the primary contributors to excessive housing costs. The Removal of Regulatory Barriers to Affordable Housing Act, 42 U.S.C. §§ 12705a-12705d, implements the Commission's recommendations. It provides grants to state and local governments to pursue barrier removal strategies and establishes a Regulatory Barriers Clearinghouse, both as recommended by the Commission. Section 12705b excludes rent controls from the definition of "regulatory barriers." Also excluded are "policies that have served to create or preserve . . . housing for low-and very low-income families, including displacement protections, demolition controls, replacement housing requirements, relocation benefits, housing trust funds, dedicated funding sources, waiver of local property taxes and builder fees, inclusionary zoning, rental zoning overlays, long-term use restrictions, and rights of first refusal." The excluded policies and techniques are ineligible for grant funding under the Act.

For a useful collection of papers on the Commission report, see Downs, *The Advisory Commission on Regulatory Barriers to Affordable Housing: Its Behavior and Accomplishments,* 2 Hous. Pol'y Debate 1095 (1991), together with comments by William Fischel, Chester Hartman and Bernard Siegan, *id.* 1139-1178. See also Regulatory Impediments to the Development and Placement of Affordable Housing, Hearing Before the Subcomm. on Policy Research and Insurance of the House Comm. on Banking, Finance and Urban Affairs, 101st Cong., 2d Sess. (1990).

4. For discussion of the application of the Fair Housing Act to zoning see Federal Land Use Law, *supra,* § 3.04; Schwartz, *The Fair Housing Act and "Discriminatory Effect": A New Perspective,* 11 Nova L.J. 71 (1987); Ford, *The Boundaries of Race: Political Geography in Legal Analysis,* 107 Harv. L. Rev. 1841, 1894-97 (1994).

D. DISCRIMINATION AGAINST GROUP HOMES FOR THE HANDICAPPED

Congress in 1988 amended the Fair Housing Act to prohibit discrimination against group homes for the handicapped. The amendments prohibit a number of discriminatory practices in the sale or rental of housing, but they also apply to discrimination in zoning ordinances. By adopting the case-by-case approach to zoning discrimination against group homes, Congress opened up a pandora's box of litigation which has not clarified community responsibility under the Act. Below are some of the major features of the Act. The important question is the effect the amendments have on zoning restrictions and the zoning process. It is an important example of a congressional override on local zoning, and has prompted calls for revision from local government organizations.

Definition of handicap.—The Act does not apply to all group homes, only to homes for the handicapped. Congress explicitly adopted the definition used in the Rehabilitation Act of 1973. 20 U.S.C. § 794. The statute defines "handicap" as a "physical or mental impairment which substantially limits one or more of such person's major life activities." 42 U.S.C. § 3602(h). The definition includes alcoholism, drug addiction and persons with AIDS. See *Bragdon v. Abbott,* 524 U.S. 624 (1998) (persons with AIDS). It does not cover all of the group homes that often are subject to discriminatory restrictions under zoning law. Discrimination in zoning against these group homes has been litigated under other statutes, such as the Americans with Disabilities Act (discussed in note 6, *infra*).

Application to zoning.—The Act does not explicitly include zoning, but it includes language borrowed from elsewhere in the Act that prohibits acts that "otherwise make unavailable or deny" a dwelling because of a handicap. 42 U.S.C. § 3604(f)(1). The courts have made it clear in racial discrimination cases that this phrase includes zoning, and the House Judiciary Committee report on the group home amendments makes it clear they are to apply to "zoning decisions and practices." These include special requirements and conditional and special use permits "that have the effect of limiting the ability of such individuals to live in the residence of their choice in the community." H.R. Rep. No. 711, 100th Cong., 2d Sess. 24 (1988). The legislative history indicates courts are to apply an effects test to discrimination against the handicapped by zoning ordinances.

The Act also includes as discrimination the refusal to make reasonable accommodations in rules, policies and practices when such accommodations are necessary to afford handicapped persons an opportunity to use and enjoy a dwelling. 42 U.S.C. § 3604(f)(3)(B). This provision is limited to this part of the Fair Housing Act, and could be a powerful requirement as applied to zoning.

Facial vs. as-applied attacks.—State statutes and local zoning ordinances can violate the Fair Housing Act in two ways: they may be facially in conflict with the Act, or they may violate the Act as applied. One example of a requirement that may conflict facially with the Act are zoning ordinances and statutes that contain density, spacing and quota requirements for group homes. The presence of provisions of this type in group home statutes and ordinances raises important questions about the use of quotas in land use regulation. Similar quotas for the spacing of housing based on racial occupancy are unthinkable. The following case considers the validity of this type of requirement under the Fair Housing Act ("as-applied" cases are discussed in note 4, *infra*).

LARKIN v. STATE OF MICHIGAN DEPARTMENT OF SOCIAL SERVICES

89 F.3d 285 (6th Cir. 1996)

ALDRICH, DISTRICT JUDGE. . . .

I.

Geraldine Larkin sought a license to operate an adult foster care (AFC) facility which would provide care for up to four handicapped adults in Westland, Michigan. The Michigan Adult Foster Care Licensing Act (MAF-CLA), M.C.L. §§ 400.701 et seq., governs the issuance of such licenses. It prevents the issuance of a temporary license if the proposed AFC facility would "substantially contribute to an excessive concentration" of community residential facilities within a municipality. M.C.L. § 400.716(1). Moreover, it requires compliance with section 3b of the state's zoning enabling act, codified as M.C.L. § 125.583b. M.C.L. § 400.716(3). Section 3b of the zoning act provides in part:

> At least 45 days before licensing a residential facility [which provides resident services or care for six or fewer persons under 24-hour supervision], the state licensing agency shall notify the council . . . or the designated agency of the city or village where the proposed facility is to be located to review the number of existing or proposed similar state licensed residential facilities whose property lines are within a 1,500-foot radius of the property lines of the proposed facility. The council of a city or village or an agency of the city or village to which the authority is delegated, when a proposed facility is to be located within the city or village, shall give appropriate notification . . . to those residents whose property lines are within a 1,500-foot radius of the property lines of the proposed facility. A state licensing agency shall not license a proposed residential facility if another state licensed residential facility exists within the 1,500-foot radius of the proposed location, unless permitted by local zoning ordinances or if the issuance of the license would substantially contribute to an excessive concentration of state licensed residential facilities within the city or village.

M.C.L. § 125.583b(4). MAFCLA also requires notice to the municipality in which the proposed AFC facility will be located. M.C.L. § 400.732(1).

Michigan Department of Social Services (MDSS) notified Westland of Larkin's application in accordance with MAFCLA. Westland determined that there was an existing AFC facility within 1,500 feet of the proposed facility and so notified MDSS. It also notified MDSS that it was not waiving the spacing requirement, so that MDSS could not issue a license to Larkin. When MDSS informed Larkin of Westland's action, Larkin withdrew her application. . . .

[On cross-motions for summary judgment the district court ruled that the Michigan statutes were preempted by the Fair Housing Act and violated the federal Equal Protection Clause. The department appealed.]

III.

. . . [The court reviewed the provisions of the federal act.]

A. Preemption

. . . [The court noted that "[i]n this case, the FHAA expressly provides that any state law 'that purports to require or permit any action that would be a discriminatory housing practice under this subchapter shall to that extent be invalid.'" 42 U.S.C. § 3615. It thus treated the case as one of express preemption and actual conflict between the federal and state law.]

B. Discrimination

This brings us to the crux of the case: whether the statutes at issue discriminate against the disabled in violation of the FHAA. The district court held that two different aspects of MAFCLA violate the FHAA: (1) the 1500-foot spacing requirement of M.C.L. § 125.583b(4); and (2) the notice requirements of M.C.L. §§ 125.583b(4) & 400.732(1). . . . [The court noted that most courts applying the Fair Housing Act have analogized it to Title VII of the Civil Rights Act, and have concluded a violation can be shown through disparate treatment or disparate effect.]

Here, the challenged portions of MAFCLA are facially discriminatory. The spacing requirement prohibits MDSS from licensing any new AFC facility if it is within 1500 feet of an existing AFC facility. The notice requirements require MDSS to notify the municipality of the proposed facility, and the local authorities to then notify all residents within 1500 feet of the proposed facility. By their very terms, these statutes apply only to AFC facilities which will house the disabled, and not to other living arrangements. As we have previously noted, statutes that single out for regulation group homes for the handicapped are facially discriminatory. Accordingly, this is a case of intentional discrimination or disparate treatment, rather than disparate impact.

MDSS argues that the statutes at issue cannot have a discriminatory intent because they are motivated by a benign desire to help the disabled. This is incorrect as a matter of law. The Supreme Court has held in the employment context that "the absence of a malevolent motive does not convert a facially discriminatory policy into a neutral policy with a discriminatory effect." [*International Union, United Auto. Aerospace & Agricultural Implement Workers v.*] *Johnson Controls,* 499 U.S. [187] at 199 (1991). Following *Johnson Controls*, all of the courts which have considered this issue under the FHAA have concluded the defendant's benign motive does not prevent the statute from being discriminatory on its face. MDSS relies on *Familystyle of St. Paul, Inc. v. City of St. Paul,* 728 F. Supp. 1396 (D. Minn. 1990), *aff'd,* 923 F.2d 91 (8th Cir. 1991), for the proposition that proof of a discriminatory motive is required for a finding of discriminatory intent. However, both decisions in *Familystyle* preceded the Supreme Court's opinion in *Johnson Controls.* Thus, they have been implicitly overruled by *Johnson Controls* in this regard.

Because the statutes at issue are facially discriminatory, the burden shifts to the defendant to justify the challenged statutes. However, it is not clear how much of a burden shifts. MDSS urges us to follow the Eighth Circuit and rule that discriminatory statutes are subject to a rational basis scrutiny, i.e., they will be upheld if they are rationally related to a legitimate government objective. *See Familystyle,* 923 F.2d at 94. Plaintiffs urge us to reject the rational basis test and adopt the standard announced by the Tenth Circuit, which requires the defendant to show that the discriminatory statutes either (1) are justified by individualized safety concerns; or (2) really benefit, rather than discriminate against, the handicapped, and are not based on unsupported stereotypes. *Bangerter* [*v. Orem City Corp.,* 46 F.3d [1491] at 1503–04 [(10th Cir. 1995).]

Although we have never explicitly decided the issue, we have held that in order for special safety restrictions on homes for the handicapped to pass muster under the FHAA, the safety requirements must be tailored to the particular needs of the disabled who will reside in the house. *Marbrunak* [*v. City of Stowe],* 974 F.2d [43] at 47 [(6th Cir. 1992)]. We rejected the ordinances at issue in that case because they required nearly every safety requirement that one might think of as desirable to protect persons handicapped by any disability—mental or physical; and all the requirements applied to all housing for developmentally disabled persons, regardless of the type of mental condition that causes their disabilities or of the ways in which the disabilities manifest themselves.

Id. Therefore, in order for facially discriminatory statutes to survive a challenge under the FHAA, the defendant must demonstrate that they are "warranted by the unique and specific needs and abilities of those handicapped persons" to whom the regulations apply. *Id.*

MDSS has not met that burden. MDSS claims that the 1500-foot spacing requirement integrates the disabled into the community and prevents "clustering" and "ghettoization." In addition, it argues that the spacing requirement also serves the goal of deinstitutionalization by preventing a cluster of AFC facilities from recreating an institutional environment in the community.

As an initial matter, integration is not a sufficient justification for maintaining permanent quotas under the FHA or the FHAA, especially where, as here, the burden of the quota falls on the disadvantaged minority. The FHAA protects the right of individuals to live in the residence of their choice in the community. *Marbrunak,* 974 F.2d at 45. If the state were allowed to impose quotas on the number of minorities who could move into a neighborhood in the name of integration, this right would be vitiated.

MDSS argues that the state is not imposing a quota because it is not limiting the number of disabled who can live in a neighborhood, it is merely limiting the number of AFC facilities within that neighborhood. However, as we have previously noted, disabled individuals who wish to live in a community often have no choice but to live in an AFC facility. Alternatively, if the disabled truly have the right to live anywhere they choose, then the limitations on AFC facilities do not prevent clustering and ghettoization in any meaningful way. Thus, MDSS's own argument suggests that integration is not the true reason for the spacing requirements.

Moreover, MDSS has not shown how the special needs of the disabled warrant intervention to ensure that they are integrated. MDSS has produced no evidence that AFC facilities will cluster absent the spacing statute. In fact, this statute was not enforced from 1990 to 1993, and MDSS has offered no evidence that AFC facilities tended to cluster during that period.

Instead, MDSS simply assumes that the disabled must be integrated, and does not recognize that the disabled may choose to live near other disabled individuals. The result might be different if some municipalities were forcing the disabled to segregate, or cluster, in a few small areas. However, Michigan already prohibits such behavior:

In order to implement the policy of this state that persons in need of community residential care shall not be excluded by zoning from the benefits of a normal residential surroundings, a state licensed residential facility providing supervision or care, or both, to 6 or less persons shall be considered a residential use of property for purposes of zoning and a permitted use in all residential zones, including those zoned for single family dwellings, *and shall not be subject to a special use or conditional use permit or procedure different from those required for other dwellings of similar density in the same zone.*

M.C.L. § 125.583b(2) (emphasis added). The only clustering or segregation that will occur, then, is as the result of the free choice of the disabled. In other words, the state's policy of forced integration is not protecting the disabled from any forced segregation; rather, the state is forcing them to integrate based on the paternalistic idea that it knows best where the disabled should choose to live.

In contrast, deinstitutionalization is a legitimate goal for the state to pursue. However, MDSS does not explain how a rule prohibiting two AFC facilities from being within 1500 feet of each other fosters deinstitutionalization in any real way. Two AFC facilities 500 feet apart would violate the statute without remotely threatening to recreate an institutional setting in the community. In fact, the spacing requirement may actually inhibit the goal of deinstitutionalization by limiting the number of AFC facilities which can be operated within any given community.

MDSS relies again on *Familystyle*, where both the district court and the Eighth Circuit found that the goal of deinstitutionalization justified facially discriminatory spacing requirements. However, *Familystyle* is distinguishable from the present case. In *Familystyle*, the plaintiff already housed 119 disabled individuals within a few city blocks. The courts were concerned that the plaintiffs were simply recreating an institutionalized setting in the community, rather than deinstitutionalizing the disabled.

Here, however, Larkin seeks only to house four disabled individuals in a home which happens to be less than 1500 feet from another AFC facility. The proposed AFC facility, and many more like it that are prohibited by the spacing requirement, do not threaten Michigan's professed goal of deinstitutionalization. Because it sweeps in the vast majority of AFC facilities which do not seek to recreate an institutional setting, the spacing requirement is too broad, and is not tailored to the specific needs of the handicapped. . . .

MDSS also has failed to provide an adequate justification for the notice requirements. MDSS merely offers the same justifications for the notice requirements as it offers for the spacing requirements, i.e., integration and deinstitutionalization. Notifying the municipality or the neighbors of the proposed AFC facility seems to have little relationship to the advancement of these goals. In fact, such notice would more likely have quite the opposite effect, as it would facilitate the organized opposition to the home, and animosity towards its residents. Furthermore, MDSS has offered no evidence that the needs of the handicapped would warrant such notice. We find that the notice requirements violate the FHAA and are preempted by it.

By this holding, we in no way mean to intimate that the FHA, as amended by the FHAA, prohibits reasonable regulation and licensing procedures for AFC facilities. As was stated in *Marbrunak*, "the FHAA does not prohibit the city from imposing *any* special safety standards for the protection of developmentally disabled persons." *Marbrunak,* 974 F.2d at 47 (emphasis in original). Rather, it merely prohibits those which are not "demonstrated to be warranted

by the unique and specific needs and abilities of those handicapped persons."
Id. . . .

For the foregoing reasons, the judgment of the district court is

Affirmed.

NOTES AND QUESTIONS

1. *When zoning conflicts.* Compare the court's review of the statutory requirements in the *Larkin* case with the court's analysis of the zoning denial
in the *Huntington* case, reproduced *supra.* In what ways are they similar?
Different? Notice that the court in *Larkin* finds a deinstitutionalization policy
in the federal law and then applies it to invalidate the state statutes. Compare
that policy with the desegregation policy implicit in *Huntington.* Do the courts
treat the burden of proof issue the same way in both cases?

2. *Limitations on occupancy.* Occupancy limitations are important to group
homes because restrictive limitations can make a group home impracticable.
Chapter 3 considered a similar issue concerning limitations in zoning ordinances on the number of unrelated people who can live together. Occupancy
limitations in zoning ordinances that apply to group homes also present a
problem of facial conflict with the federal Act.

Oxford House-C v. City of St. Louis, 77 F.3d 249 (8th Cir.), *cert. denied,* 519
U.S. 816 (1996), upheld an ordinance that allowed eight unrelated persons
in a group home and only three unrelated persons in a single family dwelling.
This limitation effectively prohibited group homes that had to have more than
eight residents to be financially successful. The court relied on the Supreme
Court's *Belle Terre* case, reproduced *supra,* to hold that the legitimate goals
of decreasing traffic, congestion and noise in residential areas justified the
ordinance. Is this case contrary to *Larkin,* at least in spirit? Some district
courts disagree with the *St. Louis* case. *Children's Alliance v. City of Bellevue,*
950 F. Supp. 1491 (W.D. Wash. 1997) (invalidating ordinance limiting group
home to six residents, not more than two caretakers, plus minor children of
residents and caretakers).

However, courts will invalidate ordinances that exclude group homes from
residential areas, either through the definition of "family," *Oxford House, Inc.
v. Town of Babylon,* 819 F. Supp. 1179 (N.D.N.Y. 1993), or by placing onerous
restrictions that have the effect of excluding group homes, *Children's Alliance,*
supra.

3. *Statutory exemption for occupancy restrictions.* The statute contains an
exemption that permits "reasonable . . . restriction[s] regarding the maximum number of occupants permitted to occupy a dwelling." 42 U.S.C.
§ 3607(b)(1). In *City of Edmonds v. Oxford House, Inc.,* 115 S. Ct. 1776 (1995),
the city's zoning ordinance defined "family" as a household either "related by
genetics, adoption or marriage," or consisting of no more than five unrelated
persons; this definition blocked a group home. The city argued that the
ordinance definition was permitted by § 3607(b)(1) as a reasonable occupancy
restriction.

The Court disagreed. Justice Ginsburg distinguished between *occupancy limits*, normally found in a housing code, which restrict the number of persons who may live in a dwelling, and *use restrictions*, such as the limitation to single-family use at issue before the court. The definition of family, she held, was ancillary to this *use restriction*, and thus not covered by the exemption applicable to occupancy limits. Congress provided the occupancy limit exemption, the Court held, because in another provision of the 1988 Amendments, it had prohibited discrimination against families with children, and it did not want to leave municipalities unable to prevent overcrowding. The Edmonds ordinance exactly inverted this concern, permitting families of any number but limiting unrelated groups.

True occupancy restrictions are covered by the exemption. *Fair Hous. Advocates Ass'n v. City of Richmond Heights,* 998 F. Supp. 825 (N.D. Ohio) (upholding occupancy restriction based on number of square feet in unit).

4. *Exceptions and variances.* Zoning ordinances commonly require group homes to obtain exceptions or variances. These zoning techniques, which are discussed in the next chapter, require some (usually discretionary) approval from a zoning agency. A refusal to grant a variance or exception is a potential as-applied violation of the federal Act.

Baxter v. City of Belleville, 720 F. Supp. 720 (S.D. Ill. 1989), indicates how courts have handled cases where there is a refusal to grant approval. The court held a refusal to grant a special use permit for a hospice for terminally ill AIDS patients was an intentional violation of the Act because the evidence showed that irrational fear of AIDS was at least a motivating factor in the decision. The court also found the refusal had a discriminatory impact on people with AIDS again because it was based on fear of AIDS. Compare *Cleburne, reproduced supra,* Ch. 3.

Courts will uphold a denial of a variance or exception when there is a legitimate reason for the denial. See *Gamble v. City of Escondido,* 104 F.3d 300 (9th Cir. 1997) (proposed building too large for lot and did not conform in size and bulk with neighborhood structures). An interesting question is the extent to which the Fair Housing Act modifies the usual rules for exceptions and variances. One court held a proposed group home was not entitled to a special exception in a business zone when traditional homes would also have been denied an exception in this zone. *Forest City Daly Hous., Inc. v. Town of N. Hempstead,* 175 F.3d 144 (2d Cir. 1999). Compare *Hovson's, Inc. v. Township of Brick,* 89 F.3d 1096 (3d Cir. 1996) (refusal to grant variance in residential area violated reasonable accommodation requirement when group homes for handicapped were not allowed in these areas as-of-right).

Challenging individual denials of special uses and other land use approvals is a time-consuming, expensive and uncertain strategy, however. Could it be argued that the very requirement of a special use or other approval violates the Act because of the stigma it attaches to group homes for the handicapped? The court thought not in *United States v. Village of Palatine,* 37 F.3d 1230 (7th Cir. 1994):

> In this case the burden on the inhabitants of [the group home] imposed by the public hearing — which they need not attend — does not outweigh the Village's interest in applying its facially neutral law to all

applicants for a special use approval. Public input is an important aspect of municipal decision making; we cannot impose a blanket requirement that cities waive their public notice and hearing requirements in all cases involving the handicapped. [*Id.* at 1234.]

5. *Amendments to the zoning ordinance.* An even more difficult problem is whether the "reasonable accommodation" provision requires a municipality to amend its zoning ordinance to allow for a group home. In one case, a court of appeals remanded so the district court could determine whether this provision required an amendment to a zoning ordinance to allow midsized group homes in residential areas. On remand, the court rejected claims by the city that an amendment would fundamentally alter its zoning policy. The court of appeals affirmed but limited the number of residents to nine. *Smith & Lee Assocs. v. City of Taylor (II),* 102 F.3d 781 (6th Cir. 1996). Another case did not require a rezoning to an increased multi-family density to accommodate a multi-family group home. Although there were multi-family buildings at the requested density in the surrounding area, the court held they did not compel a rezoning for the group home because otherwise every residential area would have to be rezoned to the highest density of any lot. *Hemisphere Bldg. Co. v. Village of Richton Park,* 171 F.3d 437 (7th Cir. 1999). If this is a correct statement of zoning law, on what basis could the Fair Housing Act require a modification?

6. *The Americans with Disabilities and Rehabilitation Acts.* Group homes not covered by the Fair Housing Act may be able to bring suits claiming zoning discrimination under these acts. Both statutes prohibit municipalities denying disabled persons the benefits of "services, programs or activities." See 42 U.S.C. 12132 (ADA). *Innovative Health Systems, Inc. v. City of White Plains,* 117 F.3d 37 (2d Cir. 1997), held that this language included zoning, and held the plaintiff stated a claim that these statutes had been violated by a refusal to issue a building permit for an alcohol-and drug-dependent treatment center based on "stereotypes and generalized fears."

7. *Some final comments.* The Fair Housing Act amendments that cover group homes for the handicapped have resulted in substantial changes in zoning practices as they apply to these homes. Do you agree with the balance the courts have struck? How does the effect the Fair Housing Act has on zoning for group homes compare with the effect of exclusionary zoning doctrines on zoning for affordable housing?

8. For additional discussion see Connor, *How the Federal Fair Housing Act Protects Persons with Handicaps in Group Homes,* Land Use L. & Zoning Dig., Vol. 50, No. 1, at 3 (1998); Elliott, *The Fair Housing Act's "Reasonable Accommodation" Requirement,* Land Use L. & Zoning Dig., Vol. 52, No. 4, at 3 (2000); Schonfeld, *"Reasonable Accommodation" Under the Federal Fair Housing Amendments Act,* 25 Fordham Urb. L.J. 413 (1998); Note, *Not In My Backyard: The Disabled's Quest For Rights in Local Zoning Disputes Under the Fair Housing, the Rehabilitation, and the Americans with Disabilities Acts,* 33 Val. U. L. Rev. 581-642 (1999).

Chapter 5

THE ZONING PROCESS: EUCLIDEAN ZONING GIVES WAY TO FLEXIBLE ZONING

A. THE ROLE OF ZONING CHANGE

We have so far considered the traditional, or Euclidean, zoning system, so named for the U.S. Supreme Court case that upheld the constitutionality of zoning by districts. Euclidean zoning contemplates the division of the community into districts, in which land uses are allowed as-of-right. The administrative process should be quite simple:

> The originators of zoning anticipated a fairly simple administrative process. They thought of the zoning regulation as being largely "self-executing." After the formulation of the ordinance text and map by a local zoning commission and its adoption by the local governing body, most administrations would require only the services of a building official who would determine whether proposed construction complied with the requirements. This official was not expected to exercise discretion or sophisticated judgment. Rather, he was to apply the requirements to the letter. In the case of new construction, he was to compare the builder's plans with the requirements governing the particular land and either grant or deny a permit. Even today, this nondiscretionary permit process is at the heart of zoning administration. [Building the American City 202 (Report of the Nat'l Comm'n on Urban Problems, 1968).]

The Standard Zoning Act also provided for discretionary administrative procedures as well as a process through which the zoning ordinance could be amended, as the following article points out. Some of these procedures were intended to provide relief from the land use restrictions of the zoning ordinance.

MANDELKER, DELEGATION OF POWER AND FUNCTION IN ZONING ADMINISTRATION, 1963 Washington University Law Quarterly 60, 61–63

As elsewhere in public administration, the basic problem in zoning is to achieve as clear a differentiation as possible between policy-making and policy-application. On this score the Standard State Zoning Enabling Act, on which a majority of the state statutes are modeled, failed to make tenable distinctions. Policy-making was confided to the governing body of the locality, which was given the authority to adopt the zoning ordinance. Administration was given to the zoning administrator, often the building inspector, who has the power to issue zoning permits. But ambiguity comes in the introduction of two agencies, the plan commission and the board of adjustment, known also

423

as the board of zoning appeals. Both the commission and the board exercise functions that are partly legislative and partly administrative.

The plan commission is to advise on the enactment and amendment of the original ordinance. In theory, zoning amendments are to be made in response to substantial changes in environmental conditions or in other instances in which a policy change is indicated. Instead, amendments have often been employed to take care of limited changes in use, usually confined to one lot, a technique that has disapprovingly been called "spot zoning." Spot zoning for one parcel, vigorously opposed by adjacent neighbors, takes on adversary characteristics that give it a distinctly adjudicative cast.

The agency originally intended to provide a safety valve from the zoning ordinance is the board of adjustment. This board was authorized to grant both variances and [special] exceptions. . . . The variance is an administratively authorized departure from the terms of the zoning ordinance, granted in cases of unique and individual hardship, in which a strict application of the terms of the ordinance would be unconstitutional. The grant of the variance is meant to avoid an unfavorable holding on constitutionality.

By way of contrast, an exception is a use permitted by the ordinance in a district in which it is not necessarily incompatible, but where it might cause harm if not watched. Exceptions are authorized under conditions which will insure their compatibility with surrounding uses. Typically, a use which is the subject of a special exception demands a large amount of land, may be public or semi-public in character and might often be noxious or offensive. Not all of these characteristics will apply to every excepted use, however. Hospitals in residential districts are one example, because of the extensive area they occupy, and because of potential traffic and other problems which may affect a residential neighborhood. A filling station in a light commercial district is another example because of its potentially noxious effects.

NOTES AND QUESTIONS

1. Try to work out as clearly as you can the difference between a zoning amendment, a variance, and a special exception. The difficulty is that the owner of a small lot who wishes to have the applicable zoning restrictions changed as they apply to his property might conceivably make use of any of these techniques. He can ask the governing body for a map amendment to apply a different zoning classification. He might also be able to ask for a variance. He can also apply for a special exception if the use he proposes is listed as a special exception use in the zoning district in which his land is located. Under what circumstances might any or all of these alternatives be available? This is the problem addressed by the materials in this chapter.

The nature of the zoning change problem also varies with the nature of the area in which the landowner's property is located. In built-up areas, his property is likely to be an "infill" piece of vacant property surrounded by developed uses. The question is whether his proposed use fits in with this built-up land use environment. In suburban and developing areas, the problem is different. Here the surrounding area is likely to be undeveloped or sparsely developed. The landowner may own a substantial piece of land on which he plans to build a major development, such as a shopping center or a large residential development.

In suburban and developing areas, as *Building the American City* pointed out, the community may not intend its zoning ordinance to guide future development. Typically, such land use is zoned just below what it is anticipated that the market will demand, requiring all developers to come before a local zoning body to request some kind of zoning change. This type of zoning was called "wait-and-see" zoning, *id.* at 206; the zone is often referred to as a "holding zone," in that the municipality is holding open its options. Under a wait-and-see zoning system, all land development requires some type of permission, and zoning becomes a discretionary decisionmaking process rather than a system in which land uses are permitted as-of-right. Are the "taking" cases an impediment to this approach? Do you see other potential constitutional problems? Is this system of zoning administration rational? Well-organized? The American Planning Association has proposed model legislation that provides a major overhaul of the zoning administration process. Am. Plan. Ass'n, Model Planning Legislation Ch. 10 (2000 draft).

2. This chapter covers the variance, special exception and amendment, which are the traditional statutory techniques through which landowners secure a change in the zoning restrictions applicable to their property. It also covers the floating zone and contract zoning, which are newer forms of flexible zoning, and the role of site-plan review and the comprehensive plan in the zoning process. A concluding section considers the role of the initiative and referendum in zoning. For a discussion of the zoning process and wait-and-see zoning, see Krasnowiecki, *Abolish Zoning,* 31 Syracuse L. Rev. 719 (1980).

———

Proceedings before zoning boards lack the formality and controls of a judicial proceeding. The following fictitious transcript of a zoning variance hearing, written by the late Marlin Smith, illustrates how this process works. Marlin claimed that every statement made in this hearing was based on an actual occurrence!

PROCEEDINGS BEFORE THE PLANNING AND ZONING BOARD OF THE CITY OF SAN CIBOLA

THE DOCKET

Case No. 80-V-8: Application of Bullion Bank & Trust for a variance for a drive-up banking window.

The Members of the Board:

Wilbert Wawfull, Chairperson

Greta Greenbelt Grotheplanne

Oliver Oldmoney

Preston Pettefogg

Mark Multilist

[The chairperson called the proceedings to order and immediately recognized Mr. Giltedge, who rose to speak:]

Giltedge: I'm Gilbert Giltedge, President of Bullion Bank & Trust. You've got our variation application at the very end of the agenda and I know it's not going to be controversial. On the other hand it looks like some of the matters tonight are going to take a long time and I don't see why we can't get my simple little variation out of the way and let me go home.

Wawfull: That seems reasonable to me.

Grotheplanne: Mr. Chairman, that seems to me to be highly irregular. The bank's application for a variance was filed only a little more than two weeks ago and it is the last item on the agenda.

Wawfull: That doesn't really matter. It's the Chairman's prerogative to take these things up in the order he thinks best, and there's just no sense to making an important person like Mr. Giltedge sit here through all these other matters.

Grotheplanne: Well, I've only been on this Board for eight months and no one has given me a copy of the rules yet, but I can't believe that they permit you to decide to hear cases out of order without the consent of the Board.

Wawfull: But we don't really have any rules. We just try to do what's fair and it doesn't seem fair to me to ask Mr. Giltedge to wait when his matter won't take very long.

Grotheplanne: How do you know that?

Wawfull: Why, he told me all about it when we had dinner before the meeting.

Giltedge: This is a very simple matter. We want to build a drive-up teller window in the parking lot alongside our bank on Main Street. We applied for a building permit, but the Zoning Administrator gave us some foolishness about drive-ins not being a permitted use and he said we would have to get a variance from this Board. I've got some plans here showing how we propose to do it. If you look at the plans, you'll see that we would put the drive-up facility along the west side of the bank. Cars would still enter the existing parking lot from Main Street, and then they could proceed either to a parking place or to the drive-up window. There would still be two exits, one on Central Avenue and one on Main Street. Most banks have these drive-up facilities now, and we're just trying to stay abreast of the times and provide modern conveniences for our customers.

Pettefogg: I don't know whether we've got any rules, but if we have let's waive them.

Oldmoney: I agree.

Wawfull: It's settled then, we'll hear Mr. Giltedge.

Giltedge: This new drive-up window will be architecturally harmonious with the rest of the bank and we think it will be a credit to the downtown area.

Wawfull: That sounds like a fine idea, Mr. Giltedge. Anybody got any questions or objections?

Multilist: I don't seem to have a copy of the application.

Wawfull: That's because we just received it tonight.

Grotheplanne: Then how could the zoning administrator prepare the notice? There was a notice published, wasn't there?

Wawfull: Oh yes. Mr. Codebook just took down the information for the notice from Mr. Giltedge.

Multilist: (Puzzled) I'm looking at the notice now and it appears to me the legal description is not right. It refers to Lot 5 in the River Trails Subdivision.

Giltedge: That fool Codebook must've copied from the wrong piece of paper.

Wawfull: Well, that's just a little technical problem. The street address is right and everybody knows where the Bullion Bank is.

Pettefogg: I agree. We can't let technicalities stand in the way of progress.

Grotheplanne: Your idea sounds fine, Mr. Giltedge, but I wonder if you are aware of the standards in the zoning ordinance for variances?

Giltedge: Codebook gave me some forms, but I didn't have time to pay much attention to a lot of bureaucratese.

Grotheplanne: Well, to be specific the ordinance requires that you establish five points to the satisfaction of this Board showing that the restrictions in the ordinance cause you an unnecessary hardship.

Wawfull: Greta, if you are in one of your technical moods, we're going to be here all night.

Grotheplanne: Don't be snide, Wilbert. Now as I was saying, there are five standards. First, the property cannot yield a reasonable return if it can be used only in accord with the regulations in the zoning district. Second, the plight of the owner is due to unique circumstances. Third, the variance will not serve merely as a convenience to the applicant, but will alleviate some demonstrable and unusual hardship. Fourth, the alleged hardship has not been created by anyone presently having a proprietary interest in the property. Fifth, the proposed variance will not alter the essential character of the area, cause congestion in the streets, injure the value of nearby property, or adversely affect the health, safety, or welfare of the public. I don't recall, Mr. Giltedge, that anything you said dealt with any of those matters.

Oldmoney: Really, Greta, you'd think Mr. Giltedge was a newcomer to our town. Why that bank has been in his family for three generations. My own family has done business with them since Mr. Giltedge's grandfather founded it. Surely you don't believe a Giltedge would do anything that would not be good for San Cibola?

Grotheplanne: (Somewhat waspishly) I don't see anything in the zoning ordinance that says Giltedges are exempt from it.

Giltedge: (Placatingly) Now, Ms. Grotheplanne, I think that I can set your mind at ease. There won't be any traffic congestion because there won't be any additional traffic. We will have the same customers, but some will use the drive-up window. The bank is in the downtown business district and our drive-up window will be just another commercial use. There will not be any injurious effect on the value of any nearby property. After all, our bank is the closest property and we would not want to injure the value of our own property. The variance is not a convenience for us, it's a convenience for our customers. Our bank didn't create this hardship; it was created by the changing nature of the banking business. You could say our situation is unique because you've already given the Fourth Bank and Trust and Fidelity Savings & Loan variances for drive-up windows. And if you want to talk about a reasonable rate of return, let me tell you that if we can't stay competitive, we're not going to be able to stay in the downtown area very long.

Wawfull: Maybe we had better vote.

Bill Bottomline: Doesn't the public get a chance to say anything? I thought that this was supposed to be a public hearing.

Wawfull: Sure you do. What would you like to say?

Bottomline: My name is Bill Bottomline. I'm the Chief Accountant at the San Cibola plant of Bliteland Metals. You folks let the Fourth Bank and Trust Co. put in a drive-up window last year and it created a terrible mess on Front Street because the cars stack up in the street waiting to get in to the drive-up window. Some mornings it can take 10 minutes to go one block on Front Street. You are going to have the same kind of traffic jam if you let the Bullion Bank do the same thing on Main Street. Why can't you make them close the entrance on Main and enter from Central Avenue, which is the side street? Then there would be room for cars to line up on the parking lot and if some backed up into the street, it still would not create as much of a problem.

Giltedge: We couldn't do that — Central is a one-way street and people coming from the east would have to drive all the way to Bluff Boulevard and then come back to turn into Central. Besides, that would make it difficult for cars to get into and out of parking spaces and it wouldn't be energy efficient.

Grotheplanne: I am a little concerned that the exhaust from cars standing in line may have more pollutants in it than moving vehicles do. I think that we should have some air quality information before we act upon this variance application.

Wawfull: Well, I don't know about that. It would just delay the bank and we like to move these matters along. I think we're ready to vote.

Multilist: Aren't we going to have any discussion?

Wawfull: Sure, Mark. What did you want to say?

Multilist: I think that this Board ought to know that people from Bullion Bank & Trust have been in my real estate office to inquire about available land out near the new regional shopping mall. It seems to me that if Bullion Bank & Trust are not allowed to put in their drive-up window downtown, then they may move their main banking facilities out to the mall and build the drive-up facility out there. So if we don't want to see businesses moving out of downtown and deterioration set in, we should not be too fussy about a little modernization that will benefit the City.

Wawfull: Any more discussion? (Pause) I'll entertain a motion based on the findings of fact to grant the variance.

Grotheplanne: What findings of fact?

Wawfull: That there is unnecessary hardship.

Grotheplanne: There isn't anything resembling evidence of hardship.

Wawfull: When Mr. Giltedge says our zoning ordinance creates a hardship for him, I believe him. It's not his fault that the ordinance does not list drive-in banks as a permitted use.

Multilist: I move we grant the variance.

[Oldmoney seconded the motion and all voted in favor except Grotheplanne.]

NOTES AND QUESTIONS

1. *Due process?* This variance proceeding raises both substantive and procedural problems. What procedural problems do you see? Variances and their substantive requirements are discussed in the next section. What if the zoning ordinance required drive-in teller windows to be approved as a special exception? Would this be constitutional? Would the bank be entitled to a special exception? Could this problem be handled through an amendment to the zoning ordinance? How? Consider this question as you study special exceptions and zoning amendments later in this section. Also consider, when you review the material on site plans, *infra,* whether a site plan would help resolve the problems raised by the bank's application.

2. *The parties to land use litigation.* In most of the cases studied so far, either a landowner or a third party in interest, such as a housing organization, has brought the case to court. Landowners can also appeal zoning decisions that deny them a zoning change, but if the change is granted it is the neighbors who will appeal. This type of case raises somewhat different problems, so at this point it will be helpful to make some distinctions in the way in which zoning cases get to court and who the real parties in interest are. Professor Williams' discussion of the "three parties in interest" in land use litigation makes the point:

> Zoning litigation arises when a developer wishes to do something which requires a change in the rules, or perhaps an interpretation of them. The normal starting point for a zoning case is therefore a request for relaxation of some of the restrictions applying to the land in question. If the municipal authorities refuse to authorize such a relaxation, the developer may either accept this decision, or challenge it by suing the municipality. In the latter instance, the result is the

first type of zoning case — often referred to below as a "developer's case." The question in such a case is whether the municipal decision has unreasonably restricted the developer's property right to make use of his land. In the opposite situation, if the municipality decides to go along with a relaxation of the preexisting rules, neighboring landowners may (and often do) object, and may bring an action challenging this decision to relax the rules; and the result is a "neighbors' case." In such a case the plaintiff is a neighboring landowner, and the real defendant is the developer; in this instance the municipality ends up siding with the developer. In one sense, therefore, the municipality is not a separate party in interest in land use conflicts, but merely the ally of one or the other of two primary parties in interest.

In many states the courts handle these two types of cases quite differently, either explicitly (by different doctrine) or implicitly (by a markedly different pattern of decisions). As for the latter, the states vary sharply in their attitude towards claims by developers; but in almost all states the neighbors usually lose, with a few striking exceptions. [1 N. Williams, American Land Planning Law 71–72 (Rev. ed. 1988).]

Professor Williams also states that the legal issues in developer cases are "fairly well defined," and that it is in these cases that the states "split sharply." In neighbor cases "the legal technology is relatively primitive," with no clearly established rules nationwide. He adds that the major zoning states have used a good deal of ingenuity in applying various doctrines to give neighbors some standing to raise issues in court. *Id.* at 73–74.

The next group of cases primarily considers neighbor cases in which neighbors challenge a zoning change the municipality has provided for a developer. When reviewing the materials in this section, consider whether the distinctions Professor Williams makes between developer and neighbor cases are correct.

Who are the third party interests in zoning litigation? Professor Williams refers to these third party interests as "third-party nonbeneficiaries of the entire system." Their interests may be severely affected, but they "rarely appear in the case law." An example are the racial and economic minorities often excluded from a community by exclusionary zoning, who were considered in the last chapter.

PROBLEM

Excellent views of the snow-covered Del Pedro Mountains are available from all parts of Metro City. Proposals by developers to build several high-rise office buildings on the outskirts of Metro City threaten to spoil these views for Metro City residents. To prevent this from happening, the Metro City Council amended its comprehensive plan to include View Protection Guidelines (VPG) for areas of the city where view-threatening development is imminent. The VPG recommend as limits a 100-foot height and a 100-foot width for any new buildings in the area covered by the VPG. Metro City's zoning regulations are authorized by the State of Metro Zoning Act, which is modeled on the Standard Zoning Enabling Act.

Mesa Development Company owns a vacant block in an area covered by the VPG which is zoned C-N Commercial. The C-N Commercial district allows commercial (but not office) uses subject to a height limit of 40 feet and 35-foot setbacks from the lot edge. The four-block area surrounding the Mesa site is also zoned C-N Commercial and is almost fully developed with commercial buildings that conform to the height and setback restrictions. Mesa has applied to have its site rezoned from the C-N Commercial to the O-2 Office District, which allows office buildings without any restrictions on height. Mesa plans an office building 200 feet in height to be built to the lot lines.

(1) Assume the Metro City Council grants Mesa's rezoning application without restriction. The planning commission report recommending the rezoning states it is needed to help fill a growing demand for office space in the city. An owner of an adjacent commercial building has sued to have the rezoning declared invalid. What result? What if the O-2 Office District has the same setbacks as the C-N Commercial District? Mesa now applies for a variance from the setback requirement so it can build to the lot lines. Should the variance be granted?

(2) Now assume that after Mesa applied for the rezoning the city planning department informed Mesa the city council would grant the rezoning if Mesa agreed to record an easement on its property that would limit the building's height to 100 feet and its width to 40 feet. Mesa accepted the planning department's recommendation and recorded the easement. The city council then rezoned the Mesa site to O-2. Is the rezoning valid?

(3) Now assume an office building is authorized as a conditional use in a C-N zone. The height and setback restrictions of the C-N zone apply to any approved conditional use. The zoning ordinance authorizes the Zoning Board of Adjustment to approve an authorized conditional use if it finds the use is compatible with adjacent and permitted uses, will have adequate off-street parking and loading facilities and will be adequately served by public facilities. The Board holds a hearing and decides Mesa's conditional use meets all of these requirements except the compatibility requirement. The Board denies the conditional use and Mesa appeals to a state court. What result?

B.   THE ZONING VARIANCE

PURITAN-GREENFIELD IMPROVEMENT ASS'N v. LEO

7 Mich. App. 659, 153 N.W.2d 162 (1967)

LEVIN, JUDGE:

Defendant-appellant John L. Leo claims the circuit judge erred in setting aside a use variance granted by the Detroit Board of Zoning Appeals.

Leo owns a one-story, one-family dwelling at the northwest corner of Puritan avenue and Prest avenue, located in the northwest section of Detroit in an R-1 (single family residence) zoning district. On application and after hearing, the board granted Leo a variance to permit the use of the property as a dental and medical clinic (an RM-4 use) and to use the side yard for off-street parking on certain conditions.

The order of the board states that immediately to the west of the westerly boundary of Leo's property is a gasoline service station (at the corner of Puritan and Greenfield); that there was testimony Leo had not received any offers from residence-use buyers during the period of over a year the property had been listed and offered for sale; and, in the event a variance was granted, it was intended to preserve the present exterior of the building without significant alteration so that it would continue to appear to be a one-family dwelling.

The appeal board's dominant finding was:

> "That the board found unnecessary hardship and practical difficulty because of the heavy traffic and the closeness to the business section immediately to the west."

The board also found that the proposed use would not alter the essential character of the neighborhood, would not be injurious to the contiguous property, would not be detrimental to the surrounding neighborhood, and would not depreciate property values.

Plaintiff-appellee, Puritan-Greenfield Improvement Association, filed a complaint with the circuit court which was treated by the court as one for superintending control. The matter was heard by the circuit judge on the record made before the board. The circuit judge reversed the decision of the board, stating *inter alia* that it had not been shown the land could not yield a reasonable return or be put to a proper economic use if used only for a purpose allowed by existing zoning and that such showing of hardship as had been made was of "self-created" hardship attributable to the character of the structure thereon.

The applicable enabling act provides for a board of zoning appeals authorized to grant a variance upon a showing of practical difficulties or unnecessary hardship. The Detroit ordinance requires evidence of special conditions and unnecessary hardship or practical difficulties.

. . . The minimum constitutional standard establishes the scope of review. The circuit judge and we are required by the Michigan constitution to determine whether the findings of the board and its order are authorized by law and whether they are supported by competent, material, and substantial evidence on the whole record.

Although there has been a great deal of judicial effort expended in Michigan in considering challenges to the reasonableness or constitutionality of zoning as applied to individual properties, we find no Michigan appellate decisions construing the words "unnecessary hardship or practical difficulties."

The first modern zoning regulations were adopted by the city of New York and the phrase "practical difficulties or unnecessary hardship" was fashioned as the applicable standard to guide New York's board of appeals in considering applications for variances. A comparison of the relevant language of the applicable Michigan enabling act with that of the original New York city legislation shows that the Michigan provision authorizing the vesting in a board of zoning appeals the authority to grant variances parallels the corresponding New York city provision.

It appears that most State enabling acts, and ordinances based thereon, use "unnecessary hardship" as the governing standard. In those States (like Michigan and New York) where the applicable standard is "unnecessary hardship *or* practical difficulties," the phrase "practical difficulties" had been regarded as applicable only when an area or a dimension variance is sought, and in determining whether a use variance will be granted the decisive words are "unnecessary hardship." In the light of this history, we have turned for guidance to decisions of other States applying the "unnecessary hardship" standard.

A text writer, Rathkopf, states that courts have held, variously, that a property owner seeking a variance on the ground of "unnecessary hardship" must show credible proof that the property will not yield a reasonable return if used only for a purpose allowed by the ordinance or must establish that the zoning gives rise to hardship amounting to virtual confiscation or the disadvantage must be so great as to deprive the owner of all reasonable use of the property. He concedes that the showing required "is substantially equivalent to that which would warrant a court in declaring the ordinance confiscatory, unreasonable, and unconstitutional in its application to the property involved." 2 Rathkopf, The Law of Zoning and Planning, p. 45-14.

These principles also find expression in the frequently stated generalizations that variances should be sparingly granted, that it is not sufficient to show that the property would be worth more or could be more profitably employed if the restrictions were varied to permit another use, and that the board of appeals, being without legislative power, may not in the guise of a variance amend the zoning ordinance or disregard its provisions.

The judicial attitudes so expressed could well have been influenced by the early history of the boards of zoning appeal and the need to declare more precise standards than the somewhat nebulous "unnecessary hardship." When zoning was in its infancy it was thought by some that without a board of zoning appeals the individual declarations of zoning ordinance invalidity would be so numerous it would become necessary to declare the legislation void as a whole and, thus, "the chief value of the board of appeals in zoning is in protecting the ordinance from attacks upon its constitutionality." That view of the purpose of the board of zoning appeals has been said to require a standard related to the reasonableness of the zoning:

> "The hardship contemplated in this legislation has constitutional overtones, and it is the purpose of the variance to immunize zoning legislation against attack on the ground that it may in some instances operate to effect a taking of property without just compensation." *R.N.R. Associates v. City of Providence Zoning Board of Review* (1965), R.I., 210 A.2d 653, 654.

It has been said that the function of a board of zoning appeals is to protect the community against usable land remaining idle and it is that purpose which gives definition to "unnecessary hardship."

"Since the main purpose of allowing variances is to prevent land from being rendered useless, 'unnecessary hardship' can best be defined as a situation where in the absence of a variance no feasible use can be made of the land." 74 Harv. Law Rev. p.1401 [1961].

Whatever the rationale may be, it has been held that a variance should not be granted until it appears the property cannot be put reasonably to a conforming use; or the application of the ordinance is so unreasonable as to constitute an arbitrary and capricious interference with the basic right of private property; or that the property cannot be used for a conforming purpose.

"An unnecessary hardship exists when all the relevant factors taken together convince that the plight of the location concerned is unique in that it cannot be put to a conforming use because of the limitations imposed upon the property by reason of [its] classification in a specific zone." *Peterson v. Vasak,* [76 N.W.2d at 426 (Neb. 1956)].

The authors of a number of scholarly studies appear to agree that an applicant desiring a variance must show

"(a) that if he complies with the provisions of the ordinance, he can secure no reasonable return from, or make no reasonable use of, his property; (b) that the hardship results from the application of the ordinance to his property; (c) that the hardship of which he complains is suffered by his property directly, and not merely by others; (d) that the hardship is not the result of his own actions; and (e) that the hardship is peculiar to the property of the applicant." Green, The Power of the Zoning Board of Adjustment to Grant Variances from the Zoning Ordinance (1951), 29 N.C. Law Rev. 245, 249.

The New York Court of Appeals has stated:

"Before the Board may exercise its discretion and grant a [use] variance upon the ground of unnecessary hardship, the record must show that (1) the land in question cannot yield a reasonable return if used only for a purpose allowed in that zone; (2) that the plight of the owner is due to unique circumstances and not to the general conditions in the neighborhood which may reflect the unreasonableness of the zoning ordinance itself; and (3) that the use to be authorized by the variance will not alter the essential character of the locality." *Otto v. Steinhilber* (1939), 282 N.Y. 71, 24 N.E.2d 851.

The *Otto* definition has been adopted by other courts.

We find overwhelming support for the proposition — expressed in *Otto* — that the hardship must be unique or peculiar to the property for which the variance is sought. . . .

Under these definitions even if the land cannot yield a reasonable return if used only for a purpose permitted by existing zoning, a use variance may not be granted unless the landowner's plight is due to unique circumstances and not to general conditions in the neighborhood that may reflect the unreasonableness of the zoning.

This limitation on the board's powers is related to the third limitation expressed in *Otto* — that a use authorized by a variance shall not alter the essential character of the locality. In this connection we note that the Detroit ordinance prohibits a variance that would be contrary to the public interest or inconsistent with the spirit of the ordinance.

> "If it [the hardship] affects a whole area, then his remedy lies in seeking an amendment to the zoning ordinance. This is true even where the applicant's property is situated in an area where none of the properties can be put to any reasonable beneficial use owing to zoning restrictions. It is not for the board in these circumstances to bestow liberties upon one single member of this group of property holders. The legislature must be the body to make decisions of this sort even in cases where the most severe hardship can be shown." Pooley, Planning Zoning in the United States, op. cit. at p. 59 [1961].

The Rhode Island Supreme Court has stated that once the right to a variance becomes established the only matter remaining is the scope and character of the relief to be granted, which must be effectuated in a manner consistent with the public interest; but if a considerable number of property owners are similarly affected, it might well appear contrary to the spirit of the ordinance to grant relief to one while denying it to another, and in such a case it has been said that relief should be withheld until it can be decreed by the governing body or, if necessary, by the courts.

While we have discussed the foregoing statements that the hardship must be unique and that there are limitations on a zoning appeal board's power to frame a remedy when the hardship is shared with others — such statements being so inextricably a part of judicial, text and scholarly definitions of "unnecessary hardship" that the construction of that term could not accurately be discussed without reference to those statements — we do not here express our views thereon, as it is not necessary to do so in order to decide this case. We limit our holding to that expressed in the next paragraph.

Our review of the authorities leads us to hold that a use variance should not be granted unless the board of zoning appeals can find on the basis of substantial evidence that the property cannot reasonably be used in a manner consistent with existing zoning. In *Otto* the New York Court of Appeals stated that one seeking a variance must show that the land in question cannot yield a *reasonable return* if used only for a purpose allowed in the relevant zoning district. It will be noted that we have used the word "property" (i.e., including improvements) rather than "land," reserving to a later day the decision whether we wish to adopt that aspect of the *Otto* definition. It will also be noted that our holding speaks in terms of "reasonable use" rather than "reasonable return." Whether property usable in trade or business or held for the production of income can reasonably be used for a purpose consistent with existing zoning will, no doubt, ordinarily turn on whether a reasonable return can be derived from the property as then zoned. While any property, including a single family residence, may be made to produce income if a tenant can be found therefor, it would in our opinion be unrealistic as to all properties (without regard to their varying utility) to resolve the question solely on the basis of the return that can be derived from the property.

In the case of Leo's property, we perceive the question to be whether the property can continue reasonably to be used as a single family residence. The appeal board made no determination in that regard, resting its finding of unnecessary hardship solely on the "heavy traffic and the closeness to the business section immediately to the west."

Leo's property has been used for some time as a single family residence. While the board found there was "testimony" that Leo had not received any offers from residence-use buyers during the period of over a year the property had been listed and offered for sale, the asking price for the house and adjoining lot was $38,500 in a neighborhood where, according to the only record evidence, houses generally sell for $20,000 to $25,000. There was no evidence of efforts to sell the property at any price lower than $38,500; indeed, there was no testimony at all as to the extent of the sales effort or the income that could be derived from the property as zoned.

Testimony that the house and lot could not be sold for $38,500 in a neighborhood where houses generally sell for substantially less than that amount does not, in our opinion, constitute any evidence that the property could not continue reasonably to be used as a single family residence.

Thus there was not only a failure to find that the property could not reasonably be used in a manner consistent with existing zoning, but, as we read the record, there was no evidence upon which such a finding could have been based. In this connection, it should be remembered that the fact that the property would be worth more if it could be used as a doctor's clinic and that the corner of Puritan and Prest has disadvantages as a place of residence does not authorize the granting of a variance. Heavy traffic is all too typical of innumerable admittedly residential streets. Adjacency to gasoline stations or other commercial development is characteristic of the end of a business or commercial district and the commencement of a residential district. "A district has to end somewhere." *Real Properties, Inc. v. Board of Appeal of Boston* (Mass. 1946), 65 N.E.2d 199, 201.

It can readily be seen that unless the power of the board of zoning appeals to grant a use variance is defined by objective standards, the appeal board could [and we do not in any sense mean to suggest this would be deliberate] rezone an entire neighborhood — a lot or two lots at a time. The variance granted in response to one "hardship" may well beget or validate another claim of hardship and justify still another variance. If it is a hardship to be next to a gasoline station, it could be a hardship to be across from one, to be behind one, or diagonally across from one. If heavy traffic is a valid basis, variances might become the rule rather than the sparingly granted exception.

We do not wish to be understood as challenging the judgment of the board of zoning appeals. A doctor's office with the appearance of a single family residence on a busy street which already has other commercial uses may very well be a logical, sensible and unobjectionable use. However the question before us is not whether the board of zoning appeals has acted reasonably, but whether on the proofs and findings the board could grant a variance on the ground of unnecessary hardship. We have concluded that neither the proofs nor the findings justified the variance granted.

We have given careful consideration to the considerable number of cases we found where the result was based on the reviewing court's conclusion that the appeal board had not abused the discretion confided to it. If there is substantial evidence to support the necessary findings, such a decision is, indeed, the correct one. However, there must be such evidence and such findings.

We have considered and rejected appellee's contention that a board of zoning appeals may not grant a use variance. We have also considered appellee's contention that the board's action should be reversed because the hardship alleged by Leo was "self-created." However, the hardship found by the board in this case could not be said to have been self-created — Leo neither created the traffic conditions on Puritan nor the gasoline station immediately to the west of his property.

Affirmed. Costs to appellee.

NOTES AND QUESTIONS

1. *The role of variances.* The Standard Zoning Act provided a single standard for variances, but over time a distinction has grown up between so-called "use" variances, in which a change in the use permitted in the district is sought, and "area" variances, in which relaxation of physical requirements (lot size, setbacks, height, etc.) is sought. Area variances are described, *infra.*

The principal case adopts and applies the usual tests that are used to review use variances. What are they? How would you define a "use" variance? For an extensive discussion of the role of use variances see *Cromwell v. Ward,* 651 A.2d 424 (Md. App. 1995).

What effect does the granting of a variance have on the property and on the underlying zoning? Although the personal circumstances of the applicant affected the court's decision in the principal case, it is clear that personal need cannot be the basis for a variance. *Larsen v. Zoning Bd. of Adjustment,* 543 Pa. 415 (Pa. 1996) (variance requested to provide play area for children). Moreover, a variance runs with the land and is not personal to the applicant who receives one, because zoning deals with the use, not the users. Although the granting of a variance does not change the applicable zoning restrictions, a new owner can continue to rely on the terms of the variance. See *Stop & Shop Supermarket Co. v. Board of Adjustment of Springfield,* 744 A.2d 1169 (N.J. 2000) (variance for parking in residential zone). Under what conditions might the underlying zoning be applied?

Some of the requirements for a use variance are the result of judicial interpretation, not explicit statutory language. The authority to grant variances derives from § 7 of the Standard Zoning Act, which most states have adopted. The Standard Act is reproduce in Chapter 3, Section A.2. Some states have adopted standards for variances that are more detailed than the Standard Act. E.g., Pa. Stat. Ann. tit. 53, § 10910.2. New Jersey authorizes a "special reasons" variance, which is more like a special exception because hardship is not required. N.J. Stat. § 40:55D-70(d). Note also that the statute and court-adopted standards impose a multi-factor test, and that all elements of the test must be met if a variance is to be granted.

Although the courts may interpret the statutory criteria, most courts hold that the statutory criteria for a variance may not be modified by the zoning ordinance. See *Nelson v. Donaldson*, 50 So. 2d 244 (Ala. 1951). Indeed, an ordinance provision that any variance granted must be the minimum variance necessary to provide the landowner with a reasonable return on his investment has been held invalid as an additional standard not included in the statute. See *Celantano v. Board of Zoning Appeals*, 184 A.2d 49 (Conn. 1962); *Coderre v. Zoning Bd. of Review*, 230 A.2d 247 (R.I. 1967).

2. *Variance standards. Otto v. Steinhilber,* cited and quoted in the principal case, is undoubtedly the leading case on standards for granting zoning variances. In *Steinhilber* the court distinguished situations where a variance should be granted from those where zoning regulations as applied to a substantial area should be held invalid, as follows:

> The object of a variance granted by the Board of Appeals in favor of property owners suffering unnecessary hardship in the operation of a zoning law, is to afford relief to an individual property owner laboring under restrictions to which no valid general objection may be made. Where the property owner is unable reasonably to use his land because of zoning restrictions, the fault may lie in the fact that the particular zoning restriction is unreasonable in its application to a certain locality or the oppressive result may be caused by conditions peculiar to a particular piece of land. In the former situation, the relief is by way of direct attack upon the terms of the ordinance. . . . In order to prevent the oppressive operation of the zoning law in particular instances, when the zoning restrictions are otherwise generally reasonable, the zoning laws usually create a safety valve under the control of a Board of Appeals, which may relieve against "unnecessary hardship" in particular instances. [24 N.E.2d at 852.]

Some states have codified the uniqueness rule. Cal. Gov't Code § 65906.

Most courts follow the New York decisions and refuse to approve a variance if it appears that the variance is based on conditions general to the neighborhood. *Nance v. Town of Indialantic*, 419 So. 2d 1041 (Fla. 1982); *Priest v. Griffin*, 222 So. 2d 353 (Ala. 1969). Compare *Wolfman v. Board of Appeals*, 444 N.E.2d 943 (Mass. App. 1983) (soil conditions justified variance to avoid height increase). Of course, when "unnecessary hardship" is a result of conditions general to the neighborhood, it would be proper for the local governing body to amend the ordinance, either on its own initiative or on the request of the landowners in the neighborhood.

Otto v. Steinhilber also states that the use allowed by a variance should not "alter the essential character of the locality." Some courts have adopted this limitation, and refer to it as the negative criterion. See *Commons v. Westwood Zoning Bd. of Adjustment*, 410 A.2d 1138 (N.J. 1980). How should this requirement be applied? Is it redundant? In *Medici v. BPR Co.*, 526 A.2d 109 (N.J. 1987), the court expanded on this approach by requiring an "enhanced quality of proof" in use variance cases: "Such proofs and findings must satisfactorily reconcile the grant of a use variance with the ordinance's continued omission of the proposed use from those permitted in the zone." Approval of a four-story motel in an industrial zone was overturned. Conversely, a use variance cannot be granted just because it is less intensive than uses permitted by the zoning ordinance. *Klein v. Hamilton County Bd. of Zoning Appeals,* 716 N.E.2d 268 (Ohio App. 1998) (insurance office).

The Standard Act requirement, that the spirit of the ordinance be observed and "substantial justice" done has not received much attention in the cases. But see *Belanger v. City of Nashua,* 430 A.2d 166 (N.H. 1966). However, statutes and ordinances often include this requirement as one factor to consider in deciding whether to grant a variance.

3. *No reasonable return.* What is the significance of the distinction drawn by Judge Levin, in the principal case, between proof that the land in question "cannot yield a *reasonable return* if used only for a purpose allowed in the relevant zoning district" and proof that no reasonable use of the property can be made unless a variance is granted? This distinction is rarely made in the variance cases from other states, and courts seem to use the two formulas interchangeably. Typical of judicial statements with respect to the "unnecessary hardship" test is the following language from *MacLean v. Zoning Bd. of Adjustment,* 185 A.2d 533 (Pa. 1962), where the court affirmed the board's refusal to grant a variance to permit construction of a gasoline service station in a residential area:

> [T]he real owner of this property, testified that the "best use" of this property would be as a gasoline service station, [so] it is obvious that his definition of "best use" is that use which would be most productive of economic profit. An examination of this record clearly shows that the request for a variance is not based upon any lack of feasibility of the use of this property for residential purposes but rather upon the expectation that the property will be productive of greater financial gain if used as a gasoline service station. This is the type of "economic hardship" which time and again we have stated does not constitute an "unnecessary hardship" sufficient to justify the grant of a variance. [*Id.* at 536.]

Accord *Lovely v. Zoning Bd. of Appeals,* 259 A.2d 666 (Me. 1969). See also *State v. Winnebago County,* 540 N.W.2d 6 (Wis. App. 1995) (variance cannot be granted to maximize value of the property).

4. *What about Lucas?* Is the *Puritan-Greenfield* case consistent with the Supreme Court's *Lucas* decision, which held a taking occurs per se when a land use regulation denies a property owner all economically productive use of his land? Is the variance standard adopted in that case, though it does not use the same terminology, virtually the same test? Presumably, if the *Lucas* test is met, a variance should follow automatically. See, *Village Bd. v. Jarrold,* 423 N.E.2d 385 (N.Y. 1981), holding pre-*Lucas* that the "no reasonable return" rule applied in variance cases is similar to the rule applied to takings claims.

5. *Efforts to sell.* The court's concern in the principal case about the landowner's efforts to sell the property reflect the rule adopted in *Forrest v. Evershed,* 164 N.E.2d 841 (N.Y. 1959), that a landowner applying for a variance must show that he made diligent efforts to sell his property without success. Should this rule be part of variance law? Isn't the value of the property dependent on conditions in the neighborhood, not on the unique circumstances of the land? If so, isn't the "attempt to sell" rule inconsistent with the uniqueness requirement? In *Valley View Civic Ass'n v. Zoning Bd. of Adjustment,* 462 A.2d 637 (Pa. 1983), the court rejected this rule but noted that evidence of inability to sell "has unquestionable probative value."

6. *Self-inflicted hardship.* If the landowner's hardship is "self-inflicted," courts will set aside any variance granted on the ground of hardship. Hardship is clearly self-inflicted if a landowner or developer proceeds to build in willful or accidental violation of the zoning ordinance and the municipal authorities insist that the violation be corrected. Hardship is also self-inflicted when it is "manufactured" — e.g., where the landowner or developer has torn down a residential structure and then claims that his property cannot profitably be put to residential use, or where he has deliberately carved a triangular lot out of a larger tract and then claims that development for residential use is not feasible. *Baker v. Connell,* 488 A.2d 1303 (Del. 1985). Similarly, when a developer pays a premium price for land, and then seeks a variance on the ground of financial hardship, the hardship has been held to be self-inflicted. *Josephson v. Autry,* 96 So. 2d 784 (Fla. 1957).

Some courts also have held that the purchase of property with knowledge of the zoning restrictions gives rise to self-inflicted hardship even if, arguably, the vendor could have established sufficient hardship to justify a variance. See *Sanchez v. Board of Zoning Adjustments,* 488 So. 2d 1277 (La. App. 1986). Such a broad rule is difficult to justify, since it results in a requirement that any landowner who has a legitimate claim to a hardship variance must himself obtain the variance before selling his property, even though he has no intention of developing the property himself; otherwise, the purchaser will be barred from obtaining a variance and, presumably, must attempt to have the zoning restrictions declared invalid as applied to his property if no reasonable return on a conforming use is possible.

Other courts have rejected the rule that purchase alone is self-created hardship, *Spence v. Board of Zoning Appeals,* 496 S.E.2d 61 (Va. 1998), while yet others hold that it is only one factor to consider. *Chirichello v. Zoning Bd. of Adjustment,* 397 A.2d 646 (N.J. 1979). See Reynolds, *Self-Induced Hardship in Zoning Variances: Does a Purchaser Have No One But Himself to Blame?,* 20 Urb. Law. 1 (1988).

7. *Use variances.* So-called "use" variances have been recognized as valid in the great majority of states, and the litigated cases on variances usually involve use variances. See *Matthew v. Smith,* 707 S.W.2d 411 (Mo. 1986). In a few states, however, the courts have refused to recognize the validity of use variances on the ground that to grant a variance that changes the uses permitted in a zoning district is, in substance, to amend the zoning ordinance, and thus to usurp the legislative power of the local governing body. *Josephson v. Autry,* 96 So. 2d 784 (Fla. 1957); *Bray v. Beyer,* 166 S.W.2d 290 (Ky. 1942); *Leah v. Board of Adjustment,* 37 S.E.2d 128 (N.C. 1946). The California zoning enabling act also prohibits use variances: "[a] variance shall not be granted for a parcel of property which authorizes a use or activity which is not otherwise expressly authorized by the zone regulation governing the parcel of property." Cal. Gov't Code § 65906.

8. *Conditions.* Most courts hold that the zoning board of adjustment (or appeals) has the power to attach appropriate conditions to the grant of any variance, although the Standard State Zoning Enabling Act and enabling statutes modeled on it do not expressly confer such power. It is arguable that the power to impose conditions can be implied from the final phrase in the Standard Act's authorization for the granting of variances — "so that the spirit of the ordinance shall be observed and substantial justice be done." Municipal zoning ordinances often expressly authorize the board of adjustment (or appeals) to impose conditions upon the grant of a variance, and in some cases the courts have considered this authorization to be significant. See also *Town of Burlington v. Jencik,* 362 A.2d 1338 (Conn. 1975) (conditions alleviate possible harm from use allowed by variance).

Not all conditions will be upheld. Conditions affecting the development of the site, such as conditions requiring landscaping, paving and access, are usually upheld. *Wright v. Zoning Bd. of Appeals,* 391 A.2d 146 (Conn. 1978). What about a condition terminating a variance if there is a change in the person using the property? See *St. Onge v. Donovan,* 522 N.E.2d 1019 (N.Y. 1988) (held invalid). Why allow the one but not the other?

9. *Findings.* Should boards of adjustment be required to make formal findings in variance cases? A few statutes require findings. E.g., 65 Ill. Comp. Stat. Ann. 5/11-13-11. Even without a statutory requirement, some courts require formal findings in order to provide for effective judicial review. A leading case is *Topanga Ass'n for a Scenic Community v. County of Los Angeles,* 522 P.2d 12 (Cal. 1974), noted, 1975 Urb. L. Ann. 349.

10. *Abuse.* The variance was initially considered an important "safety valve" in the administration of zoning ordinances. However, because of lack of expertise, political influence, and — in some of the larger cities — far too heavy a case load, many zoning boards of adjustment (or appeals) have long shown a regrettable tendency to ignore the standards prescribed by statute and by judicial decision for the granting of variances, as the drive-in bank case at the beginning of this section illustrates. Two substantial empirical studies of variance procedures both concluded that the boards in the communities under study did not, in a majority of cases, insist that the statutory and case law standards for variances be satisfied. See Dukeminier & Stapleton, *The Zoning Board of Adjustment: A Case Study in Misrule,* 50 Ky. L.J. 273 (1962); Comment, 50 Cal. L. Rev. 101 (1962). For a more recent study reaching similar conclusions, see Contemporary Studies Project, *Rural Land Use in Iowa: An Empirical Analysis of County Board of Adjustment Practices,* 68 Iowa L. Rev. 1083 (1983). But see Johannessen, *Zoning Variances: Unnecessarily an Evil,* 41 Land Use L. & Zoning Dig., No. 7, at 3 (1989).

A court can reverse a board that grants or denies a variance for reasons not based on the statutory criteria. See *Arkules v. Board of Adjustment,* 728 P.2d 657 (Ariz. App. 1986) (color variance invalidated).

11. *Sources.* See Reynolds, *The "Unique Circumstances" Rule in Zoning Variances—An Aid in Achieving Greater Prudence and Less Leniency,* 31 Urb. Law. 127 (1999); Reynolds, *Self-Induced Hardship in Zoning Variances: Does a Purchaser Have No One But Himself to Blame?,* 20 Urb. Law. 1 (1988); Comment, *A Constitutional Safety Valve: The Variance in Zoning and Land-Use Based Environmental Controls,* 22 B.C. Envtl. Aff. L. Rev. 307 (1995).

A NOTE ON AREA OR DIMENSIONAL VARIANCES

Much of the preceding material on zoning makes it clear that area, bulk and density regulations are often more important to the land developer than use regulations. This is especially so with residential district regulations. Most communities have several residential zones, and the distinctions between the zones are usually based on density rather than use. Density, in turn, may be controlled in a variety of ways, often used in combination: limitations on the number of dwelling units per acre, height limitations, restrictions on the percentage of lot that can be covered, and provisions requiring a minimum amount of open space for each residential unit. A developer can obtain a modification of these regulations through what are known as dimensional, area or site variances.

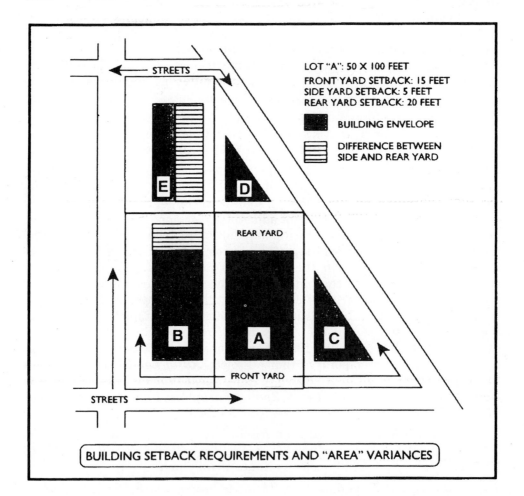

LOT "A": 50 X 100 FEET

FRONT YARD SETBACK: 15 FEET
SIDE YARD SETBACK: 5 FEET
REAR YARD SETBACK: 20 FEET

BUILDING ENVELOPE

DIFFERENCE BETWEEN SIDE AND REAR YARD

BUILDING SETBACK REQUIREMENTS AND "AREA" VARIANCES

A developer may request a dimensional variance for a number of reasons. She may need only a minor adjustment in a setback regulation. She may also seek a more fundamental increase in density. Getting a density increase is important to the developer because it increases her return.

The Standard Zoning Act provided a single "unnecessary hardship" test for all variances. A number of zoning statutes and ordinances have modified the Standard Act by providing that a variance may be granted for "practical difficulties" as well as for unnecessary hardship. Many cases hold that this type of statute does not create a dual standard and apply the unnecessary hardship test and other tests to both use and area variances. *City & Borough of Juneau v. Thibodeau,* 595 P.2d 626 (Alaska 1979) is a leading decision. Other statutes apply only a "practical difficulties" test for area variances. Me. Rev Stat. tit. 30-A, § 4353(4).

Courts have adopted a variety of tests for area variances when they do not apply the unnecessary hardship test. They indicate that the difference between the tests for use and area variances is a matter of degree, but emphasize that the test for area variances is less stringent. Courts usually apply a set of factors to determine when the practical difficulties test justifies an area variance. These usually include the significance of the economic injury, the magnitude of the variance sought, whether the difficulty was self-created, and whether other feasible alternatives could avoid the difficulty. Statutes and ordinances may also contain different standards, such as requiring only "adverse impact," and may also impose a "uniqueness" requirement. See *Cromwell v. Ward,* 651 A.2d 414 (Md. App. 1995) (summarizing the cases).

Husnander v. Town of Barnstead, 660 A.2d 477 (N.H. 1995), illustrates a typical situation in which courts will uphold an area variance. The court upheld a setback variance under a statutory provision similar to the Standard Act that contained an unnecessary hardship requirement. The building envelope allowed by the permitted setback was an elongated, curved strip roughly seventy feet long. One end was approximately thirty feet wide, but more than half of the strip was only fifteen feet wide. The owner conceded the allowable building envelope contained adequate square footage to construct a dwelling of the same size even if she did not get a variance, but contended that "the odd-shaped result from such construction would make the living space dysfunctional." The court found sufficient evidence of unnecessary hardship. For a similar case see *Lang v. Zoning Bd. of Adjustment,* 733 A.2d 464 (N.J. 1999) (variance for in-ground pool).

Area versus use variances.—It is not always clear what the courts mean when they speak of an area variance, which matters if the area standard is more permissive than the use standard. For instance, the New York court has held that a variance is an area variance even though it results in an increase in density. *Wilcox v. Zoning Bd. of Appeals,* 217 N.E.2d 633 (N.Y. 1966). This was an apartment case. Other courts have not been as lenient. *O'Neill v. Zoning Bd. of Adjustment,* 254 A.2d 12 (Pa. 1969). Here the property was located in an apartment zone, but the developer secured a variance permitting him to increase the floor space in his building by two and one-half times. While admitting that it might be willing to relax its rules for space variances, the court held that this was not such a case and that a change of this magnitude had to be made legislatively. The variance was set aside. Of similar import is *Mavrantonis v. Board of Adjustment,* 258 A.2d 908 (Del. 1969), where the court set aside a variance which would have reduced the side yard for a

12-story apartment building. The court noted that there were "sound reasons" for side yards.

If a court does not take this view and is willing to treat "density" variances like "area" variances for the purpose of applying the "practical difficulties" standard rather than the "unnecessary hardship" standard, it seems likely that it would treat height and similar variances in the same manner. However, in *Taylor v. District of Columbia Bd. of Zoning Adjustment,* 308 A.2d 230 (D.C. 1973), the landowner was denied a variance from height, side yard, court and lot occupancy requirements which would have allowed him to build twenty-seven townhouses instead of ten detached single-family dwellings on his property. The court noted that "while the requested variance may not be a use variance in its 'purest form,' it was a hybrid variance which would drastically alter the character of the zoned district" and could be characterized as "a use-area variance." *Id.* at 233. See also *Board of Adjustment v. Willie,* 511 S.W.2d 591 (Tex. Civ. Cas. 1974), reversing a height variance granted by the board of adjustment.

This problem can arise in other contexts. *Jenney v. Durham,* 707 A.2d 752 (Del. Super.), *aff'd,* 1997 Del. LEXIS 194 (Del. 1997), held a variance from a steep slope ordinance to allow the building of two homes was a use variance, because the ordinance did not allow residences as a permitted use in the prohibitive steep slope district in which the proposed homes would be located. *Hertzberg v. Zoning Bd. of Adjustment,* 721 A.2d 43 (Pa. 1998), upheld a variance to allow the owner of a dilapidated vacant building in a rundown area to convert it to a homeless shelter was an area variance. The court held a court may consider factors in deciding whether to grant area variances that include "economic detriment if the variance is denied, financial hardship created by work necessary to bring a building into strict zoning compliance, and the character of the surrounding neighborhood." Any other standard, it held, would inhibit neighborhood rehabilitation by prohibiting a variance that would allow the rehabilitation of a dilapidated building.

What policy factors in the administration of zoning ordinances appear to control these cases? How could a zoning ordinance deal with these important problems?

C. THE SPECIAL EXCEPTION, SPECIAL USE PERMIT, OR CONDITIONAL USE

BOARD OF SUPERVISORS OF FAIRFAX COUNTY v. SOUTHLAND CORP.

224 Va. 514, 297 S.E.2d 718 (1982)

RUSSELL, J., delivered the opinion of the Court:

In this zoning case, we must decide whether a local zoning ordinance may constitutionally distinguish "quick-service food stores" from other grocery stores and similar retail uses. The Southland Corporation brought a motion for declaratory judgment against the Board of Supervisors of Fairfax County, seeking an adjudication that certain parts of the Fairfax County Zoning Ordinance were unconstitutional and void as applied to it. The trial court, after hearing the evidence ore tenus, in a written opinion found for Southland. It held that the ordinance, as applied to Southland, violates the due process and equal protection provisions of the Virginia and United States Constitutions, as well as Code § 15.1-488, which requires the uniform application of zoning laws within zoning districts.

Southland operates a nationwide chain of retail food and convenience stores known as "7-Eleven." These are typically located in free-standing buildings containing less than 500 square feet, on small parcels of land fronting on heavily traveled roads, and feature drive-in parking immediately in front of the entrance. The majority of the stores contain 2500 square feet of net floor area.

The Fairfax County Zoning Ordinance, art. 20, § 20-300 classifies "any building which contains less than 5000 square feet of net floor area and which is used for the retail sale of food and other items" as a "quick-service food store." Quick-service food stores are permitted in free-standing buildings as a matter of right in three zoning districts: planned development housing (PDH), planned development commercial (PDC), and planned residential community (PRC), but these in turn require a development plan individually approved by the Board of Supervisors. Such stores are also permitted as a matter of right in certain shopping centers (in C-6, C-7, and C-8 districts), but only if they are located under the roof of a shopping center which contains at least six other stores and meets certain highway access criteria. They are permitted in free-standing buildings in C-5, C-6, C-7, C-8, I-5, and I-6 commercial and industrial districts, but only if they obtain a special exception from the Board. They share this special exception requirement with twenty-two other uses classified as "Commercial and Industrial Uses of Special Impact." *Id.* art. 9, § 9-500, 501. These are defined as uses "which by their nature or design can have an undue impact upon or be incompatible with other uses of land within a given zoning district." *Id.* art. 9, § 9-001. The Board reserves the right to deny any application for a special exception for one of these uses if it deems such use to be incompatible with existing or planned development in the district. The Board may also impose such "conditions and restrictions" as it thinks proper to insure that such a use will be homogeneous with the neighborhood. *Id.*

Southland points out that the effect of these provisions is to deny it the right to construct or operate a free-standing quick-service food store in any commercial district in Fairfax County. It contends that the special exception process to which it is thus subjected costs about $4,000.00 in application fees, attorneys fees, engineering and other costs for each site, increases construction costs substantially, and delays each store's opening for nine to twelve months. As Southland says, many other commercial uses, permitted by right, are exempt from the special exception process. Among these are grocery stores over 5000 square feet in floor area, restaurants, retail stores, shopping centers, banks, theaters, churches, hotels, motels, and schools. Southland argued, and the trial court found, that quick-service food stores of the "7-Eleven" type would have less adverse impact upon neighboring properties, the environment, and traffic than would some uses permitted by right, and that the ordinance was therefore an unreasonable classification as applied to South-land. [The court held that it had jurisdiction under the declaratory judgment statute to decide this attack on the ordinance.] . . .

We now turn to the merits. The power to regulate the use of land by zoning laws is a legislative power, residing in the state, which must be exercised in accordance with constitutional principles. This power may be delegated to the political subdivisions of the state. Code § 15.1-486 authorizes the governing bodies of Virginia counties to adopt local zoning ordinances. Section 15.1-491(c) authorizes such governing bodies to reserve unto themselves the right to issue "special exceptions under suitable regulations and safeguards."

The terms "special exception" and "special use permit" are interchangeable. Both terms refer to the delegated power of the state to set aside certain categories of uses which are to be permitted only after being submitted to governmental scrutiny in each case, in order to insure compliance with standards designed to protect neighboring properties and the public. The legislature may require certain uses, which it considers to have a potentially greater impact upon neighboring properties or the public than those uses permitted in the district as a matter of right, to undergo the special exception process. Each site is to be examined by public officials, guided by standards set forth in the ordinance, for the impact the use will have if carried out on that site. Although the uses in such special exception categories are permissible under the ordinance,[2] such permission is to be granted subject to such limitations and conditions as public officials may impose in order to reduce the impact of the use upon neighboring properties and the public to the level which would be caused by those uses permitted as a matter of right.

Whether a legislative body has reserved unto itself the power to grant or deny special exceptions or use permits, or has delegated the power to a Board of Zoning Appeals, we have consistently held the exercise of that power to be a legislative, rather than an administrative act.[3] A fortiori, the decision of the legislative body, when framing its zoning ordinance, to place certain uses in the special exception or conditional use category, is a legislative action. It involves the same balancing of the consequences of private conduct against the interests of public welfare, health, and safety as any other legislative decision.

The parameters of the judicial review of legislative zoning decisions are well settled. The action of the local governing body in enacting or amending its zoning ordinance is presumed to be valid. Inherent in the presumption of legislative validity is a presumption that the classification that the ordinance contains, and the distinctions which it draws, are not arbitrary, not capricious, but reasonable. Where such presumptive reasonableness is challenged by probative evidence of unreasonableness, the ordinance cannot be sustained unless the governing body meets the challenge with some evidence of reasonableness. But the governing body is not required to go forward with evidence

---

[2] This distinguishes the special exception from the variance. The latter authorizes a use which would otherwise be prohibited by the ordinance. Zoning ordinances usually delegate to public officials the power to grant variances where literal enforcement would result in unnecessary hardship. Code § 15.1-495(b). Public officials, passing upon requests for variances, act in an administrative, rather than a legislative, capacity.

[3] This appears to be a minority view.

sufficient to persuade the fact-finder of reasonableness by a preponderance of the evidence. The burden is less stringent. If evidence of reasonableness is sufficient to make the question "fairly debatable," the ordinance must be sustained.

Applying the foregoing principles to the evidence before us, we conclude that the County was entitled to a presumption of legislative validity, which Southland challenged by probative evidence tending to show unreasonableness. Although the evidence touched upon such problems as glare from night lighting and run-off from storm drainage, the principal dispute was the relative amount of highway traffic congestion caused by quick-service food stores, compared to that caused by the uses permitted by right. It is unnecessary to review the evidence in detail, except to observe that it was sufficient to overcome the County's initial presumption of legislative validity. It is self-evident, for example, that large shopping centers and supermarkets generate more total traffic than 2500 square foot convenience stores.

The County, however, responds with evidence of two countervailing considerations. First, actual traffic counts showed that the peak hours of vehicle activity entering and leaving quick-service food stores tended to coincide with the peak hours of traffic on the adjacent roads, particularly the morning rush hour. The peak hours in the larger commercial uses permitted by right tended to occur in mid-morning, or at other times when the roads were less congested. Second, the intensity of traffic activity in relation to land area was far greater in the case of small convenience markets. They were found to generate 506 "trips" per 1000 square feet, while neighborhood shopping centers generated only 65 such "trips." A "trip" was defined as a vehicle either entering or leaving the site between 7:00 a.m. and 7:00 p.m.

This might have little significance in itself, but it was coupled with the fact that the small convenience markets, situated on much smaller parcels of land, had little flexibility in the location of entrances and "curb cuts." If such a store were to be sited at the corner of a busy intersection, for example, it would precipitate a substantial amount of traffic directly into the most congested part of the traffic pattern, at the most congested hours. While entrances and "curb cuts" may be reasonably regulated in the exercise of the police power, access may not be entirely denied, absent a "taking" for public use and the resulting constitutional necessity for the payment of just compensation.

Larger shopping centers and supermarkets, by contrast, being located on larger tracts of land, may be subjected to far more traffic control before the point of confiscatory regulation is reached. Their greater size permits more flexibility in providing service roads, deceleration lanes, and other means of access control. Even if they are to be provided only with simple entrances, these may more readily be kept away from congested intersections and other danger points by reason of the greater land area involved.

We shall not undertake to resolve the controversy posed by the foregoing arguments because they demonstrate that the question whether quick-service food stores should be required to obtain a special exception is "fairly debatable." "Given the human tendency to debate any question, an issue may be said to be fairly debatable when the evidence offered in support of the opposing views would lead objective and reasonable persons to reach different conclusions." *Fairfax County v. Williams*, 216 S.E.2d 33, 40 (Va. 1975). Thus the County has presented evidence sufficient to render the reasonableness of the ordinance "fairly debatable," and it must therefore be sustained. . . .

NOTES AND QUESTIONS

1. *What they are.* The issue of what uses can be classified as special exceptions has surprisingly not received extensive consideration in the courts. Compare this statement in a leading case with the holding in the principal case:

> [C]ertain uses, considered by the local legislative body to be essential or desirable for the welfare of the community . . ., are entirely appropriate and not essentially incompatible with the basic uses in any zoning . . ., but not at every or any location . . . or without conditions being imposed by reason of special problems the use . . . presents from a zoning standpoint. . . . [*Tullo v. Millburn Twp.*, 149 A.2d 620, 624, 625 (N.J. App. Div. 1959).]

Could the drive-in bank that was the subject of a variance application in the hypothetical hearing, sec. A *supra*, be classified as a conditional use? What about a landfill? See *Bierman v. Township of Taymouth*, 383 N.W.2d 235 (Mich. App. 1985) (can classify junkyards but not landfills as special exceptions in agricultural district). Contra *Ackman v. Board of Adjustment*, 596 N.W.2d 96 (Iowa 1999). See Blaesser, *Special Use Permits: The "Wait-and-See" Weapon of Local Communities*, 21 Zoning & Plan. L. Rep. 69 (1998).

It is clear that the zoning pioneers did not intend the "special exception" to be anything more than a supplement to the basic technique of "pre-zoning" a municipality into a number of different use and density districts. *Rockhill v. Chesterfield Twp.*, 128 A.2d 473 (N.J. 1956), makes it clear that the special exception technique, combined with low density and "wait-and-see" zoning, cannot be used as the primary method by which a municipality controls its growth and development.

2. *Who may grant?* Note that the Standard Zoning Act, § 7, largely left to the governing body the decision on what standards to adopt for special exceptions. It provides:

> [T]he . . . board of adjustment may, in appropriate cases and subject to appropriate conditions and safeguards, make special exceptions to the terms of the ordinance in harmony with its general purpose and intent and in accordance with general or specific rules contained therein.

Many states have adopted this language verbatim. Compare the present New Jersey statute, which authorizes the planning board to grant special exceptions "according to definite specifications and standards which shall be clearly set forth with sufficient certainty and definiteness to enable the developer to know their limit and extent." N.J. Stat. Ann. § 40:55D-67(a). Why do you suppose the legislature made this change? See also Idaho Code § 67-6512(e) (may require social, economic, fiscal and environmental studies).

As Judge (later Justice) Hall said in *Tullo*, "special use" or "special use permit" would be a more accurate term than "special exception" to describe the uses specified in the zoning ordinance as permitted in a given district with the approval of a designated local zoning board or agency. The term "conditional use" or "conditional use permit" is sometimes used in zoning enabling acts and local zoning ordinances. See Cal. Gov't Code § 65901(a).

3. *Which agency?* Zoning ordinances often delegate the authority to grant special exceptions to the planning commission or local governing body, probably because these agencies almost always will receive advice on the special exception from the planning staff. See the model zoning ordinance, Ch. 3 *supra.* In states that have adopted the Standard Zoning Act § 7, the courts hold this arrangement impermissible, because of the specific delegation to the board of adjustment. See *Depue v. City of Clinton,* 160 N.W.2d 860 (Iowa 1968). Delegation to these bodies is allowable when the statute leaves open the authority to grant special exceptions. See *Kotrich v. County of Du Page,* 166 N.E.2d 601 (Ill.), *appeal dismissed,* 364 U.S. 475 (1960).

The planning commission is authorized by statute to grant special exceptions in some states. See Neb. Rev. Stat. § 19-929(3) (council may also retain power). Some states allow more than one agency to grant special exceptions. Cal. Gov't Code § 65902 (board of adjustment or zoning administrator). A state that authorizes hearing examiners may give them the authority to grant special exceptions. Nev. Rev. Stat. Ann. § 278.262.

4. *Delegation of power.* It is clear that a zoning board of adjustment (or appeals) acts "administratively" when it grants or denies a special exception, special use permit, or conditional use. Moreover, where the final decision is made by the local governing body upon recommendation of the board of adjustment (or appeals), the courts have generally held that the governing body acts "administratively" rather than "legislatively." The principal case is contra, and a distinct minority. Thus, in theory, the zoning ordinance should contain standards adequate to guide the exercise of administrative discretion by the board of adjustment (or appeals).

Judicial treatment of ordinance standards for special exceptions, special use permits, and conditional uses is summarized as follows in American Law Institute, Model Land Development Code, Tentative Draft No. 2, Note to § 2-207 (1970):

> Mandelker's review of cases shows that "nuisance standards" — negatively phrased standards directing that uses will not be allowed as exceptions if they create nuisance type external costs — have been approved overwhelmingly. Ordinances without any standards — simply authorizing an administrative board to issue an exception — generally have been held to delegate legislative authority invalidly. But most zoning ordinances provide general welfare standards and here judicial reaction is mixed. (Usually the ordinance allows the board to permit any of the enumerated special uses if such action would be in accord with the purposes and intent of the ordinance and be conducive to the general welfare.) Many cases sustain such standards without any critical comment. Some courts attempt to evaluate such standards and conclude that they are certain enough in view of

the technological complexities of zoning administration. A number of cases hold such standards unconstitutional or ultra vires. Confusingly, courts in the same jurisdiction, and even the same courts, render inconsistent opinions on similar standards in different cases. The problems raised by exceptions are like those raised by variances. At base it is the fear that without somewhat concrete standards landowners will be vulnerable to discrimination. In addition, there is the desire to have policy made by a representative body and to assure neighborhood status quo. And as with variances, courts have not been able to take solace in procedural regularity because enabling acts and ordinances have not required administrative agencies to state in detail the reasons for granting or denying exceptions.

"Mandelker's review of cases" can be found in Mandelker, *Delegation of Power and Function in Zoning Administration,* 1963 Wash. U. L.Q. 60.

5. *Discretion to deny or approve.* How much discretion does a local zoning agency have to grant or deny a special exception use? Note that the standards for special exceptions can be quite broad, e.g., in the general welfare or public interest. Consider the following from *Archdiocese of Portland v. County of Wash.,* 458 P.2d 682 (Or. 1969):

> [T]he ordinance itself reveals the legislative plan forecasting the likelihood that certain specified uses will be needed to maximize the use of land in the zone for residential purposes. The Board's discretion is thus narrowed to those cases in which an application falls within one of the specified uses. The fact that these permissible uses are predefined and have the legislative endorsement of the governing body of the county as a tentative part of the comprehensive plan for the area limits the possibility that the Board's action in granting a permit will be inimical to the interests of the community. The suspicion which is cast upon the approval of a change involving an incompatible use . . . is not warranted where the change has been anticipated by the governing body. Therefore, unlike the spot zoning cases the granting of permits for conditional uses is not likely to cause the "erosive effect upon the comprehensive zoning plan" described in *Smith v. County of Washington* [406 P.2d 545 (Or. 1965)]. [*Id.* at 686.]

Does this analysis suggest that zoning boards have limited discretion to deny a special exception?

The following case indicates how courts review decisions by zoning boards on special exception applications:

CROOKED CREEK CONSERVATION AND GUN CLUB, INC. v. HAMILTON COUNTY NORTH BOARD OF ZONING APPEALS

677 N.E.2d 544 (Ind. App. 1997)

SULLIVAN, JUDGE

Appellant Crooked Creek Conservation & Gun Club, Inc. (Crooked Creek) sought a special exception from appellee Hamilton County North Board of Zoning Appeals (BZA) in order to build a trap and skeet shooting range in Hamilton County. Following a public hearing during which remonstrators opposed Crooked Creek's plans, the BZA refused to grant the special exception. Crooked Creek petitioned the trial court for a writ of certiorari and the trial court affirmed the BZA's decision.

Crooked Creek now appeals, presenting the following restated issues for our review:

(1) Did the trial court err in affirming the BZA's refusal to grant the special exception? . . .

Crooked Creek has operated a trap and skeet shooting club in Marion County for over 45 years. Concerned with the increased urbanization of the area in which its present facilities are located, Crooked Creek found what it believed to be a more suitable parcel of land upon which to conduct its activities in rural Hamilton County. The property is zoned "A-2," a designation which contemplates agricultural, large-lot residential, and flood plain uses. The Hamilton County Zoning Ordinance (HCZO) provides that gun clubs may be permitted in A-2 districts as special exceptions to the above-delineated uses. Hamilton Co. Zoning Ord. (hereinafter HCZO) Art. 15(B) § 1. A special exception is simply a use permitted under a zoning ordinance upon the showing of certain criteria set forth in the ordinance. The HCZO provides that the BZA must determine that the specially excepted use will fulfill three separate requirements before the BZA may grant the exception. As HCZO Art. 15(A) § 2 states:

> Upon hearing, in order for a special exception to be granted, the board must find, in writing, that:
>
> a. The establishment, maintenance, or operation of the special exception will not be injurious to the public health, safety, morals, or general welfare of the community;
>
> b. The special exception will not affect the use and value of other property in the immediate area in a substantially adverse manner;
>
> c. The establishment of the special exception will be consistent with the character of the district (particularly that area immediately adjacent to the special exception) and the land use permitted therein.

In March, 1994, Crooked Creek applied to the Hamilton County North Board of Zoning Appeals for a special exception for its trap and skeet shooting operation. On April 26, 1994, the Hamilton County North Board of Zoning Appeals convened to review and take public comments upon Crooked Creek's application. Crooked Creek presented testimonial evidence and submitted a comprehensive package of documentary evidence in support of its application. Crooked Creek's evidence generally supported its assertion that its shooting operation would satisfy the three above-mentioned requirements for the granting of a special exception. The remonstrators, however, presented evidence, both documentary and testimonial, which suggested, among other things, that Crooked Creek's trap and skeet shooting activities would be detrimental to public health and would decrease property values in the area. After both sides completed their presentations, the BZA tabled the matter so that the board members could consider the documentary evidence supporting and opposing Crooked Creek's application. The BZA indicated that it would come to a conclusion at the following meeting to be held May 24, 1994.

When the BZA reconvened on May 24, Crooked Creek asked the BZA to consider additional documentary evidence compiled by Crooked Creek assertedly rebutting the evidence presented by the remonstrators at the April 26 meeting. The BZA refused to consider this additional evidence, indicating that the time for submission of evidence ended upon the adjournment of the April 26 meeting, and then voted three to one to deny Crooked Creek's application. The BZA members voting against the application found, generally, that the lead shot used in trap and skeet shooting presented potential public health hazards, and that gun noise could adversely impact property values in the otherwise bucolic surroundings.

When reviewing a decision of a zoning board, an appellate court is bound by the same standard of review as the certiorari court. Under this standard, a reviewing court, whether at the trial or appellate level, is limited to determining whether the zoning board's decision was based upon substantial evidence. The proceeding before the certiorari court is not intended to be a trial de novo, and neither that court nor the appellate court may reweigh the evidence or reassess the credibility of witnesses; rather, reviewing courts must accept the facts as found by the zoning board.

I.

Crooked Creek argues that the trial court erred in failing to reverse the BZA's decision to deny Crooked Creek's application. Crooked Creek first contends that since it presented substantial evidence to show that it would comply with the three criteria for special exceptions, the BZA was required to grant the exception. Crooked Creek also argues that the remonstrators presented insufficient evidence to support the BZA's conclusion that the trap and skeet shooting operations would not meet the special exception criteria.

Crooked Creek claims that the award of a special exception is mandatory upon the applicant's presentation of evidence that its proposed use satisfies the statutory prerequisites set forth in the zoning ordinance. It is often true, as Crooked Creek notes, that if a petitioner for a special exception presents sufficient evidence of compliance with relevant statutory requirements, the exception must be granted. *Town of Merrillville Bd. of Zoning Appeals v. Public Storage, Inc.*, 568 N.E.2d 1092, 1095 (Ind. App. 1991) trans. denied. However, the *Town of Merrillville* case was careful to note that while some special exception ordinances are regulatory in nature and require an applicant to show compliance with certain regulatory requirements (e.g. structural specifications), providing the zoning board with no discretion, some special exception ordinances provide a zoning board with a discernable amount of discretion (e.g. those which require an applicant to show that its proposed use will not injure the public health, welfare, or morals). *Id.* at n.3. Crooked Creek's position that a board of zoning appeals must grant a special exception upon the applicant's submission of substantial evidence of compliance with the relevant criteria is true only as to ordinances falling within the former category. In other words, when the zoning ordinance provides the board of zoning appeals with a discernable amount of discretion, the board is entitled, and may even be required by the ordinance, to exercise its discretion. When this is the case, the board is entitled to determine whether an applicant has demonstrated that its proposed use will comply with the relevant statutory requirements.

The ordinance implicated in the present case confers upon the Hamilton County North Board of Zoning Appeals a significant amount of discretion. The ordinance requires the board to find a variety of facts before issuing a special exception. For example, the board must find that the specially excepted use "will not be injurious to the public health, safety, morals, or general welfare of the community" and that the use "will not affect the use and value of other property in the immediate area in a substantially adverse manner; . . ." HCZO Art. 15(A) § 2. It is clear that these criteria, having no absolute objective standards against which they can be measured, involve discretionary decision making on the part of the board. Thus, the BZA was entitled to determine whether Crooked Creek satisfied the requirements for the grant of a special exception.

Crooked Creek nevertheless maintains that the evidence presented by the remonstrators was not sufficiently substantial to support the BZA's determination. We must note here that the burden of demonstrating satisfaction of the relevant statutory criteria rests with the applicant for a special exception. This court has accordingly been cautious to avoid the imposition upon remonstrators of an obligation to come forward with evidence contradicting that submitted by an applicant. Crooked Creek bore the burden to show that its trap and skeet shooting operation would comply with the three above-mentioned criteria. Neither those opposed to Crooked Creek's application, nor the BZA, were required to negate Crooked Creek's case.

Since remonstrators need not affirmatively disprove an applicant's case, a board of zoning appeals may deny an application for a special exception on the grounds that an applicant has failed to carry its burden of proving compliance with the relevant statutory criteria regardless of whether remonstrators present evidence to negate the existence of the enumerated factors.[1]

---

[1] This court previously noted the apparent dilemma thus presented for boards of zoning appeals. A zoning board may in its discretion determine that an applicant has not presented substantial evidence to demonstrate that its proposed use will comply with statutory requirements even in the absence of contrary evidence submitted by remonstrators. The difficulty arises when the zoning board attempts to support its determination. This court has indicated that it would be inappropriate to require the board to provide a detailed explanation as to why the criteria have not been met, for to do so would either force those who object to the exception to come forward with specific evidence in opposition, or would compel the board to explain how the criteria should or could have been met. Both options, we have noted, improperly remove the burden from the applicant to affirmatively prove compliance with the criteria. This dilemma is not squarely before us because the remonstrators presented evidence that Crooked Creek's proposed use would not meet the criteria set forth in the zoning ordinance, and because the BZA expressly rested its conclusion on this evidence. However, in the event that boards of zoning appeals deny applications for special exceptions upon grounds that the applicant has failed to carry its burden to show compliance with relevant statutory criteria, boards would be well advised to at least state as much in their findings and to point out what they see as any deficiency in the applicant's evidence. Boards should be able to perform this task without improperly assuming the burden of negating the applicant's case.

However, since the BZA determined that Crooked Creek was not entitled to a special exception, and based its determination upon evidence presented by the remonstrators, we will determine whether the BZA's decision was based upon substantial evidence by examining the sufficiency of the evidence presented by the remonstrators.

When determining whether an administrative decision is supported by substantial evidence, the reviewing court must determine from the entire record whether the agency's decision lacks a reasonably sound evidentiary basis. Thus, we have noted that evidence will be considered substantial if it is more than a scintilla and less than a preponderance. In other words, substantial evidence is such relevant evidence as a reasonable mind might accept as adequate to support a conclusion. We think that the certiorari court's conclusion that the BZA's determination was supported by substantial evidence was not error.

The remonstrators presented substantial evidence that the lead shot used in trap and skeet shooting presents a public health hazard, and that noise from gunfire could impair local property values. The remonstrators submitted a letter signed by Thomas F. Long, described in the letter and by the letterhead as a Senior Toxicologist with the Environmental Toxicology Section of the Illinois Department of Public Health, explaining the effects of lead shot used in target shooting upon human health. The letter stated that when lead shot is discharged from a shotgun into a target, "it tends to be pulverized into a fine dust." This dust, according to the letter, "tends to be mobile and moves easily in the environment on wind or in water." Finally, the letter concluded that lead is a very dangerous, although often subtle, poison absorbed by the gut and lung. In humans, lead primarily attacks the nervous system with children being at highest risk. Children exposed to excessive levels of lead can suffer damage as subtle as a loss of IQ and developmental delays or as serious as mental retardation and death. Adults may also experience nervous system damage as a result of lead exposure although it is generally not as devastating as is seen in children. Additionally, lead will attack the digestive system, the blood, the kidneys, and the reproductive system. Since lead can damage both male and female reproduction and will cross the placenta, miscarriage and birth defects can result. The opinion of Mr. Long constitutes sufficient evidence to justify the Board's conclusion in this regard.

The remonstrators also presented testimony from a qualified and experienced real estate appraiser who gave his opinion that the location of a gun club in the community would reduce demand for the property, thereby decreasing its value. Another remonstrator, a builder and developer of a local subdivision, testified that one individual made an offer to purchase one of the builder's properties upon the condition that Crooked Creek's plans were denied. The builder also stated his belief that the presence of a gun club would negatively impact property values in the area. Moreover, many of the remonstrators who testified at the April 24 meeting expressed their concern with respect to the noise level of Crooked Creek's activities, expressing the fear that the noise of gunfire would take away from the quiet, rural character which attracted them to the area. Crooked Creek's own real estate appraisal expert testified that the value of property is driven by the demand for that property. Substantial evidence was adduced at the April 26 meeting to support the BZA's conclusion that a gun club could reduce the value of land in the area by taking away its only apparent attraction, the peace and quiet of the rural neighborhood.

Crooked Creek disputes these contentions and submitted evidence to the effect that the lead involved in trap and skeet shooting poses no threat to human health in its normal usage, and that the presence of the gun club would not tend to reduce property values in the area. However, the zoning board was under no obligation to give the evidence presented by Crooked Creek more weight than that of the remonstrators. As we have noted, a board of zoning appeals has the discretion to deny a special exception if the board determines that the applicant has not met the relevant criteria. Moreover, when both the applicant and remonstrators present substantial evidence in support of their respective positions, it is the function of the board of zoning appeals, with its expertise in zoning questions, to determine which side shall prevail. Since the board's determination in either case would be supported by substantial evidence, it should not be disturbed upon appeal.

The remonstrators presented evidence to support the BZA's conclusion that the lead discharged during trap and skeet shooting posed a public health hazard, and that the gun club would negatively impact local property values. The BZA, as it was entitled to do, credited that evidence and determined that Crooked Creek was not entitled to a special exception because it found that the lead shot used in target shooting could be hazardous to human health and that property values could be negatively impacted by the existence of a gun club in the area. . . .

The decision of the trial court affirming the BZA is affirmed.

NOTES AND QUESTIONS

1. *The standards issue.* The *Crooked Creek* case makes an important distinction between standards that confer discretion on zoning boards and those that do not. What do you think of this distinction? In the *Merrillville* case, which is discussed in *Crooked Creek,* the board denied a conditional use for a public storage facility when neighbors objected. The court reversed because it found the use complied with the criteria contained in the ordinance.

The Merrillville board found the use would violate a requirement that it not have an adverse effect on property values. Opponents to the use had expressed fears on this issue but did not present evidence. The court held that was not the point: "Once a petitioner has established its right to a special exception by presenting sufficient evidence of compliance with relevant statutory requirements, the exception must be granted." *Id.* at 1095. The court also held the use would not violate an ordinance requirement that it would impede the development of the area, which was a mixed-use urban strip. The board had again relied only on remarks by objectors to find that the development of the area would be impeded. How does the evidence in *Crooked Creek* differ?

Objections by neighbors to conditional use applications are common, especially when the proposed use is considered undesirable. Why were the fears of neighbors acceptable in *Crooked Creek* but not in *Merrillville?* How should courts distinguish between legitimate neighbor concerns and spurious objections? In *Washington State Dep't of Corrections v. City of Kennewick,* 937 P.2d 1119 (Wash. App. 1997), the court held that whereas in nuisance cases the fears of neighbors were a factor in finding the existence of a nuisance, the rule did not apply in zoning cases; the court reversed a decision to deny a conditional use for a work release facility.

2. *What if?* Given the court's treatment of the evidence in the principal case, can you imagine any state of facts under which the gun club could have prevailed? (Both it and the court seem to assume that lead shot is the only ammunition available.) If not, what point is there in listing gun clubs as a "special exception"?

3. *More on standards.* The typical conditional use case is concerned with "compatibility," the ability of the "special" use to harmonize with its neighbors. See *Amoco Oil Co. v. City of Minneapolis,* 395 N.W.2d 115 (Minn. App. 1986) (reversing denial of conditional use for 24-hour gas station and grocery store; restrictions to minimize late night noise, glare and traffic held sufficient despite residential neighbors' objections). If the compatibility standard is met, a board cannot deny a proposed conditional use because it is more intensive than a previous use on the property. *State ex rel. Presbyterian Church v. City of Washington,* 911 S.W.2d 697 (Mo. App. 1995). Does this make sense?

Although the *Crooked Creek* case held that ordinance standards can confer discretion on zoning boards, courts may find them vague and unenforceable if they confer too much discretion. In *C.R. Invs., Inc. v. Village of Shoreview,* 304 N.W.2d 320 (Minn. 1981), the court reversed the denial of a special exception for nineteen "quad" apartments to be built adjacent to single-family homes located across a road. It relied for reversal on policies in its comprehensive plan, but the court reversed and held the policies were "unreasonably vague" and "unreasonably subjective." The plan standards required an applicant to demonstrate that the proposed use was "an improvement on the plan and consistent with the plan's general intent and purpose" and that the proposed use was "equal to or better than, single-family usage." How do these policies compare with the ordinance standards in *Crooked Creek?*

4. *Evidentiary matters and findings.* The *Crooked Creek* case applies the accepted rule, that the applicant carries the burden of proof in conditional use cases. Note, however, that the zoning board is in an awkward position because it is the decision-making body, not a party. Do you agree with the court's suggestions in footnote 1? Don't they contradict the rule that boards must make findings of fact?

Must local zoning agencies make findings of fact when they grant or deny special exceptions? *Tullo, supra,* said yes. Compare *Archdiocese of Portland, supra,* in which the court held that its function was to determine only whether the zoning agency acted arbitrarily or capriciously. "The basis for that action need not be found in 'evidence' as we use that term in connection with the trial of cases before a court."

In *Kotrich, supra,* the court held there was no need for "written findings of fact" when a legislative rather than an administrative body grants a special exception. In such a case, "judicial review is had in an independent action on a new record made in court." Does this make sense? Are "written findings of fact" more or less important in special exception than in variance cases? Note that the courts are divided on whether standards are required when a legislative body exercises administrative functions under the zoning ordinance, such as the review of special exceptions. See *State v. Guffey,* 306 S.W.2d 552 (Mo. 1957) (standards required). Should the decision on standards affect the court's view on whether findings of fact are required?

5. *Reforming procedures.* Draft Chapter 10 of the American Planning Association model legislation provides a carefully scripted application and hearing process for administrative decisions on conditional use and other similar applications. An application must be considered complete by the local government. If a record hearing is held, the notice of the hearing must state the land development regulations and comprehensive plan elements that apply to the application, and detailed findings and a decision by the hearing board are required. Section 10-615(d) authorizes the court to reverse the decision if it "is not supported by evidence that is substantial when viewed in light of the record before the court." Would the model law have required a different result in *Crooked Creek*?

6. *Conditions.* The Standard Zoning Act, and the state zoning acts that follow it, expressly authorize conditions on special exceptions. Should this affect the discretion of the zoning agency under a special exception provision? The law on special exception conditions is similar to the law on variance conditions. Compare *Water Dist. No. 1 v. City Council,* 871 P.2d 1256 (Kan. 1994) (upholding condition on operation of sludge lagoon), with *Sandbothe v. City of Olivette,* 647 S.W.2d 198 (Mo. App. 1983) (invalidating conditions restricting hours of operation and prohibiting drive-through facility for fast food restaurant). What additional conditions could be validly imposed in the *Amoco* case, *supra* note 3, where the business included a car wash, large trucks deliver gasoline to the site, customers' cars arrive with headlights on and (the facts established) there was another 24-hour convenience store in the same block?

D. THE ZONING AMENDMENT

The zoning amendment is probably the most straightforward way in which a landowner can secure a change in zoning that will allow a land use not permitted by the existing zoning classification. Indeed, the drafters of the Standard Zoning Act appear to have considered the zoning amendment as the principal method for making changes in the land use classifications in the zoning ordinance. Reread the provisions in the Standard Act, reproduced in Ch. 3 *supra,* on the zoning amendment. Note that the Act provides no standards for zoning amendments. Why do you suppose this was done?

The zoning amendment can be used to make comprehensive changes in the zoning ordinance, including a comprehensive revision of the zoning text or map or a revision affecting a substantial part of the community. In the more usual case, the landowner seeks only a map amendment for his tract of land, which may be as small as a quarter-acre city lot or smaller. He usually requests a map amendment to make a textual zoning classification applicable to his land that will permit a more intensive land use. In this discussion, this type of zoning amendment will be called an upzoning. (A downzoning, by contrast, moves the site towards a less intense permitted use.)

The distinction between a comprehensive zoning ordinance amendment and a tract or "spot" amendment is important, as these materials will indicate. Note also that the spot upzoning amendment accomplishes the same result as a variance or special exception. Consider the differences between these zoning techniques when you study these materials.

1. ESTOPPEL AND VESTED RIGHTS

Assume a developer buys a tract of land zoned for multi-family use. He plans to build a multi-family project, enters into contracts for site plans and architectural drawings, and begins preliminary site preparation. Neighborhood opposition develops and the city council, in response, downzones his land to single-family use. Is the developer protected from this downzoning change?

The answer to this question lies in a doctrine known variously as the "estoppel" or "vested rights" doctrine, although most courts use these terms interchangeably and the two doctrines do not always produce different results. Estoppel and vested rights problems have become increasingly important as disputes over land use have become aggravated in many communities. The following case indicates how the courts apply estoppel and vested rights theories to protect developers from zoning change.

WESTERN LAND EQUITIES, INC. v. CITY OF LOGAN

617 P.2d 388 (Utah 1980)

STEWART, JUSTICE:

Defendants appeal from a ruling of the district court that the City of Logan unlawfully withheld approval of plaintiff's proposed residential plan and was estopped from enforcing a zoning change that prohibits plaintiffs' proposed use. We affirm the trial court's order. . . .

[Plaintiffs planned to build a moderately priced single-family housing project on 18.53 acres of land zoned M-1, in which both manufacturing and single-family development was allowed. The planning commission rejected a proposed subdivision of the land after going on record in opposition of single-family development in M-1 zones. The plaintiffs unsuccessfully appealed the planning commission's decision to the municipal council and then filed a complaint in the trial court. The court granted and then lifted a restraining order prohibiting the city from amending the zoning ordinance. After the order was lifted, the council adopted a zoning amendment prohibiting single-family development in M-1 zones.]

It is established that an owner of property holds it subject to zoning ordinances enacted pursuant to a state's police power. With various exceptions legislative enactments, other than those defining criminal offenses, are not generally subject to the constitutional prohibitions against retroactive application. The legality of retroactive civil legislation is tested by general principles of fairness and by due process considerations.[1] . . .

[T]he rule generally accepted in other jurisdictions [is] that an applicant for a building permit or subdivision approval does not acquire any vested right under existing zoning regulations prior to the issuance of the permit or official approval of a proposed subdivision. Generally, denial of an application may be based on subsequently-enacted zoning regulations.

However, for the reasons discussed below, we are of the view that the majority rule fails to strike a proper balance between public and private interests and opens the area to so many variables as to result in unnecessary litigation. We hold instead that an applicant for subdivision approval or a building permit is entitled to favorable action if the application conforms to the zoning ordinance in effect at the time of the application, unless changes in the zoning ordinances are pending which would prohibit the use applied for, or unless the municipality can show a compelling reason for exercising its police power retroactively to the date of application.

In the present case, the trial court found that plaintiffs had acquired a vested development right by their substantial compliance with procedural requirements and that the city was estopped from withholding approval of the proposed subdivision. The court used the language of zoning estoppel, a principle that is widely followed.[2] That principle estops a government entity from exercising its zoning powers to prohibit a proposed land use when a property owner, relying reasonably and in good faith on some governmental act or omission, has made a substantial change in position or incurred such extensive obligations or expenses that it would be highly inequitable to deprive the owner of his right to complete his proposed development.[3]

The focus of zoning estoppel is primarily upon the conduct and interests of the property owner. The main inquiry is whether there has been substantial reliance by the owner on governmental actions related to the superseded zoning that permitted the proposed use. The concern underlying this approach is the economic hardship that would be imposed on a property owner whose development plans are thwarted. Some courts hold that before a permit is issued no action of the owner is sufficient reliance to bar application of changes in zoning ordinances because there has been no governmental act sufficient to support an estoppel. Accordingly, a landowner is held to have no vested right in existing or anticipated zoning. *Avco Community Developers, Inc. v. South Coast Regional Comm'n,* 553 P.2d 546 (Cal. 1976). Other courts consider any substantial change of position in determining the estoppel issue. This Court in *Wood v. North Salt Lake,* 390 P.2d 858 (Utah 1964), held a zoning ordinance change requiring larger lots unenforceable because water mains

---

[1] See discussion of retroactive legislation in Cunningham and Kremer, *Vested Rights, Estoppel, and the Land Development Process,* 29 Hastings L.J. 623, 660 *et seq.* (1978).

[2] See *People v. County of Cook,* 206 N.E.2d 441 (Ill. App. 1965); Heeter, *Zoning Estoppel: Application of the Principles of Equitable Estoppel and Vested Rights to Zoning Disputes,* 1971 Urban L. Ann. 63.

[3] These requirements are discussed in Heeter, *supra* n.2, and Delaney and Kominers, *He Who Rests Less, Vests Best: Acquisition of Vested Rights in Land Development,* 23 St. Louis U. L.J. 219 (1979).

and sewer connections had already been provided for lots that conformed in size to a previous ordinance. The Court stated that enforcement of the new ordinance in those circumstances would be unfair and inequitable.

Generally, "substantial reliance" is determined by various tests employed by the courts — for example, the set quantum test, the proportionate test, and a balancing test. The set quantum test, used by the majority of courts, determines that an owner is entitled to relief from new, prohibitory zoning if he has changed his position beyond a certain point, measured quantitatively. A related test is the proportionate test, which determines the percentage of money spent or obligations incurred before the zoning change as compared with the total cost. The problem with both of these tests is that there is no predictable point short of adjudication which separates reliance that is less than "substantial" from the reliance sufficient to result in a vested right or to support an estoppel.

The balancing test, although likely to produce a more fair outcome in a particular case, also results in little predictability. The test weighs the owner's interest in developing his property and the reasonableness of his proposed use against the interests of public health, safety, morals, or general welfare. If the gain to the public is small when compared to the hardship that would accrue to the property owner, the actions of the owner in preparation for development according to a formerly permitted use may be seen as sufficiently substantial to justify the issuance of a permit or continuation of development despite an amendment to the zoning ordinances. See *Nott v. Wolff,* 163 N.E.2d 809 (Ill. 1960).

An additional requirement generally considered in zoning estoppel cases is that of the existence of some physical construction as an element of substantial reliance. Preconstruction activities such as the execution of architectural drawings or the clearing of land and widening of roads are not sufficient to create a vested right, nor generally are activities that are not exclusively related to the proposed project.

If the substantial reliance requirement of zoning estoppel were applied to the facts of the present case, we could not agree with the trial court that plaintiffs' "substantial compliance" with procedural requirements justified the estoppel of the city's enforcement of a new zoning ordinance. Although plaintiffs allege they proceeded with subdivision plans and incurred significant costs with the encouragement of certain city officials, they had not yet received official approval of their plan, and their expenditures were merely for surveying and preliminary plans. The record indicates that plaintiffs spent $1,335 for a boundary survey and $890 for the preparation of a preliminary subdivision plat. The boundary survey has value regardless of the city's approval or disapproval of the plaintiffs' proposal. The expenditure of $890 for the plat is not significant in relation to the size of the parcel and is not substantial enough to justify an estoppel with regard to the enforcement of valid zoning ordinances that became effective before official approval of plaintiffs' proposed subdivision.

In rejecting the zoning estoppel approach in this matter, we are not prepared to state that it would never be relevant to a determination of the validity of the retroactive application of a zoning ordinance. We are of the view, however, that the relevant public and private interests are better accommodated in the first instance by a different approach.

A number of other approaches have been followed or suggested as alternatives to zoning estoppel in an effort to promote fairness and consistency. . . .

Courts in several states have adopted the view . . . that an application for a building permit creates a vested right as of the time of application. Pennsylvania, one of these states, initially followed the general rule that a vested right accrued when an owner could show substantial reliance, made in good faith, on a validly issued permit.[4] *Schechter v. Zoning Board of Adjustment,* 149 A.2d 28 (Pa. 1959). . . . At the present time Pennsylvania follows what is termed the "pending ordinance rule." This rule provides that an application for a permitted use cannot be refused unless a prohibiting ordinance is pending at the time of application. *Boron Oil Co. v. Kimple,* 284 A.2d 744 (Pa. 1971), stated the applicable test as follows:

> [A]n ordinance is pending when a Borough Council has resolved to consider a particular scheme of rezoning and has advertised to the public its intention to hold public hearings on the rezoning. The pending ordinance rule reflected the court's attempt to. . . balance the interest of the municipality in effecting a change in its zoning laws free from the perpetuation of nonconforming uses against the interest of the individual property owner to be free from lengthy restraints upon the use of his property.

The court in *Boron Oil Co.,* also imposed a duty of good faith on the part of the municipality:

> [I]t is to be emphasized that the various governmental authorities charged with the responsibility of proposing, promulgating and administering local zoning and planning laws are under a basic duty to act reasonably. In sum, a building permit may be properly refused in situations such as the one at bar *only* when the municipality acts initially in good faith to achieve permissible ends and thereafter proceeds with reasonable dispatch in considering the proposed rezoning.

The Pennsylvania cases do not indicate whether an owner need show substantial reliance on the permitted zoning prior to the advertisement of a zoning change as an element of acquiring a vested development right. Nor is there a time limit on an owner's right to develop in accordance with a superseded use pursuant to the pending ordinance rule. . . .

The State of Washington has also refused to follow the general rule that building permits are not protected against revocation by subsequent zoning change unless a permittee has gained a vested right through a substantial change in position in reliance on the permit. As stated in *Hull v. Hunt,* 331 P.2d 856, 859 (Wash. 1958):

---

[4] The Pennsylvania experience with the vested zoning rights issue is analyzed in Keiter, *Emerging from the Confusion: Zoning and Vested Rights in Pennsylvania,* 83 Dickinson L. Rev. 515 (1979).

Notwithstanding the weight of authority, we prefer to have a date certain upon which the right vests to construct in accordance with the building permit. We prefer not to adopt a rule which forces the court to search through (to quote from . . . [an earlier Washington case], "the moves and countermoves of . . . parties . . . by way of passing ordinance and bringing actions for injunctions" — to which may be added the stalling or acceleration of administrative action in the issuance of permits — to find that date upon which the substantial change of position is made which finally vests the right. The more practical rule to administer, we feel, is that the right vests when the party, property owner or not, applies for his building permit, if that permit is thereafter issued. This rule, of course, assumes that the permit applied for and granted be consistent with the zoning ordinances and building codes in force at the time of application for the permit.

The court met the argument that its rule would result in speculation in building permits by noting that the cost of preparing plans and meeting permit requirements was such that an applicant would generally have a good faith expectation of proceeding according to his application, and, furthermore, that the city building code renders a permit null and void if work authorized by the permit does not commence within 180 days.

A "rule of irrevocable commitment" was suggested as an appropriate standard in an extensive treatment of the vested development rights problem in Cunningham and Kremer, *Vested Rights, Estoppel, and the Land Development Process, supra,* n.1. This approach would protect from new laws any project to which the developer has made a "reasonable and irrevocable commitment of resources." The scope of the protection granted would be determined by a detailed analysis of the resources committed, the planned objectives of the project, and the concerns of the general welfare. If the investment made in the project prior to passage of a new prohibitory zoning regulation could be utilized for another legitimate use, there would be less need to protect the developer's right to proceed than if significant expenditures were uniquely related to the original project. . . .

A vested right in a particular development scheme may be created by statute. For example, in Pennsylvania, § 508(4) of the Municipalities Planning Code confers a vested right on property owners who have previously received approval of a subdivision plan in which the lots are too small to conform to the requirements of a newly-enacted ordinance. This vested right has a three-year duration. . . .

In our view the tests employed by most other jurisdictions tend to subject landowners to undue and even calamitous expense because of changing city councils or zoning boards or their dilatory action and to the unpredictable results of burdensome litigation. The majority rule permits an unlimited right to deny permits when ordinances are amended after application and preliminary work. It allows government in many cases broader power with regard to land regulation than may be justified by the public interests involved. A balancing test, though geared toward promoting fairness, must be applied on a case-by-case basis and offers no predictable guidelines on which landowners can intelligently base their decisions regarding extensive development projects. Tests currently followed by the majority of states are particularly unsatisfactory in dealing with the large multistage projects. The threat of denial of a permit at a late stage of development makes a developer vulnerable to shifting governmental policies and tempts him to manipulate the process by prematurely engaging in activities that would establish the substantial reliance required to vest his right to develop when inappropriate.

The economic waste that occurs when a project is halted after substantial costs have been incurred in its commencement is of no benefit either to the public or to landowners. In a day when housing costs have severely escalated beyond the means of many prospective buyers, governmental actions should not be based on policies that exacerbate a severe economic problem without compelling justification. Governmental powers should be exercised in a manner that is reasonable and, to the extent possible, predictable.

On the other hand, a rule which vests a right unconditionally at the time application for a permit is made affords no protection for important public interests that may legitimately require interference with planned private development. If a proposal met zoning requirements at the time of application but seriously threatens public health, safety, or welfare, the interests of the public should not be thwarted.

The above competing interests are best accommodated in our view by adopting the rule that an applicant is entitled to a building permit or subdivision approval if his proposed development meets the zoning requirements in existence at the time of his application and if he proceeds with reasonable diligence, absent a compelling, countervailing public interest. Furthermore, if a city or county has initiated proceedings to amend its zoning ordinances, a landowner who subsequently makes application for a permit is not entitled to rely on the original zoning classification.

This rule . . . is intended to strike a reasonable balance between important, conflicting public and private interests in the area of land development. A property owner should be able to plan for developing his property in a manner permitted by existing zoning regulations with some degree of assurance that the basic ground rules will not be changed in midstream. Clearly it is desirable to reduce the necessity for a developer to resort to the courts. An applicant for approval of a planned and permitted use should not be subject to shifting policies that do not reflect serious public concerns.

At the same time, compelling public interests may, when appropriate, be given priority over individual economic interests. A city should not be unduly restricted in effectuating legitimate policy changes when they are grounded in recognized legislative police powers. There may be instances when an application would for the first time draw attention to a serious problem that calls for an immediate amendment to a zoning ordinance, and such an amendment would be entitled to valid retroactive effect. It is incumbent upon a city, however, to act in good faith and not to reject an application because the application itself triggers zoning reconsiderations that result in a substitution of the judgment of current city officials for that of their predecessors. Regardless of the circumstances, a court must be cognizant of legitimate public concerns in considering whether a particular development should be protected from the effects of a desirable new law.

In the present case, the zoning of the property in question was found by the trial court to have permitted the proposed use at the time of the application. The owners had received encouragement from city officials, although no official approval was rendered. After the application, the city council members decided to reexamine the pertinent zoning regulation and thereafter voted to amend or "clarify" the zoning ordinance to disallow subdivisions in an M-1 zone and permit residences only by special permit. Their actions may have had a reasonable basis. It was argued that fire protection would be undermined because of limited access roads, but it does not appear the problem would be any less serious if the unarguably-permitted manufacturing facilities were erected instead of single-family houses. Objections as to inadequate sidewalks and other problems can be handled by requiring modification of specifications that do not meet city subdivision requirements. Indeed, the order of the trial court stated that the developers must comply with all the reasonable requirements of the city's subdivision ordinance.

We do not find the reasons given by the city for withholding approval of plaintiffs' proposed subdivision to be so compelling as to overcome the presumption that an applicant for a building permit or subdivision approval is entitled to affirmative official action if he meets the zoning requirements in force at the time of his application.

NOTES AND QUESTIONS

1. *The issues.* The principal case reviews the competing rules and policy considerations applied and considered by the courts in estoppel and vested rights cases. The rule of the principal case, that rights can vest even though no building permit has been issued, is a minority view. Note the varying views the courts take, and the extent to which they put the parties at the risk of uncertain judicial interpretations.

What are the real issues in these cases? As the article by Heeter, which is cited in the principal case, points out, the theory on which relief is awarded to the landowner is not entirely clear:

> The defense of estoppel is derived from equity, but the defense of vested rights reflects principles of common and constitutional law. Similarly their elements are different. Estoppel focuses on whether it would be inequitable to allow the government to repudiate its prior conduct; vested rights upon whether the owner acquired real property rights which cannot be taken away by governmental regulation. [*Id.* at 64-65.]

Do these doctrines isolate the issues courts should consider in cases of this type? Did the principal case cut through both doctrines and consider policy issues that are more important in these cases? If so, what policy issues did the court consider? What other policy issues should it have considered? Do you agree with the rule the court adopted? Do you see a relationship between vested rights doctrine and the protection courts provide to nonconforming uses?

As the principal case indicates, the long-term trend in the decisions has been toward greater protection for the landowner and consideration of the "equities." See *Tremarco Corp. v. Garzio,* 161 A.2d 241 (N.J. 1960). The court found an estoppel, noting that the municipality changed its zoning regulations only after neighborhood residents protested and that there were no zoning reasons that justified the change.

2. *A majority rule?* The estoppel-vested rights rule is usually stated as follows:

> A court will preclude a municipality from changing its regulations as they apply to a particular parcel of land when a property owner in good faith, upon some act or omission of the government, has made a substantial change in position or has incurred such extensive obligations and expenses that it would be highly inequitable and unjust to destroy the right he acquired. [*Florida Cos. v. Orange County,* 411 So. 2d 1008, 1010 (Fla. App. 1982).]

The act or omission requirement has been the biggest stumbling block for developers. As the principal case indicates, the majority rule requires a building permit as the governmental "act." *Avco Community Builders,* cited in the principal case, is a leading decision on this point. As the *Avco* court noted, protecting a developer who has not been issued a building permit would impair the right of government to "control land use policy." Why? Does the principal case convince you that a building permit should not be required?

Some cases take an intermediate view and find estoppel when a landowner relies on some government act other than a building permit. In *Town of Largo v. Imperial Homes Corp.,* 309 So. 2d 571 (Fla. App. 1975), the town knew "that the purchase of the land by Imperial was contingent upon obtaining multiple-family zoning." The town rezoned to the developer's satisfaction, the developer purchased the land, and the court held that the town was estopped from a subsequent downzoning to a restrictive single-family classification. Is it enough if the developer makes informal inquiries at the zoning office and is told to "go ahead"? Compare *Nemmers v. City of Dubuque,* 716 F.2d 1194 (8th Cir. 1983) (estoppel found when city made road improvements to serve development and was receptive to development proposal), with *Colonial Inv. Co. v. City of Leawood,* 646 P.2d 1149 (Kan. App. 1982) (contra, when developer relied on advice from planning staff). What policy reason is there for requiring a building permit as the basis for an estoppel?

3. *Substantial reliance.* As the principal case indicates, the courts disagree on how much "substantial reliance" by the developer is required. The Maryland court has a high threshold. "[T]he work done must be recognizable, on inspection of the property by a reasonable member of the public, as the commencement of a building for a use permitted under the then current zoning." *Sterling Homes Corp. v. Anne Arundel County,* 695 A.2d 1238, 1249 (Md. App. 1997) (marina bathhouse and parking lot; grading, bulkhead and revetment construction not enough).

Preliminary expenditures may not be enough unless the developer enters into preliminary contractual obligations. See *County Council v. District Land Corp.,* 337 A.2d 712 (Md. 1975). The courts divide on whether site excavation is enough, *Prince George's County v. Sunrise Dev. Ltd. Partnership,* 623 A.2d 1296 (Md. 1993), and the purchase of land is usually not sufficient. Compare *Tremarco, supra,* rejecting a quantitative rule and applying a test that balances the interests of the developer against the interests of the municipality. See also *Clackamas County v. Holmes,* 508 P.2d 190 (Or. 1973) (relaxed substantial reliance test and applied equitable factors); *Even v. City of Parker,* 597 N.W.2d 670 (S.D. 1999) (finding reliance when a person of humble means spent a small amount on a building). Does the equitable nature of estoppel suggest that equitable "balancing" is the better rule?

4. *Good faith.* The principal case did not have much to say on the "good faith" requirement. The courts apply either an objective or a subjective good faith test, with the objective courts more likely to find good faith. Obviously, a developer who rushes to complete his project knowing that a zoning change may be made runs a serious risk that he will be found in bad faith. Note how the Pennsylvania cases discussed in the principal case handled the good faith problem when an ordinance proposing a zoning change was pending. The courts also have held that a mere expectation of a political change that will bring about a revision of the zoning ordinance is not enough for a finding of bad faith. See *Sakolsky v. City of Coral Gables,* 151 So. 2d 433 (Fla. 1963).

5. *Illegal building permit.* What if the municipality issues a building permit but it turns out later that the building permit was illegally issued because the project violates the zoning ordinance? May the municipality later revoke the permit? There are competing policy considerations in these cases. The developer may have been "innocent," yet the zoning ordinance theoretically embodies the "general welfare," and the common good arguably should be allowed to prevail. Note the qualified nature of both these statements. A sophisticated developer (as opposed to an amateur home remodeler) may be as capable of reading the relevant ordinances as a clerk in the building department. Most ordinances, in truth, embody only one of many solutions to the "general welfare." Is it possible to state a categorically "fair" rule? Most courts allow revocation in this situation. See, e.g., *Parkview Assocs. v. City of New York,* 519 N.E.2d 1372 (N.Y. 1988). Contra *Town of W. Hartford v. Rechel,* 459 A.2d 1015 (Conn. 1983).

6. *Phased developments.* Very large residential projects, usually known as planned unit developments (PUDs), are usually completed in phases over a period of time. What if a municipality issues building permits for Phase I of a PUD, the developer completes Phase I, but the municipality then refuses to issue building permits for Phase II even though it had approved the plans for the entire project earlier? *Avco, supra,* is a PUD case indicating that preliminary approvals such as the approval of project plans are not enough, and that rights do not vest until the municipality issues a building permit. Contra *Village of Palatine v. LaSalle Nat'l Bank,* 445 N.E.2d 1277 (Ill. App. Ct. 1983):

> We regard Palatine's approval of the original site plan, the issuance of building permits for Phase I, and the continuing treatment of [the project] as a PUD "in fact" as the type of affirmative acts of public officials upon which a landowner is entitled to rely. [*Id.* at 1283.]

Is this decision correct, or should the multi-phase developer be "at risk" until he receives building permits for each phase of his project? Some states provide statutory protection in this situation. See "A Note on Development Agreements," *infra*. For discussion of PUDs, see Ch. 6, sec. C. The ripeness problems raised by a phased development are reviewed in the Supreme Court's *Hamilton Bank* case, reproduced in Chapter 2, *infra*.

7. *The developer's dilemma.* One court, discussing a rule making building permits revocable, saw the problem this way:

> The permittee could win immunity from such "ex post facto" revocation only by constructing a substantial portion of the structure authorized by his permit in good faith reliance upon the prior law. A permittee who delayed construction in the face of an impending amendment to the zoning laws might find that he had not progressed far enough in time to qualify for immunity; one who proceeded with unseemly haste ran the risk that his conduct might bear the stigma of bad faith. No facile formula informed the permittee how to strike the delicate balance which would afford the desired immunity. [*Russian Hill Imp. Ass'n v. Board of Permit Appeals,* 423 P.2d 824, 828–29 (Cal. 1967).]

The court enforced a revocation based on a newly enacted height limit.

8. *Statutory and ordinance protection.* Several states have adopted statutes enacting vested rights protection. Most of them follow the Washington rule, now codified by statute, that confers protection as of the date an application is filed. The Oregon statute states it simply:

> If the application [e.g., for a permit or zone change] was complete when first submitted or the applicant submits the requested additional information within 180 days of the date the application was first submitted and the city has a comprehensive plan and land use regulations acknowledged under [the state land use law], approval or denial of the application shall be based upon the standards and criteria that were applicable at the time the application was first submitted. [Ore. Rev. Stat. § 227.178(3).]

Note that the statute requires a "complete" application. This is designed to preclude vesting based on vague proposals, hastily drafted to beat a change in the law. For the Washington law see Wash. Rev. Code Ann. § 19.27.095. See Overstreet & Kircheim, *The Quest for the Best Test to Vest: Washington's Vested Rights Doctrine Beats the Rest,* 23 Seattle U.L. Rev. 1043 (2000). What are the benefits of dating vested rights protection from the time an application is submitted? Does this tip the scales too much in favor of developers?

Other statutes provide protection from the time of submission of applications for site plan, subdivision or similar approvals. E.g., Cal. Gov't Code § 66498.1 to 66498.3; Colo. Rev. Stat. § 24-68-102.5; Mass. Gen. Laws ch. 40A, § 6. A Virginia statute codifies the court-made law of vested rights. Va. Code § 15.2-2307. Some of these statutes specify the regulations covered by the vested rights protection, and some have time limits.

Sources.—See C. Siemon and W. Larsen, Vested Rights (1982); Campanella, Elliott & Merriam, *New Vested Property Rights Legislation: States Seek to*

Steady a Shaky Judicial Doctrine, 11 Zoning & Plan. L. Rep. 81 (1988); Delaney, *Vesting Verities and the Development Chronology: A Gaping Disconnect,* 3 Wash. U. J.L. & Pol'y 603 (2000); Delaney & Vaias, *Recognizing Vested Development Rights as Protected Property in Fifth Amendment Due Process and Taking Claims,* 49 J. Urb. & Contemp. L. 27 (1996); Dennison, *Estoppel as a Defense to Enforcement of Zoning Ordinance,* 19 Zoning & Plan. L. Rep. 69 (1996).

A NOTE ON DEVELOPMENT AGREEMENTS

The development agreement is an alternative to a reliance on judicially protected vested rights. It removes uncertainty in the development process by providing the developer with an assurance that development regulations that apply to his project will not change. A number of states have now adopted statutes that authorize development agreements, beginning with California as a response to the *Avco* decision, *supra,* and as an alternative to legislation providing greater protection for vested rights. Cal. Gov't Code §§ 65864-65869.5. See also, e.g., Fla. Stat. Ann. §§ 163.3220 to 163.3243; Hawaii Rev. Stat. §§ 46-121 to 46-132; Nev. Rev. Stat. §§ 278.0201 to 278.0207.

> The statutes . . . authorize local governments to enter into agreements with developers and to make local land use and development regulations in place at the time of the agreement a part of the contract. The statutes direct the local government to hold public hearings prior to approving an agreement or making subsequent modifications. They also require periodic review of the development project and allow the governing body to modify or terminate the agreement if the developer is unable to comply with its terms. The governing body may also modify the agreement if circumstances arise which threaten the public interest. Unless the statute provides a special remedy for the enforceability of the agreement, the parties may use common law contract remedies. [Moore, *A Comparative Analysis of Development Agreement Legislation in Hawaii, Nevada and Florida,* 11 Newsl. of the Plan. & L. Div. of the Am. Plan. Ass'n, No. 3, at 19 (1987).]

The "approval freeze" is an important element of development agreements because it prevents the local government from making changes in development regulations that apply to the project. Here is what the Florida statute provides:

> (2) A local government may apply subsequently adopted laws and policies to a development that is subject to a development agreement only if the local government has held a public hearing and determined: (a) They are not in conflict with the laws and policies governing the development agreement and do not prevent development of the land uses, intensities, or densities in the development agreement; (b) They are essential to the public health, safety, or welfare, and expressly state that they shall apply to a development that is subject to a development agreement; (c) They are specifically anticipated and provided for in the development agreement; (d) The local government demonstrates that substantial changes have occurred in pertinent

conditions existing at the time of approval of the development agreement; or (e) The development agreement is based on substantially inaccurate information supplied by the developer. [Fla. Stat. Ann. § 163.3233.]

Without an "approval freeze," a municipality is free to disregard an agreement and downzone property that is subject to an agreement. *Sprenger, Grubb & Assocs., Inc. v. City of Hailey,* 903 P.2d 741 (Idaho 1995).

The "approval freeze" provisions of development agreement statutes are their most critical feature but raise a number of constitutional questions. The most important is whether the statutes authorize an unconstitutional bargaining-away of the police power. *Stephens v. City of Vista,* 994 F.2d 650 (9th Cir. 1993), held a city can guarantee development density while retaining review of the design features of a development without surrendering control of its land use powers. In an analogous situation, the courts upheld agreements in which a landowner agrees to annex to a municipality in return for a municipality's promise to provide public services. See *Morrison Homes Corp. v. City of Pleasanton,* 130 Cal. Rptr. 196 (Cal. App. 1976). These cases support the constitutionality of similar provisions in development agreements, but a freeze on existing zoning restrictions is more doubtful. Compare *City of Louisville v. Fiscal Court,* 623 S.W.2d 219 (Ky. 1981) (annexation agreement in which city agreed to cooperate in rezoning held invalid), with *Mayor & City Council v. Crane,* 352 A.2d 786 (Md. 1976) (city bound by agreement providing for density increase in exchange for developer's donation of land to city).

Development agreements may also require improvements from the developer and can be used to impose exactions, a practice which has been approved in some states. See Crew, *Development Agreements After Nollan v. California Coastal Commission,* 22 Urb. Law. 23 (1990).

NOTES AND QUESTIONS

1. *How much certainty?* A development agreement statute is not an "open sesame" to guaranteed protection against changes in land use regulations. For one thing, developer performance of the agreement is essential. For another, statutes require very specific details on the development the developer plans to carry out. For example, the Florida statute requires details as to "the development uses permitted on the land, including population densities, and building intensities and height; a description of public facilities that will service the development, including who shall provide such facilities; the date any new facilities, if needed, will be constructed; and a schedule to assure public facilities are available concurrent with the impacts of the development; a description of any reservation or dedication of land for public purposes." Fla. Stat. Ann. § 163.3227. This is typical. Exaction requirements are subject, of course, to the exaction tests discussed in Chapter 6, *infra*.

Here's the dilemma: In the large, long-term projects for which development agreements are most suited, changes in the project and marketing possibilities may make the original development agreement obsolete. An amendment is then necessary, and it is not guaranteed. Similar problems arise in planned unit developments. See Chapter 6, Section C, *infra*.

Nor do development agreement statutes guarantee that no change can occur in existing regulations. Note the provisions in the Florida law authorizing the application of subsequent laws to a development agreement. For a California case upholding the adoption of ordinances under the health and safety exception that rescinded a development agreement see *216 Sutter Bay Associates v. County of Sutter,* 68 Cal. Rptr. 2d 492 (Cal. App. 1997). On balance, how do development agreements compare with relying on vested rights doctrine?

2. *Bargaining and the comprehensive plan.* Development agreements are an example of bargaining over land development regulations. Conditional zoning, which is discussed later in this chapter, is another example. How does this kind of bargaining compare with the bargaining over land use restrictions that is reviewed in Chapter 1, *supra?* In answering that question, keep in mind that many of the development agreement statutes require agreements to be consistent with the comprehensive plan. See Haw. Rev. Stat. § 46-129. Consider how effective this control might be after you review the materials on consistency of zoning with the comprehensive plan later in this chapter.

3. *Sources.* See Curtin & Edelstein, *Development Agreement Practice in California and Other States,* 22 Stetson L. Rev. 961 (1993); Delaney, *Development Agreements: The Road from Prohibition to "Let's Make a Deal!",* 25 Urb. Law. 49 (1993); Taub, *Development Agreements,* Land Use L. & Zoning Dig., Vol. 42, No. 10, at 3 (1990).

2. "SPOT" ZONING

KUEHNE v. TOWN OF EAST HARTFORD

136 Conn. 452, 72 A.2d 474 (1950)

MALTBIE, C.J.:

. . . . [A substantial part of the opinion is omitted. — Eds.]

Main Street in East Hartford runs substantially north and south. The petitioner before the town council, Langlois, owned a piece of land on the east side of it which he had been using for growing fruit and vegetables, and he has had upon it a greenhouse and a roadside stand for the sale of products of the land. The premises, ever since zoning was established in East Hartford in 1927, had been in an A residence district. Langlois made an application to the town council to change to an A business district a portion of the tract fronting on Main Street for about 500 feet and extending to a depth of 150 feet. He intended, if the application was granted, to erect upon the tract a building containing six or eight stores, apparently in the nature of retail stores and small business establishments calculated to serve the needs of residents in the vicinity. Starting at a business district to the north and extending for almost three miles to the town boundary on the south, the land along Main Street and extending to a considerable depth on each side of it has been, ever since zoning was established in the town, in an A residence district, with certain exceptions hereinafter described. Seven hundred feet north of the

Langlois property is a small business district lying on both sides of Main Street; the land on the east side is used for a fruit and vegetable stand, a milk bar and a garage and gas station; and the land on the west side, with an area a little larger than the Langlois tract in question, is now unoccupied. About 500 feet south of the Langlois property is another small business district in which is located a grill and restaurant, a drugstore, a cleaning and dyeing business and a large grocery and meat market. Formerly the land about the tract in question was used quite largely for agricultural purposes, but within the last few years a large residential community, comprising some one thousand houses, has grown up in the vicinity.

The application to the town council was based upon the claim that residents in the vicinity need the stores and services which could be located in the building Langlois proposed to erect. There was, for example, a petition filed with the council in support of the application signed by fifty-one of those residents which asked it to allow such a change as might be necessary to permit for their benefit a shopping center on the property. None of the signers, however, owned property on Main Street or in the immediate vicinity of the Langlois property. On the other hand, the application was opposed by the owner of property directly opposite the tract in question and by the owners of the two properties fronting on Main Street immediately south of the Langlois land.

The council voted that the application "be granted for the general welfare and the good of the town in that section." In *Bartram v. Zoning Commission* (Conn.), 68 A.2d 308, we recently had before us an appeal from the granting by a zoning commission of an application to change a lot in Bridgeport even smaller than the tract here in question from a residence to a business zone, and we sustained the action of the commission. We said: "A limitation upon the powers of zoning authorities which has been in effect ever since zoning statutes were made applicable generally to municipalities in the state is that the regulations they adopt must be made 'in accordance with a comprehensive plan.' 'A "comprehensive plan" means "a general plan to control and direct the use and development of property in a municipality or a large part of it by dividing it into districts according to the present and potential use of the properties."'" Action by a zoning authority which gives to a single lot or a small area privileges which are not extended to other land in the vicinity is in general against sound public policy and obnoxious to the law. It can be justified only when it is done in furtherance of a general plan properly adopted for and designed to serve the best interests of the community as a whole. The vice of spot zoning lies in the fact that it singles out for special treatment a lot or a small area in a way that does not further such a plan. Where, however, in pursuance of it, a zoning commission takes such action, its decision can be assailed only on the ground that it abused the discretion vested in it by the law. To permit business in a small area within a residence zone may fall within the scope of such a plan, and to do so, unless it amounts to unreasonable or arbitrary action, is not unlawful." It appeared in that case that the change was granted by the commission in pursuance of a policy to encourage decentralization of business in the city and to that end to permit neighborhood stores in outlying districts. It is true that we said in that opinion that if the commission decided, "on facts affording a sufficient basis and in the exercise of a proper discretion, that it would serve the best interests of the community as a whole to permit a use of a single lot or small area in a different way than was allowed in surrounding territory, it would not be guilty of spot zoning in any sense obnoxious to the law." We meant by that statement to emphasize the fact that the controlling test must be, not the benefit to a particular individual or group of individuals, but the good of the community as a whole, and we did not mean in any way to derogate from our previous statement that any such change can only be made if it falls within the requirements of a comprehensive plan for the use and development of property in the municipality or a large part of it.

In the case before us it is obvious that the council looked no further than the benefit which might accrue to Langlois and those who resided in the vicinity of his property, and that they gave no consideration to the larger question as to the effect the change would have upon the general plan of zoning in the community. In fact, the controlling consideration seems to have been that Langlois intended to go ahead at once with his building rather than any consideration of the suitability of the particular lot for business uses, because there is no suggestion in the record that the council considered the fact that only some 700 feet away was a tract of land already zoned for business which, as appears from the zoning map in evidence, was more easily accessible to most of the signers of the petition than was the Langlois land.

In *Strain v. Mims,* (Conn.), 193 A. 754, we said "One of the essential purposes of zoning regulation is to stabilize property uses." In this case it is significant that the change was opposed by the owners of three properties so situated as to be most affected by it, while those who supported it were the owner of the tract and residents who did not live in its immediate vicinity. It should also be noted that the petition they signed contained a provision that it should not be construed as supporting permission for the use of the premises as a liquor outlet, but at the hearing before the council the attorney for Langlois in effect conceded that the zoning regulations permitted such a use in an A business district; and if that is so and the change were granted, it is quite possible that the premises would be sooner or later converted to such a use.

The action of the town council in this case was not in furtherance of any general plan of zoning in the community and cannot be sustained. . . .

There is error, the judgment is set aside and the case is remanded to be proceeded with according to law. . . .

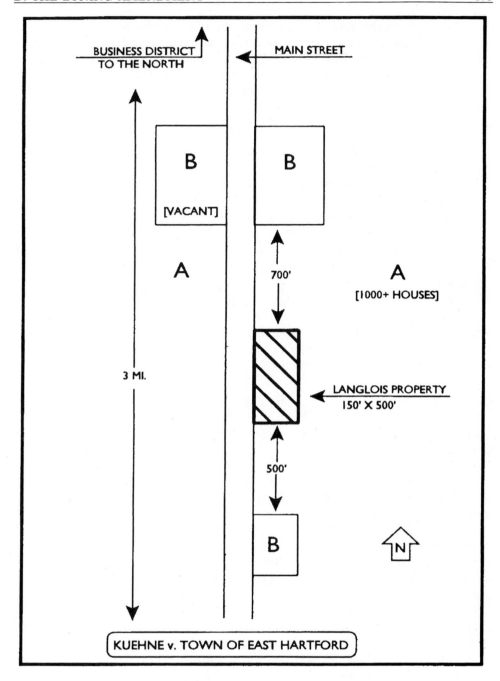

BUSINESS DISTRICT TO THE NORTH

MAIN STREET

B

[VACANT]

B

A

700'

A

[1000+ HOUSES]

3 MI.

LANGLOIS PROPERTY
150' X 500'

500'

B

N

KUEHNE v. TOWN OF EAST HARTFORD

NOTES AND QUESTIONS

1. *The problem.* The principal case is a typical spot zoning decision. Notice how a rezoning differs from a variance or conditional use. Statutory standards govern variances, while standards in the zoning ordinance govern the conditional use. No standards govern a rezoning, which is a legislative act in most states. But what is spot zoning? One court defined spot zoning as descriptive of the process of singling out a small parcel of land for a use classification different and inconsistent with the surrounding area, for the benefit of the owner of such property and to the detriment of the rights of other property owners. [*Burkett v. City of Texarkana,* 500 S.W.2d 242, 244 (Tex. Civ. App. 1973).]

Well and good, but what is the constitutional basis for attacking spot zoning? Substantive due process? Equal protection? Why?

The principal case makes the point that spot zoning violates the statutory requirement that zoning be "in accordance with" a comprehensive plan. This requirement comes from the Standard Zoning Act, § 3, and has been adopted in most states. Note that the principal case finds the "comprehensive plan" in the policies of the zoning ordinance. What is there in the opinion that supports this conclusion? A minority of states now require the adoption of a comprehensive plan and the consistency of zoning with that plan. See sec. G *infra.* Consistency with the plan, however, does not necessarily defeat a spot zoning claim, though consistency is a factor in considering the claim. See *Griswold v. City of Homer,* 925 P.2d 1015 (Alaska 1996). Should it be?

The cases sometimes emphasize that spot zoning rules are flexible and that "spot zoning" is merely a descriptive term. The ultimate test is the reasonableness of the zoning as determined by a number of factors such as compatibility with adjacent uses and consistency with the comprehensive plan. *Chrismon v. Guilford County,* 370 S.E.2d 579 (N.C. 1988); *Smith v. Town of St. Johnsbury,* 554 A.2d 233 (Vt. 1988). But courts vary somewhat in how they state spot zoning rules, which leads to inconsistent decisions.

2. *An erratic rule?* Was the Connecticut court persuasive in distinguishing the principal case from *Bartram v. Zoning Comm'n* on the ground that, in *Bartram,* "the change was granted by the commission in pursuance of a policy to encourage decentralization of business in the city and to that end to permit neighborhood stores in outlying districts"? Perusal of the *Bartram* opinion indicates that only one commission member testified that the commission had adopted such a policy; the court, however, said, "nowhere in the record is there any suggestion that this testimony is not true," and apparently gave significant weight to it. Assuming that the zoning commission, in fact, had formulated such a policy in *Bartram*, does it rise to the dignity of "a comprehensive plan" within the meaning of the Standard State Zoning Enabling Act and the Connecticut zoning statute? The *Bartram* opinion does not indicate that the zoning commission had adopted any standards or guidelines to be applied when landowners sought rezoning to permit establishment of business uses in areas zoned for residential use. The zoning commission justified the business rezoning in *Bartram* as follows:

> The location is on Sylvan Avenue, a sixty-foot street, and there is no shopping center within a mile of it. To the north of this tract there is a very large development but only small nonconforming grocery stores to serve people. 2. There is practically only one house, adjacent to this tract on the north, which will be directly affected by this change of zone. 3. Business Zone No. 3 regulations, with their thirty-foot setback and liquor restrictions, were designed to meet conditions like

this and help alleviate the great congestion in the centralized shopping districts.

Do any of these findings demonstrate that the land rezoned was, in fact, the best location for a new neighborhood shopping center in the general area involved in the case? Would a refusal to rezone be an improper use of zoning to control competition?

Courts sometimes say they are applying the fairly debatable rule in spot zoning cases. *MC Props., Inc. v. City of Chattanooga,* 994 S.W.2d 132 (Tenn. App. 1999). Are they?

3. *Rezoning for commercial use.* The differing results in the Connecticut cases indicate the ad hoc nature of spot zoning and the ad hoc way in which courts consider spot zoning claims. The difficulty is that a spot zoning is necessarily piecemeal and at odds with a comprehensive planning and zoning regime for a municipality.

Spot commercial rezonings illustrate this point. In *Griswold, supra,* for example, the city, having agonized for years over whether to allow auto sales lots in their central business district, passed a zoning ordinance prohibiting them in this area, but then adopted a rezoning for this use on 13 lots, primarily to help out a lot owner who lost his "grandparented" rights to such a business. The court upheld the rezoning, citing tax, employment, infill and convenience benefits. Not all courts recognize tax benefits. E.g., *Little v. Winborn,* 518 N.W.2d 384 (Iowa 1994). Why should they?

The issues are tougher when a commercial zoning is in a residential district on a small lot. Some courts see this as zoning anathema and invalidate the rezoning. *Bossman v. Village of Riverton,* 684 N.E.2d 427 (Ill. App. 1997). Other courts are impressed with the tax and job gain and uphold the rezoning. *Rando v. Town of N. Attleborough,* 692 N.E.2d 544 (Mass. App. 1998).

4. *Rezoning of large tracts.* The courts usually acknowledge that the size of a rezoned tract is an important factor in spot zoning cases, but they caution that it is not determinative. With this comment in mind, consider the following cases:

(a) *Chrobuck v. Snohomish County,* 480 P.2d 489 (Wash. 1971). The county rezoned 635 acres out of a 7680-acre tract of land located in a prime residential and recreational area to allow the construction of an oil refinery. The court invalidated the rezoning. The county based the rezoning on the potential tax revenue of the project and the reluctance of the oil refinery company to consider another site. The planning department's report recommended against the rezoning and noted that the refinery site was in the "wrong place." It was located "in the midst of an outstanding residential area without adequate road or rail access and could possibly have an effect on water and land resources." But see *Save Our Rural Env't v. Snohomish County,* 662 P.2d 816 (Wash. 1983) (upholding business park rezoning partly because it would broaden the industrial base of the region and produce energy and travel savings for employees).

(b) *Little v. Winborn,* 518 N.W.2d 384 (Iowa 1994). The court invalidated a rezoning of 223 acres from an A-1 to an A-2 agricultural district to permit the construction of two uninhabited structures and a shoot club. The tract was surrounded by agricultural land, and there was no reason for the rezoning other than the benefit to the club members. The A-1 district was adopted to prevent the intrusion of non-agricultural uses in agricultural areas, while the A-2 zone was a holding zone adopted as a transition to urban development.

(c) *Save Our Forest Action Coalition, Inc. v. City of Kingston*, 675 N.Y.S.2d 451 (App. Div. 1998). The court upheld a rezoning of 107 acres in a residential district to industrial use. "[T]he primary motivation for the zoning amendment was to support local economic development through retention of the City's largest employer and to reap associated economic and tax benefits in connection with the development of a business park." The court also noted the zoning was adopted after an extensive review that considered the impact on adjoining residential areas, consistency with existing zoning plans, alternative sites and environmental concerns. Why didn't the city just carry out a comprehensive rezoning for industrial uses? See also *Willott v. Village of Beachwood,* 197 N.E.2d 201 (Ohio 1964) (court applied fairly debatable rule to uphold rezoning of 80-acre tract in residential area for a shopping center, even though objectors claimed no change in conditions, "drastic depreciation" in the value of their homes, and dangers from traffic, noise and other nuisances).

5. *Purpose and need.* In some cases in which a rezoning from single-family to multi-family use has been granted, the courts rely on a need for multi-family housing to justify the rezoning. See *Lee v. District of Columbia Zoning Comm'n,* 411 A.2d 635 (D.C. 1980), holding that rezonings of this kind are "not disturbed . . . when a need for housing exists and injury to the land is minimal." Accord *City of Pharr v. Tippitt,* 616 S.W.2d 173 (Tex. 1981), holding that evidence of a need for multi-family housing was "evidence that rezoning would benefit and promote the general welfare of the community." Is this view consistent with the definition of spot zoning in Note 1 *supra?*

6. *The change-mistake rule.* The courts in spot zoning cases often give weight to whether a change in conditions has occurred that justifies the rezoning. See *Pierrepont v. Zoning Comm'n,* 226 A.2d 659 (Conn. 1967) (rezoning for apartments). Compare *Zoning Comm'n v. New Canaan Bldg. Co.,* 148 A.2d 330 (Conn. 1959), invalidating a downzoning from multi-family to single-family use. The court noted that no change in conditions had occurred that justified the rezoning and that "[t]hose who buy property in a zoned district have the right to expect that the classification made in the ordinance will not be changed unless a change is required for public good."

Maryland has gone one step farther. In that state a rezoning must be justified either by an original mistake in the zoning ordinance or by a change in conditions. See *Wakefield v. Kraft,* 96 A.2d 27 (Md. 1953). A few states have adopted the change-mistake rule, e.g., *Lewis v. City of Jackson,* 184 So. 2d 384 (Miss. 1966), but other states have expressly rejected it. See *King's Mill Homeowners Ass'n v. City of Westminster,* 557 P.2d 1186 (Colo. 1976). Maryland has codified the rule. Md. Ann. Code art. 66B, § 4.05.

Unless there was a mistake in the original zoning ordinance, the change-mistake rule requires the court to find some change in conditions in the surrounding area that justifies the zoning amendment. This determination requires the courts to make planning judgments. In apartment zoning cases, for example, the Maryland courts have had to determine whether apartments are appropriate as buffer zones between residential and nonresidential districts, and whether a new highway or improved public facilities are changes in conditions that justify an apartment rezoning. For a review of the Maryland apartment rezoning change-mistake cases, see D. Mandelker, The Zoning Dilemma 87-105 (1971). Is the change-mistake rule based on a misunderstanding of the planning process? Are there cases where piecemeal change in the zoning ordinance is justified?

7. *Sources.* For discussion of the zoning amendment, see Burke, *The Change-Mistake Rule and Zoning in Maryland,* 26 Am. U. L. Rev. 631 (1976); Haar, Sawyer & Cummings, *Computer Power and Legal Rezoning: A Case Study of Judicial Decision Prediction in Zoning Amendment Cases,* 1977 Am. B. Found. Res. J. 651; Reynolds, *"Spot Zoning"—A Spot That Could Be Removed from the Law,* 48 Wash. U. J. Urb. & Contemp. L. 117 (1995).

3. QUASI-JUDICIAL VERSUS LEGISLATIVE REZONING

Some observers of the zoning process believe it is an error to characterize the rezoning decision as legislative because it does not allow the courts enough control of decisionmaking. One way to deal with this problem is to recharacterize the zoning process as quasi-judicial, which allows courts to modify the usual standards of judicial review. The Florida case that follows is an example of this approach:

BOARD OF COUNTY COMMISSIONERS OF BREVARD COUNTY v. SNYDER

627 So. 2d 469 (Fla. 1993)

GRIMES, J.:

. . . Jack and Gail Snyder owned a one-half acre parcel of property on Merritt Island in the unincorporated area of Brevard County. The property is zoned GU (general use) which allows construction of a single-family residence. The Snyders filed an application to rezone their property to the RU-2-15 zoning classification which allows the construction of fifteen units per acre. The area is designated for residential use under the 1988 Brevard County Comprehensive Plan Future Land Use Map. Twenty-nine zoning classifications are considered potentially consistent with this land use designation, including both the GU and the RU-2-15 classifications.

After the application for rezoning was filed, the Brevard County Planning and Zoning staff reviewed the application and completed the county's standard "rezoning review worksheet." The worksheet indicated that the proposed multifamily use of the Snyders' property was consistent with all aspects of the comprehensive plan except for the fact that it was located in the one-hundred-year flood plain in which a maximum of only two units per acre was permitted. For this reason, the staff recommended that the request be denied.

At the planning and zoning board meeting, the county planning and zoning director indicated that when the property was developed the land elevation would be raised to the point where the one-hundred-year-flood plain restriction would no longer be applicable. Thus, the director stated that the staff no longer opposed the application. The planning and zoning board voted to approve the Snyders' rezoning request.

When the matter came before the board of county commissioners, Snyder stated that he intended to build only five or six units on the property. However, a number of citizens spoke in opposition to the rezoning request. Their primary concern was the increase in traffic which would be caused by the development. Ultimately, the commission voted to deny the rezoning request without stating a reason for the denial.

The Snyders filed a petition for certiorari in the circuit court. Three circuit judges, sitting *en banc*, reviewed the petition and denied it by a two-to-one decision. The Snyders then filed a petition for certiorari in the Fifth District Court of Appeal.

The district court of appeal acknowledged that zoning decisions have traditionally been considered legislative in nature. Therefore, courts were required to uphold them if they could be justified as being "fairly debatable." Drawing heavily on *Fasano v. Board of County Commissioners,* 507 P.2d 23 (Or. 1973), however, the court concluded that, unlike initial zoning enactments and comprehensive rezonings or rezonings affecting a large portion of the public, a rezoning action which entails the application of a general rule or policy to specific individuals, interests, or activities is quasi-judicial in nature. Under the latter circumstances, the court reasoned that a stricter standard of judicial review of the rezoning decision was required. The court went on to hold:. . .

[The court below held "that the governmental agency (by whatever name it may be characterized) applying legislated land use restrictions to particular parcels of privately owned lands, must state reasons for action that denies the owner the use of his land and must make findings of fact and a record of its proceedings, sufficient for judicial review." The court also held the landowner has the burden to show that his proposal "complies with the reasonable procedural requirements of the ordinance and that the use sought is consistent with the applicable comprehensive zoning plan." At this point "the landowner is presumptively entitled to use his property in the manner he seeks unless the opposing governmental agency asserts and proves by clear and convincing evidence that a specifically stated public necessity requires a specified, more restrictive, use." If this showing is made, the landowner has the burden to show that this more restrictive use is a taking of his property."]

Applying these principles to the facts of the case, the court found (1) that the Snyders' petition for rezoning was consistent with the comprehensive plan; (2) that there was no assertion or evidence that a more restrictive zoning classification was necessary to protect the health, safety, morals, or welfare of the general public; and (3) that the denial of the requested zoning classification without reasons supported by facts was, as a matter of law, arbitrary and unreasonable. The court granted the petition for certiorari. . . .

Historically, local governments have exercised the zoning power pursuant to a broad delegation of state legislative power subject only to constitutional limitations. Both federal and state courts adopted a highly deferential standard of judicial review early in the history of local zoning. In *Village of Euclid v. Ambler Realty Co.,* 272 U.S. 365 (1926), the United States Supreme Court held that "if the validity of the legislative classification for zoning purposes be fairly debatable, the legislative judgment must be allowed to control." 272 U.S. at 388. This Court expressly adopted the fairly debatable principle in *City of Miami Beach v. Ocean & Inland Co.,* 3 So. 2d 364 (1941).

Inhibited only by the loose judicial scrutiny afforded by the fairly debatable rule, local zoning systems developed in a markedly inconsistent manner. Many land use experts and practitioners have been critical of the local zoning system. Richard Babcock deplored the effect of "neighborhoodism" and rank political influence on the local decision-making process. Richard F. Babcock, *The Zoning Game* (1966). Mandelker and Tarlock recently stated that "zoning decisions are too often ad hoc, sloppy and self-serving decisions with well-defined adverse consequences without off-setting benefits." Daniel R. Mandelker and A. Dan Tarlock, *Shifting the Presumption of Constitutionality in Land-Use Law,* 24 Urb. Law. 1, 2 (1992).

Professor Charles Haar, a leading proponent of zoning reform, was an early advocate of requiring that local land use regulation be consistent with a legally binding comprehensive plan which would serve long range goals, counteract local pressures for preferential treatment, and provide courts with a meaningful standard of review. Charles M. Haar, *"In Accordance With A Comprehensive Plan,"* 68 Harv. L. Rev. 1154 (1955). In 1975, the American Law Institute adopted the Model Land Development Code, which provided for procedural and planning reforms at the local level and increased state participation in land use decision-making for developments of regional impact and areas of critical state concern.

Reacting to the increasing calls for reform, numerous states have adopted legislation to change the local land use decision-making process. As one of the leaders of this national reform, Florida adopted the Local Government Comprehensive Planning Act of 1975. Ch. 75-257, Laws of Fla. This law was substantially strengthened in 1985 by the Growth Management Act. Ch. 85-55, Laws of Fla.

Pursuant to the Growth Management Act, each county and municipality is required to prepare a comprehensive plan for approval by the Department of Community Affairs. The adopted local plan must include "principles, guidelines, and standards for the orderly and balanced future economic, social, physical, environmental, and fiscal development" of the local government's jurisdictional area. § 163.3177(1), Fla. Stat. (1991). At the minimum, the local plan must include elements covering future land use; capital improvements generally; sanitary sewer, solid waste, drainage, potable water, and natural ground water aquifer protection specifically; conservation; recreation and open space; housing; traffic circulation; intergovernmental coordination; coastal management (for local government in the coastal zone); and mass transit (for local jurisdictions with 50,000 or more people). *Id.* at § 163.3177(6).

Of special relevance to local rezoning actions, the future land use plan element of the local plan must contain both a future land use map and goals, policies, and measurable objectives to guide future land use decisions. This plan element must designate the "proposed future general distribution, location, and extent of the uses of land" for various purposes. *Id.* at § 163.3177(6)(a). It must include standards to be utilized in the control and distribution of densities and intensities of development. In addition, the future land use plan must be based on adequate data and analysis concerning the local jurisdiction, including the projected population, the amount of land needed to accommodate the estimated population, the availability of public services and facilities, and the character of undeveloped land. *Id.* at § 163.3177(6) (a).

The local plan must be implemented through the adoption of land development regulations that are consistent with the plan. *Id.* at § 163.3202. In addition, all development, both public and private, and all development orders approved by local governments must be consistent with the adopted local plan. *Id.* at § 163.3194(1) (a). Section 163.3194(3), Florida Statutes (1991), explains consistency as follows:

> (a) A development order or land development regulation shall be consistent with the comprehensive plan if the land uses, densities or intensities, and other aspects of development permitted by such order or regulation are compatible with and further the objectives, policies, land uses, and densities or intensities in the comprehensive plan and if it meets all other criteria enumerated by the local government. . . .

Because [under the statute. — Eds.] an order granting or denying rezoning constitutes a development order and development orders must be consistent with the comprehensive plan, it is clear that orders on rezoning applications must be consistent with the comprehensive plan.

The first issue we must decide is whether the Board's action on Snyder's rezoning application was legislative or quasi-judicial. A board's legislative action is subject to attack in circuit court. However, in deference to the policy-making function of a board when acting in a legislative capacity, its actions will be sustained as long as they are fairly debatable. On the other hand, the rulings of a board acting in its quasi-judicial capacity are subject to review by certiorari and will be upheld only if they are supported by substantial competent evidence.

Enactments of original zoning ordinances have always been considered legislative. . . .

It is the character of the hearing that determines whether or not board action is legislative or quasi-judicial. Generally speaking, legislative action results in the formulation of a general rule of policy, whereas judicial action results in the application of a general rule of policy. In *West Flagler Amusement Co. v. State Racing Commission,* 165 So. 64, 65 (1935), we explained:

> A judicial or quasi-judicial act determines the rules of law applicable, and the rights affected by them, in relation to past transactions. On the other hand, a quasi-legislative or administrative order prescribes what the rule or requirement of administratively determined duty shall be with respect to transactions to be executed in the future, in order that same shall be considered lawful. But even so, quasi-legislative and quasi-executive orders, after they have already been entered, may have a quasi-judicial attribute if capable of being arrived

at and provided by law to be declared by the administrative agency only after express statutory notice, hearing and consideration of evidence to be adduced as a basis for the making thereof.

Applying this criterion, it is evident that comprehensive rezonings affecting a large portion of the public are legislative in nature. However, we agree with the court below when it said:

> Rezoning actions which have an impact on a limited number of persons or property owners, on identifiable parties and interests, where the decision is contingent on a fact or facts arrived at from distinct alternatives presented at a hearing, and where the decision can be functionally viewed as policy application, rather than policy setting, are in the nature of . . . quasi-judicial action . . . .

Therefore, the board's action on Snyder's application was in the nature of a quasi-judicial proceeding and properly reviewable by petition for certiorari.

We also agree with the court below that the review is subject to strict scrutiny. In practical effect, the review by strict scrutiny in zoning cases appears to be the same as that given in the review of other quasi-judicial decisions. See *Lee County v. Sunbelt Equities, II, Ltd. Partnership,* 619 So. 2d 996 (Fla. 2d DCA 1993) (The term "strict scrutiny" arises from the necessity of strict compliance with comprehensive plan.). This term as used in the review of land use decisions must be distinguished from the type of strict scrutiny review afforded in some constitutional cases.

At this point, we depart from the rationale of the court below. In the first place, the opinion overlooks the premise that the comprehensive plan is intended to provide for the future use of land, which contemplates a gradual and ordered growth. See *City of Jacksonville Beach,* 461 So. 2d at 163, in which the following statement from *Marracci v. City of Scappoose,* 552 P.2d 552, 553 (Or. Ct. App. 1976), was approved:

> [A] comprehensive plan only establishes a long-range maximum limit on the possible intensity of land use; a plan does not simultaneously establish an immediate minimum limit on the possible intensity of land use. The present use of land may, by zoning ordinance, continue to be more limited than the future use contemplated by the comprehensive plan.

Even where a denial of a zoning application would be inconsistent with the plan, the local government should have the discretion to decide that the maximum development density should not be allowed provided the governmental body approves some development that is consistent with the plan and the government's decision is supported by substantial, competent evidence.

Further, we cannot accept the proposition that once the landowner demonstrates that the proposed use is consistent with the comprehensive plan, he is presumptively entitled to this use unless the opposing governmental agency proves by clear and convincing evidence that specifically stated public necessity requires a more restricted use. We do not believe that a property owner is necessarily entitled to relief by proving consistency when the board action is also consistent with the plan. . . .

This raises a question of whether the Growth Management Act provides any comfort to the landowner when the denial of the rezoning request is consistent with the comprehensive plan. It could be argued that the only recourse is to pursue the traditional remedy of attempting to prove that the denial of the application was arbitrary, discriminatory, or unreasonable. Yet, the fact that a proposed use is consistent with the plan means that the planners contemplated that that use would be acceptable at some point in the future. We do not believe the Growth Management Act was intended to preclude development but only to insure that it proceed in an orderly manner.

Upon consideration, we hold that a landowner seeking to rezone property has the burden of proving that the proposal is consistent with the comprehensive plan and complies with all procedural requirements of the zoning ordinance. At this point, the burden shifts to the governmental board to demonstrate that maintaining the existing zoning classification with respect to the property accomplishes a legitimate public purpose. In effect, the landowners' traditional remedies will be subsumed within this rule, and the board will now have the burden of showing that the refusal to rezone the property is not arbitrary, discriminatory, or unreasonable. If the board carries its burden, a landowner's only remaining recourse will be to demonstrate that the existing zoning classification of the property is confiscatory and thereby constitutes a taking.

While they may be useful, the board will not be required to make findings of fact. However, in order to sustain the board's action, upon review by certiorari in the circuit court it must be shown that there was competent substantial evidence presented to the board to support its ruling. . . . [The court quashed the decision below but allowed the landowners an opportunity to file a new application for rezoning.] BARKETT, C.J., and OVERTON, MCDONALD, KOGAN and HARDING, J.J., concur. SHAW, J., dissents.

NOTES AND QUESTIONS

1. *Snyder* made several major changes in the rules governing judicial review of the zoning process. The presumption of constitutionality is reversed, the burden of proof is shifted to the municipality, and the plan becomes the standard under which the zoning amendment is judged. Of course, a court could adopt the quasi-judicial approach to zoning amendments, yet not make the zoning ordinance or some other standard the basis for judicial review. See *Woodland Hills Conserv., Inc. v. City of Jackson*, 443 So. 2d 1173 (Miss. 1983) (change-mistake and public need tests applied in that state make rezoning quasi-judicial). The point is that there must be a standard or policy communities can apply in the zoning process.

You should note the influence of the mandatory planning requirement on the court's decision. This subject is taken up in detail in sec. G, *infra*. In a departure from usual practice, Florida (as the court notes) characterizes decisions on land use applications as "development orders." This is consistent with administrative practice in state agencies.

2. *Why should zoning be quasi-judicial?* The *Fasano* case, which is discussed in *Snyder*, adopted this view because it believed the zoning process was

controlled by developers who pressured municipalities into rezonings that impaired the comprehensive plan. Characterizing the zoning process as quasi-judicial and reversing the presumption of constitutionality is a way to control this problem. Richard Babcock described the problem:

> The roots of this judicial restlessness lie in the mess of local zoning administration. In those zoning jurisdictions where the final local zoning decisions are legislative, . . . the courts are torn between their traditional judicial reluctance to explore the motives of legislators and their suspicion that, as one appellate judge put it, "there's a lot of hanky-panky we suspect but cannot find in the record." [R. Babcock, The Zoning Game 104 (1966).]

Yet, as one report pointed out:

> The private citizen probably stands to gain the most from the quasi-judicial approach. As a party, a citizen has the right of full participation in the hearing. . . . Well armed with the facts, the citizen can be quite effective against the most sophisticated developer. [Housing for All Under Law 272 (Report of the American Bar Ass'n Advisory Comm'n on Housing & Urban Growth, R. Fishman ed. 1978).]

The article by Professors Mandelker and Tarlock, which is quoted in the *Snyder* decision, builds a case for presumption-shifting based in part on developer capture of the local government zoning process.

3. *Other reasons for adopting the quasi-judicial view.* The Idaho Supreme Court provided a different reason in *Cooper v. Board of County Comm'rs,* 614 P.2d 947 (Idaho 1980):

> The great deference given true legislative action stems from its high visibility and widely felt impact, on the theory that the appropriate remedy can be had at the polls. . . . This rationale is inapposite when applied to a local zoning body's decision as to the fate of an individual's application for rezon[ing]. Most voters are unaware or unconcerned that fair dealing and consistent treatment have been sacrificed. [*Id.* at 950.]

What kind of remedy at the polls is the court talking about? Voting out the council members? A referendum on a zoning ordinance? On the use of referenda in zoning, see sec. H, *infra.* Note the trade-off here. Only local legislative actions are subject to referendum, so that a holding that a rezoning is quasi-judicial means that a referendum on the rezoning is not available. But see *Margolis v. District Court,* 638 P.2d 297 (Colo. 1981) (rezoning held quasi-judicial for purposes of judicial review but legislative for purposes of referendum). Is this a good compromise?

Other states have adopted the quasi-judicial view. See, e.g., *Tate v. Miles,* 503 A.2d 187 (Del. 1986); *Golden v. City of Overland Park,* 584 P.2d 130 (Kan. 1978); *Lowe v. City of Missoula,* 525 P.2d 551 (Mont. 1974) (downzoning).

4. *Is every rezoning quasi-judicial?* The answer obviously is "no" because, as the *Snyder* case held, a rezoning is quasi-judicial only when the local governing body *applies* policy through the rezoning ordinance. Would a rezoning covering a substantial tract of land be legislative because the area is so large that the rezoning amounts to a change in land use policy for the municipality?

The Oregon Supreme Court considered this question in *Neuberger v. City of Portland,* 603 P.2d 771 (Or. 1979). The city rezoned a 601-acre parcel of land for a development of more than 1000 single-family homes at a more intensive density. The court indicated when and why a land use decision would be held quasi-judicial:

> [O]ur land use decisions indicate that when a particular action by a local government is directed at a relatively small number of persons, and when that action also involves the application of existing policy to a specific factual setting, the requirement of quasi-judicial procedures has been implied. [*Id.* at 775.]

The court stated that quasi-judicial procedures are necessary when relatively few individuals are involved to provide "the safeguards of fair and open procedures." When pre-existing criteria are applied, quasi-judicial procedures are necessary "in order to assure that factual determinations will be made correctly."

The court then considered whether the rezoning was a "free choice among competing policies" or the "application of existing policy." Both types of decisionmaking were present. The rezoning required a policy decision because the development was so large that it would have a major impact on municipal services and other local government jurisdictions. Yet the rezoning also was quasi-judicial because it required the application of statutory rezoning criteria and the state planning goals. The Court concluded that the action was quasi-judicial, but that the municipality had met its burden; the rezoning was upheld.

Is the amendment of a comprehensive plan quasi-judicial? In *Martin County v. Yusem,* 690 So. 2d 1288 (Fla. 1997), the Florida Supreme Court reaffirmed *Snyder* as applied to the type of zoning at issue in that case, but held that amendments to the comprehensive plan are legislative. It held that an amendment to the plan "required the County to engage in policy reformulation of its comprehensive plan and to determine whether it now desired to retreat from the policies embodied in its future land use map for the orderly development of the County's future growth." What about an amendment to a comprehensive plan that only affects a small tract? See also *Stuart v. Board of County Comm'rs,* 699 P.2d 978 (Colo. App. 1985) (plan amendment held legislative when the development and its impact authorized by the plan was not known).

5. *The quasi-judicial view rejected.* Several courts refused to follow *Fasano's* holding that a rezoning map amendment is quasi-judicial. See, e.g., *Wait v. City of Scottsdale,* 618 P.2d 601 (Ariz. 1980); *Hall Paving Co. v. Hall County,* 226 S.E.2d 728 (Ga. 1976); *State v. City of Rochester,* 268 N.W.2d 885 (Minn. 1978). The most elaborate rejection of *Fasano* came in *Arnel Dev. Co. v. City of Costa Mesa,* 620 P.2d 565 (Cal. 1980), although the court did not expressly mention *Fasano.* Voters had adopted an initiative ordinance downzoning land on which a developer planned to build a moderate-income housing development that was allowable under the zoning ordinance before the initiative was passed. The California court said in part:

The factual setting of the present case illustrates the problems courts will face if we abandoned past precedent and attempted to devise a new test distinguishing legislative and adjudicative decisions. The Court of Appeal, for example, found here that the instant initiative was an adjudicative act because it rezoned a "relatively small" parcel of land. It is not, however, self-evident that 68 acres is a "relatively small" parcel; some cities have entire zoning classifications which comprise less than 68 acres. The size of the parcel, moreover, has very little relationship to the theoretical basis of the Court of Appeal holding — the distinction between the making of land-use policy, a legislative act, and the asserted adjudicatory act of applying established policy. The rezoning of a "relatively small" parcel, especially when done by initiative, may well signify a fundamental change in city land-use policy.

Plaintiffs alternatively urge that the present initiative is adjudicatory because it assertedly affects only three landowners. But this is a very myopic view of the matter; the proposed construction of housing for thousands of people affects the prospective tenants, the housing market, the residents living nearby, and the future character of the community. The number of landowners whose property is actually rezoned is as unsuitable a test as the size of the property rezoned. Yet without some test which distinguishes legislative from adjudicative acts with clarity and reasonable certainty, municipal governments and voters will lack adequate guidance in enacting and evaluating land-use decisions.

In summary, past California land-use cases have established generic classifications, viewing zoning ordinances as legislative and other decisions, such as variances and subdivision map approvals, as adjudicative. This method of classifying land-use decisions enjoys the obvious advantage of economy; the municipality, the proponents of a proposed measure, and the opponents of the measure can readily determine if notice, hearings, and findings are required, what form of judicial review is appropriate, and whether the measure can be enacted by initiative or overturned by referendum. [*Id.* at 572.]

The court also held that adopting the quasi-judicial view was not necessary to protect the public interest in "orderly land use planning," noting that California requires consistency with the land use plan and that the California court adopted a "regional general welfare" rule that limits exclusionary zoning. Absent these two safeguards, would you agree with the court's conclusions?

6. *Sources.* For discussion of the Florida cases and problems of quasi-judicial decision making in zoning see Lincoln, *Executive Decisionmaking by Local Legislatures in Florida: Justice, Judicial Review and the Need for Legislative Reform,* 25 Stetson L. Rev. 627 (1996); Sullivan & Kressel, *Twenty Years After: Renewed Significance of the Comprehensive Plan Requirements,* 9 Urb. L. Ann. 33 (1975); Note, *Trying to Fit an Elephant in a Volkswagen: Six Years of the Snyder Decision in Florida Land Use Law,* 52 Fla. L. Rev. 217 (2000).

A NOTE ON PROCEDURAL DUE PROCESS IN
LAND USE DECISIONS

Due process requirements under state law.—The procedural responsibilities of zoning agencies are not well-developed in state law. The Standard Zoning Act and most state acts provide rudimentary procedural requirements, such as requirements for notice and a hearing before legislative and administrative bodies, but this is usually about all. Failure to give adequate notice can be fatal. *American Oil Corp. v. City of Chicago,* 331 N.E.2d 67 (Ill. App. 1975).

A failure to provide an opportunity for a hearing is also fatal, *Bowen v. Story County Bd. of Supvrs.,* 209 N.W.2d 569 (Iowa 1973). There are no requirements for the adequacy of a hearing in states that classify a rezoning as legislative, but see *Pendley v. Lake Harbin Civic Ass'n,* 198 S.E.2d 503 (Ga. 1973) (post-midnight hearing inadequate). When a hearing is administrative, courts may require the right to present evidence, the right to cross-examine witnesses, the right to respond to written submissions, the right to counsel and a decision on the record with stated reasons. These rights are not unlimited. *Crispin v. Town of Scarborough,* 736 A.2d 241 (Me. 1999) (upholding limitation of initial comments to three minutes in light of number of people at hearing).

Complainants may find it difficult to sustain claims of procedural due process violations. Litigants may have to defeat the presumption that local authorities performed their duties properly, prove that they were prejudiced by the failure to provide due process, *White v. Town of Hollis,* 589 A.2d 46 (Me. 1991), and preserve their rights by objecting to procedural due process violations at the hearing level.

Courts will not usually allow the taking of ex parte evidence by an administrative board, *Rodine v. Zoning Bd. of Adjustment,* 434 N.W.2d 124 (Iowa 1988). See also *Blaker v. Planning & Zoning Comm'n,* 562 A.2d 1093 (Conn. 1989) (rezoning and special permit; receipt of ex parte evidence shifts burden of proof). Site visits can be a problem; adequate notice of the meeting must be provided. *Nazarko v. Conservation Comm'n,* 717 A.2d 853 (Conn. App. 1998) (notice inadequate). See Comment, *Ex Parte Communications in Local Land Use Decisions,* 15 B.C. Envtl. Aff. L. Rev. 81 (1987).

As noted earlier, neighborhood opposition is often a factor in the denial of applications for rezonings, conditional uses and the like. Courts often set aside a zoning decision if they believe that neighborhood opposition tainted the zoning action with an improper motive or purpose. *Chanhassen Estates Residents Ass'n v. City of Chanhassen,* 342 N.W.2d 335 (Minn. 1984), is a leading case. See Ellis, *Neighborhood Opposition and the Permissible Purposes of Zoning,* 7 J. Land Use & Envtl. L. 275 (1992).

Open meetings.—All states have open meeting laws, which usually apply to planning commissions and boards of adjustment. A closed meeting can void a zoning decision if one is required. *Town of Palm Beach v. Gradison,* 296 So. 2d 473 (Fla. 1974) (comprehensive rezoning void because citizens advisory committee appointed by a town board to assist with ordinance held closed meetings). All of the meeting must be open. A board cannot hold an evidentiary hearing and then go into closed session to make a decision. *Beck v. Crisp*

County Zoning Bd. of Appeals, 472 S.E.2d 558 (Ga. App. 1996). See Note, *The Changing Weather Forecast: Government in the Sunshine in the 1990s — An Analysis of State Sunshine Laws,* 71 Wash. U. L.Q. 1165 (1993).

Federal law.—The federal law on procedural due process requirements is better developed and at the same time more flexible. *Cloutier v. Town of Epping,* reproduced *supra* Ch. 2, is an example of a federal decision in which procedural due process problems were raised. Like the state courts, the federal courts apply procedural due process requirements only to administrative actions, but after that the federal law varies:

> Procedural due process requirements apply only to an entitlement to a property interest, not to an expectancy. A landowner has an entitlement:
>
> a. if he has a vested right in a particular use of his land; or
>
> b. if his land use is permitted at the time he makes an application for a permit or requests development approval, and the land use agency does not have the discretion to deny the permit or request for approval. . . .
>
> The federal courts apply a balancing test [based on *Matthews v. Eldridge,* 424 U.S. 319 (1976)] to administrative decision-making to determine whether an administrative decision violates procedural due process. . . . [T]hey consider:
>
> a. the private interest affected by the official action;
>
> b. the risk of an erroneous deprivation of such an interest through the procedures used and the probable value of additional or substitute procedural safeguards; and
>
> c. the government's interest, including the function involved and fiscal and administrative burdens that the additional or substitute procedures require. [Land Use and the Constitution 40–41, 43 (B. Blaesser & A. Weinstein eds. 1989).]

Most of the federal cases have not found procedural due process violations, see *Cloutier v. Town of Epping, supra* Ch. 2, holding that a full judicial hearing was not required. But see *Herrington v. County of Sonoma,* 857 F.2d 567 (9th Cir. 1988), *cert. denied,* 489 U.S. 1090 (1989), holding that notice and hearing for a subdivision denial were inadequate.

NOTES AND QUESTIONS

1. *An example.* Review the proceedings in the drive-in bank variance application in the hypothetical hearing, *supra.* Are there procedural due process violations under state law? Under federal law? Since under federal law there must be an entitlement in order to trigger procedural due process requirements, and since under state law most land use approvals are discretionary, will the application of federal procedural due process be limited? Which land use approval techniques are likely to create "entitlements" under federal law? See *Yale Auto Parts, Inc. v. Johnson,* 758 F.2d 54 (2d Cir. 1985) (junkyard permit discretionary).

The Supreme Court took a somewhat different view of distinguishing legislative from administrative actions in a case in which it held that legislative bodies were immune from suit under § 1983. In *Bogan v. Scott-Harris*, 523 U.S. 44 (1998), the court held that whether an act is legislative turns, not on the motive of the legislators, but on whether the act was "formally legislative" and within the "traditional sphere of legislative activity." In this case an ordinance terminating an employee position was legislative because it was a "discretionary, policymaking decision" that could well have prospective effect.

2. *Bias and conflict of interest.* The law of bias and conflict of interest developed by the state courts also provides a control on decision making in the zoning process but is generally applied only to administrative decisions. A few states have also adopted legislation on this problem that attempts to codify the common law rules. E.g., N.J. Stat. Ann. § 40:55D-23b. Board members are disqualified for bias when they make outspoken public statements on matters they subsequently hear, *Lage v. Zoning Bd. of Appeals*, 172 A.2d 911 (Conn. 1961), but campaign statements are an exception. *City of Farmers Branch v. Hawnco, Inc.*, 435 S.W.2d 288 (Tex. Civ. App. 1968).

Pecuniary interest based on the ownership of property is the typical conflict of interests case. See *Griswold v. City of Homer*, 925 P.2d 1015 (Alaska 1996), where the court found a conflict of interest when a council member owned one of 13 lots in a central business district that was rezoned to allow auto sales. Is ownership of property in the municipality enough to disqualify from voting on a plan amendment eliminating a proposed floating zone for mining? *Segalla v. Planning Bd.*, 611 N.Y.S.2d 287 (App. Div. 1994), held no, because everybody in the municipality is equally affected and any benefit from the rezoning is speculative. But see *Clark v. City of Hermosa Beach*, 56 Cal. Rptr. 2d 223 (Cal. App. 1996) (council member who lived one block away from a housing project he opposed was disqualified), *cert. denied*, 520 U.S. 1167 (1996).

Close business or personal relationships can also create a conflict of interest. A board member was disqualified when his nephew was a member of the law firm that represented the applicant. *Kremer v. City of Plainfield*, 244 A.2d 335 (N.J. 1968). Accord *Dick v. Williams*, 452 S.E.2d 172 (Ga. App. 1994). What if a commissioner's wife was occasionally employed by an applicant who received a site plan approval which the commissioner opposed and voted against? The court found no problem in *Petrick v. Planning Bd.*, 671 A.2d 140 (N.J. App. Div. 1996), because the conflict was too remote and speculative. Was there bias or a conflict of interest in the hypothetical drive-in bank variance hearing?

An effective solution for the bias and conflict of interest problems is elusive. Individual residents of a community may own property, have well-defined views on land use issues, and relatives employed in a variety of occupations. Should they be disqualified from serving on zoning agencies, and if they serve, should they be disqualified when apparent conflict or bias emerges?

For discussion see Baker, *Ethical Limits on Attorney Contact with Represented and Unrepresented Officials: The Example of Municipal Zoning Boards Making Site-Specific Land Use Decisions*, 31 Suffolk U. L. Rev. 349 (1997);

Dyas, *Conflicts of Interest in Planning and Zoning Cases,* 17 J. Legal Prof. 219 (1993); Tarlock, *Challenging Biased Zoning Board Decisions,* 10 Zoning & Plan. L. Rep. 97 (1987); Vietzen, *Controlling Conflicts of Interest in Land Use Decisions,* 38 Land Use L. & Zoning Dig., No. 1, at 3 (1986).

3. *The hearing process.* Oregon legislation provides some useful insights on how the quasi-judicial procedural "revolution" affects the land use decision making process. Ore. Rev. Stat. § 197.763. Detailed requirements are included for giving notice. The notice must "explain the nature of the application and the proposed use or uses which could be authorized, [and] list the applicable criteria from the ordinance and the plan that apply to the application at issue." This limits the basis for the hearing.

All documents and evidence submitted by the applicant must be available to the public. "Any staff report used at the hearing shall be available at least seven days prior to the hearing." A statement must be made at the commencement of the hearing that lists the applicable substantive criteria and "states that failure to raise an issue accompanied by statements or evidence sufficient to afford the decision maker and the parties an opportunity to respond to the issue precludes appeal to the board based on that issue." The statute also provides for continuances. The American Planning Association model legislation contains similar requirements for hearings and applications for development permits. § 10-207 (draft 2000).

A NOTE ON BRIBERY AND CORRUPTION IN ZONING

Conflict of interest and bias problems are only part of a larger problem of bribery and corruption in the zoning process. The following comment, which especially applies to land use regulation, shows why this issue is important:

> A major strand in thinking about corruption is curtailing the role of special interest groups within the political and governmental process. Susan Rose-Ackerman's landmark study of corruption provides a helpful framework. [Corruption: A Study in Political Economy (1978).] She describes our system of making allocative choices as a "mixed" one in which "both market and nonmarket mechanisms clearly have important allocative roles to play." The democratic political system is the preferred mechanism for allocating public goods. However, "wealth and market forces can undermine whatever dividing line has been fixed. Thus, political decisions that are made on the basis of majority preferences may be undermined by wide use of an illegal market as the method of allocation." The result is political corruption. [Brown, *Putting Watergate Behind Us — Salinas, Sun-Diamond, and Two Views of the Anticorruption Model,* 74 Tul. L. Rev. 747, 752 (2000).]

Corruption in zoning was the subject of a multi-volume study by the Stanford Research Institute, Corruption in Land Use and Building Regulation (1978). Bribery was the major culprit, as the study of Fairfax County, Virginia indicates. The county is part of the Washington, D.C. metropolitan area.

> In the 1960s, some developers and their lawyers apparently began to work together with several of the members of the Board of

Supervisors in order to ensure that rezonings needed for high-profit development were approved by the Board of Supervisors. Subsequent investigations during this period indicated that lawyers representing some developers provided money to supervisors to rezone a factory site, approve sites for apartment complexes, and approve a shopping center complex. . . . Some members of the county planning staff were also involved in some deals. . . . It appears that the loosely run land-use regulatory system existing in the county during this time encouraged these abuses; the practices continued until the land-use system was overhauled after scandals surfaced. [Vol. I, An Integrated Report of Conclusions 41 (1978).]

The Fairfax County example illustrates the heavy involvement of developers and construction interests in local politics, and the cooperative relationship that can emerge between these interests and local decision makers. For a detailed account of this kind of symbiotic relationship in a Long Island, New York suburb, see M. Gottdiener, Planned Sprawl: Private and Public Interests in Suburbia (1977).

These problems have not disappeared with time. For some recent successful prosecutions against local officials for accepting bribes in zoning matters, see *Evans v. United States*, 504 U.S. 255 (1992) (federal officer impersonated developer); *State v. Leevre,* 972 P.2d 1021 (Ariz. App. 1998); *Sawyer v. State,* 583 N.E.2d 795 (Ind. App. 1991).

As Professor Brown indicates in his article, *supra,* the answer to these problems in the post-Watergate era has been to tighten restrictions on public officials and step up criminal prosecutions. This approach was taken in a companion report to the corruption study, sponsored by the American Planning Association, that recommended a number of zoning reforms to reduce corruption. See J. Getzels & C. Thurow, An Analysis of Zoning Reforms: Minimizing the Incentive for Corruption (1978). Many of these reforms have been discussed in these pages, such as the use of quasi-judicial procedures and hearing examiners and a requirement that land use decisions be consistent with a comprehensive plan. One of the major themes of the Stanford corruption report was that opportunities for corruption decrease when decision making is highly visible. If this is so, then more formal and open procedures in the decision making process should help.

Yet Professor Brown notes a reaction to heightened efforts at dealing with the "scandal" problem:

Numerous academic and policy experts have spearheaded a formidable reaction to what they see as the excessive zeal of the post-Watergate approach. The office of independent counsel is their favorite target, but others include the overcriminalization of ethical matters, the need for greater concern about the rights of public officials, and the advantages of a pluralistic system in which interest groups voice their concern within a process mediated by institutions such as political parties. [*Id.* at 810.]

Consider these comments in view of the discussion of market solutions to land use conflicts in Chapter 1, and the comment there that reliance on the market may motivate some participants to try to bribe decision makers.

4. DOWNZONING

STONE v. CITY OF WILTON

331 N.W.2d 398 (Iowa 1983)

McGiverin, Justice:

Plaintiffs Alex and Martha Stone appeal from the dismissal of their petition for declaratory judgment, injunctive relief and damages in an action regarding defendant City of Wilton's rezoning from multi-family to single-family residential of certain real estate owned by plaintiffs. The issues raised by plaintiffs focus on the validity of the rezoning ordinance and the trial court's striking of plaintiffs' claim for lost profits. We find no error in [the] trial court's rulings and affirm its decision.

This appeal is a zoning dispute involving approximately six acres of land in the city of Wilton, Iowa. Plaintiffs purchased the undeveloped land in June 1979 with the intent of developing a low income, federally subsidized housing project. The project was to consist of several multi-family units; therefore, feasibility of the project depended upon multi-family zoning of the tract. At the time of the purchase approximately one-fourth of plaintiffs' land was zoned R-1, single-family residential, and the remainder was zoned R-2, multi-family residential.

After the land was purchased, plaintiffs incurred expenses for architectural fees and engineering services in the preparation of plans and plats to be submitted to the city council and its planning and zoning commission. In addition, plaintiffs secured a Farmers' Home Administration (FHA) loan commitment for construction of the project.

This suit is based primarily on actions of city officials between December 1979 and June 1980. We will discuss only the most pertinent events now and will relate other facts later when we consider the issues raised by plaintiffs.

In December 1979 plaintiffs filed a preliminary plat for the project with the city clerk. In March 1980, following a public meeting, the planning and zoning commission recommended to the city council that land in the northern part of the city be rezoned to single-family residential due to alleged inadequacies of sewer, water and electrical services. The rezoning recommendation affected all of plaintiffs' property plus tracts owned by two other developers. Plaintiffs' application on May 21, 1980, for a building permit to construct multi-family dwellings was denied due to the pending rezoning recommendation.

In May 1980, plaintiffs filed a petition against the city seeking a declaratory judgment invalidating any rezoning of their property, temporary and permanent injunctions to prohibit passage of any rezoning ordinance, and in the event of rezoning, $570,000 damages for monies expended on the project, anticipated lost profits and alleged reduction in the value of plaintiffs' land. The temporary injunction was denied.

In accordance with the recommendation of the planning and zoning commission, the city council passed an ordinance rezoning the land from R-2 to R-1 in June 1980. . . .

This action proceeded to trial in November 1980. . . .

I. *Scope of Review*

[The court held the case was "best treated as one in equity" and that review was de novo.]

II. *Validity of the Rezoning Ordinance*

. . . .

Land use restrictions (such as at issue here) reasonably related to the promotion of the health, safety, morals, or general welfare repeatedly have been upheld even though the challenged regulations destroyed or adversely affected recognized real property interests or flatly prohibited the most beneficial use of the property. Hence, such laws, when justifiable under the police power, validly enacted and not arbitrary or unreasonable, generally are held not to be invalid as taking of property for public use without compensation. However, some instances of government regulation are "so onerous as to constitute a taking which constitutionally requires compensation." *Goldblatt v. Town of [Hempstead]*, 369 U.S. 590, 594 (1962).

A.

We focus initially on the general claims which plaintiffs make concerning the validity of the rezoning. Controlling our review of the enactment's validity is the principle that the validity of a police power enactment, such as zoning, depends on its reasonableness; however, "[the Supreme Court] has often said that 'debatable questions as to reasonableness are not for the courts but for the legislature. . . .'" *Goldblatt*, 369 U.S. at 595.

The zoning ordinance at issue was passed as a general welfare measure. It affected not only Stones' proposed housing project, but also land owned by Land, Ltd. and Wilton Sunset Housing Corporation, which intended to erect multi-family housing for the elderly. The city council's stated reasons for rezoning this section of the city from R-2 to R-1 were as follows: (1) The existing zoning was no longer appropriate to the current and anticipated growth and development of the area; (2) the existing zoning would create a greater density than now appropriate; (3) the existing zoning would create a traffic and pedestrian flow too great for the existing street and sidewalk systems in the area; and (4) the city's electrical, water and sewer systems were inadequate for a concentration of multi-family dwellings in that area of town.

Plaintiffs, however, claim the above were mere pretext. They contend that the council disregarded its comprehensive plan. They further argue that the council was prompted by a desire to advance the private economic interests of a member of the planning and zoning commission and by racial discrimination against the "type" of persons who might live in plaintiffs' housing project. The trial court disagreed and so do we. "If the [city council] gave full consideration to the problem presented, including the needs of the public, changing conditions, and the similarity of other land in the same area, then it has zoned in accordance with a comprehensive plan." *Montgomery v. Bremer*

County Board of Supervisors, 299 N.W.2d 687, 695 (Iowa 1980). On the record in this case, we cannot conclude that the council's stated reasons, which are recognized as valid reasons for zoning, Iowa Code §§ 414.2, .3 (1981), were mere pretext. . . .

Plaintiffs also suggested that questions concerning the "types" of tenants in the housing project were racially motivated and affected the council's decision to rezone. The evidence is clear that the Wilton city council was faced with a number of competing concerns in regard to the proper zoning of the area of the city in which plaintiffs' land was situated. It is precisely because legislative bodies, like this city council, are faced with balancing numerous competing considerations that courts refrain from reviewing the merits of their decisions if at least a debatable question exists as to the reasonableness of their action.

"But racial discrimination is not just another competing consideration. When there is a proof that a discriminatory purpose has been a motivating factor in the decision, this judicial deference is no longer justified." *Village of Arlington Heights v. Metropolitan Housing Development Corp.,* 429 U.S. 252, 265–66 (1977). We are unable to find sufficient evidence in the record to conclude that plaintiffs carried their burden of proof. We find that discriminatory purpose was not a motivating factor in the council's decision to rezone.

In sum, zoning is not static. A city's comprehensive plan is always subject to reasonable revisions designed to meet the ever-changing needs and conditions of a community. We conclude that the council rationally decided to rezone this section of the city to further the public welfare in accordance with a comprehensive plan. . . .

Affirmed

NOTES AND QUESTIONS

1. *Downzoning issues.* The principal case indicates some of the special characteristics of a downzoning amendment. The city takes away what the landowner had before, and the action looks arbitrary and discriminatory. Yet the Iowa court applied the usual "fairly debatable" rule to uphold the downzoning and rejected the racial discrimination claim. Note that an upzoning amendment discriminates in favor of the landowner while the downzoning amendment discriminates against the landowner. Should the courts treat these discrimination claims differently?

The downzoning cases are closely related to the vested rights cases, even though the landowner has no vested right in the continuation of a pre-existing zoning classification. Should this relationship strengthen the landowner's challenge to a downzoning? The court in the principal case rejected a vested rights claim made by the landowner in a portion of the decision which is not reproduced. For an account of how Virginia's vested rights statute was a response to downzoning problems see Prichard & Riegle, *Searching For Certainty: Virginia's Evolutionary Approach to Vested Rights,* 7 Geo. Mason L. Rev. 983 (1999).

Some courts do not apply the usual presumption of validity to downzonings. With the principal case compare *Trust Co. of Chicago v. City of Chicago,* 96 N.E.2d 499 (Ill. 1951). The court invalidated a downzoning of a lot from multi-family to single-family use in an area generally zoned and developed for multi-family use. The court noted that the downzoning was "not made for the public good" but "for the benefit only of those residents of the block who desired to exclude" apartments. Can you distinguish this case from the principal case? A court may also invalidate a downzoning if it appears directed at a particular developer. See *A.A. Profiles, Inc. v. City of Fort Lauderdale,* 850 F.2d 1483 (11th Cir. 1988) (downzoning followed revocation of building permit). For discussion of downzoning generally, see Williamson, *Constitutional and Judicial Limitations on the Community's Power to Downzone,* 12 Urb. Law. 157 (1980).

2. *Good or bad?* Is there anything inherently good or bad about a piecemeal downzoning? In the *Wilton* case, the downzoning was done to block lower-income housing development. See also *Gregory v. County of Harnett,* 493 S.E.2d 786 (N.C. App. 1997), where the court reversed a downzoning done to block the extension of a mobile home park, holding that fear of crime from residents of the park was not a sufficient justification. How would the discrimination claim in *Wilton* be analyzed under *Huntington, supra* Ch. 4? (Recall that *Huntington* departs significantly from the *Arlington Heights* test, upon which the principal case relies.)

Two courts have adopted rules that make it more difficult to justify downzonings. *Parkridge v. City of Seattle,* 573 P.2d 359 (Wash. 1978), held that downzonings were quasi-judicial actions, dropped the presumption of constitutionality, and placed the burden to prove the validity of the downzoning on the municipality. In *Board of Supvrs. v. Snell Constr. Corp.,* 202 S.E.2d 889 (Va. 1974), the court applied a variant of the Maryland change-mistake rule to piecemeal downzonings that weakened the usual presumption of constitutionality. If a piecemeal downzoning is not justified by changed circumstances, the municipality must introduce evidence of mistake, fraud, or changed circumstances sufficient to make the downzoning a reasonably debatable issue.

Yet one commentator argues that downzoning is useful in lower-income and minority neighborhoods as a means of eliminating undesirable uses. Arnold, *Planning Milagros: Environmental Justice and Land Use Regulation,* 76 Denv. U.L. Rev. 1, 108–14 (1998). For example, in *Smith Inv. Co. v. Sandy City,* 958 P.2d 245 (Utah App. 1998), the court upheld a downzoning of 16 unused acres in a shopping center to residential use, noting it was a reasonably debatable way of limiting business concentration in an area surrounded on three sides by homes. The court also noted that the adjacent residential areas were undergoing "deteriorating housing and high turnover of owners," and that the downzoning might help stabilize the area by encouraging additional residential development. See also *Ex parte City of Jacksonville,* 693 So. 2d 465 (Ala. 1996) (upholding downzoning from multi-family to single family residential in a neighborhood that had been developing as single family homes).

3. *Comprehensive downzonings.* As in the spot "upzoning" cases, a question to ask in the piecemeal downzoning cases is why a comprehensive downzoning was not done? These should survive attack. A leading case is *Norbeck Village*

Joint Venture v. Montgomery County Council, 254 A.2d 700 (Md. 1969). The court upheld a downzoning of fifty square miles to two-acre lots. The purpose of the downzoning was to implement a comprehensive plan based on a regional plan by creating a low density development area that would isolate a town center identified in the plan from urban sprawl. The court expressly relied on the plan as a basis for upholding the downzoning. See also *Carty v. City of Ojai,* 143 Cal. Rptr. 506 (Cal. App. 1978) (upheld downzoning of land zoned for outlying shopping center to implement plan calling for protection of downtown business district).

Would the courts have upheld these downzonings if they had not been supported by a comprehensive plan? See *Pace Resources, Inc. v. Shrewsbury Twp. Planning Comm'n,* 492 A.2d 818 (Pa. Commw. 1985) (invalidating downzoning inconsistent with comprehensive plan).

4. *Takings.* The court in *Norbeck, supra* note 3, also rejected a taking claim that had been made against the downzoning, finding that the land as rezoned could be put to a reasonably profitable use. Taking claims are often made in downzoning cases. As in cases brought to challenge any zoning restriction, the courts will consider whether the land use allowed by the downzoning is compatible with the surrounding area. Compare *Grimpel Assocs. v. Cohalan,* 361 N.E.2d 1022, 1024 (N.Y. 1977) (invalidating downzoning where the residential use would be an "'inappropriate and unjustifiable island' surrounded by business operations and major vehicular thoroughfares"), with *McGowan v. Cohalan,* 361 N.E.2d 1025 (N.Y. 1977) (approving another part of same downzoning, where area was mix of residential, commercial and industrial uses, but Town's goal of encouraging residential use was reasonable and achievable), and *A.A. Profiles, supra* (recognizing taking claim). Of course, a court will not find a taking if the downzoning results only in a decrease in the value of the property. See *Spenger, Grubb & Assocs. v. City of Hailey,* 903 P.2d 741 (Idaho 1995).

5. *Purposes.* The principal case suggests that the purpose to be achieved by a downzoning may be an important factor bearing on its constitutionality. Courts have frequently upheld downzonings for the purpose of conforming the zoning of a site to uses compatible with the surrounding area. See *Lum Yip Kee, Ltd. v. City & County of Honolulu,* 767 P.2d 815 (Hawaii 1989).

Consider the following cases:

Mountcrest Estates v. Mayor & Twp. Comm., 232 A.2d 674 (N.J. App. Div.), *cert. denied,* 234 A.2d 402 (N.J. 1967). The township passed a downzoning ordinance increasing lot sizes in its B residential district. Mountcrest argued that the downzoning was invalid because eighty-five percent of the lots in the B district were built upon or platted at the previous higher density. This argument did not impress the court, which upheld the downzoning. Existing uses were a factor to consider, but the plan evidenced by the zoning ordinance was mutable and a presumption of validity attached to the amended ordinance. "The municipality's problems with respect to congestion, overcrowding and inability to provide public facilities due to the population explosion will be lessened because between 180 and 250 fewer homes can be built in the B district under the amended ordinance than could have been built before the amendments — a possible difference in population of from 500 to 1,000 persons." *Id.* at 677. Accord *Chucta v. Planning & Zoning Comm'n,* 225 A.2d 822 (Conn. 1967).

Kavanewsky v. Zoning Bd. of Appeals, 279 A.2d 567 (Conn. 1971). A town doubled the minimum lot size in one of the two zoning districts into which it was divided. The court noted that the downzoning was "'made in demand of the people to keep Warren a rural community with open spaces and keep undesirable businesses out.' We agree, . . . that the reason given . . . is not in accordance with the requirements of" the purposes provision of the state zoning enabling act, which followed the Standard Act. *Id.* at 571. The downzoning was invalidated.

Sullivan v. Town of Acton, 645 N.E.2d 700 (Mass. App. 1995). The town downzoned a nine-acre parcel at the intersection of two highways which had been used since 1940 for agricultural and residential purposes, though it was zoned for general business use. The downzoning occurred after a comprehensive planning effort recommended changes for uses along the highway. Its purpose was to control strip development along the highway by restricting further commercial development; to preserve and encourage residential development; to focus new commercial growth in two defined historic "villages"; and to limit traffic growth and congestion.

The court rejected a "spot zoning" challenge, noting that several large and undeveloped parcels along the highway had been rezoned to residential use. "A comprehensive plan designed to preserve a mixture of uses over a substantial area of a municipality does not necessarily run afoul of the uniformity principle expressed in spot zoning law." The purposes for the downzoning were also reasonable. Accord on similar facts *Spenger, Grubb & Assocs. v. City of Hailey,* 903 P.2d 741 (Idaho 1995).

6. *Acquisitory intent.* In a related type of case, a municipality may plan to acquire a tract of land for a park or other public facility. It then downzones the property in order to depress its value in advance of acquisition. Courts uniformly hold this kind of zoning invalid. See, e.g., *Burrows v. City of Keene,* 432 A.2d 15 (N.H. 1981); *Ripley v. City of Lincoln,* 330 N.W.2d 505 (N.D. 1983). Can you see why these cases are consistent with the Supreme Court's 1987 taking trilogy? These cases often award compensation to the successful landowner. Is this consistent with the Supreme Court's decision in *First English*?

E.   OTHER FORMS OF FLEXIBLE ZONING

1.   WITH PRE-SET STANDARDS: THE FLOATING ZONE

RODGERS v. VILLAGE OF TARRYTOWN

302 N.Y. 115, 96 N.E.2d 731 (1951)

FULD, JUDGE:

This appeal, here by our permission, involves the validity of two amendments to the General Zoning Ordinance of the Village of Tarrytown, a suburban area in the County of Westchester, within twenty-five miles of New York City.

Some years ago, Tarrytown enacted a General Zoning Ordinance dividing the village into seven districts or zones — Residence A for single family dwellings, Residence B for two-family dwellings, Residence C for multiple dwellings and apartment houses, three business districts and an industrial zone. In 1947 and 1948, the board of trustees, the village's legislative body, passed the two amendatory ordinances here under attack.

The 1947 ordinance creates "A new district or class of zone . . . [to] be called 'Residence B-B,'" in which, besides one-and two-family dwellings, buildings for multiple occupancy of fifteen or fewer families were permitted. The boundaries of the new type district were not delineated in the ordinance but were to be "fixed by amendment of the official village building zone map, at such times in the future as such district or class of zone is applied, to properties in this village." The village planning board was empowered to approve such amendments and, in case such approval was withheld, the board of trustees was authorized to grant it by appropriate resolution. In addition, the ordinance erected exacting standards of size and physical layouts for Residence B-B zones: a minimum of ten acres of land and a maximum building height of three stories were mandated; set-back and spacing requirements for structures were carefully prescribed; and no more than 15% of the ground area of the plot was to be occupied by buildings.

A year and a half after the 1947 amendment was enacted, defendant Elizabeth Rubin sought to have her property, consisting of almost ten and a half acres in the Residence A district, placed in a Residence B-B classification. After repeated modification of her plans to meet suggestions of the village planning board, that body gave its approval, and, several months later, in December of 1948, the board of trustees, also approving, passed the second ordinance here under attack. In essence, it provides that the Residence B-B district "is hereby applied to the [Rubin] property . . . and the district or zone of said property is hereby changed to 'Residence B-B' and the official Building Zone Map of the Village of Tarrytown is hereby amended accordingly [by specification of the various parcels and plots involved]."

Plaintiff, who owns a residence on a six-acre plot about a hundred yards from Rubin's property, brought this action to have the two amendments declared invalid and to enjoin defendant Rubin from constructing multiple dwellings on her property. The courts below, adjudging the amendments valid and the action of the trustees proper, dismissed the complaint. We agree with their determination.

While stability and regularity are undoubtedly essential to the operation of zoning plans, zoning is by no means static. Changed or changing conditions call for changed plans, and persons who own property in a particular zone or use district enjoy no eternally vested right to that classification if the public interest demands otherwise. Accordingly, the power of a village to amend its basic zoning ordinance in such a way as reasonably to promote the general welfare cannot be questioned. Just as clearly, decision as to how a community shall be zoned or rezoned, as to how various properties shall be classified or reclassified, rests with the local legislative body; its judgment and determination will be conclusive, beyond interference from the courts, unless shown to be arbitrary, and the burden of establishing such arbitrariness is imposed upon him who asserts it. . . .

By that test, the propriety of the decision here made is not even debatable. In other words, viewing the rezoning in the case before us, as it must be viewed, in the light of the area involved and the present and reasonably foreseeable needs of the community, the conclusion is inescapable that what was done not only accorded with sound zoning principles, not only complied with every requirement of law, but was accomplished in a proper, careful and reasonable manner.

The Tarrytown board of trustees was entitled to find that there was a real need for additional housing facilities; that the creation of Residence B-B districts for garden apartment developments would prevent young families, unable to find accommodations in the village, from moving elsewhere; would attract business to the community; would lighten the tax load of the small home owner, increasingly burdened by the shrinkage of tax revenues resulting from the depreciated value of large estates and the transfer of many such estates to tax-exempt institutions; and would develop otherwise unmarketable and decaying property.

The village's zoning aim being clear, the choice of methods to accomplish it lay with the board. Two such methods were at hand. It could amend the General Zoning Ordinance so as to permit garden apartments on any plot of ten acres or more in Residence A and B zones (the zones more restricted) or it could amend that ordinance so as to invite owners of ten or more acres, who wished to build garden apartments on their properties, to apply for a Residence B-B classification. The board chose to adopt the latter procedure. That it called for separate legislative authorization for each project presents no obstacle or drawback — and so we have already held. Whether we would have made the same choice is not the issue; it is sufficient that the board's decision was neither arbitrary nor unreasonable.

As to the requirement that the applicant own a plot of at least ten acres, we find nothing therein unfair to plaintiff or other owners of smaller parcels. The board undoubtedly found, as it was privileged to find, that garden apartments would blend more attractively and harmoniously with the community setting, would impose less of a burden upon village facilities, if placed upon larger tracts of land rather than scattered about in smaller units. Obviously, some definite acreage had to be chosen, and, so far as the record before us reveals, the choice of ten acres as a minimum plot was well within the range of an unassailable legislative judgment.

Nor did the board, by following the course which it did, divest itself or the planning board of power to regulate future zoning with regard to garden apartments. The mere circumstance that an owner possesses a ten-acre plot and submits plans conforming to the physical requirements prescribed by the 1947 amendment will not entitle him, *ipso facto,* to a Residence B-B classification. It will still be for the board to decide, in the exercise of a reasonable discretion, that the *grant* of such a classification accords with the comprehensive zoning plan and benefits the village as a whole. And — while no such question is here presented — we note that the board may not arbitrarily or unreasonably *deny* applications of other owners for permission to construct garden apartments on their properties. The action of the board must in all cases be reasonable and, whether a particular application be granted or denied, recourse may be had to the courts to correct an arbitrary or capricious determination.

The charge of illegal "spot zoning" — levelled at the creation of a Residence B-B district and the reclassification of defendant's property — is without substance. Defined as the process of singling out a small parcel of land for a use classification totally different from that of the surrounding area, for the benefit of the owner of such property and to the detriment of other owners, "spot zoning" is the very antithesis of planned zoning. If, therefore, an ordinance is enacted in accordance with a comprehensive zoning plan, it is not "spot zoning," even though it (1) singles out and affects but one small plot, or (2) creates in the center of a large zone small areas or districts devoted to a different use. Thus, the relevant inquiry is not whether the particular zoning under attack consists of areas fixed within larger areas of different use, but whether it was accomplished for the benefit of individual owners rather than pursuant to a comprehensive plan for the general welfare of the community. Having already noted our conclusion that the ordinances were enacted to promote a comprehensive zoning plan, it is perhaps unnecessary to add that the record negates any claim that they were designed solely for the advantage of defendant or any other particular owner. Quite apart from the circumstance that defendant did not seek the benefit of the 1947 amendment until eighteen months after its passage, the all-significant fact is that that amendment applied to the entire territory of the village and accorded each and every owner of ten or more acres identical rights and privileges.

By the same token, there is no basis for the argument that "what has been done by the board of trustees" constitutes a device for "the granting of a 'variance.'" As we have already shown, the village's zoning aim, the statute's purpose, was not to aid the individual owner but to permit the development of the property for the general welfare of the entire community. That being so, the board of trustees followed approved procedure by changing the General Zoning Ordinance itself. Accordingly, when the board was called upon to consider the reclassification of the Rubin property under the 1947 amendment, it was concerned, not with any issue of hardship, but only with the question of whether the property constituted a desirable location for a garden apartment.

We turn finally to the contention that the 1947 ordinance is invalid because, in proclaiming a Residence B-B district, it set no boundaries for the new district and made no changes on the building zone map. The short answer is that, since the ordinance merely prescribed specifications for a new use district, there was no need for it to do either the one or the other. True, until boundaries are fixed and until zoning map changes are made, no new zone actually comes into being, and neither property nor the rights of any property owner are affected. But it was not the design of the board of trustees by that enactment to bring any additional zone into being or to affect any property or rights; the ordinance merely provided the mechanics pursuant to which property owners might in the future apply for the redistricting of their property. In sum, the 1947 amendment was merely the first step in a reasoned plan of rezoning, and specifically provided for further action on the part of the board. That action was taken by the passage of the 1948 ordinance which fixed the boundaries of the newly created zone and amended the zoning map accordingly. It is indisputable that the two amendments, read together as they must be, fully complied with the requirements of the Village Law and accomplished a rezoning of village property in an unexceptionable manner.

In point of fact, there would have been no question about the validity of what was done had the board simply amended the General Zoning Ordinance so as to permit property in Residence A and Residence B zones — or, for that matter, in the other districts throughout the village — to be used for garden apartments, provided that they were built on ten-acre plots and that the other carefully planned conditions and restrictions were met. It may be conceded that, under the method which the board did adopt, no one will know, from the 1947 ordinance itself, precisely where a Residence B-B district will ultimately be located. But since such a district is simply a garden apartment development, we find nothing unusual or improper in that circumstance. The same uncertainty — as to the location of the various types of structures — would be present if a zoning ordinance were to sanction garden apartments as well as one-family homes in a Residence A district — and yet there would be no doubt as to the propriety of that procedure. . . . Consequently, to condemn the action taken by the board in effectuating a perfectly permissible zoning scheme and to strike down the ordinance designed to carry out that scheme merely because the board had employed two steps to accomplish what may be, and usually is, done in one, would be to exalt form over substance and sacrifice substance to form.

Whether it is generally desirable that garden apartments be freely mingled among private residences under all circumstances, may be arguable. In view, however, of Tarrytown's changing scene and the other substantial reasons for the board's decision, we cannot say that its action was arbitrary or illegal. While hardships may be imposed on this or that owner, "cardinal is the principle that what is best for the body politic in the long run must prevail over the interests of particular individuals." *Shepard v. Village of Skaneateles* (N.Y.), 89 N.E.2d 619, 620.

The judgment of the Appellate Division should be affirmed, with costs.

NOTES AND QUESTIONS

1. *Why use a floating zone?* The *Tarrytown* case is a classic, and deserves careful study. What advantage was there, from the municipality's viewpoint, in using the "floating zone" amendment technique to introduce garden apartments into the village instead of simply amending the General Zoning Ordinance "so as to permit property in Residence A and Residence B zones — or, for that matter, in the other districts throughout the village — to be used for garden apartments, provided that they were built on ten-acre plots and that the other carefully planned conditions and restrictions were met"? The court may have supplied a partial answer when it said: "The mere

circumstance that an owner possesses a ten-acre plot and submits plans conforming to the physical requirements prescribed by the 1947 amendment will not entitle him, *ipso facto*, to a Residence B-B classification. It will still be for the [planning] board to decide, in the exercise of a reasonable discretion, that the *grant* of such a classification accords with the comprehensive zoning plan and benefits the village as a whole." But what standards are to guide the "exercise of a reasonable discretion"? Is it enough to say, as the New York court did, that "the board may not arbitrarily or unreasonably *deny* applications of other owners for permission to construct garden apartments on their properties"?

2. *Pros and cons.* One commentator has summarized the advantages of floating zones:

> The floating zone. . . can be tailored to site specific land uses, as well as performance and design objectives. It forms the host for a variety of flexible zoning districts. Moreover, it can be applied more quickly and easier than Euclidean zoning and therefore responds better to market forces and provides for more streamlined regulation. For these very reasons, however, the floating zone is viewed with suspicion by community groups and political pressure often discourages its use. [Tierney, *Bold Promises by Basic Steps: Maryland's Growth Policy in the Year 2020,* 23 U. Balt. L. Rev. 461 (1994).]

Professor Arnold has another view in his *Planning Milagros* article, *supra.* He points out that "[f]loating zones pose an uncertain threat to local residents and landowners, who do not know whether a neighboring property will be chosen for a floating zone use. . . . Furthermore, floating zones appear to be used most often for either industrial uses or high-density residential uses." *Id.* at 120. Note that the ordinance in *Tarrytown* did not resolve this problem because there were no controls on the location of multi-family developments. Land use attorney Brian Blaesser suggests that the comprehensive plan should contain policies to guide decisions on floating zones. Discretionary Zoning § 7.08[2]. Plans could then adopt policies on location.

3. *Other states.* Courts elsewhere have accepted the reasoning of the *Tarrytown* case and have approved floating zones. *Sheridan v. Planning Bd.,* 266 A.2d 396 (Conn. 1969); *Bellemeade Co. v. Priddle,* 503 S.W.2d 734 (Ky. 1974); *Huff v. Board of Zoning Appeals,* 133 A.2d 83 (Md. 1957) (light manufacturing zone).

A Missouri court upheld the floating zone in a sweeping decision in which land was rezoned from M-3 planned industrial to C-8 planned commercial. *Treme v. St. Louis County,* 609 S.W.2d 706 (Mo. App. 1980). The court said in part:

> We find the reasoning of the cases which have upheld the "floating zone" to be persuasive. . . . There has been no delegation of legislative authority to rezone here. Rezoning to C-8 can be accomplished only by legislative act. . . .
>
> We further find no objection to the fact that the ordinance does not spell out in detail the standards upon which a determination to rezone to C-8 is to be made. The section does provide for general standards

which are to be considered by the legislative body. Rezoning cannot, by its very nature, be based upon precise and inflexible standards, for each plot of ground is different and the environment in which it lies is different. [*Id.* at 712.]

Is this case consistent with *Tarrytown?*

4. *Comparison with the special exception.* Does the floating zone have an advantage as a means for "flexible" zoning? Surely the special exception technique does not give any greater advance notice to landowners of the possible intrusion of a new use in an area previously restricted against such use. Nor is the expertise of the zoning board of adjustment, which normally administers the special exception procedure, likely to be greater than the combined expertise of the planning board and the local governing body, which usually administer the floating zone procedure. And it is hard to see how the standards generally held sufficient to guide the exercise of administrative discretion in special exception cases are really more definite than the statutory standards which govern the amending process. Moreover, the floating zone procedure results in a change of the zoning map to reflect the change in classification, while the special exception procedure does not. Does the landowner acquire any greater "entitlement" to have the proposed use approved under one approach or the other?

5. *Hybrids.* In *Carron v. Board of County Comm'rs,* 976 P.2d 359 (Colo. App. 1998), the ordinance created Foothills and Valley zoning districts. Initially, the boundaries of these districts were identical, and all land was presumed to be in the Valley district until a landowner applied to have his land moved to the Foothill district, which allowed more intensive development. A zoning amendment was not required. The court held the procedure was similar to that adopted for special uses and did not violate the statutory districting requirement. What were the benefits of this procedure? Note that the floating zone concept is the basis for other flexible zoning techniques, such as the planned unit development, discussed in Chapter 6.

2. WITHOUT PRE-SET STANDARDS: CONTRACT AND CONDITIONAL ZONING

COLLARD v. INCORPORATED VILLAGE OF FLOWER HILL

52 N.Y.2d 594, 421 N.E.2d 818, 439 N.Y.S.2d 326 (1981)

JONES, JUDGE:

Where a local municipality conditions an amendment of its zoning ordinance on the execution of a declaration of covenants providing, in part, that no construction may occur on the property so rezoned without the consent of the municipality, absent a provision that such consent may not be unreasonably withheld the municipality may not be compelled to issue such consent or give an acceptable reason for failing to do so.

Appellants now own improved property in the Village of Flower Hill. In 1976, the then owners of the subject premises and appellants' predecessors in title, applied to the village board of trustees to rezone the property from a General Municipal and Public Purposes District to a Business District.[1] On October 4 of that year the village board granted the rezoning application by the following resolution:

"Resolved that the application of Ray R. Beck Company for a change of Zone of premises known and designated as Section 6, Block 73, Lots 9, 12 and 13 on the land and tax map of Nassau County from General Municipal and Public Purposes District be and the same hereby is granted upon the following conditions:

"(a) The Subject Premises and any buildings, structures and improvements situated or to be situated thereon, will be erected, altered, renovated, remodeled, used, occupied and maintained for the following purposes and no other:

"(i) Offices for the practice of the professions of medicine, dentistry, law, engineering, architecture or accountancy;

"(ii) Executive offices to be used solely for the management of business concerns and associations and excluding therefrom, but without limitation, retail or wholesale sales offices or agencies, brokerage offices of all types and kinds, collection or employment agencies or offices, computer programming centers or offices, counseling centers or offices and training offices or business or trade schools.

"(b) No more than four separate tenancies or occupancies are to be permitted on the subject premises or in any building, structure or improvement situated therein at any one time.

"(c) No building or structure or any portion thereof situated or to be situated on the Subject Premises is to be occupied by more than one person (excluding visitors, clients or guests of any tenant or occupant of such building or structure) for each 190 square feet of the gross floor area of such building or structure.

"(d) No building or structure situated on the Subject Premises on the date of this Declaration of Covenants will be altered, extended, rebuilt, renovated or enlarged without the prior consent of the Board of Trustees of the Village.

"(e) There will be maintained on the Subject Premises at all times, no less than twenty-six paved off-street, onsite parking spaces for automobiles and other vehicles, each such parking space to be at least 9' X 20' in dimensions and will be served by aisles and means of ingress

---

[1] Prior to 1964 the subject premises, then vacant, had been zoned for single-family dwellings with a minimum lot size of 7,500 square feet. In that year the then owners applied to the village board to rezone a portion of the property and place it in the General Municipal and Public Purposes District so that a private sanitarium might be constructed. Concurrently with that application a declaration of covenants restricting the use of the property to a sanitarium was recorded in the county clerk's office. The village board then granted the rezoning application, but limited the property's use to the purposes set forth in the declaration of covenants. The 1976 rezoning application, which as conditionally granted is the subject of this suit, was made because the private sanitarium had fallen into disuse and it was asserted that without rezoning the property could neither be sold nor leased.

and egress of sufficient width to permit the free movement and parking of automobiles and other vehicles.

"(f) Trees and shrubs installed on the Subject Premises pursuant to a landscape plan heretofore filed with the Village in or about 1964, will be maintained in compliance with said landscape plan."

Subsequently, appellants' predecessors in title entered into the contemplated declaration of covenants which was recorded in the office of the Clerk of Nassau County on November 29, 1976. Consistent with paragraph (d) of the board's resolution, that declaration provided that "[n]o building or structure situated on the Subject Premises on the date of this Declaration of Covenants will be altered, extended, rebuilt, renovated or enlarged without the prior consent of the Board of Trustees of the Village."

Appellants, after acquiring title, made application in late 1978 to the village board for approval to enlarge and extend the existing structure on the premises. Without any reason being given that application was denied. Appellants then commenced this action to have the board's determination declared arbitrary, capricious, unreasonable, and unconstitutional and sought by way of ultimate relief an order directing the board to issue the necessary building permits.

Asserting that the board's denial of the application was beyond review as to reasonableness, respondent moved to dismiss the complaint for failure to state a cause of action. Special Term denied the motion, equating appellants' allegation that the board's action was arbitrary and capricious with an allegation that such action was lacking in good faith and fair dealing — an allegation which it found raised triable issues of fact. The Appellate Division reversed and dismissed the complaint, holding that the allegation of arbitrary and capricious action by the board was not the equivalent of an allegation that the board breached an implied covenant of fair dealing and good faith. We now affirm.

At the outset this case involves the question of the permissibility of municipal rezoning conditioned on the execution of a private declaration of covenants restricting the use to which the parcel sought to be rezoned may be put. Prior to our decision in *Church v. Town of Islip,* (N.Y.), 168 N.E.2d 680 in which we upheld rezoning of property subject to reasonable conditions, conditional rezoning had been almost uniformly condemned by courts of all jurisdictions — a position to which a majority of States appear to continue to adhere. Since *Church,* however, the practice of conditional zoning has become increasingly widespread in this State, as well as having gained popularity in other jurisdictions.

Because much criticism has been mounted against the practice, both by commentators and the courts of some of our sister States,[3] further exposition is in order.

---

[3] See, e. g., Comment, The Use and Abuse of Contract Zoning, 12 UCLA L. Rev. 897. For judicial criticism, see, e. g., Baylis v. City of Baltimore, (Md.), 148 A.2d 429; Hartnett v. Austin, 93 So. 2d 86 (Fla.); Houston Petroleum Co. v. Automotive Prods. Credit Ass'n, (N.J.), 87 A.2d 319. [Several citations are omitted. — Eds.]

Probably the principal objection to conditional rezoning is that it constitutes illegal spot zoning, thus violating the legislative mandate requiring that there be a comprehensive plan for, and that all conditions be uniform within, a given zoning district. When courts have considered the issue, the assumptions have been made that conditional zoning benefits particular landowners rather than the community as a whole and that it undermines the foundation upon which comprehensive zoning depends by destroying uniformity within use districts. Such unexamined assumptions are questionable. First, it is a downward change to a less restrictive zoning classification that benefits the property rezoned and not the opposite imposition of greater restrictions on land use. Indeed, imposing limiting conditions, while benefiting surrounding properties, normally adversely affects the premises on which the conditions are imposed. Second, zoning is not invalid per se merely because only a single parcel is involved or benefited; the real test for spot zoning is whether the change is other than part of a well-considered and comprehensive plan calculated to serve the general welfare of the community (*Rodgers v. Village of Tarrytown*). Such a determination, in turn, depends on the reasonableness of the rezoning in relation to neighboring uses — an inquiry required regardless of whether the change in zone is conditional in form. Third, if it is initially proper to change a zoning classification without the imposition of restrictive conditions notwithstanding that such change may depart from uniformity, then no reason exists why accomplishing that change subject to condition should automatically be classified as impermissible spot zoning.

Both conditional and unconditional rezoning involve essentially the same legislative act — an amendment of the zoning ordinance. The standards for judging the validity of conditional rezoning are no different from the standards used to judge whether unconditional rezoning is illegal. If modification to a less restrictive zoning classification is warranted, then a fortiori conditions imposed by a local legislature to minimize conflicts among districts should not in and of themselves violate any prohibition against spot zoning.

Another fault commonly voiced in disapproval of conditional zoning is that it constitutes an illegal bargaining away of a local government's police power. Because no municipal government has the power to make contracts that control or limit it in the exercise of its legislative powers and duties, restrictive agreements made by a municipality in conjunction with a rezoning are sometimes said to violate public policy. While permitting citizens to be governed by the best bargain they can strike with a local legislature would not be consonant with notions of good government, absent proof of a contract purporting to bind the local legislature in advance to exercise its zoning authority in a bargained-for manner, a rule which would have the effect of forbidding a municipality from trying to protect landowners in the vicinity of a zoning change by imposing protective conditions based on the assertion that that body is bargaining away its discretion, would not be in the best interests of the public. The imposition of conditions on property sought to be rezoned may not be classified as a prospective commitment on the part of the municipality to zone as requested if the conditions are met; nor would the municipality necessarily be precluded on this account from later reversing or altering its decision.

Yet another criticism leveled at conditional zoning is that the State enabling legislation does not confer on local authorities authorization to enact conditional zoning amendments. On this view any such ordinance would be *ultra vires*. While it is accurate to say there exists no explicit authorization that a legislative body may attach conditions to zoning amendments, neither is there any language which expressly forbids a local legislature to do so. Statutory silence is not necessarily a denial of the authority to engage in such a practice. Where in the face of nonaddress in the enabling legislation there exists independent justification for the practice as an appropriate exercise of municipal power, that power will be implied. Conditional rezoning is a means of achieving some degree of flexibility in land use control by minimizing the potentially deleterious effect of a zoning change on neighboring properties; reasonably conceived conditions harmonize the landowner's need for rezoning with the public interest and certainly fall within the spirit of the enabling legislation.

One final concern of those reluctant to uphold the practice is that resort to conditional rezoning carries with it no inherent restrictions apart from the restrictive agreement itself. This fear, however, is justifiable only if conditional rezoning is considered a contractual relationship between municipality and private party, outside the scope of the zoning power — a view to which we do not subscribe. When conditions are incorporated in an amending ordinance, the result is as much a "zoning regulation" as an ordinance, adopted without conditions. Just as the scope of all zoning regulation is limited by the police power, and thus local legislative bodies must act reasonably and in the best interests of public safety, welfare and convenience, the scope of permissible conditions must of necessity be similarly limited. If, upon proper proof, the conditions imposed are found unreasonable, the rezoning amendment as well as the required conditions would have to be nullified, with the affected property reverting to the preamendment zoning classification.

Against this backdrop we proceed to consideration of the contentions advanced by appellants in the appeal now before us. It is first useful to delineate arguments which they do not advance. Thus, they do not challenge the conditional zoning change made in 1976 at the behest of their predecessors in title; no contention is made that the village board was not authorized to adopt the resolution of October 4, 1976, conditioned as it was on the execution and recording of the declaration of covenants, or that the provisions of that declaration were in 1976 arbitrary, capricious, unreasonable or unconstitutional. [4] The reason may be what is apparent, namely, that any successful challenge to the adoption of the 1976 resolution would cause appellants' premises to revert to their pre-1976 zoning classification — a consequence clearly unwanted by them.

The focus of appellants' assault is the provision of the declaration of covenants that no structure may be extended or enlarged "without the prior consent of the Board of Trustees of the Village." Appellants would have us

---

[4] Inasmuch as no contention is made that the adoption of the 1976 resolution by the village board constituted impermissible spot zoning or that the action of the board at that time was otherwise unreasonable or constituted an impermissible exercise of its zoning powers, we do not reach or consider such issues.

import the added substantive prescription — "which consent may not be unreasonably withheld." Their argument proceeds along two paths: first, that as a matter of construction the added prescription should be read into the provision; second, that because of limitations associated with the exercise of municipal zoning power the village board would have been required to include such a prescription.

Appellants' construction argument must fail. The terminology employed in the declaration is explicit. The concept that appellants would invoke is not obscure and language to give it effect was readily available had it been the intention of the parties to include this added stipulation. Appellants point to no canon of construction in the law of real property or of contracts which would call for judicial insertion of the missing clause. Where language has been chosen containing no inherent ambiguity or uncertainty, courts are properly hesitant, under the guise of judicial construction, to imply additional requirements to relieve a party from asserted disadvantage flowing from the terms actually used.

The second path either leads nowhere or else goes too far. If it is appellants' assertion that the village board was legally required to insist on inclusion of the desired prescription, there is no authority in the court to reform the zoning enactment of 1976 retroactively to impose the omitted clause. Whether the village board at that time would have enacted a different resolution in the form now desired by appellants is open only to speculation; the certainty is that they did not then take such legislative action. On the other hand, acceptance of appellants' proposition would produce as the other possible consequence the conclusion that the 1976 enactment was illegal, throwing appellants unhappily back to the pre-1976 zoning of their premises, a destination which they assuredly wish to sidestep.

Finally, we agree with the Appellate Division that the allegation of the complaint that the village board in denying appellants' application acted in an arbitrary and capricious manner is not an allegation that the board acted in bad faith or its equivalent.

For the reasons stated the Board of Trustees of the Incorporated Village of Flower Hill may not now be compelled to issue its consent to the proposed enlargement and extension of the existing structure on the premises or in the alternative give an acceptable reason for failing to do so. Accordingly, the order of the Appellate Division should be affirmed, with costs.

NOTES AND QUESTIONS

1. *Contract zoning.* The principal case discusses the major objections to "contract" zoning. Did the court actually decide that the rezoning in the case was valid? See footnote 4 of the opinion. The court seems to hold that a contract zoning is tested by the same rules applicable to a zoning amendment without a contract. This is a minority view. Do you agree with it? For a recent case holding contract zoning invalid see *Hale v. Osborn Coal Enters.*, 729 So. 2d 853 (Ala. Civ. App. 1997). *Dacy v. Village of Ruidoso*, 845 P.2d 793 (N.M. 1992), is another extensive discussion of the rules governing contract zoning. Note that conditions applied to the property in the form of private covenants

will bind future owners only if they touch and concern the land. See *City of New York v. Delafield 246 Corp.,* 662 N.Y.S.2d 286 (App. Div. 1997).

2. *Good or bad?* The court in the principal case does not tell us when contract zoning is invalid. One distinction often made is that contract zoning is invalid while "conditional" zoning is valid. Another distinction is that "bilateral" zoning is invalid while "unilateral" zoning is valid. Consider the usefulness of these distinctions in view of the following cases, which raise typical contract zoning problems.

(a) In *Carlino v. Whitpain Investors,* 453 A.2d 1385 (Pa. 1982), a developer brought an action to restrain a municipality from conditioning a rezoning on the elimination of an access road in a buffer area. The court held that this was improper "contractually conditioned zoning" because the municipal police power cannot be subjected to agreements that condition rezoning. The court also agreed with *Houston Petroleum Co.,* cited in footnote 3 of the principal opinion, that contracts "have no place in a zoning plan." Compare *State ex rel. Zupancic v. Schimenz,* 174 N.W.2d 533 (Wis. 1970), holding valid an agreement executed between a landowner-developer and his neighbors. The court held that rezoning is not invalid contract zoning when the rezoning is motivated by land use agreements made by others.

(b) In *Bartsch v. Planning & Zoning Comm'n,* 506 A.2d 1093 (Conn. App. 1986), the commission approved a zone change conditioned on the filing of a restrictive covenant limiting the use of the premises to a medical office building and requiring the creation of a green belt buffer area. The court held that "the commission has grossly violated the statutory uniformity requirement." *Id.* at 1095. Accord, *Dacy v. Village of Ruidoso,* 845 P.2d 793 (N.M. 1992).

(c) In *Cross v. Hall County,* 235 S.E.2d 379 (Ga. 1977), a rezoning resolution stated that it was passed provided the landowner resurfaced a road. The court held that conditional zoning was valid when the conditions are imposed "for the protection or benefit of neighbors to ameliorate the effects of the zoning change." When the conditional zoning is "otherwise valid," these conditions cannot be attacked by these neighbors.

(d) In *Giger v. City of Omaha,* 442 N.W.2d 182 (Neb. 1989), the court upheld a rezoning for a mixed-use development that included four agreements executed by the city and the developer that incorporated a development plan. The court found the distinction between contract and conditional zoning irrelevant and held that the critical question was whether the conditions on the rezoning advanced the public health, safety and welfare. The city was entitled to make agreements with developers concerning their plans to avoid difficult enforcement problems. The court did not find a bargaining away of the police power because the agreement required city approval of variances from the plan and because the plan was more stringent than the zoning ordinance. See also *Sylvania Elec. Prods., Inc. v. City of Newton,* 183 N.E.2d 118 (Mass. 1962).

Are any of these cases distinguishable, or do some of them conflict? What rule can you derive from these decisions?

3. *Bargaining in the zoning process.* Like development agreements, "contract" zoning is another example of bargaining in the zoning process. Unlike development agreements, however, a zoning "contract" is attached to a zoning change. Contract zoning is attractive because it provides an opportunity to tailor the requirements of a zoning ordinance more specifically to the property in question, as in *Collard.* Compare the floating zone and a conditioned special use, which permit a similar "tailoring" in the formal decision making process, without an agreement. Which is preferable?

If the justification for imposing collective decisionmaking on the land use process is that an "efficient" result cannot always be achieved by purely private bargaining, what (if anything) is wrong with a hybrid scheme in which the government, as representative of the collective interest, explicitly bargains with the affected private party or parties? Can you decipher this tortured sentence from the principal case, in which the court appears to be considering this question?

> While permitting citizens to be governed by the best bargain they can strike with a local legislature would not be consonant with notions of good government, absent proof of a contract purporting to bind the local legislature in advance to exercise its zoning authority in a bargained-for manner, a rule which would have the effect of forbidding a municipality from trying to protect landowners in the vicinity of a zoning change by imposing protective conditions based on the assertion that that body is bargaining away its discretion, would not be in the best interests of the public.

Are those courts which prohibit or restrict contract zoning implicitly expressing misgivings about the underlying theory of land use controls?

4. *Concomitant Agreement Zoning.* Professor Bruce M. Kramer, noting that "[t]he contract-conditional zoning dichotomy is little more than a semantic game," has suggested an alternative analysis. *Contract Zoning — Old Myths and New Realities,* 34 Land Use L. & Zoning Dig., No. 8, at 4 (1982). He suggests the approach adopted by the Washington Supreme Court, which calls this device concomitant agreement zoning, or CAZ. *State ex rel. Myhre v. City of Spokane,* 422 P.2d 790 (Wash. 1969):

> [T]his neutral term would allow courts to analyze the underlying validity of each CAZ rather than merely concluding that contract zoning is invalid and conditional zoning is valid. This more *ad hoc* approach would allow the courts to view what most CAZs attempt to achieve — namely, the minimization of negative externalities caused by certain types of new developments that are otherwise beneficial to the community and its neighborhood. [*Id.* at 5.]

Do you agree with this suggestion? Does it explain the cases discussed in Note 2 *supra?* Would any of these cases come out differently under Professor Kramer's test? Professor Kramer reviews all of the contract zoning cases. He notes states in which contract zoning is either per se valid or invalid, states that are "schizophrenic," and states in which there are "muddy waters."

5. *Effect of invalidity.* Suppose there is no challenge by third parties to a conditional rezoning and that the landowner later refuses to observe the land use restrictions contained in a recorded covenant because they violate the statutory mandate that all zoning regulations "shall be uniform for each class or kind of buildings throughout each district." If the court should accept this argument, would it be likely simply to hold that the added restrictions were invalid, or that the entire rezoning transaction was void so that the land would revert to its prior zoning classification? See Comment, *Contract and Conditional Zoning: A Tool for Zoning Flexibility,* 23 Hastings L.J. 825, 836 (1972), observing that, where a municipality seeks to enforce the added restrictions and the landowner resists, the courts generally either sustain the added restrictions or hold them invalid without deciding the validity of the rezoning amendment itself, although a court clearly has the discretion to invalidate both the amendment and the added restrictions. How does the principal case handle this issue?

In *Cross,* Note 2 *supra,* the court said: "The owner of the rezoned land may be estopped from objecting to the conditions by having proposed or consented to them. And the conditions may be upheld against the unestopped landowner as being sustainable under the police power." 235 S.E.2d at 383 n.2. For a case holding a developer estopped to challenge a rezoning as illegal contract zoning see *City of Cedar Rapids v. McConnell-Stevely-Anderson Architects & Planners,* 423 N.W.2d 17 (Iowa 1988) (developer requested and city granted zoning change and special use permit).

6. *Statutory authority.* Some statutes confer the authority to do conditional zoning. See Ariz. Rev. Stat. Ann. § 11-832 (zoning conditioned on development schedule and specific uses; board may revoke zoning if property not developed at end of scheduled period); R.I. Gen. Laws § 45-24-53(H) (similar). This type of statute at least deals with the uniformity problem. *Sweetman v. Town of Cumberland,* 364 A.2d 1277 (R.I. 1976), held that the statute authorized the local governing body to limit the application of the conditions imposed to those parcels which are rezoned, and that identical conditions need not be imposed on land in the same use classification but not covered by the rezoning amendment.

A Maryland statute confers a more limited power:

> On the zoning or rezoning of any land, a local legislative body may retain or reserve the power to approve or disapprove the design of buildings, construction, landscaping, or other improvements, alterations, and changes made or to be made on the land being zoned or rezoned to assure conformity with the intent and purpose of this article and of the local jurisdiction's zoning ordinance. [Md. Code Ann. Art. 66B, § 4.01.]

Board of County Comm'rs v. H. Manny Holtz, Inc., 501 A.2d 489 (Md. App. 1985), held that this statute did not authorize conditional use zoning. Its purpose was to "assure design conformity within the subject area" and authorized only the imposition of "additional structural or architectural limitations . . . necessary to achieve such conformity." *Id.* at 492.

7. *Reverters.* One problem with conditional zoning is that the developer may not proceed as planned. Can a statute or the agreement provide that the zoning will revert if development does not begin by a stated time? In *Scrutton v. County of Sacramento,* 79 Cal. Rptr. 872 (Cal. App. 1969), the court invalidated an automatic reversion clause that provided that the land would revert to its original classification if the landowner breached any of the covenants in the conditional zoning agreement. The court held that the reversion would be a second rezoning and would violate statutory requirements that rezoning be accomplished through notice, hearing and planning commission inquiry. The automatic reversion would also violate substantive limitations on the zoning power. The court characterized the automatic reversion as a "forfeiture rather than a legislative decision on land use." Accord *Spiker v. City of Lakewood,* 603 P.2d 130 (Colo. 1979).

Compare *Colwell v. Howard County,* 354 A.2d 210 (Md. App. 1976). The court upheld a "use it or lose it" clause under which the property would revert to its original classification unless the property owner applied for a site plan within two years of the rezoning, applied for a building permit within one year of the approval of the site plan, and commenced substantial construction within three years of the permit's issuance. The court noted that the issuance of a building permit in Maryland does not create a vested right until substantial construction is begun. For this reason, "it does no violence to his constitutional rights to require through a generally applied, properly enacted law, that a zoning change be utilized within a reasonable time period." *Id.* at 216. Are the cases distinguishable? Are they correct?

8. *Sources.* For discussion of contract zoning, reverters and other flexible zoning devices, see 2 Ziegler, Rathkopf's Law of Zoning and Planning ch. 29A; Wegner, *Moving Toward the Bargaining Table: Contract Zoning, Development Agreements, and the Theoretical Foundations of Government Land Use Deals,* 65 N.C. L. Rev. 957 (1987); Note, *Concomitant Agreement Zoning: An Economic Analysis,* 1985 U. Ill. L. Rev. 89.

F. SITE PLAN REVIEW

Site plan review is another technique available to land use agencies to review the details of a land development project. Site plan review may give the municipality its only opportunity to review the design specifics of a development that is a permitted use and can be built "as of right." Of course, it may also be applied to developments that require a zoning change, or a separate approval, such as a conditional use permit or a subdivision approval. Site plan review is an almost invariable feature in planned unit development (PUD) zoning provisions. See Ch. 6.

The purposes of site plan review are indicated by the following New York statute, which authorizes site plan review:

> Site plans shall show the arrangement, layout and design of the proposed use of the land on said plan. The ordinance or local law shall specify the land uses that require site plan approval and the elements to be included on plans submitted for approval. The required site plan elements which are included in the zoning ordinance or local law may include, where appropriate, those related to parking, means of access, screening, signs, landscaping, architectural features, location and dimensions of buildings, adjacent land uses and physical features meant to protect adjacent land uses as well as any additional elements

specified by the town board in such zoning ordinance or local law. [New York Town Law § 274-a(2)(a).]

See also N.J. Stat. Ann. § 40:55D-41 (includes elements listed in New York law and adds preservation of existing natural resources on site and conservation of energy and use of renewable energy resources). Only a few states authorize site plan review, but in the absence of statute most courts find this authority implied in the general terms of land use legislation. See *Y.D. Dugout, Inc. v. Board of Appeals,* 255 N.E.2d 732 (Mass. 1970); *Town of Grand Chute v. U.S. Paper Converters, Inc.,* 600 N.W.2d 33 (Wis. App. 1999).

Site plan review serves many of the same purposes as conditions attached to a rezoning to the extent that it controls the details of a development, except that the statute or ordinance limits the contents of the site plan. In addition, a site plan does not contain enforceable textual limitations on the use of the property. In the case that follows, the site plan questions arise in the absence of specific statutory authority, but the case is otherwise typical of the concerns that local boards have.

CHARISMA HOLDING CORP. v. ZONING BOARD OF APPEALS OF THE TOWN OF LEWISBORO

266 App. Div. 2d 540, 699 N.Y.S.2d 89 (1999)

DECISION & ORDER

The petitioner Charisma Holding Corp. (hereinafter Charisma) is the owner of commercially-zoned real property in the respondent Town of Lewisboro. The property is the site of an automobile dealership and is abutted to the north and east by residentially-zoned property. In January 1988 Charisma petitioned the respondent Zoning Board of Appeals of the Town of Lewisboro (hereinafter ZBA) for various relief, including an area variance to build a 3,000 square-foot six-bay garage. One bay was to be used for washing vehicles, another for spray-painting vehicles, and the remaining four for repairs and service. Although such a garage is a permitted use of the property under the relevant zoning regulations, an area variance was needed because it would bring the developed area of the property to 69% of the total area, and the relevant regulations permit development of no more than 60%. The petitioner proposed to locate the garage on the northern end of its property. During the review process, which included three public meetings and two visits to the property, residential neighbors to the north and east voiced various objections to the location of the proposed garage. One property owner in particular noted that the proposed location would place it within 100 feet of her kitchen window and would result, inter alia, in exhaust and paint fumes, and additional noise and traffic.

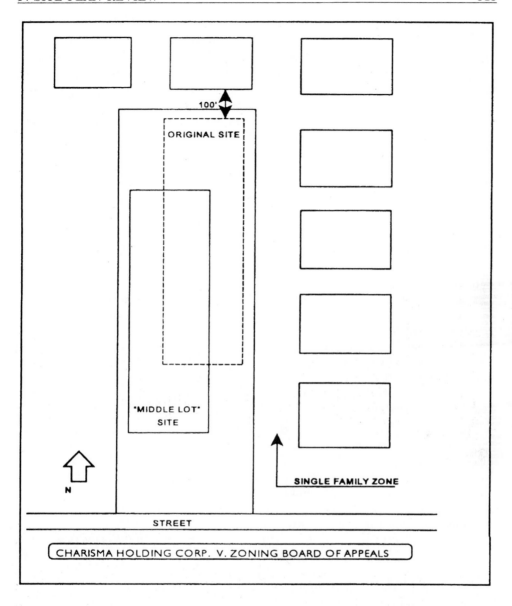

CHARISMA HOLDING CORP. V. ZONING BOARD OF APPEALS

Based on such concerns, the ZBA considered two alternative sites for the garage. After various inquiries, the ZBA noted a preference for what they designated as site No. 3 (hereinafter the middle lot), which they determined would create significantly less impact on the surrounding residential properties. The petitioner, asserting various additional costs and concerns in building the garage on that site, pressed its preference for the site originally proposed. By determination dated April 27, 1998, the ZBA denied the petitioner's request for an area variance for the site as proposed. The ZBA found that a grant of the area variance as requested would result in a substantial undesirable change in the character of the residential neighborhood to the north, that there would be a substantial detriment to the nearby properties, and that there was an alternative site. The ZBA found that the benefit to the petitioner if the area variance was granted as requested was outweighed by the detriment to the health, safety, and welfare of the neighborhood community (see, Town Law § 267-b). However, the ZBA granted an area variance to the petitioner based on locating the garage on the middle lot, finding no similar concerns. In the judgment appealed from, the Supreme Court directed the ZBA to grant the requested area variance as proposed by the petitioner. The court held that because the garage was a permitted use of the property and otherwise conformed with all relevant zoning restrictions, the sole issue properly before the ZBA was the development of 69%, as opposed to 60%, of the total lot area. Thus, the court held, the ZBA's denial of the variance as requested was based on a matter not relevant to its considerations, that is, the proposed use of the additional area. Accordingly, the court determined that because the ZBA implicitly found that the use of the additional area should be permitted, the variance should have been granted as requested. We reverse.

Judicial review of the denial of the area variance is limited to whether the determination was illegal, arbitrary, or an abuse of discretion. If the determination is supported by substantial evidence and has a rational basis, it will not be disturbed. Here, review of the record reveals that the ZBA properly considered and weighed the relevant statutory criteria, and that its determination was supported by substantial evidence and had a rational basis (see, Town Law § 267-b). We disagree with the Supreme Court that the relevant statutory balancing test can be properly applied without consideration of the proposed use. Accordingly, the respondents' denial of the area variance as requested is confirmed.

The petitioner, characterizing the determination of the ZBA as a grant of the requested area variance with a condition that the garage be built on an alternative site, argues that the ZBA usurped the role of the Planning Board by considering the location of the garage. The petitioner argues that the authority to consider the placement of buildings is vested solely with the Planning Board pursuant to its authority to approve a site plan, which includes consideration of "parking, means of access, screening, signs, landscaping, architectural features, *location and dimensions of buildings,* adjacent land uses and physical features meant to protect adjacent land uses" (see Town Law § 274-a[2] [emphasis supplied]). However, even accepting the petitioner's characterization of the ZBA's determination as correct, the determination may nonetheless be upheld. In granting use and area variances, the ZBA is expressly authorized to impose "such reasonable conditions and restrictions as are directly related to and incidental to the proposed use of the property" that are "consistent with the spirit and intent of the zoning ordinance or local law" and that shall minimize "any adverse impact such variance may have on the neighborhood or community" (Town Law § 267-b[4]). The petitioner has not cited, and research does not reveal, any case law which holds that there may be no overlap between matters that might be properly considered by a Planning Board on review of a site plan and conditions that might be properly imposed by a zoning board in granting an area variance. Rather, the conclusion to be drawn from the case law is to the contrary. The Court of Appeals has held that conditions imposed by a zoning board in granting a variance or special permit "might properly relate 'to fences, safety devices, landscaping, screening and access roads relating to period of use, screening, outdoor lighting and noises, and enclosure of buildings and relating to emission of odors, dust, smoke, refuse matter, vibration noise and other factors incidental to comfort, peace, enjoyment, health or safety of the surrounding area'" (*Matter of St. Onge v Donovan*, 522 N.E.2d 1019.) Further, the Court of Appeals has held that the rezoning of property for commercial uses had been properly conditioned on the requirement that the owners thereof "execute and record restrictive covenants relating to the maximum area to be occupied by buildings, the erection of a fence, and the planting of shrubbery" (*Matter of St. Onge v Donovan, supra*, citing *Church v Town of Islip*.) Such conditions both implicitly and expressly overlap with considerations relevant to review of a site plan (see, Town Law § 274-a[2]. [The court cited appellate division cases holding a variance for a fence was properly granted on conditions that a portion of the fence be located five feet from the property line and that certain specified green plantings be maintained; that a use variance was properly granted on condition that there be no change to the exterior design or appearance of the building; and that variances were properly granted on condition, inter alia, that petitioner remove a shed on the property and return the area to green space.] Accordingly, here, the ZBA did not exceed its authority in considering the location of the petitioner's proposed garage in rendering a determination on the requested area variance.

NOTES AND QUESTIONS

1. *Authority to review.* Only a few states authorize site plan review, but in the absence of statute most courts imply this authority from the general terms of land use legislation. *Y.D. Dugout, Inc. v. Board of Appeals*, 255 N.E.2d 732 (Mass. 1970); *Town of Grand Chute v. U.S. Paper Converters, Inc.*, 600 N.W.2d 33 (Wis. App. 1999). The principal case is different only in that New York authorizes site plan review but assigns it to a different body. Suppose the court had upheld the denial of the variance as initially proposed but then held that site plan issues were beyond the ZBA's jurisdiction. The applicant could have presented the "middle lot" site plan to the planning board, but that proposal also required a variance, which the planning board could not grant. Are the town and the applicant doomed to the failure of a land use proposal that, in the end, was satisfactory to both? The court's actual holding permits an efficient and equitable outcome. Some modern statutes allow boards to exercise each other's jurisdiction under some circumstances so that the application can be considered in a single proceeding. See, e.g., N.J.S.A. § 40:55D-76.

2. *Permitted uses as a site plan issue.* In *Sherman v. City of Colorado Springs Planning Comm.*, 680 P.2d 1302 (Colo. App. 1983), the parties stipulated that a proposed 14-story residential building was in all respects a permitted use in the district under the zoning code. The site plan application was denied because of neighborhood opposition based on height and traffic. The court held that

> Where, as here, the zoning body has determined that the health, safety, and general welfare are best promoted by zoning land for residential high-rise purposes with specified set back, height, and bulk

limitations, that body may not thereafter attempt to reserve to itself
the discretion to decide which of the complying land uses will be permitted. To interpret this development plan ordinance as giving the city
the power to deny a lawful use of property runs contrary to the
requirement of adequate standards. [*Id.* at 1304]

Other courts agree. See *Kosinski v. Lawlor*, 418 A.2d 66 (Conn. 1979) (retail
complex rejection as a "poor use of the site" reversed); *S.E.W. Friel v. Triangle
Oil Co.*, 543 A.2d 863 (Md. App. 1988) (cannot disapprove site plan because
permitted use is not compatible with surrounding area). If this were not the
general rule, would there be any difference between site plan review and the
special permit approach? Why do you suppose municipalities try to use site
plan review to block projects permitted by the zoning ordinance? *Compare City
of Colorado Springs v. Securecare Self Storage, Inc.*, 10 P.3d 1244 (Colo. 2000)
(interpreting zoning ordinance to allow rejection of use in site plan review that
is authorized by the zoning ordinance).

3. *Off-site conditions.* Site plan review is intended as a review of conditions
arising on the site. See *Coscan Washington, Inc. v. Maryland-National Capital
Park & Planning Comm'n*, 590 A.2d 1080 (Md. App. 1991) (building materials). In *Lionel's Appliance Center, Inc. v. Citta*, 383 A.2d 773 (N.J.L. Div. 1978),
the reason given for rejection of an office complex site plan was, as is often
the case, off-site traffic congestion. The court held that off-site traffic problems
were a proper factor for consideration in the approval of variances and special
exceptions, but not in site plan review. A site plan could be denied "only if
the ingress and egress proposed by the plan creates an unsafe and inefficient
vehicular condition." The court did hold that the site plan statute authorized
a contribution from the developer for off-site improvements. Accord *PRB
Enters., Inc. v. South Brunswick Planning Bd.*, 518 A.2d 1099 (N.J. 1987);
Moriarty v. Planning Bd., 506 N.Y.S.2d 184 (App. Div. 1986) (inadequate fire
protection).

Attorney Brian Blaesser argues that site plan review "should not address
off-site conditions except to the extent that on-site conditions affect off-site
conditions." Discretionary Zoning, *supra,* at § 5.03[4]. A number of courts
support this position. *Southland Corp. v. Mayor & City Council*, 541 A.2d 653
(Md. App. 1988) (can deny site plan because of traffic hazards). However, isn't
a consideration of off-site conditions an implicit reconsideration of the status
of a project as a permitted use under the zoning ordinance? Note that the New
York statute, reproduced *supra,* authorizes site plan elements "meant to
protect adjacent land uses." How should this provision be interpreted?

This issue also arises under subdivision control ordinances. See Ch. 6.
Compare *Robbins Auto Parts, Inc. v. City of Lanconia*, 371 A.2d 1167 (N.H.
1977) (followed subdivision control cases to hold that site plan review may
require contribution for facilities needed by subdivision), with *Riegert Apartments Corp. v. Planning Bd.*, 441 N.E.2d 1076 (N.Y. 1982) (contra).

G. THE ROLE OF THE COMPREHENSIVE PLAN IN THE
ZONING PROCESS

Although the Standard Zoning Act and many state acts that follow it provide
that zoning must be "in accordance with a comprehensive plan," most courts

do not give this requirement its literal meaning. The leading case is *Kozesnik v. Montgomery Twp.*, 131 A.2d 1 (N.J. 1957). The court held that this requirement did not require a comprehensive plan in some "physical form" outside the zoning ordinance. The court held that the intent of this requirement was to prevent a capricious exercise of the zoning power. The court noted that

> "plan" connotes an integrated product of a rational process and "comprehensive" requires something beyond a piecemeal approach, both to be revealed by the ordinance considered in relation to the physical facts and the [statutory] purposes. [*Id.* at 7.]

Most courts still take this position. See *Sasich v. City of Omaha,* 347 N.W.2d 93 (Neb. 1984). New Jersey legislation, N.J. Stat. Ann. § 40:55D-62, partially overrules *Kozesnik* by requiring elements of a formal plan and consistency unless this requirement is set aside by a majority vote of the full membership of the local governing body.

The first break with this interpretation came in an Oregon case, *Fasano v. Board of County Comm'rs,* 507 P.2d 23 (Or. 1973), which held that any zoning change must be consistent with the comprehensive plan. *Fasano* is considered in connection with the *Snyder* case, *supra.* Oregon later adopted legislation establishing a state planning program that requires planning by local governments and the consistency of zoning with an adopted and state-approved plan.

A number of states now mandate comprehensive planning by statute and some also require that zoning be consistent with the plan. California is a leading example. It mandates planning and requires zoning ordinances to be consistent with the comprehensive plan. Consistency is defined to mean that

> [t]he various land uses authorized by the [zoning] ordinance are compatible with the objectives, policies, general land uses and programs specified in such a plan. [Cal. Gov't Code § 65860(a) (ii).]

Florida legislation provides a more comprehensive definition. It is reproduced in the *Snyder* case, reproduced *infra.* The *Snyder* decision gave weight to the comprehensive plan by making the presumption of constitutionality of a zoning change depend on the plan.

Why consistency?—Note how the consistency requirement changes the rules under which the zoning ordinance and zoning changes are judicially reviewed. Without a consistency requirement, for example, a rezoning amendment is subject to the ad hoc rules that govern spot zoning. See sec. D2, *supra.* With a consistency requirement, a rezoning will be governed by the policies of the plan. Why this change?

One answer has been provided by the Minnesota Supreme Court:

> The essence of constitutional zoning with no due process or equal protection problems is generally recognized to be demonstrated by the existence of a plan which uniformly, without discrimination and without unreasonable restrictions, promotes the general welfare. [*Amcon Corp. v. City of Eagan,* 348 N.W.2d 66, 74 (Minn. 1984).]

What does the court mean by "due process and equal protection" problems? One answer is that the court is concerned with the "fundamental fairness" in land use decisionmaking which is demanded by these constitutional limitations.

This point is made in Mandelker, *Should State Government Mandate Local Planning? . . . Yes,* 44 Planning, No. 6, at 14 (1978). The article notes two aspects of the fundamental fairness problem. One is the need to prevent arbitrary decisionmaking in the land use process, a concern dominant in the Oregon cases mandating consistency with the plan. The other is the need to resolve the "conflicting societal pressures" that land use programs make on the use of land. The article concludes that

> the courts prefer the advance statement of principle for land use decisions [through plans] to the ad hoc adjustments that commonly take place when these principles are not provided. [*Id.* at 16.]

Planning Professor Lawrence Susskind took the opposing view in this debate. *Should State Government Mandate Local Planning? . . . No, id.,* at 17. Susskind argued that attempts to mandate local planning would fail because difficulties in winning support for planning are not taken into account and because planning is not adequately funded. He also argued that state planning standards cannot take community differences into consideration, that the planning profession cannot agree on what constitutes a good plan, and that it is "almost impossible" to ensure consistency among the elements of the plan and between a plan and subsequent zoning decisions.

NOTES AND QUESTIONS

1. *Who won the planning debate?* Many of the arguments against mandatory planning concentrate on the inadequacies of the plan and the planning process. See J. DiMento, The Consistency Doctrine and the Limits of Planning 48–51 (1980) (author favors mandatory planning). Consult Ch. 1 for a discussion of the strengths and weaknesses of planning. For more detailed arguments supporting mandatory planning and the consistency requirement, see Mandelker, *The Role of the Comprehensive Plan in Land Use Regulation,* 74 Mich. L. Rev. 899 (1976). For discussion of the reasons behind the language used in the Standard Act and a review of statutory consistency requirement see Meck, *The Legislative Requirement that Zoning and Land Use Controls be Consistent with an Independently Adopted Comprehensive Plan,* 3 Wash. U. J.L. & Pol'y 295 (2000).

2. *A middle view.* Some courts, although not adopting the view that consistency with the plan is required, at least give presumptive weight to the plan if one exists. *Udell v. Hass,* 235 N.E.2d 897 (N.Y. 1968), is a leading case. A small suburban village downzoned a property from commercial to residential uses after it became apparent that the owner of the property intended to build commercially. The village had consistently zoned this property commercial. The court invalidated the downzoning and held that local zoning authorities must pay more than "mock obeisance" to the statutory "in accordance with the comprehensive plan" requirement. The plan was not to be defined as "any particular document," and rezonings "should not conflict with

the fundamental land use policies and development plans of the community." The court noted that these policies could be found in the comprehensive plan of the community if one has been adopted. Accord *Palatine Nat'l Bank v. Village of Barrington,* 532 N.E.2d 955 (Ill. App. 1988).

A few courts also have held that the presumption of validity usually accorded zoning is shifted or weakened in the absence of a comprehensive plan. See *Forestview Homeowners Ass'n v. County of Cook,* 309 N.E.2d 763 (Ill. App. 1974) (rezoning for apartments held invalid). However, in *First Nat'l Bank v. Village of Vernon Hills,* 371 N.E.2d 659 (Ill. App. 1977), the court held the relevant issue was whether the municipality had given "care and consideration to the use and development of the land within its boundaries, not whether it had a piece of paper in the form of a comprehensive plan." Where does this leave us?

3. *Takings.* The *Amcon* case, in the excerpt quoted in the text *supra,* did not make reference to the role of the plan as a defense to taking of property objections. For a case relying on a local plan to reject taking objections to a local growth-management program, see the *Ramapo* case, reproduced *infra,* Ch. 7.

How is a court likely to interpret the consistency requirement when there is an apparent conflict between the comprehensive plan and a zoning amendment? The following case considers this question.

HAINES v. CITY OF PHOENIX

151 Ariz. 286, 727 P.2d 339 (1986)

HATHAWAY, CHIEF JUDGE:

Appellant contests the trial court's granting of summary judgment in affirmance of the City of Phoenix's (city) authority to rezone the parcel in controversy. Appellees cross-appeal and challenge the trial court's finding that the city has adopted a general or specific plan of urban development. We agree with the trial court on both counts and affirm.

On January 1, 1974, Arizona's Urban Environment Management Act (act) became effective. The act requires municipalities to adopt long-range, general plans for urban development. A.R.S. § 9-461.05(A). The act also authorizes specific plans. A.R.S. § 9-461.08. The act requires municipal zoning ordinances be consistent with the general plans. § 9-462.01(E). On July 3, 1979, the city adopted two plans — the Phoenix Concept Plan 2000 and the Interim 1985 Plan. It is disputed whether these plans are general or specific plans as defined by the statute.

This action arose from the Phoenix City Council's granting of a "height waiver" for a highrise office project that is proposed to be constructed by appellee Adams Group on 14.48 acres of land on Central Avenue between Glenrosa and Turney avenues in Phoenix. The property was zoned C-2H-R (intermediate commercial highrise) and subject to a 250-foot highrise limitation. The 1985 plan also limits to 250 feet buildings in the area in which this parcel is located.

On July 29, 1983, the Adams Group submitted an application to amend the city zoning ordinance to permit a building on the parcel in excess of the 250-foot height limitation. The rezoning application was heard by the planning commission on November 16, 1983. That body recommended denial by a 3 to 2 vote. Pursuant to § 108-J.1 of the city zoning ordinance the Adams Group requested the city council to hold a public hearing on the application and not to adopt the planning commission's recommendation. Two hearings were held, on December 19, 1983 and February 6, 1984. On February 6, the city council approved a rezoning which allowed the Adams Group to erect a 500-foot building. Appellant then filed this action alleging the city council's action is inconsistent with the general or specific plans and therefore is in violation of A.R.S. § 9.462.01(E). Appellees argue that the city had not adopted either a general or specific plan at the time of the city council action and the only issue before the city council was whether there was compliance with § 412-B.2-F(1) of the Phoenix Zoning Ordinance, permitting height amendments.

It is without dispute that the city council complied with § 412-B.2-F(1). The trial court, on August 17, 1984, granted appellant partial summary judgment finding that the city had adopted a general or specific plan. On November 26, 1984, however, the trial court entered summary judgment finding that the city council's action did not violate A.R.S. § 9-462.01(E), and therefore dismissed appellant's complaint. Appellant appealed and appellees cross-appealed.

Appellant raises one issue on appeal: The trial court erred in finding that the rezoning was in compliance with A.R.S. § 9-462.01(E). Appellees raise two issues on appeal: (1) Phoenix has not adopted a general or specific plan and is not subject to the limitations of § 9-462.01(E) and (2) in any event, the actions of the city council were in compliance with both the Concept Plan 2000 and the 1985 plan.

I. *Has the City Adopted a General or Specific Plan?*

. . . .

A.R.S. § 9-461(1) states a general plan means: ". . . [A] municipal statement of land development policies, which may include maps, charts, graphs and text which set forth objectives, principles and standards for local growth and redevelopment enacted under the provisions of this article or any prior statute." A.R.S. § 9-461(5) states a specific plan means: ". . . [A] detailed element of the general plan enacted under the provisions of this article or a prior statute."

It is clear that both the Concept Plan 2000 and the Interim Plan 1985 meet the definition for a general plan. Additionally, Interim Plan 1985 could be viewed as a specific plan for the implementation of the general plan pronounced in Concept Plan 2000. Concept Plan 2000 establishes the policy of dividing the city into villages, each containing a core, gradient and periphery. Interim Plan 1985 establishes specific criteria for the implementation of that policy in the Encanto Area in which this dispute occurred. Additionally, there is not any evidence that these two plans were not adopted under the provisions of the article pursuant to A.R.S. § 9-461.06. The real debate concerns A.R.S. § 9-461.05, which enunciates the scope of a general plan.

A.R.S. § 9-461.05(C) and (D) require the general plan to contain nine distinct elements. Those elements are:

1. A land use element.

2. Circulation element.

3. Conservation element.

4. Recreation element.

5. Public services and facility element.

6. Public buildings element.

7. Housing element.

8. Conservation rehabilitation and redevelopment element.

9. Safety element.

A review of the two plans establishes that some of the above required elements have not been addressed by either the Concept Plan 2000 or the Interim Plan 1985. . . . [We hold that] the missing elements . . . are irrelevant to the existence of a plan. . . .

While these plans are probably not satisfactory in their completeness, they are clearly plans according to the statutory definition. Appellees' reasoning would permit the city to perpetually avoid urban planning by leaving out any element or any subdivision of an element defined in § 9-461.05. This would produce the untenable result of the slightest omission causing the city to have no plan. . . .

II. Was the Rezoning in Conformity with the Plan?

A. Applicability of A.R.S. § 9-462.01(E).

A.R.S. § 9-462.01(E) states: "All zoning ordinances or regulations adopted under this article shall be consistent with the adopted general or specific plans of the municipality. . . ."

We must consider whether an amendment to a rezoning ordinance, such as we have in the current situation, falls under the mandate of this statute which only specifically states it applies to "zoning ordinances or regulations." While there are no Arizona decisions on point, other jurisdictions have held the requirement of conformity to the general plan is applicable to amendments as well as to the original zoning ordinance. [The decisions cited included *Udell v. Haas,* discussed *supra.*] The above decisions [reason] that the legislature intended to protect landowners in the populace from arbitrary and impulsive use [of] the zoning power and that such a safeguard would be meaningless unless applied to amendments of the ordinance. Other jurisdictions have held, however, that where the amendment itself constitutes a change in the comprehensive plan the limiting statute is not applicable. The current situation is controlled by the first line of cases inasmuch as the record supports no such intention by the city council. Therefore, the present amendment is valid only if it is consistent with the general and specific plans. . . .

B. *Is the amendment consistent with the general and specific plan?*

Normally the level of judicial review of a zoning ordinance or amendment is the rational basis test. This test is utilized because zoning or rezoning is a legislative act not a quasi-judicial act. Under the rational basis test if the court can hypothesize any rational reason why the legislative body made the choice it did, the statute or ordinance is constitutionally valid. This test validates statutes even if the legislative body did not consider the reasons articulated by the court. The reason for the adoption of the rational basis test was to prevent courts from sitting as super-legislatures and thereby prevent infringement upon the separation of powers. Of course, when fundamental constitutional liberties are at stake, courts will use a higher level of scrutiny.

If we were to apply the rational basis review to the current situation, we would presume the rezoning to be valid and would uphold its validity if we could hypothesize any reason why the city council may have believed the rezoning was consistent with the general plan. Some courts have taken this approach to deciding whether a zoning amendment is consistent with a general plan. Appellant argues, however, that the passage of § 9-462.01(E) vitiates the above normal level of review. He argues that if rational basis review is utilized, the legislative mandate requiring consistency between zoning and the general plan is without any force. Appellant argues instead that, due to the statute, there be no presumption of legislative validity and the city council be required to make written findings and articulate reasons for any deviation from the general plan. There is support for this approach.

We, however, reject both of the above approaches. By the enactment of § 9-462.01(E), the legislature has provided a standard by which to review zoning decisions in addition to the usual constitutional standard. That standard is consistency with the general plan. In our review, however, we will not substitute our judgment for that of the duly elected legislative body, the city council. Therefore our review will consist of viewing the record that was before the city council and determining if, from that evidence, the council could have decided that despite the deviation from the letter of the plan there was consistency. The burden of proof will still be on the plaintiff to show inconsistency.

Consistency has been defined as "basic harmony." J. Di Mento, The Consistency Doctrine and the Limits of Planning (1980). Therefore in the current situation if from the evidence before it the city council could have determined that the rezoning was in basic harmony with the general plan, the rezoning is valid. Of course in cases where the rezoning does not deviate from the general plan, rational basis review will still be utilized.

This rezoning did deviate from the general plan in that it surpassed by a large margin the 250-foot height restriction. The plan, however, has other goals for that area. The plan does provide that gradient areas where this proposed building lies will have some concentrations of land use in sub cores. Also there is a provision for commercial development of the Central Avenue corridor. The building height restrictions are only stated in precatory language. Additionally, the plan provided for open space in the gradient, encouragement of landscaping, areas for people to enjoy and commercial development. The city council had before it evidence that this building would be commercially beneficial, would provide open spaces and recreational areas, landscaping, etc. The council also heard testimony that the developer could build two 20-story buildings which would leave less open space and less potential recreational areas. In viewing the above evidence, we cannot say the city council was wrong in finding the rezoning in basic harmony with the general plan. We do not need specific findings by the council to come to this conclusion since we have viewed the same evidence the council viewed. Certainly written findings would be preferable, but they are not mandatory.

C. Spot zoning.

Although not argued by appellant, the issue of spot zoning must be addressed. Spot zoning is not per se invalid and validity turns on the circumstances of the particular situation. Courts have held that there is not illegal spot zoning when the zoning ordinance is in accordance with the general or comprehensive plan designed to promote general welfare. As we have held above, the amendment granted by the city council was in compliance with the general plan of the city. Therefore this amendment did not constitute illegal spot zoning.

Affirmed.

HOWARD, P.J., Specially Concurring. [Omitted.]

NOTES AND QUESTIONS

1. *The consistency issue.* Do you agree with the court's interpretation of the plan in the principal case? If the plan is ambiguous and requires judicial interpretation, the court and not the local government will determine what the planning policy really is. Does this displacement of authority provide the fundamental fairness that advocates of the consistency requirement demand? One way out of this dilemma is to require more specific plans. The plan would then resemble the zoning ordinance. Is this much specificity in plans desirable?

The judicial review standard courts apply in their review of the consistency requirement has a major effect on the outcome of a consistency case. This issue is discussed in the principal case, which appeared to apply the usual presumption in favor of the municipality. See accord *Fritz v. Lexington-Fayette Urban County Gov't,* 986 S.W.2d 456 (Ky. App. 1998). Should the consistency requirement alter the traditional "fairly debatable" standard? See the *Snyder* case, reproduced *supra.*

2. *Interpreting plans.* The presumption courts apply in favor of municipalities usually allows local zoning agencies considerable discretion in the interpretation of comprehensive plans. See *Greenebaum v. City of Los Angeles,* 200 Cal. Rptr. 237 (Cal. App. 1984) (accepting contention by city that land use decisions need only be in agreement or harmony with the plan). Courts also find consistency when the plan is amorphous and gives the municipality more discretion. *Sequoyah Hills Homeowners Ass'n v. City of Oakland,* 29 Cal. Rptr. 2d 182 (Cal. App. 1993). What does this say about plan drafting?

In *Holmgren v. City of Lincoln,* 256 N.W.2d 686 (Neb. 1977), the court held that a multi-family rezoning was consistent with a plan that indicated single-family zoning for the tract. It held that the plan was intended only as a guide. The use designated by the rezoning was residential, as provided by the plan, even though it permitted a higher density. Courts upholding rezonings as consistent with a plan sometimes rely on the legislative character of the rezoning, which is accorded presumptive validity. See *Dade County v. Inversiones Rafamar, S.A.,* 360 So. 2d 1130 (Fla. App. 1978).

3. *Consistency not found.* Courts may sometimes find an inconsistency, especially where there is a clear conflict between the plan and the land use decision. See *Families Unafraid to Uphold Rural Eldorado County v. Board of Supervisors,* 74 Cal. Rptr. 2d 1 (Cal. App. 1998) (conflict with growth management policy).

In *Gillis v. City of Springfield,* 611 P.2d 355 (Or. App. 1980), the plan called for medium-density residential development. The rezoning allowed predominantly commercial development, though at the same density. The court held that comparability in intensity of use did not make the rezoning consistent with the plan. Should the use make any difference if the density is the same? Compare *Allius v. Marion County,* 668 P.2d 1242 (Or. App. 1983) (density policy in plan did not mandate minimum lot size requirement in zoning ordinance), with *Board of Supvrs. v. Jackson,* 269 S.E.2d 381 (Va. 1980) (upholding interpretation of ambiguous residential infill policy in plan).

In *Mira Dev. Co. v. City of San Diego,* 252 Cal. Rptr. 825 (Cal. App. 1988), a proposed rezoning was consistent with the land use designation in the plan but violated a planning policy requiring adequate public facilities. The city denied the rezoning and the court affirmed. Is this correct? See also *Philipi v. City of Sublimity,* 662 P.2d 325 (Or. 1983) (court upheld denial of residential development in area zoned residential because plan favored retention of productive farm land in this area until it was needed for development). Some courts require specific findings as the basis for judicial review of consistency. *Love v. Board of County Comm'rs,* 671 P.2d 471 (Idaho 1983).

4. *Effect on zoning.* To what extent does the consistency requirement limit the discretion of a local government in the zoning process? In *Baker v. City of Milwaukie,* 533 P.2d 772 (Or. 1975), the court ordered a downzoning to compel compliance with a density policy in the plan. Does this mean a court can order an upzoning? The court thought not in *Marracci v. City of Scappoose,* 552 P.2d 552 (Or. App. 1976). The court held that a plan's designation of a more intensive future land use did not require a rezoning to allow that use.

In *Bone v. City of Lewiston,* 693 P.2d 1046 (Idaho 1984), the city refused to rezone the plaintiff's land from a residential use to a commercial use shown on the comprehensive plan. The plaintiff brought an action in mandamus to compel the city to rezone its property in accordance with the comprehensive plan. The court held the action would not lie:

> It is illogical to say that what has been projected as a pattern of projected land uses is what a property owner is entitled to have zoned today. The land use map is not intended to be a map of present zoning uses, nor even a map which indicates what uses are presently appropriate. Its only purpose is that which [the statute] mandates — to

indicate "suitable projected land uses." Therefore, we hold that a city's land use map does not require a particular piece of property, as a matter of law, to be zoned exactly as it appears on the land use map. [*Id.* at 1052.]

The court added that the statutory "in accordance with a comprehensive plan" requirement does not allow governing bodies to ignore their comprehensive plan when adopting or amending zoning ordinances. They must determine as a matter of fact whether a requested zoning ordinance or amendment reflects the goals of the plan and takes the plan into account in light of the factual circumstances surrounding the request. The court indicated that an aggrieved landowner could appeal this factual decision. On what basis could a court review a factual decision not to rezone to a more intensive use shown on the plan? Compare *Nova Horizon, Inc. v. City Council,* 769 P.2d 721 (Nev. 1989) (council decision refusing to rezone in accordance with plan held improper).

5. *Conditional uses.* Must conditional uses be consistent with the plan in states that have a consistency requirement? This issue was considered in *Neighborhood Action Group v. County of Calaveras,* 203 Cal. Rptr. 401 (Cal. App. 1984). Although the statute did not require conditional use permits to be consistent with the plan, that requirement could be implied "from the hierarchical relationship of land use laws." The court reasoned that zoning ordinances must be consistent with the plan and that the validity of conditional use permits, which are governed by the zoning regulations, depends derivatively on "the general plan's conformity with statutory criteria." *Id.* at 407. For an Oregon case contra, see *Kristensen v. City of Eugene Planning Comm'n,* 544 P.2d 591 (Or. App. 1976).

Are there policy reasons for exempting conditional uses from compliance with the comprehensive plan? Conditional uses are similar to those in the district in which they are allowed, and are approved subject to standards in the zoning ordinance. If so, isn't it enough that the zoning ordinance complies with the plan? What about floating zones? And subdivision controls? See Cal. Gov't Code § 65567 (subdivision map must be consistent with plan).

6. *Judicial review of plan adequacy.* To what extent will the courts review a comprehensive plan to determine whether it meets the statutory requirements? The California courts require "actual compliance" with the planning statute but hold a plan inadequate only if the local government acted arbitrarily. See *Twain Harte Homeowners Ass'n v. County of Tuolumne,* 188 Cal. Rptr. 233 (Cal. App. 1983) (reviewing the cases). The court found the land use element of the plan inadequate because it did not express densities in terms of population and the circulation element inadequate because transportation facilities were not correlated with land use. The analysis of housing needs in the housing element was held adequate. See also *Bounds v. City of Glendale,* 170 Cal. Rptr. 342 (Cal. App. 1980) (housing element need not contain action program for condominium conversion). Judicial review of plans in California should be deferential under a statutory amendment providing the adoption of a plan is a legislative act. Cal. Gov't Code § 65301.5. Recall that the amendment of a plan is legislative in Florida.

Some states attempt to deal with internal conflicts in plans by statute. Cal. Gov't Code § 65300.5 requires a plan to "comprise an integrated, internally consistent and compatible statement of policies." For a case applying this provision to hold a plan internally inconsistent see *Concerned Citizens of Calaveras County v. Calaveras County Bd. of Supvrs.*, 212 Cal. Rptr. 273 (Cal. App. 1985). Internal conflicts in a plan may also support a decision that a zoning change is inconsistent with the plan. See *Bridger Canyon Property Owners' Ass'n v. Planning & Zoning Comm'n*, 890 P.2d 1268 (Mont. 1995).

7. *Spot planning.* What if a municipality amends the zoning ordinance to allow a land use and at the same time amends the comprehensive plan for the affected property to make the plan consistent with the rezoning? This is called spot planning. The courts have been willing to accept spot planning in states that do not have a consistency requirement. See *Cheney v. Village No. 2 at Mt. Hope, Inc.*, 241 A.2d 81 (Pa. 1968). Compare *Dalton v. City & County of Honolulu*, 462 P.2d 199 (Hawaii 1969). The court invalidated a contemporaneous rezoning and plan amendment for medium-density housing. It held that plan amendments must be accompanied by studies showing the need for the housing, that the housing should be located at the site, and that this location was the "best site."

A state may also limit the number of times a plan may be amended during any one year. See Cal. Gov't Code § 65358(b) (four times a year). This limitation should allow the municipality to consider together any plan amendments that affect a particular area in the community.

8. *Does the consistency requirement work?* E. Netter & J. Vranicar, Linking Plans and Regulations (American Planning Ass'n, Planning Advisory Serv. Rep. No. 363, 1981), reports field studies of six jurisdictions in two states, California and Florida, that have consistency requirements. The study found that some communities satisfied the consistency requirement by adopting detailed land use plans with land use districts identical to those contained in the zoning ordinance. Some jurisdictions had more general plans that permitted considerable flexibility in interpreting the consistency requirement. Other communities adopted detailed subarea plans in addition to a general community plan and relied on the subarea plans as the basis for requiring consistency. This technique helps preserve the general policy nature of the comprehensive plan while allowing the adoption of subarea plans as needed to provide more planning guidance.

The report concluded:

> [T]he political pressures and concerns that developers and citizens previously brought on the zoning ordinance seems to have shifted to the plan itself. . . . [With one exception] the experiences of the six communities . . . do not appear to be inspiring communities to break new ground in resolving the tension between planning and regulation. . . . Even with a consistency requirement, there will always be a struggle to achieve a reasonable, workable balance between flexibility and predictability when land-use decisions are made. [*Id.* at 21.]

The American Planning Association model land use legislation requires local planning agencies to prepare an advisory report on whether proposed land use actions, such as zoning amendments, are consistent with the comprehensive plan and whether the proposal should be approved, denied or changed. § 8-104(2) (2000 Draft). In his article, *supra,* Stuart Meck, who was the director of the model legislation project, argues that this proposal introduces a process that can substantially improve the application of the consistency requirement.

9. *Sources.* See Cobb, Mandatory Planning: An Overview, (Am. Plan. Ass'n, PAS Memo, Feb. 1994); Brooks, *The Law of Plan Implementation in the United States,* 16 Urb. L. Ann. 225 (1979); Bross, *Circling the Squares of Euclidean Zoning: Zoning Predestination and Planning Free Will,* 6 Envtl. L. 97 (1975); Stach, *Zoning — To Plan or Protect?,* 2 J. Plan. Lit. 472 (1987); Sullivan & Pelham, *The Evolving Role of the Comprehensive Plan,* 29 Urb. Law. 363 (1997).

A NOTE ON SIMPLIFYING AND COORDINATING THE DECISION MAKING PROCESS

This is probably a good place to discuss this problem. You will have noticed the Standard Act and statutes that follow it do not provide for one single permit that can authorize a development project. A mixed use project may require a rezoning for a zoning map amendment, a conditional use permit for some of its uses, and a variance if setback and other requirements are troublesome. As a result, the review of a proposed development is not a point-to-point process but a series of single-issue reviews. See the *Charisma* decision, reproduced *supra.*

There have been many proposals for some time to modify this process to make it more coordinated because delay and lack of coordination are expensive, both for the developer and the municipality. The model legislation proposed by the American Planning Association remedies this problem by authorizing a single development permit that covers all of the approvals a development requires. See Chapter 10 (2000 Draft). This follows Florida practice. See Fla. Stat. Ann. § 163.3164(8). A rezoning is included in the development permit in states where a rezoning is quasi-judicial rather than legislative. A single permit requirement can eliminate multiple hearings on single-issue problems, such as whether a variance is needed.

In addition, the model legislation authorizes a Consolidated Permit Review Process under which an applicant can apply at one time for all of the development permits or zoning map amendments required for a project. § 10-208. The advantage of this process is that it includes zoning map amendments in states where they are legislative. Appointment of a permit coordinator is authorized, and she is authorized to issue a master permit for the development. See also Ore. Rev. Stat. § 215.416(2); Wash. Rev. Code § 36.70B.120.

Additional changes can be made in the decision making process to simplify it and make it more coordinated. See Bassert, *Streamlining the Development Approval Process,* Land Development, Vol. 12, No. 4, at 14 (1999); McClendon, *Simplifying and Streamlining Zoning,* Inst. on Plan. Zoning & Eminent Domain 45, 76–95 (1982). Ms. Bassert, who is a senior land use planner with the National Association of Homebuilders, makes a number of proposals, such as a central information desk and one-stop permitting, clearly stated submittal requirements, approval process checklists and flow charts, time limits on decisions, fast-tracking for simple projects, and combined inspections.

Unified development codes.—Some municipalities have experimented with combining all their land use ordinances into one unified development code. See M. Brough, A Unified Development Ordinance (1985). The advantage of a unified code is that it provides consistency of standards for all advisory and governing bodies and simplifies the development review process. One important feature is the combination of zoning with subdivision ordinances, discussed in the next chapter, so that the code applies even though a subdivision is not required. For discussion, with examples from several cities, see Morris, *Zoning and Subdivision Codes Unite! Lessons from Four Communities with Unified Development Codes,* Planning, Vol. 59, No. 11, at 12 (1993).

The application process.—Section 10-202 of the American Planning Association model law requires local governments to specify the contents of development applications in detail, while § 10-203 requires a completeness determination, which has time limits and is carefully described. For example, if a local government finds an application incomplete it must specify in detail what will make it complete. For similar requirements see Cal. Gov't Code § 65943 et seq.

Time limits.—The model legislation also has other time limits, such as those limiting time for decisions following hearings, § 10-210. See also Cal. Gov't Code § 69590; N.J. Stat. Ann. 40:55D-61 (120-day period for planning board actions). Under this kind of provision, a project not approved within the statutory time limit is deemed approved. One problem with this kind of approach is that more complex projects may take longer to consider. To deal with the problem, the model law provides that the time limits will not run during any period, which is suggested not to exceed 30 days, "in which a local government requests additional studies or information concerning a development permit application."

Project hierarchies.—Local governments in Oregon have adopted project hierarchies that divide proposed developments according to their complexity. The simpler projects are fast-tracked, while the more complex projects require a full hearing.

For additional suggestions see J. Vranicar, W. Sanders, & D. Mosena, Streamlining Land Use Regulation: A Guidebook for Local Governments (1980). This kind of tightening in the land use process obviously works a major change over current practice in most states. What are the downsides?

H. INITIATIVE AND REFERENDUM

Early in the twentieth century, many states began to adopt constitutional and statutory provisions authorizing the initiative and referendum. This reform reflected the dominant populism of the period, which favored a number of changes that would return government to the people. It also reflected a serious concern over the domination of state legislatures by interest groups and lobbyists. Today, almost all states have constitutional provisions authorizing the referendum at the state and local level, while about half the states have constitutional provisions authorizing the initiative at both governmental levels. Initiatives and referenda may also be authorized by statute or by local charters.

Recent years have seen renewed interest in the initiative and referendum as part of the local zoning process. The reasons for this development, and the pros and cons of the initiative and referendum as it applies to zoning, are summarized in the following student note:

> This recent trend in the direction of increased public participation in land use decisionmaking is both understandable and desirable. Heightened community sensitivity to the quality of the environment and increasing voter skepticism of the judgment of public officials provide much of the impetus for referenda. Moreover, such popular decisionmaking is consistent with the cardinal principle of our democratic system that decisions be made with the consent of the governed.
>
> At the same time, however, the use of the referendum to override the rezoning decisions of public bodies carries with it certain disadvantages. An individual landowner who seeks a rezoning may not be able to rely upon the electorate to make a reasoned decision that takes into account all the relevant information concerning the proposal and its impact on the municipality. Moreover, communities recognize now more than ever before the importance of planning coordinated and rational land use decisions, a goal that may be inconsistent with the referendum process. [Note, *The Proper Use of Referenda in Zoning*, 29 Stan. L. Rev. 819 (1977).]

As applied to the zoning process, a referendum follows a zoning action by the legislative body and may either be mandatory or permissive. If the referendum is permissive, a zoning ordinance will not be submitted to popular vote unless a voter petition for a referendum is filed. In some states, the legislative body may also propose a referendum. Frequently, the referendum is used to block zoning amendments that provide for a more intensive use of a single piece of property; in some communities it has developed a distinctive anti-growth bias. Referenda have also been used to block subsidized, low-income and moderate-income housing projects.

A zoning initiative is a voter-initiated zoning proposal which in some states is placed directly on the ballot following submission of a petition carrying the required number of voters' signatures. Under a variant of this process, the legislative body is first given an opportunity to accept or reject the measure before the election is held. Although it is unlikely that something as comprehensive as community-wide rezoning would be proposed through an initiative, this process has been used to propose specific zoning amendments such as height restrictions and growth moratoria. In many cases the initiative is also used as a substitute for the referendum, which is possible in most states. If the legislative body enacts a zoning amendment which the voters wish to challenge, an initiative proposal may be filed calling for the repeal of the amendment and reinstatement of the prior zoning. This approach may be used if the period of time for filing a referendum is limited, as it may not be possible to collect all the signatures necessary for a referendum in the time provided.

The kinds of zoning actions that are subject to the initiative and referendum are about as wide as the zoning process, with the limitation that only legislative and not administrative zoning actions may be subject to electoral review. This limitation will restrict the use of the initiative and referendum in states in which the zoning amendment has been characterized as a quasi-judicial and not a legislative action. Even if a court does not go quite this far, the detailed notice and hearing procedures which the zoning enabling legislation requires prior to the enactment of any zoning measure may be viewed as a bar to the availability of the initiative and referendum. The case that follows considers the validity of a zoning referendum under state law.

TOWNSHIP OF SPARTA v. SPILLANE

125 N.J. Super. 519, 312 A.2d 154 (1973), *petition
for certification denied,* 64 N.J.
493, 317 A.2d 706 (1974)

CARTON, P.J.A.D.:

The issue to be resolved in these appeals is whether the referendum procedure provided for in the Faulkner Act applies to an amendment to the zoning ordinance of a municipality which has adopted the provisions of that act. The Township of Sparta and Township of Mount Olive cases involve this identical issue. Consequently they will be considered together, although they have not been formally consolidated.

Sparta has operated since 1960 under the Council-Manager Plan B of the Faulkner Act, N.J.S.A. 40:69A-99 et seq. On April 12, 1972 the township council adopted an amendment to its zoning ordinance authorizing a Planned Unit Development (P.U.D.) pursuant to N.J.S.A. 40:55-55 to 67. The plans for the P.U.D. were originally proposed by a subsidiary of a large corporation owning about 2,000 acres in Sparta.

The amendatory ordinance was referred to and acted upon favorably by the planning board after extended public hearings. Thereafter defendants in the Sparta action filed a petition with the municipal clerk seeking a referendum pursuant to N.J.S.A. 40:69A-185. The petition was found sufficient by the township clerk to comply with N.J.S.A. 40:69A-187, whereupon Sparta Township sought a declaratory judgment to determine whether the referendum provisions of the Faulkner Act were applicable to amendments of a zoning ordinance. The trial judge granted the township's motion for summary judgment, holding that such provisions were not applicable.

Mount Olive Township operated under the Mayor and Council Plan E of the Faulkner Act, N.J.S.A. 40:69A-68 to 73. On August 25, 1972 the township council, over strong opposition, adopted an ordinance amending the township zoning ordinance by establishing a new zone denominated C-R (Commercial-Recreational). Permissible uses in this zone included permanent year-round or seasonal amusement parks. Two of the defendants in the Mount Olive case own about two-thirds of the land in the newly created C-R zone on which they intend to construct and operate a major amusement park. The lands in question are located near Interstate Route 80 and were originally zoned for industrial uses.

The amendment was approved by the mayor after its passage by the council. On September 18 the plaintiffs in the Mount Olive case filed a petition with the township clerk for a referendum on the amendatory ordinance. This petition was found to comply with the statutory requirement.

As in the Sparta action, a declaratory judgment was sought by the municipality as to the applicability of the referendum procedures to the ordinance. The trial judge ruled in this case, as did the trial judge in the Sparta litigation, that the referendum procedure was not applicable.

The issue raised here presents a question not directly decided before in New Jersey. The Faulkner Act, in pertinent part, provides:

> The voters shall also have the power of referendum which is the power to approve or reject at the polls any ordinance submitted by the council to the voters or any ordinance passed by the council, against which a referendum petition has been filed as herein provided. No ordinance passed by the municipal council, except when otherwise required by general law or permitted by the provisions of section 17-32(b) of this act, shall take effect before twenty days from the time of its final passage and its approval by the mayor where such approval is required. . . . [N.J.S.A. 40:69A-185]

A companion section of the statute (N.J.S.A. 40:69A-184) provides a slightly different procedure for expressing public participation in municipal government through the initiative process:

> The voters of any municipality may propose any ordinance and may adopt or reject the same at the polls, such power being known as the initiative. . . .

The Faulkner Act was adopted in order to encourage public participation in municipal affairs in the face of normal apathy and lethargy in such matters. The act gave municipalities the option of choosing one form or another of local government best suited to its needs. It was a legislative demonstration of the democratic ideal of giving the people the right of choosing the form of government they preferred and the opportunity to exercise the powers under that form to the furthest limits. Some 76 of the 567 municipalities of this State have adopted one form or another of the forms of government authorized under the Faulkner Act.

The initiative and referendum processes authorized by the act comprise two useful instruments of plebiscite power and provide a means of arousing public interest. Ordinary rules of construction would, of course, dictate that such provisions should be liberally construed. See 5 McQuillin, Municipal Corporations, § 16.48 at 199-200 (1969), where the author advocates that these procedures should be respected and given wide use if possible. It should be noted, however, that he adds a caveat that any grant of the power of initiative and referendum and its exercise are subject to and must be construed with governing constitutional and statutory provisions. 5 McQuillin, *supra* at § 16.50.

Undeniably, zoning issues often are of great public interest and some, as in the present case, may concern the entire population of the municipality involved. In both the cases before us it has been argued forcefully that the proposed ordinances change or alter the complexion of the municipalities. Thus, the ultimate question is whether major decisions should be made by the planning boards and governing bodies, with only voiced public approval or dissent as prescribed in the Zoning Act, or whether they should be open to a final decision by the vote of the entire population. This issue pits the philosophy of comprehensive zoning planned by a panel of experts and adopted by elected and appointed officials, against the philosophy of a wider public participation and choice in municipal affairs.

Other states faced with similar problems of referendum provisions have arrived at conflicting determinations. However, the decisions of other states furnish little aid here since the laws of the states involved differ in substantial respects from the New Jersey statutes.

Our consideration of the applicability of the referendum provided for in the Faulkner Act to the zoning procedure logically should begin with an examination of the treatment accorded by our courts to the companion process of the initiative. *Smith v. Livingston Tp.*, 256 A.2d 85 (Ch. Div. 1969), *aff'd o.b.* 257 A.2d 698 (1969), held that the initiative was not applicable to amendatory zoning ordinances. In so holding, Judge Mintz found that the zoning statutes represented an exclusive grant of power by the Legislature to municipalities generally and was not impliedly superseded by the later adopted Faulkner Act. He noted that the Zoning Act is specific in detailing the manner in which zoning ordinances may be amended; that steps in the zoning procedure include consideration by the municipal planning board, the opportunity of property owners to object, and approval by the governing body. He also pointed out that in the event of objection by the property owners involved, a vote of two-thirds of the governing body is required to effect a change in the zoning ordinance (N.J.S.A. 40:55-34 to 35). He likewise observed that the initiative and referendum provisions in the Faulkner Act contain no specific reference to zoning. He concluded that if the initiative procedure were allowed to be applied to zoning matters, it would "disregard the valuable expertise of the planning board, and permit the electorate to defeat the beneficent purpose of the comprehensive zoning ordinance."

Appellants argue that a referendum is sufficiently dissimilar to an initiative as to justify treating it differently. They stress the fact that a referendum merely adds an additional stage which follows the governing body's approval and does not, as in the case of the initiative, provide a substitute for legislative action by the governing body. Consequently, they reason, a proposed zoning change should no more than any other legislative act be immune from further public examination. They point also to the fact that the planning board would not be altogether by-passed as in the case of initiative since a referendum begun by a petitioner would not occur until after the adoption of the zoning amendment and such adoption could not occur until the planning board had reviewed the amendment and made its recommendation. N.J.S.A. 40:55-35 and N.J.S.A. 40:69A-185.

These arguments have some cogency. However, we conclude that essentially the same considerations which bar application of the initiative process to zoning ordinance amendments apply in the case of the referendum.

Zoning is intended to be accomplished in accordance with a comprehensive plan and should reflect both present and prospective needs of the community. Among other things, the social, economic and physical characteristics of the community should be considered. The achievement of these goals might well be jeopardized by piecemeal attacks on the zoning ordinances if referenda were permissible for review of any amendment. Sporadic attacks on a municipality's comprehensive plan would tend to fragment zoning without any overriding concept. That concept should not be discarded because planning boards and governing bodies may not always have acted in the best interest of the public and may not, in every case, have demonstrated the expertise which they might be expected to develop.

The spirit and thrust of *Smith v. Livingston Tp.* requires treatment of both processes in the same fashion in their relation to the zoning procedure. Such considerations stem from the exclusivity and uniqueness of the Zoning Act itself (and the related Planning Act) and the Legislature's evident intention of providing uniformity of procedure for all municipalities in the State in zoning matters.

Thus, the Legislature has authorized governing bodies of municipalities to establish administrative agencies to assist them in the performance of functions in this area and has laid down very specific and detailed procedure to be followed by all governmental bodies in carrying out such functions. Such comprehensive and precise treatment demonstrates the special concern of the Legislature in this important area of municipal regulation.

Moreover, certain aspects of the zoning statute seem inherently incompatible with the referendum process. N.J.S.A. 40:55-35 provides three avenues by which an amendment to a zoning ordinance may be effected; first, following approval by the planning board the governing body passes the amended ordinance; second, upon rejection by the planning board the amended ordinance may be approved by two-thirds of the governing body; third, should at least 20% of the landowners directly or contiguously affected by the proposed amendment object, the governing body must pass the amended ordinance by a two-thirds vote. A zoning ordinance amendment does not become operative unless the planning board and governing body have acted. Whether the referendum stems from a submission of an ordinance by the governing body directly to the voters or by a referendum petition filed by the necessary number of voters, the so-called veto power of the planning board or protesting landowners would be rendered meaningless. A simple majority of the voters would be all that was necessary to approve or disapprove the ordinance.

We are not satisfied that the publicity which might accompany the referendum campaign and the exposure and discussion of the issues generated thereby justify disregarding these procedural requirements. In this connection we note that the zoning statute requires public notice of proposed zoning changes (N.J.S.A. 40:55-34). Moreover, from common experience we know that zoning amendments of a controversial nature, especially those which may greatly affect the entire population of the community, are often widely discussed and vigorously debated at the public hearings prior to adoption. . . .

Both judgments appealed from are affirmed.

NOTES AND QUESTIONS

1. *Referendum.* The principal case details most of the objections state courts have to allowing the use of the referendum in zoning. New Jersey has now exempted zoning ordinances and amendments from both the initiative and referendum. N.J. Stat. Ann. § 40:55D-62(b). For cases agreeing with the principal case on statutory conflict grounds and reviewing cases elsewhere, see *Elliott v. City of Clawson,* 175 N.W.2d 821 (Mich. App. 1970), and *I'On, L.L.C. v. Town of Mt. Pleasant,* 526 S.E.2d 716 (S.C. 2000), which holds that allowing referenda "could nullify a carefully established zoning system or master plan developed after debate among many interested persons and entities, resulting in arbitrary decisions and patchwork zoning with little rhyme or reason."

The New Jersey court did not consider possible due process objections to the referendum which might arise because the referendum, by definition, precludes observance of the notice and hearing requirements contained in zoning enabling legislation. Since the referendum occurs after the zoning amendment has been enacted by the legislative body following the statutory notice and hearing, most state courts have either not perceived or have not found a due process violation on this account. See *City of Ft. Collins v. Dooney,* 496 P.2d 316 (Colo. 1972), upholding the application of a referendum to a zoning map amendment and noting that "[t]he fact that due process requirements may be met in one manner when the change is by council action does not preclude other procedures from meeting due process requirements. . . ." *Id.* at 319. Quoting from another case, the court then added that "'[t]he election campaign, the debate and airing of opposing opinions, supplant a public hearing prior to the adoption of an ordinance by the municipal governing body.'" *Id.* How realistic is this assumption?

The *Ft. Collins* case relied on the nature of the referendum as a "fundamental right" of the people in holding that a home rule charter provision allowing a referendum on "all" ordinances could not be construed to exempt zoning amendments. The court added that its holding was not intended to strip the property owner of his constitutional rights. "We can conceive of situations where the court might hold that the action of the electorate was arbitrary and capricious." *Id.*

For other cases holding that zoning is subject to referendum on zoning map amendments, see *Queen Creek Land & Cattle Corp. v. Yavapi County Bd. of Supvrs.,* 501 P.2d 391 (Ariz. 1972), noting that the referendum does not change the zoning as an initiative does and that the notice and hearing process is accomplished prior to the referendum; *Cook-Johnson Realty Co. v. Bertolini,* 239 N.E.2d 80 (Ohio 1968), upholding a permissive referendum and noting that the only effect of a successful referendum is to restore the zoning to what it was before the map amendment was requested; and *Florida Land Co. v. City of Winter Springs,* 427 So. 2d 171 (Fla. 1983), rejecting due process objections on the authority of *Eastlake, infra.* See also *State ex rel. Wahlmann v. Reim,* 445 S.W.2d 336 (Mo. 1969), rejecting the statutory conflict argument and upholding a referendum on a newly enacted comprehensive zoning ordinance though noting that it might not be available on "isolated amendments." Accord *Wilson v. Manning,* 657 P.2d 251 (Utah 1982).

2. *Legislative vs. administrative.* Referenda are available only for administrative, not legislative, actions. See *State ex rel. Srovnal v. Linton,* 346 N.E.2d 764 (Ohio 1976), holding that a special exception is administrative. It would have been thought that the adoption of a comprehensive plan is a legislative act, as the court held in *O'Loane v. O'Rourke,* 42 Cal. Rptr. 283 (Cal. Ct. App. 1965):

> It is apparent that the plan is, in short, a constitution for all future development within the city. . . . To argue that property rights are not affected by the general plan (as the city so asserts) as adopted ignores that which is obvious. Any zoning ordinance adopted in the future would surely be interpreted in part by its fidelity to the general plan as well as by the standards of the process. [*Id.* at 288.]

The court took a different view in *Fritz v. City of Kingman,* 957 P.2d 337 (Ariz. 1998), where it said that "the city's General Plan is a statement of broad policies, goals, and principles. It enacts nothing definite or specific nor does it implement any law, purpose, or policy previously declared by the legislative body."

What about a zoning map amendment? Recall that most courts hold a zoning map amendment a legislative act. In *Fritz, supra,* the question was whether a zoning map amendment that allowed four dwelling units to the acre was administrative because it implemented very specific policies in the comprehensive plan that provided a density range of one to four units per acre for the parcel. The court held no. Because the plan was not a legislative act, rezonings that implemented the plan were not administrative. See also *Camden Community Dev. Corp. v. Sutton,* 5 S.W.3d 439 (Ark. 1999) (rejection of zoning map amendment held an administrative act not subject to initiative).

Utah has a statute that expressly exempts "individual property zoning decisions" from referenda. Utah Code Ann. § 20A-7-101. The Utah court adopted a multi-factor test to apply the exemption that considers whether there was sufficient notice so that voters would know they could ask for a referendum, whether there was a material variance from the basic zoning law, and whether the zoning change implicated a policy-making decision amenable to voter control. *Citizen's Awareness Now v. Marakis,* 873 P.2d 1117 (Utah 1994), noted, 1995 Utah L. Rev. 325. Would these tests be helpful even without such a statute? How does the decision on whether a zoning map amendment is subject to referendum differ from whether the amendment is quasi-judicial for purposes of judicial review?

3. *Initiative.* Most cases have held the initiative is not available to enact a zoning ordinance. Unlike the referendum, which follows legislative adoption of a zoning measure in which statutory notice and hearing requirements have been observed, a successful initiative will result in the enactment of a zoning measure without the statutory notice and hearing. For this reason, courts may find that the zoning initiative violates the statutory notice and hearing procedures, and some courts have found a denial of procedural due process as well. See, e.g., *Transamerica Title Ins. & Trust v. City of Tucson*, 757 P.2d 1055 (Ariz. 1988); *Kaiser Hawaii Kaii Dev. Co. v. City & County of Honolulu*, 777 P.2d 244 (Hawaii 1989); *Gumprecht v. City of Coeur D'Alene*, 661 P.2d 1214 (Idaho 1983). Most of these cases considered the use of the initiative as a means of repealing a zoning amendment applicable to a single parcel of land, and this fact may have led these courts to emphasize notice and hearing problems. Some courts have approved the use of the referendum in the zoning process but disapprove the use of the initiative. Can you see why?

4. *The initiative in California. Associated Homebuilders, Inc. v. City of Livermore*, 557 P.2d 473 (Cal. 1976), upheld an initiative ordinance that enacted a growth moratorium for the city. It held that the initiative procedure did not conflict with the notice and hearing and other provisions of the zoning enabling act on the ground that no such conflict was intended. The court noted the right to the initiative was reserved in the constitution, and that the zoning act might be unconstitutional if it were construed to bar the initiative. *Id.* at 479-80. It also referenced a constitutional provision authorizing the initiative as "[d]rafted in light of the theory that all power of government ultimately resides in the people," *id.* at 477. Accord *State ex rel. Hickman v. City Council*, 690 S.W.2d 799 (Mo. App. 1985).

The availability of the initiative in zoning has led to an explosion of voter-initiated measures adopting growth management controls as well as other restrictions in California communities, often over the objections of council and planning staff. In *Devita v. County of Napa*, 889 P.2d 1019 (Cal. 1995), the court held the initiative is available to amend a general plan. In that case, the voters had amended the plan to substantially prevent any development of land in agricultural areas for 30 years without approval by the vote of the people. Has the court gone too far? What happens to planning in this kind of political environment? See Alperin & King, *Ballot Box Planning: Land Use Planning Through the Initiative Process in California*, 21 Sw. U. L. Rev. 1 (1992).

5. *Good or bad?* Some critics of the initiative and referendum claim that voter control of zoning will lead to excesses that will escape judicial review. See *Ranjel v. City of Lansing*, 417 F.2d 321 (6th Cir. 1969). Compare the arguments for the initiative and referendum in the following student note:

> The initiative process contains adequate safeguards against arbitrary decisionmaking; the open process of a political campaign is likely to reveal to the voters adequate information upon which to make an intelligent decision. Even if some prejudice may be suffered by individual property owners, courts should consider the unique educational and participatory values represented by the initiative. Moreover, the protection of property owners may be accomplished by means other than categorically prohibiting the initiative's use. Courts should consider the possibility of heightened judicial scrutiny of the substance of initiative measures which seem to focus on an individual parcel rather than on broad community objectives; this type of review would be in accord with the close judicial scrutiny of "spot-zoning" discussed

above. Courts concerned about forcing property owners to wage both a political campaign and a subsequent legal challenge may wish to consider relaxing the traditional judicial reluctance to rule on the validity of an initiative measure prior to passage. [Comment, *The Initiative and Referendum's Use in Zoning,* 64 Calif. L. Rev. 74, 93 (1976).]

In *Arnel Dev. Co. v. City of Costa Mesa,* 178 Cal. Rptr. 723 (Cal. App. 1981), the court held invalid an initiative that repealed a zoning amendment for moderate-income housing. The court subjected the initiative to the same tests applicable to a municipally adopted zoning ordinance. It found no change in conditions or circumstances that justified the repeal by initiative and held it was adopted for the sole and specific purpose of defeating the housing development. Neither did the initiative accommodate the regional interest in the provision of moderate-income housing, as required in California. But see *Northwood Homes, Inc. v. Town of Moraga,* 265 Cal. Rptr. 363 (Cal. App. 1989) (distinguishing *Arnel*).

6. *Sources. See* Callies, Neuffer & Calibaoso, *Ballot Box Zoning: Initiative, Referendum and the Law,* 39 Wash. U. J. Urb. & Contemp. L. 53 (1991); Freilich & Guemmer, *Removing Artificial Barriers to Public Participation in Land-Use Policy: Effective Zoning by Initiative and Referenda,* 21 Urb. Law. 511 (1989); Ziegler, *Limitations on Use of Initiative and Referendum Measures in Controlling Land Use Disputes,* 13 Zoning & Plan. L. Rep. 17 (1990); Comment, *Land Use By, For, and of the People: Problems With the Application of Initiatives and Referenda to the Zoning Process,* 19 Pepp. L. Rev. 99 (1991).

The previous case considered the validity of a zoning referendum under state law. Constitutional objections to the initiative and referendum may also be raised in federal courts. They were given consideration in the following Supreme Court decision, which deals with a mandatory zoning referendum. When reading this decision remember that it does not preclude a different view of either the referendum or the initiative in a state court.

CITY OF EASTLAKE v. FOREST CITY ENTERPRISES, INC.

426 U.S. 668 (1976)

CHIEF JUSTICE BURGER delivered the opinion of the Court:

The question in this case is whether a city charter provision requiring proposed land use changes to be ratified by 55% of the votes cast violates the due process rights of a landowner who applies for a zoning change.

The city of Eastlake, Ohio, a suburb of Cleveland, has a comprehensive zoning plan codified in a municipal ordinance. Respondent, a real estate developer, acquired an eight-acre parcel of real estate in Eastlake zoned for "light industrial" uses at the time of purchase.

In May 1971, respondent applied to the City Planning Commission for a zoning change to permit construction of a multifamily, high-rise apartment building. The Planning Commission recommended the proposed change to the City Council, which under Eastlake's procedures could either accept or reject the Planning Commission's recommendation. Meanwhile, by popular vote, the voters of Eastlake amended the city charter to require that any changes in land use agreed to by the Council be approved by a 55% vote in a referendum.[1] The City Council approved the Planning Commission's recommendation for reclassification of respondent's property to permit the proposed project. Respondent then applied to the Planning Commission for "parking and yard" approval for the proposed building. The Commission rejected the application, on the ground that the City Council's rezoning action had not yet been submitted to the voters for ratification.

Respondent then filed an action in state court, seeking a judgment declaring the charter provision invalid as an unconstitutional delegation of legislative power to the people. While the case was pending, the City Council's action was submitted to a referendum, but the proposed zoning change was not approved by the requisite 55% margin. Following the election, the Court of Common Pleas and the Ohio Court of Appeals sustained the charter provision.

The Ohio Supreme Court reversed. Concluding that enactment of zoning and rezoning provisions is a legislative function, the court held that a popular referendum requirement, lacking standards to guide the decision of the voters, permitted the police power to be exercised in a standardless, hence arbitrary and capricious manner. Relying on this Court's decisions in *Washington ex rel. Seattle Trust Co. v. Roberge,* 278 U.S. 116 (1928), *Thomas Cusack Co. v. Chicago,* 242 U.S. 526 (1917), and *Eubank v. Richmond,* 226 U.S. 137 (1912), but distinguishing *James v. Valtierra,* 402 U.S. 137 (1971), the court concluded that the referendum provision constituted an unlawful delegation of legislative power.

We reverse.

I

The conclusion that Eastlake's procedure violates federal constitutional guarantees rests upon the proposition that a zoning referendum involves a delegation of legislative power. A referendum cannot, however, be characterized as a delegation of power. Under our constitutional assumptions, all power derives from the people, who can delegate it to representative instruments which they create. See, *e.g.,* Federalist Papers, No. 39 (Madison). In establishing legislative bodies, the people can reserve to themselves power to deal directly with matters which might otherwise be assigned to the legislature. *Hunter v. Erickson,* 393 U.S. 385, 392 (1969).

The reservation of such power is the basis for the town meeting, a tradition which continues to this day in some States as both a practical and symbolic

---

[1] As adopted by the voters, Art. VIII, § 3, of the Eastlake City Charter provides in pertinent part: "That any change to the existing land uses or any change whatsoever to any ordinance . . . cannot be approved unless and until it shall have been submitted to the Planning Commission, for approval or disapproval. That in the event the city council should approve any of the preceding changes, or enactments, whether approved or disapproved by the Planning Commission it shall not be approved or passed by the declaration of an emergency, and it shall not be effective, but it shall be mandatory that the same be approved by a 55% favorable vote of all votes cast of the qualified electors of the City of Eastlake at the next regular municipal election, if one shall occur not less than sixty (60) or more than one hundred and twenty (120) days after its passage, otherwise at a special election falling on the generally established day of the primary election. . . ."

part of our democratic processes. The referendum, similarly, is a means for direct political participation, allowing the people the final decision, amounting to a veto power, over enactments of representative bodies. The practice is designed to "give citizens a voice on questions of public policy." *James v. Valtierra, supra,* at 141.

In framing a state constitution, the people of Ohio specifically reserved the power of referendum to the people of each municipality within the State.

> The initiative and referendum powers are hereby reserved to the people of each municipality on all questions which such municipalities may now or hereafter be authorized by law to control by legislative action. . . . Ohio Const., Art. II, § 1f.

To be subject to Ohio's referendum procedure, the question must be one within the scope of legislative power. The Ohio Supreme Court expressly found that the City Council's action in rezoning respondent's eight acres from light industrial to high-density residential use was legislative in nature.[7] Distinguishing between administrative and legislative acts, the court separated the power to zone or rezone, by passage or amendment of a zoning ordinance, from the power to grant relief from unnecessary hardship. The former function was found to be legislative in nature.[9]

II

The Ohio Supreme Court further concluded that the amendment to the city charter constituted a "delegation" of power violative of federal constitutional guarantees because the voters were given no standards to guide their decision. Under Eastlake's procedure, the Ohio Supreme Court reasoned, no mechanism existed, nor indeed could exist, to assure that the voters would act rationally in passing upon a proposed zoning change. This meant that "appropriate legislative action [would] be made dependent upon the potentially arbitrary and unreasonable whims of the voting public." 324 N.E.2d, at 746. The potential for arbitrariness in the process, the court concluded, violated due process.

Courts have frequently held in other contexts that a congressional delegation of power to a regulatory entity must be accompanied by discernible standards, so that the delegatee's action can be measured for its fidelity to the legislative will. Assuming, *arguendo,* their relevance to state governmental functions, these cases involved a delegation of power by the legislature

---

[7] The land use change requested by respondent would likely entail the provision of additional city services, such as schools and police and fire protection. Cf. James v. Valtierra, 402 U.S. 137, 143 n. 4 (1971). The change would also diminish the land area available for industrial purposes, thereby affecting Eastlake's potential economic development.

[9] The power of initiative or referendum may be reserved or conferred "with respect to any matter, legislative or administrative, within the realm of local affairs. . . ." 5 E. McQuillan, Municipal Corporations § 16.54, p. 208 (3d ed., 1969). However, the Ohio Supreme Court concluded that only land use changes granted by the City Council when acting in a legislative capacity were subject to the referendum process. Under the court's binding interpretation of state law, a property owner seeking relief from unnecessary hardship occasioned by zoning restrictions would not be subject to Eastlake's referendum procedure. For example, if unforeseeable future changes give rise to hardship on the owner, the holding of the Ohio Supreme Court provides avenues of administrative relief not subject to the referendum process.

to regulatory bodies, which are not directly responsible to the people; this doctrine is inapplicable where, as here, rather than dealing with a delegation of power, we deal with a power reserved by the people to themselves.[10]

In basing its claim on federal due process requirements, respondent also invokes *Euclid v. Ambler Realty Co.,* but it does not rely on the direct teaching of that case. Under *Euclid,* a property owner can challenge a zoning restriction if the measure is "clearly arbitrary and unreasonable, having no substantial relation to the public health, safety, morals, or general welfare." If the substantive result of the referendum is arbitrary and capricious, bearing no relation to the police power, then the fact that the voters of Eastlake wish it so would not save the restriction. As this Court held in invalidating a charter amendment enacted by referendum:

> The sovereignty of the people is itself subject to those constitutional limitations which have been duly adopted and remained unrepealed. *Hunter v. Erickson,* 393 U.S., at 392.

But no challenge of the sort contemplated in *Euclid v. Ambler Realty* is before us. The Ohio Supreme Court did not hold, and respondent does not argue, that the present zoning classification under Eastlake's comprehensive ordinance violates the principles established in *Euclid v. Ambler Realty.* If respondent considers the referendum result itself to be unreasonable, the zoning restriction is open to challenge in state court, where the scope of the state remedy available to respondent would be determined as a matter of state law, as well as under Fourteenth Amendment standards. That being so, nothing more is required by the Constitution.

Nothing in our cases is inconsistent with this conclusion. Two decisions of this Court were relied on by the Ohio Supreme Court in invalidating Eastlake's procedure. The thread common to both decisions is the delegation of legislative power, originally given by the people to a legislative body, and in turn delegated by the legislature to a *narrow segment* of the community, not to the people at large. In *Eubank v. City of Richmond,* the Court invalidated a city ordinance which conferred the power to establish building setback lines upon the owners of two-thirds of the property abutting any street. Similarly, in *Washington ex rel. Seattle Title Trust Co. v. Roberge,* the Court struck down an ordinance which permitted the establishment of philanthropic homes for the aged in residential areas, but only upon the written consent of the owners of two-thirds of the property within 400 feet of the proposed facility.

Neither *Eubank* nor *Roberge* involved a referendum procedure such as we have in this case; the standardless delegation of power to a limited group of property owners condemned by the Court in *Eubank* and *Roberge* is not to

---

[10] The Ohio Supreme Court's analysis of the requirements for standards flowing from the Fourteenth Amendment also sweeps too broadly. Except as a legislative history informs an analysis of legislative action, there is no more advance assurance that a legislative body will act by conscientiously applying consistent standards than there is with respect to voters. For example, there is no certainty that the City Council in this case would act on the basis of "standards" explicit or otherwise in Eastlake's comprehensive zoning ordinance. Nor is there any assurance that townspeople assembling in a town meeting, as the people of Eastlake could do, will act according to consistent standards. The critical constitutional inquiry, rather, is whether the zoning restriction produces arbitrary or capricious results.

be equated with decisionmaking by the people through the referendum process. The Court of Appeals for the Ninth Circuit put it this way:

> A referendum, however, is far more than an expression of ambiguously founded neighborhood preference. It is the city itself legislating through its voters — an exercise by the voters of their traditional right through direct legislation to override the views of their elected representatives as to what serves the public interest. *Southern Alameda Spanish Speaking Organization v. City of Union City, California,* 424 F.2d 291, 294 (1970).

Our decision in *James v. Valtierra,* upholding California's mandatory referendum requirement, confirms this view. Mr. Justice Black, speaking for the Court in that case, said:

> This procedure ensures that *all the people* of a community will have a voice in a decision which may lead to large expenditures of local governmental funds for increased public services. . . . 402 U.S., at 143 (emphasis added).

Mr. Justice Black went on to say that a referendum procedure, such as the one at issue here, is a classic demonstration of "devotion to democracy. . . ." *Id.,* at 141. As a basic instrument of democratic government, the referendum process does not, in itself, violate the Due Process Clause of the Fourteenth Amendment when applied to a rezoning ordinance.[13] Since the rezoning decision in this case was properly reserved to the people of Eastlake under the Ohio Constitution, the Ohio Supreme Court erred in holding invalid, on federal constitutional grounds, the charter amendment permitting the voters to decide whether the zoned use of respondent's property could be altered.

The judgment of the Ohio Supreme Court is reversed, and the case is remanded for further proceedings not inconsistent with this opinion.

Reversed and remanded.

JUSTICE POWELL, dissenting:

There can be no doubt as to the propriety and legality of submitting generally applicable legislative questions, including zoning provisions, to a popular referendum. But here the only issue concerned the status of a single small parcel owned by a single "person." This procedure, affording no realistic

---

[13] The fears expressed in dissent rest on the proposition that the procedure at issue here is "fundamentally unfair" to landowners; this fails to take into account the mechanisms for relief potentially available to property owners whose desired land use changes are rejected by the voters. First, if hardship is occasioned by zoning restrictions, administrative relief is potentially available. Indeed, the very purpose of "variances" allowed by zoning officials is to avoid "practical difficulties and unnecessary hardship." 8 E. McQuillan, Municipal Corporations § 25.159, p. 511 (3d ed. 1965). As we noted, remedies remain available under the Ohio Supreme Court's holding and provide a means to challenge unreasonable or arbitrary action.

The situation presented in this case is not one of a zoning action denigrating the use or depreciating the value of land; instead, it involves an effort to *change* a reasonable zoning restriction. No existing rights are being impaired; new use rights are being sought from the City Council. Thus, this case involves an owner's seeking approval of a new use free from the restrictions attached to the land when it was acquired.

opportunity for the affected person to be heard, even by the electorate, is fundamentally unfair. The "spot" referendum technique appears to open disquieting opportunities for local government bodies to bypass normal protective procedures for resolving issues affecting individual rights.

JUSTICE STEVENS, with whom JUSTICE BRENNAN joins, dissenting:

[Most of Justice Stevens' dissent is omitted, but his views on the zoning process and the fair procedures required in that process are of interest.]

The expectancy that particular changes consistent with the basic zoning plan will be allowed frequently and on their merits is a normal incident of property ownership. . . .

The fact that an individual owner (like any other petitioner or plaintiff) may not have a legal right to the relief he seeks does not mean that he has no right to fair procedure in the consideration of the merits of his application. The fact that codes regularly provide a procedure for granting individual exceptions or changes, the fact that such changes are granted in individual cases with great frequency, and the fact that the particular code in the record before us contemplates that changes consistent with the basic plan will be allowed, all support my opinion that the opportunity to apply for an amendment is an aspect of property ownership protected by the Due Process Clause of the Fourteenth Amendment. . . .

[W]hen the record indicates without contradiction that there is no threat to the general public interest in preserving the city's plan — as it does in this case, . . . I think the case should be treated as one in which it is essential that the private property owner be given a fair opportunity to have his claim determined on the merits. . . .

NOTES AND QUESTIONS

1. *Federal issues.* The *Eastlake* case put to rest the federal constitutional objections to a zoning referendum. The Supreme Court's view of the referendum process was the decisive factor. How does it contrast with the view of state courts that zoning referenda are undesirable? Should the Supreme Court have held that a referendum denies due process because it results "in arbitrary decisions and patchwork zoning with little rhyme or reason," as the South Carolina Supreme Court holds? Or is it really a procedural due process question, as Justice Stevens' dissent suggests?

Would the court's disposition of this case have been aided by acknowledging the debate in state courts over whether zoning amendments are "legislative" or "quasi-judicial"? Or does the Ohio Supreme Court's labeling dispose of that issue? Is it an answer to an attack on the process through which zoning amendments are enacted that the landowner has a substantive opportunity to overturn a zoning restriction that is unconstitutionally applied to him? Could he do so in a variance proceeding, as Chief Justice Burger suggests? See accord *Taylor Props. v. Union County,* 583 N.W.2d 638 (S.D. 1998) (non-mandatory referendum). For discussion of the *Eastlake* decision, see Note, *The Proper Use of Referenda in Zoning,* 29 Stan. L. Rev. 819, 825–44 (1977).

The student Note makes a series of criticisms of the use of mandatory referenda in the zoning process. Voters are likely to be uninformed about the zoning proposal, and so incapable of making an informed choice. If the referendum result is judicially reviewed the court will not have a record of any kind on which it can base its decision. See *Ranjel v. City of Lansing,* 417 F.2d 321, 324 (6th Cir. 1969), in which the court refused to upset an unfavorable referendum on a zoning change which would have allowed a subsidized housing project. It suggested that judicial review of the referendum "would entail an intolerable invasion of the privacy that must protect an exercise of the franchise."

The student Note also suggests that developers forced to face a mandatory referendum will bypass the local legislative body entirely and seek an electoral zoning change directly through the initiative. If this occurs there will be no opportunity for the mutual bargaining between the municipality and the developer which is often necessary to adjust the developer's proposal. Mandatory referenda also delay the development process, interfere with comprehensive planning and frustrate attempts by the municipality to zone for regional needs. What is your evaluation of these criticisms? Would they be entirely eliminated if the referendum were made permissive and not mandatory, as the student Note also suggests?

2. *A racial perspective.* Earlier Supreme Court cases considering claims of racial discrimination in the referendum process can provide a better perspective on *Eastlake:*

Hunter v. Erickson, 393 U.S. 385 (1969). The city of Akron, Ohio, enacted a fair housing ordinance that prohibited discrimination in the sale or rental of housing. After plaintiff filed a complaint under the ordinance, the city charter was amended to require a referendum on any ordinance of this type. The city also had a long-standing referendum procedure under which a referendum could be had on almost any city ordinance following the filing of a petition by ten percent of the electors.

The charter provision mandating a referendum on fair housing ordinances was held unconstitutional, as it was "an explicitly racial classification treating racial housing matters differently from other racial and housing matters." *Id.* at 389. The court noted that while the law applied on its face to both majority and minority groups its impact fell on the minority. *Id.* at 391. Because the mandatory referendum was based on a racial classification it bore a heavier burden of justification than other classifications. It was not justified by "insisting that a State may distribute legislative power as it desires and that the people may retain for themselves the power over certain subjects . . . [as there is a violation of] the Fourteenth Amendment." *Id.* at 392. The concurring opinion noted that the optional referendum procedure was grounded upon "general democratic principle," and that procedures of this type "do not violate the Equal Protection clause simply because they occasionally operate to disadvantage Negro political interests." *Id.* at 394.

James v. Valtierra, 402 U.S. 137 (1971). The Court upheld an amendment to the California state constitution that mandated a referendum on all local public housing projects. These projects are built by local agencies and governments and receive federal subsidies. The Court distinguished *Hunter* because the amendment "requires referendum approval for any low-rent public housing project, not only for projects which will be occupied by a racial minority."

There was no support in the record for "any claim that a law seemingly neutral on its face is in fact aimed at a racial minority." *Id.* at 141.

Justice Black also noted that California had provided extensively for mandatory referenda on a variety of subjects, and that there was justification for mandating the referendum in this case because localities in which public housing projects are located might be subject to large expenditures for public services needed by these projects. In a footnote, Black noted that public housing projects were exempt by federal law from local property taxation and that in-lieu payments required as a substitute for local taxation were ordinarily less than the taxes that otherwise would have been levied. Was the Court correct in ignoring the racial impact of the referendum in *Eastlake?* For discussion of these cases see Comment, *Restoring Accountability at the Municipal Level: The "Save Miami Beach" Zoning Referendum,* 53 U. Miami L. Rev. 541 (1999).

Referenda on zoning and on proposed subsidized housing projects have been invalidated under the Fair Housing Act, which requires only proof of racially discriminatory effect rather than intent. *United States v. City of Birmingham,* 727 F.2d 560 (6th Cir.), *cert. denied,* 469 U.S. 821 (1984); *United States v. City of Parma,* 494 F. Supp. 1049 (N.D. Ohio 1980) (restrictive land use regulations), *aff'd,* 661 F.2d 562 (6th Cir. 1981), *cert. denied,* 456 U.S. 962 (1982). Note that these cases were as-applied rather than facial attacks. Does this suggest a strategy for attacking the referendum requirement in *Eastlake?*

3. *Delegations to neighbors. Eubank* and *Roberge* hold that a delegation to neighbors, a "narrow segment" of the community, to establish land use rules is unconstitutional. Does *Eastlake* convince you that a referendum is qualitatively different from this type of delegation? The third case in the *Eubank-Roberge* trilogy, *Cusak,* cited but not discussed in the principal case, held that a similar delegation to *waive* restrictions in an ordinance established legislatively (there, a flat prohibition against billboards) is constitutional.

The legislate/waive dichotomy in these old cases has defied scholarly attempts at reconciliation. For a sophisticated tour over this terrain, see Michelman, *Political Markets and Community Self-Determination,* 53 Ind. L.J. 145, 164–77 (1977–78). Notwithstanding these doubts, state courts sometimes flirt with the distinction. See *Howard Twp. Bd. of Trustees v. Waldo,* 425 N.W.2d 180 (Mich. App. 1988) (approving in principle a requirement of neighborhood consent for waiver of mobile home prohibition, citing *Eastlake,* but disapproving specific ordinance because consent of 100 percent of neighbors required). Accord *Cary v. City of Rapid City,* 559 N.W.2d 891 (S.D. 1997) (invalidating statute giving veto power to landowners).

Instead of the referendum procedure approved in *Eastlake,* could the municipality have required the applicant to have sought a waiver and subjected that process to neighborhood approval? See *Rispo Inv. Co. v. City of Seven Hills,* 629 N.E.2d 3 (Ohio App. 1993) (upholding charter requiring approval of zoning change by voters in ward in which property was located).

4. *The Eastlake model.* The mandatory referendum required in *Eastlake* is unusual and controversial. An Ohio court upheld a city charter provision authorizing mandatory referenda for zoning. *Kure v. City of North Royalton,*

517 N.E.2d 1016 (Ohio App. 1986). For discussion of this practice in Ohio see Rosenburg, *Referendum Zoning: Legal Doctrine and Practice,* 53 Cinn. L. Rev. 381 (1984).

The extra-majority requirement in *Eastlake* is also somewhat unusual, although it is often used in bond issue elections. The Supreme Court held that an extra-majority voting requirement for municipal bond elections did not violate the Court's one person-one vote rule. *Gordon v. Lance,* 403 U.S. 1 (1971).

Chapter 6

CONTROLLING RESIDENTIAL DEVELOPMENT

This chapter changes direction somewhat by reviewing a number of land use controls that apply primarily to the residential development of land. These controls differ from zoning, which divides the community into land use districts. Residential development controls apply when raw land is converted to residential use. Subdivision controls that apply to the subdivision of land for development are an example.

Planned unit development (PUD) regulations are an innovative technique that combines elements of zoning and subdivision controls. PUD regulations authorize the review of development plans for residential projects in a review process in which the design, intensity, and uses proposed for the development are considered at one time. Planned unit developments can also include commercial uses.

PROBLEM

The State of Metro has adopted Sections 13 and 14 of the Standard State Planning Enabling Act, which are reproduced *infra*. Metro County has adopted a subdivision control ordinance under the authority of this statute. It includes design standards for new subdivisions, including standards for the arrangement, dimension and orientation of lots, and requirements for roads and drainage and storm sewers. Sewer and water facilities must be provided in the subdivision if connection to public systems is not possible. The ordinance also authorizes the county to require the dedication of land for the widening of adjacent roads.

Ace Development Company owns 500 acres of land in an outlying area of Metro County that has been growing rapidly. A recently developed subdivision is located just to the south, but farmland borders the tract on all of its other sides. Ace has submitted a preliminary subdivision plat to the county for approval that contains 1000 lots for single-family homes. Lot sizes and densities comply with the zoning ordinance. The Ace tract is bordered on two sides by narrow two-lane county roads.

The county ordinance authorizes the planning department to review subdivision plat proposals and submit a report to the planning commission, which holds a hearing on the plat and decides whether to approve or reject it. The planning department approved the plat for the Ace subdivision and forwarded it to the planning commission, with a recommendation that Ace dedicate 50 feet of land to the county to widen the adjacent county roads. This requirement will reduce the number of homes that Ace can build in the subdivision.

The planning commission held a hearing and approved the preliminary plat and the dedication requirement, but with a condition that Ace redesign the subdivision "to provide a residential design compatible with the historic design features typical of Metro County." In its finding approving the subdivision the commission noted it disapproved of the cul-de-sac design used in the subdivision, and preferred a neotraditional design that would use a gridiron street pattern.

The President of Ace has come to you for advice. Would you advise that the design condition is not authorized by the statute? By the ordinance? That it is unconstitutional? Is the dedication requirement authorized by the statute? Is it constitutional?

A. SUBDIVISION CONTROLS

In addition to zoning, the early Model Acts also authorized controls over new subdivisions. In practice, subdivision controls apply in most states only to new single-family residential development. Originally intended to require the provision of streets and other necessary facilities, subdivision controls in many states now include other elements, such as floodplain control requirements, and may even implement growth management programs.

Another important development is the use of subdivision controls to shift the cost of providing public facilities, such as roads, to developers. This occurs through an exaction requirement that obliges subdividers to dedicate land for public facilities, or to pay a fee in lieu of the exaction that municipalities can use to provide the facilities themselves. Exactions have grown in importance in recent years because tax and debt limits have restricted government spending for infrastructure, and because communities see exactions as a way of shifting public facility costs away from existing residents to new residents and developers. Impact fees, imposed on developers at the time a building permit is issued, are another form of exaction. The Supreme Court's *Nollan* case, reproduced in Ch. 2, and its *Dolan* case, reproduced in this chapter, have had important effects on exaction law.

History of Subdivision Controls.—The need for subdivision controls arises because raw land that is to be converted to residential use usually is held in comparatively large tracts. Before it can be developed it must be subdivided into lots and blocks suitable for building.

Subdivision controls first were adopted in rudimentary form as land platting legislation toward the end of the nineteenth century to remedy conveyancing problems. Land had been conveyed by metes and bounds boundary descriptions. This conveyancing method requires a reference to boundary markers, distances, and directions that often are confusing and unreliable, leading to disputes over land ownership and titles. To avoid these problems, land developers prepared so-called plats of subdivisions on which the blocks and lots were shown. Once a plat was recorded, parcel conveyance could be by reference to blocks and lots within the plat, e.g., "Lot 5 in Block 4 of Milligan's Addition to the City of Indian Falls." The early platting laws simply required the recording of these subdivision plats in the appropriate records office, after which the conveyance of lots within the plat could be made with reference to the plat in the manner just indicated. Many of these early laws mandated the recording of subdivision plats before conveyances with reference to the plat could be made.

It soon became apparent that the subdivision control process could accomplish substantive objectives as well. Many of the early subdivisions were cursed poor design and layout and inadequate streets and facilities. Often the subdivider would leave his development with badly constructed streets that would soon crumble, leaving the homeowners to be assessed the cost of necessary street improvements. Other problems arose when subdividers planned their subdivisions independently, with the result that streets did not connect properly from one subdivision to the next. This practice has not disappeared. A survey of new subdivisions in Jefferson County, Missouri, which did not then have subdivision control, found several hundred dead-end subdivision streets ending at hills, gullies, and other unlikely places.

Modern Enabling Legislation.—Some states amended their subdivision platting legislation late in the nineteenth century to require subdivision streets to conform to the municipal street system plan. When the Standard State Planning Enabling Act was drafted in the 1920s, these early subdivision platting statutes were used as a model for subdivision control provisions included in the Act. The scope of public control over subdivisions contemplated at that time is indicated by the text of the Standard Act, which incorporated these early statutory requirements and added others requiring the provision of on-site facilities necessary to service the subdivision development:

> Section 13. Whenever a planning commission shall have adopted a major street plan . . . [which is on file in the office of the county recorder], then no plat of a subdivision of land . . . shall be filed or recorded until it shall have been approved by such planning commission. . . .

> Section 14. Before exercising . . . [subdivision control] powers . . . the planning commission shall adopt regulations governing the subdivision of land within its jurisdiction. Such regulations may provide for the proper arrangement of streets in relation to other existing or planned streets and to the master plan, for adequate and convenient open spaces for traffic, utilities, access of firefighting apparatus, recreation, light and air, and for the avoidance of congestion of population, including minimum width and areas of lots.

> Such regulations may include provisions as to the extent to which streets and other ways shall be graded and improved and to which water and sewer and other utility mains, piping, or other facilities shall be installed as a condition precedent to the approval of the plat. [Standard City Planning Enabling Act (U.S. Dep't of Commerce, 1928).]

For early discussions of subdivision control legislation, which are still helpful, see Melli, *Subdivision Control in Wisconsin,* 1953 Wis. L. Rev. 389; Reps, *Control of Land Subdivision by Municipal Planning Boards,* 40 Cornell L.Q. 258 (1955); Note, *Land Subdivision Control,* 65 Harv. L. Rev. 1226 (1952); Note, *Platting, Planning and Protection, A Summary of Subdivision Statutes,*

36 N.Y.U. L. Rev. 1205 (1961). In many states the subdivision control legislation is still based on the provisions of the Standard Act.

More modern subdivision control legislation extends the substantive requirements applicable to new subdivisions in several directions, and tends to view the act of subdividing as a triggering event that calls into play a range of controls that shape and give character to newer development in the community. This shift in direction needs emphasis. Subdivision control has gradually evolved from a simple control over the recording of new subdivision plats to an extensive set of controls over new land development.

This newer legislation has added a variety of requirements to the provisions of the Standard Act. The number of on-site facilities required has been extended, new subdivisions have been restricted in floodplains and on environmentally sensitive land, and the phasing of new development has been controlled in connection with the provision of public facilities. In addition, many states now have legislation authorizing exactions.

The Connecticut subdivision control enabling legislation is a modern example:

> Conn. Gen. Stat. § 8-18. *Definitions.* . . . "Commission" means a planning commission; . . . "subdivision" means the division of a tract or parcel of land into three or more parts or lots . . . for the purpose, whether immediate or future, of sale or building development expressly excluding development for municipal, conservation or agricultural purposes, and includes resubdivision. . . .

> § 8-25(a). *Subdivision of land.* No subdivision of land shall be made until a plan for such subdivision has been approved by the commission. . . . [A fine of $500 is imposed for any person making subdivision without approval.] . . . Before exercising the powers granted in this section, the commission shall adopt regulations covering the subdivision of land. . . . Such regulations shall provide that the land to be subdivided shall be of such character that it can be used for building purposes without danger to health or the public safety, that proper provision shall be made for water, sewerage and drainage, including the upgrading of any downstream ditch, culvert or other drainage structure which, through the introduction of additional drainage due to such subdivision, becomes undersized and creates the potential for flooding on a state highway and, in areas contiguous to brooks, rivers or other bodies of water subject to flooding, including tidal flooding, that proper provision shall be made for protective flood control measures and that the proposed streets are in harmony with existing or proposed principal thoroughfares shown in the plan of conservation and development . . . especially in regard to safe intersections with such thoroughfares, and so arranged and of such width, as to provide an adequate and convenient system for present and prospective traffic needs.

> Such regulations shall also provide that the commission may require the provision of open spaces, parks and playgrounds when, and in places, deemed proper by the planning commission, which open spaces,

parks and playgrounds shall be shown on the subdivision plan. Such regulations may, with the approval of the commission, authorize the applicant to pay a fee to the municipality or pay a fee to the municipality and transfer land to the municipality in lieu of any requirement to provide open spaces. Such payment or combination of payment and the fair market value of land transferred shall be equal to not more than ten per cent of the fair market value of the land to be subdivided prior to the approval of the subdivision. . . . [Open space requirements do not apply to transfers within a family or if subdivision is for affordable housing.]

Such regulations . . . shall provide that proper provision be made for soil erosion and sediment control. . . . [Regulations shall not impose regulations on manufactured homes constructed under federal standards that are "substantially different from conditions and requirements imposed on single-family dwellings and lots containing single-family dwellings."] The commission may also prescribe the extent to which and the manner in which streets shall be graded and improved and public utilities and services provided [and may accept a bond in lieu of completion of such work.]

(b) The regulations adopted under subsection (a) of this section shall also encourage energy-efficient patterns of development and land use, the use of solar and other renewable forms of energy, and energy conservation. . . .

NOTES AND QUESTIONS

1. *What is required?* How has the Connecticut statute expanded the subdivision control requirements contained in the Standard Act? Note the extensive environmental controls. See also Cal. Gov't Code § 66474(e) (subdivision design must not cause substantial environmental damage). For a more extensive provision, see Ariz. Rev. Stat. Ann. § 9-463.01(C)(4), which authorizes municipalities to

[d]etermine that certain lands may either not be subdivided, by reason of adverse topography, periodic inundation, adverse soils, subsidence of the earth's surface, high water table, lack of water or other natural or man-made hazard to life or property, or control the lot size, establish special grading and drainage requirements, and impose other regulations deemed reasonable and necessary for the public health, safety or general welfare on any lands to be subdivided affected by such characteristics.

Does this statute provide an alternative to the prohibition of development on these lands? What is it? Many subdivision control enabling acts require the adoption of subdivision regulations by the governing body in ordinance form. Some acts give the power to approve subdivision plats to the local governing body.

2. *Health requirements.* Many states also provide authority to state health and environmental agencies to regulate on-site wells and on-site sewage disposal through septic tanks and similar facilities. E.g., Mich. Stat. Ann. § 26.430(105)(g), requiring the approval of all subdivisions to be conditioned

on compliance with the rules of the state department of environmental quality "relating to suitability of groundwater for on-site water supply for subdivisions not served by public water or to suitability of soils for subdivisions not served by public water and public sewers;" N.H. Rev. Stat. Ann. § 485-A:4(IX), authorizing a state agency to specify standards, procedures and criteria for sewage or waste disposal systems in subdivisions.

Acceptability of on-site systems under these laws is usually based on the ability of the soil to handle waste disposal. See also Mich. Stat. Ann. § 26.430(109)(a) (no approval of subdivision of less than one acre unless public water and sewer available or approved on-site alternative). Denial of a state permit will foreclose development of the site unless the developer ties in with public facilities. The importance of these state health laws in the development of new subdivisions is often neglected. Note also that the state permit law adds another approval stage to the subdivision control process.

A NOTE ON SUBDIVISION COVENANTS AND OTHER PRIVATE CONTROL DEVICES

What they are.—The act of subdivision is usually the point in the development process at which the developer decides whether to restrict the newly created lots with rights and duties other than those contained in a formal system of land use controls, such as zoning. This Note briefly explores the complex subject of easements, covenants, and equitable servitudes, full consideration of which is usually found in Property or Real Estate Transactions courses. Over the centuries this area of the law has acquired mindbreaking layers of complexity, often in order to preserve (or avoid) the rigid distinction between actions at law and in equity, or to fit within the arcane pigeonholes of the common law writ system. For a useful introduction to the modern effort to simplify this law, see Restatement of the Law, Property (Servitudes), T.D. No. 1 at xix-xxviii (1989). For a survey of the traditional rules, see R. Cunningham, W. Stoebuck & D. Whitman, The Law of Property Ch. 8 (2d ed. 1993).

For present purposes, a few very general points will suffice. To function the way a zoning ordinance or other land use regulation does, the servitudes (we use the modern collective term espoused by the Restatement, *supra,* although it has not yet found general acceptance) must survive the individual parties who create them so that they can be enforced by and against whoever holds the land in question. This is permitted if the benefits and burdens can be shown to be sufficiently related to the land itself, or to a recognized estate in land, a requirement sometimes (but not always) embodied in the familiar phrases, "running with the land," and "touching and concerning the land." As might be expected, a substantial body of law addresses these terms. See, e.g., *Peterson v. Beekmere, Inc.,* 283 A.2d 911 (N.J. L.Div. 1971) (covenant to pay annual assessment does not "touch or concern" land because money not required to be expended for benefit of the subdivision).

Because England did not have recording systems, the early law of covenants abounds in complex notice rules. While notice remains a requirement, in America it is normally satisfied by compliance with state recording acts. For use in

modern subdivisions and condominiums, the developer usually originates
elaborate covenants, which are either recorded with the subdivision plat and
incorporated by reference in the individual conveyances or set out in full in
each conveyance. State subdivision and condominium statutes often regulate
the form and content of this process.

Finally, in order to be enforceable, covenants must be "lawful," that is to
say, they must be on a subject appropriate for private parties to agree upon
and they must not be contrary to public policy. The best known example is,
of course, *Shelley v. Kraemer,* 334 U.S. 1 (1947) (invalidating racially restrictive covenants). This is an area where the law appears to be changing.
Compare *West Hill Baptist Church v. Abbate,* 261 N.E.2d 196 (Ohio Misc.
1969) (invalidating covenant prohibiting church), with *Riley v. Stone,* 526 P.2d
747 (Ariz. App. 1974) (upholding age-restrictive covenant). See Comment, *Resolving a Conflict: Ohana Zoning and Private Covenants,* 6 U. Hawaii L. Rev.
177 (1984). The courts also recognize the constitutionally protected right to
contract by enforcing the more restrictive land use provision when a conflict
arises between a covenant and a zoning ordinance.

Review the materials in Ch. 1. What are the potential strengths and weaknesses of a privately organized system of controls, such as that described in
this Note? If the Restatement's position on public policy limitations gains
general acceptance, is the effect to shift ultimate decisionmaking responsibility from legislative bodies to courts?

A great deal of the complexity in the law in this area arose from the
distinction between actions at law and in equity, and the consequent distinction between monetary and injunctive relief. In practice, the modern litigant
seeks to enforce (or avoid) the effects of servitudes through injunctive relief,
rather than damages, and the law has generally accommodated this approach,
without regard to labels. Review the nuisance cases in Ch. 2, *supra,* particularly *Boomer* and *Spur Industries.* What do those cases suggest about the
proper relationship between legal and equitable remedies in land use control
cases? Reconsider also the "taking" cases in Ch. 2. Historically, the courts'
approach to servitudes has varied with society's attitude towards the utility
of constraints on land use. Note the parallel in the current debate over
regulatory takings. Should private and public constraints on land use be viewed
the same way?

Architectural controls.—It is common for subdivision developers to impose
restrictions that prohibit erection of certain kinds of buildings or to alter
existing buildings without the permission of a majority of the lot owners or,
where a homeowners' association has been created, the permission of the
association's board of directors or a committee appointed by the board of
directors. Because of their "consensual" nature, these restrictions are generally upheld by the courts, often with a loosely worded good faith qualification.
See *Goode v. Village of Woodgreen Homeowners Ass'n,* 662 So. 2d 1064, 1077
(Miss. 1995) (announcing a nearly absolute rule in favor of architectural
approval covenants). However, decisions by architectural control committees
are the largest class of cases in which courts are likely to intervene. See, e.g.,
Young v. Tortoise Island Homeowners Ass'n, 511 So. 2d 381 (Fla. App. 1987)
(rejecting disapproval of flat roof; board's power to consider aesthetics,

harmony, and balance held too personal and vague); *Town & Country Estates Ass'n v. Slater,* 740 P.2d 668 (Mont. 1987) (overturning rejection of plans when committee could not articulate a design standard).

Changing social and judicial attitudes toward private covenants and their enforcement may lead to more judicial intervention. See also Brower, *Communities Within the Community: Consent, Constitutionalism, and Other Failures of Legal Theory in Residential Associations,* 7 J. Land Use & Envtl. L. 203 (1992), arguing for judicial review that considers substantive values, and Sterk, *Minority Protection in Residential Private Governments,* 77 B.U. L. Rev. 273 (1997).

For comprehensive discussions of the use of private agreements to achieve private residential governments, see Ellickson, *Cities and Homeowner Associations,* 130 U. Penn. L. Rev. 1519 (1982); Reichmann, *Residential Private Governments: An Introductory Survey,* 43 U. Chi. L. Rev. 253 (1976). See also R. Cunningham, W. Stoebuck & D. Whitman, The Law of Property §§ 8.13–8.33 (2d ed. 1993). Houston, Texas, has never had a comprehensive zoning ordinance, although it has a subdivision ordinance and building and housing codes. Because the location of different land uses is not controlled by any ordinance, private restrictive covenants are extensively used in Houston, and actually enforced by the city. For a fuller discussion, see Siegan, *Non-Zoning in Houston,* 13 J.L. & Econ. 71, 142–43 (1970). See also Goodrich, *Private Land Restrictions in Texas: A Need for Greater Legislative Control,* 15 St. Mary's L.J. 575 (1984). Houston last rejected a zoning ordinance in 1993.

1. THE STRUCTURE OF SUBDIVISION CONTROLS

DRUCKER, LAND SUBDIVISION REGULATION, in THE PRACTICE OF LOCAL GOVERNMENT PLANNING 198, 200-35 (F. So & J. Getzels eds., 1988)

Purposes of subdivision regulation.

Over time, subdivision regulation has come to be regarded as a means of determining who will finance capital improvements needed to serve new growth, but it serves a number of other purposes as well. By requiring the platting, or mapping, of newly created lots, streets, easements, and open areas, regulation requirements help to ensure the creation and preservation of adequate land records. . . .

Ensuring that subdivisions are properly designed is another key function of the subdivision review process. The manner in which land is subdivided, streets are laid out, and lots and houses are sold sets the pattern of community development for years to come. . . .

Subdivision review also allows a local government the opportunity to ensure that a new subdivision is properly equipped and that a public agency or private party will be responsible for maintaining the subdivision improvements that the developer provides. . . .

Subdivision regulations can also be viewed as consumer protection measures. At least in urban areas, lot purchasers rarely know what water line size or system pumping capacity will ensure adequate water pressure for their future homes. Nor are they likely to be able to evaluate the base and paving materials used to construct the streets that serve their houses. Establishing minimum standards for subdivision improvements and design is the traditional way to protect purchasers, who generally lack the specialized knowledge to evaluate improvements and design. . . .

The regulatory setting. . . .
Organizational arrangements within local government.

The organizational arrangements for administering subdivision regulations vary substantially from jurisdiction to jurisdiction and from state to state. Most states have followed the suggestion of the Standard City Planning Enabling Act by delegating the power to regulate subdivisions to locally appointed planning commissions or boards. In some states (e.g., Connecticut) planning commissions are authorized both to adopt subdivision regulations and to review plats. Elsewhere, such a commission may serve as the plat approval agency, but the local legislative body actually adopts regulations. In some states, (e.g., Arizona), the governing board both adopts ordinances and approves plats, which means that it serves in a legislative as well as an administrative capacity. Not all jurisdictions rely on elected or appointed boards for plat approval. In many states, plat approval authority is delegated to staff technical review committees. . . .

Elements of subdivision design.

Properly handled, subdivision plat review can afford a community an outstanding opportunity to encourage the creation of attractive sites and visually appealing neighborhoods, to ensure that traffic circulation is efficient and convenient, to protect residential and other uses from traffic and incompatible land uses, to determine that individual lots are appropriately arranged and oriented, and to require that public improvements and facilities are coordinated with community plans and the character of surrounding areas. Unfortunately, many communities do not take sufficient advantage of the opportunity to influence the design of new subdivisions. . . .

[The article then discusses a number of components of subdivision design, including attention to the natural hazard and critical environmental areas, stormwater management, soil erosion and sedimentation control, water quality, landscaping and aesthetics, and street, block, and lot layout. Does the Standard Planning Act authorize control of all of these design elements? The Connecticut act? The article also notes that "[o]ne of the most fundamental requirements of a subdivision ordinance is that new lots conform to the lot size and other lot-related standards of the zoning ordinance."]

Administering subdivision regulations.

The fundamental steps that most local governments follow in reviewing a subdivision plat have not changed substantially over the years . . . [but in recent years critics] have attacked the development review process as too complicated, too slow, too unpredictable, and unfair. . . .

A number of communities have attempted to reform the subdivision review process. In some cases, regulations have been simplified to reduce the time needed to review a plat, thereby influencing one of the factors that increases the price of housing. Other reforms have been made to reduce the work load for elected and appointed public officials or to make the review process more open to the public and to make officials more accountable. Some communities have simplified procedures to gain a competitive edge in attracting new development.

The other major change in subdivision review involves the exercise of discretion by plat approval agencies. Subdivision review has always involved negotiation among developers, staff, and reviewing agencies, but as long as the review focused on the impact of the proposal within the subdivision, the approval of a typical subdivision plat was a relatively straightforward and predictable matter. Innovative and flexible growth management techniques have broadened the focus of subdivision review to encompass wider, even community wide impacts. Standards have become more general, and plat approval agencies now tend to wield more discretionary power. As the subdivision review process has come to include more bargaining and negotiation, the outcome of the process has become more uncertain. . . .

Preapplication.

Early consultation between developers and staff familiarizes developers with local development requirements and staff with proposed plans, reduces errors and omissions in applications, clarifies the proposal's impact on public facilities, and reveals possible conflicts with other projects, with past precedents, and with community feeling. Relatively little detail should be expected from the subdivider at this stage; one of the local government's objectives should be to help the subdivider to avoid the later redesign of the project. . . . [Some subdivision ordinances require the submittal of a sketch plat before a preliminary plat is submitted. A sketch plat presents the general concept of the subdivision proposal so that the developer can receive input and suggestions from the municipality. It is not a binding document. —Eds.]

Preliminary plat review.

The next important step in the review process is often the submission of a preliminary plat of the proposed subdivision, along with other documentation and plans. (In some communities this is the first step.) To call a subdivision map submitted at this stage "preliminary" is somewhat misleading, since the plat will, in large measure, fix the nature, design, and scope of the subdividing activity to follow. Furthermore, it serves as a general blueprint for whatever improvements or facilities the developer is to provide. Ordinarily, the subdivider will not be required to submit a site plan or building elevations to obtain subdivision plat approval, particularly if the subdivision is intended for single-family detached residences; but if construction of housing units is allowed before final site plan review, the site plan may be reviewed as if it were a preliminary plat. However, a final recordable plat is always required. . . .

The customary practice is for a board to approve a plat, approve it with conditions, or deny approval. Several alternatives are possible if changes are required to bring the preliminary plat into conformity with the regulations or if conditions are added that may require the redesign of the plat. The board can require the applicant to withdraw the plat, redesign the subdivision to incorporate the required changes, and then resubmit the revised plat. Alternatively, the board can approve the preliminary plat subject to the condition that the required changes be incorporated into the final plat. . . . One compromise may be for the board to delegate to staff the authority to approve redesigned preliminary plans prior to the submission of final plans.

Most regulations require final plans to be submitted and approved within a certain time (often a year or two) after the preliminary plat is approved. Approval of the preliminary plat generally implies approval of a final plat conforming substantially to the preliminary version, even if subdivision and zoning standards change during the intervening period. . . .

Final plat review.

The final plat is submitted in much the same way as the preliminary plat, with adequate copies for distribution to interested departments and to agencies that made recommendations or approved plans earlier in the process. Final plat review ensures that the recordable plat is in substantial accordance with plans approved earlier and that whatever subdivision improvements have been constructed conform to those plans. . . .

Guaranteed developer performance.

Generally, a developer may not begin to construct subdivision improvements until the preliminary plat is approved. Although installation or construction of improvements may begin with approval of the preliminary plat, most jurisdictions do not require that improvements be completed before final plat approval. . . .

Most jurisdictions allow a subdivider to install or construct some or all of the required improvements after final plat approval, provided that the jurisdiction has a financial guarantee or some other form of leverage to ensure that the tasks will be performed. [The subdivider can guarantee completion of improvements by obtaining a performance bond or irrevocable letter of credit, placing cash or real or personal property in escrow, or by entering into a three-party agreement with his lender and the local government.]

NOTES AND QUESTIONS

1. *What subdivision control covers.* Note that subdivision control applies in Connecticut, as is usually the case, only when there is a subdivision of land. (Consult again the definition in the statute *supra.*) This requirement creates a regulatory gap problem. Major developments that do not require subdivision, such as multifamily projects, shopping centers, and industrial parks, are outside the subdivision control process. This gap is one reason for site plan review (described in Ch. 5) and planned unit development controls, *infra*, either of which apply a similar review process to projects on single sites and to major residential developments. Note also that the Connecticut definition of subdivision creates an opportunity for evasion because a developer can build on a single lot at a time without having to comply with the subdivision ordinance. Why is this so? The purpose requirement in statutes worded like Connecticut's also can be a problem. See *Slavin v. Ingraham,* 339 N.E.2d 157 (N.Y. 1975) (no showing that developers were selling individual lots collectively for residential purposes or holding themselves out as subdividers).

Most courts hold that a municipality may not modify the definition of a subdivision contained in the enabling act. See, e.g., *State v. Visser,* 767 P.2d 858 (Mont. 1988). For a clever (and successful) example of avoiding even a broadly worded subdivision ordinance, see *Vinyard v. St. Louis County,* 399 S.W.2d 99 (Mo. 1966) (creation of access road through residential lots to serve landlocked apartment development).

Section 12 of the Standard Act authorized subdivision regulation in an extraterritorial area five miles beyond the municipal limits. Most states confer extraterritorial powers. See *Petterson v. City of Naperville,* 137 N.E.2d 371 (Ill. 1956) (upholding extraterritorial delegation).

For model subdivision ordinances see R. Freilich & J. Levi, Modern Subdivision Control Regulations (2d ed. 1995); D. Listokin & C. Walker, The Subdivision and Site Plan Handbook (Ordinance) (1989).

2. *Exemptions and minor subdivisions.* Most statutes contain exemptions from subdivision control. The subdivision of land for agricultural purposes is one example. N.J. Stat. Ann. § 40:55D-7 (over five acres). Cal. Gov't Code 1126 § 66426 contains a typical list of exemptions. They include subdivisions of less than five acres when each parcel fronts on a maintained public street or highway and no dedications or improvements are required; subdivisions with parcels of 20 acres or more that front on a maintained public street or highway; and subdivisions with parcels of 40 acres or more. Exemptions of this kind make it difficult to prevent development in areas prohibited from development in growth management programs. See Chapter 7.

Providing special procedures for minor subdivisions under a certain size, such as eliminating the preliminary plat stage, is another possibility. Condominiums are usually held not to be subdivisions but some subdivision control statutes include them.

3. *Vested rights.* The subdivision approval process can be long and time-consuming. At what stage in this process does the right to develop vest? A mere recording of the subdivision plat without a street dedication is not enough. *In re McCormick Mgt. Co.,* 547 A.2d 1319 (Vt. 1988). Neither is an approval of the preliminary plat, when the statute is silent on the effect of an approval. *Boutet v. Planning Bd.,* 253 A.2d 53 (Me. 1969). Substantial expenditure may be required.

Some states require approval of the final plat if it meets the requirements imposed on the approval of the preliminary plat. Cal. Gov't Code § 66458. The approval of the final plat may then become a judicially enforceable ministerial act. *Youngblood v. Board of Supvrs.,* 586 P.2d 556 (Cal. 1979). Other states protect a finally approved subdivision for a period of time against subsequent changes in zoning and other land use regulations. See Pa. Stat. Ann. tit. 53, § 10508(4) (protection applies from time application filed). What does all this indicate about the risks and uncertainties of the subdivision approval process? What risks does a subdivider face? What changes would you recommend in subdivision enabling legislation?

4. *Variances.* The subdivision control statute may authorize variances. N.J. Stat. Ann. § 40:55D-51(a). See *South E. Prop. Owners & Residents Ass'n v. City Plan Comm'n,* 244 A.2d 394 (Conn. 1968) (statutory authority required). The criteria are similar to those applicable to zoning variances. There has been little case law, but see *Baum v. Lunsford,* 365 S.E.2d 739 (Va. 1988) (assumed subdivision variance requires lesser proof than zoning variance and held variance may not be granted to prevent financial loss).

5. *Evasion and enforcement.* Evasion is possible for the small developer who wishes to build on one lot at a time. Even the developer of a large residential subdivision can evade the ordinance by conveying through a metes and bounds boundary description. The Connecticut statute, *supra,* attempts to avoid this problem by prohibiting subdivision unless the subdivision plat has been approved. Note the indirect sanction in the Standard Act, § 16. The Act authorizes a monetary penalty when land is sold "by reference to or exhibition" of a plat if the subdivision is not approved. Why this language?

A number of other alternatives to prevent evasion are possible:

(a) The statute provides that "no lands shall be conveyed" until the subdivision plat is "approved and recorded." See *Kass v. Lewin,* 104 So. 2d 572 (Fla. 1958) (held unconstitutional as a restraint on alienation).

(b) The statute authorizes the denial of a building permit for buildings in unapproved subdivisions. But see *Keizer v. Adams,* 471 P.2d 938 (Cal. 1970) (may not withhold permit from innocent purchaser). Compare Wash. Rev. Code Ann. § 58.17.210 (grantee has option to void deed).

(c) The statute prohibits the issuance of a building permit except on a lot abutting a street suitably improved to the satisfaction of the municipality. See *Brous v. Smith,* 106 N.E.2d 503 (N.Y. 1952) (upheld). Why might this remedy be effective?

(d) The statute authorizes an injunction against the sale of lots in an unapproved subdivision. N.Y. Town Law § 268(2). See also *Lake County v. Truitt,* 758 S.W.2d 529 (Tenn. App. 1988) (court enjoined selling of lots in unapproved subdivision but did not order subdivider to bring subdivision into compliance).

Which of these remedies do you prefer? Why? See Note, *Prevention of Subdivision Control Evasion in Indiana,* 40 Ind. L.J. 445 (1965).

A NOTE ON THE SUBDIVISION REVIEW PROCESS

The process of review and negotiation afforded by the subdivision control ordinance creates an entirely different climate for the review of land development proposals than the zoning ordinance. In zoning administration, the outcome of the zoning process is a decision either permitting or not permitting the use of land proposed by the developer. Such a clear outcome easily triggers a constitutional claim when the development is disallowed. In subdivision control, the planning agency administers a large number of development standards, none of which is sufficiently significant on its own to have a drastic impact on development costs. This fact, the substantial amount of discretion usually built into the administration of the ordinance, and the opportunities for compromise and negotiation in the review process, usually allow for a working out of differences and forestall judicial attacks by developers unhappy with the outcome of a subdivision review.

For example, assume the subdivision ordinance requires a minimum pavement width of 24 feet for local service streets and allows the planning board to require a greater width if "the demands of present or future traffic make it desirable." Assume that the board decides to require a greater width of 26 feet, but after negotiation with the developer reduces the requirement to 25 feet. The developer is unlikely to appeal. Because of the discretion accorded the board in imposing this added requirement, a court decision overturning the additional pavement width is not likely. In addition, the extra cost of the additional pavement is sufficiently marginal from the developer's perspective so that an appeal is not worthwhile. These characteristics of the subdivision control process explain why litigation over subdivision control review is less frequent than litigation over zoning restrictions.

Planners like the process of negotiation and compromise built into subdivision review because it allows them to review proposed subdivisions for assurances on what really interests them — who the developer is, whether it has a good track record in the community, whether it can be depended on to complete the project, and the like. Discretionary standards built into subdivision control ordinances also allow for considerable control in the planning agency over subdivision design, another issue of great interest to planners.

The chart that follows illustrates the subdivision review procedure. The map that follows is a Preliminary Subdivision Layout that shows land contours, other natural features (the circles are large trees), and existing features such as roads. How is this information relevant?

SUGGESTED PROCEDURES FOR SUBDIVISION REVIEW

OPTIONAL PROCEDURES

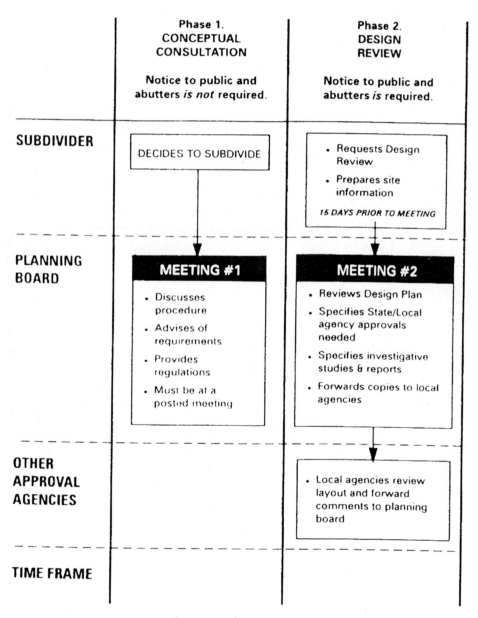

(continued on next page)

SUGGESTED PROCEDURES FOR SUBDIVISION REVIEW
(continued from previous page)

REQUIRED PLAT PROCEDURE

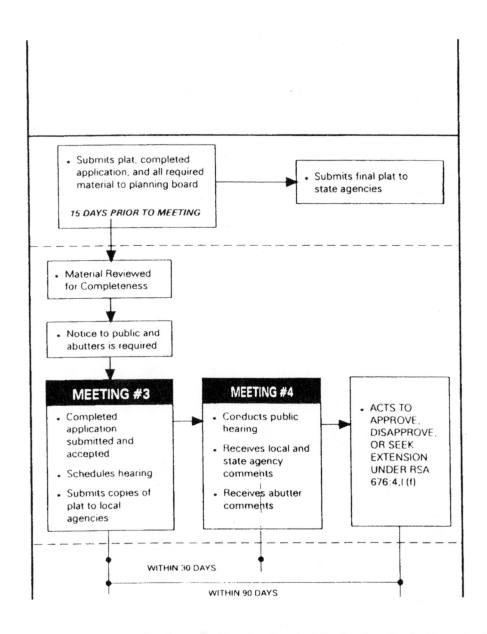

Adapted from "Handbook . . . for Planning Boards & Zoning Boards of Adjustments"
Southern New Hampshire Planning Commission

PRELIMINARY SUBDIVISION LAYOUT

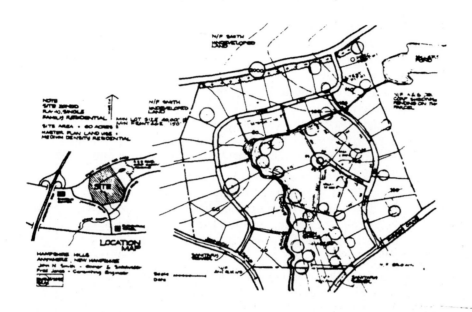

Source: Office of State Planning, State of New Hampshire, Handbook of
Subdivision Practice 26 (1972)

2. SUBSTANTIVE CONTROLS AND REQUIREMENTS

GARIPAY v. TOWN OF HANOVER

116 N.H. 34, 351 A.2d 64 (1976)

GRIFFITH, JUSTICE:

This is an appeal under RSA 36:34 (Supp. 1975) [now codified as
§ 674:36(II) (A) — Eds.] from a decision of the planning board of the town
of Hanover denying plaintiffs' agents' request for preliminary approval of a
subdivision in that town. The issues were submitted to the trial court on an
agreed statement of facts and transferred without ruling by *Johnson, J.* The
planning board's denial of the request for approval of the subdivision was
based on a finding that Hemlock Road, the access road connecting the
proposed subdivision to the main network of town roads, would be inadequate
to handle the increased traffic created by forty-nine new homes. The question
presented to us is whether the planning board is authorized under RSA ch.
36 and the town ordinances to reject a subdivision proposal which intrinsically
conforms to the requirements of the town zoning ordinance and regulations
solely because of the inadequacy of an offsite, town-owned road.

The dangers posed by the inadequacy of Hemlock Road to accommodate
increased traffic demands are discussed at length in the minutes of the
planning board meetings of December 18, 1973, January 8, 1974, and January

15, 1975. The location of the proposed subdivision is on top of a hill to which Hemlock Road provides the only access. This road is described as "narrow, steep and winding, having a width of fourteen to sixteen feet, shoulders only two feet wide, a grade which at times exceeds 15%," and a course which results in "at least one horseshoe curve." Consequently, the planning board found that the road would pose "a serious danger to both pedestrian and vehicular traffic." The town police chief expressed "serious reservations about [his] department being able to respond to an emergency in this area, in the winter-time." There was evidence that in winter the steepness of the road often forces residents to leave their cars at the foot of the hill, and that while the limited available space can accommodate the present vehicles, congestion created by further abandoned cars from the subdivision could cause serious hazards.

The plaintiffs do not contest the accuracy of these findings. Their argument is that the planning board is precluded from considering offsite factors and must limit its investigation to whether the subdivision internally complies with state and town requirements. In our opinion both the state-enabling legislation and the Hanover subdivision regulations provide authority for the board's decision.

RSA 36:21 provides that town planning boards may promulgate regulations which "provide against such scattered or premature subdivision of land as would involve danger or injury to health, safety, or prosperity by reason of the lack of . . . transportation . . . or other public services, or necessitate an excessive expenditure of public funds for the supply of such services." Pursuant to this statute, Hanover has enacted article III (B) of its subdivision regulations, which uses language identical to that quoted above. These provisions plainly empower the planning board to take offsite factors into its consideration, insofar as they render subdivisions "scattered or premature."

The plaintiffs argue that the proposed subdivision cannot be deemed "scattered or premature" because there are already some eighteen homes in the area. Plaintiffs further maintain that such a finding is precluded by language on a map contained in the Hanover master plan, which designates the site "to be developed after 1970." According to this argument once an area is found not to be premature for a particular degree of development, it must be found ripe for all levels of development. In other words, where there are presently some homes in the area, the planning board may not find that an addition of forty-nine homes would be premature, regardless of the amount of public services available.

We reject this interpretation as too narrow, for prematurity is a relative rather than an absolute concept. The statute, by defining a "scattered and premature" development as one which poses a danger to the public through insufficiency of services, sets up a guide for the planning board's determination. The board must ascertain what amount of development, in relation to what quantum of services available, will present the hazard described in the statute and regulations. At the point where such a hazard is created, further development becomes premature. Thus in the instant case, although the available services suffice to meet the need of the present eighteen homes, when an additional forty-nine homes will endanger the well-being of residents both within and contiguous to the development, the statute and regulations authorize the planning board to find the subdivision premature. Thus the action of the Hanover Planning Board was within its statutory mandate.

Case law in other jurisdictions recognizes that absent specific statutory authority a planning board is authorized to reject a proposed subdivision because of an inadequate offsite access road under a general statutory mandate such as that found in RSA 36:21 "[Planning board regulations] generally may include provisions which will tend to create conditions favorable to health, safety, convenience, or prosperity." *Mtr. of Pearson Kent Corp. v. Bear,* 271 N.E.2d 218 (N.Y. 1971). "Subdivision controls are imposed on the supportable premise that a new subdivision is not an island, but an integral part of the whole community which must mesh efficiently with the municipal pattern of streets, sewers, water lines and other installations which provide essential services and vehicular access. . . . [O]ffsite circumstances may be considered by the reviewing board, and may provide the basis for denying approval of a plat." 3 R. Anderson, American Law of Zoning § 19.36 (1968).

Appeal dismissed.

BAKER v. PLANNING BOARD

353 Mass. 141, 228 N.E.2d 831 (1967)

KIRK, JUSTICE:

In the Superior Court the judge entered a decree that the planning board of Framingham (the board) had exceeded its authority in disapproving the definitive plan for the subdivision of approximately eleven acres of land owned by the plaintiff (Baker). The decree annulled the decision of the board and directed that it promptly take further proceedings under the subdivision control law consistent with the applicable statutes and the decree. The board's appeal brings the case to us.

. . . The only questions presented . . . are (1) whether the findings of the master are contradictory, mutually inconsistent or plainly wrong, and (2) whether the decree is within the scope of the pleadings and supported by the facts found.

We summarize the admissions made in the pleadings and the facts found by the master which, in light of the standard of review and the arguments made, are pertinent to the issues to be resolved. In December, 1934, Baker and her husband granted to the town by recorded deed an easement (ten feet wide), through land owned by them, for the purpose of constructing and maintaining a pipe drain or excavating and maintaining a ditch of "sufficient depth to permit without interruption the flow of surface water and drainage" through the Baker land. The town excavated a ditch which received water accumulating on Brook Street and channeled the water across Baker's land to land of another where it entered a fifteen inch drain controlled by the town, and thence was carried to the Sudbury River. Because of the development of land in the area since the easement was granted, including the construction of a church with a large paved parking lot, the volume of water now accumulating on Brook Street during heavy rainstorms has greatly increased. The ditch

Taking?

cannot carry off the increased volume of water to the drain pipe on the adjoining land, and the drain pipe, in turn, cannot carry away the water which is collected in and over the ditch. The result is that the Baker land becomes flooded for a considerable area on both sides of the ditch, and the land consequently serves as a flood control or "retention area" for the town, to the extent of 16,200 cubic feet of water, during and after heavy rains and thaws.

Baker's definitive plan was submitted on February 26, 1965. A preliminary plan had been submitted earlier. The board of health approved the definitive plan. G.L. c. 41, §§ 81M, 81U. The planning board did not modify the definitive plan but, by majority vote, disapproved it and stated its reasons. G.L. c. 41, § 81U. In summary, the board's reasons for disapproval relate to the sewerage and water drainage systems proposed in the definitive plan. The sewerage system would require the construction and maintenance of a lift or pumping station to tie in with the town's sewerage system, whereas the board favored a gravity system which would not require a lift station. The proposed water drainage system, although adequate for the subdivision, would deprive the town of the retention area on Baker's land and, in consequence, would overtax the downstream drainage system outside the subdivision. The board stated that neither the preliminary nor the definitive plan, as submitted, delineated the town's drainage easement across the Baker land. The board disapproved on the additional ground that "[a]pproval . . . would not be in the best interest of the Town, since it would negate the PURPOSE of section 81-M" . . . [of the subdivision control enabling act which makes] special reference to ". . . securing safety in cases of . . . flood, . . . securing adequate provision for water, sewerage, drainage and other requirements where necessary in a subdivision."

Additional findings by the master were that the majority of the board believed that they were justified in disapproving the plan because of the additional expense which the town would incur by the enlargement of the town's drainage system to compensate for the loss of use of the Baker land as a water retention area, and by the construction and maintenance of the lift station for the sewerage system. The plan with respect to the sewerage and drainage systems for the subdivision met all of the requirements of the statutes and of the rules and regulations of the board. The town already operates several lift or pumping stations in its sewerage system. The omission from the plans of the town's easement across Baker's land did not deceive and was not intended to deceive the board, but was the result of an understanding between the town engineer and Baker's engineer that the town probably would reroute its drainage system through pipes on one of the streets shown on the plans.

The master's ultimate finding was that the board "had but a single reason for disapproving the . . . [definitive] plan, namely, the extra cost to the Town of handling the sewage and surface drainage produced by the subdivision." We think that the ultimate finding of the master cannot be said to be plainly wrong and that his subsidiary findings are consistent with it.

The decree based on the master's report was right. Our decisions dealing with the powers of planning boards as clarified by G.L. c. 41 § 81M, hold that, having exercised due regard for insuring compliance with the applicable zoning by-law, approval under § 81U should be given to a plan if it complies with the recommendations of the board of health and the reasonable rules and regulations of the planning board.* The zoning by-law is not an issue; the board of health has given its approval; there is no violation of, or failure to comply with, existing rules and regulations. Obviously a planning board may not exercise its authority to disapprove a plan so that a town may continue to use the owner's land as a water storage area and thereby deprive the owner of reasonable use of it. The board's action appears to be based on the assumption that it may disapprove a plan when it considers that "the best interest of the Town" or "the public interest" would be served by the disapproval of installations which meet the established requirements. This is an erroneous assumption . . . . It was beyond the board's authority to disapprove the plan.

Decree affirmed.

---

* Section 81U states that "the planning board shall approve, or, if such plan does not comply with the subdivision control law or the rules and regulations of the planning board or the recommendations of the health board or officer, shall modify and approve or shall disapprove such plan." — Eds.

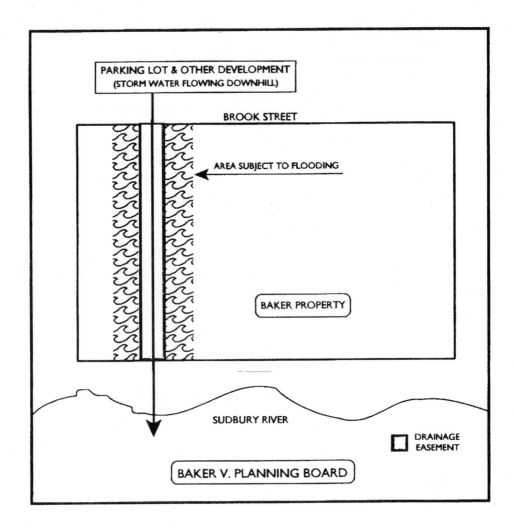

NOTES AND QUESTIONS

1. *The scope of controls.* Both *Baker* and *Garipay* raise questions about the use of subdivision control to monitor growth within the community, and the validity of denying subdivision approval on the basis of conditions not intrinsic to the subdivision. Would the planning commission in *Garipay* have been within the scope of its authority if the New Hampshire statute had not specifically prohibited the "scattered or premature subdivision of land"?

In *Pearson Kent Corp. v. Bear,* 271 N.E.2d 218 (N.Y. 1971), "[t]he [planning] commission denied petitioner's development approval, not because it regarded the plan itself as intrinsically not acceptable but because the project was so located as to create danger to nearby residents in the inadequate approaches to the development from the greatly increased demands to be exerted on the existing approaches." *Id.* at 219. In a brief opinion, the court noted that while the local charter and subdivision control law were "addressed to approval or disapproval internal to the subdivision" the commission was not prevented from considering "the impact of the proposed development on adjacent territory and property within its jurisdiction. . . . These matters are the routine functions of the commission." *Ibid.*

Do these holdings improperly give control over new subdivisions to municipalities through the power to withhold improvements to off-site public facilities? If the developer because of these decisions is forced to make off-site improvements, is this a valid exercise of the subdivision control power? Was this the vice of the *Baker* case? In *North Landers Corp. v. Planning Bd.*, 416 N.E.2d 934 (Mass. 1981), the court said that all courts were in agreement "that the condition of adjacent public ways must be considered in the board's deliberations."

The present version of the statute considered in *Garipay* authorizes a prematurity determination based on a lack of a number of facilities, including water supply, fire protection and schools. N.H. Rev. Stat. § 674:36(II)(A). Despite the statutory language, the court invalidated a prematurity denial based on inadequate schools in *Ettlingen Homes v. Town of Derry*, 681 A.2d 97 (N.H. 1996). It held the authority conferred by the statute was exceeded because the decision "plainly was taken to control growth." Chapter 7 discusses ordinances that authorize the denial of development approval when public facilities are inadequate.

When a municipality disapproves a subdivision because of on-site problems, the disapproval usually is upheld. In *Hamilton v. Planning Bd.*, 343 N.E.2d 906 (Mass. App. 1976), the court upheld a disapproval because of a failure to remedy flooding problems by providing adequate drainage on the subdivision site. The court distinguished the case

> from those in which a planning board had disapproved a plan adequate for the proposed subdivision solely because it would overtax existing municipal facilities or otherwise adversely affect the public interest. [*Id.* at 907, citing *Baker*.]

See also *Durant v. Town of Dumbarton*, 430 A.2d 140 (N.H. 1981) (upholding disapproval based partly on potential problems with subsurface septic systems).

2. *Design and access issues.* These pose much less of a problem since they relate directly to the subdivision. In fact, the adequacy of the subdivider's plans for streets and highways is an important factor in the review process. Planning commissions will often require, as a condition to subdivision approval, that internal streets be of sufficient width and satisfactory design, and that access be adequate.

In *Forest Constr. Co. v. Planning & Zoning Comm'n*, 236 A.2d 917 (Conn. 1967), a subdivision was denied approval because only one access was provided for 110 lots, thereby causing all traffic from the subdivision to be discharged at one intersection. The denial was found to be within the commission's authority to reject applications for development that would be hazardous to the health and welfare of the community. See also *Burke & McCaffrey, Inc. v. City of Merriam*, 424 P.2d 483 (Kan. 1967) (upholding denial of subdivision because of plan's cul-de-sac design); *Isabelle v. Town of Newbury*, 321 A.2d

570 (N.H. 1974) (upholding denial of subdivision because lot ownership pattern jeopardized access in case of fire).

✓ **3.** *Authority to deny or approve.* As *Baker* indicates, statutory authority questions can be serious in subdivision control cases. Subdivision control legislation is much more specific than zoning legislation, and does not provide the broad grants of authority that often allow courts to take a lenient view of scope of authority problems in zoning cases. Lack of statutory authority has limited the use of subdivision control as a basis for disapproving subdivisions because they impose an excessive burden on schools or other public facilities. *Beach v. Planning & Zoning Comm'n,* 103 A.2d 814 (Conn. 1954).

Recall that the Standard Act and most state acts require the planning commission to adopt subdivision regulations. The general enabling authority in the subdivision acts requires the commission to spell out in more detail the criteria for subdivision review. A court may hold that a municipality may not rely on the general purposes of a land use law as the basis for disapproving a subdivision but must base disapprovals on standards contained in the subdivision ordinance. See *Pizzo Mantin Group v. Township of Randolph,* 645 A.2d 89 (N.J. 1994).

Courts will reverse a subdivision denial if it is based on a reason not authorized by the statute or the subdivision regulations. See *Richardson v. City of Little Rock Planning Comm'n,* 747 S.W.2d 116, 117 (Ark. 1988) (statute did not authorize denial for "marginal development potential" because of unusual lot shapes and means for access); *Interladco, Inc. v. Billings,* 538 P.2d 496 (Colo. Ct. App. 1975) (county "did not want a development of single-family residences isolated from other developed urban areas"). Compare *Garipay.* Are these cases consistent? See also *Smith v. City of Mobile,* 374 So. 2d 305 (Ala. 1979) (may not disapprove subdivision because it was "out of character" with other lots in area), and *Hixon v. Walker County,* 468 S.E.2d 744 (Ga. 1996) (may not base disapproval on statement of purpose to protect character and social and economic stability of county).

A court can also hold that the factual record does not support the subdivision disapproval. See *Christopher Estates, Inc. v. Parish of E. Baton Rouge,* 413 So. 2d 1336 (La. App. 1982) (no proof that smaller lots in subdivision would lower property values in neighborhood). Nor may a delay in the disapproval decision help. *Norco Constr. Inc. v. King County,* 649 P.2d 103 (Wash. 1982) (county could not delay decision beyond ninety-day decision period because subdivision not in compliance with proposed plan and zoning ordinance).

Why not just put the actual criteria in the subdivision control regulations? Would there then be a problem with court approval? For example, would a court uphold a standard authorizing the disapproval of a subdivision if the development potential is marginal, as in the *Richardson* case, *supra?* In *Richardson,* the site was steep and making the Board's changes would have reduced the number of lots from 15 to 12, for which the developer "stood to lose $100,000 to $150,000." 747 S.W.2d at 119 (dissenting opinion). Do you suppose that neighborhood opposition is often a factor in subdivision disapproval in the cases cited in this Note?

Kaufman v. Planning & Zoning Comm'n, 298 S.E.2d 148 (W. Va. 1982), illustrates these problems. The commission disapproved a subdivision for subsidized housing in a decision that considered property depreciation, the project's "rental nature, [and] the economic class of the proposed occupants." The court held these factors unauthorized by a statute authorizing consideration of the harmonious development of the community, which it held too vague in the absence of more specific regulations. See Reynolds, *Local Subdivision Regulations: Formulaic Constraints in an Age of Discretion,* 24 Ga. L. Rev. 525 (1990).

4. *Zoning and the comprehensive plan.* The potential overlap between subdivision control and zoning is clear. Some subdivision statutes require compliance with the zoning ordinance. N.J. Stat. Ann. § 40:55D-38(b) (1). Can the subdivision control ordinance also include regulations commonly found in zoning ordinances? In *Town of Sun Prairie v. Storms,* 327 N.W.2d 642 (Wis. 1983), the court held that the subdivision statute authorized a minimum lot size requirement and then held that this requirement was properly adopted as a subdivision control:

> [Z]oning and subdividing are complementary land planning devises. Subdivision control is concerned with the initial division of undeveloped land, while zoning more specifically regulates the further use of the land. [*Id.* at 646–47.]

Do you agree? Why have a minimum lot size requirement in both ordinances? A municipality may reject a subdivision because it does not comply with the zoning ordinance, *Krawski v. Planning & Zoning Comm'n,* 575 A.2d 1036 (Conn. App. 1990), and may require zoning compliance in its subdivision control ordinance, *Benny v. City of Alameda,* 164 Cal. Rptr. 776 (Cal. App. 1980). How do these limitations affect the exercise of discretion in subdivision review?

The Standard Act required the adoption of a master street plan before a subdivision ordinance could be adopted. Some states go further and require consistency with the local comprehensive plan. Cal. Gov't Code § 66474(a). *Board of County Comm'rs v. Ghaster,* 401 A.2d 666 (Md. 1979), held that the board could disapprove a subdivision not consistent with a comprehensive plan even though the subdivision complied with the zoning ordinance. Other statutes go further and require subdivisions to be consistent with the local comprehensive plan. E.g., Cal. Gov't Code §66474(a). See *Lake City Corp. v. City of Mequon,* 558 N.W.2d 100 (Wis. 1997). What kind of policies on new development should a plan contain?

5. *Who pays?* Lurking behind some of these cases is an attempt by municipalities to manipulate the subdivision control process by forcing developers to provide services and facilities not properly chargeable to the subdivision. Courts have held that the developer cannot be forced to resolve problems common to the community for which it is not responsible. In *Baltimore Plan Comm'n v. Victor Dev. Co.,* 275 A.2d 478 (Md. 1971), the court held that the commission could not reject the subdivision on the ground that the occupancy of apartments proposed for the subdivision would create an increase in the local population, which would in turn cause the public schools to be overcrowded.

In *Florham Park Inv. Assocs. v. Planning Bd.,* 224 A.2d 352 (N.J. L. Div. 1966), the municipality denied approval of a subdivision because the later construction of a planned highway across the subdivision would make lots in the subdivision substandard as defined by local regulations. The court reversed, noting that "[t]o deprive plaintiff of the right to use and improve its property for an indefinite time, while awaiting the final action of a third party which may come in one year or ten or never, is arbitrary and unreasonable." *Id.* at 356. The court placed some weight on the indefinite nature of the highway agency's plans for the highway. What if the route were permanently fixed and known? Would this be a reason for denial? See also *Divan Bldrs., Inc. v. Planning Bd.*, 300 A.2d 883 (N.J. L. Div. 1973) (developer could not be made to contribute to construction cost of off-site municipal drainage system as condition to subdivision approval). On the question of whether municipalities may condition development approval on the availability of municipal facilities and services, see Chapter 7.

B.   DEDICATIONS, EXACTIONS, AND IMPACT FEES

Exactions require that developers provide, or pay for, some public facility or other amenity as a condition for receiving permission for a land use that the local government could otherwise prohibit. [Been, *Exit as a Constraint on Land Use Exactions: Rethinking the Unconstitutional Conditions Doctrine*, 91 Colum. L. Rev. 473, 478–79 (1991).]

Supreme Court taking decisions have made exactions a major battleground in land use law. Exactions started quite simply. Communities asked developers only to provide streets and other internal improvements, which are facilities required by new developments. Exactions requirements soon expanded. Communities saw they could use the subdivision control process to provide for parks and schools, so park and school dedications were added. Developers were also asked to dedicate land or make cash payments for adjacent street widenings and for off-site facilities, such as sewage and drainage facilities, that served the subdivision. Cash payments are sometimes called in-lieu fees. A community may require a fee, for example, when a residential development creates a need for additional recreation space, but there is no land within the development that can be dedicated for this purpose.

Another form of exaction is levied outside the subdivision control process as an impact fee. The fee is usually collected at the time the building permit is issued and is used to construct or improve off-site facilities, such as water and sewage facilities.

Exactions are even more important in an age of municipal financial austerity. In California, after voter adoption of Proposition 13 amended the constitution to drastically limit local property taxes, municipalities turned to impact fees to make up the revenue shortfall. Fee increases have been substantial. Rapid growth has stimulated the widespread use of impact fees on new development in Florida. Exactions in Florida are now tied to a mandatory planning process.

All of this activity has led to substantial increases in the amount of exactions and their percentage of the value of a home. Impact fees as high as $25,000 or more are common in some areas. This, in turn, has also led to developer protests when they believe exactions are too high. Developers believe that the legality of exactions is one of the most important legal issues in land use controls.

Although exactions and impact fees are, in one sense, a land use control, they also raise critical questions about public responsibility for public services. Who should pay? The taxpayers, through general revenues, or new development through exactions and impact fees? Note also the equity problems. Do exactions and impact fees make an inequitable distinction between old and new residents? Between rich and poor? These questions concerning the distribution of fiscal responsibility for municipal services should be kept in mind when reviewing the materials in this section.

1. THE TAKINGS CLAUSE AND THE NEXUS TEST

The takings clause is the legal crucible in which the legality of subdivision exactions is tested. State courts traditionally had tested the validity of exactions under a nexus test: a relationship between the exaction and some need for public facilities created by the subdivision had to be shown. For example, if a new subdivision reduced service levels by causing congestion on an adjacent road, a dedication of subdivision land to widen the road could be required.

The Supreme Court's decisions in *Nollan* and *Dolan v. City of Tigard*, 512 U.S. 374 (1994), substantially changed the law of exactions because Supreme Court cases apply, of course, in state courts and override state land development policies. However, recognizing that "state courts have been dealing with this question a good deal longer than we have," 512 U.S. at 389, Chief Justice Rehnquist in *Dolan* provided a useful summary of the different approaches taken by various states, with which we begin:

> In some States, very generalized statements as to the necessary connection between the required dedication and the proposed development seem to suffice. See, e.g., *Billings Properties, Inc. v. Yellowstone County*, 394 P. 2d 182 (Mont. 1964); *Jenad, Inc. v. Scarsdale*, 218 N.E.2d 673 (N.Y. 1966). We think this standard is too lax to adequately protect petitioner's right to just compensation if her property is taken for a public purpose.
>
> Other state courts require a very exacting correspondence, described as the "specifi[c] and uniquely attributable" test. The Supreme Court of Illinois first developed this test in *Pioneer Trust & Savings Bank v. Mount Prospect*, 176 N. E. 2d 799, 802 (1961). Under this standard, if the local government cannot demonstrate that its exaction is directly proportional to the specifically created need, the exaction becomes "a veiled exercise of the power of eminent domain and a confiscation of private property behind the defense of police regulations." *Id.*, at 802. We do not think the Federal Constitution requires such exacting scrutiny, given the nature of the interests involved.
>
> A number of state courts have taken an intermediate position, requiring the municipality to show a "reasonable relationship" between the required dedication and the impact of the proposed development. Typical is the Supreme Court of Nebraska's opinion in *Simpson*

v. North Platte, 292 N.W.2d 297, 301 (1980), where that court stated: "The distinction, therefore, which must be made between an appropriate exercise of the police power and an improper exercise of eminent domain is whether the requirement has some reasonable relationship or nexus to the use to which the property is being made or is merely being used as an excuse for taking property simply because at that particular moment the landowner is asking the city for some license or permit." Thus, the court held that a city may not require a property owner to dedicate private property for some future public use as a condition of obtaining a building permit when such future use is not "occasioned by the construction sought to be permitted." *Id.,* at 302.

Some form of the reasonable relationship test has been adopted in many other jurisdictions. [citing cases]. [512 U.S. at 389–90.]

Reread or refresh your memory of the *Nollan* case, reproduced in Ch. 2. *Nollan* reaffirmed the nexus test but indicated courts should apply it more stringently. The next case is a post-*Nollan* case that applies the nexus test to a street widening exaction. Although this case is not a subdivision control case, the court treats the subdivision exaction decisions as controlling.

ROHN v. CITY OF VISALIA

214 Cal. App. 3d 1463, 263 Cal. Rptr. 319 (1989)

BAXTER, ASSOCIATE JUSTICE:

Introduction

We are called upon to determine whether the City of Visalia may condition approval of a site plan review and issuance of a building permit on dedication of 14 percent of respondents' land to correct the alignment of Court Street at its intersection with Tulare Avenue consistent with its general plan. Since there is no reasonable relationship between the dedication condition and the converted use of the property, we affirm the trial court's judgment deleting the condition.

Facts and Proceedings Below

Court Street runs north and south and intersects Tulare Avenue, which runs east and west. The intersection is within the city limits of Visalia. The portion of Court Street south of Tulare Avenue is skewed to the east; it does not line up perfectly with the continuation of Court Street as it crosses Tulare to the north. It appears that this imperfect intersection came into existence during the original planning development of the area.

In 1978, the city amended its general plan and approved the . . . eventual connection of Court and Locust north of Tulare Avenue. The decision was not made based on the projected future use of the adjacent parcels, but because of the general need "to plan for the future growth needs of the City of Visalia." The proposal also included a plan to correct the imperfect alignment of Court

Street at its intersection with Tulare Avenue by curving Court slightly to the west to match the northern corners. The city has not begun work on either the connection or the realignment.

Respondents own real property at the southwest corner of Court Street and Tulare Avenue. A single family residence was on the property and it was zoned for either single or multi-family residences. On May 14, 1985, respondents applied to the city for an amendment to the general plan to change the land use designation from residential to professional administrative offices. The owners intended to convert the house to an office building.

On July 22, 1986, the planning division prepared a report for the Visalia Planning Commission discussing the impact of the conversion. It compared the potential traffic that would be generated by apartments, which could be built without an amendment or zoning change, and by the proposed office building. Two other sites adjoining the property were also considered as potential office buildings. The planning staff determined that the conversion of the three parcels to professional offices would appear "to generate less traffic impact than their development to existing multiple family zoning potential." The report also noted that the proposed Court Street realignment "will necessitate the dedication of additional right-of-way along the northeast corner of the subject property. However, staff does not feel that this will create a constraint on the future conversion of the existing structure." There was no indication that the dedication was required because of increased traffic from the conversion, when the dedication would be demanded, or the exact amount of property that would be required for the dedication. . . .

[The planning commission held hearings on and approved the amendment to the general plan. "A member of the planning staff stated that professional offices would not create any greater traffic than multi-family developments for which the site was already zoned." The existing single family dwelling, known as the McSwain Mansion, was then placed on the historic register. Next the city council held a hearing on the proposed plan amendment and considered an environmental impact report which included a statement that the conversion would not create significant traffic impacts. The council unconditionally adopted the plan amendment. The respondent then applied for a rezoning amendment, which was approved by the Historic Preservation Advisory Board. The city council approved the rezoning on condition that respondents dedicate part of their land for a realignment of Court Street.]

The city staff presented a precise dedication proposal on March 28, 1986. The proposed dedication consists of a triangular piece of land on the east edge of the property. At its widest point, the triangle is approximately 25 feet wide. The entire property is 24,259.6 square feet; the proposed dedication is for 3,401.6 square feet. The proposed dedication represents 14 percent of the entire property. Respondents claim that the land proposed for dedication is worth $25,000. [The planning commission and city council rejected respondent's challenge to the dedication.]. . .

On June 25, 1986, respondents filed a petition in Tulare County Superior Court for a writ of mandamus ordering the city to delete its dedication condition to the issuance of the building permit. On August 2, 1988, the trial court issued its order granting the writ of mandamus. The court determined that the increased traffic flow in the area caused by the professional development was of a "very minuscule nature." The court acknowledged the city's power to require the dedication of land as a condition of development but ruled that . . . there was no reasonable relation between the required dedication and the use for which the building permit was requested.

The city appeals the order granting the writ of mandamus on the [basis] that . . . the dedication was a reasonable requirement of the site plan and building permit due to increased traffic from the conversion. Respondents claim there is no reasonable relationship between the issuance of a building permit and the dedication of 14 percent of their property.

Discussion

May the City Condition Approval of the Site Plan and Issuance of the Building Permit on Respondents' Dedication of the Land for the Realignment of Court Street?

A dedication involves the uncompensated transfer of an interest in private property to a public entity for public use. A regulatory body may constitutionally require a dedication of land as a condition of development, and such a requirement is not viewed as an act of eminent domain.

The government is limited, however, in its power to impose conditional dedications. A grant of public privilege, such as a building permit, may not be conditioned upon the deprivation of constitutional protections. *Scrutton v. County of Sacramento,* 79 Cal. Rptr. 872 (1969). "An arbitrarily conceived exaction will be nullified as a disguised attempt to take private property for public use without resort to eminent domain or as a mask for discriminatory taxation." *Ibid.* If the applicant must donate property for a public use that bears no relationship to the benefit conferred on the applicant or the burden imposed on the public, there is a taking of property. *Remmenga v. California Coastal Com.,* 209 Cal. Rptr. 628 (1985). "Conversely, if there is such a rational relationship, the requirement of dedication of property . . . is a validly imposed condition." *Ibid.*

Any government action, including a dedication requirement, which deprives the owner of all reasonable use of his property amounts to a taking which must be compensated. Where the conditions imposed are not reasonably related to the landowner's proposed use, but are imposed by a public entity to shift the burden of providing the cost of a public benefit to one not responsible, or only remotely or speculatively benefiting from it, there is an unreasonable exercise of police power.

Whether there has been a reasonable exercise of the police power is a question for the court. The relationship between the condition exacted by the public entity and the use proposed by the landowner presents a factual inquiry for the trial court.

An entity may conditionally approve a subdivision map on condition the subdivider dedicate property for streets or parks. Dedications of land for streets, in order to provide reasonable traffic flow for the general welfare of lot owners and the public, is not a taking under the power of eminent domain because it is reasonably related to the increased traffic and other needs of the proposed subdivision. . . .

[The court distinguished an earlier California case, *Associated Home Builders Etc., Inc. v. City of Walnut Creek,* 484 P.2d 606 (Cal. 1971), which had upheld an impact fee for parks.]

Dedications and easements also have been required as a condition of obtaining coastal development permits. In *Liberty v. California Coastal Com., supra,* plaintiff sought to demolish an existing structure and erect a restaurant across from a beach. The California Coastal Commission approved the plan on condition that plaintiff provide adequate parking for the patrons. He was also required to record a deed restriction to provide free parking until 5 p.m. in the restaurant's lot for 30 years to offset the need for public parking near the beach. The area required additional public parking because of an earlier planning failure to require other restaurants to provide sufficient parking. Plaintiff challenged the condition as an abuse of discretion and a taking without just compensation.

The court agreed with the commission's determination that parking was a problem near the beach. While the commission was authorized to require adequate parking for the restaurant, it could not require "a landowner to dedicate property for free public parking far beyond his own land use requirements. . . ."

Conditions imposed on land use applications "are valid if reasonably conceived to fulfill public needs emanating from the landowner's proposed use." *Liberty v. California Coastal Com., supra.* "Various factors are taken into consideration by courts in determining whether in a given situation there is a proper exercise of the police power, in which case, . . ., the landowner must yield 'uncompensated obedience' or whether a governmental exercise of the power of eminent domain is masquerading in the guise of the police power. The determining factor, . . ., is fairness." *Id.* While it was appropriate for the commission to require ample parking for the intended use, it was unfair to go beyond that and require plaintiff to provide free parking for the beach and other restaurants for which sufficient parking had not been originally planned or provided. "The State Commission is here attempting to disguise under the police power its actual exercise of the power of eminent domain. That it cannot do." *Id.* To impose the burden on one property owner to an extent beyond his own use "shifts the government's burden unfairly to a private party." *Ibid.*

The United States Supreme Court recently reviewed the validity of an easement required by the California Coastal Commission as a condition of obtaining a building permit. [The court then discussed the *Nollan* decision and its nexus holding in some detail.]. . .

The disagreement in the instant case is whether there is a sufficient nexus or relationship between the condition imposed and respondents' proposed conversion. The authority relied upon by the city to impose the conditional dedication is section 7429 of its zoning regulations. Section 7429 permits the city to grant the planned development permit on condition the applicant dedicate, among other things, all necessary rights-of-way to widen a bordering or traversing major street to its ultimate width established as the standard for such major street. Section 7429 provides:

> "REQUIRED IMPROVEMENTS. Because of changes which may occur in a local neighborhood *due to increased vehicular traffic generated by facilities requiring a planned development permit,* and upon the principle that *such developments should be required to provide street dedications and improvements proportionate to such increased vehicular traffic,* the following dedications and improvements may be deemed necessary by the Site Plan Review Committee and may be required as a condition to the approval of any site plan. Residential developments should not, however, be required to provide such street facilities for non-related vehicular traffic." (Emphasis added.)

By its terms, the premise of section 7429 is to require developers to provide various street dedications to offset the increased vehicular traffic resulting from the development. The ordinance represents a valid exercise of the police power in requiring developers to compensate for the increased burden placed on local traffic patterns by the influx of additional residents or traffic.

The trial court determined that there was not a reasonable relationship between the condition imposed and the use of the property. The dedication requirement is based on a 1978 amendment to the general plan to alter existing traffic patterns in southeastern Visalia. The underlying purpose was to plan for general future growth needs of the city by providing a thoroughfare between Court and Locust Street. The major part of the plan calls for a curved arterial near Locust Street, which is well north of respondents' property. As part of this general plan amendment, the council also decided to realign Court Street at its intersection with Tulare Avenue, which, as a result of an earlier planning failure, is imperfectly aligned. The plan was not designed because of projections on the future traffic needs of the Court/Tulare area, or its development as a major professional enclave, but as part of the general plan for the growth of the community. The correction of the original imperfect intersection was included as part of the street conversion. [The city staff report, which is discussed *supra,* was then summarized.]. . .

The trial court had substantial evidence from which to conclude that there is no reasonable relationship between the conditional dedication and the proposed use of respondents' property. It is clear that the Court Street realignment was made necessary by an instance of poor planning during the original development of the intersection. There is nothing in the record to indicate that development of professional offices, both on respondents' property and the two adjoining parcels, would generate such "increased vehicular traffic" that respondents should provide street dedications which are clearly not "proportionate to such increased vehicular traffic" pursuant to section 7429 of the zoning regulations. Appellant argues, pursuant to *Associated Home Builders,* that the conditional dedication need not be based on the impact caused by the proposed development. The recreation dedication required by *Walnut Creek,* however, was part of the city's overall plan to offset increased residential development by reserving open spaces for parks that might otherwise succumb to additional development. The court concluded that present and future residents of the subdivision would benefit both directly and indirectly by the existence of parks in settled locations throughout the city.

In the instant case, the conditional dedication resembles the public parking easement required in *Liberty*. The condition is not related to the proposed professional development but is a "means of shifting the burden of providing the cost of a public benefit to another not responsible for or only remotely or speculatively benefiting from it." *Liberty v. California Coastal Com., supra.* The proposed dedication bears absolutely no relationship, either direct or indirect, to the present or future use of the property. The city's attempt to condition the building permit on the dedication of 14 percent of respondents' property is merely an attempt to "disguise under the police power its actual exercise of the power of eminent domain." *Id.* The administrative record indicates that the city purchased the property necessary to proceed with an earlier project to widen Walnut Avenue and intends to purchase additional property to accomplish the Court/Locust connection to the east and west. The way the ultimate dedication requirement evolved is also revealing. It appeared, almost like an afterthought, in the Engineering Department's Site Plan Review: "We could need some additional [right of way] at the cor[ner]. . . ."

Appellant argues that the required nexus exists because respondents' project imposes a greater traffic burden and creates the need for the street widening and realignment. This argument is based on "common sense," which indicates that the proposed conversion will result in an increased traffic flow and therefore contribute to the overall traffic problem. "The change in use imposes a greater traffic burden on the City's streets, and in particular on the streets immediately adjacent to the subject property."

The city contends that as long as there is some nexus, the amount of property required for dedication is unlimited. We need not reach this issue because there is no such nexus between the dedication condition and the alleged traffic burden created by the conversion. Contrary to appellant's contentions, the record disputes that the change in use of the property will impose a significant traffic burden in the area or the city's streets in general. The EIR [Environmental Impact Report — Eds.] concluded that the conversion of the property would impose no significant traffic problems in the area. The planning report acknowledged that conversion of the property, and others in the area, to professional use would decrease the potential that could result if the zoning remained the same and apartments were built. The dedication required by the Site Plan Review was not based on any such traffic problems, but as a means of implementing the 1978 Court/Locust connection and the long-awaited realignment of Court Street at its intersection with Tulare Avenue. The determination of whether a legitimate state interest is being substantially advanced by the dedication condition is "more than a pleading requirement." *Nollan v. California Coastal Com'n.* The record fails to present the required nexus.

Our review of the record indicates that the city viewed the landowners' application for rezoning and site plan review as the "hook" it needed to acquire this property for nothing, even though the reasons for the dedication existed long before the conversion of the McSwain Mansion was proposed. The "hook," however, is unavailable. As in *Nollan,* the city may proceed with its general traffic plan, but if it wants 3,400 square feet of respondents' property for a street project lacking any relation to the proposed conversion, it must pay for it. . . .

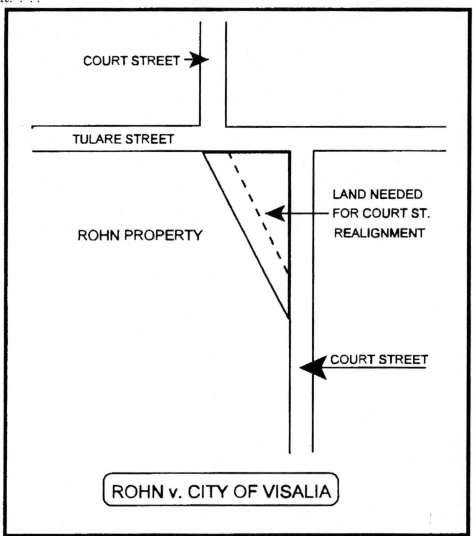

ROHN v. CITY OF VISALIA

NOTES AND QUESTIONS

1. *Defining nexus.* What does the principal case tell us about the nexus test? As this test is sometimes formulated, the dedication must be proportional to the need created by and the benefits conferred on the subdivision. See *Land/ Vest Properties, Inc. v. Town of Plainfield,* 379 A.2d 200 (N.H. 1977). Does the principal case adopt this statement of the test? Why doesn't the general plan provide a nexus? What if the landowner in the principal case owned 20 historic homes on Court Street and planned to convert them to office use? Would that make a difference? Would it make a difference if the conversions increased traffic substantially? Would that justify a dedication for a street widening to improve traffic flow? For a similar case see *Board of Supvrs. v. Fiechter,* 566 A.2d 370 (Pa. Commw. 1989) (partition of 25-acre lot into two lots and its development does not justify dedication of 8 foot of road frontage for adjacent street widening).

Note that the court compares traffic generated by the site after the old house becomes professional offices to traffic *potentially* generated by a totally new multi-family development, as permitted by the zoning. Why not compare present use to proposed use? Is the court saying that conversion to a more intensive use permitted by the ordinance will never justify an exaction?

Does *G. Dunbar, Inc. v. Toledo Plan Comm'n,* 367 N.E.2d 1192 (Ohio App. 1976), help explain the principal case? The city's street plan showed a major highway through a subdivision but the city had not approved a definite right-of-way and had no immediate plans for construction. The court held that the dedication for the highway was unconstitutional, as the city could not require a dedication for a major highway that would serve community needs. The dedication would have covered about one-third of the subdivision. Neither could the dedication be upheld as a freeze on the property. For another pre-*Nollan* case holding a highway dedication invalid see *181 Inc. v. Salem County Planning Bd.,* 336 A.2d 501 (N.J.L. Div. 1975) (development would not burden abutting road with increased traffic). What is the cost-shifting rationale these cases adopt for road dedications?

What about exactions for environmental purposes? See *Leroy Land Dev. v. Tahoe Regional Planning Agency,* 939 F.2d 696 (9th Cir. 1991) (upholding exaction to mitigate environmental impact of development); *Grogan v. Zoning Bd. of Appeals,* 633 N.Y.S.2d 809 (App. Div. 1995) (same; conservation easement required as condition to development of property); *Gardner v. New Jersey Pinelands Comm'n,* 547 A.2d 725 (N.J. Ch. Div. 1988) (upholding exaction restricting housing in agricultural area of Pinelands to agricultural use). Why wasn't there an "environmental" purpose in *Visalia?*

2. *Relationship to development.* As *Visalia* indicates, the nexus test is not satisfied when an exaction is not related to the development. For example, in *Paradyne Corp. v. State Dep't of Transp.,* 528 So. 2d 921 (Fla. App. 1988), the Department required Paradyne to redesign its road connection as a condition to a road connection permit. The Department also required Paradyne to provide joint access across its property for an adjacent property. The court upheld the redesign requirement but not the joint access requirement. Can you see why? See also *Surfside Colony, Ltd. v. California Coastal Comm'n,* 277 Cal. Rptr. 371, (Cal. App. 1991) (invalidating beach access requirement as condition to permission to build revetment because no showing that revetment would cause erosion).

3. *Variations on the nexus test.* As noted by Chief Justice Rehnquist, the Illinois Supreme Court adopted a test for exactions that is more stringent than the "reasonableness" test. It held that a municipality could impose an exaction on a developer only if it was "specifically and uniquely attributable" to his activity. *Pioneer Trust & Sav. Bank v. Village of Mount Prospect,* 176 N.E.2d 799 (Ill. 1961). This test has a limited following. See *Aunt Hack Ridge Estates, Inc. v. Planning Comm'n,* 273 A.2d 880 (Conn. 1970) (upholding lot fee for parks). Illinois has now adopted a road improvement impact fee statute codifying the "specifically and uniquely attributable" test. *Northern Illinois Homebuilders Ass'n, Inc. v. County of Du Page,* 649 N.E.2d 384 (Ill. 1995).

Are the "reasonableness" and "nexus" tests the same? Two commentators reviewed the tests the courts apply and concluded "[a]s a matter of dictionary definition, it is difficult to see any differences between them." Kayden & Pollard, *Linkage Ordinances and Traditional Exactions Analysis: The Connection Between Office Development and Housing,* 50 Law & Contemp. Probs. 127, 128 n.3 (1987). Do you agree? The *Surfside* case, *supra,* held that *Nollan* had heightened the judicial review standard for exactions.

4. *Dedications vs. conditions.* In *City of Annapolis v. Waterman,* 745 A.2d 1000 (Md. 2000), the city required a subdivider to set aside one lot for recreational space to be used by residents of the subdivision. The court held this was a condition on the subdivision subject only to regulatory taking tests, and not a dedication subject to the tests for exactions "because the proposed recreational space is not for general public use; it is intended only for the use of those residing within the Parkway development." *Id.* at 1011. See also *Clark v. City of Albany,* 904 P.2d 185 (Ore. App. 1995), where the city imposed a condition requiring a traffic-free area as part of an approval of a site plan for a fast food restaurant. The court held this was a traffic regulation, not a dedication.

Is there a relationship between these cases and cases that always uphold requirements for improvements internal to a subdivision? See *Pima County v. Arizona Title Ins. & Trust Co.,* 565 P.2d 524 (Ariz. App. 1977) (street paving); *Garvin v. Baker,* 59 So. 2d 360 (Fla. 1952) (width of streets).

Compare *Parking Ass'n v. City of Atlanta,* 450 S.E.2d 200 (Ga. 1994). A city ordinance applied to all parking lots of more than 30 spaces in downtown and midtown zoning districts, and required ten percent of the lot to be landscaped and one tree for every eight spaces. The court held the exaction tests did not apply. "Here the city made a legislative determination with regard to many landowners and it simply limited the use the landowners might make of a small portion of their lands. Moreover, the city demonstrated a 'rough proportionality' between the requirements and objectives of the ordinance." *Id.* at 203, n.3 What were the objectives? Does the *Annapolis* test apply?

The Supreme Court denied certiorari, 515 U.S. 1116 (1995), but Justices Thomas and O'Connor dissented from the denial because they believed legislative acts should be subject to the exaction tests. This issue is discussed *infra.*

5. *Small lots.* For very small lots, it is possible a dedication could meet the nexus test yet require the dedication of a substantial portion of the landowner's land. In the principal case, for example, the landowner was required to dedicate 14 percent of the property. Was this important to the decision? The court invalidated a requirement that all developers dedicate 7.5 percent of their land to the community as extortion in *J.E.D. Assocs. v. Town of Atkinson,* 432 A.2d 12 (N.H. 1982), because it was not based on a showing of need.

6. *Dedications in the zoning process.* Courts have also upheld compulsory dedications in the zoning process. In *Bringle v. Board of Supvrs.,* 351 P.2d

765 (Cal. 1960), the court upheld a variance granted on the condition that an easement be dedicated for the widening of a street. The court held that reasonable conditions may be attached to a variance to preserve the purpose and intent of the zoning ordinance. See also *Southern Pac. Co. v. City of Los Angeles,* 51 Cal. Rptr. 197 (Cal. App. 1966) (same; building permit). As in subdivision control, the need for the improvement must be created by the development. *Bethlehem Evangelical Lutheran Church v. City of Lakewood,* 626 P.2d 668 (Colo. 1981) (condition attached to building permit). California now imposes this requirement by statute. Cal. Gov't Code § 65909(a). See also *Mayor & City Council v. Brookeville Tpk. Constr. Co.,* 228 A.2d 263 (Md. 1967) (may impose compulsory dedication when land annexed to municipality).

Some courts do not allow compulsory dedications outside the subdivision control process. *City of Corpus Christi v. Unitarian Church,* 436 S.W.2d 923 (Tex. Civ. App. 1968); *Board of Supvrs. v. Rowe,* 216 S.E.2d 199 (Va. 1975).

7. *Sources.* See A. Altshuler & J Gomez-Ibanez, Regulation for Revenue: The Political Economy of Land Use Exactions (1993); J. Frank, Development Exactions (1987); Cordes, *Legal Limits on Development Exactions: Responding to Nollan and Dolan,* 15 N. Ill. U.L. Rev. 513 (1995); Kayden, *Land-Use Regulations, Rationality, and Judicial Review: The RSVP in the Nollan Invitation,* 23 Urb. Law. 301 (1991); Morgan, *Exactions as Takings: Tactics for Dealing With Dolan,* Land Use L. & Zoning Dig., Vol. 46, No. 9, at 3 (1994); Stroud & Trevarthen, *Defensible Exactions After Nollan v. California Coastal Commission and Dolan v. City of Tigard,* 25 Stetson L. Rev. 719 (1996); Sullivan, *Dolan and Municipal Risk Assessment,* 12 J. Envtl. L. & Litigation 1 (1997).

A NOTE ON THE PRICE EFFECTS OF EXACTIONS: WHO PAYS?

Exactions have price effects on housing markets. Dedications of land or fees are costs to developers they will have to absorb unless they can pass them on. Costs can be passed forward to buyers who purchase dwelling units in a development subject to exactions or backward to landowners who sell land to developers. Costs can also be shared among all three of these market participants.

Several studies have examined the price effects of exactions with inconclusive results. All studies agree that who finally pays for the exaction depends on how competitive the housing and land markets are and the elasticity of supply and demand. Developers will not be able to pass exaction costs on to homebuyers if there is alternative and equally attractive housing in jurisdictions that do not charge exactions. In this situation, developers will have to pass the cost of exactions back to sellers of land by demanding lower prices. Sellers of land can resist price reductions in markets where they have monopoly power because the area has unique features that make it more attractive to consumers. Sellers may also resist price reductions because they do not consider the time-value of money and have a reservation price below which they will not sell.

One study notes that long-run market adjustments may be more important than the ability to set price:

In competitively organized markets, housing prices and developer costs are market-determined. Since under most market conditions they are not price-setters, homebuilders cannot simply factor development fees into their production process in a way that results in a substantially higher price for their finished product. They can, however, reduce their annual production if high fees were to reduce profits substantially below the long term industry standard. . . . [B]uilding starts would decline in high-fee areas and housing demand would eventually exceed the available supply [if builders cannot pass fees backward to sellers of land or forward to buyers]. The excess demand would force prices upward, eventually to levels that restore post-development-fee profits to their pre-fee levels. In the long run, therefore, it is very unlikely that the homebuilding industry will absorb development fees in the form of lower returns. [T. Snyder & M. Stegman, Paying for Growth 106 (1986).]

The conclusion is that the cost of exactions is passed on to consumers of housing. For other studies reaching the same conclusion see Huffman, Nelson, Smith & Stegman, *Who Bears the Burden of Impact Fees?*, 54 J. Am. Plan. Ass'n 49 (1988); Singell & Lillydahl, *An Empirical Examination of the Effect of Impact Fees on the Housing Market,* 66 Land Econ. 82 (1990).

What effect should these studies have on the constitutionality of exactions? Some studies note that exactions provide a windfall to the owners of existing homes because increases in the price of new homes allow owners of existing homes to raise their prices. Should this be considered?

For additional studies of the price incidence of exactions see Downing & McCaleb, *The Economics of Development Exactions,* in Development Exactions 42 (J. Frank & R. Rhodes eds., 1987); Weitz, *Who Pays Infrastructure Benefit Charges: The Builder or the Home Buyer,* in The Changing Structure of Infrastructure Finance, 94 (J. Nicholas ed., 1985); Delaney & Smith, *Development Exactions: Winners and Losers,* 17 Real Estate L.J. 195 (1989). Yinger, *Who Pays for Development Fees?* in Local Government Tax and Land Policies in the United States, ch. 11 (H. Ladd ed., 1998), finds some of the empirical studies flawed, but agrees that the incidence of exactions is likely to fall on sellers of land in many cases.

2. THE "ROUGH PROPORTIONALITY" TEST

DOLAN v. CITY OF TIGARD

512 U.S. 374 (1994).

CHIEF JUSTICE REHNQUIST delivered the opinion of the Court:

Petitioner challenges the decision of the Oregon Supreme Court which held that the city of Tigard could condition the approval of her building permit on the dedication of a portion of her property for flood control and traffic improvements. We granted certiorari to resolve a question left open by our decision in Nollan v. California Coastal Comm'n, of what is the required degree of connection between the exactions imposed by the city and the projected impacts of the proposed development.

I

. . . Petitioner Florence Dolan owns a plumbing and electric supply store located on Main Street in the Central Business District of the city. The store covers approximately 9,700 square feet on the eastern side of a 1.67-acre parcel, which includes a gravel parking lot. Fanno Creek flows through the southwestern corner of the lot and along its western boundary. The year-round flow of the creek renders the area within the creek's 100-year floodplain virtually unusable for commercial development. The city's comprehensive plan includes the Fanno Creek floodplain as part of the city's greenway system.

Petitioner applied to the city for a permit to redevelop the site. Her proposed plans called for nearly doubling the size of the store to 17,600 square feet, and paving a 39-space parking lot. The existing store, located on the opposite side of the parcel, would be razed in sections as construction progressed on the new building. In the second phase of the project, petitioner proposed to build an additional structure on the northeast side of the site for complementary businesses, and to provide more parking. The proposed expansion and intensified use are consistent with the city's zoning scheme in the Central Business District.

The City Planning Commission granted petitioner's permit application subject to conditions imposed by the city's CDC [the Community Development Code, required by Oregon's comprehensive land use management statute]. The CDC establishes the following standard for site development review approval: "Where landfill and/or development is allowed within and adjacent to the 100-year floodplain, the city shall require the dedication of sufficient open land area for greenway adjoining and within the floodplain. This area shall include portions at a suitable elevation for the construction of a pedestrian/bicycle pathway within the floodplain in accordance with the adopted pedestrian/bicycle plan." . . . The dedication required by that condition encompasses approximately 7,000 square feet, or roughly 10% of the property. In accordance with city practice, petitioner could rely on the dedicated property to meet the 15% open space and landscaping requirement mandated by the city's zoning scheme. The city would bear the cost of maintaining a landscaped buffer between the dedicated area and the new store. . . .

[Dolan's challenge to the conditions was unsuccessful in state administrative and judicial proceedings.]

II

The Takings Clause of the Fifth Amendment of the United States Constitution, made applicable to the States through the Fourteenth Amendment, *Chicago, B. & Q. R. Co. v. Chicago*, 166 U.S. 226, 239 (1897), provides: "[N]or shall private property be taken for public use, without just compensation."[5]

---

[5] Justice Stevens' dissent suggests that this case is actually grounded in "substantive" due process, rather than in the view that the Takings Clause of the Fifth Amendment was made

One of the principal purposes of the Takings Clause is "to bar government from forcing some people alone to bear public burdens which, in all fairness and justice, should be borne by the public as a whole." *Armstrong v. United States*, 364 U.S. 40, 49 (1960). Without question, had the city simply required petitioner to dedicate a strip of land along Fanno Creek for public use, rather than conditioning the grant of her permit to redevelop her property on such a dedication, a taking would have occurred. *Nollan, supra*, at 831. Such public access would deprive petitioner of the right to exclude others, "one of the most essential sticks in the bundle of rights that are commonly characterized as property." *Kaiser Aetna v. United States*, 444 U.S. 164, 176 (1979).

On the other side of the ledger, the authority of state and local governments to engage in land use planning has been sustained against constitutional challenge as long ago as our decision in *Euclid v. Ambler Realty Co.*, 272 U.S. 365 (1926). "Government hardly could go on if to some extent values incident to property could not be diminished without paying for every such change in the general law." *Pennsylvania Coal Co. v. Mahon*, 260 U.S. 393, 413 (1922). A land use regulation does not effect a taking if it "substantially advance[s] legitimate state interests" and does not "den[y] an owner economically viable use of his land." *Agins v. Tiburon*, 447 U.S. 255, 260 (1980).[6]

The sort of land use regulations discussed in the cases just cited, however, differ in two relevant particulars from the present case. First, they involved essentially legislative determinations classifying entire areas of the city, whereas here the city made an adjudicative decision to condition petitioner's application for a building permit on an individual parcel. Second, the conditions imposed were not simply a limitation on the use petitioner might make of her own parcel, but a requirement that she deed portions of the property to the city. In *Nollan, supra*, we held that governmental authority to exact such a condition was circumscribed by the Fifth and Fourteenth Amendments. Under the well-settled doctrine of "unconstitutional conditions," the government may not require a person to give up a constitutional right—here the right to receive just compensation when property is taken for a public use—in exchange for a discretionary benefit conferred by the government where the property sought has little or no relationship to the benefit. See *Perry v. Sindermann*, 408 U.S. 593 (1972); *Pickering v. Board of Ed. of Township High School Dist.*, 391 U.S. 563, 568 (1968).

Petitioner contends that the city has forced her to choose between the building permit and her right under the Fifth Amendment to just compensation for the public easements. Petitioner does not quarrel with the city's authority to exact some forms of dedication as a condition for the grant of a building permit, but challenges the showing made by the city to justify these exactions. She argues that the city has identified "no special benefits"

---

applicable to the States through the Fourteenth Amendment. But there is no doubt that later cases have held that the Fourteenth Amendment does make the Takings Clause of the Fifth Amendment applicable to the States, [citing Penn Central and Nollan]. Nor is there any doubt that these cases have relied upon Chicago, B. & Q. R. Co. v. Chicago, 166 U.S. 226 (1897), to reach that result. . . .

[6] There can be no argument that the permit conditions would deprive petitioner "economically beneficial us[e]" of her property as she currently operates a retail store on the lot. Petitioner assuredly is able to derive some economic use from her property.

conferred on her, and has not identified any "special quantifiable burdens" created by her new store that would justify the particular dedications required from her which are not required from the public at large.

III

In evaluating petitioner's claim, we must first determine whether the "essential nexus" exists between the "legitimate state interest" and the permit condition exacted by the city. *Nollan*, 483 U.S., at 837. If we find that a nexus exists, we must then decide the required degree of connection between the exactions and the projected impact of the proposed development. We were not required to reach this question in *Nollan*, because we concluded that the connection did not meet even the loosest standard. Here, however, we must decide this question.

A

We addressed the essential nexus question in *Nollan*. [The Court described the "nexus" analysis of *Nollan*.] . . . The absence of a nexus left the Coastal Commission in the position of simply trying to obtain an easement through gimmickry, which converted a valid regulation of land use into "an out-and-out plan of extortion." *Ibid*, quoting *J. E. D. Associates, Inc. v. Atkinson*, 432 A. 2d 12, 14–15 (N.H. 1981).

No such gimmicks are associated with the permit conditions imposed by the city in this case. Undoubtedly, the prevention of flooding along Fanno Creek and the reduction of traffic congestion in the Central Business District qualify as the type of legitimate public purposes we have upheld. It seems equally obvious that a nexus exists between preventing flooding along Fanno Creek and limiting development within the creek's 100-year floodplain. Petitioner proposes to double the size of her retail store and to pave her now-gravel parking lot, thereby expanding the impervious surface on the property and increasing the amount of stormwater run-off into Fanno Creek.

The same may be said for the city's attempt to reduce traffic congestion by providing for alternative means of transportation. In theory, a pedestrian/ bicycle pathway provides a useful alternative means of transportation for workers and shoppers: "Pedestrians and bicyclists occupying dedicated spaces for walking and/or bicycling . . . remove potential vehicles from streets, resulting in an overall improvement in total transportation system flow." A. Nelson, *Public Provision of Pedestrian and Bicycle Access Ways: Public Policy Rationale and the Nature of Private Benefits* 11, Center for Planning Development, Georgia Institute of Technology, Working Paper Series (Jan. 1994). See also, Intermodal Surface Transportation Efficiency Act of 1991, Pub. L. 102–240, 105 Stat. 1914; (recognizing pedestrian and bicycle facilities as necessary components of any strategy to reduce traffic congestion).

B

The second part of our analysis requires us to determine whether the degree of the exactions demanded by the city's permit conditions bear the required relationship to the projected impact of petitioner's proposed development. *Nolan*, supra, at 834, quoting *Penn Central*, 438 U.S. 104, 127 (1978) ("'[A] use restriction may constitute a taking if not reasonably necessary to the effectuation of a substantial government purpose'"). Here the Oregon Supreme Court deferred to what it termed the "city's unchallenged factual findings" supporting the dedication conditions and found them to be reasonably related to the impact of the expansion of petitioner's business.

The city required that petitioner dedicate "to the city as Greenway all portions of the site that fall within the existing 100-year floodplain [of Fanno Creek] . . . and all property 15 feet above [the floodplain] boundary." In addition, the city demanded that the retail store be designed so as not to intrude into the greenway area. The city relies on the Commission's rather tentative findings that increased stormwater flow from petitioner's property "can only add to the public need to manage the [floodplain] for drainage purposes" to support its conclusion that the "requirement of dedication of the floodplain area on the site is related to the applicant's plan to intensify development on the site."

The city made the following specific findings relevant to the pedestrian/ bicycle pathway: "In addition, the proposed expanded use of this site is anticipated to generate additional vehicular traffic thereby increasing congestion on nearby collector and arterial streets. Creation of a convenient, safe pedestrian/bicycle pathway system as an alternative means of transportation could offset some of the traffic demand on these nearby streets and lessen the increase in traffic congestion."

The question for us is whether these findings are constitutionally sufficient to justify the conditions imposed by the city on petitioner's building permit. Since state courts have been dealing with this question a good deal longer than we have, we turn to representative decisions made by them. [The Court's discussion of state cases is reprinted, *supra*, pp. 591-592.]

We think the "reasonable relationship" test adopted by a majority of the state courts is closer to the federal constitutional norm than either of those previously discussed. . . . But we do not adopt it as such, partly because the term "reasonable relationship" seems confusingly similar to the term "rational basis" which describes the minimal level of scrutiny under the Equal Protection Clause of the Fourteenth Amendment. We think a term such as "rough proportionality" best encapsulates what we hold to be the requirement of the Fifth Amendment. No precise mathematical calculation is required, but the city must make some sort of individualized determination that the required dedication is related both in nature and extent to the impact of the proposed development. [8]

---

[8] Justice Stevens' dissent takes us to task for placing the burden on the city to justify the required dedication. He is correct in arguing that in evaluating most generally applicable zoning regulations, the burden properly rests on the party challenging the regulation to prove that it constitutes an arbitrary regulation of property rights. Here, by contrast, the city made an adjudicative decision to condition petitioner's application for a building permit on an individual parcel. In this situation, the burden properly rests on the city. This conclusion is not, as he suggests, undermined by our decision in Moore v. East Cleveland, 431 U.S.494 (1977), in which we struck down a housing ordinance that limited occupancy of a dwelling unit to members of a single family as violating the Due Process Clause of the Fourteenth Amendment. The ordinance at issue in Moore intruded on choices concerning family living arrangements, an area in which the usual deference to the legislature was found to be inappropriate. Id., at 499.

Justice Stevens' dissent relies upon a law review article for the proposition that the city's conditional demands for part of petitioner's property are "a species of business regulation that heretofore warranted a strong presumption of constitutional validity." But simply denominating a governmental measure as a "business regulation" does not immunize it from constitutional challenge on the grounds that it violates a provision of the Bill of Rights. In *Marshall v. Barlow's, Inc.*, 436 U.S. 307 (1978), we held that a statute authorizing a warrantless search of business premises in order to detect OSHA violations violated the Fourth Amendment. And in *Central Hudson Gas & Electric Corp. v. Public Service Comm'n of N.Y.*, 447 U.S. 557 (1980), we held that an order of the New York Public Service Commission, designed to cut down the use of electricity because of a fuel shortage, violated the First Amendment insofar as it prohibited advertising by a utility company to promote the use of electricity. We see no reason why the Takings Clause of the Fifth Amendment, as much a part of the Bill of Rights as the First Amendment or Fourth Amendment, should be relegated to the status of a poor relation in these comparable circumstances. We turn now to analysis of whether the findings relied upon by the city here, first with respect to the floodplain easement, and second with respect to the pedestrian/bicycle path, satisfied these requirements.

It is axiomatic that increasing the amount of impervious surface will increase the quantity and rate of storm-water flow from petitioner's property. Therefore, keeping the floodplain open and free from development would likely confine the pressures on Fanno Creek created by petitioner's development. In fact, because petitioner's property lies within the Central Business District, the Community Development Code already required that petitioner leave 15% of it as open space and the undeveloped floodplain would have nearly satisfied that requirement. But the city demanded more — it not only wanted petitioner not to build in the floodplain, but it also wanted petitioner's property along Fanno Creek for its Greenway system. The city has never said why a public greenway, as opposed to a private one, was required in the interest of flood control.

The difference to petitioner, of course, is the loss of her ability to exclude others. As we have noted, this right to exclude others is "one of the most essential sticks in the bundle of rights that are commonly characterized as property." *Kaiser Aetna*, 444 U.S., at 176. It is difficult to see why recreational visitors trampling along petitioner's floodplain easement are sufficiently related to the city's legitimate interest in reducing flooding problems along Fanno Creek, and the city has not attempted to make any individualized determination to support this part of its request.

The city contends that recreational easement along the Greenway is only ancillary to the city's chief purpose in controlling flood hazards. It further asserts that unlike the residential property at issue in *Nollan*, petitioner's property is commercial in character and therefore, her right to exclude others is compromised. The city maintains that "[t]here is nothing to suggest that preventing [petitioner] from prohibiting [the easements] will unreasonably impair the value of [her] property as a [retail store]." *PruneYard Shopping Center v. Robins*, 447 U.S. 74, 83 (1980).

Admittedly, petitioner wants to build a bigger store to attract members of the public to her property. She also wants, however, to be able to control the time and manner in which they enter. The recreational easement on the Greenway is different in character from the exercise of state-protected rights of free expression and petition that we permitted in *PruneYard*. In *PruneYard*, we held that a major private shopping center that attracted more than 25,000 daily patrons had to provide access to persons exercising their state constitutional rights to distribute pamphlets and ask passersby to sign their petitions. *Id.* at 85. We based our decision, in part, on the fact that the shopping center "may restrict expressive activity by adopting time, place, and manner regulations that will minimize any interference with its commercial functions." *Id.*, at 83. By contrast, the city wants to impose a permanent recreational easement upon petitioner's property that borders Fanno Creek. Petitioner would lose all rights to regulate the time in which the public entered onto the Greenway, regardless of any interference it might pose with her retail store. Her right to exclude would not be regulated, it would be eviscerated.

If petitioner's proposed development had somehow encroached on existing greenway space in the city, it would have been reasonable to require petitioner to provide some alternative greenway space for the public either on her property or elsewhere. See *Nollan*, 483 U.S., at 836 ("Although such a requirement, constituting a permanent grant of continuous access to the property, would have to be considered a taking if it were not attached to a development permit, the Commission's assumed power to forbid construction of the house in order to protect the public's view of the beach must surely include the power to condition construction upon some concession by the owner, even a concession of property rights, that serves the same end.") But that is not the case here. We conclude that the findings upon which the city relies do not show the required reasonable relationship between the floodplain easement and the petitioner's proposed new building.

With respect to the pedestrian/bicycle pathway, we have no doubt that the city was correct in finding that the larger retail sales facility proposed by petitioner will increase traffic on the streets of the Central Business District. The city estimates that the proposed development would generate roughly 435 additional trips per day.[9] Dedications for streets, sidewalks, and other public ways are generally reasonable exactions to avoid excessive congestion from a proposed property use. But on the record before us, the city has not met its burden of demonstrating that the additional number of vehicle and bicycle trips generated by the petitioner's development reasonably relate to the city's requirement for a dedication of the pedestrian/bicycle pathway easement. The city simply found that the creation of the pathway "could offset some of the traffic demand. . . and lessen the increase in traffic congestion."[10]

---

[9] The city uses a weekday average trip rate of 53.21 trips per 1000 square feet. Additional Trips Generated = 53.21 X (17,600 - 9720).

[10] In rejecting petitioner's request for a variance from the pathway dedication condition, the city stated that omitting the planned section of the pathway across petitioner's property would conflict with its adopted policy of providing a continuous pathway system. But the Takings Clause requires the city to implement its policy by condemnation unless the required relationship between the petitioner's development and added traffic is shown.

As Justice Peterson of the Supreme Court of Oregon explained in his dissenting opinion, however, "[t]he findings of fact that the bicycle pathway system *'could* offset some of the traffic demand' is a far cry from a finding that the bicycle pathway system *will*, or is *likely to*, offset some of the traffic demand." 854 P.2d, at 447 (emphasis in original). No precise mathematical calculation is required, but the city must make some effort to quantify its findings in support of the dedication for the pedestrian/bicycle pathway beyond the conclusory statement that it could offset some of the traffic demand generated.

IV

Cities have long engaged in the commendable task of land use planning, made necessary by increasing urbanization particularly in metropolitan areas such as Portland. The city's goals of reducing flooding hazards and traffic congestion, and providing for public greenways, are laudable, but there are outer limits to how this may be done. "A strong public desire to improve the public condition [will not] warrant achieving the desire by a shorter cut than the constitutional way of paying for the change." *Pennsylvania Coal*, 260 U.S., at 416.

The judgment of the Supreme Court of Oregon is reversed, and the case is remanded for further proceedings consistent with this opinion.

JUSTICE STEVENS, with whom JUSTICE BLACKMUN and JUSTICE GINSBURG join, dissenting:

. . . .

IV

The Court has made a serious error by abandoning the traditional presumption of constitutionality and imposing a novel burden of proof on a city implementing an admittedly valid comprehensive land use plan. Even more consequential than its incorrect disposition of this case, however, is the Court's resurrection of a species of substantive due process analysis that it firmly rejected decades ago. . . .

This case inaugurates an even more recent judicial innovation than the regulatory takings doctrine: the application of the "unconstitutional conditions" label to a mutually beneficial transaction between a property owner and a city. . . . Although it is well settled that a government cannot deny a benefit on a basis that infringes constitutionally protected interests—"especially [one's] interest in freedom of speech," *Perry v. Sindermann*, 408 U.S. 593, 597 (1972)—the "unconstitutional conditions" doctrine provides an inadequate framework in which to analyze this case.[12] Dolan has no right to be

---

[12] Although it has a long history, see Home Ins. Co. v. Morse, 20 Wall. 445, 451 (1874), the "unconstitutional conditions" doctrine has for just as long suffered from notoriously inconsistent application; it has never been an overarching principle of constitutional law that operates with equal force regardless of the nature of the rights and powers in question. See, e.g., Sunstein, Why the Unconstitutional Conditions Doctrine is an Anachronism, 70 B. U. L. Rev. 593, 620 (1990) (doctrine is "too crude and too general to provide help in contested cases"); [Other citations omitted]. As the majority's case citations suggest, modern decisions invoking the doctrine have

compensated for a taking unless the city acquires the property interests that she has refused to surrender. Since no taking has yet occurred, there has not been any infringement of her constitutional right to compensation.

Even if Dolan should accept the city's conditions in exchange for the benefit that she seeks, it would not necessarily follow that she had been denied "just compensation" since it would be appropriate to consider the receipt of that benefit in any calculation of "just compensation." See *Pennsylvania Coal Co. v. Mahon*, 260 U.S. 393, 415 (1922) (noting that an "average reciprocity of advantage" was deemed to justify many laws); *Hodel v. Irving*, 481 U.S. 704, 715 (1987) (such "'reciprocity of advantage'" weighed in favor of a statute's constitutionality). Particularly in the absence of any evidence on the point, we should not presume that the discretionary benefit the city has offered is less valuable than the property interests that Dolan can retain or surrender at her option. But even if that discretionary benefit were so trifling that it could not be considered just compensation when it has "little or no relationship" to the property, the Court fails to explain why the same value would suffice when the required nexus is present. In this respect, the Court's reliance on the "unconstitutional conditions" doctrine is assuredly novel, and arguably incoherent. The city's conditions are by no means immune from constitutional scrutiny. The level of scrutiny, however, does not approximate the kind of review that would apply if the city had insisted on a surrender of Dolan's First Amendment rights in exchange for a building permit. One can only hope that the Court's reliance today on First Amendment cases, . . . [such as *Perry v. Sindermann*], and its candid disavowal of the term "rational basis" to describe its new standard of review, do not signify a reassertion of the kind of superlegislative power the Court exercised during the Lochner era. . . .

[Justice Souter's separate dissent concluded with the following paragraph:

"In any event, on my reading, the Court's conclusions about the city's vulnerability carry the Court no further than *Nollan* has gone already, and I do not view this case as a suitable vehicle for taking the law beyond that point. The right case for the enunciation of takings doctrine seems hard to spot."

He amplified this conclusion by arguing there was an ample nexus between the greenway and the flood control problem, that the public's "incidental recreational use [of the greenway] can stand or fall with the bicycle path," and that the city had met its burden under *Nollan* of showing a nexus between the bikeway and the traffic congestion rationale. He appeared to agree with Justice Stevens that, *Nollan* having been satisfied, there was no need to subject the city's conditions to an additional "rough proportionality" test.]

---

most frequently involved First Amendment liberties [citations omitted]. The necessary and traditional breadth of municipalities' power to regulate property development, together with the absence here of fragile and easily "chilled" constitutional rights such as that of free speech, make it quite clear that the Court is really writing on a clean slate rather than merely applying "well-settled" doctrine.

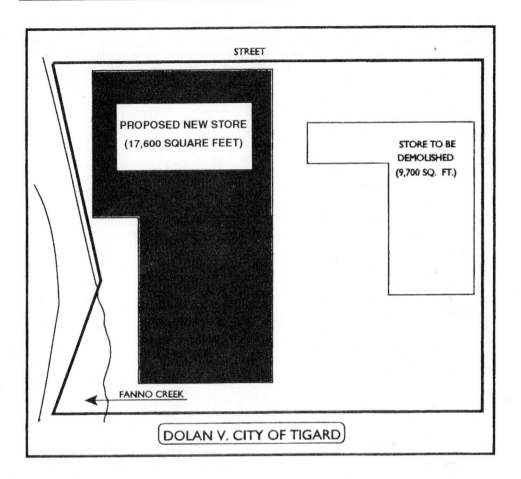

DOLAN V. CITY OF TIGARD

NOTES AND QUESTIONS

1. *What does Dolan mean?* Perhaps the most important holding in *Dolan* is the decision to adopt a new "rough proportionality" rule for exactions. How will this rule be applied? Professor Freilich argues that courts "would do well to avoid reading the *Dolan* test as establishing a rigid requirement, but instead interpret the circumstances of a dedication in terms of a general reasonableness standard, and applying heightened scrutiny to a dedication which is required as the result of an adjudicative or administrative determination." *"Thou Shalt Not Take Title Without Adequate Planning:" The Takings Equation After Dolan v. City of Tigard,* 27 Urb. Law. 187, 200, 201. (1995). Do you agree?

The majority is careful to emphasize that the state nexus cases from which it takes guidance are not dispositive of federal law (compare the use of "background principles" of state nuisance law in the *Lucas* case, reproduced in Ch. 2.) After *Dolan,* however, an exaction justified on a "weak" nexus theory is presumably invalid under federal law, thus essentially narrowing the range of state nexus tests to "strict" and "stricter."

2. *Is a unified theory of takings possible?* Since the revival of interest in regulatory takings doctrine in the mid-1960s, commentators have struggled to articulate a general theory that explains where the line should be drawn between compensation and no compensation for the adverse effects of regulations. Until Justice Scalia's arrival, by contrast, the Supreme Court tended to approach the problem as, in Justice Brennan's oft-quoted phrase from the *Penn Central* opinion, a series of "essentially ad hoc, factual inquiries." First with the heightened "nexus" test of *Nollan* and then with the *per se* rule of *Lucas,* Justice Scalia seemed to be guiding the court towards an objectified, property-rights theory of regulatory takings. How does *Dolan*'s "individualized determination" requirement differ, if at all, from Justice Brennan's "essentially ad hoc, factual" inquiry? Is individualized determination consistent with implementing a general theory of takings?

3. *Nexus.* Many commentators and courts interpreted *Nollan* as applying heightened scrutiny to the nexus requirement. If that is so, what does *Dolan* add? In *Nollan,* Justice Scalia concluded there was absolutely no nexus at all between the lateral beachfront easement and the loss of visual access occasioned by the new development. After *Dolan,* would it be more accurate to say that there was a nexus of sorts in *Nollan* (as Justice Brennan argued) but that it was too tenuous to satisfy the "rough proportionality" test? Or does *Nollan* mean that there is a zone of *de minimis* nexus that is tantamount to a *per se* taking? (Notice the parallel to the open question of whether *Lucas*'s *per se* test applies in a zone where the regulation leaves the property with some residual, but *de minimis* use and value.) See Morgan, *Exactions as Takings: Tactics for Dealing with Dolan,* Land Use L. & Zoning Dig., Vol. 46, No. 9, at 3 (1994).

4. *The "right to exclude."* Both *Dolan* and *Nollan* emphasize the compulsory conveyance of a property interest to the public, the beachfront easement of passage in *Nollan,* the greenway and bikeway easements in *Dolan.* Earlier Supreme Court cases held that physical occupancy is a *per se* taking. Why is that not the end of the inquiry in *Dolan,* without going on to the nexus analysis at all, or at least to the new second step? Is there constitutional significance in the fact that Mrs. Dolan applied for a land use permit, while the property owners in the physical occupation cases did not?

5. *Dedications.* Consider the greenway and bikeway requirements separately.

a. *Greenway.* Insofar as flood control is concerned, it would appear that the city could obtain all that it is entitled to have by restricting development within the floodplain and leaving title in Dolan. Can you think of any reason why the city would have to have title solely to protect against flooding? If Dolan retained title, could she argue for a reduction in the taxable value of the land based on its unavailability for development? If the city, at a later date, condemned an easement of way through the greenbelt for the benefit of the public, could it argue that the property taken had only nominal value because of the legitimate restriction on its use? Cf. *Preseault v. ICC,* 494 U.S. 1 (1990).

On these matters, consider an omitted portion of Justice Stevens' dissent:

Given the commercial character of both the existing and the proposed use of the property as a retail store, it seems likely that potential customers "trampling along petitioner's floodplain," are more valuable than a useless parcel of vacant land. Moreover, the duty to pay taxes and the responsibility for potential tort liability may well make ownership of the fee interest in useless land a liability rather than an asset. That may explain why Dolan never conceded that she could be prevented from building on the floodplain.

b. *Bikeway.* Whatever the fate of the greenway dedication, the bikeway would be pointless without public access. But even if there is an essential nexus of appropriate nature and extent between the bikeway and traffic generated by the new stores, is there one between Dolan's traffic and recreational users of the bikeway? How far does the majority's analysis reach? Why, to pose a more typical example, can a municipality require a subdivider to dedicate internal streets and sidewalks when it is clear that many of the users will not actually be traveling to or from the properties in the subdivision? Should the landowner be able to opt for private streets if desired, and require the public to pay for any public access? The majority seems to assume that an uncompensated dedication is constitutional once the nexus is established. Is this deference to the traditional way of doing things simply a further example of the extent to which takings theory is becoming a loosely connected series of *ad hoc* rules?

6. *Burden of proof.* A very important aspect of *Dolan* is the shifting of the burden of proof to the government to justify the exaction. Why might this be so? Consider the following:

a. *Trial strategy.* Is the majority demanding of the city anything more than that it prepare its justification more carefully (avoiding soft words such as "could," for instance, when defending the bikeway requirement)? How likely is it that the "nature" and "extent" of the "essential nexus" required by the court are susceptible of proof by hard evidence? Is Justice Stevens correct when he says that "predictions on such matters [as bikeway usage] are nothing more than estimates"? In representing the city, how would you attempt to reformulate the record on remand? Even if not many of Mrs. Dolan's customers used the bikeway (carrying away plumbing fixtures on two wheels is not easy), would it be sufficient to show that the bikeway reduced road usage otherwise, making room for Mrs. Dolan's customers?

b. *The rights hierarchy.* In citing cases such as *Perry v. Sindermann,* does the majority mean that the constitution protects property rights to the same extent that it protects free speech and other aspects of individual liberty? (See also Justice Scalia's footnote 3 in *Nollan,* reproduced in Chapter 2, *supra.*) Is this what justifies the shift in the burden of proof? How does this relate to the debate between the majority and Justice Stevens over substantive due process? Consider also the care the court takes to differentiate "rough proportionality" from the federal constitutional law of minimum scrutiny "rational basis" tests. Do *Nollan* and *Dolan* lay the foundation for the Court to eventually reexamine the different levels of judicial review based on the distinction between economic rights and individual liberties established by footnote four of *U.S. v. Carolene Products,* 304 U.S. 144 (1938)?

In their concurrence in *U.S. v. Carlton,* 512 U.S. 26, 41 (1994), cited in footnote 13 of Justice Stevens' dissent, Justices Scalia and Thomas are much blunter: "The picking and choosing among various rights to be accorded 'substantive due process' protection is alone enough to arouse suspicion; but the categorical and inexplicable exclusion of so-called 'economic rights' (even though the Due Process Clause explicitly applies to 'property') unquestionably involves policymaking rather than neutral legal analysis."

c. *The commercial/residential distinction.* Another way to evaluate both the "rights hierarchy" problem and the question of whether a uniform theory is possible is to consider the distinction between commercial and non-commercial exactions suggested by Justice Stevens. The majority notes, with a faint tinge of scorn, that he relies on a law review article for this argument. The article includes the following key language which Justice Stevens quotes:

> The subdivider is a manufacturer, processor, and marketer of a product; land is but one of his raw materials. In subdivision control disputes, the developer is not defending hearth and home against the king's intrusion, but simply attempting to maximize his profits from the sale of a finished product. As applied to him, subdivision control exactions are actually business regulations. [Johnston, *Constitutionality of Subdivision Control Exactions: The Quest for a Rationale,* 52 Cornell L.Q. 871, 923 (1967).]

How does the Chief Justice answer this point? Are separate rules for commercial regulation workable? Inescapable under *Carolene Products*? Note that if takings and free speech doctrines are indeed analogous, as the majority implies, the separate treatment of "commercial speech" has been steadily eroded by the court in recent years.

7. *Legislative vs. adjudicative.* What is the significance of characterizing the city's action as "adjudicative," rather than "legislative?" Dissenting on this point, Justice Souter said, "[T]he permit conditions were imposed pursuant to Tigard's Community Development Code. The adjudication here was of Dolan's requested variance from the permit conditions otherwise required to be imposed by the Code. This case raises no question about discriminatory, or 'reverse spot' zoning, which 'singles out a particular parcel for different, less favorable treatment than the neighboring ones.' [*Penn Central*]" Did the Court mean that every application of a legislative rule is adjudicative? Further developments on this issue are discussed in the next section.

3. *DOLAN* APPLIED

The task of applying *Dolan* has been complicated by its failure to discuss whether the rough proportionality test applies only when a contribution of property or cash is required incident to a land use approval or whether it applies to all regulatory takings claims and also, within the category of contributions, whether it applies only to physical dedications of land. The actual case involved an "exaction," in which a property interest in the land itself was required to be dedicated to the public. Another very common technique is to require payment of a cash "impact fee," levied in the subdivision control process or at the time a building permit issues, to finance public facilities, on-or off-site, that are needed because of the new development. Or municipalities may levy an "in-lieu" fee, which is paid in cash in lieu of a dedication of land. Many important takings cases (*Penn Central, Loretto, Nollan*) have either said explicitly or implied that physical intrusion under the guise of regulation will increase the likelihood of there being a taking. Is *Dolan*'s "rough proportionality" test triggered only by exactions, which "take" a property interest, or does it apply across the board?

Del Monte Dunes.—The heated debate over the reach of *Dolan* was at least partially settled by the Supreme Court in *City of Monterey v. Del Monte Dunes, Ltd.*, 526 U.S. 687 (1999). *Del Monte* was an inverse condemnation case in which the claim was that the development had been rejected altogether; neither exactions nor impact fees were at issue. The court held (without much explanation) that the "rough proportionality" test of *Dolan* did not apply:

> Although in a general sense concerns for proportionality animate the Takings Clause, we have not extended the rough-proportionality test of *Dolan* beyond the special context of exactions — land-use decisions conditioning approval of development on the dedication of property to public use. The rule applied in *Dolan* considers whether dedications demanded as conditions of development are proportional to the development's anticipated impacts. It was not designed to address, and is not readily applicable to, the much different questions arising where, as here, the landowner's challenge is based not on excessive exactions but on denial of development. We believe, accordingly, that the rough-proportionality test of *Dolan* is inapposite to a case such as this one. [*Id.* at 702–03.]

Read literally, the court would seem to mean that the *Dolan* test applies *only* when physical dedications of land are required as an exaction. Some state courts had taken the same position. See, e.g., *McCarthy v. City of Leawood*, 894 P.2d 836 (Kan. 1995). See also Ansson, *Dolan v. Tigard's Rough Proportionality Standard: Why This Standard Should Not be Applied to an Inverse Condemnation Claim Based Upon Regulatory Denial*, 10 Seton Hall Const. L.J. 417 (2000). But the court also connects "rough proportionality" to "the development's anticipated impacts." Is there reason to apply stricter scrutiny when land, as opposed to cash, is demanded? Does *Loretto* help answer this question?

Impact fees and rough proportionality.—Even if, for the sake of argument, one applies *Dolan* to impact fees as well as exactions, it is clear that impact fees can more easily satisfy the rough proportionality test:

> Perhaps the exactions most at risk from an attack under *Dolan* are subdivision regulations requiring the contribution of land and facilities to assure adequacy of roadways, water, wastewater and drainage (the so-called "hard services") to serve the project. Such traditional land use regulations are applied almost universally by municipalities large and small. Typically, as in *Dolan*, exactions are guided by a master plan that identifies approximate locations and dimensions of system facilities necessary to serve the community. Such location-based exactions do not readily lend themselves to proportionality tests. . . .

On the other hand, demand-based exaction programs, such as impact fees, are designed to measure the impacts created by a development on community facilities and to convert such demand to a value expressed as monetary fees. . . . Because . . . impact fees were developed in the context of judicially crafted proportionality standards, . . . [they] should satisfy "rough proportionality" tests from the outset. [Morgan, Shortlidge & Watson, *Right-of-Way Exactions and Rough Proportionality,* Mun. Law., Vol. 40, No. 1, at 28 (1999).]

Review the *Visalia* case, reproduced *supra,* in view of these comments.

Legislative vs. adjudicative.—Now assume that *Del Monte* is read literally, so that *Dolan* applies only in exactions cases. Questions still remain because it is unclear whether the rough proportionality test applies only when an exaction is imposed adjudicatively (as in *Dolan* itself), or also when an exaction is imposed legislatively. A review of the cases finds that the courts have divided since *Dolan* on this question, and are also divided in how to characterize the nature of an exaction. Note, *The Distinction Between Legislative and Adjudicative Decisions in Dolan v. City of Tigard,* 75 N.Y.U. L. Rev. 242, 253–259 (2000). Compare *Curtis v. Town of South Thomaston,* 708 A.2d 657, 660 (Me. 1998) (legislative nature of exaction only one factor in applying *Dolan*), and *Schultz v. City of Grants Pass,* 884 P.2d 569 (Ore. App. 1994) (dedication imposed on a landowner is adjudicative though required by the provisions of the local ordinance), with *Ehrlich v. City of Culver City,* 911 P.2d 429, 438 (Cal. 1996) (concluding that *Nollan* and *Dolan* only apply to cases of regulatory "leveraging" where conditions are imposed on land use approvals), *cert. denied,* 519 U.S. 929 (1996). The court added that "the heightened standard of scrutiny is triggered by a relatively narrow class of land use cases—those exhibiting circumstances which increase the risk that the local permitting authority will seek to avoid the obligation to pay just compensation." *Id.* at 439. Does this distinction make sense? Accord *Home Builders Ass'n of Central Arizona v. City of Scottsdale,* 930 P.2d 993 (Ariz. 1997).

The difficulties in distinguishing between legislative and adjudicative decisions in the exactions context reflect the difficulties typically encountered in making these distinctions generally in the land use decision making process, as discussed in Chapter 5. Surveys of municipal practices show an almost even split between exactions that are formula-based, those that use a legislative standard with some flexibility, and those that are based on case-by-case adjudication. Purdum & Frank, *Community Use of Exactions: Results of a National Survey*, in Development Exactions 128 (J. Frank & R. Rhodes eds., 1987). Does this complicate the characterization problem? Note that in *Dolan* the dedication was imposed under the development code but was determined administratively. Would it be best to apply *Dolan* to all exactions, even though imposed legislatively?

a. Dedications of Land

The following case illustrates how courts apply the rough proportionality test to dedications of land. The term "short plat" used by the court refers to a subdivision of less than five lots. See Wash. Rev. Code § 58.17.020(6), (8).

SPARKS v. DOUGLAS COUNTY

127 Wn.2d 901, 904 P.2d 738 (1995)

SMITH, J.—Petitioner Douglas County seeks review of a decision by the Court of Appeals, Division Three, reversing a ruling of the Douglas County Superior Court which upheld action of the Board of Commissioners of Douglas County conditioning approval of short plat applications by Respondents Herschel and Elizabeth Sparks upon dedication of rights of way for road improvements. We granted review. We reverse.

QUESTION PRESENTED

The question presented in this case is whether the action by Douglas County conditioning approval of the Sparkses' short plat applications upon dedication of rights of way for road improvements was arbitrary and capricious and constitutes an unconstitutional taking of property.

STATEMENT OF FACTS

On March 29, 1990, Herschel and Elizabeth Sparks (Sparkses) filed four short plat applications with the Douglas County Planning Office, designated as plats 2, 3, 4 and 5. Plat 2 covers 9.19 acres located East of Empire Avenue and North of 30th Street Northwest in unincorporated Douglas County near East Wenatchee (Sparks 2). Plat 3 is located immediately South of Plat 2, East of Empire Avenue and North of 29th Street Northwest, covering 9.5 acres (Sparks 3). Plat 4 consists of 6.72 acres between Empire Avenue and Fir Street Northwest, north of 32nd Street Northwest (Sparks 4). Plat 5 is located on 5.6 acres between Empire Avenue and Fir Street Northwest and adjacent to 32nd Street Northwest on the south (Sparks 5). Each of the proposed short plats contains four residential lots.

The planning director reviewed the plat applications and determined the streets bordering the plats were deficient in right of way width by county standards and thus would not accommodate future construction of street improvements. The director also determined that 32nd Street did not meet fire code requirements for safe access.

The matter was referred to the Subdivision Review Committee, which met on June 21, 1990. Its findings were consistent with those of the planning director. It approved the short plat applications subject to certain conditions, which included dedication of rights of way for future improvements along the public roads bordering the plats. The committee specifically required a 10-foot right of way along the portion of plat 2 bordering Empire Avenue; a 10-foot right of way along the portion of plat 3 bordering Empire Avenue and a 5-foot right of way along the portion of that plat adjacent to 29th Street; a 25-foot right of way along the portion of plat 4 abutting Fir Street; and dedication of 25-foot rights of way along the portions of plat 5 bordering Fir Street and 32nd Street.

Respondents Sparks appealed the decision of the Subdivision Review Committee to the Douglas County Regional Planning Commission, which held a hearing on August 22, 1990. The Commission upheld the conditional approval of plats 2 and 3, but disapproved plats 4 and 5 based upon noncompliance with fire code provisions for adequate roadway.

Respondents then appealed the decision of the Planning Commission to the Douglas County Board of County Commissioners during a hearing on April 1, 1991. The Commissioners, reinstating the decision of the Subdivision Review Committee, approved all the short plat applications subject to the dedication requirements. As to Empire Avenue, the Board concluded:

> 9. Empire Avenue NW has been determined to have deficiencies regarding pavement width and pavement condition by Urban Arterial Board Standards.

> 10. Existing pavement width on NW Empire is 16' to 17' wide. Since the time of . . . this finding, Empire has been improved to 20 feet of width by a maintenance project.

> 11. Urban Arterial Board standards require an improved roadway section of a minimum 24 feet of paving, ditches, and backslopes which can only be accomplished in a minimum of 50 feet of right-of-way.

> 12. Adequate right-of-way is not available to allow future improvements for safe access based on the existing average daily traffic (ADT) 220 ADT, nor the increase in traffic that may be generated by this short plat.

The commissioners also concluded that 29th Street is deficient in right of way and road surfacing; that Fir Street "is deficient in standards for right of way width to allow future street improvements"; and that 32nd Street "does not meet Uniform Fire Code requirements for safe access" and is "deficient in right-of-way width, road surface, and pavement width." Based upon these findings, the Commissioners determined that the plats could be approved only if the Sparkses dedicated sufficient rights of way to allow the roads to be improved according to county standards.

Respondents Sparks sought a writ of review in the Superior Court of Douglas County, arguing that the required dedications were unconstitutional takings of property without compensation. The Superior Court, the Honorable John E. Bridges, affirmed the County Commissioners' action on June 18, 1992. Consistent with the Commissioners' findings, the court determined the streets bordering the plats were deficient in paved surface and in width of right of way. Comparing the County's traffic counts on each of the access streets with the projected average daily trips the developments would generate, the court found the developments would approximately double traffic in the area. It concluded Respondents Sparks did not establish that the County Commissioners' action was arbitrary or capricious.

The Court of Appeals reversed in a split decision on December 14, 1993. The majority (Chief Judge Philip J. Thompson writing) determined there was no evidence that residential development of the Sparkses' properties would have an adverse impact which would necessitate widening the adjacent roads. The court concluded that requiring dedication of rights of way as a condition for plat approval was an unconstitutional taking.

On January 13, 1994, Douglas County filed a petition for review in this Court. Consideration was deferred pending a decision of the United States Supreme Court in *Dolan v. Tigard*. The Supreme Court has now ruled in that case. We granted the petition on September 7, 1994.

DISCUSSION

. . .

The *Dolan* Test of Constitutionality

The statement of the law by the Court of Appeals conflicts with the United States Supreme Court's recent ruling in *Dolan v. Tigard*. The Court of Appeals stated a dedication is permissible only if it "reasonably prevents or compensates for, in a specific and proportional fashion, adverse public impacts of the proposed development." *Dolan* found such exacting scrutiny unacceptable. . . . [The court then discussed the *Dolan* case.]

The approach adopted by the United States Supreme Court in *Dolan* can be applied in consonance with Washington law. RCW 82.02.020 permits dedications as a condition for subdivision approval if the local government can show the conditions are "reasonably necessary as a direct result of the proposed development or plat to which the dedication of land or easement is to apply." Reviewing agencies must consider adequacy of access to a proposed subdivision, and may condition approval on provision of adequate access. Short subdivision plats may not be approved unless the legislative body finds, among other things, that appropriate provisions are made "for the public health, safety, and general welfare and for . . . open spaces, drainage ways, streets or roads. . . ."

But the fact that the dedications in this case were imposed, in part, to accommodate anticipated future improvement of the roads makes application of the *Dolan* standard less certain. It is not clear whether, under *Dolan*, municipalities may take into account future developments and their anticipated cumulative impacts. A Nebraska case cited in *Dolan* as representative of the "reasonable relationship" standard held that a local government may not require a property owner to dedicate private property for future public use as a condition for obtaining a building permit when that future use is not "occasioned by the construction sought to be permitted." [Simpson v. North Platte, 292 N.W.2d 297, 302 (Neb. 1980).] At any rate, the determinative issue in this case is not future use, but the degree of connection between the County's exaction and the impact of the developments.

Rough Proportionality

Addressing the first step of the *Dolan* test, the Sparkses have conceded that a "nexus" exists between requiring dedication of rights of way and the County's legitimate interest in promoting road safety. The next step—determining whether a reasonable relationship also exists between the dedications and the impact created by the developments—is disputed in this case.

The pivotal issue under the *Dolan* approach is whether the exactions demanded by Douglas County are roughly proportional to the impact of the Sparkses' proposed developments. Respondents Sparks argue that the determination by the Court of Appeals that the new land use has no adverse impact on road safety demonstrates an absence of rough proportionality between development impact and exactions. Respondents also claim there is no way to truly measure whether the conditions demanded by the County are proportionate to the impact of the development.

While *Dolan* disregarded precise calculations in analyzing development impacts, it ruled that local government must make some effort to quantify its findings to support its permit conditions. In this case, the findings made by the County were more than mere conclusory statements of general impact. They were the result of the kind of individualized analysis required under *Dolan*. The report prepared by the Planning Office for each of the short plats documented the deficiencies in right of way width and surfacing of the adjoining streets. Douglas County's records also reflect calculation of increase in traffic and the specific need for dedication of rights of way based upon the individual and cumulative impacts of the series of short subdivisions.

The findings upon which the County relies reflect the required rough proportionality between the exactions and the impact of the Respondents' proposed developments. It is undisputed that the developments would generate increased traffic on adjacent roads which are not adequate for safe access under county standards. The County has, in the process of individualized analysis, satisfied the final step of the Dolan test.

Respondents argue that the substandard conditions of the roads existed even prior to the Sparkses' plat applications and cannot therefore be caused by their proposed developments. But it has been established that the increase in traffic generated by those plats on already unsafe roads would require additional right of way and reconstruction to accommodate the overflow. Empire Avenue, in particular, has been listed in the County's six-year road improvement plan, and the county engineer testified the developments themselves necessitate upgrading of that road. The adverse impact created by the plats on adjacent roads was concluded by the trial court upon substantial evidence and need not be re-examined by this Court. . . .

We reverse the decision of the Court of Appeals which reversed the Douglas County Superior Court ruling upholding the action by Petitioner Douglas County conditioning approval of plat applications by Respondents Sparks on dedication of rights of way for road improvements.

ALEXANDER, J. (dissenting in part) — . . . Admittedly, the County's traffic predictions are detailed, scientifically based, and individualized calculations concerning the specific area surrounding the proposed developments. I am, nonetheless, satisfied that the exactions are constitutionally deficient with respect to the right-of-way along Empire Way because the County has not demonstrated that the extent of the exactions along this street are roughly proportional to the impact that it anticipates will be caused by the developments.

In reviewing a challenged exaction, a court must first identify the starting point from which to measure the extent of the exaction as a necessary predicate to calculating whether an exaction is proportional to an impact. In regard to Empire Way, at least, it cannot be presumed that the current condition of the roadway is the appropriate reference point for calculating the extent of the exaction. I reach this conclusion because Douglas County had previously made a formal announcement of its commitment to make certain improvements to Empire Way. Once these planned improvements are factored into the equation, the exaction of land from the developer for right-of-way cannot be said to be related in any extent, let alone proportionally related, to the traffic impacts arising from the development. Because the County has effectively said that Empire Way needed improvement, even before the Sparkses applied for permits to develop their land adjoining Empire Way, the impacts that logically relate to that development are only those that require roadway improvements in addition to those already planned. When the County failed to show that its already planned improvements could not accommodate the additional traffic generated by the development, the County failed to show that the exaction of any right-of-way is related, in extent, to the development.

The record shows that Douglas County had placed Empire Way on its six-year development plan prior to the date that either the Planning Commission or the Board of County Commissioners considered the Sparkses' plat application. It also reveals that the County had been unsuccessful in earlier attempts to obtain funding for the project. By its earlier action, the County determined that it was necessary to improve Empire Way to meet specifications contained in that plan. It is a pure fortuity that the Sparkses decided to develop their properties before the County completed these planned improvements. Had they delayed submitting their application for development permits until after the County was able to carry out its roadway improvement plan, the County, presumably, would have been required to obtain the necessary frontage by negotiation or by invoking its power of eminent domain. In either case, the affected property owners would have been compensated for their involuntary contribution to the public good. Unfortunately, under the majority's opinion, the County is rewarded for its delay, and the Sparkses are penalized for a mere happenstance of timing. The protections afforded by the due process clause of the Fifth Amendment to the United States Constitution should not hinge on such fortuities. . . .

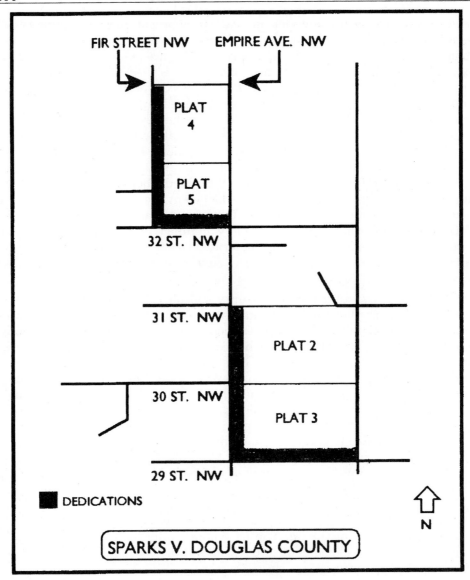

NOTES AND QUESTIONS

1. *Defending dedications. Sparks* indicates the difficulties in defending dedications of land for roads and other facilities. Should it have been a defense to the exaction that the improvements to Empire Way were included in the county's comprehensive plan? See the article by Morgan et al, *supra*. Should planning for roadway improvements necessarily invalidate any exactions for such improvements? Is this the dissent's argument? Reconsider the *Visalia* case, reproduced *supra*.

Compare *Amoco Oil Co. v. Village of Schaumburg,* 661 N.E.2d 380 (Ill. App. 1995), *cert. denied,* 519 U.S. 976 (1996), where the court invalidated the approval of a site plan for the razing and rebuilding of a gasoline station conditioned on dedications that would improve an adjacent congested intersection. The court said:

> Schaumburg attempted to expropriate over twenty percent (20%) of Amoco's property without a legitimate reason. In fact, the record is replete with evidence showing that the required dedication had little or no relationship to the anticipated impact of the proposed development. For example, in addition to the testimony cited by the circuit court, Kenneth Hemstreet also testified that Amoco's proposed improvements would have had no effect on the need to increase the number of lanes for both Golf and Roselle roads. In fact, according to Hemstreet, IDOT [the state transportation agency]. recommended widening the streets notwithstanding the redevelopment of Amoco's property. [*Id.* at 939.]

See also *J.C. Reeves Corp. v. Clackamas County,* 887 P.2d 360 (Ore. App. 1994). The landowner was required to provide surfacing, stormwater, curb and sidewalk improvements along an existing roadway. The court invalidated this requirement because the county did not make "the appropriate comparison . . . between the traffic and other effects of the subdivision and the subdivision frontage improvements that the county has required." *Id* at 365. Merely stating the relationship between subdivision-generated traffic and the need for improvements is not enough.

2. *Future use and development.* In most subdivision dedication cases, the development that will occur on the subdivided land and its impact on the roadway system is clear. But that is not always the case. In *Schultz v. City of Grants Pass,* 884 P.2d 569 (Ore. App. 1994), the city conditioned the partitioning of one lot into two with a requirement that the subdivider dedicate land for adjacent roadways. It based this requirement on an assumption that the property would be developed for at least 15 to 17 homes, as allowed by the zoning ordinance. The court reversed because the dedication was based on a "worst-case scenario" that assumed the development of the tract to its "full development potential." A dedication requirement could only take into account the proposal in question, which was the division of one lot into two. But see *State by & Through Dep't of Transp. v. Altimus,* 905 P.2d 258 (Ore. App. 1995), holding in a condemnation case that the jury could consider the effect of a hypothetical dedication requirement on a condemnation award.

Goss v. City of Little Rock, 151 F.3d 861 (8th Cir. 1998), *cert. denied,* 526 U.S. 1050 (1999), considered a similar problem when a dedication was attached to a rezoning. The court relied on the district court opinion to invalidate a rezoning to a commercial use district on condition that the landowner dedicate 22% of the land for the expansion of an adjacent roadway. The district court found that the nexus test was satisfied but not the rough proportionality test. It concluded that "Little Rock's assessment of the impact of rezoning was too speculative because that assessment was based on traffic that could, as said by the city's witness, 'conceivably' be generated at some unknown point in the future if a strip mall were erected on Goss's land, although there are no plans to build a strip mall on the property and there is no reason to expect one to be built." *Id.* at 863.

Note the difficulties this decision creates for municipalities. As Chapter 5 pointed out, an application for a rezoning amendment is an application for a zoning map change, not an application for a particular use or development. Is there a way out of this dilemma?

b. Impact Fees

The Supreme Court's *Del Monte* decision seems to have held that impact fees are not subject to the *Dolan* rough proportionality test. If *Dolan* applies, however, impact fees must satisfy this test. *F & W Assocs. v. County of Somerset,* 648 A.2d 482 (N.J. App. 1994), is an important case applying a statutory rational nexus test to uphold a traffic impact fee based on trip generation studies that determined each developer's share of needed traffic improvements in the township.

There have been few impact fee cases post-*Dolan,* but they have usually been favorable to municipalities. In *Ehrlich v. City of Culver City,* 911 P.2d 429 (Cal. 1996), after the plaintiff demolished a private recreational facility, the city approved an office building on the site subject to a condition that the plaintiff pay a recreational mitigation fee to be used for additional recreational facilities to replace those lost when the plaintiff demolished the facility. The city also required payment of an "art in public places" fee.

The court held the discontinuance of a private use could have significant impacts justifying a monetary exaction to alleviate it. It also held the city's findings on the relationship between the monetary exaction and the withdrawal of land restrictively zoned for private recreational use satisfied the nexus test, but it remanded the case because the record did not support the amount of the fee required. That fee should be based on the loss of land reserved for recreational use, not the loss of plaintiff's facilities, which were privately owned. The court upheld the "art in public places" fee because "[t]he requirement of providing art in an area of the project reasonably accessible to the public is, like other design and landscaping requirements, a kind of aesthetic control well within the authority of the city to impose."

National Ass'n of Home Builders of the United States v. Chesterfield County, 907 F. Supp. 166 (E.D. Va. 1995), *aff'd without opinion,* 92 F.3d 1180 (4th Cir. 1996), upheld a county policy the court interpreted as specifying a maximum contribution for public facilities. The amount required was based on county-wide averages. The court held there was nothing in the policy that prevented its application in accordance with the *Dolan* requirements.

A case decided after *Del Monte* applied the *Dolan* tests to uphold an impact fee for roadway improvements, but described these tests as a "reasonable relationship" test and did not discuss the *Del Monte* decision. *Home Builders Ass'n of Dayton v. City of Beavercreek,* 729 N.E.2d 349 (Ohio 2000). The fee was based on an accepted methodology similar to that described in the Morgan article, *supra.* The court held the choice of methodology was primarily for the local legislature and said "a court must only determine whether the methodology used is reasonable based on the evidence presented." It then held that the decision of the trial court, which had upheld the fee, was supported by sufficient evidence in the record. The impact was contained in an ordinance, but the court did not indicate whether this qualified as a legislative action.

Park and school fees.—Impact fees for parks and schools can present a more serious problem because these facilities are used by both new and old residents, and facility needs created by new developments are more difficult to identify. If the fee is not earmarked for projected needs created by new development, a court may hold it invalid. See *Weber Basin Home Bldrs. Ass'n v. Roy City,* 487 P.2d 866 (Utah 1971) (proceeds of building permit fee went into city's general fund).

In *St. John's County v. Northeast Florida Builders Ass'n,* 583 So. 2d 635 (Fla. 1991), decided after *Nollan,* the court upheld an impact fee for new schools levied on new residential development. The court required a showing of a rational nexus between the need for new schools and the population growth the subdivision generated, and between the expenditure of the fees and the benefits accruing to the subdivision. To satisfy this requirement, funds had to be earmarked to benefit residents of the subdivisions where fees would be collected. The court rejected a claim that the fee was invalid because it would be collected for homes that would never have school children. Is the fee valid after *Dolan? Contra, West Park Ave., Inc. v. Ocean Twp.,* 224 A.2d 1, 3–4 (N.J. 1966) (schools traditionally are the responsibility of the entire community, including undeveloped land taxed in prior years).

For an elaborate test that requires municipalities to equalize the relative tax burdens borne by new and existing properties see *Banberry Dev. Corp. v. South Jordan City,* 631 P.2d 899 (Utah 1981), applied and explained in *Home Builders Ass'n v. City of American Fork,* 973 P.2d 425 (Utah 1999). The test is based on an article by Professor Ellickson, *Suburban Growth Controls: An Economic and Legal Analysis,* 86 Yale L.J. 385 (1977), who argues that "if a municipality mixes special and general revenues in financing a service, the portion financed by general revenues should presumptively be distributed equally per dwelling unit." *Id.* at 460.

Could a state statute or municipal ordinance provide that the municipal contribution to facilities such as sewers should in no case be excessive, and authorize an appropriate increase in developer contributions on a case-by-case basis to avoid excessive municipal contributions? See *Land/Vest Properties, Inc. v. Town of Plainfield,* 379 A.2d 200 (N.H. 1977) (applying statute enacting this requirement).

How to do it right.—*Morgan* et al, *supra,* provide a method for calculating an impact fee for roadways that meets the rough proportionality test. The objective is to measure "the consumption of vehicular capacity of the municipality's thoroughfare system by a particular development, and [convert] this demand into dollars." The first step is to determine the type of roads to be included in the network used to simulate travel demand. Total travel on the road network associated with the new development must then be estimated. This is a two-part determination involving trip generation and trip length.

"The roadway capacity consumed by a new development is the number of trips generated during a selected time period multiplied by the average trip length." The next step is to determine the value of the road capacity consumed by the proposed development. Dividing the cost of the roadway by its carrying capacity provides an average cost per thoroughfare mile-trip. This average cost is then multiplied by the number of thoroughfare mile-trips the development will generate.

The final step is to establish a value for the developer's contributions of land and facilities that are required as an exaction. The municipality can demand the exaction in full if the cost of providing the facility is equal to or greater than the value of the exaction. *Id.* at 37–38. Notice that this method requires a case-by-case adjudication of each exaction, although it would seem that an ordinance should establish the criteria for making these determinations. How does this method fit under the *Dolan* rules?

NOTES AND QUESTIONS

1. *Variants on impact fees.* In *J.W. Jones Cos. v. City of San Diego,* 203 Cal. Rptr. 580 (Cal. App. 1984), the court upheld an interesting variant of the impact fee as applied to finance municipal improvements required in the city's growth-management program. The city levied a facilities benefit assessment (FBA) on undeveloped property in a growth area, "to pay in the future for public facilities to be installed in the future at a cost measured in 1980 dollars [adjusted for inflation]." *Id.* at 587. The FBA calculation allocated aggregated facilities costs on the basis of "net equivalent dwelling units" permitted by zoning, rather than making separate calculations for each component facility. The court recognized that the FBA was a distant cousin to the special assessment and "does not mirror general state law." *Id.*

The court rejected an argument that the FBA did not confer a special benefit because "some of the facilities are remote and any benefit must therefore be indirect." *Id.* at 588. The FBA was levied in proportion to benefit, and contiguity was not essential. The exclusion of developed property from the FBA did not violate equal protection because developed property in the area was presently served with adequate facilities. The court added:

> The undeveloped perimeters of urban centers require to be controlled in their growth not on a street by street basis looking to adjacent properties to bear improvement costs, but from the perspective of future communities planned to be complete in themselves. The vision of San Diego's future . . . is attainable only through the comprehensive financing scheme contemplated by the FBA. [*Id.* at 589.]

2. *Fee vs. tax.* Arguments are often made that impact fees are taxes and that communities may not levy them because there is no statutory authority for a tax of this type. In *Hillis Homes, Inc. v. Snohomish County,* 650 P.2d 193 (Wash. 1983), for example, two counties levied fees for waste disposal facilities, parks, roads, and sheriff's services. The court held that the characterization of the fees would turn on their primary purpose. The fees would not be taxes if they were "merely tools in the regulation of land subdivision." They would be taxes if their primary purpose was to raise money. The court held that "[t]here can be no question" that the primary purpose of the fees was to raise revenue. The fees were clearly "to be applied to offset the costs of providing specified services." No provision was made for regulating residential development. *Id.* at 195–96. Accord *Country Joe, Inc. v. City of Eagan,*

560 N.W.2d 681 (Minn. 1997). Contra, *Contractors & Builders Ass'n v. City of Dunedin,* 329 So. 2d 314 (Fla. 1976), *cert. denied,* 444 U.S. 867 (1979).

Is this reasoning in *Hillis Homes* helpful? Can you provide an alternative test for determining when an impact fee is a tax? Courts will also find that a fee is a tax if it produces revenue in excess of the reasonable costs of providing the services or facilities for which the fee is levied. See *Building Indus. Ass'n v. City of Oxnard,* 198 Cal. Rptr. 63 (Cal. App. 1984) (applying this reasoning to "growth requirement development fee" levied as 2.8 percent of building valuation of development). Washington has since enacted legislation authorizing impact fees. Comment, *Subdivision Exactions in Washington: The Controversy Over Imposing Fees on Developers,* 59 Wash. L. Rev. 289 (1984).

3. *The tax option.* When statutory authority is present, a municipality can levy an impact fee for new facilities as a tax. The tax is then subject to the relaxed equal protection rules applied to non-property taxes. See *Cherry Hills Farms v. City of Cherry Hills,* 670 P.2d 778 (Colo. 1983) (service-expansion fee held to be excise tax); *Oregon State Homebuilders Ass'n v. City of Tigard,* 604 P.2d 886 (Or. App. 1979) (system development charge held to be tax reasonably related to cost of providing new services); *Paul L. Smith, Inc. v. Southern York County School Dist.,* 403 A.2d 1034 (Pa. Commw. 1979) (school privilege tax). If all this sounds too easy, keep in mind that municipal power to levy taxes is limited in many states. See *Rancho Colorado, Inc. v. City of Broomfield,* 586 P.2d 659 (Colo. 1978) (service-expansion fee held not to be valid occupation tax); Etahier & Weiss, *Development Excise Taxes: An Exercise in Cleverness and Imagination,* 42 Land Use L. & Zoning Dig., No. 2, at 3 (1990).

4. *Sources.* See, e.g., Private Supply of Public Services (R. Alterman ed., 1988); Cordes, *Legal Limits on Development Exactions: Responding to Nollan and Dolan,* 15 N. Ill. U. L. Rev. 513 (1995); Gerry, *Parity Revisited: An Empirical Comparison of State and Lower Federal Court Interpretations of Nollan v. California Coastal Commission,* 23 Harv. J.L. & Pub. Pol'y 233 (1999); Morgan, *Exactions as Takings: Tactics for Dealing With Dolan,* Land Use L. & Zoning Dig., Vol. 46, No. 9, at 3 (1994); Stroud & Trevarthen, *Defensible Exactions After Nollan v. California Coastal Commission and Dolan v. City of Tigard,* 25 Stetson L. Rev. 719 (1996); Note, *Taking Sides: The Burden of Proof Switch in Dolan v. City of Tigard,* 71 N.Y.U. L. Rev. 1301 (1996); Note, *Exactions for Transportation Corridors After Dolan v. City of Tigard,* 29 Loy. L.A. L. Rev. 247 (1995).

A NOTE ON STATUTORY AUTHORITY FOR DEDICATIONS, IN-LIEU FEES AND IMPACT FEES

The statutory authority problem.—The Standard Planning Act did not authorize the imposition of dedications or in-lieu fees in subdivision control, and this led some courts to hold there was no statutory authority to impose dedications. *Hylton Enters. v. Board of Supvrs.,* 258 S.E.2d 577 (Va. 1979). Other courts held to the contrary, *Divan Bldrs., Inc. v. Planning Bd.,* 334 A.2d 30 (N.J. 1975) (fee for off-site improvements), and some found the authority to require dedication in constitutional home rule powers, *City of College Station v. Turtle Rock Corp.,* 680 S.W.2d 802 (Tex. 1984).

The problem of finding sufficient authority for impact fees can also be troubling. See *Amherst Builders Ass'n v. City of Amherst,* 402 N.E.2d 1181 (Ohio 1980) (home rule powers confer authority to levy impact fee). Failure to comply with enabling legislation can lead to invalidation. See *Washington Sub. San. Comm'n v. C.I. Mitchell & Best Co.,* 495 A.2d 30 (Md. 1985). Local impact fees may also be preempted by conflicting legislation authorizing the funding of public facilities. See *Albany Area Builders Ass'n v. Town of Guilderland,* 546 N.E.2d 920 (N.Y. 1989) (local transportation impact fee preempted by state highway funding law).

Fees in lieu of dedications also fall under attack as taxes not authorized by state legislation. See *Haugen v. Gleeson,* 359 P.2d 108 (Or. 1961) (unauthorized tax because fees not earmarked for benefit of subdivision). In *Jenad, Inc. v. Scarsdale,* 218 N.E.2d 673 (N.Y. 1966), the court stated that fees in lieu of dedication are not taxes but are "fees imposed on the transaction of obtaining plat approval." *Id.,* at 676. In *Jenad* the fees were earmarked for park purposes but not for use within the contributing subdivision. Contra, *Town of Longboat Key v. Lands End, Ltd.,* 433 So. 2d 574 (Fla. App. 1983) (in-lieu fee held a tax because not earmarked for benefit of subdivision).

Statutory authority.—To resolve the statutory problem, several states have authorized dedications and in-lieu fees. E.g., Colo. Rev. Stat. § 30-28-133(4)(a) (park and school sites or fees reasonably necessary to serve subdivision); Vt. Stat. Ann. tit. 24, § 4417(5) (dedication limited to fifteen percent of plat).

Almost half the states have also adopted legislation authorizing impact fees, and this legislation has become a major factor in the use of these fees and in litigation. Some of this legislation is brief, and merely contains enabling authority, but most of the laws contain elaborate requirements for impact fee programs. These may include the preparation of a capital improvements plan, detailed accounting requirements and time limits on the expenditure of fees collected. These statutes often codify the constitutional nexus test. See *Homebuilder's Ass'n of Central Arizona v. City of Scottsdale,* 930 P.2d 993 (Ariz. 1997).

The California legislation, which is typical, applies to fees imposed on "development projects," authorizes the preparation of a capital improvement plan and requires the identification of the purpose of the fee, which may refer to the plan. The municipality must find a "reasonable relationship" between the need for the public facility and the type of development project on which the fee is imposed. The fee must not exceed the reasonable cost of establishing the facility. Special accounting is required, and fees must be spent for the project for which they are collected. Unspent fees not properly accounted for must be returned to developers. Cal. Gov't Code §§ 66000-66008. The statute expressly states that its purpose is to codify existing "constitutional and decisional law." *Id.* § 66005.

Texas also has an elaborate impact fee statute. Tex. Local Gov't Code Ann. §§ 395.001-395.081. The statute enacts the nexus test by authorizing impact fees "to generate revenue for funding or recouping the costs of capital improvements or facility expansions necessitated by and attributable to . . . new development." Detailed provisions are included for calculating and assessing the fee. Before it can levy a fee, a local government must adopt findings on "land use assumptions," which are "a description of the service area and projections of changes in land uses, densities, intensities, and population in the service area over at least a 10-year period." Why do you suppose the statute contains this requirement?

For additional legislation see Ga. Code Ann. § 36-71-1 to § 36-71-13; Haw. Rev. Stat. § 46-141 to § 46-148; Me. Rev. Stat. tit. 30-A, § 4354. Some statutes exempt affordable housing from impact fees. Is this justified?

Here is a typical statutory statement of the standard for levying impact fees:

> County governments affected by the construction of new development projects are hereby authorized to require the payment of fees for any new development projects constructed therein in the event any costs associated with capital improvements or the provision of other services are attributable to such project. Such fees shall not exceed a proportionate share of such costs required to accommodate any such new development. Before requiring payment of any fee authorized hereunder, it must be evident that some reasonable benefit from any such capital improvements will be realized by any such development project. [W. Va. Code § 7-20-4.]

For discussion of impact fee legislation see Blaesser & Kentopp, *Impact Fees: The "Second Generation,"* 38 Wash. U.J. Urb. & Contemp. L. 55 (1990); Leitner & Schoettle, *A Survey of State Impact Fee Enabling Legislation,* 25 Urb. Law. 491 (1993).

A NOTE ON OFFICE-HOUSING LINKAGE PROGRAMS

What they are.—A number of cities have adopted exaction programs requiring office developers either to construct low-or moderate-income housing or pay an in-lieu fee to the city to be used for the construction of such housing. The programs are based on the assumption that new office space creates new jobs that attract new office workers who create pressures on the housing market. Programs in Boston and San Francisco are leading examples. These programs can be mandatory whenever a new office development is built, or can apply only when a developer requests a discretionary approval, such as a variance or special use. For discussion of the San Francisco program see Goetz, *Office-Housing Linkage in San Francisco,* 55 J. Am. Plan. Ass'n 66 (1989). The program has produced a substantial number of affordable housing units.

Authority to adopt.—San Francisco relied on powers derived from a municipal code section that gives the planning commission discretion to grant or deny permits. Share & Diamond, *San Francisco's Office-Housing Production Program,* 35 Land Use L. & Zoning Dig., No. 10, at 4, 6 (1983). After *Bonan v. City of Boston,* 496 N.E.2d 640 (Mass. 1986), suggested the need for legislation to authorize the Boston program, the legislature passed enabling legislation specifically authorizing the program as it then existed. Mass. Gen. Laws ch. 665, §§ 15–20.

For an unusual resolution of the statutory authority issue, see *Holmdel Bldrs. Ass'n v. Township of Holmdel,* 583 A.2d 277 (N.J. 1990). Although there was no explicit state legislative authorization, the court held that approval of housing impact fees was implicit in the state's authorization to adopt inclusionary zoning ordinances. Before fees could actually be collected, however, it required that implementing regulations be adopted by the state's affordable housing agency.

However, in *San Telmo Assocs. v. City of Seattle,* 715 P.2d 673 (Wash. 1987), a city ordinance required owners of low-income housing who demolish it to convert the property to nonresidential use, give the current tenants relocation notices and assistance, and replace a specified percentage of the low-income housing with other suitable housing. The owner could contribute to a low-income housing replacement fund in lieu of providing replacement housing. The court held that the low-income housing requirements were an unauthorized tax:

> Quite simply, the municipal body cannot shift the social costs of development on to a developer under the guise of a regulation. Such cost shifting is a tax, and absent specific legislative pronouncement, the tax is impermissible and invalid. [*Id.* at 675.]

See also *Nunziato v. Planning Bd.,* 541 A.2d 1105 (N.J. App. Div. 1988) invalidating a developer's contribution for affordable housing in return for site plan approval of an office building. It held the board's action was arbitrary and capricious because the contribution was made to induce approval of the building. Without legislative standards the possibilities for abuse in this situation were unlimited, and the free-wheeling dealing in this case was grossly inimical to sound land use regulation.

Is it an exaction?—This question is moot if impact fees do not fall under *Dolan,* as *Del Monte Dunes* seems to hold. Otherwise, the tests for exactions apply. In the *San Telmo* case, *supra,* the court said:

> [T]he City may not constitutionally pass on the social costs of the development of the downtown Seattle area to current owners of low income housing. The problem must be shared by the entire city, and those who plan to develop their property from low income housing to other uses cannot be penalized by being required to provide more housing. [*Id.* at 675.]

The court also suggested the ordinance would be a taking of property because the developer would have to build a new, comparable housing project or contribute approximately $1.5 million to the low-income housing fund. The court seriously questioned whether that levy would allow the developer to make a profitable use of its property. See *Sintra, Inc. v. City of Seattle (II),* 935 P.2d 555 (Wash. 1997) (taking found on remand).

However, in *Commercial Bldrs. of Northern California v. City of Sacramento,* 941 F.2d 872 (9th Cir. 1991), *cert. denied,* 504 U.S. 931 (1992), the Ninth Circuit upheld a linkage fee for building permits on noncommercial buildings. The city based the fee on a study of the need for lower-income housing, and the amount required to offset the impact of nonresidential use on such housing. The court held that the *Nollan* rule of stricter scrutiny did not apply, and that the fee was based on careful study and conservatively assessed only part of the need for lower-income housing to developers. See also *Terminal Plaza Corp. v. City & County of San Francisco,* 223 Cal. Rptr. 739 (Cal. App. 1986) (upholding affordable housing exaction on hotel owners who planned to convert residential hotels to another use).

Holmdel, supra, considered the question raised by *San Telmo* by holding that new developments consume land that could otherwise be used for affordable housing: "The scarcity of land as a resource bears on the opportunity and means to provide affordable housing." 583 A.2d at 285, citing Major, *Linkage of Housing and Commercial Development: The Legal Issues,* 15 Real Estate L.J. 328, 331 (1987). How does the dwindling supply of land specially affect the provision of affordable housing? Recall, in this connection, Chief Justice Wilentz' statement in *Mount Laurel II, supra*: "The state controls the use of land, *all* of the land." Does a diminished supply of land support development fees for other, non-housing, purposes?

Sources.—For an analysis suggesting the Boston linkage program meets the subdivision exaction nexus test, see Kayden & Pollard, *Linkage Ordinances and Traditional Exactions Analysis: The Connection Between Office Development and Housing,* 50 Law & Contemp. Probs. 127 (1987). See also Inclusionary Zoning Goes Downtown (D. Merriam, D. Brower & P. Tegeler eds., 1985); Downtown Linkages (D. Porter ed., 1985); Merrill & Lincoln, *Linkage Fees and Fair Share Regulations: Law and Method,* 25 Urb. Law. 223 (1993); Schukoske, *Housing Linkage: Regulating Development Impact on Housing Costs,* 76 Iowa L. Rev. 1011 (1991).

C. PLANNED UNIT DEVELOPMENTS (PUDs) AND PLANNED COMMUNITIES

Council Turns Down PUD!

Cosconing, May 22nd. — Voting at two o'clock a.m. last night, the town council again turned down a proposed PUD to have been built by Fauna Realty Company. Zoning on the Company's tract stands at its original one-acre level. Spokesmen for the Company indicate that they will now build identical dwellings on the tract. "If cheesebox design is what they want, that's what they'll get," one company official said.

Fauna's proposal called for townhouses and apartments placed in an original design around a man-made lake. Densities would have gone up. The design would have preserved attractive features of the site, which is in the fashionable Upper Seatack neighborhood. Plans for the townhouses and apartments had been drawn by a nationally respected architectural firm.

None of this appeased residents in the area. Organized as the Save Our Seatack (SOS) association, they turned out by the hundreds at last night's meeting. George Pepone, President of SOS, spoke out against the higher densities. "We bought here because this was an aesthetic, suburban community," he told the council. "We want to keep it that way." Highlight of the meeting was a parade of neighborhood children carrying signs reading "STOP PUD." The council's unanimous vote denying the PUD was contrary to the recommendation of its planning commission and planning director.

Exclusionary zoning? Racial discrimination? Hardly. The townhouses and apartments the developer proposed for its Cosconing PUD were priced for the upper-income market. Then why all the fuss? An answer to this question requires an explanation of the PUD concept and what it means for the land use control process.

Conventional zoning divides land uses into fixed categories. Zoning ordinances divide communities into zoning districts that roughly separate incompatible uses. Subdivision controls divide land into lots and blocks. They tend to produce uniform developments in basic cell patterns, in which all of the land is used and all of the building lots are of the same size.

This approach to land development may have fit the building practices of the early twentieth century, when residential development proceeded slowly and houses were built one at a time. (It also met the judicial penchant for equal treatment.) With the coming of the post-war years, the pattern of residential development shifted. Large-scale developers, building hundreds of homes at a time on large tracts, became common. This kind of development prompted the need for a control system in which the entire development could be reviewed as an entity and advantage taken of the design and other opportunities which large-scale development creates. For examples, see S. Tomioka & E. Tomioka, Planned Unit Developments: Design and Regional Impact (1984).

Today, it is common to refer to PUDs as planned communities, or master-planned communities. However, this section will use the term PUD because that term is the one most commonly used in court decisions and ordinances.

The advantages of PUD regulations.—PUD regulations have several advantages over conventional land use controls. The PUD is reviewed as an entity without the restrictions imposed by fixed yard and height requirements. This provides an opportunity for better project design. Lower costs are possible because PUDs usually reallocate project densities. Higher densities in one part of the project are offset by common open areas in another. The opportunity to concentrate development lowers street and utility costs.

The PUD also has several land use advantages. Land saved by the reduction of side and front yards can be set aside as more useful common open space for all the residents. Building types can be mixed as a PUD may include both multifamily and single-family dwellings. This breakdown in building type separation is hard to achieve under traditional zoning. PUD review can also allow for higher densities, which may be offset by the provision of common open space or improved project design. Attention can also be given to the preservation of natural resource features, such as wetlands and woodlands, in the design of PUD projects. See S. Van der Ryn & S. Cowan, Ecological Design (1995).

PUD types.

Density Transfer Systems.—The simplest and least controversial of the planned development techniques, the "density transfer," is best exemplified by cluster development. Under this system, minimum lot sizes (and usually yard requirements) are smaller than those normally required by the zoning ordinance. The permitted building types, however, are unaffected — a density transfer system will not allow apartments in a single-family zone. Nor does a density transfer system affect the over-all density of development — the area "saved" through lot-size reductions is merely retained within the development, most often being designated as common open space. [For an interesting case sustaining the transfer of development rights in the context of a PUD ordinance see *Dupont Circle Citizens Ass'n v. District of Columbia Zoning Comm'n*, 355 A.2d 550 (D.C. App. 1976).]

Varying Residential Types; No Increase in Density.—Some planned development ordinances allow multi-family or single-family structures (or both), but still prohibit any increase in density. The provision of common open space, though not unusual, may not be required by such an ordinance.

Varying Residential Types; Density Increases Allowed.—Some of the ordinances which allow a variety of residential types also authorize an increase in density. Ordinarily, these increases are subject to standards contained in the ordinance.

Mixed-Use Projects.—To a variety of dwelling types the planned development ordinance may also add other uses, such as ancillary shopping or even a neighborhood or community shopping center. Industrial uses may also be allowed. Increases in residential density may or may not be permitted. If the scale of a mixed-use project is sufficiently extensive, it can take on the character of an entire planned community or "new town." [D. Mandelker, Controlling Planned Residential Developments 8–9 (1966).]

The PUD concept today.—The PUD concept is a technique for approving development projects as an entity. It can be used for master-planned communities with thousands of residents or for small-scale residential projects. For a review of master-planned community development see A. Schmitz & L. Bookout, Trends and Innovations in Master-Planned Communities (1998). Financing and marketing problems, however, lead many developers to prefer smaller projects, often called cluster development. See Knack, *Master Planned Lite,* Planning, Vol. 61, No. 10, at 4 (1995). For a review of cluster development design principles see James, *Getting the Most Out of Compact Development,* Land Development, Vol. 13, No. 3, at 23 (2000). James suggests a number of design principles for compact development to achieve greater variety, such as splitting large lots into smaller parcels with open space, varying cluster shapes for individuality and intrigue, and varying garage locations and setbacks for a "soft streetscape." *Id.* at 25. Note how this type of design presents challenges for the PUD approval process. Some communities attempt to influence the size of their PUDs by setting minimum sizes for PUD developments.

NOTES AND QUESTIONS

1. *PUD issues.* Map 1 on the following page illustrates a simple density transfer planned unit residential development and illustrates the regulatory problems presented by this kind of project. What has happened is that open space areas have been provided throughout the development for common use. Lot sizes have been reduced for the individual lots, but this apparent increase in density is offset by the open space areas; there is no net density increase in the development. Under variants of the PUD approach, as discussed in the excerpt, densities could have been increased as well, and new building types such as townhouses and apartments added. If this were a larger PUD, a retail shopping area could also have been included.

MAP 1. A RESIDENTIAL DENSITY TRANSFER PLANNED UNIT DEVELOPMENT

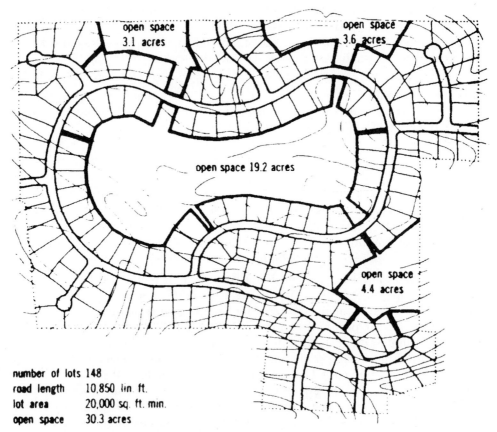

number of lots 148
road length   10,850 lin. ft.
lot area   20,000 sq. ft. min.
open space   30.3 acres

Source: Office of State Planning, State of New Hampshire, Handbook of Subdivision Practice 82 (1972).

An initial thought is that the project shown by Map 1 does not look all that bad. Then why all the fuss in the Cosconing news story at the beginning of this section? Richard Babcock, the late well-known Chicago zoning lawyer, may have the answer:

> The initial response is one of enthusiasm for the novel plot plan. It does have a catchy design. The local commissioner is as intrigued as he would be by four-color copy in an ad in the New Yorker magazine. The emotional empathy rises. Then there is a pause. This proposal represents people, not tonic water. The emotional graph levels off. And down it zooms as some practical soul asks: "What kind of nut would move to Wedgewood and not want his own backyard?"
>
> Another client asks: "Well, if your costs are less, then, of course, you expect to reduce your prices?" With that the jig is up. [R. Babcock, The Zoning Game 31–32 (1966).]

Although most PUDs emphasize residential uses and are sometimes called PRDs, it is also possible to have either Planned Commercial (PCD) or Planned Industrial (PID) Developments. See, e.g., N.J. Stat. Ann. § 40:55D-6. See *City of Little Rock v. Pfeifer*, 887 S.W.2d 296 (Ark. 1994); *Singer v. Fairborn*, 598 N.E.2d 806 (Ohio App. 1991). How might the PUD goals of flexibility and better design be applied in non-residential PUDs?

2. *The PUD review and approval process.* The zoning ordinance must provide a method for approving PUDs. One way to do this is to map all the PUD districts in advance. Under a more common method, the PUD regulations are included in the zoning ordinance, but PUDs are mapped individually as applications for approval are made. This procedure resembles a floating zone.

The next consideration is "the extent to which the PUD regulations will be driven by the development standards of the base zoning districts or contain separate standards." B. Blaesser, Discretionary Zoning § 6.10 (2000). The first approach is process-oriented, and gives the decision maker the opportunity to modify existing standards on a case-by-case basis. The second approach provides a separate set of standards that can be specifically tailored to guide the approval of PUDs. Either approach raises the spectre of arbitrary decision making if standards are not adequate.

To avoid this problem, careful attention must be given to setting PUD standards. Standards should be provided for land uses, densities, project design, and site development, such as height and spacing requirements. PUD ordinances may also contain purpose clauses requiring, for example, that a PUD must provide a "harmonious residential environment superior to what would be provided under" the zoning restrictions that would otherwise apply. The ordinance should make it clear whether the purpose clause is a substantive standard that must be satisfied before a PUD can be approved. See *Dupont Circle Citizens Ass'n v. District of Columbia Zoning Comm'n*, 426 A.2d 327 (D.C. 1981) (purpose clause containing requirement of this type held not to require a comparison of PUDs with conventional developments).

The ordinance must also select the zoning agency which is to conduct PUD reviews. This can present problems under the Standard Zoning Act. One alternative is to have the planning commission carry out PUD reviews under the standards in the ordinance once PUDs are mapped. The legislative body may have to approve individual PUDs under the PUD standards, especially if PUD land uses and densities are different from those allowed by the previous applicable zoning district. Why?

Problems may then arise because the Standard Zoning Act does not authorize the case-by-case review by these zoning agencies that the PUD process requires. However, a simple density transfer PUD that does not require changes in land uses or densities could be approved by the planning commission in the subdivision control process.

Approval procedures may take time if review is required by more than one local body. One study found that developers criticized the PUD approval process because of the length and complexity of the approval process, the lack of sophistication of local officials authorized to approve PUDs, and problems created by community opposition. C. Moore & C. Siskin, PUDs in Practice 40–44 (1985)

3. *The uniformity issue.* Recall that the Standard Zoning Act requires that all zoning regulations be uniform throughout each zoning district.

> Because single-use districts are a fairly common feature of conventional zoning practice, many have inferred that the uniform regulation requirement when applied to use regulations means that only one kind of land use may be permitted within a given district. Thus the argument goes that the mixture of uses contemplated by the typical PUD ordinance is beyond the power of the local legislature. [F. So, D. Mosena, & F. Bangs, Planned Unit Development Ordinances 48 (American Soc'y of Planning Officials, Planning Advisory Service Rep. No. 291, 1973).]

It was also thought that the courts might recoil against the flexible case-by-case approval that is inherent in the PUD process, and that the courts might object to sensitive zoning that would react specifically to the particularized development plans of an individual developer. See Krasnowiecki, *Legal Aspects of Planned Unit Development,* in Theory and Practice in Frontiers of Planned Unit Development 99, 101–02 (R. Burchell ed., 1973).

The following case indicates how one court reacted to claims that a PUD review process was not authorized by a state zoning statute based on the Standard Act. Note the date. The case was decided at a time when PUDs were becoming popular as a form of development, but the authority to adopt PUD regulations under statutes based on the Standard Zoning Act had not been tested.

CHENEY v. VILLAGE 2 AT NEW HOPE, INC.

429 Pa. 626, 241 A.2d 81 (1968)

ROBERTS, JUSTICE:

. . . [After explaining the PUD concept, the court detailed the enactment of a PUD district by the Borough of New Hope. On the same day the Borough council adopted the district it also rezoned a large tract of land known as the

Rauch Farm from low density residential to PUD. The planning commission then approved a plan for the PUD and building permits were issued. Neighboring property owners brought an action challenging the adoption of the PUD and the PUD rezoning, and the lower court held the ordinances invalid "for failure to conform to a comprehensive plan and for vesting too much discretion in the New Hope Planning Commission."

[The supreme court reversed. It held that the PUD was consistent with the plan and that it was not improper spot zoning. The court then considered the approval procedure authorized by the PUD ordinance.]

The court below next concluded that even if the two ordinances were properly passed, they must fall as vesting authority in the planning commission greater than that permitted under Pennsylvania's zoning enabling legislation. More specifically, it is now contended by appellees that complete project approval by the planning commission under ordinance 160 requires that commission to encroach upon legislative territory whenever it decides where, within a particular PUD district, specific types of buildings should be placed.

In order to appreciate fully the arguments of counsel on both sides it is necessary to explain in some detail exactly what is permitted within a PUD district, and who decides whether a particular land owner has complied with these requirements. Admittedly the range of permissible uses within the PUD district is greater than that normally found in a traditional zoning district. Within a New Hope PUD district there may be: single family attached or detached dwellings; apartments; accessory private garages; public or private parks and recreation areas including golf courses, swimming pools, ski slopes, etc. (so long as these facilities do not produce noise, glare, odor, air pollution, etc., detrimental to existing or prospective adjacent structures); a municipal building; a school; churches; art galleries; professional offices; certain types of signs; a theatre (but not a drive-in); motels and hotels; and a restaurant. The ordinance then sets certain overall density requirements. The PUD district may have a maximum of 80% of the land devoted to residential uses, a maximum of 20% for the permitted commercial uses and enclosed recreational facilities, and must have a minimum of 20% for open spaces. The residential density shall not exceed 10 units per acre, nor shall any such unit contain more than two bedrooms. All structures within the district must not exceed maximum height standards set out in the ordinance. Finally, although there are no traditional "set back" and "side yard" requirements, ordinance 160 does require that there be 24 feet between structures, and that no townhouse structure contain more than 12 dwelling units.

The procedure to be followed by the aspiring developer reduces itself to presenting a detailed plan for his planned unit development to the planning commission, obtaining that body's approval and then securing building permits. Of course, the planning commission may not approve any development that fails to meet the requirements set forth in the ordinance as outlined above.

We begin with the observation that there is nothing in the borough zoning enabling act which would prohibit council from creating a zoning district with this many permissible uses. The applicable section of the borough code is 53

P.S. § 48201. Under this section, council is given the power to regulate and restrict practically all aspects of buildings themselves, open spaces, population density, location of structures, etc., the only limitation on this power being that it be exercised so as to promote the "health, safety, morals or the general welfare" of the borough. Under the same act, 53 P.S. § 46601 empowers council to adopt ordinances to govern the use of public areas, such as streets, parks, etc., again with the only limitation being that such ordinances create "conditions favorable to the health, safety, morals and general welfare of the citizens." Thus, if council reasonably believed that a given district could contain *all* types of structures, without *any* density requirements whatsoever, so long as this did not adversely affect health, safety and morals, such a district could be created. In fact, it is common knowledge that in many industrial and commercial districts just such a wide range of uses is permitted. Given such broad power to zone, we cannot say that New Hope Borough Council abrogated its legislative function by creating a PUD district permitting the mixture of uses outlined supra, especially given the density requirements.

We must next examine the statutory power of the borough planning commission to determine whether such an administrative body may regulate the internal development of a PUD district. The Act, 53 P.S. § 46155 requires that all plans for land "laid out in building lots" be approved by the planning commission before they may be recorded. Thus, the traditional job of the commission has been to examine tract plans to determine whether they conform to the applicable borough ordinances. The ordinances most frequently interpreted and applied by the planning commission are those dealing with streets, sewers, water and gas mains, etc., i.e., the so-called public improvements. However, the statute contains no language which would prohibit the planning commission from approving plans with reference to ordinances dealing with permissible building uses as well. The primary reason that planning commissions have not traditionally interpreted this type of ordinance is that such regulations do not usually come into play until the landowner wishes to begin the actual construction of a particular building. By this time, the relevant subdivision plan has already been approved by the commission; thus the task of examining the plans for a particular structure to see whether it conforms to the regulations for the zoning district in which it will be erected devolves upon the local building inspector who issues the building permit.

However, in the case of a PUD the entire development (including specific structures) is mapped out and submitted to the administrative agency at once. Accordingly, the requirements set forth in a PUD ordinance must relate not only to those areas traditionally administered by the planning commission, but also to areas traditionally administered by the building inspector. Therefore, quite logically, the job of approving a particular PUD should rest with a single municipal body. The question then is simply which one: Borough Council (a legislative body), the Planning Commission (an administrative body), or the Zoning Board of Adjustment (an administrative body)?

There is no doubt that it would be statutorily permissible for council itself to pass a PUD ordinance and simultaneous zoning map amendment so specific that no details would be left for any administrator. The ordinance could specify where each building should be placed, how large it should be, where the open spaces are located, etc. But what would be the practical effect of such an ordinance? One of the most attractive features of Planned Unit Development is its flexibility; the chance for the builder and the municipality to sit down together and tailor a development to meet the specific needs of the community and the requirements of the land on which it is to be built. But all this would be lost if the Legislature let the planning cement set before any developer could happen upon the scene to scratch his own initials in that cement. Professor Krasnowiecki has accurately summed up the effect on planned unit development of such legislative planning. The picture, to be sure, is not a happy one:

> "The traditional refuge of the courts, the requirement that all the standards be set forth in advance of application for development, does not offer a practical solution to the problem. The complexity of pre-established regulations that would automatically dispose of any proposal for planned unit development, when different housing types and perhaps accessory commercial areas are envisaged, would be quite considerable. Indeed as soon as various housing types are permitted, the regulations that would govern their design and distribution on every possible kind of site, their relationship to each other and their relationship to surrounding properties must be complex unless the developer's choice in terms of site, site plan, and design and distribution of housing is reduced close to zero. It is not likely . . . that local authorities would want to adopt such a set of regulations." Krasnowiecki, Planned Unit Development: A Challenge to Established Theory and Practice of Land Use Control, 114 U. Pa. L. Rev. 47, 71 (1965).

Left with Professor Krasnowiecki's "Hobson's choice" of no developer leeway at all, or a staggering set of legislative regulations sufficient to cover every idea the developer might have, it is not likely that Planned Unit Development could thrive, or even maintain life, if the local legislature assumed totally the role of planner.

The remaining two municipal bodies which could oversee the shaping of specific Planned Unit Developments are both administrative agencies, the Zoning Board of Adjustment and the Planning Commission. As this Court views both reality and the zoning enabling act, the Zoning Board of Adjustment is not the proper body. The Act, 53 P.S. § 48207(g) specifically sets forth the powers of a borough zoning board of adjustment. These powers are three in number, and only three. The board may (1) hear and decide appeals where there is an alleged error made by an administrator in the enforcement of the enabling act or any ordinance enacted pursuant thereto; (2) hear and decide special exceptions; and (3) authorize the grant of variances from the terms of existing ordinances. These powers in no way encompass the authority to review and approve the plan for an entire development when such plan is neither at variance with the existing ordinance nor is a special exception to it; nor does (1) above supply the necessary power since the board would not be reviewing an alleged administrative error.

Moreover, from a practical standpoint, a zoning board of adjustment is, of the three bodies here under discussion, the one least equipped to handle the problem of PUD approval. Zoning boards are accustomed to focusing on one lot at a time. They traditionally examine hardship cases and unique uses proposed by landowners. As Professor Krasnowiecki has noted: "To suggest that the board is intended, or competent, to handle large scale planning and design decisions is, I think, far fetched." Technical Bulletin 52, Urban Land Institute, p. 38 (1965). We agree.

Thus, the borough planning commission remains the only other body both qualified and statutorily permitted to approve PUD. Of course, we realize that a planning commission is not authorized to engage in actual re-zoning of land. But merely because the commission here has the power to approve more than one type of building for a particular lot within the PUD district does not mean that the commission is usurping the zoning function. Indeed, it is acting in strict *accordance* with the applicable zoning ordinance, for that ordinance, No. 160, *permits* more than one type of building for a particular lot. To be sure, if the commission approved a plan for a PUD district where 30% of the land were being used commercially, *then* we would have an example of illegal re-zoning by an administrator. But no one argues in the present case that appellant's plan does not conform to the requirements of ordinance 160.

Nor is this Court sympathetic to appellees' argument that ordinance 160 permits the planning commission to grant variances and special exceptions. We fail to see how a development such as appellant's that meets every single requirement of the applicable zoning ordinance can be said to be the product of a variance or a special exception. The very essence of variances and special exceptions lies in their *departure* from ordinance requirements, not in their compliance with them. We therefore conclude that the New Hope Planning Commission has the power to approve development plans submitted to it under Ordinance 160. . . .

NOTES AND QUESTIONS

1. *The delegation problem.* Carefully review the provisions of the PUD ordinance in *Cheney.* The ordinance specified densities and uses. Does this exhaust legislative policy making? If so, does this explain the court's decision upholding the authority of the planning commission to approve PUD plans? What if the ordinance left the determination of densities and uses to the planning commission? *Sheridan Planning Ass'n v. Board of Sheridan County Comm'rs,* 924 P.2d 988 (Wyo. 1996), held that delegation of approval of a final PUD plan was not an improper delegation when the plan could be approved only if it complied with a schematic plan previously approved by the legislative body.

2. *PUD approval procedures. Chrinko v. South Brunswick Twp. Planning Bd.,* 187 A.2d 221 (N.J.L. Div. 1963), is another case holding that PUD ordinances may be enacted under a zoning statute based on the Standard Act. The township enacted a density transfer PUD ordinance with power to approve in the planning board, which is the New Jersey term for planning commission. Although noting that the zoning act did not "in so many words" authorize PUD ordinances, the court held that

> such an ordinance reasonably advances the legislative purposes of securing open spaces, preventing overcrowding and undue concentration of population, and promoting the general welfare. Nor is it an

objection that uniformity of regulation is required within a zoning district. Such a legislative technique accomplishes uniformity because the option is open to all developers within a zoning district, and escapes the vice that it is compulsory. [*Id.* at 225.]

What if the PUD procedures are compulsory? In *Porpoise Point P'ship v. St. John's County,* 532 So. 2d 727 (Fla. App. 1988), the court invalidated a PUD the county adopted for a development on its own initiative. The court held that planned unit development was a voluntary procedure intended to provide development flexibility not possible under the zoning ordinance, but that it cannot be forced on a developer who simply wants a rezoning of its land.

Other courts have easily rejected challenges to PUD ordinances based on a lack of uniformity. In *Orinda Homeowners Comm. v. Board of Supvrs.,* 90 Cal. Rptr. 88 (Cal. App. 1970), the court had this to say on the uniformity requirement:

> [The zoning enabling statute] provides that the *regulations* shall be uniform for each class or kind of building or use of land throughout the zone. It does not state that the units must be alike even as to their character, whether single family or multi-family. In conventional zoning, where apartment houses are permitted in a particular zone, single family dwellings, being regarded (whether rightly or wrongly) as a "higher" use, are also allowed. This causes no conflict with . . . [the statute]. [*Id.* at 90–91.]

An argument related to the uniformity requirement may arise out of the bargaining and negotiation that usually precede a PUD approval. In *Rutland Envtl. Protection Ass'n v. Kane County,* 334 N.E.2d 215 (Ill. App. 1975), the argument was made that this kind of negotiation was invalid as contract zoning. The argument was rejected, the court noting that "[s]ince the overall aims of . . . [PUD] zoning cannot be accomplished without negotiations and because conferences are indeed mandated by the regulating ordinance, the conduct of the . . . [county] cannot be read as contributing to contract zoning." *Id.* at 219. Note that the PUD is usually conditioned because it must comply with specific development requirements contained in the approved PUD development plan. How is it that the legislative body can approve the PUD plan and yet avoid arguments that it has illegally conditioned the exercise of legislative power? Krasnowiecki, *supra,* at 102, suggests that "zoning changes granted at the request of a particular applicant can be limited by ordinance to the proposal as described in the plans and oral testimony presented by the applicant in support of his request," citing *Albright v. Town of Manlius,* 268 N.E.2d 785 (N.Y. 1971).

3. *Which zoning agency. Cheney* approved PUD approvals by the planning commission. What problems might arise if the PUD ordinance provides for PUD approval by other zoning agencies? Consider the following cases:

In re Moreland, 497 P.2d 1287 (Okla. 1972). Acting under a local PUD ordinance, the board of adjustment approved a PUD for a mobile home park and retail shopping center. The ordinance was upheld as falling within the provisions of the state zoning act allowing the board to grant special exceptions. Since the board's function was to determine whether the PUD complied with the provisions of the ordinance, it was acting in a quasi-judicial and not a legislative capacity. No revision of the local comprehensive plan or zoning ordinance could be carried out by the board, and the ordinance required that any approved PUDs be devoted primarily to residential purposes and only secondarily to nonresidential uses. The ordinance provided a series of design standards, and also required that approved PUDs conform to the intent and purposes of the local zoning ordinance and the local and regional comprehensive plans.

Chandler v. Kroiss, 190 N.W.2d 472 (Minn. 1972). The PUD ordinance authorized the legislative body to grant special permits for PUDs. Since the PUD contemplated multifamily development, which was not a permitted use under the zoning ordinance, an argument was made that a variance should have been requested. The court rejected this argument, noting that the PUD ordinance provided for a hybrid procedure combining the variance and special exception. "To the extent that the result of the proceeding for approval of a planned unit development thus alters the established, allowed land usages of the village, it has the same effect as would a succession of variances or rezonings." *Id.* at 476.

Lutz v. City of Longview, 520 P.2d 1374 (Wash. 1974). This case considered a floating zone PUD. The planning commission was authorized to approve PUDs as authorized by the PUD provision of the zoning ordinance, and in this case approved a PUD for multi-family use in a single-family area. Holding that such a change in use is a legislative function, the court held that PUD approval under the ordinance could not be delegated to the planning commission. Is this case consistent with the principal case?

Compare *City of Waukesha v. Town Bd.,* 543 N.W.2d 515 (Wis. App. 1995). The court invalidated an ordinance allowing the plan commission to approve a PUD because the ordinance did not specify where a PUD could be located, and authorized a PUD approval allowing uses not authorized in the zoning district.

Town of N. Hempstead v. Village of N. Hills, 342 N.E.2d 566 (N.Y. 1975). The PUD ordinance provided for the approval of PUDs as a floating zone through the amendment of the zoning map. Relying on its earlier floating zone case, *Rodgers v. Village of Tarrytown,* reproduced *supra,* Ch. 5, the court upheld this procedure. Neither was the ordinance discriminatory because PUDs were allowed only in one residential zone. The court noted that eighty percent of the land in this community was in this zone.

4. *Density transfers.* In *Prince George's County v. M & B Constr. Co.,* 297 A.2d 683 (Md. 1972), a PUD ordinance was adopted that delegated approval of PUDs to the planning commission. Amendments were made both to the zoning and subdivision control ordinances to allow PUDs. Single-family dwellings and townhouses were allowed in PUDs, which were a permitted use in residential zones. Reductions in lot sizes were allowed subject to a minimum lot size requirement, but existing densities and building bulk in approved PUDs were to remain the same. The court held that the approval of PUDs was properly delegated to the planning commission as part of its subdivision control powers. PUDs authorized by this ordinance appear to fall in the density transfer category. Does this help support the court's opinion?

A provision in one of the early model planning acts authorizing density transfer PUDs has been adopted in a few states. For discussion of the New York version of this provision, see *Rouse v. O'Connell,* 353 N.Y.S.2d 124 (N.Y. Sup. 1974) (trial court). See generally on the problems raised in these Notes, Aloi, *Legal Problems in Planned Unit Development: Uniformity, Comprehensive Planning, Conditions, and the Floating Zone,* 1 Real Est. L.J. 5 (1972).

5. *The comprehensive plan.* What is the role of the comprehensive plan in the PUD approval process? *Lutz, supra,* indicated that the lack of specific guidelines for PUDs in the comprehensive plan did not mean that a PUD approval would be invalid as spot zoning. In *Amcon Corp. v. City of Eagan,* 348 N.W.2d 66 (Minn. 1984), the planning board refused to grant a business rezoning supplementary to a PUD approval even though the rezoning would have been consistent with the comprehensive plan. The court held that the failure to follow the plan was "strong evidence of arbitrary action" and remanded with directions ordering a rezoning.

6. In view of these cases, how would you evaluate the observation of many commentators that an amendment of land use control legislation is not necessary in order to adopt and implement a PUD ordinance? Do the cases allow sufficient flexibility in the adoption of PUD ordinances to carry out all the objectives of PUD procedures? Is there sufficient flexibility in the selection of the local agency to review and approve a PUD?

The PUD approval process often requires the approval of a general development plan followed by the approval of a more precise plan. The extent to which the legislative body must participate in the approval of these plans is not always clear, as the following case indicates.

MILLBRAE ASS'N FOR RESIDENTIAL SURVIVAL v. CITY OF MILLBRAE

262 Cal. App. 2d 222, 69 Cal. Rptr. 251 (1968)

MOLINARI, PRESIDING JUSTICE:

. . . .

Findings of Fact

The specific findings of fact of the trial court were as follows: in 1959 the City Council of the City of Millbrae duly adopted and enacted Ordinance No. 161, which amended the basic zoning ordinance of the City of Millbrae (Ordinance 42) to provide for a classification of land use known as Planned Unit Development or PD District. In 1960 the Trousdale Construction Company filed with the City of Millbrae an application to rezone approximately 52 acres of R-1 land (single family residence) to PD district. The "Project General Plan" accompanying said application divided said 52 acres of land into 8 sections, numbered from Section A to Section I. After due notice and public hearings on the question, the City Planning Commission adopted Resolution No. 12 approving the rezoning of all 8 sections of the property described in the application of the "Project General Plan" from R-1 to PD zoning. The City

Council, after giving due notice and holding public hearings on the zoning described in Resolution No. 12 and in the accompanying "Project General Plan," adopted Ordinance No. 182 on August 1, 1961, rezoning only Section A (approximately 13 acres) of the total property from R-1 to PD district. The "Project General Plan" submitted at that time provided for construction of seven six-story apartment buildings on the property. . . .

On April 6, 1962, interveners acquired an option to purchase the subject property including the rezoned Section A. Shortly thereafter the then owners of the property applied to the City to amend the "Project General Plan" described in Ordinance 182 to provide for three high-rise apartment buildings and seven quadplexes instead of the seven six-story buildings originally contemplated. The City Planning Commission held public hearings on the amendment and then adopted Resolution No. 22 approving the changes subject to four conditions, which were, briefly, that Vallejo and Connejo Drives be connected; that off-street parking be provided in a ratio of .75 to 1; that a water tank be provided; and that the developer incorporate into the PD district property which he owned immediately east of the district. After due notice was given and public hearings held, the City Council on August 7, 1962, approved the amendment of the "Project General Plan" subject to the foregoing conditions and requested interveners to present their "Project Precise Plan" reflecting the changes. . . .

On February 20, 1963, pursuant to the terms of Ordinance 161, the owners of the property filed with the City Planning Commission an application for approval of their "Project Precise Plan." At four regular public meetings, the Planning Commission reviewed and ultimately, on April 22, 1963, approved the Precise Plan. No public hearings as such were held, although local newspapers carried stories about the proceedings. While the Planning Commission was reviewing the Precise Plan, the City Council requested copies thereof and reviewed said plans at a public meeting on March 19, 1963, but took no formal action thereon. The Precise Plan was approved April 22, 1963, and changed the "Amended Project General Plan" of August 7, 1962, as follows: seven apartment units were added to the high-rise buildings; part of a proposed pitch and putt golf course was eliminated; parking spaces were increased; and two of the three high-rise buildings, buildings A-1 and A-2, were substantially relocated. The Precise Plan relocated building A-2 from 70 feet distant to 35 feet distant from the property line of plaintiffs Robert J. and Patricia M. Lloyd, who had made a deposit on their property adjacent to the PD district around February of 1963 and moved into their residence in February 1964.

On May 27, 1963, the subject property was conveyed to interveners. . . .

Interveners' Appeal [10]

A. *The Validity of the Planning Commission's Approval of Interveners' "Project Precise Plan"*

As previously noted, the Planning Commission approved interveners' "Project Precise Plan" on April 22, 1963, without holding public hearings as such and without the City Council taking any formal action, although the City Council did request copies of the Plan and reviewed the same at a public meeting on March 19, 1963. The trial court found that the respects in which the "Project Precise Plan" deviated from the "Amended Project General Plan" constituted substantial changes. The question for our decision is whether the trial court erred in concluding that the Precise Plan is invalid as an attempt by the Planning Commission at de facto rezoning. . . .

The "general plan" with which we are here concerned, as conceded by the parties, is that provided for in section 3.7-E-3 of Ordinance No. 161 providing for the initiation of a change of classification to PD district. In order to have property rezoned PD an applicant must, in accordance with the procedure for securing an amendment to the zoning ordinance, submit to the Planning Commission and to the City Council a general plan of his proposed development, on the basis of which plan the City Council must approve or disapprove the application. (Ord. 161, §§ 3.7-E-3, 3.7-E-4.) Said general plan must show the proposed site of the project and "the character and use of adjoining property; the general size, location and use of all proposed buildings and structures to be placed on the site; the location and dimensions of streets, parking areas, open areas and other public and private facilities and users." (Ord. 161, § 3.7-E-3.)

After having secured the rezoning of his property as PD, the applicant may nevertheless not begin development of the site unless he secures approval of a "Precise Plan" which must include certain specified data such as the total development plan, engineering site plans and landscaping plans, architectural drawings and/or sketches demonstrating the design and character of the proposed structure, uses and facilities, and other pertinent information necessary to determine whether the contemplated arrangements or use make it desirable to apply regulations and requirements differing from those ordinarily applicable. (Ord. 161, §§ 3.7-E-4, 3.7-E-7.) In order to grant approval of a "Precise Plan," the Planning Commission must make certain findings indicating that the proposed development is in conformity to certain specified standards. [11] Under the ordinances the approval of this "Precise

---

[10] Interveners appeal from that portion of the modified judgment of the trial court which reads:

"Project Precise Plan approved by the Planning Commission on April 22, 1963, is invalid since it is not in accord with the Amended Project General Plan dated August 7, 1962 and the City of Millbrae and the City Building Inspector thereof are hereby enjoined and restrained from issuing permits for buildings pursuant to said invalid Project Precise Plan dated April 22, 1963."

[11] These findings are as follows:

"1. That the proposed development will produce an environment of stable and desirable character, and

"2. That the proposed development provides over-all standards of population densities, of open

Plan" is wholly delegated to the Planning Commission, and the holding of public meetings thereon is optional. (Ord. 161, §§ 3.7-E-6 to 3.7-E-10.) . . .

Essentially, the parties agree that if the approval of such a Precise Plan is the same sort of administrative function as the issuance of a conditional use permit or the granting of a variance, then the Planning Commission has the authority to grant such approval, independently of the City Council and without any mandatory public hearings. Likewise, the parties agree that the Planning Commission may not rezone property or otherwise effectuate any changes in the Millbrae zoning ordinances without acting in conjunction with the City Council in compliance with the notice and hearing procedures expressly required by Millbrae Ordinance 42, sections 4.6, 4.62, 4.63, 4.64 and former Government Code sections 65500-65805. . . .

Before proceeding further, it will be necessary to review the concept of planned unit development or PD districting in use of the City of Millbrae at all times here relevant. The technique of planned unit development is the development of land as a unit where it is desirable to apply regulations more flexible than those pertaining to other zoning classifications and to grant diversification in the location of structures and other site qualities. It should be particularly noted that the PD district established constitutes a separate zoning district in addition to the more conventional types of zoning districts such as R-1 (single family residential) and C-1 (light commercial). (See Millbrae Ord. 161, § 2.1.) The Millbrae zoning ordinances do not prescribe any specific use standards, restrictions, nor requirements applicable to PD districts other than limiting such districts to a minimum size of four acres and restricting the uses to those permitted in the other types of zoning districts existing in Millbrae, the significant feature of the PD district being that the several uses may be commingled. (See Ord. 161, §§ 3.7-2, 3.7-E-5.) . . .

[I]n the present case at the time the Planning Commission was called upon to approve the "Project Precise Plan" the subject property was zoned PD district limited to the construction of three high-rise apartments and seven quadplexes of a general size and at locations designated in the general plan and subject to the location and dimensions of the streets, parking areas and other open spaces as specified in the general plan. We note, further, that the four conditions imposed by the Planning Commission and the City Council upon which the zoning was made contingent were performed by interveners and that the evidence establishing such performance is sustained in the record.

Our immediate inquiry, therefore, is to ascertain the nature of the plan which was designated as the "Project Precise Plan." The thrust of our inquiry is whether, in addition to the matters which were properly the subject of the precise plan provided for in the ordinance and solely for the consideration of

---

space, of circulation and offstreet parking, and other general conditions of use at least equivalent to those required by the terms of this ordinance in districts where similar uses are permitted, and

"3. That the proposed Precise Plan shall represent a development of sufficient harmony within itself and with adjacent areas to justify any exceptions to the normal regulations within this ordinance." (Ord. 161, § 3.7-E-8.)

the Planning Commission, there was included therein substantial changes which were tantamount to a rezoning of the PD district as is contended by plaintiffs. As already noted, interveners urge that provision in the "Project Precise Plan" for seven additional apartments in the high-rise buildings, the reduction in size of the golf course, the increase in the number of parking spaces, and the relocation of two of the high-rise buildings amounted to nothing more than the issuance of a use permit or the granting of a variance, matters solely for the Planning Commission's determination. This determination is a question of law. . . .

In our view, while the change in the number of apartments in each of the high-rise buildings would properly be the subject of the precise plan under the ordinance so long as it did not increase the "general size" of the buildings as delineated in the general plan, the other changes amount to a substantial alteration of the general plan since they materially and fundamentally change the location of two of the high-rise buildings and the size of the parking areas and the open areas. These were specific elements of the general plan incident to the zoning of the PD district and their change and alteration amounted to a rezoning of the district. We are persuaded to this conclusion by the very nature of the PD district. Although the creation of such a district allows for greater flexibility and diversification in the location of structures and other site qualities and their uses, once these elements are delineated in the general plan they constitute material and indispensable attributes of the district itself. In other words, the zoning characteristics of the district consist not only in the classification of the district to PD but in the components of the general plan accompanying the application for the creation of the district and any subsequent amendments to the plan that may properly be adopted. Accordingly, any substantial change or alteration in the actual physical characteristics of the district and its configuration amount to a rezoning of the district and may only be accomplished pursuant to the provisions of the state statutes and the local ordinances consistent therewith providing for zoning and rezoning.

The argument urged by interveners that the subject changes are analogous to the granting of a use permit or a variance is not applicable here. The cases cited by them apply to situations where the property is validly zoned for a particular purpose and the variances or conditional uses are permitted as being within the scope and purpose of the zoning ordinance. Here, aside from the addition in the number of apartments to be contained within the size of authorized buildings, the proposed changes do not constitute "use permits" amounting to permissible variances but are substantial alterations in the zoning which is peculiarly indigenous to the established zoning district. . . .

NOTES AND QUESTIONS

1. *Amending PUDs.* As the principal case indicates, there can be considerable confusion about the land use restrictions that control an approved PUD. Where were the controlling restrictions in the principal case? In the zoning ordinance or the general plan? What was being amended? Note also the similarities between the "general" and "precise" plans at issue in the principal case and the conventional practice of requiring "preliminary" and "final" subdivision and site plan approvals. Are the legal considerations different, however? Does *Millbrae* throw any light on what questions in the initial approval of a PUD must be decided by the legislative body? The approval process for PUDs described in *Millbrae* illustrates one method of PUD review that is still common today.

The PUD ordinance can resolve uncertainties in the amendment process by distinguishing between minor and major changes and providing that minor changes can be made administratively. See *Foggy Bottom Association v. District of Columbia Zoning Commission*, 639 A.2d 578 (D.C. App. 1994). These distinctions do not necessarily bind the court, as the principal case indicates. See also *McCarty v. City of Kansas City*, 671 S.W.2d 790 (Mo. App. 1984) (use change requires rezoning).

The planned unit development ordinance can specifically provide that the approved PUD plan takes the place of the regulations contained in the zoning ordinance, which then is no longer in effect, as in the principal case. *City of New Smyrna Beach v. Andover Dev. Corp.*, 672 So. 2d 618 (Fla. 1996), points out the implications of this situation:

> The plan submitted incorporates the developer's recommendation as to what the setbacks, the percentage of open space, the height of buildings, etc. should be and, once accepted by the governmental agency, these recommendations become fixed as the PUD classification is molded over and around the approved plan. The PUD classification, therefore, although flexible in concept, becomes rigid in application. . . . [T]here remains no "unused" development authority in the PUD. . . . Therefore, if the plan is to be subsequently amended, the PUD classification, by necessity, must also be amended. [*Id.* at 620.]

2. *PUD decision making.* Is the approval of a PUD by a legislative body a legislative or an administrative act? The standards that apply to PUD reviews may be a factor in answering this question. Note the general standards in the *Millbrae* ordinance, as quoted in footnote 11 of the opinion. The standards would probably be upheld against delegation of power objections. See *Tri-State Generation & Transmission Co. v. City of Thornton*, 647 P.2d 670 (Colo. 1982) (upholding similar standards).

When the approval of a PUD is characterized as a rezoning, or when the approval decision is delegated to the legislative body, most courts characterize the approval decision as legislative even though specific criteria control the approval of a PUD. See *State ex rel. Helujon, Ltd. v. Jefferson County*, 964 S.W.2d 531 (Mo. App. 1998) (held legislative even though site plan included in approval). Courts may especially be influenced to hold the approval decision legislative if the PUD accomplishes a major change in land use from what the zoning ordinance previously allowed. *Todd-Mart, Inc. v. Town Bd.*, 370 N.Y.S.2d 683 (N.Y. App. Div. 1975) (large commercial PUD); *Peachtree Dev. Co. v. Paul*, 423 N.E.2d 1087 (Ohio 1981) (PUD included multi-family and commercial uses in district zoned single-family).

3. *What is the scope of judicial review?* This will depend on how the decision is made, and the standards contained in the ordinance. When the decision is made by the legislative body, especially when it is adopted as a rezoning, courts can apply the usual deferential standard to denials and approvals. *Ford Leasing Dev. Co. v. Board of County Comm'rs,* 528 P.2d 237 (Colo. 1974) (upholding denial based on incompatibility with surrounding area); Moore v. City of Boulder, 484 P.2d 134 (Colo. App. 1971) (rezoning); *Home Bldg. Co. v. City of Kansas City,* 666 S.W.2d 816 (Mo. App. 1984) (refusal to rezone).

If the PUD application is reviewed through a conditional use procedure, the usual standards of review again apply. *BECA of Alexandria, L.L.P. v. County of Douglas by Bd. of Comm'rs,* 607 N.W.2d 459 (Minn. App. 2000). There is no discretion to deny when the approval requirements in the ordinance are specific, and the applicant has met all of these requirements. *C.C. & J. Enters., Inc. v. City of Asheville,* 512 S.E.2d 766 (N.C. App. 1999). There is more discretion to reject when the ordinance contains generalized health, safety and general welfare requirements. *Dore v. County of Ventura,* 28 Cal. Rptr.2d 299 (Cal. App. 1994) (upholding denial based on safety and incompatibility findings). A PUD proposal must be consistent with the zoning ordinance, *Citizens for Mount Vernon v. City of Mount Vernon,* 947 P.2d 1208 (Wash. 1997), and must comply with the comprehensive plan if the ordinance requires this. *Cathedral Park Condominium Committee v. District of Columbia Zoning Comm'n,* 743 A.2d 1231 (D.C. App. 2000). What do these decisions indicate about how to draft a PUD ordinance?

4. *The standards problem again.* The cases on judicial review indicate that the way in which PUD review standards are drafted is a critical element in the administration of a PUD ordinance. The old problem of how to ensure flexibility while preventing arbitrary decision making again rears its head. For example, open-ended review standards give the reviewing agency the flexibility it needs to ensure well-done PUD development, but may foreclose effective judicial review and may provide an opportunity to use the PUD review procedures in an exclusionary manner. Recall the Cosconing story at the beginning of this section. What kind of standards would support the decision to deny the PUD in that example?

RK Dev. Corp. v. City of Norwalk, 242 A.2d 781 (Conn. 1968) indicates how the standards adopted for reviewing PUDs can affect judicial review. The governing body denied a PUD "for the sake of the children up there; the welfare of the community and also the health hazards." It did not indicate how the PUD failed to comply with rather specific site planning standards in the ordinance that required adequate traffic access and circulation and the dispersal of open space and recreational areas "to insure the safety and welfare of resident children." The court held the denial invalid. See also *Woodhouse v. Board of Comm'rs,* 261 S.E.2d 882 (N.C. 1980) (reversing denial because applicant satisfied ordinance standards).

Yet the adoption of precise PUD review standards may rigidly limit PUD design, and may be resisted by municipalities that want the greatest amount of discretion possible in the PUD review process. Drafting sufficiently precise PUD review standards also has its difficulties. What do you think of the following standard? How much discretion does it give the municipality? Is it an improper delegation of legislative power?

> The council may approve the final development plan if it provides for safe, efficient, convenient and harmonious groupings of structures,

uses and facilities; for appropriate relation of space inside and outside buildings to intended uses and natural and structural features; and for preservation of desirable natural and environmental features and minimum disturbance to the natural environment.

5. *Marketing problems.* A governing body may sometimes deny a PUD because it believes the market will not support it, reasoning that approval and subsequent abandonment of the PUD by the developer would present serious problems. Can the municipality deal with this problem directly? In *Soble Constr. Co. v. Zoning Hearing Bd.,* 329 A.2d 912 (Pa. Commw. 1974), the ordinance provided that "[t]he proposed developer shall demonstrate that a sufficient market exists for the type, size and character of the development proposed."

The court held this requirement invalid because market-sufficiency showing was not related to the general welfare. A municipality may not "zone or refuse to zone land for the purpose of limiting competition with existing commercial facilities." The court added that "[i]f the developer is willing to accept the risk of constructing this project and complies with all of the other valid requirements of the zoning ordinance, the application should not be denied merely because the zoning board believes that the development will not be profitable." *Id.* at 917. This appears to be an application of the rule that zoning may not be used to control competition. See Chapter 3. Is it correct?

6. *Model planned development legislation.* Model legislation specifically authorizing the enactment of PUD ordinances was proposed in the mid-1960s. The model act is reproduced in Babcock, Krasnowiecki & McBride, *The Model State Statute,* 114 U. Pa. L. Rev. 140 (1965). The model act specified a detailed adjudicatory review process and provided a detailed set of PUD approval standards.

A few states adopted the act, usually with modifications. See, e.g., Pa. Stat. Ann. tit. 53, §§ 10701–10711, which was amended and reenacted in 1988. New Jersey, which originally adopted the act, later repealed it and redistributed its provisions to various sections of the land use law. A few states also have less sophisticated legislation simply authorizing planned unit development controls. E.g., § 65 Ill. Comp. Stat. 5/11-13-1.1 (authorizing planned developments as special use).

The American Planning Association model legislation proposes a more open-ended enabling act that defines a PUD, requires consistency with the comprehensive plan and minimum provisions, and authorizes approval as a conditional use or subdivision depending on the PUD's size. § 8-303 (draft 2000). Site planning standards "may vary the density or intensity of land use" based on factors such as the provision of common open space and the physical character of the PUD, and may also authorize neotraditional neighborhood development.

7. *New towns.* A variant and more ambitious example of large-scale development based on the planned unit development principle is the new town. First tried in Great Britain, the new town idea was heralded in the United States as an approach to the development of entire new communities that could achieve significant design and planning objectives that otherwise would not be possible.

The new town was envisaged as an entire new community, built from the ground up and complete with shopping and industrial areas as well as residential neighborhoods. One advantage of the new community was that it was to be planned, developed, and managed under a single or unified management pursuant to a comprehensive development plan. The plan would incorporate the highest design principles, and would provide opportunities for lower-income housing in its residential areas. Part of the new town promise was the hope that employment opportunities within the new town would be available for a large proportion of its residents, thus reducing work-trip commuting.

Development control problems in new towns have been handled to some extent by expanded versions of planned unit development ordinances. Reston, a new town in the suburban Virginia sector of the Washington, D.C., metropolitan area was built under a specially tailored planned unit development provision. For discussion, see Christensen, *Land Use Control for the New Community,* 6 Harv. J. on Legis. 496 (1969). The regulatory problems are similar to those raised under more limited PUD ordinances.

In Great Britain, many of the new towns have been sold and some have failed. In the United States, a federal program of financial assistance for new towns was terminated because of marketing and financial difficulties after several new towns had been started. New towns continue to be built in the United States by private developers, often under the PUD concept, and some major new towns are under construction in Dallas, Texas and elsewhere. For a thorough discussion of the new town idea, see Note, *New Communities: In Search of Cibola — Some Legislative Trails,* 12 Urb. L. Ann. 177 (1976).

8. *Sources.* See Frontiers of Planned Unit Development (R. Burchell ed., 1973); W. Sanders, The Cluster Subdivision: A Cost-Effective Approach (American Planning Association, Planning Advisory Serv. Rep. No. 356) (1981); Symposium, *Planned Unit Development,* 114 U. Pa. L. Rev. 3 (1965); Gudder, *A Primer on Planned Unit Development,* 21 Zoning & Plan. L. Rep. 18, 25 (1998). Forrest, *Planned Unit Development and Takings Post Dolan,* 15 N. Ill. U. L. Rev. 571 (1995), discusses the impact of Supreme Court cases on exactions demanded in the PUD approval process.

PROBLEM

You are the city attorney of a city of 100,000 with substantial areas of undeveloped land remaining. The city operates under the standard zoning act. You have been asked by the city council to draft an ordinance authorizing the approval of planned unit developments. Based on these materials, which zoning agency would you choose to administer the PUD approval process? What kind of PUDs would you allow? What approval standards would you require? What procedures would you specify for the initial approval and subsequent amendment of PUDs?

Chapter 7

GROWTH MANAGEMENT

A. AN INTRODUCTION TO GROWTH MANAGEMENT

The Future of the San Leandro Region

The San Leandro region, which includes the city of San Leandro, is an urban region on the Pacific Coast with a population of 4.3 million. By 2020, the region is likely to number well over six million. Where will these people go? While the overall historic density in the region is 7.7 housing units per acre, right now the region is adding units at only 3.7 units per acre on fresh suburban land, including land to be developed for multifamily housing. Low densities mean suburban sprawl.

Schools and other public facilities can't keep up with demand. Highways are congested, but this new population will need another 1,300 lane miles of freeways because each new person adds 1.29 vehicles to the roads. This means six more freeways that will duplicate a major freeway already in place. In addition, 37 square miles of parking must be provided for each new million people added to the region.

Sprawl: Definitions, Costs and Solutions.—This brief description, which is based on data for San Diego at the millennium, illustrates the problems growth management tries to solve. Note the major characteristics of this growth scenario. The growth problem is residential development at low densities, though the densities in San Diego are higher than in other areas of the country, where lots up to three acres are typical in suburban areas. This kind of low density growth is called sprawl. One of the best indicators of sprawl is the relationship between land consumption in urbanized areas and population growth. In the Chicago urbanized area, for example, population increased by nine percent from 1990 to 1996, while the developed land area grew by 40%.

Sprawl was high on the political agenda as the millennium turned, and since sprawl is a major target of growth management it is important to begin with this concept and try to define it. Although there is no universally accepted definition of sprawl, critics usually define it as low density development that expands in leapfrog, noncontiguous steps from the core of a metropolitan area. Regulations for the state land use planning program in Florida provide a somewhat more technical definition: they define urban sprawl as the premature and poorly planned conversion of urban land, and as development unrelated to adjacent land uses that does not make maximum use of existing public facilities. Fla. Admin. Code § 9J-5.003(134).

Sprawl, and the rapid growth that usually goes with it, create a number of serious economic and social problems. These include excessive higher capital and operating costs for public facilities, higher transportation costs and traffic congestion, air pollution, the excessive conversion of agricultural and sensitive lands to new development, and an inability to provide public services and facilities as development occurs. These are suburban problems, but they also affect the growth and livability of the urban region in which sprawl occurs. Are these problems likely to occur in the San Leandro region? Some commentators claim that sprawl also contributes to inner city decline, but one study did not find this relationship. See Downs, *Some Realities About Sprawl and Urban Decline,* 10 Housing Pol'y Debate 955, 961 (1999).

Growth management policies attempt to deal with these problems. One type of growth management program concentrates only on the capital facility and service delivery problem. It proposes techniques that require the provision of new services and facilities when new development occurs. This remedy solves the timing problem, but does not solve problems such as fragmented growth and excessive land consumption that sprawl creates. Early growth management programs were often limited to timing controls.

A more comprehensive solution for the problems of urban sprawl requires attention to problems of urban form. The usual solution is a more dense and more compact form of development than present development patterns create, as the San Leandro example illustrates. Indeed, to some extent the battle over growth management is a battle over residential density and the form and structure of urban regions. Excessive costs drive the move toward more compact form. Though contested, studies consistently show that urban sprawl will cost up to 20 percent more for public facilities than a more compact form of development.

Controls over urban form require more than controls limited to the timing of new public facilities. One program for achieving this objective is the urban growth boundary, which limits the area in which new development can occur. Complementary controls that preserve agricultural and sensitive lands are also critical.

Defining Growth Management.—A multi-dimensional program like growth management is difficult to define, but a definition may provide context for the kinds of control techniques that growth management includes. Here is a typical definition:

> Growth management is active and dynamic. . .; it seeks to maintain an ongoing equilibrium between development and conservation, between various forms of development and concurrent provision of infrastructure, between the demands for public services generated by growth and the supply of revenues to finance these demands, and between progress and equity. [Chinitz, *Growth Management: Good for the Town, Bad for the Nation?*, 56 J. Am. Plan. Ass'n 3, 6 (1990)].

This definition suggests that growth management programs are a response to failures in the standard planning and zoning acts. These acts, as Chapters 2 and 3 explained, provide a process for adopting comprehensive plans and zoning ordinances, but do not require particular planning and zoning policies for land use problems. As a result, the traditional zoning system is not able to handle growth management problems.

Zoning assumes that growth will occur and primarily regulates its location and intensity. Zoning does place implicit limits on growth because the density and location assignments of the zoning ordinance place a nominal cap on development in the community, but the ease with which ordinances can be amended (see Chapter 5) makes this process somewhat more theoretical than real. Zoning also uses a variety of techniques, such as low-density residential zones, to implement growth-staging policies. Development occurs as the community shifts its low-density zones to more intensive uses. But traditional zoning does not include explicit growth-management controls.

> All of this means that the zoning map is not a very useful tool for planning such capital improvements as new highways, parks, and schools. Few communities are rich enough to build major roads and trunk sewer and water lines into all their undeveloped areas. Thus, to the extent that a community wants to invest in infrastructure for future needs, public officials would like to know where and when growth will occur. Because the zoning map does not guarantee what development will take place in what location, many communities simply wait to see what will occur before making such improvements. However, the result of that very practical policy is that such improvements are not available before development takes place. [E. Kelly, Community Growth: Policies, Techniques, and Impacts 20 (1993).]

Growth management programs fill this gap by requiring planning and land use regulation programs to deal with problems of rapid growth and urban sprawl. The next selection describes commonly used growth management techniques in more detail.

E. KELLY, PLANNING, GROWTH, AND PUBLIC FACILITIES: A PRIMER FOR LOCAL OFFICIALS 16
(American Planning Association, Planning Advisory Service Report No. 447, 1993)

Types of Growth Management Programs . . .

 • *Adequate public facilities programs* establish criteria to prohibit development except where adequate public facilities are available. Good programs carefully define the meaning of the term "adequate," usually using level-of-service standards to measure acceptable performance levels for traffic, school, fire, and other systems with flexible capacities. These programs directly address the availability of public facilities to serve a particular development. . . .

 • *Phased-growth programs* supplement zoning controls by defining when development can take place in a particular location. The capacity of public facilities, environmental issues, and general community growth policies help to determine the phasing patterns. In addition, some communities may find that establishing adequate public facilities standards for facilities like schools can be difficult because there is no precise way to measure capacity limits. In such communities, a growth-phasing program can encourage growth in areas that generally have the most available capacity in such facilities. . . .

 • *Urban growth boundary programs* attempt to regulate the shape of the community by drawing a line around it and limiting or prohibiting development outside that line. The focus of such programs is typically the elimination of "sprawl" and the protection of agricultural and other open lands. . . . . [Urban service lines, that define a boundary within which urban services will be provided, are a similar technique.—Eds.]

• *Rate-of-growth programs* establish a defined growth area, either as a percentage or as a number. [Petaluma, California was a famous example of such a program. The city adopted a quota of 500 dwelling units a year which it allocated under a point system. The Petaluma plan is discussed later in the chapter.—Eds.]

NOTES AND QUESTIONS

1. *Putting it all together.* Professor Kelly provides a typology of growth management programs that can be used individually or in combination. A number of programs are profiled in D. Porter, Profiles in Growth Management (1996). One of the best-known of these programs is the program in Montgomery County, Maryland, adjacent to Washington, D.C. It combines a number of elements that include comprehensive and special area planning based on a corridor plan concept adopted for the entire region, an adequate public facilities program, a farmland protection program, an inclusionary housing program, and a transit-oriented development program. See *id.* at 71–80, and D. Porter, Managing Growth in America's Communities 33–42 (1997). Each of these programs is discussed in this chapter. For discussion of inclusionary housing, see Chapter 4, *supra.*

One study confirmed the intuitive assumption that adequate public facilities programs help reduce sprawl, while low density zoning, caps on building and a heavy reliance on the property tax encourage it. Pendall, *Do Land-Use Controls Cause Sprawl?*, 26 Envtl. & Plan. Bull. 555 (1999).

2. *The costs of sprawl.* Critics claim that capital facilities and services cost more in a sprawl pattern of development because lower densities drive up costs for transportation and other public facilities. A number of studies have attempted to quantify the costs of sprawl. The results vary, but they indicate a savings of 20–25 percent for road costs and 15–20 percent for utility infrastructure costs in planned and compact developments as compared with sprawl. Try applying these cost reductions to the San Leandro region cost forecasts. For a monograph reviewing these studies see Transit Cooperative Research Program, Rep. 39, The Costs of Sprawl — Revisited (1998). The reference in the title is to an earlier study, Real Estate Research Corp., The Costs of Sprawl (1974). See also Burchell, *Economic and Fiscal Costs (and Benefits) of Sprawl*, 29 Urb. Law. 159 (1997).

Sprawl is not universally condemned. Its defenders claim that a dispersed pattern of suburban development offers advantages, such as meeting the demand for travel flexibility through use of the automobile, the privacy offered by low density development, quality schools and a sense of community security. Fina & Shabman, *Some Unconventional Thoughts on Sprawl,* 23 Wm. & Mary Envtl. L. & Pol'y Rev. 739 (1999). Other observers claim the sprawl problem is overrated because the sprawl index is declining, urban development does not threaten agriculture, the effect of suburban development on local government costs is exaggerated, and air quality deteriorates at higher densities. S. Staley, The Sprawling of America: In Defense of the Dynamic City (Reason Pub. Pol'y Inst. Policy Paper 251, 1999). The impact of the sprawl debate on growth management programs is considerable. How the courts view programs intended to manage growth will depend to a great extent on how they view the urban sprawl menace. How do the data on land inventories presented in Chapter 1 bear on this debate?

3. *Externalities and the pricing alternative.* From another perspective, the costs of sprawl are simply another example of the kind of market externality that free markets cannot internalize. These issues were explored in Chapter 1. The argument is that new residents who settle in suburban areas in sprawl development do not pay the costs of their development, which are forced on the public sector in the form of additional highways, congestion, air pollution and the like. The assumption is that new entrants should pay the marginal cost of their development, not just the average cost of providing services and facilities over the region.

Programs that would shift the cost of new development to new residents could include impact fees on new development, which were reviewed in the previous chapter; peak-hour road tolls on major commuting highways; and a development tax on land converted from agricultural to urban use. How practical and effective these suggestions are is another matter. Anthony Downs points out that impact fees have not stopped sprawl where they are used, and that the other proposals are not likely to be adopted. Downs, *supra,* at 962. If government must intervene in growth management because the market cannot supply alternatives, is the basis for intervention different than when government intervenes to resolve potential land use conflicts in a community through a zoning ordinance? Is Coasian bargaining another alternative?

✓ **4.** *Exclusion.* Is growth management really an example of exclusionary zoning adopted by affluent, socially stratified suburbs? The studies do not provide a clear answer. Most find that broad community characteristics, such as rate of growth and whether a community emphasizes homeowner interests or economic growth, determine whether a community adopts growth controls. Belief in governmental activism and concern about government's handling of land use issues are also positively related to growth controls. See, e.g., Albrecht, Bultena & Hoeberg, *Constituency of the Antigrowth Movement: A Comparison of the Growth Orientations of Urban Status Groups,* 21 Urb. Aff. Q. 607 (1986); Logan & Zou, *The Adoption of Growth Controls in Suburban Communities,* 71 Soc. Sci. Q. 118 (1990); Neiman & Fernandez, *Local Planners and Limits on Local Residential Development,* 66 J. Am. Plan. Ass'n 295 (2000). These factors are less important in counties, and the extent of urbanization is a dominant factor in counties adopting growth controls. Steel & Lovrich, *Growth Management Policy and County Government: Correlates of Policy Adoption Across the United States,* 32 State & Local Gov't Rev. 7 (2000).

A recent empirical study found that low density zoning below eight units to the acre limited the number of black and Hispanic residents by consistently reducing the amount of rental housing. Building permit caps also limited the number of Hispanic residents. Other growth controls, such as urban growth boundaries, adequate public facilities ordinances and moratoria, had a more limited effect on housing types and racial distribution. Pendall, *Local Land Use Regulation and the Chain of Exclusion,* 66 Am. Plan. Ass'n J. 125 (2000).

5. *Growth management and market monopoly.* Some critics argue that communities can impose growth controls that restrict development or make it more expensive only if there is no market substitute for the housing opportunities the community provides. See, e.g., Ellickson, *Suburban Growth Controls: An Economic and Legal Analysis,* 86 Yale L.J. 384, 425–35 (1977). See also the argument in Chapter 4, sec. B1, *supra,* that only communities with a market monopoly can engage in exclusionary zoning.

The conventional view is that monopoly is unlikely in a suburban area fragmented into numerous suburban communities. Paradoxically, suburban fragmentation and the absence of regional coordination through regional planning usually create the pressures that lead to the adoption of growth controls. See Gottdiener, *Some Theoretical Issues in Growth Control Analysis,* 18 Urb. Aff. Q. 565, 567 (1983). See also M. Baldassare, The Growth Dilemma 139 (1981) (small unconnected suburban governments not well organized to compete with growth). Is this a reason to support or to oppose growth management?

Both the Ramapo and Petaluma growth control programs discussed later in this chapter were adopted by communities in fragmented suburban areas. Is it possible that numerous suburban communities, nominally in competition, hold sufficiently similar social and economic views that they act in tandem (consciously or otherwise), thus creating a de facto monopoly despite their fragmentation? A Florida study showing that growth management controls had a negative impact on construction activity may support the monopoly thesis. See Feiock, *The Political Economy of Growth Management,* 22 Am. Pol. Q. 208 (1994) (also suggesting that environmental gains may offset economic losses).

6. *Price effects.* Like exclusionary zoning, growth management is problematic if it increases the price of housing above the market price that would prevail in its absence. Proving the price increase hypothesis empirically is difficult because it is difficult to control for the many variables that determine housing price. For example, housing price increases may be caused by an increase in income levels, which in turn inflates demand. Growth management affects housing price in several ways. Growth staging can increase prices by placing artificial restrictions on the supply of land for housing. Urban growth boundaries create major differences in price levels inside and outside the boundary, and higher density and more exclusive housing inside the boundary may be not be affordable by lower income groups.

Some empirical studies have found that growth controls significantly affect the price of housing. E.g., Katz & Rosen, *The Interjurisdictional Effects of Growth Controls on Housing Prices,* 30 J.L. & Econ. 149 (1987) (prices 17% to 38% higher); Pollakowski & Wachter, *The Effects of Land Use Constraints on Housing Prices,* 66 Land Econ. 315 (1990). For a review of these studies see S. Staley, J. Edgens & G. Mildner, A Line in the Land: Urban-Growth Boundaries, Smart Growth and Housing Affordability (1999) (finding that housing prices increase); Lillydahl & Singell, *The Effect of Growth Management on the Housing Market: A Review of the Theoretical and Empirical Evidence,* 9 J. Urb. Aff. 63 (1987).

However, the evidence is conflicting. Elliott, *The Impact of Growth Control Regulations on Housing Prices in California,* 9 J. Am. Real Est. & Urb. Econ. Ass'n 115 (1981), found that growth controls increased housing prices only when housing was strongly regulated throughout a housing market. An extensive California study found that formal growth controls were so weak that the effect on housing prices was minimal. Landis, *Do Growth Controls Work? A New Assessment,* 58 J. Am. Plan. Ass'n 489 (1992). Price increases may also reflect the additional amenities in the community that growth controls create. See Bruekner, *Growth Controls and Land Values in an Open City,* 66 Land Econ. 237 (1990).

The monopoly position of a community may be critical. "In most communities subject to competition within the region, economists believe that market limits on development cost increases ultimately will drive prices down." D. Porter, Managing Growth in America's Communities 264 (1997). Developers in these areas may be able to escape to communities that do not have growth controls, where new housing they build will compete with housing in growth-controlled communities. Downsizing housing or shifting to multifamily construction may also minimize price increases in growth-controlled communities.

7. *Sources.* For discussion of urban sprawl and growth management programs see F. Benfield, M. Raimi & D. Chen, Once There Were Greenfields (1999); R. Freilich, From Sprawl to Smart Growth (1999); A. Nelson & J. Duncan, Growth Management Principles & Practices (1995); D. Rusk, Inside Game/Outside Game (1999); Sierra Club, The Dark Side of the American Dream (1998); U.S. General Accounting Office, Extent of Federal Influence on "Urban Sprawl" is Unclear (1999); Buzbee, *Urban Sprawl, Federalism, and the Problem of Institutional Complexity,* 68 Fordham L. Rev. 57 (1999).

PROBLEM

River County is a rural county that includes Metro City, a major regional center with a population of 250,000 which is located at the western edge of the county. Most of the county is undeveloped. The county consists of rolling hills and an attractive river valley along the Swimming River, for which the county is named. There is a county seat, River City, approximately at the middle of the county, which has a population of 25,000. River City is served with a public sewer and water system, but the rest of the county is not. There are no other incorporated municipalities in the county and, until recently, no other areas of urban settlement.

Urban growth from Metro City is beginning to spill into River County. A number of scattered residential developments have been developed in the past few years within the county and just over the border from Metro City. These developments are served by on-site water and sewer systems, but schools are overcrowded and county roads in the area are congested and do not provide adequate levels of service. The state has designated a corridor in this area for a limited-access connection to an Interstate highway, but construction is not scheduled for years. The county is authorized to but does not provide water and sewer service.

The county planning department has asked your advice on how to prepare a growth management program for the county. The planners have told you they prefer a program that will allow a moderate expansion of River City and the creation of additional population centers at appropriate points throughout the county. Time is needed to bring public facilities and services up to standard, and the planners wish to avoid scattered development that will make the provision of facilities and services inefficient. The county has a conventional zoning ordinance, but the comprehensive plan is out of date. What would you advise? How will your answer be affected by the statutory authority available for planning and land use controls?

B. MORATORIA AND INTERIM CONTROLS

A moratorium is a regulation that prohibits new development. Municipalities often adopt moratoria in order to forestall inappropriate development during the time they are considering new growth management controls, which may include a revision of the zoning ordinance or the adoption of new control techniques. For example, San Leandro may want to consider an urban growth boundary or an increase in densities. A community may also adopt a development moratorium to prohibit development when public facilities are inadequate. Development moratoria can use a number of land use control techniques. They include:

- A freeze on the extension of public facilities to new areas.
- A freeze on new connections to utilities.
- A freeze on building permits.
- A freeze on subdivision approvals.
- A freeze on rezonings to higher densities.
- A reduction or quota allocation for any of the above measures.

The terms "moratorium" and "interim controls" (or "interim zoning") are often given interchangeable, or at least interrelated, meanings. The substance of an "interim zoning" ordinance may in fact be a freeze on development, in which case it could more properly be called a "moratorium." Generally speaking, cases and commentary that use the word "moratorium" will emphasize the "freeze" aspect of the problem, while those that use the word "interim" are more likely to emphasize a "pause" in development during which rational planning to solve the underlying land use problem can take place, or a service deficiency remedied. Try to decide, as you read the materials in this section, whether a "moratorium" can ever be justified other than as an "interim control" along the way to a new plan.

The takings issue.—Prior to the Supreme Court's 1987 trilogy of takings cases, the courts had pretty much accepted the constitutionality of moratoria when they had a legitimate public purpose and when they were not unreasonably long. The 1987 cases raised some new issues, especially because *First*

English involved a moratorium imposed to prohibit development in a flood-plain and held that temporary takings are compensable. At the same time, a dictum in *First English* also indicated that moratoria could be constitutional without compensation, because the Court said that "normal delays" caused by the processing of applications for development approval are not compensable. Cases after *First English* upheld development moratoria. E.g., *Jackson Court Condominiums v. City of New Orleans,* 874 F.2d 1070 (5th Cir. 1989) (moratorium on time share condominiums; developer had other uses); *Tocco v. New Jersey Council on Affordable Housing,* 576 A.2d 328 (N.J. App. Div. 1990) (18-month development moratorium).

The takings landscape changed with the Court's 1992 decision in *Lucas,* which held a per se taking occurs when a land use regulation denies a landowner all economically beneficial use of her land, even though the regulation serves a legitimate governmental purpose. (Recall that *Lucas* was in effect a "temporary taking" case because the regulation banning coastal development had been amended by the time the case was decided.) Development moratoria may be vulnerable under *Lucas* because they prohibit all development during the moratorium period, even if justified by the need to gain time to remedy public facility plans or develop a new plan or land use ordinance. The case that follows examines these problems:

TAHOE-SIERRA PRESERVATION COUNCIL, INC. v. TAHOE REGIONAL PLANNING AGENCY

216 F.3d 764 (9th Cir. 2000)

REINHARDT, CIRCUIT JUDGE:

This case involves approximately 450 plaintiffs who own property in the Lake Tahoe Basin. The lead plaintiff, Tahoe-Sierra Preservation Council, Inc. (TSPC), is an association of Tahoe-area property owners. Each individual property owner has alleged, inter alia, that each of several land-use regulations enacted in the 1980s by the Tahoe Regional Planning Agency (TRPA) constituted a "taking" of his property under the Fifth and Fourteenth Amendments. The principal question on this appeal is whether a temporary planning moratorium, enacted by TRPA to halt development while a new regional land-use plan was being devised, effected a taking of each plaintiff's property under the standard set forth in *Lucas v. South Carolina Coastal Council.* . . .

FACTUAL BACKGROUND

Lake Tahoe is a large alpine lake located in the northern Sierra Nevada mountains. The lake is unique, both aesthetically and ecologically, because of its size, depth, and the astounding clarity of its water. Indeed, it is one of the clearest large lakes in the world. The unusual clarity of Lake Tahoe results from the fact that it historically was "oligotrophic" — that is, very low in nutrients and lacking a steep temperature gradient that would prevent deep circulation and mixing. Since mid-century, however, the lake has been undergoing "eutrophication," a process by which the nutrient loading in the lake increases dramatically, due to nitrogen and phosphorus (contained in soil) being washed into the lake. The excessive enrichment of the lake by these nutrients encourages the growth of algae. As algal growth in the lake increases, the lake loses its clarity and color, becoming green and opaque. In addition to destroying the water's visual perfection, the algae also depletes its oxygen content, thereby jeopardizing the survival of fish and other lake-dwelling animal life. In short, the eutrophication of the lake is causing serious, and effectively permanent, environmental damage.

The dramatic increase in Lake Tahoe's nutrient levels has been caused by the rapid development of environmentally sensitive land in the Lake Tahoe Basin. The land in the basin drains into the lake, and artificial disturbances of the land — the destruction of vegetation, the creation of impervious objects such as roads and houses, etc. — greatly increase the flow of nutrients into the lake. Of course, the degree to which the development of a particular parcel of land in the basin increases the nutrient flow into the lake depends on the particular characteristics of that property. In general, the development of steeper land leads to more environmental damage, because steeper land is susceptible to more rapid soil erosion. Along with steepness, other land characteristics also affect the amount of damage caused to the lake by development. For example, certain areas near streams and other wetlands, known as Stream Environment Zones (SEZs), act as filters for much of the nutrient loading that runoff carries. Disturbance of SEZ lands can lead to the rapid release of these stored nutrients into the lake. In addition, disturbance of SEZ lands may prevent them from performing their natural filtering function, thereby permitting more of the nutrients contained in runoff from higher elevations to reach the lake. Accordingly, SEZ lands are considered especially sensitive to the impact of development. . . .

[The court noted the creation of the Tahoe Regional Planning Agency (TRPA) by Congress. TRPA then adopted land-use Ordinance No. 4, which, "classified the land in the basin according to its susceptibility to environmental damage." Dissatisfaction with this ordinance led to an amendment to the interstate Compact creating TRPA which] directed TRPA (1) to adopt "environmental threshold carrying capacities" within eighteen months of the date on which the Compact became effective; (2) to adopt a new regional plan within twelve months of the adoption of the carrying capacities; and (3) to review all projects and establish temporary restrictions on development in the basin pending the enactment of a new regional plan.

[TRPA then adopted Ordinance 81–5, that "temporarily prohibited most residential and all commercial construction on both Class 1–3 and SEZ lands." The moratorium was to expire when TRPA adopted the new regional plan. On August 26, 1982, TRPA adopted environmental threshold carrying capacities and began to develop the new regional plan. When it became clear the plan would not be completed within twelve months of the adoption of carrying capacities, as required by the Compact, TRPA adopted Resolution 83–21, which suspended all permitting activities "pending adoption of the new regional plan." This resolution was extended until the new plan was adopted on April 16, 1984. In another lawsuit brought by the State of California, the district court enjoined the issuance of any new building permits until a new plan was adopted. The injunction was upheld on appeal and was in effect until a revised plan was adopted in 1987. The moratorium was in effect for 32 months.]

PROCEDURAL HISTORY

. . .

[Property owners in the present litigation also sued after TRPA adopted the 1984 Plan. Following trials and a series of appeals, the district court held on remand that "Ordinance 81-5 and Resolution 83–21 were facially invalid because they constituted a categorical taking of the plaintiffs' property." Defendants appealed.] . . .

DISCUSSION

I. TIME PERIODS I & II . . .

A.

[The Court discussed the takings rules of *Penn Central* and *Lucas*. The only question before the court was whether *Lucas* applied. Plaintiffs did not argue that a taking had occurred under the *Penn Central* "balancing test."]

Our focus is also narrowed by the fact that the plaintiffs bring only a facial challenge to Ordinance 81-5 and Resolution 83–21. In facial takings claims, our inquiry is limited to "whether the mere enactment of the [regulation] constitutes a taking." [citing *Agins*.] For that reason, we look only to the regulation's "'general scope and dominant features,'" rather than to the effect of the application of the regulation in specific circumstances. In this connection, "since it is difficult to demonstrate that [the] 'mere enactment' of a piece of legislation" amounts to a taking, the Court has recognized that facial takings challenges "face an uphill battle." [citing *Suitum v. Tahoe Reg'l Planning Agency*, discussed in Chapter 8.]

B.

The plaintiffs contend that, for purposes of determining whether the regulations constitute a categorical taking under *Lucas*, we should not treat the plaintiffs' properties as the fee interests that they are. Instead, they argue, we should define narrowly, as a separate property interest, the temporal "slice" of each fee that covers the time span during which Ordinance 81-5 and Resolution 83–21 were in effect. It is this carved-out piece of each plaintiff's property interest, the plaintiffs assert, that has been "taken" by the regulations. . . .

At base, the plaintiffs' argument is that we should conceptually sever each plaintiff's fee interest into discrete segments in at least one of these dimensions — the temporal one — and treat each of those segments as separate and distinct property interests for purposes of takings analysis. Under this theory, they argue that there was a categorical taking of one of those temporal segments.

While Supreme Court precedent has not over the years been entirely uniform in its treatment of the conceptual severance question, most modern case law rejects the invitation of property holders to engage in conceptual severance, except in cases of physical invasion or occupation. . . . [The court discussed *Penn Central* and its holding that takings jurisprudence "does not divide a single parcel into discrete segments and attempt to determine whether rights in a particular segment have been entirely abrogated," and then discussed other Supreme Court cases that examined this issue.]

To not reject the concept of temporal severance, we would risk converting every temporary planning moratorium into a categorical taking. Such a result would run contrary to the Court's explanation that it is "relatively rare" that government "regulation denies all economically beneficial or productive use of land." [citing *Lucas*.]

More important, the widespread invalidation of temporary planning moratoria would deprive state and local governments of an important land-use planning tool with a well-established tradition. Land-use planning is necessarily a complex, time-consuming undertaking for a community, especially in a situation as unique as this. In several ways, temporary development moratoria promote effective planning. First, by preserving the status quo during the planning process, temporary moratoria ensure that a community's problems are not exacerbated during the time it takes to formulate a regulatory scheme. Relatedly, temporary development moratoria prevent developers and landowners from racing to carry out development that is destructive of the community's interests before a new plan goes into effect. Such a race-to-development would permit property owners to evade the land-use plan and undermine its goals. Finally, the breathing room provided by temporary moratoria helps ensure that the planning process is responsive to the property owners and citizens who will be affected by the resulting land-use regulations. Absent the pressure of trying to out-speed developers who are attempting to circumvent the planning goals, the "planning and implementation process may be permitted to run its full and natural course with widespread citizen input and involvement, public debate, and full consideration of all issues and points of view." Given the importance and long-standing use of temporary moratoria, courts should be exceedingly reluctant to adopt rulings that would threaten the survival of this crucial planning mechanism. . . .Contrary to the plaintiffs' suggestion, however, the [Supreme] Court's holding in *First English* was not that temporary moratoria are "temporary takings." In fact, the opposite is true. The *First English* Court very carefully defined "'temporary' regulatory takings [as] those regulatory takings which are ultimately invalidated by the courts." What is "temporary," according to the Court's definition, is not the regulation; rather, what is "temporary" is the taking, which is rendered temporary only when an ordinance that effects a taking is struck down by a court. In other words, a permanent regulation leads to a "temporary" taking when a court invalidates the ordinance after the taking.

C.

Having determined that the property interest at stake is just what one would expect it to be — the plaintiffs' fee interests — we must evaluate whether Ordinance 81-5 and Resolution 83–21 effected a categorical taking of each plaintiff's property. For purposes of this analysis, two features of these provisions are relevant. First, the provisions effectively placed a moratorium on the development of the plaintiffs' property. The second relevant feature of the provisions is that the moratorium they effected was intended to be temporary — the regulations were designed to institute a temporary moratorium that would remain in effect only until a new regional land-use plan could be adopted.

To determine whether the temporary moratorium instituted by TRPA's regulations denies "all economically beneficial or productive use" of the plaintiffs' land, we must first consider the meaning of the phrase "economically beneficial or productive use." The phrase's precise meaning is elusive, and has not been clarified by the Supreme Court. The central confusion over its meaning centers on the relationship between the "use" of property and its "value." Clearly, the economic value of property provides strong evidence of the availability of "economically beneficial or productive uses" of that property. Nevertheless, there are instances in which certain kinds of "value" may be poor measures of the existence of such uses. In any event, we need not resolve the sticky issues surrounding the meaning and proof of the existence of "economically beneficial or productive uses," because it is clear from the "general scope and dominant features" of Ordinance 81-5 and Resolution 83–21 that the temporary moratorium imposed by these regulations did not deprive the plaintiffs' land in the Lake Tahoe Basin of either all of its "value" or all of its "use."

First, as amici Cities and Counties of California note, basic principles of economics show that the moratorium did not render the plaintiffs' property valueless. The moratorium was temporary — it was designed to and did dissolve upon the adoption of a new regional plan. Given that the ordinance and resolution banned development for only a limited period, these regulations preserved the bulk of the future developmental use of the property. This future use had a substantial present value.

Of course, were a temporary moratorium designed to be in force so long as to eliminate all present value of a property's future use, we might be compelled to conclude that a categorical taking had occurred. We doubt, however, that a true temporary moratorium would ever be designed to last for so long a period. Certainly, the moratorium at issue here was not. The temporary moratorium was designed to suspend development only until a new regional land-use plan could be formulated — a process that the 1980 Compact intended would take thirty months. While the completion of the regional plan actually took forty months (which led to the temporary moratorium remaining in effect for eight months longer than expected), the moratorium still was in effect for only thirty-two months.

Moreover, there is no evidence that owners or purchasers of property in the basin anticipated that the temporary moratorium would continue indefinitely. Nor would they have had reason to: the district court found that TRPA worked diligently to complete the regional plan as quickly as possible. Thus, while the temporary moratorium surely had a negative impact on property values in the basin, we cannot conclude that the interim suspension of development wiped out the value of the plaintiffs' properties.

Furthermore, the temporary moratorium did not deprive the plaintiffs of all "use" of their property. The "use" of the plaintiffs' property runs from the present to the future. (This is a simple corollary of our earlier conclusion that the plaintiffs' property interests may not be temporally severed.) By instituting a temporary development moratorium, TRPA denied the plaintiffs only a small portion of this future stream; the thirty-two months during which the moratorium was in effect represents a small fraction of the useful life of the Tahoe properties.

Because the temporary development moratorium enacted by TRPA did not deprive the plaintiffs of all of the value or use of their property, we hold that it did not effect a categorical taking. Indeed, given the above analysis, it is equally clear that the district court was correct to conclude that the moratorium did not constitute a taking under the *Penn Central* test. Thus, while the district court was correct as to this latter point, we reverse its holding that a categorical taking occurred. In reaching this conclusion, we preserve the ability of local governments to do what they have done for many years — to engage in orderly, reasonable land-use planning through a considered and deliberative process. To do otherwise would turn the Takings Clause into a weapon to be used indiscriminately to penalize local communities for attempting to protect the public interest.

NOTES AND QUESTIONS

1. *The takings issue.* *Lake Tahoe* is the first major case to uphold development moratoria after *Lucas,* which had cast considerable doubt on their constitutionality. *Lake Tahoe* thus becomes another case that refuses to apply *Lucas* to find a taking under its categorical rule.

The conceptual severance problem decided by the court is similar to the denominator problem that arises when courts must determine whether property can be conceptually severed for takings clause analysis. See the Note on the *Lucas* exceptions in Chapter 2. Do you agree with the court's analysis of severance over time? Although the case was a facial attack on the ordinance, the court seemed to hold that a moratorium of reasonable length would not be a taking as applied.

For cases taking a similar view of moratoria see *Williams v. City of Central,* 907 P.2d 701 (Colo. App. 1995), and *Woodbury Place Partners v. City of Woodbury,* 492 N.W.2d 258 (Minn. App. 1992). For a discussion of land use programs for Lake Tahoe see Pryor, *Tahoe Untangled,* Planning, Vol. 65, No. 8, at 14 (1999). The clarity of the lake has continued to decline one foot per year, but a $900 million environmental improvement program is planned.

2. *Inadequate public facilities.* What do you make of the court's additional statement that a temporary moratorium would be a taking if it was "designed to be in force so long as to eliminate all present value of a property's future use." How could this happen? Public facility problems are often a reason for growth management programs, so when facilities are inadequate a local government may adopt a moratorium to allow time to remedy the problem. The cases recognize this as a sufficient reason for adopting a moratorium, but require that it be limited in time and that inadequacies be remedied during the moratorium period. *Smoke Rise, Inc. v. Washington Suburban Sanitary Comm'n,* 400 F. Supp. 1369 (D. Md. 1975), is a leading case, decided pre-*Lucas,* that upheld a moratorium on sewer hook-ups in an area of rapid growth around Washington, D.C. The court held there was no indication the moratorium was intended to prevent the area from accepting a fair share of the region's growth when plans were being implemented to improve facility capacity, and when the moratorium was reasonable in length. See also the California court's decision on remand from the Supreme Court in *First English II*, 258 Cal. Rptr. 893 (Cal. App. 1989), which upheld the moratorium because its purpose was to protect public safety; *Kaplan v. Clear Lake City Water Auth.*, 794 F.2d 1059 (5th Cir. 1986); and *Capture Realty Corp. v. Board of Adjustment*, 313 A.2d 624 (N.J. L. Div. 1993), *aff'd*, 336 A.2d 30 (N.J. App. Div. 1995).

The cases usually invalidate public facilities moratoria when there is no necessity for the moratorium. See *Lockary v. Kayfetz, supra* (no water shortage); *Q.C. Constr. Co. v. Gallo*, 649 F. Supp. 1331 (D.R.I. 1986), *aff'd without opinion*, 836 F.2d 1340 (1st Cir. 1987) (invalidating sewer moratorium when no remedial measures planned); *Tisei v. Town of Ogunquit*, 491 A.2d 564 (Me. 1985) (temporary moratorium on development must be justified by service emergency). What if a municipality consistently refuses to budget funds to improve sewer facilities and then imposes a moratorium on development because the facilities are inadequate? Would a court invalidate? See Note, *Sometimes There's Nothing Left to Give: The Justification for Denying Water Service to New Consumers to Control Growth*, 44 Stan. L. Rev. 429 (1992).

3. *Equal protection and pretext.* A moratorium can raise equal protection problems if a community adopts it to stall plans by a developer. See *Mont Belvieu Square, Ltd. v. City of Mont Belvieu*, 27 F. Supp. 2d 935 (S.D. Tex. 1998) (moratorium adopted to block lower-income housing developer). However, in *Kaplan v. Clear Lake City Water Auth.*, 794 F.2d 1059 (5th Cir. 1986), a water and sewer district adopted a moratorium on sewer connections because capacity was inadequate and refused service to a proposed multifamily development. The court applied deferential federal doctrine to reject due process and equal protection objections. Compare *Begin v. Inhabitants of Town of Sabbatus*, 409 A.2d 1269 (Me. 1979) (slow-growth ordinance applicable only to mobile homes held to violate equal protection), and *Pritchett v. Nathan Rogers Constr. & Realty Co.*, 379 So. 2d 545 (Ala. 1979) (invalidating refusal to connect to sanitary sewer when tap-ins denied on an arbitrary, case-by-case basis). *Kawaoka v. City of Arroyo Grande*, 17 F.3d 1227 (9th Cir.), *cert. denied*, 513 U.S. 870 (1994), is an interesting case rejecting a claim that a moratorium adopted because of lack of water was pretextual.

4. In view of this discussion, when would the adoption of a moratorium for growth management purposes be abusive? Note that an extended moratorium can have the effect of limiting growth in a community because development is likely to meet housing demand by going elsewhere during the moratorium period. Can the courts correct for this problem? What about legislation?

Moratoria are often needed when a community considers a growth management program because revisions in its comprehensive plan and zoning ordinance are usually necessary, and it is important to prohibit new development during the transition period that would be incompatible with the new plan and zoning regulations. The article that follows discusses the problems that should be considered when an ordinance of this kind is adopted:

GARVIN & LEITNER, DRAFTING INTERIM DEVELOPMENT ORDINANCES: CREATING TIME TO PLAN, Land Use Law & Zoning Digest, Vol. 48, No. 6, at 3–5 (1996)

Thorough planning takes time and community involvement. While this is occurring, development applications are often still being submitted and the existing problem(s) may be exacerbated before they are solved. To temporarily stem the tide of applications while creating time for a complete (and useful) planning process, communities are increasingly relying on some form of interim development controls (IDC). . . . [This is a type of moratorium.—Eds.]

Nature and Purposes of IDC

An IDC may temporarily restrict the zoning of land, new subdivision approval, and/or development permit issuance for a reasonable period of time in certain geographic areas until a new plan for the area is developed. The intent of the IDC is to preserve, temporarily, the status quo pending the adoption of the plan and permanent implementing ordinances. This is accomplished by allowing only such development as will be clearly in accord with the proposed changes and prohibiting other development approvals. . . .

To achieve this goal, the IDC should serve three functions. First, and perhaps most important, is protecting the planning process during its formulation and development. . . . Second, and corollary to protecting the planning process, is preventing new nonconforming uses during the planning period. This will ensure that the effectiveness of the planning is not destroyed prior to implementation, and should serve to stem the flood of new development applications that may be submitted in anticipation of a change to the existing plan and land-use regulations. Third, the IDC should foster public debate on the issues, goals and policies of the plan, and permanent development controls to be adopted upon the expiration of the IDC. . . .

[The] next task is to discern the needs of the underlying planning process and translating its needs into the terms of the IDC. Needs of the planning process that must be drafted into the IDC language relate to: (1) the length of the planning process; (2) the timing of initiation of the planning process; (3) the geographic area of the community to be subject to the new plan; (4) the type of development to be subject to the new plan; and (5) the type of development applications to be subject to the new plan. . . .

Type of Development, Duration, and Approvals

In each geographic area in which the IDC will apply, the community will also have to decide which land uses should be affected. The range of options is very broad — all land uses — to application to only a single land-use type, *e.g.,* residential development less than a specified [density]. . .

If the IDC is applied by area and subarea, the time period that it remains in effect to different areas may vary.

NOTES AND QUESTIONS

1. *The moratorium ordinance.* As this article indicates, a moratorium requires a careful evaluation of the problems it is adopted to remedy and careful drafting. Does the moratorium adopted in the *Tahoe* case, reproduced *supra*, meet the criteria specified in the article? How does the structure and content of a moratorium affect the takings issue?

2. *Authority to adopt.* The authority to adopt a moratorium is an issue in states that have zoning legislation based on the Standard Act, because it does not authorize moratoria. However, most courts have found an implied authority to adopt moratoria and interim zoning ordinances under zoning statutes based on the Act. See *Arnhold Bernhard & Co. v. Planning & Zoning Comm'n,* 479 A.2d 801 (Conn. 1984); *Collura v. Town of Arlington,* 329 N.E.2d 733 (Mass. 1975) (citing cases). See also *Dill v. Board of County Comm'rs of Lincoln County,* 928 P.2d 809 (Colo. App. 1996) (implying power to adopt moratorium from sewer facilities act). But see *Board of Supervisors v. Horne,* 215 S.E.2d 453 (Va. 1975) (county did not have implied authority to adopt an interim development order suspending the approval of subdivisions).

Municipalities may use procedural shortcuts when they adopt moratoria because development proposals they want to stop may be imminent. When that happens, a court will invalidate the moratorium if the municipality adopted it without following the formal notice and hearing requirements of the zoning statute. See *Deighton v. City Council,* 902 P.2d 426 (Colo. App. 1995)).

3. *The zoning freeze.* A common form of interim zoning simply freezes existing zoning regulations until changes in the zoning ordinance can be made. This kind of interim zoning has usually been upheld by the courts. See, e.g., *Walworth County v. City of Elkhorn,* 133 N.W.2d 257 (Wis. 1965). The prevailing rule was stated in *State ex rel. SCA Chem. Waste Serv., Inc. v. Konigsberg,* 636 S.W.2d 430 (Tenn. 1982):

> Assuming that the municipality has the legislative authority to adopt such [interim] ordinances, and assuming that such an ordinance or resolution is of limited duration for a period of time that is reasonable under the circumstances and has been enacted in good faith and without discrimination, such ordinances have generally been upheld, . . . so long as the purpose is to study and to develop a comprehensive zoning plan which does in fact proceed promptly, culminating in the expeditious adoption of appropriate zoning ordinances when the study is completed. [*Id.* at 435.]

In this case, a county adopted an interim ordinance prohibiting the issuance of building permits for hazardous waste treatment plants to preserve the status quo until a previously adopted zoning ordinance could take effect. For other cases upholding the reasonableness of time periods in moratoria see *Guinanne v. City & County of San Francisco,* 241 Cal. Rptr. 787 (Cal. App. 1987) (more than one year); *Almquist v. Town of Marshan,* 245 N.W.2d 819 (Minn. 1975) (six months). Compare *Morales v. Haines,* 349 F. Supp. 684 (N.D. Ill. 1972) (one-year suspension of building permits for subsidized housing held to violate equal protection). Does a zoning freeze escape takings problems?

4. *Downzoning during moratorium.* A landowner may have a successful as-applied claim when a community downzones her property during the moratorium period. The cases pro and con are collected in Annot., 30 A.L.R.3d 1196, 1235–50 (1970). Although the landowner cannot usually claim a zoning estoppel in these cases, a court may hold an interim ordinance inapplicable if it is impressed with the equities of the landowner's case.

A good case illustrating these problems is *Ogo Assocs. v. City of Torrance,* 112 Cal. Rptr. 761 (Cal. App. 1974). Plaintiff applied for a building permit to build a federally subsidized housing project in a mixed use area in which the plaintiff's property had been zoned to permit this use for eight years. The city next enacted an ordinance placing a moratorium on all new construction in the area and a permanent ordinance in the interim period changing the zoning on plaintiff's tract to a use not allowing the proposed project. It then refused to issue plaintiff a building permit. Although plaintiff had not satisfied all of the conditions for the building permit prior to the adoption of the moratorium ordinance, the court remanded the case to allow plaintiff to prove its claim of racial and economic discrimination in the adoption of the moratorium ordinance and permanent zoning change. For discussion, see Mandelker, *Downzoning to Control Growth Draws a Close Look by the Courts,* 3 Real Est. L.J. 402 (1975). For seemingly contrary opinions by the Minnesota Supreme Court in fact situations roughly comparable to the *Ogo* case, compare *Almquist v. Town of Marshan,* 245 N.W.2d 819 (Minn. 1976) (interim moratorium may be applied to pending development), with *Alexander v. City of Minneapolis,* 125 N.W.2d 583 (Minn. 1963) (contra).

A NOTE ON STATUTES AUTHORIZING MORATORIA AND INTERIM ZONING

Concern about how moratoria can affect development opportunities and the supply of affordable housing have led a number of states to adopt statutes that specify when and for how long a moratorium can be in place. Examples are Cal. Gov't Code § 65858 (limiting the duration of the ordinance and prohibiting uses that may be in conflict with contemplated zoning when there is a threat to health, safety and welfare); Minn. Stat. Ann. § 394.34 (limited to one year when revision in comprehensive plan or land use regulations pending); Mont. Code Ann. § 76-2-206 (limited to one year); Utah Code Ann. § 17-27-404 (counties, six-month interim ordinance); cf. Wash. Rev. Code Ann. § 36.70.790 (no time limit).

Some statutes authorize development moratoria but limit the authorization to threats to public health. For example, N.J. Stat. Ann. § 40:55D-90 authorizes a six-month moratorium, but only when there exists "a clear imminent danger to the health of the inhabitants." The statute modifies prior case law on moratoria. See *Toll Bros. v. West Windsor Twp.,* 712 A.2d 266 (N.J. App. Div. 1998) (ordinance authorizing timed growth controls held to be a moratorium prohibited by the statute). A California statute provides that a quota on residential development is presumed to have an impermissible effect on the regional housing supply, but exempts from this limitation "a moratorium, to protect the public health and safety, on residential construction for a specified period of time." Cal. Evid. Code § 669.5.

Do these limitations deal with takings problems or with other constitutional limitations? If so, which ones? Do they effectively preclude a constitutional attack on a moratorium adopted under the statutory provisions?

The most extensive statutory restrictions on development moratoria have been adopted in Oregon. The statute authorizes a moratorium only "to prevent a shortage of public facilities which would otherwise occur during the effective period of the moratorium." Or. Rev. Stat. § 520(2). A moratorium not justified by a shortage of facilities must be justified by a demonstration of "compelling need." For urban and urbanizable land, this demonstration requires the following:

(A) That application of existing development ordinances or regulations and other applicable law is inadequate to prevent irrevocable public harm from development in affected geographical areas;

(B) That the moratorium is sufficiently limited to ensure that a needed supply of affected housing types and the supply of commercial and industrial facilities within or in proximity to the city, county or special district are not unreasonably restricted by the adoption of the moratorium;

(C) Stating the reasons alternative methods of achieving the objectives of the moratorium are unsatisfactory;

(D) That the [local government] . . . has determined that the public harm which would be caused by failure to impose a moratorium outweighs the adverse effects on other affected local governments, including shifts in demand for housing or economic development, public facilities and services and buildable lands, and the overall impact of the moratorium on population distribution; and

(E) That the [local government] proposing the moratorium has determined that sufficient resources are available to complete the development of needed interim or permanent changes in plans, regulations or procedures within the period of effectiveness of the moratorium. [Or. Rev. Stat. § 197.520(3).]

Urban and urbanizable land is land within urban growth boundaries.

To what extent does this statute remedy the problems with moratoria identified in the case law? See *Davis v. City of Bandon*, 805 P.2d 709 (Ore. App. 1991) (moratorium justified by need to preserve valuable wildlife habitat). *Gisler v. Deschutes County*, 945 P.2d 1051 (Ore. App. 1997), held a denial of a subdivision application because it did not meet local approval standards was not a moratorium as defined by the statute.

C. GROWTH MANAGEMENT CONTROL STRATEGIES

In the sections that follow we discuss the different types of growth management programs outlined by Professor Kelly, *supra*. When reading these materials, keep in mind that the two key issues in these programs are the adequacy of public facilities and services for new development, and the location and rate at which growth occurs. The programs handle and relate these issues in different ways.

1. PHASED GROWTH PROGRAMS

As Professor Kelly pointed out, a phased growth program defines when development can take place in a particular location. It does not necessarily place a limit on the rate of growth, nor does it usually place limits on the expansion of an urban area.

An early phased growth program adopted by the Town of Ramapo, New York, made residential development dependent on the availability of public facilities and services. Ramapo, located west of the Hudson River, experienced accelerated growth after construction of a thruway bridge opened up commuting to New York City and adjacent suburbs. The highest New York court upheld the program in a landmark decision that has provided the legal basis for growth management ever since. The decision was all the more remarkable because one or two scattered New York cases had invalidated early forms of staged growth control. See *Albrecht Realty Co. v. Town of New Castle*, 167 N.Y.S.2d 843 (Sup. Ct. 1957) (invalidating building permit quota).

When reading this decision keep in mind that Ramapo is a New York town, a unit of local government that is usually limited in size and includes both unincorporated areas and incorporated villages, although the growth control program included only the unincorporated areas because the villages are distinct legal units. This type of local government is unusual and found only in a few states. The growth management program provided for a total build-out of the town during the growth management period, again an unusual strategy that is not possible in larger jurisdictions.

The program included a unique special permit requirement for new residential development that linked the permit to the availability of adequate public facilities. It assigned points to new development based on distance from a list of public facilities and required a minimum number of points before a permit could be granted.

GOLDEN v. RAMAPO PLANNING BOARD

30 N.Y.2d 359, 285 N.E.2d 291,
appeal dismissed, 409 U.S. 1003 (1972)

SCILEPPI, JUDGE:

Both cases arise out of the 1969 amendments to the Town of Ramapo's Zoning Ordinance. [Property owners and a builders's association brought a facial attack on the ordinance. The town planning board had denied subdivision approval for some of the property owners because they had not obtained the special development permit. The court treated the action as a facial attack and held that the alleged harm was sufficient to raise a justiciable issue concerning the validity of the ordinance.] . . .

Experiencing the pressures of an increase in population and the ancillary problem of providing municipal facilities and services,[1] the Town of Ramapo,

---

[1] The Town's allegations that present facilities are inadequate to service increasing demands goes uncontested. We must assume, therefore, that the proposed improvements, both as to their nature and extent, reflect legitimate community needs and are not veiled efforts at exclusion.

as early as 1964, made application for [a federal] grant . . . to develop a master plan. [This federal program has since been terminated. — Eds.] The plan's preparation included a four-volume study of the existing land uses, public facilities, transportation, industry and commerce, housing needs and projected population trends. The proposals appearing in the studies were subsequently adopted pursuant to section 272-a of the Town Law, in July, 1966 and implemented by way of a master plan. The master plan was followed by the adoption of a comprehensive zoning ordinance. Additional sewage district and drainage studies were undertaken which culminated in the adoption of a capital budget, providing for the development of the improvements specified in the master plan within the next six years. Pursuant to section 271 of the Town Law, authorizing comprehensive planning, and as a supplement to the capital budget, the Town Board adopted a capital program which provides for the location and sequence of additional capital improvements for the 12 years following the life of the capital budget. The two plans, covering a period of 18 years, detail the capital improvements projected for maximum development and conform to the specifications set forth in the master plan, the official map and drainage plan.

Based upon these criteria, the Town subsequently adopted the subject amendments for the alleged purpose of eliminating premature subdivision and urban sprawl. Residential development is to proceed according to the provision of adequate municipal facilities and services, with the assurance that any concomitant restraint upon property use is to be of a "temporary" nature and that other private uses, including the construction of individual housing, are authorized.

The amendments did not rezone or reclassify any land into different residential or use districts,[2] but, for the purposes of implementing the

---

In the period 1940–1968 population in the unincorporated areas of the Town increased 285.9%. Between the years of 1950–1960 the increase, again in unincorporated areas, was 130.8%; from 1960–1966 some 78.5%; and from the years 1966–1969 20.4%. In terms of real numbers, population figures compare at 58,626 as of 1966 with the largest increment of growth since the decennial census occurring in the undeveloped areas. Projected figures, assuming current land use and zoning trends, approximate a total Town population of 120,000 by 1985. Growth is expected to be heaviest in the currently undeveloped western and northern tiers of the Town, predominantly in the form of submission development with some apartment construction. A growth rate of some 1,000 residential units per annum has been experienced in the unincorporated areas of the Town.

[2] As of July, 1966, the only available figures, six residential zoning districts with varying lot size and density requirements accounted for in excess of nine tenths of the Town's unincorporated land area. Of these the RR classification (80,000 square feet minimum lot area) plus R-35 zone (35,000 square feet minimum lot area) comprise over one half of all zoned areas. The subject sites are presently zoned RR-50 (50,000 square feet minimum lot area). The reasonableness of these minimum lot requirements is not presently controverted, though we are referred to no compelling need in their behalf. . . . Under present zoning regulations, the population of the unincorporated areas could be increased by about 14,600 families (3.5 people) when all suitable vacant land is occupied. Housing values as of 1960 in the unincorporated areas range from a modest $15,000 (approx. 30%) to higher than $25,000 (25%), with the undeveloped western tier of Town showing the highest percentage of values in excess of $25,000 (41%). Significantly, for the same year only about one half of one per cent of all housing units were occupied by nonwhite families. Efforts at adjusting this disparity are reflected in the creation of a public housing authority and the authority's proposal to construct biracial low-income family housing. . . .

proposals appearing in the comprehensive plan, consist, in the main, of additions to the definitional sections of the ordinance, section 46-3, and the adoption of a new class of "Special Permit Uses," designated "Residential Development Use." "Residential Development Use" is defined as "The erection or construction of dwellings [on] any vacant plots, lots or parcels of land" (§ 46-3, as amd.); and, any person who acts so as to come within that definition, "shall be deemed to be engaged in residential development which shall be a separate use classification under this ordinance and subject to the requirement of obtaining a special permit from the Town Board" (§ 46-3, as amd.).

The standards for the issuance of special permits are framed in the terms of the availability to the proposed subdivision plat of five essential facilities or services; specifically (1) public sanitary sewers or approved substitutes; (2) drainage facilities; (3) improved public parks or recreation facilities, including public schools; (4) State, county or town roads — major, secondary or collector; and, (5) firehouses. No special permit shall issue unless the proposed residential development has accumulated 15 development points, to be computed on a sliding scale of values assigned to the specified improvements under the statute. Subdivision is thus a function of immediate availability to the proposed plat of certain municipal improvements; the avowed purpose of the amendments being to phase residential development to the Town's ability to provide the above facilities or services.

Certain savings and remedial provisions are designed to relieve of potentially unreasonable restrictions. Thus, the board may issue special permits vesting a present right to proceed with residential development in such year as the development meets the required point minimum, but in no event later than the final year of the 18-year capital plan. The approved special use permit is fully assignable, and improvements scheduled for completion within one year from the date of an application are to be credited as though existing on the date of the application. A prospective developer may advance the date of subdivision approval by agreeing to provide those improvements which will bring the proposed plat within the number of development points required by the amendments. And applications are authorized to the "Development Easement Acquisition Commission" for a reduction of the assessed valuation. Finally, upon application to the Town Board, the development point requirements may be varied should the board determine that such a variance or modification is consistent with the on-going development plan.

The undisputed effect of these integrated efforts in land use planning and development is to provide an over-all program of orderly growth and adequate facilities through a sequential development policy commensurate with progressing availability and capacity of public facilities. While its goals are clear and its purposes undisputably laudatory, serious questions are raised as to the manner in which these ends are to be effected, not the least of which relates to their legal viability under present zoning enabling legislation, particularly sections 261 and 263 of the Town Law. The owners of the subject premises argue, and the Appellate Division has sustained the proposition, that the primary purpose of the amending ordinance is to control or regulate population growth within the Town and as such is not within the authorized objectives of the zoning enabling legislation. We disagree.

In enacting the challenged amendments, the Town Board has sought to control subdivision in all residential districts, pending the provision (public or private) at some future date of various services and facilities. A reading of the relevant statutory provisions reveals that there is no specific authorization for the "sequential" and "timing" controls adopted here. That, of course, cannot be said to end the matter, for the additional inquiry remains as to whether the challenged amendments find their basis within the perimeters of the devices authorized and purposes sanctioned under current enabling legislation. Our concern is, as it should be, with the effects of the statutory scheme taken as a whole and its role in the propagation of a viable policy of land use and planning. . . .

[The court analyzed the provisions of the New York Town Law authorizing zoning ordinances. These provisions are based on the Standard Zoning Enabling Act, and the court found that the power "to restrict and regulate" conferred by the Town Law includes "by way of necessary implication, the authority to direct the growth of population for the purposes indicated, within the confines of the township. It is the matrix of land use restrictions, common to each of the enumerated powers and sanctioned goals, a necessary concomitant to the municipalities' recognized authority to determine the lines along which local development shall proceed, though it may divert it from its natural course." The court then considered an argument that the program was invalid because it authorized the prohibition of subdivision, a power not delegated to the town. — Eds.]

[T]o say that the Planning Board lacks the authority to deny subdivision rights is to mistake the nature of our inquiry which is essentially whether development may be conditioned pending the provision by the municipality of specified services and facilities. Whether it is the municipality or the developer who is to provide the improvements, the objective is the same — to provide adequate facilities, off-site and on-site; and in either case subdivision rights are conditioned, not denied.[7]

Experience, over the last quarter century, however with greater technological integration and drastic shifts in population distribution has pointed up serious defects and community autonomy in land use controls has come under increasing attack by legal commentators, and students of urban problems alike, because of its pronounced insularism and its correlative role in producing distortions in metropolitan growth patterns, and perhaps more importantly, in crippling efforts toward regional and State-wide problem solving, be it pollution, decent housing, or public transportation.

---

[7] . . . The reasoning, as far as it goes, cannot be challenged. Yet, in passing on the validity of the ordinance on its face, we must assume not only the Town's good faith, but its assiduous adherence to the program's scheduled implementation. We cannot, it is true, adjudicate in a vacuum and we would be remiss not to consider the substantial risk that the Town may eventually default in its obligations. Yet, those are future events, the staple of a clairvoyant, not of a court in its deliberations. The threat of default is not so imminent or likely that it would warrant our prognosticating and striking down these amendments as invalid on their face. When and if the danger should materialize, the aggrieved landowner can seek relief by way of an article 78 proceeding, declaring the ordinance unconstitutional as applied to his property. Alternatively, should it arise at some future point in time that the Town must fail in its enterprise, an action for a declaratory judgment will indeed prove the most effective vehicle for relieving property owners of what would constitute absolute prohibitions.

Recognition of communal and regional interdependence, in turn, has resulted in proposals for schemes of regional and State-wide planning, in the hope that decisions would then correspond roughly to their level of impact. Yet, as salutary as such proposals may be, the power to zone under current law is vested in local municipalities, and we are constrained to resolve the issues accordingly. What does become more apparent in treating with the problem, however, is that though the issues are framed in terms of the developer's due process rights, those rights cannot, realistically speaking, be viewed separately and apart from the rights of others "'in search of a [more] comfortable place to live.'"

There is, then, something inherently suspect in a scheme which, apart from its professed purposes, effects a restriction upon the free mobility of a people until sometime in the future when projected facilities are available to meet increased demands. Although zoning must include schemes designed to allow municipalities to more effectively contend with the increased demands of evolving and growing communities, under its guise, townships have been wont to try their hand at an array of exclusionary devices in the hope of avoiding the very burden which growth must inevitably bring. Though the conflict engendered by such tactics is certainly real, and its implications vast, accumulated evidence, scientific and social, points circumspectly at the hazards of undirected growth and the naive, somewhat nostalgic imperative that egalitarianism is a function of growth.

Of course, these problems cannot be solved by Ramapo or any single municipality, but depend upon the accommodation of widely disparate interests for their ultimate resolution. To that end, State-wide or regional control of planning would insure that interests broader than that of the municipality underlie various land use policies. Nevertheless, that should not be the only context in which growth devices such as these, aimed at population assimilation, not exclusion, will be sustained; especially where, as here, we would have no alternative but to strike the provision down in the wistful hope that the efforts of the State Office of Planning Coordination and the American Law Institute will soon bear fruit. [The reference is to legislation proposed by the Institute and the state office calling for state review of local land use control decisions. — Eds.]

Hence, unless we are to ignore the plain meaning of the statutory delegation, this much is clear: phased growth is well within the ambit of existing enabling legislation. And, of course, it is no answer to point to emergent problems to buttress the conclusion that such innovative schemes are beyond the perimeters of statutory authorization. These considerations, admittedly real, to the extent which they are relevant, bear solely upon the continued viability of "localism" in land use regulation; obviously, they can neither add nor detract from the initial grant of authority, obsolescent though it may be. The answer which Ramapo has posed can by no means be termed definitive; it is, however, a first practical step toward controlled growth achieved without forsaking broader social purposes.

The evolution of more sophisticated efforts to contend with the increasing complexities of urban and suburban growth has been met by a corresponding reluctance upon the part of the judiciary to substitute its judgment as to the plan's over-all effectiveness for the considered deliberations of its progenitors. Implicit in such a philosophy of judicial self-restraint is the growing awareness that matters of land use and development are peculiarly within the expertise of students of city and suburban planning, and thus well within the legislative prerogative, not lightly to be impeded. To this same end, we have afforded such regulations the usual presumption of validity attending the exercise of the police power, and have cast the burden of proving their invalidity upon the party challenging their enactment. Deference in the matter of the regulations' over-all effectiveness, however, is not to be viewed as an abdication of judicial responsibility, and ours remains the function of defining the metes and bounds beyond which local regulations may not venture, regardless of their professedly beneficent purposes.

The subject ordinance is said to advance legitimate zoning purposes as it assures that each new home built in the township will have at least a minimum of public services in the categories regulated by the ordinance. The Town argues that various public facilities are presently being constructed but that for want of time and money it has been unable to provide such services and facilities at a pace commensurate with increased public need. It is urged that although the zoning power includes reasonable restrictions upon the private use of property, exacted in the hope of development according to well-laid plans, calculated to advance the public welfare of the community in the future, the subject regulations go further and seek to avoid the increased responsibilities and economic burdens which time and growth must ultimately bring.

It is the nature of all land use and development regulations to circumscribe the course of growth within a particular town or district and to that extent such restrictions invariably impede the forces of natural growth. Where those restrictions upon the beneficial use and enjoyment of land are necessary to promote the ultimate good of the community and are within the bounds of reason, they have been sustained. "Zoning [, however,] is a means by which a governmental body can plan for the future — it may not be used as a means to deny the future." [Citing *National Land & Inv. Co. v. Kohn,* 215 A.2d 597, 610 (Pa. 1965).] Its exercise assumes that development shall not stop at the community's threshold, but only that whatever growth there may be shall proceed along a predetermined course. It is inextricably bound to the dynamics of community life and its function is to guide, not to isolate or facilitate efforts at avoiding the ordinary incidents of growth. What segregates permissible from impermissible restrictions depends in the final analysis upon the purpose of the restrictions and their impact in terms of both the community and general public interest. The line of delineation between the two is not a constant, but will be found to vary with prevailing circumstances and conditions.

What we will not countenance, then, under any guise, is community efforts at immunization or exclusion. But, far from being exclusionary, the present amendments merely seek, by the implementation of sequential development and timed growth, to provide a balanced cohesive community dedicated to the efficient utilization of land. The restrictions conform to the community's considered land use policies as expressed in its comprehensive plan and represent a bona fide effort to maximize population density consistent with orderly growth. True other alternatives, such as requiring off-site improvements as a prerequisite to subdivision, may be available, but the choice as how best to proceed, in view of the difficulties attending such exactions, cannot be faulted.

Perhaps even more importantly, timed growth, unlike the minimum lot requirements recently struck down by the Pennsylvania Supreme Court as exclusionary [See, e.g., *National Land & Inv. Co. v. Kohn,* 215 A.2d 597 (Pa. 1965) — Eds.] does not impose permanent restrictions upon land use. Its obvious purpose is to prevent premature subdivision absent essential municipal facilities and to insure continuous development commensurate with the Town's obligation to provide such facilities. They seek, not to freeze population at present levels but to maximize growth by the efficient use of land, and in so doing testify to this community's continuing role in population assimilation. In sum, Ramapo asks not that it be left alone, but only that it be allowed to prevent the kind of deterioration that has transformed well-ordered and thriving residential communities into blighted ghettos with attendant hazards to health, security and social stability — a danger not without substantial basis in fact.

We only require that communities confront the challenge of population growth with open doors. Where in grappling with that problem, the community undertakes, by imposing temporary restrictions upon development, to provide required municipal services in a rational manner, courts are rightfully reluctant to strike down such schemes. The timing controls challenged here parallel recent proposals put forth by various study groups and have their genesis in certain of the pronouncements of this and the courts of sister States. While these controls are typically proposed as an adjunct of regional planning, the preeminent protection against their abuse resides in the mandatory on-going planning and development requirement, present here, which attends their implementation and use.

We may assume, therefore, that the present amendments are the product of foresighted planning calculated to promote the welfare of the township. The Town has imposed temporary restrictions upon land use in residential areas while committing itself to a program of development. It has utilized its comprehensive plan to implement its timing controls and has coupled with these restrictions provisions for low and moderate income housing on a large scale. Considered as a whole, it represents both in its inception and implementation a reasonable attempt to provide for the sequential, orderly development of land in conjunction with the needs of the community, as well as individual parcels of land, while simultaneously obviating the blighted aftermath which the initial failure to provide needed facilities so often brings.

The proposed amendments have the effect of restricting development for onwards to 18 years in certain areas. Whether the subject parcels will be so restricted for the full term is not clear, for it is equally probable that the proposed facilities will be brought into these areas well before that time. Assuming, however, that the restrictions will remain outstanding for the life of the program, they still fall short of a confiscation within the meaning of the Constitution.

An ordinance which seeks to permanently restrict the use of property so that it may not be used for any reasonable purpose must be recognized as a taking: The only difference between the restriction and an outright taking in such a case "is that the restriction leaves the owner subject to the burden of payment of taxation, while outright confiscation would relieve him of that burden" (*Arverne Bay Constr. Co. v. Thatcher*, [15 N.E.2d 587 (N.Y. 1938).]) An appreciably different situation obtains where the restriction constitutes a *temporary* restriction, promising that the property may be put to a profitable use within a reasonable time. The hardship of holding unproductive property for some time might be compensated for by the ultimate benefit inuring to the individual owner in the form of a substantial increase in valuation; or, for that matter, the landowner might be compelled to chafe under the temporary restriction, without the benefit of such compensation, when that burden serves to promote the public good.

We are reminded, however, that these restrictions threaten to burden individual parcels for as long as a full generation and that such a restriction cannot, in any context, be viewed as a temporary expedient. The Town, on the other hand, contends that the landowner is not deprived of either the best use of his land or of numerous other appropriate uses, still permitted within various residential districts, including the construction of a single-family residence, and consequently, it cannot be deemed confiscatory. Although no proof has been submitted on reduction of value, the landowners point to obvious disparity between the value of the property, if limited in use by the subject amendments and its value for residential development purposes, and argue that the diminution is so considerable that for all intents and purposes the land cannot presently or in the near future be put to profitable or beneficial use, without violation of the restrictions.

Every restriction on the use of property entails hardships for some individual owners. Those difficulties are invariably the product of police regulation and the pecuniary profits of the individual must in the long run be subordinated to the needs of the community. The fact that the ordinance limits the use of, and may depreciate the value of the property will not render it unconstitutional, however, unless it can be shown that the measure is either unreasonable in terms of necessity or the diminution in value is such as to be tantamount to a confiscation. Diminution, in turn, is a relative factor and though its magnitude is an indicia of a taking, it does not of itself establish a confiscation.

Without a doubt restrictions upon the property in the present case are substantial in nature and duration. They are not, however, absolute. The amendments contemplate a definite term, as the development points are designed to operate for a maximum period of 18 years and during that period, the Town is committed to the construction and installation of capital improvements. The net result of the on-going development provision is that individual parcels may be committed to a residential development use prior to the expiration of the maximum period. Similarly, property owners under the terms of the amendments may elect to accelerate the date of development by installing, at their own expense, the necessary public services to bring the parcel within the required number of development points. While even the best of plans may not always be realized, in the absence of proof to the contrary, we must assume the Town will put its best effort forward in implementing the physical and fiscal timetable outlined under the plan. Should subsequent events prove this assumption unwarranted, or should the Town because of some unforeseen event fail in its primary obligation to these landowners, there will be ample opportunity to undo the restrictions upon default. For the present, at least, we are constrained to proceed upon the assumption that the program will be fully and timely implemented.

Thus, . . . the present amendments propose restrictions of a certain duration and founded upon estimate determined by fact. Prognostication on our part in upholding the ordinance proceeds upon the presently permissible inference that within a reasonable time the subject property will be put to the desired use at an appreciated value. In the interim assessed valuations for real estate tax purposes reflect the impact of the proposed restrictions. The proposed restraints, mitigated by the prospect of appreciated value and interim reductions in assessed value, and measured in terms of the nature and magnitude of the project undertaken, are within the limits of necessity.

In sum, where it is clear that the existing physical and financial resources of the community are inadequate to furnish the essential services and facilities which a substantial increase in population requires, there is a rational basis for "phased growth" and hence, the challenged ordinance is not violative of the Federal and State Constitutions. . . .

[Judge Breitel's dissenting opinion is omitted.]

NOTES AND QUESTIONS

1. *Point systems.* Growth management programs using a point system to link the approval of new development with public facilities are no longer common. A modified version of this kind of program, that requires adequate public facilities to be available before development can be approved, is discussed in Section 3, *infra.* The Ramapo program ran into trouble. Unexpected flooding resulting from hurricanes in 1971 and 1972 forced the town to appropriate 1.5 million dollars to remedy storm damage. Much of the work scheduled on capital facilities was deferred in these years. Emanuel, *Ramapo's Managed Growth Program,* 4 Planners' Notebook, No. 5, at 1 (1974). The town abandoned the program in 1983. For discussion of the program by the person who designed it see R. Freilich, From Sprawl to Smart Growth 39–65 (1999).

2. *Putting limits on timing programs.* The Ramapo program was never attacked as-applied, but the New York court indicated how it would handle as-applied attacks on growth management programs in *Charles v. Diamond,* 360 N.E.2d 1295 (N.Y. 1977). A local ordinance required developers to connect with a village sewer system. The village authorized a connection but the state environmental agency informed the developer that it could not connect to the system until system deficiencies were corrected. The state agency also instructed the county health department to disapprove a system connection. The developer then brought an action against the state and county agencies and the village, contending that their actions amounted to a taking of property.

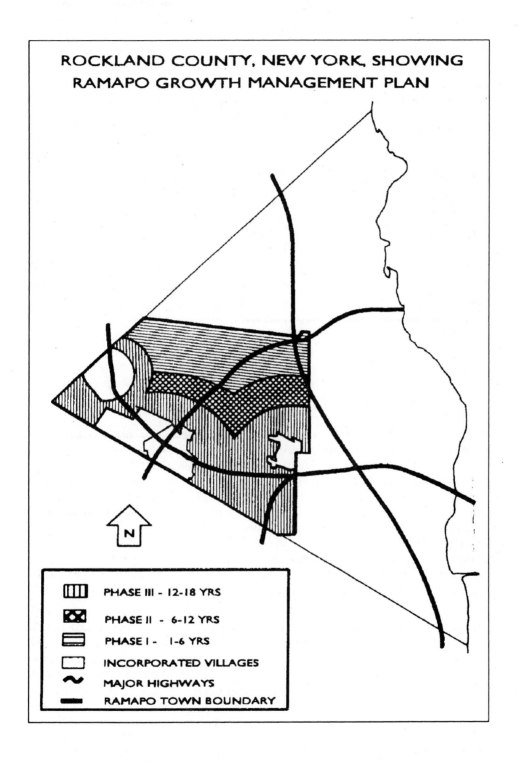

ROCKLAND COUNTY, NEW YORK, SHOWING
RAMAPO GROWTH MANAGEMENT PLAN

N

PHASE III - 12-18 YRS
PHASE II - 6-12 YRS
PHASE I - 1-6 YRS
INCORPORATED VILLAGES
MAJOR HIGHWAYS
RAMAPO TOWN BOUNDARY

Although it remanded the case for trial because the record had not been sufficiently developed to decide the constitutional issues, the court noted that temporary restrictions on development because of service difficulties were justified but that permanent restrictions were not. It adopted a set of factors to determine how long a restriction on development for this reason could last, including the extent of the service problem, the ability of the community to raise the necessary capital, and the role of the state and federal governments. An extensive delay would be justified "only if the remedial steps are of sufficient magnitude to require extensive preparations, including preliminary studies, applications for assistance to other governmental entities, the raising of large amounts of capital, and the letting of work contracts." *Id.* at 1301.

Noting that it had accepted development delays of up to eighteen years in the *Ramapo* decision, the court added that "the crucial factor, perhaps even the decisive one, is whether the ultimate cost of the benefit is being shared by the members of the community at large, or, rather, is being hidden from the public by the placement of the entire burden upon particular property owners." *Id.* at 1300. Is this statement a further extension of the court's dictum in footnote 7 of the *Ramapo* decision? Recall that *Ramapo* did not consider the growth management plan as applied to a particular property owner. The court in *Charles* also noted, again citing *Ramapo,* that a municipality "must be committed firmly to the construction and installation of the necessary improvements." *Id.* at 1301. Do *Ramapo* and *Charles* create a Catch-22 situation for a municipality attempting a growth management plan of this type? The municipality must be firmly committed to a reasonable time schedule in providing necessary public facilities, but making this commitment may be difficult if not undesirable because it locks the municipality into a rigid, long-range plan.

3. *How would the Ramapo program fare under the Lucas case?* A post-*Lucas* court probably would not be impressed by the town's "commitment" to the program. Would the residual single family use be enough? In *Petersen v. City of Decorah,* 259 N.W.2d 553 (Iowa App. 1977), the court invalidated an agricultural use district "intended to reserve areas suitable for nonagricultural use until the land is needed for development in accordance with a future land use plan." The city denied a rezoning for a shopping center because it was holding the land for future industrial development. The court noted that no industry had been attracted to the city since 1964, that the city admitted the property was suitable for a shopping center, and that the land was not suitable for agricultural purposes.

4. *Statutory authority.* The Ramapo permit system was not explicitly authorized by the New York law, which was based on the Standard Zoning Act. Do you agree with the New York court's decision that it is implicitly authorized? This issue has not been extensively litigated elsewhere. In *Beck v. Town of Raymond,* 394 A.2d 847 (N.H. 1978), the court held that a growth control ordinance enacted as a general ordinance was not a valid exercise of delegated statutory police powers. But see *Boulder Bldrs. Group v. City of Boulder,* 759 P.2d 752 (Colo. 1988) (growth management program including quota authorized as an exercise of home rule).

A New Jersey case held a sophisticated timed growth scheme was, in fact, a moratorium that was prohibited by the state planning legislation. *Toll Bros.,*

Inc. v. West Windsor Township, 712 A.2d 266 (N.J. App. Div. 1998). See Buchsbaum, *Timed Growth Ordinances Rejected in New Jersey,* 31 Urb. Law. 823 (1999).

5. *Exclusion issues.* H. Franklin, *Controlling Growth—But for Whom?* (Potomac Inst. 1973), pointed out that in the 1970 census Ramapo was about six percent black, but that ninety-one percent of the blacks lived in a village not included in the growth management program. Franklin also noted that very few blacks lived in Ramapo's public housing and that sixty-five percent of the vacant land in the town was covered by large lot zoning with required minimum lot areas of 25,000 to 80,000 square feet. Development would have been postponed until 1986 on forty-eight percent of the vacant land available under the zoning ordinance just prior to the time the Ramapo plan was adopted. No zoning district was set aside for multifamily housing, and no additional public housing was planned.

Subsequent to *Ramapo,* in a case arising in nearby Westchester County, *Berenson v. Town of New Castle,* 341 N.E.2d 236 (N.Y. 1975), a developer attacked a town zoning ordinance that required one-acre and two-acre minimum lots in two of its residential districts. The ordinance also excluded multifamily dwellings. *Berenson* is discussed in Ch. 4, *supra.*

Although noting that in *Ramapo* it had held "that a town may permissibly adopt a program for phased growth," the court in *Berenson* also pointed out that in *Ramapo* "we were careful to note that 'community efforts at immunization or exclusion' would not be countenanced." *Id.* at 241. The court in *Berenson* then held that a multifamily development exclusion would be unconstitutional if it prevented a municipality from meeting its share of regional housing need. Does *Berenson* qualify *Ramapo?* The *Mount Laurel I* court also treated *Ramapo* cautiously. See 336 A.2d 713, 732 n.20.

Is it important under *Berenson* that the Ramapo growth control program also was fairly consistent with applicable state and regional plans? It concentrated intensive new development in the villages by maintaining low density zoning in the unincorporated areas of the town. In *Beck v. Town of Raymond, supra* Note 4, the court stated, in dictum, that growth controls must be reasonable and nondiscriminatory, that they must be a product of careful study and must be reexamined constantly with a view toward relaxation or termination, and that they must be accompanied by good faith efforts to "increase the capacity of municipal services." *Id.* at 852. The court added that growth controls "must not be imposed simply to exclude outsiders, especially outsiders of any disadvantaged social or economic group." *Ibid.*

New Hampshire later codified the *Beck* holding in a statute authorizing local governments to "control the timing of development":

> Any ordinance imposing such a control may be adopted only after . . . adoption . . . of a master and a capital improvement program and shall be based on a growth management process intended to assess and balance community development needs and consider regional development needs. [N.H. Rev. Stat. Ann. § 674:22.]

Stoney-Brook Dev. Corp. v. Town of Fremont, 474 A.2d 561 (N.H. 1984), applied the statute to invalidate a growth management program based on a three percent growth rate as arbitrary and not based on careful study. *Rancourt v. Town of Barnstead,* 523 A.2d 55 (N.H. 1986), held the town could not base a disapproval of a subdivision on its master plan when it had not adopted a capital improvement program or growth management ordinance as required by the statute. The court rejected a trial court finding that a three percent growth rate adopted in the master plan had a "solid, scientific, statistical basis." Would the Ramapo plan be upheld under this statute?

6. *How fair was the Ramapo point system?* Although the New York court upheld the Ramapo point system, some problems with the system indicate why this type of control is difficult to adopt. One problem was that not all of the public facilities on which points were awarded were under the control of the town. The county was responsible for the construction of interceptor sewers, and firehouses were provided by special districts formed by local residents.

Does the Supreme Court's nexus test for exactions apply to the Ramapo program? If it does, is there a "rough proportionality" between the growth program and the points requirement, which was based on the availability of public services?

The point system utilized by the ordinance was to some extent based on the distance of the required facilities from "each separate lot or plot capable of being improved with a residential dwelling." For example, points for service from fire houses were assigned as follows:

Within 1 mile	3 points
Within 2 miles	1 point
Further than 2 miles	0 points

Compare Department of Planning and Community Development: A Report of Population Growth in the City of Aurora [Colorado] 41 (1973), noting that "[t]he safety zone within which a fire station can adequately serve an area can be viewed as a diamond, with the station at the center." Fire protection, according to this report, is measured by distance from the station in time, with five minutes being the outer limit for safety purposes. Obviously, the time it takes for a fire truck to reach a fire depends on the nature of the road network and topography. Did points for firehouse meet the "rough proportionality" requirement?

Points for drainage were based on "Percentage of Required Drainage Capacity Available." This rating was based on the capacity of the drainage system to handle peak drainage at points along the system, not on the incremental impact of a new development. The first developer in an area, in order to get the maximum number of points, had to make an improvement that provided adequate drainage for future development in the entire area. Did this requirement satisfy the "rough proportionality" test? Was the point system acceptable under the rough proportionality test because the amount of development it permitted was reasonable in relationship to the town's service capacity? The entire Ramapo ordinance is reproduced in 24 Zoning Dig. 68 (1972).

7. *What the Ramapo program accomplished.* A study of the Ramapo program while it was in effect indicated that it substantially reduced growth in the town, that it shifted development to nearby communities, and that it reduced the price of land not qualified for development under the point system. S. Seidel, Housing Costs & Government Regulations: Confronting the Regulatory Maze 218–22 (1978). Seidel believed the weak point in the program was the fragmented governmental authority over the public facilities on which the point system was based. He concluded that the program "has proven neither useful nor accurate as a planning device, and that it has also failed to improve the township's municipal fisc." *Id.* at 222. He also noted that the town's property tax had increased at a faster rate after the program was adopted than before, even though the relative increase in expenditures had declined.

8. For discussion of the Ramapo program, see Bosselman, *Can the Town of Ramapo Pass a Law to Bind the Whole World?,* 1 Fla. St. U. L. Rev. 234 (1973); Note, *Phased Zoning: Regulation of the Tempo and Sequence of Land Development,* 26 Stan. L. Rev. 585 (1974); Note, *A Zoning Program for Phased Growth: Ramapo Township's Time Controls on Residential Development,* 47 N.Y.U. L. Rev. 723 (1972).

2. RATE-OF-GROWTH PROGRAMS: GROWTH CAPS AND QUOTAS

a. How These Programs Work

This is another type of growth management program described by Professor Kelly. These programs differ from phased growth programs, like the Ramapo program, because they place an explicit limitation on growth through quotas and growth caps. The point system in the Ramapo program limited the rate of growth by making development approval depend on the availablity of facilities and services, but this limit was implicit rather than explicit.

Rate-of-growth programs are not common. A survey of 1,168 communities found only 45 with rate-of-growth program in place, and most of these were in California. *Growth Controls and Affordable Housing: Results from a National Survey,* Am. Plan. Ass'n, PAS Memo, Jan. 1995, at 3. Here is how this type of control works:

> Each system places a carefully selected numerical limit or quota on the amount of development which will be approved during a designated time frame. Development proposals are then evaluated and ranked based upon the degree that they satisfy criteria designed to ensure consistency with the system's objectives and goals. The quota is then allocated to the developments in accordance with their ranking until all proposals are approved or the quota for the time period is exhausted. [Chinn & Garvin, *Designing Development Allocation Systems*, Land Use L. & Zoning Digest, Vol. 44, No. 2, at 3 (1992).]

Communities evaluate and rank development proposals to determine which ones will receive an allotment under the quota. Point systems, like those in the Ramapo program, are one way of doing this. Developments receive a set number of points for satisfying the ranking criteria. Quota allocations are then assigned to developments with the most points. The use of point systems seems to be declining, however, as they have proved complicated and difficult to administer. Communities more frequently use flexible systems under which development allocation awards are based on community policies or simply awarded by lottery or on a first-come, first-served basis. See Chinn & Garvin, *supra*. Notice that these programs do not usually consider the location of new development when they make development allocations, although the Petaluma plan, discussed below, contained geographic priorities.

b. Taking and Other Constitutional Issues: The *Petaluma* Case

Quota and growth cap programs raise constitutional issues similar to those raised by timing phasing programs like the Ramapo program. The takings issue is one. Assume a developer is denied a development allocation in a given year because he does not meet community development objectives. He can reapply, of course, the next year. Is the one-year delay a compensable temporary taking? Is it a "normal" delay under *First English*? Presumably it is a categorical per se taking under *Lucas* if there is no economically productive use during the one-year delay period, but on this point see the *Lake Tahoe* case, reproduced *supra*. Is the case unripe because no final decision has been made on the development application and the developer can simply reapply the following year? See *Long Beach Equities, Inc. v. County of Ventura*, 282 Cal. Rptr. 877 (Cal. App. 1991), *cert. denied*, 505 U.S. 1219 (1992) (dismissing facial takings claim against timing and quota program and holding an as-applied takings claim unripe). What if points are awarded for land dedications for parks and schools? Does this raise a *Nollan* or *Dolan* problem?

The landmark case on quota programs is *Construction Industry Ass'n v. City of Petaluma*, 522 F.2d 897 (9th Cir. 1975), *cert. denied*, 424 U.S. 934 (1976), which considered a substantive due process challenge to a point system that allocated a quota of 500 new dwelling units per year, and was concerned primarily with the exclusionary effects of the program. The court described the allocation procedure:

> At the heart of the allocation procedure is an intricate point system, whereby a builder accumulates points for conformity by his projects with the City's general plan and environmental design plans, for good architectural design, and for providing low and moderate income dwelling units and various recreational facilities. The Plan further directs that allocations of building permits are to be divided as evenly as feasible between the west and east sections of the City and between single-family dwellings and multiple residential units (including rental units), that the sections of the City closest to the center are to be developed first in order to cause "infilling" of vacant area, and that 8 to 12 per cent of the housing units approved be for low and moderate income persons. [*Id.* at 901.]

The court found that the primary purpose of the plan was to limit Petaluma's demographic and market growth rate in housing and "the immigration of new residents." The court concluded that the plan, if adopted throughout the region, would lead to a housing shortfall that would affect housing quality and mobility and the choice of housing available to lower income families. There was no evidence, however, that these negative impacts would occur in

Petaluma, especially as the plan increased the number of multifamily and low-income units, which the court said were rarely built in the days before the plan. The court then held the plan constitutional:

> Although we assume that some persons desirous of living in Petaluma will be excluded under the housing permit limitation and that, thus, the Plan may frustrate some legitimate regional housing needs, the Plan is not arbitrary or unreasonable. We agree with appellees that unlike the situation in the past most municipalities today are neither isolated nor wholly independent from neighboring municipalities and that, consequently, unilateral land use decisions by one local entity affect the needs and resources of an entire region. It does not necessarily follow, however, that the due process rights of builders and landowners are violated merely because a local entity exercises in its own self-interest the police power lawfully delegated to it by the state. If the present system of delegated zoning power does not effectively serve the state interest in furthering the general welfare of the region or entire state, it is the state legislature's and not the federal courts' role to intervene and adjust the system. . . . [T]he federal court is not a super zoning board and should not be called on to mark the point at which legitimate local interests in promoting the welfare of the community are outweighed by legitimate regional interests. [*Id.* at 906.]

NOTES AND QUESTIONS

1. *Litigation strategy.* Plaintiff's lawyers in *Petaluma* brought the case on a right-to-travel claim, which they won in the district court but lost in the court of appeal. The idea was, of course, to get the court to raise the constitutional standard of review to strict scrutiny by asserting a fundamental constitutional right. By shifting to substantive due process, the court was able to fall back on the deferential review of land use regulations federal courts give under the substantive due process clause. It is extremely difficult to win a land use case on substantive due process grounds in federal court. D. Mandelker, T. Sullivan & J. Gerard, Federal Land Use Law § 2.02. Similarly, an equal protection claim also is difficult to win in federal court. The right to travel theory is discussed further in note 9 *infra.*

2. *More on Petaluma.* Some additional aspects of the Petaluma Plan at the time of the decision are not covered by the court's opinion and illustrate typical components of a rate-of-growth system. McGivern, *Putting a Speed Limit on Growth*, 38 Plan. 263 (1972) (author was planning director of Petaluma). Part of the purpose of the plan was to redistribute new growth equally between an older western and a newer eastern section of the city. The council could also require that between 8 and 12 percent of each annual quota must be lower-income housing.

A Residential Development Evaluation System was utilized to determine which developers would receive the annual quota of allowable dwelling units, based on a point system similar to Ramapo's. From zero to five points were awarded for each of the following public facilities factors:

1. the capacity of the water system to provide for the needs of the proposed development without system extensions beyond those normally installed by the developer;

2. the capacity of the sanitary sewers to dispose of the wastes of the proposed development without system extensions beyond those normally installed by the developer;

3. the capacity of the drainage facilities to adequately dispose of the surface runoff of the proposed development without system extensions beyond those normally installed by the developer;

4. the ability of the Fire Department of the city to provide fire protection according to the established response standards of the city without the necessity of establishing a new station or requiring addition of major equipment to an existing station;

5. the capacity of the appropriate school to absorb the children expected to inhabit a proposed development without necessitating adding double sessions or other unusual scheduling or classroom overcrowding;

6. the capacity of major street linkage to provide for the needs of the proposed development without substantially altering existing traffic patterns or overloading the existing street systems, and the availability of other public facilities (such as parks and playgrounds) to meet the additional demands for vital public services without extension of services beyond those provided by the developer.

The evaluation system was utilized to require substantial contributions from developers for citywide facilities such as water, sewer, drainage, and fire protection. Would this be constitutional under *Dolan*?

The second review category was based on site and architectural design quality and a number of developer contributions. Some of the criteria on which developers were assigned points were the following:

4. the provision of public and/or private usable open space and/or pathways along the Petaluma River or any creek;

5. contributions to and extensions of existing systems of foot or bicycle paths, equestrian trails, and the greenbelt provided for in the Environmental Design Plan;

6. the provision of needed public facilities such as critical linkages in the major street system, school rooms, or other vital public facilities;

7. the extent to which the proposed development accomplishes an orderly and contiguous extension of existing development as against "leap frog" development;

8. the provision of units to meet the city's policy goal of 8 percent to 12 percent low-and moderate-income dwelling units annually.

As an alternative, what about distributing development permits under a quota on a first-come, first-served basis. Is this preferable to the elaborate scoring system Petaluma used? Would it stimulate a race to propose poorly planned developments?

3. *What happened in Petaluma.* In the first several years the Petaluma program slowed down residential growth but did not increase the number of multifamily dwellings. S. Seidel, Housing Costs & Government Regulations: Confronting the Regulatory Maze 222-28 (1978). Another study of this early period found the price of housing had increased significantly more in Petaluma than in one nearby comparison city but not in another, and that small, low-priced houses practically disappeared. Schwartz, Hansen & Green, *Suburban Growth Controls and the Price of New Housing*, 8 J. Envtl. Econ. & Mgt. 313 (1981).

Another review is critical:

> Petaluma's point system did not work well. Developers had difficulty understanding the complex point system. City staff had difficulty administering it despite a computer program designed to compute points. Projects which met minimum standards eventually obtained approvals. The time-consuming and costly ranking process had little impact on actual approval or denial of projects. In order to achieve minimum numbers of points, developers included in their projects some expensive features, probably not wanted by occupants or really needed by the city. As a few large developers came to dominate homebuilding in Petaluma, and as the pattern of approvals became clear, developers submitted projects which were adequate, but not excellent. In addition, it was difficult to get a majority of the evaluation committee to meet. Finally, one member could unduly skew the total points awarded and complicate the approval process by ranking a project very low or very high. [LeGates, *The Emergence of Flexible Growth Management Systems in the San Francisco Bay Area*, 24 Loyola L.A. L. Rev. 1035, 1060 (1991).]

4. *Petaluma today.* The residential Development Growth Management System with its annual quota of 500 units is still in effect. Not all of the allocation is normally used, and the city has been averaging about 380 units a year. The yearly allocation process is initiated with the development of Residential Development Objectives in the first quarter of every year. The city council establishes criteria for approving applications and weighs applications against the criteria. Examples of objectives that have been identified in the past include providing more affordable housing for families and the disabled, providing more of an equal number of units between the east and the west portions of the community, providing high-density market rate housing, and providing residential development in mixed-use projects. The staff and the city council look at vacancy rates and the perception of housing need in the community in formulating these criteria.

Despite this program, Petaluma has continued to grow, with urban sprawl using up surrounding farmland and new development creating traffic congestion. In early 1998, voters adopted an urban growth boundary as the city neared an urban limits line established in 1969. A quarter of the city's central area remains vacant, but the city is developing a new plan to revive the central area. See Lockwood, *Pioneering Petaluma*, Planning, Vol. 64, No. 10, at 16 (1998).

What does the Petaluma experience say about the design and effectiveness of rate-of-growth programs? Are development allocations easier to uphold on constitutional grounds if they are based on flexible criteria rather than points? Recall the difficulty New York City has had with rigid design criteria, described in Chapter 3. Is the new program more or less constitutional than the program considered in the *Petaluma* case?

5. *The irony of quotas.* In an essay in which he makes a plea for legitimizing quotas, land use lawyer Jan Krasnowiecki states:

> The irony of it is that while standard zoning does not approve of quotas (at least until the New York court suggested otherwise in *Ramapo*), *the easiest way to run a quota system is to employ standard zoning.* All you have to do is zone all of the undeveloped areas of the municipality at a level which is just below the level at which it is economically safe to develop. If you do the job just right, no one will be able to show that he cannot develop his property yet no one will, in fact, develop until you grant him some change. . . . Thus by employing standard zoning you can run a quota system without ever stating the principles upon which it is based. [Krasnowiecki, *Legal Aspects of Planned Unit Development in Theory and Practice*, in Frontiers of Planned Unit Development 99, 105 (R. Burchell ed., 1973) (emphasis in original).]

What do you think of his argument?

6. *California legislation.* Quota programs are now limited by legislation in California. Comprehensive plans in California must contain a mandatory housing element in which communities must provide for their fair share of regional housing need. In addition, these programs must meet the following statutory requirement:

> If a county or city . . . adopts or amends a mandatory general plan element which operates to limit the number of housing units which may be constructed on an annual basis, such adoption or amendment shall contain findings which justify reducing the housing opportunities of the region. The findings shall include all of the following:
>
> (a) A description of the city's or county's appropriate share of the regional need for housing.
>
> (b) A description of the specific housing programs and activities being undertaken by the local jurisdiction to fulfill the requirements of . . . [the housing element in the plan.]
>
> (c) A description of how the public health, safety, and welfare would be promoted by such adoption or amendment.
>
> (d) The fiscal and environmental resources available to the local jurisdiction. [Cal. Gov't Code § 65302.8.]

There are hardly any cases interpreting this statute. *Lee v. City of Monterey Park*, 219 Cal. Rptr. 309 (Cal. App. 1985), held that a complaint challenging an annual building quota stated a cause of action under this statute and related statutes imposing a similar requirement. The complaint stated the city adopted the quota without considering the housing needs of the region, that the quota did not accommodate competing municipal interests, including the need for affordable housing, and that the burden on the city's public facilities were no greater than in other cities in the region.

7. *Growth cap held invalid.* A Florida court invalidated a much-publicized absolute limit on population growth in *City of Boca Raton v. Boca Villas Corp.*, 371 So. 2d 154 (Fla. App. 1979). A charter amendment adopted by popular vote imposed a development cap of 40,000 dwelling units. The city council then cut the permitted densities in all multifamily districts in half. The court found that the dwelling unit limit was supported by after-the-fact studies, was not supported in trial testimony by the planning director, and was adopted without consulting the planning department. The court also found no public service inadequacies or environmental problems that would support the population limit. This litigation is said to have cost the parties 1.5 million dollars.

8. *Quota programs in other states.* The courts in a few other cases have considered quota programs. In *Sturges v. Town of Chilmark*, 402 N.E.2d 1346 (Mass. 1980), the court upheld a growth quota ordinance adopted for Martha's Vineyard. The ordinance limited building permits over a ten-year period in new residential subdivisions to ten percent of the maximum permitted density of the lot annually. The court upheld the ordinance against substantive due process objections as a measure for restricting growth while the town studied development problems resulting from substandard soil conditions. The court noted that, in a rural environment where no showing of regional demand for primary housing had been made, the public interest in preserving the environment outweighed the social consequences of closing the doors to affluent outsiders seeking vacation homes. Do you suppose the limited time period for the quota helped the town? See also *Del Oro Hills v. City of Oceanside*, 37 Cal. Rptr. 2d 677 (Cal. App. 1995) (rejecting facial takings claim to annual quota on residential development); *Wilkinson v. Board of County Comm'rs*, 872 P.2d 1269 (Colo. App. 1993) (upholding rejection of development proposal; takings claim not ripe).

9. *The right to travel.* Because it triggers stricter scrutiny, the right to travel theory enjoyed a vogue in land use litigation, but recent decisions have followed *Petaluma* and have rejected right to travel arguments. One case had this to say about the right to travel doctrine as it affected the permit program of the interim California coastal act:

> It does not follow, however, that all regulations affecting travel, however indirect or inconsequential, constitute invasions of the fundamental right. The right may be invoked if the regulations "unreasonably burden or restrict" the freedom of movement. In a particular case the question is whether the travel inhibited is of sufficient importance to individual liberty to give rise to a constitutional violation. Thus far the United States Supreme Court has invoked the right to travel only in cases involving invidious discrimination, durational residence requirements or direct restrictions on interstate or foreign travel. . . .
>
> We fail to see how the Coastal Initiative interferes with fundamental right to travel. It is not discriminatory; it imposes no durational residence requirement; it exacts no penalty for exercising the right to travel or to select one's place of residence. In short, it has no chilling

effect on an individual's freedom of movement. [*CEEED v. California Coastal Zone Conservation Comm'n*, 118 Cal. Rptr. 315, 333 (Cal. Ct. App. 1974).]

See also *Northern Ill. Home Bldrs. Ass'n v. County of Du Page,* 649 N.E.2d 38 (Ill. 1993) (no standing to assert right to travel).

In its most recent right to travel case, the Supreme Court invalidated a California statute that limited welfare benefits paid to newly arrived residents to the benefits they had been received in the state from which they came. *Saenz v. Roe,* 526 U.S. 489 (1999). The Court held that the issue in the case was "the right of the newly arrived citizen to the same privileges and immunities enjoyed by other citizens of the same State." How does this case affect the right to travel issue in land use regulation?

3. ADEQUATE PUBLIC FACILITIES ORDINANCES AND CONCURRENCY

Adequate public facilities (APF) ordinances are close relatives to the Ramapo plan because they authorize the approval of new development only if adequate public facilities are available. They differ from the Ramapo plan, however, because that plan was a buildout of the town over a specified period of time according to a capital improvement plan. APF ordinances may or may not be based on a comprehensive plan, and may not include policies that time new development or direct it to priority areas. The typical APF ordinance authorizes a case-by-case review of new development proposals to determine if they meet criteria for adequacy contained in the ordinance.

About one-third of the communities surveyed in the growth management survey had adopted APF ordinances. Concurrency is a similar requirement that is part of the Florida and Washington state planning programs. Local governments in these states are required by state law to authorize new development only if adequate facilities will be provided concurrently.

a. Adequate Public Facilities Ordinances

How they work.—The following selection describes how APF ordinances work:

> *Linking Development to Infrastructure Capacity.* One of the most commonly used growth management techniques today makes development approvals contingent on the availability of facilities adequate to serve the proposed development. Regulations for *adequate public facilities* (APF) require evidence that capacities of public facilities are adequate to serve prospective development before subdivision plats are approved or building permits issued. . . .
>
> Most APF requirements deal only with one or two types of facilities, such as roads or sewers, that have caused critical problems in the community. A substantial number of communities, however, apply APF regulations to the full range of public facilities, although certain "problem" facilities usually become the principal focus of attention.

APF requirements may be spelled out in a few sentences or in longer sections that incorporate standards and criteria. They may be adopted as separate ordinances or, more often, as provisions in subdivision regulations. Typically, the evaluation of facility adequacy is conducted during the subdivision approval process. The evaluation will determine whether facilities impacted by the proposed subdivision have capacity to support the development. If, for example, the amount of traffic generated from a proposed project will decrease the level of service of a nearby road intersection below the established standard, then the development must be postponed until (1) public programs are scheduled or funded to improve the intersection's capacity, (2) the developer promises to institute traffic management programs to reduce traffic generation to desired levels, or (3) the developer commits to funding or constructing capacity improvements to meet the standards. The de facto moratorium on further development exists until agreement is reached on one or more solutions to the congestion problem. [D. Porter, Managing Growth in America's Communities 123 (1997).]

Implementing APF ordinances.—Unlike the Ramapo plan, APF ordinances present more difficult implementation problems because they must specify and apply standards that determine adequacy. These criteria vary. The key standard is a level of service (LOS) standard, which is defined as follows:

A LOS standard is a measurement standard that describes the capacity and performance characteristic of each facility included in the APFO. The adopted LOS standard governs the rate and amount of development approvals, the quality of infrastructure, and the magnitude of capital investments for new facilities to correct existing deficiencies and to accommodate new growth. [M. White, *Adequate Public Facilities Ordinances and Transportation Management,* 17 American Planning Association, Planning Advisory Serv. Rep. No. 465 (1996).]

A typical LOS standard for fire and emergency medical service, for example, might state: "Respond to calls within seven minutes in 85% of cases." Compare this with the distance standard in the Ramapo plan. LOS standards for traffic are based on standard service levels for highway congestion. For example, LOS A represents free flow, while LOS F represents forced or breakdown flow. Without the automatic guarantee of development approval if enough points are acquired, as in the Ramapo plan, an APF ordinance requires considerable discretion in its interpretation and may create problems in implementation, both for the municipality and for developers.

Consider the following typical program for implementing an APF ordinance in a fast-growing suburban county: The county first adopts multiple standards, one for rural areas, one for urban areas, and one for its central business district. Traffic data less then six months old is not acceptable. The county then adopts a fairly extensive study area for analysis for each development proposal. This decision substantially expands the number of critical intersections and roadway links to be considered, increases the competition among development proposals for available roadway capacity, makes it more difficult to find available capacity for each additional development, and adds to the time and cost of doing traffic studies. Changing attitudes in the level of services the public expects also affect the way in which service levels are defined.

The APF program described here is similar to programs adopted in several Maryland counties. See Baumgaertner, Guckert & Andrus, *Leveraging Growth with APFOs*, in Performance Standards for Growth Management, ch. 5 in D. Porter, ed., American Planning Association, Planning Advisory Serv. Rep. No. 461 (1996). Md. Code Ann. Art. 66B, § 10.1(a)(1) authorizes adequate public facilities ordinances. The authors point out there are a number of data issues that must be answered in determining adequacy and that require a substantial amount of discretion in decision making. These are:

> What facilities should be studied (signalized intersections, unsignalized intersections, roadway links, etc.)? Which trip generation rates should be used . . .? What existing data are acceptable and what are not? What background traffic is required? What growth rates for future traffic are acceptable? How should the study area be selected? What are valid trip generation assumptions? Can project phasing be considered, and will that require multiple traffic impact studies? [*Leveraging Growth, supra,* at 26.]

The availability of so much discretion in administering the program gives the local government considerable freedom in determining how it should be run. The study notes the following effects of APO ordinances:

> (1) growth was pushed farther into the future; (2) development densities were reduced due to newly predicted reductions in roadway capacities; or (3) individual developments were postponed indefinitely because the sites could no longer pass the APFO evaluation. [*Leveraging Growth,* at 24–25.]

The result was growth management by proxy, brought on by complexity, which leads to delay, which forces negotiation, which promotes compromise, which yields concessions. *Id.* at 28–29.

NOTES AND QUESTIONS

1. *Lessons learned.* This description of APF programs shows they can become de facto growth management programs with unintended consequences that may be undesirable. Note, for example, that facility problems can lead to density reductions to meet APF requirements. Low densities contribute to sprawl.

Problems appear to arise in APF programs because local governments abdicate control over the location and timing of development to the private sector, and public planning for and the provision of public facilities becomes reactive. Douglas Porter argues that local governments should not simply sit back "and watch developers scramble to provide facilities," but must take reasonable steps to assure that public facilities necessary to serve new development are available as needed. Managing Growth, *supra,* at 131–33.

Carlsbad, California, which is in the San Diego area, is an example of a city with a successful and fair APF program. The city adopted a capital facilities plan that projects the ultimate buildout of development and an APF ordinance that contains both quantitative and qualitative standards for defining adequacy for 11 public facilities. It also adopted threshold standards of development at which facilities would require improvement to meet adequacy standards, and defined a total of 25 zones in the city in which local facilities plans were to be prepared before additional development would be allowed. A management program to secure financing for improvements relies on sources such as impact fees and debt funding. Direct developer financing is also used in many cases. Each proposal for development within local zones is subject to a fine-grained analysis of facilities needs and funding requirement at the time of approval to determine whether the adequacy requirement has been met. One commentator terms Carlsbad's program "a rational procedure for determining facility needs," and notes its efforts "are aided by jurisdictional boundaries that provide discrete limits to future development and by a level of fiscal health that permits adequate funding of planning efforts." D. Porter et al., Profiles in Growth Management 98–106 (1993).

2. *How should "adequacy" be defined?* In *Maryland-National Capital Park & Planning Comm'n v. Rosenberg,* 307 A.2d 704 (Md. 1973), the Commission refused to approve plaintiff's subdivision because it claimed its residential development would overload the neighborhood school. The court reversed on the basis of testimony that adjacent schools had excess capacity, and that a revision of adjacent service area boundaries would remedy the overcapacity problem at the neighborhood school. There was testimony that school service areas were changed frequently. The ordinance provided that "adequate" schools had to be available within a "reasonable" distance. What does this case indicate about the administration of AFP programs? Was the Commission's decision manipulative?

3. *Are APF ordinances constitutional?* In *Schneider v. Montgomery County,* 614 A.2d 84 (Md. 1991), the court upheld a denial of a subdivision plat because transportation facilities were inadequate. The denial was based on a level of service policy that allowed development in areas where traffic congestion was higher but where the greater availability of transit services provided an alternate transportation mode. Can you see why the developer objected to this policy, and the basis for upholding it? The court rejected takings challenge because there were alternate viable uses for the property, and the APF ordinance left open the possibility of development in the future. See also *Albany Area Builders Ass'n v. Town of Clifton Park,* 576 N.Y.S.2d 932 (App. Div, 1991) (upholding an ordinance that limited the number of building permits that could be approved in a development area to 20 percent of the total units approved for any one project to remedy congested traffic conditions).

b. Concurrency

The Florida program.—Concurrency requirements in state land planning programs are similar to APF ordinances, with the difference that they are part of a state-mandated local planning process. Florida has had this requirement for the longest time. A critical element of the Florida system is a requirement that necessary public facilities be available when development is approved. The state Department of Community Affairs had adopted concurrency rules based on various goals in the state plan and a legislative statement of intent "that public facilities and services needed to support development shall be available concurrent with the impacts of such development." Fla. Stat. Ann. § 163.3177(10)(h). The 1993 legislature effectively ratified the departmental rule.

The Florida land use system, as noted in Chapter 1, requires local governments to adopt comprehensive plans. The plan must contain a "capital improvements element" that includes "[s]tandards to ensure the availability of public facilities and the adequacy of those facilities including acceptable levels of service." § 163.3177(3)(a)(3). Public facilities and services must meet or exceed the standards established in the capital improvements element, and must be available for development when needed. In addition, "a local government shall not issue a development order or permit which results in a reduction in the level of services for the affected public facilities below the level of services provided in the comprehensive plan of the local government." § 163.3202(2)(g).

The statute also contains a separate concurrency requirement. Seven public facilities are subject to concurrency, including highways, water, sanitary sewer, solid waste and drainage facilities. § 163.3180(1)(a). The statute contains requirements for determining when the concurrency requirement is met. For example, "[c]onsistent with the public welfare, and except as otherwise provided in this section, transportation facilities needed to serve new development shall be in place or under actual construction no more than 3 years after issuance by the local government of a certificate of occupancy or its functional equivalent." § 163.3180(2)(c).

The concurrency requirement for transportation facilities presented serious problems because the vast majority of local governments have a transportation facility deficit. To partly remedy this problem, and to direct development to urbanized areas, the statute allows an exemption for development consistent with the comprehensive plan, and that either promotes public transportation or is in an infill and urban redevelopment area. § 163.3180(5)(b).

The 1993 amendments also provided a method to help resolve this problem by ratifying a departmental rule that authorized the establishment of Transportation Concurrency Management Areas. The idea behind the rule was to provide for areas in which the level of service for transportation facilities, such as highways, could be averaged throughout the area to determine compliance with the concurrency requirement. Averaging helps to obtain compliance because average service levels may be adequate throughout a management area even though they might be inadequate in specific locations where development is contemplated.

The statute codifies the rule by authorizing areawide level-of-service averaging in "a compact geographic area with an existing network of roads where multiple, viable alternative travel paths or modes are available for common trips." § 163.3180(7). In addition, "[e]ach local government may adopt as a part of its plan a long-term transportation concurrency management system with a planning period of up to 10 years for specially designated districts where significant backlogs exist." The state Department may extend this period to 15 years for "good and sufficient cause." § 163.3180(9). Finally, a local government may allow development to proceed even though transportation levels of service are inadequate if the development is consistent with an approved comprehensive plan, a fair share of the cost of transportation facilities is assessed against the landowner, and he has made a binding commitment to pay them. § 163.3180(11).

How the program has worked.—An advantage of the Florida concurrency requirement is that it is part of a state land use program in which the state can review and recommend modifications in local plans and so coordinate local planning efforts. However, the emphasis on adequacy of facilities without attention to urban form had undesirable effects on growth and development patterns similar to those that occurred in areas without state planning programs. Developers created urban sprawl by getting approval of projects in outlying areas where, because of sparse development, service levels were adequate to meet concurrency requirements.

The state agency attempted to deal with this problem with an urban sprawl policy codified in 1994 in a departmental rule. Fla. Admin. Code § 9J-5.006(5). The rule specifies "indicators" of urban sprawl in local comprehensive plans, such as allowance of low density development, rural development at a substantial distance from urban areas, and a "failure to make a clear separation between urban and rural areas." These indicators, in combination with an evaluation of local land uses, conditions and development controls, form the basis for determining whether a local plan must be disapproved because it "does not discourage the proliferation of urban sprawl." For discussion of concurrency see Pelham, *Adequate Public Facilities Requirements: Reflections on Florida's Concurrency System for Managing Growth,* 19 Fla. St. U. L. Rev. 973, 976 (1992); Powell, *Back to Basics on School Concurrency,* 26 Fla. St. Univ. L. Rev. 451 (1999).

The Washington Program.—Washington's state land use program also contains a concurrency requirement limited to transportation facilities, but complements it with an urban growth boundary requirement that helps control urban form. Urban growth boundaries are discussed in the next section.

The comprehensive plan must contain service levels for transportation facilities. Wash. Rev. Code § 36.70A.070(6)(a). The concurrency requirement is as follows:

> After adoption of the comprehensive plan . . . local jurisdictions must adopt and enforce ordinances which prohibit development approval if the development causes the level of service on a locally owned transportation facility to decline below the standards adopted in the transportation element of the comprehensive plan, unless transportation improvements or strategies to accommodate the impacts of development are made concurrent with the development. These strategies may include increased public transportation service, ride sharing programs, demand management, and other transportation systems

> management strategies. For the purposes of this subsection (6) "concurrent with the development" shall mean that improvements or strategies are in place at the time of development, or that a financial commitment is in place to complete the improvements or strategies within six years. [*Id.* § 36.70A.070(6)(b).]

The statute encourages concurrency on other public services and facilities, but does not indicate how to achieve this goal. *Id.* § 36.70A.020(12).

Professor Settle has noted several problems unresolved by the statute:

> The transportation concurrency requirement leaves central issues unresolved. Are there state-mandated limits on LOS standards a local government may adopt? May a city choose congestion as a strategy to induce motorists to use public transportation? What constitutes an adequate financial commitment? And "within six years" of what? Regulatory approval? Completion of construction? [Settle, *Washington's Growth Management Revolution Goes to Court*, 23 Seattle U. L. Rev. 5, 18 (1999).]

How would you handle these problems? How do the requirements in the Washington statute differ from those in the Florida statute? From the programs that are typical in local APF ordinances? Which do you prefer? For additional discussion see Walsh & Pearce, *The Concurrency Requirement of the Washington State Growth Management Act,* 16 Puget Sound L. Rev. 1025 (1993).

PROBLEM

Review the River County Problem at the beginning of this chapter.

Would you recommend that the county adopt any of the growth management programs discussed in this section? Would the Ramapo plan be useful? The Petaluma plan? An adequate public facilities ordinance? How would a state concurrency requirement work in this setting? Remember that the fixed point system and certainty of the Ramapo plan helped sustain it in court. Programs that do not have those features, and that require the exercise of discretion in their administration, may not be as well-received.

4.   URBAN GROWTH BOUNDARIES

The growth control programs discussed so far make the approval of new development dependent on the availablity of facilities and services or other criteria, such as the provision of affordable housing. An urban growth boundary (UGB) is a growth management strategy that is not tied to the provision of facilities and services.

A UGB is a boundary that is placed around an urbanized area that marks the limits of urban growth. Development can occur within, but is not allowed outside, a boundary. The UGB is a growth control strategy that can stop sprawl if the UGB is drawn and administered so that all new growth occurs inside the boundary, and growth outside the boundary is effectively stopped. UGBs can be adopted for counties or metropolitan areas.

A surprising 68% of the local governments who responded to the growth management survey, and who were not surrounded on all sides by other municipalities, had UGBs in place. UGB programs are also included in some of the state growth management programs. The best-known statewide UGB requirement is part of the Oregon state land use program. Washington, Tennessee and Maine also have UGB requirements in their state land use programs. Urban growth boundaries in Oregon are adopted for municipalities. They are a county responsibility in Washington and Tennessee. A variant of the UGB is the designation of an urban service area, and the limitation of public service availability to land inside that area.

Urban growth boundary programs present a number of problems. Decisions must be made on how much land to include within the growth area boundary, the shape the urban boundary should take and how to expand the boundary as growth occurs. Regulating growth just outside the boundary line to prevent future development until the boundary is extended is another problem. Development permission denials outside the growth boundary clearly raise takings problems.

The materials that follow discuss the urban growth boundary program in Oregon, which has been in effect since the early 1970s and is well-documented:

MANDELKER, MANAGING SPACE TO MANAGE GROWTH, 23 William and Mary Environmental Law and Policy Review 801, 811–17 (1999)

Oregon's state land use and urban growth boundary (UGB) programs are well-known growth management systems. A set of state planning goals adopted by the state Land Conservation and Development Commission (LCDC) are its critical elements. LCDC reviews local plans and land use regulations and approves them if they comply with the state goals. Local land use regulations and decisions must be consistent with the approved plan. A special tribunal, the Land Use Board of Appeals (LUBA), hears appeals on land use decisions after appellants exhaust all local appeals.

The principal state planning goal that mandates growth management is an urbanization goal that requires incorporated municipalities to adopt urban growth boundaries. Local governments must draw a clear line between areas that can urbanize and areas that must remain nonurban. Local governments must apply seven factors contained in the urbanization goal [which is goal 14] to decide on the size of the urban growth boundary. Incorporated municipalities apply these factors to designate enough growth within their UGB to provide an adequate land supply for twenty years. A UGB can, and usually does, extend beyond municipal boundaries. The Portland regional planning agency [the Metropolitan Council] administers this program in the Portland metropolitan area and is responsible for making decisions about the boundary. The state housing goal, supplemented by legislation, requires local governments to provide needed affordable housing within UGB boundaries.

[The seven factors are: (1) the demonstrated need to accommodate long-range urban population growth requirements consistent with LCDC goals; (2) the need for housing, employment opportunities, and livability; (3) the orderly and economic provision for public facilities and services; (4) the maximum efficiency of land uses within and on the fringe of the existing urban area; (5) the environmental, energy, economic, and social consequences; (6) the retention of agricultural land as defined, with Class I the highest priority for retention and Class VI the lowest priority; and (7) the compatibility of the proposed urban uses with nearby agricultural activities. Department of Land Conservation & Dev., Oregon's Statewide Planning Goals and Guidelines (1995). The first two factors are called the "need" factors.]

A key purpose of the state program is the preservation of the Willamette Valley in western Oregon, which has most of the state's valuable agricultural land and most of its population. [A state agricultural goal requires the preservation of agricultural land, and is reinforced by exclusive farm use zones and a required 80-acre lot size in these zones.] . . . Growth can occur outside UGBs in agricultural areas known as "exception lands." These are lands either committed to urbanization or needed for other uses. [Or. Rev. Stat. § 197.732(1)(a)(c).]

Observers agree that the preservation of agricultural and other natural resource areas were the primary motivation behind the urbanization goal and the UGB policy. These priorities mean that the UGB . . . is not primarily a measure to shape urban growth. The state planning goals also do not include a strategy for allocating development within a UGB.

An important measure of the program's success is the extent to which growth has occurred inside, rather than outside, UGBs. . . . Portland provides public facilities and subsidies inside the urban growth boundary to encourage development, although highway congestion is a problem. Studies of the UGBs, some limited to Portland, do find that a substantial portion of new development has occurred within UGBs. A study of development inside the UGBs also showed a substantial amount of development occurring in or next to the urban core, as intended. [Weitz & Moore, *Development Inside Urban Growth Boundaries: Oregon's Empirical Evidence of Contiguous Urban Form*, 64 J. Am. Plan. Ass'n 424, 429 tbl. 4 (1998).] Density increases inside the Portland UGB are impressive, but densities are lower than the program intended. Lower densities have occurred though zoning that discourages housing or makes it more costly is prohibited by statute, [§ 197.307(6)] and though LCDC requires six to ten units per acre for the Portland area on undeveloped, residentially designated lands. [Or. Admin. R. 660-07-035.]

One of the reasons why higher-density development has not occurred inside the UGBs is that opposition to this type of development has become increasingly common. Developers became disillusioned when they could not build at the expected densities promised by the program at its adoption.

Development has continued to occur at low densities in so-called exception areas outside UGBs, often as spurious farms. [Or. Rev. Stat. § 197.732.] These are areas already developed for rural residential homesites or for commercial or industrial uses, or are areas "committed" to development because of parcelization or installation of services or because surrounding development makes farming and forestry impracticable. This development is substantial and undercuts the urban growth boundary program, though it has slowed in recent years. The conversion of land contiguous to UGBs to low density development is especially troublesome because it makes the extension of UGBs difficult. If low density development occurs on land next to the UGB, it will not be available for high-density development when the boundary expands. The UGB must then expand further than it should have been, and higher-density development must leapfrog over the low-density development that is in the expansion area. This is the very type of urban sprawl the urban growth boundary program tries to prevent.

Oregon legislation [§ 195.145] now allows local governments to designate "urban reserve areas" that are next to UGBs. These areas provide for the long-term urban expansion and cost-effective provision of public facilities and services when UGB expands. Local governments are to give priority to urban reserve areas when expanding urban growth boundaries. [§ 197.298]. . . .

A significant problem in the Oregon UGB program is deciding where development should occur and at what densities. Development at low densities inside the UGBs accelerates demands for boundary expansion, which can damage the goal of preserving agricultural and forest lands. Higher densities within the UGB reduce demand for boundary expansion but create opposition from existing neighborhoods. Housing at higher densities inside the UGB can be expensive and push lower-income housing outward. Balancing these competing claims requires a carefully orchestrated strategy, which is more difficult to secure. The statutes now authorize density increases within a UGB to meet housing needs as an alternative to a boundary expansion. [§ 197.296(4)(b).]

To help resolve these conflicting pressures, the Portland regional planning agency has adopted an urban growth management plan as part of its Metro 2040 Growth Concept, although opposition has slowed implementation. The plan requires local governments to increase housing densities and meet housing capacity standards set by the plan. The Growth Concept, and the statute giving priority to urban reserve areas in boundary expansions, are the basis for agency regulations for the review of growth boundary expansions. These regulations supplement the state planning goals.

The regulations create a category of "first tier urban reserves" that have a priority in boundary expansions because they are areas where urban services are most effectively provided. A proposed boundary expansion amendment also requires an urban reserve plan that provides for an average minimum residential density of ten dwelling units to the acre and a diversity of housing stock. Plans must ensure the orderly, economic and efficient provision of urban services through annexation to a city, a city and county agreement on planning and zoning, or an urban services agreement. These regulations reinforce the UGB program by giving priority in boundary expansions to adjacent lands and by requiring reasonable densities with assurances that adequate services are available.

NOTES AND QUESTIONS

1. *Evaluating Portland.* As this discussion of the Portland UGB indicates, managing urban growth boundaries requires delicate balancing. Population growth puts pressure on local growth boundaries. One option is to expand the

boundary, but this may create new sprawl. Higher densities within the boundary can avoid expansion, but may lead to opposition from residents who oppose high density development in their neighborhoods. This has happened in Portland. Many jurisdictions follow the Oregon model by including a "market factor" in their boundary designations to provide up to 25 percent of vacant buildable land for future growth. See Dearborn & Gygi, *Planner's Panacea or Pandora's Box: A Realistic Assessment of the Role of Urban Growth Areas in Achieving Growth Management Goals,* 16 U. Puget Sound L. Rev. 975 (1993). But this helps only so long as land within the boundary is not fully developed. See also Lassar & Porter, *Urban Rural Boundaries: The Limits of Limits,* Urban Land, vol. 49, no.12, at 32 (1990).

One review notes the success of the UGB, and praises Portland as "a place where the downtown has a thousand retail stores, the outlying neighborhoods are healthy and growing, and the sprawl ends at a greenbelt 20 minutes from the city line." Ehrenhalt, *The Great Wall of Portland,* Governing, May 1997, at 20. But he notes the criticism that housing prices have been rising rapidly, though he admits they have been rising more in cities that do not have a UGB.

Higher density is the key. The Director of Legislative Affairs for the Oregon Building Industry Association notes that the average lot size in the Portland metropolitan area is 6,500 square feet, creating a density just under five units to the acre. Chandler, *The State of Planning in Oregon,* 12 Land Development 15, 18 (2000). Yet the regional planning agency assumed, in its decision to expand the UGB, that average density in the expansion areas would be ten units to the acre. It also assumed that 30 per cent of growth over the next 20 years would occur in existing neighborhoods through infill and redevelopment. *Id.* The question is whether residents will accept this.

What planning and regulatory techniques can help provide for higher densities? Note that upzonings to provide higher densities may lead to political lobbying and successful "spot zoning" lawsuits by objecting neighbors. This problem is hard to remedy if objection to higher density runs deep. One problem may be that the UGB concept was accepted as an overlay on existing land use controls systems with not enough thought given to providing secondary strategies that can support UGB objectives, such as high density development. One solution is more attention to planning for urbanized areas that can indicate where new development should occur. The village plans developed for the Seattle, Washington area are an example. See D. Porter, Profiles in Growth Management 230–55 (1996).

Providing adequate public facilities for higher density development in urbanized areas is another problem. Is there a role for adequate public facilities ordinances here? Impact fees?

2. *The push for farmland preservation.* Preserving agricultural land was a major incentive for adopting UGBs, but Chandler notes: "[T]o preserve farmland, development is pushed into the hills, where it is more expensive to develop infrastructure; therefore development occurs at lower density, resulting in a larger amount of land consumed. This pattern makes it more difficult to deliver affordable housing and makes it more likely that traffic problems will be exacerbated." *Id.* at 19. Portland is surrounded by hills, which creates this problem. How might similar problems arise in an area that does not have this geography?

On the hills development issue see *Collins v. Land Conservation & Dev. Comm'n,* 707 P.2d 599 (Or. App. 1985) (cannot include hillsides that are not urbanizable in a UGB because city wants aesthetic backdrop and wants to create area where no urbanization can occur). Does this case put municipalities in a catch-22 in view of Mr. Chandler's comments? For more on agricultural preservation, see Section E, *infra,*

3. *The Portland UGB expansion.* In 1999 Portland's Metropolitan Service District (Metro) approved a major expansion of the UGB, only to have it invalidated by the Land Use Borad of Appeal (LUBA) because Metro did not properly apply its urban reserve rule. The court of appeals affirmed LUBA. *D S. Parklane Dev., Inc. v. Metro,* 994 P.2d 1205 (Or. App. 2000). The rule requiring priority in urban expansions to first tier reserves has now been revoked, apparently because it created an expectancy that these areas would be included within a UGB boundry expansion. See also *Hummel v. Land Conservation & Dev. Comm'n,* 954 P.2d 824 (Ore. App. 1998) (holding expansion of UGB was proper on the facts, and that development had to go into hillside areas); *Baker v. Marion County,* 852 P.2d 254 (Or. App. 1993) (affirming denial of UGB expansion when no need shown).

4. *UGBs and takings.* A UGB can create takings problems because of its total restriction on development outside the boundary. Traditional zoning regulations, such as large lot zoning and agricultural zoning, which is discussed later in this chapter, are one way to prevent development from occurring outside the boundary. Will there be a taking if the restriction is permanent? What if the delay is temporary, which can occur, for example, with respect to land located in an urban reserve area in Portland? Is the temporary delay in development a taking? Reconsider the cases on moratoria discussed earlier in this chapter. Do they apply? What about the argument that a takings challenge on land a substantial distance from a boundary is not likely because a landowner may believe that "the discounted development value of her land at a future date is worth more than what she might recover as compensation in a takings suit"? *Managing Space, supra,* at 821.

5. *Alternate urban forms.* An urban boundary that prohibits development outside and increases densities inside the boundary contradicts the standard American development pattern, in which densities gradually slope downward as development moves out. The Oregon UGBs provide an alternate urban form, which is usually an inner urbanized area surrounded by a circular growth boundary. There are other alternatives. One consists of an urbanized core with development allowed along major corridors leading outward from the core. The corridors can contain public transit links. This is the pattern adopted for the Washington, D.C. metropolitan area in its 1965 Year 2000 Plan. A second alternative does not have corridors but complements the urbanized core with satellite nodes or centers developed at urban densities. How would the legal controls needed to create and maintain these alternate urban forms differ from the UGB program?

6. For discussion of UGBs and the Oregon program see V. Easley, *Staying Inside the Lines: Urban Growth Boundaries,* American Planning Association,

Planning Advisory Serv. Rep. No. 444 (1992); G. Knaap & A Nelson, The Regulated Landscape: Lessons on State Land Use Planning from Oregon (1992); A. Nelson & J. Duncan, Growth Management Principles and Practices, ch. 6 (1995); D. Porter, Managing Growth in America's Communities 61–74 (1997); Farquhar, *Zoning Fallout: The Implications of Urban Growth Area Designations,* Am. Plan. Ass'n Zoning News, Mar. 1999; Lang & Hornburg, *Planning Portland Style: Pitfalls and Possibilities,* 8 Hous. Pol'y Debate 1 (1997); Liberty, *Oregon's Comprehensive Growth Management Program: An Implementation Review and Lessons for Other States,* 22 Envtl. L. Rep. 10367 (1992). See also Sullivan, *Reviewing the Reviewer: The Impact of the Land Use Board of Appeals on the Oregon Land Use Program 1979–1999* (forthcoming); Sullivan, *Marking the Twenty-Fifth Anniversary of SB 100,* 77 Or. L. Rev. 813 (1998).

A NOTE ON TIERS AND URBAN SERVICE AREAS

Tiers.—Tier systems are an alternate strategy that links the approval of new development to the availability of public facilities through a staging process. Robert Freilich describes this concept:

> A more sophisticated application of the UGB approach is the use of a "tier system," which has been applied in San Diego, California, and Minneapolis, Minnesota. A principal tenet of the "tier" system involves the geographic and functional division of the planning area into subareas ("tiers"). . . .Tiers within the growth category are commonly designated "Urbanized" and "Planned Urbanizing." The tiers within the limited growth category would be "Rural/Future Urbanizing," "Agricultural," and "Conservation/Open Space." Each of the tiers has specific geographical boundaries and is capable of being mapped. The Urbanized tier consists of those areas which are at or near build out and served by public facilities. The Planned Urbanizing area represents the "new" growth area. The Rural/Future Urbanizing area may be a permanent rural density development area or may be a temporary "holding" zone until the growth areas are built out. The Rural/Future Urbanizing tier generally contains lands that are presently unsewered and which have a lower population density. The Agriculture tier is intended to identify those lands which should be preserved either temporarily or permanently for agricultural production. The Conservation/Open Space tier consists of lands containing natural resources or environmentally sensitive areas. [Freilich, *The Land-Use Implications of Transit-Oriented Development: Controlling the Demand Side of Transportation Congestion and Urban Sprawl,* 30 Urb. Law. 547, 559–560 (1998).]

One difference between tier systems and UGBs is that the tiers do not contain an explicit boundary between areas where growth can and cannot occur. They are an extension of the Ramapo plan, and may contemplate the eventual build-out of the tiered areas unless conservation and agricultural areas are permanently preserved. For discussion of the San Diego tiers, which Professor Freilich authored, see *Managing Space, supra,* at 805–11. Political pressures in that city led to accelerated conversion of the planned urbanizing tier. For additional discussion of tiered systems see R. Freilich, From Sprawl to Smart Growth (1999).

Urban service areas (USAs).—The USA is an area beyond which a local government will not provide basic services or invest in significant road improvements. Its primary purpose is to ensure an efficient, orderly and cost-effective delivery of services and infrastructure. Staging is achieved by timing extensions of the USA with the availablity of urban public facilities. The rural area beyond the urban service limit line may be allowed to develop at densities and with uses that do not require urban services and that will not overload road capacity.

Lexington-Fayette County, Kentucky has the oldest USA in the country. It has been successful in keeping growth within the urban service area limits and in protecting rural areas outside these limits. Complementary plans direct growth within the service area limits and protect the rural area through level of service standards. See From Sprawl to Smart Growth, *supra,* at 125–30.

The case that follows considers the tensions that can arise in a UGB program between the need to contain growth boundaries, and the need to provide additional land for economic growth and development:

BENJFRAN DEVELOPMENT, INC. v. METROPOLITAN SERVICE DISTRICT

95 Ore. App. 22, 767 P.2d 467 (1989)

RICHARDSON, PRESIDING JUDGE:

Petitioner seeks review of LUBA's affirmance of the Metropolitan Service District (Metro) denial of an amendment to its acknowledged metropolitan urban growth boundary (UGB). The amendment would have added an area of approximately 500 acres, which petitioner wished to use as the site of an "advance performance standards regional industrial park." That project, according to petitioner, would attract industry and jobs to the region, is akin to an industrial marketing technique which is coming into use in comparable metropolitan areas and cannot be located on any existing sites within the UGB. Metro concluded that petitioner had failed to establish a "need" to amend the UGB. LUBA agreed. We do, too, and affirm.

Goal 14 states seven factors on which the establishment and change of UGBs must be based. The first two, which are commonly described as the "need factors," require that, for land to be added to a UGB, there must be:

"(1) Demonstrated need to accommodate long-range urban population growth requirements consistent with LCDC goals;

"(2) Need for housing, employment opportunities and livability."

Petitioner's first assignment is that Metro and LUBA misapplied factor (2). Petitioner's premise is that Metro based its decision on what petitioner describes as a "sufficient growth" test, under which need for a UGB amendment cannot be demonstrated if the economic growth which is taking place within the UGB is consistent with or adequate for the year 2000 population projections which were made when the UGB was established. Petitioner contends:

> "[A]ccording to Metro and LUBA, the application for the UGB amendment was properly denied on the grounds that [petitioner] failed to show that insufficient growth was occurring to meet the projections of needs relied upon in the establishment of the UGB. The decision can only be interpreted as requiring an applicant to answer the fundamental questions of whether economic development opportunities are needed, whether the people of a region need employment opportunities, and whether growth beyond projections should occur. LUBA's ruling permits the local government to then hide behind the constraints imposed by projections which were intended simply to provide a basis, a starting point, for establishing a UGB, and to say that all a region 'needs' is to meet projections.". . .

> "[A]t least where the proposed use is a legitimate economic developmental activity, projections are irrelevant to the determination of need in the consideration of a proposal for a UGB amendment. The need for economic development statewide has been determined as a matter of policy by the state legislature by the enactment of the Economic Development Law, ORS 197.707 et seq. Under this statute (and Statewide Goal 9, which the statute was enacted to bolster), a local government does not have the discretion to find that the region it serves does not need economic development."

Goal 9 states that its purpose is "[t]o diversify and improve the economy of the state." It also defines these terms:

DIVERSIFY — refers to increasing the variety, type, scale and location of business, industrial and commercial activities.

IMPROVE THE ECONOMY OF THE STATE — refers to a beneficial change in those business, industrial and commercial activities which generate employment, products and services consistent with the availability of long term human and natural resources.

[Section 197.07 states that "[i]t was the intent of the Legislative Assembly in enacting . . . [the planning laws] not to prohibit, deter, delay or increase the cost of appropriate development, but to enhance economic development and opportunity for the benefit of all citizens." The other relevant provision in the Economic Development Law is § 197.712, which is discussed later in the opinion.]

Although petitioner does not so state, the core of its argument is that ORS 197.707 *et seq.* and Goal 9 require local governments to treat economic development as a *per se* need to expand their UGBs and that developmental objectives either supersede the first two factors of Goal 14 or are incorporated into the second as the prevailing consideration. LUBA responded:

> "Metro is not required to amend its UGB to provide appropriate land to accommodate every new industrial land marketing technique

enjoying success in other major urban real estate markets. As Metro noted, such an extreme view of its obligation under Goal 14 is not warranted even if the amendment would attract industrial firms that may otherwise go elsewhere. Indeed, petitioner's view would require Metro to amend the UGB without consideration of whether loss of such firms threatens the industrial and employment growth Metro assumed would occur when it drew the UGB. . . .

"Second, we fail to understand how Metro's decision is not consistent with Goal 9. That is, we find nothing to suggest that Metro has ignored or violated Goal 9 by declining to accept petitioner's view of the desirability of enlarging its UGB to accommodate an APS Regional Industrial Park."

We agree. Whatever the full relationship may be between the statutory and regulatory economic development provisions and the Goal 14 need factors, the former do not completely preempt the latter, as petitioner seems to postulate. Under petitioner's theory, local governments would be required to find a need to urbanize land to accommodate *every* developmental proposal, regardless of the adequacy of currently urbanized or urbanizable land to serve the economic development requirements of the locality. Petitioner suggests no reason why *its* proposal answers a need or why the current economic circumstances within Metro's UGB leave a need to be answered. Stated differently, petitioner's argument can succeed only if Goal 9, ORS 197.707 *et seq.* or the implementing provisions which localities must adopt pursuant to the statutes mandate the approval of every land use proposal with potential beneficial economic effects. We hold that the argument does not succeed.

Although what we have said suffices to answer petitioner's first assignment, there are other difficulties with its argument which call for some discussion. . . . Petitioner assumes that the local economic development regulations that the statutes require must necessarily provide for particular UGB amendments which particular proponents seek at particular times. That assumption may well be incorrect. ORS 197.712(2)(g) provides:

"Local governments shall provide:

"(A) Reasonable opportunities to satisfy local and rural needs for residential and industrial development and other economic activities *on appropriate lands outside urban growth boundaries,* in a manner consistent with conservation of the state's agricultural and forest land base; and

"(B) Reasonable opportunities for urban residential, commercial and industrial needs *over time* through changes to urban growth boundaries." (Emphasis supplied.)

Petitioner's argument also treats factor (2) as existing in a vacuum and as providing a basis for a finding of need, without reference to the first Goal 14 factor. As LUBA correctly noted, in response to [a related] argument [made by] another party to this case:

"We add, *1000 Friends of Oregon*'s view of population projections and its narrow application of Goal 14, Factor 1 ignore the final

enjoinder in Factor 1 that the UGB include land needed to accommodate the population 'consistent with LCDC goals.' The goals expressly include goals for housing (Goal 10), and economic development and employment opportunities (Goal 9). Further, most goals
address liveability, whether directly or indirectly. In our view, rigid
separation of Factors 1 and 2 into independent mandatory criteri[a]
ignores the obvious overlaps between the two factors."

Similarly, petitioner's emphasis on the "employment opportunities" and
"liveability" criteria of factor (2) lead it to disregard the standards of other
goals which are incorporated into factor (1), e.g., the resource land preservation and orderly urbanization requirements of [other state planning goals.]. . .

Affirmed.

NOTES AND QUESTIONS

1. *Containment v. growth.* This case arose at a time when Oregon was in
recession. Do you see what the disagreement was between the petitioner and
LUBA? How did the court handle it? Section 197.712(2) (a), which is discussed
in the opinion, provides that "[c]omprehensive plans shall include an analysis
of the community's economic patterns, potentialities, strengths and deficiencies as they relate to state and national trends." Is this provision relevant to
the problem presented in the principal case? The court of appeals has affirmed
Benjfram's holding that the economic objectives of Goal 9 do not prevail over
other goals. *Port of St. Helens v. Land Conserv. & Dev. Comm'n,* 996 P.2d 1014
(Or. App. 2000).

1000 Friends of Oregon, which is mentioned in the principal case, is a major,
statewide citizens' organization dedicated to supporting the state land use
program. It frequently intervenes in court cases. There are now similar
organizations in other states.

2. *Oregon's affordable housing policies.* Studies have found a significant
deterioration in housing affordablity in Portland in recent years, although it
is not clear that the UGB is entirely responsible. See, e.g., Portland State
Univ. Center for Urban Studies, Impact of the Urban Growth Boundary on
Metropolitan Housing Markets (1996). Affordable housing policies in the state
land use program are intended to offset any impact the UGBs may have on
housing prices. They include LCDC's adoption of the New Jersey fair share
rule. *Seaman v. City of Durham,* 1 L.C.D.C. 283 (1978). Later LCDC issued
its so-called "St. Helen's" policy, which requires communities to provide sufficient buildable land to meet housing need. LCDC also struck down building
moratoria. In *1000 Friends of Oregon v. City of Lake Oswego,* 2 L.C.D.C. 138
(1981), LCDC found that building densities were too low to meet regional
housing needs. These actions implemented the Housing Goal, No. 10, which
provides:

> [P]lans shall encourage the availability of adequate numbers of
> housing units at price ranges and rent levels which are commensu-
> rate with the financial capabilities of Oregon households and allow
> for flexibility of housing location, type and density.

Minimum densities are also mandated in the Portland metropolitan area. See *Managing Growth, supra.*

The legislature codified the St. Helen's policy in 1981. Or. Rev. Stat. §§ 197.295-197.314. One important provision mandates that approval standards, special conditions and approval procedures for needed housing must be "clear and objective and shall not have the effect, either in themselves or cumulatively, of discouraging needed housing through unreasonable cost or delay." § 197.307(6). "Needed" housing includes multi-family and manufactured housing. The purpose of this provision is to prohibit the adoption of standards that can be used to deny approval to this kind of housing. See *Rogue Valley Ass'n of Realtors v. City of Ashland,* 970 P.2d 685 (Or. App. 1999).

The exclusion of any type of housing from residential zones is prohibited and equal treatment for subsidized housing is required. § 197.312. Moratoria are strictly limited, as noted in Section A. §§ 197.505-197.540. LCDC has also indicated that communities must have a formal rezoning process in which land can be rezoned to higher densities to meet the housing goal. City of Milwaukie Comprehensive Plan and Implementing Measures, Acknowledgment Order, Jan. 21, 1981.

3. *A statutory model for UGBs.* The American Planning Association's model legislation for UGBs notes that when UGBs are adopted by individual jurisdictions the effect may be to shift development to other communities or to the next tier of developable land, which causes sprawl. To prevent these problems, the model legislation requires adoption of UGBs by a regional agency, the provision of additional land to accommodate growth, the establishment and maintenance of a land monitoring system, and periodic five-year reviews of the boundary to ensure an adequate supply of buildable land. American Planning Association, Legislative Guidebook Phases I & II, Interim Edition, at 6-53 to 6-59 (1998). Is this a good statutory model?

4. *Affordable housing in other growth management programs.* Thirty-six percent of the local government respondents to the growth management survey reported they had at least one program to stimulate private sector affordable housing production. *Growth Controls and Affordable Housing, supra,* at 4. Programs included the use of city funds or staff to support nonprofit housing development agencies, assistance to local public housing authorities to build or rehabilitate housing, and inclusionary zoning. The stock of affordable housing was higher in communities with aggressive affordable housing programs.

A NOTE ON TRANSIT-ORIENTED DEVELOPMENT

What it is.—One important lesson from these materials is that higher densities in urbanized areas are an important strategy in a program intended to prevent sprawl and contain growth. Yet opposition to higher densities has occurred in areas, like Portland, where urban growth boundaries have been in effect for some time. High density development around public transit stations with appropriate design treatments is one strategy for winning over opponents. Transit-oriented development, or TOD, has especially achieved importance with the construction of new public transit systems around the country. The following definition of TOD in the transportation planning rule of the Oregon Land Conservation and Development Commission captures the idea:

> "Transit-Oriented Development (TOD)" means a mix of residential, retail and office uses and a supporting network of roads, bicycle and pedestrian ways focused on a major transit stop designed to support a high level of transit use. The key features of transit oriented development include:
>
> (a) A mixed use center at the transit stop, oriented principally to transit riders and pedestrian and bicycle travel from the surrounding area;
>
> (b) High density residential development proximate to the transit stop sufficient to support transit operation and neighborhood commercial uses within the TOD;
>
> (c) A network of roads, and bicycle and pedestrian paths to support high levels of pedestrian access within the TOD and high levels of transit use. [Oregon Admin. R. § 660-012-005(23).]

What do you think this kind of development would look like?

TOD requires a transit and pedestrian-friendly site design, which includes convenient paths and connections to transit stops and other destinations, and a continuous network of streets and pathways to minimize travel distances. The pedestrian environment should be improved through measures such as security, lighting and heightened visibility; protection from traffic; adequate space for pedestrians and bicycles; weather protection; and transit shelters. See M. Morris, ed., Creating Transit-Supportive Land-Use Regulations, ch. 1, American Planning Association, Planning Advisory Serv. Rep. No. 468 (1996). The report also discusses other aspects of TOD, such as appropriate parking design, reduction of parking spaces to discourage automobile use, mixed-use development, and density increases to support transit. See also Pollock, A Framework for Transit-Oriented Development Planning, Am. Plan. Ass'n, PAS Memo, Feb. 1996.

Robert Freilich explains what should be contained in a TOD ordinance:

> TOD regulations govern the amount of development because they tend to permit higher densities of development proximate to transit stations. TOD regulations govern the type of development by permitting a richer variety of land-uses within a given area. TOD regulations are spatial in that they attempt to minimize the distance between intensive land uses and public transit facilities, thereby encouraging persons living or working in the area to utilize transit facilities. TOD regulations are relational in that they use innovative urban design guidelines to insure not only compatibility between mixed land uses, but also that those land uses relate functionally to the transit system. [Land-Use Implications, supra, at 551.]

What land use regulations would you adopt or modify to implement these objectives?

Studies of TOD found that market support is the most important element in a successful TOD, and that the role of local government is critical but is still not well developed in many areas. Porter, *Transit-Focused Development: A Progress Report,* 64 J. Am. Plan. Ass'n 475 (1998) (study of 19 regions, including Portland). A study in San Diego found that constraints imposed by existing rights-of-way, difficulties in land assembly in developed areas, market conditions and fiscal and economic disincentives can impede TOD. Boarnet & Compin, *Transit-Oriented Development in San Diego County,* 65 J. Am. Plan. Ass'n 80 (1999). These studies suggest that active local government participation through land acquisition and joint development that is integrated with the transit facility may be necessary. Joint development programs may require land acquisition by the local government and public financing to provide necessary public improvements. For the full report see D. Porter, Transit-Focused Development (TCRP, 1999). See also *Land-Use Implications, supra,* at 561–564.

Does TOD help with sprawl?—TOD is thought to provide important local benefits by creating a transit-supportive and pedestrian-friendly environment. The regional impact of TOD on travel modes is another matter. A recent analysis holds that the impact of transportation systems on urban development will be diminished in the future because investment in new transportation facilities will be marginal to existing systems. Pickrell, Transportation and Land Use, in Essays in Transportation Economics and Policy 403, 416 (J. Gomez-Ibanez et al. eds., 1999). The growing number of multiple-worker households and shorter job durations also diminish incentives to reduce commuting costs. Niles & Nelson, Measuring the Success of Transit-Oriented Development, Paper prepared for the American Planning Association National Planning Conference, April 24–28, 1999, cite studies finding insufficient evidence that TOD on a regional scale, even with large transit investments, is likely to produce regional benefits. In the San Francisco Bay area, for example, nine percent of residents lived within a half mile of a transit station, yet only 18% of these station-area residents commuted to work by rail transit. See also Giuliano, *The Weakening Transportation-Land-Use Connection,* 6 Access 3–11 (Spring 1995).

Pickrell also finds a weak relationship between transportation systems and land use characteristics, such as residential and employment density, mixed-use development and the jobs-housing balance. *Id.* at 422–32. In addition, changes in living patterns necessary to produce significant declines in automobile travel are unlikely. Densities of over 7,500 people per square mile, which is typically 12 to 15 units per acre, would be required, but these are densities found only in central city neighborhoods of the largest urban areas. They are not likely to be achieved in suburban areas. However, Davis & Seskin, *Impacts of Urban Form on Travel Behavior,* 29 Urb. Law. 215 (1997), discuss studies finding that central business district employment density, and station area employment and residential density, have modest but significant impacts on transit use. What do these studies suggest about the desirability of TOD? Crane, *The Influence of Urban Form on Travel: An Interpretive Review,* 15 J. Plan. Lit. 3 (2000), carefully reviews studies of this problem and finds that any definite conclusions are problematic.

A NOTE ON GROWTH MANAGEMENT PROGRAMS IN OTHER STATES

In addition to Oregon, other states have UGB or similar requirements in their state land use programs. A discussion of three of the more interesting programs follows:

(1) VERMONT

How it works.—Vermont's state land use law, adopted in 1970, and known as Act 250 for its chapter number, is an early state growth management program that has attracted considerable national attention. It was a response to growing development pressures on an environmentally vulnerable state arising out of the opening of an interstate highway. Vermont is a rural state with no major urban center. Apart from nine small cities, the state is organized into 237 towns, New England local government units with authority over settled and rural areas within their jurisdiction. The statute includes a permitting requirement that is tied, to some extent, to growth management criteria.

State permitting.—Act 250 requires a state permit for all developments and subdivisions. Vt. Stat. Ann. tit. 10, § 6081(a). Development means commercial and industrial development and development for governmental purposes on ten or more acres of land, and housing projects of ten or more units. Commercial or industrial development on one or more acres is covered in towns that do not have land use regulations. *Id.* § 6001(3). State permits are also required for subdivisions of any size. Act 250 thus provides an overlay on local planning and zoning. The Act creates three District Environmental Commissions that hear applications for development approvals and decide whether to issue a permit. Appeals are to a state Environmental Board or a trial court and from there to the Supreme Court, *Id.* § 6089.

The Act originally contained ten criteria to govern permit applications that require consideration of environmental impacts, the adequacy of governmental services and consistency with local plans. *Id.* § 6086(a). The courts uphold permit denials based on substantial evidence. *In re Killington, Ltd.,* 616 A.2d 241 (Vt. 1992) (upholding permit denial). In 1973 the legislature added policies contained in a Land Use Capability and Development Plan for land use and development, the conservation and use of natural resources and linkages between government services and growth rates.

Two of these policies have growth management implications. One requires consideration of whether a proposed development would "significantly affect" a town or region's financial capacity to "reasonably accommodate" growth. *In re Wal-Mart Stores, Inc.,* 702 A.2d 397 (Vt. 1997) upheld a decision by the Environmental Board invalidating a permit for a Wal-Mart store under this policy. The court held the Board had properly concluded the store's impact on market competition was a relevant factor under this criterion. The court noted the project's impact on existing stores would negatively affect the tax base and thus the ability to pay for public services. See Recent Development, 54 Wash. U.J. Urb. & Contemp. L. 323 (1998).

The second policy requires consideration of whether the additional costs of public services and facilities caused by "scattered development" outweigh the tax revenue and other public benefits of the development, including increased employment opportunities. *In re Pyramid Mall Co.* (Vt. Dist. Envtl. Comm'n No. 4, No. 4C0281, 1978) held that a proposed shopping center located six miles from the central business district of Burlington, the largest city in the state, did not satisfy this policy. Studies submitted in the case indicated the development would have a negative impact on Burlington by attracting 40 percent of the existing businesses in the downtown business district. The Pyramid Mall developers appealed to a trial court, which dismissed the case but granted an interlocutory appeal, which the supreme court dismissed. *In re Pyramid Co.,* 449 A.2d 915 (Vt. 1982). The developer then withdrew its action in the trial court. The Pyramid Mall litigation attracted national attention. See Brooks, *Fiscal Impact Analysis and the Pyramid Mall Case,* 12 Pol'y Stud. J. 511 (1984); *Two Sides of a Pyramid,* 45 Planning, No. 5, at 3 (1980).

State planning.—The Growth Management Act of 1988 strengthened the state and regional planning process, provided a set of state planning goals partly incorporating Act 250's development approval criteria, and provided for the approval of local plans by regional planning commissions for consistency with the state planning goals. Approval by the commissions carries incentives, such as additional state funding and a requirement that state agency plans comply with the local plan. Vt. Stat. Ann. tit. 24, §§ 4301–4387; tit. 3, § 4020. However, the state planning program has fallen into a state of benign neglect, and there no longer is a state planning office.

A state permit program like Vermont's is obviously not a serious possibility in larger and more complex states. You might want to consider the advantages of programs, like the Oregon and Washington programs, that delegate responsibilities to the local level subject to state supervision. What are the disadvantages?

For discussion of the Vermont program see R. Brooks, Toward Community Sustainability: Vermont's Act 250 (1996); J. DeGrove, Planning & Growth Management in the States, ch. 5 (1992).

(2) WASHINGTON

How it works.—This state adopted a Growth Management Act in 1993 that combines the urban growth boundary concept of the Oregon program with the concurrency requirement of the Florida program. Professor Settle has described the program. *Washington's Growth Management Revolution Goes to Court,* 23 Seattle U.L. Rev. 5 (1999). The Act requires local governments to adopt comprehensive land use plans to guide development consistent with the statutory goals, and then implement the plan with consistent regulations. All growing counties must participate in the program, and others have opted in. The Washington program provides for local administration subject to review by three regional Growth Management Hearings Boards, rather than for administrative review by a state agency.

Counties designate Urban Growth Areas (UGAs), the equivalent of Oregon's UGBs. Development within UGAs is to be at "urban densities." Land outside city limits can be included in a UGA only if it is "already characterized by urban growth," is "adjacent to" such areas, or is a "new and fully contained community." Wash. Rev. Code § 36.70A.110. These requirements are intended to prevent leapfrog development by requiring UGAs to be contiguous to city limits. The statute requires a "rural element" in comprehensive plans and contains detailed guidance for development that is allowed in rural areas. *Id.* § 36.70A.070(5). Its concurrency requirement, unlike Florida's, specifically applies only to transportation facilities. *Id.* § 36.70A.070(6)(e). The statute also requires county plans to include a process for identifying and siting "essential public facilities" that are typically difficult to site, such as airports and correctional facilities. *Id.* § 36.70A.200. See Settle, *Washington's Growth Management Revolution Goes to Court,* 23 Seattle U.L. Rev. 5 (1999).

Experience so far.—A report on the Washington UGAs found evidence that they had achieved their objectives of preserving natural areas, encouraging investment in downtowns and older neighborhoods and, in some cases, encouraging higher densities. Fulton, *Ring Around the Region,* Planning, vol. 65, no. 3, at 18 (1999). There has also been an increase in annexations, prompted in part by the requirement that all incorporated municipalities must be within a GMA. However, some outlying areas have resisted compliance, resentment has developed in some areas over the authority of the Growth Management Hearings Boards, and some areas have attempted to secede from existing counties in order to get control over land use policy. For additional discussion see *Symposium: Guidance for Growth,* 16 U. Puget Sound L. Rev. 863 (1993); Note, *The Land Use Study Commission and the 1997 Amendments to Washington State's Growth Management Act,* 22 Harv. Envtl. L. Rev. 559 (1998).

Land use in the UGA.—In *City of Redmond v. Central Puget Sound Growth Mgt. Hearings Bd.,* 959 P.2d 1091 (Wash. 1998), the city designated land as agricultural within its UGA that was currently zoned agricultural and suitable by soil type for agricultural use but that had not been used for agricultural purposes for many years. The statute defined "agricultural land" as land "primarily devoted" to commercial agriculture with "long-term significance for agricultural production." The owners of the land opposed the agricultural designation and had acquired it with the intent to develop it for more intensive uses. They petitioned the Growth Hearings Board to have the agricultural designation changed, and the Board agreed, holding that the landowners' current or intended use was conclusive and that the land had not been devoted to agricultural use.

The court reversed. It held the land was properly designated agricultural under the statutory definition, which applied to land capable of being put to agricultural use even though it was not presently being used for that purpose. It also held that to allow "landowner intent" to control the designation of agricultural land would frustrate the statutory goal of preserving natural resource lands because that goal would be frustrated by each landowner's current use of her land. However, the court held the city had not provided for a transfer of development rights program for agricultural land as required by statute when agricultural land is designated within UGAs. Why do you suppose this requirement is in the statute?

A concurring opinion argued the decision undercut the statute by prohibiting the conversion of land not presently used for agriculture to urban uses.

How does this case compare with the *Benjfran* decision, *supra?* The *Collins* decision, *supra?* Is there a valid policy reason for allowing agricultural land within a UGA? Doesn't this contribute to urban sprawl?

(3) MARYLAND

How it works.—In 1992 the legislature adopted a new planning act that requires local governments to adopt comprehensive plans that incorporate seven "vision" or policy statements included in the legislation, which include the concentration of development in suitable areas and the protection of sensitive lands. Md. Ann. Code, art. 66B, § 3.06(b). A Smart Growth Areas Act followed in 1997. This act contains programs for the acquisition of farmland and open space and for neighborhood conservation, but the key strategy is the concept of priority funding areas. See Md. State Fin. & Proc. Code § 5-7B-01 to -10. Douglas Porter explains how this concept works:

> [It] requires that growth-related spending on infrastructure, housing, economic development, and other programs be targeted to development of existing communities, municipalities, and areas designated for growth. It is intended to implement the visions calling for concentration of growth in suitable areas and protection of sensitive and resource areas. The act identifies existing municipalities and certain areas designated by existing state programs as growth areas. In addition, it allows counties to voluntarily certify additional growth areas as "priority funding areas." [See *id.* § 5-7B-03.]

> The act spells out several criteria for determining priority funding areas. These criteria emphasize the goals of developing compactly around existing developed areas and maintaining and revitalizing existing developed areas through infrastructure improvements and infill and redevelopment activities. Although no formal state approval of priority funding areas is required, counties may elect to submit proposed areas to [the state planning office] for comments before formal certification. [Porter, Maryland's "Smart Growth" Program: An Evaluation and Recommendations, Am. Plan. Ass'n PAS Memo, Aug. 1999, at 2, 3.]

Porter notes that vagueness in the statutory vision policies and the absence of a requirement for state approval may weaken the program. For an assessment of the program see Gurwitt, *The State vs. Sprawl*, Governing, Vol. 12, No. 4, at 21 (1999). Ellison, *The Challenge of Smart Growth in Charles County, Maryland,* Land Development, Vol. 12, No. 2, at 13 (1999), reports a defeat in smart growth planning. The county adopted a smart growth plan and zoning ordinance that called for concentrated higher densities, but drastically rewrote the zoning ordinance to eliminate higher density housing after citizens protested the smart growth policies. The author notes that effective smart growth planning requires a clear consensus on what it does and adequate advance funding of public facilities and services.

NOTES AND QUESTIONS

1. *Georgia: the land use-transportation connection.* Georgia's program is limited to the Atlanta area. Severe problems of urban sprawl, air pollution and traffic congestion there led to the adoption of a Regional Transportation Authority Act in 1999 to deal with these problems. Official Code of Ga. Ann. §§ 50-32-1 to 50-32-70. The state had earlier amended its planning legislation to mandate and improve the local planning process. The new regional authority will coordinate transportation planning and infrastructure, and can compel the 13 counties in the metropolitan area to pay for transportation improvements. The authority can also veto projects proposed by local governments and the state transportation department, although a local government can override the veto by a three-fourths vote of the governing body. *Id.* § 50-32-14. This Act is an innovative attempt to deal with transportation and land use problems through a centralized authority at the regional level.

2. *Hawaii: The Quiet Revolution.* State land use programs with UGB or similar requirements are the successors to earlier state land use programs, adopted in the 1960s and 1970s that were termed the "Quiet Revolution" in land use controls. F. Bosselman & D. Callies, The Quiet Revolution in Land Use Controls (1971), review the early legislation.

The Oregon and Vermont programs, described above, were part of the Quiet Revolution. Another was in Hawaii whose program, like Vermont's, was prompted by environmental problems. It involves a unique, state-centered program adopted soon after statehood that provides a land use allocation overlay for the entire state. See D. Callies, Preserving Paradise (1994). A state Land Use Commission divides the state into urban, agricultural, rural and conservation districts. Preservation of agricultural land was a major reason for the legislation. There is no growth management component. There is a state plan, and the statute requires amendments to the land use districts to comply with the plan, which is a set of legislatively adopted goals. See Hawaii Rev. Stat. ch. 226, § 2-5-16.

3. *Evaluating the state programs.* Growth management planner Douglas Porter has provided a critique of the state programs. *State Growth Management: The Intergovernmental Experiment,* 13 Pace L. Rev. 481 (1993). He notes the programs have promoted increased attention to state and regional interests and have improved planning and coordination efforts. He also notes that state programs have not recognized differences in the size, growth rates or other characteristics of local governments that affect their planning needs and their ability to respond to state mandates. He suggests that state planning goals need further definition to provide adequate guidance to determine the consistency of state and local plans. Porter adds that the programs have been negatively affected by political instability at the state level and a failure to provide adequate financial assistance. He concludes that evaluations in Florida and Oregon show that results "on the ground" fall short of desired objectives in controlling urban development and protecting environmental resources. Porter recommends that states adopt the Oregon strategy for the Portland area of requiring minimum densities for local plans. A later article highlights serious local tensions between state agencies and local officials, and calls for more regional management of growth management programs along the lines of the Portland model. Porter, *Reinventing Growth Management for the 21st Century,* 23 Wm. & Mary Envtl. L. & Pol'y Rev. 705 (1999).

4. *Sources.* For additional discussion of state land use programs and their growth management requirements see American Planning Association,

Planning Communities for the 21st Century (1999); J. Weitz, Sprawl Busting: State Programs to Guide Growth (1999); State & Regional Comprehensive Planning (P. Buchsbaum & L. Smith eds., 1993); Gale, *Eight State-Sponsored Growth Management Programs: A Comparative Analysis,* 58 J. Am. Plan. Ass'n 425 (1992); Weitz, *From Quiet Revolution to Smart Growth: State Growth Management Programs, 1960 to 1999,* 14 J. Plan. Lit. 257 (CPL Bibliography 355/356/357, 1999); Wickersham, *The Quiet Revolution Continues: The Emerging New Model for State Growth Management Statutes,* 18 Harv. Envtl. L. Rev. 433 (1994).

D. CONTROLLING GROWTH THROUGH PUBLIC SERVICES AND FACILITIES

Many of the growth management strategies reviewed so far manage growth by linking the approval of new development to the availability of public services and facilities. This section looks at opposite strategies that manage growth through controls over public facilities and services. One strategy manages growth by limiting the availability of urban services to areas where growth is planned to occur. A second strategy influences growth by designating corridors where land is reserved for the construction of highway and other transportation facilities. A major purpose of corridor preservation is to prevent new development from occurring where future transportation facilities are to be constructed. Corridor preservation can also be an important growth management strategy because the highway network is such an important element in shaping urban growth. The following materials discuss both of these strategies.

1. LIMITING THE AVAILABILITY OF PUBLIC SERVICES

Several legal problems arise when local governments attempt to manage urban growth by controlling the availability of urban services:

DATELINE BUILDERS, INC. v. CITY OF SANTA ROSA

146 Cal. App. 3d 520, 194 Cal. Rptr. 258 (1983)

WHITE, PRESIDING JUSTICE:

On this appeal by Dateline Builders, Inc. (Builders) from a judgment in favor of the City of Santa Rosa (City), the major question is whether the City was required to connect its existing sewer trunk line to Builders' proposed "leap frog" housing development beyond the City's boundaries. For the reasons set forth below we have concluded that the City reasonably exercised its police power because Builders' proposed housing development was not consistent with the City's compact land use and development policy as set forth in the City and County's previously adopted General Plan.

The pertinent facts substantially as found below and revealed by the record are as follows: Builders, a California corporation, held an option on a parcel of real property located beyond the limits of the city boundary, on Todd Road in an undeveloped rural area known as the Santa Rosa Plain. The City is a charter city located in Sonoma County (County).

The County Board of Supervisors determined that: (1) there was a need for development of sewer facilities in the Santa Rosa Plain; (2) it was in the public interest to avoid the proliferation of small and scattered un-unified sewer treatment facilities by a cooperative effort with the City to create a single regional facility to be owned and operated by the City. On October 17, 1964 the City and County entered into the "Plains Agreement," a mutual expression of policy and intent to exercise their police powers cooperatively for the orderly development of the Santa Rosa Plain, and to prevent a proliferation of fragment sewer districts and systems.

Paragraph 10 of the Plains Agreement provided that both the City and County would adopt a policy that the areas in the Santa Rosa Plain adaptable to urban type development, would be developed consistent with the City and County's General Plan[4] and with the development standards of the City. To implement this policy the City and County agreed to enact subdivision, building, zoning and other property development regulations "to prevent haphazard or substandard property development." Paragraph 10 further provided that any development proposal in the Santa Rosa Plain be accompanied by proof that the proposed development was consistent with the City and County's joint General Plan and consistent with the City's development standards and regulations.

To implement one of the policies of the Plains Agreement the City Council adopted a procedure that required the proponent of a development to apply for and receive a certificate of compliance (certificate) prior to the extension of new service outside the city; the certificate then served as proof of compliance with the city's development standards.

The General Plan adopted by the City and County in 1967 had as its goals, inter alia: (1) to encourage a compact growth pattern and discourage inefficient sprawl through out the planning area; (2) to provide safe convenient traffic ways linking living areas with shopping and employment centers and recreation areas; (3) to further develop the public utility system in a manner to serve the growing metropolitan area most economically and efficiently; (4) to schedule utility extensions in a manner to help insure compact, efficient growth patterns with maximum economy; and (5) to encourage cooperation between all governmental agencies responsible for development occurring in the planning area. The Plan envisioned that utilities will be extended when it is economically feasible and "in accordance with *orderly development instead of urban sprawl.*"

Builders wanted to subdivide and develop its Todd Road property as a single family moderate and low income home tract. The Todd Road property was not contiguous with the City but was contiguous to one of the City's trunk sewer lines. Builders had obtained FHA approval for the project under a loan program for homes in communities of less than 10,000 population. The sewer hookup was not a condition for the availability of the federal funds. Builders planned to build 66 single family homes and submitted a tentative subdivision

---

[4] The General Plan covered the 120 square mile area of the City's potential expansion.

map to the County in 1971. At that time, the Todd Road property was zoned for agricultural use. On December 16, 1971, the County conditionally approved the tentative map but attached 24 conditions, including sewer hookup approval from the City and rezoning[5] of the property to R-1 residential use by the County. For a project of the size contemplated by Builders, the County required a sewer system rather than septic tanks. After that date, Builders never performed any of these conditions or took any steps to do so.

Builders' application for a certificate was reviewed by the City for consistency with its plan, and development policies and standards. The City determined that Builders' proposed development in an agricultural area well beyond the city boundaries represented "leap-frog" development inconsistent with the city's plans, policies and standards.[6] On December 9, 1971, the City denied the request without prejudice; Builders never submitted a subsequent or renewed application for a certificate. Builders appealed the determination to the City Council. On January 4, 1972 the City Council heard the appeal and refused to issue the certificate, on the same grounds, i.e., inconsistent with the City's General Plan and standards for compact development.

On March 2, 1972, the City Council reiterated its refusal and explained that the Builders' proposed development was in conflict with the 1967 General Plan of compact growth. The staging concept would provide utility services to undeveloped and partially developed areas immediately surrounding the urban core before such services would be available to areas more removed from the urban core. The City's lack of sewer capacity was not a reason for the city's denial of the certificate. No environmental review pursuant to the state's Environmental Quality Act was prepared for the proposed development. The County's tentative approval of Builders' subdivision map expired on June 16, 1973 by operation of law. Builders commenced the instant action in May 1972.

The trial court concluded that: (1) Builders was neither a third party beneficiary of, nor entitled to, enforce the Plains Agreement; (2) the City was not liable for breach of the Plains Agreement; (3) the City was not a public utility charged with providing sewer connections to the Builders proposed development; (4) the City's urban development strategy in the implementation of its General Plan, development policies and standards involved fundamental policy decisions in an exercise of the police power; (5) as a result of Builders' failure to perform any of the conditions attached to the county's approval of the tentative subdivision map, Builders were never in a position to receive any benefit from an approval of their application to the City for a certificate; (6) the City acted reasonably in determining that Builders' proposed development was inconsistent with its adopted land use plan and policies, and then denying the certificate; and (7) under the circumstances, the granting of a certificate would have been an abuse of discretion.

On appeal, the Builders argue that: (1) the court below, as a matter of law, erred in construing the Plains Agreement, and by concluding that Builders was neither a third party beneficiary nor entitled to damages under that

---

[5] The rezoning for single family residential use was contemplated by the General Plan and the property was eligible for rezoning. However, the City had no jurisdiction over zoning and could not override the County Planning Commission.

[6] Builders' response merely emphasized the low cost aspects of its proposed subdivision.

agreement; (2) in the alternative, even in the absence of a contract, since the City was acting in its proprietary capacity as a public utility and was the only provider of utility services for the Santa Rosa Plain, the City's refusal to grant the certificate was arbitrary and constituted unjust and unlawful discrimination as a matter of law; and (3) the City had no power to act beyond its boundaries.

We turn first to Builders' contention that as third party beneficiaries of the Plains Agreement, they were entitled to damages as the City's refusal to issue the certificate constituted a breach. . . .

[The court held that the builders were not entitled to sue as third party beneficiaries.]

The parties agree that the major questions here presented have not been the subject of a published opinion by a California appellate court.

Preliminarily we turn to the appropriate standard of review. After a careful review of the arguments on rehearing and the record, we are convinced there was no constitutionally suspect basis for the City's action. We hold therefore that the proper test is whether the City's action was a reasonable exercise of its police power, and whether, in fact, it bears a reasonable relationship to the public welfare. (Cf. *Associated Home Builders v. City of Livermore* (1976) 557 P.2d 473.) The concept of public welfare is sufficiently broad to encompass the City's desire to grow at an orderly pace and in a compact manner.

Builders rely on, and urge us to follow, *Robinson v. City of Boulder* (Colo. 1976) 547 P.2d 228 and *Delmarva Enterprises, Inc. v. Mayor and Council of the City of Dover* (Del. 1971) 282 A.2d 601. In both *Robinson* and *Delmarva, supra,* the owners of property outside of the city limits successfully argued that each city had unlawfully discriminated against them by refusing to hook up their properties to the city's exclusive water and sewer services. Both the Delaware and Colorado courts reasoned that: (1) as the exclusive supplier of these services, each city acting in a proprietary capacity as a public utility, was held to the same standards as a private utility, and therefore could refuse to do so only for utility-based reasons, such as insufficient capacity; and (2) each city was bound by the rule that a municipality is without jurisdiction over territory beyond its limits in the absence of legislation. In *Boulder,* however, the court did not reach the City's argument that the rules applicable to private utilities should not apply to a governmental utility authorized to implement governmental objectives such as the adoption of a Masterplan. The City of Boulder and the county in which it was located had jointly developed and adopted a Boulder Valley comprehensive plan to provide for discretionary land use decisions. The court specifically noted that the proposed Boulder development complied with the county zoning regulations and that the county, rather than the city, had the ultimate responsibility for the approval of the proposed development.

Builders argue that the *Boulder* case, *supra,* is on all fours with the facts of the instant case. Builders, however, ignore the fact that its Todd Road project had the tentative approval of the county conditioned, inter alia, upon a change in zoning and other conditions with which Builders admittedly did not attempt to comply. However, we do not base our holding only on this factual distinction. By failing to seek rezoning from the County or meet the other 23 conditions imposed by the County in its tentative approval of the subdivision map, and then pursuing this action against the City, Builders was trying to play off against each other, the City and County who had agreed to cooperative planning. Basically, Builders argues that because a City cannot exercise its police power beyond its boundaries, the City was prevented from using the denial of the sewer hookup as a planning tool.

Builders ignores the joint policy of the City and County as expressed in the Plains Agreement, for orderly growth in conformance with the guidelines of the jointly adopted General Plan. Agreements such as that here in issue that lead to joint planning by cities and counties should and have been encouraged by the Legislature.[10] The complex economic, political and social factors involved in land use planning are compelling evidence that resolution of the important housing and environmental issues raised here, is the domain of the Legislature. Unfortunately, the experience of many communities in this state has been that when planning is left to developers, the result is urban sprawl. The City's express and reiterated reason for denying the certificate was that Builders' proposed development violated its policy of orderly compact development from the urban core, and would result in a "leap-frog" development and "urban sprawl." A municipality cannot be forced to take a stake in the developer's success in the area. (Cf. *Reid Dev. Corp. v. Parsippany-Troy Hills Tp.* (N.J. 1954) 107 A.2d 20, at 23.) Neither common law nor constitutional law inhibits the broad grant of power to local government officials to refuse to extend utility service so long as they do not act for personal gain nor in a wholly arbitrary or discriminatory manner. (See authorities cited in *Control of the Timing and Location of Government Utility Extensions* (1974) 26 Stanford L. Rev. 945–963.)

Builders rely on the line of California authorities holding that where a municipality provides a public utility service "[g]enerally it is true that where the scope of a project transcends the boundaries of a municipality it ceases to be for a municipal purpose." . . . These authorities, of course, predate *Associated Home Builders, etc., Inc. v. City of Livermore, supra.* We agree with the City that unlike the situation in the past, most municipalities today are neither isolated nor wholly independent from neighboring entities, and consequently, land use decisions by one local unit affect the needs and resources of the entire region. The Plains Agreement and the General Plan demonstrate that the City and County were aware of these realities.

---

[10] Around the time of the Plains Agreement, Legislature enacted many provisions encouraging the joint and cooperative planning by cities and counties and regions. For example, see Government Code sections 65061–65061.4 (Creation of Regional Planning Districts), sections 65300, 65307 (Authority and scope of General Plans). Since 1951 all cities and counties have been required to prepare and adopt a general plan. (Gov. Code, § 65300). In 1965 charter cities were exempted from some of the local planning requirements; they are not exempt from the planning elements prescribed by article 5 (commencing with Government Code section 65300) if a general plan is adopted under their charter. (Gov. Code, § 65700). Government Code section 65302 as originally enacted required a land use element (which included population density) and a circulation element. The "housing element" which shall make adequate provision for the housing needs of all economic segments of the community, was added by Statutes 1967, chapter 1658, section 1. Since then Government Code section 65302 has been amended repeatedly to require more detailed general plan elements of charter cities.

Builders recognize that in this state, as elsewhere, publicly owned municipal utilities are not regulated by the Public Utilities Commission (PUC) or any other supervisory agency in the absence of a legislative grant of authority while privately owned utilities are. It has long been the rule in this state that when operating a municipal utility, a city retains its character as a municipal corporation. Reasons must be found for holding it liable to the same extent as a private utility corporation. Builders here argue that there were sufficient reasons here because the City was the only supplier, could not act beyond its boundaries and could not use sewer hookup as a planning device. We do not agree.

In *Associated Home Builders, etc., Inc. v. City of Livermore, supra,* our Supreme Court intimated that in California a city may enact restrictions that are effective beyond its boundaries. *Associated Home Builders* also reiterated the desirability of regional planning. As to a city's alleged inability to act beyond its boundaries, we note that Government Code section 65859 set forth below,[11] a part of the same enactment as Government Code section 65300 and 65302 . . . expressly provides otherwise.

Builders' contention that denial of the certificate could not be used as a planning device overlooks a fundamental distinction between such a decision as an improper initial use of the police power, and as here, a necessary and proper exercise of the power once the planning decision had been made. Here, of course, the adoption of the General Plan with its policy of orderly and compact growth to avoid urban sprawl was made in 1967. The policy was a proper exercise of the police power for the general welfare previously adopted by the City Council and the County. (Cf. *Golden v. Ramapo.*) Builders' argument that only zoning may be used for planning sits poorly in its mouth as they never sought to rezone the property or meet any of the County's other conditions.

The judgment is affirmed.

NOTES AND QUESTIONS

1. *Services as a growth control.* Plans like the Ramapo plan and adequate public facilities ordinances, discussed *supra* in this chapter, link the approval of new development to facility and service adequacy. *Dateline Builders* dealt with the converse problem: the authority of a municipality to deny services as a method of controlling growth. This authority is crucial. As a practical matter, no human-use development can take place unless water and sewers can be provided at reasonable cost, either publicly or privately; conversely, once services are in place, it is usually only a matter of time before development follows, no matter what the current regulatory pattern. These

---

[11] § 65859. A city *may prezone unincorporated territory adjoining the city for the purpose of determining the zoning* that will apply to such property in *the event of subsequent annexation to the city.* The method of accomplishing such prezoning shall be as provided by this chapter for zoning within the city. Such zoning shall become effective at the same time that the annexation becomes effective.

If a city has not prezoned territory which is annexed, it may adopt an interim ordinance in accordance with the provisions of § 65858. (Emphasis added.)

implications of service provision issues are lost neither on municipalities nor developers, and resolution of service issues is often of more practical importance than is the formal zoning of the land.

2. *The precedents.* In the *Boulder* and *Delmarva* cases, relied on by the plaintiffs in the *Dateline* litigation, each city's refusal of service was held invalid. In both cases, the landowner was located in an area where the doctrines of "extraterritoriality" and "duty to serve," discussed below, obligated the city to provide water and sewer service. In the *Boulder* case, the proposed development was also found to be consistent with the controlling comprehensive plan, that of the county. In *Dateline Builders* the refusal to serve was also extraterritorial. Did the court successfully distinguish these cases, or was it holding that they did not apply under California law?

3. *Extraterritoriality.* Extraterritorial refusals to serve may present a problem if a municipal utility has the authority to provide service in extraterritorial areas but the local government does not have extraterritorial land use powers. This omission was fatal in the *Boulder* case because the city could not rely on its growth-management program as a basis for a service refusal in an extraterritorial area. How does the *Dateline* case resolve this problem? *County of Del Norte v. City of Crescent City,* 84 Cal. Rptr. 2d 179 (Cal. App. 1999), followed *Dateline* and upheld the city's refusal to extend water service to extraterritorial customers to implement a growth management policy.

Some states have conferred statutory extraterritorial zoning powers, and these statutes have been upheld. See D. Mandelker, Land Use Law §§ 4.22– 4.23 (4th ed. 1997). For an argument that the availability of extraterritorial zoning powers in Wisconsin would support a refusal to provide services to implement a growth management program, see Comment, *Utility Extension: An Untested Control on Wisconsin's Urban Sprawl,* 1977 Wis. L. Rev. 1132.

4. *The duty to serve rule.* Whether controls over public service extensions can be used as a growth management device depends on a variety of interlocking legal principles. Although use of the governmental/proprietary distinction has been much criticized in the law of local government, many courts nonetheless begin their analysis by asking whether the municipal public service function is governmental or proprietary. If the function is proprietary, municipally owned utilities are subject to the duty to serve obligation imposed on private utilities. They may not be able to refuse service to new customers in order to implement a growth management program. Did the *Boulder* decision take this view? What did the *Dateline* case hold on this issue?

The duty to serve rule applies if a court holds that the provision of public services is a proprietary function. A court may hold that the public service function in extraterritorial areas is proprietary, as in *Delmarva,* because the utility is serving customers who are not residents of the city and who do not have a political voice in public service decisions. Courts apply the rule that the provision of services is proprietary to curb the monopoly power of utilities:

> [T]he consumer of utility services still cannot pick and choose his supplier of water as he does his grocer. The utility consumer is thus at the mercy of the monopoly and, for this reason, utilities, regardless of the character of their ownership, should be, and have been, subjected to control under the common-law rule forbidding unreasonable

discrimination. [*City of Texarkana v. Wiggins,* 246 S.W.2d 622, 625 (Tex. 1952) (invalidating discriminatory municipal extraterritorial rates).]

Some courts have adopted a more lenient rule. They hold that municipal utilities have the discretion to refuse service and that an exercise of discretion to refuse service may be overturned only if it is arbitrary. Whether the authority to refuse service is wider under the exercise of discretion rule is not clear. Note, *Control of the Timing and Location of Government Utility Extensions,* 26 Stan. L. Rev. 945 (1974), cited in the *Dateline* case, argues that the discretion to refuse service is wider under this rule. Did *Dateline* adopt this view?

Characterizing the municipal public service function as governmental may not always support the use of that function in growth management programs. In *Levy Court v. City of Dover,* 333 A.2d 161 (Del. 1975), a city agreed to join a county sewer system in return for the county's promise not to provide service in areas outside the city's growth limits. The court held that the county's provision of sewer services was a governmental function requiring the exercise of discretion and could not be bargained away by contract. The court distinguished its earlier *Delmarva* decision; there, the city acted in a "proprietary" capacity outside its boundaries, whereas the county acted "governmentally" within its boundaries. Is there a principled basis for this distinction? Note that the court in *Dateline* relied on an agreement between the city and county in upholding the refusal to provide service. Is this reliance consistent with *Levy Court?*

5. *Utility-related reasons.* As the *Boulder* case indicates, the duty to serve rule is usually applied to require the provision of services in areas where the utility has held itself out as a service provider. A utility may refuse to provide services under this rule only for utility-related reasons, such as economic or practicable infeasibility, insufficient expected return, or supply shortages. See Note, *The Duty of a Public Utility to Render Adequate Service: Its Scope and Enforcement,* 62 Colum. L. Rev. 312 (1962).

A utility may sometimes rely on utility-related reasons to implement a growth management policy. In *Swanson v. Marin Mun. Water Dist.,* 128 Cal. Rptr. 485 (Cal. App. 1976), the district placed a moratorium on new water extensions because the safewater yield of the district was below future consumption. The court upheld the moratorium as an emergency measure, holding that the district had the statutory authority to conserve water supply to avoid a future emergency. See Note, *Sometimes There's Nothing Left to Give: The Justification for Denying Water Service to New Customers to Control Growth,* 44 Stan. L. Rev. 429 (1992).

6. *Planning reasons.* Despite the duty to serve rule, other courts have upheld planning reasons for refusing to provide utility services. Compare *Okemo Trailside Condominiums v. Blais,* 380 A.2d 84 (Vt. 1977). The court held that a village could exercise its discretion to determine whether it had excess capacity to service condominiums located outside the village limits. The court seemed to approve a planning reason for a service denial, noting that "[o]vercommitment outside the municipal limits might . . . increase the impact of necessary additional construction on the local zoning law." *Id.* at

86. Accord *Denby v. Brown,* 199 S.E.2d 214 (Ga. 1973). See also, *Town of Rocky Mount v. Wenco, Inc.,* 506 S.E.2d 17 (Va. 1998), holding that the provision of sewer service to a retail store on a trunk sewer line intended to permit development in a highway corridor was a planning decision and did not constitute consent to provide services to others in the area. The holding out rule did not apply.

7. *Sources.* For additional discussion, see Biggs, *No Drip, No Flush, No Growth: How Cities Can Control Growth Beyond Their Boundaries by Refusing to Extend Utility Services,* 22 Urb. Law. 285 (1992); Stone, *The Prevention of Urban Sprawl Through Utility Extension Control,* 14 Urb. Law. 357 (1982).

2. CORRIDOR PRESERVATION

These materials have indicated the importance of highway and other transportation facilities to growth management and the prevention of sprawl. Yet highway and transportation facilities can take years to plan, especially since the availability of federal construction funding requires detailed environmental review. The preservation of corridors from development while the planning and environmental review process is carried on is essential because land needed for these projects must be kept undeveloped until they can be constructed.

The program strategy that can preserve highway and transportation corridors from development is known as corridor preservation, which is

> a concept utilizing the coordinated application of various measures to obtain control of or otherwise protect the right-of-way for a planned transportation facility. [Report of the AASHTO Task Force on Corridor Preservation 1–2 (1990).]

As the Report explained, corridor preservation should be applied as early as possible in the identification of a transportation corridor to prevent inconsistent development; minimize or avoid environmental, social, and economic impacts; prevent the foreclosure of desirable location options; allow for the orderly assessment of impacts; permit orderly project development; and reduce costs. *Id.*

Corridor preservation can confer a number of benefits:

> Corridor preservation can play a significant role in the transportation planning and project development process and in the avoidance of environmental damage. Corridor preservation seeks to control development that may occur within a proposed corridor so that needed improvements can be provided. Studies done as the basis for corridor preservation should also result in the selection of transportation corridors that not only minimize environmental harm but also provide opportunities for environmental enhancements. A new location not only may not serve transportation needs as well as the original corridor but also may be more damaging environmentally.

> Corridor preservation can also provide major benefits to local governments in their planning and land use control programs, and to the development community by providing more predictability in the

marketplace. By fixing the location of important transportation corridors that are a major determinant of new development, corridor preservation can allow developers to adjust their development strategies accordingly and thereby encourage more orderly and appropriate development in metropolitan and rural areas. In other words, uncertainties about the location of transportation facilities that otherwise would frustrate local planning and land use regulation are removed by corridor preservation. The designation of transportation corridors in a corridor preservation program provides certainty by indicating where major transportation improvements will be located. Developers and local governments can rely on these corridor designations when they plan and review new development projects. [D. Mandelker & B. Blaesser, Corridor Preservation: Study of Legal and Institutional Barriers 2 (Federal Highway Admin., 1995).]

Corridor preservation began under a very different name in the Standard Planning Enabling Act, §§ 21–25, which contained statutory authority for the adoption of an official street map by local governments. These local roads were vitally important in the days before major intercity highways, and so the official street map had the same function as the more sophisticated corridor preservation programs of today. Local governments exercising this authority mapped the right-of-way for future streets, thereby keeping development out of the right-of-way until the street was completed.

The following excerpt explains official map laws and more recent legislation authorizing corridor preservation by state transportation agencies:

MANDELKER, LAND RESERVATION LEGISLATION, in Land Use Law § 10.11 (4th ed. 1997)

The Standard Planning Act's provision for official maps was based on earlier legislation adopted in New York and other states. The Act required compensation to landowners whose land was reserved for future streets, denied compensation for any buildings built in mapped streets, and did not contain a variance provision. It authorized the local governing body to set a time limit on an official map reservation. Some official map legislation is based on the Standard Planning Act model. [*E.g.*, Pa. Stat. Ann. tit. 53, §§ 22777–22779.]

Two model acts published after the Standard Planning Act also included legislative authority for official maps. The model acts differ in detail, but their statutory authority for official maps is similar. The model acts rely on the police power and do not authorize compensation to landowners whose land is reserved for acquisition in an official map. The acts prohibit the development of land reserved on an official map unless the municipality grants a variance. The model acts make the adoption of a street plan an explicit or implicit condition for the adoption of an official street map. Some official map legislation that authorizes official maps is based on one of the model acts. [*E.g.,* Mass. Gen. Laws Ann. ch. 41, §§ 81E-81J; N.Y. Gen. City Law §§ 26, 29, 33–36.] Official map legislation in other states is similar to but not based directly on the model acts. [*E.g.,* La Rev. Stat. Ann. § 33:116.] The model acts and most state official map acts do not authorize the adoption of a time limit for an official map reservation.

Some subdivision control statutes and ordinances also authorize the reservation of land for acquisition for a public facility. They may also prohibit the development of the land during the reservation period. [Ala. Code §§ 11-52-50 to 11-52-54.]

A number of states authorize the state transportation agency to adopt maps for transportation corridors or for the location of future highway rights-of-way. A comprehensive state mapping law will require public hearings and comments on planned corridors, the preparation and recording of official maps of the corridors, and local government referral to the state transportation agency of any application to develop land within the corridor. The state transportation agency must then find either that the development proposal has an impact on the preservation of the corridor or does not have an impact. If the proposed development is found to have an impact on the corridor, the state transportation agency must negotiate with the developer either for the purchase of its land or for a modification in development plans that will protect the corridor. [Cal Sts. & High. Code §§ 740, 741; 605 Ill. Comp. Stat. 5/4-510; Neb. Rev. Stat. §§ 39-1311 to 39-1311.05; N.H. Rev. Stat. Ann §§ 230-a:1 to 230-a:14; N.J. Stat. Ann. §§ 27:7-66, 27:7-67.]

NOTES

As this excerpt points out, both local governments and state transportation agencies can be involved in corridor preservation programs. Local governments can exercise the regulatory powers conferred by an official map or similar law to preserve corridors. States do not have land use control powers, and must depend on local governments for the implementation of a corridor preservation law. This difference may make a difference when corridor preservation is challenged under the takings clause, as the next case indicates.

Federal legislation also requires the preparation and adoption of regional and state transportation plans. 23 U.S.C. §§ 134, 135. The designation of highway corridors in these plans can provide a basis for corridor preservation programs.

The case that follows reviews the constitutionality of corridor preservation:

PALM BEACH COUNTY v. WRIGHT

641 So. 2d 50 (Fla. 1994)

GRIMES, C.J.

We review *Palm Beach County v. Wright,* 612 So. 2d 709 (Fla. 4th DCA 1993), in which the court certified the following as a question of great public importance:

IS A COUNTY THOROUGHFARE MAP DESIGNATING CORRIDORS FOR FUTURE ROADWAYS, AND WHICH FORBIDS LAND USE ACTIVITY THAT WOULD IMPEDE FUTURE CONSTRUCTION OF A ROADWAY, ADOPTED INCIDENT TO A COMPREHENSIVE COUNTY LAND USE PLAN ENACTED UNDER THE LOCAL GOVERNMENT COMPREHENSIVE PLANNING AND LAND DEVELOPMENT REGULATION ACT,

FACIALLY UNCONSTITUTIONAL UNDER *Joint Ventures, Inc. v. Department of Transportation,* 563 So. 2d 622 (Fla. 1990)? . . .

The thoroughfare map referred to in the certified question is a portion of the traffic circulation element of the Palm Beach County Comprehensive Plan as adopted in Ordinance 89-17. The map defines certain transportation corridors along specified roadways throughout Palm Beach County as well as certain other locations designated for future roadway construction. The traffic circulation element of the Comprehensive Plan provides that the "County shall provide for protection and acquisition of existing and future right-of-way consistent with the adopted Thoroughfare Right-of-Way Protection Map." *Wright,* 612 So. 2d at 710–11 (Anstead, J., concurring specially). The traffic circulation element continues by providing that the "Map is designed to protect identified transportation corridors from encroachment by other land use activities." *Id.* at 711 (Anstead, J., concurring specially). The map applies to all land development activities within unincorporated Palm Beach County. The land development activities are defined as including but not limited to residential, commercial, institutional, or industrial purposes. All development is required to be consistent with and provide for the transportation right-of-way shown on the thoroughfare map. The land use element of the Comprehensive Plan provides that no land use activity may be permitted within any roadway designated on the thoroughfare map that would impede future construction of the roadway. The land use element further provides that all development approvals and actions by the county must be consistent with the provisions contained in the Comprehensive Plan.

The roadway corridors are located on the thoroughfare map in varying widths from 80 to 240 feet. The thoroughfare map contains a 220-foot right-of-way corridor which includes Southern Boulevard, an existing roadway in Palm Beach County. Because Southern Boulevard is bound on the south by a canal, the future alignment of the right-of-way corridor would be measured northward from the existing south property line of Southern Boulevard. Respondents own property on the north side of Southern Boulevard. Therefore, a portion of their property lies within the corridor of the thoroughfare map.

The respondents filed suit attacking the constitutionality of the thoroughfare map. The trial court entered summary judgment against the county finding that the map as implemented by the land use element and traffic circulation element of the Comprehensive Plan was facially unconstitutional. The court determined that the map was in violation of the Fifth Amendment of the United States Constitution and article X, section 6 of the Florida Constitution. The court reasoned that the map was not a valid police regulation furthering the county's planning function for future growth and that it did not substantially advance a legitimate state interest. The court also held that the adoption of the map constituted a temporary taking of the respondents' property within the right-of-way corridor and ordered a jury trial to determine compensation for the taking. In a split decision, the district court of appeal affirmed the judgment. The appellate court reasoned that the thoroughfare map was functionally indistinguishable from the reservation map this Court declared invalid in *Joint Ventures, Inc. v. Department of Transportation,* 563 So. 2d 622 (Fla. 1990). The court also agreed that a taking had occurred.

Subsequent to the decision of the district court of appeal, this Court issued its opinion in *Tampa-Hillsborough County Expressway Authority v. A.G.W.S. Corp.,* [640 So.2d 54 (Fla. 1994)], which has a substantial bearing on this case. In *A.G.W.S.,* we held that landowners with property inside the boundaries of maps of reservation invalidated by *Joint Ventures, Inc.,* are not legally entitled to receive per se declarations of taking. We explained that subsections 337.241(2) and (3), Florida Statutes (1987), which authorized the filing of the maps of reservation, were held invalid because they did not meet the requirements of due process, not because the filing of such a map always resulted in a taking. Whether the filing of a map of reservation resulted in a taking of particular property would depend upon whether its effect was to deny the owner of substantially all of the economically beneficial or productive use of the land.

[The statute cited authorized the state Department of Transportation (DOT) to file maps of reservation to designate proposed rights-of-way for the widening of existing roads. The maps were to designate building setback lines from the center of any existing road, and for a period of five years prohibited development permits for "new construction of any type." It also prohibited the "renovation of an existing commercial structure that exceeds 20 percent of the appraised value of the structure."

[DOT argued that the statute was a valid use of the police power because prohibiting development in the reserved right-of-way would reduce the cost of land acquisition, but the court held the statute was a "thinly-veiled" attempt to acquire land without going through the statutory eminent domain procedures. The court found no distinction between this statutory "freezing" of property values and a deliberate attempt to depress land values in advance of acquisition.]

If the filing of a map of reservation under subsections 337.241(2) and (3) did not constitute a per se taking, it is clear that the adoption of the Palm Beach County thoroughfare map which designates corridors for future roadways would not constitute a per se taking. Therefore, at least one portion of the final judgment will have to be reversed. There remains, however, the question of whether the thoroughfare map is unconstitutional. On this point, the parties differ with respect to the applicability of *Joint Ventures, Inc.*

The respondents assert that the practical effect of the thoroughfare map is the same as that of the maps of reservation held invalid in *Joint Ventures* in that the thoroughfare map does not permit land use or activity within the designated corridors which would impede future roadway construction. However, the county argues that section 337.241, which prohibited construction within the limits of the recorded maps of reservation, was enacted for the sole purpose of reducing the future acquisition costs of roads. By contrast, the county's thoroughfare map is an unrecorded long-range planning tool tied to a comprehensive plan that outlines general roadway corridors and does not on its face delineate the exact routes of future roadways.

The county contends that the plan provides sufficient flexibility so that it cannot be determined whether a taking has occurred within the roadway corridors until the property owner submits a development approval application. When this occurs, the county asserts that it will be in the position to work with the property owner to (1) assure the best routes through the land that maximize the development potential; (2) offer development opportunities for clustering the increasing densities at key nodes and parcels off the corridors; (3) grant alternative and more valuable uses; (4) avoid loss of value that results in taking by using development rights transfer and credit for impact fees; and, if necessary, (5) alter or change the road pattern.

The county points out that the effect of designating road corridors is to increase most property values. Often, the increase in value of abutting property will more than offset any loss occasioned by the owner's inability to use land within the corridor. Therefore, the county argues that a determination of whether a taking has occurred within the corridor can only be made when a county has acted upon an application for development approval.

Palm Beach County's comprehensive plan was adopted pursuant to the requirements of the Local Government Comprehensive Planning and Land Development Regulation Act. Section 163.3177(6)(b), Florida Statutes (1991), requires the comprehensive plan to contain "[a] traffic circulation element consisting of the types, locations, and extent of existing and proposed major thoroughfares and transportation routes." Palm Beach County was further required by Florida Administrative Code Rule 9J-5.007(3)(b)(4) and (c)(4), promulgated by the Department of Community Affairs and approved by the legislature in section 163.3177(10), Florida Statutes (1991), to place measures in the comprehensive plan to protect existing and future rights-of-way from building encroachments and to preserve and acquire existing and future rights-of-way. One of the purposes of the thoroughfare map is to place property owners on notice as to the necessity and location of future roads. According to the comprehensive plan, this "allows land developers adequate time to plan their developments with proper road interfacing requirements."

There are many public benefits to be achieved through comprehensive planning of future road development.

> Since the infrastructure of many of America's cities demands extensive redevelopment along sewer and transportation networks, the opportunity arises for a comprehensive integration of land use and transportation planning. Where mass and rapid transit is envisioned, the area from one-quarter to one-half of a mile in radius from stops should be planned for redevelopment. These areas should be developed at densities sufficient to sustain the planned transportation facility. . . .
>
> . . . Additionally, commercial and industrial siting should follow this pattern so that sites may be concentrated along transportation corridors and thus facilitate access to employment and decreased energy consumption and automobile usage. The resulting pattern of community development would allow transit and other aspects of the infrastructure to take advantage of economics of scale.

James A. Kushner, *Urban Transportation Planning,* 4 Urb. L. & Pol'y 161, 173 (1981). Thus, there can be no question that the planning for future growth must include designation of the areas where roads are likely to be widened and future roads are to be built.

We are persuaded that the Palm Beach County thoroughfare map as implemented by the comprehensive plan is not facially invalid. At least with respect to existing streets, the roadway corridors are analogous to set-back requirements. Many years ago this Court held that a city may establish building set-back lines through the exercise of police power and without compensation to the property owners. *City of Miami v. Romer,* 58 So. 2d 849 (Fla. 1952). Furthermore, the owners most likely to benefit from planned road construction are those whose properties are adjacent to transportation corridors. Under the concurrency requirements of section 163.3177(10)(h), Florida Statutes (1991), development will be curtailed unless roads are available to accommodate the impact of such development. Therefore, projects closest to new roads are likely to benefit the most from construction of the roads even if a portion of the owner's property must be reserved for road construction.

The thoroughfare map differs in several ways from the maps of reservation invalidated by *Joint Ventures.* The thoroughfare map only limits development to the extent necessary to ensure compatibility with future land use. The thoroughfare map is not recorded as were maps of reservation and may be amended twice a year. The road locations within the transportation corridors shown on the thoroughfare map have not been finally determined. Unlike the Department of Transportation which recorded the maps of reservation, Palm Beach County is a permitting authority which has the flexibility to ameliorate some of the hardships of a person owning land within the corridor. Section 337.241 precluded the issuance of all development permits for land within the recorded map. Moreover, the only purpose of that statute was to freeze property so as to depress land values in anticipation of eminent domain proceedings. While the Palm Beach County thoroughfare map can have the effect of adversely affecting land values of some property, it also serves as an invaluable tool for planning purposes. Thus, we hold that the adoption of the thoroughfare map is the proper subject of the county's police power which substantially advances a legitimate state interest. In fact, the county's ability to plan for future growth would be seriously impeded without the thoroughfare map.

At the same time, we recognize that as applied to certain property, the thoroughfare map may result in a taking. . . . [The court quoted the three-factor takings test adopted in the Supreme Court's *Penn Central* case.]

Therefore, we are convinced that the taking issue may only be determined upon an individualized basis because the various property owners' interests will be different and will be affected by the thoroughfare map in a differing manner. . . . Normally, we would expect the issue to be precipitated by a property owner's application for a development permit. By virtue of the county's response, the owner will then know what can be done with the property. In any event, an aggrieved owner may always bring an inverse condemnation proceeding which if successful will result in a payment for the taking as well as the recovery of attorney's fees.

We answer the certified question in the negative and quash the decision below.

It is so ordered.

NOTES AND QUESTIONS

1. *The constitutional issues.* Corridor preservation is really a type of moratorium with a clear prohibition on development within the corridor prior to land acquisition. There is the added complication, as noted in *Joint Ventures,* that corridor preservation looks a lot like the use of the police power to depress the value of land before acquisition, which is always held invalid. For example, in *People ex rel. Dep't of Transp. v. Diversified Props. Co. III,* 17 Cal. Rptr.2d 676 (Cal. App. 1993), a city cooperated with the state to deny approval of development plans on property the state intended to acquire for a freeway. The court held that the delay due to these unreasonable precondemnation activities amounted to a de facto taking.

On the other side of the problem, as *Palm Beach* noted, a corridor reservation for a street widening is like a street setback, which the courts uniformly uphold. This analogy does not work, of course, if a corridor is reserved for a highway or street on a new location.

Although *Palm Beach* refers to *Joint Ventures* as a due process, not a takings, case, it is clear from a reading of the *Joint Ventures* decision that the court had takings in mind. This distinction aside, what features of the *Palm Beach* program led the court to hold it constitutional? The absence of a "real" official map? The availability of the county's land use regulation authority? A change of heart in the court? If so, on what issues?

2. *Pre-Lucas takings cases.* The Supreme Court's *Lucas* decision threatens corridor preservation programs because it held a categorical taking occurs when a land use regulation deprives a landowner of all economically viable use of his land. Even prior to *Lucas,* however, some courts held that official maps were a taking of property.

For example, in *Jensen v. City of New York,* 369 N.E.2d 1179 (N.Y. 1977), the court invalidated an official map reservation for streets that it viewed as including all of the landowner's property. The landowner had not exhausted administrative remedies by applying for a variance, but the court held that an application for a variance was unnecessary. The plaintiff only wanted to sell the land, but the property was "virtually unsalable" and banks were unwilling to finance repairs because of the official map. This was "no less a deprivation of the use and enjoyment" of the property than if the plaintiff had applied for and been denied a building permit. The dissent would have applied the rule that a depreciation in property value resulting from project planning is not a taking. See also *Urbanizador Versalles, Inc. v. Rivera Rios,* 701 F.2d 993 (1st Cir. 1983) (invalidating official map reservation for highway that had been in effect for 14 years); *Miller v. City of Beaver Falls,* 82 A.2d 34 (Pa. 1951) (invalidating reservation for parks and playgrounds though reservation for streets previously upheld). For a post-*Lucas* case see *Ward v. Bennett,* 625 N.Y.S.2d 609 (App. Div. 1995) (all economically viable use of property denied for 50 years).

Kingston E. Realty Co. v. State, 330 A.2d 40 (N.J. App. Div. 1975), upheld a reservation for a highway under a state corridor preservation law. The municipality refused to issue a permit for an office research laboratory complex. The state law mandated the issuance of a permit if the state agency did not take any action to acquire the property during a 120-day period. The state agency took no action to acquire the property. The court held that no temporary taking of the plaintiff's property had occurred during the time the statute stayed the building permit while the agency was allowed to consider acquisition, noting that the reservation was for a short period of time and was not absolute. It held that "similar measures," such as zoning moratoria, "have been recognized under narrow circumstances as reasonable regulations in the exercise of governmental powers." The court noted that the highway reservation law was "reasonably designed to reduce the cost of public acquisition." How important were the provisions for the review of development contained in the law? Contra *Lackman v. Hall,* 364 A.2d 1244 (Del. Ch. 1976). For discussion of the taking issues raised by official maps see Mandelker, *Interim Development Controls in Highway Programs: The Taking Issue,* 4 J. Land Use & Envtl. L. 167 (1989).

3. *As-applied takings.* The court in *Palm Beach* indicated that corridor preservation could be a taking as applied. How can this occur? See *Rochester Bus. Inst. v. City of Rochester,* 267 N.Y.S.2d 274 (App. Div. 1966), upholding a street widening reservation on an official map that increased the cost of construction by six percent because the height of the building was increased to make up for the loss of the land. What if the official map reservation covered 90 percent of the property?

4. *Subdivision reservations.* It is also possible to reserve land for future acquisition for public facilities as part of the process of subdivision approval. Development may not occur on reserved land for a specified number of years, and the local government is required to compensate the landowner when the land is acquired for a public facility. See, e.g., Ariz. Rev. Stat. § 9-463.01 (D)-(F).

A Maryland law illustrates the use of this technique. Md. Ann. Code art. 28, § 7-116(a) (4). Ordinances implementing the law in Montgomery and Prince George's counties base subdivision reservations on general county and area plans, which are in turn carried forward to detailed plans showing lot lines and ownerships. Reservations are limited to three years, and property taxes are abated during this period. Maryland cases have held that such reservations are not a taking of property. *Howard County v. JJM, Inc.,* 482 A.2d 908 (Md. 1984). But see *Maryland-National Capital Park & Planning Comm'n v. Chadwick,* 405 A.2d 241 (Md. 1979) (taking occurred when only permitted "use" during reservation period was weed and trash removal).

For a case holding unconstitutional a right-of-way reservation required as part of subdivision approval see *Lomarch Corp. v. Mayor & Common Council,* 237 A.2d 881 (N.J. 1968), codified in N.J. Stat. Ann. § 40:55D-44 (requiring compensation for the "option to purchase" during the period when the reservation is in effect).

5. *Land acquisition and access management.* Mention should be made of two additional programs that can be useful in corridor preservation. Advance acquisition of land, either through condemnation or voluntary purchase, is one possibility. A federal statute, 23 U.S.C. § 108, provides federal funding for advance acquisition programs in the states.

Access management is another option. A number of states have adopted access management programs. These programs regulate access points so that traffic flow is kept at acceptable levels or improved, which maintains highway capacity and helps avoid the construction of new highways. Some statutes authorize access management. See N.J. Stat. Ann. § 27:7-91.

6. *Model corridor map legislation.* The American Planning Association model land use legislation includes a model corridor map act. The model legislation authorizes the adoption of a corridor map for transportation facilities, but it specifies that "this Section does not forbid or restrict the use of any reserved land that does not constitute the development of that land, nor does this Section forbid or restrict development on the unreserved portion of any reserved land." American Planning Association, Legislative Guidebook Phases I & II, Interim Edition, at 7-245 (1998). Will this solve any takings problems? Like much of the state corridor preservation legislation, the model law requires a development permit before any development can occur in the reserved corridor. Commentary to the model law explains how the local government is to proceed after receiving an application:

> If a landowner applies for a permit for development on reserved land, there must be a hearing, open to the public, on the permit application. The local planning commission, planning agency, or a hearing officer may conduct the hearing, and after the hearing recommends a determination of the case from a list of options. These include (1) approving the permit, (2) approving it conditionally, (3) denying it, (4) staying the determination for a specific period of time, (5) modifying the permit application and then granting it as modified, (6) eliminating or altering the reservation, (7) compensating the owner through TDRs or other similar mechanisms, (8) taking the right-of-way by eminent domain, (9) obtaining voluntarily or by eminent domain a negative easement over the reserved land — that is, a contractual duty, running with the land, on the part of the owner not to build on the land, akin to a conservation easement, or purchasing an option on the land. Its recommendations are forwarded to the local legislative body, which can adopt or reject the recommendations or remand the matter for further hearings. [*Id.* at 7-241.]

What are the benefits of this approach, both from a constitutional standpoint and as a method of implementing the law? For the text of the model law see *Id.*, at 7-241 to 7-251. See also Thomas & Payne, *Long-Range Highway Corridor Preservation: Issues, Methods and Model Legislation,* 13 BYU J. Pub. L. 1 (1998).

E. PRESERVING AGRICULTURAL LAND

1. THE PRESERVATION PROBLEM

The preservation of agricultural land is critical in growth management programs when productive agricultural areas are contiguous to urbanized areas, as in Oregon. The program must contain regulatory and other measures to prevent urban development that would destroy and interfere with agricultural production. The other reason for agricultural preservation is a larger fear (which some say is unfounded) that America's farmlands are under attack, and are disappearing at so alarming a rate that the production of food to feed the nation's population is threatened.

Agricultural land preservation is a major policy problem that gained national prominence with the publication of the Final Report of the National Agricultural Lands Study in 1981. This massive, interagency, federally funded study found a crisis in the conversion of agricultural land: "Annually [between 1967 and 1975], nearly three million acres of agricultural land were converted. . . . About 70 percent of this land was converted to urban, built-up and transportation uses, and 30 percent to man-made reservoirs, lakes, and other water-impounding facilities" (Final Report, at 35). The study indicated that one-third of the agricultural land converted was prime farm land and that, if these trends continued, our reserve of agricultural land would be exhausted in a generation.

Although the 1981 study received much criticism, a more recent study confirms that farmland loss remains a serious problem. A. Sorenson, R. Green & K. Russ, American Farmland Trust, Farming on the Edge (1997). This study focused on the geographic relationship between high quality farmland and development pressure by examining conversion patterns from 1982 to 1992, and also focused on geographic regions that had homogenous characteristics related to farming. The study found that four million acres of prime farmland during this period were converted to more intensive land uses, and that a substantial amount of the best farmland was under significant development pressure. A worst case scenario predicted that this country would become a net importer of food within 60 years. *Id.* at 2.

There are dissenters. The Reason Public Policy Institute claims that farmland loss has moderated significantly since the 1960s, that cropland has remained stable for decades despite farmland loss, that only about 26% of cropland loss is caused by urbanization, and that land accounts for only 18% of agricultural productivity and has been declining. S. Staley, The "Vanishing Farmland" Myth and the Smart-Growth Agenda (Policy Brief No. 12, Jan. 2000). See also Klein & Reganold, *Agricultural Changes and Farmland Protection in Western Washington*, 52 J. Soil & Water Conservation, Jan.-Feb. 1997, at 6 (suburban expansion led to decrease in number of farms but increase in farm earnings); Lockeretz, *Secondary Effects on Midwestern Agriculture of Metropolitan Development and Decreases in Farmland*, 65 Land Econ. 205 (1989) (studies fail to support conclusion that metropolitan expansion has adverse effect on farmland).

NOTES AND QUESTIONS

1. *Urban sprawl and agriculture.* Urban sprawl that introduces urban development among farm uses has the expected problems. A study in the Chicago suburbs found that scattered development that fragmented agricultural areas did not pay enough taxes to pay for education costs and road maintenance. Extending water and sewer services to this kind of development was risky because buildout at sufficiently rapid rates was not assured. The study also found that police response times were 600 percent longer and ambulance response times as much as 50 percent longer in scattered development area. A. Sorensen & J. Esseks, Living on the Edge: The Costs and Risks of Scatter Development (American Farmland Trust, 1999).

2. *The structure of American farming.* Changes in the size of farms and the character of American farming also affect the preservation of agricultural land. The number of farms continues to decline, and their average size continues to increase. Data from 1992 show that fewer than one-third of all farms produce over four-fifths of the country's farm products. So-called hobby farms that produced less than $10,000 a year in sales make up about half of all farms but produce only three percent of total farm produce. The smallest farms of less than 10 acres had decreased in numbers by 11.3 percent in the previous decade, while the largest farms, with 2000 or more acres, had increased by 9.9 percent. T. Daniels & D. Bowers, Holding Our Ground 63–64 (1997). These trends are expected to continue, and raise questions about the purpose of agricultural preservation programs, which to some extent were adopted to protect the family farm.

3. *A market solution?* Classic market theorists make another argument against interventionist programs that seek to retard farmland conversion. They argue that competition for land in the open market will prevent the excessive withdrawal of farmland, presumably because the demand price for agricultural land will be sufficiently high to bid it away from potential urban users. This argument overlooks a set of externalities that occur when agricultural land is withdrawn from production. Fewer acres will be farmed, and maximizing production on a reduced agricultural acreage may lead to negative environmental impacts such as soil erosion and compaction, declining groundwater supplies, and a loss of wildlife habitat. It also overlooks the problem of distributional equity inherent in reliance on the mechanism of price. How likely is it that agricultural users will outbid urbanizers? Is there, in effect, a ceiling price on agricultural land, determined by how much less affluent consumers can afford to pay for the food grown on that land? How would an economist solve this problem?

Intergenerational problems are also disregarded in the classic market calculus. Because we value the consumption needs of future generations less than our own, we are not likely to take the agricultural land needs of future generations into account. Market economists sometimes concede this difficulty, but argue that technological innovation will compensate for declining agricultural resources. See Book Review, 48 J. Am. Planning A. 112 (1982).

2. PROGRAMS FOR THE PRESERVATION OF AGRICULTURAL LAND

The key issues in agricultural land preservation programs are determining what farmland will be subject to preservation programs and deciding on what programs to adopt. The decision on what farmland to preserve is made in urban growth boundaries, as in Oregon, that divide urban from agricultural land. The decision on what land to protect can be more difficult when there is no clearcut boundary decision.

Church, *Farmland Conversion: The View From 1986,* 1986 U. Ill. L. Rev. 521, notes that the uncertain rate of agricultural land conversion suggests a number of criteria for agricultural land preservation programs. They should concentrate on the direction rather than the quantity of conversion, should not provide cropland protection for only a temporary period because this will only divert conversion elsewhere, and should concentrate on areas not now under pressure. *Id.* at 559–60. Even without an urban growth boundary, of course, an agricultural land preservation program becomes a de facto growth control to the extent that it prohibits urban development on reserved land.

The federal government plays a limited role in the preservation of agricultural land. The following article describes state and local programs:

CORDES, TAKINGS, FAIRNESS AND FARMLAND PRESERVATION, 60 Ohio St. L.J. 1033, 1045–1049 (1999)

[*Property Tax Relief*]

One of the earliest and most common techniques for farmland preservation is state programs providing various types of tax-relief to owners of agricultural land. Today all fifty states have some form of tax relief provisions for agricultural land. The most common of these are preferential-assessment statutes, which assess land at a reduced value when used for agriculture, and deferred taxation programs, which provide lower assessment for farmland but require partial or total repayment of tax savings if the land is later converted to other uses. The obvious purpose of both types of legislation is to provide financial incentives for farmers to offset the financial pressures posed by conversion. [See, e.g., Ariz. Rev. Stat. Ann. §§ 42-12004, 42-15004; Iowa Code Ann. § 441.21; W. Va. Code § 11-1A-10. — Eds.]

[*Right-to-Farm Laws*]

A second type of farmland preservation program, also found in all fifty states, are right-to-farm laws. These statutes provide farmers protection against certain nuisance actions, typically in "coming to the nuisance" situations, where development has moved out to agricultural areas and created conflicting uses. Slightly less than half the states also provide protection against local government efforts to zone out existing agricultural uses, again typically in "coming to the nuisance" scenarios. They do not permit expansion of existing uses, but provide protection for the level of agricultural activity in existence when development arrived. These right-to-farm statutes do not guarantee preservation, but provide protection to farmers who desire to continue farming in the face of approaching development. [See, e.g., Ala. Code § 6-5-127; 740 Ill. Comp. Stat. Ann. §§ 70/1 to 5; Ind. Code Ann. § 34-1-52-4. — Eds.]

[*Agricultural Districting*]

A third and less common type of preservation program is agricultural districting. Currently recognized in approximately fifteen states, agricultural districting involves the voluntary creation of special agricultural districts, which require that the land be used for agricultural purposes. Districts are established for a limited period of time, such as five to ten years, which can then be renewed. In exchange for the requirement that the land stay agricultural, landowners receive a number of benefits, depending on the particular authorizing statute. Some are similar to benefits conferred by other statutes, such as differential tax assessments and right-to-farm provisions. Others are more unique to the district, and might include [purchase of development rights] provisions, limitations on the exercise of eminent domain against farm property, and restrictions on special assessments and government annexations. [See, e.g., Md. Code Ann., Agric. §§ 2-501 to 516; Minn. Stat. Ann. §§ 473 H.01-473 H.18; N.J. Stat. Ann. §§ 4:1C-1 to 55; Utah Code Ann. §§ 17-41-101 to 406. — Eds.]

. . . [T]he voluntary nature of all of the above programs significantly limits their effectiveness. Right-to-farm laws are only effective in preventing involuntary conversion against a landowner's wishes; they provide little basis to preserve farmland when a farmer desires to convert. Although tax incentives and agricultural districting can both provide some temporary relief from conversion pressures, neither is sufficient to offset the financial incentive of conversion when significant development pressure exists. Indeed, in some instances they simply help subsidize farmland while waiting for development. Such programs play an important role in a comprehensive preservation program, but by themselves will often be ineffective in establishing long-term farmland preservation.

[Agricultural Zoning]

For that reason, effective farmland preservation programs will need to restrict a landowner's ability to convert by relying on techniques that place decisionmaking authority elsewhere, most notably the government. The most common and least expensive way this can be done is by some type of public restriction placed on the land, typically in the form of agricultural zoning. Fourteen states currently have statutes which specifically address and authorize particular forms of "agricultural protection zoning," but as a practical matter agricultural zoning clearly falls within local government's general zoning power, even in the absence of a special statute. Because it can preclude conversion of farmland even when significant financial incentives exist, zoning is a widely and increasingly used farmland preservation technique at the local government level. [For statutes authorizing agricultural zoning see, e.g., Ky. Rev. Stat. Ann. § 100.187; Or. Rev. Stat. § 215.203 (1991 & Supp. 1998); Vt. Stat. Ann. tit. 24, §§ 4301-4496. — Eds.]

NOTES AND QUESTIONS

1. *Differential property tax assessment.* The following excerpt explains the way in which differential property tax assessments are handled under state legislation:

> Differential assessment laws are usually categorized as falling into one of three categories: preferential assessment, deferred taxation, and restrictive agreement. Preferential assessment laws produce an

abatement of taxes by authorizing assessors simply to assess eligible land on the basis of farm use value, rather than on market value. Deferred taxation laws add an additional feature and impose a sanction requiring owners of eligible land who convert it to non-eligible uses to pay some or all the taxes which they were excused from paying for a number of years prior to conversion. Restrictive agreement laws include both preferential assessment and, in all states except Vermont, a sanction in the form of a payment of back taxes. In addition, they require the owner to sign a contract spelling out his rights and duties, and preventing him from converting the land to an ineligible use for a specified term of years. [Keene, *Differential Assessment and the Preservation of Open Space,* 14 Urb. L. Ann. 11, 14 (1977).]

Critics claim that the differential tax programs simply make it easier for speculators to buy and hold farmland until it can be developed because the tax reduction reduces holding costs. The following commentary provides some insight into this problem:

Differential assessment operates primarily on one of the supply factors, by reducing the income squeeze which farmers in rural-urban fringe areas experience as a result of rising property taxes. It has a secondary impact on the demand side because it permits farmer-buyers, speculators and developers either to offer somewhat more for the land or to buy more land at the same price because their carrying costs are reduced. This latter effect is difficult to appraise, but it is likely to be marginal because the buyer will normally be simply exchanging tax costs on the land for interest costs on the money he has to borrow either to pay the higher price or to buy additional land. [Council on Environmental Quality, Untaxing Open Space 77-78 (1976).]

Differential property tax assessment increases the price of farmland because the lower tax is capitalized in the selling price, providing a windfall to farmland owners at the time the assessment goes into effect. The lower tax burden may not reduce the land costs for new farmers. Future farmer-buyers, as the excerpt indicates, may find reduced taxes offset by the higher carrying costs of purchasing farmland. The property tax reduction is lost when farmland is converted to urban use, depressing the price of farmland for urban development. Agricultural zoning may moderate these equity effects by keeping differentially taxed farmland in agricultural use. For additional discussion, see Property Tax Preferences for Agricultural Land. (N. Roberts & H. Brown eds., 1980).

Another criticism is that voluntary differential property tax assessment programs do not achieve the preservation of agricultural land in urbanizing areas close to cities. A study reported in Note, *Farmland and Open Space Preservation in Michigan: An Empirical Analysis,* 19 U. Mich. J.L. Reform 1107 (1986), reaches similar conclusions. The study found that the program was successful in enrolling a substantial amount of farm acreage in the state but was not successful in attracting enrollment near urban areas, where development pressures are the greatest. See also, Comment, *The State of Agricultural Land Preservation in California in 1997: Will the Agricultural Land*

Stewardship Program Solve the Problems Inherent in the Williamson Act?, 7 San Joaqin Agric. L. Rev. 135 (1998); *Evaluating the Effectiveness of Use-Value Programs,* 7 Prop. Tax J. 157 (1988) (program slowed rate of farm conversion in three of four Virginia counties studied).

2. *Agricultural districts.* A review of agricultural district programs in New York state shows they can be helpful in preserving farmland but have their limitations. White, *Beating Plowshares Into Townhomes: The Loss of Farmland and Strategies For Slowing Its Conversion to Nonagricultural Uses,* 28 Envtl. L. 113 (1998). As of 1996, 8.48 million acres of land were protected in 411 districts. About two-thirds of this acreage was being used for agricultural production. However, farmland loss in New York has been substantial, and over half of the state's agricultural production land is within developing areas. In addition, agricultural districts may not preserve agricultural land because counties can terminate them when agricultural production ceases, and the districts have very little effect on local zoning. As a result, farmland conversions may occur incrementally within a district, which will allow a county to terminate it under the law because its character has changed. See also Nolo, *The Stable Door is Open: New York's Statutes to Protect Farm Land,* 67 N.Y. St. B.J. 36 (1995). A Long Island county has supplemented the district program with a purchase of development rights program. These are discussed *infra.*

3. *The Federal Farmland Policy Protection Act.* In response to the agricultural conversion problems identified by the National Agricultural Lands Study, Congress enacted the Farmland Policy Protection Act, 7 U.S.C. §§ 4201–4209 (1981). The Department of Agriculture, in cooperation with other federal agencies, is to "develop criteria for identifying the effects of Federal programs on the conversion of farmland to nonagricultural uses." 7 U.S.C. § 4202(a). The Act then provides:

> Departments, agencies, independent commissions, and other units of the Federal Government shall use the criteria established under subsection (a) of this section, to identify the quantity of farmland actually converted by Federal programs, and to identify and take into account the adverse effects of Federal programs on the preservation of farmland; consider alternative actions, as appropriate, that could lessen such adverse effects; and assure that such Federal programs, to the extent practicable, are compatible with State, unit of local government, and private programs and policies to protect farmland. [7 U.S.C. § 4202(b).]

Federal agencies must review their policies and regulations to determine whether they are consistent with the Act and must develop "proposals for action" to bring their "programs, authorities, and administrative activities" into compliance with the Act. 7 U.S.C. § 4203.

All of this sounds quite formidable, but the Act expressly declares that it does "not authorize the Federal Government in any way to regulate the use of private or non-Federal land, or in any way affect the property rights of owners of such land." 7 U.S.C. § 4208(a). Regulations of the Department of Agriculture indicate the Act is not an absolute bar to development. 7 C.F.R. § 658.3(c). A federal agency need only take any adverse effects on farmland into account and develop alternative actions that could mitigate these effects. It is not required to disapprove a development if its effects on agricultural land are adverse. *Id.* See Johnson & Fogleman, *The Farmland Protection Policy Act: Stillbirth of a Policy?*, 1986 U. Ill. L. Rev. 563. But see *Eagle Found., Inc. v. Dole,* 813 F.2d 798 (7th Cir. 1987) (Act requires Secretary of Transportation to consider impact on agriculture when approving highway route).

4. *Sources.* For additional discussion of agricultural land preservation programs see Alterman, *The Challenge of Farmland Preservation: Lessons From a Six-Nation Comparison,* 63 J. Am. Plan. Ass'n 220 (1997); Duncan, *Agriculture as a Resource: Statewide Land Use Programs for the Preservation of Farmland,* 14 Ecology L.Q. 401 (1987); Pope, *A Survey of Governmental Response to the Farmland Crisis: States' Application of Agricultural Zoning,* 11 U. Ark. Little Rock L.J. 515 (1988–89).

A NOTE ON PURCHASE OF DEVELOPMENT RIGHTS AND EASEMENT PROGRAMS

How they work.—Professor Cordes' article briefly mentions the purchase of development rights as an agricultural preservation program. A number of states have purchase of development rights programs. See, e.g., Cal. Pub. Rev. Code §§ 10200 to 10277; Conn. Gen. Stat. Ann. §§ 22-26aa to 26jj; N.J. Stat. Ann. §§ 4:1C-1 to 55; Vt. Stat. Ann. tit. 24, §§ 4301 to 4495. In these programs, a government entity buys the development rights on agricultural land, and pays the difference between the land's value for development and its value when restricted to agricultural uses. Often the conveyance of a temporary or permanent easement restricting the development of the land is required in return for the development rights payment.

At the federal level, purchase of development rights programs are included in federal farm legislation. These programs are usually available to owners of agricultural land who agree to carry out conservation or preservation measures in compliance with approved plans. Examples are the Wetland Reserve Program, 16 U.S.C. §§ 3837 et seq., which provides funding for the conveyance of permanent or thirty-year easements and restoration cost agreements for wetlands protection. Another program, the Conservation Reserve Program, most commonly relies on contractual provisions rather than easements to protect environmentally sensitive land. 16 U.S.C. §§ 3831 et seq. Expenditures in the Conservation Reserve Program are in the billions, and have removed millions of acres of highly erodible and other sensitive cropland from production for ten-year periods. This program requires periodic renewal. For descriptions of these programs see Comment, *Biodiversity and Federal Land Ownership: Mapping A Strategy for the Future,* 25 Ecology L.Q. 229, 294–298 (1998).

For discussion of purchase of development rights and easement programs see Protecting the Land: Conservation Easements Past, Present and Future (J. Gustanski & R. Squires eds., 2000); Quinn, *Preserving Farmland With Conservation Easements: Public Benefit or Burden?,* 1992/1993 Ann. Surv. Am. L. 235 (1993). White, *Beating Plowshares Into Townhomes: The Loss of*

Farmland and Strategies for Slowing Its Conversion to Nonagricultural Uses, 28 Envtl. L. 113, 140–144 (1998), surveys a purchase of development rights program in Lancaster County, Pennsylvania, and notes the fairly high expense of preserving a limited number of acres. See also Thompson, *"Hybrid" Farmland Protection Programs: A New Paridigm for Growth Management,* 23 Wm. & Mary Envtl. L. & Pol'y Rev. 831 (1999) (discussing hybrid program in which purchase of development rights works in tandem with a transfer of development rights program to preserve agricultural land).

Purchase vs. regulation.—This casebook has concentrated on regulation as the method of implementing land use policies. The purchase of easements and development rights are an alternative. Which is preferable? Jordan, *Perpetual Conservation: Accomplishing the Goal Through Preemptive Federal Easement Programs*, 43 Case W. Res. L. Rev. 401, 435–438 (1993), argues there are problems with agricultural land use regulation. She claims that the productivity costs of regulation are difficult to assess because productivity varies annually, and because costs may also be offset by gains from regulation that protect the ecological quality of farms. She argues that farmers may not be able to pass the costs of regulation on to consumers because agricultural producers cannot set prices, which are determined by the marketing chain. She also claims that regulation impairs competition in agriculture. Farmers are not equally affected by regulation because the distribution of environmentally sensitive agricultural lands varies geographically. Are these appropriate factors to consider in a regulatory program?

Another commentator finds fault with purchase programs:

> However, there are several important drawbacks to such programs. First, from a regulatory standpoint, direct payments to landowners may establish a troublesome compensation precedent. Such a precedent, if firmly established, would create an atmosphere of entitlement and redefine the concept of property rights in a much more protective manner than is currently accepted. A political atmosphere that precluded regulatory mechanisms could negatively impact biodiversity preservation and other goals of current regulatory programs. Moreover, government resources are too limited to turn easement acquisitions and cooperative agreements into the sole methods of regulating land-use. [*Biodiversity and Federal Land Ownership, supra*, at 293.]

The author also claims that, at the federal level, the limited duration of some easements, the need to reauthorize annual payments, and high administration and monitoring costs also weaken these programs. Experience with a long-standing conservation easement program along the Great River Road in Wisconsin illustrates other problems. Ohm, *The Purchase of Scenic Easements and Wisconsin's Great River Road,* 66 J. Am. Plan. Ass'n 177 (2000). Landowners subject to easements have requested modifications as development pressures have increased, but the state agency requires landowners must buy back development rights before it will grant variances from easement restrictions. Determining the value of the buyback raises the same kind of compensation problems that arise in temporary takings cases. Termination of easement restrictions through legislation or because of changed conditions is another problem, although this has not occurred in Wisconsin.

A NOTE ON NONPOINT SOURCE AGRICULTURAL
WATER POLLUTION

Agricultural activities are not entirely beneficial. Runoff pollution from farming carries sediment, insecticides and other pollutants that can impair water quality. Runoff pollution from confined animal feedlots is another major contributor. Agricultural activities are known as nonpoint sources of water pollution because they are diffuse. Nonpoint source pollution from mining, forestry, urban development and stormwater is also a major problem, but nonpoint source pollution from agriculture is a major contributor in many parts of the country.

The federal role.—Federal agencies have been spending about $3 billion annually in 35 programs to address nonpoint source pollution. U.S. General Accounting Office, Federal Role in Addressing — and Contributing to — Nonpoint Source Pollution 25-42 (1999). Many of these programs provide grants to governments and private entities such as farmers to address land management practices.

The federal Clean Water Act, which is administered by the Environmental Protection Agency (EPA), contains requirements for state nonpoint pollution programs that apply to agricultural sources. A regional planning program contained in § 208, 33 U.S.C. § 1288, required regional planning agencies to develop nonpoint source controls, but funding for this program ended in 1980 and the voluntary programs adopted under this section were ineffective.

Amendments to the Act in 1987 added a new nonpoint source program in § 319, 33 U.S.C. § 1329. This program requires the states to prepare an assessment of their nonpoint sources that indicates controls needed to remedy nonpoint pollution problems and then develop a management program for these sources. EPA must approve the assessment but not the management program, which leaves the adoption of controls for nonpoint sources to the states. This was a deliberate congressional choice. Congress provides funding for the program, which has been used for a wide variety of activities such as education, technology transfer and demonstration projects, but critics claim the program has been ineffective. See Note, *Agriculture, Nonpoint Source Pollution, and Regulatory Control: The Clean Water Act's Bleak Present and Future,* 20 Harv. Envtl. L. Rev. 515 (1996) (not enough carrots and sticks, not enough funding, consequences of noncompliance insignificant).

The national Coastal Zone Management Act requires states to develop coastal nonpoint source pollution controls, but this Act has a requirement that state programs must contain "management measures for nonpoint source pollution to restore and protect coastal waters." 16 U.S.C. 1455b(a)(1). The program must serve as an expansion of programs adopted under § 319, and states must coordinate the program closely with state and local water quality programs.

State and local programs.—Nonpoint pollution is usually regulated through a variety of controls known as best management practices (BMPs), which are to be included in the management program required by the federal law. BMPs for agricultural nonpoint pollution include the provision of vegetative cover, crop production practices that reduce erosion, controls of nutrients and pesticides, and erosion and sedimentation controls. See V. Novotny & G. Chesters, Handbook of Nonpoint Pollution: Sources and Management ch. 11 (1981).

Federal assistance in sharing the costs of adopting best management practices is available through county soil and water conservation districts. The districts operate under statutes based on federally drafted model legislation that includes land use regulation authority in some states. For a comprehensive review of such legislation in the Midwest, see Massey, *Land Use Regulatory Power of Conservation Districts in the Midwestern States for Controlling Nonpoint Source Pollutants,* 33 Drake L. Rev. 35 (1983–84). Some of this legislation merely authorizes land use regulation, but in some states the districts are required to enact regulations adopted by a state agency. Mandatory regulations usually require soil erosion and sedimentation controls.

A takings claim against the application of soil erosion controls to farm land was rejected in *Woodbury County Soil Conserv. Dist. v. Ortner,* 279 N.W.2d 276 (Iowa 1979), *noted,* 65 Iowa L. Rev. 1035 (1980). The owner of the farm was required either to seed the land to permanent pasture or hay, or to terrace it. Noting that the impact of the regulation on the farming operations was conflicting, the court held:

> While this imposes an extra financial burden on defendants, it is one the state has a right to exact. The importance of soil conservation is illustrated by the state's willingness to pay three-fourths of the cost. . . . The argument that one must make substantial expenditures to comply with regulatory statutes does not raise constitutional barriers. [*Id.* at 279.]

How might the *Lucas* case affect this decision?

Sources.—For discussion of nonpoint pollution control programs see S. Jeer et al., Nonpoint Source Pollution: A Handbook for Local Governments, Am. Plan. Ass'n, Planning Advisory Serv. Rep. No. 476 (1997); Envtl. L. Inst., Enforceable State Mechanisms for the Control of Nonpoint Source Water Pollution (1997); Mandelker, *Controlling Nonpoint Source Water Pollution: Can It Be Done?,* 65 Chi.-Kent L. Rev. 479 (1990); Sivas, *Groundwater Pollution from Agricultural Activities: Policies for Protection,* 7 Stan. Envtl. L.J. 117 (1987–88).

3. AGRICULTURAL ZONING

Limitations in programs like preferential tax assessment and agricultural districts that rely on incentives to preserve farmland indicates that direct regulation through zoning may be necessary as an additional program. Professor Cordes describes how agricultural zoning works:

CORDES, TAKINGS, FAIRNESS AND FARMLAND PRESERVATION, 60 Ohio St. L.J. 1033, 1047–1048 (1999)

Fourteen states currently have statutes which specifically address and authorize particular forms of "agricultural protection zoning," but as a practical matter agricultural zoning clearly falls within local government's general zoning power, even in the absence of a special statute. Because it can preclude conversion of farmland even when significant financial incentives exist, zoning is a widely and increasingly used farmland preservation technique at the local government level. [For statutes authorizing agricultural zoning see, e.g., Ariz. Rev. Stat. Ann. § 9-462.01; Neb. Rev. Stat. §§ 19-903 to 916; Or. Rev. Stat. § 215.203. — Eds.]

Agricultural zoning can take several basic forms. On the one hand, local governments can impose what is often referred to as "exclusive agricultural zoning," which prohibits any use other than agricultural. Even this type of zoning will permit certain compatible or accessory buildings, such as barns, on the property; fundamentally, however, exclusive agricultural zoning is designed to limit the property to agricultural use only.

A more common approach to agricultural zoning is to permit non-farm uses, most notably residential, but in effect to establish agricultural restrictions through severe density limitations. This is often done through large minimum-lot size requirements, where the minimum lot size typically corresponds to "the minimum size of commercial farms . . . in the area." Thus, minimum lot sizes might range from one house per 40 acres to one house per 160 acres. The obvious effect is to limit the property to agricultural use. Agricultural zoning might also impose density restrictions but permit small lot "clustering" of actual development on the property. This permits a greater overall density level, such as one dwelling per ten acres, but leaves a significant area of land to be completely free for farming.

Whatever its form, agricultural zoning serves the purpose of significantly limiting development on farmland property, thus preserving the property's farmland status. Importantly, by placing public restrictions on the property the landowner is not free to sell the land for nonagricultural use when development pressure and attendant financial incentives become great. The result is to place the cost of preservation as reflected in diminution in land value on the restricted landowner.

GARDNER v. NEW JERSEY PINELANDS COMMISSION

125 N.J. 193, 593 A.2d 251 (1991)

The opinion of the Court was delivered by HANDLER, J.

The central issue in this case is whether the application of state regulations that limit the use of land in an environmentally-sensitive area constitutes an unconstitutional taking of private property. The regulations strictly limit residential development on such land and require that all remaining undeveloped acreage be subject to a recorded deed restriction limiting it to agriculture and related uses. A farmer contends that the application of this regulatory scheme to his farm effects a partial taking of his property without compensation.

Hobart Gardner lived and worked for almost seventy years on a 217-acre farm that had been owned by his family since 1902. The farm is located in Shamong Township, Burlington County, a part of the pinelands region subject to the regulations. Gardner, now deceased, and his son, who lives on the farm today, cultivated sod and grain. The farm includes a two-family house, barns, and out-buildings.. . . .

[Gardner brought an inverse condemnation action claiming the regulations an unlawful taking, and also claimed the regulations were an unlawful exaction and a denial of equal protection. All actions were brought under the New Jersey constitution. The trial court granted summary judgment for defendants on plaintiff's inverse condemnation claim and the appellate division affirmed.]

I

The value of the unique ecological, economic, and cultural features of the New Jersey Pine Barrens, or Pinelands, has been recognized for decades. Protection of the area, however, did not begin in earnest until Congress enacted the National Parks and Recreation Act of 1978, establishing over one-million acres as the Pinelands National Reserve. . . .

[The court described the Pinelands as a wilderness of pine-oak forests and wild and scenic rivers that overlies a major aquifer.] There has been very little development within the Pinelands; there are no major retail centers, and developed property comprises only one to two percent of the land in most areas. Agriculture in the Pinelands, especially the cultivation of cranberries and blueberries, is particularly important both nationally and locally.

In recent years, anxiety over the loss of farming and the fragile ecology of the Pinelands has produced increasingly stringent federal and state regulation. Both the federal and the implementing state legislation make clear that conservation, preservation, and protection are the principal ends of governmental regulation of land use in the Pinelands. . . .

[The court described the creation of the New Jersey Pinelands Commission and its mandate "to develop a 'comprehensive management plan' (CMP) to serve as the land-use blueprint for the region." Counties and municipalities are required to conform their master plans and zoning ordinances to the CMP and to have such plans and ordinances approved by the Commission. If plans and ordinances do not conform, the Commission will exercise direct control over local land use.]

Reflecting the aims of the federal and state statutes, the goals of the CMP include the "continuation and expansion of agricultural and horticultural uses." N.J.S.A. 13:18A-9(b)(3). The original CMP, adopted by the Commission in November 1980, stressed that agriculture contributes both to the unique characteristics of the Pinelands and to the environment "by creating open space, terrestrial and aquatic habitats, and wild-life feeding areas." It also stated that suburban development contributes to "an unfavorable economic environment for farmers through escalating taxes, enactment of inhibiting local ordinances, and increased trespassing and vandalism." Consequently, the original CMP called for several programs to accomplish the objective of agricultural preservation. It identified eight "Pinelands Management Areas" of varying ecological sensitivity, including a Preservation Area District, Forest Areas, Agricultural Production Areas, and Regional Growth Areas.

The original CMP restricted residential development in Agricultural Production Areas, reserving them primarily for farm and farm-related purposes.

Section 5-304 of the plan allowed residential units on lots with 3.2 acres as long as the applicant met certain stringent conditions. The original CMP also permitted ten-acre residential zoning, that is, one residential unit per ten acres, "provided that the dwelling unit is accessory to an active agricultural operation, and is intended for the use of the owners or employees of the agricultural operation."

The Commission further created a development-rights transfer program, under which it would award Pinelands Development Credits (PDCs) to landowners for recording permanent deed restrictions on their property limiting the land to specific uses set forth in the CMP. The PDC program seeks to channel development by permitting holders of PDCs to transfer them to owners who wish to increase densities in specially-designated Regional Growth Areas. PDCs may be sold privately at market prices; according to the Assistant Director for Development Review at the Commission, Burlington County has a PDC bank that routinely pays $10,000 per credit. A landowner in an Uplands Agricultural Production Area — the designation that apparently includes the Gardner farm — receives two PDCs per thirty-nine acres.

In the fall of 1987, Gardner explored the possibility of subdividing his property into fourteen to seventeen ten-acre "farmettes" in accordance with the CMP option allowing one farm-related residential unit per ten acres of land. Before the application was submitted, the Commission completed a periodic revision and amendment of the CMP, as required by the Act. The Commission determined, according to an affidavit submitted by its Assistant Director for Development Review, that the ten-acre farm option had deteriorated into a ten-acre subdivision requirement with no guarantee that the land actually would be used for farming, and had led in some situations "to the cessation of agricultural operations," "effectively eliminating existing agricultural uses, and threatening significant agricultural use of adjoining areas."

The revised CMP permits only three options for residential development of farmland in Agricultural Production Areas: (1) second-generation Pinelands residents or persons whose livelihood depends on traditional Pinelands economic activities may build homes on 3.2-acre lots; (2) a home may be constructed on a ten-acre lot for an operator or employee of the farm, but that option may be exercised only once every five years; or (3) homes may be constructed at a density of one unit per forty acres, but only if the residences are clustered on one-acre lots and the remaining thirty-nine acres allocated to each residence are permanently dedicated to agricultural use by a recorded deed restriction. The restriction of residential development to forty-acre tracts prompted the filing of Gardner's complaint.

II

Land use regulations span a wide spectrum, from conventional zoning, to particularized restrictions on property with special characteristics, [citing *Penn Central*]. The Pinelands Protection Act virtually fills the entire spectrum. It imposes comprehensive and complex regulatory land-use controls over an extensive geographic region with distinctive natural, economic, cultural, and historic characteristics. . . .

[The court held "the Pinelands scheme is fundamentally a regime of zoning," discussed federal takings law, and concluded:] Essentially, then, application of takings principles requires a fact-sensitive examination of the regulatory scheme, focusing on whether it substantially advances a legitimate public purpose and whether it excessively interferes with property rights and interests.

A

There is not the slightest quarrel that the Act substantially advances several interrelated legitimate and important public purposes. . . . [The court noted the legislative declaration of purpose to protect the Pinelands, and added that the comprehensive management plan] reiterates that purpose, recognizing especially the importance of agriculture because of its capacity to contribute to the special character of the Pinelands and to the environment "by creating open space, terrestrial and aquatic habitats, and wildlife feeding areas," as well as adding "to the cultural, historical, social, visual, and economic characteristics of the Pinelands." . . .

The preservation of agriculture and farmland constitutes a valid governmental goal. N.J. Const. art. VIII, § 1, para. 1(b) (lands used for agriculture or horticulture entitled to favorable tax treatment). The Act and the land-use regulations directly advance agricultural preservation, particularly through the limitation of residential development by large-tract requirements and complementary deed restrictions on undeveloped, nonresidential land. Cf. *Barancik v. County of Marin,* 872 F.2d 834, 837 (9th Cir. 1988), *cert. denied,* 493 U.S. 894 (1989) (upholding county plan that restricts housing density to one residence per sixty acres in a valley used for agriculture); *Gisler v. County of Madera,* 112 Cal. Rptr. 919 (Cal. App. 1974) (upholding ordinance providing for exclusive agricultural use and prohibiting sales of parcels less than eighteen acres); *Wilson v. County of McHenry,* 416 N.E.2d 426 (Ill. App. 1981) (upholding 160-acre minimum lot size in agricultural zones); *Codorus Township v. Rodgers,* 492 A.2d 73 (Pa. Commw. 1985) (upholding ordinance prohibiting division of productive farmland into tracts of less than fifty acres).

The Act further advances a valid public purpose by preventing or reducing harm to the public. That is exemplified most dramatically by its measures to safeguard the environment and protect the water supply by severely limiting development. The Legislature specifically determined that "pressures for residential, commercial and industrial development" and the "current pace of random and uncoordinated development" pose an "immediate threat" to a region of vital public importance. N.J.S.A. 13:18A-2.

The health, safety and morals or general welfare may be promoted by prohibiting certain uses of land.

That land itself is a diminishing resource cannot be overemphasized. Environmentally-sensitive land is all the more precious. Hence, a proposed development that may constitute only a small insult to the environment does not lessen the need to avoid such an offense. The cumulative detrimental impact of many small projects can be devastating. . . .

B

The critical remaining question is whether the regulations impair to an impermissible degree valuable property rights and interests. . . . A regulatory scheme will be upheld unless it denies "all practical use" of property, or "substantially destroys the beneficial use of private property," or does not allow an "adequate" or "just and reasonable" return on investment. [Citing cases] Significantly, our courts have applied the standard that focuses on the beneficial or economic uses allowed to a property owner in the context of particularized restraints designed to preserve the special status of distinctive property and sensitive environmental regions, such as the Pinelands.

Plaintiff acknowledges that preserving agriculture is a legitimate governmental objective that can be achieved through land-use regulation. He contends, nonetheless, that the land-use regulations, including the required deed restrictions of the revised CMP, interfere to an intolerable degree with his right and freedom to use and enjoy his farmland property. The response to that contention is found in *Penn Central*. [The court discussed *Penn Central*]. . . .

Plaintiff's claim fails under the *Penn Central* analysis. The CMP does not change or prohibit an existing use of the land when applied to plaintiff's farm. Like Penn Central, plaintiff may continue the existing, admittedly beneficial use of the property. Further, although whether Penn Central could again make use of all of its property, particularly the airspace over its terminal, was unclear, plaintiff may gainfully use all of his property, including the right to build five homes clustered together on the restricted land. There also is no showing that the economic impact of the regulations interferes with distinct investment-backed expectations. In addition, Penn Central could offset its loss by transferring valuable property rights to other properties, even if such transfers did not fully compensate it. Plaintiff possesses the similar right to offsetting benefits; it may receive Pinelands Development Credits in return for recording the deed restrictions. Finally, there is no invidious or arbitrary unfairness in the application of the regulatory scheme. Gardner's neighbors in Uplands Agricultural Areas are burdened by exactly the same restrictions, and other landowners in the Pinelands must abide by comparable regulations as part of an integrated comprehensive plan designed to benefit both the region and the public. . . .

In sum, plaintiff retains several viable, economically-beneficial uses of his land under the revised CMP. That those uses do not equal the former maximum value of the land in a less- or un-regulated state is not dispositive, for there exists no constitutional right to the most profitable use of property. We conclude that the restriction on lands to farmland and related uses, given the distinctive and special characteristics of the Pinelands, does not deprive plaintiff of the economic or beneficial use of all or most of his property, sufficiently diminish the value or profitability of his land, or otherwise interfere with his ownership interest to constitute a taking of property without just compensation.

III

Plaintiff contends that the regulations constitute a form of illegal "exaction," in effect requiring Pinelands farmers to pay the costs of zoning benefits for the public at large. . . .

On a conceptual level, applying the nexus requirement that governs responsibility for off-site improvements in connection with a single private development to a comprehensive environmental protection scheme that limits the use of land is difficult, if not impossible. Moreover, in the exactions cases, the development constitutes a lawful, permitted use; in that situation, the critical issue is the validity of imposing on the permissible development the costs for off-site improvements or for overcoming burdens occasioned by the development. In contrast, regulations that lawfully impose land-use constraints on an ecologically-sensitive area can validly disallow the development itself. If, in that context, the developer could not claim that the regulation effects an unlawful taking, it cannot claim that it constitutes an unlawful exaction.

Furthermore, unlike exactions for off-site improvements that unfairly or disproportionately penalize a developer and benefit the general public, the uniform land-use restrictions in the CMP are part of a comprehensive scheme. The CMP creates eight areas within the vast Pinelands region, prescribing different land uses according to the environmental, ecological, economic, and cultural characteristics of the respective areas. The CMP distributes and allocates the economic burdens among all property owners in order to promote the public good. Thus, plaintiff and his neighbors within the Uplands Agricultural Production Area are subject to identical development restrictions; that the impact of such a broad scheme may affect particular property differently does not impugn the scheme. Plaintiff and his neighbors, as well as the general public, also share the benefits from the preservation of the natural environment and the protection of the water supply. . . .

STEIN, J., concurring. [Omitted.]

NOTES AND QUESTIONS

1. *The constitutionality of agricultural zoning.* The *Gardner* decision is a ringing endorsement of agricultural zoning. Although certain features of the Pinelands program reinforced the zoning restrictions, such as the transfer of development rights program and the comprehensive plan and regulatory system, the decision should support any well-conceived agricultural zoning program. Note the citations to other cases upholding agricultural zoning. Although *Gardner* was decided before the Supreme Court's *Lucas* decision, it is consistent with that decision and indicates the New Jersey court would not have found that the agricultural zoning was a categorical per se taking.

Note how the court rejects the takings argument by holding that the landowner retained economically viable uses. This conclusion should always be possible when land restricted to agricultural use is agriculturally viable. Note also how the court handled the exactions argument. Did it adopt a version of the reciprocity of advantage rule toward the end of the opinion?

Landowners may also claim that agricultural zoning is an as-applied taking. A court could find a taking per se under the Supreme Court's *Lucas* decision

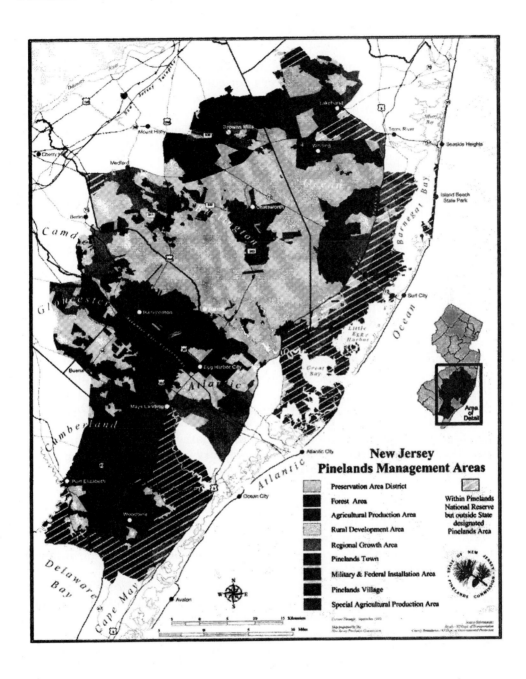

New Jersey
Pinelands Management Areas

Preservation Area District

Forest Area

Agricultural Production Area

Rural Development Area

Regional Growth Area

Pinelands Town

Military & Federal Installation Area

Pinelands Village

Special Agricultural Production Area

Within Pinelands
National Reserve
but outside State
designated
Pinelands Area

if the zoning left a specific property owner without an economically feasible use of the land. See *Racich v. County of Boone,* 625 N.E.2d 1095 (Ill. App. 1993); *City Nat'l Bank v. County of Kendall,* 489 N.E.2d 486 (Ill. App. 1986).

The Pinelands comprehensive plan was clearly an important factor in the *Gardner* decision. Similarly, Oregon's agricultural zoning program is carried out in the context of that state's comprehensive planning requirements. The American Planning Association's model planning legislation authorizes an extensive Agriculture and Forest Preservation Element in local comprehensive plans. American Planning Association, Legislative Guidebook Phases I & II, Interim Edition, § 7-212 (1998).

2. *Area-based allocation zoning.* This is an alternate form of agricultural zoning that allows landowners to build one dwelling for each specified unit of land that they own. The dwelling allowance can be fixed and will allow one dwelling unit for a specified number of acres. No dwelling units are allowed on remainders less than a specified number of acres. For example, the ordinance could allow one dwelling unit for each forty acres. Dwelling units must be built on small lots, usually less than three acres, so that the rest of the land is available for farm use. Other area-based allocation ordinances use a sliding scale in which the number of acres allowed usually decreases as farm size increases. Under this approach, smaller tracts are allowed more units on the theory that smaller acreage is more difficult to farm.

Defenders of area-based allocation zoning consider it a more legally defensible zoning technique that preserves farm land while allowing limited development, but the allocation system can trigger legal attacks. In *Hopewell Township Bd. of Supervisors v. Golla,* 452 A.2d 1337 (Pa. 1982), the Pennsylvania Supreme Court struck down an ordinance that allowed only five dwelling units on prime agricultural land whatever the size of the farm. It held the ordinance arbitrary and discriminatory because the dwelling cap had the effect of allowing a greater percentage of land for housing on smaller tracts. The court believed that a straight linear scale would not preserve agricultural land properly.

Three years later the court upheld a similar ordinance with a nonlinear sliding scale that also allowed more dwelling units on smaller parcels. The ordinance also imposed a maximum of two dwellings on prime farm land no matter what the size of the parcel, but the court upheld this limitation as part of the broader scheme. *Boundary Drive Assocs. v. Shrewsbury Township Bd. of Supervisors,* 491 A.2d 86 (Pa. 1985). Do you think that area-based allocation zoning really is more defensible legally than exclusive agricultural zoning? For discussion see Hartzell, *Agricultural and Rural Zoning in Pennsylvania— Can You Get There From Here?,* 10 Vill. Envtl. L.J. 245 (1999); Pivo, Small & Wolfe, *Rural Cluster Zoning: Survey and Guidelines,* Land Use L. & Zoning Dig., vol. 42, No.9, at 3 (1990).

3. *Oregon's Exclusive Farm Use (EFU) zoning.* Oregon has one of the most comprehensive agricultural land preservation programs in the country. State land use Goal 3 requires in part that agricultural lands "shall be preserved and maintained for farm use, consistent with existing and future needs for agricultural products . . . and open space," and includes factors local governments must consider before agricultural land can be converted to urbanizable land. This goal made mandatory a program for Exclusive Farm Use (EFU) Zones the legislature had authorized earlier. Land in EFU zones can be used only for farming. New farm and nonfarm dwellings are regulated, minimum lot sizes of 80 acres are mandatory, and land classified EFU must meet exacting statutory criteria before it can be reclassified. Land in EFU zones receives preferential property tax assessment. For the lot size requirement see Ore. Rev. Stat. § 215.780.

The EFU program is extensive. Half the private land in the state is in an EFU zone, but pressures on the program have limited its effectiveness. Urban growth boundary expansions consume EFU land. Another major threat is the extensive list of nonfarm uses permitted in EFU zones, which includes several types of dwelling units. See, e.g., Ore. Rev. Stat. § 215.203. Other uses include greyhound kennels, golf courses, and solid waste disposal sites.

The state Land Conservation and Development Commission has now adopted a rule that provides more stringent requirements for nonfarm uses than the statute does. The supreme court upheld the rule in *Lane County v. Land Conservation & Dev. Comm'n,* 942 P.2d 278 (1997). The court of appeals strengthened the minimum lot size requirement by holding that it prevented the division of farm land into parcels that violate the minimum. *Dorvinen v. Crook County,* 957 P.2d 180 (Ore. App. 1998). See also *Still v. Board of County Comm'rs,* 600 P.2d 433 (Ore. App. 1979) (nonfarm residential development not allowable in an EFU zone if it violates the state's statutory agricultural preservation policy, even if it is economically unfeasible to farm the land, and even if it does not interfere with farming).

Many of the problems in the Oregon program are created by urbanites who want the rural living style and who try to comply with EFU zoning by getting approval for spurious "martini" farms. The problem is difficult to solve because legislation must allow some flexibility, but this makes it difficult to control the program at the county level because it makes weak enforcement difficult to identify. What changes would you suggest in the Oregon program? For discussion see Rasche, *Protecting Agricultural Lands in Oregon: An Assessment of the Exclusive Farm Use Zone System,* 77 Or. L. Rev. 993 (1998); White, *supra,* at 118–125.

4. *Agricultural zoning in growth management programs.* As the Oregon program shows, growth management programs that restrict land from development can rely on agricultural zoning as a regulatory strategy. One problem is that agricultural lands near the urban edge will be under heavy pressure to develop, often at low densities. Reread the *Managing Growth* article in section C4, *supra.* How can agricultural zoning help deal with this problem?

A NOTE ON THE TRANSFER OF DEVELOPMENT RIGHTS AS A TECHNIQUE FOR PROTECTING AGRICULTURAL AND NATURAL RESOURCE AREAS

As the *Gardner* case indicates, transfer of development rights (TDR) programs can be a helpful supplement to agricultural land preservation programs. The objective is to avoid taking of property problems and achieve a fairer distribution of the burdens and benefits of regulation. In addition to the Pinelands, a highly successful TDR program that helps implement an agricultural preservation program is in effect in Montgomery County, Maryland, adjacent to Washington, D.C. The text that follows reviews these programs. Takings and other problems in TDR programs are discussed in the section on historic preservation in Chapter 8.

Montgomery County.—The county adopted a plan for the preservation of agriculture and rural open space land, which it implemented through a downzoning of 91,591 acres in an agricultural reserve area to a twenty-five-acre lot minimum from an original five-acre requirement. This minimum lot size was considered necessary to sustain farming on a cash crop basis. One development right for residential development can be transferred in the TDR program for every five acres of land, so that five times as much development can occur if development rights are transferred. The county has designated receiving sites for transferred development rights in nine communities.

Zoning at the receiving sites has two maximum densities, one for development without TDR and one for development in which transferred development rights are used. A developer is not guaranteed the maximum density, however, because the Planning Board can require a lower density if there are site constraints and environmental limitations. In addition, there is a minimum density of at least two-thirds of the allowable density increase. This requirement was adopted to prevent developers from building at reduced densities on large sites. Easements with land use restrictions must be placed on the transfer site. The county initially established but then terminated a TDR fund for buying development rights. As of 1994, the county had saved one-third of the land zoned as farmland through the TDR program. See R. Pruetz, Saved by Development 210–214 (1997).

The Pinelands.—The *Gardner* decision contains a brief description of the Pineland Development Credits (PDC) program. It was created for areas in the Pinelands that are covered by severe development restrictions. The number of PDCs allocated to a sending area depends on its development potential and the environmental sensitivity of the land. A New Jersey Pinelands Development Credit Bank now acts as a buyer of last resort and has been active in purchasing and holding PDCs. It may sell PDCs only if there is sufficient demand to justify a sale, and only if the sale would not impair the private sale of PDCs. Applications for PDC transfer are submitted to the Pinelands Commission first and then to the receiving community.

To be certain there would be enough land to receive transferred credits, the Pinelands plan designated receiving areas capable of receiving twice the number of PDCs available. In each receiving community the zoning code designates the extra density available when PDCs are used, and these are available as a matter of right. There has been substantial activity in this program, and as of December, 1994 there were 275 receiving site developments that had been built, approved or were pending approval. Modifications in the program have attempted to improve the transfer process and have made funding available for sewer improvements in receiving areas that can make higher densities possible. See Pruetz, *supra,* at 217–223.

NOTES AND QUESTIONS

The Montgomery County and Pinelands TDR programs are among the most successful in the country. What elements in these programs do you think contributed to their success?

1. *Montgomery County.* In *West Montgomery County Citizens Ass'n v. Maryland-Nat'l Capital Park & Planning Comm'n,* 522 A.2d 1328 (Md. 1987), the court invalidated the original Montgomery County TDR program. The court held that the zoning ordinance amendment adopting the TDR program improperly delegated unlimited authority concerning land to be designated as receiving parcels and the increased density to be assigned to these parcels to the planning board. The ordinance failed because the board did not have the necessary zoning authority to carry out this function:

> What appears to have been contemplated by the District Council in its attempts to implement the receiving area prong of the TDR concept is the creation of zoning subclassification systems within the designated single family zones. These subclassifications would contain the properties approved as TDR receiving areas, grouped according to the density level assigned. . . . Proper implementation of that structure would result in uniformity of zones, and informative identification of the precise classification of the property on the zoning map. [*Id.* at 1337.]

The system was subsequently amended to incorporate the district concept.

2. *The Pinelands.* A county development bank program in the Pinelands was upheld by a trial court in *Matlack v. Board of Chosen Freeholders,* 466 A.2d 83 (N.J.L. Div. 1983). The trial judge upheld the price set by the county for a PDC, and reviewed and approved the PDC program. For discussion, see Randle, *The National Reserve System and Transferable Development Rights: Is the New Jersey Pinelands Plan an Unconstitutional "Taking"?*, 10 B.C. Envtl. Aff. L. Rev. 183 (1982).

3. *Sources.* For additional discussion of the Montgomery County and Pinelands programs, see Johnston & Madison, *From Landmarks to Landscapes: A Review of Current Practice in the Transfer of Development Right,* 63 J. Am. Plan. Ass'n 365 (1997); Pizor, *Making TDR Work,* 52 J. Am. Plan. Ass'n 203 (1986). See also Juergensmeyer, Nichols & Leebrick, *Transferable Development Rights and Alternatives After Suitum,* 30 Urb. Law. 441 (1998).

4. RIGHT-TO-FARM LAWS

Right-to-farm laws, which have been adopted in all 50 states, are a popular attempt to preserve agricultural land by modifying the law of nuisance. The most popular version of these laws provides that a farming operation shall not be or become a public or private nuisance if it was not a nuisance at the time it began operation, even though conditions change in the surrounding area. Usually the agricultural use must have been in place for one year. Some laws protect the agricultural use even if it changes, but some remove the statutory protection once there is a change or expansion.

This type of law is an attempt to protect farming from disruptive nuisance suits filed by invading residential neighbors. It does so by legislating the "coming to the nuisance" rule that some courts apply in private nuisance suits. See Chapter 2. The rule means that a plaintiff may not successfully sue to prevent a nuisance if the nuisance was in existence when the plaintiff purchased her property. The effect of the statute is that a preexisting agricultural use acquires an implicit negative easement that prohibits development on surrounding property, because it prevents adjacent property owners suing to prohibit the use as an agricultural nuisance.

The following article explains other requirements in these laws and how they vary among the states:

> State RTF laws differ considerably on the activities that are covered by the statutory nuisance protection. While some laws specifically delineate coverage to farms and farming operations, other laws cover roadside markets and the manufacturing of animal feed. Generally, RTF laws cover the growing and harvesting of crops, the feeding, breeding, and management of livestock, and other agricultural and horticultural uses.

> Prerequisites concerning location and practices also restrict RTF laws' coverage of agricultural operations. Many RTF laws only apply to commercial activities so that hobbyists or non-farmers do not qualify for the nuisance protection. Some states require agricultural producers to be in an agricultural district before they can qualify for the nuisance protection. A law may require that the activity at issue be a sound agricultural practice before it qualifies for legal protection. Other provisions say that improper and negligent agricultural activities are not protected. . . .

> Provisions in most of the RTF laws do not affect other causes of action in tort or obviate the requirements of other statutes. Agricultural producers remain subject to zoning ordinances, building codes, and local and state laws. RTF laws do not impact environmental laws or pollution legislation, thus, producers must comply with legislation governing clean water and the disposal of animal manure. Further, the RTF laws do not offer protection to the operation or the operator if the activities or actions constitute negligence or trespass or violate other legal provisions. For causes of action for negligence, many of the RTF laws specifically provide that any negligent or improper operation at an agricultural facility is not protected. Other provisions in RTF laws may state that the laws do not affect any other right to sue for damages. [Centner, *Anti-Nuisance Legislation: Can the Derogation of Common-Law Nuisance Be a Taking?*, 30 Envtl. L. Rep. 10253, 10254 (2000).]

An initial question under right-to-farm laws is to determine when an agricultural activity is protected from nuisance litigation. The following case considers this question:

BUCHANAN v. SIMPLOT FEEDERS LIMITED PARTNERSHIP

134 Wash. 2d 673, 952 P.2d 610 (Wash. 1998)

DOLLIVER, J.—The certified question in this case stems from the Buchanans' federal lawsuit against Defendants Simplot Feeders Limited Partnership (Simplot) and IBP, Inc. (IBP). The lawsuit complains of manure dust, flies, and odors allegedly emanating from Defendants' feedlot and meat processing plant adjacent to the Buchanans' farm.

Our summary of the facts behind this lawsuit is based solely on the parties' motions and pleadings. The following summary should not be construed as an endorsement of any of the parties' factual claims. The Buchanans own and operate a 320-acre farm near Pasco, Washington. They have farmed and lived on the land since 1961. When they purchased the property, the adjacent properties were primarily used as rangeland. In approximately 1969, a small cattle feeding operation opened on land to the southeast of the Buchanan farm. The Buchanans allege Simplot purchased the feedlot in fall 1992. The Simplot operation now allegedly covers over 580 acres of pens and holds over 40,000 cows. The Buchanans allege Simplot's operation of the lot since 1992 has resulted in a significant increase of flies and foul and obnoxious odors.

The Buchanans allege a small meat processing plant began operation on property to the southeast of the Buchanan farm on or about 1970. They allege IBP purchased and has operated the facility since 1976. The Buchanans claim IBP has significantly expanded its meat processing and rendering plant since 1993, adding a new, large wastewater storage lagoon, a new, large storage pond for brine, and several new "cookers." The Buchanans allege this expansion has resulted in a significant increase in foul and obnoxious odors crossing onto the Buchanans' farm and residence.

The Buchanans sued Simplot and IBP in federal court, alleging nuisance, trespass and negligence. Under the trespass action, the Buchanans complained of flies and manure dust which were damaging the Buchanans' crops. Under the nuisance claim, they complained of the foul and obnoxious odors.

As to the nuisance claim, Simplot and IBP argued to the federal court that their operations were exempt from nuisance suits under RCW 7.48.305, a "right-to-farm" statute. RCW 7.48.305 declares certain agricultural activities do not constitute a nuisance under certain conditions.

The Buchanans disputed Defendants' reliance on RCW 7.48.305. They argued to the federal court that the statute cannot apply since the Buchanan farm allegedly was in operation before Defendants' activities. . . . [The federal court certified a question concerning an interpretation of the law, but the state court decided it must first determine whether the law was available as defense in this case.]

During the 1970s and early 1980s, every state except South Dakota enacted what are generally referred to as right-to-farm statutes. Right-to-farm statutes were created to address a growing concern that too much farmland was being overtaken by urban sprawl. As more urban dwellers moved into agricultural areas, nuisance lawsuits by those urbanites threatened the existence of many farms. Nuisance suits frustrated farming operations and encouraged farmers to sell to developers, continuing the cycle.

Most of the right-to-farm statutes adopted across the country codified the common law defense of "coming to the nuisance." Plaintiffs who purchase or improve property, after the establishment of a local nuisance activity, have "come to the nuisance." While this fact did not absolutely bar the plaintiff's nuisance action, it was one factor to be considered in whether to grant the plaintiff relief. Restatement (Second) of Torts sec. 840D (1977).

The Washington State Legislature embraced the right-to-farm issue in 1979, when it passed an act entitled "Agricultural Activities—Protection from Nuisance Lawsuits." Laws of 1979, ch. 122 (codified at RCW 7.48.300-.310 & .905). We will refer to this legislation as the Right-to-Farm Act, or the Act.
. . .

The Right to Farm Act was intended to protect existing farms from the pressures associated with urbanization. Urbanization is not at issue in this case. Instead, it is the Buchanan family farm that is being forced out by the expanding cattle feedlot and industrial-like beef processing facility. The Right to Farm Act neither expressly nor impliedly applies to this situation.

The Buchanans further argued RCW 7.48.305 applies only to the following situation:

> If a farm or agricultural activity pre-exists at a particular location and then a non-farm activity, such as a residential community, moves into the area, the non-farm activity is precluded from bringing an action for nuisance against the pre-existing farm.

Since the Buchanan farm allegedly does not constitute "encroaching urbanization," and since the Buchanans' farm was allegedly in operation before Defendants' activities giving rise to the nuisance, the Buchanans argued the Defendants should not be able to raise RCW 7.48.305 as a defense.

In their memoranda submitted to the federal court, Simplot and IBP argued they can rely on RCW 7.48.305. They claimed the only time a farm is not exempt from a nuisance suit under the statute is if the farm locates in preexisting urban areas. Simplot and IBP assert their activities were established before any surrounding nonagricultural activities, allowing them to rely on RCW 7.48.305 as a defense. The record shows no indication of any nonagricultural activities existing in the area. . . .

As written, RCW 7.48.305 is not very structured. The statute provides:

> Notwithstanding any other provision of this chapter, agricultural activities conducted on farmland and forest practices, if consistent with good agricultural and forest practices and established prior to surrounding nonagricultural and nonforestry activities, are presumed to be reasonable and shall not be found to constitute a nuisance unless the activity has a substantial adverse effect on the public health and safety.

> If those agricultural activities and forest practices are undertaken in conformity with all applicable laws and rules, the activities are

presumed to be good agricultural and forest practices not adversely affecting the public health and safety for purposes of this section and RCW 7.48.300. An agricultural activity that is in conformity with such laws and rules shall not be restricted as to the hours of the day or days of the week during which it may be conducted.

Nothing in this section shall affect or impair any right to sue for damages.

Three conditions can be derived from this statute. An agricultural activity is presumed to be reasonable and shall not constitute a nuisance when: (1) the activity does not have a substantial adverse effect on public health and safety; (2) the activity is consistent with good agricultural practices, laws, and rules; and (3) the activity was established prior to surrounding nonagricultural activities. The Legislature itself has read RCW 7.48.305 in a similar way. See 52d Wash. State Leg., 1991 Final Legislative Report 133 (describing the Right-to-Farm Act as allowing nuisance immunity when those three circumstances are present).

The third condition requires the challenged agricultural activity to have been established prior to surrounding nonagricultural activities before the nuisance exemption applies. This condition also suggests an established farm may not be able to institute a new or radically expanded "activity" and maintain nuisance immunity, because the language of the statute focuses on agricultural activity that has been established prior to the urban encroachment. Cf. *Payne v. Skaar,* 900 P.2d 1352, 1355 (Idaho 1995) (Idaho Right-to-Farm Act does not protect an established feedlot from nuisance suits if the nuisance arises because of expansion of the agricultural activity). This third condition presents an ambiguity within the structure of RCW 7.48.305: One would assume the statute's nuisance exemption is limited to situations where the nuisance suit arises *because of* the subsequent surrounding nonagricultural activities, since the Legislature expressly states the statute is designed to protect farms *"in urbanizing areas"* from nuisance suits. RCW 7.48.300 (emphasis added). The language of the statute, however, does not explicitly make this connection between the nuisance suit and the urbanization.

Since the statute contains an ambiguity, this court must look to legislative intent when applying the statute. When analyzing the ambiguous language in RCW 7.48.305 along with the Legislature's finding and purpose in RCW 7.48.300, it becomes clear the nuisance immunity should be allowed just in those cases where the nuisance suit arises because of urban encroachment into an established agricultural area.

Our ability to interpret and apply the Right-to-Farm Act is enhanced by the Legislature's express statement of findings and purpose. See RCW 7.48.300. The first sentence of the statute clearly connects the design of the Act to protecting farms in urbanizing areas:

> The legislature finds that agricultural activities conducted on farmland and forest practices in urbanizing areas are often subjected to nuisance lawsuits, and that such suits encourage and even force the premature removal of the lands from agricultural uses and timber production.

RCW 7.48.300. The second sentence of the statute, however, offers a more sweeping statement:

> It is therefore the purpose of RCW 7.48.300 through 7.48.310 and 7.48.905 to provide that agricultural activities conducted on farmland and forest practices be protected from nuisance lawsuits.

RCW 7.48.300. This second sentence broadly offers nuisance protection for all agricultural activities. In their arguments to the federal court, Defendants focused on this second sentence.

When determining the legislative intent of the nuisance exemption, we cannot blindly focus on the second sentence — we must read it in context with the first sentence. . . . The Legislature is concerned farmlands in urbanizing areas are prematurely being closed to agricultural use because of nuisance lawsuits in those urbanizing areas. This first sentence expresses the specific problem the Legislature intended to address. We read the second sentence in a narrow sense as responding to the specific problem of farming operations being threatened by urbanization.

The Legislature's stated purpose of the Right-to-Farm Act supports a narrow interpretation of RCW 7.48.305. A narrow reading is also supported by the legislative history of the statute, which is an important tool to ascertain intent. The Senate floor debate concerning passage of the Right-to-Farm Act clearly shows RCW 7.48.305 was intended to protect farms in urbanizing areas from nuisance suits.

Senator Rasmussen, who was the only senator to vote against passage of the law, posed several hypothetical situations in the attempt to criticize the bill. In defense of the bill, Senator Gaspard stated:

> We are really trying to state a policy that farm lands are disappearing from this Puget Sound region and those farm lands that have been established *before urban areas and suburban areas have surrounded them* are having a very difficult time staying where they are. I think that it is more a statement of policy by the state than anything else." 46th Wash. State Leg., Senate Journal 514 (1979) (emphasis added).

Senator Bottiger also stated:

> "An answer that Senator Gaspard didn't give, and that I think turns the case against Senator Rasmussen, is the question *who was there first.* If the dog kennel was there first and you chose to come with your subdivision and build all around it, then you bought with the dog kennel next door to you and you can't bring a nuisance action to get rid of them. . . ."

Id. at 515 (emphasis added). Senator Bottiger's statement supports finding Washington's Right-to-Farm Act codifies the coming to the nuisance defense, and it justifies a narrow application of the nuisance exemption. . . .

The express legislative purpose and the legislative history behind the Right-to-Farm Act support this court's reading the phrase "established prior to surrounding nonagricultural . . . activities" as including the premise that the only nuisance suits barred by RCW 7.48.305 are those which arise because of subsequent nonagricultural development and which are filed by one of those nonagricultural activities referenced in the language of the statute. This narrow reading of the ambiguous condition serves the narrowly tailored legislative intent of protecting farms "in urbanizing areas" from nuisance lawsuits which arise because of the encroaching urbanization.

Additionally, we find public policy considerations urge a narrow application of the Act. The protection afforded by the nuisance exemption is similar to a prescriptive easement. When a farm establishes a particular activity which potentially interferes with the use and enjoyment of adjoining land, and urban developments subsequently locate next to the farm, those developers presumably have notice of those "farm" activities. The Right-to-Farm Act gives the farm a quasi easement against the urban developments to continue those nuisance activities.

A farm obtains this quasi easement much more easily under the Act than if the farm was required to meet the strict requirements for a prescriptive easement. See *Bradley v. American Smelting & Refining Co.*, 709 P.2d 782 (Wash. 1985) (prescriptive easement claimant must show (1) open, notorious, uninterrupted use for 10 years which is (2) adverse to the title owner, and (3) the owner was aware of the adverse use and had the opportunity to enforce the owner's rights). The Right-to-Farm Act does not even set a minimum time period for which a farm activity must be established in order to be exempt from nuisance suits. Compare *Payne v. Skaar*, 900 P.2d 1352, 1355 (Idaho 1995) (Idaho Right-to-Farm Act requires the agricultural activity to be "in operation for more than one (1) year" before nuisance exemption applies); see also Neil D. Hamilton & David Bolte, *Nuisance Law and Livestock Production in the United States: A Fifty-State Analysis*, 10 J. Agric. Tax'n & L. 99, 101 (1988) (most right-to-farm statutes require the challenged agricultural activity predates changes in the neighborhood by at least one year). Just as prescriptive rights are difficult to obtain, and are not favored in law, we hold the nuisance protection afforded by the Right-to-Farm Act must be applied cautiously and narrowly. RCW 7.48.305 should not be read to insulate agricultural enterprises from nuisance actions brought by an agricultural or other rural plaintiff, especially if the plaintiff occupied the land before the nuisance activity was established. See Neil D. Hamilton, *Right-To-Farm Laws Revisited: Judicial Consideration of Agricultural Nuisance Protections*, 14 J. Agric. Tax'n & L. 195, 217 (1992) ("A right-to-farm law does not give farmers the power to inflict any hardship on neighbors just because an agricultural facility is involved, especially when the neighbors are there first.").

We have commented on the issue of who may raise RCW 7.48.305 as a defense only because we find no case law clarifying the ambiguous statute. We are unprepared to rule on the merits of Defendants' reliance on the statute in this case, nor does the certified question ask for such a ruling. Our analysis is solely intended to aid the federal court in deciding the question when the federal proceedings resume. . . .

ALEXANDER, J. (dissenting) [Omitted.]

NOTES AND QUESTIONS

1. *What does the right-to-farm law protect?* The *Simplon* case raises some important questions about the protection offered by a right-to-farm (RTF) law.

Do you agree with the holding that the law only protects against "urbanization"? If so, what is "urbanization"? What about a neighboring "cocktail farm"? Notice that the court does not really consider the factual situation in the case, which would have prevented the application of the statute because the defendant's use had changed.

The court takes the position that the application of the law must be based on fairness. Note, however, that the Washington law did not require a farm to be in existence for a designated period of time before it was protected from a nuisance suit. Is this a correct statement of how the law works? If so, do you agree that the law serves a proper purpose? Can you say the law is fair because the presence of agricultural uses in an area places any incoming land use on notice that a nuisance suit is not available to prohibit an agricultural use?

2. *Change and expansion.* Notice that the Washington law does not protect a farm use once it changes or expands. See also *Swedenberg v. Phillips,* 562 So.2d 170 (Ala. 1990) (law did not apply when plaintiffs were residing on their land before defendant's agricultural operations began); *Herrin v. Opatut,* 281 S.E.2d 275 (Ga. 1981) (law not a defense for changes in agricultural operations occurring after changes occurred in surrounding area). This is a serious limitation, because change and expansion occur in agricultural uses as they do in any use. This type of law will probably protect an agricultural use only for a limited period of time if change and expansion are inevitable. It may actually have a negative effect on agricultural activities if farmers avoid changes in operations because they know that such actions will remove the protection of the law. In this respect, RTF operates differently from traditional non-conforming use doctrine, discussed in Chapter 3, *supra,* where restrictive rules are intended to encourage a shift to a different use over time.

Some RTF laws allow expansion of an agricultural use. E.g., Or. Rev. Stat. § 30.936. A few offer some nuisance protection for limited changes. Fla. Stat. Ann. § 823.14(4) (changes allowed to comply with best management practices).

3. *Zoning.* Many of the RTF laws provide that zoning and other local ordinances cannot make a protected farm a nuisance. E.g., Ala. Code § 6-5-127(c). Some laws also preempt the application of zoning ordinances, but most do not. *Villari v. Zoning Bd. of Adjustment,* 649 A.2d 98 (N.J. App. Div. 1994). When zoning ordinances apply, they can limit the protection afforded by the RTF law. See *City of Troy v. Papadelis,* 572 N.W.2d 246 (Mich. App. 1997) (RTF law does not bar application of zoning ordinance to a residential parcel that had not established a prior nonconforming use); *Wellington Farms, Inc. v. Township of Silver Spring,* 679 A.2d 267 (Pa. Commw. 1996) (poultry slaughterhouse not protected by RTF law). What are the arguments pro and con for making zoning ordinances applicable?

4. *The takings issue.* The *Simplon* case referred to the protection provided by the RTF law as a quasi-easement. In *Bormann v. Board of Supervisors,* 584 N.W.2d 309 (Iowa 1998), *cert. denied,* 525 U.S. 1172 (1999), the court held the statutory immunity from nuisance suits conferred by an RTF law was a taking without compensation. It created an easement over the land of others that allowed protected agricultural uses to carry out activities that would otherwise be a nuisance. The court noted the *Lucas* per se takings rule, and held a nontrespassory invasion could be a per se taking. How is the statutory immunity's effect on property value any different from the effect of a zoning ordinance that restricts the use of land?

Unlike other RTF laws, the Iowa law conferred protection from nuisance suits even if the agricultural activity expanded, and did not require the protected use to follow sound agricultural practices. For a trial court case refusing to apply *Bormann* because the RTF law applied only when a state agency found that an agricultural practice is sound, see *Pure Air & Water, Inc. v. Davidsen,* No. 2690–97 (N.Y. Sup. Ct. May 25, 1999). For discussion of *Bormann* see Centner, *supra;* Pearson, *Immunities as Easements as "Takings": Bormann v. Board of Supervisors,* 48 Drake L. Rev. 53 (1999).

A Maine law authorizes the registry of farmland in local registers, and provides that "No owner of abutting land may undertake or allow any inconsistent development upon or use of land within 100 feet of properly registered farmland." The statute also prohibits the issuance of building permits for development prohibited under this section. Me. Rev. Stat. Ann. tit. 7, § 56. Any taking problems?

5. *Good or bad?* Whether RTF laws are good or bad social policy is contested. Farmers, of course, claim that these laws are essential to protect them from disruptive nuisance litigation. A student Note, *The Right to Farm: Hog-Tied and Nuisance-Bound,* 73 N.Y.U. L. Rev. 1694 (1998), takes a different position. The author argues that RTF laws assume that those who come to a nuisance are to blame for their troubles. He then argues that protected uses may be operators that do not contribute to the goals of RTF laws, that typical plaintiffs are not new residents in the area, and that the number of nuisance suits is exaggerated. Some protected agricultural uses can be environmental polluters, although some RTF statutes authorize nuisance actions against agricultural uses that pollute streams or other bodies of water that cross a plaintiff's property. E.g., Ark. Code Ann. § 2-4-106. Finally, the author notes the shift to larger farms, and claims that larger farm units can remedy nuisance-creating activity, and are able to provide buffers between their offensive land uses and neighbors because their farms are bigger.

How would you draft a right-to-farm law to deal with these criticisms? How would your evaluation of nuisance law, discussed in Chapter 2, affect your recommendations? What about bargaining between neighbors as an alternative, as recommended in the classic Coase article discussed in Chapter 1?

6. *Sources.* For additional discussion of RTF Laws see Burgess-Jackson, *The Ethics and Economics of Right-to-Farm Statutes,* 9 Harv. J.L. & Pub. Pol'y 481 (1986); Grossman & Fischer, *Protecting the Right to Farm: Statutory Limits on Nuisance Actions Against the Farmer,* 1983 Wis. L. Rev. 95; Hand, *Right-to-Farm Laws: Breaking New Ground in the Preservation of Farmland,* 45 U. Pitt. L. Rev. 289 (1984).

Chapter 8

AESTHETICS: DESIGN AND ADVERTISING CONTROLS AND HISTORIC PRESERVATION

The set of land use programs loosely defined as aesthetic is the focus of this chapter. They include the regulation of outdoor advertising, design review and design plans, and historic preservation. Each of these programs rests on aesthetic considerations because each is concerned with aesthetic appearance or visual character of structures, buildings or areas of a city. Aesthetic controls have spread rapidly in recent decades and have been accepted in court decisions. One important qualification is necessary. Free speech concerns affect the regulation of outdoor advertising and qualify the state case law that traditionally dominated this field.

A. AESTHETICS AS A REGULATORY PURPOSE

A majority of courts now recognize "aesthetics alone" as a proper regulatory purpose in land use controls, but it was not always that way. Judicial recognition of aesthetic regulation occurred in three stages. Courts early in the century held that aesthetics was not a proper basis for land use control. This early view, coming from a strict view of the police power, is illustrated by *City of Passaic v. Paterson Bill Posting, Adv. & Sign Painting Co.*, 62 A. 267 (N.J. 1905), invalidating a statute imposing setback and height restrictions on signs:

> Aesthetic considerations are a matter of luxury and indulgence rather than necessity, and it is necessity alone which justifies the exercise of the police power to take private property without compensation. [*Id.* at 268.]

Courts moved to an intermediate view in the second stage, which recognized that aesthetics alone was not enough to justify a land use regulation but that it was sufficient if supported by other factors. A Texas case upholding the regulation of junkyards illustrates this intermediate view:

> [L]eaving flammable materials in a collection of junked cars increases the possibility of fire. Wrecked cars have jagged edges of metal that are dangerous to playing children who have access to them. Leaving vehicles in a large unenclosed area facilitates theft. Because of these facts and because of the unsightliness of such operations wrecking yards must inevitably have a depreciating effect on the value of other property in the vicinity. [*City of Houston v. Johnny Frank's Auto Parts, Inc.*, 480 S.W.2d 774, 778 (Tex. Civ. App. 1972).]

This case illustrates the typical "other factors" recognized in the second stage that support a land use regulation that also is motivated by aesthetic concerns. Note the reliance on health and safety problems as well as the effect on property values. The economic side of aesthetic regulation was put even more forcefully in a leading billboard prohibition case, *United Adv. Corp. v. Borough of Metuchen,* 198 A.2d 447 (N.J. 1964):

> There are areas in which aesthetic and economics coalesce, areas in which a discordant sight is as hard an economic fact as an annoying odor or sound. We refer not to some sensitive or exquisite preference but to concepts of congruity held so widely that they are inseparable from the enjoyment and hence the value of property. [*Id.* at 449.]

The court added that even "the recognition of different residential districts" rests on aesthetic considerations. Why?

An important dictum by Justice Douglas in *Berman v. Parker,* 348 U.S. 26 (1954), accelerated the third and final stage in which courts accepted "aesthetics alone" as a regulatory justification. Justice Douglas said:

> [W]e emphasize what is not in dispute. . . . [T]his Court has recognized, in a number of settings, that States and cities may enact land-use restrictions or controls to enhance the quality of life by preserving the character and desirable aesthetic features of a city. . . . [*Id.* at 129.]

State v. Miller, 416 A.2d 821 (N.J. 1980), a sign ordinance case in which New Jersey moved to the third stage, illustrates the majority state court view on the acceptance of aesthetic purposes in land use control:

> Consideration of aesthetics in municipal land use planning is no longer a matter of luxury and indulgence. . . . The development and preservation of natural resources and clean salubrious neighborhoods contribute to psychological and emotional stability and well-being as well as stimulate a sense of civic pride. [*Id.* at 824.]

See also *Kucera v. Lizza,* 69 Cal. Rptr. 2d 582 (Cal. App. 1997) (upholding ordinance regulating tree growth to preserve views and sunlight).

Some courts continue to express doubts about aesthetic regulation. See *Sun Oil Co. v. City of Upper Arlington,* 379 N.E.2d 266 (Ohio App. 1977) (aesthetic considerations must be limited to situations where maintenance of a free-standing sign "would be patently offensive to [the] surrounding area rather than merely [a] matter of taste"); *White Adv. Metro, Inc. v. Zoning Hearing Bd.,* 453 A.2d 29 (Pa. Commw. 1982) (reversing denial of conditional use for advertising sign and holding that "purely aesthetic judgments are far too subjective to alone carry the burden of showing detriment to the public interest" though aesthetic goals were legitimate part of protection of public welfare).

NOTES AND QUESTIONS

1. *As-applied attacks.* Cases like *State v. Miller* make it clear that a facial attack on aesthetic regulation based on substantive due process objections will not stand, but as-applied attacks are still a possibility. A few cases have considered the as-applied problem. In *People v. Goodman,* 280 N.E.2d 139 (N.Y. 1972), the court upheld an ordinance placing restrictions on business signs on Fire Island, a congressionally designated seashore area. The court held that an ordinance regulating aesthetics must be reasonably related to community policy and must not be unduly oppressive. The regulatory setting is an important factor. "Indeed, regulation in the name of aesthetics must bear *substantially* on the economic, social and cultural patterns of the community or district." *Id.* at 141 (emphasis in original).

State v. Jones, 290 S.E.2d 675 (N.C. 1982), adopted a balancing test. The court stated that "[t]he test focuses on the reasonableness of the regulation by determining whether the aesthetic purpose to which the regulation is reasonably related outweighs the burdens imposed on the private property owner by the regulation." *Id.* at 681. Does this help?

2. *Doubts about the second stage?* Some commentators are critical of the intermediate "other factors" view of aesthetic regulation, noting that the other factors are simply derived from the aesthetic impact. See, e.g., Rowlett, *Aesthetic Regulation Under the Police Power: The New General Welfare and the Presumption of Constitutionality,* 34 Vand. L. Rev. 603 (1981). Rowlett notes that

> the alleged economic, health, or safety benefits are often nonexistent or at least unproven. Because land use restrictions are presumed constitutional . . ., the courts rarely require proof of the "nonaesthetic" economic, health, or safety justifications. [*Id.* at 607.]

She argues that this approach to aesthetic regulation allows the courts to escape critical analysis. What does this say about the holding in *Metuchen, supra?*

3. *A skeptical view.* Other commentators take the view that the aesthetic justification is really meaningless:

> [T]he words "beautiful as well as healthy" have become something of a talisman for courts forced to decide the validity of regulations that serve solely or predominantly aesthetic purposes. Rather than inquire into the nature of the individual and community interests at stake, courts have used the discretion that *Berman* [*v. Parker*] affords state and local governing bodies as a basis for upholding almost any aesthetic regulation. [Williams, *Subjectivity, Expression, and Privacy: Problems of Aesthetic Regulation,* 62 Minn. L. Rev. 1, 2 (1977).]

In the same vein, a provocative article by John Costonis rejects the visual beauty rationale and examines an alternative cultural stability rationale for aesthetic regulation. Costonis, *Law and Aesthetics: A Critique and a Reformulation of Policy,* 80 Mich. L. Rev. 355 (1980). See also J. Costonis, *Icons and Aliens* (1989).

4. *Void for vagueness.* Although most courts may now be willing to accept aesthetic controls as a valid regulatory purpose, subjectivity again becomes an issue when aesthetic regulations are challenged as unconstitutionally vague. Most courts reject vagueness claims to aesthetic regulation by relying on common meaning and understanding. See *Asselin v. Town of Conway,* 628 A.2d 247 (N.H. 1993) (ordinance prohibiting interior illumination of signs).

Some courts take a different view. In *City of Independence v. Richards,* 666 S.W.2d 1 (Mo. App. 1984), the court struck down an ordinance prohibiting the accumulation of refuse in an unsightly manner. Though conceding that regulation for aesthetic purposes was acceptable, the court held that "the ordinance term *unsightly* [does] not conjure a concept of visual incongruity so generally held that no further definition is required." Neither does the "momentary blight" of unsightly trash "concern the police power." *Id.* at 8. Accord *Morristown Rd. Assocs. v. Mayor & Common Council,* 394 A.2d 157 (N.J.L. Div. 1978) (design review ordinance requiring harmonious visual relationship held void for vagueness). Vagueness problems are more serious when aesthetic regulations are challenged under the free speech clause.

5. *Sources.* The literature on aesthetic regulation is substantial. The classic article is still Dukeminier, *Zoning for Aesthetic Objectives: A Reappraisal,* 20 Law & Contemp. Probs. 218 (1955). See also C. Duerksen & M. Goebel, *Aesthetics, Community Character, and the Law,* (Am. Plan. Ass'n, Planning Advisory Serv. Rep. No. 490, 1999); Karp, *The Evolving Meaning of Aesthetics in Land Use Controls,* 15 Colum. J. Envtl. L. 31 (1990); Susong & Pearlman, *Regulating Beauty: A Review of Recent Law Journal Literature,* 14 J. Plan. Lit. 637 (2000); Ziegler, *Visual Environment Regulation and Derivative Human Values: The Emerging Rational Basis for Modern Aesthetic Doctrine,* 9 Zoning & Plan. L. Rep. 17 (1986); Note, *You Can't Build That Here: The Constitutionality of Aesthetic Zoning and Architectural Review,* 58 Fordham L. Rev. 1013 (1990).

B. OUTDOOR ADVERTISING REGULATION

PROBLEM

You are the city attorney of Metro City, a city of 500,000 with the usual variety of commercial, industrial and residential areas. The city council has asked your opinion on a sign regulation ordinance it plans to adopt. The ordinance would prohibit all billboards, defined as signs not advertising goods sold or manufactured on the property. Signs would be allowed for on-premise businesses that advertise the business being conducted on the premises. Portable signs would be prohibited. The ordinance would also regulate the size, number and location of on-premise signs. For example, each business would be allowed only one pole or ground sign, and height and area limitations for these signs would vary depending on the zoning district in which the business is located. Political campaign signs would be allowed before, during and after an election. Is the ordinance constitutional under state law? Under the free speech clause of the federal constitution? How would you define the various signs the ordinance would regulate? If the ordinance is unconstitutional for any reason, what changes would you recommend to make it constitutional?

1. IN THE STATE COURTS

The business of outdoor advertising on a commercial basis dates from the 1880s. Under the common law, advertising posters considered offensive or dangerous were dealt with under the common law of nuisance. Prohibitory local ordinances became common from the 1890s onward, when the large-scale commercial promotion of billboard advertising became so aggressive and its methods so crude that municipal regulation was considered necessary. In the early years, the courts were generally hostile to these prohibitory ordinances and declared many of them unconstitutional. These judicial attitudes reflected the early hostility to aesthetic regulation.

The decision generally credited with having the greatest influence in changing judicial attitudes toward billboard regulations is *St. Louis Gunning Adv. Co. v. City of St. Louis,* 137 S.W. 929 (Mo. 1911), *appeal dismissed,* 231 U.S. 761 (1913). In an opinion covering 124 pages, the Missouri court discussed the evolution of the law up to that time and sustained a municipal ordinance regulating the size, height, and location of billboards. In an oft-quoted passage, the court said:

> The signboards upon which this class of advertisements are displayed are constant menaces to the public safety and welfare of the city; they endanger the public health, promote immorality, constitute hiding places and retreats for criminals and all classes of miscreants. They are also inartistic and unsightly.
>
> In cases of fire they often cause their spread and constitute barriers against their extinction; and in cases of high wind, their temporary character, frail structure and broad surface, render them liable to be blown down and to fall upon and injure those who may happen to be in their vicinity. The evidence shows and common observation teaches us that the ground in the rear thereof is being constantly used as privies and the dumping ground for all kinds of waste and deleterious matters, and thereby creating public nuisances and jeopardizing public health; the evidence also shows that behind these obstructions the lowest form of prostitution and other acts of immorality are frequently carried on, almost under public gaze; they offer shelter and concealment for the criminal while lying in wait for his victim; and last, but not least, they obstruct the light, sunshine and air, which are so conducive to health and comfort. [*Id.* at 942.]

Although the Missouri court, in the passage set out above, expressly mentioned the fact that signboards are inartistic and unsightly, it made clear at a later point in its opinion that, in its view, aesthetic considerations alone were insufficient to justify the regulatory ordinance. *Id.* at 961. Commentators have tended to deride the public safety arguments in the *Gunning* case, and certainly the modern billboard, placed high above the ground and made of sturdy and noncombustible materials, does not match the court's description. But this line of argument can be carried too far. The day after one of the editors made this argument to a class in land use law, a young telephone operator was raped and stabbed behind a billboard in the central area of the city in which the class was held.

Modern courts are usually willing to uphold billboard prohibitions, although other non-aesthetic factors often help provide the basis for the decision. One of the best of these cases is the California Supreme Court decision in *Metromedia, Inc. v. City of San Diego,* which is reproduced next. This case was appealed to the U.S. Supreme Court, which reversed on free speech grounds the state court found unpersuasive. The California court's holding on the aesthetic regulation issues is still important, and provides a basis for understanding the free speech implications of billboard control considered in the next section.

A note on sign types.—When reading the cases and materials that follow, it is important to understand the differences between different types of signs. One distinction is between off-premise signs, usually called billboards, which are not located on the site of a business, and on-premise signs, which are located at the business site. Another distinction is between signs attached to walls and signs located on the ground, usually known as pole or ground signs, which may be either off-or on-premise. Then there are signs displayed for temporary periods of time, such as those displayed during political campaigns. Portable signs are signs that are not permanent. Sign regulations typically regulate all of these sign types, though we will see that free speech law has eroded some of these categories and has made others questionable.

METROMEDIA, INC. v. CITY OF SAN DIEGO

26 Cal. 3d 848, 610 P.2d 407, 164 Cal. Rptr. 510 (1980),
rev'd on other grounds, 453 U.S. 490 (1981)

TOBRINER, JUSTICE:

The City of San Diego enacted an ordinance which bans all off-site advertising billboards and requires the removal of existing billboards following expiration of an amortization period. Plaintiffs, owners of billboards affected by the ordinance, sued to enjoin its enforcement. Upon motion for summary judgment, the superior court adjudged the ordinance unconstitutional, and issued the injunction as prayed.

We reject the superior court's conclusion that the ordinance exceeded the city's authority under the police power. We hold that the achievement of the purposes recited in the ordinance — eliminating traffic hazards and improving the appearance of the city — represent proper objectives for the exercise of the city's police power, and that the present ordinance bears a reasonable relationship to those objectives. [The court held that the ordinance did not violate the free speech clause, but that it was preempted by state law to the extent it required the uncompensated removal of nonconforming billboards protected by the federal law. The court remanded for a determination of which billboards fell within the preemptive scope of the state law.]. . . .

1. Summary of proceedings in the trial court.

The present case concerns the constitutionality of San Diego Ordinance No. 10795 (New Series), enacted March 14, 1972. With limited exceptions specified in the footnote[1] the ordinance as subsequently amended prohibits all off-site

---

[1] The original ordinance permitted the following off-site signs: Signs maintained in the discharge of a governmental function; bench advertising signs; commemorative plaques, religious symbols, holiday decorations and similar such signs; signs located within shopping malls not visible from any point on the boundary of the premises; signs designating premises for sale, rent or lease; public service signs depicting time, temperature or news; signs on vehicles conforming to city regulations; and temporary off-premises subdivision directional signs.

"outdoor advertising display signs."[2] Off-site signs are defined as those which do not identify a use, facility or service located on the premises or a product which is produced, sold or manufactured on the premises. All existing signs which do not conform to the requirements of the ordinance must be removed following expiration of an amortization period, ranging from 90 days to 4 years depending upon the location and depreciated value of the sign.

Plaintiffs, Metromedia, Inc., and Pacific Outdoor Advertising Co., Inc., are engaged in the outdoor advertising business and own a substantial number of off-site billboards subject to removal under Ordinance No. 10795. Plaintiffs filed separate actions against the city, attacking the validity of the ordinance. The actions were consolidated by stipulation. After extensive interrogatories and requests for admission had been answered all parties moved for summary judgment.

To facilitate the determination of the motion for summary judgment the parties entered into a stipulation of facts. The following portions of that stipulation are particularly pertinent to the present appeal: "2. If enforced as written Ordinance No. 10795 will eliminate the outdoor advertising business in the City of San Diego. . . . 13. Each of the plaintiffs are the owners of a substantial number of outdoor advertising displays (approximately 500 to 800) in the City of San Diego. . . . 17. The displays have varying values depending upon their size, nature and location. 18. Each of the displays has a fair market value as a part of an income-producing system of between $2,500 and $25,000. 19. Each display has a remaining useful income-producing life in excess of 25 years. 20. All of the signs owned by plaintiffs in the City of San Diego are located in areas zoned for commercial and industrial purposes. . . . 28. Outdoor advertising increases the sales of products and produces numerous direct and indirect benefits to the public. Valuable commercial, political and social information is communicated to the public through the use of outdoor advertising. Many businesses and politicians and other persons rely upon outdoor advertising because other forms of advertising are insufficient, inappropriate and prohibitively expensive. . . . 31. Many of plaintiffs' signs are within 660 feet and others are within 500 feet of interstate or federal primary highways. . . . 34. The amortization provisions of Ordinance No. 10795 have no reasonable relationship to the fair market value, useful life or income generated by the signs and were not designed to have such a relationship."

As originally enacted, the ordinance contained no exception for political signs. On October 19, 1977, the city counsel amended the ordinance to permit "Temporary political campaign signs, including their supporting structures, which are erected or maintained for no longer than 90 days and which are removed within 10 days after the election to which they pertain." (Ord. No. 12189 (New Series).) This amendment may have been prompted by the decision of the Ninth Circuit in Baldwin v. Redwood City (1976) 540 F.2d 1360, in which that court held an ordinance regulating temporary signs to be an unconstitutional restriction upon political speech.

[2] [The court noted that the ordinance did not define the term "outdoor advertising display signs," and that the exceptions did not exclude many "noncommercial signs that present no significant aesthetic blight or traffic hazard." That failure, and the failure to define the signs that were prohibited, might permit a construction of the ordinance to prohibit noncommercial signs such as political signs. To avoid that danger, which would create a "risk of constitutional overbreadth," the court adopted a narrow construction limiting the ordinance to "the intendment of the enactment," which was to prohibit commercial signs only.]

The trial court filed a memorandum opinion stating that the ordinance was invalid as an unreasonable exercise of police power and an abridgment of First Amendment guaranties of freedom of speech and press. The court then entered judgment enjoining enforcement of the ordinance. The city appeals from that judgment.

2. The summary judgment cannot be sustained on the ground that the San Diego ordinance exceeds the city's authority under the police power.

The San Diego ordinance, as we shall explain, represents a proper application of municipal authority over zoning and land use for the purpose of promoting the public safety and welfare. The ordinance recites the purposes for which it was enacted, including the elimination of traffic hazards brought about by distracting advertising displays and the improvement of the appearance of the city. Since these goals are proper objectives for the exercise of the city's police power, the city council, asserting its legislative judgment, could reasonably believe the instant ordinance would further those objectives.

Plaintiffs cannot question that a city may enact ordinances under the police power to eliminate traffic hazards. They maintain, however, that the city failed to prove in opposition to plaintiffs' motion for summary judgment that the ordinance reasonably relates to that objective. We could reject plaintiffs' argument on the simple ground that plaintiffs, as the parties asserting the unconstitutionality of the ordinance, bear the burden of proof and cannot rely upon the city's failure of proof. To avoid unnecessary litigation upon remand of this cause, however, we have probed plaintiffs' broader argument: We hold as a matter of law that an ordinance which eliminates billboards designed to be viewed from streets and highways reasonably relates to traffic safety.

Billboards are intended to, and undoubtedly do, divert a driver's attention from the roadway. Whether this distracting effect contributes to traffic accidents invokes an issue of continuing controversy.[7] But as the New York Court of Appeals pointed out, "mere disagreement" as to "whether billboards or other advertising devices . . . constitute a traffic hazard . . . may not cast doubt on the statute's validity. Matters such as these are reserved for legislative judgment, and the legislative determination, here expressly announced, will not be disturbed unless manifestly unreasonable." (*New York State Thruway Auth. v. Ashley Motor Ct.* (1961), 176 N.E.2d 566.) Many other decisions have upheld billboard ordinances on the ground that such ordinances reasonably relate to traffic safety; we cannot find it manifestly unreasonable for the San Diego City Council to reach the same conclusion. As the Kentucky Supreme Court said in *Moore v. Ward* (1964) 377 S.W.2d 881, 884: "Even assuming [plaintiffs] could produce substantial evidence that billboard signs

---

[7] "No matter what one's position on the sign and safety issue one can find the study to support it . . . . [D]espite the insights provided by statistical analyses, the case for the hazards of private signs rests largely upon common sense and the informed judgments of traffic engineers and other experts. The arguments are complex and sometimes highly technical, but on the whole, the courts are increasingly likely to conclude that regulation of private signs may be reasonably expected to enhance highway safety." (Dowds, Private Signs and Public Interests, in 1974 Institute on Planning, Zoning and Eminent Domain, p. 231.)

do not adversely affect traffic safety, . . . the question involves so many intangible factors as to make debatable the issue of what the facts establish. Where this is so, it is not within the province of courts to hold a statute invalid by reaching a conclusion contrary to that of the legislature."

We further hold that even if, as plaintiffs maintain, the principal purpose of the ordinance is not to promote traffic safety but to improve the appearance of the community, such a purpose falls within the city's authority under the police power. . . .

Because this state relies on its scenery to attract tourists and commerce, aesthetic considerations assume economic value. Consequently any distinction between aesthetic and economic grounds as a justification for billboard regulation must fail. "Today, economic and aesthetic considerations together constitute the nearly inseparable warp and woof of the fabric upon which the modern city must design its future."

[A contrary] holding also conflicts with present concepts of the police power. Most jurisdictions now concur with the broad declaration of Justice Douglas in *Berman v. Parker* (1954) 348 U.S. 26: "The concept of the public welfare is broad and inclusive. [Citation.] The values it represents are spiritual as well as physical, aesthetic as well as monetary. It is within the power of the legislature to determine that the community should be beautiful as well as healthy, spacious as well as clean, well-balanced as well as carefully pa-trolled." (*Id.* at p. 33.) Although Justice Douglas tendered this description in a case upholding the exercise of the power of eminent domain for community redevelopment, it has since been recognized as a correct description of the authority of a state or city to enact legislation under the police power. As the Hawaii Supreme Court succinctly stated: "We accept beauty as a proper community objective, attainable through use of the police power." (*State v. Diamond Motors, Inc.* (1967), 429 P.2d 825, 827.)

Present day city planning would be virtually impossible under a doctrine which denied a city authority to legislate for aesthetic purposes under the police power. Virtually every city in this state has enacted zoning ordinances for the purpose of improving the appearance of the urban environment and the quality of metropolitan life. Many municipalities engage in projects of one type or another designed to beautify their communities. . . . But as the New York Court of Appeals pointed out, "Once it be conceded that aesthetics is a valid subject of legislative concern the conclusion seems inescapable that reasonable legislation designed to promote that end is a valid and permissible exercise of the police power. . . . [W]hether such a statute or ordinance should be voided should depend upon whether the restriction was 'an arbitrary and irrational method of achieving an attractive . . . community — and *not* upon whether the objectives were primarily aesthetic.'" [*People v. Stover,* 191 N.E.2d 272 (N.Y. 1963).]

In a subsequent decision, the New York Court of Appeals confirmed that aesthetic considerations may justify the exercise of the police power to ban all off-site billboards in a community. *Suffolk Outdoor Adv. Co., Inc. v. Hulse* (1977), 373 N.E.2d 263, *app. dism.,* 439 U.S. 808. "It cannot be seriously argued," the New York court said, "that a prohibition of this nature is not reasonably related to improving the aesthetics of the community." (373 N.E.2d at p. 266.) The fact that the ordinance bans billboards in commercial and industrial areas, and that it permits on-site signs, does not demonstrate that the ordinance as a whole lacks a reasonable relationship to improving community appearance. "[T]he notion that an extensively commercial or industrial area will be made more attractive by the absence of billboards is open to debate. Since the issue is debatable, however, the modern judicial presumption in favor of legislation [requires the court] to uphold the ordinance as a rational means of enforcing the legislative purpose of preserving aesthetics." (Lucking, *The Regulation of Outdoor Advertising: Past, Present and Future* (1977) 6 Environmental Aff. 179, 188.)

If the San Diego ordinance reasonably relates to the public safety and welfare, it should logically follow that the ordinance represents a valid exercise of the police power. Plaintiffs contend, however, that the police power is subject to an additional limiting doctrine: That regardless of the reasonableness of the act in relation to the public health, safety, morals and welfare[,] the police power can never be employed to prohibit completely a business not found to be a public nuisance. . . .

For the reasons we shall offer, however, we believe that this doctrine, too, conflicts with reality and with current views of the police power. The distinction between prohibition and regulation in this case is one of words and not substance. "[E]very regulation necessarily speaks as a prohibition." *Goldblatt v. Hempstead* (1962) 369 U.S. 590, 592.) In the present case, for example, plaintiffs describe the ordinance as a *prohibition of off-site advertising,* while the city describes it as a *regulation of advertising,* one which limits advertising to on-site signs. Surely the validity of the ordinance does not depend on the court's choice between such verbal formulas.

Rather than strive to develop a logical distinction between "regulation" and "prohibition," and to find themselves embroiled in language rather than fact, courts of other jurisdictions in recent decisions have held that a community can entirely prohibit off-site advertising. These decisions fall within the general principle that a community may exclude any or all commercial uses if such exclusion reasonably relates to the public health, safety, morals or general welfare. As the Oregon Supreme Court explained in *Oregon City v. Hartke,* 400 P.2d 255, "[I]t is within the police power of the city wholly to exclude a particular use if there is a rational basis for the exclusion. . . . It is not irrational for those who must live in a community from day to day to plan their physical surroundings in such a way that unsightliness is minimized. The prevention of unsightliness by wholly precluding a particular use within the city may inhibit the economic growth of the city or frustrate the desire of someone who wishes to make the proscribed use, but the inhabitants of the city have the right to forego the economic gain and the person whose business plans are frustrated is not entitled to have his interest weighed more heavily than the predominant interest of others in the community." (400 P.2d p. 263.)

Plaintiffs stress that most of the cases upholding a community ban on billboards or other commercial uses have involved small, predominantly residential, towns or rural localities. Recently, however, the Massachusetts Supreme Judicial Court upheld an ordinance similar to the one at issue here involving a total prohibition of billboards in a densely populated town with a sizable business and industrial district. (*John Donnelly & Sons, Inc. v. Outdoor Advertising Bd.,* 339 N.E.2d 709.) The court there stated that "We believe that it is within the scope of the police power for the town to decide that its total living area should be improved so as to be more attractive to both its residents and visitors. Whether an area is urban, suburban or rural should not be determinative of whether the residents are entitled to preserve and enhance their environment. Urban residents are not immune to ugliness." (P. 720.) . . .

Nor do we perceive how we could rationally establish a rule that a city's police power diminishes as its population grows, and that once it reaches some unspecified size it no longer has the power to prohibit billboards. San Diego, for example, has already prohibited billboards within *97 percent of its limits* — a region which in area and population far surpasses most California cities. Plaintiffs claim that a ban covering 97 percent of the city is a "regulation," while the extension of that ban to the remaining 3 percent of the city is a "prohibition," but such sophistry is a mere play upon words.

Thus the validity of Ordinance No. 10795 under the police power does not turn on its regulatory or prohibitory character, nor upon the size of the city which enacted it, but solely on whether it reasonably relates to the public safety and welfare. As we have explained, the ordinance recites that it was enacted to eliminate traffic hazards, improve the appearance of the community, and thereby protect property values. The asserted goals are proper objectives under the police power, and plaintiffs have failed to prove that the ordinance lacks a reasonable relationship to the achievement of those goals. We conclude that the summary judgment cannot be sustained on the ground that the ordinance exceeds the city's authority under the police power. . . .

To hold that a city cannot prohibit off-site commercial billboards for the purpose of protecting and preserving the beauty of the environment is to succumb to a bleak materialism. We conclude with the pungent words of Ogden Nash:

"I think that I shall never see
"A billboard lovely as a tree.
"Indeed, unless the billboards fall,
"I'll never see a tree at all."

The Judgment is reversed.

CLARK, JUSTICE, dissenting:

[Omitted. Justice Clark would have held that the ordinance "unconstitutionally prohibits speech protected by the First Amendment."]

NOTES AND QUESTIONS

1. Is the principal case an acceptance of the "aesthetics alone" rule of aesthetic regulation or does it require the presence of "other factors"? What factors does the court accept, or does the court simply decide the case with presumptions? All courts have accepted a traffic safety improvement justification despite the conflicting evidence on the effect of signs on traffic safety.

In *Opinion of the Justices,* 169 A.2d 762 (N.H. 1961), the court said that signs "may reasonably be found to increase the danger of accidents, and their regulation along highways clearly falls within the police power." *Id.* at 764.

What about tourism? Why does this factor justify a billboard prohibition? The California court quotes the New York *Stover* decision's dictum that an arbitrary and irrational method of achieving an attractive community would be unconstitutional. Can you give an example? What do you think of the court's rejection of the *prohibit* vs. *permit* distinction?

2. *The regulatory setting of billboard controls.* Exclusions from residential areas have not been a problem. See *Naegele Outdoor Adv. Co. v. Village of Minnetonka,* 162 N.W.2d 206 (Minn. 1968). The total exclusion of commercial billboards from a community is more problematic when the community has commercial and industrial areas to which the exclusion applies. In *United Adv. Corp. v. Borough of Metuchen,* 198 A.2d 447 (N.J. 1964), the court upheld a total community exclusion as applied to billboards in non-residential areas. It stressed that Metuchen was a small and primarily residential community and that the purpose of the regulation was "to achieve the maximum degree of compatibility with the residential areas." Accord *John Donnelly & Sons v. Outdoor Adv. Bd.,* discussed in the principal case.

For a contrary view, see *Combined Commun. Corp. v. City & County of Denver,* 542 P.2d 79 (Colo. 1975), striking down a total billboard exclusion in the city. The court held that the prohibition of an entire industry in a major city was not authorized, at least when the industry was not a public nuisance. It relied on statutory and charter provisions that authorized the city only to regulate and restrict land uses. Compare the *Metromedia* case on this point.

What if a local government rezones land to a commercial use solely for the display of billboards? The courts have thrown this kind of zoning out when it has been challenged, though they will uphold rezoning for billboards that is part of a comprehensive rezoning. See *Kunz v. State,* 913 P.2d 765 (Utah App. 1996) (rezoning held invalid).

3. *On-premise sign exemption.* The San Diego ordinance did not prohibit on-premise signs and billboards advertising the business conducted on the premises. Almost all the cases uphold this exemption, usually relying on the importance of on-premise signs to the business and disregarding problems of aesthetic uniformity in sign control. See *Metuchen, supra,* and *City of Lake Wales v. Lamar Adv. Ass'n,* 414 So. 2d 1030 (Fla. 1982). Does the on-premise sign exemption make aesthetic sense?

4. *On-premise sign regulation.* The courts have upheld limitations on the size and number of on-premise signs, recognizing that their cumulative impact can have an undesirable visual effect. See *Westfield Motor Sales Co. v. Town of Westfield,* 324 A.2d 113 (N.J. Super. Ct. L. Div. 1974), (size limits), noted, 11 Urb. L. Ann. 295 (1976); *Tunis-Huntingdon Dodge, Inc. v. Horn,* 290 N.Y.S.2d 7 (N.Y. App. Div. 1968) (number of signs). See also *Kenyon Peck, Inc. v. Kennedy,* 168 S.E.2d 117 (Va. 1969) (upholding prohibition on moving signs); *Schaffer v. City of Omaha,* 248 N.W.2d 764 (Neb. 1977) (portable signs prohibited). The last two cases relied heavily on the presumption of constitutionality. Courts not fully recognizing aesthetics as a public purpose may take a contrary view. *Mayor & City Council v. Mano Swartz, Inc.,* 299 A.2d 828 (Md. 1973) (ordinance prohibiting roof signs, moving and flashing signs and painted signs).

Regulations for on-premise signs are not usually well-drafted and may consist of an ad hoc mixture of limitations, some of which may not make aesthetic sense. For example, it is customary to make the size of a sign dependent on the linear footage of the lot on which a building stands. For a simple but effective model sign ordinance proposed for small communities, see E. Kelly & G. Raso, *Sign Regulations for Small and Midsize Communities: A Planners Guide and A Model Ordinance,* American Planning Association, Planning Advisory Serv. Rep. No. 419 (1989).

Street Graphics, a more complex but aesthetically more effective method for controlling on-premise signs, was proposed in a book published in 1971 and later updated. D. Mandelker & W. Ewald, Street Graphics and the Law (rev. ed. 1988). A model street graphics ordinance included in the 1971 publication was adopted in a number of cities and revised in the 1988 edition.

The street graphics system is based on performance standards which adopt a proportionality rule for on-premise signs. Free-standing signs are related to the width of adjacent streets and to traffic speed; signs can be larger as streets get wider and traffic moves more quickly. Wall signs are related to building mass and may occupy only a stated percentage of wall area. More restrictive regulations apply when residential areas are adjacent.

The model ordinance also limits the number of items of information on a sign. An item of information is defined as

> A syllable of a word, an initial, a logo, an abbreviation, a number, a symbol, or a geometric shape.

The purpose of this restriction is to limit communication overload. Is it constitutional? Does it raise free speech problems? A local sign control ordinance based on the Street Graphics system is reproduced in an appendix to *National Adv. Co. v. City of Bridgeton,* 626 F. Supp. 837 (E.D. Mo. 1985). The court rejected free speech objections to the ordinance. For an analysis of the ordinance from an urban design perspective see Amy Mandelker, *Writing Urban Spaces: Street Graphics and the Law as Postmodern Design and Ordinance,* 3 Wash. U. J.L. & Pol'y 403 (2000).

5. *The takings issue.* Prior to the Supreme Court's 1987 takings trilogy, most courts held that billboard prohibitions were not restrictive enough as a limitation on land use to amount to a taking. *Inhabitants of Boothbay v. National Adv. Co.,* 347 A.2d 419 (Me. 1975); *Newman Signs, Inc. v. Hjelle,* 268 N.W.2d 741 (N.D. 1978) (applying balancing test). For example, *Jackson v. City Council,* 659 F. Supp. 470 (W.D. Va. 1987), held that an ordinance prohibiting commercial billboards was not a taking because the "only damages" were lost business opportunities and a reduction in the value of the signs. See also *New York State Thruway Auth. v. Ashley Motor Court, Inc.,* cited in the principal case, holding that the construction of a highway provides the opportunity for outdoor advertising so that a sign regulation "takes" only the value the highway added to the land. Is this holding still good law?

Since the trilogy, the courts have continued to hold that sign regulation advances legitimate governmental purposes and does not deny property owners all economically viable use. E.g., *Summey Outdoor Adv. v. County of Henderson*, 386 S.E.2d 439 (N.C. App. 1989). The Fourth Circuit adopted a multi-factor balancing test based on the Supreme Court's 1987 takings trilogy. It applies the "whole parcel" rule by looking at the area in which a company's billboards are displayed to determine the appropriate number of billboards to consider when determining whether a taking has occurred. *Naegele Outdoor Advertising, Inc. v. City of Durham*, 844 F.2d 172 (4th Cir. 1988).

What effect will the *Lucas* per se takings rule have? Could a court hold that an ordinance prohibiting billboards is a per se taking of the severable property interest in the lease or license? See *Wilson v. City of Louisville*, 957 F. Supp. 948 (W.D. Ky. 1997), holding that restrictions on the size, height and hours of display of small freestanding signs did not deprive the owner of the economically viable use of the property. The court noted that 80% of the business was outside the city, where the plaintiff could still market these signs. The court also applied dicta from *Lucas*, that the takings clause does not protect personal property, such as signs, from regulation. For discussion see Floyd, *The Takings Issue in Billboard Control*, 3 Wash. U. J.L. Pol'y 357 (2000).

6. *The billboard business today.* It has changed. One trend is the increasing consolidation in the business, though 65% of advertising is still controlled by local and regional companies outside big cities. Technology has changed, as the painted billboard has given way to brilliant four-color panels produced by computerized machines, which can be animated with changing displays. There are still three standard sizes: The bulletin, which is 14x48, or 672 square feet; the poster, which is 12x25 or 300 square feet, and the junior poster, which is 6x12, or 72 square feet. Finally, tobacco and liquor advertising no longer dominate; they have been replaced by advertisers of mainstream consumer brands. How should these trends affect judicial reception of billboard regulation?

A NOTE ON THE FEDERAL HIGHWAY BEAUTIFICATION ACT

Federal legislation, first enacted in 1958 and strengthened in 1965, requires the states to prohibit all billboards within 660 feet of the right-of-way of federal interstate and primary highways. 23 U.S.C. § 131. In rural areas, billboards must not be visible from the highway. The federal act exempts on-premise signs. It also authorizes an exemption for commercial and industrial areas under agreements between the states and the federal Secretary of Transportation. States not complying with the federal law are subject to a penalty of ten percent of their state federal-aid highway funds. This penalty has seldom been imposed. As the court also noted in *Markham Adv. Co. v. State*, 439 P.2d 248 (Wash. 1965), the federal act does not preempt state controls. Noncomplying states are subject only to the federal penalty. That states may adopt more stringent regulations also is clear. The state laws controlling billboards along federal highways have all been upheld. The decisions often rely on a traffic safety rationale. See, e.g., *Moore v. Ward,* 377 S.W.2d 881 (Ky. 1964).

The federal act has always authorized the removal of nonconforming signs. Compensation is required, and the federal government must share seventy-five percent of the cost. Despite the compensation requirement, local governments continued to use amortization to remove nonconforming signs on federal highways after the federal act was adopted. See *Vermont v. Brinegar*, 379 F. Supp. 606 (D.Vt. 1974) (unsuccessful claim that compensation requirement is moot if state law permits removal without compensation). In 1978, an amendment to the federal law prohibited the use of amortization by local governments, and many states now prohibit local governments from amortizing nonconforming signs on federal highways; some of these laws include all signs. Is it a denial of equal protection to pay compensation for nonconforming billboards on federal highways while amortizing nonconforming billboards not on federal highways? The California Supreme Court in *Metromedia* said no. For discussion of amortization, see Chapter 3, *supra*.

State outdoor advertising laws usually authorize local regulation along highways. Some courts rely on this authority to hold that the state law does not prohibit more stringent local regulation. See *City of Doraville v. Turner Commun. Co.,* 223 S.E.2d 798 (Ga. 1976) (500-foot local prohibition). Compare *Southeastern Displays, Inc. v. Ward,* 414 S.W.2d 573 (Ky. 1967) (state highway agency decision prohibiting sign preempts local ordinance under which it was permitted). For discussion of the federal Highway Beautification Act, see C. Floyd & P. Shedd, Highway Beautification (1979); Albert, *Your Ad Goes Here: How the Highway Beautification Act of 1965 Thwarts Highway Beautification*, 48 U. Kan. L. Rev. 463 (2000).

2. FREE SPEECH ISSUES

The free speech problem.—The United States Supreme Court accepted an appeal from the California Supreme Court's *Metromedia* decision, reproduced *supra,* a development foreshadowed by Court decisions in the 1970s that brought commercial speech under the protection of the free speech clause. The application of the free speech clause to sign regulation raises a number of critical and to some extent unresolved constitutional issues:

> Free speech law weighs the constitutional interest in free expression against the governmental interests advanced by sign regulation. These governmental interests are the same aesthetic and traffic safety interests that provide a basis for sign ordinances absent free speech objections. The difference is that sign ordinances enjoy a presumption of constitutionality when the courts do not consider free speech values. When the courts consider free speech values, they reverse the presumption of constitutionality and examine more rigorously the governmental interests that justify sign ordinances. [D. Mandelker & W. Ewald, Street Graphics and the Law 179 (Rev. ed. 1988).]

Commercial speech.—First Amendment law that protects free speech is complicated and, to some extent, inconsistent. We cannot explore all of free speech law here, but we can study some of the major principles that determine how the law of free speech affects sign regulation. Chapter 3 considered free speech issues as they apply to adult uses. The same basic principles apply to sign regulation, but there are some differences.

A major distinction in First Amendment law that affects sign regulation is the different treatment courts give to commercial as compared with noncommercial speech. The Supreme Court applies the free speech clause less rigorously to the regulation of commercial speech. Signs with commercial messages are a form of commercial speech. In *Central Hudson Gas & Elec. Corp. v. Public Serv. Comm'n,* 447 U.S. 667 (1980), the Court adopted a three-part test for laws affecting commercial speech:

> At the outset, we must determine [1] whether the expression is protected by the First Amendment. For commercial speech to come within that provision, it at least must [a] concern lawful activity and [b] not be misleading. Next, [if the speech is protected] we ask [2] whether the asserted governmental interest is substantial. If both inquiries yield positive answers, we must determine [3] whether the regulation directly advances the governmental interest asserted, and [4] whether it is not more extensive than is necessary to serve that interest. [*Id.* at 563.]

Note how the fourth part of this test modifies the presumption of constitutionality. But see *Board of Trustees v. Fox,* 492 U.S. 459 (1989) (*Central Hudson* did not adopt "less restrictive alternative" test; only "reasonable fit" required between ends and means). There is some indication the Court may revise the *Central Hudson* test. In *44 Liquormart, Inc. v. State of Rhode Island,* 517 U.S. 484 (1996), a plurality held that commercial speech doctrine does not apply to a prohibition of "truthful, nonmisleading commercial messages for reasons unrelated to the preservation of a fair bargaining process." If that holding applies to sign regulation it may mean that this type of regulation is no longer a regulation of commercial speech.

Content vs. viewpoint neutrality.—This distinction has a major impact on the constitutionality of sign regulation under free speech doctrine. A law that regulates the subject matter of speech regulates its content. Examples are laws regulating political speech (regardless of the speaker's political position) and laws regulating particular words, such as sign ordinances permitting the government to post otherwise-impermissible "No Parking" signs. A law regulates viewpoint if it regulates the point of view expressed, such as an ordinance prohibiting signs opposing nuclear power, but not those supporting it. Laws regulating viewpoint are more easily invalidated under the free speech clause than laws regulating content, but the Supreme Court has not been consistent in its treatment of content and viewpoint neutrality. Recall also that the *Renton* decision, reproduced in Chapter 3, held that whether a regulation is content-neutral is determined by its legislative purpose as well as its terms.

In order to understand content neutrality it is important to understand the difference between commercial and noncommercial speech. The distinction is obvious, although traditional speech might be a better term than noncommerical. Traditional messages that might be placed on signs include ideological messages, such as "Save the Whales," and political campaign messages. The important point to make is that sign regulations may not identify the messages they regulate by their content, whether it is commercial or noncommercial speech.

Time, place and manner regulations.—This type of regulation does not regulate speech because of its content but instead protects governmental interests unrelated to the content of speech, such as a law regulating parades to prevent traffic problems. Time, place and manner regulations are usually given greater deference by courts than laws directly regulating speech. Sign regulations that regulate the location, number, height and size of signs fall in this category.

Overbreadth.—The overbreadth doctrine is another free speech doctrine that affects the constitutionality of sign regulations. This doctrine prevents governmental regulation from sweeping so far that it restricts protected as well as unprotected speech. See the discussion by the California Supreme Court in footnote 1 of its *Metromedia* opinion, reproduced *supra.*

These doctrines provide the conceptual framework for the Supreme Court's *Metromedia* decision, which is reproduced next:

METROMEDIA, INC. v. CITY OF SAN DIEGO

453 U.S. 490 (1981)

Justice White announced the judgment of the Court and delivered an opinion, in which Justice Stewart, Justice Marshall, and Justice Powell joined. . . .

I

Stating that its purpose was "to eliminate hazards to pedestrians and motorists brought about by distracting sign displays" and "to preserve and improve the appearance of the City," San Diego enacted an ordinance to prohibit "outdoor advertising display signs." The California Supreme Court subsequently defined the term "advertising display sign" as "a rigidly assembled sign, display, or device permanently affixed to the ground or permanently attached to a building or other inherently permanent structure constituting, or used for the display of, a commercial or other advertisement to the public." "Advertising displays signs" include any sign that "directs attention to a product, service or activity, event, person, institution or business."

The ordinance provides two kinds of exceptions to the general prohibition: onsite signs and signs falling within 12 specified categories. Onsite signs are defined as those

> "designating the name of the owner or occupant of the premises upon which such signs are placed, or identifying such premises; or signs advertising goods manufactured or produced or services rendered on the premises upon which such signs are placed."

The specific categories exempted from the prohibition include: government signs; signs located at public bus stops; signs manufactured, transported, or stored within the city, if not used for advertising purposes; commemorative historical plaques; religious symbols; signs within shopping malls; for sale and for lease signs; signs on public and commercial vehicles; signs depicting time, temperature, and news; approved temporary, off-premises, subdivision directional signs; and "[temporary] political campaign signs." Under this scheme, onsite commercial advertising is permitted, but other commercial advertising and noncommercial communications using fixed-structure signs are everywhere forbidden unless permitted by one of the specified exceptions. . . .[The Court described the outdoor advertising business and the way in which outdoor advertising is usually purchased.]

III. . .

[The Court noted that "at times First Amendment values must yield to other societal interests."]. . . Each method of communicating ideas is "a law unto itself" and that law must reflect the "differing natures, values, abuses and dangers" of each method. We deal here with the law of billboards.

Billboards are a well-established medium of communication, used to convey a broad range of different kinds of messages. . . . [The court quoted from the dissenting opinion in the California Supreme Court and the stipulation of facts, which noted that billboards convey noncommercial as well as commercial messages.]

But whatever its communicative function, the billboard remains a "large, immobile, and permanent structure which like other structures is subject to . . . regulation." 610 P.2d, at 419. Moreover, because it is designed to stand out and apart from its surroundings, the billboard creates a unique set of problems for land-use planning and development.

Billboards, then, like other media of communication, combine communicative and noncommunicative aspects. As with other media, the government has legitimate interests in controlling the noncommunicative aspects of the medium, but the First and Fourteenth Amendments foreclose a similar interest in controlling the communicative aspects. Because regulation of the noncommunicative aspects of a medium often impinges to some degree on the communicative aspects, it has been necessary for the courts to reconcile the government's regulatory interests with the individual's right to expression. . . . Performance of this task requires a particularized inquiry into the nature of the conflicting interests at stake here, beginning with a precise appraisal of the character of the ordinance as it affects communication.

As construed by the California Supreme Court, the ordinance restricts the use of certain kinds of outdoor signs. That restriction is defined in two ways: first, by reference to the structural characteristics of the sign; second, by reference to the content, or message, of the sign. Thus, the regulation only applies to a "permanent structure constituting, or used for the display of, a commercial or other advertisement to the public." 610 P. 2d, at 410, n. 2. Within that class, the only permitted signs are those (1) identifying the premises on which the sign is located, or its owner or occupant, or advertising the goods produced or services rendered on such property and (2) those within one of the specified exemptions to the general prohibition, such as temporary political campaign signs. To determine if any billboard is prohibited by the ordinance, one must determine how it is constructed, where it is located, and what message it carries.

Thus, under the ordinance (1) a sign advertising goods or services available on the property where the sign is located is allowed; (2) a sign on a building or other property advertising goods or services produced or offered elsewhere is barred; (3) noncommercial advertising, unless within one of the specific exceptions, is everywhere prohibited. The occupant of property may advertise his own goods or services; he may not advertise the goods or services of others, nor may he display most noncommercial messages.

IV

Appellants' principal submission is that enforcement of the ordinance will eliminate the outdoor advertising business in San Diego and that the First and Fourteenth Amendments prohibit the elimination of this medium of communication. Appellants contend that the city may bar neither all offsite commercial signs nor all noncommercial advertisements and that even if it may bar the former, it may not bar the latter. . . . Because our cases have consistently distinguished between the constitutional protection afforded commercial as opposed to noncommercial speech, in evaluating appellants' contention we consider separately the effect of the ordinance on commercial and noncommercial speech. . . . [The Court discussed decisions, including *Central Hudson,* indicating that commercial speech receives less protection than noncommercial speech.]

Appellants agree that the proper approach to be taken in determining the validity of the restrictions on commercial speech is that which was articulated in *Central Hudson,* but assert that the San Diego ordinance fails that test. We do not agree.

There can be little controversy over the application of the first, second, and fourth criteria. There is no suggestion that the commercial advertising at issue here involves unlawful activity or is misleading. Nor can there be substantial doubt that the twin goals that the ordinance seeks to further — traffic safety and the appearance of the city — are substantial governmental goals. It is far too late to contend otherwise with respect to either traffic safety, *Railway Express Agency, Inc. v. New York,* 336 U.S. 106 (1949), or esthetics, [citing *Penn Central, Belle Terre* and *Berman v. Parker.*] Similarly, we reject appellants' claim that the ordinance is broader than necessary and, therefore, fails the fourth part of the *Central Hudson* test. If the city has a sufficient basis for believing that billboards are traffic hazards and are unattractive, then obviously the most direct and perhaps the only effective approach to solving the problems they create is to prohibit them. The city has gone no further than necessary in seeking to meet its ends. Indeed, it has stopped short of fully accomplishing its ends: It has not prohibited all billboards, but allows onsite advertising and some other specifically exempted signs.

The more serious question, then, concerns the third of the *Central Hudson* criteria: Does the ordinance "directly advance" governmental interests in traffic safety and in the appearance of the city? It is asserted that the record

is inadequate to show any connection between billboards and traffic safety.
. . . [The Court discussed the holding of the California court on the traffic
issue.] We likewise hesitate to disagree with the accumulated, commonsense
judgments of local lawmakers and of the many reviewing courts that billboards are real and substantial hazards to traffic safety. There is nothing here
to suggest that these judgments are unreasonable. As we said in a different
context, *Railway Express Agency, Inc. v. New York,* supra, at 109:

> "We would be trespassing on one of the most intensely local and
> specialized of all municipal problems if we held that this regulation
> had no relation to the traffic problem of New York City. It is the
> judgment of the local authorities that it does have such a relation. And
> nothing has been advanced which shows that to be palpably false."

We reach a similar result with respect to the second asserted justification
for the ordinance — advancement of the city's esthetic interests. It is not
speculative to recognize that billboards by their very nature, wherever located
and however constructed, can be perceived as an "esthetic harm." San Diego,
like many States and other municipalities, has chosen to minimize the
presence of such structures. Such esthetic judgments are necessarily subjective, defying objective evaluation, and for that reason must be carefully
scrutinized to determine if they are only a public rationalization of an
impermissible purpose. But there is no claim in this case that San Diego has
as an ulterior motive the suppression of speech, and the judgment involved
here is not so unusual as to raise suspicions in itself.

It is nevertheless argued that the city denigrates its interest in traffic safety
and beauty and defeats its own case by permitting onsite advertising and other
specified signs. Appellants question whether the distinction between onsite
and offsite advertising on the same property is justifiable in terms of either
esthetics or traffic safety. The ordinance permits the occupant of property to
use billboards located on that property to advertise goods and services offered
at that location; identical billboards, equally distracting and unattractive, that
advertise goods or services available elsewhere are prohibited even if permitting the latter would not multiply the number of billboards. Despite the
apparent incongruity, this argument has been rejected, at least implicitly, in
all of the cases sustaining the distinction between offsite and onsite commercial advertising. We agree with those cases and with our own decisions in
[earlier cases].

In the first place, whether onsite advertising is permitted or not, the
prohibition of offsite advertising is directly related to the stated objectives of
traffic safety and esthetics. This is not altered by the fact that the ordinance
is underinclusive because it permits onsite advertising. Second, the city may
believe that offsite advertising, with its periodically changing content, presents a more acute problem than does onsite advertising. Third, San Diego has
obviously chosen to value one kind of commercial speech — onsite advertising
— more than another kind of commercial speech — offsite advertising. The
ordinance reflects a decision by the city that the former interest, but not the
latter, is stronger than the city's interests in traffic safety and esthetics. The
city has decided that in a limited instance — onsite commercial advertising
— its interests should yield. We do not reject that judgment. As we see it,

the city could reasonably conclude that a commercial enterprise — as well as the interested public — has a stronger interest in identifying its place of business and advertising the products or services available there than it has in using or leasing its available space for the purpose of advertising commercial enterprises located elsewhere. It does not follow from the fact that the city has concluded that some commercial interests outweigh its municipal interests in this context that it must give similar weight to all other commercial advertising. Thus, offsite commercial billboards may be prohibited while onsite commercial billboards are permitted.

The constitutional problem in this area requires resolution of the conflict between the city's land-use interests and the commercial interests of those seeking to purvey goods and services within the city. In light of the above analysis, we cannot conclude that the city has drawn an ordinance broader than is necessary to meet its interests, or that it fails directly to advance substantial government interests. In sum, insofar as it regulates commercial speech the San Diego ordinance meets the constitutional requirements of *Central Hudson,* supra.

V

It does not follow, however, that San Diego's general ban on signs carrying noncommercial advertising is also valid under the First and Fourteenth Amendments. The fact that the city may value commercial messages relating to onsite goods and services more than it values commercial communications relating to offsite goods and services does not justify prohibiting an occupant from displaying its own ideas or those of others.

As indicated above, our recent commercial speech cases have consistently accorded noncommercial speech a greater degree of protection than commercial speech. San Diego effectively inverts this judgment, by affording a greater degree of protection to commercial than to noncommercial speech. There is a broad exception for onsite commercial advertisements, but there is no similar exception for noncommercial speech. The use of onsite billboards to carry commercial messages related to the commercial use of the premises is freely permitted, but the use of otherwise identical billboards to carry noncommercial messages is generally prohibited. The city does not explain how or why noncommercial billboards located in places where commercial billboards are permitted would be more threatening to safe driving or would detract more from the beauty of the city. Insofar as the city tolerates billboards at all, it cannot choose to limit their content to commercial messages; the city may not conclude that the communication of commercial information concerning goods and services connected with a particular site is of greater value than the communication of noncommercial messages.

Furthermore, the ordinance contains exceptions that permit various kinds of noncommercial signs, whether on property where goods and services are offered or not, that would otherwise be within the general ban. A fixed sign may be used to identify any piece of property and its owner. Any piece of property may carry or display religious symbols, commemorative plaques of recognized historical societies and organizations, signs carrying news items or telling the time or temperature, signs erected in discharge of any governmental function, or temporary political campaign signs. No other noncommercial or ideological signs meeting the structural definition are permitted, regardless of their effect on traffic safety or esthetics.

Although the city may distinguish between the relative value of different categories of commercial speech, the city does not have the same range of choice in the area of noncommercial speech to evaluate the strength of, or distinguish between, various communicative interests. With respect to noncommercial speech, the city may not choose the appropriate subjects for public discourse: "To allow a government the choice of permissible subjects for public debate would be to allow that government control over the search for political truth." *Consolidated Edison Co.* [*v. Public Service Comm'n,*] 447 U.S. [530], at 538 [1980]. Because some noncommercial messages may be conveyed on billboards throughout the commercial and industrial zones, San Diego must similarly allow billboards conveying other noncommercial messages throughout those zones.[20]

Finally, we reject appellees' suggestion that the ordinance may be appropriately characterized as a reasonable "time, place, and manner" restriction. The ordinance does not generally ban billboard advertising as an unacceptable "manner" of communicating information or ideas; rather, it permits various kinds of signs. Signs that are banned are banned everywhere and at all times. We have observed that time, place, and manner restrictions are permissible if "they are justified without reference to the content of the regulated speech, . . . serve a significant governmental interest, and . . . leave open ample alternative channels for communication of the information." *Virginia Pharmacy Board v. Virginia Citizens Consumer Council,* 425 U.S. [748], at 771 [1978]. Here, it cannot be assumed that "alternative channels" are available, for the parties stipulated to just the opposite:. . . A similar argument was made with respect to a prohibition on real estate "For Sale" signs in *Linmark Associates, Inc. v. Willingboro,* 431 U.S. 85 (1977), and what we said there is equally applicable here:

> "Although in theory sellers remain free to employ a number of different alternatives, in practice [certain products are] not marketed through leaflets, sound trucks, demonstrations, or the like. The options to which sellers realistically are relegated . . . involve more cost and less autonomy then . . . signs[,] . . . are less likely to reach persons not deliberately seeking sales information[,] . . . and may be less effective media for communicating the message that is conveyed by a . . . sign. . . . The alternatives, then, are far from satisfactory." *Id.* at 93.

---

[20] Because a total prohibition of outdoor advertising is not before us, we do not indicate whether such a ban would be consistent with the First Amendment. . . .

Similarly, we need not reach any decision in this case as to the constitutionality of the federal Highway Beautification Act of 1965. That Act, like the San Diego ordinance, permits onsite commercial billboards in areas in which it does not permit billboards with noncommercial messages. However, unlike the San Diego ordinance, which prohibits billboards conveying noncommercial messages throughout the city, the federal law does not contain a total prohibition of such billboards in areas adjacent to the interstate and primary highway systems. As far as the Federal Government is concerned, such billboards are permitted adjacent to the highways in areas zoned industrial or commercial under state law or in unzoned commercial or industrial areas. Regulation of billboards in those areas is left primarily to the States. . . .

It is apparent as well that the ordinance distinguishes in several ways between permissible and impermissible signs at a particular location by reference to their content. Whether or not these distinctions are themselves constitutional, they take the regulation out of the domain of time, place, and manner restrictions. . . .

VII

Because the San Diego ordinance reaches too far into the realm of protected speech, we conclude that it is unconstitutional on its face. The judgment of the California Supreme Court is reversed, and the case is remanded to that court. [26]

It is so ordered.

[Justice Brennan concurred in an opinion joined by Justice Blackmun. He believed the ordinance was a total ban and would uphold a total ban that sufficiently served a governmental interest when a more narrowly drawn restriction would not promote that goal. However, this ordinance was unconstitutional. There was no evidence that billboards impaired traffic safety, its interest in aesthetics was not sufficiently substantial in the industrial and commercial areas, and "San Diego has failed to demonstrate a comprehensive coordinated effort in its commercial and industrial areas to address other obvious contributors to an unattractive environment." Even a total ban only on commercial billboards would raise free speech problems because it would give the city the right to determine whether a proposed message was commercial or noncommercial. However, he would not read the exemption for on-site signs as limited solely to commercial speech.

[Justice Stevens dissented, though he agreed with Parts I through IV of the plurality opinion. He believed a city could totally ban all commercial and noncommercial billboards because "the essential inquiry is the same throughout the city." He believed the impact of the ordinance on signs that were on-site was speculative and need not be considered. There was no evidence of the use of on-site premises for noncommercial signs, and it was "safe to assume that such uses in the future will be at best infrequent." The exceptions for various signs contained in the ordinance were constitutional because they were viewpoint-neutral.

[Chief Justice Burger also dissented. He believed the plurality's decision had "trivialized" the First Amendment and had improperly substituted its judgment for that of the city, and that the ordinance was constitutional because it was viewpoint-neutral. The exceptions for various signs "did not remotely endanger freedom of speech," and the city was not required to allow on-site signs to display noncommercial as well as commercial speech. Justice Rehnquist agreed substantially with the other dissenting opinions, and believed that aesthetic justifications alone were enough to justify a total ban on billboards. He described the opinions in the case as a Tower of Babel.]

---

[26] [The Court considered whether the unconstitutional parts of the ordinance could be severed and added:] Since our judgment is based essentially on the inclusion of noncommercial speech within the prohibitions of the ordinance, the California courts may sustain the ordinance by limiting its reach to commercial speech, assuming the ordinance is susceptible to this treatment.

NOTES AND QUESTIONS

1. *What Metromedia held.* The plurality opinion requires content neutrality in sign regulation, which creates troublesome problems for local governments. Try to decide what it was about the ordinance that was fatal to the plurality opinion, and note how questions of content neutrality, about time, place and manner regulation, and about the distinction between commercial and non-commercial speech affected the decision. On remand, the California Supreme Court was unable to sever the constitutional from the unconstitutional parts of the San Diego ordinance and invalidated all of it. 649 P.2d 902 (Cal. 1982).

Although *Metromedia* did not consider the constitutionality of the federal Highway Beautification Act, lower federal courts have relied on aesthetic and traffic safety purposes to uphold state laws implementing the act. See *National Advertising Co. v. City of Denver,* 912 F.2d 405 (10th Cir. 1990); *Wheeler v. Commissioner of Highways,* 822 F.2d 566 (6th Cir. 1987). For additional discussion of *Metromedia* see Blumoff, *After Metromedia: Sign Controls and the First Amendment,* 28 St. Louis U. L.J. 171 (1984).

2. *Discovery Network.* The Supreme Court considered and explained *Metromedia* in *City of Cincinnati v. Discovery Network, Inc.,* 507 U.S. 410 (1993). The Court invalidated an ordinance that prohibited newsracks that displayed commercial handbills but allowed newsracks that displayed newspapers. The Court assumed the ordinance banned commercial but allowed noncommercial speech, and found there was no close fit between the regulation's goals and its purposes because this distinction bore no relationship to the purposes of the ordinance. The Court distinguished *Metromedia*:

> Unlike this case, which involves discrimination between commercial and noncommercial speech, the "offsite-onsite" distinction [in *Metromedia*] involved disparate treatment of two types of commercial speech. Only the onsite signs served both the commercial and public interest in guiding potential visitors to their intended destinations; moreover, the plurality concluded that a "city may believe that offsite advertising, with its periodically changing content, presents a more acute problem than does onsite advertising." (citation omitted) [*Id.* at 425 n.20.]

The Court in *Discovery Network* indicated its holding was narrow and that a city might be able to justify the differential treatment of commercial and noncommercial newsracks. In this case, however, the very basis for the news-rack regulation was the difference in content. Does *Discovery Network* suggest that regulations affecting noncommercial signs are more likely to be struck down?

3. *The Vincent case.* A few years after *Metromedia,* in *Members of City Council v. Taxpayers for Vincent,* 466 U.S. 789 (1984), a majority of the Court upheld an ordinance prohibiting the posting of signs on public property, as applied to prevent the posting of temporary political campaign signs. The Court reaffirmed that traffic safety and aesthetic interests are sufficient to justify a sign ordinance under the Free Speech clause, and that the ordinance in *Vincent* was a "reasonable regulation of time, place, or manner" that was no broader than necessary. Alternate methods were available to distribute the messages on these signs.

Several aspects of the *Vincent* decision help support sign regulation. The Court was willing to accept alternate means of communication as adequate, and may have indicated that sign regulations need only be viewpoint-neutral, which contradicts the *Metromedia* plurality. The Court also referred to the "substantive evil" of "visual blight. . .[as] created by the medium of expression itself" — i.e., the sign.

4. *Off-premise v. on-premise signs.* Sign ordinances that make this distinction remain problematic. Municipalities have been able to avoid the *Metromedia* holding that ordinances may not prohibit on-premise noncommercial speech by amending their ordinances to allow this kind of speech on-premise. The courts have upheld these ordinances. See *Major Media of the Southeast v. City of Raleigh,* 792 F.2d 1269 (4th Cir. 1986), *cert. denied,* 479 U.S. 1102 (1987). This court rejected an argument that owners of commercial premises would want to display only commercial signs. It held that this would be the decision of the individual property owner and had nothing to do with the ordinance.

Defining off-premise signs can be difficult to do without violating content neutrality rules. A typical definition is that an off-premise sign is one with messages not related to business or activity on the premises, which arguably is content-related because the nature of the message defines the sign. However, *Messer v. City of Douglasville,* 975 F.2d 1505 (11th Cir. 1992), *cert. denied,* 508 U.S. 930 (1993), upheld an ordinance with this definition even though the city had to read the sign to determine whether it was an off-premise sign. It held the ordinance regulated signs based on location, not viewpoint.

Total bans on off-premise signs are also problematic. The problem is whether the ordinance improperly discriminates against noncommercial speech. A total ban on off-premise commercial signs is not underinclusive even though noncommercial off-premise signs are exempt. *Lavey v. City of Two Rivers,* 171 F.3d 1110 (7th Cir. 1999). However, it is difficult to ban only commercial off-premise signs because billboards showing noncommercial messages may still be erected, and some courts uphold total bans on both off-premise commercial and noncommercial signs. E.g., *Georgia Outdoor Advertising, Inc. v. City of Waynesville,* 833 F.2d 43 (4th Cir. 1987) (relying on a provision allowing noncommercial messages on all signs permitted under the ordinance). Contra *National Advertising Co. v. City of Orange,* 861 F.2d 246 (9th Cir. 1988) (not enough that both types of speech are treated equally). What is it in *Metromedia* that creates this contradictory authority? See also *Ackerley Communications v. City of Cambridge,* 88 F.3d 33 (1st Cir. 1996) (invalidating ordinance treating different kinds of noncommercial speech differently).

For a more limited view see *Messer, supra,* where an ordinance banned commercial and noncommercial off-premise signs in an historic district. The court held *Metromedia* did not consider this problem, and upheld the ordinance because it was viewpoint-neutral, because the ban was limited to the historic district, and because aesthetic interests are especially important in such areas.

Southlake Property Assocs., Ltd. v. City of Morrow, 112 F.3d 1114 (11th Cir. 1998), *cert. denied,* 525 U.S. 280 (1998), eases the off-site v. on-site problem by holding that all noncommercial speech occurs on-site. Under this view, all off-premise signs display only commercial speech. A provision allowing noncommercial speech on all signs permitted by the ordinance can also help avoid free speech problems. See *Outdoor Systems, Inc. v. City of Mesa,* 997 F.2d 604 (9th Cir. 1993).

5. *Content neutrality and exemptions.* The *Metromedia* plurality's conclusion that the "ban with exemptions" approach to noncommercial billboards was unconstitutional presents another serious problem for sign regulators. Reread the exemptions. Aren't some of them necessary, such as the exemption for government signs? The Court had also held that municipalities could not ban "For Sale" or "For Rent" signs. *Linmark Assocs., Inc. v. Township of Willingboro,* 431 U.S. 85 (1977). San Diego's provision exempting political signs was added after a federal court in California struck down a political sign ordinance as too restrictive. *Baldwin v. Redwood City,* 540 F.2d 1360 (9th Cir. 1976). Is the plurality saying that because some noncommercial speech must be permitted, *all* noncommercial speech must be permitted?

The *Metromedia* plurality holding on exemptions continues to be troublesome. Some courts invalidate exemptions like those in *Metromedia* by relying on the plurality opinion. E.g., *National Advertising Co. v. Town of Niagara,* 941 F.2d 145 (2d Cir. 1991). Other courts refuse to follow the *Metromedia* plurality by combining decisions by other Justices in the case that would have upheld these exemptions. E.g., *Scadron v. City of Des Plaines,* 737 F. Supp. 1437 (N.D. Ill. 1990), *aff'd mem.,* 989 F.2d 502 (7th Cir. 1993). See also *Messer, supra* (upholding exemptions because they were more limited and only applied to permit requirement); *National Adv. Co. v. Town of Babylon,* 900 F.2d 551 (2d Cir.), *cert. denied,* 498 F.2d 852 (1990) (relying on *Linmark* to uphold exemption of "for sale" signs). The Fourth Circuit held the *Metromedia* plurality was no longer good law and adopted its own free speech test for sign regulation, but invalidated the exemptions in the ordinance. *Rappa v. New Castle County,* 18 F.3d 1043 (4th Cir. 1994).

Content neutrality problems also arise when municipalities define the signs they want to regulate. For example, an ordinance may authorize signs providing directions on business premises or advertising the sale or rental of property. This kind of definition is unconstitutional if courts continue to apply the requirement that sign ordinances must be content-neutral. See *North Olmsted Chamber of Commerce v. City of North Olmsted,* 86 F. Supp.2d 755 (N.D. 2000), striking down an ordinance that contained numerous definitions based on the content of the sign that also determined what sign regulations applied. Even benign definitions will be struck down as content-based. See *Flying J Travel Plaza v. Transportation Cabinet,* 928 S.W.2d 344 (Ky. 1996) (invalidating ordinance authorizing time and temperature signs). But see *Penn Advertising of Baltimore, Inc. v. Mayor & Council,* 63 F.3d 1318 (4th Cir. 1995), *modified & adhered to,* 101 F.3d 332 (4th Cir. 1996) (prohibiting cigarette advertising where it would be visible to minors); *Anheuser-Busch,*

Inc. v. Schmoke, 63 F.3d 1305 (4th Cir. 1995), *adhered to on remand,* 101 F.3d 325 (4th Cir. 1996) (same; liquor).

A NOTE ON FREE SPEECH PROBLEMS WITH OTHER TYPES OF SIGN REGULATIONS

Restrictions on size, height, number and method of display.—These restrictions have usually been upheld as reasonable time, place and manner regulations. See *Donrey Communications Co. v. City of Fayetteville,* 660 S.W.2d 900 (Ark. 1984), upholding a restriction on the size of signs over an objection that it prevented the display of the standard 300 square foot poster. Courts have also upheld regulations limiting the height, *City of Albuquerque v. Jackson,* 684 P.2d 543 (N.M. App. 1984) (26 feet); *South-Suburban Housing Center v. Greater South Suburban Bd. of Realtors,* 935 F.2d 868 (7th Cir. 1991), *cert. denied,* 502 U.S. 1074 (1992) and illumination of signs, *Asselin v. Town of Conway,* 628 A.2d 247 (N.H. 1993). Contra *State v. Calabria,* 693 A.2d 949 (N.J. App. Div. 1997) (prohibition of neon signs violates free speech). Ordinances restricting or prohibiting price information on signs violate the free speech clause. *H & H Operations, Inc. v. City of Peachtree City,* 283 S.E.2d 867 (Ga. 1981), *cert. denied,* 456 U.S. 961 (1982).

Portable signs.—Some of the cases immediately after *Metromedia* struck down bans on portable signs. Portable signs are often displayed on moveable carriages in front of businesses, and can be ugly, but the courts could not see an aesthetic difference between these signs and permanent signs.

Harnish v. Manatee County, 783 F.2d 1535 (11th Cir. 1986), relied on *Vincent* to uphold a prohibition on the display of portable signs. The court noted that the county had an "aesthetically appealing and fragile environment" and that local residents complained at workshops held on the portable sign ordinance that these signs were "inherently ugly." The court interpreted *Vincent* as holding that a municipality must have discretion to determine how much aesthetic regulation is necessary and the best method for achieving aesthetic protection. The court also read *Vincent* to hold that the Constitution does not mandate judicial speculation on how a municipality should revise regulations to tailor them narrowly to achieve governmental goals while leaving alternative means of communication available. The court held it could not engage in this kind of speculation because the portable sign prohibition reasonably advanced aesthetic objectives. The evidence in the case did not indicate that the city could adopt less restrictive means to accomplish this objective.

Note how the court narrowed the application of the "less restrictive alternatives" requirement to sign controls. Does this limit too severely the application of free speech protection to sign control ordinances? Accord *Lindsay v. City of San Antonio,* 821 F.2d 1103 (5th Cir. 1987), *cert. denied,* 484 U.S. 1010 (1988).

Political and campaign signs.—In *Vincent,* Justice Stevens stated that to create an exception for political speech "might create a risk of engaging in constitutionally forbidden content discrimination." This problem arises with temporary campaign signs. The reason is that an ordinance defining campaign signs as "signs displaying the names of candidates" is content-based. If the ordinance then provides more stringent regulations for these signs than for other temporary signs there is a serious risk a court will hold it unconstitutional. Prior to *Metromedia,* state and lower federal courts overturned a number of restrictions on campaign signs. *Blumoff, supra,* at 191–98. Restrictions limiting the amount of time a campaign sign can be displayed before an election are particularly vulnerable. *Baldwin v. Redwood City,* 540 F.2d 1360 (9th Cir. 1976), is an early leading case.

Whitton v. City of Gladstone, 54 F.3d 1400 (8th Cir. 1994), illustrates the tough view courts can take toward restrictions on political campaign signs. The court struck down an ordinance that limited the display of these signs to 30 days before an election, prohibited their external illumination, and made the candidate prima facie responsible for their erection, placement and removal. Relying heavily on *Discovery Network,* the court held that all these provisions were content-based and did not pass the strict scrutiny test required to uphold them. How would you remedy the problems created by cases like this? Could you simply include campaign signs in regulations for all temporary signs but then impose some different requirements? What would they be?

Some courts uphold requirements that campaign signs must be removed within a certain time after an election. See *Messer, supra,* upholding ten-day requirement. Contra *Outdoor Systems, Inc. v. City of Merriam,* 67 F. Supp.2d 1258 (D. Kan. 1999).

Signs on residential property: The Ladue Case.—In *City of Ladue v. Gilleo,* 512 U.S. 43 (1994), an exclusive St. Louis residential suburb prohibited homeowners from displaying any signs except residence identification, "for sale," and safety hazard warning signs. However, it permitted commercial business, churches and nonprofit organizations to display signs not allowed at residences. The Court held the ordinance violated the free speech clause in a case brought by a homeowner prohibited from displaying in her window an 8½ by 11 inch sign stating "For Peace in the Gulf." The city had defended the ordinance as an attempt to improve aesthetics by limiting the number of signs in residential areas. The Court endorsed both the plurality and concurring opinions in *Metromedia.*

The Court accepted the city's argument the ordinance was content-and viewpoint-neutral because it was aimed at the secondary effects of signs. But it held Ladue's interest in minimizing visual clutter was not a sufficient "compelling" reason for prohibiting residential message signs completely. By limiting restrictions on signs to residential areas, the city had "diminished the credibility" of the claim that it was interested in aesthetics. Ladue had "almost completely foreclosed" a venerable, unique and important means of communication to political, religious, or personal messages.

The Court rejected Ladue's argument that the prohibition on residential message signs was a mere "time, place, or manner" regulation because residents had alternate means for conveying their messages. It held that displaying a sign from a residence carried a "quite distinct" message because it provides information about the identity of the speaker. In addition, residential signs are "an unusually cheap and convenient form of communication."

Respect for individual liberty in the home, the Court concluded, has long been part of our culture and law. It suggested that Ladue could adopt "more temperate measures" to meet its regulatory needs, and noted that not every kind of sign must be permitted in residential areas.

Cleveland Area Bd. of Realtors v. City of Euclid, 88 F.3d 382 (6th Cir. 1996), relied on *Ladue* to strike down an ordinance prohibiting all yard signs except those displaying the residents' name and address and pertinent security information. It held the ordinance burdened substantially more speech than necessary because it completely foreclosed an inexpensive and autonomous way to communicate. Accord *Pica v. Sarno,* 907 F. Supp. 795 (D.N.J. 1995). What about allowing one permanent six-foot square sign on each residential premise with no restrictions on what can be displayed?

Sources.—See D. Mandelker & W. Ewald, Street Graphics and the Law ch. 11 (1987); D. Mandelker, J. Gerard & T. Sullivan, Federal Land Use Law ch. 7; Gerard, *Election Signs and Time Limits,* 3 Wash. U. J.L. & Pol'y 379 (2000); Comment, *Billboard Regulation After Metromedia and Lucas,* 31 Hous. L. Rev. 1555 (1995); Note, *Municipal Regulation of Political Signs: Balancing First Amendment Rights Against Aesthetic Concerns,* 45 Drake L. Rev. 767 (1997); Note, *Unsightly Politics: Aesthetics, Sign Ordinances, and Homeowners' Speech in City of Ladue v. Gilleo,* 20 Harv. Envtl. L. Rev. 473 (1996).

C. REGULATING DESIGN

Design elements are a factor in all land use regulation. Zoning ordinances that separate residential from commercial uses, for example, do so because of different design elements in these different types of uses. The regulations considered in this section explicitly take the visual elements of design into account. This section first considers appearance codes and then discusses more broadly based design review ordinances. A final section discusses urban design plans.

PROBLEM

Metro City, a desert city with a population of about one million, has just adopted an extensive design review code for the entire city. The code includes a set of design "principles" that require consideration of (1) context, or relationship to setting; (2) amenity, including shaded areas, courtyards and other elements to provide respite from a desert climate; (3) visual interest; and (4) views.

The design review code contains three sets of criteria. "Requirements" are one set. They are mandatory. For example:

> All roof-top equipment and satellite dishes must be screened to the height of the tallest equipment and/or integrated with the building design.

"Considerations" are optional and have no legal force. For example:

> The building facade should be designed to provide a sense of human scale at ground level.

"Presumptions" are just that. Designers must follow them unless they can make a good case based on the design "principles" for not following a presumption. For example:

Overhangs and canopies should be integrated in the building design along all pedestrian thoroughfares.

Assume your client is interested in constructing a three-story office building adjacent to the downtown area of Metro City. Do the "principles" provide enough design guidance for this development? What would you have to know about the surrounding area? Would you modify the principles, and if so, how? Now assume you are the staff attorney to the plan commission and are asked for an opinion on the constitutionality of the design code. Based on these examples, what opinion would you give? [This problem is based on the City of Phoenix design review process. It is described in Gammage, *Design Review Comes to Phoenix* in Design Review: Challenging Urban Aesthetic Control ch. 8 (B. Scheer & W. Preiser eds., 1994).]

1. APPEARANCE CODES

Appearance codes were an early form of design review. They are usually adopted in suburban or small communities, usually apply only to residential dwellings, and authorize the creation of review boards that must approve the appearance of new residences before they can be built. The following case is an early decision considering the validity of aesthetic considerations in design review under a local appearance code:

STATE ex rel. STOYANOFF v. BERKELEY

458 S.W.2d 305 (Mo. 1970)

PRITCHARD, COMMISSIONER:

. . . [The trial court issued a summary judgment ordering a writ of mandamus to compel the issuance of a building permit to the Stoyanoffs because it held the Ladue ordinance deprived the owners of their property without due process of law.] Relators' petition pleads that they applied to appellant Building Commissioner for a building permit to allow them to construct a single family residence in the City of Ladue, and that plans and specifications were submitted for the proposed residence, which was unusual in design, "but complied with all existing building and zoning regulations and ordinances of the City of Ladue, Missouri."

It is further pleaded that relators were refused a building permit for the construction of their proposed residence upon the ground that the permit was not approved by the Architectural Board of the City of Ladue. Ordinance 131, as amended by Ordinance 281 of that city, purports to set up an Architectural Board to approve plans and specifications for buildings and structures erected within the city and in a preamble to "conform to certain minimum architectural standards of appearance and conformity with surrounding structures, and that unsightly, grotesque and unsuitable structures, detrimental to the stability of value and the welfare of surrounding property, structures and residents, and to the general welfare and happiness of the community, be avoided, and that appropriate standards of beauty and conformity be fostered and encouraged." . . . [The petition claimed the ordinances were unconstitutional because "they are vague and provide no standard nor uniform rule by which to guide the architectural board," and there was no statutory authority for them.]

Relators filed a motion for summary judgment and affidavits were filed in opposition thereto. Richard D. Shelton, Mayor of the City of Ladue, deponed that the facts in appellant's answer were true and correct, as here pertinent: that the City of Ladue constitutes one of the finer suburban residential areas of Metropolitan St. Louis, the homes therein are considerably more expensive than in cities of comparable size, being homes on lots from three fourths of an acre to three or more acres each; that a zoning ordinance was enacted by the city regulating the height, number of stories, size of buildings, percentage of lot occupancy, yard sizes, and the location and use of buildings and land for trade, industry, residence and other purposes; that the zoning regulations were made in accordance with a comprehensive plan "designed to promote the health and general welfare of the residents of the City of Ladue," which in furtherance of said objectives duly enacted said Ordinances numbered 131 and 281. Appellant also asserted in his answer that these ordinances were a reasonable exercise of the city's governmental, legislative and police powers, as determined by its legislative body, and as stated in the above-quoted preamble to the ordinances. It is then pleaded that relators' description of their proposed residence as "'unusual in design' is the understatement of the year. It is in fact a monstrosity of grotesque design, which would seriously impair the value of property in the neighborhood."

The affidavit of Harold C. Simon, a developer of residential subdivisions in St. Louis County, is that he is familiar with relators' lot upon which they seek to build a house, and with the surrounding houses in the neighborhood; that the houses therein existent are virtually all two-story houses of conventional architectural design, such as Colonial, French Provincial or English; and that the house which relators propose to construct is of ultra-modern design which would clash with and not be in conformity with any other house in the entire neighborhood. It is Mr. Simon's opinion that the design and appearance of relators' proposed residence would have a substantial adverse effect upon the market values of other residential property in the neighborhood, such average market value ranging from $60,000 to $85,000 each.

As a part of the affidavit of Russell H. Riley, consultant for the city planning and engineering firm of Harland Bartholomew & Associates, photographic exhibits of homes surrounding relators' lot were attached. To the south is the conventional frame residence of Mrs. T. R. Collins. To the west is the Colonial two-story frame house of the Lewis family. To the northeast is the large brick English Tudor home of Mrs. Elmer Hubbs. Immediately to the north are the large Colonial homes of Mr. Alex Cornwall and Mr. L. Peter Wetzel. In substance Mr. Riley went on to say that the City of Ladue is one of the finer residential suburbs in the St. Louis area with a minimum of commercial or industrial usage. The development of residences in the city has been primarily by private subdivisions, usually with one main lane or drive leading therein (such as Lorenzo Road Subdivision which runs north off of Ladue Road in which relators' lot is located). The homes are considerably more expensive than average homes found in a city of comparable size. The ordinance which has been adopted by the City of Ladue is typical of those which have been adopted by a number of suburban cities in St. Louis County and in similar cities throughout the United States, the need therefor being based upon the protection of existing property values by preventing the construction of houses that are in complete conflict with the general type of houses in a given area. The intrusion into this neighborhood of relators' unusual, grotesque and nonconforming structure would have a substantial adverse effect on market values of other homes in the immediate area. According to Mr. Riley the standards of Ordinance 131, as amended by Ordinance 281, are usually and customarily applied in city planning work and are: "(1) whether the proposed house meets the customary architectural requirements in appearance and design for a house of the particular type which is proposed (whether it be Colonial, Tudor English, French Provincial, or Modern), (2) whether the proposed house is in general conformity with the style and design of surrounding structures, and (3) whether the proposed house lends itself to the proper architectural development of the City; and that in applying said standards the Architectural Board and its Chairman are to determine whether the proposed house will have an adverse effect on the stability of values in the surrounding area."

Photographic exhibits of relators' proposed residence were also attached to Mr. Riley's affidavit. They show the residence to be of a pyramid shape, with a flat top, and with triangular shaped windows or doors at one or more corners. . . .

[On the statutory issue, the court then quoted § 89.020, which is identical to § 1 of the Standard Zoning Enabling Act, reproduced in Ch. 3, sec. A *supra*. This section authorizes the regulation of land use. The court also quoted § 89.040, which is identical to § 3 of the Standard Act, "Purposes in View." The court italicized the following language from § 3: "Such regulations shall be made with reasonable consideration . . . to the character of the district and its particular suitability for particular uses, and with a view to conserving the values of buildings and encouraging the most appropriate use of land throughout such municipality."] . . .

As is clear from the affidavits and attached exhibits, the City of Ladue is an area composed principally of residences of the general types of Colonial, French Provincial and English Tudor. The city has a comprehensive plan of zoning to maintain the general character of buildings therein. . . . [T]he italicized portion [of § 89.040] relating to the character of the district, its suitability for particular uses, and the conservation of the values of buildings therein. . . . are directly related to the general welfare of the community. [The court quoted cases holding that the police power includes regulations to promote the public convenience or general welfare, and that stabilizing property values is "probably the most cogent reason" for zoning ordinances.] The preamble to Ordinance 131, quoted above in part, demonstrates that its purpose is to conform to the dictates of § 89.040, with reference to preserving values of property by zoning procedure and restrictions on the use of property.

This is an illustration of what was referred to in *Deimeke v. State Highway Commission,* Mo., 444 S.W.2d 480, 484, as a growing number of cases recognizing a change in the scope of the term "general welfare." In the *Deimeke* case on the same page it is said, "Property use which offends sensibilities and debases property values affects not only the adjoining property owners in that vicinity but the general public as well because when such property values are destroyed or seriously impaired, the tax base of the community is affected and the public suffers economically as a result."

Relators say further that Ordinances 131 and 281 are invalid and unconstitutional as being an unreasonable and arbitrary exercise of the police power. It is argued that a mere reading of these ordinances shows that they are based entirely on aesthetic factors in that the stated purpose of the Architectural Board is to maintain "conformity with surrounding structures" and to assure that structures "conform to certain minimum architectural standards of appearance." The argument ignores the further provisos in the ordinance: ". . . and that unsightly, grotesque and unsuitable structures, *detrimental to the stability of value and the welfare of surrounding property, structures, and residents,* and *to the general welfare and happiness of the community,* be avoided, and that appropriate standards of beauty and conformity be fostered and encouraged." (Italics added.) Relators' proposed residence does not descend to the "'patently offensive character of vehicle graveyards in close proximity to such highways'" referred to in the *Deimeke* case, *supra* (444 S.W.2d 484). Nevertheless, the aesthetic factor to be taken into account by the Architectural Board is not to be considered alone. Along with that inherent factor is the effect that the proposed residence would have upon the property values in the area. In this time of burgeoning urban areas, congested with people and structures, it is certainly in keeping with the ultimate ideal of general welfare that the Architectural Board, in its function, preserve and protect existing areas in which structures of a general conformity of architecture have been erected. The area under consideration is clearly, from the record, a fashionable one. In *State ex rel. Civello v. City of New Orleans,* 97 So. 440, 444 (La.), the court said, "If by the term 'aesthetic considerations' is meant a regard merely for outward appearances, for good taste in the matter of the beauty of the neighborhood itself, we do not observe any substantial reason for saying that such a consideration is not a matter of general welfare. The beauty of a fashionable residence neighborhood in a city is for the comfort and happiness of the residents, and it sustains in a general way the value of property in the neighborhood.". . .

In the matter of enacting zoning ordinances and the procedures for determining whether any certain proposed structure or use is in compliance with or offends the basic ordinance, it is well settled that courts will not substitute their judgments for the city's legislative body, if the result is not oppressive, arbitrary or unreasonable and does not infringe upon a valid preexisting nonconforming use. The denial by appellant of a building permit for relators' highly modernistic residence in this area where traditional Colonial, French Provincial and English Tudor styles of architecture are erected does not appear to be arbitrary and unreasonable when the basic purpose to be served is that of the general welfare of persons in the entire community.

In addition to the above-stated purpose in the preamble to Ordinance 131, it establishes an Architectural Board of three members, all of whom must be architects. Meetings of the Board are to be open to the public, and every application for a building permit, except those not affecting the outward appearance of a building, shall be submitted to the Board along with plans, elevations, detail drawings and specifications, before being approved by the Building Commissioner. The Chairman of the Board shall examine the application to determine if it conforms to proper architectural standards in appearance and design and will be in general conformity with the style and design of surrounding structures and conducive to the proper architectural development of the city. If he so finds, he approves and returns the application to the Building Commissioner. If he does not find conformity, or has doubt, a full meeting of the Board is called, with notice of the time and place thereof given to the applicant. The Board shall disapprove the application if it determines the proposed structure will constitute an unsightly, grotesque or unsuitable structure in appearance, detrimental to the welfare of surrounding property or residents. If it cannot make that decision, the application shall be returned to the Building Commissioner either with or without suggestions or recommendations, and if that is done without disapproval, the Building Commissioner may issue the permit. If the Board's disapproval is given and the applicant refuses to comply with recommendations, the Building Commissioner shall refuse the permit. Thereafter provisions are made for an appeal to the Council of the city for review of the decision of the Architectural Board. Ordinance 281 amends Ordinance 131 only with respect to the application initially being submitted to and considered by all members of the Architectural Board.

Relators claim that the above provisions of the ordinance amount to an unconstitutional delegation of power by the city to the Architectural Board. It is argued that the Board cannot be given the power to determine what is unsightly and grotesque and that the standards, "whether the proposed structure will conform to proper architectural standards in appearance and design, and will be in general conformity with the style and design of surrounding structures and conducive to the proper architectural development of the City . . ." and "the Board shall disapprove the application if it determines that the proposed structure will constitute an unsightly, grotesque or unsuitable structure in appearance, detrimental to the welfare of surrounding property or residents . . . ," are inadequate. . . . Ordinances 131 and 281 are sufficient in their general standards calling for a factual determination of the suitability of any proposed structure with reference to the character of the surrounding neighborhood and to the determination of any adverse effect on the general welfare and preservation of property values of the community. Like holdings were made involving Architectural Board ordinances in *State ex rel. Saveland Park Holding Corp. v. Wieland*, 69 N.W.2d 217 (Wis.), and *Reid v. Architectural Board of Review of the City of Cleveland Heights*, 192 N.E.2d 74 (Ohio App.).

The judgment is reversed.

NOTES AND QUESTIONS

1. *Stoyanoff* is a "second stage" aesthetic regulation case decided in the days before courts held that aesthetics alone is a sufficient basis for a land use regulation. The court relied on other zoning purposes besides aesthetic purposes to uphold the ordinance. What were they? Why do you suppose the property owners' attorney moved for summary judgment? Was this wise?

What were the ordinance standards in this case? One of them required "general conformity with the style and design of surrounding structures." This is known as a similarity requirement: The proposed dwelling must be similar to surrounding dwellings. What about the mixed styles in the area surrounding the proposed dwelling in *Stoyanoff*? *Saveland Park*, cited in the principal case, upheld a similarity ordinance intended to prevent "substantial depreciation in the property values" of neighborhoods. The court said that the protection of property values clearly fell within the police power. It was immaterial whether the ordinance was grounded solely on this objective or whether this was one of several legitimate objectives.

In *Stoyanoff*, the proposed pyramid dwelling was out of keeping with the surrounding neighborhood. *Reid*, also cited in *Stoyanoff*, was a similar case in which the property owner planned "a flat-roofed complex of twenty modules" in a residential area of "dignified, stately and conventional structures." The court upheld the ordinance, which contained generalized standards requiring a review of architectural design.

Is a similarity requirement in an appearance code simply the familiar zoning compatibility requirement in a slightly different guise? If so, is this kind of design review ordinance really so unique? Compare *Hankins v. Borough of Rockleigh*, 150 A.2d 63 (N.J. App. Div. 1959) (invalidating ordinance prohibiting flat roofs as applied in area where flat-roofed dwellings already existed).

2. *Dissimilarity.* Another variant in appearance codes requires architectural dissimilarity. New dwellings must not be too similar to existing dwellings. What do you suppose is the reason behind the dissimilarity requirement? If a municipality disapproved the dwelling in *Stoyanoff* under a dissimilarity requirement, would a court reverse?

In *Village of Hudson v. Albrecht, Inc.*, 458 N.E.2d 855 (Ohio 1984), the court upheld an ordinance that contained both a similarity and dissimilarity requirement, as well as general design review standards. The court noted that the ordinance did not rely solely on aesthetic considerations but "also reflects a concern for the monetary interests of protecting real estate from impairment and destruction of value." *Id.* at 857. The dissent claimed the building modification under review would not affect property values because it was a store located in a shopping center.

3. *Do appearance codes stifle creative architecture?* The dwelling disapproved in *Stoyanoff* was a triangular three-story pyramid with corner windows; the upper stories were to be design studios. It won praise from an architectural magazine. The dwelling disapproved in *Reid* also was a radical architectural design. Does this suggest that design review is applied to suppress creative architecture?

If this is so, does architectural design review raise free speech problems? The dissents in *Reid* and *Village of Hudson* thought so. The first question is whether architectural expression is a form of speech. If it is, could you argue that the proposed dwelling in the *Stoyanoff* case was so intrusive on its neighbors that it justified a restriction on that expression. Would the impairment of property values justification used in *Stoyanoff* be enough to save a design review ordinance from a free speech challenge? How about an argument that a disapproved architectural style could be built elsewhere.

In *Novi v. City of Pacifica,* 215 Cal. Rptr. 439 (Cal. App. 1985), the city rejected a site development permit because an ordinance prohibited approval where "there is insufficient variety in the design of the structure and grounds to avoid monotony in the external appearance." The court held the provision was not unconstitutionally vague and that the U.S. Supreme Court's free speech decision in *Metromedia* did not require objective criteria for aesthetic land use regulation:

> The legislative intent is obvious: the Pacifica city council wishes to avoid "ticky-tacky" development of the sort described by songwriter Malvina Reynolds in the song, "Little Boxes." No further objective criteria are required. . . . [*Id.* at 441.]

See also Breneric Assocs. v. City of Del Mar, 81 Cal. Rptr.2d 324 (Cal. App. 1998) (upholding denial of permit for addition to residence because inconsistent with existing structure and surrounding neighborhood). For criticism of this case see Weinberg & McGuire, *Design Regulation and Architecture: Collision Course?,* 22 Zoning & Plan. L. Rep. 89 (1999).

2. DESIGN REVIEW

What it is.—Design review goes beyond appearance. Land use attorney Brian Blaesser describes urban design review as a process "where the focus is the urban fabric — light, air, views, open space, and spatial and functional relationships within a city." Discretionary Land Use Controls § 8.03 (2000). Design review can apply to individual land uses, such as residences, commercial uses and signs, or to particular areas of a city, such— as the downtown or historic districts, or to the entire city.

Design review standards.—Design review standards go beyond the simple design criteria used in appearance codes. How should they be drafted? *Anderson v. City of Issaquah,* 851 P.2d 744 (Wash. App. 1993), considered an urban design review program in a suburb of Seattle, Washington. Here are some of the design standards the ordinance contained:

> 1. Evaluation of a project shall be based on quality of its design and relationship to the natural setting of the valley and surrounding mountains.

> 2. Building components, such as windows, doors, eaves and parapets, shall have appropriate proportions and relationship to each other, expressing themselves as a part of the overall design.

3. Colors shall be harmonious, with bright or brilliant colors used only for minimal accent.

4. Design attention shall be given to screening from public view all mechanical equipment, including refuse enclosures, electrical transformer pads and vaults, communication equipment, and other utility hardware on roofs, grounds or buildings.

5. Exterior lighting shall be part of the architectural concept. Fixtures, standards, and all exposed accessories shall be harmonious with the building design.

6. Monotony of design in single or multiple building projects shall be avoided. Efforts should be made to create an interesting project by use of complementary details, functional orientation of buildings, parking and access provisions and relating the development to the site. In multiple building projects, variable siting of individual buildings, heights of buildings, or other methods shall be used to prevent a monotonous design. [*Id.* at 746–47.]

The plaintiff proposed to build a structure for several retail tenants with off-white stucco facing and a blue metal roof in a "modern" style with an unbroken "warehouse" appearance in the rear and large retail windows in the front. The city refused design approval for a number of reasons, including an objection to the front facade and an objection that the building did not fit with the "image" of Issaquah. The plaintiff redesigned the building to change the roof to tile, change the color to gray with blue trim and add brick to the front facade and later added wood trim and trees to break up the rear facade. Again the city rejected the design, noting in part that the building was not "sensitive to the unique character of our Signature Street."

The court held the ordinance was vague. It agreed with a brief filed by several associations of architects that the ordinance provisions "'do not give effective or meaningful guidance' to applicants, to design professionals, or to the public officials of Issaquah who are responsible for enforcing the code." *Id.* at 751. The court added that, in interpreting the code, "the commissioners charged with that task were left with only their own individual, subjective 'feelings' about the 'image of Issaquah' and as to whether this project was 'compatible' or 'interesting'." *Id.* at 752.

NOTES AND QUESTIONS

1. *The delegation issue.* The cases are about divided on whether design standards are constitutional as a delegation of power. Compare the holding in *Issaquah* with the contrary holding in *Stoyanoff,* and note how the cases on vagueness and delegation of power are a replay in a different setting of the aesthetic purpose issue.

2. *Can standards be precise?* A recent review of design ordinances found that roughly three-quarters of the ordinances surveyed used criteria such as "encourage retention of existing vegetation," "favor site-specific response to topography," and similar criteria. Lightner, Survey of Design Review Practices 4 (American Planning Association, PAS Memo, Jan. 1993). In the *Issaquahah* case, the city relied primarily on procedural safeguards in the code, arguing that aesthetic considerations are "subjective in concept" and cannot be reduced "to a formula or a number." This argument did not impress the court, but perhaps the city was right:

> The problem with any quest for *precise* standards in design review is simply that there are some varieties of "aesthetic" regulation for which *sensible* details are impossible to prescribe without defeating the very purpose of the regulation. . . . Precise standards direct the attention of design communities to the superficialities of style instead of to the basic aspects of design that are likely to affect community life. [Introduction to Highland Park, Illinois Appearance Code, as quoted in P. Glassford, Appearance Codes for Small Communities 4 (Am. Planning Association, Planning Advisory Serv. Rep. No. 379 (1983)) (Report reviews details of design review ordinances in several communities.) (Emphasis in original.).]

See also the classic article by Jesse Dukeminier, *Zoning for Aesthetic Objectives: A Reappraisal,* 20 Law & Contemp. Probs. 218, 226–27 (1955) (planners should abandon the "cry for precise criteria" and develop "a satisfactory set of operations describing what is beautiful").

3. *Better standards.* M. Hinshaw, Design Review (American Planning Association, Planning Advisory Serv. Rep. No. 454 (1995)), makes a case for more specific design guidelines. He urges the use of visual drawings to supplement written standards, a practice that is increasingly common. He suggests that guidelines, as a minimum, should address overall site design, landscaping, building orientation and form, signage and public spaces. He includes the following guideline on building orientation and form from Boston, Massachusetts as an example:

> Tall buildings, particularly the newer generation of office buildings with large areas per floor, can appear to loom over the city due to their bulk. This effect can be mitigated, if not eliminated, by design strategies that attempt to break up the mass by the use of offsets and other methods to articulate the horizontal and vertical planes of buildings. [*Id.* at 27.]

Do you understand what this guideline means, and how it should be applied in practice? What about the standards and guidelines in the Problem at the beginning of this section? For suggestions on the drafting of design review ordinances see C. Duerksen & R.M. Goebel, *Aesthetics, Community Character, and the Law* 35 (American Planning Association, Planning Advisory Serv. Rep. No. 489/490 (1999)).

4. *Big box retail.* These stores, such as Wal-Mart and similar stores, create serious design problems because of their box-like look and their sterile, windowless exterior faces. Communities are beginning to adopt design guidelines for these stores that require architectural treatments and awnings that break up faceless facades. See Duerksen, *Site Planning for Large-Scale Retail Stores,* (American Planning Association, PAS Memo, Apr. 1996).

5. *Does discretionary review improve design?* A study in Columbus, Ohio looked at design results in a city neighborhood before and after the city extended the jurisdiction of its design review board to this area. Surprisingly, projects approved before discretionary review were considered more compatible and preferable by neighborhood residents. Physical inventory evaluations showed the discretionary review projects as slightly more compatible, but not at the level of statistical significance. Nassar & Grannis, *Design Review Reviewed: Administrative v. Discretionary Methods,* 65 J. Am. Plan. Ass'n 424 (1999). Other studies reached similar results.

6. Compare design review ordinances with historic preservation ordinances. Is the "standards" problem less severe, for instance, in an historic district? Should courts skeptical about design review generally review historic preservation ordinances more generously? Preservation issues are considered in sec. D, *infra.*

7. *Sources.* For discussion of design review ordinances, see Design Review: Challenging Urban Aesthetic Control (B. Scheer & W. Preiser eds., 1994); Note, *You Can't Build Here: The Constitutionality of Aesthetic Zoning and Architectural Review,* 58 Fordham L. Rev. 1013 (1990). See also Barnett & Hack, Urban Design in the Practice of Local Government Planning ch. 13 (C. Hoch, L. Dalton & F. So eds., 3d ed. 2000); Bross, *Taking Design Review Beyond the Beauty Part: Aesthetics in Perspective,* 9 Envtl. L. 211 (1979).

A NOTE ON VIEW PROTECTION

View protection is a form of aesthetic control that can be incorporated in design review or legislated in a stand-alone ordinance. Here is how it works:

Preserving Viewsheds. Perhaps the most common category of view protection ordinance focuses on preserving viewsheds — those grand, scenic vistas, visible from many vantage points, that encompass a multitude of elements, both natural and man-made, and that give communities their special identity.

There are two common types of viewshed ordinances. The first allows new development subject to some kind of design review [which can include height limitations.] . . . A stricter type of viewshed ordinance sharply curtails the types of new development allowed in viewsheds in order to preserve the scenic areas in a relatively undisturbed state. These ordinances require sensitive siting or screening of any buildings allowed in the viewshed. . .

Preserving View Corridors. . . . [V]iew corridors [are] openings in the urban fabric that allow either quick glimpses or more extended views of important constructed resources . . . or natural features. . . . View corridor regulations [can] . . . attempt to prevent shadows from falling onto important view corridors and public places. . . .View corridor regulations also may be more complex, as is the case with Denver and Austin programs that rely on mathematical formulas to calculate allowable building heights. [Duerksen & Goebel, *supra,* at 44–45.]

Notice that view protection can be carried out through discretionary design review or legislated through specific standards, which can be complex. For example, the Austin, Texas formula to protect views of the state capital "establishes height allowance in each [view] corridor defined by sightline elevations from the viewpoints to the base of the capital dome." *Id.* at 46. For a case rejecting a constitutional attack on a view protection ordinance see *Landmark Land Co., Inc. v. City & County of Denver,* 728 P.2d 1281 (Colo. 1986) (ordinance served legitimate governmental purposes and was not a taking because the properties involved were still extremely valuable), *appeal dismissed,* 483 U.S. 1001 (1987). Identify an area where you live that could benefit from view protection and consider what regulations you think should be adopted.

3. URBAN DESIGN PLANS

Urban design plans are a more comprehensive application of the design review concept. These plans cover an area of a community in which the character, form, scale, and visual attractiveness of new development are a community concern. Downtown areas are an important example. Design plans can also be adopted for other areas of the city such as commercial growth corridors, residential areas undergoing transition and projects grouped around a development node, such as a major street intersection.

The design plan is a subarea plan similar to the comprehensive plan but contains detailed policies relating to form, character and visual elements. Depending on the scale of the plan, building types and forms and pedestrian and traffic elements may be explicitly indicated. The framework policies for the Seattle, Washington 1985 Land Use and Transportation Plan indicate the type of policies that can be included:

1. Enhancing the relationship of downtown to its spectacular setting of water, hills and mountains;

2. Preserving important public views;

3. Ensuring light and air at street levels and in public parks;

4. Establishing a high quality pedestrian oriented street environment;

5. Reinforcing the vitality and special character of downtown's many parts;

6. Creating new downtown parks and open spaces at strategic locations; and

7. Preserving downtown's historic buildings to provide tangible links to the past. [J. Puntner, Design Guidelines in American Cities 32 (1999).]

The design plan can be implemented through a variety of techniques. Design review that applies the policies of the plan to individual development applications is common. The zoning ordinance can also include height limitations and building bulk standards that implement the plan. Other useful implementation measures are incentive zoning that provides increased density in return for designated design features, historic preservation controls, and transfer of development rights programs. See sec. D of this chapter. The San Antonio River Corridor plan reproduced on the following page is a typical example of an urban design plan. A classic text on urban design is H. Shirvani, Urban

Design Review: A Guide for Planners (1981). See also J. Nasar, The Evaluative Image of the City (1998).

San Francisco.— Rapid and intensive office development in downtown San Francisco led to the adoption of the first comprehensive downtown design plan in the country in 1972. This was a major planning effort carried out as part of the comprehensive planning process, and enlisted important national design specialists as consultants. For an account of the struggles over the plan by the city's former planning director, see A. Jacobs, Making City Planning Work ch. 8 (1978). A number of legislative actions implemented the plan, including historic district designations, design review and a new zoning ordinance in 1979.

Continued opposition to high-rise office development, marked by a series of anti-high-rise voter initiatives that failed, provided the political background for a second plan adopted in 1985. The new plan made some major revisions in the 1972 plan, but retained many of the same policies, such as restricting the scale and intensity of development, requiring shorter, thinner and more finely detailed buildings, preserving architecturally significant buildings, encouraging open spaces and increasing the supply of affordable housing.

San Francisco voters adopted an initiative in 1986 that modifies the downtown plan by putting a cap on downtown office development. It also required each development proposal to be tested for compliance with priority policies such as neighborhood preservation, landmark and open space preservation and affordable housing. This requirement led to a "beauty contest" for the approval of new development, which faded when an oversupply of office space led to a building recession. Design issues are no longer as paramount in the city, but the San Francisco experience remains important as the first major attempt at design planning for downtown areas. For discussion of the downtown plan see T. Lassar, Carrots and Sticks: New Zoning Downtown ch. 4 (1989); *Punter, supra*, ch.4. See also Griffith & Fleming, *San Francisco's Downtown Plan: Blueprint for the 1990s,* 18 Urb. Law. 1063 (1986); Comment, *San Francisco's Downtown Plan: Environmental and Urban Design Values in Central Business District Regulation,* 12 Ecology L.Q. 511 (1985).

Vancouver.—Bringing residential development back to city centers is a major policy problem. Vancouver, British Columbia has adopted an ambitious plan to encourage downtown housing. Beasley, "Living First" in Downtown Vancouver, Am. Plan. Ass'n, Zoning News, April 2000. The basic principles are to extend the "fabric, patterns and character of the existing city," and to develop complete mixed-use neighborhoods at the pedestrian scale. *Id.* at 2. Design guidelines complement these policies. They require thin towers with small floor plates, the separation of retail and other on-street uses to manage noise, a prohibition on blank walls, street landscaping, limited vehicle crossings of sidewalks, and underground parking. The regulatory process was then modified so that the plan is implemented through a highly discretionary regulatory framework.

Urban design plans clearly require a careful integration of planning and design policy with regulatory controls. An interesting exercise might be to develop a set of design policies for the downtown area of your city, and then

PLAN FOR REVITALIZATION AND CONSERVATION STRATEGIES
SAN ANTONIO RIVER CORRIDOR

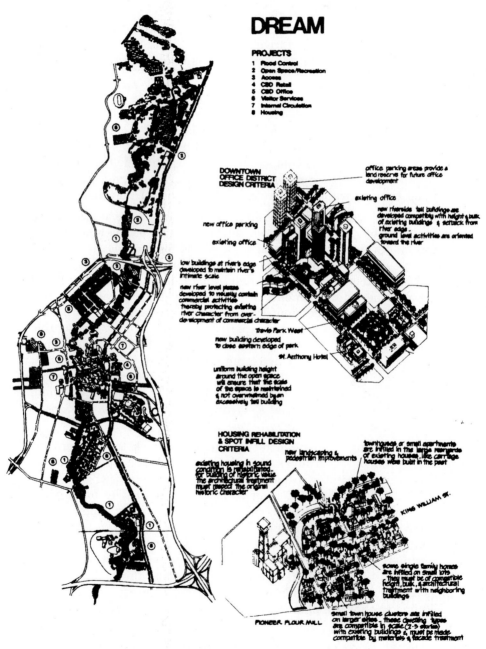

Source: The Practice of Local Government Planning 366 (F. So., I. Stollman, F. Beal & D. Arnold eds., 1979).

decide on what kinds of regulatory controls can best implement them, taking into account any possible constitutional objections.

D. HISTORIC PRESERVATION

Historic preservation is a major land use control. Thousands of historic listings are on the National Register of Historic Places, federal legislation requires federal agencies to take historic resources into account, and historic preservation programs are widespread at the local level. This section reviews historic district regulation and historic landmark protection, which are the two major local regulatory programs. It also reviews the use of development rights transfers as an historic preservation technique.

What is historic?—The term certainly means any building that is old, although even that limitation no longer is meaningful as buildings less than fifty years old can be listed on the National Register. A special historic architectural style is another important attribute, but a historic building may also be humble or not even architecturally interesting. The buildings in Honolulu's Chinatown are undistinguished architecturally but have important historic associations. Is this an aesthetic regulatory problem?

Some assistance is provided by the criteria for listing historic districts and buildings on the National Register. The criteria require a "quality of significance in American history" for districts, sites and buildings

(a) that are associated with events that have made a significant contribution to the broad patterns of our history; or

(b) that are associated with the lives of persons significant in our past; or

(c) that embody the distinctive characteristics of a type, period, or method of construction, or that represent the work of a master, or that possess high artistic values, or that represent a significant and distinguishable entity whose components may lack individual distinction; or

(d) that have yielded, or may be likely to yield, information important in prehistory or history. [36 C.F.R. § 60.4.]

What is preservation?—Federal regulations define "preservation" as "the act or process of applying measures to sustain the existing form, integrity, and material of a building." 36 C.F.R. § 68.2(b). What does this definition really mean? Integrity may be the key word. For the most part, historic preservation ordinances maintain integrity by preserving the historic character of building exteriors. This objective distinguishes historic preservation from traditional zoning, which regulates land use, and reinforces the constitutionality of historic preservation. Takings problems are less severe because the use of building interiors is not affected so long as the exterior is maintained. Of course, historic preservation regulation may include more than this: it usually requires the maintenance and rehabilitation of historic buildings and may also prohibit their demolition. Occasionally, preservation of interiors is also required. Cf. *Sameric Corp. v. City of Philadelphia, infra.* These requirements raise additional constitutional problems.

The leading case on historic preservation is *Penn Central Transp. Co. v. City of New York,* 438 U.S. 104 (1978), reproduced in Ch. 2. The Supreme Court upheld the designation of Grand Central Terminal as a historic landmark against objections based on substantive due process, takings of property, and equal protection. *Penn Central* settled many but not all of the legal questions raised by historic preservation. This section reviews these unsettled questions as well as the treatment of the issues considered by *Penn Central* in the state courts.

1. HISTORIC DISTRICTS

Historic district ordinances and legislation.—States have enacted enabling legislation for historic districts that is separate from the Standard Zoning Act. Most of this legislation merely includes historic preservation as one of the purposes of zoning or authorizes historic districts but leaves implementation details to municipalities. See N.M. Stat. Ann.§ 3-22-2; N.Y. Gen. Mun. Law § 86-a. In most municipalities, historic districts are usually established and administered separately from the zoning ordinance as a separate "overlay" district.

This practice is recognized in some historic district legislation, which is more detailed and specifies the regulatory powers and procedures for historic district regulations. See Mass. Gen. L. ch. 40C; Mich. Comp. Laws Ann. §§ 399.172 to 300.215. This type of legislation authorizes local governments to establish historic district commissions, which can conduct historic area surveys and make recommendations for historic districts to the governing body, which designates historic districts. The historic district ordinance also contains controls to be applied within an historic district. The most important control requires owners of buildings within historic districts to secure a "certificate of appropriateness" from the historic district commission for the exterior alteration or demolition of structures. Owners of vacant land must secure a certificate of appropriateness for new construction. Maintenance and repair requirements may also be included. Some statutes authorize the commission to approve construction on nearby property that affects the district. See *Reiter v. City of Beloit,* 947 P.2d 425 (Kan. 1997) (upholding zoning change for commercial use adjacent to historic residence).

Notice how the certificate of appropriateness requirement shapes the legal issues that arise in historic districts. Legal challenges to historic district ordinances necessarily become as-applied claims that a refusal to allow the demolition or modification of an historic structure violated the takings or some other constitutional clause. Note how the constitutional issues change here because an existing building is affected, not a proposal to develop vacant land.

Coordination with zoning is necessary if the historic district is not part of the zoning ordinance, which is usually the case. Coordination is difficult in some communities. See *Heritage Hill Ass'n v. City of Grand Rapids,* 211 N.W.2d 77 (Mich. 1977) (variance granted to allow demolition of building in historic district). Interagency agreements are one possibility. Another approach is to place the historic district regulations in the zoning ordinance. See *City of Santa Fe v. Gamble-Skogmo, Inc.,* 389 P.2d 13 (N.M. 1964) (zoning enabling act authorized historic district controls). New Jersey's enabling act mandates a notice procedure between boards. N.J. Stat. Ann. § 40:55D-110.

First generation districts.—The first decisions considered historic districts adopted for showplace historic settlements, and the courts had no difficulty upholding their constitutionality. In *Opinion of the Justices,* 128 N.E.2d 557 (Mass. 1955), the court upheld a historic district for the town of Nantucket. It noted "the sedate and quaint appearance of the old island town [that] has to a large extent still remained unspoiled." See also *City of New Orleans v. Pergament,* 5 So. 2d 129 (La. 1941) (Vieux Carré); *Opinion of the Justices,* 128 N.E.2d 563 (Mass. 1955) (Beacon Hill in Boston).

Second generation districts.—The rationale for historic districts shifted as the historic district movement spread to include areas that were not old, quaint, and revered. In *Bohannon v. City of San Diego,* 106 Cal. Rptr. 333 (Cal. App. 1973), the court upheld the designation of the city's "Old Town" as a historic district. The court stressed the importance of the Old Town image as "a visual story of the beginning of San Diego" and "an educational exhibit of the birth place of California." The court also stressed benefits to tourism.

The following case illustrates the rationale courts use when the area preserved has architectural or historic merit but is neither singular nor unique:

FIGARSKY v. HISTORIC DISTRICT COMMISSION

171 Conn. 198, 368 A.2d 163 (1976)

BARBER, ASSOCIATE JUSTICE:

The plaintiffs, owners of a house and lot located within the Norwich historic district, appealed to the Court of Common Pleas from a decision of the defendant commission denying their application for a certificate of appropriateness which would permit them to demolish the house. The court rendered judgment dismissing the appeal and the plaintiffs, upon the granting of certification, have appealed to this court.

The undisputed facts of the case are as follows: The Norwich historic district, established by the city of Norwich in 1967, pursuant to §§ 7-147a through 7-147m of the General Statutes, consists of the Norwichtown Green, which dates back to colonial days, and about one hundred buildings and lots surrounding, or in close proximity to, the green. The plaintiffs' property, which they purchased in 1963, is a two-story building zoned for commercial uses and is located just inside the bounds of the district. The property faces the green but is bounded on two sides by a McDonald's hamburger stand and parking lot. The building is in need of some repairs, which the Norwich building inspector has ordered the plaintiffs to undertake. Rather than make the repairs, however, the plaintiffs would prefer to demolish the building. In August, 1972, the plaintiffs applied to the building inspector for a demolition permit. The building inspector informed the plaintiffs that before such a permit could be issued a certificate of appropriateness was required. The plaintiffs, therefore, applied to the defendant for a certificate, filing their application with the building inspector on November 29, 1972. The defendant held a public hearing on the application on January 25, 1973. The hearing was attended by more than 100 persons, none of whom, except for the plaintiffs and their attorney, spoke in favor of granting the application. On the following day, the commission voted unanimously to deny the plaintiffs' application.

The plaintiffs maintain that the costs of the repairs necessary for the building are prohibitive. The building inspector has ordered the plaintiffs to repair the foundation and replace a door sill and hall floor, and the health department has ordered the plaintiffs to tie in to a newly accessible public sewer. At the hearing before the commission, the plaintiffs offered the testimony of a local contractor to the effect that the cost of these repairs, together with the cost of reroofing the building, would amount to between $15,000 and $18,000. The plaintiffs offered no evidence of the value of the house without repairs, its value if repaired, or the value of the lot if the building were razed. Nor did the plaintiffs disclose to the commission the use which they intended to make of the lot if the building were razed.

The commission also received numerous opinions from the plaintiffs' neighbors and from the Connecticut historical commission, the southeastern Connecticut regional planning agency, and the Connecticut society of architects, as to the historic value of the premises. The consensus of these opinions was that although the building itself is of little historic value or interest, it does, by virtue of its location, perform an important screening function, separating the green from an encroaching commercial district, and its preservation is important in maintaining the character of the historic district.[1] The commission stated its reasons for denying the application as follows: "The Commission is of the opinion that the building in question significantly contributes to the importance of the Norwichtown Green as an historic landmark, and the Commission would have violated its responsibilities as defined in [§§ 7-147a — 7-147k] to have permitted its demolition. In weighing

---

[1] A communication from the state historical commission stated, in part: "Competent authority has placed the date of construction in or about 1760 and identified the owner at that period as keeping an inn where lawyers at the nearby Court of Norwich were accommodated. On the exterior at least, the structure has undergone considerable alteration over the years but still retains its essential form and proportions, wholly in keeping with the scale and appearance of numerous other old buildings that border the Green area. Aside from the house proper, its site is of historic interest as occupying the original home lot of the Reverend James Fitch, religious leader of the first settlers. It often happens that buildings forming a recognizable grouping, as around a green, may not individually be especially notable for architecture or historical association. But together as a unified whole they constitute a significant entity, no part of which can be removed without a definite and usually adverse effect upon the character and appearance of the entire area. This is the condition that obtains in Norwich town.

"The commercially zoned district south and southeast of the site under consideration exhibits the unattractive characteristics of so many such areas, with disparate structures of poor design uncoordinated with one another and obtrusive advertising signs. It stands close upon the boundaries of the local historic district. If the property at 86 Town Street were demolished, it would remove the most important screening element between these evidences of low-grade commercialism and the attractiveness of the largely unspoiled Green. State recognition of the importance of this land has recently been affirmed by the erection of a historical marker under auspices of this Commission, which details the history of early years in Norwich and the central role of the Green in that history. Nomination of the entire area has been made to the National Register of Historic Places maintained by the Office of Archeology and Historic Preservation, National Park Service, United States Department of the Interior, under the National Historic Preservation Act of 1966, Public Law 89-665."

all the considerations concerning this Application, the Commission was cognizant of [§ 7-147g, pertaining to permissible variations], but concluded that the hardships presented by the Applicant were not of sufficient magnitude to warrant granting approval for demolition."

Procedure upon an appeal from any decision of a historic district commission is the same as that for appeals from zoning boards. The controlling question which the trial court had to decide was whether the historic district commission had acted, as alleged in the appeal, illegally, arbitrarily and in abuse of the discretion vested in it. Since the trial court decided the appeal solely on the record returned by the commission and made only a limited finding of facts on the issue of aggrievement, review by this court must be based on the record of the proceedings before the commission to determine whether the commission's decision is reasonably supported by the record.

In their appeal, the plaintiffs allege that they will be forced to undergo economic hardship and loss as a result of not being permitted to demolish their building, and that the historic district commission, in denying their application for a certificate of appropriateness, acted illegally, arbitrarily and in abuse of its discretion. Several claims of law which were overruled by the trial court are assigned as error. . . .

The plaintiffs' principal claim is that the Norwich historic district ordinance, implementing the state enabling act, is unconstitutional as applied to them, and that the denial of their application for a certificate of appropriateness to demolish their building amounts to a taking of their property for public use without compensation. More specifically, they contend that the ordinance is "vague aesthetic legislation," incapable of application in accordance with mandates of due process, and that because of the denial of their application they will be forced to expend large sums in the maintenance of their property without being able to put it to any practical use.

Neither the constitution of the United States, amendments five and fourteen, nor the constitution of Connecticut, article first, § 11, deny the state the power to regulate the uses to which an owner may devote his property. . . .

[At this point the court, citing *Euclid v. Ambler Realty Co.*, stated the usual police power maxims: all property is subject to the police power; regulations restricting the use of property "to some extent" are not a taking; courts will not substitute their judgment for a fairly debatable legislative judgment. The court also quoted the dictum from *Berman v. Parker*, which endorsed aesthetic regulation.] It is apparent from the language of the enabling statute[2] that the General Assembly, in enacting those statutes, was cognizant not only of the intangible benefits to be derived from historic districts, such as an increase in the public's awareness of its New England heritage, but of the economic benefits to be reaped as well, by augmenting the value of properties located within the old sections of the state's cities and towns, and encouraging tourism within the state. In a number of recent cases, it has been held that the

---

[2] "[General Statutes]' § 7-147a. Historic districts authorized. . . . to promote the educational, cultural, economic and general welfare of the public through the preservation and protection of buildings, places and districts of historic interest by the maintenance of such as landmarks in the history of architecture, of the municipality, of the state or of the nation, and through the development of appropriate settings for such buildings, places and districts. . . ."

preservation of a historical area or landmark as it was in the past falls within the meaning of general welfare and, consequently, the police power. We cannot deny that the preservation of an area or cluster of buildings with exceptional historical and architectural significance may serve the public welfare.

The plaintiffs argue that the Norwich ordinance constitutes "vague aesthetic legislation," and point to our statement in *DeMaria v. Planning & Zoning Commission,* 271 A.2d 105, 108, that "vague and undefined aesthetic considerations alone are insufficient to support the invocation of the police power,". . . . The "aesthetic considerations" involved in the Norwich ordinance are not, however, "vague and undefined"; § 7-147f of the General Statutes, incorporated by reference into the ordinance, sets out with some specificity the factors to be considered by the commission in passing upon an application for a certificate of appropriateness.[3] Nor . . . do "aesthetic considerations alone" provide the basis for the ordinance. . . . Although we need not directly decide the issue in the present case, we note that other jurisdictions have recognized that "aesthetic considerations alone may warrant an exercise of the police power."

Having determined that the ordinance creating the Norwich historic district constitutes a valid exercise of the state's police power, we are left with the question of whether the application of that ordinance to the plaintiffs' property amounts to an unconstitutional deprivation of their property without compensation. In this context, it has often been noted that the police power, which regulates for the public good the uses to which private property may be put and requires no compensation, must be distinguished from the power of eminent domain, which takes private property for a public use and requires compensation to the owner. The difference is primarily one of degree, and the amount of the owner's loss is the basic criterion for determining whether a purported exercise of the police power is valid, or whether it amounts to a taking necessitating the use of the power of eminent domain. See Sax, "Takings and the Police Power," 74 Yale L.J. 36. "A regulation which otherwise constitutes a valid exercise of the police power may, as applied to a particular parcel of property, be confiscatory in that no reasonable use may be made of the property and it becomes of little or no value to the owner.["]

Whether the denial of the plaintiffs' application for a certificate of appropriateness to demolish their building has rendered the Norwich ordinance, as applied to them, confiscatory, must be determined in the light of their particular circumstances as they have been shown to exist. In regulating the

---

[3] "[General Statutes]' §7-147f. Considerations in determining appropriateness. If the commission determines that the proposed erection, construction, restoration, alteration, razing or parking will be appropriate, it shall issue a certificate of appropriateness. In passing upon appropriateness as to exterior architectural features the commission shall consider, in addition to any other pertinent factors, the historical and architectural value and significance, architectural style, general design, arrangement, texture and material of the architectural features involved and the relationship thereof to the exterior architectural style and pertinent features of other structures in the immediate neighborhood. In passing upon appropriateness as to parking, the commission shall take into consideration the size of such parking area, the visibility of cars parked therein, the closeness of such area to adjacent buildings and other similar factors. A certificate of appropriateness may be refused for any building or structure, the erection, reconstruction, restoration, alteration or razing of which, or any parking which, in the opinion of the commission, would be detrimental to the interest of the historic district."

use of land under the police power, the maximum possible enrichment of a particular landowner is not a controlling purpose. It is only when the regulation practically destroys or greatly decreases the value of a specific piece of property that relief may be granted, provided it promotes substantial justice. "The extent of that deprivation must be considered in light of the evils which the regulation is designed to prevent."

The plaintiffs had the burden of proving that the historic district commission acted illegally, arbitrarily, in a confiscatory manner or in abuse of discretion. This the plaintiffs failed to do. The plaintiffs went no further than to present evidence that their house was unoccupied and in need of extensive repairs. There was no evidence offered that the house, if repaired, would not be of some value, or that the proximity of the McDonald's hamburger stand rendered the property of practically no value as a part of the historic district.

The Norwich historic district commission, after a full hearing, lawfully, reasonably and honestly exercised its judgment. The trial court was correct in not substituting its own judgment for that of the commission.

NOTES AND QUESTIONS

1. *Average reciprocity?* In *Penn Central,* Justice Brennan indicated that historic district legislation was constitutional because it produced "an equitable distribution of benefits and burdens." This comment is an apparent reference to the "average reciprocity of advantage" that supports zoning ordinances. All landowners in a zoning district are burdened by a restrictive zoning regulation, but they also benefit from the protection the zoning ordinance provides.

How does this rationale apply when, as in *Figarsky,* the land uses in a historic district apparently are mixed? Could you argue that allowing the demolition in *Figarsky* would have an unraveling effect that would destroy the historic integrity of the district? Is the balancing test adopted by the court still good law after the Supreme Court's *Lucas* decision?

Does preventing demolition confer an "average reciprocity of advantage"? See Gold, The *Welfare Economics of Historic Preservation,* 8 Conn. L. Rev. 348 (1976). What if the owner of the house in *Figarsky* had been willing to build a new building identical in exterior facade?

2. *Historic residential neighborhoods.* Additional insight on these questions is provided by *A-S-P Assocs. v. City of Raleigh,* 258 S.E.2d 444 (N.C. 1979). A declaratory judgment was brought challenging the designation as a historic district of the "only intact neighborhood . . . composed primarily of Victorian houses" in the city. The neighborhood was undergoing revitalization. Although it did not fully embrace the "aesthetics is enough" rationale, the court upheld the ordinance, relying on *Penn Central* and *Berman v. Parker.* It added to the catalog of reasons for historic preservation, noting that it could stimulate revitalization and foster architectural creativity. Why?

Plaintiffs claimed the historic district was unreasonable as applied to them because they owned a vacant lot on which they planned to construct an office building. The court replied by relying on the *tout ensemble* doctrine adopted by the Louisiana courts. This doctrine recognizes that it is important to protect the setting or scene in which historic buildings are situated. Neither were property owners prohibited from constructing new buildings. "They are only required to construct them in a manner that will not result in a structure incongruous with the historic aspects of the Historic District." *Id.* at 451. What does this say about average reciprocity?

The court dismissed an equal protection argument based on the exclusion of adjacent historic buildings from the district. It relied on the usual rational relationship standard of equal protection review. The court also found no improper delegation of power, and followed the traditional view that the required statutory comprehensive plan could be found in the zoning regulations.

3. *Value enhancement.* Compare the holding in *M & N Enters., Inc. v. City of Springfield,* 250 N.E.2d 289 (Ill. App. 1969). The city designated a four-block area around Abraham Lincoln's Springfield home as a historic district. A majority of the area was residential and was zoned residential. Plaintiffs were denied a rezoning to construct a motel prior to the adoption of the historic district. They then applied for a conditional use and variance to construct a commercial wax museum and gift shop. The city took no action on this application, even though plaintiffs represented that the building would have architectural features appropriate to the district. The court held the district constitutional:

> From our review of this record, we must conclude that the enhanced value of the plaintiff's property is directly related to . . . [the creation of the historic district]. The proximity of the property to the Lincoln Home increases its value, and yet it is clear that use not in conformity with the existing zoning would be detrimental to the Lincoln Home Area and the total concept of the municipality relating to historical preservation. When property has an enhanced value by reason of planning and zoning for historical preservation, the zoning ordinances to implement the planning can hardly be said to be confiscatory or unreasonable or unconstitutional simply because the owners seek to use it for commercial purposes to exploit the visitors and tourists attracted, in part at least, by the creation of the Historical District. [*Id.* at 293.]

Would the Supreme Court accept this rationale?

4. *Due process-takings problems.* Here are some examples of the problem likely to arise under historic district ordinances:

(a) The property owner seeks to build or remodel a building but does not wish to conform with architectural restrictions imposed in the historic district. This problem arose in *Gamble-Skogmo, supra.* Gamble-Skogmo wished to remodel their building in the historic district of the city but did not want to comply with a requirement that window panes not exceed thirty inches square. It argued that "such a minute detail of construction is only an attempt by the city to impose its idea of an aesthetic detail of architecture." The court answered:

They ignore the fact that the window pane requirement is only one of very many details of the historical architectural style which it is said has evolved within the City of Santa Fe from about the year 1600 to the present, which the ordinance seeks to protect and preserve. So far as the record discloses, the window design is as much a part of the Santa Fe style as are flat roofs, projecting vigas, and wooden lintels. [*Id.* at 17.]

What kind of restriction on architectural detail is justified if styles in the historic district are mixed? Cf. *Parker v. Beacon Hill Arch. Ass'n,* 536 N.E.2d 1108 (Mass. 1989) (upholding denial of additional floor on row house because it would be inimical to historic appearance of building and diminish picturesque silhouette of row houses in this location). See also *Globe Newspaper Co. v. Beacon Hill Architectural Ass'n,* 659 N.E.2d 710 (Mass. 1996) (statute held to authorize ban on street furniture on Beacon Hill).

(b) The historic district ordinance contains a requirement that buildings in the district must be maintained to prevent deterioration. An objection to this kind of requirement was raised in *Maher v. City of New Orleans,* 516 F.2d 1051 (5th Cir. 1975). The court simply held that "[o]nce it has been determined that the purpose of the Vieux Carré legislation is a proper one, upkeep of buildings appears reasonably necessary to the accomplishment of the goals of the Ordinance. . . . It may be that, in some set of circumstances, the expense of maintenance under the Ordinance — were the city to exact compliance — would be so unreasonable as to constitute a taking." *Id.* at 1066–67.

(c) A property owner in a historic district is ordered to repair a building that is in a deteriorated condition. In *Lafayette Park Baptist Church v. Scott,* 553 S.W.2d 856 (Mo. App. 1977), the church owned and sought to demolish a double-entry townhouse in a historic district that was in a deteriorated condition. Permission to demolish was denied by the board of adjustment, which noted that it was feasible to restore the building. This decision was reversed in a muddled opinion, the court noting that historic district regulations were akin to zoning and that "economic considerations cannot be wholly discounted." The ordinance "must be interpreted to authorize demolition when the condition of the structure is such that the economics of restoration preclude the landowner from making any reasonable use of the property." *Id.* at 862. The court also noted that the cost of rehabilitation would exceed $50,000 and "that this cost was economically unwarranted for the end product which would result." *Id.* at 863.

On what basis does the court reach this conclusion? If all of the dwellings in the historic area are rehabilitated is it possible that their value after rehabilitation will be more than their existing value plus the cost of repair? Accord *Keeler v. Mayor & City Council,* 940 F. Supp. 879 (D. Md. 1996) (taking when no economically feasible rehabilitation plan possible). But see *City of Pittsburgh, Historic Review Comm'n v. Weinberg,* 676 A.2d 207 (Pa. 1996) (cost of renovation would not exceed value after renovation, owner knew of historic designation when bought property and could sell it for a profit). For discussion of historic preservation in declining neighborhoods, see Gold, *supra,* at 357–61.

(d) A property owner wishes to demolish his building so that he can put his land to a more profitable use. The principal case and *Maher, supra,* considered this problem. In *Maher* the court held:

> An ordinance forbidding the demolition of certain structures, if it serves a permissible goal in an otherwise reasonable fashion, does not seem on its face constitutionally distinguishable from ordinances regulating other aspects of land ownership, such as building height, set back or limitations on use. . . . Nor did Maher demonstrate . . . that a taking occurred because the ordinance so diminished the property value as to leave Maher, in effect, nothing. In particular, Maher did not show that the sale of the property was impracticable, that commercial rental could not provide a reasonable rate of return, or that other potential use of the property was foreclosed. [*Id.* at 1066.]

Wolk v. Reisen, 413 N.Y.S.2d 60 (App. Div. 1979), overturned a denial of permission to demolish a historic house that was vacant and vandalized and was set on fire, and found by the local building official to be unsafe and dangerous. The court held that vital interests in public health and safety took precedence over aesthetic and historic concerns. But see *Park Home v. City of Williamsport,* 680 A.2d 835 (Pa. 1996) (refusal to allow demolition upheld; owners did not consider sale of property as alternative).

How does the Supreme Court's decision in *Lucas* affect the cases in this Note? *Lucas* presumably means the Court will pay no attention to regulatory objectives if there is a denial of all beneficial or productive use. In which of the cases discussed above would this be true?

5. *Delegation of power objections.* Courts have usually rejected these claims. *A-S-P Assocs., supra* Note 2, is typical. The court upheld a "congruity" standard contained in the ordinance for the review of exterior building changes. It characterized this standard as "contextual" and added that the "incongruity" standard derived its meaning from "the total physical environment of the historic district." *Id.* at 54. The architectural "melange" in the district did not make the standard meaningless. How does this holding compare with the holding in *Stoyanoff? Issaquah?* Accord *Mayes v. City of Dallas,* 747 F.2d 325 (5th Cir. 1984) (facade and landscape standards).

2. HISTORIC LANDMARKS

In addition to historic districts, municipalities also commonly have programs for the designation of individual historic landmarks not located in historic districts. Some states have adopted historic landmark legislation, which may authorize historic landmark regulation in a separate ordinance, see Cal. Gov't Code §§ 25373, 37361, or in the zoning ordinance, see N.J. Stat. Ann. § 40:55D-65.1.

Local controls for historic landmark preservation are similar to those for historic districts. Landmark preservation ordinances and statutes authorize landmark designation and require a certificate of appropriateness for any exterior changes and for demolition. Landmark owners may be required to keep them in good repair. To avoid takings problems, restrictions on landmarks may not apply if they do not allow the owner a reasonable return. Hardship variances also may be authorized.

The takings issue.—Takings questions in landmark preservation present special problems. Reciprocity of advantage may not help avoid a takings claim because historic landmarks usually are isolated and, as in *Penn Central,* surrounded by buildings that make more intensive use of the land. Historic landmark regulation may then present the classic case of a regulation that benefits the general public but whose burdens are concentrated on a single landowner.

Takings law on historic landmarks is limited. *Maher v. City of New Orleans,* 516 F.2d 1051 (5th Cir. 1975), *cert. denied,* 426 U.S. 905 (1986), and *Penn Central Transp. Co. v. City of New York,* reproduced in Ch. 2, are the principal cases that have considered takings questions raised by historic landmark regulation. *Maher* held that a refusal to allow the demolition of a landmark is not a taking if a reasonable use of the property remains. See also *900 G Street Assocs. v. Department of Hous. & Community Dev.,* 430 A.2d 1387 (D.C. 1981).

Penn Central did not consider a proposed demolition of a historic building. The Court found a taking had not occurred partly because the owners of Grand Central Station could continue its use, which they admitted was profitable. The Court also noted that the station owners could reapply for a less intrusive building over the station, and that the opportunity to transfer development rights somewhat offset their takings claim. These cases seem consistent with the Supreme Court's per se takings rule in *Lucas.* Compare *Mayor & Aldermen v. Anne Arundel County,* 316 A.2d 807 (Md. 1974) (court upheld refusal to permit demolition of historic church), with *Texas Antiquities Comm. v. Dallas Community College Dist.,* 554 S.W.2d 924 (Tex. 1977) (allowing demolition of deteriorated historic building when cost of restoration was economically prohibitive).

NOTES AND QUESTIONS

1. *The Sameric case.* In *Sameric Corp. v. City of Philadelphia,* 558 A.2d 155 (Pa. Cmwlth. 1989), an intermediate appellate court sustained the "historic" designation of a moving picture theatre, described as a substantially intact "Art Deco movie palace." The designation applied to both the exterior and the interior of the theatre. Although the theatre owner provided evidence that the exterior's Art Deco design had undergone "substantial alteration" the court had little difficulty in sustaining the "historic" designation with respect to the exterior. The "historic" designation of the interior presented a more difficult problem because the historic landmark ordinance only gave the Philadelphia Historical Commission authority to designate "buildings, structures, sites and objects" as "historic" landmarks. The court upheld the "historic" designation of the theatre's interior after concluding that the City Council intended the term "building" to include "both interior and exterior" because it considered the interior to be "an essential part of the community's historic and esthetic values."

On appeal, the Pennsylvania Supreme Court reversed. *United Artists' Theater Circuit, Inc. v. City of Philadelphia,* 635 A.2d 612 (Pa. 1994). It held there was "no 'clear and unmistakable' authority to designate the interior of a building." The supreme court also receded from an earlier opinion in which it had held that the historic designation (exterior as well as interior) was a taking. The court applied earlier Pennsylvania precedent holding that an independent analysis of constitutional issues is required under the Pennsylvania constitution, although "an examination of related federal precedent may be useful."

On the "taking without compensation" issue the court held that a constitutional amendment recognizing a right to the preservation of historic and other resources expressed a general public interest in historic landmark designation. The court rejected the use of eminent domain as an impracticable alternative. Finally, the court held that the owner of the historic landmark had not been deprived of all profitable use. The City of Philadelphia conceded defeat on the interior designation; the owner subsequently remodeled it into a modern quadriplex theater. Brin, "Preservation Endorsed by Supreme Court," The Legal Intelligencer, Friday, November 12, 1993.

2. *Religious uses.* The courts have had a difficult time with challenges by religious organizations to landmark designation. The New York Court of Appeals reached somewhat inconsistent results in two cases in which churches wished to demolish buildings so they could erect new buildings on the site. In *Lutheran Church in America v. City of N.Y.,* 316 N.E.2d 305 (N.Y. 1974), the court allowed demolition because the existing building was no longer adequate for its use. Later, in *Society of Ethical Culture v. Spatt,* 415 N.E.2d 922 (N.Y. 1980), decided after *Penn Central,* the court reached a contrary result on similar facts.

An important Second Circuit case rejected "taking" and "free exercise of religion" issues. In *St. Bartholemew's Church v. City of New York,* 728 F. Supp. 958 (S.D.N.Y.1989), *aff'd,* 914 F.2d 348 (2d Cir.1990), *cert. denied,* 499 U.S. 905 (1991), the Church challenged the New York Landmarks Commission's refusal to allow the Church to demolish its seven-story "community house," located on the same lot as the Church itself, and to construct a high-rise office building in its place. The Church argued that the Commission's action effected a "taking" because it deprived the Church of its ability to earn a "reasonable return" on its investment, and that it violated the "free exercise" clause because it "impaired the Church's ability to carry on and expand the ministerial and charitable activities that are central to its religious mission."

On the "free exercise" issue, the Court of Appeals held that the Landmarks Law was "a facially neutral regulation of general applicability within the meaning of Supreme Court decisions" which, "as applied," did not violate the "free exercise" clause since there was no showing of discriminatory motive, coercion with respect to religious practice, or deprivation of the Church's ability to carry out its religious mission in its existing facilities. The Court of Appeals also rejected the "takings" claim, holding the Church had failed to show it could no longer conduct its charitable activities or carry out its religious mission in its existing facilities. The court based this holding explicitly on *Penn Central,* where, said the Court of Appeals, the Supreme Court held that "the constitutional question is whether the land use regulation impairs the continued operation of the property in its originally expected use."

In reaching its decision on the "takings" issue, the Court of Appeals rejected the Church's arguments that (1) the amount and configuration of usable space in its Community House was "insufficient to accommodate the Church's various programs," and (2) that "the necessary repairs to the physically deteriorating Community House would be prohibitively expensive" and beyond the Church's financial ability if it were to continue its other programs.

Other recent cases have refused to recognize free exercise claims. See *First Church of Christ, Scientist v. Ridgefield Historic Dist. Comm'n,* 738 A.2d 224 (Super. Ct. 1998), *aff'd,* 737 A.2d 989 (Conn. App. 1999) (upholding refusal to allow church to install vinyl clad siding in historic district).

3. *Cases protecting religious uses.* In *First Covenant Church of Seattle v. City of Seattle,* 787 P.2d 1352 (Wash. 1990), the Church challenged the City's designation of its church structure as a "landmark" pursuant to the city's landmarks preservation ordinances. The Washington Supreme Court held the Church was entitled to a declaratory judgment invalidating the designation because, on its face, the ordinances violated the Church's rights under both the First Amendment and under Washington's state constitution.

The City then sought a writ of certiorari from the United States Supreme Court, which granted the writ, vacated the state court judgment, and remanded the case to the Washington Supreme Court "for further consideration in light of *Employment Division, Dept. of Human Resources of Oregon v. Smith,* 494 U.S. 872 (1990)." *Smith* is the famous "peyote" case where the Court held that government may constitutionally restrict certain activities associated with the practice of religion, pursuant to its general regulatory power, by a non-discriminatory, generally applicable law that happens to prohibit religiously motivated actions.

On remand, the Washington Supreme Court again struck down the landmark preservation ordinances as they affected the Church, in an extended set of opinions reported in 840 P.2d 174 (Wash. 1992). The Washington court distinguished both *Smith* and *St. Bartholemew's Church* and, by a 4-3 vote, invalidated the City's landmark preservation ordinances, both on First Amendment grounds and because the ordinances violated the "right to religious liberty" guaranteed by Article 1, § 11 of the Washington constitution. That provision, said the Washington court, expressly provides that "only the government's interest in peace or safety or in preventing licentious acts can excuse an imposition on religious liberty." See also *Society of Jesus v. Boston Landmarks Comm.,* 564 N.E.2d 571 (Mass. 1990) (designation of church interior as landmark violates Free Exercise clause when adopted to prevent renovation).

Is there a convergence in the takings and free exercise cases? Do both cases turn on how courts view the "burdens" placed on religious uses by land use regulations? See Homer, *Landmarking Religious Institutions: The Burden of Rehabilitation and the Loss of Religious Freedom,* 28 Urb. Law. 327 (1996); Weinstein, *The Myth of Ministry vs. Mortar: A Legal and Policy Analysis of Landmark Designation of Religious Institutions,* 65 Temp. L. Rev. 91 (1992).

Less frequently, historic preservation laws may raise "establishment clause" problems. See Cal. Gov't Code §§ 35373, 37361, which prohibit landmarking any noncommercial structure owned by a religiously affiliated entity over the owner's objection, upon a showing of "substantial hardship." A court of appeal held these sections did not violate the establishment clause. *East Bay Asian Local Development Corp. v. State of California,* 81 Cal. Rptr. 2d 908 (Cal. App. 1999) (review granted and depublished).

4. *Religious Freedom Restoration Acts.* The religious use cases were affected by the Religious Freedom Restoration Act, adopted by Congress in 1993, that restored the "compelling" governmental interest test the Supreme Court had previously required to justify governmental action affecting the free exercise of religion. *City of Boerne v. Flores,* 521 U.S. 507 (1997), held the act unconstitutional as beyond the power of Congress. The Act did not mention zoning, but it was clear from the legislative history that Congress intended the Act to apply to zoning actions. See H.R. Rep. 103–88, 103d Cong., 1st Sess. 6, n. 14 (1993) (disapproving *St. Bartholomew's Church* decision). Congress enacted a new religious freedom act in August 2000 that applies specifically to land use regulation. A constitutional challenge to the act is expected.

A few states have adopted religious freedom restoration acts modeled on the federal act the Supreme Court held unconstitutional, and other states are considering such legislation. *E.g.,* Fla. Stat. Ann. § 761.03; 775 Ill. Comp. Stat. Ann. §§ 35/15 to 35/25; R.I. Gen. Laws. §§ 42-80.1-1 to 42-80.1-4; S.C. Code §§ 1-32-10 to 1-32-60; Tex. Civ. Practice & Remedies Code §§ 110.001-110.012. See *City of Chicago Heights v. Living Word Outreach Full Gospel Church & Ministries, Inc.,* 707 N.E.2d 53 (Ill. App. 1999) (special use requirement for church does not violate act).

5. *Incentives for historic preservation.* Regulation alone may not be enough to accomplish historic preservation. One alternative is the use of historic conservation easements on the exterior facade. The easement gives a private organization or a government agency the right to review any changes in the exterior building facade. Compensation is paid for the easement. More than half the states have legislation authorizing easements for conservation or historic purposes, and elsewhere the common law of easements allows similar restrictions. A federal tax deduction is available. Easements provide savings on federal income and estate taxes.

Property tax abatements, exemptions, and assessment freezes for historic buildings also have been authorized in more than half the states. Property tax relief can offset any decline in value resulting from the landmark designation of a historic property and can avoid property tax increases resulting from rehabilitation or renovation.

The basis for property tax relief varies, and the effectiveness of tax relief programs is mixed, as there is considerable variation in the amount of tax abatement allowed. See Stockford, *Property Tax Abatement of Conservation Easements,* 17 B.C. Envtl. Aff. L. Rev. 823 (1990).

6. For additional reading on historic preservation, see Linder, *New Directions for Preservation Law: Creating an Environment Worth Experiencing,* 20 Envtl. L. 4 (1990); Netter & Barry, *Zoning for Historic Preservation,* 13 Zoning & Plan. L. Rep. 9 (1990); Comment, *The Free Exercise Clause and Historic Preservation Law: Suggestions For a More Coherent Free Exercise Analysis,* 72 Tul. L. Rev. 1767 (1998).

A NOTE ON FEDERAL HISTORIC PRESERVATION PROGRAMS

The National Historic Preservation Act (NHPA).—This Act, 16 U.S.C. §§ 470-470w, requires federal agencies to take into account the effect of federal "undertakings" on historic districts, sites and buildings listed on the National Register. 16 U.S.C. § 470f. It also establishes a National Register of Historic Places and a National Advisory Council on Historic Preservation and authorizes state historic preservation programs headed by a State Historic Preservation Officer.

Regulations of the Advisory Council require federal agencies to determine whether an undertaking "has the potential to cause effects on historic properties." See 36 C.F.R. Pt. 800. The agency shall then apply "criteria of adverse effect to historic properties within the area of potential effects." If an adverse effect is found, there must be consultation "to develop and evaluate alternatives or modifications to the undertaking that could avoid, minimize or mitigate adverse effects on historic properties." A Memorandum of Agreement can be agreed to that resolves any identified adverse effects. If no Memorandum of Agreement is reached, the Advisory Council may comment on the adverse effects on historic properties, and the agency shall take them in to account in making its decision. The regulations allow compliance with section 106 to be incorporated into the NEPA documentation process while preserving the legal requirements of each statute. Only a few of the federal undertakings considered each year are considered by the Council. For discussion see Comment, *Old Stuff is Good Stuff: Federal Agency Responsibilities Under Section 106 of the National Historic Preservation Act,* 7 Admin. L.J. Am. U. 697 (1993–94).

Income Tax Credit.—The Internal Revenue Code provides investment tax credits for certified rehabilitation expenses on historic buildings. The tax credit generated a substantial amount of historic building renovation until the law was amended in the 1986 Tax Reform Act by placing restrictions on who can claim the credit and by limiting the income the credit can offset. As a result, the number of rehabilitation projects that have used the credit has declined substantially. See Note, *Rehabilitation Tax Credit: Does It Still Provide Incentives?,* 10 Va. Tax Rev. 167 (1990).

Other federal legislation.—This legislation includes the Historic Sites Act of 1935, 16 U.S.C. §§ 461–67, which authorizes the Department of Interior to conduct surveys and acquire property; the Antiquities Act of 1906, 16 U.S.C. §§ 431–33, which authorizes the President to designate and implement a permit system for national monuments; and § 4(f) of the Department of Transportation Act, 49 U.S.C. § 303(c). Section 4(f) requires a review process similar to a NEPA review when a federally funded transportation project, such as a highway, crosses or affects a historic site or other designated environmental area, such as parks. The difference from NEPA is that the Department may not approve a project affecting a historic site unless there is no feasible or prudent alternative. This is a substantive requirement that creates a judicially protected presumption that protected areas must be avoided. *Citizens to Preserve Overton Park v. Volpe,* 401 U.S. 402 (1971).

3. TRANSFER OF DEVELOPMENT RIGHTS AS A HISTORIC PRESERVATION TECHNIQUE

Transfer of development rights programs (TDR) are an imaginative concept that attempt to avoid takings problems by compensating landmark owners through the sale of development rights on landmark properties. Although TDR first attracted attention when the constitutionality of landmark preservation was problematic, the problem is more than constitutional, as the following comment indicates:

> Because the typical landmark building makes only partial use of the floor area allotted to its site, it often cannot compete for survival in an overheated real estate market. Intense development pressure means higher land values that present an irresistible economic temptation to owners of small parcels. Because zoning bonuses [available through incentive zoning — Eds.] can be efficiently exploited only on large parcels, developers hasten to assemble a number of smaller parcels to realize the greatest possible advantage from the system. The result . . . is inevitable: demolition of what remains of our architectural heritage. [Note, *Development Rights Transfer and Landmarks Preservation — Providing a Sense of Orientation,* 9 Urb. L. Ann. 131, 139 (1975).]

What TDR does.—The TDR concept is straightforward. Development rights available under the zoning ordinance on an underdeveloped historic landmark site are purchased by the owner of another site, where they may be used to supplement the development rights available under existing zoning at that site. The landmark site is called the sending site and the site to which the development rights are transferred is called the receiving or transfer site.

TDR programs may contain additional features to ensure their successful operation. The owner of a landmark on a sending site may be required to convey preservation restrictions to the city, for which the owner receives a property tax abatement. A development rights bank may be established to sell and buy development rights. The bank serves as a backstop for the TDR market, which may not always operate in a satisfactory manner. The development rights that can be utilized at the transfer site may be limited to avoid excessive densities in areas where the development rights are transferred. Valuation of the development rights transferred also is a problem. For historic landmarks, one technique is to base valuation on the excess building bulk allowable at the sending site under the zoning ordinance. Whether the landmark owner must receive compensation equivalent to that which is constitutionally required under the takings clause is not clear.

The New York program.—New York City has had a TDR program for historic landmarks for some years, but the concept first attracted national attention when law professor John Costonis proposed a TDR program for Chicago landmarks in Space Adrift (1974). Chicago did not adopt the program, and TDR has been slow to catch on as a historic preservation technique although a few cities use TDR programs to implement downtown design plans. TDR is more widely used in the preservation of agricultural and other environmental resource areas, and this use of TDR is discussed in Ch. 7, *supra.*

Under the New York program, development rights transfer is allowed from sites occupied by historic landmarks to adjacent lots, which, generally, may be contiguous lots or lots across a street. Transfers are approved by the City Planning Commission through a special permit process. An application for a transfer must include a program providing for the maintenance of the landmark, a report from the Landmarks Preservation Commission and plans for the development of the receiving site.

The maximum amount transferable is the maximum floor area allowed for the site, less existing built floor area. Twenty percent above the floor area ratio is the maximum increase allowed for the transfer site. The Planning Commission must find that the program providing for the maintenance of the landmark will result in its preservation, and that the transfer will not cause planning problems in the transfer area. An instrument of transfer and deed restrictions prohibiting building in the transferred air rights are executed. Only about a dozen buildings have been preserved under the New York program, probably because other options for increasing building density are available, such as zoning incentives. See R. Pruetz, Saved by Development, 223–225 (1997), which also discusses TDR programs for historic preservation in San Francisco and other cities. See also Comment, *Transferring Development Rights: Purpose, Problem, and Prospects in New York,* 17 Pace L. Rev. 319 (1996).

Statutory authority.—Although municipalities can adopt TDR programs under their zoning powers, enabling legislation for TDR can provide the necessary statutory authority, and can provide statutory guidelines that ensure that TDR will be used fairly and effectively. Some state legislation simply authorizes the TDR without providing detailed implementation requirements. *E.g.,* Idaho Code § 67-4619; S.D. Codified Laws § 1-19B-26; Wash. Rev. Code § 36.70A.090 (comprehensive plan should provide for innovative techniques, including TDRs).

Other states provide detailed guidance. For example, New York legislation for its municipalities requires that a TDR ordinance must be in accordance with a comprehensive plan, that a receiving district must have adequate public facilities and other resources to accommodate the transferred development rights, that the impact of the TDR program on affordable housing must be considered and adjusted, and that a generic environmental impact statement for the receiving area must be maintained under the state environmental review law. Sending and receiving areas must be specifically designated, and transfer procedures must be provided. An easement transferring development rights at the sending parcel and a certificate documenting the development rights transferred to the receiving parcel must be prepared and recorded. A development rights bank is authorized, and the assessed value of land affected by a TDR must be adjusted. See, e.g., N.Y. Gen. City Law § 20-f. For other detailed legislation see, e.g., 65 Ill. Comp. Stat. Ann. §§ 5/11-48.2-1 to 48.2-7; Ky. Rev. Stat. Ann. § 100.208. The statutes usually authorize TDR programs for environmental land preservation as well as historic preservation. Consider, as you review the materials that follow, how a statute of this type can affect the constitutional issues. See Bredin, *Transfer of Development Rights: Cases, Statutes, Examples,* Am. Plan. Ass'n PAS Memo, Nov. 1998.

NOTES AND QUESTIONS

1. Professor Kayden points out some of the limitations of TDR programs. *Market-Based Regulatory Approaches: A Comparative Discussion of Environmental and Land Use Techniques in the United States*, 19 B.C. Envtl. Aff. L. Rev. 565 (1992). The demand for and price of development rights are a function of a city's planning and zoning policy. Demand for rights will be created in receiving districts only if the city regulates land use in these districts tightly. Zoning must also be stable because sellers and buyers will not be willing to create a market for development rights if they do not have confidence in the stability and integrity of a city's zoning. Transaction costs are high because time-consuming negotiation is required and the valuation of development rights is troublesome. The seller will want to receive a price equal to the capitalized value of the development foregone, while the value to the buyer depends on his site plans.

2. *Constitutional problems at the transfer site.* Many of the constitutional problems raised by TDR have centered on takings problems raised by the owners of sending sites. These problems are considered in the case that follows these notes. Constitutional problems also arise at the transfer site:

(a) *Uniformity.* TDR imposes a dual standard on lots in the transfer district. Developers may build at existing zoning levels without purchasing development rights, but may build more intensively only if development rights are purchased. Is there a uniformity problem? Dean Costonis argues that the uniformity objection has no merit, and relies on cases sustaining the constitutionality of PUD ordinances against uniformity objections. See Ch. 6, sec. D. "A development transfer district is, in effect, a special development district in which bulk is redistributed in accordance with the density zoning technique. It encompasses an area of the community that is unique because of the concentration there of many of the community's landmark buildings." Costonis, *The Chicago Plan: Incentive Zoning and the Preservation of Landmarks*, 85 Harv. L. Rev. 574, 623 (1971). Does this argument hold if TDR is used for purposes other than landmark preservation?

(b) *Due process and takings.* The requirement that lot owners at transfer sites purchase additional development rights in order to carry out more intensive development may raise due process and takings problems:

> If the existing zoning is sound, it may be claimed, relaxing bulk restrictions on transferee sites will overload public services and distort the urban landscape. . . . If it is too stringent, the proper course is to raise prevailing bulk limitations within the area generally and, in the process, to remove unwarranted public restrictions on the rights of property owners there. [Costonis, *supra* at 628.]

Costonis argues against this conclusion, pointing out that "it invests the numbers in the zoning code with an aura of scientific exactitude that is largely without foundation in fact." *Id.* at 629. Therefore, "the bulk increments allotted to development rights purchasers fall within a range that is defensible in planning terms." *Id.* at 630. In other words, communities may set zoning densities within a higher and lower range. If densities are set at the lower range, so that purchase of development rights is required to build at the higher range, no constitutional problem results. What do these problems indicate for the marketing problems discussed in Note 1? For arguments that the cost of development rights to the transfer owner is justified as a way of eliminating externalities in development and as a tax on unearned increment see Costonis, *Development Rights Transfer: Description & Perspectives for a Critique,* Urb. Land, Vol. 34, No. 1, at 5, 9 (1975).

Due process and takings problems at transfer sites may be more serious if the community must first downzone existing densities in order to make a market for the purchase of development rights at these sites. For a discussion of downzoning, see Ch. 5. How do the Supreme Court's recent takings cases affect the answer to these problems? See the discussion of the *Suitum* case in Note 4 following the next principal case.

Consider *Barancik v. County of Marin,* 872 F.2d 834 (9th Cir. 1988), *cert. denied,* 493 U.S. 894 (1989). A zoning ordinance required a 60-acre lot minimum in a ranching area but included a TDR program under which owners of land in the area could acquire additional development rights. A rancher wanted to build on 20-acre lots, but was unwilling to pay enough to purchase the additional rights necessary for this density. He sued after the county denied a rezoning to a 20-acre lot size. The court held the TDR program did not increase the total amount of development in the area, was rationally related to agricultural preservation, and was not an exaction falling under the *Nollan* case because payment was to a private owner, not the state.

3. *Price and marketing problems.* What price developers will pay for development rights at the transfer site is analyzed in Field & Conrad, *Economic Issues in Programs of Transferable Development Rights,* 51 Land Econ. 331 (1975). The authors point out that the transfer price of development rights at the transfer site will depend on how the market for development rights is organized, and the extent to which the public agency intervenes to manage the development rights price. In a poorly organized market, with little or no public intervention, purchasers of development rights may be able to seek out holders of rights with low reservation prices and contract for their rights at these prices. Questions may then arise concerning the adequacy of compensation to the restricted owners.

If the development right charge raises the price of land in the transfer district, will this excess charge be passed on to tenants and purchasers of buildings constructed on the transfer site? "This depends on the degree of competition in markets for comparable developments, both within the planning area and in adjacent areas. The lower the degree of competition, . . . the higher the likelihood that development rights costs can be passed on to future occupants." *Id.* at 338.

If the cost of development rights is passed on, can TDR be faulted on equity grounds?

> [TDR] costs are even more inequitably skewed when compared to the total proportion of a given population that is beneficiary to TDR's presumed preservation services. Theoretically, a protected resource such as scenic open space or a historic mansion is a public good. That is, it is a commodity which, "if available to anyone, is equally available

to all others." To be sure, in practice TDR's preserved resources are not likely to be equally accessible to *all* income or age groups in a jurisdiction. But it is just as certain that those who do have access and can visually enjoy a verdant meadow or an Italianate Victorian townhouse compose a considerably larger population than the burdened groups identified under compensatory and redistributive TDR measures. Therefore, it would seem compellingly apparent that TDR schemes of whatever stripe are likely to fail a test of equitability based on the criterion of benefits derived. [Gale, *The Transfer of Development Rights: Some Equity Considerations,* 14 Urb. L. Ann. 81, 94 (1977).]

For discussion of how to value transferred development rights see Danner, *TDRs — Great Idea But Questionable Value,* 65 Appraisal J. 133 (1997).

4. *Does TDR avoid a taking?* Simulated market analysis of TDR plans casts additional light on whether the value of TDRs will fully compensate owners who are restricted from the full development of their land in TDR programs. Berry & Steiker, *An Economic Analysis of Transfer of Development Rights,* 17 Nat. Resources J. 55 (1977) examine a hypothetical TDR system in which the entire jurisdiction is subject to a TDR program and no development may occur without the purchase of development rights from landowners in areas restricted from development. The authors are skeptical that the transfer value of development rights under this kind of system will provide adequate compensation to owners of restricted land. A number of factors will determine whether exchange values for these rights will fully compensate these restricted owners, including "the revenues generated and costs associated with development, the amount of land put in the no-growth zone, and the number of development rights created." *Id.* at 73. However, if applied on a limited scale, as in site-to-site transfer situations such as those contemplated in the *French* and *Penn Central* cases, the exchange value of development rights can be expected to approach full compensation so long as the local land market is relatively active. *Id.*

The authors also note that in order for the exchange value of development rights to yield sufficient compensation to restricted owners, the supply of those rights must be carefully managed with reference to the market demand for those rights. This kind of management requires public intervention to withhold rights from the market:

> The withholding action may be by 1) public purchase of development rights at some "parity price," 2) refusing to give out (or create) all the development rights in the first place, or 3) only the agency selling development rights and limiting sales so as to gain a high rent; the monopolist would then distribute the rents to the landowners in the no-growth zone in proportion to their losses of exchange value. All three remedies require administrative costs and the first requires a large initial expenditure (or bond issue) before substantial revenue from sales can be obtained. [*Id.* at 64 n.23.]

Note that management problems may be serious even in a site-to-site TDR program aimed at protecting historic landmarks. As the number of landmarks protected by the program increases, the impact of the sale of development rights from these landmarks on the land market will also increase and substantial public management may be necessary in order to guarantee full compensation to restricted landmark owners. See Conrad & LeBlanc, *The Supply of Development Rights: Results From a Survey in Hadley, Massachusetts,* 55 Land Econ. 269 (1979). The survey indicated that transferred development rights would sell at a price close to the cost of full acquisition. They suggest alternative strategies, such as acquisition with resale after the development rights have been removed. See also Thorsnes & Simons, *Letting The Market Preserve Land: The Case For a Market-Driven Transfer of Development Rights Program,* 17 Contemp. Econ. Pol'y 256 (1999).

One purpose of TDR programs is to avoid the takings objections that can be leveled against landmark preservation. Will TDR always eliminate these objections? The following case may provide some answers.

FRED F. FRENCH INVESTING CO. v. CITY OF NEW YORK

39 N.Y.2d 587, 350 N.E.2d 381, *appeal dismissed,* 429 U.S. 990 (1976)

BREITEL, CHIEF JUDGE:

Plaintiff Fred F. French Investing Co., purchase money mortgagee of Tudor City, a Manhattan residential complex, brought this action to declare unconstitutional a 1972 amendment to the New York City Zoning Resolution and seeks compensation as for "inverse" taking by eminent domain. The amendment purported to create a "Special Park District," and rezoned two private parks in the Tudor City complex exclusively as parks open to the public. It further provided for the granting to the defendant property owners of transferable development (air) rights usable elsewhere. It created the transferable rights by severing the above-surface development rights from the surface development rights, a device of recent invention. . . .

Tudor City is a four-acre residential complex built on an elevated level above East 42nd Street, across First Avenue from the United Nations in mid-town Manhattan. Planned and developed as a residential community, Tudor City consists of 10 large apartment buildings housing approximately 8,000 people, a hotel, four brownstone buildings, and two 15,000 square-foot private parks. The parks, covering about 18 2% of the area of the complex, are elevated from grade and located on the north and south sides of East 42nd Street, with a connecting viaduct. . . .

[The Tudor City complex was conveyed and] the new owner announced plans to erect a building, said to be a 50-story tower, over East 42nd Street between First and Second Avenues. This plan would have required New York City Planning Commission approval of a shifting of development rights from the parks to the proposed adjoining site and a corresponding zoning change. Alternatively, the owner proposed to erect on each of the Tudor City park sites a building of maximum size permitted by the existing zoning regulations.

There was immediately an adverse public reaction to the owner's proposals, especially from Tudor City residents. After public hearings, the City Planning Commission recommended, over the dissent of one commissioner, and on

December 7, 1972 the Board of Estimate approved, an amendment to the zoning resolution establishing Special Park District "P." By contemporaneous amendment to the zoning map, the two Tudor City parks were included within Special Park District "P."

Under the zoning amendment, "only passive recreational uses are permitted" in the Special Park District and improvements are limited to "structures incidental to passive recreational use." When the Special Park District would be mapped, the parks are required to be open daily to the public between 6:00 a.m. and 10:00 p.m.

The zoning amendment permits the transfer of development rights from a privately owned lot zoned as a Special Park District, denominated a "granting lot," to other areas in midtown Manhattan, bounded by 60th Street, Third Avenue, 38th Street and Eighth Avenue, denominated "receiving lots." Lots eligible to be receiving lots are those with a minimum lot size of 30,000 square feet and zoned to permit development at the maximum commercial density. The owner of a granting lot would be permitted to transfer part of his development rights to any eligible receiving lot, thereby increasing its maximum floor area up to 10%. Further increase in the receiving lot's floor area, limited to 20% of the maximum commercial density, is contingent upon a public hearing and approval by the City Planning Commission and the Board of Estimate. Development rights may be transferred by the owner directly to a receiving lot or to an individual or organization for later disposition to a receiving lot. Before development rights may be transferred, however, the Chairman of the City Planning Commission must certify the suitability of a plan for the continuing maintenance, at the owner's expense, of the granting lot as a park open to the public.

It is notable that the private parks become open to the public upon mapping of the Special Park District, and the opening does not depend upon the relocation and effective utilization of the transferable development rights. Indeed, the mapping occurred on December 7, 1972, and the development rights have never been marketed or used. . . .

[The court held that the zoning amendment "deprives the owner of all his property rights, except the bare title and a dubious future reversion of full use" and then considered whether the TDR program offset this deprivation:]

It is recognized that the "value" of property is not a concrete or tangible attribute but an abstraction derived from the economic uses to which the property may be put. Thus, the development rights are an essential component of the value of the underlying property because they constitute some of the economic uses to which the property may be put. As such, they are a potentially valuable and even a transferable commodity and may not be disregarded in determining whether the ordinance has destroyed the economic value of the underlying property.

Of course, the development rights of the parks were not nullified by the city's action. In an attempt to preserve the rights they were severed from the real property and made transferable to another section of mid-Manhattan in the city, but not to any particular parcel or place. There was thus created floating development rights, utterly unusable until they could be attached to some accommodating real property, available by happenstance of prior ownership, or by grant, purchase, or devise, and subject to the contingent approvals of administrative agencies. In such case, the development rights, disembodied abstractions of man's ingenuity, float in a limbo until restored to reality by reattachment to tangible real property. Put another way, it is a tolerable abstraction to consider development rights apart from the solid land from which as a matter of zoning law they derive. But severed, the development rights are a double abstraction until they are actually attached to a receiving parcel, yet to be identified, acquired, and subject to the contingent future approvals of administrative agencies, events which may never happen because of the exigencies of the market and the contingencies and exigencies of administrative action. The acceptance of this contingency-ridden arrangement, however, was mandatory under the amendment.

The problem with this arrangement, as Mr. Justice Waltemade so wisely observed at Special Term, is that it fails to assure preservation of the very real economic value of the development rights as they existed when still attached to the underlying property. By compelling the owner to enter an unpredictable real estate market to find a suitable receiving lot for the rights, or a purchaser who would then share the same interest in using additional development rights, the amendment renders uncertain and thus severely impairs the value of the development rights before they were severed (see Note, the Unconstitutionality of Transferable Development Rights, 84 Yale L.J. 1101, 1110–1111). Hence, when viewed in relation to both the value of the private parks after the amendment, and the value of the development rights detached from the private parks, the amendment destroyed the economic value of the property. It thus constituted a deprivation of property without due process of law.

None of this discussion of the effort to accomplish the highly beneficial purposes of creating additional park land in the teeming city bears any relation to other schemes, variously described as a "development bank" or the "Chicago Plan" (see Costonis, The Chicago Plan: Incentive Zoning and the Preservation of Urban Landmarks, 85 Harv. L. Rev. 574; Costonis, Development Rights Transfer: An Exploratory Essay, 83 Yale L.J. 75, 86–87). For under such schemes or variations of them, the owner of the granting parcel may be allowed just compensation for his development rights, instantly and in money, and the acquired development rights are then placed in a "bank" from which enterprises may for a price purchase development rights to use on land owned by them. Insofar as the owner of the granting parcel is concerned, his development rights are taken by the State, straightforwardly, and he is paid just compensation for them in eminent domain. The appropriating governmental entity recoups its disbursements, when, as, and if it obtains a purchaser for those rights. In contrast, the 1972 zoning amendment short-circuits the double-tracked compensation scheme but to do this leaves the granting parcel's owner's development rights in limbo until the day of salvation, if ever it comes. . . .

It would be a misreading of the discussion above to conclude that the court is insensitive to the inescapable need for government to devise methods, other than by outright appropriation of the fee, to meet urgent environmental needs of a densely concentrated urban population. It would be equally simplistic to ignore modern recognition of the principle that no property has value except as the community contributes to that value. The obverse of this principle is, therefore, of first significance: no property is an economic island, free from contributing to the welfare of the whole of which it is but a dependent part. The limits are that unfair or disproportionate burdens may not, constitutionally, be placed on single properties or their owners. The possible solutions undoubtedly lie somewhere in the areas of general taxation, assessments for public benefit (but with an expansion of the traditional views with respect to what are assessable public benefits), horizontal eminent domain illustrated by a true "taking" of development rights with corresponding compensation, development banks, and other devices which will insure rudimentary fairness in the allocation of economic burdens.

Solutions must be reached for the problems of modern zoning, urban and rural conservation, and last but not least landmark preservations, whether by particular buildings or historical districts. Unfortunately, the land planners are now only at the beginning of the path to solution. In the process of traversing that path further, new ideas and new standards of constitutional tolerance must and will evolve. It is enough to say that the loose-ended transferable development rights in this case fall short of achieving a fair allocation of economic burden. Even though the development rights have not been nullified, their severance has rendered their value so uncertain and contingent, as to deprive the property owner of their practical usefulness, except under rare and perhaps coincidental circumstances.

The legislative and administrative efforts to solve the zoning and landmark problem in modern society demonstrate the presence of ingenuity. That ingenuity further pursued will in all likelihood achieve the goals without placing an impossible or unsuitable burden on the individual property owner, the public fisc, or the general taxpayer. These efforts are entitled to and will undoubtedly receive every encouragement. The task is difficult but not beyond management. The end is essential but the means must nevertheless conform to constitutional standards.

NOTES AND QUESTIONS

1. *Penn Central TDR upheld.* A mandatory TDR plan was also part of the landmarks designation program considered in the Supreme Court's *Penn Central* decision. The TDR program was extensively considered in the state court decision, 366 N.E.2d 1271 (N.Y. 1977), which upheld it with the following comments:

> Development rights, once transferred, may not be equivalent in value to development rights on the original site. But that, alone, does not mean that the substitution of rights amounts to a deprivation of property without due process of law. Land use regulation often diminishes the value of the property to the landowner. Constitutional standards, however, are offended only when that diminution leaves the owner with no reasonable use of the property. The situation with transferable development rights is analogous. If the substitute rights

received provide reasonable compensation for a landowner forced to relinquish development rights on a landmark site, there has been no deprivation of due process. The compensation need not be the "just" compensation required in eminent domain, for there has been no attempt to take property.

The case at bar, like the *French* case, fits neatly into this analysis. In *French* the development rights on the original site were quite valuable. The regulations deprived the original site of any possibility of producing a reasonable return, since only park uses were permitted on the land. And, the transferable development rights were left in legal limbo, not readily attachable to any other property, due to a lack of common ownership of the rights and a suitable site for using them. Hence, plaintiffs were deprived of property without due process of law. The regulation of Grand Central Terminal, by contrast, permitted productive use of the terminal site as it had been used for more than half a century, as a railroad terminal. In addition, the development rights were made transferable to numerous sites in the vicinity of the terminal, several owned by Penn Central, and at least one or two suitable for construction of office buildings. Since this regulation and substitution was reasonable, no due process violation resulted. [*Id.* at 1278.]

Little consideration was given to the TDR program in the Supreme Court because the court held a taking had not occurred. The court did note that the transferable development rights might not have constituted just compensation if a taking had occurred, but added that these rights mitigated whatever financial burdens the landmark designation imposed and were to be taken into account in considering the impact of this regulation. *Id.* at 137.

2. *Distinguishing the cases.* What further light does the *Penn Central* case shed on the "fairness" that Judge Breitel requires in TDR programs? In a speech commenting on his *French* and *Penn Central* opinions, Judge Breitel noted that in TDR programs "it becomes fairly clear that, to the extent that they [the transferable development rights] are necessary to compensate the owner of the original site, they must be either in cash, acceptable in kind, or be sufficiently translatable into cash." Breitel, *A Judicial View of Transferable Development Rights,* 30 Land Use L. & Zoning Dig., No. 2, at 5, 6 (1978). He then distinguished the two cases as follows:

In the *Fred F. French* case, the owner at one point had been offered a tremendous price for those development rights somewhere else in mid-Manhattan. But by the time the case was decided, mid-Manhattan was terribly overbuilt and the value of the TDRs had dropped. That really isn't an accidental circumstance. This is the nature of our economy. This is the reason why the TDR transfers were found insufficient in *Fred F. French* and why, on the other hand, we found them of some value in *Penn Central.* [*Ibid.*]

Judge Breitel also noted, apparently with reference to *Penn Central,* that the neighboring properties were so profitable in their present use that development rights transferred to those properties would have to be heavily discounted. Nevertheless, he added that if TDR is going to be accepted "we have to abandon the fiction or pretense that we are going to give the owner of the original site full value of that part which we take away from him, let alone the full fee interest; and, . . . that the TDR is not even going to come anywhere close to the exploitative value of the air rights over his land." *Id.* at 5.

Dean Costonis does not believe the two cases can be distinguished. *The Disparity Issue: A Context for the Grand Central Terminal Decision,* 91 Harv. L. Rev. 402 (1977). He notes that both programs were mandatory and that both offered transfer districts with numerous sites suitable for development of the type desired. He states that the only difference was that the landowner in *French* did not own land within the transfer district, but that this difference did not negate the value of the transfer rights. *Id.* at 419–20. Do you agree? On the basis of these decisions, how would you formulate a TDR program for historic landmarks that would win judicial approval? How do the Supreme Court's recent takings cases, particularly *Lucas,* affect this problem?

3. *A beachfront TDR.* The court upheld a TDR program in *City of Hollywood v. Hollywood, Inc.,* 432 So. 2d 1332 (Fla. App. 1983). A developer owned sixty-five acres of a ninety-two-acre tract on the coast. The eastern coastal portion was zoned as single family residential at seven units to the acre, for a total of 79 units. The western portion of the tract was zoned multi-family. Under the TDR plan, the coastal portion of the tract would remain open and unbuilt, but the multi-family zoning on the western portion would be intensified to allow an increase of 368 multi-family residential units.

Penn Central, the court said, required it to consider the character of the governmental action, the economic impact of the regulation and whether a taking had occurred. The court noted it had "found the government action to be proper and reasonably related to a valid public purpose." It did not disapprove of the economics of the TDR trade-off, noting that the loss of single-family units would be offset by the gain in multi-family units, that the developer owned both parcels, and that the value "of all the multifamily units will be enhanced because the buildings will have an uninterrupted ocean-front position and view." *Id.* at 1338.

What does *Hollywood* indicate about the constitutionality of a TDR program for landmark sites? For a discussion of the *Hollywood* case by the lawyer who helped design the program, see Freilich & Senville, *Takings, TDRs, and Environmental Preservation: "Fairness" and the Hollywood Beach Case,* 35 Land Use L. & Zoning Dig., No. 9, at 4 (1983).

The TDR program in *Hollywood* required the developer to dedicate the beach front by deed. The court upheld this requirement as a quid pro quo for the density transfer. When there is no dedication or property restriction a court may decide later that restrictive zoning on an historic landmark or environmental site should be lifted. See *Francis v. City & County of Denver,* 418 P.2d 45 (Colo. 1966) (landmark was vandalized and demolished).

4. *Suitum.* In *Suitum v. Tahoe Regional Planning Agency,* 520 U.S. 725 (1997), a property owner claimed that a restriction on environmentally sensitive land was a taking, even though an option to transfer development rights was available. The case was decided by the Supreme Court on a ripeness issue, but Justice Scalia examined the takings issue in a concurring opinion. He argued that the availability of TDRs can help determine the compensation due a property owner, but should not affect the question of whether a taking had occurred. Otherwise, the availability of a development rights transfer could completely eliminate a takings claim by providing enough compensation to a landowner to support an argument that substantial value remained in the property. Justice Scalia distinguished *Penn Central* because the landowner owned some of the lots to which development rights were to be transferred.

What practical effect would the Court's adoption of Justice Scalia's argument have on TDR programs? Do you agree with his distinction of *Penn Central?* See Juergensmeyer, Nicholas & Leebrick, *Transferable Development Rights and Alternatives After Suitum,* 30 Urb. Law. 441 (1998).

5. *Sources.* See Miller, *Transferable Development Rights in the Constitutional Landscape: Has Penn Central Failed to Weather the Storm,* 39 Nat. Res. J. 459 (1999); Note, *Banking on TDRs: The Government's Role as Banker of Transferable Development Rights,* 73 N.Y.U. L. Rev. 1329 (1998); Note, *Caught Between Scalia and the Deep Blue Lake: The Takings Clause and Transferable Development Rights Programs,* 83 Minn. L. Rev. 815 (1999); Note, *Past, Present, and Future Constitutional Challenges to Transferable Development Rights,* 74 Wash. L. Rev. 825 (1999).

TABLE OF CASES

[Principal cases appear in capitals; references are to pages.]

[Principal cases appear in capitals; references are to pages.]

[Principal cases appear in capitals; references are to pages.]

[Principal cases appear in capitals; references are to pages.]

[Principal cases appear in capitals; references are to pages.]

[Principal cases appear in capitals; references are to pages.]

[Principal cases appear in capitals; references are to pages.]

[Principal cases appear in capitals; references are to pages.]

[Principal cases appear in capitals; references are to pages.]

[Principal cases appear in capitals; references are to pages.]

[Principal cases appear in capitals; references are to pages.]

[Principal cases appear in capitals; references are to pages.]

[Principal cases appear in capitals; references are to pages.]

[Principal cases appear in capitals; references are to pages.]

[Principal cases appear in capitals; references are to pages.]

Principal cases appear in capitals; references are to pages.

INDEX

[References are to pages.]

[References are to pages.]

[References are to pages.]

[References are to pages.]

[References are to pages.]

[References are to pages.]

[References are to pages.]